RESEARCH UPDATES

In addition to these exciting new media elements, *Psychology: Concepts and Connections* has many new research updates and new modern examples. Some key updates include:

■ Chapter 2—A new figure that shows the relationship between cells, chromosomes and DNA as well as a section containing new research (2006) about heredity and human behavior and updated (2004) information on the International Human Genome Sequencing Consortium.

■ Chapter 2—A new figure showing different brain scans, how the brain scan machines work, and corresponding updated information on brain imaging techniques.

■ Chapter 3—A new **A Closer Look** box that discusses the challenges of bridging adolescence in the United States.

■ Updated coverage of adulthood and aging including new information on patterns for aging, sex, and ethnicity in the new **A Closer Look** box.

■ Chapter 4—A new chapter opening vignette that includes coverage of the movie *The Matrix* as it relates to sensation and perception.

■ Chapter 4—A new figure that shows the perception of color.

■ Chapter 4—A new **A Closer Look** box that talks about animal instinct and how many animals sensed the 2005 tsunami days and hours before humans did.

■ Chapter 5—A new **A Closer Look** box discussing the controversy around biological functioning for people with brain injury especially as it relates to the case of Terri Schiavo.

■ Chapter 5—A new section called "Altering Consciousness by Going Online". Coverage includes Internet addiction and contains an applied section designed to help students reduce the amount of time they spend online.

■ Chapter 6—A new opening vignette that ties the topic of learning violence in video games.

■ Chapter 6—A new **A Closer Look** box that discusses how researchers are using operant conditioning to teach rats how to search for disaster survivors.

■ Chapter 7—A new chapter opening vignette that teaches students how reliant we have become on things like cellular phones to remember important things.

■ Chapter 7—A new section that covers the biology of memory including a new figure illustrating long-term potentiation.

■ Chapter 8—A new figure showing MRI results of great apes revealing possible language centers in the brain.

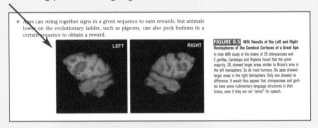

❖ Apes can string together signs in a given sequence to earn rewards, but animals lower on the evolutionary ladder, such as pigeons, can also peck buttons in a certain sequence to obtain a reward.

FIGURE 8.5 MRI Results of the Left and Right Hemispheres of the Cerebral Cortexes of a Great Ape
In their MRI study of the brains of 25 chimpanzees and 2 gorillas, Cantalupo and Hopkins found that the great majority, 20, showed larger areas similar to Broca's area in the left hemisphere. So do most humans. Six apes showed larger areas in the right hemisphere. Only one showed no difference. It would thus appear that chimpanzees and gorillas have some rudimentary language structures in their brains, even if they are not "wired" for speech.

■ Chapter 11—A new chapter opening vignette that discusses popular online personality tests.

■ Chapter 11—A new **A Closer Look** box that discusses the creation of heroes by the media and how Americans react to heroes.

■ Chapter 11—A new **A Closer Look** box on positive psychology and Trait Theory.

■ Chapter 12—A new **A Closer Look** box on pheromones and sexual orientation including a figure showing differences in the hypothalamus as it "lights up" depending on sexual orientation.

■ Chapter 13—A new chapter opening vignette that tells the story of two survivors of Hurricane Katrina as their experiences relate to stress and health.

■ Chapter 14—Updated material on classifying psychological disorders.

■ Chapter 14—Updated research covering the prevalence of psychological disorders including a new table that illustrates past year and lifetime prevalence rates as well as median age of onset.

■ Chapter 14—A new figure uses MRI to show the rate of gray matter loss in schizophrenic people versus non-schizophrenic people.

■ Chapter 15—A new opening vignette highlights the usage and effectiveness of virtual reality therapy.

■ Chapter 15—A new **A Closer Look** box covers EMDR therapy.

■ Chapter 16—A new opening vignette tackles the topic of social psychology as it relates to terrorist attacks.

■ Chapter 16—A new **A Closer Look** box on suicide terrorists and fundamental attribution error.

Psychology

Concepts & Connections

Ninth Edition

Media & Research Update

Spencer A. Rathus

New York University

THOMSON

WADSWORTH ™

Australia • Brazil • Canada • Mexico • Singapore • Spain • United Kingdom • United States

THOMSON
WADSWORTH

Psychology: Concepts & Connections, Media and Research Update, Ninth Edition
Spencer A. Rathus

Publisher: Michele Sordi

Senior Development Editor: Kate Barnes

Managing Assistant Editor: Dan Moneypenny

Editorial Assistant: Erin Miskelly

Technology Project Manager: Lauren Keyes

Marketing Manager: Sara Swangard

Marketing Assistant: Natasha Coats

Marketing Communications Manager: Linda Yip

Project Manager, Editorial Production: Megan Hansen

Art Director: Vernon Boes

Print Buyer: Doreen Suruki

Permissions Editor: Sarah D'Stair

Production Service: Newgen–Austin

Photo Researcher: Eric Schrader

Copy Editor: Matt Darnell

Cover Designer: Denise Davidson

Cover Images: Portrait of a woman ©Veer/ImageSource Photography; Woman smiling ©Veer/ImageSource Photography; Woman wearing headphones ©Taxi/Claudia Goepperi; Businessman resting chin ©Stone/Bruce Ayres; Woman smiling, close-up ©PhotoDisc Red/Amos Morgan; Toddler girl, smiling, portait ©PhotoDisc Green/Amos Morgan; Portrait of two smiling women ©Digital Vision; Portrait of two Goths ©Digital Vison; Portrait of couple holding hands ©Digital Vision; Portrait of teenage boy ©PhotoDisc Green; Portrait of teenage girl in classroom ©PhotoDisc Green; Father teaching boy to play guitar ©Charles Gupton/CORBIS

Compositor: Newgen

Printer: Transcontinental–Beauceville

Printed in Canada
1 2 3 4 5 6 7 11 10 09 08 07

For more information about our products, contact us at:
Thomson Learning Academic Resource Center
1-800-423-0563
For permission to use material from this text or product,
submit a request online at
http://www.thomsonrights.com
Any additional questions about permissions can be submitted by
e-mail to thomsonrights@thomson.com.

ExamView® and ExamView Pro® are registered trademarks of FSCreations, Inc. Windows is a registered trademark of the Microsoft Corporation used herein under license. Macintosh and Power Macintosh are registered trademarks of Apple Computer, Inc. Used herein under license.

Library of Congress Control Number: 2006932928

ISBN 0-495-09800-0

For Lois, Jill, Allyn, Jordan, and Taylor

BRIEF CONTENTS

CONTENTS

Chapter 4

Sensation and Perception 140

Chapter 7

Memory: Remembrance of Things Past—and Future 264

Chapter 8

Cognition and Language 306

Chapter 11

Personality: Theory and Measurement 398

Chapter 12

Gender and Sexuality 434

Chapter 13

Stress, Health, and Adjustment 478

Chapter 16

Social Psychology 592

Appendix A

Statistics A–1

Appendix B Answer Keys to Self-Assessments and Active Reviews A–18

FEATURES

Concept Review

 ## Self-Assessment

CONTROVERSY IN PSYCHOLOGY

Psychology: Concepts and Connections

My favorite psychology professor told the class, "You probably judge how well you did in the course by your grade. I judge how well *I* did in the course in terms of how many additional psychology courses you sign up for."

Now, it's my turn. Users of this textbook will judge what they have obtained from it in various ways. I will consider myself to have been successful if it inspires students to take additional courses in psychology.

I had several goals in writing this introductory textbook: They include painting psychology as the rigorous science it is, teaching students how to think critically, and introducing students to the various fields of psychology and the concepts they investigate. But it was also essential to me to inspire students with the subject matter. Thus I have tried to use a warm, engaging writing style, including humor and personal anecdotes, rather than a dry one. I also believed it is important to show students how psychology connects with important issues in their own lives. Psychology is not just "out there"; its many concepts provide information and ideas that all students can apply for their own benefit and that of those whom they care about.

Psychology: Concepts and Connections–More Than Just a Title

All academic disciplines have their own concepts, and psychology is no exception. One of the key tasks of any introductory course is to acquaint students with the basic concepts of the discipline. Students of introductory psychology are probably not surprised that concepts such as *intelligence, personality, stress, mental illness* (which we refer to as *psychological disorder*), and *psychotherapy* are important to the discipline. They may be surprised to learn that psychologists debate whether some familiar concepts, such as *psychoanalysis,* have a place—other than a historic place—in psychology as a science. Students are unlikely to be surprised that the concepts of *personality* and *learning* and *memory* are found in psychology, but they may find that these concepts—as defined and used by psychologists—are not quite what they thought they were. Students may also be somewhat surprised that the very concept they had of the field of psychology—of what psychology *is*—probably makes up less than half of what they will find in this textbook.

All this is very good. Psychology consists of things that are familiar and things that are new. One of the purposes of this course is to set the record straight, to show students what does and what does not belong within the science of psychology.

Thinking Critically about Psychology–In Life and in the Classroom

Another goal of this course is to show that psychologists, like other scientists, are open minded. They thrive on debate. They do not even necessarily agree on the definitions of the topics they discuss. For example, there is no one definition of *psychology* that all psychologists agree on. When we approach the topic of learning, we will similarly see that experts in that field disagree as to how to define *learning*.

Later we will see that psychologists disagree as to what *intelligence* is, and as to whether there is one kind of general intelligence or there are several "intelligences." As if this were not enough, we will see that there is also major controversy over the origins of intelligence.

Again, all of this is very good. Scientific debate should not be confused with pointless argument. Honest debate helps psychologists—and students—come ever closer to the truth. Students will of course memorize standard definitions; however, it is more important that they come away from this course with an understanding of the true scientific nature of psychology and of the controversies within psychology. Critical thinking is the key to understanding these controversies. I believe too many individuals blindly follow the demands of the media and authority figures, and it is my goal to help students hone their critical thinking skills so that they can evaluate the arguments they hear in the media and from authority figures. In fact, I have incorporated numerous Critical Thinking exercises throughout the text to get students thinking critically about the content they encounter in the text and the situations they encounter in their lives.

Because of the value of critical thinking, every Learning Connections section within each chapter contains a **_Critical Thinking_** item. Here is a sampling:

◆ From Chapter 1, "What Is Psychology?": Do you believe that the richness and complexity of human behavior can be explained as the summation of so many instances of learning? Explain.

◆ From Chapter 2, "Biology and Psychology": Why was Darwin reluctant to publish his theory of evolution? Do you believe that this textbook, and other textbooks, should present the theory of evolution?

◆ From Chapter 5, "Consciousness": Is it possible to study the consciousness of another person?

◆ From Chapter 14, "Psychological Disorders": When does a psychological problem become a "psychological disorder"? Is the border clearly defined?

◆ From Chapter 16, "Social Psychology": Critical thinkers do not overgeneralize. Most people would probably agree that it is good for children to be obedient. But is it always good for children—and for adults—to be obedient? As an individual, how can you determine whether or not it is good for *you* to be obedient? How do we define the limits?

Come into this course as you will. Leave this course as a skeptic. Believe nothing about psychology until you have had an opportunity to see and evaluate the evidence—for yourself.

Making Life Connections

One of the wonderful things about psychology is how the topics in the field relate to your daily life. These connections are pointed out throughout the text and also in a special section at the end of every chapter.

Given that the first chapter is about psychology as a science, it should come as no surprise that the "Life Connections" section focuses on distinguishing between true sciences such as psychology, chemistry, and physics, and false sciences (called *pseudo*sciences) such as clairvoyance and astrology.

Consider two more examples of "Life Connections." Chapter 4 is about "Sensation and Perception"—how people make sense (excuse the pun) of the world in which they dwell. The "Life Connections" section in that chapter is about a fortunate and unfortunate aspect of sensation and perception: pain—how and why we experience pain (it can serve a positive function as well as being a, well, pain), and what we can do to alleviate pain. After reading this section, students may go to the psychology cabinet as well as the medicine cabinet for relief.

Chapter 10 is about the closely related topics of "Motivation and Emotion." The chapter discusses one of our most pressing motives—the hunger drive. The chapter's "Life Connections" section discusses obesity, which for too many people creates a perpetual battle with the hunger drive. It explores reasons why too many people in the United States overeat and offers concrete advice as to what to do about it.

Making Learning Connections

My emphasis on making connections is also reflected in the book's pedagogical package. Psychology is a robust science with a lengthy research tradition; therefore, there is a good deal of subject matter in *Psychology: Concepts and Connections*. The book's pedagogy is designed to help students understand the concepts presented so they *take away* more of that knowledge from the book. *Psychology: Concepts and Connections* fully integrates the PQ4R method in every chapter to help students learn and retain the subject matter.

PQ4R—A Complete Pedagogical Package

PQ4R is the acronym for Preview, Question, Read, Reflect, Review, and Recite, a method that is related to the work of educational psychologist Francis P. Robinson. PQ4R is more than the standard built-in study guide. It goes well beyond a few pages of questions and exercises that are found at the ends of the chapters of many textbooks. It is an integral part of every chapter. It flows throughout every chapter. It begins and ends every chapter, and it accompanies the student page by page.

PQ4R discourages students from believing that they are sponges who will automatically soak up the subject matter in the same way that sponges soak up water. The PQ4R method stimulates students to *actively* engage the subject matter. Students are encouraged to become *proactive* rather than *reactive*.

CHAPTER PREVIEWS Previewing the material helps shape students' expectations. It enables them to create mental templates or "advance organizers" into which they categorize the subject matter. Each chapter of *Psychology: Concepts and Connections* previews the subject matter with a **Truth or Fiction?** section and a chapter **Preview.** The *Truth or Fiction?* items stimulate students to delve into the subject matter by challenging folklore and common sense (which is often common nonsense). Then the *Preview* outlines the material in the chapter, creating mental categories that guide students' reading.

Following is a sampling of challenging *Truth or Fiction?* items from various chapters:

- Your genetic code overlaps 25% with that of a carrot.
- Fear can give you indigestion.
- A brain cell can send out hundreds of messages each second—and manage to catch some rest in between.
- It may be easier for you to recall the name of your first-grade teacher than the name of someone you just met at a party.
- If you study with the stereo on, you would probably do better to take the test with the stereo on.
- Opposites attract.
- A man shot the president of the United States in front of millions of television witnesses, yet was found not guilty by a court of law.
- In the Middle Ages, innocent people were drowned to prove that they were not possessed by the Devil.
- It is abnormal to feel anxious.

QUESTION Devising questions about the subject matter, before reading it in detail, is another feature of the PQ4R method. Writing questions gives students goals: They attend class or read the text *in order to answer the questions.* Questions are placed in all primary sections of the text to help students use the PQ4R method most effectively. They are printed in purple. When students see a question, they can read the following material in order to answer that question. If they wish, they can also write the questions and answers in their notebooks, as recommended by Robinson.

READ Reading is the first R in the PQ4R method. Although students will have to read for themselves, they are not alone. The text helps them by providing:

- **Previews** that help them organize the material,
- **Truth or Fiction?** sections that stimulate students by challenging common knowledge and folklore,
- Presentation of the subject matter in clear, stimulating prose,
- A **running glossary** that defines key terms in the margin of the text, near where the terms appear in the text, and
- Development of **concepts** in an orderly fashion so that new concepts build on previously presented concepts.

I have chosen a personal writing style. It speaks directly to the student and employs humor and personal anecdotes designed to motivate and stimulate students.

REVIEW The second R in PQ4R stands for Review. Regular reviews of the subject matter help students learn. Therefore, Reviews are incorporated into ***Learning Connections*** sections that follow all major sections in the text.

Learning Connections contain three types of items that foster active learning, retention, and critical thinking. The ***Active Review*** is the first type of item. It is called an *Active Review* because it is presented in a fill-in-the-blank format that asks students to *produce,* not simply *recognize,* the answer. The fill-in blanks are numbered and the answers are provided in the Appendix B. For example, the *Active Review* on "The Endocrine System" in the chapter on "Biology and Psychology" reads as follows:

> ***Active Review*** (1) The _____ secretes hormones that regulate the pituitary gland. (2) The pituitary hormone _____ regulates maternal behavior in lower animals and stimulates production of milk in women. (3) The thyroid hormone _____ affects the metabolism. (4) Corticosteroids are secreted by the adrenal _____ and promote development of muscle mass and increase resistance to stress. (5) Epinephrine is secreted by the adrenal _____ and is involved in emotional arousal.

Because reviewing the subject matter is so important and because of the value of visual cues in learning, ***Concept Reviews*** are also found throughout the text. *Concept Reviews* are presented in dynamic layouts that readily communicate the key concepts and the relationships among concepts. Here is a sampling of the *Concept Reviews* found throughout the text:

Chapter 2, "Biology and Psychology": The Endocrine System

Chapter 7, "Memory": The Relationships among the Various Kinds of Memories

Chapter 11, Personality: "Perspectives on Personality"

Chapter 14, "Psychological Disorders": Psychological Disorders

Chapter 15, "Methods of Therapy": Methods of Therapy

REFLECT Students learn more effectively when they *reflect* (the third "R" in PQ4R is for "Reflect") on, or relate to, what they are learning. Psychologists who study learning and memory refer to reflection on subject matter as *elaborative rehearsal.* One way of reflecting on a subject is to *relate* it to things they already know about, whether it be academic material or events in their own lives (Willoughby et al., 1994[1]). Reflecting on, or relating to, the material makes it meaningful and easier to remember (Woloshyn et al., 1994[2]). It also makes it more likely that students will be able to *apply* the information to their own lives (Kintsch, 1994[3]). Through effective reflection, students can embed material firmly in their memory so that rote repetition is unnecessary.

Because reflecting on the material is intertwined with relating to it, the second kind of item in each **Learning Connections** section is termed ***Reflect and Relate.*** Here is the *Reflect and Relate* item from Chapter 2's *Learning Connections* section on the endocrine system:

> ***Reflect and Relate:*** Have you heard that adolescents are "hormonal" or affected by "glands"? If so, which glands would they be?

The following *Reflect and Relate* items are found in Chapter 9, "Intelligence and Creativity":

> ***Reflect and Relate:*** When did you form an impression of how intelligent you are? Has this impression helped you or hurt you? Explain.

> ***Reflect and Relate:*** You have probably taken a number of intelligence tests, most of which were group tests. What were the experiences like? Were you informed as to how well you did on the tests? Do you believe that the test assessed you fairly or arrived at an accurate estimate of your intelligence?

A number of ***mini-experiments*** are part of the *Reflect and Relate* feature and are also found elsewhere throughout the text. Psychologists have found that one important avenue to learning is doing. Mini-experiments offer hands-on opportunities for students to enhance their mastery of the subject matter.

Here is a mini-experiment from the section on persuasion in the chapter on "Social Psychology":

> Keep a log of radio or TV commercials you hear or see for a few days. Which ones grab your attention? Why? Which ones do you believe? Why? Which ones tempted you to consider buying or trying a product? Why?

These mini-experiments as well as other applications-oriented material are catalogued in the index provided on the inside back cover of the book.

RECITE The PQ4R method recommends that students recite the answers to the questions aloud. Reciting answers aloud helps students remember them by means of repetition, by stimulating students to produce concepts and ideas they have learned, and by associating them with spoken words and gestures (Dodson & Schacter, 2001).[4]

Recite sections are found at the end of each chapter. They help students summarize the material, but they are active summaries. For this reason, the sections are termed ***Recite—An Active Summary™.*** They are written in question-and-answer format. To provide a sense of closure, the active summaries repeat the questions found within the chapters and are, again, printed in purple. The answers are concise but include most of the key terms found in the text.

---

[1]Willoughby, T., Wood, E., & Khan, M. (1994). Isolating variables that impact on or detract from the effectiveness of elaboration strategies. *Journal of Educational Research, 86,* 279–289.

[2]Woloshyn, V. E., Paivio, A., & Pressley, M. (1994). Use of elaborative interrogation to help students acquire information consistent with prior knowledge and information inconsistent with prior knowledge. *Journal of Educational Psychology, 86,* 79–89.

[3]Kintsch, W. (1994). Text comprehension, memory, and learning. *American Psychologist, 49,* 294–303.

[4]Dodson, C. S., & Schacter, D. L. (2001). "If I had said it I would have remembered it": Reducing false memories with a distinctiveness heuristic. *Psychonomic Bulletin & Review, 8*(1), 155–161.

The *Recite—An Active Summary™* sections are designed in two columns so that students can cover the second column (the answers) as they read the questions. (You can use the perforated bookmark at the front of this book to cover the second column.) Students can recite the answers as they remember or reconstruct them and then check what they have recited against the answers they had covered. Students should not feel that they are incorrect if they have not exactly produced the answer written in the second column; their individual approach might be slightly different, even more inclusive. The answers provided in the second column are intended to be a guide, to provide a check on students' learning. They are not carved in stone.

Students can also access interactive versions of the Learning Connections (including drag-and-drop fill-in Active Reviews) and the PQ4R method of studying on the companion book Web site. These Web resources are indicated in the book by a Web icon like the one you see to the left. On the companion Web site students will also find quizzing as well as interactive versions of the Concept Reviews and animated versions of key figures called Power Visuals.

Features

Psychology: Concepts and Connections includes a number of features that are intended to motivate students, enhance learning, and foster critical thinking. These include "Controversies in Psychology," emphasis on the evolutionary perspective, emphasis on diversity, "A Closer Look" features, Self-Assessments, and "In Profile" features.

Controversies in Psychology

The field of psychology does not shy away from controversy, and neither does *Psychology: Concepts and Connections*. Psychologists welcome controversy as a vehicle for enhancing knowledge and stimulating critical thinking. "Controversy in Psychology" features are found throughout the text and are set off by a special header like the one to the left.

Some of the controversies exist between psychologists from various schools of psychology. For example, a controversy in the chapter on learning is titled "How Should We Define Learning?" We see at the outset of the chapter that behaviorists and cognitive psychologists define learning in different ways and that their definitions affect their entire view of the subject matter of learning. We continue the theme with another controversy in the same chapter: "Should Children Be Punished for Misbehavior?" We see that punishment has many consequences, some of them unintended, and that the issue is more complex than most readers might expect.

Emphasis on the Evolutionary Perspective

The influence of various schools of psychology has changed over the generations. In Chapter 1 we see that we can trace psychology's roots to the Golden Age of Greece and beyond. In the early part of the 20th century, there were multiple schools and emphases, including behaviorism (brought to prominence by John B. Watson and others), psychoanalysis (based mainly on the theory of Sigmund Freud), and Gestalt psychology (which focused on perception and cognitive processes). In the second half of the 20th century, learning theory broadened to include behaviorism and cognitive views. Cognitive–developmental theory (as propounded by theorists such as Jean Piaget and Lawrence Kohlberg) gained importance. Humanistic–existential psychology developed, to some degree, as an answer to feelings of alienation following the horrors of World War II. Work in cognitive psychology mushroomed in the laboratory and the clinic. The overlaps of biology and psychology exploded in the forms of neuroscience (the study of the nervous system) and endocrinology (the study of hormones).

By now you will not be surprised to learn that few psychologists would agree as to the relative importance of these various perspectives. But perhaps most would agree that there is a current surge of interest in evolutionary psychology. Psychology today recognizes the influence of evolution not only on physical traits, but also on behavior and mental processes. *Psychology: Concepts and Connections* addresses the impact of the evolutionary perspective throughout the text, as catalogued, in part, by the Evolutionary Psychology index provided on the inside back cover of this book. The evolutionary perspective receives the full emphasis it deserves in the current edition, while still providing thorough coverage of other traditional and contemporary perspectives. Some examples of new evolutionary coverage are as follows:

- Chapter 2: Begins with the section "Evolution and Evolutionary Psychology: 'Survivor' Is More Than Just a Game."
- Chapter 4: The evolutionary perspective on how pain and the location of taste buds are adaptive and promote survival.
- Chapter 6: Discussion of the evolutionary value of taste aversions, spontaneous recovery, generalization and discrimination, and cognitive learning.
- Chapter 10: Discussion of evolution and instinct, stimulus motives, aggression, and universal recognition of facial expressions.
- Chapter 12: Discussion of the possible roles of evolution in gender typing, gender differences in mate selection, gender differences in pursuit of casual sexual relationships, and sexual aggression.
- Chapter 13: Discussion of gender differences in response to threats—such as the (predominantly male?) tendency for "fight or flight" as compared with the (predominantly female?) tendency to "tend and befriend."
- Chapter 14: Discussion of how evolutionary forces might have favored the survival of individuals who were predisposed toward acquiring fears of large animals, spiders, snakes, heights, entrapment, sharp objects, and strangers.
- Chapter 16: Discussion of the evolutionary benefits of altruism and self-sacrifice.

Emphasis on Diversity

Although the profession of psychology focuses mainly on the individual's behavior and mental processes, we cannot understand people's behavior and mental processes without reference to their diversity—diversity in terms of ethnic background, gender, socioeconomic status, age, and other factors. When we consider perspectives other than our own, it's important that we understand the role of a culture's beliefs, values, and attitudes in behavior and mental processes. Our knowledge of the science of psychology is enriched by acknowledging and studying why people from diverse cultures behave and think in different ways.

You will find reference to human diversity integrated within the main body of the text. For example, a study in Chapter 2, "Biology and Psychology," discusses the relationships between perception of people of different races and activity in the limbic system of the brain. A section of Chapter 14, "Psychological Disorders," discusses possible reasons for the greater incidence of depression among women than men. When diversity is discussed in the text, you will find a diversity icon that looks like the one to the right. These topics are also cataloged in the Diversity index on the inside back cover of this text.

Some discussions of human diversity are found in "A Closer Look" features, which we describe next.

"A Closer Look"

"A Closer Look" boxes, which are new to this edition, highlight certain topics, allowing students to pursue them in greater depth. These features can be grouped according to certain themes. A number of these boxes, as noted, underscore the indispensability of human diversity within the field of psychology. For example, Chapter 3's "Aging, Gender, and Ethnicity: Different Patterns of Aging" discusses why women tend to outlive men and why people from certain ethnic groups tend to outlive people from other ethnic groups.

Other "A Closer Look" boxes stimulate critical thinking. For example, Chapter 2's "Are You a Human or a Mouse (or a Chimp or a Carrot)? Some Fascinating Facts about Genes" shows that we may be related to other forms of life more closely than we think. Chapter 6's "Contingency Theory" compares and contrasts the behaviorist view of conditioning with a cognitive perspective. Chapter 9's "Just What Do Lie Detectors Detect?" examines what lie detectors actually measure and how these measurements are (or are not) related to lying. Still other "A Closer Look" features focus on topics of high interest such as Chapter 2's "Steroids, Behavior, and Mental Processes," Chapter 9's "Wired—The Awesome Future of Artificial Intelligence," and Chapter 14's "The Insanity Plea."

Some boxes serve other functions. For example, Chapter 3's "How Child Abuse May Set the Stage for Psychological Disorders in Adulthood" follows the methodology of a key research study in detail.

Self-Assessments

Self-Assessment boxes are another aspect of the way in which the text connects with students. One of the more fascinating features consists of the psychological tests and measurements that help psychologists, and individuals, learn about their personality, behavior, and mental processes. The Self-Assessments stimulate student interest by helping them satisfy their curiosity about themselves and enhance the relevance of the text to their lives. Following is a sampling of the Self-Assessments found in the text:

◆ Chapter 1: Dare You Say What You Think? The Social Desirability Scale.
◆ Chapter 5: Sleep Quiz: Are You Getting Your Z's?
◆ Chapter 9: The Remote Associates Test (a self-test of creativity).
◆ Chapter 11: Do You Strive to Be All That You Can Be? (A self-test of whether or not one is a self-actualizer).
◆ Chapter 13: The Locus of Control Scale.
◆ Chapter 14: Do You Speak Your Mind or Do You Wimp Out? The Assertiveness Schedule.

These boxes are cataloged, along with other applied topics, in the Applications index on the inside back cover of this book. Furthermore, students can access interactive versions of these Self-Assessments on their student companion website.

"In Profile" Features

The "In Profile" feature is one of the most popular features in the text. It paints people of importance to the history (and current practice) of psychology as flesh-and-blood human beings. For example, Ivan Pavlov, the Russian biologist who discovered classical conditioning, took one of a pair of his wife's favorite shoes with him on a trip. She feared the shoe had been lost, only to discover that Ivan had taken it as a remembrance of her. Charles Darwin, the originator of the modern theory of evolution, kept his theory a secret for 20 years because he feared it would bring scorn upon his family. He only published it when he learned that another scientist was about to publish a similar theory of evolution. Mary Whiton Calkins refused the doctoral degree that was offered her by Radcliffe, Harvard's "sister" college. She had completed her work at Harvard at a time before Harvard formally accepted women students, and she refused to accept a degree that did not fully recognize her accomplishments. The psychiatrist Aaron Beck assisted in surgical operations as a way of overcoming his own fear of blood. And so it goes. Scientists are people, and when we learn about them as people, we see that they are in many ways like us—driven by emotion as well as intellect.

A Major Revision

Psychology: Concepts and Connections is quite new, a major revision. In addition to containing a new pedagogical system and new features, every chapter has undergone major updating, both in terms of the currency of the research and the coverage of topics. Following is a sampling of what is new in each chapter:

Chapter 1: What Is Psychology?

◆ New coverage of the contributions of Mary Salter Ainsworth, Elizabeth Loftus, Susan Nolen-Hoeksema, Mamie Phipps Clark, Nancy Boyd-Franklin, Tony Strickland, Lillian Comas-Diaz, Martha Bernal, and Richard Suinn to psychology.

◆ New Self-Assessment: "Dare You Say What You Think? The Social-Desirability Scale."

◆ New Life Connections feature: "Critical Thinking, Science, and Pseudoscience."

◆ New Concept Reviews on "Historic Schools of Psychology" and "Research Methods."

Chapter 2: Biology and Psychology:

◆ Chapter reorganized to go from broader issues, such as evolution, to narrower issues, such as the makeup of the neuron and, finally, the endocrine system.

◆ Expanded coverage of evolution and evolutionary psychology, including natural selection, selective breeding, and instinctive behavior.

◆ Expanded coverage of heredity to include molecular genetics, genetics and psychological traits, genotypes and phenotypes, twin studies, and adoptee studies.

◆ New "A Closer Look: Are You a Human or a Mouse (or a Chimp or a Carrot)? Some Fascinating Facts about Genes."

◆ New Self-Assessment: "Symptoms of PMS."

◆ New Concept Reviews on "Key Neurotransmitters and Their Functions" and "The Endocrine System."

Chapter 3: Voyage through the Life Span:

◆ New coverage of the way in which the study of motor development provides a "laboratory" for the nature–nurture controversy.

◆ New coverage of the views of the Russian psychologist Lev Semenovich Vygotsky in the area of cognitive development.

◆ New coverage of the "uninvolved" parenting style.

◆ New Concept Reviews on "Piaget's Stages of Cognitive Development," "Kohlberg's Levels and Stages of Moral Development," and "Erikson's Stages of Psychosocial Development."

Chapter 4: Sensation and Perception:

◆ New coverage of the classic case study of the African pygmy Kenge.

◆ New research is reported on how lizards use the sense of smell to identify the sex of another lizard and how women may use body odor as a way of determining preferences for men.

◆ New coverage of the debate over the number of primary taste qualities in humans.

◆ New mini-experiments that, for example, help students determine the sensitivity of their sense of touch and the use of kinesthesis.

◆ New Concept Reviews on "Cues for Depth Perception" and "The Senses."

Chapter 5: Consciousness:

◆ Expanded coverage of biological and circadian rhythms.

◆ New coverage of Internet addiction.

◆ New cross-cultural feature: "A Closer Look: Dreams across Cultures—From Forests to Rainshowers to 'The Dreaming.' "

◆ New feature on researching the content of dreams *in rats:* "A Closer Look: When Rats Dream, It Seems, It's after a Day at the Mazes."

◆ A new feature on the risks of steroids: "A Closer Look: With No Answers on Risks, Steroid Users Still Say 'Yes.' "

Chapter 6: Learning:

◆ New research on the effects of punishment.

◆ New research on the roles of parents and peers in socialization.

◆ Updated coverage of the effects of violence in the media.

◆ A new Concept Review on "Kinds of Learning."

Chapter 7: Memory:

◆ New research on the associations between priming and neural activity.

◆ New "In Profile" on Elizabeth Loftus.

◆ New feature on how the reconstruction of memory makes life more pleasant: "A Closer Look: Life Is Pleasant—and Memory Helps to Keep It That Way!"

◆ New research on the *déjà vu* experience.

◆ New research on the effects of stress hormones on memory.

Chapter 8: Cognition and Language:

◆ New research on cross-cultural aspects of concepts.

◆ Expanded coverage of apes and language.

◆ New research on the linguistic-relativity hypothesis.

Chapter 9: Intelligence and Creativity:

◆ New section on "Creativity and Intelligence."

◆ Completely revised section on culture-free intelligence tests.

◆ New "Life Connections" feature on "Enhancing Intellectual Functioning."

Chapter 10: Motivation and Emotion:

◆ Completely revised section on aggression, with new information about the evolutionary perspective.

◆ New section "'Is Evvvvrybody Happy?' An Excursion into Positive Psychology" that challenges the commonly held view that happiness is largely unrelated to income.

Chapter 11: Personality:

◆ New Concept Review on "Perspectives on Personality."

◆ New "Life Connections" feature on "Understanding and Enhancing Self-Esteem."

Chapter 12: Gender and Sexuality:

◆ New Concept Review on "Gender-Typing."

◆ Updated information on the evolutionary theory of mate selection, including the desire for sexual variety.

◆ Updated information on genetic factors in sexual orientation.

◆ New information on how people seeking other people present themselves and develop feelings of attraction online ("virtual attraction").

Chapter 13: Stress, Health, and Adjustment:

◆ New recent and classic research on the effects of conflict.

◆ New "A Closer Look: The Atkins 'Diet Revolution': Prescription for Heart Health or Heart Disease?"

◆ New research on how prolonged psychological conditions such as depression or stress may heighten the risk of cancer by depressing the functioning of the immune system.

Chapter 14: Psychological Disorders:

◆ Expanded coverage of the evolutionary theory of phobias and of neurotransmitters and phobias.

◆ Expanded coverage of dissociative disorders and abuse in childhood.

◆ New coverage of the connection between somatoform disorders and rumination.

◆ New coverage of the connection between excessive self-blame and physical illness.

◆ New discussion of borderline personality disorder.

◆ New Concept Review on "Psychological Disorders."

Chapter 15: Methods of Therapy:

◆ New "In Profile" on both Aaron Beck and Albert Ellis.

◆ New research on the effects of cognitive therapy on anxiety, depression, and personality disorders.

◆ New research on the effects of selective serotonin reuptake inhibitors (SSRIs) on disorders other than depression.

◆ New Concept Review on "Methods of Therapy."

Chapter 16: Social Psychology:

◆ New mini-experiments, including one on attribution theory (observing an argument and applying attribution theory to interpret the outcome) and one on body language.

◆ New research on gender differences in protecting the environment.

♦ New research on the effects of crowding in submarines.

♦ New research on the effects of crowding on people in collectivist and individualist cultures.

Appendix A: Statistics:

♦ New "Life Connections" feature: "Thinking Critically about 'Junk Statistics.' "

Ancillaries

Psychology: Concepts and Connections is accompanied by a wide array of supplements prepared for both the instructor and student. Many are available free to professors or students. Others can be packaged with this text at a discount. For more information on any of the listed resources, please call the Thomson Learning™ Academic Resource Center at 800-423-0563.

For the Instructor

Instructor's Resource Manual Written by Cameron John of Utah Valley State College, this manual contains chapter-specific lecture outlines; annotated lists of suggested readings, films, and Web sites; and student learning objectives. The manual has suggested student activities and projects for each chapter. These activities include ideas for in and out of class, for large lecture classes and small discussion sections. The manual's *Resource Integration Guide* will help you coordinate the many teaching and learning supplements available for this text. In addition, the *Instructor's Resource Manual* includes general teaching strategies, references, and other helpful materials, such as handout masters.

Test Bank Written by Anne M. Cooper of St. Petersburg College, the test bank consists of 2,000 multiple-choice questions, over 300 fill-in questions, over 150 true-false questions, and essay questions for each chapter, all with page references. Each multiple-choice item is labeled with question type (factual, application or conceptual) and level of difficulty. The Test Bank also includes a midterm and final exam.

ExamView® Computerized Testing Create, deliver, and customize printed and online tests and study guides in minutes with this easy-to-use assessment and tutorial system. ExamView includes a Quick Test Wizard and an Online Test Wizard to guide instructors step by step through the process of creating tests. The test appears on screen exactly as it will print or display online. Using ExamView's complete word processing capabilities, instructors can enter an unlimited number of new questions or edit questions included with ExamView.

Alternate ExamView, Computerized Testing This additional ExamView product offers over 1,400 more test items written by Dan Bellack of Trident Technical College.

Instructor's Edition Each *Instructor's Edition* of *Psychology: Concepts and Connections* includes a "Resource Integration Guide" to help you seamlessly integrate all of the online, CD-ROM, and print resources offered with this text.

Wadsworth Media Guide for Introductory Psychology This booklet lists hundreds of video and feature film recommendations for all major topics for the Introductory Psychology course. Each entry has a clear description of the content and length of the video and select feature film entries also provide discussion questions and specific scene analyses.

Classroom Presentation Tools for the Instructor

Transparency Acetates More than 100 acetates feature full-color figures from the text to enhance lecture presentations.

Multimedia Manager: A Microsoft® PowerPoint® Link Tool. With the one-stop digital library and presentation tool, instructors can assemble, edit, and present custom lectures with ease. The Multimedia Manager contains a selection of digital media from Wadsworth's latest titles in introductory psychology, including figures and tables. Also included are animations, CNN video clips, and preassembled Microsoft PowerPoint lecture slides based on each specific text. Instructors can use the material or add their own material for a truly customized lecture presentation.

Instructor's Resource CD This one-stop instructor houses electronic files for the Instructor's Resource Manual Notebook, ExamView and Alternate ExamView, as well as the Multimedia Manager.

***CNN Today* Videos for Introductory Psychology** Illustrate the relevance of psychology to everyday life with this exclusive series of videos for the introductory psychology course. Jointly created by Wadsworth and CNN, each video consists of approximately 45 minutes of footage originally broadcast on CNN and specifically selected to illustrate important introductory psychology concepts. The videos are divided into short two- to seven-minute segments, perfect for use as lecture launchers or as illustrations of key concepts. Special adoption conditions apply.

> *CNN Today: Introductory Psychology, Volume I* (ISBN: 0-534-36634-1)
> *CNN Today: Introductory Psychology, Volume II* (ISBN: 0-534-50420-5)
> *CNN Today: Introductory Psychology, Volume III* (ISBN: 0-534-50749-2)
> *CNN Today: Introductory Psychology, Volume IV* (ISBN: 0-534-50751-4)

Psychology Digital Video Library CD-ROM This CD-ROM provides access to over 100 video clips that feature a broad range of materials, such as classic footage of prominent psychologists, demonstrations and simulations of important experiments, and selections from the *CNN Today* videos.

Wadsworth Psychology Film and Video Library This large selection of thought-provoking films is available to instructors based on adoption size. Contact your Thomson/Wadsworth representative or Wadsworth Academic Resource Center for a more detailed video list, more information on the video policy, and more information on ordering products from the Wadsworth Film and Video Library.

***Psychology: Careers for the Twenty-First Century* Video** Wadsworth has an exclusive agreement with the American Psychological Association to offer this dynamic 13-minute video free to adopters of *Psychology: Concepts and Connections*. The video, which was produced by the APA, gives students an overview of the emerging growth opportunities in the field of psychology and advice about how to choose a career path.

For the Student

Study Guide Written by Lisa Valentino of Seminole County Community College, the *Study Guide* is designed to promote active learning through a guided review of the important principles and concepts in the text. The *Study Guide* is closely aligned with the PQ4R learning model found in the text. The materials for each chapter include a chapter summary and a comprehensive multiple-choice self-test, as well as critical thinking, Internet, and InfoTrac® College Edition exercises that challenge students to think about and to apply what they have learned.

***Connections* Student Notebook** This collection of lecture outlines allows the student to follow along with the instructor and take notes. It also includes selected images from the text for note taking.

Psyk.Trek™ 2.0: A Multimedia Introduction to Psychology *Psyk.Trek's* visual learning environment delivers course content in a brand-new way that reinforces key concepts. This CD-ROM includes 62 interactive learning modules that present the core content of psychology with real-time video, animated graphics, and hundreds of photos and illustrations. Students using *Psyk.Trek* will take part in experiments using simulations and then quiz themselves on the content. *Psyk.Trek* also includes interactive concept checks and a multimedia glossary with an audio pronunciation guide.

PsychNow! Interactive Experiences in Psychology 2.0. *PsychNow!* provides a dynamic multimedia experience that goes beyond the boundaries of the classroom. Graphics and animations, interesting video clips, interactive exercises, and Web links bring psychology to life. This CD-ROM also allows students to conduct 15 different interactive research experiments in areas such as neurocognition, perception, and memory.

Internet-Based Supplements Resources.

InfoTrac® College Edition With InfoTrac College Edition, instructors can stimulate discussion and supplement lectures with the latest developments in introductory psychology. Available as a free option with newly purchased texts, InfoTrac College Edition gives instructors and students four months of free access to an extensive database of reliable, full-length articles (not just abstracts) from hundred of top academic journals and popular periodicals. In-text exercises suggest search terms to make the most of this resource.

Wadsworth Psychology Resource Center http://psychology.wadsworth.com At this Web site, students and instructors have access to a rich array of teaching and learning resources you won't find anywhere else, including some classic simulations and demonstrations, online experiments and self-assessments for active student participation, links to the Career center, Wadsworth Online Lecture series, Author Insights, Vmentor, and more!

Web site for *Psychology: Concepts and Connections.* The *Connections* companion book site features interactive activities that support the main text's active learning system, PQ4R (Preview, Question, Read, Reflect, Review, Recite):

- *Review boxes online:* Students can answer the review questions from their text online and get instant feedback.
- *Reflect and Relate questions online:* The thought-provoking "Reflect" questions that encourage students to apply the concepts they're learning to their own lives are linked to the interactive Bulletin Board. This allows for class and individual discussion.
- *Recite feature online:* Students can check their understanding of each chapter through the interactive version of the chapter summary, presented through flash cards.

◆ *Interactive quizzing:* Chapter-by-chapter interactive quizzes include multiple-choice, true/false, fill-in-the-blank, matching, essay, and critical thinking questions with a direct-to-professor email function.

◆ *Power visuals:* Figures of key concepts from the text are presented in an interactive, drag-and-drop mode for study and drill of key concepts and terms.

◆ *Web links:* This area provides links to other psychology-related sites on the Internet.

Web Tutor™ Advantage on WebCT and Blackboard This Web-based software for students and instructors takes a course beyond the classroom to an anywhere, anytime environment. Students gain access to a full array of study tools, including chapter outlines, chapter-specific quizzing material, interactive games, and videos. With WebTutor Advantage, instructors can provide virtual office hours, post syllabi, track student progress with the quizzing material, and even customize content to meet their needs. Instructors can also use the communication tools to set up threaded discussions and conduct "real-time" chats. "Out of the box" or customized, WebTutor Advantage provides a powerful tool for instructors and students alike. For details, visit http://webtutor.thomsonlearning.com.

MyCourse 2.1 This free online course builder can greatly enhance course administration. With *MyCourse 2.1,* you can easily create a custom course Web site that allows you to assign, track, and report on student progress, load your syllabus, and more. Contact your Thomson/Wadsworth sales representative for details or visit http://mycourse.thomsonlearning.com for more information.

Supplementary Books

There are several other supplementary books that offer help to students.

Challenging Your Preconceptions: Thinking Critically about Psychology, Second Edition This paperbound book (ISBN: 0-534-26739-4), written by Randolph Smith, helps students strengthen their critical thinking skills. Psychological issues such as hypnosis and repressed memory, statistical seduction, the validity of pop psychology, and other topics arc used to illustrate the principles of critical thinking.

Writing Papers in Psychology: A Student Guide The fifth edition of *Writing Papers in Psychology* (ISBN: 0-534-52975-5), by Ralph L. Rosnow and Mimi Rosnow, is a valuable "how-to" manual for writing term papers and research reports. This new edition has been updated to reflect the latest APA guidelines. The book covers each task with examples, hints, and two complete writing samples. Citation ethics, how to locate information, and new research technologies are also covered.

College Survival Guide: Hints and References to Aid College Students This fourth edition of Bruce Rowe's *College Survival Guide* (ISBN: 0-534-35569-2) is designed to help students succeed. Rowe provides valuable tips on how to finance an education, how to manage time, how to study for and take exams, and more. Other sections focus on maintaining concentration, credit by examination, use of the credit/no credit option, cooperative education programs, and the importance of a liberal arts education.

Cross-Cultural Perspectives in Psychology How well do the concepts of psychology apply to various cultures? What can we learn about human behavior from cultures different from our own? These questions lie behind a collection of original articles written by William F. Price and Rich Crapo. The fourth edition of *Cross-Cultural Perspectives in Psychology* (ISBN: 0-534-54653-6) contains articles on North American ethnic groups as well as cultures from around the world.

Culture and Psychology: People around the World, second edition David Matsumoto's unique book (ISBN: 0-534-35436-X) discusses similarities and differences in research findings in the United States and other cultures. By doing so, it helps students see psychology and their own behavior from a broader, more culturally aware perspective.

Psychology Resources on the World Wide Web This handy guide is designed to serve as a directory for students who may be conducting research via the Internet. The author, Edward P. Kardas, presents an up-to-date, comprehensive book that is organized topically (similar to that of a typical introductory psychology text) and includes a chapter on how to perform research on the Web (ISBN: 0-534-35941-8).

Psychology: Careers for the Twenty-First Century This 30-page pamphlet describes the field of psychology, as well as how to prepare for a career in psychology. This is available through an agreement with the American Psychological Association and includes a discussion of career options and resources.

Acknowledgments

Writers of novels and poems may secrete themselves in their studies and complete their work in solitude. Not so the textbook author. Writing a textbook is a partnership—partnership between the author and peers who review the manuscript at every step of the way to make sure that it is accurate and covers the topics it should be covering. My partners for the current edition of *Psychology: Concepts and Connections* included:

R. Peter Johnson, Mid-Plains Community College
H. Mitzi Doane, University of Minnesota, Duluth
Cameron John, Utah Valley State College
Kathy Sexton-Radek, Elmhurst College
Fred Whitford, University of Montana, Bozeman
Richard Townsend, Miami-Dade Community College
Kerrie Baker, Cedar Crest College
J. Davis Mannino, Santa Rosa City College
Christine Panyard, University of Detroit, Mercy
Michael McBride, Gonzaga University
Dan Bellack, Trident Technical College
David Yells, Utah Valley State College
Larry Ludewig, Kilgore College
Jim Hail, McLennan Community College
Sal Macias, University of South Carolina, Sumter
Trisha Folds-Bennett, College of Charleston
Karl Andreasson, Spokane Falls Community College
Valerie Keffala, Kirkwood Community College
Nancy Fuentes, Austin Community College
Lisa Valentino, Seminole Community College
Jennifer Gibson, Tarleton State University
Victor Duarte, North Idaho College
Julie Stokes, Cal State Fullerton
Stephen Buggie, University of New Mexico–Gallup

Jack Hartnett, Virginia Commonwealth University
N.L. Ashton, Stockton College of New Jersey
Rick Froman, John Brown University
Vince Lembo, Tarrant County College
Penny Wolfe, Elmhurst College

In addition to the reviewers for the current edition, I would like to extend my continued gratitude to the reviewers of previous editions who have helped shaped my book over the years:

Holiday E. Adair, California University of Pennsylvania; Ambrose Akinkunle, Olive Harvey College; Marilyn Andrews, Hartnell College; Mark H. Ashcraft, Cleveland State University; Lynn Haller Augsbach, Morehead State University; Gladys J. Baez-Dickreiter, St. Phillip's College; Anne Barich, Lewis University; Patricia Barker, Schenectady County Community College; Barbara Basden, California State University; Alan Bates, Snead State Community College; Melita Bauman, Glendale Community College; James Beaird, Western Oregon State University; Connie Beddingfield, Jefferson State Community College; William Bell, Olivet Nazarene University; Thomas L. Bennett, Colorado State University; John Benson, Texarkana College; Otto Berliner, SUNY–Alfred; Tom Billimek, San Antonio College; Joyce Bishop, Golden West College; Richard A. Block, Montana State University; C. Robert Boresen, Wichita State University; Theodore N. Bosack, Providence College; Charles M. Bourassa, University of Alberta; Betty Bowers, North Central Technical Institute; Peter J. Brady, Clark Technical College; Jack Brennecke, Mount San Antonio College; Thomas Brothen, University of Minnesota; Evelyn Brown, Austin Community College; Conald Buckley, Cumberland Community College; Carol Burk-Braxton, Austin Community College; Robert Cameron, Fairmont State College; Lucy B. Champion, Southern Union State Community College; Garvin Chastain, Boise State University; Stephen Chew, Samford University; John Childers, East Carolina University; John Clark, William Rainey Harper College; Samuel L. Clay II, Morehead State University; Michael Connor, Long Beach Community College; Lauren Coodley, Napa Valley College; Miki A. Cook, Gadsden State Community College; Terry Daniel, University of Arizona; Richard Day, Manchester Community College; Donald L. Daoust, Southern Oregon State College; Carl L. Denti, Dutchess County Community College; Robert DeStefano, Rockland Community College; Mary Dezindolet, Cameron University; Steve Donohue, Grand Canyon University; Carol Doolin, Henderson County Junior College; Gene Douglas, Cameron University; Wendy L. Dunn, Coe College; Eve Efird, Johnston Community College; Jeanette Engles, Southwestern Oklahoma State University; Warren Fass, University of Pittsburgh at Bradford; Lawrence A. Fehr, Widener University; Jose Feito, St. Mary's College, California; Gloria Foley, Austin Community College; John Foust, Parkland College; Bob Freudenthal, Moraine Valley Community College; Mary Rita Freudenthal, Moraine Valley Community College; Morton P. Friedman, University of California at Los Angeles; William Rick Fry, Youngstown State University; Michael Garza, Brookhaven College; David A. Gersh, Houston Community College; Marian Gibney, Phoenix College; Colleen Gift, Highland Community College; Ron Gilkerson, Waubonsee Community College; Michael Goodstein, Moraine Valley Community College; Bernard Gorman, Nassau County Community College; Richard Gottwald, Indiana University at South Bend; Peter Gram, Pensacola Junior College; Nancy Grayson, McLennan Community College; Vincent J. Greco, Weschester Community College; Beverly Greene, St. John's University; John C. Greenwood, Lewis University; Gloria Griffith, Tennessee Technological University; Richard Griggs, University of Florida; Sandra L. Groeltz, DeVry Institute of Technology at Chicago; Lydia Guerra, Olive Harvey College; Arthur Gutman,

Florida Institute of Technology; Jim Hail, McLennan Community College; Algea O. Harrison, Oakland University; Myra Harville, Holmes Community College; Robert W. Hayes, Boston University; Alylene Hegar, Eastfield College; Lisa R. Hempel, Columbia Basin College; George Herrick, SUNY–Alfred; Sidney Hochman, Nassau Community College; Morton Hoffman, Metropolitan State College; Betsy Howton, Western Kentucky University; John H. Hummel, University of Houston; Sam L. Hutchinson, Radford University; Gayle Y. Iwamasa, Oklahoma State University; Jarvel Jackson, McClellan Community College; Ed James, Purdue University–Calumet; Rafael Art Javier, St. John's University; Chwan-Shyang Jih, Lewis University; Robert L. Johnson, Umpqua Community College; Timothy Johnston, University of North Carolina at Greensboro; Eve Jones, Los Angeles City College; Karen Jones, University of the Ozarks; Kenneth Kallio, SUNY–Genesco; Charles Karis, Northwestern University; Ed Kearney, Lewis University; Kevin Keating, Broward Community College; Mary Louise Keen, University of California at Irvine; Judith Keith, Tarrant County Junior College; Richard Kellogg, SUNY–Alfred; Shirin Khosropour, Austin Community College; Dan Kimble, University of Oregon; Gary King, Rose State College; Richard A. King, University of North Carolina at Chapel Hill; Norman Kinney, Southeast Missouri State University; Dwight Kirkpatrick, Purdue University–Calumet; Jane Klingberg, Moraine Valley Community College; Mike Knight, Central State University; Wolanyo Kpo, Chicago State University; Velton Lacefield, Prairie State College; Alan Lanning, College of DuPage; Daniel Lapsley, University of Notre Dame; Mary Ann Larson, Fullerton College and Rancho Santiago College; Marliss Lauer, Moraine Part Technical College; John D. Lawry, Marymount College; Patsy Lawson, Volunteer State Community College; Charles A. Levin, Baldwin-Wallace College; Charles Levinthal, Hofstra University; Marc Levy, Southern Oregon University; William Levy, Manchester Community College; Erica Lilleleht, Seattle University; Robert G. Lowder, Bradley University; Robert MacAleese, Spring Hill College; Ricardo A. Machon, Loyola Marymount University; Daniel Madsen, University of Minnesota–Duluth; Adam Maher, Austin Community College; John Malone, University of North Carolina at Greensboro; George Martin, Mount San Antonio College; A. W. Massey, Eastfield College; S. R. Mathews, Converse College; Elaine Mawhinney, Horry-Georgetown Technical College; Michael M. Mayall, Tarrant County Junior College; James McCaleb, South Surburban College; Richard McCaberty, Lorain College; Barbara McFarland, Lehigh University; Joseph McNair, Miami–Dade Community College; Juan Mercado, McLennan Community College; Leroy Metze, Western Kentucky University; Joseph Miele, East Stroudsberg University; Richard E. Miller, Navarro College; Thomas Minor, SUNY–Stony Brook; Thomas Moeschl, Broward Community College; Christopher F. Monte, Manhattanville College; Luis Montesinos, Montclair State University; Joel Morgovsky, Brookdale Community College; Walena C. Morse, Westchester University; Dave Murphy, Waubonsee Community College; Basil Najjar, College of DuPage; Robbye Nesmith, Navarro College; Jeffrey S. Nevid, St. John's University; John W. Nichols, Tulsa Junior College; Nora Noel, University of North Carolina at Wilmington; Joseph Paladino, Indiana State University at Evansville; Ursula Palmer, Eastfield College; Carol Pandey, L. A. Pierce College; Fred Patrizi, East Central University; John Pennachio, Adirondack Community College; Terry Pettijohn, Ohio State University–Marion; Gregory Pezzetti, Rancho Santiago College; Walter Pieper, Georgia State University; Carole Pierce, Austin Community College; Shane Pitts, Birmingham Southern College; Terrie Potts, Navarro College; Donis Price, Mesa Community College; Rosemary Price, Rancho Santiago College; Gerald Pudelko, Olympic College; Richard A. Rare, University of Maine; Rose Ray, Purdue University–Calumet; Bernard Rechlicz, Olive Harvey College; Victoria Reid, Olive Harvey College; Beth Rienzi, California State University, Bakersfield; Vicki Ritts, St. Louis Community College; Ross Robak, Pace University; Valda Robinson, Hillsborough Community College; James Roll, William Rainey Harper College; Laurie Rotando, Westchester Community College; George

S. Rotter, Montclair State University; Patrick J. Ryan, Tompkins-Cortland Community College; Catherine Sanderson, Amherst College; H. R. Schiffman, Rutgers University; Sharon Sexton, McLennan Community College; Joseph Shaver, Fairmont State College; Larry J. Siegel, University of Lowell; Paul Silverstein, L. A. Pierce College; Pamela Simon, Baker College; Patricia J. Slocum, College of DuPage; Ron Smith, Navarro College; Susan Spooner, McLennan Community College; William Sproull, Texas Christian University South; Frank Stanicek, South Surburban College; Jacob Steinberg, Fairleigh Dickinson University; Joanne Stephenson, Union University; Doris Stevens, McLennan Community College; Valerie Stratton, Pennsylvania State University–Altoona; Elizabeth Street, Central Washington University; Adolph Streng, Eastfield College; Hugh Stroube, Navarro College; Ann Swint, North Harris County College; Sherrill Tabing, Los Angeles Harbor College; Robert S. Tacker, East Carolina University; Francis Terrell, North Texas State University; Harry A. Tiemann, Mesa State College; Larry M. Till, Fullerton College and Cerritos College; Linda Truesdale, Midland Technical College; Lisa Valentino, Seminole Community College; Mary Vandendrope, Lewis University; Frank J. Vattano, Colorado State University; Benjamin Wallace, Cleveland State University; Douglas Wallen, Mankato State University; Cathrine Wambach, University of Minnesota; Glen Weaver, Calvin College; Charles Weichert, San Antonio College; Paul Wellman, Texas A & M University; Richard Whinery, Ohio University–Chillicothe; Mary P. Whitney, St. Joseph College; Kenneth Wildman, Ohio Northern University; Robert Williams, William Jewel College; Rob Winningham, McLennan Community College; Keith A. Wollen, Washington State University; and Walter Zimmerman, New Hampshire College.

Finally, I would like to thank the fine group of publishing professionals at Wadsworth/Thomson Learning. They handled editorial duties and details too numerous to mention which somehow took a printed manuscript and transformed it into the colorful book you are now holding in your hands.

They include new friends and old friends, a glorious combination: Susan Badger, President, whom I knew in her days in the Northeast, and who moved to the West Coast to take charge of Wadsworth; Sean Wakely, Senior Vice President, who one time in Boston refused to let me leave a room until I signed a contract (he won, but he also had two other editors with him); Eve Howard, Editor in Chief, my oldest (but young!) friend in publishing, whom I met by chance in El Paso, Texas, and then with whom I worked in New York, Fort Worth, and now, California; Michele Sordi, Editor, another transplant from the Northeast to California, who has elicited my respect, admiration, and friendship in a relatively brief period; Kate Barnes, Developmental Editor, who has the misfortune of living on the Monterey peninsula, and who has organized the unorganizable and pushed me into some of the best work of my career; Paula Berman, Production Editor, whose voice I most enjoy hearing on the telephone (Sorry, everyone else); Dan Moneypenny, Assistant Editor, who has overseen all aspects of the supplements package; Michelle Vardeman, Technology Project Manager, who has organized the creation of the CD-ROM and Web site for my book; and Chris Caldeira, Marketing Manager, who exudes enough zest to fill a medium-sized continent.

—Spence Rathus

Psychology

Truth or Fiction?

T F More than 2,000 years ago, Aristotle wrote a book on psychology, with contents similar to the book you are now holding.

T F The ancient Greek philosopher Socrates suggested a research method that is still used in psychology.

T F As psychologist Wilhelm Wundt lay on his deathbed, his main concern was to analyze the experience of dying.

T F Men receive the majority of doctoral degrees in psychology.

T F Even though she had worked to complete all the degree requirements, the first female president of the American Psychological Association turned down the doctoral degree that was offered to her.

T F You could survey millions of voters and still not accurately predict the outcome of a presidential election.

T F In many experiments, neither the subjects nor the researchers know who is receiving the real treatment and who is not.

T F A psychologist could write a believable personality report about you without interviewing you, testing you, or even knowing who you are.

 Go to **http://psychology.wadsworth.com/ rathus_pcc9e** to answer and score this Truth or Fiction quiz.

What Is Psychology?

Preview

■ Human Courage and Self-Sacrifice What do we find when we look in the mirror? People may have their negative qualities, including aggressiveness, but hundreds of firefighters and police officers sacrificed themselves to save others by racing into the blazing towers of the World Trade Center on September 11, 2001. Why do people care for others? What motivates people to care for their children and protect their families and the community at large?

"What a piece of work," wrote William Shakespeare. He was writing about you: "How noble in reason! How infinite in faculty! In form and moving how express and admirable! In action how like an angel! In apprehension how like a god! The beauty of the world! The paragon of animals!"

You probably had no trouble recognizing yourself in this portrait—"noble in reason," "admirable," unlimited in understanding, head and shoulders above other animals. Consider some of the noble and admirable features of human behavior:

◆ The human abilities to think and solve problems have allowed us to build cathedrals and computers and to scan the interior of the body without surgery. Yet just what is "thinking"? How do we solve problems?

◆ The human ability to create led to the writing of great works of literature and the composition of music from opera to rap. Yet what exactly is creativity?

◆ Human generosity and charity have encouraged us to care for older people, people who are ill, and people who are less advantaged than we are—even to sacrifice ourselves for those we love. Why do we care for others? What motivates us to care for our children and protect our families?

Some human behavior is not as noble or admirable as these examples suggest. In fact, human behavior varies greatly and some of it is downright puzzling. Consider some more examples:

◆ Although people can be generous, most adults on crowded city streets will not stop to help a person lying on the sidewalk. Why?

◆ Most people who overeat or smoke cigarettes know they are jeopardizing their health. Yet they continue their bad habits. Why?

◆ A person claims to have raped, killed, or mutilated a victim because of insanity. The person was overcome by an irresistible impulse, or by "another personality" that took control. What is insanity? What is an irresistible impulse?

Human behavior has always fascinated people. Sometimes we are even surprised at ourselves. We have thoughts or impulses that seem to be out of character, or we cannot recall something that seems to be hovering on the "tip of the tongue." Psychologists, like other people, are also intrigued by the mysteries of behavior, but for them the scientific study of behavior is their life's work. **Question: What is psychology?**

Psychology as a Science

Psychology is the scientific study of behavior and mental processes. Topics of interest to psychologists include the nervous system, sensation and perception, learning and memory, intelligence, language, thought, growth and development, personality, stress and health, psychological disorders, ways of treating those disorders, sexual behavior, and the behavior of people in social settings such as groups and organizations.

Sciences have certain goals. **Question: What are the goals of psychology?** Psychology, like other sciences, seeks to describe, explain, predict, and control the events it studies. Psychology thus seeks to describe, explain, predict, and control behavior and mental processes.

What do psychologists mean by "controlling" behavior and mental processes?

"Controlling" behavior and mental processes doesn't mean to psychologists what it may sound like to most people. Some erroneously think that psychologists seek ways to make people do their bidding, like puppets on strings. This is

Psychology The science that studies behavior and mental processes.

not so. Psychologists are committed to a belief in the dignity of human beings, and human dignity demands that people be free to make their own decisions and choose their own behavior. Psychologists are learning more about the influences on human behavior all the time, but they use this knowledge only on request and in order to help people clarify and meet their own goals.

When possible, descriptive terms and concepts are interwoven into **theories.** Theories are formulations of apparent relationships among observed events. They allow us to derive explanations and predictions. Many psychological theories combine statements about behavior (such as eating or aggression), mental processes (such as attitudes and mental images), and biological processes. For instance, many of our responses to drugs such as alcohol and marijuana can be measured as overt behavior, and they are presumed to reflect the actions of these drugs and of our (mental) expectations about their effects.

A satisfactory psychological theory allows us to predict behavior. For instance, a theory of hunger should allow us to predict when people will or will not eat. If our observations cannot be adequately explained by, or predicted from, a given theory, we should consider revising or replacing it.

The remainder of this chapter presents an overview of psychology as a science. You will see that psychologists have diverse interests and fields of specialization. We discuss the history of psychology and the major perspectives from which today's psychologists view behavior. Finally, we consider the research methods psychologists use to study behavior and mental processes.

Your Turn: Now that we have introduced psychology as a science, enhance your mastery of the material with the nearby "Learning Connections." Review the material by filling in the blanks, reflect on the material by relating it to other things you know, and think critically about it.

Learning Connections | PSYCHOLOGY AS A SCIENCE

ACTIVE REVIEW (1) Psychology is defined as the study of _____ and mental processes. (2) Psychology seeks to describe, explain, _____, and control behavior. (3) Behavior is explained through psychological _____, which are sets of statements that involve assumptions about behavior.

REFLECT AND RELATE How would you have defined psychology before you began this course?

CRITICAL THINKING What is the difference between the way that scientists view the world and laypeople view the world?

Go to **http://psychology.wadsworth.com/ rathus_pcc9e** for an interactive version of this Learning Connections unit.

What Psychologists Do: Something for Everyone?

Psychologists share a keen interest in behavior; but, in other ways, they may differ markedly. **Question: Just what do psychologists do?** Psychologists engage in research, practice, and teaching. Some researchers engage primarily in basic, or pure, research. **Pure research** has no immediate application to personal or social problems and therefore has been characterized as research for its own sake. Others engage in **applied research,** which is designed to find solutions to specific personal or social problems. Although pure research is sparked by curiosity and the desire to know and understand, today's pure research frequently enhances tomorrow's way of life. Pure research on learning and motivation in pigeons, rats, and monkeys done early in the 20th century has found applications in today's school systems. It has shown, for example, that learning often takes time and repetition and profits form "booster shots" (that is, repetition even after the learning goal has been reached). Pure research into the workings of the nervous system has enhanced knowledge of disorders such as epilepsy, Parkinson's disease, and Alzheimer's disease.

Theory A formulation of relationships underlying observed events.

Pure research Research conducted without concern for immediate applications.

Applied research Research conducted in an effort to find solutions to particular problems.

Many psychologists do not conduct research. Instead, they *practice* psychology by applying psychological knowledge to help individuals change their behavior so that they can meet their own goals more effectively. Still other psychologists engage primarily in teaching. They share psychological knowledge in classrooms, seminars, and workshops. Some psychologists engage in all three: research, practice, and teaching.

Fields of Psychology: From the Clinic to the Colosseum

Psychologists are found in a number of different specialties. Although some psychologists wear more than one hat, most of them carry out their functions in the following fields.

Clinical psychologists help people with psychological disorders adjust to the demands of life. People's problems may range from anxiety and depression to sexual dysfunctions to loss of goals. Clinical psychologists evaluate these problems through interviews and psychological tests. They help their clients resolve their problems and change self-defeating behavior. Clinical psychologists are the largest subgroup of psychologists (Kyle & Williams, 2000; see Figure 1.1). These psychologists differ from psychiatrists in that *psychiatrists* are *medical* doctors who specialize in the study and treatment of psychological disorders.

Counseling psychologists, like clinical psychologists, use interviews and tests to define their clients' problems. Their clients typically have adjustment problems but not serious psychological disorders. For example, clients may have trouble making academic or vocational decisions or making friends in college. They may experience marital or family conflicts, have physical disabilities, or have adjustment problems such as those encountered by people who lose their jobs because of mergers or downsizing. Counseling psychologists help clients clarify their goals and overcome obstacles and are often employed in college and university counseling and testing centers. As suggested by Figure 1.1, more than half of doctoral students in psychology are enrolled in clinical or counseling psychology programs.

School psychologists are employed by school systems to identify and assist students who have problems that interfere with learning. Such problems range from social and family problems to emotional disturbances and learning disorders. They help schools make decisions about the placement of students in special classes.

Educational psychologists, like school psychologists, attempt to facilitate learning. But they usually focus on course planning and instructional methods for a school system rather than on individual children. Educational psychologists research theoretical issues related to learning, measurement, and child development. For example, they study how learning is affected by psychological factors such as motivation and intelligence, sociocultural factors such as poverty and acculturation, and teacher behavior. Some educational psychologists prepare standardized tests such as the Scholastic Assessment Tests (SATs).

Developmental psychologists study the changes—physical, cognitive, social, and personality—that occur throughout the life span. They attempt to sort

FIGURE 1.1

Students Enrolled in Doctoral Programs in Fields of Psychology

Nearly half (47%) of the doctoral students who enrolled in doctoral programs in psychology in 1998–1999 enrolled in clinical programs. (Current enrollments were used because they are the best indicator of the current directions of psychology.) The next most popular field was counseling psychology. The figure combines students enrolled in public and private institutions.

Source: Kyle, T. M., & Williams, S. (2000, May). Results of the 1998–1999 APA survey of graduate departments of psychology, Tables 13A & 13B. APA Research Office. Washington, D.C.: American Psychological Association.

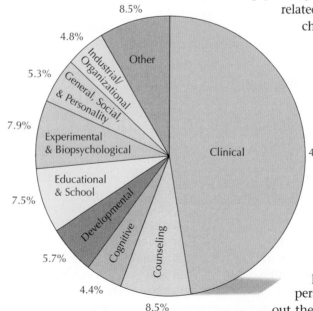

8.5% Other
4.8% Industrial/Organizational
5.3% General, Social, & Personality
7.9% Experimental & Biopsychological
7.5% Educational & School
5.7% Developmental
4.4% Cognitive
8.5% Counseling
47.4% Clinical

out the influences of heredity and the environment on development. Developmental psychologists conduct research on issues such as the effects of maternal use of drugs on an embryo, the outcomes of various patterns of child rearing, children's concepts of space and time, conflicts during adolescence, and problems of adjustment among older people.

Personality psychologists focus on goals such as identifying and measuring human traits; determining influences on human thought processes, feelings, and behavior; and explaining psychological disorders. They are particularly concerned with issues such as anxiety, aggression, and gender roles.

Social psychologists are primarily concerned with the nature and causes of individuals' thoughts, feelings, and behavior in social situations. Whereas personality psychologists tend to look within the person for explanations of behavior, social psychologists tend to focus on external or social influences.

Environmental psychologists study the ways in which people and the environment—the natural environment and the human-made environment—influence one another. For example, we know that extremes of temperature and loud noises interfere with learning in school. Some generations ago, people seemed to be at the mercy of the environment, but in recent years we have gained the capacity to do significant harm to the environment. As a result, environmental psychologists study ways to encourage people to recycle and to preserve bastions of wilderness. We have learned that initial resistance to recycling, for example, usually gives way to cooperation as people come to accept it as the norm.

© Jeff Greenberg/PhotoEdit

■ **Developmental Psychology** Developmental psychologists study the changes that occur throughout the life span. They attempt to sort out the influences of heredity and the environment. Their concerns range from the effects of day care on infants to the adjustment issues of older people.

Psychologists in all specialties may conduct experiments. However, those called *experimental psychologists* specialize in basic processes such as the nervous system, sensation and perception, learning and memory, thought, motivation, and emotion. For example, experimental psychologists have studied what areas of the brain are involved in processing math problems or listening to music. They have used animals such as pigeons and rats to study processes of learning in the laboratory.

Industrial psychology and organizational psychology are closely related fields. *Industrial psychologists* focus on the relationships between people and work. *Organizational psychologists* study the behavior of people in organizations such as businesses. *Human factors psychologists* make technical systems such as automobile dashboards and computer keyboards more user-friendly. *Consumer psychologists* study the behavior of shoppers in an effort to predict and influence their behavior. They advise store managers how to lay out the aisles of a supermarket in ways that boost impulse buying, how to arrange window displays to attract customers, and how to make newspaper ads and TV commercials more persuasive.

Health psychologists examine the ways in which behavior and mental processes such as attitudes are related to physical health. They study the effects of stress on health problems such as headaches, cardiovascular disease, and cancer. Health psychologists also guide clients toward healthier behavior patterns—such as exercising and quitting smoking—and diets.

Sport psychologists help people improve their performance in sports. They help athletes concentrate on their performance and not on the crowd, use cognitive strategies such as positive visualization (imagining themselves making the right moves) to enhance performance, and avoid choking under pressure (Van Raalte & Brewer, 2002).

Your Turn: Now that we have discussed what psychologists do, focusing on the various fields of psychology, enhance your mastery of the material with the nearby "Learning Connections." Review the material by filling in the blanks, reflect on the material by relating it to other things you know, and think critically about it.

Learning Connections | WHAT PSYCHOLOGISTS DO

ACTIVE REVIEW (4) Some psychologists engage in basic, or _____, research, which has no immediate applications. (5) Other psychologists engage in _____ research, which seeks solutions to specific problems. (6) Clinical psychologists help people resolve problems through _____. (7) _____ psychologists work with individuals who have adjustment problems but do not show seriously abnormal behavior. (8) _____ psychologists assist students with problems that interfere with learning. (9) _____ psychologists are more concerned with theoretical issues concerning human learning. (10) _____ psychologists study the changes that occur throughout the life span. (11) _____ psychologists study the nature and causes of our thoughts, feel-ings, and behavior in social situations. (12) _____ psychologists conduct research into basic psychological processes, such as sensation and perception, learning and memory, and motivation and emotion. (13) _____ psychologists focus on the relationships between people and work.

REFLECT AND RELATE Think of a friend who either has experienced a problem or is experiencing one now. Would you advise him or her to see a psychologist? Why or why not? If so, what kind of psychologist?

CRITICAL THINKING What unites all the various fields of psychology?

 Go to **http://psychology.wadsworth.com/ rathus_pcc9e** for an interactive version of this Learning Connections unit.

Where Psychology Comes From: A History

Know then thyself, presume not God to scan,
The proper study of mankind is man. . . .
Created half to rise, and half to fall,
Great lord of all things, and yet a prey to all;
Sole judge of truth, in endless error hurled;
The glory, jest, and riddle of the world!

From "An Essay on Man," Alexander Pope

The English poet Alexander Pope advised "Know then thyself" in the 1700s. He was not the first. The ancient Greek philosopher Socrates, more than 2,000 years earlier, also advised "Know thyself." Psychology, which is in large part the endeavor to know ourselves, is as old as history and as modern as today. Knowledge of the history of psychology allows us to appreciate its theoretical conflicts, its place among the sciences, the evolution of its methods, and its social and political roles.

In Profile | ARISTOTLE

His father was physician to a king. He himself was trained as a physician and was a student of Plato. He tutored the child who would become Alexander the Great. He founded what has been considered the world's first university—the Lyceum. The Greek philosopher Aristotle (384–322 BCE) is also the first philosopher to treat extensively topics that would later become part of the science of psychology.

How do we number Aristotle's contributions to psychology? He was a proponent of *empiricism*—the view that science could rationally treat only information gathered by the senses. He numbered the so-called five senses of vision, hearing, smell, taste, and touch. He explored the nature of cause and effect. He pointed out that people differ from other living things in their capacity for rational thought. He explained how the imagination and dreaming contained images that survived the stimulation that caused them. And he outlined laws of *associationism* that have lain at the heart of learning theory for more than 2,000 years.

These are but a few of the topics Aristotle touched upon within the province of psychology. How daunting is it, then, to consider that he also made significant contributions to logic, physics, biology (he was the first to note that whales are mammals), politics, ethics, and rhetoric? But in one way, Aristotle would agree with some contemporary students: He did not believe that mathematics was all that important.

 Go to **http://psychology.wadsworth.com/ rathus_pcc9e** to access more information about Aristotle.

Question: Who were some of the ancient contributors to psychology? One of them is the ancient Greek philosopher Aristotle. **Truth or Fiction Revisited:** It is true that more than 2,000 years ago, Aristotle wrote a book on psychology, with contents similar to the book you are now holding. In fact, the outline for this textbook could have been written by Aristotle. One of Aristotle's works, *Peri Psyches,* translates as "About the Psyche." Like this book, *Peri Psyches* begins with a history of psychological thought and historical perspectives on the nature of the mind and behavior. Aristotle argued that human behavior, like the movements of the stars and the seas, is subject to rules and laws. Then he delved into his subject matter topic by topic: personality, sensation and perception, thought, intelligence, needs and motives, feelings and emotion, and memory. This book presents these topics in a different order, but each is here.

Aristotle also declared that people are motivated to seek pleasure and avoid pain. This view remains as current today as it was in ancient Greece.

Other ancient Greek philosophers also contributed to psychology. Around 400 BCE, Democritus suggested that we could think of behavior in terms of a body and a mind. (Contemporary psychologists still talk about the interaction of biological and mental processes.) He pointed out that our behavior is influenced by external stimulation. Democritus was one of the first to raise the question of whether there is free will or choice. Putting it another way, where do the influences of others end and our "real selves" begin?

Plato (c. 427–347 BCE) was a disciple of the great philosopher Socrates. **Truth or Fiction Revisited:** It is true that Socrates suggested a research method that is still used in psychology. It is based on Socrates' advice to "Know thyself," which has remained a motto of psychology ever since. Socrates claimed that we could not attain reliable self-knowledge through our senses, because the senses do not mirror reality exactly. Because the senses provide imperfect knowledge, Socrates suggested that we should rely on processes such as rational thought and **introspection**—careful examination of one's own thoughts and emotions—to achieve self-knowledge. He also pointed out that people are social creatures who influence one another.

Had we room enough and time, we could trace psychology's roots to thinkers even farther back in time than the ancient Greeks, and we could trace its development through the great thinkers of the Renaissance. As it is, we must move on to the development of psychology as a laboratory science during the second half of the 19th century. Some historians set the marker date at 1860. It was then that Gustav Theodor Fechner (1801–1887) published his landmark book *Elements of Psychophysics,* which showed how physical events (such as lights and sounds) are related to psychological sensation and perception. Fechner also showed how we can scientifically measure the effect of these events. Most historians set the debut of modern psychology as a laboratory science in the year 1879, when Wilhelm Wundt established the first psychological laboratory in Leipzig, Germany.

Structuralism: The Elements of Experience

Like Aristotle, the German psychologist Wilhelm Wundt (1832–1920) saw the mind as a natural event that could be studied scientifically, like light, heat, and the flow of blood. Wundt used introspection to try to discover the basic elements of experience. When presented with various sights and sounds, he and his colleagues tried to look inward as objectively as possible to describe their sensations and feelings.

Wundt and his students founded the school of psychology called **structuralism. Question: What is structuralism?** Structuralism attempted to break conscious experience down into *objective* sensations, such as sight or taste, and *subjective* feelings, such as emotional responses, will, and mental images like memories or dreams. Structuralists believed that the mind functions by combining objective and subjective elements of experience.

Introspection Deliberate looking into one's own cognitive processes to examine one's thoughts and feelings.

Structuralism The school of psychology that argues that the mind consists of three basic elements—sensations, feelings, and images—that combine to form experience.

In Profile | WILHELM WUNDT

The German psychologist Wilhelm Wundt was born in 1832, in a time when people used candles to light their homes and horses for travel. Several of Wundt's brothers died when he was young, and Wundt left home to live with a village pastor. At first he did poorly in school—his mind would wander—and he had to repeat a grade. Eventually he attended medical school because he wanted to earn a good living. He did not like working with patients, however, and dedicated himself to philosophy and psychology. He became such a workaholic that his wife and family received only one paragraph in his autobiography.

Truth or Fiction Revisited: In keeping with his theory of structuralism, he became preoccupied with trying to analyze the experience of dying during a serious illness. He kept an extensive diary of his conscious experiences, breaking them down into *objective* sensations such as what he was seeing and smelling, and into *subjective* feelings such as his depressive (although busy!) emotional responses, his will to live, and his memories of childhood and recent events, even his dreams. It is ironic, however, that he recovered and went on to live a long life. As a result, his diary of dying was "reduced" to becoming a diary of an illness. Wundt eventually died in 1920, in a time when people lit their homes with electricity and traveled by automobile and airplane.

Go to **http://psychology.wadsworth.com/ rathus_pcc9e** to access more information about Wilhelm Wundt.

Functionalism: Making Psychology a Habit

I wished, by treating Psychology like a natural science, to help her become one.
William James

Toward the end of the 19th century, William James was a major figure in the development of psychology in the United States. He focused on the relation between conscious experience and behavior. He argued, for example, that the stream of consciousness is fluid and continuous. Introspection convinced him that experience cannot be broken down into objective sensations and subjective feelings as the structuralists maintained.

James was a founder of the school of **functionalism. Question: What is functionalism?** The school of functionalism focused on behavior in addition to the mind or consciousness. Functionalists looked at how our experience helps us function more adaptively in our environments—for example, how habits help us cope with common situations. (When eating with a spoon, we do not create an individual plan to bring each morsel of food to our mouths.) They also turned to the laboratory for direct observations as a way to supplement introspection. The structuralists tended to ask, "What are the pieces that make up thinking and experience?" In contrast, the functionalists tended to ask, "How do behavior and mental processes help people adapt to the requirements of their lives?"

James was also influenced by Charles Darwin's (1809–1882) theory of evolution. Earlier in the 19th century, the British naturalist Darwin had argued that organisms with adaptive features—that is, the "fittest"—survive and reproduce. Functionalists adapted Darwin's theory and proposed that adaptive behavior pat-

Functionalism The school of psychology that emphasizes the uses or functions of the mind rather than the elements of experience.

In Profile | WILLIAM JAMES

William James (1842–1910), brother of the novelist Henry James, has been called the first true American psychologist. He came from a wealthy family, and his home was visited regularly by the likes of Ralph Waldo Emerson; Henry David Thoreau; Nathaniel Hawthorne; Alfred, Lord Tennyson; and John Stuart Mill. James received an M.D. degree from Harvard University but never practiced medicine. He made his career teaching at Harvard—first in physiology, then in philosophy, and finally in psychology. He described his views in the first modern psychology textbook, *The Principles of Psychology,* a huge two-volume work that was published in 1890. Two years later he came out with a brief edition, which students affectionately called the "Jimmy." He was often seen strolling across Harvard Yard, talking animatedly with students, in an era when most professors were more formal. James was also fascinated by religious experience and occult phenomena such as extrasensory perception. He once brought the young Helen Keller an ostrich feather—a gift he believed the blind and deaf girl could appreciate.

Go to **http://psychology.wadsworth.com/ rathus_pcc9e** to access more information about William James.

Archives of the History of American Psychology

terns are learned and maintained. Maladaptive behavior patterns tend to drop out, and only the "fittest" behavior patterns survive. These adaptive actions tend to be repeated and become habits. James wrote that "habit is the enormous flywheel of society." Habit keeps the engine of civilization running.

Habits include such deceptively simple acts as how we lift a spoon to our mouth or turn a doorknob. At first, these acts require our full attention. If you are in doubt, stand by with paper towels and watch a baby's first efforts at eating oatmeal by himself. Through repetition, the movements that make up self-feeding become automatic, or habitual. The multiple acts involved in learning to drive a car also become routine through repetition, so we can focus on other matters such as telling a joke to our passenger, changing the CD, or talking on the phone. (Many state legislatures have concluded, however, that it is too dangerous for drivers to use handheld phones.) This idea of learning by repetition is also basic to the behavioral tradition in psychology.

Behaviorism: Practicing Psychology in Public

Imagine you have placed a hungry rat in a maze. It meanders down a pathway that ends in a T. It can then turn left or right. If you consistently reward the rat with food for turning right at this choice point, it will learn to turn right when it arrives there, at least when it is hungry. But what does the rat *think* when it is learning to turn right? "Hmm, last time I was in this situation and turned to the right, I was given some Purina rat chow. Think I'll try that again"?

Does it seem absurd to try to place yourself in the "mind" of a rat? So it seemed to John Broadus Watson (1878–1958), the founder of American behaviorism. We will talk more about behaviorism shortly, but Watson was asked to consider the contents of a rat's "mind" as one of the requirements for his doctoral degree, which he received from the University of Chicago in 1903. Functionalism was the dominant view of psychology at the University of Chicago, and functionalists were concerned with the stream of consciousness as well as observable behavior. But Watson (1913) believed that if psychology was to be a natural science, like physics or chemistry, it must limit itself to observable, measurable events—that is, to behavior alone—hence the term *behaviorism.*

Question: What is behaviorism? **Behaviorism** is the school of psychology that focuses on the learning and effects of observable behavior. "Observable" does not only mean visible to the eye. Yes, observable behavior does include activities such

Behaviorism The school of psychology that defines psychology as the study of observable behavior and studies relationships between stimuli and responses.

In Profile   JOHN B. WATSON

He was the son of a Southern farmer and tended to get into fights in his youth. Later—much later—he taught rats to find their way through a miniature maze that was modeled on the maze at King Henry VIII's retreat in the London suburbs.

Watson's aim was to show how most human behavior and emotional reactions—other than a few inborn reflexes—resulted from conditioning. Perhaps his most renowned experiment was with "Little Albert," an infant who was conditioned by Watson and his student, Rosalie Rayner, to develop a fear of furry white animals (see Chapter 5). Watson was later forced to resign by the president of Johns Hopkins University when it was discovered he and Rayner were having an affair. His wife had written the university president about the affair, assuming that the president would compel Watson to change his ways. But her letter did not have the effect she sought when the president forced Watson to

resign and the couple were divorced. Watson then married Rayner, and the couple eventually had two sons.

After leaving the university, Watson and Rayner moved to New York, where he worked as a psychologist for the J. Walter Thompson advertising agency. He grew wealthy through successful ad campaigns for products such as Camel cigarettes, Johnson & Johnson Baby Powder, and Maxwell House Coffee—in which he introduced the idea of the "coffee break."

Tragically, his wife died from dysentery in her 30s and Watson, 58, never married again. He continued to work sporadically and was awarded a gold medal from the APA for his lifetime contributions to psychology one year before he died at the age of 80. He had let himself go following his wife's death. He put on weight and paid little attention to his appearance. His children had to "pull him together" and dress him for his final appearance before the APA, which he attended, so to speak, as a "bundle of nerves."

Go to **http://psychology.wadsworth.com/ rathus_pcc9e** to access more information about John B. Watson.

■ **The Power of Reinforcement** In the photo on the left, we see a feathered friend that has learned to drop shapes into their proper places through reinforcement. In the photo on the right, "Air Raccoon" shoots a basket. Behaviorists teach animals complex behaviors such as shooting baskets by first reinforcing approximations to the goal (or target behavior). As time progresses, closer approximations are demanded before reinforcement is given.

as pressing a lever, turning left or right, eating and mating, and dilation of the pupils of the eyes. But it also includes behaviors that are observable by means of specialized instruments, such as the heart rate, the blood pressure, and the emission of brain waves. All of these behaviors are *public*. They can be measured by simple observation or by laboratory instruments, and different observers would readily agree about their existence and features. Given their focus on behavior, it should come as no surprise that behaviorists define psychology as the scientific study of *behavior*, not of *behavior and mental processes*.

Another major modern contributor to behaviorism was Harvard University psychologist B. F. Skinner (1904–1990). He believed that organisms learn to behave in certain ways because they have been **reinforced** for doing so—that is, their behavior has a positive outcome. He demonstrated that laboratory animals can be trained to carry out behaviors through strategic use of reinforcers, such as food. He trained rats to turn in circles, climb ladders, and push toys across the floor. Because Skinner demonstrated that remarkable combinations of behaviors could be taught by means of reinforcement, many psychologists adopted the view that, in principle, one could explain complex human behavior in terms of thousands of instances of learning through reinforcement.

Gestalt Psychology: Making Psychology Whole

In the 1920s, another school of psychology—**Gestalt psychology**—was prominent in Germany. In the 1930s, the three founders of the school—Max Wertheimer (1880–1943), Kurt Koffka (1886–1941), and Wolfgang Köhler (1887–1967)—left Europe to escape the Nazi threat. They carried on their work in the United States, giving further impetus to the growing American ascendance in psychology.

Question: What is Gestalt psychology? Gestalt psychologists focused on perception and on how perception influences thinking and problem solving. The German word *Gestalt* translates roughly to "pattern" or "organized whole." In contrast to the behaviorists, Gestalt psychologists argued that we cannot hope to understand human nature by focusing only on overt behavior. In contrast to the structuralists, they claimed that we cannot explain human perceptions, emotions, or thought processes in terms of basic units. Perceptions are *more* than the sums of their parts: Gestalt psychologists saw our perceptions as wholes that give meaning to parts, as we see in Figure 1.2.

Gestalt psychologists illustrated how we tend to perceive separate pieces of information as integrated wholes, depending on the contexts in which they occur. In Figure 1.2A, the dots in the centers of the configurations are the same size, yet we may perceive them as being of different sizes because of what surrounds them. The second symbol in each line in part B is identical, but in the top row we may perceive it as a B and in the bottom row as the number 13. The symbol has not changed, but the context in which it appears has. The inner squares in part C are equally bright, but they do not appear so because of their contrasting backgrounds. There are many examples of this in literature and everyday life. In *The Prince and the Pauper*, Mark Twain dressed a peasant boy as a prince, and the kingdom bowed to him. Do clothes sometimes make the man or woman? Try wearing cutoffs for a job interview!

Gestalt psychologists believed that learning could be active and purposeful, not merely responsive and mechanical as in Watson's and Skinner's experiments. They

Reinforcement A stimulus that follows a response and increases the frequency of the response.

Gestalt psychology The school of psychology that emphasizes the tendency to organize perceptions into wholes and to integrate separate stimuli into meaningful patterns.

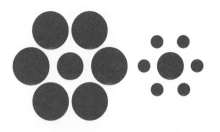
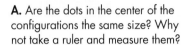

A. Are the dots in the center of the configurations the same size? Why not take a ruler and measure them?

B. Is the second symbol in each line the letter B or the number 13?

C. Which one of the gray squares is brighter?

FIGURE 1.2 **The Importance of Context**
Gestalt psychologists have shown that our perceptions depend not only on our sensory impressions but also on the context of our impressions. You will interpret a man running toward you very differently depending on whether you are on a deserted street at night or at a track in the morning.

demonstrated that much learning, especially in problem solving, is accomplished by **insight,** not by mechanical repetition, as we see in a classic experiment that took place early in the last century.

Wolfgang Köhler was marooned during World War I on one of the Canary Islands, where the Prussian Academy of Science kept a colony of apes, and his research while there gave him, well, insight into the process of learning by insight. Have you ever pondered a problem for quite a while and then, suddenly, seen the solution? Did the solution seem to come out of nowhere? In a "flash"? Consider the chimpanzee in Figure 1.3. At first, it is unsuccessful in reaching for bananas suspended from the ceiling. Then it suddenly stacks the boxes and climbs up to reach the bananas. It seems the chimp has experienced a sudden reorganization of the mental elements of the problem—that is, it has had a "flash of insight." Köhler's findings suggest that we often manipulate the elements of problems until we group them in such a way that we believe we will be able to reach a goal. The manipulations may take quite some time as mental trial and error proceeds. Once the proper grouping has been found, however, we seem to perceive it all at once as a clear pattern or whole.

Psychoanalysis: Digging Beneath the Surface

Psychoanalysis, the school of psychology founded by Sigmund Freud (1856–1939), differs from the other schools in both background and approach. Freud's theory has invaded popular culture, and you may be familiar with a number of its concepts. For example, perhaps a friend has tried to "interpret" a slip of the tongue you made or has asked you what you thought might be the meaning of an especially vivid dream.

Insight In Gestalt psychology, the sudden reorganization of perceptions, allowing the sudden solution of a problem.

FIGURE 1.3 **Some Insight into Insight**
At first, the chimpanzee cannot reach the bananas hanging from the ceiling. After some time has passed, it has an apparent "flash of insight" and piles the boxes on top of one another to reach the fruit.

Psychoanalysis The school of psychology that emphasizes the importance of unconscious motives and conflicts as determinants of human behavior.

Question: What is psychoanalysis? **Psychoanalysis** is the name given to the theory of personality and to the method of therapy originated by Sigmund Freud. As a theory of personality, psychoanalysis was based on the idea that much of our lives are governed by unconscious ideas and impulses that have their origins in childhood

Concept Review   HISTORIC SCHOOLS OF PSYCHOLOGY

School/Major Proponent(s)	Key Concepts	Current Status
Structuralism Wilhelm Wundt	The mind can be studied scientifically by using introspection to discover the basic elements of experience. Conscious experience can be broken down into *objective* sensations such as sight or taste, and *subjective* feelings such as emotional responses, will, and mental images like memories or dreams.	We do not encounter structuralists today, but cognitive and experimental psychologists study related topics such as sensation and perception, emotion, memory, and states of consciousness (including dreams).
Functionalism William James	There is a relationship between consciousness and behavior. Consciousness is fluid and streamlike. Experience cannot be broken down into objective sensations and subjective feelings. Functionalists focused on how experience helps us function more adaptively in our environments.	We do not have pure functionalists today, but functionalism preceded behaviorism in its interest in how habits are formed by experience and help us adapt. Behavior is seen as evolving: Adaptive behavior is maintained, whereas maladaptive behavior tends to drop out.
Behaviorism John B. Watson, B. F. Skinner	Psychology must limit itself to observable, measurable events—to behavior, not mental processes. Organisms learn to behave in certain ways because of the effects of their behavior.	Some "pure" behaviorists remain, but behaviorism more generally has contributed to experimental psychology, the psychology of learning, and methods of therapy (behavior therapy). Although many contemporary psychologists argue that it is desirable to study consciousness and mental processes, the behaviorist influence has encouraged them to base many of their conclusions on measurable behaviors.
Gestalt Psychology Max Wertheimer, Kurt Koffka, Wolfgang Köhler	Gestalt psychologists focused on perception, thinking, and problem solving. Whereas structuralists tried to isolate basic elements of experience, Gestalt psychologists focused on the tendency to see perceptions as wholes that give meaning to parts.	Gestalt principles continue to be studied in the field of sensations and perception. Other Gestalt ideas, such as those involving thinking and problem solving, continue to be studied by cognitive psychologists and experimental psychologists. Gestalt therapy—which aims to help people integrate conflicting parts of their personalities—remains in use.
Psychoanalysis Sigmund Freud, Carl Jung, Alfred Adler, Karen Horney, Erik Erikson	Visible behavior and conscious thinking are influenced by unconscious ideas and conflicts. People are motivated to gratify primitive sexual and aggressive impulses, even if they are unaware of their true motives. Unconscious processes are more influential than conscious thought in determining human behavior.	Psychoanalytic thinking remains quite alive in the popular culture. Among psychologists, many discount psychoanalysis altogether, because many of its concepts cannot be studied by scientific means. Modern psychoanalytic therapists tend to place more emphasis on the roles of conscious motives, conscious thinking, and decision making.

John B. Watson

B. F. Skinner

A. Are the dots in the center of the configurations the same size? Why not take a ruler and measure them?

Sigmund Freud

Karen Horney

Erik Erikson

Go to **http://psychology.wadsworth.com/ rathus_pcc9e** to access a drag-and-drop version of this Concept Review designed to help you test yourself on the major topics provided here.

conflicts. As a method of psychotherapy, psychoanalysis aims to help patients gain insight into their conflicts and to find socially acceptable ways of expressing wishes and gratifying needs (see Chapter 15).

Your Turn: Now that we have discussed the history of psychology, enhance your mastery of the material with the nearby "Learning Connections." Review the material by filling in the blanks, reflect on the material by relating it to other things you know, and think critically about it.

Learning Connections — WHERE PSYCHOLOGY COMES FROM: A HISTORY

ACTIVE REVIEW The Greek philosopher (14) _____ was among the first to argue that human behavior is subject to rules and laws. (15) _____ proclaimed "Know thyself" and suggested the use of introspection to gain self-knowledge. (16) _____ founded the school of structuralism. (17) William James founded the school of _____, which dealt with behavior as well as conscious experience. (18) _____ founded the school of behaviorism. (19) _____ psychologists saw our perceptions as wholes that give meaning to parts. (20) _____ founded the school of psychoanalysis.

REFLECT AND RELATE Psychologist William James visited Helen Keller as a child and brought her an ostrich feather. If you had been Helen Keller, would you have appreciated this gift? Explain.

CRITICAL THINKING Do you believe that the richness and complexity of human behavior can be explained as the summation of so many instances of learning? Explain.

 Go to **http://psychology.wadsworth.com/ rathus_pcc9e** for an interactive version of this Learning Connections unit.

How Today's Psychologists View Behavior and Mental Processes

Today we no longer find psychologists who describe themselves as structuralists or functionalists. Although the school of Gestalt psychology gave birth to current research approaches in perception and problem solving, few would consider themselves Gestalt psychologists. On the other hand, we do find Gestalt therapists who focus on helping clients integrate conflicting parts of their personality (making themselves "whole"). The numbers of orthodox behaviorists and psychoanalysts have been declining (Robins et al., 1999). Many contemporary psychologists in the behaviorist tradition look on themselves as social cognitive[1] theorists, and many psychoanalysts consider themselves neoanalysts rather than traditional Freudians.

The history of psychological thought has taken many turns, and contemporary psychologists differ in their approaches. Today there are several broad, influential perspectives in psychology: the biological, cognitive, humanistic–existential, psychodynamic, learning, and sociocultural perspectives. Each emphasizes different topics of investigation. Each approaches its topics in its own ways.

The Evolutionary and Biological Perspectives: It's Only Natural

Psychologists are interested in the roles of evolution and heredity in behavior and mental processes such as psychological disorders, criminal behavior, and thinking. Generally speaking, our heredity provides a broad range of behavioral and mental possibilities. Environmental factors interact with inherited factors to determine specific behavior and mental processes. **Question: What is the evolutionary perspective?**

Modern evolutionary psychologists focus on the evolution of behavior and mental processes. Charles Darwin argued that in the age-old struggle for existence, only the "fittest" (most adaptive) organisms manage to reach maturity and reproduce. For example, fish that swim faster or people who are naturally immune to certain diseases

[1]Formerly termed *social-learning theorists*.

are more likely to survive and transmit their **genes** to future generations. Individuals die, but species tend to evolve in adaptive directions. Evolutionary psychologists suggest that much human social behavior, such as aggressive behavior and mate selection, has a hereditary basis. People may be influenced by social rules, cultural factors, even personal choice, but evolutionary psychologists believe that inherited tendencies sort of whisper in people's ears and tend to move them in certain directions.

When we ask the question "What evolves?", we answer biological processes and structures. These processes and structures may give rise to ideas and behaviors, but it is not believed that ideas and behavior exist in the absence of biological substance. Psychologists assume that thoughts, fantasies, and dreams—and the inborn or **instinctive** behavior patterns of various species—are made possible by the nervous system and especially by the brain. **Question: What is the biological perspective?** Psychologists with a biological perspective seek the links between the electrical and chemical activity of the brain, the chemical activity of hormones, and heredity, on the one hand, and behavior and mental processes on the other. They use techniques such as CAT scans and PET scans to show what parts of the brain are involved in such activities as language, mathematical problem solving, and music. We have learned how natural chemical substances in the brain are involved in the formation of memories. Experiments have shown that, among some animals, electrical stimulation of parts of the brain prompts the expression of "prewired," or inborn, sexual and aggressive behaviors.

Biological psychologists are also concerned with the influences of the endocrine system on behavior and mental processes. The endocrine system consists of glands that secrete hormones and release them into the bloodstream. In people, for instance, the hormone prolactin stimulates production of milk. In rats, however, prolactin also gives rise to maternal behavior. In many animals, sex hormones determine whether mating behavior will follow stereotypical masculine or feminine behavior patterns. In humans, sex hormones regulate the menstrual cycle and are also connected with feelings of psychological well-being.

The biological perspective tends to focus on events that occur below the level of consciousness. The cognitive perspective is the essence of consciousness. **Question: What is the cognitive perspective?**

The Cognitive Perspective: Keeping Psychology "In Mind"

Psychologists with a **cognitive** perspective venture into the realm of mental processes to understand human nature (Sperry, 1998). They investigate the ways in which we perceive and mentally represent the world, how we learn, remember the past, plan for the future, solve problems, form judgments, make decisions, and use language (Basic Behavioral Science Task Force, 1996a). Cognitive psychologists, in short, study those things we refer to as the *mind*.

The cognitive tradition has roots in Socrates' advice to "Know thyself" and in his suggested method of introspection. We also find cognitive psychology's roots in structuralism, functionalism, and Gestalt psychology, each of which, in its own way, addressed issues that are of interest to cognitive psychologists. In general, cognitive science has experienced a rapid expansion in the past couple of decades and continues to attract interest and inspire research.

The Humanistic–Existential Perspective: The Search for Meaning

The humanistic–existential perspective is cognitive in flavor, yet it emphasizes more the role of subjective (personal) experience. **Question: What is the humanistic–existential perspective?** Let us consider each of the parts of this perspective: *humanism* and *existentialism*. **Humanism** stresses the human capacity for self-fulfillment and the central roles of consciousness, self-awareness, and decision making. Humanistic psychology considers personal, or subjective, experience to be the most important event in psychology. Humanists believe that self-awareness, experience, and choice permit us, to a large extent, to "invent ourselves" and our ways of relat-

Genes The basic building blocks of heredity.

Instinctive An inborn pattern of behavior that is triggered by a particular stimulus.

Cognitive Having to do with mental processes such as sensation and perception, memory, intelligence, language, thought, and problem solving.

Humanism The philosophy and school of psychology that asserts that people are conscious, self-aware, and capable of free choice, self-fulfillment, and ethical behavior.

ing to the world as we progress through life. Humanistic–existential psychologists stress the importance of subjective experience and assert that people have the freedom to make choices. Consciousness—our sense of being in the world—is seen as the force that unifies our personalities. **Existentialism** views people as free to choose and be responsible for choosing ethical conduct.

Humanistic–existential psychologists stress the importance of subjective experience and assert that people have the freedom to make real choices. Grounded in the work of Carl Rogers (1951) and Abraham Maslow (1970), the humanistic perspective continues to find many contemporary adherents (Moss, 2002; Schneider et al., 2001).

The Psychodynamic Perspective: Still Digging

Many modern psychologists continue to embrace the diverse theories descended from Sigmund Freud. In fact, in the 1940s and 1950s, psychodynamic theory dominated the practice of psychotherapy and was influential in scientific psychology and the arts. Most psychotherapists were psychodynamically oriented. Many renowned artists and writers consulted psychodynamic therapists as a way to liberate the expression of their unconscious ideas. Today, Freud's influence continues to be felt, although it no longer dominates methods of psychotherapy.

Question: What is the role of psychoanalysis today? Contemporary psychologists who follow theories derived from Freud are likely to call themselves *neoanalysts*. Famous neoanalysts such as Karen Horney (1885–1952) and Erik Erikson (1902–1994) focused less on unconscious processes and more on conscious choice and self-direction. The same is true of modern neoanalysts today, such as former APA president Dorothy Cantor.

Let us note also that many Freudian ideas are retained in some form by the population at large. For example, sometimes we have ideas or desires that seem unusual for us. We may even say that it sometimes seems as if some unconscious idea or impulse is trying to get the better of us. In the Middle Ages, such thoughts and impulses were usually attributed to the devil or to demons. Dreams, likewise, were thought to enter us magically from the spirit world. Followers of Sigmund Freud tend to attribute dreams and unusual ideas or desires to unconscious processes, and dreams are commonly viewed this way in popular culture.

Perspectives on Learning: From the Behavioral to the Cognitive

Many contemporary psychologists study the effects of experience on behavior. Learning, to them, is the essential factor in describing, explaining, predicting, and controlling behavior. The term *learning* has different meanings to psychologists of different persuasions, however. Some students of learning find roles for consciousness and insight. Others do not. This distinction is found today among those who adhere to the behavioral and social cognitive perspectives. **Question: What are the two major perspectives on learning?**

For the founder of American behaviorism, John B. Watson (1878–1958), behaviorism was an approach to life as well as a broad guideline for psychological research. Not only did Watson despair of measuring consciousness and mental processes in the laboratory, he also applied behavioral analysis to virtually all situations in his daily life. He viewed people as doing things because of their learning histories, their situations, and rewards rather than because of conscious choice.

Like Watson, contemporary behaviorists emphasize environmental influences and the learning of habits through repetition and reinforcement. Modern **social cognitive theorists** (previously termed *social-learning theorists*), in contrast, suggest that people can modify or even create their environments. They also grant **cognition** a key role. They note that people engage in intentional learning by observing others. Since the 1960s, social cognitive theorists have gained influence in the areas of personality development, psychological disorders, and psychotherapy.

Existentialism The view that people are free and responsible for their own behavior.

Social cognitive theory A school of psychology in the behaviorist tradition that includes cognitive factors in the explanation and prediction of behavior. Formerly termed *social-learning theory*.

Cognition The use of mental processes to perceive and mentally represent the world, think, and engage in problem solving and decision making.

The Sociocultural Perspective: How Do You Complete the Sentence "I Am . . ."?

Sociocultural perspective The view that focuses on the roles of ethnicity, gender, culture, and socioeconomic status in behavior and mental processes.

Ethnic group A group characterized by common features such as cultural heritage, history, race, and language.

Gender The culturally defined concepts of *masculinity* and *femininity*.

The profession of psychology focuses mainly on the individual and is committed to the dignity of the individual. However, many psychologists today believe we cannot understand people's behavior and mental processes without reference to their diversity (Basic Behavioral Science Task Force, 1996b). Studying perspectives other than their own helps psychologists understand the role of a culture's beliefs, values, and attitudes in behavior and mental processes. It helps them perceive why people from diverse cultures behave and think in different ways, and how the science of psychology is enriched by addressing those differences (Denmark, 1998; Reid, 1994).

Question: What is the sociocultural perspective? The **sociocultural perspective** addresses many of the ways in which people differ from one another. It studies the influences of ethnicity, gender, culture, and socioeconomic status on behavior and mental processes (Allen, 1993; Lewis-Fernández & Kleinman, 1994). For example, what is often seen as healthful, self-assertive, outspoken behavior by most U.S. women may be interpreted as brazen behavior in Latino and Latina American or Asian American communities.

ETHNICITY One kind of diversity involves people's ethnicity. Members of an **ethnic group** are united by their cultural heritage, race, language, and common history. The experiences of various ethnic groups in the United States highlight the impact of social, political, and economic factors on human behavior and development (Basic Behavioral Science Task Force, 1996b; Phinney, 1996).

The probing of human diversity enables students to appreciate the cultural heritages and historical problems of various ethnic groups. This textbook considers many psychological issues related to ethnicity, such as the representation of ethnic minority groups in psychological research studies, substance abuse among adolescents from various ethnic minority groups, bilingualism, ethnic differences in intelligence test scores, the prevalence of suicide among members of different ethnic groups, ethnic differences in vulnerability to physical problems and disorders ranging from obesity to hypertension and cancer, multicultural issues in the practice of psychotherapy, and prejudice.

GENDER **Gender** refers to the culturally defined concepts of *masculinity* and *femininity*. Gender is not fully defined by anatomic sex. It involves a complex web of cultural expectations and social roles

Larry Williams/CORBIS

■ **The Sociocultural Perspective** The United States is a mosaic of people from various ethnic backgrounds. The sociocultural perspective teaches that we cannot understand the hopes and problems of people from a particular ethnic group without understanding that group's history and cultural heritage. The sociocultural perspective helps us understand and appreciate the scope of behavior and mental processes.

that affect people's self-concepts and hopes and dreams as well as their behavior. How can sciences such as psychology and medicine hope to understand the particular viewpoints, qualities, and problems of women if most research is conducted with men and by men (Matthews et al., 1997)?

Just as members of ethnic minority groups have experienced prejudice, so too have women. Even much of the scientific research on gender roles and gender differences assumes that male behavior represents the norm (Ader & Johnson, 1994).

Your Turn: Now that we have discussed contemporary perspectives on psychology, enhance your mastery of the material with the nearby "Learning Connections." Review the material by filling in the blanks, reflect on the material by relating it to other things you know, and think critically about it.

Our discussion of the sociocultural perspective naturally leads us to reflect—in the following section—on the roles of women and people from various racial and ethnic backgrounds in psychology.

 Learning Connections | **HOW TODAY'S PSYCHOLOGISTS VIEW BEHAVIOR AND MENTAL PROCESSES**

ACTIVE REVIEW (21) _____ oriented psychologists study the links between behavior, the brain, hormones, and heredity. (22) _____ psychologists note that only the fittest organisms reach maturity and reproduce, thereby transmitting their genes to future generations and causing species to evolve in adaptive directions. (23) _____ psychologists study the ways in which we perceive and mentally represent the world. (24) Humanistic–_____ psychologists stress the importance of self-awareness and people's freedom to make choices. (25) _____ cognitive theorists are in the behaviorist tradition but also find roles for intentional learning and note that people can create or modify their environments. (26) The _____ perspective fosters the consideration of matters of ethnicity, gender, culture, and socioeconomic status in psychology.

REFLECT AND RELATE Which contemporary perspective on human behavior has the most personal appeal to you? Why?

CRITICAL THINKING Should we teach Freud's ideas? Many psychologists argue that Freud's views have not been supported by research evidence and are thus of no more than historic interest. Therefore, Freud's ideas should not be emphasized in psychology textbooks. Some psychologists would even exclude Freud from a scientific textbook. What do you think?

 Go to **http://psychology.wadsworth.com/ rathus_pcc9e** for an interactive version of this Learning Connections unit.

Gender, Ethnicity, and Psychology: Real People in the Real World

It's all about access. **Question: How have access to education and the field of psychology historically influenced the participation of women and people from various ethnic and racial backgrounds?** Until the 20th century, women and people of color were systematically excluded from most institutions of higher learning. Thus it is not surprising that the overwhelming majority of psychologists in the 1800s and early 1900s were European and European American males. Nevertheless, a few pioneering women and individuals from various racial and ethnic backgrounds were able to open the door to an education and to the field of psychology.

Women in Psychology: Opening the Floodgates

Although American women have only attended college since 1833, when Oberlin College opened its doors to women, most American college students today are in fact women. Women now receive nearly three-quarters of the undergraduate degrees in psychology and two-thirds of the doctoral degrees (Kohout & Williams, 1999). **Truth or Fiction Revisited:** Women now actually receive the majority of doctoral degrees in psychology.

Mary Whiton Calkins, who is profiled nearby, is one of thousands of women who have made indispensable contributions to psychology. Consider also Christine

In Profile   MARY WHITON CALKINS

She just said no. Mary Whiton Calkins (1863–1930) had completed all the requirements for the Ph.D., but accepting the degree would endorse prejudice against women. So she turned it down. Calkins studied psychology at Harvard University. However, she had to attend Harvard as a "guest student," because Harvard was not yet admitting women. It did not matter that William James considered Calkins to be his brightest student. When she completed her degree requirements, Harvard would not award her the degree because of her gender. Instead, Harvard offered to grant her a doctorate from its sister school, Radcliffe. She declined the offer.

Truth or Fiction Revisited: It is therefore true that the first female president of the American Psychological Association turned down the doctoral degree that was offered to her.

Calkins' story is typical of those of talented, self-assertive women who pressed for political rights and economic independence at the turn of the century—that is, the turn of the 19th century into the 20th. At a time when men dominated the discipline of psychology, Calkins was one of the pioneers who fought the male-centered bias and encouraged psychology to incorporate the values of the "new woman" (Minton, 2000). Calkins fought mightily for many of the rights that women in the United States can take for granted today.

Even without a doctorate, Calkins went on to pioneer research in memory at Wellesley College, where she founded a psychology laboratory in 1891. She introduced the method of paired associates, discovered the primacy and recency effects, and engaged in research into the role of the frequency of repetition in the vividness of memories (Madigan & O'Hara, 1992). In 1905 she became the first female president of the American Psychological Association—doctorate or no.

Go to **http://psychology.wadsworth.com/ rathus_pcc9e** to access more information about Mary Whiton Calkins.

Ladd-Franklin (1847–1930). She, like Calkins, was born during an era in American history in which women were expected to remain in the home and were excluded from careers in science (Minton, 2000). She nevertheless pursued a career in psychology, taught at Johns Hopkins and Columbia Universities, and formulated a theory of color vision.

Margaret Floy Washburn (1871–1939) was the first woman to receive a Ph.D. in psychology. Washburn wrote *The Animal Mind,* a work containing many ideas that would later become part of behaviorism. Helen Bradford Thompson (1874–1947) was the first psychologist to study psychological gender differences. Her 1903 book *The Mental Traits of Sex* analyzed the performance of 25 women and 25 men on tests of intellect, emotional response, and sensation and perception (Milar, 2000). Thompson was ahead of her time in her conclusion that gender differences in these areas appeared to be strongly influenced by the social environment from infancy through adulthood.

In more recent years, Mary Salter Ainsworth (1913–1999) revolutionized our understanding of attachment between parents and children by means of her cross-cultural studies and her innovation of the Strange Situation method (see Chapter 3). Elizabeth Loftus (e.g., Loftus, 2001; Thomas & Loftus, 2002) has shown that our memories are not snapshots of the past. Instead, they often consist of something old (what actually happened), something new (that is, influenced by more recent events), something borrowed (for example, further shaped by our biases and prejudices), and something blue (altered by tinges of color or emotion) (Chapter 7). Susan Nolen-Hoeksema (e.g., 2003) is contributing to our understanding of the ways in which self-destructive ruminating (that is, going back and forth repeatedly over the same issues) prevents us from making decisions and heightens feelings of depression (Chapter 14). The number of women making such contributions today is truly countless.

Ethnicity and Psychology

Like women, individuals from various ethnic and racial groups have also struggled for recognition in psychology. Back in 1901, Gilbert Haven Jones was the first African American to receive a Ph.D. in psychology, but he had to do so in Germany. J. Henry Alston engaged in research on perception of heat and cold and was the first African American psychologist to be published in a major psychology journal (the year was 1920).

In Profile   KENNETH B. CLARK AND MAMIE PHIPPS CLARK

Kenneth Bancroft Clark was born in 1914, the son of West Indian parents. He earned his bachelor's degree from Howard University in Washington, D.C., where he also met and married Mamie Phipps (1917–1983). Although Mamie was the daughter of a physician, she attended a segregated school in her hometown in Arkansas and was compelled to use public facilities labeled for "coloreds only."

Kenneth Clark and Mamie Phipps Clark earned their doctorates in psychology at Columbia University. (Kenneth was the first African American to receive a Ph.D. in psychology from Columbia.) The couple were committed to children's welfare (Lal, 2002). In the 1940s, the Clarks founded the Northside Center for Child Development and conducted research that showed the negative effects of school segregation on African American children. In one such study, African American children were shown white and brown dolls and asked to "Give me the pretty doll," or "Give me the doll that looks bad." Most children's choices showed that they preferred the white dolls over the brown ones. The Clarks concluded that the children had swallowed the larger society's prejudiced views that favored European Americans.

The Clarks were activists as well as psychologists (Keppel, 2002; Lal, 2002). In the 1950s, Kenneth Clark began working with the NAACP to end school segregation. Clark's research was cited by the Supreme Court in 1954 when it overturned the "separate but equal" schools doctrine that had actually allowed inequalities in school services for various ethnic groups. Clark went on to study the quality of education and juvenile delinquency. He was among the first to recommend education for preschoolers, after-school programs, and community participation in educational decision making.

 Go to **http://psychology.wadsworth.com/ rathus_pcc9e** to access more information about Kenneth B. Clark and Mamie Phipps Clark.

Library of Congress

The most well-known African American psychologists may be Kenneth Clark and Mamie Phipps Clark (see the nearby In Profile feature). They played important roles in desegregation and in the education of African American children.

Today African Americans continue to have a powerful impact on the profession of psychology. For example, psychologist Robert Williams—sometimes referred to as the "father of Ebonics"—has offered us insight into language differences that are often found between European Americans and African Americans (see Chapter 8). Psychologist Claude Steele (e.g., Blascovich et al., 2001) has shown that many African Americans sabotage their own performance on intelligence tests because of *stereotype threat* (Chapter 9). That is, rather than focus on the test items, they worry about the stereotype, or widespread belief, that African Americans are not as intelligent as European Americans. As a result, they hurt their own performance. According to Steele, this phenomenon can apply to any negatively stereotyped group as well—to women in mathematics, for example. African American psychologist Nancy Boyd-Franklin (e.g., Franklin & Boyd-Franklin, 2000) is on the faculty at Rutgers University and studies group and family therapy with African Americans. African American psychologist Tony Strickland (e.g., Stein & Strickland, 1998; Strickland et al., 1998) studies the effects of psychoactive drugs on individuals with and without psychological disorders. He has discovered that people from different ethnic groups may respond to drugs in different ways.

Latino and Latina American and Asian American psychologists have also made their mark. Jorge Sanchez was among the first to show how intelligence tests are culturally biased—to the disadvantage of Mexican American children. Latina American psychologist Lillian Comas-Diaz (e.g., 2001) edits a journal on multicultural mental health. Latina American psychologist Martha Bernal (e.g., 1999) studies the development of ethnic identity among Mexican American children. Asian American psychologist Stanley Sue (e.g., Chang & Sue, 2003; Lam & Sue, 2001) directed the National Research Center on Asian American Mental Health in Los Angeles and has shown that discrimination may be connected with racial differences in intelligence and achievement (Chapter 9). Asian American psychologist Richard Suinn (e.g., 2001) studies mental health and the development of identity among Asians and Asian Americans.

The contributions of women and members of diverse ethnic and racial groups have broadened our understanding of the influences of gender and ethnicity on behavior and mental processes. They have taught us that what is true for men may not always be true for women (that is, what is sauce for the goose may not always be sauce for the gander). What is true for European Americans may not be true for

Americans from other backgrounds. The presence of women and individuals from diverse ethnic backgrounds has given us the grand mosaic that is psychology today.

African Americans make up 6% to 7% of first-year students in doctoral departments in psychology; 6% are Asian American; 5% are Latino and Latina Americans; and about 1% are Native American (American Psychological Association Research Office, 2000). Even though these percentages do not yet reflect these groups' numbers in the general population, psychology is being enriched as it increasingly attracts a diverse population (Kite et al., 2001).

By now we have a sense of the various fields of psychology, the history of psychology, and the ways in which today's psychologists look at behavior and mental processes. Basically, psychology has sought to be the scientific study of behavior and mental processes. Like other scientists, psychologists rely on research to find answers to the questions that interest them.

Your Turn: Now that we have discussed gender, ethnicity, and psychology, enhance your mastery of the material with the nearby "Learning Connections." Review the material by filling in the blanks, reflect on the material by relating it to other things you know, and think critically about it.

Learning Connections — GENDER, ETHNICITY, AND PSYCHOLOGY: REAL PEOPLE IN THE REAL WORLD

ACTIVE REVIEW (27) _____ introduced the method of paired associates and discovered the primacy and recency effects. (28) _____ formulated a theory of color vision. (29) Kenneth B. _____ influenced a key United States Supreme Court decision on desegregation in the schools. (30) _____ has been referred to as the "father of Ebonics."

REFLECT AND RELATE Consider your own gender and ethnic background. What would it have been like for you to try to study psychology in the United States a century ago?

CRITICAL THINKING Women now receive the majority of undergraduate and graduate degrees in psychology. Review the fields in psychology and speculate as to why this may be so.

 Go to **http://psychology.wadsworth.com/ rathus_pcc9e** for an interactive version of this Learning Connections unit.

How Psychologists Study Behavior and Mental Processes

Consider some questions of interest to psychologists: Does alcohol cause aggression? Why do some people hardly ever think of food, whereas others are obsessed with it and snack all day long? Why do some unhappy people attempt suicide, whereas others seek ways of coping with their problems? Does having people of different ethnic backgrounds collaborate in their work serve to decrease or increase feelings of prejudice?

Many of us have expressed opinions—maybe even some strong opinions—on questions like these. Various psychological theories also suggest possible answers. Modern psychology aims to be an *empirical* science, however. In an empirical science, we cannot test assumptions about the behavior of cosmic rays, chemical compounds, cells, or people unless we observe and measure that behavior. Assumptions must be supported by evidence. Strong arguments, reference to authority figures, even tightly knit theories are not adequate as scientific evidence. The guiding principle behind this kind of skepticism is the scientific method.

The Scientific Method: Putting Ideas to the Test

Question: What is the scientific method? The scientific method is an organized way of using experience and testing ideas in order to expand and refine knowledge. Psychologists do not necessarily follow the steps of the scientific method as we might follow a recipe in a cookbook. However, modern research ideally is guided by certain principles.

Correlational method A mathematical method of determining whether one variable increases or decreases as another variable increases or decreases. For example, there is a correlation between intelligence test scores and grades in school.

Hypothesis In psychology, a specific statement about behavior or mental processes that is tested through research.

Correlation An association or relationship among variables, as we might find between height and weight or between study habits and school grades.

In Profile SIR FRANCIS GALTON

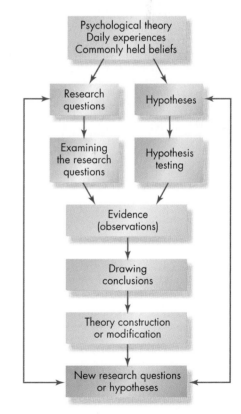

© The Granger Collection, New York

His parents named him Francis. I think of him as Mr. Measurement.

The Englishman Sir Francis Galton (1822–1911) was reading and writing by the age of 2½. He read Shakespeare for pleasure at the age of 7. He invented weather maps and coined the now-familiar terms *high*, *low*, and *front*. He innovated the use of fingerprinting for purposes of identification. He was also Charles Darwin's cousin. Independently wealthy, young Galton attended medical school for a while and then dropped out. He traveled in the Middle East and Africa and mapped out previously uncharted territories. He assumed that intelligence could be measured by means of sensory sharpness (it cannot) and constructed devices to measure the keenness of the senses. He also believed that intelligence was inherited and founded the *eugenics* movement, which proposed that only bright people should mate. In fact, he wanted the British government to pay people who shared desirable traits to marry and bear children. These misguided views have since caused him to be branded as exclusionary and racist.

But Galton's fascination with measurement led to many positive innovations in the field of psychology, such as the use of questionnaires and twin studies. He invented the use of the **correlational method** so that there would be a mathematical way to see what goes with what—that is, the relationship between variables, as discussed on page 28. For example, he sought ways to measure the amount of boredom in the audience at scientific lectures—an undertaking that probably did not heighten his popularity with his fellow scientists. He also sought to measure the effectiveness of prayers (he concluded that they were ineffective) and to determine which nation had the world's most attractive women. He chose his native England, mistakenly assuming that the local standards for beauty were universal.

Despite Galton's missteps, observation and the measurement of observations are keys to the scientific method. Much of what Galton taught, such as the use of questionnaires and the correlational method, remains in use today.

 Go to **http://psychology.wadsworth.com/ rathus_pcc9e** to access more information about Sir Francis Galton.

Psychologists usually begin by *formulating a research question*. Research questions can have many sources. Our daily experiences, psychological theory, even folklore all help generate questions for research. Consider some questions that may arise from daily experience. Daily experience in using day-care centers may motivate us to conduct research on whether day care affects the development of social skills or the bonds of attachment between children and mothers. Social cognitive principles of observational learning may prompt research on the effects of TV violence.

Research questions may also arise from common knowledge. Consider familiar adages such as "misery loves company," "opposites attract," and "seeing is believing." Psychologists may ask, *does* misery love company? *Do* opposites attract? *Can* people believe what they see?

A research question may be studied as a question or reworded as a hypothesis (see Figure 1.4). A **hypothesis** is a specific statement about behavior or mental processes that is tested through research. One hypothesis about day care might be that preschoolers who are placed in day care will acquire greater social skills in relating to peers than preschoolers who are cared for in the home. A hypothesis about TV violence might be that elementary school children who watch more violent TV shows tend to behave more aggressively toward their peers.

Psychologists next examine the research question or *test the hypothesis* through controlled methods such as the experiment. For example, we could take a group of preschoolers who attend day care and another group who do not, and introduce each to a new child in a controlled setting such as a child-research center. We could then observe how children in each group interact with the new acquaintance.

Psychologists draw conclusions about their research questions or the accuracy of their hypotheses on the basis of their observations or findings. When their observations do not bear out their hypotheses, they may modify the theories from which the hypotheses were derived. Research findings often suggest refinements to psychological theories and, consequently, new avenues of research.

In our research on day care, we would probably find that children in day care show greater social skills than children who are cared for in the home (Belsky et al., 2001). We would probably also find that more aggressive children spend more time watching TV violence.

As psychologists draw conclusions from research evidence, they are guided by principles of critical thinking. For example, they try not to confuse **correlations**—

FIGURE 1.4 **The Scientific Method**

The scientific method is a systematic way of organizing and expanding scientific knowledge. Daily experiences, common beliefs, and scientific observations all contribute to the development of theories. Psychological theories explain observations and lead to hypotheses about behavior and mental processes. Observations can confirm the theory or lead to its refinement or abandonment.

Flowchart:
Psychological theory / Daily experiences / Commonly held beliefs → Research questions / Hypotheses → Examining the research questions / Hypothesis testing → Evidence (observations) → Drawing conclusions → Theory construction or modification → New research questions or hypotheses

Selection factor A source of bias that may occur in research findings when subjects are allowed to choose for themselves a certain treatment in a scientific study.

Replicate Repeat, reproduce, copy.

Generalize To extend from the particular to the general; to apply observations based on a sample to a population.

Sample Part of a population.

Population A complete group of organisms or events.

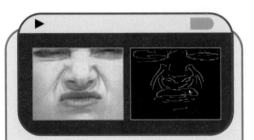

Video Connections—Facial Analysis—The Scientific Method in Action Will you soon be using your camera cell phone to snap a picture of someone, send it to a lab for analysis, and get a report back on the person? To understand more about the scientific method in action, go to your companion website and click on the "Facial Analysis" video link.

or associations—between findings with cause and effect. Although more aggressive children apparently spend more time watching violent TV shows, it may be erroneous to conclude from this kind of evidence that TV violence *causes* aggressive behavior. Perhaps a **selection factor** is at work—because the children studied choose (select) for themselves what they will watch. Perhaps more aggressive children are more likely than less aggressive children to tune in to violent TV shows.

To better understand the effects of the selection factor, consider a study on the relationship between exercise and health. Imagine that we were to compare a group of people who exercised regularly with a group of people who did not. We might find that the exercisers were physically healthier than the couch potatoes. But could we conclude without doubt that exercise is a causal factor in good health? Perhaps not. The selection factor—the fact that one group chose to exercise and the other did not—could also explain the results. Perhaps healthy people are more likely to *choose* to exercise.

Some psychologists include publication of research reports in professional journals as a crucial part of the scientific method. Researchers are obligated to provide enough details of their work so that others will be able to repeat or **replicate** it to see whether the findings hold up over time and with different subjects. Publication of research also permits the scientific community at large to evaluate the methods and conclusions of other scientists.

Samples and Populations: Hitting the Target Population

Consider a piece of history that never quite happened: The Republican candidate Alf Landon defeated the incumbent president, Franklin D. Roosevelt, in 1936. Or at least Landon did so in a poll conducted by a popular magazine of the day, the *Literary Digest.* In the actual election, however, Roosevelt routed Landon by a landslide of 11 million votes. **Truth or Fiction Revisited:** It is true that you could survey millions of voters and still not predict the outcome of a presidential election. In effect, the *Digest* accomplished something like this when they predicted a Landon victory. How was so great a discrepancy possible?

The *Digest,* you see, had surveyed voters by phone. Today telephone sampling is a widely practiced and reasonably legitimate polling technique. But the *Digest* poll was taken during the Great Depression, when people who had telephones were much wealthier than those who did not. People at higher income levels are also more likely to vote Republican. No surprise, then, that the overwhelming majority of those sampled said they would vote for Landon.

Question: How do psychologists use samples to represent populations? The *Digest* poll failed because of its method of sampling. Samples must be drawn so that they accurately *represent* the population they are intended to reflect. Only representative samples allow us to **generalize**—or *extend*—our findings from research samples to populations.

In surveys such as that conducted by the *Literary Digest,* and in other research methods, the individuals who are studied are referred to as a **sample.** A sample is a segment of a **population** (the group that is targeted for study). Psychologists and other scientists need to ensure that the people they observe *represent* their target population, such as U.S. voters, and not subgroups such as southern Californians or European American members of the middle class.

PROBLEMS IN GENERALIZING FROM PSYCHOLOGICAL RESEARCH

All generalizations are dangerous, even this one.
Alexandre Dumas

Many factors must be considered in interpreting the accuracy of the results of scientific research. One is the nature of the research sample.

Later in the chapter we consider research in which the subjects were drawn from a population of college men who were social drinkers. That is, they tended to drink at social gatherings but not when alone. Whom do college men represent, other than themselves? To whom can we extend, or generalize, the results? For one thing, the results may not extend to women, not even to college women. In the chapter on consciousness, for example, we will learn that alcohol affects women more quickly than men.

Also, compared to the general adult male population, college men tend to be younger and score higher on intelligence tests. We cannot be certain that the findings extend to older men or to those with lower intelligence test scores, although it seems reasonable to assume they do. Social drinkers may also differ biologically and psychologically from alcoholics, who have difficulty controlling their drinking. Nor can we be certain that male college social drinkers represent people who do not drink at all.

By and large, we must also question whether findings of research with men can be generalized to women and whether research with European American men can be extended to members of ethnic minority groups. For example, personality tests completed by European Americans and by African Americans may need to be interpreted in diverse ways if accurate conclusions are to be drawn. The well-known Kinsey studies on sexual behavior (Kinsey et al., 1948, 1953) did not adequately represent African Americans, low-income people, older people, and numerous other groups.

RANDOM AND STRATIFIED SAMPLING One way to achieve a representative sample is by means of **random sampling.** In a random sample, each member of a population has an equal chance of being selected to participate. Researchers can also use a **stratified sample,** which is selected so that identified subgroups in the population are represented proportionately in the sample. For instance, 13% of the American population is African American. A stratified sample would thus be 13% African American. As a practical matter, a large randomly selected sample will show reasonably accurate stratification. A random sample of 1,500 people will represent the broad American population reasonably well. A haphazardly drawn sample of 20 million, however, might not.

Large-scale magazine surveys of sexual behavior have asked readers to fill out and return questionnaires. Although many thousands of readers completed the questionnaires and sent them in, did the survey respondents represent the American population? Probably not. These studies and similar ones may have been influenced by **volunteer bias.** People who offer or volunteer to participate in research studies differ systematically from people who do not. In the case of research on sexual behavior, volunteers may represent subgroups of the population—or of readers of the magazines in question—who are willing to disclose intimate information and therefore may also be likely to be more liberal in their sexual behavior (Rathus et al., 2005). Volunteers may also be more interested in research than other people, as well as have more spare time. How might such volunteers differ from the population at large? How might such differences slant or bias the research outcomes?

Another bias in the case study and survey methods is social desirability. That is, many people involved in research studies tend to tell the interviewer what they think the interviewer would like to hear and not what they really think. You can gain insight into whether you tend to express your genuine feelings or socially desirable answers by completing the nearby Social-Desirability Scale.

Methods of Observation: The Better to See You With

Many people consider themselves experts on behavior and mental processes. How many times, for example, have you or someone else been eager to share a life experience that proves some point about human nature?

Indeed, we see much during our lifetimes. However, our personal observations tend to be fleeting and unsystematic. We sift through experience for the things that interest us. We often ignore the obvious because it does not fit our assumptions about the way things ought to be. Scientists, however, have devised more controlled

Random sample A sample drawn so that each member of a population has an equal chance of being selected to participate.

Stratified sample A sample drawn so that identified subgroups in the population are represented proportionately in the sample. How can stratified sampling be carried out to ensure that a sample represents the ethnic diversity we find in the population at large?

Volunteer bias A source of bias or error in research reflecting the prospect that people who offer to participate in research studies differ systematically from people who do not.

Self-Assessment | Dare You Say What You Think? The Social-Desirability Scale

One of the problems researchers encounter during surveys and case studies is that of social desirability. That is, people being interviewed may tell the researcher what they think the researcher wants to hear and not what they really believe. In doing so, they may provide the so-called socially desirable answer—the answer they believe will earn the approval of the researcher. Falling prey to social desirability may cause us to distort our beliefs and experiences in interviews and psychological tests. The bias toward responding in socially desirable directions is a source of error in the case study and survey methods.

What about you? Do you say what you think, or do you tend to misrepresent your beliefs to earn the approval of others? Do you answer questions honestly, or do you say what you think other people want to hear?

You can complete the Social-Desirability Scale devised by Crowne and Marlowe to gain insight into whether you have a tendency to produce socially desirable responses.

Directions: Read each item and decide whether it is true (T) or false (F) for you. Try to work rapidly and answer each question by circling the T or the F. Then turn to the scoring key in the appendix to interpret your answers.

T F   1. Before voting, I thoroughly investigate the qualifications of all the candidates.

T F   2. I never hesitate to go out of my way to help someone in trouble.

T F   3. It is sometimes hard for me to go on with my work if I am not encouraged.

T F   4. I have never intensely disliked anyone.

T F   5. On occasions I have had doubts about my ability to succeed in life.

T F   6. I sometimes feel resentful when I don't get my way.

T F   7. I am always careful about my manner of dress.

T F   8. My table manners at home are as good as when I eat out in a restaurant.

T F   9. If I could get into a movie without paying and be sure I was not seen, I would probably do it.

T F   10. On a few occasions, I have given up something because I thought too little of my ability.

T F   11. I like to gossip at times.

T F   12. There have been times when I felt like rebelling against people in authority even though I knew they were right.

T F   13. No matter whom I'm talking to, I'm always a good listener.

T F   14. I can remember "playing sick" to get out of something.

T F   15. There have been occasions when I have taken advantage of someone.

T F   16. I'm always willing to admit it when I make a mistake.

T F   17. I always try to practice what I preach.

T F   18. I don't find it particularly difficult to get along with loudmouthed, obnoxious people.

T F   19. I sometimes try to get even rather than forgive and forget.

T F   20. When I don't know something I don't mind at all admitting it.

T F   21. I am always courteous, even to people who are disagreeable.

T F   22. At times I have really insisted on having things my own way.

T F   23. There have been occasions when I felt like smashing things.

T F   24. I would never think of letting someone else be punished for my wrongdoings.

T F   25. I never resent being asked to return a favor.

T F   26. I have never been irked when people expressed ideas very different from my own.

T F   27. I never make a long trip without checking the safety of my car.

T F   28. There have been times when I was quite jealous of the good fortune of others.

T F   29. I have almost never felt the urge to tell someone off.

T F   30. I am sometimes irritated by people who ask favors of me.

T F   31. I have never felt that I was punished without cause.

T F   32. I sometimes think when people have a misfortune they only got what they deserved.

T F   33. I have never deliberately said something that hurt someone's feelings.

Source: D. P. Crowne and D. A. Marlowe, A new scale of social desirability independent of pathology, *Journal of Consulting Psychology,* 24 (1960): 351. Copyright 1960 by the American Psychological Association.

ways of observing others. **Question: What methods of observation are used by psychologists?** In this section we consider three methods of observation widely used by psychologists and other behavioral scientists: the case study, survey, and naturalistic observation methods.

CASE STUDY We begin with the case study method because our own informal ideas about human nature tend to be based on **case studies,** or information we collect about individuals and small groups. But most of us gather our information haphazardly. We often see only what we want to see. Unscientific accounts of people's behavior are referred to as *anecdotes*. Ideally, psychologists attempt to gather information about individuals more carefully.

Case studies are sometimes used to investigate rare occurrences, as in the case of "Eve," immortalized in the film *The Three Faces of Eve*. Eve was an example of a person with multiple personalities (technically termed *dissociative identity disorder*). "Eve White" was a mousy, well-intentioned woman who had two other "personalities" living inside her. One of them was "Eve Black," a promiscuous personality who emerged now and then to take control of her behavior. The third personality, "Jane," was a well-adjusted woman who integrated parts of Eve White and Eve Black.

Case studies can provide compelling portraits of individuals, but they also have some sources of inaccuracy. For example, there are gaps and factual inaccuracies in people's memories (Azar, 1997a). People may also distort their pasts to please the interviewer or because they want to remember things in certain ways. Interviewers may also have certain expectations and may subtly encourage subjects to fill in gaps in ways that are consistent with these expectations. Psychoanalysts, for example, have been criticized for guiding people who seek their help into viewing their own lives from the psychodynamic perspective (Hergenhahn, 2001). No wonder, then, that many people provide "evidence" that is consistent with psychodynamic theory—such as, "My parents' inept handling of my toilet training is the source of my compulsive neatness." However, interviewers and other kinds of researchers who hold *any* theoretical viewpoint run the risk of indirectly prodding people into saying what they want to hear.

THE SURVEY In the good old days, we had to wait until the wee hours of the morning to learn the results of local and national elections. Throughout the evening and early morning hours, suspense would build as ballots from distant neighborhoods and states were tallied. Nowadays, we are barely settled with an after-dinner cup of coffee on election night when reporters announce that a computer has examined the ballots of a "scientifically selected sample" and predicted the next president of the United States. All of this may occur with less than 1% of the vote tallied.

Just as computers and pollsters predict election results and report national opinion on the basis of scientifically selected samples, psychologists conduct **surveys** to learn about behavior and mental processes that cannot be observed in the natural setting or studied experimentally. Psychologists conducting surveys may employ questionnaires and interviews or examine public records. One of the advantages of the survey is that by distributing questionnaires and analyzing answers with a computer, psychologists can study many thousands of people at a time.

Alfred Kinsey of Indiana University and his colleagues published two surveys of sexual behavior, based on interviews, that shocked the nation. These were *Sexual Behavior in the Human Male* (1948) and *Sexual Behavior in the Human Female* (1953). Kinsey reported that masturbation was virtually universal in his sample of men at a time when masturbation was still widely thought to impair health. He also reported that about 1 woman in 3 who was still single at age 25 had engaged in premarital intercourse.

Surveys, like case studies, have various sources of inaccuracy. People may recall their behavior inaccurately or purposefully misrepresent it. Some people try to ingratiate themselves with their interviewers by answering in what they perceive to be the

Case study A carefully drawn biography that may be obtained through interviews, questionnaires, and psychological tests.

Survey A method of scientific investigation in which a large sample of people answer questions about their attitudes or behavior.

socially desirable direction. The Kinsey studies all relied on male interviewers, for example. It has been speculated that female interviewees might have been more open and honest with female interviewers. Similar problems may occur when interviewers and the people surveyed are from different ethnic or socioeconomic backgrounds. Other people may falsify their attitudes and exaggerate their problems in order to draw attention to themselves or intentionally foul up the results.

Consider some examples of survey measurement errors caused by inaccurate self-reports of behavior (Barringer, 1993). If people brushed their teeth as often as they claimed, and used the amount of toothpaste they indicated, three times as much toothpaste would be sold in the United States as is actually sold. People also appear to overreport church attendance and to underreport abortions (Barringer, 1993). Why do you think this is so?

NATURALISTIC OBSERVATION You use **naturalistic observation**—that is, you observe people in their natural habitats—every day. So do psychologists and other scientists. Naturalistic observation has the advantage of allowing psychologists and other scientists to observe behavior where it happens, or "in the field." In doing so, researchers use *unobtrusive* measures to avoid interfering with the behaviors they are observing. For example, Jane Goodall has observed the behavior of chimpanzees in their natural environment to learn about their social behavior, sexual behavior, use of tools, and other facts of chimp life. Her observations have shown us that (1) we were incorrect to think that only humans use tools; and (2) kissing on the lips, as a greeting, is apparently used by chimpanzees as well as by humans (Goodall, 2000).

Correlation: On How Things Go Together—Or Not

Are people with higher intelligence more likely to do well in school? Are people with a stronger need for achievement likely to climb higher up the corporate ladder? What is the relationship between stress and health?

Such questions are often answered by means of the correlational method. **Question: What is the correlational method?** Correlation follows observation. By using the correlational method, psychologists investigate whether observed behavior or a measured trait is related to, or correlated with, another. Consider the variables of intelligence and academic performance. These variables are assigned numbers such as intelligence test scores and academic averages. Then the numbers are mathematically related and expressed as a **correlation coefficient.** A correlation coefficient is a number that varies between +1.00 and −1.00.

Naturalistic observation A scientific method in which organisms are observed in their natural environments.

Correlation coefficient A number between +1.00 and −1.00 that expresses the strength and direction (positive or negative) of the relationship between two variables.

■ **The Naturalistic-Observation Method** Jane Goodall has observed the behavior of chimpanzees—our closest genetic relatives—in the field, "where it happens." She has found that chimps use sticks to grub for food and that they apparently kiss each other as a social greeting. Scientists who use this method try not to interfere with the animals or people they observe, even though this sometimes means allowing an animal to be mistreated by other animals or to die from a curable illness.

Michael K. Nichols/National Geographic Society

Studies report **positive correlations** between intelligence test scores and academic achievement, as measured, for example, by grade point averages. Generally speaking, the higher people score on intelligence tests, the better their academic performance is likely to be. The scores attained on intelligence tests tend to be positively correlated (about +0.60 to +0.70) with academic achievement (see Figure 1.5). But factors *other* than performance on intelligence tests also contribute to academic success. These include achievement motivation, adjustment, and common sense (Collier, 1994; Sternberg et al., 1995).

Many correlations are *negative;* that is, as one variable increases, the other variable decreases. There is a **negative correlation** between stress and health. As the amount of stress affecting us increases, the functioning of our immune system decreases. Under high levels of stress, many people show poorer health.

What kinds of correlations (positive or negative) would you expect to find among behavior patterns such as the following: Churchgoing and crime? Language ability and musical ability? Level of education and incidence of teenage pregnancy? Grades in school and delinquency? Why?

Correlational research may suggest but does not prove cause and effect. For instance, it may seem logical to assume that high intelligence makes it possible for children to profit from education. Research has also shown, however, that education contributes to higher scores on intelligence tests. Preschoolers who are placed in stimulating Head Start programs later attain higher scores on intelligence tests than age-mates who did not have this experience. The relationship between intelligence and academic performance may not be as simple as we might think. What of the link between stress and health? Does stress impair health, or is it possible that people in poorer health encounter more stress? (See Figure 1.6.)

The Experimental Method: Trying Things Out

Question: What is the experimental method? Most psychologists agree that the preferred method for answering questions about cause and effect is the experiment. In an **experiment,** a group of subjects obtains a **treatment,** such as a dose of alcohol, a change in room temperature, perhaps an injection of a drug. The subjects are then observed carefully to determine whether the treatment makes a difference in their behavior. Does alcohol alter the ability to take tests, for example? What about differences in room temperatures and level of background noise?

Experiments are used whenever possible because they allow psychologists to control the experiences of subjects and draw conclusions about cause and effect. A psychologist may theorize that alcohol leads to aggression because it reduces fear of consequences or because it energizes the activity levels of drinkers. She or he

Positive correlation A relationship between variables in which one variable increases as the other also increases.

Negative correlation A relationship between two variables in which one variable increases as the other decreases.

Experiment A scientific method that seeks to confirm cause-and-effect relationships by introducing independent variables and observing their effects on dependent variables.

Treatment In experiments, a condition received by subjects so that its effects may be observed.

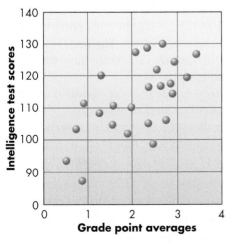

Positive correlation, as found between intelligence and academic achievement

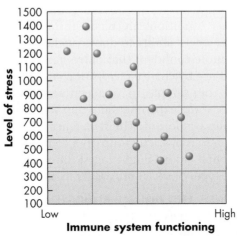

Negative correlation, as found between stress and functioning of the immune system

FIGURE 1.5 **Positive and Negative Correlations** When there is a positive correlation between variables, as there is between intelligence and achievement, one increases as the other increases. By and large, the higher people score on intelligence tests, the better their academic performance is likely to be, as in the diagram to the left. (Each dot represents an individual's intelligence test score and grade point average.) But there is a negative correlation between stress and health. As the amount of stress we experience increases, the functioning of our immune system tends to decrease. Correlational research may suggest but does not demonstrate cause and effect.

FIGURE 1.6 Correlational Relationships, Cause, and Effect

Correlational relationships may suggest but do not demonstrate cause and effect. In part A, there is a correlation between variables X and Y. Does this mean that either variable X causes variable Y or that variable Y causes variable X? Not necessarily. Other factors could affect both variables X and Y. Consider the examples of academic grades (variable X) and juvenile delinquency (variable Y) in part B. There is a negative correlation between the two. Does this mean that poor grades contribute to delinquency? Perhaps. Does it mean that delinquency contributes to poor grades? Again, perhaps. But there could also be other variables—such as a broken home, lack of faith in the educational system, or peer influences—that contribute both to poor grades and delinquency.

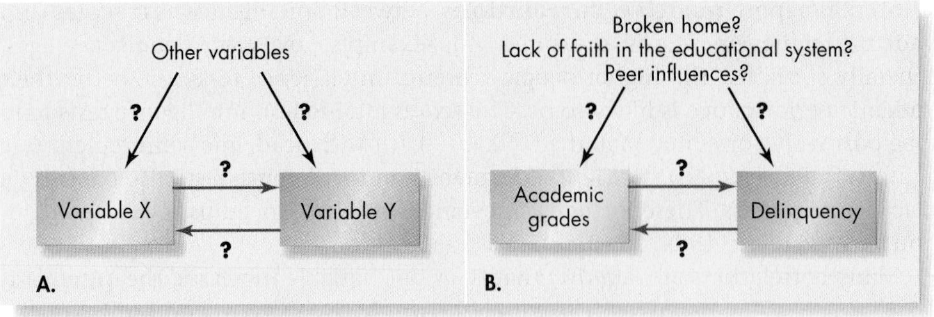

may then hypothesize that a treatment in which subjects receive a specified dosage of alcohol will lead to increases in aggression. Let us follow the example of the effects of alcohol on aggression to further our understanding of the experimental method.

INDEPENDENT AND DEPENDENT VARIABLES In an experiment to determine whether alcohol causes aggression, subjects are given an amount of alcohol and its effects are measured. In this case, alcohol is an **independent variable.** The presence of an independent variable is manipulated by the experimenters so that its effects may be determined. The independent variable of alcohol may be administered at different levels, or doses, from none or very little to enough to cause intoxication or drunkenness.

The measured results, or outcomes, in an experiment are called **dependent variables.** The presence of dependent variables presumably depends on the independent variables. In an experiment to determine whether alcohol influences aggression, aggressive behavior would be a dependent variable. Other dependent variables of interest might include sexual arousal, visual-motor coordination, and performance on intellectual tasks such as defining words or doing numerical computations.

In an experiment on the relationships between temperature and aggression, temperature would be an independent variable and aggressive behavior would be a dependent variable. We could set temperatures from below freezing to blistering hot, and study its effects on aggression. We could also use a second independent variable such as social provocation. That is, we could insult some subjects but not others and see whether insults affect their level of aggression. This method would allow us to study the ways in which two independent variables—temperature and social provocation—affect aggression, singly and/or together.

EXPERIMENTAL AND CONTROL GROUPS Ideal experiments use "experimental groups" and "control groups." Subjects in **experimental groups** obtain the treatment. Members of **control groups** do not. Every effort is made to ensure that all other conditions are held constant for both groups. This method enhances the researchers' ability to draw conclusions about cause and effect. The researchers can be more confident that outcomes of the experiment are caused by the treatments and not by chance factors or chance fluctuations in behavior.

For example, in an experiment on the effects of alcohol on aggression, members of the experimental group would ingest alcohol, and members of the control group would not. The researcher would then measure how much aggression was expressed by each group. In a complex version of this experiment, different experimental groups might ingest different dosages of alcohol and be exposed to different types of social provocations as well.

BLINDS AND DOUBLE BLINDS One experiment on the effects of alcohol on aggression (Boyatzis, 1974) reported that men at parties where beer and liquor were served acted more aggressively than men at parties where only soft drinks were served. But subjects in the experimental group *knew* they had drunk alcohol, and those in the control group *knew* they had not. Aggression that appeared to result from alcohol

Independent variable A condition in a scientific study that is manipulated so that its effects may be observed.

Dependent variable A measure of an assumed effect of an independent variable.

Experimental groups In experiments, groups whose members obtain the treatment.

Control groups In experiments, groups whose members do not obtain the treatment, while other conditions are held constant.

might not have reflected drinking per se. Instead, it might have reflected the subjects' *expectations* about the effects of alcohol. People tend to act in stereotypical ways when they believe they have been drinking alcohol. For instance, men tend to become less anxious in social situations, more aggressive, and more sexually aroused. To what extent do these behavior patterns reflect the direct effects of alcohol on the body, and to what extent do they affect people's *beliefs* about the effects of alcohol?

In medicine, physicians have sometimes given patients **placebos** (or "sugar pills") when the patient insisted on having a medical cure but the physician did not believe that one was necessary. When patients report that placebos have helped them, it is because they expected the pills to be of help and not because of the direct effect of the pills on their bodies. Psychologists and other researchers have adopted the lore of the "sugar pill" to sort out the effects of actual treatments from people's expectations about the effects of those treatments. Placebos are not actually limited to pills made of sugar. When subjects in psychological experiments are given placebos such as tonic water, but they think they have drunk alcohol, we can conclude that changes in their behavior stem from their beliefs about the effects of alcohol, not from the alcohol itself.

Well-designed experiments control for the effects of expectations by creating conditions under which subjects are unaware of, or **blind** to, the treatment (Day & Altman, 2000). Yet researchers may also have expectations. They may, in effect, be "rooting for" a certain treatment. For instance, tobacco company executives may wish to show that cigarette smoking is harmless. In such cases, it is useful if the people measuring the experimental outcomes are unaware of which subjects have received the treatment. Studies in which neither the subjects nor the experimenters know who has obtained the treatment are called **double-blind studies.**

Truth or Fiction Revisited: It is true that neither the subjects nor the researchers know who is receiving the real treatment in many experiments. For example, the Food and Drug Administration requires double-blind studies before it allows the marketing of new drugs. The drug and the placebo look and taste alike. Experimenters assign the drug or placebo to subjects at random. Neither the subjects nor the observers know who is taking the drug and who is taking the placebo. After the final measurements have been made, a neutral panel (a group of people who have no personal stake in the outcome of the study) judges whether the effects of the drug differed from those of the placebo.

In one double-blind study on the effects of alcohol, Alan Lang and his colleagues (1975) pretested a highball of vodka and tonic water to determine that it could not be discriminated by taste from tonic water alone. They recruited college men who described themselves as social drinkers to participate in the study. Some of the men drank vodka and tonic water. Others drank tonic water only. Of the men who drank vodka, half were misled into believing they had drunk tonic water only (Figure 1.7). Of those who drank tonic water only, half were misled into believing their drink contained vodka. Thus, half the subjects were blind to their treatment. Experimenters who measured the men's aggressive responses were also blind concerning which subjects had drunk vodka.

The research team found that men who believed that they had drunk vodka responded more aggressively to a provocation than men who believed that they had drunk tonic water only. The actual content of the drink was immaterial. That is, the men's *belief* about what they drank affected their aggressive

■ **What Are the Effects of Alcohol?** Psychologists have conducted numerous studies to determine the effects of alcohol. Questions have been raised about the soundness of research in which people *know* that they have drunk alcohol. Why would such research be questioned, and how can we keep people blind to the fact that they have drunk alcohol?

Placebo A bogus treatment that has the appearance of being genuine.

Blind In experimental terminology, unaware of whether or not one has received a treatment.

Double-blind study A study in which neither the subjects nor the observers know who has received the treatment.

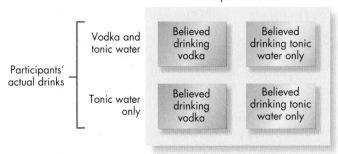

FIGURE 1.7 **The Experimental Conditions in the Lang Study**
The taste of vodka cannot be discerned when vodka is mixed with tonic water. For this reason, it was possible for subjects in the Lang study on the effects of alcohol to be kept "blind" as to whether or not they had actually drunk alcohol. Blind studies allow psychologists to control for the effects of subjects' expectations.

Concept Review RESEARCH METHODS

Method	What Happens	Comments
Case Study	The researcher uses interviews and records to gather in-depth information about an individual or a small group.	The accuracy of case studies is compromised by gaps and mistakes in memory and by subjects' tendency to present themselves in a socially desirable manner.
The Survey	The researcher uses interviews, questionnaires, or public records to gather information about large numbers of people.	Surveys can include thousands of people but are subject to the same limitations as case studies. People who volunteer to participate in surveys may also differ from people who do not. There may thus be problems in generalization of results to people who do not participate.
Naturalistic Observation	The researcher observes behavior where it happens—"in the field."	Researchers try to avoid interfering with the behaviors they are observing by using *unobtrusive* measures.
Correlation	The researcher uses statistical (mathematical) methods to reveal positive and negative relationships between variables.	The correlational method does not show cause and effect. Correlation coefficients vary between $+1.00$ (a perfect positive correlation) and -1.00 (a perfect negative correlation).
Experiment	The researcher manipulates independent variables and observes their effects on dependent variables.	Experimental groups obtain the treatment; control groups do not. Researchers use *blinds* to control for the effect of expectations. With *double blinds*, neither the subjects nor the observers know which subject has received which treatment. The experimental method allows researchers to draw conclusions about cause and effect.

Go to **http://psychology.wadsworth.com/ rathus_pcc9e** to access a drag-and-drop version of this Concept Review designed to help you test yourself on the major topics provided here.

behavior more than what they actually consumed. The results of the Lang study differ dramatically from those reported by Boyatzis, perhaps because the Boyatzis study did not control for the effects of expectations or beliefs about alcohol. The nearby Concept Review will enhance your understanding of all the research methods you have just learned about.

Your Turn: Now that we have discussed the ways in which psychologists study behavior and mental processes, you can further enhance your mastery of the material with the nearby "Learning Connections." Review the material by filling in the blanks, reflect on the material by relating it to other things you know, and think critically about it.

Learning Connections HOW PSYCHOLOGISTS STUDY BEHAVIOR AND MENTAL PROCESSES

ACTIVE REVIEW (31) Scientists often test a specific statement, or _____, about behavior or mental processes. (32) Samples must accurately represent the target _____. (33) In a _____ sample, each member of a population has an equal chance of being selected to participate. (34) A _____ study is a carefully drawn biography. (35) In the _____, a large sample of people answer questions about their attitudes or behavior. (36) The _____-observation method observes individuals in their natural habitats. (37) The _____ method investigates whether behaviors or traits are related to others. (38) Correlational research does not reveal _____ and effect. (39) An _____ is conducted in an effort to determine cause and effect. (40) The _____ variable is manipulated by the experimenters so that its effects may be determined. (41) Ideal experiments use experimental and _____ groups. (42) Well-designed experiments control

for the effects of expectations by creating conditions under which subjects are unaware of, or _____ to, the treatment they have received.

REFLECT AND RELATE Why not try out the naturalistic observation method for yourself? The next time you eat at a fast-food restaurant, look around. Pick out slender people and overweight people and note whether they eat differently—even when they select the same foods. Do overweight people eat more rapidly? Do they chew less frequently? Do they leave less food on their plates? What conclusions can you draw?

CRITICAL THINKING People who exercise are generally healthier than people who do not. Does this fact show that exercise is a causal factor in good health? Why or why not?

Go to **http://psychology.wadsworth.com/ rathus_pcc9e** for an interactive version of this Learning Connections unit.

Ethical Issues in Psychological Research and Practice

The researchers in the Lang study gave some participants alcohol to drink and deceived the entire group about the purposes and methods of the study. Was their method **ethical?** We'll return to this question, but let's first address a broader one. **Question: What are the ethical issues that concern psychological research and practice with humans?**

Psychologists adhere to a number of ethical standards that are intended to promote individual dignity, human welfare, and scientific integrity. The standards are also intended to ensure that psychologists do not undertake research methods or treatments that are harmful.

Research with Humans

If the Lang group were running their experiment today rather than in the 1970s, they might have been denied permission to do so by a university ethics review committee. Why? Because in virtually all institutional settings, including colleges, hospitals, and research foundations, ethics review committees help researchers consider the potential harm of their methods and review proposed studies according to ethical guidelines. When such committees find that proposed research might be unacceptably harmful to subjects, they may withhold approval until the proposal has been modified. Ethics review committees also weigh the potential benefits of research against the potential harm.

Today individuals must provide **informed consent** before they participate in research (American Psychological Association, 2002). Having a general overview of the research and the opportunity to choose not to participate apparently gives them a sense of control and decreases the stress of participating (Dill et al., 1982). Is there a way in which subjects in the Lang study could have provided informed consent? What do you think?

Psychologists treat the records of research subjects and clients as confidential (Smith, 2003a, 2003c). This is because they respect people's privacy and also because people are more likely to express their true thoughts and feelings when researchers or therapists keep their disclosures confidential. Sometimes conflicts of interest arise, however; for example, this can happen when a client threatens to harm someone and the psychologist feels an obligation to warn that person (Follingstad & McCormick, 2002).

Ethics also limit the types of research that psychologists may conduct. For example, how can we determine whether early separation from one's mother impairs social development? One way would be to observe the development of children who were separated from their mothers at an early age for reasons such as the death of the mother or court-ordered protective custody. It is difficult to draw conclusions from such research, however, because of the selection factor. That is, the same factors that led to the separation—such as family tragedy or irresponsible parents—and *not* the separation, may have led to the outcome. Scientifically, it would be more sound to run experiments in which researchers separate children from their mothers at an early age and compare their development with that of other children. But psychologists would not undertake such research because of the ethical issues they pose. Yet, they run experiments in which infant animals are separated from their mothers, which has brought criticism from animal-rights groups.

CONTROVERSY IN PSYCHOLOGY

Is it ethical for psychologists to deceive research participants about the methods and objectives of their research?

Some studies could not be done if subjects knew what the researchers were trying to find out, or which treatment they had received (e.g., a new medicine or a "sugar pill"). As you can imagine, psychologists have long debated

Ethical Moral; referring to one's system of deriving standards for determining what is moral.

Informed consent A subject's agreement to participate in research after receiving information about the purposes of the study and the nature of the treatments.

Debrief To elicit information about a completed procedure.

the ethics of deceiving subjects. According to the American Psychological Association's (2002) *Ethical Principles of Psychologists and Code of Conduct,* psychologists may use deception only when they believe the benefits of the research outweigh its potential harm, they believe the individuals might have been willing to participate if they had understood the benefits of the research, and subjects are **debriefed.** Debriefing means that the purposes and methods of the research are explained afterward.

Return to the Lang (Lang et al., 1975) study on alcohol and aggression. In this study, the researchers (1) misinformed subjects about the beverage they were drinking and (2) misled them into believing they were giving other subjects electric shock when they were actually only pressing switches on a dead control board. (*Aggression* was defined as pressing these switches in the study.) In the Lang study, students who believed they had drunk vodka were "more aggressive"—that is, selected higher levels of shock—than students who believed they had not.

What do you think? Was it ethical to deceive participants in the Lang study as to what they were drinking? Why or why not?

Research with Nonhuman Animals

Psychologists and other scientists frequently use animals to conduct research that cannot be carried out with humans (Carroll & Overmier, 2001). For example, experiments on the effects of early separation from the mother have been done with monkeys and other animals. Such research has helped psychologists investigate the formation of attachment bonds between parent and child.

Question: What are the ethical issues that concern research with animals? Experiments with infant monkeys highlight some of the ethical issues faced by psychologists and other scientists who contemplate potentially harmful research. Psychologists and biologists who study the workings of the brain destroy sections of the brains of laboratory animals to learn how they influence behavior. For instance, a lesion in one part of a brain structure causes a rat to overeat. A lesion elsewhere causes the rat to go on a crash diet. Psychologists generalize to humans from experiments such as these in the hope of finding solutions to problems such as eating disorders. Proponents of the use of animals in research argue that major advances in medicine and psychology could not have taken place without them (Bekoff, 2002). For example, we would know much less about how experimental drugs affect cancerous growths and the brain.

The majority of psychologists disapprove of research in which animals are exposed to pain or killed (Plous, 1996). According to the ethical guidelines of the American Psychological Association, animals may be harmed only when there is no alternative and when researchers believe that the benefits of the research justify the harm (American Psychological Association, 2002; Smith, 2003b, 2003c).

■ **The Ethics of Using Animals in Research** Is it ethical for researchers to harm animals in order to obtain knowledge that may benefit humans?

© Claus Meyer/Black Star Publishing/Picture Quest

Your Turn: Now that we have discussed ethics in psychology, enhance your mastery of the material with the nearby "Learning Connections." Review the material by filling in the blanks, reflect on the material by relating it to other things you know, and think critically about it.

Learning Connections | ETHICAL ISSUES IN PSYCHOLOGICAL RESEARCH AND PRACTICE

ACTIVE REVIEW (43) Psychologists adhere to _____ standards that help promote the dignity of the individual, maintain scientific integrity, and protect subjects or clients from harm. (44) In order to help avoid harm, human subjects must provide _____ consent. (45) Ethics require that subjects who are deceived be _____ afterward to help eliminate misconceptions and anxieties about the research. (46) Researchers use _____ to conduct research that cannot be carried out with humans.

REFLECT AND RELATE Is it ethical to harm animals in conducting research when the results may be beneficial

to humans? Researchers often use animals to conduct research that they could not carry out with people. Do you agree with the practice? Why or why not?

CRITICAL THINKING Should psychologists ever break confidences? Psychologists are expected to keep things that clients tell them confidential. However, if a client in therapy were to tell his psychologist that he was thinking of hurting you, should the psychologist tell you about it? Why or why not?

 Go to **http://psychology.wadsworth.com/ rathus_pcc9e** for an interactive version of this Learning Connections unit.

Life Connections

Critical Thinking, Science, and Pseudoscience

Nonsense and pseudoscience (false science) beckon us from the tabloids at supermarket checkout counters. Each week, there are 10 new sightings of Elvis and 10 new encounters with extraterrestrials. There are 10 new "absolutely proven effective" ways to take off weight and 10 new ways to beat stress and depression. There are 10 new ways to tell if your partner has been cheating and, of course, 10 new predictions by astrologers and psychics. For example, Mick Jagger was supposed to be elected to Parliament in 1977, and Elvis was supposed to be returned to Earth by aliens in 2002.

Neither event took place—at least, not that we know of. But will those facts dissuade people who believe in psychics and astrologers? Clairvoyance and astrology are pseudosciences, not true sciences. Unfortunately, a survey of 1,574 adults by the National Science Foundation (2002) found that 70% of Americans do not understand the scientific process.

Let us look at the world through the eyes of the psychologist. Psychologists are guided by scientific principles, and one hallmark of science is *critical thinking*. **Question: What is critical thinking?** Critical thinking has many meanings. On one level, it means taking nothing for granted. It means not believing

things just because they are in print or because they were uttered by authority figures or celebrities. It means not necessarily believing that it is healthful to express all of your feelings just because a friend in "therapy" urges you to do so. On another level, critical thinking refers to a process of thoughtfully analyzing and probing the questions, statements, and arguments of others. It means examining definitions of terms, examining the premises or assumptions behind arguments, and then scrutinizing the logic with which arguments are developed.

A group of psychologists (McGovern, 1989) defined the goals of critical thinking as fostering the following thinking skills:
• Development of skepticism about explanations and conclusions.
• The ability to inquire about causes and effects.
• Increased curiosity about behavior.
• Knowledge of research methods.
• The ability to analyze arguments critically.

Principles of Critical Thinking

Let us consider some principles of critical thinking that can be of help to you in college and beyond:
1. *Be skeptical:* Keep an open mind. Politicians and advertisers try to persuade

you. Even research reported in the media or in textbooks may take a certain slant. Extend this principle to yourself. Are some of your own attitudes and beliefs superficial or unfounded? Accept nothing as the truth until you have examined the evidence.
2. *Examine definitions of terms:* Some statements are true when a term is defined in one way but not when it is defined in another way. Consider the statement, "Head Start programs have raised children's IQs." The correctness of the statement depends on the definition of "IQ." (You will see later in the text that *IQ* has a specific meaning and is not exactly the same as *intelligence*.)
3. *Examine the assumptions or premises of arguments:* Consider the statement that one cannot learn about human beings by engaging in research with animals. One premise in the statement seems to be that human beings are not animals. We are, of course. (Would you rather be a plant?)
4. *Be cautious in drawing conclusions from evidence:* For many years, studies had shown that most clients who receive psychotherapy improve. It was therefore generally assumed that psychotherapy worked. Some 40 years ago, however, a psychologist named Hans Eysenck pointed out that most psychologically troubled people who did *not*

receive psychotherapy also improved. The question thus becomes whether people receiving psychotherapy are *more* likely to improve than those who do not. Current research on the effectiveness of psychotherapy therefore carefully compares the benefits of therapy techniques to the benefits of other techniques or of no treatment at all. Be especially skeptical of anecdotes. When you hear "I know someone who—", ask yourself whether this one person's reported experience is satisfactory as evidence.

5. *Consider alternative interpretations of research evidence:* Does alcohol cause aggression? We reported evidence that there is a clear *connection,* or "correlation," between alcohol and aggression. For example, many people who commit violent crimes have been drinking. But what of the experiment by Lang and his colleagues? Does the evidence show that drinking causes aggression? Might other factors, such as gender, age, or willingness to take risks, account for both drinking and aggressive behavior?

6. *Do not oversimplify:* Most human behavior involves complex interactions of genetic and environmental influences. Also consider the issue of whether psychotherapy helps people with psychological problems. A broad answer to this question—a simple yes or no—might be oversimplifying. It is more worthwhile to ask, What *type* of psychotherapy, practiced by *whom,* is most helpful for *what kind of problem?*

7. *Do not overgeneralize:* Consider the statement that one cannot learn about human beings by engaging in research with nonhuman animals. Is the truth of the matter an all-or-nothing issue? Are there certain kinds of information we can obtain about people from research with animals? What kinds of things are you likely to be able to learn only through research with people?

8. *Apply critical thinking to all areas of life:* A skeptical attitude and a demand for evidence are not only useful in college but are of value in all areas of life. Be skeptical when you are bombarded by TV commercials, when political causes try to sweep you up, when you

see the latest cover stories about Elvis and UFO sightings in supermarket tabloids. How many times have you heard the claim "Studies have shown that . . ."? Perhaps such claims sound convincing, but ask yourself: Who ran the studies? Were the researchers neutral scientists, or were they biased toward obtaining certain results?

These are the kinds of principles that guide psychologists' thinking as they observe behavior, engage in research, or advise clients as to how to improve the quality of their lives. Perhaps these principles will help you improve the quality of your own life.

Critical Thinking and Astrology

Let's apply principles of critical thinking to one pseudoscience—astrology. But first read this personality report. I wrote it about you:

> You have your strengths and your weaknesses, but much of the time, you do not give yourself enough credit for your strengths. You are one of those people who has the inner potential for change, but you need to pay more attention to your own feelings so that you can determine the right direction for yourself.
>
> You have many times found yourself to be in conflict as your inner impulses have run up against the limits of social rules and moral codes. Most of the time you manage to resolve conflict in a way that makes sense to you, but now and then you have doubts and wonder whether you have done the right thing. You would often like to be doing two or more things at the same time, and you occasionally resent the fact that you cannot.
>
> There is an inner you known to you alone, and you often present a face to the world that does not quite reflect your genuine thoughts and feelings. And now and then you look at the things you have done and the path that you have taken, and you have

some doubt as to whether it is all worth it.

That's you to a tee, isn't it? It probably sounds familiar enough. The tendency to believe a generalized (but phony) personality report is called the *Barnum effect,* after circus magnate P. T. Barnum, who once declared that a good circus had a "little something for everybody." **Truth or Fiction Revisited:** The Barnum effect allows generalized personality reports to sound perfectly accurate and also allows fortune-tellers to make a living. That is, most of us have enough in common so that a fortune-teller's "revelations" about us may ring true. A Mexican study found that students overwhelmingly endorse generalized personality reports about them, especially when they are favorable (Pulido & Marco, 2000).

Most of us have personality traits in common. But what do tea leaves, bird droppings, palms (of your hands, not on the tropical sands), and the stars have in common? Let us see.

P. T. Barnum also once declared, "There's a sucker born every minute." The tendency to believe generalized personality reports has made people

■ **The Lure of Astrology** Astrology has been shown to be a pseudoscience, not a real science. How, then, do we account for its allure to so many millions of people?

© Gregg Mancuso/Stock Boston LLC

vulnerable to phonies throughout history. It enriches the pocketbooks of astrologists who offer to "read your personality" and predict your future based on the movements of the stars and planets (Browne, 1995). Astrology has been popular for centuries. Gallup and Newport (1991) report that one person out of four in the United States believes in astrology. Another one in four to five are not sure. Even in an age in which science has proved itself capable of making significant contributions to people's daily lives and health, more people are likely to check their horoscope than seek scientific information when they have to make a decision.

Astrology is based on the notion that the positions of the sun, the moon, and the stars affect human temperament and human affairs. For example, people born under the sign of Jupiter are believed to be jovial, or full of playful good humor. People born under the sign of Saturn are thought to be gloomy and morose (saturnine). And people born under the sign of Mars are believed to be warlike (martial). One supposedly can also foretell the future by studying the positions of these bodies.

Astrologers maintain that the positions of the heavenly bodies at the time of our birth determine our personality and destiny. They prepare forecasts called *horoscopes* that are based on our birthdates and indicate what it is safe for us to do. If you get involved with someone who asks for your "sign" (for example, Aquarius or Taurus), he or she is inquiring about your birthdate in astrological terms. Astrologers claim that your sign, which reflects the month during which you were born, indicates whom you will be compatible with. You may have been wondering whether you should date someone of another religion. If you start to follow astrology, you may also be wondering whether it is safe for a Sagittarius to be dating a Pisces or a Gemini.

Although psychologists and other scientists consider astrology to be a pseudoscience, it has millions of followers. The National Science Foundation

(2002) found that astrology is rejected by 60% of Americans, but 43% still check their horoscopes from time to time. How do we account for astrology's allure? What can we tell people who believe in it?

The allure of astrology is understandable in that people generally want to know about themselves and about the world. One could argue that understanding one's abilities and limits and the nature of the world fosters the survival of the individual. Evolutionary forces would thus favor the survival of individuals who are curious. It is not much of a stretch to speculate that curiosity is embedded in our genes and transmitted from generation to generation. Research and theory do suggest that people are drawn to astrology and other pseudosciences as a way of understanding the self and the world—especially unexpected events (Lillqvist & Lindeman, 1998; Lindeman, 1998). But it becomes a bit self-serving, because people are most likely to believe in astrology when the descriptions they hear about their personalities are favorable (Hamilton, 2001; MacDonald & Standing, 2002). It seems to go like this: The "validity" of astrology is confirmed when the astrologer—or palm reader, or reader of tea leaves, or reader of Tarot cards, or even the reader of bird droppings—says something positive about the individual. If the message is bad, there goes the validity of the messenger!

Believers in astrology also tend to provide arguments such as the following:

- Astrology has been practiced for many centuries and is a time-honored aspect of human history, tradition, and culture.

- Astrology seems to provide a path to the core meaning in the universe for people who are uneducated and, for a fortunate few with limited means, a road to riches.

- People in high positions in government have followed the advice of astrologers. (Nancy Reagan, wife of former president Ronald Reagan, is reported to have consulted an astrologer in arranging her husband's schedule.)

- One heavenly body (the moon) is powerful enough to sway the tides of the seas. The pulls of heavenly bodies are therefore easily capable of affecting people's destinies.

- Astrology is a special art and not a science. Therefore, we shouldn't subject astrology to the rigors of scientific testing.

- Astrology has been shown to work.

Think critically about the claims of astrologers. Does the fact that there may be a long-standing tradition in astrology affect its scientific merit? Does Nancy Reagan's (or anyone else's) belief in astrology affect its scientific merit? Psychology is an *empirical* science. In an empirical science, beliefs about the behavior of cosmic rays, chemical compounds, cells, people—or the meaning of bird droppings or the movements of the stars—must be supported by evidence. Persuasive arguments and reference to authority figures are *not* scientific evidence. Pseudoscientists have made specific forecasts of events, and their accuracy—or lack of it—provides a means of evaluation. Mick Jagger was *not* elected to Parliament in 1997, and Elvis did *not* come back to planet Earth in 2002. Astrological predictions are no more likely to come true than predictions based on chance (Crowe, 1990; Munro & Munro, 2000). That is fact, but does it matter?

Maybe not. Magical predictions tend to keep their allure. For one thing, scientists make predictions about groups, not individuals. They may say that obesity heightens the risk of heart disease but may not be able to predict with certainly whether a given individual will develop heart disease. Individuals may turn to "psychics" to find out—even if they are fed false knowledge. In addition, many people just want some magic in their lives (Munro & Munro, 2000). Sad to say, even in our age of scientific enlightenment, many people are more comfortable with fanciful stories and leaps of faith than they are with objective evidence and statistical probabilities.

But what about you? Will you be more skeptical in the future?

Recite — An Active Summary™

Want to study on the go? Go to your companion website and download an audio version of this review section to your media player.

1. What is psychology?

Psychology is the scientific study of behavior and mental processes.

2. What are the goals of psychology?

Psychology seeks to describe, explain, predict, and control behavior and mental processes. Behavior and mental processes are explained through psychological theories, which are sets of statements that involve assumptions about behavior. Explanations and predictions are derived from theories. Theories are revised, as needed, to accommodate new observations.

3. What do psychologists do?

Psychologists engage in research and practice. Research can be pure or applied. Basic or pure research has no immediate applications. Applied research seeks solutions to specific problems. Psychologists also specialize in various fields. Clinical psychologists help people with psychological disorders adjust to the demands of life. Counseling psychologists work with people with adjustment problems. School psychologists assist students with problems that interfere with learning. Developmental psychologists study the changes that occur throughout the life span. Personality psychologists study influences on our thought processes, feelings, and behavior. Social psychologists focus on the nature and causes of behavior in social situations. Experimental psychologists conduct research into basic psychological processes such as sensation and perception, learning and memory, and motivation and emotion. Industrial psychologists focus on the relationships between people and work. Health psychologists study the ways in which behavior and mental processes such as attitudes are related to physical health.

4. Who were some of the ancient contributors to psychology?

The ancient Greek philosopher Aristotle declared that people are motivated to seek pleasure and avoid pain. Another Greek, Democritus, suggested that we could think of behavior in terms of a body and a mind and raised the question of whether there is free will or choice. Plato recorded Socrates' advice to "Know thyself," primarily by means of introspection.

5. What is structuralism?

Structuralism, founded by Wilhelm Wundt, used introspection to study the objective and subjective elements of experience. Wundt also established the first psychological laboratory in Leipzig, Germany, in 1879.

6. What is functionalism?

Functionalism is the school founded by William James. It dealt with observable behavior as well as conscious experience and focused on the importance of habit.

7. What is behaviorism?

Behaviorism, founded by John B. Watson, argues that psychology must limit itself to observable behavior and not attempt to deal with subjective consciousness. Behaviorism focuses on learning by conditioning, and B. F. Skinner introduced the concept of reinforcement as an explanation of how learning occurs.

8. What is Gestalt psychology?

Gestalt psychology is the school of psychology founded by Wertheimer, Koffka, and Köhler. It is concerned with perception and argues that the wholeness of human experience is more than the sum of its parts.

9. What is psychoanalysis?

Psychoanalysis was founded by Sigmund Freud. The school asserts that people are driven by hidden impulses and that they distort reality to protect themselves from anxiety.

10. What is the evolutionary perspective?

The evolutionary perspective is based on the work of Charles Darwin, who argued that in the age-old struggle for survival, only the "fittest" organisms reach maturity and reproduce, thereby transmitting the traits that enable them to survive to their offspring.

11. What is the biological perspective?

The biological perspective studies the links between behavior and mental processes on the one hand, and heredity, the nervous system, and the endocrine system on the other. The endocrine system releases hormones into the bloodstream.

12. What is the cognitive perspective?

The cognitive perspective is concerned with the ways in which we mentally represent the world and process information. Cognitive psychologists study how we learn, remember the past, plan for the future, solve problems, form judgments, make decisions, and use language.

13. What is the humanistic–existential perspective?

Humanistic–existential psychologists stress the importance of subjective experience and assert that people have the freedom to make choices.

14. What is the role of psychoanalysis today?

Contemporary psychoanalysts often call themselves *neoanalysts* because they focus less on unconscious processes and more on conscious choice and self-direction. Psychoanalysis remains popular in the culture at large.

15. What are the two major perspectives on learning?

The two key perspectives on learning are the behavioral perspective and the social cognitive perspective. Behaviorism focuses on environmental influences on learning. Social cognitive theory argues that psychologists can address thought processes, that people engage in intentional learning, and that people are free to modify and create environments.

16. What is the sociocultural perspective?

The sociocultural perspective focuses on the roles of ethnicity, gender, culture, and socioeconomic status in behavior and mental processes.

17. How have access to education and the field of psychology historically influenced the participation of women and people from various ethnic and racial backgrounds?

Women have made major contributions to psychology in the United States for more than a century. Calkins studied memory and heightened awareness of prejudice against women. Ladd-Franklin formulated a theory of color vision. Washburn's views presaged behaviorism. Ainsworth has made key contributions to the field of child development (attachment theory), and Loftus is a major figure in the psychology of memory. Nolen-Hoeksema has shown how people's cognitive styles can prolong feelings of depression. People from ethnic minority groups have contributed to all areas of psychology, but some, like Kenneth Clark, Mamie Phipps Clark, Robert Williams, and Jorge Sanchez, have heightened awareness of issues concerning their groups, such as prejudice and Ebonics.

18. What is the scientific method?

The scientific method is an organized way of expanding and refining knowledge. Psychologists reach conclusions about their research questions or the accuracy of their hypotheses on the basis of their research observations or findings.

19. How do psychologists use samples to represent populations?

The individuals who participate in research are referred to as a sample. A sample is a segment of a population. Samples must accurately represent the population they are intended to reflect. In a *random sample*, each member of a population has an equal chance of being selected to participate. Researchers can also use a *stratified sample*, which is selected so that identified subgroups in the population are represented proportionately in the sample.

20. What methods of observation are used by psychologists?

The methods used include the case study, the survey, and naturalistic observation. Case studies gather information about the lives of individuals or small groups. The survey method uses interviews, questionnaires, or public records to gather information about behavior that cannot be observed directly. The naturalistic observation method observes behavior where it happens—"in the field."

21. What is the correlational method?

The correlational method reveals relationships between variables, but does not determine cause and effect. In a positive correlation, variables increase simultaneously. In a negative correlation, one variable increases while the other decreases.

22. What is the experimental method?

Experiments are used to discover cause and effect—that is, the effects of independent variables on dependent variables. Experimental groups receive a specific treatment, whereas control groups do not. Blinds and double blinds may be used to control for the effects of the expectations of the subjects and the researchers. Results can be generalized only to populations that have been adequately represented in the research samples.

23. What are the ethical issues that concern psychological research and practice with humans?

The ethical standards of psychologists are intended to protect subjects in research and clients in practice from harm. Records of human behavior are kept confidential. Ethics review committees judge the harmfulness of proposed research and help make it less

Recite—An Active Summary™

harmful. Human subjects are required to give informed consent prior to participating in research and are debriefed afterward.

24. What are the ethical issues that concern research with animals?

Some research can be conducted only with animals. Ethical standards require that animals may be harmed only if there is no alternative and the benefits justify the harm.

25. What is critical thinking?

Critical thinking is a hallmark of psychologists and of scientists in general. Critical thinking is associated with skepticism. It involves thoughtfully analyzing the questions, statements, and arguments of others. It means examining the definitions of terms, examining the premises or assumptions behind arguments, and scrutinizing the logic with which arguments are developed. Critical thinking also refers to the ability to inquire about causes and effects, as well as knowledge of research methods. Critical thinkers are cautious in drawing conclusions from evidence. They do not oversimplify or overgeneralize.

Go to **http://psychology.wadsworth.com/rathus_pcc9e** to access an interactive version of this active summary.

Key Terms

Psychology (p. 4)
Theory (p. 5)
Pure research (p. 5)
Applied research (p. 5)
Introspection (p. 9)
Structuralism (p. 9)
Functionalism (p. 10)
Behaviorism (p. 11)
Reinforcement (p. 12)
Gestalt psychology (p. 12)
Insight (p. 13)
Psychoanalysis (p. 14)
Genes (p. 16)
Instinctive (p. 16)
Cognitive (p. 16)

Humanism (p. 16)
Existentialism (p. 17)
Social cognitive theory (p. 17)
Cognition (p. 17)
Sociocultural perspective (p. 18)
Ethnic group (p. 18)
Gender (p. 18)
Correlational method (p. 22)
Hypothesis (p. 22)
Correlation (p. 22)
Selection factor (p. 24)
Replicate (p. 24)

Generalize (p. 24)
Sample (p. 24)
Population (p. 24)
Random sample (p. 25)
Stratified sample (p. 25)
Volunteer bias (p. 25)
Case study (p. 27)
Survey (p. 27)
Naturalistic observation (p. 28)
Correlation coefficient (p. 28)
Positive correlation (p. 29)
Negative correlation (p. 29)
Experiment (p. 29)

Treatment (p. 29)
Independent variable (p. 30)
Dependent variable (p. 30)
Experimental groups (p. 30)
Control groups (p. 30)
Placebo (p. 31)
Blind (p. 31)
Double-blind study (p. 31)
Ethical (p. 33)
Informed consent (p. 33)
Debrief (p. 34)

Active Learning Resources

Visit your Companion Website for Video, Quizzing, and Self-Assessment!

http://psychology.wadsworth.com/rathus_pcc9e

On this site you can access the Facial Analysis video highlighted by the Video Connections icon on p. 24. In addition there are many quizzing opportunities including interactive versions of the fill-in-the-blank Active Review sections in your book. You can also fill out and score the Self-Assessment on p. 26.

Study on the Go!

Don't have time to study right now? You can study on the go! Visit your companion website an download an audio version of the Recite—An Active Summary section to your media player.

ThomsonNOW

http://www.thomsonedu.com

Need help studying? This site is your one-stop study shop. Take a Pre-Test and Thomson NOW will generate a Personalized Study Plan based on your test results. The Study Plan will identify the topics you need to review and direct you to online resources to help you master those topics. You can then take a Post-Test to determine the concepts you have mastered and what you still need to work on.

Author Blog

What does your author have to say about the state of psychology? Visit your companion website every Tuesday and click on "Author Blog," where he'll talk about the most recent controversies and hot topics in psychology.

Truth or Fiction?

T F Charles Darwin was nearly excluded from the voyage that led to the development of his theory of evolution because the captain of the ship did not like the shape of his nose.

T F Your genetic code overlaps 25% with that of a carrot.

T F Neanderthals are not necessarily extinct; they may be lurking in your genes.

T F The human brain is larger than that of any other animal.

T F One cell can stretch all the way from your spine to your toe.

T F Messages travel in the brain by means of electricity.

T F A brain cell can send out hundreds of messages each second—and manage to catch some rest in between.

T F Fear can give you indigestion.

T F If a surgeon were to stimulate a certain part of your brain electrically, you might swear that someone had stroked your leg.

T F A hormone turns a disinterested male rodent into a doting father.

T F Some women eliminate PMS by eliminating their periods. Period.

 Go to **http://psychology.wadsworth.com/ rathus_pcc9e** to answer and score this Truth or Fiction quiz.

© Peter Saloutos/CORBIS

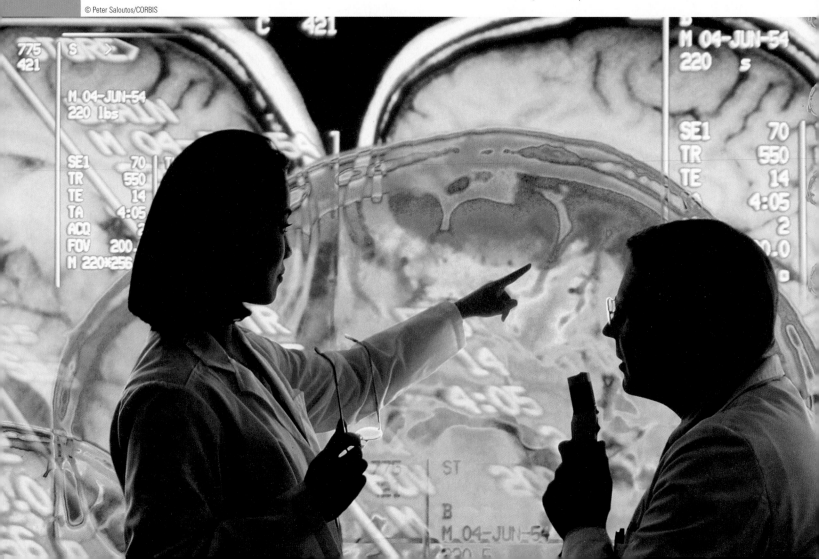

Biology and Psychology

Preview

He almost missed the boat. Literally. The British naturalist Charles Darwin had volunteered to serve as the scientist for an expeditionary voyage on H.M.S. *Beagle,* but the captain, Robert Fitz-Roy, objected to Darwin because of the shape of his nose. **Truth or Fiction Revisited:** Thus it is true that Darwin was nearly prevented from undertaking his historic voyage due to the shape of his nose. Fitz-Roy believed that you could judge a person's character by the outline of his facial features, and Darwin's nose didn't fit the . . . bill. But Fitz-Roy relented, and in the 1830s, Darwin undertook the historic voyage to the Galápagos Islands that led to the development of his theory of evolution.

In Profile — CHARLES DARWIN

Charles Darwin was a dabbler who, in one of history's coincidences, was born on the same day as Abraham Lincoln (February 12, 1809). Darwin's father was a well-known physician, and his mother was Susannah Wedgwood, of the chinaware family. His cousin was Sir Francis Galton (see Chapter 1), who made many innovations in psychological measurement. Unlike Galton, Darwin gave no early signs of genius. He did so poorly in school that his father feared that he would disgrace himself and the family. Nevertheless, Darwin went on to change the face of modern thought.

Darwin enjoyed collecting and classifying plants, minerals, and animals. He tried medical school, entered Cambridge University to become an Anglican priest, and eventually graduated with a degree in science. Because he was independently wealthy, Darwin undertook the five-year volunteer position aboard H.M.S. *Beagle.* The ship stopped at the Galápagos Islands, where Darwin observed how species of lizards, tortoises, and plants varied from island to island. Although Darwin undertook his voyage as a believer in the Book of Genesis account of creation, his observations convinced him that the organisms he observed shared common ancestors but had *evolved* in different directions.

In midlife Darwin almost missed the boat again. From his observations of sea lions and tortoises and insects and plants, he was ready to formulate his theory of evolution upon his return from his voyage. Reading Thomas Malthus's *Essay on the Principle of Population,* which had been written back in 1798, also helped. Malthus pointed out that the earth's food supply was increasing mathematically (1, 2, 3, 4, 5, 6, and so on) while population

was increasing geometrically (1, 2, 4, 8, 16, 32, and so on). Therefore, the world's population would outstrip the world's ability to feed it, except for tragic events such as war, famine, and plague. Darwin applied Malthus's ideas to all species:

> In October 1838 . . . I happened to read for amusement Malthus on *Population,* and being well prepared to appreciate the struggle for existence which everywhere goes on from long-continued observation of the habits of animals and plants, it at once struck me that under these circumstances favourable variations would tend to be preserved and unfavourable ones to be destroyed. The result of this would be the formation of new species. Here, then, I had at last got a theory by which to work; but I was so anxious to avoid prejudice, that I determined not for some time to write even the briefest sketch of it. (F. Darwin, 1892/1958, pp. 42–43)

Because he was "anxious to avoid prejudice," Darwin did not want his theory of evolution to be published until after his death. He feared it would be immensely unpopular, because it contradicted religious views, and that it would bring scorn on his family. He shared his ideas with a few fellow scientists, but he finally published his ideas more broadly 20 years later when he learned that other scientists, including Alfred Russel Wallace, were about to present similar ideas on evolution. Wallace, a scientist who had worked in the Amazon, was about to publish his own views, which were very similar to Darwin's. Papers by both theorists were read at the Linnaean Society, and Darwin's *On the Origin of Species by Natural Selection* (1859) was published shortly thereafter. The public's interest in evolutionary theory had been aroused, and the first printing of Darwin's book sold out on the first day. Needless to say, Darwin's views became better known than those of Wallace. (Have you ever heard of Wallace's theory of evolution?)

Go to **http://psychology.wadsworth.com/ rathus_pcc9e** to access more information about Charles Darwin.

Evolution and Evolutionary Psychology: "Survivor" Is More Than Just a Game

In 1871 Darwin published *The Descent of Man,* which made the case that humans, like other species, were a product of evolution. He argued that the great apes (chimpanzees, gorillas, and so on) and humans shared a common primate ancestor (see Figure 2.1). Many ridiculed Darwin's views because they were displeased with the notion that they might share ancestry with apes. Darwin's theory also contradicted the Book of Genesis, which stated that humans had been created in one day in the image of God.

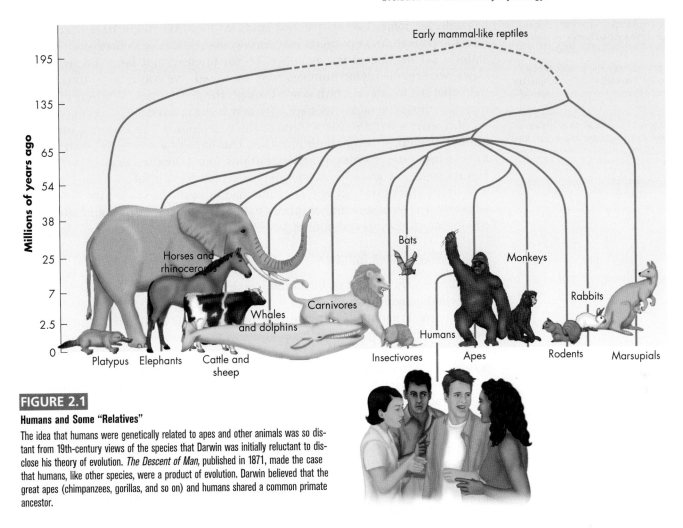

FIGURE 2.1

Humans and Some "Relatives"

The idea that humans were genetically related to apes and other animals was so distant from 19th-century views of the species that Darwin was initially reluctant to disclose his theory of evolution. *The Descent of Man,* published in 1871, made the case that humans, like other species, were a product of evolution. Darwin believed that the great apes (chimpanzees, gorillas, and so on) and humans shared a common primate ancestor.

At the Galápagos Islands, Darwin found himself immersed in the unfolding of a huge game of "Survivor." But here the game was for real, and the rewards had nothing to do with fame or fortune. The rewards were reaching sexual maturity and transmitting one's genes into subsequent generations.

Question: What are some of the basic concepts in the theory of evolution? The concept of a *struggle for existence* lies at the core of the theory of evolution. The universe is no bed of roses. Since the beginning of time, the universe has been changing. For billions of years, microscopic particles have been forming immense gas clouds in space. Galaxies and solar systems have been condensing from the clouds, sparkling for some eons, then winking out. Change has brought life and death and countless challenges to survival. As described by evolutionary theory, some creatures have adapted successfully to these challenges, and their numbers have increased. Others have not met the challenges and have fallen back into the distant mists of time. The species that prosper and those that fade away are thus determined by **natural selection.**

When we humans first appeared on planet earth, our survival required a different sort of struggle than it does today. We fought or fled from predators such as

Natural selection A core concept of the theory of evolution that holds that adaptive genetic variations among members of a species enable individuals with those variations to survive and reproduce. As a result, such variations tend to be preserved, whereas nonadaptive variations tend to drop out.

■ **Dinosaurs** Long ago and right here on planet earth, dinosaurs once ruled the day. However, they–along with 99.99% of all species that ever existed–are now extinct. Evidence that they existed, and when they existed, is found in the fossil record.

Mutation A sudden variation in an inheritable characteristic, as distinguished from a variation that results from generations of gradual selection.

Evolutionary psychology The branch of psychology that studies the ways in which adaptation and natural selection are connected with mental processes and behavior.

Species A category of biological classification consisting of related organisms who are capable of interbreeding. *Homo sapiens*—humans—make up one species.

Instinct A stereotyped pattern of behavior that is triggered by a particular stimulus and nearly identical among members of a species, even when they are reared in isolation.

leopards. We foraged across parched lands for food. We might have warred with humanoid creatures very much like ourselves—creatures who have since become extinct. But because of the evolution of our intellect, not fangs nor wings nor claws, we prevailed. Our numbers have increased. We continue to transmit the traits that led to our selection down through the generations by means of genetic material whose chemical codes are only now being cracked.

Just what is handed down through the generations? The answer is biological, or physiological, structures and processes. Our biology serves as the material base for our behaviors, emotions, and cognitions (our thoughts, images, and plans). Biology somehow gives rise to specific behavioral tendencies in some organisms, such as the chick's instinctive fear of the shadow of the hawk. But the behavior of many species, especially higher species such as humans, is flexible and affected by environmental factors and choice, as well as by heredity.

"Doing What Comes Naturally"

According to the theory of evolution, there is a struggle for survival as various species and individuals compete for the same resources. There are small variations—random genetic variations called **mutations**—that lead to differences among individuals in physical traits. Those individuals whose traits are better adapted to their environments are more likely to survive (that is, to be "naturally selected"). Survival permits them to reach sexual maturity, to reproduce, and to transmit their features or traits to the next generation. What began as chance variation becomes embedded in more and more individuals over the generations—if it fosters survival. Chance variations that hinder survival are likely to disappear from the gene pool.

Evolutionary Psychology

These same concepts of *adaptation* and *natural selection* have also been applied to psychological traits and are key concepts in **evolutionary psychology. Question: What is evolutionary psychology?** Evolutionary psychology studies the ways in which adaptation and natural selection are connected with mental processes and behavior (Buss, 2000; Cory, 2002). Over the eons evolution has provided organisms with advantages such as stronger fins and wings, sharper claws, and camouflage. Human evolution has given rise to various physical traits and also to such diverse activities as language, art, committed relationships, and warfare.

One of the concepts of evolutionary psychology is that not only physical traits but also patterns of behavior, including social behavior, evolve and are transmitted genetically from generation to generation. In other words, behavior patterns that help an organism to survive and reproduce are likely to be transmitted to the next generation (Fisher, 2000). Such behaviors are believed to include aggression, strategies of mate selection, even altruism (that is, self-sacrifice of the individual to help perpetuate the family grouping) (Bruene & Ribbert, 2002; McAndrew, 2002). The behavior patterns are termed *instinctive* or *species-specific* because they evolved within certain **species.**

Question: What is meant by an "instinct"? An **instinct** is a stereotyped pattern of behavior that is triggered in a specific situation. Instinctive behavior is nearly identical among the members of the species in which it appears. It tends to resist modification, even when it serves no purpose (as in the interminable barking of some breeds of dogs) or results in punishment. Instinctive behavior also appears when the individual is reared in isolation from others of its kind and thus cannot learn the behavior from experience.

Consider some examples of instinctive behavior. If you place an egg from the nest of a goose a few inches in front of her, she will roll it back to the nest with her beak. However, she won't retrieve it if it's farther away—in the "not my egg" zone. If you rear a white-crowned sparrow in isolation from other sparrows, it will still sing a recognizable species-specific song when it matures. The male stickleback fish instinctively attacks fish (or pieces of painted wood) with the kinds of red bellies that are

© David Thompson/OSF/Animals, Animals

■ **Instinctive Behavior** The male stickleback instinctively attacks fish (or pieces of painted wood) with the kinds of red bellies that are characteristic of other male sticklebacks. Sticklebacks will show the stereotyped instinctive behavior even when they are reared in isolation from other members of their species. Rearing an organism in isolation prevents it from learning from another member of its species.

characteristic of other male sticklebacks. Many psychologists consider language to be "instinctive" among humans. Psychologists are trying to determine what other kinds of human behavior may be instinctive. However, even instinctive behavior can be modified to some degree by learning, and most psychologists agree that the richness and complexity of human behavior are made possible by human learning ability.

Your Turn: Now that we have discussed evolution and evolutionary psychology, enhance your mastery of the material with the nearby "Learning Connections." Review the material by filling in the blanks, reflect on the material by relating it to other things you know, and think critically about it.

 Learning Connections | **EVOLUTION AND EVOLUTIONARY PSYCHOLOGY: "SURVIVOR" IS MORE THAN JUST A GAME**

ACTIVE REVIEW (1) Darwin's first book on evolution was titled *On the Origin of Species by Natural* _____. (2) The concept of a struggle for _____ lies at the core of the theory of evolution. (3) Darwin believed that mutations occur at _____ but are subject to natural selection. (4) Individuals whose traits are better _____ to their environments are more likely to survive and reproduce. (5) _____ psychology studies the ways in which adaptation and natural selection are connected with mental processes and behavior. (6) Stereotypical behavior patterns that have evolved within certain species are called _____.

REFLECT AND RELATE Have you known family pets that have engaged in instinctive behavior? What was the behavior? Why do you believe it was instinctive?

CRITICAL THINKING Why was Darwin reluctant to publish his theory of evolution? Do you believe that this textbook, and other textbooks, should present the theory of evolution?

Go to **http://psychology.wadsworth.com/ rathus_pcc9e** for an interactive version of this Learning Connections unit.

Heredity: The Nature of Nature

Consider some facts of life:

◆ People cannot breathe underwater (without special equipment).
◆ People cannot fly (again, without rather special equipment).
◆ Fish cannot learn to speak French or do an Irish jig even if you rear them in enriched environments and send them to finishing school.
◆ Chimpanzees and gorillas can use sign language but cannot speak.

People cannot breathe underwater or fly (without oxygen tanks, airplanes, or other devices) because of their **heredity. Question: What is meant by "heredity"?** Heredity defines one's *nature*—which is based on one's biological structures and processes. Heredity refers to the biological transmission of traits that have evolved from generation to generation. Fish are limited in other ways by their natural traits. Chimpanzees and gorillas can understand many spoken words and express some concepts through nonverbal symbol systems such as American Sign Language. However, apes cannot speak. They have probably failed to inherit humanlike speech areas of the brain. Their nature differs from ours. Our speech mechanisms have evolved differently.

Genetics and Behavioral Genetics

Heredity both makes behaviors possible and places limits on them. **Question: What is meant by "genetics"?** The subfield of biology that studies heredity is called **genetics. Behavioral genetics** bridges the sciences of psychology and biology. It is concerned with the genetic transmission of traits that give rise to patterns of behavior.

The field of genetics looks at both species-specific behavior patterns (instincts) and individual differences among the members of a species. Behavioral genetics

Heredity The transmission of traits from parent to offspring by means of genes.

Genetics The area of biology that focuses on heredity.

Behavioral genetics The area of biology and psychology that focuses on the transmission of traits that give rise to behavior. Behavioral genetics also addresses individual differences in behavior.

Gene A basic unit of heredity, which is found at a specific point on a chromosome.

Chromosome A microscopic rod-shaped body in the cell nucleus carrying genes that transmit hereditary traits from generation to generation. Humans normally have 46 chromosomes.

DNA Abbreviation for deoxyribonucleic acid, the substance that forms the basic material of chromosomes. It takes the form of a double helix and contains the genetic code.

focuses on individual differences (Plomin & Crabbe, 2000). Psychologists are thinking in terms of behavioral genetics when they ask about the inborn reasons why individuals may differ in their behavior and mental processes. For example, some children learn language more quickly than others. Part of the reason may lie in behavioral genetics—their heredity. But some children also experience a richer exposure to language at early ages. Heredity appears to be a factor in almost all aspects of human behavior, personality, and mental processes (Plomin & Asbury, 2005). Examples include sociability, anxiety, social dominance, leadership, effectiveness as a parent or a therapist, happiness, even interest in arts and crafts (Iervolino et al., 2005; Knafo & Plomin, 2006; Leonardo & Hen, 2006). **Question: What are the roles of genes and chromosomes in heredity?**

Genes and Chromosomes: The Building Blocks of Heredity

Genes are the most basic building blocks of heredity. Genes regulate the development of specific traits. Some traits, such as blood type, are controlled by a single pair of genes. (One gene is derived from each parent.) Other traits are determined by combinations of genes. The inherited component of complex psychological traits, such as intelligence, is believed to be determined by combinations of genes. It is estimated that the cells within your body contain 20,000 to 25,000 genes (International Human Genome Sequencing Consortium, 2006).

Genes are segments of **chromosomes.** That is, chromosomes are made up of strings of genes. Each cell in the body contains 46 chromosomes arranged in 23 pairs. Chromosomes are large complex molecules of **DNA** (short for *deoxyribonucleic acid*), which has several chemical components. The tightly wound structure of DNA was first demonstrated in the 1950s by James Watson and Francis Crick. DNA takes the form of a double helix—a twisting molecular ladder (see Figure 2.2). The "rungs" of the ladder are made up of chemicals called *nucleotides* whose names are abbreviated as A, T, C, and G. A always links up with T to complete a rung, and C always combines with G. Therefore, you can describe the *genetic code* in terms of the nucleotides you find along just one of the rungs—e.g., CTGAGTCAC and so on. A single gene can contain hundreds of thousands of base pairs. So if you think of a gene as a word, it can be a few hundred thousand letters long and completely unpronounceable. A group of scientists working together around the globe—referred to as the Human Genome Project—has learned that the sequencing of

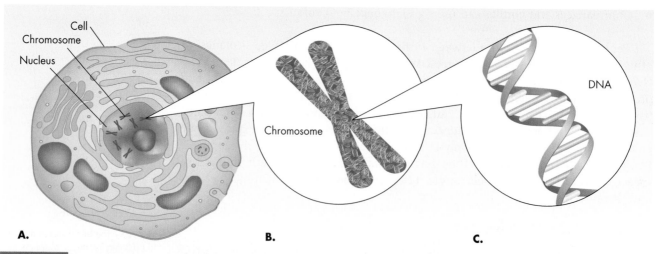

FIGURE 2.2 Cells, Chromosomes, and DNA

A. The nuclei of cells contain chromosomes. **B.** Chromosomes are made up of DNA. **C.** Segments of DNA are made up of genes that determine physical traits such as height, eye color, and whether pigs have wings (no, because of their genetic makeup, they don't). Genes are segments of chromosomes that are found with the nuclei of cells. The genetic code— that is, the order of the chemicals A, G, T, and C—determines your species and all those traits that can be inherited, from the color of your eyes to predispositions toward many psychological traits and abilities, including sociability and musical talent.

your DNA consists of about 3 billion DNA sequences spread throughout your chromosomes (Plomin & Crabbe, 2000). These sequences—the order of the chemicals we call A, T, C, and G—caused you to grow arms and not wings, and skin rather than scales. Psychologists debate the extent to which genes influence complex psychological traits such as intelligence, aggressiveness, and happiness, and the appearance of psychological disorders such as schizophrenia. Some traits, such as eye color, are determined by a single pair of genes. Other traits, especially complex psychological traits such as sociability and aggressiveness, are thought to be **polygenic**—that is, influenced by combinations of genes.

Your genetic code provides your **genotype**—that is, your full genetic potential, as determined by the sequencing of the chemicals in your DNA. But the person you see in the mirror was also influenced by your early experiences in the home, injuries, adequacy of nourishment, educational experiences, and numerous other environmental influences. Therefore, you see the outer appearance of your phenotype, including the hair styles of the day. Your **phenotype** is the manner in which your genetic code manifests itself because of your experiences and environmental circumstances. Your genotype enables you to acquire language. Your phenotype reveals that you are likely to be speaking English if you were reared in the United States or Spanish if you were reared in Mexico (or both, if you are Mexican American).

Your genotype provides what psychologists refer to as your **nature.** Your phenotype represents the interaction of you nature (heredity) and your **nurture** (environmental influences) in the origins of your behavior and mental processes. Psychologists are especially interested in the roles of nature and nurture in intelligence and psychological disorders. Our genotypes provide us with physical traits that set the stage for certain behaviors. But none of us is the result of heredity alone. Environmental factors such as nutrition, learning opportunities, cultural influences, exercise, and (unfortunately) accident and illness also determine our phenotypes, and whether genetically possible behaviors will be displayed. Behavior and mental processes represent the interaction of nature and nurture. A potential Shakespeare who is reared in poverty and never taught to read or write will not create a *Hamlet.*

We normally receive 23 chromosomes from our father's sperm cell and 23 chromosomes from our mother's egg cell (ovum). When a sperm cell fertilizes an ovum, the chromosomes form 23 pairs (Figure 2.3). The 23rd pair consists of **sex chromosomes,** which determine whether we are female or male. We all receive an X sex chromosome (so called because of the X shape) from our mother. If we also receive an X sex chromosome from our father, we develop into a female. If we receive a Y sex chromosome (named after the Y shape) from our father, we develop into a male. In the following section, we observe the unfortunate results that may

Polygenic Referring to traits that are influenced by combinations of genes.

Genotype One's genetic makeup, based on the sequencing of the nucleotides we term A, C, G, and T.

Phenotype One's actual development and appearance, as based on one's genotype and environmental influences.

Nature The inborn, innate character of an organism.

Nurture The sum total of the environmental factors that affect an organism from conception onward. (In another usage, *nurture* refers to the act of nourishing and otherwise promoting the development of youngsters.)

Sex chromosomes The 23rd pair of chromosomes, whose genetic material determines the sex of the individual.

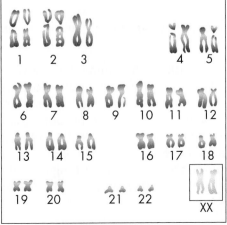

Female

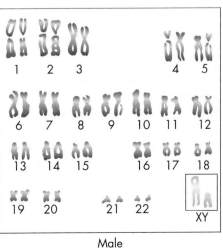

Male

FIGURE 2.3 **The 23 Pairs of Human Chromosomes**

People normally have 23 pairs of chromosomes. Whether one is female or male is determined by the 23rd pair of chromosomes. Females have two X sex chromosomes, whereas males have an X and a Y sex chromosome.

A Closer Look ARE YOU A HUMAN OR A MOUSE (OR A CHIMP OR A CARROT)? SOME FASCINATING FACTS ABOUT GENES

Truth or Fiction Revisited: Yes, it is true that your genetic code overlaps about 25% with that of a carrot. Don't be concerned. It doesn't mean you're going to turn orange, nor that you are about to enter your "salad days." So, to quote Bugs Bunny, "What's up, Doc?" What's "up" is that your genetic code, like the genetic codes of other life forms, is a sequence of four chemicals. By chance alone, then, one out of four in the sequence would be repeated in any randomly selected segments of carrot and human DNA.

The house mouse is not only in your pantry; much of it is in your genes. The genomes of humans and mice have been decoded and of the 30,000 or so genes possessed by each, about 29,700 genes in one have some counterpart in the other (Gunter & Dhand, 2002). The counterparts are not necessarily the same; for example, the mouse has more genes related to odor detection and thus a better sense of smell. The genetic difference between mice and humans results from some 75 million years of evolution along different paths from a common mammalian ancestor. When we consider how different we appear to be from the mouse, it is remarkable how similar we are in genetic makeup. But only a few hundred genes apparently explain why mice are pests (and pets). The overlap also makes mice excellent stand-ins for humans in medical research.

Our closest genetic relatives are chimpanzees, with whom we may have shared a common ancestor some 6 to 9 million years ago. Only 1.58% of the genetic code of the chimpanzee differs from our own. Putting it another way: Our genetic codes overlap with those of chimps by more than 98% (Zimmer, 2002–2003)!

The sequence of your own DNA also overlaps about 99.9% with that of other humans (Plomin & Crabbe, 2000). Yet the difference of 0.1% accounts for the differences between Mozart and Nelson Mandela and between Michelle Kwan and Oprah Winfrey. Despite this enormous overlap, people differ greatly in their skin coloration, their body shape, and their psychological makeup, including their talents and skills. Some compose symphonies and others are tone-deaf. Some tackle differential equations and others cannot add or subtract. Some figure skate in the Olympics and others trip over their own feet. Even though we differ but 0.1% in genetic code from our fellows, it often seems easier to focus on how much we differ rather than on how much we have in common.

Truth or Fiction Revisited: It is true that Neanderthals and some other ancient humanoids may not be quite as extinct as has been believed. In fact, they may be "lurking" in your own genetic code. Recent analysis of DNA suggests that modern humans—that's us—probably interbred with other humanoids for more than one hundred thousand years rather than simply replacing them (Cann, 2002). When you misbehave, you can now say it's the Neanderthal in you—although the truth could be quite the reverse.

■ **That 0.1% of Difference Can Be Quite a Difference** The genetic codes of humans overlap by 99.9%. However, the remaining 0.1% makes quite a difference, as in the cases of cellist Yo Yo Ma (left) and professional wrestler "The Rock" (right).

© Reuters New Media Inc./CORBIS

The Everett Collection

occur when people do not receive the normal complement of chromosomes from their parents.

DOWN SYNDROME When people do not have the normal number of 46 chromosomes (23 pairs), physical and behavioral abnormalities may result. Most persons with **Down syndrome,** for example, have an extra, or third, chromosome on the 21st pair. The extra chromosome is usually contributed by the mother, and the condition becomes increasingly likely as the mother's age at the time of pregnancy increases. Persons with Down syndrome have a downward-sloping fold of skin at the inner corners of the eyes, a round face, a protruding tongue, and a broad, flat nose. They are cognitively impaired and usually have physical problems that cause death by middle age (Schupf, 2000).

Down syndrome A condition caused by an extra chromosome on the 21st pair and characterized by mental deficiency, a broad face, and slanting eyes.

Kinship Studies: Is the Behavior of Relatives Related?

Question: What are kinship studies? Kinship studies are ways in which psychologists compare the presence of traits and behavior patterns in people who are biologically related or unrelated to help determine the role of genetic factors in their occurrence. The more *closely* people are related, the more *genes* they have in common. Identical twins share 100% of their genes. Parents and children have 50% of their genes in common, as do siblings (brothers and sisters). Aunts and uncles related by blood have a 25% overlap with nieces and nephews. First cousins share 12.5% of their genes. If genes are involved in a trait or behavior pattern, people who are more closely related should be more likely to show similar traits or behavior. Psychologists and behavioral geneticists are especially interested in running kinship studies with twins and adopted individuals (Plomin, 2002).

TWIN STUDIES: LOOKING INTO THE GENETIC MIRROR The fertilized egg cell (ovum) that carries genetic messages from both parents is called a *zygote*. Now and then, a zygote divides into two cells that separate, so that instead of developing into a single person, it develops into two people with the same genetic makeup. Such people are identical, or **monozygotic (MZ), twins.** If the woman releases two ova in the same month and they are both fertilized, they develop into fraternal, or **dizygotic (DZ), twins.** DZ twins, like other siblings, share 50% of their genes. MZ twins are important in the study of the relative influences of nature (heredity) and nurture (the environment) because differences between MZ twins are the result of nurture. (They do not differ in their heredity—that is, their nature—because their genetic makeup is the same.)

Twin studies compare the presence of traits and behavior patterns in MZ twins, DZ twins, and other people to help determine the role of genetic factors in their occurrence. If MZ twins show greater similarity on a trait or behavior pattern than DZ twins, a genetic basis for the trait or behavior is suggested.

Twin studies show how strongly genetic factors influence physical features. MZ twins are more likely to look alike and to be similar in height, even to have more similar cholesterol levels than DZ twins (Heller et al., 1993). This finding holds even when the identical twins are reared apart and the fraternal twins are reared together (Stunkard et al., 1990).

Other physical similarities between pairs of MZ twins may be more subtle, but they are also strong. For example, research shows that MZ twin sisters begin to menstruate about one to two months apart, whereas DZ twins begin to menstruate about a year apart. MZ twins are more alike than DZ twins in their blood pressure, brain wave patterns, even in their speech patterns, gestures, and mannerisms (Hansell et al., 2001; Lensvelt-Mulders & Hettema, 2001; Lykken et al., 1992).

MZ twins also resemble one another more strongly than DZ twins in psychological traits, such as intelligence and personality traits like sociability, anxiety, friendliness, and conformity, even happiness (Markon et al., 2002; McCourt et al., 1999; McCrae et al., 2000). David Lykken and Mike Csikszentmihalyi (2001) suggest that we inherit a tendency toward a certain level of happiness. Despite the ups and downs of life, we tend to drift back to our usual levels of cheerfulness (or irritability). We shall investigate the role of (happy?) genes in happiness in greater depth in Chapter 9. Heredity is also a key contributor to developmental factors such as cognitive functioning, autism, and early signs of attachment such as smiling, cuddling, and expression of fear of strangers (DiLalla et al., 1996; Scarr & Kidd, 1983).

MZ twins are more likely than DZ twins to share psychological disorders such as autism, depression, schizophrenia, and even vulnerability to alcoholism (McGue et al., 1992; Plomin, 2000; Veenstra-Vanderweele & Cook, 2003). In one study on autism, the concordance rate for MZ twins was about 60%. (That is, if one member

© Michael Greenlar/The Image Works

■ **Down Syndrome** Down syndrome is caused by an extra chromosome on the 21st pair and becomes more likely to occur as the mother's age at the time of pregnancy increases. Persons with Down syndrome have characteristic facial features including downward-sloping folds of skin at the inner corners of the eyes, are mentally retarded, and usually have health problems that lead to death by middle age.

Monozygotic (MZ) twins Twins that develop from a single fertilized ovum that divides in two early in prenatal development. MZ twins thus share the same genetic code. Also called *identical twins*.

Dizygotic (DZ) twins Twins that develop from two fertilized ova and who are thus as closely related as brothers and sisters in general. Also called *fraternal twins*.

of a pair of MZ twins was autistic, the other member had a 60% chance of being so.) The concordance rate for DZ twins was only 10% (Plomin et al., 1994).

Of course, twin studies are not perfect. MZ twins may resemble each other more closely than DZ twins partly because they are treated more similarly. MZ twins frequently are dressed identically, and parents sometimes have difficulty telling them apart.

One way to get around this difficulty is to find and compare MZ twins who were reared in different homes. Any similarities between MZ twins reared apart cannot be explained by a shared home environment and would appear to be largely a result of heredity. In the fascinating Minnesota Study of Twins Reared Apart (T. J. Bouchard et al., 1990; DiLalla et al., 1999; Markon et al., 2002), researchers have been measuring the physiological and psychological characteristics of 56 sets of MZ adult twins who were separated in infancy and reared in different homes. Constance Holden (1980) wrote a progress report on the study at the time when it had processed 9 pairs of MZ twins and was about to study 11 other pairs. A team of psychologists, psychiatrists, and other professionals analyzed the twins' life histories, including their interests, medical problems, abilities, and intelligence. All in all, there were some uncanny similarities between the pairs, except when there were extreme differences in their environment. Consider one pair of twins, both of whom were named Jim. Both were married and divorced. Both had been trained to become police. They each named their first sons James Allan. They drove the same kind of car and vacationed at the same beach. They each mentioned carpentry as a hobby; each had constructed a bench around a tree in the yard. There are certainly coincidences in their histories, and they were chosen for this lengthy description because of them. However, the interests in police work and carpentry are probably more than coincidental.

In sum, MZ twins reared apart are about as similar as MZ twins reared together on a variety of measures of intelligence, personality, temperament, occupational and leisure-time interests, and social attitudes. These traits thus would appear to have a genetic underpinning.

ADOPTION STUDIES The interpretation of kinship studies can be confused when relatives share similar environments as well as genes. Adoption studies offer special insight into the roles of nature and nurture in the development of traits, especially when they compare children who have been separated from their parents at an early age (or in which identical twins are separated at an early age) and reared in different environments. Psychologists look for similarities between children and their adoptive and natural parents. When children reared by adoptive parents are more similar to their natural parents in a particular trait, strong evidence exists for a genetic role in the appearance of that trait.

In later chapters we will see that psychologists have been particularly interested in the use of adoption studies to sort out the effects of nature and nurture in the development of personality traits, intelligence, and various psychological disorders. Such traits and disorders apparently represent the interaction of complex groupings of genes as well as environmental influences.

Selective Breeding: The Nurture of Nature

Under natural selection, traits that enable animals and plants to adapt better to their environments are likely to be—in Darwin's wording—"preserved." But then there is another kind of selection: selection not by nature, but by humans; and we call it *selective breeding*. **Question: What is selective breeding?**

We selectively breed plants and animals to enhance desired physical and—in the case of animals—behavioral traits. We breed cattle and chickens to be bigger and fatter so that they provide more food calories for less feed.

Dogs have been selectively bred for size, gentleness, tendencies to protect their territory, and for ease of training, including housebreaking. We haven't tried to housebreak rats, but we have selectively bred rats for maze-learning ability. In classic research, an initial group of rats was tested for maze-learning ability, as measured by the number of errors they make in repeated trials to reach a food goal (Tryon, 1940). Rats making the fewest mistakes are labeled B1, indicating high maze-learning ability. Those making the most errors are labeled D1. The distribution of errors for the first or parent generation is shown in Figure 2.4A, which shows the number of blind-alley entrances (errors) over a series of 19 runs through the maze. Note that the distribution of errors for the parent generation (part A) is rather even, ranging from very few to about 200. Rats with high maze-learning ability are then bred with other rats with high maze-learning ability; rats with low maze-learning ability are similarly bred with other "maze-dull" rats. Their offspring, the second generation (part B), begins to show dramatic differences in maze-learning ability. The offspring of the maze-bright rats (B2) are beginning to form a group that differs distinctly from the offspring of the maze-dull rats (D2). Parts C and D show that if we selectively breed subsequent generations of maze-bright and maze-dull rats, we begin to arrive at a point where the distributions of the brightest and the dullest hardly overlap at all. By the seventh generation, the maze-bright (B7) rats are making about one error per trial, whereas the maze-dull (D7) rats are making nine to ten errors per trial.

Maze-learning ability could be considered reflective of animal intelligence. It certainly requires some visual-motor skills and the ability to profit from experience. A key issue in psychology is the role of genetic factors in the behaviors and mental processes that make up intelligence in humans. We look more closely at that controversial issue in Chapter 9.

Your Turn: Now that we have discussed heredity, enhance your mastery of the material with the nearby "Learning Connections." Review the material by filling in the blanks, reflect on the material by relating it to other things you know, and think critically about it.

FIGURE 2.4 **Selective Breeding for Maze-Learning Ability in Rats**
Humans selectively breed animals and plants to achieve desired physical traits. However, in the case of animals, it is also possible to selectively breed for psychological traits and behaviors such as aggressiveness and trainability (in dogs) and maze-learning ability (in rats). In the classic Tryon (1940) study, "maze-bright" and "maze-dull" rats were selectively bred over several generations, until the distributions of their maze-learning ability barely overlapped.

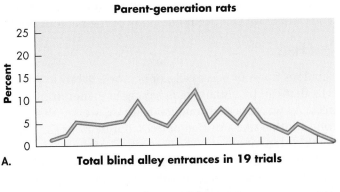
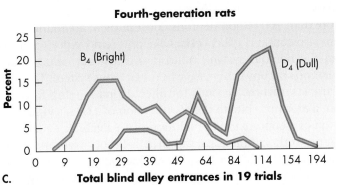
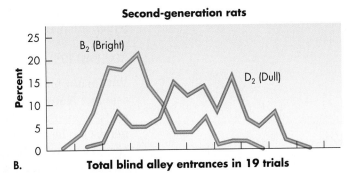
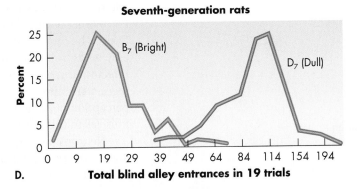

Learning Connections | HEREDITY: THE NATURE OF NATURE

ACTIVE REVIEW (7) The field of _____ genetics deals with the genetic transmission of traits that give rise to patterns of behavior. (8) _____ genetics attempts to identify specific genes that are connected with behavior and mental processes. (9) _____ are the most basic building blocks of heredity. (10) Genes are segments of _____. (11) People with _____ syndrome have an extra chromosome on the 21st pair. (12) The behavior of _____ twins is of special interest to psychologists because their genetic endowment is the same.

REFLECT AND RELATE Which family members seem to be like you physically or psychologically? Which seem to be very different? How do you explain the similarities and differences?

CRITICAL THINKING What ethical, social, and political issues would be involved in attempting to selectively breed humans for desired traits?

 Go to **http://psychology.wadsworth.com/ rathus_pcc9e** for an interactive version of this Learning Connections unit.

The Nervous System: On Being Wired

As a child, I did not think it was a good thing to have a "nervous" system. After all, if your system were not jittery, you might be less likely to jump at strange noises. Later I learned that a nervous system is not a system that is nervous. It is a system of nerves involved in thought processes, heartbeat, visual-motor coordination, and so on.

I also learned that the human nervous system is more complex than that of any other animal and that our brains are larger than those of any other animal. Now, this last piece of business is not quite true. A human brain weighs about three pounds, but the brains of elephants and whales may be four times as heavy. **Truth or Fiction Revisited:** Thus it is not true that the human brain is larger than that of any other animal. Still, our brains account for a greater part of our body weight than do those of elephants or whales. Our brains weigh about 1/60th of our body weight. Elephant brains weigh about 1/1,000th of their total weight, and whale brains are a paltry 1/10,000th of their weight. So, humans win the brain-as-a-percentage-of-body-weight contest.

The brain is only one part of the nervous system. We will see that the nervous system serves as the material base for our behaviors, emotions, and cognitions (our thoughts, images, and plans). The nervous system is composed of cells, most of which are neurons, which is where we will begin our study of the nervous system.

Neurons: Into the Fabulous Forest

Within our brains lies a fabulous forest of nerve cells, or neurons. **Question: What are neurons? Neurons** are cells that can be visualized as having branches, trunks, and roots—something like trees. As we voyage through this forest, we see that many nerve cells lie alongside one another like a thicket of trees. But neurons can also lie end to end, with their "roots" intertwined with the "branches" of the neurons that lie below. Trees receive sunlight, water, and nutrients from the soil. Neurons receive "messages" from a number of sources such as light, other neurons, and pressure on the skin, and they can pass these messages along in a complex biological dance.

We are born with more than 100 billion neurons. Most of them are found in the brain. The nervous system also contains **glial cells.** Glial cells remove dead neurons and waste products from the nervous system, nourish and insulate neurons, and direct their growth. But neurons occupy center stage in the nervous system. The messages transmitted by neurons somehow account for phenomena ranging from the perception of an itch from a mosquito bite to the coordination of a skier's vision and muscles to the composition of a concerto to the solution of an algebraic equation.

Neurons vary according to their functions and their location. Neurons in the brain may be only a fraction of an inch in length, whereas others in the legs are several feet long. A neuron is a nerve cell. Most neurons include a cell body, den-

Neuron A nerve cell.

Glial cells Cells that nourish and insulate neurons, direct their growth, and remove waste products from the nervous system.

drites, and an axon (see Figure 2.5). The cell body contains the core or *nucleus* of the cell. The nucleus uses oxygen and nutrients to generate the energy needed to carry out the work of the cell. Anywhere from a few to several hundred short fibers, or **dendrites,** extend like roots from the cell body to receive incoming messages from thousands of adjoining neurons. Each neuron has an **axon** that extends like a trunk from the cell body. Axons are very thin, but those that carry messages from the toes to the spinal cord extend several feet.

Like tree trunks, axons can branch off in different directions. Axons end in small bulb-shaped structures called *terminals* or *terminal buttons*. Neurons carry messages in one direction only: from the dendrites or cell body through the axon to the axon terminals. The messages are then transmitted from the terminal buttons to other neurons, muscles, or glands.

As a child matures, the axons of neurons become longer, and the dendrites and terminals proliferate, creating vast interconnected networks for the transmission of complex messages. The number of glial cells also increases as the nervous system develops, contributing to its dense appearance.

MYELIN: MINIATURE BRATWURST? The axons of many neurons are wrapped tightly with white, fatty **myelin** that makes them look like strings of sausages under the microscope (bratwurst, actually). The fat insulates the axon from electrically charged atoms, or ions, found in the fluids that surround the nervous system. The myelin sheath minimizes leakage of the electrical current being carried along the axon, thereby allowing messages to be conducted more efficiently.

Dendrites Rootlike structures, attached to the cell body of a neuron, that receive impulses from other neurons.

Axon A long, thin part of a neuron that transmits impulses to other neurons from branching structures called *terminal buttons*.

Myelin A fatty substance that encases and insulates axons, facilitating transmission of neural impulses.

FIGURE 2.5 **The Anatomy of a Neuron**

"Messages" enter neurons through dendrites, are transmitted along the trunklike axon, and then are sent from axon terminal buttons to muscles, glands, and other neurons. Axon terminal buttons contain sacs of chemicals called *neurotransmitters*. Neurotransmitters are released into the synaptic cleft, where many of them bind to receptor sites on the dendrites of the receiving neuron. Dozens of neurotransmitters have been identified.

Go to **http://psychology.wadsworth.com/ rathus_pcc9e** to access an interactive version of this figure.

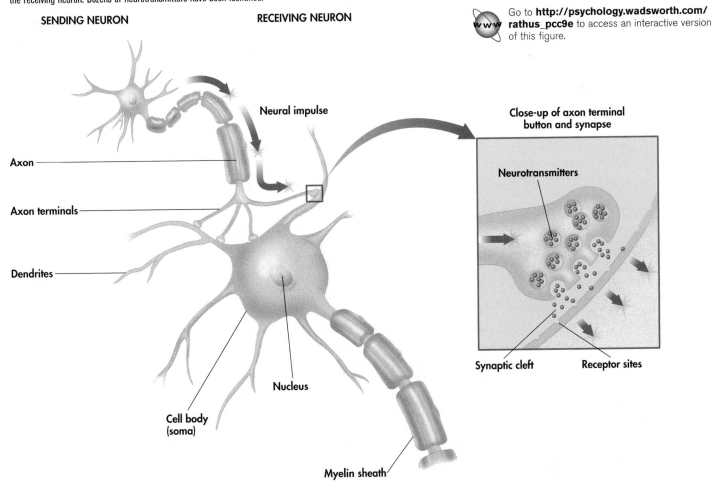

Myelination is part of the maturation process that leads to the child's ability to crawl and walk during the first year. Infants are not physiologically "ready" to engage in visual–motor coordination and other activities until the coating process reaches certain levels. In people with the disease multiple sclerosis, myelin is replaced with a hard fibrous tissue that throws off the timing of nerve impulses and disrupts muscular control.

AFFERENT AND EFFERENT NEURONS: FROM THERE TO HERE AND HERE TO THERE If someone steps on your toes, the sensation is registered by receptors or sensory neurons near the surface of your skin. Then it is transmitted to the spinal cord and brain through **afferent neurons,** which are perhaps two to three feet long. **Truth or Fiction Revisited:** Thus it is true that a single cell can stretch all the way from your spine to your toe. In the brain, subsequent messages might be conveyed by associative neurons that are only a few thousandths of an inch long. You experience the pain through this process and perhaps entertain some rather nasty thoughts about the perpetrator, who is now apologizing and begging for understanding. Long before you arrive at any logical conclusions, however, motor neurons **(efferent neurons)** send messages to your foot so that you withdraw it and begin an impressive hopping routine. Other efferent neurons stimulate glands so that your heart is beating more rapidly, you are sweating, and the hair on the back of your arms has become erect! Being a good sport, you say, "Oh, it's nothing." But considering all the neurons involved, it really is something, isn't it?

In case you think that afferent and efferent neurons will be hard to distinguish because they sound pretty much the SAME to you, remember that they *are* the "SAME." That is, *S*ensory = *A*fferent, and *M*otor = *E*fferent.

The Neural Impulse: Let Us "Sing the Body Electric"[1]

In the 18th century, the Italian physiologist Luigi Galvani (1737–1798) conducted a shocking experiment in a rainstorm. While his neighbors had the sense to remain indoors, Galvani and his wife were out on the porch connecting lightning rods to the heads of dissected frogs whose legs were connected by wires to a well of water. When lightning blazed above, the frogs' muscles contracted. This is not a recommended way to prepare frogs' legs. Galvani was demonstrating that the messages **(neural impulses)** that travel along neurons are electrochemical in nature.

Question: What are neural impulses? Neural impulses are messages that travel within neurons at somewhere between 2 (in nonmyelinated neurons) and 225 miles an hour (in myelinated neurons). This speed is not impressive when compared with that of an electrical current in a toaster oven or a lamp, which can travel at close to the speed of light—over 186,000 miles per second. Distances in the body are short, however, and a message will travel from a toe to the brain in perhaps 1/50th of a second.

AN ELECTROCHEMICAL VOYAGE (NO TICKETS NEEDED, JUST "CHARGES") The process by which neural impulses travel is electrochemical. Chemical changes take place within neurons that cause an electrical charge to be transmitted along their lengths. Neurons and body fluids contain ions—positively or negatively charged atoms. In a resting state—that is, when a neuron is not being stimulated by its neighbors—negatively charged chloride (Cl^-) ions are plentiful within the neuron, contributing to an overall negative charge in relation to the outside. The difference in electrical charge **polarizes** the neuron with a negative **resting potential** of about −70 millivolts in relation to the body fluid outside the cell membrane.

When an area on the surface of the resting neuron is adequately stimulated by other neurons, the cell membrane in the area changes its permeability to allow positively charged sodium ions to enter. Thus the area of entry becomes positively charged, or **depolarized** with respect to the outside (Figure 2.6). The permeability of the cell membrane then changes again, allowing no more sodium ions to enter.

Afferent neurons Neurons that transmit messages from sensory receptors to the spinal cord and brain. Also called *sensory neurons.*

Efferent neurons Neurons that transmit messages from the brain or spinal cord to muscles and glands. Also called *motor neurons.*

Neural impulse The electrochemical discharge of a nerve cell, or neuron.

Polarize To ready a neuron for firing by creating an internal negative charge in relation to the body fluid outside the cell membrane.

Resting potential The electrical potential across the neural membrane when it is not responding to other neurons.

Depolarize To reduce the resting potential of a cell membrane from about −70 millivolts toward zero.

[1]From Walt Whitman's *Leaves of Grass.*

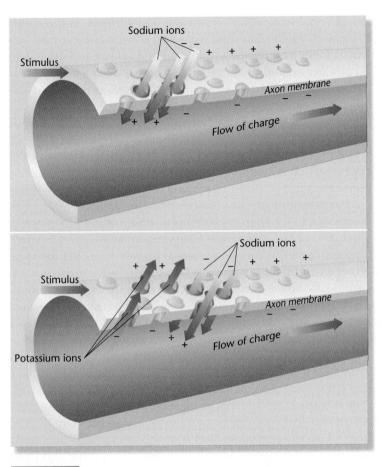

Sodium ions

Stimulus

Axon membrane

Flow of charge

A. During an action potential, sodium gates in the neuron membrane open and sodium ions enter the axon, bringing a positive charge with them.

Sodium ions

Stimulus

Axon membrane

Flow of charge

Potassium ions

B. After an action potential occurs, the sodium gates close at that point, and open at the next point along the axon. When the sodium gates close, potassium gates open and potassium ions flow out of the axon, carrying a positive charge with them.

FIGURE 2.6 The Neural Impulse

When a section of a neuron is stimulated by other neurons, the cell membrane becomes permeable to sodium ions so that an action potential of about 40 millivolts is induced. This action potential is transmitted along the axon. The neuron fires according to the all-or-none principle.

The inside of the cell axon at the disturbed area has an **action potential** of 110 millivolts. This action potential, added to the −70 millivolts that characterize the resting potential, brings the membrane voltage to a positive charge of about +30 to +40 millivolts (Figure 2.7). This inner change causes the next section of the cell to become permeable to sodium ions. At the same time, other positively charged (potassium) ions are being pumped out of the area of the cell that was previously affected, which returns the area to its resting potential. In this way, the neural impulse is transmitted continuously along an axon. Because the impulse is created anew as it progresses, its strength does not change.

Truth or Fiction Revisited: Thus it is true that messages travel in the brain by means of electricity. These are messages *within* neurons. However, communication between neurons is carried out quite differently.

Action potential The electrical impulse that provides the basis for the conduction of a neural impulse along an axon of a neuron.

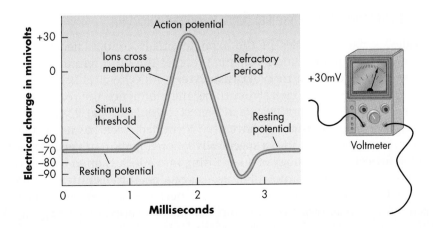

FIGURE 2.7 Changes in Electrical Charges as a Neural Impulse Is Transmitted across an Axon

The resting potential of a segment of a cell axon is about −70 millivolts. But the inside of the cell axon at the disturbed area has an action potential of about 110 millivolts. When we add this figure to the −70 millivolts that characterize the resting potential, we bring the membrane voltage to a positive charge of about +30 to +40 millivolts. This inner change causes the next section of the cell to become permeable to sodium ions. In this way, the neural impulse is transmitted continuously along an axon.

FIRING: HOW MESSAGES VOYAGE FROM NEURON TO NEURON The conduction of the neural impulse along the length of a neuron is what is meant by "firing." When a rifle fires, it sends a bullet speeding through its barrel and discharges it at more than 1,000 feet per second. **Question: What happens when a neuron fires?** Neurons also fire, but instead of a barrel, a neuron has an axon. Instead of discharging a bullet, it releases neurotransmitters.

Some neurons fire in less than 1/1,000th of a second. When they fire, neurons transmit messages to other neurons, muscles, or glands. However, neurons will not fire unless the incoming messages combine to reach a certain strength, which is defined as the *threshold* at which a neuron will fire. A weak message may cause a temporary shift in electrical charge at some point along the cell membrane, but this charge will dissipate if the neuron is not stimulated to its threshold.

Not only can a neuron fire in less than 1/1000th of a second. A neuron may also transmit several hundred messages each second. Every time a neuron fires, it transmits an impulse of the same strength. This occurrence is known as the **all-or-none principle.** That is, either a neuron fires or it doesn't. Neurons fire more often when they have been stimulated by larger numbers of other neurons. Stronger stimuli cause more frequent firing, but again, the strength of each firing remains the same.

For a few thousandths of a second after firing, a neuron is insensitive to messages from other neurons and will not fire. It is said to be in a **refractory period.** This period is a time of recovery during which sodium is prevented from passing through the neuronal membrane. When we realize that such periods of recovery might take place hundreds of times per second, it seems a rapid recovery and a short rest indeed. **Truth or Fiction Revisited:** It is therefore true that a single brain cell can send out hundreds of messages each second—and manage to catch some rest in between.

The facts that there are so many neurons and that they can fire so frequently begins to suggest how much information can be transmitted within the brain and to and from the brain. Just think: Billions of cells can each fire hundreds of times per second, sending different kinds of messages to different groups of cells each time. How can any human-made computer we know of today begin to transmit such vast quantities of information? It apparently requires such a complex system of transmission of information to begin to understand the particularly human capacities for insight and intuition.

THE SYNAPSE: ON BEING WELL-CONNECTED A neuron relays its message to another neuron across a junction called a **synapse. Question: What is a synapse?** A synapse consists of an axon terminal button from the transmitting neuron, a dendrite or the body of a receiving neuron, and a fluid-filled gap between the two that is called the *synaptic cleft* (see Figure 2.5). Although the neural impulse is electrical, it does not jump across the synaptic cleft like a spark. Instead, when a nerve impulse reaches a synapse, axon terminals release chemicals into the synaptic cleft like myriad ships being cast into the sea. Scientists have identified a few dozen of these chemicals to date. In the following section, we consider a few of them that are usually of greatest interest to psychologists.

Neurotransmitters: The Chemical Keys to Communication

Sacs called synaptic vesicles in the axon terminals contain neurotransmitters. When a neural impulse (action potential) reaches the axon terminal, the vesicles release varying amounts of **neurotransmitters**—the chemical keys to communication—into the synaptic cleft. From there, they influence the receiving neuron. **Questions: Which neurotransmitters are of interest to psychologists? What do they do?**

Dozens of neurotransmitters have been identified. Each has its own chemical structure, and each can fit into a specifically tailored harbor, or **receptor site,** on the receiving cell. The analogy of a key fitting into a lock is often used to describe this process. Once released, not all molecules of a neurotransmitter find their way into receptor sites of other neurons. "Loose" neurotransmitters are usually either broken down or reabsorbed by the axon terminal (a process called *reuptake*).

All-or-none principle The fact that a neuron fires an impulse of the same strength whenever its action potential is triggered.

Refractory period A phase following firing during which a neuron is less sensitive to messages from other neurons and will not fire.

Synapse A junction between the axon terminals of one neuron and the dendrites or cell body of another neuron.

Neurotransmitters Chemical substances involved in the transmission of neural impulses from one neuron to another.

Receptor site A location on a dendrite of a receiving neuron tailored to receive a neurotransmitter.

Some neurotransmitters act to *excite* other neurons—that is, to cause other neurons to fire. Other neurotransmitters act to *inhibit* receiving neurons. That is, they prevent them from firing. The sum of the stimulation—excitatory and inhibitory—determines whether a neuron will fire and, if so, when neurotransmitters will be released.

Neurotransmitters are involved in physical processes such as muscle contraction and psychological processes such as thoughts and emotions. Excesses or deficiencies of neurotransmitters have been linked to psychological disorders such as depression and schizophrenia. Let us consider the effects of some neurotransmitters of interest to psychologists: acetylcholine (ACh), dopamine, norepinephrine, serotonin, GABA, and endorphins.

Acetylcholine (ACh) controls muscle contractions. It is excitatory at synapses between nerves and muscles that involve voluntary movement but inhibitory at the heart and some other locations. The effects of curare highlight the functioning of ACh. Curare is a poison that is extracted from plants by native South Americans and used in hunting. If an arrow tipped with curare pierces the skin and the poison enters the body, it prevents ACh from binding to the receptor sites on neurons. Because ACh helps muscles move, curare causes paralysis. The victim is prevented from contracting the muscles used in breathing and therefore dies from suffocation. Botulism, a disease that stems from food poisoning, prevents the release of ACh and has the same effect as curare.

ACh is also normally prevalent in a part of the brain called the **hippocampus,** a structure involved in the formation of memories. When the amount of ACh available to the brain decreases, memory formation is impaired, as in Alzheimer's disease (de Toledo-Morrell, 2000). In one experiment, researchers decreased the ACh available to the hippocampus of laboratory rats. As a result, the rats were incapable of learning their way through a maze, apparently because they could not remember which way to turn at various choice points in the maze (Egawa et al., 2002).

Dopamine is involved at the level of the brain and affects voluntary movements, learning and memory, and emotional arousal. Deficiencies of dopamine are linked to Parkinson's disease, in which people progressively lose control over their muscles (Olanow, 2000; Swerdlow et al., 2003). They develop muscle tremors and jerky, uncoordinated movements. The boxer Muhammad Ali and actor Michael J. Fox are two of the better-known individuals who are afflicted with Parkinson's disease.

Video Connections—The Action Potential
A neuron's action potential is the electrical impulse that travels along its axon, enabling the conduction of a neural impulse. This difficult concept is explained and illustrated in "The Action Potential" video you will find on your companion website.

Acetylcholine (ACh) A neurotransmitter that controls muscle contractions.

Hippocampus A part of the limbic system of the brain that is involved in memory formation.

Dopamine A neurotransmitter that is involved in Parkinson's disease and that appears to play a role in schizophrenia.

■ **Former Heavyweight Champion Muhammad Ali and Actor Michael J. Fox—Two of the Many Afflicted with Parkinson's Disease**
Parkinson's disease is connected with deficiencies in the neurotransmitter dopamine, and is characterized by tremors, loss of coordination, and jerky movement. In this photo, Ali and Fox meet with two senators in the effort to secure more funding for research on the disease.

AFP Photo/Stephen Jaffe

TABLE 2.1 KEY NEUROTRANSMITTERS AND THEIR FUNCTIONS

Neurotransmitter	Functions	Comments
Acetylcholine (ACh)	Causes muscle contractions and is involved in formation of memories	Found at synapses between motor neurons and muscles; deficiencies linked with paralysis and Alzheimer's disease
Dopamine	Plays a role in movement, learning, attention, memory, and emotional response	Tremors of Parkinson's disease linked with low levels of dopamine; people with schizophrenia may *overutilize* dopamine
Norepinephrine	Accelerates the heart rate, affects eating, and is linked with activity levels, learning, and remembering	Imbalances linked with mood disorders such as depression and bipolar disorder
Serotonin	Is involved in behavior patterns and psychological problems, including obesity, depression, insomnia, alcoholism, and aggression	Drugs that block the reuptake of serotonin helpful in the treatment of depression
Gamma-aminobutyric acid (GABA)	An inhibitory neurotransmitter that may lessen anxiety	Tranquilizers and alcohol may counter anxiety by binding with GABA receptors or increasing the sensitivity of receptor sites to GABA
Endorphins	Inhibit pain by locking pain-causing chemicals out of their receptor sites	Endorphins may be connected with some people's indifference to pain, the painkilling effects of acupuncture, and the "runner's high" experienced by many long-distance runners

The psychological disorder *schizophrenia* is characterized by confusion and false perceptions, and it has been linked to dopamine. People with schizophrenia may have more receptor sites for dopamine in an area of the brain that is involved in emotional responding. For this reason, they may *overutilize* the dopamine available in the brain (Butcher, 2000; Kapur, 2003). This leads to hallucinations and disturbances of thought and emotion. The phenothiazines, a group of drugs used in the treatment of schizophrenia, inhibit the action of dopamine by blocking some dopamine receptor sites (Lidow et al., 2001). Because of their action, phenothiazines may have Parkinson-like side effects, which are usually treated by lowering the dose, prescribing additional drugs, or switching to another drug.

Norepinephrine is produced largely by neurons in the brain stem. It acts both as a neurotransmitter and as a hormone. It is an excitatory neurotransmitter that speeds up the heartbeat and other body processes and is involved in general arousal, learning and memory, and eating. Excesses and deficiencies of norepinephrine have been linked to mood disorders. Deficiencies of both ACh and norepinephrine are particularly impairing of memory (Egawa et al., 2002).

The stimulants cocaine and amphetamines ("speed") create excesses of norepinephrine (as well as dopamine) in the nervous system, increasing the firing of neurons and leading to persistent arousal. Amphetamines act by facilitating the release of these neurotransmitters and also prevent their reabsorption by the releasing synaptic vesicles—that is, their reuptake. Cocaine also blocks reuptake.

Serotonin is involved in emotional arousal and sleep. Deficiencies of serotonin have been linked to eating disorders, alcoholism, depression, aggression, and insomnia (Azar, 1997b; Leyton et al., 2000). The drug LSD decreases the action of serotonin and may also influence the utilization of dopamine. With LSD, "two no's make a yes." By inhibiting an inhibitor, it increases brain activity, in this case frequently producing hallucinations.

Gamma-aminobutyric acid (GABA) is another neurotransmitter of great interest to psychologists. One reason is that GABA is an inhibitory neurotransmitter that may help calm anxiety reactions (Stroele et al., 2002). Tranquilizers and alcohol may quell anxiety by binding with GABA receptors and amplifying its effects. One class of antianxiety drug may also increase the sensitivity of receptor

Norepinephrine A neurotransmitter whose action is similar to that of the hormone epinephrine and that may play a role in depression.

Serotonin A neurotransmitter, deficiencies of which have been linked to affective disorders, anxiety, and insomnia.

Gamma-aminobutyric acid (GABA) An inhibitory neurotransmitter that apparently helps calm anxiety.

sites to GABA. Other studies link deficiencies of GABA to depression (Sanacora et al., 2000).

Endorphins are inhibitory neurotransmitters. The word *endorphin* is the contraction of *endogenous morphine. Endogenous* means "developing from within." Endorphins occur naturally in the brain and in the bloodstream and are similar to the narcotic morphine in their functions and effects. They lock into receptor sites for chemicals that transmit pain messages to the brain. Once the endorphin "key" is in the "lock," the pain-causing chemicals are locked out. Endorphins may also increase our sense of competence, enhance the functioning of the immune system, and be connected with the pleasurable "runner's high" reported by many long-distance runners (Jonsdottir et al., 2000; Oktedalen et al., 2001). Table 2.1 reviews much of the information on neurotransmitters.

There you have it—a fabulous forest of neurons in which billions upon billions of axon terminals are pouring armadas of neurotransmitters into synaptic clefts at any given time. The process occurs when you are involved in strenuous activity. It is taking place this moment as you are reading this page. It will happen later on when you have a snack or passively watch television. Moreover, the process is repeated several hundred times every second. The combined activity of all these neurotransmitters determines which messages will be transmitted and which ones will not. You experience your sensations, your thoughts, and your control over your body as psychological events, but the psychological events somehow result from many billions of electrochemical events.

We can think of neurons as the microscopic building blocks of the nervous system. However, millions upon millions of neurons gather together to form larger, visible structures that we think of as the parts of the nervous system. We discuss those parts next, including the most human part—the brain.

The Parts of the Nervous System

Question: What are the parts of the nervous system? The nervous system consists of the brain, the spinal cord, and the **nerves** linking them to the sensory organs, muscles, and glands. As shown in Figure 2.8, the brain and spinal cord make up the **central nervous system.** If you compare your nervous system to a computer, your central nervous system would be your central processing unit (CPU).

Runner's High? Why have thousands of people taken up long-distance running? Running promotes cardiovascular conditioning, muscle strength, and weight control. But many long-distance runners also experience a "runner's high" that appears to be connected with the release of endorphins. Endorphins are naturally occurring substances that are similar in function to the narcotic morphine.

Endorphins Neurotransmitters that are composed of amino acids and that are functionally similar to morphine.

Nerve A bundle of axons from many neurons.

Central nervous system The brain and spinal cord.

FIGURE 2.8 **The Divisions of the Nervous System**

The nervous system contains two main divisions: the central nervous system and the peripheral nervous system. The central nervous system consists of the brain and spinal cord. The peripheral nervous system contains the somatic and autonomic systems. In turn, the autonomic nervous system has sympathetic and parasympathetic divisions.

 Go to **http://psychology.wadsworth.com/rathus_pcc9e** to access an interactive version of this figure.

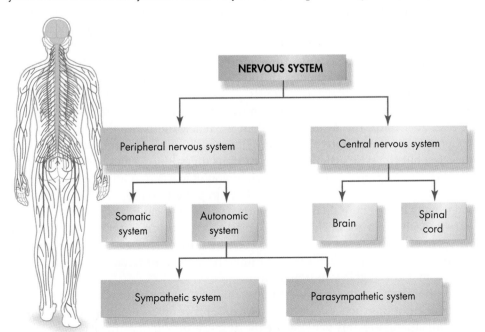

The sensory (afferent) neurons, which receive and transmit messages to the brain and spinal cord, and the motor (efferent) neurons, which transmit messages from the brain or spinal cord to the muscles and glands, make up the **peripheral nervous system.** In the comparison of the nervous system to a computer, the peripheral nervous system makes up the nervous system's peripheral devices—keyboard, mouse, CD-ROM, and so on. You would not be able to feed information to your computer's central processing unit without these *peripheral* devices. Other peripheral devices, such as your monitor and printer, allow you to follow what is happening inside your CPU and to see what it has accomplished.

THE PERIPHERAL NERVOUS SYSTEM: THE BODY'S PERIPHERAL DEVICES
Question: What are the divisions and functions of the peripheral nervous system? The peripheral nervous system consists of sensory and motor neurons that transmit messages to and from the central nervous system. Without the peripheral nervous system, our brains would be like isolated CPUs. There would be no keyboards, mouses, diskettes, or other ways of inputting information. There would be no monitors, printers, modems, or other ways of displaying or transmitting information. We would be detached from the world: We would not be able to perceive it, and we would not be able to act on it. The two main divisions of the peripheral nervous system are the *somatic nervous system* and the *autonomic nervous system.*

The **somatic nervous system** contains sensory (afferent) and motor (efferent) neurons. It transmits messages about sights, sounds, smells, temperature, body positions, and so on, to the central nervous system. As a result, we can experience the beauties and the horrors of the world, its physical ecstasies and agonies. Messages transmitted from the brain and spinal cord to the somatic nervous system control purposeful body movements such as raising a hand, winking, or running, as well as the tiny, almost imperceptible movements that maintain our balance and posture.

Autonomic means "automatic." The **autonomic nervous system (ANS)** regulates the glands and the muscles of internal organs. Thus, the ANS controls activities such as heartbeat, respiration, digestion, and dilation of the pupils of the eyes. These activities can occur automatically, while we are asleep. But some of them can be overridden by conscious control. You can breathe at a purposeful pace, for example. Methods like biofeedback and yoga also help people gain voluntary control of functions such as heart rate and blood pressure.

The ANS also has two branches, or divisions: **sympathetic** and **parasympathetic.** These branches have largely opposing effects. Many organs and glands are stimulated by both branches of the ANS (Figure 2.9). When organs and glands are simultaneously stimulated by both divisions, their effects can average out to some degree. In general, the sympathetic division is most active during processes that involve spending body energy from stored reserves, such as a fight-or-flight response to a predator or when you find out that your rent is going to be raised. The parasympathetic division is most active during processes that replenish reserves of energy, such as eating. When we are afraid, the sympathetic division of the ANS accelerates the heart rate. When we relax, the parasympathetic division decelerates the heart rate. The parasympathetic division stimulates digestive processes, but the sympathetic branch inhibits digestion.

Have you ever tried to eat a meal when you're worried or anxious about something, like a big test or a speech you will have to present to the class? At such times, food usually has no appeal; and, if you force yourself to eat, it may seem to land in your stomach like a rock. This is the sympathetic division of your ANS in action. The sympathetic division of the ANS predominates when we feel fear or anxiety, and these feelings can therefore cause indigestion. **Truth or Fiction Revisited:** Thus it is true that fear can give you indigestion.

The ANS is of particular interest to psychologists because its activities are linked to various emotions such as anxiety and love. Some people seem to have overly reactive sympathetic nervous systems. In the absence of external threats, their bodies

Peripheral nervous system The part of the nervous system consisting of the somatic nervous system and the autonomic nervous system.

Somatic nervous system The division of the peripheral nervous system that connects the central nervous system with sensory receptors, skeletal muscles, and the surface of the body.

Autonomic nervous system (ANS) The division of the peripheral nervous system that regulates glands and activities such as heartbeat, respiration, digestion, and dilation of the pupils.

Sympathetic The branch of the ANS that is most active during emotional responses, such as fear and anxiety, that spend the body's reserves of energy.

Parasympathetic The branch of the ANS that is most active during processes such as digestion that restore the body's reserves of energy.

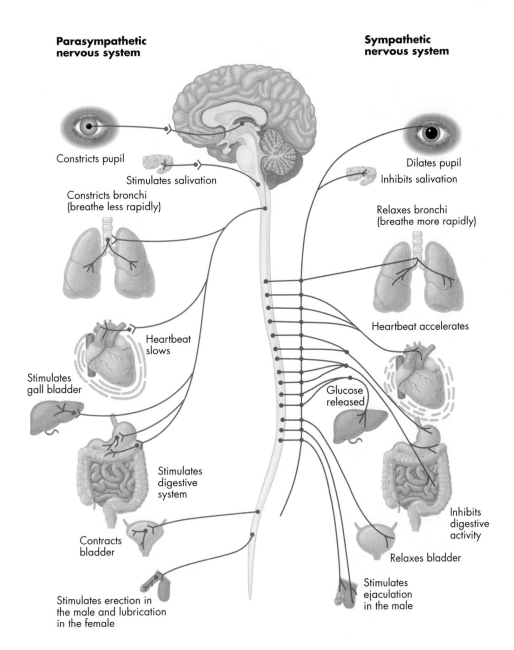

Parasympathetic nervous system

Constricts pupil

Stimulates salivation

Constricts bronchi (breathe less rapidly)

Heartbeat slows

Stimulates gall bladder

Stimulates digestive system

Contracts bladder

Stimulates erection in the male and lubrication in the female

Sympathetic nervous system

Dilates pupil

Inhibits salivation

Relaxes bronchi (breathe more rapidly)

Heartbeat accelerates

Glucose released

Inhibits digestive activity

Relaxes bladder

Stimulates ejaculation in the male

FIGURE 2.9 **The Branches of the Autonomic Nervous System (ANS)**

The parasympathetic branch of the ANS generally acts to replenish stores of energy in the body. The sympathetic branch is most active during activities that expend energy. The two branches of the ANS frequently have antagonistic effects on the organs they service.

 Go to **http://psychology.wadsworth. com/rathus_pcc9e** to access an interactive version of this figure.

still respond as though they were faced with danger. Psychologists often help them learn to relax when there is no external reason for them to feel so "wound up tight."

THE CENTRAL NERVOUS SYSTEM: THE BODY'S CENTRAL PROCESSING UNIT It is your central nervous system that makes you so special. Other species see more sharply, smell more keenly, and hear more acutely. Other species run faster, or fly through the air, or swim underwater—without the benefit of artificial devices such as airplanes and submarines. But it is your central nervous system that enables you to use symbols and language, the abilities that allow people not only to adapt to their environment but to create new environments and give them names (Bandura, 1999). **Question: What are the divisions and functions of the central nervous system?** The central nervous system consists of the spinal cord and the brain.

The **spinal cord** is a true "information superhighway"—a column of nerves about as thick as a thumb. It transmits messages from sensory receptors to the brain and from the brain to muscles and glands throughout the body. The spinal cord is also capable of some "local government." That is, it controls some responses to external stimulation through **spinal reflexes.** A spinal reflex is an unlearned response to a stimulus that may involve only two neurons—a sensory (afferent) neuron and a motor (efferent) neuron (Figure 2.10). In some reflexes, a third

Spinal cord A column of nerves within the spine that transmits messages from sensory receptors to the brain and from the brain to muscles and glands throughout the body.

Spinal reflex A simple, unlearned response to a stimulus that may involve only two neurons.

FIGURE 2.10 **The Reflex Arc**

Reflexes are inborn, stereotyped behavior patterns that have apparently evolved because they help individuals adapt to the environment even before they can understand and purposefully manipulate the environment. Here we see a cross section of the spinal cord, highlighting a sensory neuron and a motor neuron, which are involved in the knee-jerk reflex. In some reflexes, interneurons link sensory and motor neurons.

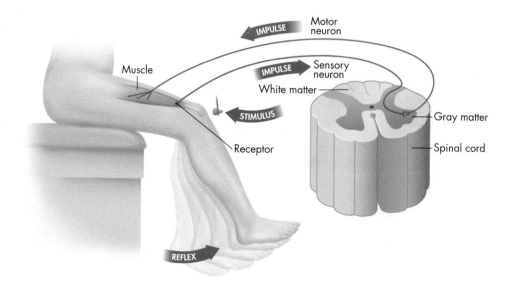

neuron, called an **interneuron,** transmits the neural impulse from the sensory neuron through the spinal cord to the motor neuron.

The spinal cord (and the brain) consists of gray matter and white matter. The **gray matter** is composed of nonmyelinated neurons. Some of these are involved in spinal reflexes. Others send their axons to the brain. The **white matter** is composed of bundles of longer, myelinated (and thus whitish) axons that carry messages to and from the brain. As you can see in Figure 2.10, a cross section of the spinal cord shows that the gray matter, which includes cell bodies, is distributed in a butterfly pattern.

We have many reflexes. We blink in response to a puff of air in our faces. We swallow when food accumulates in the mouth. A physician may tap the leg below the knee to elicit the knee-jerk reflex, a sign that the nervous system is operating adequately. Urinating and defecating are reflexes that occur in response to pressure in the bladder and the rectum. Parents typically spend weeks or months toilet-training infants—in other words, teaching them to involve their brains in the process of elimination. Learning to inhibit these reflexes makes civilization possible.

Sexual response also involves many reflexes. Stimulation of the genital organs leads to the reflexes of erection in the male and vaginal lubrication in the female (reflexes that make sexual intercourse possible), and to the reflexive muscle contractions of orgasm. As reflexes, these processes need not involve the brain, but most often they do. Feelings of passion, memories of an enjoyable sexual encounter, and sexual fantasies usually contribute to sexual response by transmitting messages from the brain to the genitals through the spinal cord.

Your Turn: Now that we have discussed the nervous system, enhance your mastery of the material with the nearby "Learning Connections." Review the material by filling in the blanks, reflect on the material by relating it to other things you know, and think critically about it.

Interneuron A neuron that transmits a neural impulse from a sensory neuron to a motor neuron.

Gray matter In the spinal cord, the grayish neurons and neural segments that are involved in spinal reflexes.

White matter In the spinal cord, axon bundles that carry messages from and to the brain.

Learning Connections   THE NERVOUS SYSTEM: ON BEING WIRED

ACTIVE REVIEW (13) Neurons transmit messages to other neurons by means of chemical substances called _____. (14) Neurons have a cell body, or soma; dendrites, which receive "messages"; and a(n)_____, which extends from the cell body. (15) The axons of many neurons have a fatty insulating sheath called _____. (16) _____ neurons conduct messages from the central nervous system that stimulate glands or cause muscles to contract. (17) The conduction of the neural impulse along the length of the neuron is called _____. (18) A(n) _____ consists of an axon terminal, a dendrite, and a fluid-filled gap between them. (19) ACh is normally prevalent in a brain structure essential to the formation of memories: the _____. (20) It is theorized that people with

_____ overutilize dopamine. (21) Deficiencies of _____ are linked to anxiety, depression, and insomnia. (22) The nervous system is made up of the _____ and central nervous systems. (23) The _____ nervous system (ANS) regulates the glands and involuntary activities such as heartbeat and digestion.

REFLECT AND RELATE Reflexes are automatic, involuntary responses. Yet the great majority of the time we engage in sexual behavior voluntarily. How, then, do we explain the fact that sexual responses like erection, vaginal lubrication, and orgasm are reflexes?

CRITICAL THINKING Psychology is the study of behavior and mental processes. Why, then, are psychologists interested in the nervous system?

 Go to **http://psychology.wadsworth.com/ rathus_pcc9e** for an interactive version of this Learning Connections unit.

The Brain: The Star of the Human Nervous System

Every show has a star, and the brain is the undisputed star of the human nervous system. The size and shape of your brain are responsible for your large, delightfully rounded head. In all the animal kingdom, you (and about 6 billion other people) are unique because of the capacities for learning and thinking residing in the human brain.

The brains of men are about 15% larger than those of women on average (Blum, 1997), which is related to the difference in body size. However, it may be that how well connected one is (in terms of synapses) is more important than size in the human brain. After all, Albert Einstein's brain was only average in size (Abraham, 2002). Moreover, women's brains "run hotter" than men's. Women metabolize more glucose (sugar) and appear to use more of their brains on a given task (Blum, 1997).

Scientists who have engaged in brain research generally agree that the mind is a function of the brain (Bogen, 1998, 2000; Voneida, 1998). **Question: How do researchers learn about the functions of the brain?**

Seeing the Brain through the Eyes of the Psychologist

Philosophers and scientists have wondered about the functions of the brain throughout history. Sometimes they have engaged in careful research that attempts to pinpoint exactly what happens in certain parts of the brain. At other times—as in the nearby profile of Phineas Gage—knowledge has almost literally fallen into

In Profile PHINEAS GAGE

Reprinted with permission from Damasio H, Gravowski T, Frank R, Galaburda AM, Damasio AR: The return of Phineas Gage: Clues about the brain from a famous patient. *Science,* 264:1102–1105, © 1994. American Association for the Advancement of Science. Photo courtesy of H. Damasio, Human Neuroanatomy and Neuroimaging Laboratory, Department of Neurology, University of Iowa

"Gage is no longer Gage," said those who had known him before the accident.

There are many key characters in the history of psychology, and some of them did not arrive there intentionally. One of these was a promising railroad worker who was helping our young nation stretch from coast to coast. His name was Phineas Gage. Gage was highly admired by his friends and his coworkers. But all that changed one day in 1848. While he was tamping down the blasting powder for a dynamite charge, Gage accidentally set the powder off. The inch-thick metal tamping rod shot upward through his cheek and brain and out the top of his head.

If the trajectory of the rod had been slightly different, Gage would have died. Although Gage fell back in a heap, he was miraculously alive. His coworkers watched in shock as he stood up a few moments later and spoke. While the local doctor marveled at the hole through Gage's head, Gage asked when he'd be able to return to work. Two months later, Gage's external wounds had healed, but the psychological aspects of the wound were now obvious. Gage had become undependable, foul-mouthed, and ill-mannered.

Generations of researchers—psychologists, physicians, biologists, neuroscientists—have wondered how the changes in Gage's personality might have been caused by the damage to his brain. Perhaps the trajectory of the rod spared parts of the frontal lobes that are involved in language and movement but damaged areas connected with personality and emotional response (Damasio, 2000).

 Go to **http://psychology.wadsworth.com/ rathus_pcc9e** to access more information about Phineas Gage.

Lesion (LEE-shun). An injury that results in impaired behavior or loss of a function.

their laps. From injuries to the head—some of them minimal, some horrendous—we have learned that brain damage can impair consciousness and awareness. Brain damage can result in loss of vision and hearing, confusion, or loss of memory. In some cases, the loss of large portions of the brain may result in little loss of function. Ironically, the loss of smaller portions in particularly sensitive locations can result in language problems, memory loss, or death. It has been known for about two centuries that damage to the left side of the brain is connected with loss of sensation or movement on the right side of the body, and vice versa. Thus it has been assumed that the brain's control mechanisms must cross over from right to left, and vice versa, as they descend into the body.

Accidents provide unplanned and uncontrolled opportunities of studying the brain. Scientists have learned more about the brain, however, through methods like experimentation, use of the electroencephalograph, and brain scans.

EXPERIMENTING WITH THE BRAIN The results of disease and accidents (as in the case of Phineas Gage) have shown us that brain injuries can be connected with changes in behavior and mental processes. Scientists have also purposefully experimented with the brain to observe the results. For example, **lesioning** (damaging) part of the brain region called the hypothalamus causes rats to overeat. Damaging another part of the hypothalamus causes them to stop eating. It is as if parts of the brain contain on–off switches for certain kinds of behavior, at least in lower animals.

Surgeon Wilder Penfield (1969) stimulated parts of human brains with electrical probes, and as a result his patients reported the occurrence of certain kinds of memories. Similar experiments in electrical stimulation of the brain have found that parts of the brain are connected with specific kinds of sensations (as of light or sound) or motor activities (such as movement of an arm or leg).

A. Computerized axial tomography (the CAT scan) passes a narrow X-ray beam through the head and measures structures that reflect the rays from various angles, enabling a computer to generate a three-dimensional image.

B. Positron emission tomography (the PET scan) injects a radioactive tracer into the bloodstream and assesses activitiy of parts of the brain according to the amount of glucose they metabolize.

C. Magnetic resonance imaging (MRI) places a person in a magnetic field and uses radio waves to cause the brain to emit signals that reveal shifts in the flow of blood which, in turn, indicate brain activity.

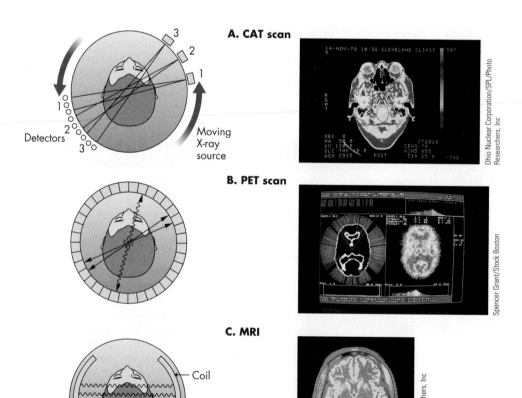

FIGURE 2.11 **Brain Imaging Techniques**
Part A shows a CAT scan, part B a PET scan, and part C, MRI.

THE ELECTROENCEPHALOGRAPH: FOLLOWING THE ELECTRIC FOOTPRINTS OF BRAINPOWER Penfield stimulated parts of the brain with an electrical current and asked people to report what they experienced as a result. Researchers have also used the electroencephalograph (EEG) to record the natural electrical activity of the brain. The EEG detects minute amounts of electrical activity—called brain waves— that pass between the electrodes. Certain brain waves are associated with feelings of relaxation and with the stages of sleep.

BRAIN-IMAGING TECHNIQUES: SEEING THE INVISIBLE When Phineas Gage had his fabled accident, the only ways to look into the brain were to drill holes or crack it open, neither of which would have contributed to the well-being of the subject. But researchers today use the computer to generate images of the parts of the brain from various sources of radiation.

As shown in Figure 2.11, the CAT (computerized axial tomograph) scan passes a narrow X-ray beam through the head and measures the structures that reflect the X-rays from various angles, generating a three-dimensional image of the brain. The CAT scan reveals deformities in shape and structure that are connected with blood clots, tumors, and other health problems. Positron emission tomography (PET scan) forms a computer-generated image of the activity of parts of the brain by tracing the amount of glucose used (or metabolized) by these parts. More glucose is metabolized in more active parts of the brain. In magnetic resonance imaging (MRI), the person lies in a powerful magnetic field and is exposed to radio waves that cause parts of the brain to emit signals, which are measured from several angles. MRI relies on subtle shifts in blood flow. (More blood flows to more active parts of the brain, supplying them with oxygen.) The PET scan and MRI have been used by researchers to see which parts of the brain are most active when we are, for example, listening to music, working out a math problem, using language, or playing chess. MRI has shown that people with schizophrenia have smaller prefrontal regions of the cortex than other people (Flashman et al., 2000) but larger ventricles (hollow spaces) in the brain (Wright et al., 2000). In Chapter 14 we discuss the implications of such findings in schizophrenia.

Research with the PET scan and MRI suggests that the prefrontal cortex of the brain may be where we process much of the information involved in making plans and solving problems (Duncan et al., 2000; Kroger et al., 2002; Rowe et al., 2001). Some researchers refer to the prefrontal cortex as the "executive center" of the brain, where decisions are made to keep information in working memory and develop solutions to various kinds of verbal and spatial problems. Figure 2.12 shows the prefrontal cortex. One prefrontal region is found in each hemisphere, a bit above the outer edge of the eyebrow.

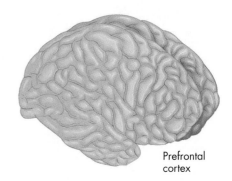

Prefrontal cortex

FIGURE 2.12 **The Prefrontal Cortex of the Brain**
The prefrontal cortex comes in pairs. One is found in each hemisphere, a bit above the outer edge of the eyebrow. The prefrontal cortex is highly active during visual and spatial problem solving. Your sense of self—your continuous sense of being in and operating on the world—may also reside largely in the prefrontal cortex.

A Voyage through the Brain: Revealing the Central Processing Unit

Perhaps you never imagined yourself as going off to foreign territory to unearth evidence about the history and functioning of the human species. But get your traveling gear, because we are about to go off on a voyage of discovery—a voyage within your own skull. We will be traveling through your brain—a fascinating archaeological site.

Your brain reveals much of what is so special about you. It also holds a record of your connectedness with other animals that have walked, swum, and flown the Earth for hundreds of millions of years. In fact, some parts of your brain—those that we meet first on our tour—are not all that different from the corresponding parts of the brains of other mammals. The "older" parts of your brain, evolutionarily speaking, also have functions very similar to those of these other species. They are involved in basic survival functions such as breathing, feeding, and the regulation of cycles of sleeping and waking. **Question: What are the structures and functions of the brain?**

Let us now begin our tour of the brain (Figure 2.13). We begin with the oldest part of our "archaeological dig"—the hindbrain, where the spinal cord rises to meet the brain. Here we find three major structures: the medulla, the pons, and the cerebellum. Many pathways that connect the spinal cord to higher levels of the brain pass through the **medulla.** The medulla regulates vital functions such as heart rate, blood pressure, and respiration. (In fact, Gage survived his accident because his medulla escaped injury.) The medulla also plays a role in sleeping, sneezing, and coughing. The **pons** is a bulge in the hindbrain that lies forward of the medulla. *Pons* is the Latin word for "bridge." The pons is so named because of the bundles of nerves that pass through it. The pons transmits information about body movement and is involved in functions related to attention, sleep and alertness, and respiration.

Behind the pons lies the **cerebellum** ("little brain" in Latin). The cerebellum has two hemispheres that are involved in maintaining balance and in controlling motor (muscle) behavior. You may send a command from your forebrain to get up and walk to the refrigerator, but your cerebellum is key to organizing the information that enables you to engage in these movements. The cerebellum allows you to place one leg in front of the other and reach your destination without tipping over. Injury to the

Medulla An oblong area of the hindbrain involved in regulation of heartbeat and respiration.

Pons A structure of the hindbrain involved in respiration, attention, and sleep and dreaming.

Cerebellum A part of the hindbrain involved in muscle coordination and balance.

FIGURE 2.13 **The Parts of the Human Brain**

This view of the brain, split top to bottom, shows some of the most important structures. Note how close the hypothalamus is to the pituitary gland. The proximity allows the hypothalamus to readily influence the pituitary gland. The "valleys" in the cerebrum are called fissures.

Go to **http://psychology.wadsworth. com/rathus_pcc9e** to access an interactive version of this figure.

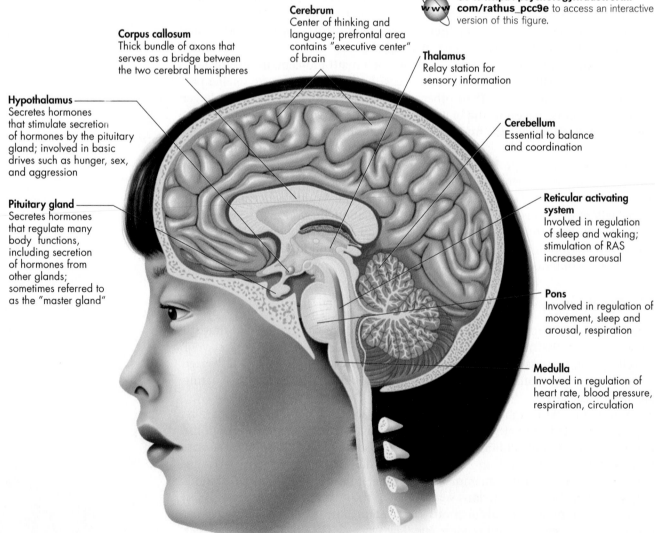

Corpus callosum
Thick bundle of axons that serves as a bridge between the two cerebral hemispheres

Cerebrum
Center of thinking and language; prefrontal area contains "executive center" of brain

Thalamus
Relay station for sensory information

Hypothalamus
Secretes hormones that stimulate secretion of hormones by the pituitary gland; involved in basic drives such as hunger, sex, and aggression

Pituitary gland
Secretes hormones that regulate many body functions, including secretion of hormones from other glands; sometimes referred to as the "master gland"

Cerebellum
Essential to balance and coordination

Reticular activating system
Involved in regulation of sleep and waking; stimulation of RAS increases arousal

Pons
Involved in regulation of movement, sleep and arousal, respiration

Medulla
Involved in regulation of heart rate, blood pressure, respiration, circulation

cerebellum may lead to lack of motor coordination, stumbling, and loss of muscle tone. Alcohol depresses the functioning of the cerebellum, so police often ask drivers suspected of drinking too much to engage in tasks that involve the cerebellum, such as touching their noses with their fingers or walking a straight line.

As we tour the hindbrain, we also find the lower part of the **reticular activating system (RAS).** That is where the RAS begins, but it ascends through the midbrain into the lower part of the forebrain. The RAS is vital in the functions of attention, sleep, and arousal. Injury to the RAS may result in a coma. Stimulation of the RAS causes it to send messages to the cerebral cortex (the large wrinkled mass that you think of as your brain), making us more alert to sensory information. In classic neurological research, Guiseppe Moruzzi and Horace Magoun (1949) discovered that electrical stimulation of the reticular formation of a sleeping cat caused it to awaken at once. But when the reticular formation was severed from higher parts of the brain, the animal fell into a coma from which it would not awaken. Drugs known as central nervous system depressants, such as alcohol, are thought to work, in part, by lowering RAS activity.

Sudden loud noises stimulate the RAS and awaken a sleeping animal or person. But the RAS may become selective through learning. That is, it comes to play a filtering role. It may allow some messages to filter through to higher brain levels and awareness while screening others out. For example, the parent who has primary responsibility for child care may be awakened by the stirring sounds of an infant, while the sounds of traffic or street noise are filtered out, even though they are louder. The other parent, in contrast, may sleep through loud crying by the infant. If the first parent must be away for several days, however, the second parent's RAS may quickly become sensitive to noises produced by the child. This sensitivity may rapidly fade again when the first parent returns.

Let's move onward and upward. Key areas of the forwardmost part of the brain, or forebrain, are the thalamus, the hypothalamus, the limbic system, and the cerebrum (see Figure 2.13). The **thalamus** is located near the center of the brain. It consists of two joined egg- or football-shaped structures. The thalamus serves as a relay station for sensory stimulation. Nerve fibers from the sensory systems enter from below; the information carried by them is then transmitted to the cerebral cortex by way of fibers that exit from above. For instance, the thalamus relays sensory input from the eyes to the visual areas of the cerebral cortex. The thalamus is also involved in controlling sleep and attention in coordination with other brain structures, including the RAS.

The **hypothalamus** lies beneath the thalamus and above the pituitary gland. It weighs only 4 grams, yet it is vital in the regulation of body temperature, concentration of fluids, storage of nutrients, and various aspects of motivation and emotion. Experimenters learn many of the functions of the hypothalamus by implanting electrodes in parts of it and observing the effects of an electrical current. They have found that the hypothalamus is involved in hunger, thirst, sexual behavior, caring for offspring, and aggression. Among lower animals, stimulation of various areas of the hypothalamus can trigger instinctual behaviors such as fighting, mating, or even nest building.

Canadian psychologists James Olds and Peter Milner (1954) made a wonderful mistake in the 1950s. They were attempting to implant an electrode in a rat's reticular formation to see how stimulation of the area might affect learning. Olds, however, was primarily a social psychologist and not a biological psychologist. He missed his target and found a part of the animal's hypothalamus instead. Olds and Milner dubbed this area the "pleasure center" because the animal would repeat whatever it was doing when it was stimulated. The term *pleasure center* is not used too frequently, because it appears to attribute human emotions to rats. Yet the "pleasure centers" must be doing something right, because rats stimulate themselves in these centers by pressing a pedal several thousand times an hour, until they are exhausted (Olds, 1969).

■ **Walking the Line** The cerebellum plays a key role in your ability to keep to the straight and narrow—that is, to walk a straight line. Because alcohol depresses the functioning of the cerebellum, police may ask suspected drivers to walk a straight line as a test of whether they have drunk too much to drive their cars safely.

Reticular activating system (RAS) A part of the brain involved in attention, sleep, and arousal.

Thalamus An area near the center of the brain involved in the relay of sensory information to the cortex and in the functions of sleep and attention.

Hypothalamus A bundle of nuclei below the thalamus involved in body temperature, motivation, and emotion.

■ **Who Is He?**
In the film *50 First Dates*, Drew Barrymore plays a woman whose ability to form new memories has been compromised by brain damage. One day she falls in love with her suitor, Adam Sandler, but she fails to recognize him upon waking the following day. The relationship manages to survive when Sandler arranges for her to see a videotape each morning that explains her situation and reintroduces him.

Limbic system A group of structures involved in memory, motivation, and emotion that forms a fringe along the inner edge of the cerebrum.

Amygdala A part of the limbic system that apparently facilitates stereotypical aggressive responses.

FIGURE 2.14 **The Limbic System**
The limbic system is made up of structures that include the amygdala, the hippocampus, and parts of the hypothalamus. It is evolved fully only in mammals and forms a fringe along the inner edge of the cerebrum. The limbic system is involved in memory and emotion, and in the drives of hunger, sex, and aggression.

 Go to **http://psychology.wadsworth.com/ rathus_pcc9e** to access an interactive version of this figure.

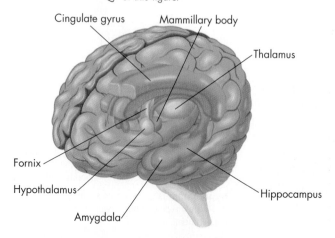

The hypothalamus is just as important to humans as it is to lower animals. Unfortunately (or fortunately), our "pleasure centers" are not as clearly defined as those of the rat. Then, too, our responses to messages from the hypothalamus are less automatic and relatively more influenced by higher brain functions—that is, cognitive factors such as thought, choice, and value systems. It is all a part of being human.

The **limbic system** forms a fringe along the inner edge of the cerebrum and is fully evolved only in mammals. (Dig in from the surface a little to find it; see Figure 2.14). It is made up of several structures, including the amygdala, hippocampus, and parts of the hypothalamus. The limbic system lies along the inner edge of the cerebrum and is fully evolved only in mammals. It is involved in memory and emotion and in the drives of hunger, sex, and aggression. People in whom surgical operations have damaged the hippocampus can retrieve old memories but cannot permanently store new information. As a result, they may reread the same newspaper day in and day out without recalling that they read it before. Or they may have to be perpetually reintroduced to people they have met just hours earlier (Squire, 1993, 1996).

The **amygdala** is near the bottom of the limbic system and looks like two little almonds. Studies using lesioning and electrical stimulation show that the amygdala is connected with aggressive behavior in monkeys, cats, and other animals. Early in the 20th century, Heinrich Klüver and Paul Bucy (1939) lesioned part of the amygdala of a rhesus monkey. Rhesus monkeys are normally a scrappy lot and try to bite or grab at intruders, but destruction of this animal's amygdala made it docile. No longer did it react aggressively to people. It even allowed people to poke and pinch it. Electrical stimulation of the part of the amygdala that Klüver and Bucy had destroyed, however, triggers a "rage response." For example, it causes a cat to hiss and arch its back in preparation to attack. The amygdala is also connected with a fear response (LeDoux, 1998). If you electrically stimulate another part of the amygdala, the cat cringes in fear when you cage it with a mouse. Not very tigerlike.

The amygdala is also connected with vigilance. It is involved in emotions, learning, and memory, and it sort of behaves like a spotlight, focusing attention on matters that are novel and important to know more about. In studies reported in 2000, researchers used fMRI to scan the amygdala while subjects were shown faces of European Americans and African Americans. One study flashed the photos by four men and four women, half European American and half African American (Hart et al., 2000). The subjects showed less activity in the amygdala when they viewed faces belonging to people of their own ethnic group, suggesting that they were more comfortable with "familiar" faces.

Other studies attempted to connect the "lighting up" of the amygdala with other racially oriented responses. In one, European American subjects were shown photos of young European Americans and African Americans (Phelps et al., 2000). Days later, the subjects were given tests to measure their responses to African Americans. For example, one test involved sitting at a computer and classifying the photos by race at the same time they were classifying words flashing on the screen as "good" or "bad." Most of the European American subjects tend to associate positive words like joy, love, and peace with European Americans and negative words like cancer, bomb, and devil with African Americans. It turned out that subjects who were more likely to associate African Americans with negative words also showed greater activity in the amygdala when presented with faces of African Americans. The researchers do not suggest that the amygdala activity—or even the word-association test—is a sign of conscious prejudice. They offer the alternative hypothesis that European Americans may simply be less familiar with faces of African Americans and that the relative lack of familiarity could trigger activity in the amygdala and negative feelings (fear of the unknown). The researchers find evidence for this interpretation in the fact that European Americans did *not* show the heightened activity of the amygdala when photos of familiar African Americans—Michael Jordan and Denzel Washington—flashed by.

And now we journey upward to the cerebrum. The **cerebrum** is the crowning glory of the brain. Only in humans does the cerebrum make up such a large part of the brain (Figure 2.15). The cerebrum is responsible for thinking and language. The surface of the cerebrum—the **cerebral cortex**—is wrinkled, or convoluted, with ridges and valleys. The convolutions allow a great deal of surface area to be packed into the brain—and surface area is apparently connected with cognitive ability. Valleys in the cortex are called *fissures*. A key fissure almost divides the cerebrum in half, creating two hemispheres with something of the shape of a walnut. The hemispheres are connected by the **corpus callosum** (Latin for "thick body" or "hard body"), a bundle of some 200 million nerve fibers.

The Cerebral Cortex: The "Bark" That Reasons

The cerebral cortex is the part of the brain that you usually think of as your brain. *Cortex* is a Latin word meaning "bark," as in the bark of a tree. Just as the bark is the outer coating of a tree, the cerebral cortex is the outer coating of the cerebrum. Despite its extreme importance and its creation of a world of civilization and culture, it is only about one-eighth of an inch thick. It is the outer edge of the brain that brings humans to their outer limits.

The cerebral cortex is involved in almost every bodily activity, including most sensations and most responses. It is also the part of the brain that frees people from the tyranny of genetic dictates and instinct. It is the seat of think-

Cerebrum The large mass of the forebrain, which consists of two hemispheres.

Cerebral cortex The wrinkled surface area (gray matter) of the cerebrum.

Corpus callosum A thick fiber bundle that connects the hemispheres of the cortex.

FIGURE 2.15 **The Geography of the Cerebral Cortex**
The cortex is divided into four lobes: frontal, parietal, temporal, and occipital. The visual area of the cortex is located in the occipital lobe. The hearing or auditory cortex lies in the temporal lobe. The sensory and motor areas face each other across the central fissure. What happens when a surgeon stimulates areas of the sensory or motor cortex during an operation?

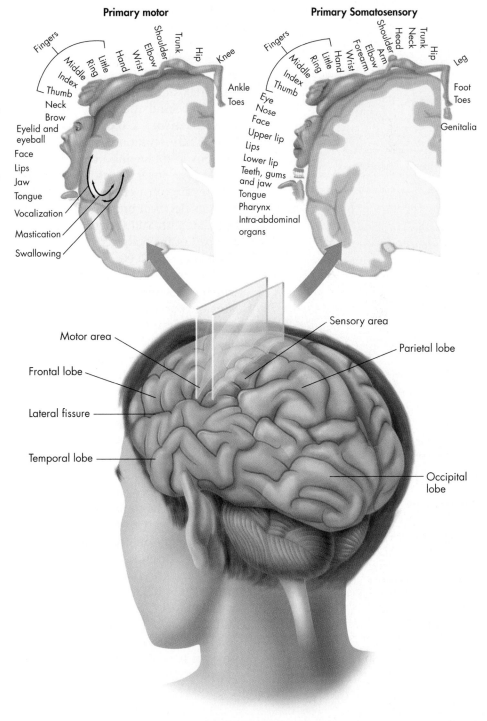

ing and language, and it enables humans to think deeply about the world outside and to make decisions. Other organisms run faster than we do, are stronger, or bite more sharply. Yet humans think faster, are intellectually "stronger," and, we might add, have a "biting" wit—all of which is made possible by the cerebral cortex.

Question: What are the parts of the cerebral cortex?

The cerebral cortex has two hemispheres, left and right. Each of the hemispheres is divided into four lobes, as shown in Figure 2.15. The **frontal lobe** lies in front of the central fissure and the **parietal lobe** behind it. The **temporal lobe** lies below the side, or lateral, fissure—across from the frontal and parietal lobes. The **occipital lobe** lies behind the temporal lobe and behind and below the parietal lobe.

When light strikes the eyes, neurons in the occipital lobe fire, and as a result, we "see" (that is, the image is projected in the brain). Direct artificial stimulation of the occipital lobe also produces visual sensations. If neurons in the occipital region of the cortex were stimulated with electricity, you would "see" flashes of light even if it were pitch black or your eyes were covered. The hearing or auditory area of the cortex lies in the temporal lobe along the lateral fissure. Sounds cause structures in the ear to vibrate. Messages are relayed from those structures to the auditory area of the cortex, and, when you hear a noise, neurons in this area are firing.

Just behind the central fissure in the parietal lobe lies an area called the **somatosensory cortex,** which receives messages from skin senses all over the body. These sensations include warmth and cold, touch, pain, and movement. Neurons in different parts of the sensory cortex fire, depending on whether you wiggle your finger or raise your leg. **Truth or Fiction Revisited:** It is quite true that, if a brain surgeon were to stimulate the proper area of your somatosensory cortex with an electrical probe, it might seem as if someone were touching your arm or leg. A Swedish MRI study found that just the expectation of being tickled in a certain part of the body activates the corresponding area of the somatosensory cortex (Carlsson et al., 2000).

But Figure 2.15 shows that the ways in which our bodies are situated or represented on the somatosensory cortex make for strange-looking humans, indeed. Our faces and our hands are huge compared with, say, our trunk and our legs. This over-representation is one of the reasons that our face, head, and hands are more sensitive to touch than other parts of the body.

Many years ago it was discovered that patients with injuries to one hemisphere of the brain would show sensory or motor deficits on the opposite side of the body below the head. This led to the recognition that sensory and motor nerves cross in the brain and elsewhere. The left hemisphere acts on, and receives inputs from, the right side of the body. The right hemisphere acts on, and receives inputs from, the left side of the body.

How do you make a monkey smile? One way is by inserting an electrical probe in its motor cortex and giving it a burst of electricity. Let us see what we mean by this.

The **motor cortex** lies in the frontal lobe, just across the valley of the central fissure from the somatosensory cortex. Neurons firing in the motor cortex cause parts of our body to move. More than 100 years ago, German scientists electrically stimulated the motor cortex in dogs and observed that muscles contracted in response (Fritsch & Hitzig, 1870/1960). Since then, neuroscientists have mapped the motor cortex in people and lower animals by inserting electrical probes and seeing which muscles contract. For example, José Delgado (1969) caused one patient to make a fist even though he tried to prevent his hand from closing. The patient said, "I guess, doctor, that your electricity is stronger than my will" (Delgado, 1969, p. 114). Delgado also made a monkey smile in this manner, many thousands of times in a row. If a surgeon were to stimulate a certain area of the right hemisphere of the motor cortex with an electrical probe, you would raise your left leg. This

Frontal lobe The lobe of the cerebral cortex that lies to the front of the central fissure.

Parietal lobe The lobe that lies just behind the central fissure.

Temporal lobe The lobe that lies below the lateral fissure, near the temples of the head.

Occipital lobe The lobe that lies behind and below the parietal lobe and behind the temporal lobe.

Somatosensory cortex The section of cortex in which sensory stimulation is projected. It lies just behind the central fissure in the parietal lobe.

Motor cortex The section of cortex that lies in the frontal lobe, just across the central fissure from the sensory cortex. Neural impulses in the motor cortex are linked to muscular responses throughout the body.

action would be sensed in the somatosensory cortex, and you might have a devil of a time trying to figure out whether you had intended to raise that leg!

We find the same overrepresentation of the face, head, and hands in the motor cortex as we find in the somatosensory cortex. The "detail" of these body parts on the cortex would appear to enable us to engage in fine muscle control over these areas of our bodies. Think of the possible human nuances of facial expression. Think of the fine motor (muscle) control we can exert as our fingers fly over the piano keyboard, or the fine motor control of the surgeon engaged in a delicate operation.

THINKING, LANGUAGE, AND THE CORTEX Areas of the cerebral cortex that are not primarily involved in sensation or motor activity are called *association areas*. They make possible the breadth and depth of human learning, thought, memory, and language. **Question: What parts of the cerebral cortex are involved in thinking and language?** As noted earlier, the association areas in the *prefrontal* region of the brain—that is, in the frontal lobes, near the forehead—could be called the brain's executive center. It appears to be where we solve problems and make plans and decisions (Chafee & Goldman-Rakic, 2000; Constantinidis et al., 2001; Duncan et al., 2000).

Executive functions like problem solving also require memory, like the memory in your computer. Association areas also provide the core of your working memory (Chafee & Goldman-Rakic, 2000; Constantinidis et al., 2001). They are connected with various sensory areas in the brain and can tap whatever kind of sensory information is needed or desired. The prefrontal region of the brain thus retrieves visual, auditory, and other kinds of memories and manipulates them—similar to the way in which a computer retrieves information from files in storage and manipulates it in working memory.

Certain neurons in the visual area of the occipital lobe fire in response to the visual presentation of vertical lines. Others fire in response to presentation of horizontal lines. Although one group of cells may respond to one aspect of the visual field and another group of cells may respond to another, association areas put it all together. As a result, we see a box or an automobile or a road map and not a confusing array of verticals and horizontals.

LANGUAGE FUNCTIONS In some ways, the left and right hemispheres of the brain duplicate each other's functions. In other ways, they differ. The left hemisphere contains language functions for nearly all right-handed people and for two out of three left-handed people (Pinker, 1994b). However, the brain remains "plastic," or changeable, through about the age of 13. As a result, children who lose the left hemisphere of the brain because of medical problems may transfer speech functions to the right hemisphere (Hertz-Pannier et al., 2002).

Two key language areas lie within the hemisphere of the cortex that contains language functions (usually the left hemisphere): Broca's area and Wernicke's area (see Figure 2.16). Damage to either area is likely to cause an **aphasia**—that is, a disruption of the ability to understand or produce language.

Wernicke's area lies in the temporal lobe near the auditory cortex. It responds mainly to auditory information (sounds). As you are reading this page, however, the visual information is registered in the visual cortex of your occipital lobe. It is then recoded as auditory information as it travels to Wernicke's area. Broca's area is located in the frontal lobe, near the section of the motor cortex that controls the muscles of the tongue, throat, and other areas of the face used when speaking (Gernsbacher & Kaschak, 2003). Broca's area processes the information and relays it to the motor cortex. The motor cortex sends the signals that cause muscles in your throat and mouth to contract. If you are "subvocalizing"—saying what you are reading "under your breath"—that is because Wernicke's area transmits information to Broca's area via nerve fibers.

Aphasia A disruption in the ability to understand or produce language.

FIGURE 2.16 Broca's and Wernicke's Areas of the Cerebral Cortex

The areas that are most involved in speech are Broca's area and Wernicke's area. Damage to either area can produce an *aphasia*—a disruption of the ability to understand or produce language.

Broca's area   Wernicke's area

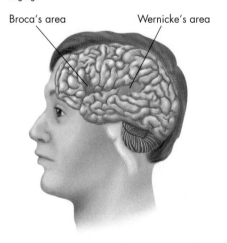

In Profile   PAUL BROCA

Culver Pictures

One of French surgeon Paul Broca's (1824–1880) hobbies was *craniometry,* or measurement of the skull. He believed that the size of the brain was related to intelligence. (Generally speaking, it isn't.) He argued that the brains of mature people were larger than those of older people, in "superior" races than in "inferior" ones, in men than in women, and in accomplished men than in run-of-the-mill men. Broca was well aware of evidence that contradicted his views. He knew that the brains of Asians were generally smaller than those of Europeans, although Asians were at least as bright. He knew of extremely intelligent women and of criminals with large brains.

Nevertheless, he and his fellow craniometrists touted their views. Upon his death, it was discovered that Broca's own brain was but a bit above average in size—nothing to brag about.

Despite his only slightly-above-average-sized brain, Broca was the first to observe a behavior problem and then locate the area of the brain that caused it. In 1861, Leborgne, a 51-year-old patient at La Bicêtre, the Paris asylum, came down with gangrene in the leg and was admitted to the surgical ward. Leborgne could understand what was said to him but could only utter the meaningless sound "tan" and sometimes blurt out "Sacred name of God!" in frustration. Leborgne had entered the asylum 21 years earlier, when he had lost the ability to speak.

Leborgne died six days later, and Broca performed an autopsy. He discovered that an egg-sized area just in front of the region of the motor cortex that regulates movement of the face on the left side of the brain had deteriorated. Broca concluded that this part of the brain was the seat of speech, and we now refer to it as *Broca's area.*

 Go to **http://psychology.wadsworth.com/ rathus_pcc9e** to access more information about Paul Broca.

People with damage to Wernicke's area may show **Wernicke's aphasia,** which impairs their abilities to comprehend speech and to think of the proper words to express their own thoughts. Ironically, they usually speak freely and with proper syntax. Wernicke's area is essential to understanding the relationships between words and their meanings. When Broca's area is damaged, people usually understand language well enough but speak slowly and laboriously, in simple sentences. This pattern is termed **Broca's aphasia.**

Some people with Broca's aphasia utter short, meaningful phrases that omit small but important grammatical words such as *is, and,* and *the.* Such an individual may laboriously say "walk dog." The phrase can have various meanings, such as "I want to take the dog for a walk" or "Take the dog out for a walk." Carroll (2004) reports the laborious, agrammatical speech of one individual with Broca's aphasia: "Yes . . . ah . . . Monday . . . er Dad and Peter H. . . . (his own name), and Dad . . . er hospital . . . and ah . . . Wednesday . . . Wednesday nine o'clock . . . and oh . . . Thursday . . . ten o'clock, ah doctors . . . two . . . an' doctors . . . and er . . . teeth . . . yah."

A part of the brain called the *angular gyrus* lies between the visual cortex and Wernicke's area. The angular gyrus "translates" visual information, as in perceiving written words, into auditory information (sounds) and sends it on to Wernicke's area. Research using MRI suggests that problems in the angular gyrus can give rise to *dyslexia,* or serious impairment in reading, because it becomes difficult for the reader to segment words into sounds (Milne et al., 2002).

Left Brain, Right Brain?

We often hear of being "left-brained" or "right-brained." **Question: What would it mean to be "left-brained" or "right-brained"?** The notion is that the hemispheres of the brain are involved in very different kinds of intellectual and emotional functions and responses. According to this view, left-brained people would be primarily logical and intellectual. Right-brained people would be intuitive, creative, and emotional. Those of us who are fortunate enough to have our brains "in balance" would presumably have the best of it—the capacity for logic combined with emotional richness.

Wernicke's aphasia A language disorder characterized by difficulty comprehending the meaning of spoken language.

Broca's aphasia A language disorder characterized by slow, laborious speech.

Like so many other popular ideas, the left-brain–right-brain notion is at best exaggerated. Research does suggest that in right-handed individuals, the left hemisphere is relatively more involved in intellectual undertakings that require logical analysis and problem solving, language, and mathematical computation (Corballis et al., 2002; Shenal & Harrison, 2003). The other hemisphere (usually the right hemisphere) is usually superior in visual–spatial functions (it's better at putting puzzles together), recognition of faces, discrimination of colors, aesthetic and emotional responses, understanding metaphors, and creative mathematical reasoning. Despite these differences, the hemispheres of the brain do not act independently such that some people are truly left-brained and others right-brained (Baynes & Gazzaniga, 2000). The functions of the left and right hemispheres overlap to some degree, and they tend to respond simultaneously as we focus our attention on one thing or another.

Now let us consider another issue involving sidedness: left-handedness. People who are left-handed are different from people who are right-handed in terms of the way they write, throw a ball, and so on. But there are interesting questions as to whether people who are left-handed are psychologically different from "righties."

Handedness: Is Being Right-Handed Right?

What do Michelangelo, Leonardo da Vinci, and Steve Young all have in common? No, they are not all artists. Only one was a football player. But they are all left-handed. Some other well-known lefties are shown in Figure 2.17. **Questions: Does it matter whether one is left-handed? Why are people right-handed or left-handed?**

FIGURE 2.17 Some Well-Known Left-Handed People

Being left-handed is connected with language problems such as dyslexia and stuttering, physical health problems such as migraine headaches and allergies, and psychological disorders like schizophrenia. However, left-handed people are also twice as likely as right-handed people to be artists, musicians, and mathematicians.

Source: Rosenbaum, D. E. (2000, May 16). On left-handedness, its causes and costs. *The New York Times*, p. F6.

From Napoleon to Oprah—Famous Lefties

Historical figures: Alexander the Great, Charlemagne, Julius Caesar, Napoleon Bonaparte, Albert Schweitzer

Napoleon Bonaparte— Soldier, emperor, and leftie

Entertainers (present): Oprah Winfrey, Whoopi Goldberg, Jay Leno, Jerry Seinfeld, Robert Redford

Oprah Winfrey—Talk show host, actor, author, and leftie

People in the news: Colin L. Powell, H. Norman Schwarzkopf, Fidel Castro, Steve Forbes, Ross Perot

Entertainers (past): Marilyn Monroe, Greta Garbo, Judy Garland, W. C. Fields, Charlie Chaplin

Authors: Mark Twain, Lewis Carroll, Eudora Welty, James Baldwin, Peter Benchley

Athletes: Ben Hogan (golf), Mark Spitz (swimming), Pelé (soccer), Bill Russell (basketball), Bruce Jenner (track)

Artists: Leonardo da Vinci, Michelangelo, Raphael, Albrecht Dürer

Music: Ludwig van Beethoven, Ringo Starr, Paul McCartney, Cole Porter, Jimi Hendrix

Law: Ruth Bader Ginsberg, Anthony M. Kennedy, Marcia Clark, Clarence Darrow, F. Lee Bailey

Criminals: John Dillinger, Billy the Kid, Boston Strangler, Jack the Ripper, John Wesley Hardin

Despite the vast success of these individuals, being left-handed was once viewed as a deficiency. Left-handed students were compelled to learn to write with the right hand, and today the language still swarms with slurs on lefties. We speak of "left-handed compliments," of having "two left feet," of strange events as "coming out of left field." The word *sinister* means "left-hand or unlucky side" in Latin. *Gauche* is a French word that literally means "left," though in English it is used to mean clumsy. The English word *adroit,* meaning "skillful," derives from the French *à droit,* "to the right." Also consider positive usages such as "being righteous" or "being on one's right side."

Overall, 8% to 10% of us are lefties. Left-handedness is more common in boys than girls (Rosenbaum, 2000). We are usually labeled right-handed or left-handed on the basis of our handwriting preferences, yet some people write with one hand and pass a football with the other. Some people even swing a tennis racket and pitch a baseball with different hands.

Being left-handed appears to provide a somewhat-greater-than-average probability of language problems, such as dyslexia and stuttering, and health problems, such as migraine headaches and allergies (Bulman-Fleming et al., 1996; Cornish, 1996; Geschwind & Galaburda, 1987). But there may also be advantages to being left-handed. According to a British study, left-handed people are twice as likely as right-handed people to be numbered among the ranks of artists, musicians, and mathematicians (Kilshaw & Annett, 1983). Figure 2.17 shows that some of the greatest artists were lefties.

The origins of handedness seem to have a genetic component. Left-handedness runs in families. In the English royal family, Queen Elizabeth II and Princes Charles and William are all left-handed, as was the Queen Mother (Rosenbaum, 2000). If both of your parents are right-handed, your chances of being right-handed are about 92%. If one of your parents is left-handed, your chances of being right-handed drop to about 80%. And if both of your parents are left-handed, your chances of also being left-handed are about 1 in 2 (Rosenbaum, 2000).

Whether we are talking about language functions, being "left-brained" or "right-brained," or handedness, we are talking about people whose hemispheres of the cerebral cortex communicate back and forth. Now let us see what happens when the major avenue of communication between the hemispheres shuts down.

Split-Brain Experiments: How Many Brains Do You Have?

A number of people with severe cases of **epilepsy** have split-brain operations in which much of the corpus callosum is severed. The purpose of the operation is to confine seizures to one hemisphere of the cerebral cortex rather than allowing a neural tempest to reverberate. Split-brain operations do seem to help people with epilepsy. **Question: What happens when the brain is split in two?**

People who have undergone split-brain operations can be thought of as winding up with two brains, yet under most circumstances their behavior remains ordinary enough. Still, some aspects of hemispheres that have stopped talking to each other are intriguing.

As reported by pioneering brain surgeon Joseph Bogen (1969, 2000), each hemisphere may have a "mind of its own." One split-brain patient reported that her hemispheres frequently disagreed on what she should be wearing. What she meant was that one hand might undo her blouse as rapidly as the other was buttoning it. A man reported that one hemisphere (the left hemisphere, which contained language functions) liked reading but the other one did not. If he shifted a book from his right hand to his left hand, his left hand would put it down. The left hand is connected with the right hemisphere of the cerebral cortex, which in most people—including this patient—does not contain language functions.

Another pioneer of split-brain research, Roger Wolcott Sperry (Bogen, 1998; Corballis, 1998), found that people with split brains whose eyes are closed may be able to verbally describe an object such as a key when they hold it in one hand, but not when they hold it in the other hand. As shown in Figure 2.18, if a person with

Epilepsy Temporary disturbances of brain functions that involve sudden neural discharges.

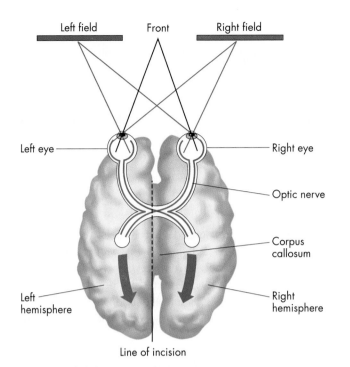

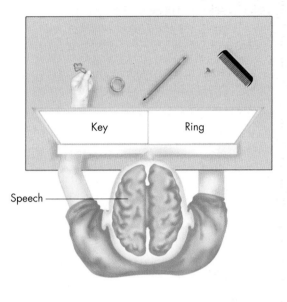

FIGURE 2.18 **A Divided-Brain Experiment**

In the drawing on the left, we see that visual sensations in the left visual field are projected in the occipital cortex of the right hemisphere. Visual sensations from the right visual field are projected in the occipital cortex in the left hemisphere. In the divided-brain experiment diagramed on the right, a person with a severed corpus callosum handles a key with his left hand and perceives the written word *key* in his left visual field. The word "key" is projected in the right hemisphere. Speech, however, is usually a function of the left hemisphere. The written word "ring," perceived by the right visual field, is projected in the left hemisphere. So, when asked what he is handling, the divided-brain subject reports "ring," not "key."

a split brain handles a key with his left hand behind a screen, tactile impressions of the key are projected into the right hemisphere, which has little or no language ability. Thus, he will not be able to describe the key. If he holds it in his right hand, he will have no trouble describing it because sensory impressions are projected into the left hemisphere of the cortex, which contains language functions. To further confound matters, if the word *ring* is projected into the left hemisphere while the person is asked what he is handling, he will say "ring," not "key."

However, this discrepancy between what is felt and what is said occurs only in people with split brains. Even so, people who have undergone split-brain operations tend to lead largely normal lives. And for the rest of us, the two hemispheres work together most of the time, even when we are playing the piano or solving math problems.

Now that we have discussed the structures and the functioning of the brain, we will return to matters of chemistry. In the next section, we see the effects on behavior and mental processes of chemicals—*hormones*—that are secreted by glands and poured directly into the bloodstream.

Your Turn: But first, enhance your mastery of the material on the brain with the nearby "Learning Connections." Review the material by filling in the blanks, reflect on the material by relating it to other things you know, and think critically about it.

Learning Connections **THE BRAIN: THE STAR OF THE HUMAN NERVOUS SYSTEM**

ACTIVE REVIEW (24) The _____ records the electrical activity of the brain. (25) In magnetic _____ imaging, radio waves cause parts of the brain to emit signals. (26) The _____ is involved in balance and coordination. (27) The _____ is involved in body tempera-ture, motivation, and emotion. (28) The hemispheres of the cerebrum are connected by the corpus _____. (29) The visual cortex is found in the _____ lobe of the cortex. (30) The executive center of the brain is found in the _____ lobe. (31) Language areas are usually

found in the (*Left*, or *Right?*) hemisphere.
(32) Left-handed people are (*More*, or *Less?*) likely than right-handed people to be artists, musicians, and mathematicians. (33) Split-brain operations sever much of the corpus callosum in order to control _____.

REFLECT AND RELATE Would you consider yourself to be more "left-brained" or "right-brained"? Explain.

CRITICAL THINKING Does the research evidence reported in this section demonstrate that the mind is a function of the brain? Why or why not?

 Go to **http://psychology.wadsworth.com/ rathus_pcc9e** for an interactive version of this Learning Connections unit.

The Endocrine System: Chemicals in the Bloodstream

The body contains two types of **glands:** glands with ducts and glands without ducts. A *duct* is a passageway that carries substances to specific locations. Saliva, sweat, tears, and breast milk all reach their destinations through ducts. Psychologists are interested in the substances secreted by ductless glands because of their behavioral effects. **Question: What is the endocrine system?** The ductless glands constitute the **endocrine system,** and they secrete **hormones** (from the Greek *horman,* meaning "to stimulate" or "to excite").

Hormones are released into the bloodstream and circulate through the body. Like neurotransmitters, hormones have specific receptor sites. That is, they act only on receptors in certain locations. Some hormones that are released by the hypothalamus influence only the **pituitary gland.** Other hormones released by the pituitary influence the adrenal cortex; still others influence the testes and ovaries, and so on (see the nearby Concept Review of the endocrine system.).

Much hormonal action helps the body maintain steady states, as in fluid levels, blood sugar levels, and so on. Bodily mechanisms measure current levels; when these levels deviate from optimal, they signal glands to release hormones. The maintenance of steady states requires feedback of bodily information to glands. This type of system is referred to as a *negative feedback loop*. That is, when enough of a hormone has been secreted, the gland is signaled to stop.

Gland An organ that secretes one or more chemical substances such as hormones, saliva, or milk.

Endocrine system The body's system of ductless glands that secrete hormones and release them directly into the bloodstream.

Hormone A substance secreted by an endocrine gland that regulates various body functions.

Pituitary gland The gland that secretes growth hormone, prolactin, antidiuretic hormone, and other hormones.

Concept Review THE ENDOCRINE SYSTEM

Hypothalamus
• Releasing hormones or factors; e.g., growth-hormone releasing factor, corticotrophin-releasing hormone (influences the pituitary gland to secrete corresponding hormones, e.g., growth hormone, adrenocorticotrophic hormone)

Pituitary
• Growth hormone (causes growth of muscles, bones, and glands)
• Adrenocorticotrophic hormone (ACTH) (regulates adrenal cortex)
• Thyrotrophin (causes thyroid gland to secrete thyroxin)
• Follicle-stimulating hormone (causes formation of egg and sperm cells)
• Luteinizing hormone (causes ovulation, maturation of egg and sperm cells)
• Prolactin (stimulates production of milk)
• Antidiuretic hormone (ADH) (inhibits production of urine)
• Oxytocin (stimulates uterine contractions during delivery and ejection of milk during nursing)

Pineal
• Melatonin (involved in regulation of sleep–wake cycle; possibly connected with aging)

Hypothalamus
Pituitary
Thyroid

Adrenal
Pancreas
Kidneys
Ovaries
Uterus
Testes

Pancreas
• Insulin (enables body to metabolize sugar; regulates storage of fats)

Thyroid
• Thyroxin (increases metabolic rate)

Adrenal
• Corticosteroids (increase resistance to stress; regulate carbohydrate metabolism)
• Epinephrine (adrenaline) (increases metabolic activity–heart and respiration rates, blood sugar level, etc.)
• Norepinephrine (noradrenaline) (raises blood pressure; acts as a neurotransmitter)

Testes
• Testosterone (promotes development of male sex characteristics; involved in sex drive and aggressiveness)

Ovaries
• Estrogen (regulates menstrual cycle; promotes development of female sex characteristics; connected with feelings of well-being)

 Go to **http://psychology.wadsworth.com/ rathus_pcc9e** to access a drag-and-drop version of this Concept Review designed to help you test yourself on the major topics provided here.

The Hypothalamus: Master of the Master Gland

The hypothalamus secretes a number of releasing hormones, or factors, that influence the pituitary gland—also called the master gland—to secrete related hormones. For example, growth-hormone-releasing factor (hGRF) causes the pituitary to produce growth hormone. A dense network of blood vessels between the hypothalamus and the pituitary gland provides a direct route of influence for these factors.

The Pituitary Gland: The Pea-Sized Governor

The pituitary gland lies below the hypothalamus. Although the pituitary is only about the size of a pea, it is so central to the body's functioning that it has been referred to as the "master gland." Despite this designation, today we know that the hypothalamus regulates much pituitary activity. (The hypothalamus could be called the "master of the master gland.") The anterior (front) and posterior (back) lobes of the pituitary gland secrete many hormones. **Growth hormone** regulates the growth of muscles, bones, and glands. Children whose growth patterns are abnormally slow may catch up to their age-mates when they obtain growth hormone. **Prolactin** largely regulates maternal behavior in lower mammals such as rats and stimulates production of milk in women. As a water conservation measure, **antidiuretic hormone (ADH)** inhibits production of urine when fluid levels in the body are low. ADH is also connected with stereotypical paternal behavior patterns in some mammals. **Truth or Fiction Revisited:** For example, ADH can transform an unconcerned male meadow vole (a mouselike rodent) into an affectionate and protective mate and father (Parker et al., 2001). The hormone is not known to have such a powerful effect with humans, however. **Oxytocin** stimulates labor in pregnant women and is connected with maternal behavior (cuddling and caring for young) in some mammals (Insel, 2000; Taylor et al., 2000b). Obstetricians may induce labor by injecting pregnant women with oxytocin. During nursing, stimulation of nerve endings in and around the nipples sends messages to the brain that cause the secretion of oxytocin. Oxytocin then causes the breasts to eject milk.

The Pineal Gland

The pineal gland secretes the hormone **melatonin,** which helps regulate the sleep–wake cycle and may affect the onset of puberty. Some researchers speculate that melatonin is also connected with aging. However, it appears that melatonin is a mild sedative and fosters sleep, and some people use it as a "sleeping pill" (Arendt, 2000; Nagtegaal et al., 2000). Melatonin may also help people adjust to jet lag (Takahashi et al., 2002).

The Thyroid Gland: The Body's Accelerator

The thyroid gland could be considered the body's accelerator. It produces **thyroxin,** which affects the body's *metabolism*—the rate at which the body uses oxygen and produces energy. Some people are overweight because of *hypothyroidism,* a condition that results from too little thyroxin. Thyroxin deficiency in children can lead to *cretinism,* a condition characterized by stunted growth and mental retardation. Adults who secrete too little thyroxin may feel tired and sluggish and may put on weight. People who produce too much thyroxin may develop *hyperthyroidism,* which is characterized by excitability, insomnia, and weight loss.

The Adrenal Glands: Coping with Stress

The adrenal glands, located above the kidneys, have an outer layer, or cortex, and an inner core, or medulla. The adrenal cortex is regulated by the pituitary hormone ACTH (adrenocorticotrophic hormone). The adrenal cortex secretes hormones known as **corticosteroids,** or cortical steroids. These hormones increase resistance to stress, promote muscle development, and cause the liver to release stored sugar, making more energy available in emergencies, as when you see another car

Growth hormone A pituitary hormone that regulates growth.

Prolactin A pituitary hormone that regulates production of milk and, in lower animals, maternal behavior.

Antidiuretic hormone (ADH) A pituitary hormone that conserves body fluids by increasing reabsorption of urine and is connected with paternal behavior in some mammals. Also called *vasopressin.*

Oxytocin A pituitary hormone that stimulates labor and lactation.

Melatonin A pineal hormone that helps regulate the sleep–wake cycle and may affect the onset of puberty.

Thyroxin The thyroid hormone that increases metabolic rate.

Corticosteroids Steroids produced by the adrenal cortex that regulate carbohydrate metabolism and increase resistance to stress by fighting inflammation and allergic reactions. Also called *cortical steroids.*

veering toward your own. Epinephrine and norepinephrine are secreted by the adrenal medulla. **Epinephrine,** also known as adrenaline, is manufactured exclusively by the adrenal glands, but norepinephrine (noradrenaline) is also produced elsewhere in the body. (We saw that norepinephrine acts as a neurotransmitter in the brain.) The sympathetic branch of the autonomic nervous system causes the adrenal medulla to release a mixture of epinephrine and norepinephrine that helps arouse the body to cope with threats and stress. Epinephrine is of interest to psychologists because it has emotional as well as physical effects. It intensifies most emotions and is crucial to the experience of fear and anxiety.

The Testes and the Ovaries

The testes and ovaries also produce steroids, among them testosterone and estrogen. If it were not for the secretion of the male sex hormone **testosterone** about six weeks after conception, we would all develop the external genital organs of females. Testosterone is produced not only by the testes but in smaller amounts by the ovaries and adrenal glands. A few weeks after conception, testosterone causes the male sex organs to develop. During puberty, testosterone stokes the growth of muscle and bone and the development of primary and secondary sex characteristics. *Primary sex characteristics* such as the increased size of the penis and the sperm-producing ability of the testes are directly involved in reproduction. *Secondary sex characteristics* such as presence of a beard and a deeper voice differentiate males from females but are not directly involved in reproduction.

The ovaries produce **estrogen** and **progesterone** as well as small amounts of testosterone. Estrogen is also produced in smaller amounts by the testes. Estrogen fosters female reproductive capacity and secondary sex characteristics such as accumulation of fat in the breasts and hips. Progesterone stimulates growth of the female reproductive organs and prepares the uterus to maintain pregnancy.

Estrogen, like testosterone, has psychological effects as well as biological effects. For one thing, higher levels of estrogen seem to be connected with optimal cognitive functioning and feelings of well-being among women (Ross et al., 2000; Yaffe et al., 2000). Women are also more interested in sexual activity when estrogen levels are high—particularly during ovulation, when they are fertile. Older women placed on estrogen replacement showed improved memory functioning and visual–spatial abilities (Duka et al., 2000). Trials are even under way to determine whether estrogen replacement can help menopausal women with Alzheimer's disease to fight the cognitive effects (memory impairment, etc.) of the disorder (Kawas, 2000; Sano, 2000). However, results to date are not very encouraging (Mulnard et al., 2000; Shaywitz & Shaywitz, 2000).

Estrogen and progesterone levels vary and regulate the woman's menstrual cycle. Following menstruation—the monthly sloughing off of the lining of the uterus—estrogen levels increase, leading to the ripening of an ovum (egg cell) and the growth of the lining of the uterus. Ovulation (release of the ovum by an ovary) occurs when estrogens reach peak blood levels. Then the lining of the uterus thickens in response to the secretion of progesterone, gaining the capacity to support an embryo if fertilization should occur. If the ovum is not fertilized, estrogen and progesterone levels drop suddenly, triggering menstruation once more.

STEROIDS, BEHAVIOR, AND MENTAL PROCESSES Steroids increase muscle mass, heighten resistance to stress, and increase the body's energy supply by signaling the liver to release sugar into the bloodstream. The steroid testosterone is connected with the sex drive in both males and females (females secrete some testosterone in the adrenal glands) (Davis, 2000).

Anabolic steroids (synthetic versions of the male sex hormone testosterone) have been used, sometimes in tandem with growth hormone, to enhance athletic prowess. Not only do they enhance athletic prowess, they are also connected with self-confidence, aggressiveness, even memory functioning (Janowsky et al., 2000).

Epinephrine A hormone produced by the adrenal medulla that stimulates sympathetic ANS activity. Also called *adrenaline.*

Testosterone A male sex hormone produced by the testes that promotes growth of male sexual characteristics and sperm.

Estrogen A generic term for several female sex hormones that promote growth of female sex characteristics and regulate the menstrual cycle.

Progesterone A female sex hormone that promotes growth of the sex organs and helps maintain pregnancy.

However, anabolic steroids are generally outlawed in sports. The lure of steroids is understandable. Sometimes the difference between an acceptable athletic performance and a great one is rather small. Thousands of athletes try to make it in the big leagues, and the edge offered by steroids—even if minor—can spell the difference between a fumbling attempt and a smashing success. If steroids help, why the fuss? Some of it is related to the ethics of competition—the idea that athletes should "play fair." But steroid use is also linked to liver damage and other health problems.

Estrogen even affects women's perceptions of who is attractive. (Really.) One study found that British women prefer feminized male faces, as shown in Figure 2.19B, during most phases of the menstrual cycle (Penton-Voak & Perrett, 2000). Women apparently associate such facial features with personality traits like warmth and honesty. However, they prefer the masculinized faces, as shown in Figure 2.19A, when they are ovulating. Perhaps they unconsciously interpret such features as indicative of reproductive capacity—that is, they instinctively see these men as likely to father children.

There are thus important links between biological factors, behavior, and mental processes. Thoughts and mental images may seem to be intangible pictures that float in our heads, but they have substance. They involve billions of brain cells (neurons) and the transmission of thousands of chemicals from one neuron to another—repeated hundreds of times per second. These countless bits of microscopic activity give rise to feelings, plans, computation, art and music, and all the cognitive activities that make us human. We pour chemicals called hormones into our own bloodstreams, and they affect our activity levels, our anxiety levels, even our sex drives. We inherit traits that make us human, that enable us to think more deeply and act more cleverly than any other organism (after all, we write the textbooks). An understanding of biology helps us grasp many psychological events that might otherwise seem elusive and without substance.

Your Turn: Now that we have discussed the endocrine system, enhance your mastery of the material with the nearby "Learning Connections." Review the material by filling in the blanks, reflect on the material by relating it to other things you know, and think critically about it.

FIGURE 2.19 **Which One Is Mr. Right?**

The answer may depend on the phase of the woman's menstrual cycle. Women are apparently more attracted to men with masculinized features when they are capable of conceiving (part A) and men with more feminized features (part B) when they are not.

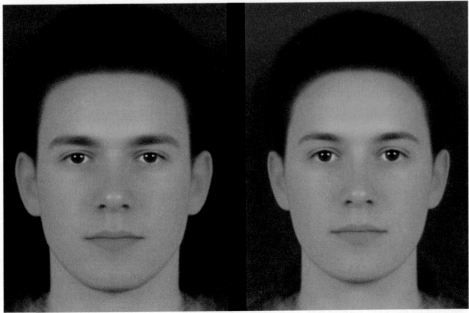

A.   B.

Science Photo Library/Photo Researchers Inc.

Learning Connections · THE ENDOCRINE SYSTEM: CHEMICALS IN THE BLOODSTREAM

ACTIVE REVIEW (34) The _____ secretes hormones that regulate the pituitary gland. (35) The pituitary hormone _____ regulates maternal behavior in lower animals and stimulates production of milk in women. (36) The thyroid hormone _____ affects the metabolism. (37) Corticosteroids are secreted by the adrenal _____ and promote development of muscle mass and increase resistance to stress. (38) Epinephrine is secreted by the adrenal _____ and is involved in emotional arousal.

REFLECT AND RELATE Have you heard that adolescents are "hormonal" or affected by "glands"? If so, which glands would they be?

CRITICAL THINKING If so many behaviors and mental processes are affected by "glands," do people have free will?

Go to **http://psychology.wadsworth.com/ rathus_pcc9e** for an interactive version of this Learning Connections unit.

Life Connections
Coping with PMS

In this "Life Connections" feature, we discuss an important issue that is related to sex hormones: premenstrual syndrome, or PMS (Burt & Stein, 2002). Psychologists study the effects of menstruation because of stereotypes about menstruating women and to help women with the discomfort that many experience. For several days prior to and during menstruation, according to the outmoded stereotype, "raging hormones" doom women to irritability and poor judgment—two traits alleged to be part of PMS. Women have historically been assumed to be more likely to commit suicide or crimes, call in sick at work, or develop physical and emotional problems during the eight-day period prior to and during menstruation. Moreover, the ability of college women to focus on academic tasks during this period has been called into question.

Now for a few facts: Studies in the United States, Spain, and Germany find that most women report *some* psychological and physical problems, such as depression, anxiety, and headaches, during the four to six days that precede menstruation (Palmero et al., 2002; Wittchen et al., 2002). However, only about 6% to 7% of women have symptoms severe enough to impair their academic, occupational, or social functioning (Brody, 1996; Wittchen et al., 2002). Women

readers may complete the nearby self-assessment to gain insight as to whether they experience PMS, and if they do, how severely.

The causes of PMS are not fully understood. It was once believed that psychological factors such as negative attitudes toward menstruation played a crucial role. Now the prevailing view is that attitudes toward menstruation—for example, conceptualizing the menstrual flow as unclean—can worsen menstrual problems, but that PMS has a biological basis. Researchers are searching out relationships between menstrual problems, including PMS, and chemical imbalances in the body. They have found that peak estrogen levels are connected with optimal cognitive functioning and psychological well-being in women (Ross et al., 2000; Yaffe et al., 2000). If peaks in female sex hormones are connected with psychological well-being, then perhaps the precipitous drop-off in hormones that precedes and accompanies menstruation is connected with discomfort (Steiner et al., 2003). But PMS is also linked with imbalances in neurotransmitters such as serotonin and beta-endorphins (Condon, 2001; Lin & Thompson, 2001; Steiner et al., 2003). Serotonin imbalances are also linked to changes in appetite, so women with PMS tend to be hungrier during part of the cycle

than other women. Sensitivity to menstrual pain may be heightened by low levels of endorphins, the body's natural painkillers (Straneva et al., 2002). PMS may reflect a complex interaction between ovarian hormones and neurotransmitters.

A generation ago, PMS was seen as something a woman must tolerate. No longer. Today there are many treatment options. These include exercise, diet (for example, eating several small meals a day rather than two or three large meals; limiting salt and sugar; and vitamin supplements), hormone treatments (usually progesterone), and medications that affect levels of neurotransmitters in the nervous system. PMS is connected with drops in serotonin levels, and drugs called selective serotonin reuptake inhibitors (SSRIs) have helped many women with PMS (Condon, 2001; Steiner & Pearlstein, 2000). SSRIs are also known as "antidepressants" because depression is also connected with low serotonin levels. The fact that these drugs help many women with PMS does not mean that the women are suffering from underlying depression, but only that serotonin is involved in both. Women who use SSRIs to help with PMS do not take them continuously, as people do to fight depression, but rather for about two weeks each month.

Self-Assessment   Symptoms of PMS

PMS is short for premenstrual syndrome, a cluster of symptoms that may affect women during a period of approximately eight days prior to and during menstruation. Research suggests that most women have some of these symptoms, but that they are usually not severe enough to interfere with their daily functioning. But some women experience severe symptoms, and they are advised to discuss their situations with their gynecologists. A great deal can be done to help women who suffer from PMS, and there is little point to simply trying to "tough it out."

Do you experience PMS? Complete the following self-assessment to gain insight into whether you do and, if so, how severely.

Directions: Following is a list of various psychological and physical symptoms of PMS. Indicate whether you encounter these symptoms and how severe they are by checking the appropriate box. Then turn to the answer key in Appendix B to assess your responses.

Part I: Psychological Symptoms of PMS	Do not have	Mild	Moderate	Severe	Disabling
Accident prone					
Depression					
Anxiety					
Panic					
Mood swings					
Crying spells					
Sudden anger					
Irritability					
Loss of interest in usual activities					
Difficulty concentrating					
Lack of energy					
Excessive use of alcohol					
Frustration					
Overeating or cravings for certain foods					
Insomnia or excessive sleeping					
Feelings of being out of control or overwhelmed					
Paranoia					
Part II: Physical Symptoms of PMS	**Do not have**	**Mild**	**Moderate**	**Severe**	**Disabling**
Migraines					
Breast tenderness					
Joint or muscle pain					
Stiffness					
Weight gain					
Feeling bloated					
Blurred vision					
Poor motor coordination					
Exhaustion					
Dark circles under the eyes					

How to Handle Menstrual Discomfort

Most women experience some degree of menstrual discomfort. Women with persistent menstrual distress may profit from the suggestions listed below. Why not adopt the techniques that sound right for you?

1. First of all, don't blame yourself. Menstrual problems were once erroneously attributed to women's "hysterical" nature. This is nonsense. Menstrual problems appear to largely reflect supersensitivity to fluctuations in levels of hormones and neurotransmitters. Researchers have not yet have fully pinpointed the causal elements and patterns, but there is no evidence that women with PMS are "hysterical."

2. Keep track of your menstrual symptoms to help you (and your doctor) identify patterns.

3. Develop strategies for dealing with days on which you experience the most distress—strategies that will enhance pleasure and minimize stress. Try things that will distract you. Go to a film or get into that novel you've been meaning to read.

4. Ask yourself whether you harbor self-defeating attitudes that might be compounding distress. Do close relatives or friends see menstruation as an illness, a time of "pollution," a "dirty thing"? Have you adopted any of these attitudes—if not verbally, then in ways that affect your behavior, as by restricting social activities during your period?

5. See a doctor about your symptoms. Severe discomfort can be caused or worsened by health problems such as endometriosis and pelvic inflammatory disease (PID). Check it out.

6. Develop nutritious eating habits— and continue them throughout the entire cycle (that means *always*). Consider limiting intake of alcohol, caffeine, fats, salt, and sweets, especially during the days preceding menstruation.

7. If you feel bloated, eat smaller meals (or nutritious snacks) throughout the day, rather than a couple of highly filling meals.

8. Vigorous exercise—jogging, swimming, bicycling, fast walking, dancing, skating, jumping rope—helps relieve premenstrual and menstrual discomfort in some women. Try it out. But why limit exercise to days prior to and during your period? Weave it into your lifestyle.

9. Check with your doctor about herbal, vitamin, and mineral supplements (chaste berry, calcium, evening primrose, magnesium, vitamin E, wild yams, and so on) (Chavez & Spitzer, 2002).

10. Ibuprofen (brand names include Medipren, Advil, and Motrin) and other medicines available over the counter may be helpful for cramping. Prescription drugs such as tranquilizers (e.g., alprazolam) and SSRIs may be of help (Condon, 2001; Lin & Thompson, 2001). Ask your doctor for a recommendation. *In these cases, you are not taking the tranquilizer to treat anxiety or the SSRI to treat depression. You are taking the drugs to treat imbalances in neurotransmitters that can also give rise to anxiety and depression.*

11. Speaking of medicines, remember that menstruation is triggered by a sharp drop-off in sex hormones. Some gynecologists prescribe estrogen replacement as a method of relieving symptoms of PMS, although this approach is not free of hazards. One method is simply to continue certain oral contraceptives for 28 days rather than 21 days and thus to forego menstruation altogether (Freeman et al., 2001; Sommerfeld, 2000). **Truth or Fiction Revisited:** It is therefore true that some women eliminate PMS by eliminating their periods. However, the pills chosen for this approach are not the same as those used for 21 days. Check with your gynecologist.

12. Remind yourself that menstrual problems are time limited. Don't worry about getting through life or a career. Just get through the next couple of days.

Recite—An Active Summary™

Want to study on the go? Go to your companion website and download an audio version of this review section to your media player.

1. What are some of the basic concepts of the theory of evolution?

The struggle for existence refers to the competition among species and among members within a species to survive and reproduce. Small random variations called mutations change organisms' ability to adapt. Mutations that enhance survival are likely to be preserved. Natural selection refers to the finding that organisms that are better adapted to their environments tend to survive and transmit their genes to subsequent generations.

2. What is evolutionary psychology?

Evolutionary psychology studies the ways in which adaptation and natural selection are connected with mental processes and behavior. Evolutionary psychologists suggest that not only physical traits but also patterns of behavior, including social behavior, evolve and are transmitted from generation to generation.

3. What is meant by an "instinct"?

An instinct is a stereotypical behavior pattern that is nearly identical among the members of a species. It occurs even when the individual is reared in isolation from others of its kind.

4. What is meant by "heredity"?

Heredity involves the biological transmission of traits from generation to generation.

5. What is meant by "genetics"?

Genetics is the area of biology that studies heredity. Behavioral genetics is concerned with the genetic transmission of traits that give rise to behavior and focuses on individual differences. Molecular genetics attempts to identify specific genes that are connected with behavior and mental processes.

Recite—An Active Summary™

6. What are the roles of genes and chromosomes in heredity?

Genes are the biochemical materials that regulate the development of traits. Genes are segments of chromosomes. Humans have 46 chromosomes arranged in 23 pairs. Chromosomes are molecules of DNA, which takes the form of a twisting ladder. We normally receive 23 chromosomes from each parent. Sex chromosomes and specific genes—e.g., SRY—determine the sex of the child. SRY is also connected with aggressive behavior. People with Down syndrome have an extra chromosome on the 21st pair.

7. What are kinship studies?

Psychologists conduct kinship studies to help determine the influences of genetic and environmental factors on behavior and mental processes. Twin studies are useful because identical (monozygotic) twins share the same genetic code; therefore, differences reflect environmental factors. When children reared by adoptive parents are more similar to their natural parents in a particular trait, evidence exists for a genetic role in the expression of that trait.

8. What is selective breeding?

In selective breeding, one breeds offspring that are closest to a desired trait and continues to breed their offspring that are yet closer to the goal. Humans have been selectively breeding many animals, including dogs, for both physical and behavioral traits.

9. What are neurons?

Neurons are cells that transmit information through neural impulses and glial cells, which mainly serve support functions. Neurons have a cell body; dendrites, which receive messages; and trunklike axons, which conduct and then transmit messages to other cells by means of chemicals called neurotransmitters. Many neurons have a myelin coating that insulates their axons, allowing for more efficient conduction of messages. Afferent neurons transmit sensory messages to the central nervous system. Efferent neurons conduct messages from the central nervous system that stimulate glands or cause muscles to contract.

10. What are neural impulses?

Neural transmission is electrochemical. An electrical charge is conducted along an axon through a process that allows sodium ions to enter the cell and then pumps them out. The neuron has a resting potential of −70 millivolts and an action potential of about +40 millivolts.

11. What happens when a neuron fires?

Neurons fire (transmit messages to other neurons, muscles, or glands) by releasing neurotransmitters. They fire according to an all-or-none principle, up to hundreds of times per second. Each firing is followed by a refractory period, during which neurons are insensitive to messages from other neurons.

12. What is a synapse?

Neurons fire across synapses, which consist of an axon terminal from the transmitting neuron, a dendrite or the body of a receiving neuron, and a fluid-filled synaptic cleft between the two.

13. Which neurotransmitters are of interest to psychologists? What do they do?

These include acetylcholine, which is involved in muscle contractions and memory; dopamine, imbalances of which have been linked to Parkinson's disease and schizophrenia; norepinephrine, which accelerates the heartbeat and other body processes; serotonin, which is involved in eating, sleep, and emotional arousal; GABA, which inhibits anxiety; and endorphins, which are naturally occurring painkillers.

14. What are the parts of the nervous system?

A nerve is a bundle of axons and dendrites. The nervous system is one of the systems that regulates the body. It is involved in thought processes, emotional responses, heartbeat, motor activity, and so on.

15. What are the divisions and functions of the peripheral nervous system?

The peripheral nervous system has two main divisions: somatic and autonomic. The somatic nervous system transmits sensory information about skeletal muscles, skin, and joints to the central nervous system. It also controls skeletal muscular activity. The autonomic nervous system (ANS) regulates the glands and activities such as heartbeat, digestion, and dilation of the pupils. The sympathetic division of the ANS helps expend the body's resources, such as when fleeing from a predator, and the parasympathetic division helps build the body's reserves.

16. What are the divisions and functions of the central nervous system?

The central nervous system consists of the brain and spinal cord. Reflexes involve the spinal cord but not the brain. The central nervous system has gray matter, which is composed of nonmyelinated neurons, and white matter, which is composed of bundles of myelinated (and thus whitish) axons.

Recite—An Active Summary™

17. How do researchers learn about the functions of the brain?

Researchers historically learned about the brain by studying the effects of accidents. They have also studied the effects of purposeful damage to the brain, made by lesions. They have seen how animals and people respond to electrical stimulations of certain parts of the brain. They have studied the waves emitted by the brain with the electroencephalograph. With CAT scans, PET scans, and MRIs, computer-generated images are made by passing radiation of some sort through the brain.

18. What are the structures and functions of the brain?

The hindbrain includes the medulla, which regulates the heart rate, blood pressure, and respiration; the pons, which is involved in movement, attention, and respiration; and the cerebellum, which is involved in balance and coordination. The reticular activating system, which is involved in wakefulness and sleep, begins in the hindbrain and continues through the midbrain into the forebrain. Important structures of the forebrain include the thalamus, which serves as a relay station for sensory stimulation; the hypothalamus, which regulates body temperature and various aspects of motivation and emotion, such as eating and sexual behavior; the limbic system, which is involved in memory, emotion, and motivation; and the cerebrum, which is the brain's center of thinking and language.

19. What are the parts of the cerebral cortex?

The outer fringe of the cerebrum is the cerebral cortex, which is divided into two hemispheres and four lobes: frontal, parietal, temporal, and occipital. The visual cortex is in the occipital lobe, and the auditory cortex is in the temporal lobe. The somatosensory cortex lies behind the central fissure in the parietal lobe, and the motor cortex lies in the frontal lobe, across the central fissure from the somatosensory cortex. The prefrontal cortex may be the executive center of the brain—making plans, solving problems, and drawing upon sensory information from other areas of the cortex as needed.

20. What parts of the cerebral cortex are involved in thinking and language?

Language areas of the cortex usually lie in the left hemisphere, near the intersection of the frontal, temporal, and parietal lobes. Wernicke's area in the temporal lobe responds mainly to auditory information. Broca's area is located in the frontal lobe and is mainly responsible for speech. Damage to either area can result in an aphasia—a problem in understanding (Wernicke's aphasia) or producing (Broca's aphasia) language.

21. What would it mean to be "left-brained" or "right-brained"?

The left hemisphere is usually relatively more involved in cognitive functions involving logical analysis and problem solving, whereas the right hemisphere is usually superior in visual–spatial functions, aesthetic and emotional responses, and creative mathematical reasoning. But the notion that some people are "left-brained" (that is, only logical and lacking completely in functions involving visual–spatial responses, and the like) and others are "right-brained" is exaggerated.

22. Does it matter whether one is left-handed? Why are people right-handed or left-handed?

About one person in ten is left-handed. Learning disabilities are somewhat more common among left-handed people, but so is creativity, as shown in the arts. Handedness appears to have a genetic component.

23. What happens when the brain is split in two?

For the most part, the behavior of people who have had split-brain operations (which sever most of the corpus callosum) is perfectly normal. However, although they may verbally be able to describe a screened-off object such as a pencil held in the hand connected to the hemisphere that contains language functions, they cannot do so when the object is held in the other hand.

24. What is the endocrine system?

The endocrine system consists of ductless glands that secrete hormones. The pituitary gland secretes growth hormone; prolactin, which regulates maternal behavior in lower animals and stimulates production of milk in women; and oxytocin, which stimulates labor in pregnant women. The pineal hormone melatonin is connected with the sleep–wake cycle and the onset of puberty. Thyroxin affects the body's metabolism, and deficiency in childhood is connected with mental retardation. The adrenal cortex produces steroids, which promote the development of muscle mass and increase activity level. The adrenal medulla secretes epinephrine (adrenaline), which increases the metabolic rate and is involved in general emotional arousal. The sex hormones are responsible for prenatal sexual differentiation. Female sex hormones regulate the menstrual cycle.

 Go to **http://psychology.wadsworth. com/rathus_pcc9e** to access an interactive version of this active summary.

Key Terms

Natural selection (p. 45)
Mutation (p. 46)
Evolutionary psychology (p. 46)
Species (p. 46)
Instinct (p. 46)
Heredity (p. 47)
Genetics (p. 47)
Behavioral genetics (p. 47)
Gene (p. 48)
Chromosome (p. 48)
DNA (p. 48)
Polygenic (p. 49)
Genotype (p. 49)
Phenotype (p. 49)
Nature (p. 49)
Nurture (p. 49)
Sex chromosomes (p. 49)
Down syndrome (p. 50)
Monozygotic (MZ) twins (p. 51)
Dizygotic (DZ) twins (p. 51)
Neuron (p. 54)
Glial cells (p. 54)
Dendrites (p. 55)
Axon (p. 55)
Myelin (p. 55)

Afferent neurons (p. 56)
Efferent neurons (p. 56)
Neural impulse (p. 56)
Polarize (p. 56)
Resting potential (p. 56)
Depolarize (p. 56)
Action potential (p. 57)
All-or-none principle (p. 58)
Refractory period (p. 58)
Synapse (p. 58)
Neurotransmitters (p. 58)
Receptor site (p. 58)
Acetylcholine (ACh) (p. 59)
Hippocampus (p. 59)
Dopamine (p. 59)
Norepinephrine (p. 60)
Serotonin (p. 60)
Gamma-aminobutyric acid (GABA) (p. 60)
Endorphins (p. 61)
Nerve (p. 61)
Central nervous system (p. 61)
Peripheral nervous system (p. 62)

Somatic nervous system (p. 62)
Autonomic nervous system (ANS) (p. 62)
Sympathetic (p. 62)
Parasympathetic (p. 62)
Spinal cord (p. 63)
Spinal reflex (p. 63)
Interneuron (p. 64)
Gray matter (p. 64)
White matter (p. 64)
Lesion (p. 66)
Medulla (p. 68)
Pons (p. 68)
Cerebellum (p. 68)
Reticular activating system (RAS) (p. 69)
Thalamus (p. 69)
Hypothalamus (p. 69)
Limbic system (p. 70)
Amygdala (p. 70)
Cerebrum (p. 71)
Cerebral cortex (p. 71)
Corpus callosum (p. 71)
Frontal lobe (p. 72)
Parietal lobe (p. 72)
Temporal lobe (p. 72)

Occipital lobe (p. 72)
Somatosensory cortex (p. 72)
Motor cortex (p. 72)
Aphasia (p. 73)
Wernicke's aphasia (p. 74)
Broca's aphasia (p. 74)
Epilepsy (p. 76)
Gland (p. 78)
Endocrine system (p. 78)
Hormone (p. 78)
Pituitary gland (p. 78)
Growth hormone (p. 79)
Prolactin (p. 79)
Antidiuretic hormone (p. 79)
Oxytocin (p. 79)
Melatonin (p. 79)
Thyroxin (p. 79)
Corticosteroids (p. 79)
Epinephrine (p. 80)
Testosterone (p. 80)
Estrogen (p. 80)
Progesterone (p. 80)

ACTIVE LEARNING RESOURCES

Visit your Companion Website for Video, Quizzing, and Self-Assessment!

http://psychology.wadsworth.com/rathus_pcc9e
On this site you can access The Action Potential video highlighted by the Video Connections icon on p. 59. In addition there are many quizzing opportunities including interactive versions of the fill-in-the-blank Active Review sections in your book. You can also fill out and score the Self-Assessment on p. 83.

Study on the Go!

Don't have time to study right now? You can study on the go! Visit your companion website and download an audio version of the Recite—An Active Summary section to your media player.

ThomsonNOW

http://www.thomsonedu.com
Need help studying? This site is your one-stop study shop. Take a Pre-Test and Thomson NOW will generate a Personalized Study Plan based on your test results. The Study Plan will identify the topics you need to review and direct you to online resources to help you master those topics. You can then take a Post-Test to determine the concepts you have mastered and what you still need to work on.

Author Blog

What does your author have to say about the state of psychology? Visit your companion website every Tuesday and click on "Author Blog," where he'll talk about the most recent controversies and hot topics in psychology.

Truth or Fiction?

T F Fertilization takes place in the uterus.

T F Your heart started beating when you were only one-fifth of an inch long and weighed a fraction of an ounce.

T F Prior to 6 months or so of age, "out of sight" is literally "out of mind."

T F Child abusers were frequently abused themselves as children.

T F Many adolescents think they are Superboy or Supergirl—invulnerable.

T F The architect Frank Lloyd Wright designed New York's innovative spiral-shaped Guggenheim Museum when he was 65 years old.

T F Alzheimer's disease is a normal part of aging.

T F Most parents suffer from the "empty-nest syndrome" when the youngest child leaves home.

T F "Successful aging" involves accepting one's limitations and avoiding new challenges.

T F Children who attend day care programs are more aggressive than children who do not.

 Go to **http://psychology.wadsworth.com/ rathus_pcc9e** to answer and score this Truth or Fiction quiz.

The Voyage through the Life Span

Preview

There is no cure for birth or death save to enjoy the interval.
George Santayana

We have a story to tell. An important story. A fascinating story. It is your story. It is about the remarkable voyage you have already taken through childhood and adolescence. It is about the unfolding of your adult life. Billions have made this voyage before. You have much in common with them. Yet you are unique, and things will happen to you, and because of you, things will happen that have never happened before.

Let us watch as Ling and Patrick Chang begin such a story by conceiving a child. On a summerlike day in October, Ling and Patrick rush to their jobs as usual. While Ling, a trial attorney, is preparing a case to present in court, a very different drama is unfolding in her body. Hormones are causing a follicle (egg container) in one of her ovaries to ovulate—that is, to rupture and release an egg cell, or ovum. Ling, like other women, possessed from birth all the egg cells she will ever have. How this particular ovum was selected to ripen and be released this month is unknown. But in any case, Ling will be capable of becoming pregnant for only a couple of days following ovulation.

When it is released, the ovum begins a slow voyage down a 4-inch-long Fallopian tube to the uterus. It is within this tube that one of Patrick's sperm cells will unite with the egg. **Truth or Fiction Revisited:** Therefore, it is not true that fertilization takes place in the uterus. The fertilized ovum, or zygote, is 1/175th of an inch across—a tiny stage for the drama that is about to unfold.

Developmental psychologists are interested in studying Patrick and Ling's new child's voyage through the life span for several reasons. The discovery of early influences and developmental sequences helps psychologists understand adults. Psychologists are also interested in the effects of genetic factors, early interactions with parents and siblings, and the school and community on traits such as aggressiveness and intelligence.

Developmental psychologists seek to learn the causes of developmental abnormalities. For instance, should pregnant women abstain from smoking and drinking? (Yes.) Is it safe for a pregnant woman to take aspirin for a headache or tetracycline to ward off a bacterial invasion? (Perhaps not. Ask your obstetrician.) What factors contribute to child abuse? Some developmental psychologists focus on adult development. For example, what conflicts and disillusionments can we expect as we voyage through our 30s, 40s, and 50s? The information acquired by developmental psychologists can help us make decisions about how we rear our children and lead our own lives.

Let us now turn to prenatal developments—the changes that occur between conception and birth. They are spectacular, but they occur "out of sight."

Prenatal Development: The Beginning of Our Life Story

The most dramatic gains in height and weight occur during prenatal development. **Question: What developments occur from conception through birth?** Within 9 months, the newly conceived organism develops from a nearly microscopic cell to a **neonate** (newborn) about 20 inches long. Its weight increases a billionfold!

During the months following conception, the single cell formed by the union of sperm and egg—the **zygote**—multiplies, becoming two cells, then four, then eight, and so on. By the time the infant is ready to be born, it contains trillions of cells.

The zygote divides repeatedly as it proceeds on its 3- to 4-day voyage to the uterus. The ball-like mass of multiplying cells wanders about the uterus for another 3 to 4 days before beginning to implant in the uterine wall. Implantation takes another week or so. The period from conception to implantation is called the **germinal stage,** or the **period of the ovum.**

The **embryonic stage** lasts from implantation until about the eighth week of development. During this stage, the major body organ systems take form. As you

Neonate A newly born child.

Zygote A fertilized ovum (egg cell).

Germinal stage The first stage of prenatal development, during which the dividing mass of cells has not become implanted in the uterine wall.

Period of the ovum Another term for the *germinal stage.*

Embryonic stage The baby from the third through the eighth weeks following conception, during which time the major organ systems undergo rapid differentiation.

can see from Figure 3.1, the growth of the head precedes that of other parts of the body. The growth of the organs—heart, lungs, and so on—also precedes the growth of the extremities. The relatively early **maturation** of the brain and the organ systems allows them to participate in the nourishment and further development of the embryo. **Truth or Fiction Revisited:** During the fourth week, a primitive heart begins to beat and pump blood—in an organism that is one-fifth of an inch long. The heart will continue to beat without rest every minute of every day for the better part of a century, perhaps longer.

By the end of the second month, the head has become rounded and the facial features distinct—all in an embryo that is about 1 inch long and weighs 1/30th of an ounce. During the second month, the nervous system begins to transmit messages. By 5 to 6 weeks, the embryo is only a quarter to half an inch long, yet nondescript sex organs have formed. By about the seventh week, the genetic code (XY or XX) begins to assert itself, causing the sex organs to differentiate. If a Y sex chromosome is present, testes form and begin to produce **androgens** (male sex hormones), which further masculinize the sex organs. In the absence of these hormones, the embryo develops sex organs typical of the female, regardless of its genetic code. However, individuals with a male genetic code would be sterile.

As it develops, the embryo is suspended within a protective **amniotic sac** in the mother's uterus. The sac is surrounded by a clear membrane and contains amniotic fluid. The fluid is a sort of natural air bag, allowing the child to move or even jerk around without injury. It also helps maintain an even temperature.

From now until birth, the embryo exchanges nutrients and wastes with the mother through the **placenta.** The embryo is connected to the placenta by the **umbilical cord.** The placenta is connected to the mother by blood vessels in the uterine wall.

The **fetal stage** lasts from the beginning of the third month until birth. By the end of the third month, the major organ systems and the fingers and toes

Maturation The process of development as guided by the unfolding of the genetic code.

Androgens Male sex hormones.

Amniotic sac A sac within the uterus that contains the embryo or fetus.

Placenta A membrane that permits the exchange of nutrients and waste products between the mother and her developing child but does not allow the maternal and fetal bloodstreams to mix.

Umbilical cord A tube between the mother and her developing child through which nutrients and waste products are conducted.

Fetal stage The baby from the third month following conception through childbirth, during which time there is maturation of organ systems and dramatic gains in length and weight.

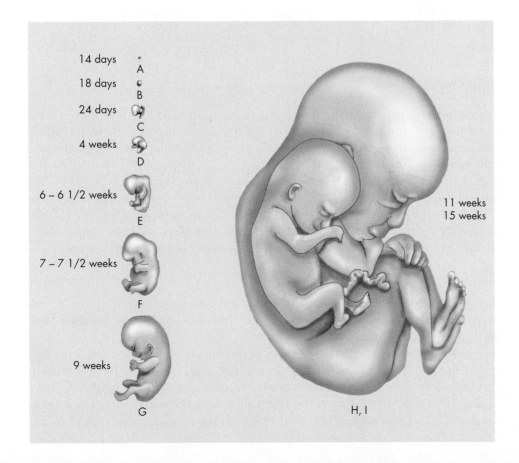

FIGURE 3.1 **Embryos and Fetuses at Various Intervals of Prenatal Development**

Development of the head (and brain) precedes that of other parts of the body. The development of the organs—heart, lungs, and so on—also precedes the development of the limbs. The relatively early maturation of the brain and the organ systems allows them to participate in the nourishment and further development of the embryo.

14 days — A
18 days — B
24 days — C
4 weeks — D
6 – 6 1/2 weeks — E
7 – 7 1/2 weeks — F
9 weeks — G
11 weeks / 15 weeks — H, I

■ **An Exercise Class for Pregnant Women** Years ago pregnant women were not expected to exert themselves. Today, it is recognized that exercise is healthful for pregnant women because it promotes fitness, which is beneficial during childbirth as well as at other times.

© Fotografia, Inc./CORBIS

have formed. In the middle of the fourth month, the mother usually detects the first fetal movements. By the end of the sixth month, the fetus moves its limbs so vigorously that mothers often feel that they are being kicked. The fetus opens and shuts its eyes, sucks its thumb, alternates between periods of being awake and sleeping, and responds to light. It also turns somersaults, which can be perceived clearly by the mother.

During the last 3 months, the organ systems of the fetus continue to mature. The heart and lungs become increasingly capable of sustaining independent life. The fetus gains about 5½ pounds and doubles in length. Newborn boys average about 7½ pounds and newborn girls about 7 pounds.

Your Turn: Now that we have discussed prenatal development, enhance your mastery of the material with the nearby "Learning Connections." Review the material by filling in the blanks, reflect on the material by relating it to other things you know, and think critically about it.

Learning Connections | PRENATAL DEVELOPMENT: THE BEGINNING OF OUR LIFE STORY

ACTIVE REVIEW (1) It is possible to become pregnant for a day or so after _____ . (2) A sperm cell combines with an ovum to form a(n) _____ . (3) The zygote implants in the wall of the _____ . (4) Prenatal development is divided into the germinal stage, the _____ stage, and the fetal stage.

REFLECT AND RELATE It is during the fourth month that most mothers begin to detect their baby's movements and feel that their baby is "alive." What is your view on when the baby is alive? What standard or standards do you use in forming your view?

CRITICAL THINKING Many researchers use terms like *zygote, embryo,* and *fetus* to refer to the human organism as it undergoes prenatal development. How do these terms differ in meaning from commonly used terms such as *baby* and *unborn child?*

 Go to **http://psychology.wadsworth.com/ rathus_pcc9e** for an interactive version of this Learning Connections unit.

Childhood

Childhood begins with birth. When my children are enjoying themselves, I kid them and say "Stop having fun. You're a child, and childhood is the worst time of life." I get a laugh because they know that childhood is supposed to be the best time of life—a time for play and learning and endless possibilities. For many children it is that, but other children suffer from problems such as malnutrition, low self-esteem, and child abuse.

Let us chronicle the events of childhood. The most obvious aspects of child development are physical. Let us therefore begin with physical development. Then we turn our attention to cognitive and social and emotional developments.

Physical Development: The Drama Continues

Physical development includes gains in height and weight, maturation of the nervous system, and development of bones, muscles, and organs. **Question: What physical developments occur during childhood?**

During infancy—the first two years of childhood—dramatic gains in height and weight continue. Babies usually double their birth weight in about 5 months and triple it by their first birthday (Kuczmarski et al., 2000). Their height increases by about 10 inches in the first year. Children grow another 4 to 6 inches during the second year and gain some 4 to 7 pounds. After that, they gain about 2 to 3 inches a year until they reach the adolescent growth spurt. Weight gains also remain fairly even at about 4 to 6 pounds per year until the spurt begins. Other aspects of physical development in childhood include reflexes and perceptual development.

REFLEXES: ENTERING THE WORLD PREWIRED Soon after you were born, a doctor or nurse probably pressed her fingers against the palms of your hands. Although you would have had no idea what to do in response, most likely you grasped the fingers firmly—so firmly that you could have been lifted from your cradle!

Grasping at birth is inborn, an example of the importance of nature in human development. Grasping is one of the neonate's many reflexes. **Reflexes** are simple, unlearned, stereotypical responses elicited by specific stimuli. Reflexes are essential to survival and do not involve higher brain functions. They occur automatically—that is, without thinking about them.

Newborn children do not know that it is necessary to eat to survive. Fortunately, they have rooting and sucking reflexes that cause them to eat. They turn their head toward stimuli that prod or stroke the cheek, chin, or corner of the mouth. This is termed **rooting.** They suck objects that touch their lips.

Neonates have numerous other reflexes that aid in survival. They withdraw from painful stimuli. This is known as the withdrawal reflex. They draw up their legs and arch their backs in response to sudden noises, bumps, or loss of support while being held. This is the startle, or Moro, reflex. They grasp objects that press against the palms of their hands (the grasp, or palmar, reflex). They fan their toes when the soles of their feet are stimulated (the Babinski reflex). Pediatricians assess babies' neural functioning by testing these reflexes.

Babies also breathe, sneeze, cough, yawn, and blink reflexively. And it is guaranteed that you will learn about the sphincter (anal muscle) reflex if you put on your best clothes and hold an undiapered neonate on your lap for a while.

MOTOR DEVELOPMENT: LABORATORY FOR THE NATURE–NURTURE CONTROVERSY The motor development of the child—that is, the progression from simple acts like lifting the head to running around—offers psychologists a wondrous laboratory for sorting out genetic and environmental influences on development. In the field of developmental psychology, genetic factors are generally discussed in terms of the concept of maturation, that is, the unfolding of traits and behavior, as determined by the genetic code. The American psychologist Arnold Gesell (1880–1961) emphasized the importance of maturation in human development and argued that all areas of development are self-regulated by the unfolding of natural plans and processes. The essential role of maturation in areas such as physical development (for example, gains in height and weight and the effects of puberty), language development, and motor development is clear. But even in these areas, environmental factors cannot be ignored. Individuals may have certain genetic potentials for body size and growth rates, but these potentials are not reached unless environmental factors such as nutrition, exposure to relatively clean air, and so on are also available. In terms of language development, we can assert that organisms do not comprehend or produce language unless their genetic codes spark the development of structures and processes in the brain that enable the use of language. But let us not downplay environmental factors: Children learn to speak the languages used in their homes, communities, and in the media that are available to them. They do not speak tongues used in foreign parts of the world without being exposed to them. Moreover, children obtain different levels of facility with their languages. Research with humans and other species leaves little doubt that maturation and experience (environmental influences) both play indispensable roles in motor development (Muir, 2000; Pryce et al., 2001; Roncesvalles et al., 2001).

Maturation of the brain is a key element in motor development. Motor development provides some of the most fascinating changes in infants, in part because so much seems to happen so quickly—and so much of it during the first year. Children gain the capacity to move about through a sequence of activities that

Reflex A simple unlearned response to a stimulus.

Rooting The turning of an infant's head toward a touch, such as by the mother's nipple.

Fixation time The amount of time spent looking at a visual stimulus.

includes rolling over, sitting up, crawling, creeping, walking, and running. The ages at which infants first engage in these activities vary, but the sequence generally remains the same (see Figure 3.2). Some children skip a step. For example, an infant may walk without ever having crawled. But by and large, the sequence remains intact. Invariant sequences are usually interpreted as reflecting the unfolding of the genetic code (maturation).

PERCEPTUAL DEVELOPMENT: ON *NOT* GOING OFF THE DEEP END Newborn children spend about 16 hours a day sleeping and do not have much opportunity to learn about the world. Yet they are capable of perceiving the world reasonably well soon after birth.

Within a couple of days, infants can follow, or track, a moving light with their eyes (Kellman & von Hofsten, 1992). By the age of 3 months, they can discriminate most colors (Banks & Shannon, 1993; Teller, 1998). Neonates are nearsighted, but, by about the age of 4 months, infants seem able to focus on distant objects about as well as adults can.

The visual preferences of infants are measured by the amount of time, termed **fixation time,** they spend looking at one stimulus instead of another. In classic research by Robert Fantz (1961), 2-month-old infants preferred visual stimuli that resembled the human face to newsprint, a bull's-eye, and featureless red, white, and yellow disks. At this age the complexity of facelike patterns may be more important than their content. For example, babies have been shown facelike patterns that differ either in the number of elements they contain or the degree to which they are organized to match the human face. Five- to 10-week-old babies fixate longer on patterns with high numbers of elements. The organization of the elements—that is, the degree to which they resemble the face—is less important. By 15 to 20 weeks, the organization of the pattern also matters. At that age babies dwell longer on facelike patterns (e.g., Haaf et al., 1983).

Infants thus seem to have an inborn preference for complex visual stimuli. However, preference for faces as opposed to other equally complex stimuli may not emerge until infants have had experience with people.

Classic research has shown that infants tend to respond to cues for depth by the time they are able to crawl (at about 6 to 8 months). Most also have the good sense to avoid crawling off ledges and table tops into open space (Campos et al., 1978). Note the setup (Figure 3.3) in the classic "visual cliff"

FIGURE 3.2 Motor Development in Infancy

Motor development proceeds in an orderly sequence, which suggests that there is a strong maturational or genetic component. However, there is considerable variation in the timing of the marker events shown in this figure. An infant who is a bit behind will most likely develop without problems, and a precocious infant will not necessarily become a rocket scientist (or gymnast).

experiment run by Walk and Gibson (1961). An 8-month-old infant crawls freely above the portion of the glass with a checkerboard pattern immediately beneath it, but hesitates to crawl over the portion of the glass beneath which the checkerboard has been dropped a few feet. Because the glass would support the infant, this is a "visual cliff," not an actual cliff.

Normal neonates hear well unless their middle ears are clogged with amniotic fluid. In such cases, hearing improves rapidly after the ears are opened up. Most neonates reflexively turn their heads toward unusual sounds, suspending other activities as they do so. This finding, along with findings about visual tracking, suggests that infants are preprogrammed to survey their environments. Speaking or singing softly in a low-pitched tone soothes infants. This is why some parents use lullabies to get infants to fall asleep.

Three-day-old babies prefer their mother's voice to those of other women, but they do not show a similar preference for their father's voice (DeCasper & Prescott, 1984; Freeman et al., 1993). Babies have, of course, had many months of "experience" in the uterus. For at least 2 or 3 months before birth, babies have been capable of hearing sounds. Because they are predominantly exposed to sounds produced by their mother, learning may contribute to neonatal preferences.

FIGURE 3.3 **The Classic Visual Cliff Experiment**
This young explorer has the good sense not to crawl out onto an apparently unsupported surface, even when Mother beckons from the other side. Rats, pups, kittens, and chicks also will not try to walk across to the other side. (So don't bother asking why the chicken crossed the visual cliff.)

The odors preferred by babies are similar to those preferred by adults. Newborn infants spit, stick out their tongue, and literally wrinkle their nose at the odor of rotten eggs. They smile and make licking motions in response to chocolate, strawberry, vanilla, and honey. The sense of smell, like the sense of hearing, may provide a vehicle for mother–infant recognition. Within the first week, nursing infants prefer to turn to look at their mother's nursing pads (which can be discriminated only by smell) rather than those of strange women (Macfarlane, 1975). By 15 days, nursing infants prefer their mother's underarm odor to those of other women (Porter et al., 1992). Bottle-fed babies do not show this preference. Shortly after birth, infants can discriminate tastes. They eagerly suck liquid solutions of sugar and milk but grimace and refuse to suck salty or bitter solutions (Petrov et al., 2001; Rosenstein & Oster, 1988).

Newborn babies are sensitive to touch. Many reflexes (including rooting and sucking) are activated by pressure against the skin. The sense of touch is an extremely important avenue of learning and communication for babies. Sensations of skin against skin appear to provide feelings of comfort and security that may contribute to the formation of affectionate bonds between infants and their caregivers.

CONTROVERSY IN PSYCHOLOGY

Is development continuous or discontinuous?

Do developmental changes tend to occur gradually (continuously)? Or do they tend to occur in major leaps (discontinuously) that dramatically alter our bodies and behavior? **Question: Does development occur gradually or in stages?**

Watson and other behaviorists viewed development as a mainly continuous process in which the effects of learning mount gradually, with no major sudden changes. Maturational theorists, however, argue that people are prewired or preset to change dramatically at certain times of life. Rapid qualitative changes can be ushered in during new stages of development. They point out that the environment, even when enriched, profits us little until we are ready, or mature enough, to develop in a certain direction. For example, newborn babies do not imitate their parents' speech, even when the parents speak clearly and deliberately. Nor does aided practice in "walking" during the first few months after birth significantly accelerate the date at which the child can walk on her own.

Stage theorists, such as Jean Piaget—whose theory of cognitive development we discuss next—and Sigmund Freud, saw development as discontinuous. Both theorists saw biological changes as providing the potential for psychological changes. Piaget's research centered on the ways in which maturation of the nervous system permits cognitive advances. Freud focused on the ways in which sexual development might provide the basis for personality development.

Certain aspects of physical development do occur in stages. For example, many of the changes that occur during prenatal development are discontinuous. For several days the dividing mass of cells that becomes the baby travels through the Fallopian tube and the uterus—literally unattached to the mother. Then it becomes implanted in the uterine wall and a whole new way of obtaining nourishment begins. Similarly, organs develop so rapidly that the fetus is clearly human-looking before the end of the first trimester. The changes from the age of 2 to the onset of puberty (the period of development during which reproduction becomes possible) are continuous, with children gradually growing larger. Then a new stage of development begins with the adolescent growth spurt. The spurt is triggered by hormones and characterized by rapid changes in structure and function (as in the development of the sex organs) as well as size.

Psychologists disagree more strongly on whether aspects of development such as cognitive development, attachment, and gender typing occur in stages. But as we see next, Jean Piaget believed that cognitive development was discontinuous and consisted of four stages of development. In this chapter we will also see that Lawrence Kohlberg's theory of moral development consists of three levels and two stages within each level. Erik Erikson's theory of psychosocial development consists of eight stages.

Cognitive Development: On the Edge of Reason?

The ways in which children mentally represent and think about the world—that is, their *cognitive development*—are explored in this section. Because cognitive functioning develops over many years, young children have ideas about the world that differ considerably from those of adults. Many of these ideas are charming but illogical—at least to adults. Let us consider three views of cognitive development. We will begin with Jean Piaget's stage theory of cognitive development. Then we will turn to the views of the Russian psychologist Lev Semenovich Vygotsky (1896–1934), whose approach is quite different from Piaget's but is enjoying a rebirth in popularity. Then we will focus on Lawrence Kohlberg's theory of moral development.

JEAN PIAGET'S COGNITIVE–DEVELOPMENTAL THEORY The Swiss biologist and psychologist Jean Piaget contributed significantly to our understanding of children's cognitive development. **Question: What are Jean Piaget's views of cognitive development?** Piaget hypothesized that children's cognitive processes develop in an orderly sequence of stages. Although some children may be more advanced than others at particular ages, the developmental sequence remains the same. Piaget (1963) identified four major stages of cognitive development: sensorimotor, preoperational, concrete operational, and formal operational (see the Concept Review of Piaget's Stages of Cognitive Development).

In Profile   JEAN PIAGET

Jean Piaget (1896–1980) was offered the curatorship of a museum in Geneva, but he had to turn it down. After all, he was only 11 at the time. Piaget's first intellectual love was biology, and he published his first scientific article at the age of 10. He then became a laboratory assistant to the director of a museum of natural history and engaged in research on mollusks (oysters, clams, snails, and such). The director soon died, and Piaget published the research findings himself. On the basis of these papers, he was offered the curatorship.

During adolescence Piaget studied philosophy, logic, and mathematics, but he earned his Ph.D. in biology. In 1920 he obtained a job at the Binet Institute in Paris, where work on intelligence tests was being conducted. His first task was to adapt English verbal reasoning items for use with French children. To do so, he had to try out the items on children in various age groups and see whether they could arrive at correct answers. The task was boring until Piaget became intrigued by the children's *wrong* answers. Another investigator might have shrugged them off, but Piaget found meaningful patterns in the children's "mistakes." The wrong answers reflected consistent, if illogical, cognitive processes. Piaget's observations led to his influential theory of cognitive development.

Piaget's original texts are difficult to read—even when translated into English. In fact, Piaget once remarked that he had the advantage of not having to read Piaget!

 Go to **http://psychology.wadsworth.com/ rathus_pcc9e** to access more information about Jean Piaget.

© Farrell Grehan/CORBIS

Assimilation and Accommodation Piaget described human thought, or intelligence, in terms of two basic concepts: assimilation and accommodation. **Assimilation** means responding to a new stimulus through a reflex or existing habit. Infants, for example, usually try to place new objects in their mouth to suck, feel, or explore. Piaget would say that the child is assimilating a new toy to the sucking schema. A **schema** is a pattern of action or a mental structure involved in acquiring or organizing knowledge.

Piaget regarded children as natural physicists who seek to learn about and control their world. In the Piagetian view, children who squish their food and laugh enthusiastically are often acting as budding scientists. In addition to enjoying the responses of their parents, they are studying the texture and consistency of their food. (Parents, of course, often wish their children would practice these experiments in the laboratory, not the dining room.)

Accommodation is the creation of new ways of responding to objects or looking at the world. In accommodation, children transform existing schemas—action patterns or ways of organizing knowledge—to incorporate new events. Children (and adults) accommodate to objects and situations that cannot be integrated into existing schemas. (For example, children who study biology learn that whales cannot be assimilated into the "fish" schema. They accommodate by constructing new schemas, such as "mammals without legs that live in the sea.") The ability to accommodate to novel stimuli advances as a result of maturation and experience.

Most of the time, newborn children assimilate environmental stimuli according to reflexive schemas, although adjusting the mouth to contain the nipple is a primitive kind of accommodation. Reflexive behavior, to Piaget, is not "true" intelligence. True intelligence involves adapting to the world through a smooth, fluid balancing of the processes of assimilation and accommodation. Let us now apply these concepts to the stages of cognitive development.

The Sensorimotor Stage The newborn infant is capable of assimilating novel stimuli only to existing reflexes (or ready-made schemas) such as the rooting and sucking reflexes. But by the time an infant reaches the age of 1 month, he or she already shows purposeful behavior by repeating behavior patterns that are pleasurable, such as sucking his or her hand. During the first month or so, an infant apparently does not connect stimuli perceived through different senses. Reflexive turning toward sources of auditory and olfactory stimulation cannot be considered purposeful searching. But within the first few months the infant begins to coordinate vision with grasping to look at the object being held or touched.

Assimilation According to Piaget, the inclusion of a new event into an existing schema.

Schema According to Piaget, a hypothetical mental structure that permits the classification and organization of new information.

Accommodation According to Piaget, the modification of schemas so that information inconsistent with existing schemas can be integrated or understood.

Video Connections—Piaget's Stages of Development How would Jean Piaget explain how nine-month-old Hayden has learned to move a large obstacle to find a more desirable toy underneath? To view children in many different stages of development, go to your companion website and click on the "Piaget's Stages of Development" video link.

Concept Review PIAGET'S STAGES OF COGNITIVE DEVELOPMENT

Stage	Approximate Age	Comments	
Sensorimotor	Birth–2 years	At first, the child lacks language and does not use symbols or mental representations of objects. In time, reflexive responding ends and intentional behavior begins. The child develops the object concept and acquires the basics of language.	© Doug Goodman/Photo Researchers, Inc.
Preoperational	2–7 years	The child begins to represent the world mentally, but thought is egocentric. The child does not focus on two aspects of a situation at once and therefore lacks conservation. The child shows animism, artificialism, and objective responsibility for wrongdoing.	
Concrete operational	7–12 years	The child develops conservation concepts, can adopt the viewpoint of others, can classify objects in series, and shows comprehension of basic relational concepts (such as one object being larger or heavier than another).	
Formal operational	12 years and above	Mature, adult thought emerges. Thinking is characterized by deductive logic, consideration of various possibilities (mental trial and error), abstract thought, and the formation and testing of hypotheses.	

Go to **http://psychology.wadsworth.com/ rathus_pcc9e** to access a drag-and-drop version of this Concept Review designed to help you test yourself on the major topics provided here.

A 3- or 4-month-old infant may be fascinated by his or her own hands and legs. The infant may become absorbed in watching him- or herself open and close the fists. The infant becomes increasingly interested in acting on the environment to make interesting results (such as the sound of a rattle) last longer or occur again. Behavior becomes increasingly intentional and purposeful. Between 4 and 8 months of age, the infant explores cause-and-effect relationships such as the thump that can be made by tossing an object or the way kicking can cause a hanging toy to bounce.

Truth or Fiction Revisited: It is true that "out of sight" is literally "out of mind" prior to the age of 6 months or so. For most infants younger than 6 months, objects are not yet represented mentally. For this reason, as you can see in Figure 3.4, a child makes no effort to search for an object that has been removed or placed behind a screen. By the age of 8 to 12 months, however, infants realize that objects removed from sight still exist and attempt to find them. In this way, they show what is known as **object permanence,** thereby making it possible to play peek-a-boo.

By the way, comparative psychologists have also studied the development of object permanence in nonhuman species, including dogs and cats . . . and magpies. Magpies are notorious thieves in the bird world, and they also hide their food to keep it safe from other animals—especially other magpies. Bettina Pollock and her colleagues (2000) found that magpies develop object permanence before they begin to hide food. Magpies would not profit from secreting away their food if out of sight meant the same thing as "out of existence."

Between 1 and 2 years of age, children begin to show interest in how things are constructed. It may be for this reason that they persistently touch and finger their parents' faces and their own. Toward the end of the second year, children begin to engage in mental trial and error before they try out overt behaviors. For instance, when they look for an object you have removed, they will no longer begin their search in the last place they saw it. Rather, they may follow you, assuming you are carrying the object even though it is not visible. It is as though they are anticipating failure in searching for the object in the place where they last saw it.

Object permanence Recognition that objects removed from sight still exist, as demonstrated in young children by continued pursuit.

FIGURE 3.4 Object Permanence

To the infant at the top, who is in the early part of the sensorimotor stage, out of sight is truly out of mind. Once a sheet of paper is placed between the infant and the toy elephant, the infant loses all interest in it. The toy is apparently not yet mentally represented. The photos on the bottom show a child later in the sensorimotor stage. This child does mentally represent objects and pushes through a towel to reach one that has been screened from sight.

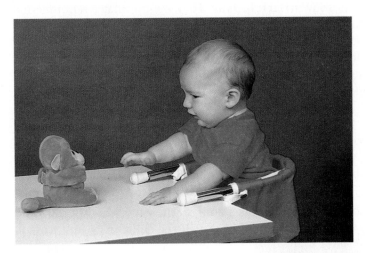
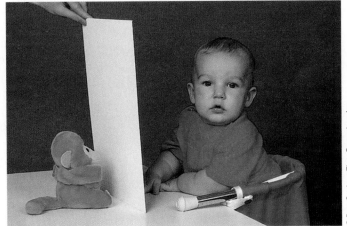

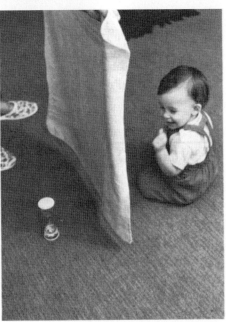

Because the first stage of development is dominated by learning to coordinate perception of the self and of the environment with motor (muscular) activity, Piaget termed it the **sensorimotor stage.** This stage comes to a close with the acquisition of the basics of language at about age 2.

The Preoperational Stage The **preoperational stage** is characterized by the use of words and symbols to represent objects and relationships among them. But be warned—any resemblance between the logic of children between the ages of 2 and 7 and your own logic is very often purely coincidental. Children may use the same words that adults do, but this does not mean their views of the world are similar to adults'. Preoperational children tend to think one-dimensionally—to focus on one aspect of a problem or situation at a time.

One consequence of one-dimensional thinking is **egocentrism.** Preoperational children cannot understand that other people do not see things the same way they do. When my daughter Allyn was 2½, I asked her to tell me about a trip to the store with her mother. "You tell me," she replied. Upon questioning, it seemed she did not understand that I could not see the world through her eyes.

To egocentric preoperational children, all the world's a stage that has been erected to meet their needs and amuse them. When asked, "Why does the sun shine?" they may say, "To keep me warm." If asked, "Why is the sky blue?" they may respond, "'Cause blue's my favorite color." Preoperational children also show **animism.** They attribute life and consciousness to physical objects like the sun and the moon. They also show **artificialism.** They believe that environmental events like rain and thunder are human inventions. Asked why the sky is blue, 4-year-olds may answer, "'Cause Mommy painted it." Examples of egocentrism, animism, and artificialism are shown in Table 3.1.

To gain further insight into preoperational thinking, find a 3- or 4-year-old and try these mini-experiments:

◆ Pour water from a tall, thin glass into a low, wide glass. Now, ask the child whether the low, wide glass contains more, less, or the same amount of water that was in the tall, thin glass. If the child says that they hold the same amount of water (with possible minor exceptions for spillage and evaporation), the child is correct. But if the child errs, why do you think this is so?

◆ Now flatten a ball of clay into a pancake, and ask the child whether you wind up with more, less, or the same amount of clay. If the child errs again, why do you think this is so?

Sensorimotor stage The first of Piaget's stages of cognitive development, characterized by coordination of sensory information and motor activity, early exploration of the environment, and lack of language.

Preoperational stage The second of Piaget's stages, characterized by illogical use of words and symbols, spotty logic, and egocentrism.

Egocentrism According to Piaget, the assumption that others view the world as one does oneself.

Animism The belief that inanimate objects move because of will or spirit.

Artificialism The belief that natural objects have been created by human beings.

TABLE 3.1 EXAMPLES OF PREOPERATIONAL THOUGHT

Type of Thought	Sample Questions	Typical Answers
Egocentrism	Why does it get dark out? Why does the sun shine? Why is there snow? Why is grass green? What are TV sets for?	So I can go to sleep. To keep me warm. For me to play in. Because that's my favorite color. To watch my favorite shows and cartoons.
Animism (attributing life and consciousness to physical objects)	Why do trees have leaves? Why do stars twinkle? Why does the sun move in the sky? Where do boats go at night?	To keep them warm. Because they're happy and cheerful. To follow children and hear what they say. They sleep like we do.
Artificialism (assuming that environmental events are human inventions)	What makes it rain? Why is the sky blue? What is the wind? What causes thunder? How does a baby get in Mommy's tummy?	Someone emptying a watering can. Somebody painted it. A man blowing. A man grumbling. Just make it first. (How?) You put some eyes on it, then put on the head.

To arrive at the correct answers to these questions, children must understand the law of **conservation.** This law holds that basic properties of substances such as mass, weight, and volume remain the same—that is, are *conserved*—when one changes superficial properties such as their shape or arrangement.

Conservation requires the ability to think about, or **center** on, two aspects of a situation at once, such as height and width. Conserving the mass, weight, or volume of a substance requires the recognition that a change in one dimension can compensate for a change in another. But the preoperational boy in Figure 3.5 focuses on only one dimension at a time. First he is shown two wide, short glasses of water and agrees that they contain the same amount of water. Then, while he watches, water is poured from a short glass into a tall, thin glass. Now he is asked which glass contains more water. After mulling over the problem, he points to the tall glass. Why? Because when he looks at the glasses he is "overwhelmed" by the fact that the thinner glass is taller. The preoperational child focuses on the most apparent dimension of the situation—in this case, the greater height of the thinner glass. He does not realize that the increased width of the squat glass compensates for the decreased height. By the way, if you ask him whether any water has been added or taken away in the pouring process, he readily says no. But if you then repeat the question about which glass contains *more* water, he again points to the taller glass. If all this sounds rather illogical, that is because it is illogical—or, in Piaget's terms, preoperational.

Piaget (1932) found that the moral judgment of preoperational children is also one-dimensional. The 5-year-olds he observed tended to be slaves to rules and authority. When you ask them why something should be done in a certain way, they may insist "Because that's the way to do it!" or "Because my Mommy says so!" Right is right and wrong is wrong. Why? "Because!"—that's why.

According to most older children and adults, an act is a crime only when there is criminal intent. Accidents may be hurtful, but the perpetrators are usually seen as blameless. But in the court of the one-dimensional, preoperational child, there is **objective responsibility.** People are sentenced (and harshly!) on the basis of the amount of damage they have done, not their motives or intentions. To demonstrate objective responsibility, Piaget would tell children stories and ask them which character was naughtier and why. John, for instance, accidentally breaks 15 cups when he opens a door. Henry breaks 1 cup when he sneaks into a kitchen cabinet to find forbidden jam. The preoperational child usually judges John to be naughtier. Why? Because he broke more cups.

The Concrete-Operational Stage By about age 7, the typical child is entering the stage of **concrete operations.** In this stage, which lasts until about age 12, children show the beginnings of the capacity for adult logic. However, their logical thoughts, or *operations,* generally involve tangible objects rather than abstract ideas. Concrete operational children are capable of **decentration;** they can center on two dimensions of a problem at once. This attainment has implications for moral judgments, conservation, and other intellectual undertakings.

Conservation According to Piaget, recognition that basic properties of substances such as weight and mass remain the same when superficial features change.

Center According to Piaget, to focus one's attention.

Objective responsibility According to Piaget, the assignment of blame according to the amount of damage done rather than the motives of the actor.

Concrete-operational stage Piaget's third stage, characterized by logical thought concerning tangible objects, conservation, and subjective morality.

Decentration Simultaneous focusing on more than one dimension of a problem, so that flexible, reversible thought becomes possible.

A.   B.   C.

FIGURE 3.5 **Conservation**
The boy in drawing A agreed that the amount of water in two identical containers is equal. As shown in drawing B, he then watched as water from one container was poured into a tall, thin container. In drawing C, he is examining one of the original containers and the new container. When asked whether he thinks the amounts of water in the two containers are now the same, he says no. Apparently, he is impressed by the height of the new container, and, prior to the development of conservation, he focuses on only one dimension of the situation at a time—in this case, the height of the new container.

Subjective moral judgment According to Piaget, moral judgment that is based on the motives of the perpetrator.

Reversibility According to Piaget, recognition that processes can be undone, that things can be made as they were.

Children now become **subjective** in their moral judgments. When assigning guilt, they center on the motives of wrongdoers as well as on the amount of damage done. Concrete-operational children judge Henry more harshly than John because John's misdeed was an accident.

Concrete-operational children understand the laws of conservation. The boy in Figure 3.5, now a few years older, would say that the tall glass still contains the same amount of water. If asked why, he might reply, "Because you can pour it back into the other one." Such an answer also suggests awareness of the concept of **reversibility**—the recognition that many processes can be reversed or undone so that things are restored to their previous condition. Centering simultaneously on the height and the width of the glasses, the boy recognizes that the loss in width compensates for the gain in height.

Children in this stage are less egocentric. They are able to take on the roles of others and to view the world, and themselves, from other people's perspectives. They recognize that people see things in different ways because of different situations and different sets of values.

During the concrete-operational stage, children's own sets of values begin to emerge and acquire stability. Children come to understand that feelings of love between them and their parents can endure even when someone feels angry or disappointed at a particular moment. We continue our discussion of Piaget's theory—his stage of formal operations—in the section on adolescence.

Evaluation of Piaget's Theory A number of questions have been raised concerning the accuracy of Piaget's views. Among them are these:

◆ *Was Piaget's timing accurate?* Some critics argue that Piaget's methods led him to underestimate children's abilities (Bjorklund, 2000; Meltzoff & Gopnik, 1997). Other researchers using different methods have found, for example, that preschoolers are less egocentric and that children are capable of conservation at earlier ages than Piaget thought.

◆ *Does cognitive development occur in stages?* Cognitive events such as egocentrism and conservation appear to develop more continuously than Piaget thought—that is, they may not occur in stages (Bjorklund, 2000; Flavell, 2000). Although cognitive developments appear to build on previous cognitive developments, the process may be more gradual than stagelike.

◆ *Are developmental sequences always the same?* Here, Piaget's views have fared better. It seems there is no variation in the sequence in which cognitive developments occur.

In sum, Piaget's theoretical edifice has been rocked, but it has not been reduced to rubble. Psychologist Andrew Meltzoff believes that "Piaget's theories were critical for getting the field of [cognitive development] off the ground, . . . but it's time to move on" (1997, p. 9). Some psychologists are moving on to *information processing*. That is, they view children (and adults) as akin to computer systems. Children, like computers, obtain information (receive "input") from their environment, store it, retrieve, manipulate it (think about it), and then respond to it overtly in terms of their behavior (produce "output") (Bjorklund, 2000). One goal of the information-processing approach is to learn just how children do these things, how their "mental programs" develop. Critical issues involve children's capacity for memory and their use of cognitive strategies, such as the ways in which they focus their attention (Bjorklund, 2000; Case, 1992; Kail, 2000). The future of cognitive development remains to be written.

Now let us consider the views of Vygotsky. Vygotsky, unlike Piaget, is not a stage theorist. Instead, he sees the transmission of knowledge from generation to generation as cumulative, and focuses on the ways in which children's interactions with their elders enhance their cognitive development.

LEV VYGOTSKY'S SOCIOCULTURAL THEORY The term *sociocultural theory* has different meanings. In Chapter 1 we saw that the term can refer to the roles of factors such as ethnicity and gender in behavior and mental processes. But Vygotsky's sociocultural theory focuses instead on the ways in which children's cognitive development is influenced by the culture in which they are reared and the individuals who help transmit information about that culture.

Vygotsky's (1978) theory focuses on the transmission of information and cognitive skills from generation to generation. The transmission of skills involves teaching and learning, but Vygotsky is no behaviorist. He does not view learning as a mechanical process that can be described in terms of the conditioning of units of behavior. Rather, he focuses more generally on how the child's social interaction with adults, largely in the home, organizes a child's learning experiences in such a way that the child can obtain cognitive skills—such as computation or reading skills—and use them to acquire information. Like Piaget, Vygotsky sees the child's functioning as adaptive (Piaget & Smith, 2000), and the child adapts to his or her social and cultural interactions.

Question: What are the key concepts of Vygotsky's theory of cognitive development? Key concepts in Vygotsky's theory include the *zone of proximal development* and *scaffolding*. The word *proximal* means "nearby" or "close," as in the words *approximate* and *proximity*. The **zone of proximal development (ZPD)** refers to a range of tasks that a child can carry out with the help of someone who is more skilled (Haenen, 2001). The "zone" refers to the relationship between the child's abilities and what she or he can do with help from others. Adults or older children best guide the child through this zone by gearing their assistance to the child's capabilities (Flavell et al., 2002).

Within the zone we find an apprenticeship in which the child works with, and learns from, others (Meijer & Elshout, 2001). When learning with others, the child tends to internalize—or bring inward—the conversations and explanations that help him or her gain skills (Prior & Welling, 2001; Vygotsky, 1962; Yang, 2000). Children not only learn the meanings of words from teachers, but also learn ways of talking to themselves about solving problems within a cultural context (DeVries, 2000). Outer speech becomes inner speech. What was the teacher's becomes the child's. What was a social and cultural context becomes embedded within the child (Moro & Rodriguez, 2000); thus the term *sociocultural theory.*

A *scaffold* is a temporary skeletal structure that enables workers to fabricate a building, bridge, or other, more permanent, structure. Cognitive **scaffolding** refers to the temporary support provided by a parent or teacher to a child who is learning to perform a task. The amount of guidance decreases as the child becomes more skilled and self-sufficient (Clarke-Stewart & Beck, 1999; Maccoby, 1992). In Vygotsky's theory, teachers and parents provide children with problem-solving methods that serve as cognitive scaffolding while the child gains the ability to function independently. A child's instructors may offer advice on sounding out letters and words that provides a temporary support until reading "clicks" and the child no longer needs the device. Children may be offered scaffolding that enables them to use their fingers or their toes to do simple calculations. Eventually, the scaffolding is removed and the cognitive structures stand alone.

A Puerto Rican study found that students also use scaffolding when they are explaining to one another how they can improve school projects, such as essay assignments (De Guerrero & Villamil, 2000). Children at first even view the value of education in terms of their parents' verbalizations about school success (Bigelow, 2001). Vygotsky's theory points out that children's attitudes toward schooling are embedded within the parent–child relationship.

The concepts of scaffolding and the zone of proximal development are illustrated in a study in which 3- and 5-year-old children were given the task of sorting doll furniture into the rooms in which they belonged (Freund, 1990). Children who were allowed to interact with their mothers performed at a higher level than children who

■ **Lev Semenovich Vygotsky** The Russian psychologist is said to have possessed the genius of a Mozart but to have lived in a time and place that was deaf to genius. In his youth he was interested in literature and philosophy. He enrolled in medical school at Moscow University, switched to law school, then returned to literature, and later became interested in psychology. After Vygotsky's death from tuberculosis in 1934, the Soviet Union repudiated his ideas, but they have since been revived. Vygotsky is known for showing how social speech becomes inner speech and how "scaffolding" by others assists children to develop the cognitive skills to succeed.

Zone of proximal development (ZPD) Vygotsky's term for the situation in which a child carries out tasks with the help of someone who is more skilled, frequently an adult who represents the culture in which the child develops.

Scaffolding Vygotsky's term for temporary cognitive structures or methods of solving problems that help the child as he or she learns to function independently.

worked alone. Furthermore, mothers adjusted the amount of help they gave to fit the child's level of competence. They gave younger children more detailed, concrete suggestions than they gave older children. When the experimenters made the task more difficult, mothers gave more help to children of both ages.

In another study, K. Alison Clarke-Stewart and Robert Beck (1999) had 31 children who were 5 years old observe a videotaped film segment with their mother, talk about it with her, and then retell the story to an experimenter. They found that the quality of the stories, as retold by the children, was related to the scaffolding strategies the mothers used. Children whose mothers focused the children's attention on the tape, who asked their children to talk about it, and discussed the feelings of the characters told better stories than children whose mothers did not use such scaffolding strategies and children in a control group who did not discuss the story at all. Children's understanding of the characters' emotional states was most strongly connected with the number of questions the mother asked and her correction of the child's misunderstandings of what he or she saw.

In a longitudinal study, Catherine Haden and her colleagues (2001) observed 21 mother–child dyads (pairs) as they engaged in specially constructed tasks when the children were 30, 36, and 42 months of age. They analyzed the children's recall of their performance 1 and 3 days afterward at all three ages.[1] It turned out that the children best recalled those aspects of the tasks they had both worked on and discussed with their mothers. Recall under these circumstances exceeded that when the activities were (1) handled jointly but talked about only by the mother or (2) handled jointly but not discussed at all.

Piaget's focus was largely maturational. It was assumed that maturation of the brain allowed the child to experience new levels of insights and suddenly develop new kinds of problem solving. Vygotsky focused on the processes in the teacher–learner relationship. To Vygotsky, cognitive development was about culture and social interaction. Let us now turn to another aspect of cognitive development—the ways in which children (and adults) arrive at judgments as to what is right and what is wrong.

LAWRENCE KOHLBERG'S THEORY OF MORAL DEVELOPMENT Question: How do children reason about right and wrong? Cognitive–developmental theorist Lawrence Kohlberg (1981) used the following tale in his research into children's moral reasoning. Before going on, why not read the tale yourself?

> In Europe a woman was near death from a special kind of cancer. There was one drug that the doctors thought might save her. It was a form of radium that a druggist in the same town had recently discovered. The drug was expensive to make, but the druggist was charging ten times what the drug cost him to make. He paid $200 for the radium and charged $2,000 for a small dose of the drug. The sick woman's husband, Heinz, went to everyone he knew to borrow the money, but he could only get together about $1,000, which was half of what it cost. He told the druggist that his wife was dying and asked him to sell it cheaper or let him pay later. But the druggist said: "No, I discovered the drug, and I'm going to make money from it." So Heinz got desperate and broke into the man's store to steal the drug for his wife. (Kohlberg, 1969)

Heinz is caught in a moral dilemma. In such dilemmas, a legal or social rule (in this case, the law forbidding stealing) is pitted against a strong human need (his desire to save his wife). Children and adults arrive at yes or no answers for different reasons. According to Kohlberg, the reasons can be classified according to the level of moral development they reflect.

As a stage theorist, Kohlberg argues that the stages of moral reasoning follow a specific sequence (see the Concept Review of Kohlberg's Levels and Stages of Moral Development). Children progress at different rates, and not all children (or adults)

---

[1] Hey, *dyad* is a technical term. Deal with it.

In Profile   LAWRENCE KOHLBERG

His car was found parked beside Boston Harbor. Three months later his body washed up onto the shore. He had discussed the moral dilemma posed by suicide with a friend, and perhaps Lawrence Kohlberg (1927–1987) had taken his own life. He was suffering from a painful parasitic intestinal disease that he had acquired 40 years earlier when he was imprisoned for smuggling Jewish refugees from Europe past the British blockade into Israel. There had also been recent disappointments in his work.

Kohlberg was born into a wealthy family in suburban New York. He graduated from Phillips Academy as World War II came to an end. Rather than go on immediately to college, he became a merchant mariner and helped save people who had been displaced by the war. Between high school and college, Kohlberg had already decided that one must attend more to one's own conscience than to law and authority figures in determining what was right and wrong.

 Go to **http://psychology.wadsworth.com/ rathus_pcc9e** to access more information about Lawrence Kohlberg.

Harvard University Archives

reach the highest stage. But the sequence is always the same: Children must go through stage 1 before they enter stage 2, and so on. According to Kohlberg, there are three levels of moral development and two stages within each level.

When it comes to the dilemma of Heinz, Kohlberg believed that people could justify Heinz's stealing of the drug or his decision not to steal it by the reasoning of any level or stage of moral development. In other words, Kohlberg was not as interested in the eventual "yes" or "no" as he was in *how a person reasoned* to arrive at yes or no.

The Preconventional Level The **preconventional level** applies to most children through about the age of 9. Children at this level base their moral judgments on the consequences of behavior. For instance, stage 1 is oriented toward obedience

Preconventional level According to Kohlberg, a period during which moral judgments are based largely on expectation of rewards or punishments.

Concept Review   KOHLBERG'S LEVELS AND STAGES OF MORAL DEVELOPMENT

	Stage of Development	Examples of Moral Reasoning That Support Heinz's Stealing the Drug	Examples of Moral Reasoning That Oppose Heinz's Stealing the Drug
Level I: Preconventional	STAGE 1: Judgments guided by obedience and the prospect of punishment (the consequences of the behavior)	It isn't wrong to take the drug. Heinz did try to pay the druggist for it, and it's only worth $200, not $2,000.	Taking things without paying is wrong because it's against the law. Heinz will get caught and go to jail.
	STAGE 2: Naively egoistic, instrumental orientation (things are right when they satisfy people's needs)	Heinz ought to take the drug because his wife really needs it. He can always pay the druggist back.	Heinz shouldn't take the drug. If he gets caught and winds up in jail, it won't do his wife any good.
Level II: Conventional	STAGE 3: Good-boy orientation (moral behavior helps others and is socially approved)	Stealing is a crime, so it's bad, but Heinz should take the drug to save his wife or else people would blame him for letting her die.	Stealing is a crime. Heinz shouldn't just take the drug, because his family will be dishonored and they will blame him.
	STAGE 4: Law-and-order orientation (moral behavior is doing one's duty and showing respect for authority)	Heinz must take the drug to do his duty to save his wife. Eventually, he has to pay the druggist for it, however.	If everyone took the law into his or her own hands, civilization would fall apart, so Heinz shouldn't steal the drug.
Level III: Postconventional	STAGE 5: Contractual, legalistic orientation (one must weigh pressing human needs against society's need to maintain social order)	This thing is complicated because society has a right to maintain law and order, but Heinz has to take the drug to save his wife.	I can see why Heinz feels he has to take the drug, but laws exist for the benefit of society as a whole and can't simply be cast aside.
	STAGE 6: Universal ethical principles orientation (people must follow universal ethical principles and their own conscience, even if it means breaking the law)	In this case, the law comes into conflict with the principle of the sanctity of human life. Heinz must take the drug because his wife's life is more important than the law.	If Heinz truly believes that stealing the drug is worse than letting his wife die, he should not take it. People have to make sacrifices to do what they think is right.

Go to **http://psychology.wadsworth.com/ rathus_pcc9e** to access a drag-and-drop version of this Concept Review designed to help you test yourself on the major topics provided here.

and punishment. Good behavior is obedient and allows one to avoid punishment. However, a child in stage 1 can decide that Heinz should or should not steal the drug.

In stage 2, good behavior allows people to satisfy their needs and those of others. (Heinz's wife needs the drug; therefore, stealing the drug—the only way of obtaining it—is not wrong.)

The Conventional Level In the **conventional level** of moral reasoning, right and wrong are judged by conformity to conventional (familial, religious, societal) standards of right and wrong. According to the stage 3, "good-boy orientation," moral behavior is that which meets the needs and expectations of others. Moral behavior is what is "normal"—what the majority does. (Heinz should steal the drug because that is what a "good husband" would do. It is "natural" or "normal" to try to help one's wife. *Or,* Heinz should *not* steal the drug because "good people do not steal.")

In stage 4, moral judgments are based on rules that maintain the social order. Showing respect for authority and doing one's duty are valued highly. (Heinz *must* steal the drug; it would be his fault if he let his wife die. He would pay the druggist later, when he had the money.) Many people do not mature beyond the conventional level.

The Postconventional Level Postconventional moral reasoning is more complex and focuses on dilemmas in which individual needs are pitted against the need to maintain the social order and on personal conscience. We discuss the postconventional level in the section on adolescence.

EVALUATION OF KOHLBERG'S THEORY Consistent with Kohlberg's theory, research suggests that moral reasoning does follow a developmental sequence (Dawson, 2002), even though most people do not reach the level of postconventional thought. Postconventional thought, when found, first occurs during adolescence. It also seems that Piaget's stage of formal operations is a prerequisite for postconventional reasoning, which requires the capacities to understand abstract moral principles and to empathize with the attitudes and emotional responses of other people (Flavell et al., 2002).

Also consistent with Kohlberg's theory, children do not appear to skip stages as they progress (Flavell et al., 2002). Classic research shows that when children are exposed to adult models who exhibit a lower stage of moral reasoning, they can be enticed to follow along (Bandura & McDonald, 1963). Children who are exposed to examples of moral reasoning above and below their own stage generally prefer the higher stage, however (Rest, 1983). The thrust of moral development would therefore appear to be from lower to higher in terms of Kohlberg's levels and stages, even if children can be influenced by the opinions of others.

Social and Emotional Development

Social relationships are crucial to us as children. When we are infants, our very survival depends on them. Later in life, they contribute to our feelings of happiness and satisfaction. In this section we discuss many aspects of social development, including Erikson's theory of psychosocial development, attachment, styles of parenting, and child abuse.

ERIK ERIKSON'S STAGES OF PSYCHOSOCIAL DEVELOPMENT According to Erik Erikson, we undergo several stages of psychosocial development (see the Concept Review on Erikson's stages). **Question: What are Erikson's stages of psychosocial development?** During Erikson's first stage, **trust versus mistrust,** we depend on our primary caregivers (usually our parents) and come to expect that our environments will—or will not—meet our needs. During early childhood and the preschool years, we begin to explore the environment more actively and try new things. At this time, our relationships with our parents and friends can encourage us to develop **autonomy** (self-direction) and initiative, or feelings of shame and guilt. During

Conventional level According to Kohlberg, a period during which moral judgments largely reflect social conventions. A "law and order" approach to morality.

Trust versus mistrust Erikson's first stage of psychosexual development, during which children do—or do not—come to trust that primary caregivers and the environment will meet their needs.

Autonomy Self-direction.

Concept Review ERIKSON'S STAGES OF PSYCHOSOCIAL DEVELOPMENT

Time Period	Life Crisis	The Developmental Task
Infancy (0–1)	Trust versus mistrust	Coming to trust the mother and the environment–to associate surroundings with feelings of inner goodness
Early childhood (1–3)	Autonomy versus shame and doubt	Developing the wish to make choices and the self-control to exercise choice
Preschool years (4–5)	Initiative versus guilt	Adding planning and "attacking" to choice, becoming active and on the move
Elementary school years (6–12)	Industry versus inferiority	Becoming eagerly absorbed in skills, tasks, and productivity; mastering the fundamentals of technology
Adolescence	Identity versus role diffusion	Connecting skills and social roles to formation of career objectives; developing a sense of who one is and what one stands for
Young adulthood	Intimacy versus isolation	Committing the self to another; engaging in sexual love
Middle adulthood	Generativity versus stagnation	Needing to be needed; guiding and encouraging the younger generation; being creative
Late adulthood	Integrity versus despair	Accepting the time and place of one's life cycle; achieving wisdom and dignity

Go to **http://psychology.wadsworth.com/ rathus_pcc9e** to access a drag-and-drop version of this Concept Review designed to help you test yourself on the major topics provided here.

the elementary school years, friends and teachers take on more importance, encouraging us to become industrious or to develop feelings of inferiority. We will see that Erikson's theory includes eight stages that straddle the life span.

Attachment: Ties That Bind

At the age of 2, my daughter Allyn almost succeeded in preventing me from finishing a book. When I locked myself into my study, she positioned herself outside the door and called, "Daddy, oh Daddy." At other times, she would bang on the door or cry outside. When I would give in (several times a day) and open the door, she would run in and say, "I want you to pick up me" and hold out her arms or climb into my lap. Although we were separate human beings, it was as though she were very much *attached* to me. **Questions: How do feelings of attachment develop? What kinds of experiences affect attachment?**

Psychologist Mary D. Salter Ainsworth (1913–1999) defined **attachment** as an emotional tie that is formed between one animal or person and another specific individual. Attachment keeps organisms together—it is vital to the survival of the infant—and it tends to endure. The behaviors that define attachment include (1) attempts to maintain contact or nearness and (2) shows of anxiety when separated. Babies and children try to maintain contact with caregivers to whom they are attached. They engage in eye contact, pull and tug at them, ask to be picked up, and may even jump in front of them in such a way that they will be "run over" if they are not picked up!

THE STRANGE SITUATION AND PATTERNS OF ATTACHMENT The ways in which infants behave in strange situations are connected with their bonds of attachment with their caregivers. Given this fact, Ainsworth and her colleagues (1978) innovated the *strange situation method* to learn how infants respond to separations and reunions with a caregiver (usually the mother) and a stranger. Using this method, Ainsworth and her colleagues (1978) identified three major types of attachment, secure attachment and two types of insecure attachment:

1. *Secure attachment.* Securely attached infants mildly protest their mother's departure, seek interaction upon reunion, and are readily comforted by her.

Attachment The enduring affectional tie that binds one person to another.

■ **Mary D. Salter Ainsworth** Ainsworth's cross-cultural studies and her innovation of the strange situation method have made her a key figure in the development of theories of the formation of bonds of attachment between children and their caregivers.

Indiscriminate attachment Showing attachment behaviors toward any person.

Initial-preattachment phase The first phase in forming bonds of attachment, characterized by indiscriminate attachment.

Attachment-in-the-making phase The second phase in forming bonds of attachment, characterized by preference for familiar figures.

Clear-cut-attachment phase The third phase in forming bonds of attachment, characterized by intensified dependence on the primary caregiver.

2. *Avoidant attachment.* Infants who show avoidant attachment are least distressed by their mother's departure. They play by themselves without fuss and ignore their mothers when they return.

3. *Ambivalent/resistant attachment.* Infants with ambivalent/resistant attachment are the most emotional. They show severe signs of distress when their mother leaves and show ambivalence upon reunion by alternately clinging to and pushing their mother away when she returns.

Attachment is connected with the quality of care that infants receive. The parents of securely attached children are more likely to be affectionate and reliable caregivers (Isabella, 1998; Posada et al., 2002). A wealth of research literature speaks of the benefits of secure attachment. For example, securely attached children are happier, more sociable, and more cooperative than insecurely attached children (Bohlin et al., 2000). Securely attached preschoolers have longer attention spans, are less impulsive, and are better at solving problems (Frankel & Bates, 1990). At ages 5 and 6, securely attached children are liked better by their peers and teachers, are more competent, and have fewer behavior problems than insecurely attached children (Granot & Mayseless, 2001; Moss & St-Laurent, 2001). In this vein, we can also note that having the primary caregiver present during stressful situations, such as pediatric exams, helps children cope with these situations (Ybarra et al., 2000).

STAGES OF ATTACHMENT Ainsworth also studied phases in the development of attachment. She and her colleagues observed infants in many societies, including the African country of Uganda. She noted the efforts of infants to maintain contact with the mother, their protests when separated from her, and their use of her as a base for exploring their environment. At first, infants show **indiscriminate attachment.** That is, they prefer being held or being with someone to being alone, but they show no preferences for particular people. Specific attachment to the primary caregiver begins to develop at about 4 months of age and becomes intense by about 7 months of age. Fear of strangers, which develops in some but not all children, follows 1 or 2 months later.

From studies such as these, Ainsworth identified three stages of attachment:

1. The **initial-preattachment phase,** which lasts from birth to about 3 months and is characterized by indiscriminate attachment.

2. The **attachment-in-the-making phase,** which occurs at about 3 or 4 months and is characterized by preference for familiar figures.

3. The **clear-cut-attachment phase,** which occurs at about 6 or 7 months and is characterized by intensified dependence on the primary caregiver.

John Bowlby (1988), a colleague of Mary Ainsworth, believed that attachment is also characterized by fear of strangers ("stranger anxiety"). That is, at about 8 to 10 months of age, children may cry and cling to their parents when strangers try to befriend them. But not all children develop fear of strangers. It therefore does not seem necessary to include fear of strangers as an essential part of the process of attachment.

THEORETICAL VIEWS OF ATTACHMENT Early in the 20th century, behaviorists argued that attachment behaviors are learned through experience. Caregivers feed their infants and tend to their other physiological needs. Thus, infants associate their caregivers with gratification of needs and learn to approach them to meet their needs. The feelings of gratification associated with the meeting of basic needs generalize into feelings of security when the caregiver is present.

Classic research by psychologist Harry F. Harlow suggests that skin contact may be more important than learning experiences. Harlow noted that infant rhesus monkeys reared without mothers or companions became attached to pieces of cloth in their cages. They maintained contact with them and showed distress when separated from them. Harlow conducted a series of experiments to find out why (Harlow, 1959).

In one study, Harlow placed infant rhesus monkeys in cages with two surrogate mothers, as shown in Figure 3.6. One "mother" was made of wire mesh from which a baby bottle was extended. The other surrogate mother was made of soft, cuddly terry cloth. The infant monkeys spent most of their time clinging to the cloth mother, even though "she" did not gratify their need for food. Harlow concluded that monkeys—and perhaps humans—have an inborn need for **contact comfort** that is as basic as the need for food. Gratification of the need for contact comfort, rather than food, might be why infant monkeys (and humans) cling to their mothers.

Harlow and Zimmerman (1959) found that a surrogate mother made of terry cloth could also serve as a comforting base from which an infant monkey could explore its environment (Figure 3.7). Toys such as stuffed bears and oversized wooden insects were placed in cages with infant rhesus monkeys and their surrogate mothers. When the infants were alone or had wire surrogate mothers for companions, they cowered in fear as long as the "bear monster" or "insect monster" was present. But when the terry cloth mothers were present, the infants clung to them for a while and then explored the intruding "monster." With human infants, too, the bonds of mother–infant attachment appear to provide a secure base from which infants feel encouraged to express their curiosity.

Other researchers, such as **ethologist** Konrad Lorenz, note that for many animals, attachment is an instinct—inborn. (Ethologists study the behavioral characteristics of various species of animals.) Attachment, like other instincts, is theorized to occur in the presence of a specific stimulus and during a **critical period** of life—that is, a period during which the animal is sensitive to the stimulus.

Some animals become attached to the first moving object they encounter. The unwritten rule seems to be, "If it moves, it must be Mother." It is as if the image of the moving object becomes "imprinted" on the young animal. The formation of an attachment in this manner is therefore called **imprinting.**

Lorenz (1981) became well known when pictures of his "family" of goslings were made public (Figure 3.8). How did Lorenz acquire his following? He was present when the goslings hatched and during their critical period, and he allowed

Contact comfort A hypothesized primary drive to seek physical comfort through contact with another.

Ethologist A scientist who studies the characteristic behavior patterns of species of animals.

Critical period A period of time when an instinctive response can be elicited by a particular stimulus.

Imprinting A process occurring during a critical period in the development of an organism, in which that organism responds to a stimulus in a manner that will afterward be difficult to modify.

Martin Rogers/Stock Boston

Martin Rogers/Woodfin Camp & Associates

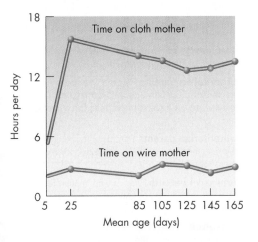

FIGURE 3.6 **Attachment in Infant Monkeys**
Although this rhesus monkey infant is fed by the wire "mother," it spends most of its time clinging to the soft, cuddly, terry cloth "mother." It knows where to get a meal, but contact comfort is apparently more important than food in the development of attachment in infant monkeys (and infant humans?).

FIGURE 3.7 Security

With its terry cloth surrogate mother nearby, this infant rhesus monkey apparently feels secure enough to explore the "bear monster" placed in its cage. But infants with wire surrogate mothers or no mothers at all cower in a corner when such "monsters" are introduced.

them to follow him. The critical period for geese and some other animals is bounded, at the younger end, by the age at which they first walk and, at the older end, by the age at which they develop fear of strangers. The goslings followed Lorenz persistently, ran to him when they were frightened, honked with distress at his departure, and tried to overcome barriers between them. If you substitute crying for honking, it all sounds rather human.

Ainsworth and Bowlby (1991) consider attachment to be instinctive in humans. However, among humans attachment is less related to issues such as locomotion and fear of strangers (which is not experienced by all humans). Moreover, the critical period with humans would be quite extended.

Another issue in social and emotional development is parenting styles. Parental behavior not only contributes to the development of attachment, but also to the development of self-esteem, self-reliance, achievement motivation, and competence.

Parenting Styles: Strictly Speaking?

Many psychologists have been concerned about the relationships between parenting styles and the personality development of the child. **Question: What types of parental behavior are connected with variables such as self-esteem, achievement motivation, and independence in children?** Diana Baumrind (1973) and her colleagues (Lamb & Baumrind, 1978) have been particularly interested in the connections between parental behavior and the development of **instrumental competence** in their children. (*Instrumental competence* refers to the ability to manipulate the environment to achieve one's goals.) Baumrind has largely focused on four aspects of parental behavior: (1) strictness; (2) demands for the child to achieve intellectual, emotional, and social maturity; (3) communication ability; and (4) warmth and involvement. She labeled the three most important parenting styles the *authoritative, authoritarian,* and *permissive* styles. Other researchers have identified and studied the *uninvolved* style. The four parenting styles are:

1. *Authoritative parents.* The parents of the most competent children rate high in all four areas of behavior (see Table 3.2). They are strict (restrictive) and demand mature behavior. However, they temper their strictness and demands with willingness to reason with their children and with love and support. They expect a lot, but they explain why and offer help. Baumrind labeled these parents **authoritative parents** to suggest that they know what they want but are also loving and respectful of their children.

2. *Authoritarian parents.* **Authoritarian parents** view obedience as a virtue to be pursued for its own sake. They have strict guidelines about what is right and wrong, and they demand that their children adhere to those guidelines. Both authoritative and authoritarian parents adhere to strict standards of conduct. However, authoritative parents explain their demands and are supportive, whereas authoritarian parents rely on force and communicate poorly with their children. Authoritarian parents do not respect their children's points of view, and they may be cold and rejecting. When their children ask them why they should behave in a certain way, authoritarian parents often answer, "Because I say so!"

3. *Permissive parents.* **Permissive parents** are generally easygoing with their children. As a result, the children do pretty much whatever they wish. Permissive parents are warm and supportive, but poor at communicating.

4. *Uninvolved parents.* **Uninvolved parents** tend to leave their children on their own. They make few demands and show little warmth or encouragement.

Research evidence shows that the children of warm parents are more likely to be socially and emotionally well-adjusted. They are also more likely to internalize moral standards—that is, to develop a conscience (MacDonald, 1992; Miller et al., 1993).

Instrumental competence Ability to manipulate one's environment to achieve one's goals.

Authoritative parents Parents who are strict and warm. Authoritative parents demand mature behavior but use reason rather than force in discipline.

Authoritarian parents Parents who are rigid in their rules and who demand obedience for the sake of obedience.

Permissive parents Parents who impose few, if any, rules and who do not supervise their children closely.

Uninvolved parents Parents who generally leave their children to themselves.

TABLE 3.2 PARENTING STYLES

Style of Parenting	Restrictiveness	Demands for Mature Behavior	Communication Ability	Warmth and Support
Authoritative	High (use of reasoning)	High	High	High
Authoritarian	High (use of force)	Moderate	Low	Low
Permissive	Low (easygoing)	Low	Low	High
Uninvolved	Low (uninvolved)	Low	Low	Low

Note: Research suggests that the children of authoritative parents develop as the most competent.

© Thomas McAvoy/Time Life Pictures/Getty Images

FIGURE 3.8 Imprinting

Quite a following? Konrad Lorenz may not look like Mommy to you, but these goslings became attached to him because he was the first moving object they perceived and followed. This type of attachment process is referred to as *imprinting.* Imprinting among goslings is an instinctive pattern of behavior that is triggered by a specific stimulus (a moving object) and which occurs during a critical period of development.

Strictness seems to pay off, provided it is tempered with reason and warmth. Children of authori*tative* parents have greater self-reliance, self-esteem, social competence, and achievement motivation than other children (Baumrind, 1991a, 1991b; Kim & Rohner, 2002). Children of authori*tarian* parents are often withdrawn or aggressive and usually do not do as well in school as children of authoritative parents (Kim & Rohner, 2002; Steinberg, 2001). Children of permissive parents seem to be the least mature. They are often impulsive, moody, and aggressive. In adolescence, lack of parental monitoring is often linked to delinquency and poor academic performance. Children of uninvolved parents tend to obtain poorer grades than children whose parents make demands on them (Ginsburg & Bronstein, 1993). The children of uninvolved parents also tend to be more likely to "hang out" with crowds who "party" a good deal and use drugs (Durbin et al., 1993). The message? Simple enough: Children appear to profit when their parents make reasonable demands, show warmth and encouragement, and spend time with them.

Child Abuse: Broken Bonds

The incidence of child abuse is underreported, but it is estimated that nearly 3 million children in the United States are neglected or abused by parents or other caregivers each year (Herman-Giddens et al., 1999). Sadly, more than half a million suffer serious injuries; thousands die.

Many factors contribute to child abuse: stress, a history of child abuse in at least one of the parents' families of origin, acceptance of violence as a way of coping with stress, failure to become attached to the children, substance abuse, and rigid attitudes toward child rearing (Belsky, 1993; Burgess & Drais, 2001). Unemployment and low socioeconomic status are common stressors that lead to abuse (Lewin, 1995).

Children who are abused are quite likely to develop personal and social problems and psychological disorders. They are less likely than other children to venture out to explore the world (Aber & Allen, 1987). They are more likely to have psychological problems such as anxiety, depression, and low self-esteem (Wagner, 1997). They are less likely to be intimate with their peers and more likely to be aggressive (Benda & Corwyn, 2002; Parker & Herrera, 1996; Rothbart & Ahadi, 1994). As adults, they are more likely to be violent toward their dates and spouses (Benda & Corwyn, 2002).

Many children are also victims of sexual abuse. The effects of child sexual abuse are variable, and it does not appear that there is a single, identifiable syndrome that results from such abuse (Saywitz et al., 2000). Nevertheless, the research literature shows that sexually abused children are more likely to develop physical and psychological health problems than unabused children (Saywitz et al., 2000). Child sexual abuse can also have lasting effects on children's relationships once they become adults.

A Closer Look | HOW CHILD ABUSE MAY SET THE STAGE FOR PSYCHOLOGICAL DISORDERS IN ADULTHOOD

One way in which child abuse may set the stage for psychological disorders in adulthood is by increasing people's bodily responses to stress. Responses to stress are typically measured in terms of the reactivity of the endocrine system (particularly stress hormones such as ACTH and cortisol) and the autonomic nervous system (e.g., heart rate). A study by Christine Heim and her colleagues (2000, 2002) recruited 49 generally healthy women with an average age of 35. Twenty-seven of the women reported childhood physical and/or sexual abuse in interviews; 22 did not. Twenty-three of the women were currently diagnosed with major depression; 26 were not. All 49 women were exposed to a stressor that has been shown to induce endocrine and autonomic reactions in a number of studies: The women anticipated and presented a public speech that included some mental arithmetic. Meanwhile, their levels of stress hormones and heart rates were being assessed. As shown in Table 3.3, the presence of depression alone did not distinguish women who were depressed (group B) from women who were not (group A). However, women who reported a history of child abuse (groups C and D) were significantly more likely to show higher blood levels of ACTH and cortisol in response to the stressor than women who did not report a history of child abuse (groups A and B). Group D, consisting of women who reported a history of abuse and who were also diagnosed with

TABLE 3.3	RESPONSES OF WOMEN WITH OR WITHOUT A HISTORY OF CHILD ABUSE TO A STRESSOR	
	Women Who Are Not Experiencing a Major Depressive Episode	**Women Who Are Experiencing a Major Depressive Episode**
Women with No History of Child Abuse	**Group A (12 Women):** *Endocrine System:* ACTH peak: 4.7 parts/liter Cortisol peak: 339 parts/liter *Autonomic Nervous System:* Heart rate: 78.4/minute	**Group B (10 Women):** *Endocrine System:* ACTH peak: 5.3 parts/liter Cortisol peak: 337 parts/liter *Autonomic Nervous System:* Heart rate: 83.8/minute
Women with a History of Child Abuse	**Group C (14 Women):** *Endocrine System:* ACTH peak: 9.3 parts/liter Cortisol peak: 359 parts/liter *Autonomic Nervous System:* Heart rate: 82.2/minute	**Group D (13 Women):** *Endocrine System:* ACTH peak: 12.1 parts/liter Cortisol peak: 527 parts/liter *Autonomic Nervous System:* Heart rate: 89.7/minute

Source of data: Heim, C., et al. (2000). Pituitary-adrenal and autonomic responses to stress in women after sexual and physical abuse in childhood. *Journal of the American Medical Association, 284,* 592–597.

major depression, showed significantly higher levels of stress hormones and heart rate than all other groups. Therefore, the combination of early abuse and current depression apparently makes the body most sensitive to stress. But even among women who were not depressed, the history of abuse was connected with greater reactivity of the endocrine system and autonomic nervous system.

The Heim study has its shortcomings: For example, it categorized women according to self-reported history of child abuse.

Not all women in the study could provide independent confirmation of abuse, such as court records. Also, it is unclear how well the stressor used in the experiment represents the types of stress people are actually exposed to in their lives. Nevertheless, the experiment suggests that child abuse may well affect bodily reactivity to stress that endures well into adulthood, and further research along these lines is certainly warranted.

Research in the United States (Newcomb & Locke, 2001; Pears & Capaldi, 2001) and Mexico (Frias-Armenta, 2002) reveals that child abuse runs in families to some degree. **Truth or Fiction Revisited:** It is true that child abusers were frequently abused themselves as children. That is, child abusers are more likely to have been abused than the general population. Even so, *most children who are abused do* not *abuse their own children as adults* (Kaufman & Zigler, 1989).

When abuse does run in families, why does it do so? There are several hypotheses. One is the generalization that child abuse is part of a poor parenting environment, and that children reared in such an environment are less likely to have resources later on that contribute to a better parenting environment (Frias-Armenta, 2002; Pears & Capaldi, 2001). Another is that parents serve as role models. According to sociologist Murray Straus (1995), "Spanking teaches kids that when someone is doing something you don't like and they won't stop doing it, you hit them." A third is that children adopt parents' strict philosophies about discipline. Exposure to violence in their own home leads some children to view abuse as normal. A fourth is that being abused can create feelings of hostility that are then expressed against others, including one's own children.

Your Turn: Now that we have discussed childhood, enhance your mastery of the material with the nearby "Learning Connections." Review the material by filling in the blanks, reflect on the material by relating it to other things you know, and think critically about it.

Learning Connections — CHILDHOOD

ACTIVE REVIEW (5) Infants double their birth weight in about *(How many?)* _____ months and triple it by the first birthday. (6) Piaget saw intelligence as including _____ (responding to events according to existing schemas) and accommodation. (7) Object permanence develops during the _____ period of cognitive development. (8) The _____-operational period is characterized by conservation and reversibility. (9) Vygotsky used the concepts of scaffolding and the _____ of proximal development to explain cognitive development. (10) Kohlberg hypothesizes that moral reasoning develops through *(How many?)* _____ "levels" and two stages within each level. (11) Erikson presents a theory of _____ development. (12) Ainsworth identified three stages of attachment: The _____ phase, which is characterized by indiscriminate attachment, the attachment-in-the-making phase, and the clear-cut-attachment phase. (13) The Harlow studies with monkeys suggest that _____ comfort is more important than conditioning in the development of attachment. (14) Ethologists argue that attachment is a(n)_____ that occurs during a critical period. (15) Baumrind labeled the three most important parenting styles _____, authoritarian, and permissive.

REFLECT AND RELATE How closely did your parents pay attention to your height and weight? Did they chart it? How did your physical development affect your self-esteem?

Remember the experiment with the child and the water reported on page 101? After you have tried that experiment, try a mini-experiment in the conservation of number. Make two rows of five pennies each. In the first row, place the pennies about half an inch apart. In the second row, place the pennies 2 to 3 inches apart. Ask a 4- to 5-year-old child which row has more pennies. What do you think the child will say? Why?

CRITICAL THINKING Which aspects of child development provide evidence for the concept of stages of development? How does the study by Christine Heim and her colleagues illustrate the ongoing interaction of nature and nurture? Go to **http://psychology.wadsworth.com/ rathus_pcc9e** for an interactive version of this Learning Connections unit.

Adolescence

Perhaps no other period of life is as exciting—and as bewildering—as adolescence. Except for infancy, more changes occur during adolescence than during any other time of life.

In our society, adolescents are "neither fish nor fowl," as the saying goes—neither children nor adults. Adolescents may be old enough to reproduce and are as large as their parents, yet they are required to remain in school through age 16, they may not be allowed to get drivers' licenses until they are 16 or 17, and they cannot attend R-rated films unless accompanied by an adult. Given the restrictions placed on adolescents, their growing yearning for independence, and a sex drive heightened by high levels of sex hormones, it is not surprising that adolescents occasionally are in conflict with their parents.

This section further chronicles human development with the changes of adolescence. **Adolescence** is a time of transition from childhood to adulthood. Like childhood, adolescence entails physical, cognitive, social, and emotional changes. Let us begin with physical changes.

Physical Development: Fanning the Flames

Following infancy, children grow about 2 to 3 inches a year. Weight gains also remain fairly even at about 4 to 6 pounds per year. **Question: What physical developments occur during adolescence?** One of the most noticeable physical developments of adolescence is a growth spurt. The adolescent growth spurt lasts for 2 to 3 years and ends the stable patterns of growth in height and weight that characterize most

Adolescence The period of life bounded by puberty and the assumption of adult responsibilities.

© 2002 Tony Anderson/Getty Images/FPG

■ **Adolescents** In our culture adolescents are "neither fish nor fowl." Although they may be old enough to reproduce and may be as large as their parents, they are often treated like children.

Puberty The period of physical development during which sexual reproduction first becomes possible.

Secondary sex characteristics Characteristics that distinguish the sexes, such as distribution of body hair and depth of voice, but that are not directly involved in reproduction.

Menarche The beginning of menstruation.

of childhood. Within this short span of years, adolescents grow some 8 to 12 inches. Most boys wind up taller and heavier than most girls.

In boys, the weight of the muscle mass increases notably. The width of the shoulders and circumference of the chest also increase. Adolescents may eat enormous quantities of food to fuel their growth spurt. Adults fighting the "battle of the bulge" stare at them in wonder as they wolf down french fries and shakes at the fast-food counter and later go out for pizza.

PUBERTY: MORE THAN "JUST A PHASE"? **Puberty** is the period during which the body becomes sexually mature. It heralds the onset of adolescence. Puberty begins with the appearance of **secondary sex characteristics** such as body hair, deepening of the voice in males, and rounding of the breasts and hips in females. In boys, pituitary hormones stimulate the testes to increase the output of testosterone, which in turn causes enlargement of the penis and testes and the appearance of body hair. By the early teens, erections become common, and boys may ejaculate. Ejaculatory ability usually precedes the presence of mature sperm by at least a year. Ejaculation thus is not evidence of reproductive capacity.

In girls, a critical body weight in the neighborhood of 100 pounds is thought to trigger a cascade of hormonal secretions in the brain that cause the ovaries to secrete higher levels of the female sex hormone, estrogen (Frisch, 1997). Estrogen stimulates the growth of breast tissue and fatty and supportive tissue in the hips and buttocks. Thus the pelvis widens, rounding the hips. Small amounts of androgens produced by the adrenal glands, along with estrogen, spur the growth of pubic and underarm hair. Estrogen and androgens together stimulate the development of female sex organs. Estrogen production becomes cyclical during puberty and regulates the menstrual cycle. The beginning of menstruation, or **menarche,** usually occurs between the ages of 11 and 14. Girls cannot become pregnant until they begin to ovulate, however, and ovulation may begin as much as two years after menarche.

Cognitive Development: The Age of Reason?

I am a college student of extremely modest means. Some crazy psychologist interested in something called "formal operational thought" has just promised to pay me $20 if I can make a coherent logical argument for the proposition that the federal government should under no circumstances ever give or lend more to needy college students. Now what could people who believe *that* possibly say by way of supporting argument? Well, I suppose they *could* offer this line of reasoning . . . (Adapted from Flavell et al., 2002)

The adolescent thinker approaches problems very differently from the elementary school child. **Question: What cognitive developments occur during adolescence?** Let us begin to answer this question by comparing the child's thought processes to that of the adolescent. The child sticks to the facts, to concrete reality. Speculating about abstract possibilities and what might be is very difficult. The adolescent, on the other hand, is able to deal with the abstract and the hypothetical. As shown in the above example, adolescents realize that one does not have to believe in the truth or justice of something in order to argue for it (Flavell et al., 2002). In this section we explore some of the cognitive developments of adolescence by referring to the theories of Jean Piaget and Lawrence Kohlberg.

THE STAGE OF FORMAL OPERATIONS According to Piaget, children typically undergo three stages of cognitive development prior to adolescence: sensorimotor, preoperational, and concrete operational. They develop from infants who respond automatically to their environment to older children who can focus on various aspects of a situation at once and solve complex problems. The stage of **formal operations** is the final stage in Jean Piaget's theory of cognitive development, and it represents cognitive maturity. For many children in Western societies, formal operational thought begins at about the beginning of adolescence—the age of 11 or 12. However, not all individuals enter this stage at this time, and some individuals never reach it.

The major achievements of the stage of formal operations involve classification, logical thought, and the ability to hypothesize. Central features are the ability to think about ideas as well as objects and to group and classify ideas—symbols, statements, entire theories. The flexibility and reversibility of operations, when applied to statements and theories, allow adolescents to follow arguments from premises to conclusions and back again. Several features of formal operational thought give the adolescent a generally greater capacity to manipulate and appreciate the outer environment and the world of the imagination: hypothetical thinking, the ability to use symbols to stand for symbols, and deductive reasoning.

Formal-operational adolescents (and adults) think abstractly. They become capable of solving geometric problems about circles and squares without reference to what the circles and squares may represent in the real world. Adolescents in this stage derive rules for behavior from general principles and can focus, or center, on many aspects of a situation at once in arriving at judgments and solving problems.

In a sense, it is during the stage of formal operations that adolescents tend to emerge as theoretical scientists—even though they may see themselves as having little or no interest in science. They become capable of dealing with hypothetical situations. They realize that situations can have different outcomes, and they think ahead, experimenting with different possibilities. Adolescents also conduct experiments to determine whether their hypotheses are correct. These experiments are not conducted in the laboratory. Rather, adolescents may try out different tones of voice and ways of carrying themselves and of treating others to see what works best for them.

ADOLESCENT EGOCENTRISM: "YOU JUST DON'T UNDERSTAND!" Adolescents in the formal-operational stage can reason deductively, or draw conclusions about specific objects or people once they have been classified accurately. Adolescents can be somewhat proud of their new logical abilities, and so a new sort of egocentrism can develop in which adolescents emotionally press for acceptance of their logic without recognizing the exceptions or practical problems that are often considered by adults. Consider this example: "It is wrong to hurt people. Company A occasionally hurts people" (perhaps through pollution or economic pressures). "Therefore, Company A must be severely punished or shut down." This thinking is logical. By impatiently pressing for immediate major changes or severe penalties, however, one may not fully consider various practical problems such as the thousands of workers who would be laid off if the company were shut down. Adults frequently have undergone life experiences that lead them to see shades of gray in situations, rather than just black or white.

The thought of preschoolers is characterized by egocentrism in which they cannot take another's point of view. Adolescent thought is marked by another sort of egocentrism, in which they can understand the thoughts of others but still have trouble separating things that are of concern to others and those that are of concern only to themselves (Elkind, 1967, 1985). Adolescent egocentrism gives rise to two interesting cognitive developments: *the imaginary audience* and the *personal fable*.

The concept of the **imaginary audience** refers to the belief that other people are as concerned with our thoughts and behavior as we are. As a result, adolescents see themselves as the center of attention and assume that other people are about as preoccupied with their appearance and behavior as they are (Milstead et al., 1993). In fact, adolescents may feel they are on stage and all eyes are focused on them.

The concept of the imaginary audience may fuel the intense adolescent desire for privacy. It helps explain why adolescents are so self-conscious about their appearance, why they worry about every facial blemish and spend long hours

Formal-operational stage Piaget's fourth stage, characterized by abstract logical thought; deduction from principles.

Imaginary audience An aspect of adolescent egocentrism; the belief that other people are as concerned with our thoughts and behaviors as we are.

■ **Adolescent Self-Consciousness** The concept of the imaginary audience may help explain why adolescents are self-conscious about their appearance, why they worry about minor facial imperfections, and why they devote so much time to grooming.

grooming. Self-consciousness seems to peak at about the age of 13 and then decline. Furthermore, girls tend to be more self-conscious than boys (Elkind & Bowen, 1979).

The **personal fable** is the belief that our feelings and ideas are special, even unique, and that we are invulnerable. **Truth or Fiction Revisited:** It is true that many adolescents think they are invulnerable, like Superboy or Supergirl. The personal fable seems to underlie adolescent behavior patterns such as showing off and taking risks (Cohn et al., 1995; Milstead et al., 1993). Some adolescents adopt an "It can't happen to me" attitude; they assume they can smoke without risk of cancer or engage in sexual activity without risk of sexually transmitted infections (STIs) or pregnancy. "All youth—rich, poor, black, white—have this sense of invincibility, invulnerability," says Ronald King (2000) of the HIV Community Coalition of Washington, D.C., explaining why many teens who apparently know the risks still expose themselves to HIV. Another aspect of the personal fable is the idea that no one else has experienced or can understand one's "unique" feelings such as needing independence or being in love. The personal fable may underlie the common teenage lament, "You just don't understand me!"

THE POSTCONVENTIONAL LEVEL OF MORAL REASONING Kohlberg's theory of moral reasoning involves three levels: preconventional, conventional, and postconventional (see the Concept Review on page 105). Individuals can arrive at the same decision—for example, as to whether or not Heinz should save his wife by taking the drug without paying for it—but they would be doing so for a different kind of reason. (Deciding not to take the drug for fear of punishment is cognitively less complex than not taking the drug because of the belief that doing so could have negative consequences for the social order.)

None of Kohlberg's levels is tied precisely to a person's age. Although postconventional reasoning is the highest level, for example, most adolescents and adults reason conventionally. However, when postconventional reasoning does emerge, it usually does so in adolescence. Kohlberg's (1969) research showed that postconventional moral judgments were clearly absent among the 7- to 10-year-olds. But by age 16, stage 5 reasoning is shown by about 20% of adolescents, and stage 6 reasoning is shown by about 5% of adolescents.

At the **postconventional level,** moral reasoning is based on the person's own moral standards. In each instance, moral judgments are derived from personal values, not from conventional standards or authority figures. In the contractual, legalistic orientation characteristic of stage 5, it is recognized that laws stem from agreed-upon procedures and that the rule of law is in general good for society; therefore, laws should not be violated. But under exceptional circumstances laws cannot bind the individual. (Although it is illegal for Heinz to steal the drug, in this case it is the right thing to do.)

Stage 6 moral reasoning demands adherence to supposed universal ethical principles such as the sanctity of human life, individual dignity, justice, and the Golden Rule ("Do unto others as you would have them do unto you"). If a law is unjust or contradicts the rights of the individual, it is wrong to obey it.

Personal fable Another aspect of adolescent egocentrism; the belief that our feelings and ideas are special and unique and that we are invulnerable.

Postconventional level According to Kohlberg, a period during which moral judgments are derived from moral principles and people look to themselves to set moral standards.

People at the postconventional level look to their conscience as the highest moral authority. This point has created confusion. To some it suggests that it is right to break the law when it is convenient. But this interpretation is incorrect. Kohlberg means that people at this level of moral reasoning must do what they believe is right even if this action runs counter to social rules or laws or requires personal sacrifice.

CONTROVERSY IN PSYCHOLOGY

Are there gender differences in moral development?

A number of studies using Heinz's dilemma have found that boys show higher levels of moral reasoning than girls. But Carol Gilligan (1982; Gilligan et al., 1989) argues that this gender difference reflects different patterns of socialization for boys and girls—not differences in morality. Gilligan points to 11-year-old Jake. Jake weighs the scales of justice like a math problem. He shows that life is worth more than property and concludes that it is Heinz's duty to steal the drug (stage 4 reasoning). Gilligan also points to 11-year-old Amy. Amy vacillates. Amy says that stealing the drug and letting Heinz's wife die are both wrong. So Amy looks for alternatives, such as getting a loan, because it wouldn't help Heinz's wife if he went to jail.

Gilligan finds Amy's reasoning to be as sophisticated as Jake's, yet Amy would be rated as showing a lower level of moral development in Kohlberg's scheme. Gilligan asserts that Amy and other girls are socialized to focus on the needs of others and forgo simplistic judgments of right and wrong. Amy is therefore more likely to show stage 3 reasoning, which focuses in part on empathy—on caring for others. Jake has been socialized to make judgments based on logic. To him, clear-cut conclusions are derived from premises.

We could argue endlessly about which form of moral reasoning—Jake's or Amy's—is "higher." Instead, let us point to a meta-analysis of the research in the area that shows that there is only a slight tendency for boys to favor Jake's "justice" approach, and a slight tendency for girls to favor Amy's "caring" approach (Jaffee & Hyde, 2000). We cannot say that the justice orientation is used predominantly by boys or the care orientation predominantly by girls.

Cognitive development blossoms markedly during adolescence. Social and emotional development also tends to change dramatically, especially in societies in which much of adolescence is characterized by having to wait before becoming a full-fledged adult, as we see in the following section.

Social and Emotional Development: Storm and Stress, Smooth Sailing, or Both?

Adolescents also differ markedly from children in their social and emotional development. **Question: What social and emotional developments occur during adolescence?** In terms of social and emotional development, adolescence has been associated with turbulence. In the 19th century, psychologist G. Stanley Hall described adolescence as a time of *Sturm und Drang*—storm and stress. More current views challenge the assumption that "storm and stress" is normal for adolescents (Griffin, 2001). Many adolescents experience a rather calm and joyous period of development. Jeffrey Arnett (1999) argues that we need to take individual differences and cultural variations into consideration. He notes that not all adolescents experience storm and stress but admits that, for those who do, it is most likely to occur during adolescence.

Certainly, many American teenagers abuse drugs, get pregnant, contract STIs, become involved in violence, fail in school, even attempt suicide (CDC, 2000b). The U.S. Centers for Disease Control and Prevention regularly survey the behavior of young people in an effort to uncover risks to health. The CDC (2000b) reported that 72% of all deaths among people aged 10 to 24 years result from only four causes: motor vehicle crashes (31%), other unintentional injuries (11%), homicide (18%), and suicide (12%). Numerous high school students engage in behaviors that increase their likelihood of death from these four causes:

◆ 16% rarely or never wear seat belts.

◆ 33% ride with drivers who have been drinking alcohol.

◆ 17% carry weapons.

◆ 50% drank alcohol during the 30 days preceding the survey.

◆ 27% used marijuana during the 30 days preceding the survey.

◆ 8% attempted suicide during the 12 months preceding the survey.

Statistics collected on the behavior of high school students revealed that:

◆ 50% had engaged in sexual intercourse.

◆ 42% of the sexually active students did not use a condom during their last sexual encounter.

◆ 2% had injected an illegal drug.

Two-thirds of all deaths among people aged 25 and above result from two causes: cardiovascular disease and cancer. The majority of risk behaviors associated with these two causes of death are initiated during adolescence. For example, 35% of high school students had smoked cigarettes within the past 30 days; 76% did not eat enough fruits and vegetables; 16% were at risk for becoming overweight; and 71% did not exercise regularly.

Hall attributed the conflicts of adolescence to biological changes. Research evidence suggests that hormonal changes affect activity levels, mood swings, and aggressive tendencies, but that sociocultural influences have a greater effect (Buchanan et al., 1992).

STRIVING FOR INDEPENDENCE As these biological changes take place, adolescents try to become more independent from their parents, which often leads to some bickering (Smetana & Gaines, 1999). They usually bicker about issues such as homework, chores, money, appearance, curfews, and dating (Galambos & Turner, 1999). Arguments are common when adolescents want to make their own choices about matters such as clothes and friends.

The striving for independence is also characterized by withdrawal from family life, at least relative to prior involvement. In one study, children ranging in age from 9 to 15 carried electronic pagers for a week so that they could report what they were doing and whom they were with when signaled (Larson & Richards, 1991). The amount of time spent with family members decreased dramatically with greater age. The 15-year-olds spent only half as much time with their families as the 9-year-olds. Yet this change does not mean that most adolescents spend their time on the streets. For 15-year-old boys in the study, time with the family tended to be replaced by time spent alone. For older girls, this time was divided between friends and solitude.

Adolescents and parents are often in conflict because adolescents experiment with many things that can be harmful to their health. Yet—apparently because of the personal fable—adolescents often do not perceive such activities to be as risky as their parents see them as being. Lawrence Cohn and his colleagues (1995) found, for example, that parents perceived drinking, smoking, failure to use seat belts, drag racing, and a number of other activities to be riskier than did their teenagers (see Table 3.4).

■ **Adolescent Relationships with Parents**
Adolescents strive for some independence from their parents, including some distancing. But most adolescents continue to feel love, respect, and loyalty toward their parents. Adolescents and parents also tend to share social, political, religious, and economic views.

TABLE 3.4 MEAN RATINGS OF PERCEIVED HARMFULNESS OF VARIOUS ACTIVITIES*

Activity	Experimental Involvement (doing activity once or twice to see what it is like)		Frequent Involvement	
	Teenager	Teenager's Parents	Teenager	Teenager's Parents
Drinking alcohol	2.6	3.5	4.4	4.8
Smoking cigarettes	3.0	3.6	4.4	4.8
Using diet pills	2.8	3.8	4.1	4.7
Not using seat belts	3.0	4.3	4.0	4.8
Getting drunk	3.2	4.2	4.4	4.8
Sniffing glue	3.6	4.6	4.6	4.9
Driving home after drinking a few beers	3.8	4.5	4.6	4.8
Drag racing	3.8	4.6	4.5	4.8
Using steroids	3.8	4.4	4.7	4.9

*Based on a scale of 1–5, with 1 being least harmful and 5 being most harmful.

Source of data: Cohn, L. D., Macfarlane, S., Yanez, C., & Imai, W. K. (1995). Risk-perception: Differences between adolescents and adults. *Health Psychology, 14,* 217–222.

Some distancing from parents is beneficial for adolescents (Galambos & Turner, 1999). After all, they do have to form relationships outside the family. But greater independence does not necessarily mean that adolescents become emotionally detached from their parents or fall completely under the influence of their peers. Most adolescents continue to feel love, respect, and loyalty toward their parents (Eberly & Montemayor, 1999). Adolescents who feel close to their parents actually show greater self-reliance and independence than do those who are distant from their parents. Adolescents who retain close ties with their parents also fare better in school and have fewer adjustment problems (Steinberg, 1996).

Despite parent–adolescent conflict over issues of control, parents and adolescents tend to share social, political, religious, and economic views (Sagrestano et al., 1999). In sum, there are frequent differences between parents and adolescents on issues of personal control. However, there is apparently less of a "generation gap" on broader matters.

EGO IDENTITY VERSUS ROLE DIFFUSION: "WHO AM I?" According to Erik Erikson, individuals undergo eight stages of psychosocial development, each of which is characterized by a certain "crisis." (See the Concept Review on page 107.) Four of these stages, beginning with that of trust versus mistrust, occur during childhood. The fifth stage, that of *ego identity versus role diffusion,* occurs during adolescence. In Western society, in which adolescents generally have a good deal of choice in determining what they will become, the creation of an adult identity is a key challenge. Much of this challenge involves learning about one's interests and abilities and connecting them with an occupation or a role in life. But identity also involves sexual, political, and religious beliefs and commitments. Will the individual be monogamous or sexually active with a number of people? Will he or she lean left or right along the political spectrum? What role will be played by religion in his or her life?

Erikson (1963) theorized that adolescents experience a life crisis of *ego identity versus role diffusion.* **Ego identity** is a firm sense of who one is and what one stands for. It can carry one through difficult times and give meaning to one's achievements.

Ego identity Erikson's term for a firm sense of who one is and what one stands for.

Role diffusion Erikson's term for lack of clarity in one's life roles (due to failure to develop ego identity).

Adolescents who do not develop ego identity may experience **role diffusion.** They spread themselves too thin, running down one blind alley after another and placing themselves at the mercy of leaders who promise to give them the sense of identity that they cannot find for themselves.

ADOLESCENT SEXUALITY—WHEN? WHAT? (HOW?) WHO? WHERE? AND WHY?—NOT TO MENTION, "SHOULD I?"

> My first sexual experience occurred in a car after the high school junior prom. We were both virgins, very uncertain but very much in love. We had been going together since eighth grade. The experience was somewhat painful. I remember wondering if I would look different to my mother the next day. I guess I didn't because nothing was said. (Adapted from Morrison et al., 1980, p. 108)

Although adolescents may not form enduring romantic relationships or be able to support themselves, the changes of puberty ready their bodies for sexual activity. High hormone levels also stir interest in sex. Adolescents therefore wrestle with issues of how and when to express their awakening sexuality. To complicate matters, Western culture sends mixed messages about sex. Teenagers may be advised to wait until they have married or at least entered into meaningful relationships, but they are also bombarded by sexual messages in films, TV and radio commercials, print advertising, and virtually every other medium.

All in all, about half of American high school students have engaged in sexual intercourse (CDC, 2000b). Adolescent girls and boys usually obtain little advice at home or in school about how to handle their emerging sexuality. Fewer than half of sexually active adolescents use contraceptives reliably (CDC, 2000b). As a result, about 800,000 teenage girls get pregnant each year, resulting in 500,000 births (CDC, 2000d).

Why is teenage pregnancy so common? Most girls become pregnant because they and their partner misunderstand reproduction and contraception or miscalculate the odds of conception. Even those who are well-informed about contraception often do not use it consistently. Peers also play an important role in determining the sexual behavior of adolescents. When teenagers are asked why they do not wait to have sexual intercourse until they are older, the top reason cited is usually peer pressure (Dickson et al., 1998).

The medical, social, and economic costs of unplanned teenage pregnancies are enormous to teenage parents and their children. Teenage mothers are more likely to have medical complications during pregnancy and to have prolonged labor. Their babies are more likely to be born prematurely and to have low birth weight. It appears that these medical problems are largely due not to the young age of the mother, but to the inadequate prenatal care and poor nutrition obtained by teenage mothers living in poverty (Fraser et al., 1995; Johnson, 2002).

Teenage parents are also less likely to graduate from high school or attend college (CDC, 2000b). Their lack of educational achievement leads to a lower standard of living and a greater need for public assistance. Few receive consistent financial or emotional help from the babies' fathers, who generally are unable to support themselves, let alone a family.

Still, there is encouraging news. The final decade of the 20th century saw a decline in the teenage pregnancy rate because of increased use of contraception and a leveling off of sexual activity among teenagers (CDC, 2000b). The teenage pregnancy rate was falling (CDC, 2000b). CDC researchers attribute the decrease in risky sexual behavior to educational campaigns in the schools, the media, churches, and communities.

Your Turn: Now that we have discussed adolescence, enhance your mastery of the material with the nearby "Learning Connections." Review the material by filling in the blanks, reflect on the material by relating it to other things you know, and think critically about it.

A Closer Look — EMERGING ADULTHOOD—BRIDGING ADOLESCENCE AND THE LIFE BEYOND

When our mothers were our age, they were engaged. They at least had some idea what they were going to do with their lives. I, on the other hand, will have a dual degree in majors that are ambiguous at best and impractical at worst (English and political science), no ring on my finger and no idea who I am, much less what I want to do. Under duress, I will admit that this is a pretty exciting time. Sometimes, when I look out across the wide expanse that is my future, I can see beyond the void. I realize that having nothing ahead to count on means I now have to count on myself; that having no direction means forging one of my own. (Page, 1999, pp. 18, 20)

—Kristen, age 22

Kristen has some work to do: She needs to forge her own direction. But what if Kristen had been born into the caste system of old England or India, into a traditional Islamic society, or into the United States of the 1950s, where the TV sitcom *Father Knows Best* was perennially in the top ten? Kristen would have had a sense of direction, but it would have been society's, not her own.

But Kristen was born into the open and challenging United States of today. She has the freedom to become whatever the interaction of her heredity and her educational and social opportunities enable her to become—and the opportunities are many. With freedom comes the need to make choices. Kristen is in the process of accumulating information about herself and about the world outside. According to psychologist Jeffrey Arnett (2000; see also Schwartz et al., 2005), she is in *emerging adulthood*. In earlier days, adolescents made a transition, for better or worse, directly into adulthood. Now many of them—especially those in affluent nations with abundant opportunities—spend time in what some theorists think of as a new period of development.

Most psychologists define adulthood in terms of what people do, not in terms of their age. The transition to adulthood is mainly marked by adjustment issues such as deciding on one's values and beliefs, accepting self-responsibility, becoming financially independent, and establishing an equal relationship with parents (Arnett, 2000).

Emerging adulthood straddles the late teens and early to middle 20s in societies that allow young people an extended opportunity to explore their life roles (Galambos et al., 2006). Such societies tend to be found in developed nations, our own among them. Parents, the government, and colleges themselves may support people through college and graduate school. This support allows young people to sort out identity issues and make meaningful life plans—even if some still don't know where they are going after they graduate from college (Reitzle, 2006; Shulman et al., 2006). On the other hand, even in the United States, many people cannot obtain the support necessary for sojourning in emerging adulthood.

When asked whether they have become adults, about 60% of individuals in their late teens and early 20s say something like, "in some respects yes and in other respects no" (Arnett, 2000; Reitzle, 2006). Many feel that they have developed beyond the conflicts and exploratory voyages of adolescence, but they may have not yet obtained the ability to assume the financial and interpersonal responsibilities they associate with adulthood.

And then, of course, there are those who remain adolescents forever.

Learning Connections — ADOLESCENCE

ACTIVE REVIEW (16) Puberty begins with the appearance of _____ sex characteristics, such as the growth of body hair, deepening of the voice in males, and rounding of the breasts and hips in females. (17) The changes of puberty are stimulated by _____ in the male and by estrogen and androgens in the female. (18) _____ operational thought is characterized by hypothetical thinking and deductive logic. (19) Adolescent egocentrism gives rise to the _____ audience and the personal fable. (20) In stage 6 moral reasoning, people consider behavior that is consistent with _____ ethical standards as right. (21) G. Stanley Hall described adolescence as a time of *Sturm und Drang*—storm and _____. (22) Erik Erikson considers the life crisis of adolescence to be ego identity versus role _____.

REFLECT AND RELATE There is a saying: "Adolescents are neither fish nor foul." Can you apply this saying to your own experiences as an adolescent?

CRITICAL THINKING Can you make the case that adolescence is a distinct stage of life? Explain.

 Go to **http://psychology.wadsworth.com/ rathus_pcc9e** for an interactive version of this Learning Connections unit.

Menopause The cessation of menstruation.

Adulthood

Development continues throughout the lifespan. Many theorists believe that adult concerns and involvements follow observable patterns, so that we can speak of "stages" of adult development. Others argue that there may no longer be a standard life cycle with predictable stages or phases. Age now has an "elastic quality"—being 50, 60, 70, 80, or even 90 no longer necessarily means loss of cognitive or physical ability, or even wrinkling. People are living longer than ever before and are freer than ever to choose their own destiny.

Physical Development: A Lifetime of Change

The most obvious aspects of development during adulthood are physical. **Question: What physical developments occur during adulthood?** Let us consider the physical developments that take place in young, or early, adulthood, which covers the ages of 20 and 40; middle adulthood, which spans 45 to 65; and late adulthood, which begins at 65.

YOUNG ADULTHOOD Most young adults are at their height of sensory sharpness, strength, reaction time, and cardiovascular fitness. On the other hand, women gymnasts find themselves lacking a competitive edge in their 20s because they are accumulating (normal!) body fat and losing suppleness and flexibility. Other athletes, such as football, baseball, and basketball players, are more likely to experience a decline in their 30s. Most athletes retire by age 40. Sexually speaking, most people in early adulthood become readily aroused. They tend to attain and maintain erections as desired and to lubricate readily.

MIDDLE ADULTHOOD In our middle years, we are unlikely to possess the strength, coordination, and stamina that we had during our 20s and 30s. The decline is most obvious in professional sports, where peak performance is at a premium. Gordie Howe still played hockey at 50, but most pros at those ages can no longer keep up with the "kids."

The years between 40 and 60 are reasonably stable. There is gradual physical decline, but it is minor and likely to be of concern only if a person competes with young adults—or with idealized memories of oneself. There are exceptions: a 20-year-old couch potato could become a 50-year-old marathoner. By any reasonable standard, people in middle adulthood can maintain excellent cardiorespiratory condition. Because the physical decline in middle adulthood is gradual, people who begin to eat more nutritious diets (e.g., decrease intake of animal fats and increase intake of fruits and vegetables) and to exercise may find themselves looking and feeling better than they did in young adulthood.

For women, **menopause** is usually considered to be the single most important change of life that occurs during middle adulthood. Menopause usually occurs during the late 40s or early 50s. Menopause is the final phase of the *climacteric,* which is caused by a decline in secretion of female sex hormones. Ovulation draws to an end, and there is some loss of breast tissue and of elasticity of the skin. Loss of bone density can lead to brittleness. During the climacteric, many women experience hot flashes, loss of sleep, and some anxiety and depression. This is all normal. Women's experiences during and following the climacteric reflect the intensity of their physical symptoms—which vary considerably—and the extent to which their self-concept was wrapped up with her reproductive capacity (Dennerstein, 2003; Hvas et al., 2004).

LATE ADULTHOOD An *agequake* is coming. With improved health care and knowledge of the importance of diet and exercise, more Americans than ever before are 65 or older (Nuland, 2005). In 1900, only 1 American in 30 was over 65. By 2030, 1 American in 5 will be 65 or older.

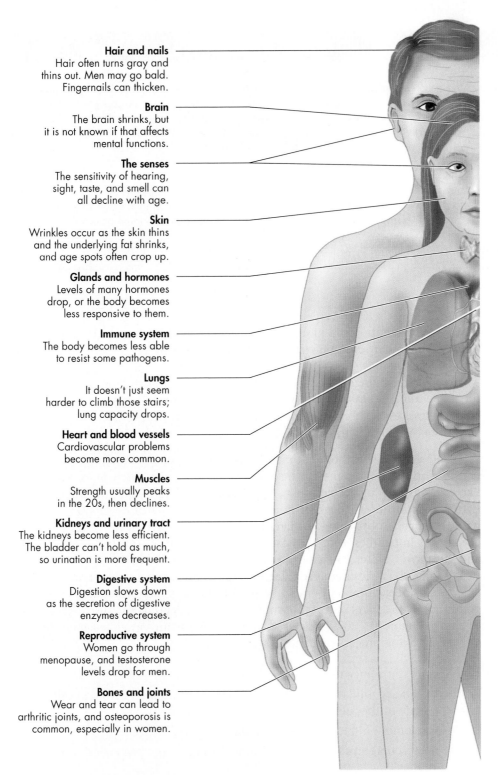

Hair and nails
Hair often turns gray and thins out. Men may go bald. Fingernails can thicken.

Brain
The brain shrinks, but it is not known if that affects mental functions.

The senses
The sensitivity of hearing, sight, taste, and smell can all decline with age.

Skin
Wrinkles occur as the skin thins and the underlying fat shrinks, and age spots often crop up.

Glands and hormones
Levels of many hormones drop, or the body becomes less responsive to them.

Immune system
The body becomes less able to resist some pathogens.

Lungs
It doesn't just seem harder to climb those stairs; lung capacity drops.

Heart and blood vessels
Cardiovascular problems become more common.

Muscles
Strength usually peaks in the 20s, then declines.

Kidneys and urinary tract
The kidneys become less efficient. The bladder can't hold as much, so urination is more frequent.

Digestive system
Digestion slows down as the secretion of digestive enzymes decreases.

Reproductive system
Women go through menopause, and testosterone levels drop for men.

Bones and joints
Wear and tear can lead to arthritic joints, and osteoporosis is common, especially in women.

FIGURE 3.9 **The Relentless March of Time**
A number of physical changes occur during the later years. However, the reasons for aging are not yet completely understood. People can also affect the pace of their aging by eating properly, exercising, maintaining a positive outlook, and finding and meeting challenges that are consistent with their abilities.

 Go to **http://psychology.wadsworth. com/rathus_pcc9e** to access an interactive version of this figure.

Various physical changes—some of them troublesome—occur during the later years (Figure 3.9). Changes in calcium metabolism increase the brittleness of the bones and heighten the risk of breaks due to falls. The skin becomes less elastic and subject to wrinkles and folds. Older people see and hear less acutely. Because of a decline in the sense of smell, they may use more spice to flavor their food. Older people need more time to respond to stimuli ("reaction time" increases). Older

A Closer Look | AGING, SEX, AND ETHNICITY: DIVERSE PATTERNS

Although Americans in general are living longer, there are sex and ethnic differences in life expectancy. **Question: What are the sex and ethnic differences in life expectancy?** For example, women in our society outlive men by five to six years (Miniño et al., 2006). European Americans and Asian Americans live longer on average than do Latino and Latina Americans, African Americans, and Native Americans (Miniño et al., 2006).

Why do women in the United States outlive men? For one thing, heart disease—

the nation's leading killer—tends to develop later in women than in men. Men are also more likely to die because of accidents, cirrhosis of the liver, strokes, suicide, homicide, AIDS, and cancer (Miniño et al., 2006). Many such deaths reflect excessive drinking and risky behavior. Many men are also reluctant to have regular physical exams or to talk to their doctors about their health problems. "In their 20s, [men are] too strong to need a doctor; in their 30s, they're too busy, and in their 40s, too scared" (Courtenay, 2000).

There is a seven-year difference in life expectancy between people in the highest income brackets and those in the lowest. Members of certain ethnic minority groups in our society are likely to be poor. Poor people tend to eat less nutritious diets, encounter more stress, and have less access to health care. We cannot control our sex and ethnic background, but we can choose whether or not to engage in more healthful behavior.

drivers, for example, need more time to respond to changing road conditions. As we grow older, our immune system functions less effectively, leaving us more vulnerable to disease.

Age-related changes affect sexual functioning, yet most people can enjoy sex for a lifetime if they remain generally healthy and adjust their expectations. Nevertheless, especially for many men, the question during late adulthood may shift from "Should I?" to "Can I?"

WHY DO WE AGE? Although it may be hard to believe it will happen to us, every person who has walked the Earth so far has aged. **Question: Why do we age?** Aging, like other aspects of development, apparently involves a complex interaction of nature and nurture (or lack of nurture). There is evidence to support a role for nature—or genes—in aging. Different species have different life spans, and longevity runs in families. People whose parents and grandparents lived into their 80s and 90s have a better chance of reaching these ages themselves. But it is unclear exactly how the genes involved in aging express themselves. There is also an obvious role for behavioral and environmental influences. Poor diet, lack of exercise, pollution, by-products of metabolism (e.g., "free radicals"), and disease contribute to aging (Kim et al., 2002). Issues such as the following provide a more detailed look at the aging process (Nuland, 2005):

1. Cells lose the ability to reproduce themselves.
2. There is an accumulation of unwanted cells, including fat cells and cells that accumulate in the joints.
3. Chromosomes mutate, leading to problems such as cancer.
4. The microscopic structures (mitochondria) in cells that produce energy for the cells mutate.
5. "Junk" accumulates within cells, leading to problems such as hardening of the arteries.
6. Junk also accumulates in the fluid outside cells, which may lead to problems such as Alzheimer's disease.
7. Proteins in the fluid outside cells undergo changes that may lead to problems such as high blood pressure.

Regular medical evaluations, proper diet (for example, consuming less animal fat), and exercise all help people live longer. Exercise helps older people maintain flexibility and cardiovascular condition. The exercise need not pound the body and

Self-Assessment   How Long Will You Live? The Life-Expectancy Scale

The life-expectancy scale is one of several used by physicians and insurance companies to estimate how long people will live. Scales such as these are far from precise—which is a good thing, if you think about it. But they make reasonable "guesstimates" based on our heredity, medical histories, and lifestyles.

Directions: To complete the scale, begin with the age of 72. Then add or subtract years according to the directions for each item.

RUNNING
TOTAL   PERSONAL FACTS:

_____ 1. If you are male, **subtract 3.**

_____ 2. If female, **add 4.**

_____ 3. If you live in an urban area with a population over 2 million, **subtract 2.**

_____ 4. If you live in a town with under 10,000 people or on a farm, **add 2.**

_____ 5. If any grandparent lived to 85, **add 2.**

_____ 6. If all four grandparents lived to 80, **add 6.**

_____ 7. If either parent died of a stroke or heart attack before the age of 50, **subtract 4.**

_____ 8. If any parent, brother, or sister under 50 has (or had) cancer or a heart condition, or has had diabetes since childhood, **subtract 3.**

_____ 9. Do you earn over $75,000* a year? If so, **subtract 2.**

_____ 10. If you finished college, **add 1.** If you have a graduate or professional degree, **add 2 more.**

_____ 11. If you are 65 or over and still working, **add 3.**

_____ 12. If you live with a spouse or friend, **add 5.** If not, **subtract 1** for every ten years alone since age 25.

LIFESTYLE STATUS:

_____ 13. If you work behind a desk, **subtract 3.**

_____ 14. If your work requires regular, heavy physical labor, **add 3.**

_____ 15. If you exercise strenuously (tennis, running, swimming, etc.) five times a week for at least a half-hour, **add 4.** If two or three times a week, **add 2.**

_____ 16. Do you sleep more than ten hours each night? **Subtract 4.**

_____ 17. Are you intense, aggressive, easily angered? **Subtract 3.**

_____ 18. Are you easygoing and relaxed? **Add 3.**

_____ 19. Are you happy? **Add 1.** Unhappy? **Subtract 2.**

_____ 20. Have you had a speeding ticket in the last year? **Subtract 1.**

_____ 21. Do you smoke more than two packs a day? **Subtract 8.** One or two packs? **Subtract 6.** One-half to one? **Subtract 3.**

_____ 22. Do you drink the equivalent of 1½ oz. of liquor a day? **Subtract 1.**

_____ 23. Are you overweight by 50 lbs. or more? **Subtract 8.** By 30 to 50 lbs? **Subtract 4.** By 10 to 30 lbs? **Subtract 2.**

_____ 24. If you are a man over 40 and have annual checkups, **add 2.**

_____ 25. If you are a woman and see a gynecologist once a year, **add 2.**

AGE ADJUSTMENT:

_____ 26. If you are between 30 and 40, **add 2.**

_____ 27. If you are between 40 and 50, **add 3.**

_____ 28. If you are between 50 and 70, **add 4.**

_____ 29. If you are over 70, **add 5.**

_____   YOUR LIFE EXPECTANCY

*This figure is an inflation-adjusted estimate.

Source: From Robert F. Allen with Shirley Linde. (1986). *Lifegain.* Human Resources Institute Press, Tempe Wick Road, Morristown, NJ.

---

produce rivers of sweat. Because older people tend to have more brittle bones and more rigid joints, fast or prolonged walking is an excellent choice (Gill et al., 2000; Hakim et al., 1998; Tanasescu et al., 2002).

Cognitive Development: Maximizing Cognitive Powers

Question: What cognitive developments occur during adulthood? As is the case with physical development, people are also at the height of their cognitive powers during early adulthood. Many professionals show the broadest knowledge of their fields at about the time they are graduating from college or graduate school. At this time their course work is freshest. They may have just recently studied for comprehensive examinations. Once they enter their fields, they often specialize. As a result, knowledge deepens in certain areas, but understanding of related areas may grow relatively superficial.

Cognitive development in adulthood has many aspects—creativity, memory functioning, and intelligence. People can be creative for a lifetime. At the age of 80, Merce Cunningham choreographed a dance that made use of computer-generated digital images (Teachout, 2000). Hans Hofmann created some of his most vibrant

AP/Wide World Photos

■ **Frank Lloyd Wright** The innovative architect created New York's unique Solomon R. Guggenheim Museum at the age of 89.

paintings at 85, and Pablo Picasso was painting in his 90s. Grandma Moses did not even begin painting until she was 78 years old. Giuseppe Verdi wrote his joyous opera *Falstaff* at the age of 79. **Truth or Fiction Revisited:** It is *not* true that the architect Frank Lloyd Wright designed New York's innovative spiral-shaped Guggenheim Museum when he was 65 years old. He was actually 89.

Memory functioning does, however, decline with age. It is common for older people to have trouble recalling the names of common objects or people they know. Memory lapses can be embarrassing, and older people sometimes lose confidence in their memories, which then lowers their motivation to remember things (Cavanaugh & Green, 1990). But declines in memory are not usually as large as people assume and are often reversible (Villa & Abeles, 2000). Memory tests usually measure ability to recall meaningless information. Older people show better memory functioning in areas in which they can apply their experience, especially their specialties, to new challenges (Graf, 1990). For example, who would do a better job of learning and remembering how to solve problems in chemistry—a college history major or a retired professor of chemistry?

You might choose the chemistry professor because of his or her crystallized intelligence, not his or her fluid intelligence. **Crystallized intelligence** represents one's lifetime of intellectual attainments. In this case we are speaking of the individual's knowledge of chemistry, but crystallized intelligence is shown more generally by vocabulary and accumulated facts about world affairs. Therefore, crystallized intelligence can increase over the decades. **Fluid intelligence** is defined as mental flexibility, demonstrated by the ability to process information rapidly, as in learning and solving problems in new areas of endeavor. It is the sort of intellectual functioning that is typically measured on intelligence tests, especially with problems that must be solved rapidly.

People also obtain the highest intelligence test scores in young adulthood (Baltes, 1997). Yet people tend to retain their verbal skills, as demonstrated by their vocabularies and general knowledge, into advanced old age. It is performance on tasks that require speed and visual–spatial skills, such as putting puzzles together, where older people tend to experience difficulty (Schaie, 1994; Zimprich & Martin, 2002).

One of the most severe assaults on intellectual functioning, especially among older people, is Alzheimer's disease.

ALZHEIMER'S DISEASE Questions: What is Alzheimer's disease? What are its origins?
Alzheimer's disease is a progressive form of mental deterioration that affects about 1% of people at age 60 and nearly 25% at age 85 (Yesavage et al., 2002). **Truth or Fiction Revisited:** Alzheimer's disease is *not* a normal part of aging. Although Alzheimer's is connected with aging, it is a disease rather than a normal progression (Yesavage et al., 2002).

Alzheimer's disease is characterized by general, gradual deterioration in cognitive processes such as memory, language, and problem solving. As the disease progresses, people may fail to recognize familiar faces or forget their names. At the most severe stage, people with Alzheimer's disease become helpless. They become unable to communicate or walk and require help in toileting and feeding. More isolated memory losses (for example, forgetting where one put one's glasses) may be a normal feature of aging (Abeles, 1997). Alzheimer's, in contrast, seriously impairs vocational and social functioning.

Alzheimer's disease is characterized by reduced levels of the neurotransmitter acetylcholine (ACh) and by the buildup of a sticky plaque that impairs neural functioning in the brain. One form of drug therapy has aimed at boosting ACh levels by slowing its breakdown (Trinh et al., 2003). This approach achieves modest benefits with many people. The plaque is formed from fragments of a body protein (beta

Crystallized intelligence One's lifetime of intellectual achievement, as shown largely through vocabulary and knowledge of world affairs.

Fluid intelligence Mental flexibility as shown in learning rapidly to solve new kinds of problems.

Alzheimer's disease (AHLTS-high-mers). A progressive form of mental deterioration characterized by loss of memory, language, problem solving, and other cognitive functions.

amyloid) (Cotman, 2000). Normally, the immune system prevents the buildup of plaque, but not effectively in the case of people with Alzheimer's disease. Thus another approach to the treatment of Alzheimer's is the development of a vaccine made from beta amyloid that will stimulate the immune system to recognize and attack the plaque more vigorously (Janus et al., 2000; Morgan et al., 2000).

Although Alzheimer's is not a normal part of aging, there are normal, gradual declines in intellectual functioning and memory among older people (Butler, 1998; Villa & Abeles, 2000). Although we understand little about why these declines occur, they appear to be connected with biological problems (Yesavage et al., 2002). However, depression and losses of sensory acuity and motivation may also contribute to lower cognitive test scores. B. F. Skinner (1983) argued that much of the falloff is due to an "aging environment" rather than an aging person. That is, the behavior of older people often goes unreinforced. This view is substantiated by a classic study of nursing home residents who were rewarded for remembering recent events and showed improved scores on tests of memory (Langer et al., 1979).

Social and Emotional Development: Growing Psychologically Healthier?

Changes in social and emotional development during adulthood are probably the most "elastic" or fluid. These changes are clearly affected by cultural expectations and individual behavior patterns. As a result, there is so much variety that it can be misleading to expect that any individual will follow a particular pattern. Nevertheless, many developmental theorists suggest that there are enough commonalities that we can speak of trends. One trend is that the outlook for older people has become much more optimistic over the past generation—not only because of medical advances but also because the behavior and mental processes of many older people are remaining younger than at any other time in history.

There is more good news. Research evidence suggests that people tend to grow psychologically healthier as they advance from adolescence through middle adulthood. Psychologists Constance Jones and William Meredith (2000) studied information on 236 participants in California growth studies who had been followed from early adolescence for about 50 years and found that they generally became more productive and had better interpersonal relationships as the years went on. Certainly there are individual differences, but many individuals, even some with a turbulent adolescence, showed dramatically better psychological health at age 62 than they had half a century earlier.

Let us now follow social and emotional developments throughout the course of adulthood, beginning with young adulthood.

YOUNG ADULTHOOD Question: What social and emotional developments occur during young adulthood? Many theorists suggest that young adulthood is the period of life during which people tend to establish themselves as independent members of society.

At some point during the 20s, many people become fueled by ambition. Many strive to advance in their careers. Those who seek professional careers may spend much of their 20s acquiring the skills that will enable them to succeed in them (Levinson et al., 1978; Levinson, 1996). It is largely during the 20s that people become generally responsible for their own support, make their own choices, and are free from parental influences. Many young adults adopt what theorist Daniel Levinson and his colleagues (1978) call **the dream**—the drive to "become" someone, to leave their mark on history—which serves as a tentative blueprint for their life.

During young adulthood, people tend to leave their families of origin and to create families of their own. Erik Erikson (1963) characterized young adulthood as the stage of **intimacy versus isolation.** (For a summary of Erikson's stages, see the Concept Review on page 107.) Erikson saw the establishment of intimate relationships as central to young adulthood. Young adults who have evolved a firm

The dream In this usage, Levinson's term for the overriding drive of youth to become someone important, to leave one's mark on history.

Intimacy versus isolation Erikson's life crisis of young adulthood, which is characterized by the task of developing abiding intimate relationships.

■ **Establishing Intimate Relationships** According to Erik Erikson, establishing intimate relationships is a central task of young adulthood.

Age-30 transition Levinson's term for the ages from 28 to 33, which are characterized by reassessment of the goals and values of the 20s.

Generativity versus stagnation Erikson's term for the crisis of middle adulthood, characterized by the task of being productive and contributing to younger generations.

Midlife transition Levinson's term for the ages from 40 to 45, which are characterized by a shift in psychological perspective from viewing ourselves in terms of years lived to viewing ourselves in terms of the years we have left.

Midlife crisis A crisis experienced by many people during the midlife transition when they realize that life may be more than halfway over and reassess their achievements in terms of their dreams.

sense of identity during adolescence are ready to "fuse" their identities with those of other people through marriage and abiding friendships. People who do not reach out to develop intimate relationships risk retreating into isolation and loneliness.

Erikson warned that we may not be able to commit ourselves to others until we have achieved ego identity—that is, established stable life roles. Achieving ego identity is the central task of adolescence. Lack of personal stability is connected with the high divorce rate for teenage marriages.

Levinson labeled the ages of 28 to 33 the **age-30 transition.** For men and women, the late 20s and early 30s are commonly characterized by reassessment: "Where is my life going?" "Why am I doing this?" During our 30s, we often find that the lifestyles we adopted during our 20s do not fit as comfortably as we had expected.

Many psychologists find that the later 30s are characterized by settling down or planting roots. Many young adults feel a need to make a financial and emotional investment in their home. Their concerns become more focused on promotion or tenure, career advancement, and long-term mortgages.

MIDDLE ADULTHOOD There are also a number of key changes in social and emotional development that tend to occur during middle adulthood. **Question: What social and emotional developments occur during middle adulthood?** Consider Erikson's views on the middle years.

Erikson (1963) labeled the life crisis of the middle years **generativity versus stagnation.** *Generativity* involves doing things that we believe are worthwhile, such as rearing children or producing on the job. Generativity enhances and maintains self-esteem. Generativity also involves helping to shape the new generation. This shaping may involve rearing our own children or making the world a better place, for example, through joining church or civic groups. *Stagnation* means treading water, as in keeping the same job at the same pay for 30 years, or even moving backward, as in moving into a less responsible and poorer paying job or removing oneself from rearing one's children. Stagnation has powerful destructive effects on self-esteem.

According to Levinson and colleagues (1978), whose research involved case studies of 40 men, there is a **midlife transition** at about age 40 to 45 characterized by a shift in psychological perspective. Previously, men had thought of their age in terms of the number of years that had elapsed since birth. Now they begin to think of their age in terms of the number of years they have left. Men in their 30s still think of themselves as older brothers to "kids" in their 20s. At about age 40 to 45, however, some marker event—illness, a change of job, the death of a friend or parent, or being beaten at tennis by their son—leads men to realize that they are a full generation older. Suddenly there seems to be more to look back on than forward to. It dawns on men that they will never be president or chairperson of the board. They will never play shortstop for the Dodgers. They mourn the passing of their own youth and begin to adjust to the specter of old age and the finality of death.

Research suggests that women may undergo a midlife transition a number of years earlier than men do (Stewart & Ostrove, 1998). Why? Much of it has to do with the winding down of the "biological clock"—that is, the abilities to conceive and bear children. For example, once they turn 35, women are usually advised to have their fetuses routinely tested for Down syndrome and other chromosomal disorders. At age 35, women also enter higher risk categories for side effects from birth control pills. Yet many women today are having children in their 40s and, now and then, beyond.

In both genders, according to Levinson, the midlife transition may trigger a crisis—the **midlife crisis.** The middle-level, middle-aged businessperson looking ahead to another 10 to 20 years of grinding out accounts in a Wall Street cubbyhole may encounter severe depression. The homemaker with two teenagers, an empty house from 8:00 AM to 4:00 PM, and a 40th birthday on the way may feel that she or he is coming apart at the seams. Both feel a sense of entrapment and loss of purpose. Some people are propelled into extramarital affairs by the desire to prove to themselves that they are still attractive.

Yet many Americans find that these years present opportunities for new direction and fulfillment. Many people are at the height of their productive powers during this period. Many or most of today's robust 45- to 55-year-olds can look forward to another 30 to 40 healthy years. Yet some people in this age group experience what Stewart and Ostrove (1998) refer to as a midcourse correction. And why not? Many decades remain for self-fulfillment.

For example, women often renew their sense of self in their 40s and 50s. Women in their early 40s are more likely than women in their early 30s to feel confident, exert an influence on their community, feel secure and committed; to feel productive, effective, and powerful, and to extend their interests beyond their family (Helson et al., 1995; Stewart et al., 2001).

 **CONTROVERSY IN PSYCHOLOGY**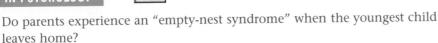

Do parents experience an "empty-nest syndrome" when the youngest child leaves home?

In earlier decades, psychologists placed great emphasis on a concept referred to as the **empty-nest syndrome.** This concept was applied most often to women. It was assumed that women experience a profound sense of loss when their youngest child goes off to college, gets married, or moves out of the home. The sense of loss was assumed to be greatest among women who had remained in the home (Stewart & Ostrove, 1998).

Truth or Fiction Revisited: However, it is *not* true that parents suffer from the empty-nest syndrome when the youngest child leaves home. Research findings paint a more optimistic picture. Certainly there can be a sense of loss when the children have left home, and the loss applies to both parents. Parents may find it difficult to let go of the children after so many years of mutual dependence. However, many mothers report increased marital satisfaction and personal changes such as greater mellowness, self-confidence, and stability once the children have left home (Stewart & Ostrove, 1998).

Abigail Stewart and her colleagues (2001; Zucker et al., 2002) have assessed four personality variables in women of various ages: identity certainty, generativity, confident power, and awareness of aging. **Identity certainty** is the feeling of having a strong and clear identity. *Generativity* is Erikson's sense of an enlarged vision of one's role in the world and increased feelings of responsibility and commitment to society. **Confident power** is the same as feelings of self-efficacy. *Awareness of aging* is self-explanatory (and all too familiar to your author!). The researchers assessed these four key variables among college women in their 40s and 50s, and retrospectively for the 30s. The evidence revealed that all of these variables grew to be more prominent in the 40s than in the 30s, and then again in the 50s than in the 40s. Yes, the older women were more aware of their aging, both because of physical changes (e.g., menopause) and psychosocial markers (e.g., the maturation of the children). However, they were also more certain as to who they were and what they stood for. They had assumed more responsibility for society at large (e.g., occupational, civic, and political activities), and were more achievement-oriented, self-confident, dominant, and self-assertive. It is as if middle age frees many women—at least educated women—from traditional gender-related shackles.

Empty-nest syndrome A sense of depression and loss of purpose felt by some parents when the youngest child leaves home.

Identity certainty A strong and clear sense of who one is and what one stands for.

Confident power Feelings of self-confidence, self-efficacy.

Ego integrity versus despair Erikson's term for the crisis of late adulthood, characterized by the task of maintaining one's sense of identity despite physical deterioration.

Wisdom Expert knowledge concerning the meaning of life, concern for people's welfare, and a push toward excellence.

LATE ADULTHOOD

It's never too late to be what you might have been.
George Eliot

Question: What social and emotional developments occur during late adulthood? Generativity does not end with middle age. Research suggests that many individuals in late adulthood continue to be creative and also to maintain a firm sense of who they are and what they stand for (Webster, 2003). The Greek philosopher Plato was so optimistic about late adulthood that he argued that one could achieve great pleasure in one's later years, engage in meaningful public service, and also achieve wisdom (McKee & Barber, 2001).

According to psychologist Erik Erikson, late adulthood is the stage of **ego integrity versus despair.** The basic challenge is to maintain the belief that life is meaningful and worthwhile as one ages and faces the inevitability of death. Erikson, like Plato, spoke of the importance of wisdom. He believed that ego integrity derives from **wisdom,** which can be defined as expert knowledge about the meaning of life, balancing one's own needs and those of others, and pushing toward excellence in one's behavior and achievements (Baltes & Staudinger, 2000; Sternberg, 2000). Erikson also believed that wisdom enables people to accept their life span as occurring at a certain point in the sweep of history and as being limited. We spend most of our lives accumulating objects and relationships, and Erikson argues that adjustment in the later years requires the ability to let go of them. Other views of late adulthood stress the importance of creating new challenges; however, biological and social realities may require older people to become more selective in their pursuits.

Successful Aging The later years were once seen mainly as a prelude to dying. Older people were viewed as crotchety and irritable. It was assumed that they reaped little pleasure from life. *No more.* Many stereotypes about aging are becoming less prevalent. **Question: How do people in the United States age today?** Despite the changes that accompany aging, most people in their 70s report being generally satisfied with their lives (Volz, 2000). Americans are eating more wisely and exercising at later ages, so many older people are robust. According to a national poll of nearly 1,600 adults by the *Los Angeles Times,* 75% of older people feel younger than their age—19 years on average (Stewart & Armet, 2000). People in their 70s and 80s felt as though they were in their 60s. People in their 60s reported feeling as though they were in their early 50s.

One aspect of successful aging is subjective well-being. A sense of well-being in late adulthood is linked to more than physical health and feeling younger than one's years. A meta-analysis of 286 studies noted three factors that are connected with subjective well-being: socioeconomic status, social network, and competence (Pinquart & Sörensen, 2000). One's level of income is more important to subjective well-being than is his or her level of education. Having social contacts with friends and one's own adult children are both related to subjective well-being. Competence enables one to take charge of one's life to fill one's days with meaningful activities and handle the problems that can arise at any age.

Developmental psychologists are using the term *successful aging* (Volz, 2000) in their study of characteristics that enable older people to lead more enjoyable and productive lives. **Truth or Fiction Revisited:** It is not true that successful aging involves accepting one's limitations and avoiding new challenges. There are three components of successful aging:

■ **"Successful Aging"?** The later years were once seen mainly as a prelude to dying. In the third millennium, however, many older people—termed "successful agers"—are seeking new challenges.

Ken Fisher/Getty Images

1. *Reshaping one's life to concentrate on what one finds to be important and meaningful.* Laura Carstensen's (1997) research on people aged 70 and above reveals that successful agers form emotional goals that bring them satisfaction. For example, rather than cast about in multiple directions, they may focus

on their family and friends. Successful agers may have less time left than younger people, but they tend to spend it more wisely (Garfinkel, 1995).

Researchers (Baltes, 1997; Schulz & Heckhausen, 1996) use terms such as "selective optimization and compensation" to describe the manner in which successful agers lead their lives. That is, successful agers no longer seek to compete in arenas best left to younger people—such as certain kinds of athletic or business activities. Rather, they focus on matters that allow them to maintain a sense of control over their own actions. Moreover, they use available resources to make up for losses. If their memory is not quite what it once was, they make notes or other reminders. If their senses are no longer as acute, they use devices such as hearing aids or allow themselves more time to take in information. There are also some ingenious individual strategies. The great pianist Arthur Rubinstein performed into his 80s, even after he had lost much of his pianistic speed. In his later years, he would slow down before playing faster passages in order to enhance the impression of speed during those passages.

2. *A positive outlook.* For example, some older people attribute occasional health problems such as aches and pains to *specific* and *unstable* factors like a cold or jogging too long. Others attribute aches and pains to *global* and *stable* factors such as aging itself. Not surprisingly, those who attribute these problems to specific, unstable factors are more optimistic about surmounting them. They thus have a more positive outlook or attitude. Of particular interest here is research conducted by William Rakowski (1995). Rakowski followed 1,400 people aged 70 or older with nonlethal health problems such as aches and pains. He found that those who blamed the problems on aging itself were significantly more likely to die in the near future than those who blamed the problems on specific, unstable factors.

3. *Self-challenge.* Many people look forward to late adulthood as a time when they can rest from life's challenges. But sitting back and allowing the world to pass by is a prescription for vegetating, not for living life to its fullest. Consider an experiment conducted by Curt Sandman and Francis Crinella (1995) with 175 people whose average age was 72. They randomly assigned subjects either to a foster grandparent program with neurologically impaired children or to a control group and followed both groups for 10 years. The foster grandparents carried out various physical challenges, such as walking a few miles each day, and also engaged in new kinds of social interactions. Those in the control group did not engage in these activities. When they were assessed by the experimenters, the foster grandparents showed improved overall cognitive functioning, including memory functioning, and better sleep patterns. Moreover, the foster grandparents showed superior functioning in these areas compared with people assigned to the control group.

The *Los Angeles Times* poll found that 25% of people who had retired believed that they had done so too soon (Stewart & Armet, 2000). Many older adults today are in what they call their "third age" (following their second or middle age). They are returning to school in record numbers, becoming entrepreneurs, volunteering, and, in many cases, continuing to work. According to retirement specialist Helen Dennis (2000),

> Work is a tremendous social environment. Generally, people spend more time at work with colleagues and friends than they do with their families. Those people who are currently retiring have had long-term experiences with an employer. They've lived through marriages, births, deaths, Christmases and Thanksgivings.

Nearly half (45%) of those polled by the *Los Angeles Times* agreed with the statement, "When you give up your job, you give up a large part of who you are" (Stewart & Armet, 2000).

Your Turn: Now that we have discussed adulthood, enhance your mastery of the material with the nearby "Learning Connections." Review the material by filling in the blanks, reflect on the material by relating it to other things you know, and think critically about it.

Learning Connections ADULTHOOD

ACTIVE REVIEW (23) In _____ adulthood, most people are at their height in sensory acuteness, reaction time, and cardiovascular fitness. (24) According to the _____ theory of aging, aging is determined by a genetic biological clock. (25) According to _____-and-tear theory, cells lose the ability to regenerate because of environmental factors such as pollution, disease, and ultraviolet light. (26) _____ intelligence refers to one's lifetime of intellectual achievement, as shown by vocabulary and general knowledge. (27) _____ intelligence is mental flexibility, as shown by the ability to solve new kinds of problems. (28) Alzheimer's disease (*Is* or *Is not?*) a normal feature of the aging process. (29) Erikson labeled the life crisis of the

middle years _____ versus stagnation. (30) Research shows that most parents (*Do* or *Do not?*) suffer from the empty-nest syndrome. (31) Erikson labeled late adulthood the stage of ego _____ versus despair.

REFLECT AND RELATE Where do you fit into the chronicle of the adult years? Do events in your own life fit with any of the research findings or theories presented in this chapter?

CRITICAL THINKING How do the factors that contribute to longevity demonstrate the essential nature of both heredity and environmental factors?

Go to **http://psychology.wadsworth.com/ rathus_pcc9e** for an interactive version of this Learning Connections unit.

On Death and Dying

Death is the last great taboo. Psychiatrist Elisabeth Kübler-Ross commented on our denial of death in her landmark book *On Death and Dying:*

> We use euphemisms, we make the dead look as if they were asleep, we ship the children off to protect them from the anxiety and turmoil around the house if the [person] is fortunate enough to die at home, [and] we don't allow children to visit their dying parents in the hospital. (1969, p. 8)

Question: What are psychological perspectives on death and dying? In her work with terminally ill patients, Kübler-Ross found some common responses to news of impending death. She identified five stages of dying through which many patients pass, and she suggested that older people who suspect that death is approaching may undergo similar stages:

1. *Denial.* In the denial stage, people feel that "It can't be happening to me. The diagnosis must be wrong."
2. *Anger.* Denial usually gives way to anger and resentment toward the young and healthy and, sometimes, toward the medical establishment—"It's unfair. Why me?"
3. *Bargaining.* Next, people may try to bargain with God to postpone their death, promising, for example, to do good deeds if they are given another six months, another year to live.
4. *Depression.* With depression come feelings of loss and hopelessness—grief at the inevitability of leaving loved ones and life itself.
5. *Final acceptance.* Ultimately, an inner peace may come, a quiet acceptance of the inevitable. Such "peace" does not resemble contentment. It is nearly devoid of feeling.

Psychologist Edwin Shneidman, who has specialized in the concerns of suicidal and dying individuals, acknowledges the presence of feelings such as those identified by Kübler-Ross, but he does not perceive them to be linked in a sequence like the one just described. Instead, he suggests that dying people show a variety of emotional and cognitive responses that tend to be fleeting or relatively stable, to ebb and flow, and to reflect pain and bewilderment. He also points out that the kinds of responses shown by individuals reflect their personality traits and their philosophies of life.

"Lying Down to Pleasant Dreams . . ."

The American poet William Cullen Bryant is best known for his poem "Thanatopsis," which he composed at the age of 18. "Thanatopsis" expresses Erik Erikson's goal of ego integrity—optimism that we can maintain a sense of trust through life. By meeting squarely the challenges of our adult lives, perhaps we can take our leave with dignity. When our time comes to "join the innumerable caravan"—the billions who have died before us—perhaps we can depart life with integrity.

"Live," wrote the poet, so that

> . . . when thy summons comes to join
> The innumerable caravan that moves
> To that mysterious realm, where each shall take
> His chamber in the silent halls of death,
> Thou go not, like the quarryslave at night,
> Scourged to his dungeon, but, sustained and soothed
> By an unfaltering trust, approach thy grave
> Like one that wraps the drapery of his couch
> About him, and lies down to pleasant dreams.

Bryant, of course, wrote "Thanatopsis" at age 18, not at 85, the age at which he died. At that advanced age, his feelings—and his verse—might have differed. But literature and poetry, unlike science, need not reflect reality. They can serve to inspire and warm us.

Your Turn: Now that we have discussed death and dying, enhance your mastery of the material with the nearby "Learning Connections." Review the material by filling in the blanks, reflect on the material by relating it to other things you know, and think critically about it.

 ## Learning Connections | ON DEATH AND DYING

ACTIVE REVIEW (32) Kübler-Ross's stages of dying include _____, anger, bargaining, depression, and final acceptance. (33) Research by Shneidman (*Supports* or *Fails to support?*) the sequence hypothesized by Kübler-Ross. (34) Kübler-Ross conducted her research with _____ ill patients.

REFLECT AND RELATE Do your own experiences with people in the final days of life fit in with the views of Kübler-Ross?

CRITICAL THINKING Erik Erikson wrote that one aspect of wisdom is the ability to visualize one's role in the march of history and to accept one's own death. Do you believe that acceptance of death is a sign of wisdom? Why or why not?

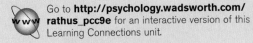 Go to **http://psychology.wadsworth.com/ rathus_pcc9e** for an interactive version of this Learning Connections unit.

Life Connections
Day Care: Blessing, Headache, or Both?

Looking for a phrase that can strike fear in the hearts of millions of American parents? Try "day care." Only a relatively small percentage of American families still fits the conventional model where the husband works and the wife stays at home and takes care of the couple's children. Nowadays the great majority of mothers, including the majority of mothers of infants, are in the workforce (Erel et al., 2000; U.S. Bureau of the Census, 2002). As a result, millions of American parents are obsessed with trying to find proper day care.

When both parents spend the day on the job, the children—at least young children—must be taken care of by others. What happens to them? Does day care affect children's bonds of attachment with their parents? Does it affect their social and cognitive development?

■ **Day Care** Because most parents in the United States are in the workforce, day care is not a luxury—it's a necessity. Day care has become a major influence on the lives of millions of children, and parents are concerned about the effects of day care on their bonds of attachment with their children and on their children's cognitive and social development.

© Bob Daemmrich/Stock, Boston/PictureQuest

How Does Day Care Affect Bonds of Attachment?

Many parents wonder whether day care will affect their children's attachment to them. Are such concerns valid? This issue has been hotly debated. Some studies have found that infants who are in day care full-time (more than 20 hours a week) are somewhat more likely than children without day care experience to show insecure attachment (Baydar & Brooks-Gunn, 1991). Some psychologists have concluded from these studies that a mother who works full-time puts her infant at risk for developing emotional insecurity (Belsky, 1990a, 1990b). Others note that infants whose mothers work may be less distressed by her departure in the strange situation and less likely to seek her out when she returns. Also keep in mind that the likelihood of insecure attachment is not much greater in infants placed in day care than in those cared for in the home. Most infants in both groups are securely attached (Booth et al., 2003; Sagi et al., 2002).

How Does Day Care Influence Social and Cognitive Development?

Day care has mixed effects on children's social and cognitive development. Infants with day care experience are more peer oriented and play at higher developmental levels than do home-reared babies. Day care children are also more likely to share their toys. They are more independent, self-confident, outgoing, and affectionate as well as more helpful and cooperative with peers and adults (Clarke-Stewart, 1991; Field, 1991). Participation in day care also is associated with better school performance during the elementary school years, especially for children from poor families (Caughy et al., 1994).

A study funded by the National Institute on Child Health and Human Development compared the development of children in "high-quality" day care with that of children in low-quality day care, and with that of children reared in the home by their mothers. The quality of the day care was defined in terms of the richness of the learning environment (availability of toys, books, and other materials), the ratio of caregivers to children (high quality meant more caregivers), the amount of individual attention received by the child (more was better), and the extent to which caregivers talked to the children and asked them questions (again: more was considered better). The researchers found high-quality day care resulted in scores on tests of language and cognitive skills that rivaled those of the children reared in the home by their mothers (Belsky et al., 2001). A study carried out in Sweden found that children placed in high-quality day care actually fared better on tests of language skills and math than children who were reared in the home (Broberg et al., 1997). It thus appears that high-quality day care enhances social and cognitive skills, but low-quality day care may be problematic.

Yet some studies find that children placed in day care are less cooperative and more aggressive toward peers and adults than children who are reared in the home. Consider findings of the National Institute on Child Health and Human Development study that went off like an H-bomb among parents in 2001. One of the findings was that the more time preschoolers spent in child care, the more likely they were to display behavioral problems in kindergarten (Belsky et al., 2001). The more time spent away from their mothers, the more likely the children were to be rated as defiant, aggressive, and disobedient once they got to kindergarten. **Truth or Fiction Revisited:** It is therefore true that children who attend day care programs are more aggressive than children who do not. However, as we will see, the differences are not all that great and the reasons for them are less than clear.

Seventeen percent of children who were in child care for more than 30 hours a week received higher scores on rating items like "gets in lots of fights," "cruelty," "talking too much," "explosive behavior," "argues a lot," and "demands a lot of attention." Only 6% of children who were in child care for fewer than 10 hours a week had these problems. The finding held regardless of the background of the child or the quality or type of child care the children received. It held for African American and European American children, for boys and for girls, for children whose parents were affluent or poor. Children who were cared for in traditional day care settings, by a grandmother, by a nanny, even by their fathers received the troublesome ratings. Could it be that Mom was the only answer?

The research findings sent shudders through millions of American homes. Nevertheless, the study also held good news for working parents. For example, it found that children who are enrolled in high-quality child care show cognitive benefits as compared with children who are in lower-quality day care or who spend more time in the home with their mothers. For example, they perform better on tests of memory, language, and knowledge.

Although the study found a positive correlation between time spent away from mothers and aggression, disobedience, and defiance in kindergarten, the reasons for the behavioral problems were not clear. For example, was it actually the time spent away from mothers that brought on the problems, or did the problems stem from other factors such as the stresses encountered by families who need two incomes? The researchers also had to admit that they did not know whether the problem behavior would continue as the children moved into higher grades. Most of them cautioned against reading too much into the study, not in the least because most of the children's behavior fell within the normal range;

even most of the aggressive behavior was not out of bounds.

Still, the findings of the National Institute of Child Health and Human Development study sent many parents into a tizzy. But a number of the researchers on the team said that if other information yielded by the study—or *not* yielded by the study—had been emphasized to the public, the reaction might have been different. Note the following:

• Although 17% of kindergartners who had been in child care acted more assertively and aggressively, that percentage is actually the norm for the general population of children. (And it remains true that 9% of the children who spent most of their time with their mothers were also rated by teachers as showing the more troubling behaviors.)

• The nature of family–child interactions had a greater impact on children's behavior than the number of hours spent in child care.

• Cruelty is never acceptable, but some other aspects of aggressiveness—and the fact that infants in day care may demand more attention as kindergartners—may in many ways be adaptive social responses to being placed in a situation in which multiple children may be competing for limited physical and human resources.

• In addition, the researchers admitted that the statistics are very modest: Yes, 17% acted aggressively and assertively, but only a few of them exhibited above-average behavior problems. Moreover, the problems were not that serious.

In any case, millions of parents have to decide not about *whether* to place their children in day care, but *where* to do so. The following section may help guide you to make the right choice.

Finding Child Care You (and Your Child) Can Live With

It's normal to be anxious. You are thinking about selecting a day care center or a private home for your precious child, and there are risks. So be a little anxious, but it may not be necessary to be

overwhelmed. You can go about the task with a checklist that can guide your considerations. Above all: Don't be afraid to open your mouth and ask questions, even pointed, challenging questions. If the day care provider doesn't like questions, or if the provider does not answer them satisfactorily, *you want your child someplace else.* So much for the preamble. Here's the checklist.

1. Does the day care center have a license? Who issued the license? What did the day care center have to do to acquire the license? (You can also call the licensing agency to obtain the answer to the last question.)

2. How many children are cared for by the center? How many caregivers are there? Remember this nursery rhyme:

There was an old woman who lived in a shoe.
She had so many children she didn't know what to do.

All right, the rhyme is sexist and ageist and maybe even shoe-ist. But it suggests that it is important for caregivers not to be overburdened by too many children, especially infants. It is desirable to have at least one caregiver for every four infants, although fewer workers are required for older children.

3. How were the caregivers hired? How were they trained? Did the center check references? What were the minimum educational credentials? Did the center check them out? Do the caregivers have any education or training in the behavior and needs of children? Do the caregivers seem to be proactive and attempt to engage the children in activities and educational experiences? Or are they inactive unless a child cries or screams? Sometimes it is impossible to find qualified day care workers, because they tend to be paid poorly— often the minimum wage, and sometimes less.

4. Is the environment child-proofed and secure? Can children stick their fingers in electric sockets? Are toys and outdoor equipment in good condition? Are sharp objects within children's reach? Can anybody walk in off the street? What is the history of children being injured or otherwise victimized in

this day care center? Is the day care provider hesitant about answering any of these questions?

5. When are meals served? Snacks? What do they consist of? Will your child find it appetizing or go hungry? Some babies are placed in day care at 6 months or younger, and parents will need to know what formulas are used.

6. Is it possible for you to meet the caregivers who will be taking care of your child? If not, why not?

7. With what children will your child interact and play?

8. Does the center seem to have an enriching environment? Do you see books, toys, games, and educational objects strewn about?

9. Are there facilities and objects like swings and tricycles that will enhance your child's physical and motor development? Are children supervised when they play with these things or are they pretty much left on their own?

10. Does the center's schedule coincide with your needs?

11. Is the center located conveniently for you? Does it appear to be in a safe location or to have adequate security arrangements? (Let me emphasize that you have a right to ask whether neighborhood or other people can walk in unannounced to where the children are. It's a fair question. You can also ask what they would do if a stranger broke into the place.)

12. Are parents permitted to visit unannounced?

13. Do you like the overall environment and feel of the center or home? Listen to your "gut."

There may be no perfect solution, but some are better than others.

Recite—An Active Summary™

Want to study on the go? Go to your companion website and download an audio version of this review section to your media player.

1. What developments occur from conception through birth?

Prenatal development occurs in stages: the germinal, embryonic, and fetal stages. During the germinal stage, the zygote divides as it travels through the Fallopian tube and becomes implanted in the uterine wall. The major organ systems are formed during the embryonic stage, and the fetal stage is characterized by maturation and gains in size.

2. What physical developments occur during childhood?

Reflexes are inborn responses to stimuli that in many cases are essential to the survival of the infant. Examples include sucking and swallowing. The motor development of the child involves the interaction of maturation and experience. Children whose experience is restricted often catch up. Early physical training does not necessarily provide important advantages. Newborn babies can see quite well and show greater interest in complex visual stimuli than in simple ones. Infants are capable of depth perception by the time they can crawl. Newborns can normally hear and show a preference for their mother's voice. Newborns show preferences for pleasant odors and sweet foods.

3. Does development occur gradually or in stages?

Stage theorists like Freud and Piaget view development as discontinuous. According to them, people go through distinct periods of development that differ in quality and follow an orderly sequence. Learning theorists, in contrast, tend to view psychological development as a more continuous process. Some aspects of development, such as the adolescent growth spurt, are discontinuous. There is controversy as to whether cognitive development is continuous or discontinuous.

4. What are Jean Piaget's views of cognitive development?

Piaget saw children as budding scientists who actively strive to make sense of the perceptual world. He defined intelligence as involving the processes of assimilation and accommodation. Piaget's view of cognitive development includes four stages: sensorimotor (prior to the use of symbols and language); preoperational (characterized by egocentric thought, animism, artificialism, and inability to center on more than one aspect of a situation); concrete operational (characterized by conservation, less egocentrism, reversibility, and subjective moral judgments); and formal operational (characterized by abstract logic).

5. What are the key concepts of Vygotsky's theory of cognitive development?

Vygotsky's key concepts include the *zone of proximal development (ZPD)* and *scaffolding*. When learning with other people, children tend to internalize conversations and explanations that help them gain skills. Children learn ways of thinking about solving problems within a cultural context.

6. How do children reason about right and wrong?

Lawrence Kohlberg hypothesized that children's moral reasoning develops through three levels, each of which consists of two stages. Moral decisions develop from being based on pain and pleasure ("preconventional"), through necessity to maintain the social order ("conventional"), to reliance on one's own conscience ("postconventional"). Not all individuals reach the postconventional level.

7. What are Erikson's stages of psychosocial development?

Erikson hypothesizes that there are eight stages of psychosocial development. Each represents a life crisis. The first of these is "trust versus mistrust," during which the crisis centers on the child's learning that the world is a good place that can meet his or her needs.

8. How do feelings of attachment develop? What kinds of experiences affect attachment?

According to Ainsworth, there are three stages of attachment: the initial-preattachment phase, the attachment-in-the-making phase, and the clear-cut-attachment phase. Bowlby adds fear of strangers as a factor in attachment. Behaviorists have argued that children become attached to their mothers through conditioning because their mothers feed them and attend to their other needs. Harlow's studies with rhesus monkeys suggest that an innate motive, contact comfort, may be more important than conditioning in the development of attachment. There are critical developmental periods during which animals such as geese and ducks become attached instinctively to (or imprinted on) an object that they follow.

9. What types of parental behavior are connected with variables such as self-esteem, achievement motivation, and independence in children?

Styles of parental behavior include the authoritative, authoritarian, and permissive styles. The children of authoritative parents are the most achievement oriented and well adjusted.

10. What physical developments occur during adolescence?

Adolescence begins at puberty and ends with assumption of adult responsibilities. Changes that lead to reproductive capacity and secondary sex characteristics are stimulated by increased levels of testosterone in the male and of estrogen and androgens in the female. During the adolescent growth spurt, young people may grow 6 or more inches in a year.

11. What cognitive developments occur during adolescence?

Formal operational thinking appears in adolescence, but not everyone reaches it. Two consequences of adolescent egocentrism are the imaginary audience and the personal fable. The imaginary audience refers to the adolescent beliefs that they are the center of attention and that other people are as concerned with their appearance and behavior as they are. The personal fable refers to the adolescent belief that one's feelings and ideas are special, even unique, and that one is invulnerable.

12. What social and emotional developments occur during adolescence?

Adolescents and parents are often in conflict because adolescents desire more independence and may experiment with things that can jeopardize their health. Despite bickering, most adolescents continue to love and respect their parents. According to Erikson, adolescents strive to forge an ego identity—a sense of who they are and what they stand for. High hormone levels stir interest in sex. Most sexually active adolescents do not use contraceptives reliably. Thus about 1 teenage girl in 10 gets pregnant each year.

13. What physical developments occur during adulthood?

People are usually at the height of their physical powers during young adulthood. Middle adulthood is characterized by a gradual decline in strength. Research suggests that most women go through menopause without great difficulty. Older people show less sensory acuity, and their reaction time lengthens. The immune system weakens.

14. What are the gender and ethnic differences in life expectancy?

Women outlive men by nearly seven years, and European and Asian Americans tend to outlive other ethnic groups in the United States. By and large, the groups who live longer are more likely to seek and make use of health care.

15. Why do we age?

Heredity plays a role in longevity. One theory (programmed senescence) suggests that aging and death are determined by our genes. Another theory (wear-and-tear theory) holds that

Recite—An Active Summary™

factors such as pollution, disease, and ultraviolet light weaken the body so that it loses the ability to repair itself. Exercise, proper diet, and *not* smoking all contribute to longevity.

16. What cognitive developments occur during adulthood?

People are usually at the height of their cognitive powers during early adulthood, but people can be creative for a lifetime. Memory functioning declines with age. People tend to retain verbal ability, as shown by vocabulary and general knowledge, into advanced old age. Crystallized intelligence—one's vocabulary and accumulated knowledge—generally increases with age. Fluid intelligence—the ability to process information rapidly—declines.

17. What is Alzheimer's disease? What are its origins?

Alzheimer's disease is characterized by cognitive deterioration in memory, language, and problem solving. On a biological level, it is connected with reduced levels of acetylcholine in the brain and with the buildup of plaque in the brain.

18. What social and emotional developments occur during young adulthood?

Young adulthood is generally characterized by efforts to advance in the business world and the development of intimate ties. Many young adults reassess the directions of their lives during the "age-30 transition."

19. What social and emotional developments occur during middle adulthood?

Many theorists view middle adulthood as a time of crisis (the "midlife crisis") and further reassessment. Many adults try to come to terms with the discrepancies between their achievements and the dreams of their youth during middle adulthood. Some middle-aged adults become depressed when their youngest child leaves home (the so-called empty-nest syndrome), but many report increased satisfaction, stability, and self-confidence.

20. What social and emotional developments occur during late adulthood?

Erikson characterizes late adulthood as the stage of ego integrity versus despair. He saw the basic challenge as maintaining the belief that life is worthwhile in the face of physical deterioration.

21. How do people in the United States age today?

Most older Americans report being generally satisfied with their lives. "Successful agers" reshape their lives to focus on what they find important, maintain a positive outlook, and find new challenges.

22. What are psychological perspectives on death and dying?

Kübler-Ross hypothesized five stages of dying among people who are terminally ill: denial, anger, bargaining, depression, and final acceptance. However, other investigators find that psychological reactions to approaching death are more varied than Kübler-Ross suggests.

 Go to **http://psychology.wadsworth. com/rathus_pcc9e** to access an interactive version of this active summary.

Key Terms

Neonate (p. 90)
Zygote (p. 90)
Germinal stage (p. 90)
Period of the ovum (p. 90)
Embryonic stage (p. 90)
Maturation (p. 91)
Androgens (p. 91)
Amniotic sac (p. 91)
Placenta (p. 91)
Umbilical cord (p. 91)
Fetal stage (p. 91)

Reflex (p. 93)
Rooting (p. 93)
Fixation time (p. 94)
Assimilation (p. 97)
Schema (p. 97)
Accommodation (p. 97)
Object permanence (p. 99)
Sensorimotor stage (p. 100)
Preoperational stage (p. 100)

Egocentrism (p. 100)
Animism (p. 100)
Artificialism (p. 100)
Conservation (p. 101)
Center (p. 101)
Objective responsibility (p. 101)
Concrete-operational stage (p. 101)
Decentration (p. 101)
Subjective moral judgment (p. 102)

Reversibility (p. 102)
Zone of proximal development (ZPD) (p. 103)
Scaffolding (p. 103)
Preconventional level (p. 105)
Conventional level (p. 106)
Trust versus mistrust (p. 106)
Autonomy (p. 106)

ACTIVE LEARNING RESOURCES

Visit your Companion Website for Video, Quizzing, and Self-Assessment!

http://psychology.wadsworth.com/rathus_pcc9e
On this site you can access the Piaget's Stages of Development video highlighted by the Video Connections icon on p. 97. In addition there are many quizzing opportunities including interactive versions of the fill-in-the-blank Active Review sections in your book. You can also fill out and score the Self-Assessment on p. 125.

Study on the Go!

Don't have time to study right now? You can study on the go! Visit your companion website and download an audio version of the Recite—An Active Summary section to your media player.

ThomsonNOW

http://www.thomsonedu.com
Need help studying? This site is your one-stop study shop. Take a Pre-Test and Thomson NOW will generate a Personalized Study Plan based on your test results. The Study Plan will identify the topics you need to review and direct you to online resources to help you master those topics. You can then take a Post-Test to determine the concepts you have mastered and what you still need to work on.

Author Blog

What does your author have to say about the state of psychology? Visit your companion website every Tuesday and click on "Author Blog," where he'll talk about the most recent controversies and hot topics in psychology.

Truth or Fiction?

T F People have five senses.

T F If we could see waves of light with slightly longer wavelengths, warm-blooded animals would glow in the dark.

T F People sometimes hear what they want to hear.

T F When we mix blue and yellow light, we obtain green light.

T F The bodies of catfish are covered with taste buds.

T F The skin is a sensory organ as well as a protective coating for the body.

T F You have a sense that keeps you an upright person.

T F Some people can read other people's minds.

T F Many people experience pain in limbs that have been amputated.

 Go to **http://psychology.wadsworth.com/ rathus_pcc9e** to answer and score this Truth or Fiction quiz.

© Erwin Redl/www.paramedia.net

Sensation and Perception

Preview

In *The Matrix* film series, our world is unreal. The people we touch, the food we taste, the distant hills we see, the sunshine we feel on our skin, the voices and traffic we hear, the perfumes and exhaust we smell, the buildings that shelter us from the wetness of the rain and the bite of winter ice—all these are nothing but software. We, too—that is, you and I—are also software.

We lead our lives in the early days of the 21st century. But according to the films, the real world is found 200 years in our future. Real people are plugged into devices that harvest their energy and provide them with simulated lives 200 years in the past. How are people given their make-believe lives? Cells in their brains are caused to fire in patterns that create illusions of reality. We think we see because the cells involved in vision are firing. We think we hear because the cells involved in hearing are firing. And so on for all our senses. The illusion is almost perfect. The great majority of us are content to dwell as software in an illusory world. Our interactions with computerized objects and other people's software selves are satisfying and convincing enough. Only a very few sense that something is wrong, but not even they are sure what it is.

The real world, such as it is, is a withered sunless specter of its former self. It is ruled by machines, whose artificial intelligence rivals or surpasses our own. People lie in pods, hooked into the virtual world of the early 2000s. The muscles in their limbs remain unused and weaken. Their eyes stay shut.

Yet sensory information is transmitted to their central nervous systems, and they piece it together to form their representations of the world outside. In *The Matrix*, the world outside is very different, but their virtual reality is created much as our "real reality" is.

Sensation and Perception: Your Tickets of Admission to the World Outside

Question: What are sensation and perception? **Sensation** is the stimulation of sensory receptors and the transmission of sensory information to the central nervous system (the spinal cord or brain). Sensory receptors are located in sensory organs such as the eyes and ears, the skin, and elsewhere in the body. Stimulation of the senses is an automatic process. It results from sources of energy, like light and sound, or from the presence of chemicals, as in smell and taste. In *The Matrix*, a step is skipped: There is no stimulation of sensory receptors in the eyes, the nose, the skin,

■ **How Do Our Senses Connect Us with the World Outside?** In *The Matrix* film series, our world is unreal. The people we touch, the food we taste, even the sun we feel on our skin are all software. In this photo, Keanu Reeves battles not only gravity but also a software program (right) who is an expert in kung fu.

Sensation The stimulation of sensory receptors and the transmission of sensory information to the central nervous system.

Warner Bros./The Kobal Collection

and so on. There is, instead, direct transmission of sensory information to the central nervous system.

Perception is not automatic. Perception is an active process in which sensations are organized and interpreted to form an inner representation of the world. Perception may begin with sensation, but it also reflects our experiences and expectations as it makes sense of sensory stimuli. A person standing 15 feet away and a 12-inch-tall doll may cast similar-sized images on the back of your eye, but whether you interpret the shape to be a foot-long doll or a full-grown person 15 feet away is a matter of perception that depends on your experience with dolls, people, and distance.

In this chapter you will see that your personal map of reality—your ticket of admission to a world of changing sights, sounds, and other sources of sensory input—depends largely on the so-called five senses: vision, hearing, smell, taste, and touch. We will see, however, that touch is just one of several "skin senses," which also include pressure, warmth, cold, and pain. There are also senses that alert you to your own body position without your having to watch every step you take. As we explore the nature of each of these senses, we will find that similar sensations may lead to different perceptions in different people—or within the same person in different situations. **Truth or Fiction Revisited:** People do have more than five senses.

Before we begin our voyage through the senses, let us consider a number of concepts that apply to all of them: absolute threshold, difference threshold, signal-detection theory, and sensory adaptation. In doing so, we will learn why we can dim the lights gradually to near darkness without anyone noticing. (Sneaky?) We will also learn why we might become indifferent to the savory aromas of delightful dinners. (Disappointing?) **Questions: How do we know when something is there? How do we know when it has changed?**

Absolute Threshold: So, Is It There or Not?

Gustav Fechner used the term **absolute threshold** to refer to the weakest amount of a stimulus that a person can distinguish from no stimulus at all. For example, the absolute threshold for light would be the minimum brightness (physical energy) required to activate the visual sensory system.

Psychophysicists look for the absolute thresholds of the senses by exposing individuals to progressively stronger stimuli until they find the minimum stimuli that the person can detect no more (and no less) than 50 percent of the time. However, it has been discovered that these absolute thresholds are not really absolute. That is, some people are more sensitive than others, and even the same person might have a slightly different response from one occasion to another.

Nevertheless, under ideal conditions, our ability to detect stimuli are amazingly sensitive. The following are measures of the absolute thresholds for the senses of vision, hearing, taste, smell, and touch:

◆ *Vision:* a candle flame viewed from about 30 miles on a clear, dark night.
◆ *Hearing:* a watch ticking from about 20 feet away in a quiet room.
◆ *Taste:* 1 teaspoon of sugar dissolved in 2 gallons of water.
◆ *Smell:* about one drop of perfume diffused throughout a small house (1 part in 500 million).
◆ *Touch:* the pressure of the wing of a fly falling on a cheek from a distance of about 0.4 inch.

It's interesting to imagine how our lives would differ if the absolute thresholds for the human senses differed. For example, if your ears were more sensitive to sounds that are low in **pitch,** you might hear the collisions among molecules of air. If you could see light with slightly longer wavelengths, you would see infrared light waves. Your world would be transformed because heat generates infrared light. **Truth or Fiction Revisited:** Moreover, if we could see waves of light with slightly longer

Perception The process by which sensations are organized into an inner representation of the world.

Absolute threshold The minimal amount of energy that can produce a sensation.

Psychophysicist A person who studies the relationships between physical stimuli (such as light or sound) and their perception.

Pitch The highness or lowness of a sound, as determined by the frequency of the sound waves.

In Profile | GUSTAV THEODOR FECHNER

Gustav Theodor Fechner (1801–1887) was interested in the occult and reported attending seances in which a bed, a table, and he himself moved in response to strange forces. He was interested in spiritual phenomena and wrote a bereaved friend that death is but a transition to another state of existence, in which one's soul merges with others to join the Supreme Spirit. Yet he advocated scientific rigor in all other matters and contributed to the precise measurement of the senses. Under the pen name of "Dr. Mises," he ridiculed unscientific thought by a tongue-in-cheek argument: (a) Insects have six legs; (b) mammals have four; and (c) birds, who ascend closest to heaven, only two. (d) Therefore, angels, higher yet, must have none. In contrast to his humorous treatise on legless angels, Fechner insisted on actually measuring things rather than just arguing about them.

The son and grandson of German village pastors, Fechner, like his father, combined religious faith with a skeptical scientific outlook.

His father scandalously installed a lightning rod on the local church at a time when it was assumed that God would take care of heavenly threats to faithful parishes. His father also ignored tradition and preached without a wig, arguing that Jesus had done the same.

Fechner obtained a degree in medicine at the University of Leipzig, but his interests turned to physics and math. He founded the discipline known as *psychophysics,* which deals with the ways in which we translate physical events such as lights and sounds into psychological experiences. For example, light and sound are types of physical energy. It may surprise you that we do not sense them directly, powerful as they may seem to us. Instead, these sources of energy are converted into neural impulses by our sensory receptors—our eyes and ears and so on. The process of transforming physical energy (in the cases of light, sound, and touch) or chemicals (in the cases of odors and tastes) into neural impulses is called *transduction.* Many of Fechner's laboratory methods remain in use today.

 Go to **http://psychology.wadsworth.com/ rathus_pcc9e** to access more information about Gustav Theodor Fechner.

wavelengths, warm-blooded animals would glow in the dark. Also, the worlds of those who are blind, deaf, or have other variations in their sensory capabilities can be substantially different. These different experiences of reality may not be viewed as losses, either. For example, some deaf people have advocated against artificial restoration of hearing through surgical means because of the beauty and value of a world of silence and sign language. (For more on deafness, see page 168.)

Difference Threshold: Is It the Same, or Is It Different?

How much of a difference in intensity between two lights is required before you will detect one as being brighter than the other? The minimum difference in magnitude of two stimuli required to tell them apart is their **difference threshold.** As with the absolute threshold, psychologists have agreed to the criterion of a difference in magnitudes that can be detected 50% of the time.

Psychophysicist Ernst Weber discovered through laboratory research that the threshold for perceiving differences in the intensity of light is about 2% (actually closer to 1/60th) of their intensity. This fraction, 1/60th, is known as **Weber's constant** for light. A closely related concept is the **just noticeable difference (jnd),** the minimum difference in stimuli that a person can detect. For example, at least 50% of the time, most people can tell if a light gets just 1/60th brighter or dimmer. Weber's constant for light holds whether we are comparing two quite bright lights or two moderately dull lights. However, it becomes inaccurate when we compare extremely bright or extremely dull lights.

Weber's constant for noticing differences in lifted weight is 1/53rd. (Round it off to 1/50th.) That means if you are strong enough to heft a 100-pound barbell, you would not notice that it was heavier until about 2 pounds were added. Yet if you are a runner who carries 1-pound dumbbells, you would definitely notice if someone slipped you dumbbells even a pound heavier because the increase would be 100%, not a small fraction.

What about sound? People are most sensitive to changes in the pitch (frequency) of sounds. The Weber constant for pitch is 1/333, meaning that on average, people can tell when a tone rises or falls in pitch by an extremely small one-third of 1%. (Singers have to be right on pitch. The smallest error makes them sound sharp or flat.) Remember this when friends criticize your singing—you may not be "tone deaf" but just slightly off. The sense of taste is much less sensitive. On

Difference threshold The minimal difference in intensity required between two sources of energy so that they will be perceived as being different.

Weber's constant The fraction of the intensity by which a source of physical energy must be increased or decreased so that a difference in intensity will be perceived.

Just noticeable difference (jnd) The minimal amount by which a source of energy must be increased or decreased so that a difference in intensity will be perceived.

In Profile | ERNST HEINRICH WEBER

His research tools included knitting needles, lamps, and the little weights druggists use to measure powders and potions. He showed that the sense of touch actually consists of several senses: pressure, temperature, and pain. He also showed that there is a "muscle sense" *(kinesthesis)* that people use to sense the movements of their arms, legs, and so on even when their eyes are closed.

Born in Wittenberg, Germany, Ernst Heinrich Weber (1795–1878) devoted himself to the study of sensation and perception. He was the third of thirteen children and one of three sons who became distinguished scientists. (If the times had been different, one wonders what the sisters would have accomplished.) He obtained his doctorate in physiology at the University of Leipzig and taught there until his retirement.

The knitting needles were used to touch people's backs. Weber would ask them to place a finger where the needle had been as a way of assessing their sensitivity to touch. Using a series of weights, he assessed the smallest difference—the *just noticeable difference (jnd)*—that people could perceive and discovered that the jnd differs for each sense.

 Go to **http://psychology.wadsworth.com/ rathus_pcc9e** to access more information about Ernst Heinrich Weber.

The Granger Collection, New York

average, people cannot detect differences in saltiness of less than 20%. That is why those low-salt chips that have 15% less salt than your favorite do not taste so bad.

Signal-Detection Theory: Is Being Bright Enough?

From the discussion so far it might seem as if people are simply switched on by certain amounts of stimulation. This is not quite so. People are influenced by psychological factors as well as by external changes. **Signal-detection theory** considers the human aspects of sensation and perception. **Question: What is signal-detection theory?**

According to signal-detection theory, the relationship between a physical stimulus and a sensory response is not just mechanical. People's ability to detect stimuli such as meaningful blips on a radar screen depends not only on the intensity of the blips but also on their training (learning), motivation (desire to perceive meaningful blips), and psychological states such as fatigue or alertness.

The intensity of the signal is just one factor that determines whether people will perceive sensory stimuli (signals) or a difference between signals. Another is the degree to which the signal can be distinguished from background noise. It is easier to hear a friend in a quiet room than in a room in which people are talking loudly and clinking glasses. The sharpness or acuteness of a person's biological sensory system is still another factor. Is sensory capacity fully developed? Is it diminished by advanced age?

Truth or Fiction Revisited: It is true that people sometimes hear what they want to hear. That is, we tend to detect stimuli we are searching for. Signal-detection theory also considers psychological factors such as motivation, expectations, and learning. For example, the place in which you are reading this book may be abuzz with signals. If you are outside, perhaps a breeze is blowing against your face. Perhaps the shadows of passing clouds darken the scene now and then. If you are inside, perhaps there are the occasional clanks and hums emitted by a heating system. Perhaps the aromas of dinner are hanging in the air, or the voices from a TV set suggest a crowd in another room. Yet you are focusing your attention on this page (I hope). Thus, the other signals recede into the background of your consciousness. One psychological factor in signal detection is the focusing or narrowing of attention to signals that the person deems important.

Feature Detectors in the Brain: Firing on Cue

Imagine that you are standing by the curb of a busy street as a bus approaches. When neurons in your sensory organs—in this case, your eyes—are stimulated by the approach of the bus, they relay information to the sensory cortex in the brain. Nobel prize winners David Hubel and Torsten Wiesel (1979) discovered that various neurons in the visual cortex of the brain fire in response to particular features

Signal-detection theory The view that the perception of sensory stimuli involves the interaction of physical, biological, and psychological factors.

DAVID OLIVER/Getty Images

■ **Signal Detection** The detection of signals is determined not only by the physical characteristics of the signals but also by psychological factors such as motivation and attention. The people in this photo are tuned into their newspapers for the moment and not to each other.

Feature detectors Neurons in the sensory cortex that fire in response to specific features of sensory information such as lines or edges of objects.

Sensory adaptation The processes by which organisms become more sensitive to stimuli that are low in magnitude and less sensitive to stimuli that are constant or ongoing in magnitude.

Sensitization The type of sensory adaptation in which we become more sensitive to stimuli that are low in magnitude. Also called *positive adaptation.*

Desensitization The type of sensory adaptation in which we become less sensitive to constant stimuli. Also called *negative adaptation.*

of the visual input. **Question: What are feature detectors?** Many cells in the brain detect (fire in response to) lines presented at various angles—vertical, horizontal, and in between. Other cells fire in response to specific colors.

Because they respond to different aspects or features of a scene, these brain cells are termed **feature detectors.** In the example of the bus, visual feature detectors respond to the bus's edges, depth, contours, textures, shadows, speed, and kinds of motion (up, down, forward, and back). There are also feature detectors for other senses. Auditory feature detectors, for example, respond to the pitch, loudness, and other aspects of the sounds of the bus.

Sensory Adaptation: Where Did It Go?

Our sensory systems are admirably suited to a changing environment. **Question: How do our sensory systems adapt to a changing environment? Sensory adaptation** refers to the processes by which we become more sensitive to stimuli of low magnitude and less sensitive to stimuli that remain the same (such as the background noises outside the window).

Consider how the visual sense adapts to lower intensities of light. When we first walk into a darkened movie theater, we see little but the images on the screen. As we search for our seats, however, we become increasingly sensitive to the faces around us and to the features of the theater. The process of becoming more sensitive to stimulation is referred to as **sensitization,** or positive adaptation.

But we become less sensitive to constant stimulation. Sources of light appear to grow dimmer as we adapt to them. In fact, if you could keep an image completely stable on the retinas of your eyes—which is virtually impossible to accomplish without a motionless image and stabilizing equipment—the image would fade within a few seconds and be very difficult to see. Similarly, at the beach we soon become less aware of the lapping of the waves. When we live in a city, we become desensitized to traffic sounds except for the occasional backfire or siren. And, as you may have noticed from experiences with freshly painted rooms, sensitivity to disagreeable odors fades quite rapidly. The process of becoming less sensitive to stimulation is referred to as **desensitization,** or negative adaptation.

Our sensitivities to stimulation provide our brains with information that we use to understand and control the world outside. This information influences our behavior and mental processes. Therefore, it is not surprising that psychologists study the ways in which we sense and perceive this information—through vision, hearing, the chemical senses, and yet other senses, as we see throughout the remainder of the chapter.

Your Turn: Now that we have discussed basic information about sensation and perception, enhance your mastery of the material with the nearby "Learning Connections." Review the material by filling in the blanks, reflect on the material by relating it to other things you know, and think critically about it.

Learning Connections | SENSATION AND PERCEPTION: YOUR TICKETS OF ADMISSION TO THE WORLD OUTSIDE

ACTIVE REVIEW (1) _____ is a mechanical process that involves the stimulation of sensory receptors and the transmission of sensory information to the central nervous system. (2) _____ is the organization of sensations into an inner representation of the world; it reflects learning and expectations, as well as sensations. (3) The _____ threshold for a stimulus, such as light, is the lowest intensity at which it can be detected. (4) The minimum difference in intensity that can be discriminated is the _____ threshold. (5) According to _____-detection theory, many factors determine perception of a stimulus: the sensory stimuli, the biological sensory system of the person, and psychological factors, such as motivation and attention.

REFLECT AND RELATE Think of times when you have been so involved in something that you didn't notice the heat or the cold. Think of times you have grown so used to sounds like those made by crickets or trains at night that you fall asleep without hearing them. How do these experiences relate to signal-detection theory?

CRITICAL THINKING Which factors in sensation and perception reflect our nature? Which reflect nurture?

Go to **http://psychology.wadsworth.com/ rathus_pcc9e** for an interactive version of this Learning Connections unit.

Vision: Letting the Sun Shine In

Our eyes are literally our "windows on the world." More than half of our brain's cerebral cortex is devoted to visual functions (Basic Behavioral Science Task Force, 1996b). Because vision is our dominant sense, blindness is considered by many to be the most debilitating type of sensory loss. To understand vision, let us first consider the nature of light.

Light: How Dazzling?

Light is fascinating stuff. It radiates. It illuminates. It dazzles. It glows. It beckons like a beacon. We speak of the "light of reason." We speak of genius as "brilliance." In almost all cultures, light is a symbol of goodness and knowledge. People who aren't in the know are said to be "in the dark." **Question: Just what is light?**

It is **visible light** that triggers visual sensations. Yet visible light is just one small part of a spectrum of electromagnetic energy that surrounds us (see Figure 4.1). All forms of electromagnetic energy move in waves, and different kinds of electromagnetic energy have signature wavelengths, as follows:

◆ *Cosmic rays:* The wavelengths of these rays from outer space are only a few *trillionths* of an inch long.
◆ *Radio waves:* Some radio signals extend for miles.
◆ *Visible light:* Different colors have different wavelengths, with violet the shortest at about 400 *billionths* of a meter in length and red the longest at 700 billionths of a meter.

Have you seen rainbows or light that has been broken down into several colors as it filtered through your windows? Sir Isaac Newton, the British scientist, discovered that sunlight could be broken down into different colors by means of a triangular solid of glass called a *prism* (Figure 4.1). When I took introductory psychology, I was taught to remember the colors of the spectrum, from longest to shortest wavelengths, by using the mnemonic device *Roy G. Biv* (red, orange, yellow, green, blue, indigo, violet). The wavelength of visible light determines its

Visible light The part of the electromagnetic spectrum that stimulates the eye and produces visual sensations.

FIGURE 4.1 **The Visible Spectrum**

By passing a source of white light, such as sunlight, through a prism, we break it down into the colors of the visible spectrum. The visible spectrum is just a narrow segment of the electromagnetic spectrum. The electromagnetic spectrum also includes radio waves, microwaves, X rays, cosmic rays, and many others. Different forms of electromagnetic energy have wavelengths which vary from a few trillionths of a meter to thousands of miles. Visible light varies in wavelength from about 400 to 700 *billionths* of a meter. (A meter = 39.37 inches.)

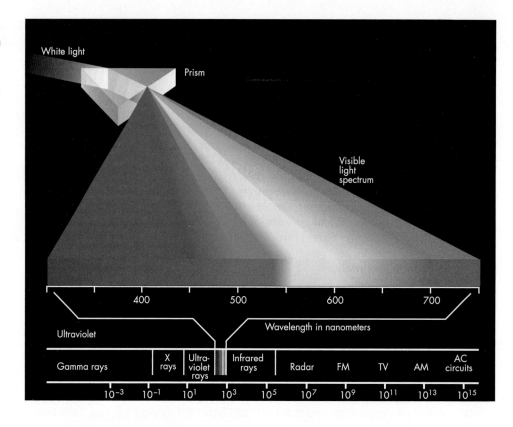

color, or **hue.** The wavelength for red is longer than the wavelength for orange, and so on through the spectrum.

The Eye: The Better to See You With

Consider that magnificent invention called the camera, which records visual experiences. In traditional cameras, light enters an opening and is focused onto a sensitive surface, or film. Chemicals on film create a lasting impression of the image that entered the camera.

Question: How does the eye work? The eye—our living camera—is no less remarkable. Look at its major parts, as shown in Figure 4.2. As with a film or TV camera, light enters through a narrow opening and is projected onto a sensitive surface. Light first passes through the transparent **cornea,** which covers the front of the eye's surface. (The "white" of the eye, or *sclera,* is composed of hard protective tissue.) The amount of light that passes through the cornea is determined by the size of the opening of the muscle called the **iris,** which is the colored part of the eye. The opening in the iris is the **pupil.** The size of the pupil adjusts automatically to the amount of light present. Therefore, you do not have to purposefully open your eyes further to see better in low lighting conditions. The more intense the light, the smaller the opening. In a similar fashion, we adjust the amount of light allowed into a camera according to its brightness. Interestingly, pupil size is also sensitive to emotional response: We can literally be "wide-eyed with fear."

Once light passes through the iris, it encounters the **lens.** The lens adjusts or accommodates to the image by changing its thickness. Changes in thickness permit a clear image of the object to be projected onto the retina. These changes focus the light according to the distance of the object from the viewer. If you hold a finger at arm's length and slowly bring it toward your nose, you will feel tension in the eye as the thickness of the lens accommodates to keep the retinal image in focus. When people squint to bring an object into focus, they are adjusting the thickness of the lens. In contrast, the lens in a camera does not accommodate to the distance of objects. Instead, to focus the light that is projected onto the film, the camera lens is moved farther from the film or closer to it, as in a zoom lens.

Hue The color of light, as determined by its wavelength.

Cornea Transparent tissue forming the outer surface of the eyeball.

Iris A muscular membrane whose dilation regulates the amount of light that enters the eye.

Pupil The apparently black opening in the center of the iris, through which light enters the eye.

Lens A transparent body behind the iris that focuses an image on the retina.

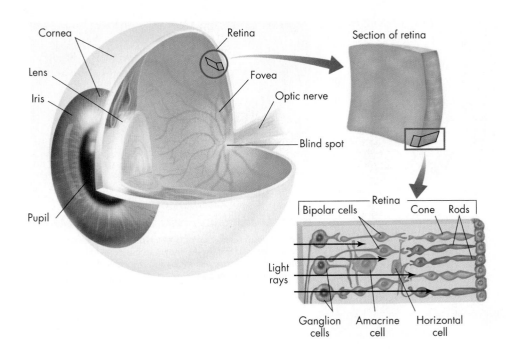

FIGURE 4.2 **The Human Eye**
In both the eye and a camera, light enters through a narrow opening and is projected onto a sensitive surface. In the eye, the photosensitive surface is called the retina, and information concerning the changing images on the retina is transmitted to the brain. The retina contains photoreceptors called rods and cones. Rods and cones transmit sensory input back through the bipolar neurons to the ganglion neurons. The axons of the ganglion neurons form the optic nerve, which transmits sensory stimulation through the brain to the visual cortex of the occipital lobe.

Go to **http://psychology.wadsworth. com/rathus_pcc9e** to access an interactive version of this figure.

The **retina** is like the film or image surface of the camera. However, the retina consists of cells called **photoreceptors** that are sensitive to light (photosensitive). There are two types of photoreceptors: *rods* and *cones*. The retina (see Figure 4.2) contains several layers of cells: the rods and cones, **bipolar cells,** and **ganglion cells.** All of these cells are neurons. The rods and cones respond to light with chemical changes that create neural impulses that are picked up by the bipolar cells. These then activate the ganglion cells. The axons of the million or so ganglion cells in our retina converge to form the **optic nerve.** The optic nerve conducts sensory input to the brain, where it is relayed to the visual area of the occipital lobe. As if this were not enough, the eye has additional neurons to enhance this process. Amacrine cells and horizontal cells make sideways connections at a level near the rods and cones and at another level near the ganglion cells. As a result, single bipolar cells can pick up signals from many rods and cones, and, in turn, a single ganglion cell is able to funnel information from multiple bipolar cells. In fact, rods and cones outnumber ganglion cells by more than 100 to 1.

RODS AND CONES As mentioned, **rods** and **cones** are the photoreceptors in the retina (see Figure 4.3). About 125 million rods and 6.4 million cones are distributed across the retina. The cones are most densely packed in a small spot at the center of the retina called the **fovea** (Fig. 3.2). Visual acuity (sharpness and detail) is greatest at this spot. The fovea is composed almost exclusively of cones. Rods are most dense just outside the fovea and thin out toward the periphery of the retina.

Rods allow us to see in black and white. Cones provide color vision. In low lighting, it is possible to photograph a clearer image with black-and-white film than with color film. Similarly, rods are more sensitive to dim light than cones. Therefore, as the illumination grows dim, as during the evening and nighttime hours, objects appear to lose their color well before their outlines fade completely from view.

In contrast to the visual acuity of the fovea is the **blind spot,** which is insensitive to visual stimulation. It is the part of the retina where the axons of the ganglion cells converge to form the optic nerve (see Figures 4.2 and 4.4).

Visual acuity (sharpness of vision) is connected with the shape of the eye. People who have to be unusually close to an object to discriminate its details are *nearsighted.* People who see distant objects unusually clearly but have difficulty focusing on nearby objects are *farsighted.* Nearsightedness can result when the

Retina The area of the inner surface of the eye that contains rods and cones.

Photoreceptors Cells that respond to light.

Bipolar cells Neurons that conduct neural impulses from rods and cones to ganglion cells.

Ganglion cells Neurons whose axons form the optic nerve.

Optic nerve The nerve that transmits sensory information from the eye to the brain.

Rods Rod-shaped photoreceptors that are sensitive only to the intensity of light.

Cones Cone-shaped photoreceptors that transmit sensations of color.

Fovea An area near the center of the retina that is dense with cones and where vision is consequently most acute.

Blind spot The area of the retina where axons from ganglion cells meet to form the optic nerve.

Visual acuity Sharpness of vision.

FIGURE 4.3 Rods and Cones

You have about 125 million rods and 6.4 million cones distributed across the retina of each eye. Only cones provide sensations of color. The fovea of the eye is almost exclusively populated by cones, which are then distributed more sparsely as you work toward the periphery of the retina.

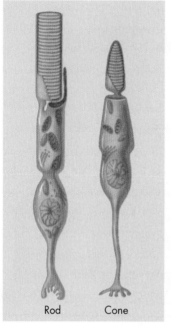

B. Each human retina contains two types of photoreceptor cells: rods and cones. As shown in this color-enhanced photo, the rods are rod-shaped in appearance and the cones are cone-shaped.

Rod   Cone

A.

eyeball is elongated so that the images of distant objects are focused in front of the retina. When the eyeball is too short, the images of nearby objects are focused behind the retina, causing farsightedness. Eyeglasses or contact lenses can be used to help nearsighted people focus distant objects on their retinas. Laser surgery can correct vision by actually changing the shape of the eye. Farsighted people usually see well enough without eyeglasses until they reach their middle years, when they may need glasses for reading.

Beginning in the late 30s to the mid-40s, the lenses start to grow brittle, making it more difficult to accommodate to, or focus on, objects. This condition is called **presbyopia,** from the Greek words for "old man" and "eyes," but presbyopia occurs by middle adulthood, not late adulthood. Presbyopia makes it difficult to perceive nearby visual stimuli. People who had normal visual acuity in their youth often require corrective lenses to read in middle adulthood and beyond.

LIGHT ADAPTATION When we walk out onto a dark street, we may at first not be able to see people, trees, and cars clearly; but, as time goes on, we are better able to discriminate the features of people and objects. The process of adjusting to lower lighting conditions is called **dark adaptation.**

Figure 4.5 shows the amount of light needed for detection as a function of the amount of time spent in the dark. The cones and rods adapt at different rates. The cones, which permit perception of color, reach their maximum adaptation to darkness in about 10 minutes. The rods, which allow perception of light and dark only, are more sensitive to dim light and continue to adapt to darkness for up to about 45 minutes.

Presbyopia A condition characterized by brittleness of the lens.

Dark adaptation The process of adjusting to conditions of lower lighting by increasing the sensitivity of rods and cones.

FIGURE 4.4 The Blind Spot

To try a "disappearing act," close your left eye, hold the book close to your face, and look at the boy with your right eye. Slowly move the book away until the pie disappears. The pie disappears because it is being projected onto the blind spot of your retina, the point at which the axons of ganglion neurons collect to form the optic nerve. Note that when the pie disappears, your brain "fills in" the missing checkerboard pattern, which is one reason that you're not usually aware that you have blind spots.

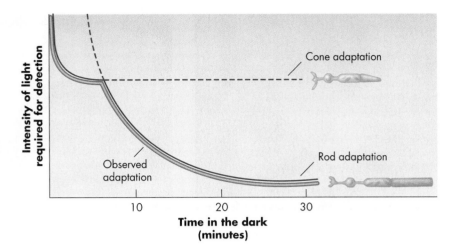

FIGURE 4.5 **Dark Adaptation**
This illustration shows the amount of light necessary for detection as a function of the amount of time spent in the dark. Cones and rods adapt at different rates. Cones, which permit perception of color, reach maximum dark adaptation in about ten minutes. Rods, which permit perception of dark and light only, are more sensitive than cones. Rods continue to adapt for up to about 45 minutes.

Go to **http://psychology.wadsworth. com/rathus_pcc9e** to access an interactive version of this figure.

Adaptation to brighter lighting conditions takes place much more rapidly. When you emerge from the theater into the brilliance of the afternoon, you may at first be painfully surprised by the featureless blaze around you. The visual experience is not unlike turning the brightness of the TV set to its maximum setting, at which the edges of objects seem to dissolve into light. Within a minute or so of entering the street, however, the brightness of the scene dims and objects regain their edges.

Color Vision: Creating an Inner World of Color

For most of us, the world is a place of brilliant colors—the blue-greens of the ocean, the red-oranges of the setting sun, the deepened greens of June, the glories of the purple rhododendron and red hibiscus. Color is an emotional and aesthetic part of our everyday lives. In this section we explore some of the dimensions of color and then examine theories about how we manage to convert different wavelengths of light into perceptions of color. **Question: What are some perceptual dimensions of color?** These include hue, value, and saturation.

The wavelength of light determines its color, or *hue*. The value of a color is its degree of lightness or darkness. The saturation refers to how intense a color appears to us. A fire-engine red will appear more saturated than a pale pinkish red.

Colors can also have psychological associations within various cultural settings. For example, in the United States a bride may be dressed in white as a sign of purity. In traditional India, the guests would be shocked, because white is the color for funerals. Here we mourn in black.

WARM AND COOL COLORS If we bend the colors of the spectrum into a circle, we create a color wheel, as shown in Figure 4.6. Psychologically, the colors on the green-blue side of the color wheel are considered to be cool in temperature. Those colors on the yellow-orange-red side are considered to be warm. Perhaps greens and blues suggest the coolness of the ocean and the sky, whereas things that are burning tend to be red or orange. A room decorated in green or blue may seem more appealing on a hot July day than a room decorated in red or orange.

COMPLEMENTARY COLORS The colors across from one another on the color wheel are labeled **complementary.** Red–green and blue–yellow are the major complementary pairs. If we mix complementary colors together, they dissolve into gray. **Truth or Fiction Revisited:** It is true, therefore, that when we mix blue and yellow light, we obtain green light.

"But wait!" you say. "Blue and yellow cannot be complementary because by mixing pigments of blue and yellow we create green, not gray."

Complementary Descriptive of colors of the spectrum that when combined produce white or nearly white light.

FIGURE 4.6

The Color Wheel

A color wheel can be formed by bending the colors of the spectrum into a circle and placing complementary colors across from one another. (A few colors between violet and red are not found in the spectrum and must be added to complete the circle.) When lights of complementary colors such as yellow and violet-blue are mixed, they dissolve into neutral gray. The afterimage of a color is its complement.

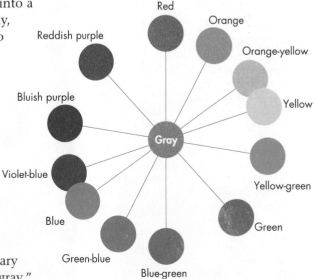

FIGURE 4.7 Additive and Subtractive Color Mixtures Produced by Lights and Pigments

Thomas Young discovered that white light and all the colors of the spectrum could be produced by adding combinations of lights of red, green, and violet-blue and varying their intensities (see Part A). Part B shows subtractive color mixtures, which are formed by mixing pigments, not light.

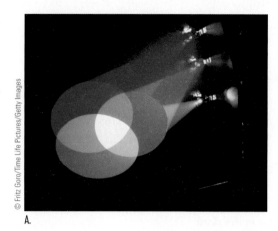
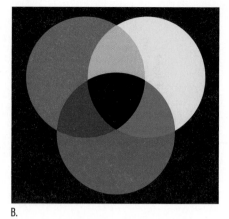

A.

B.

True enough, but we have been talking about mixing *lights,* not *pigments.* Light is the source of all color. Pigments reflect and absorb different wavelengths of light selectively. The mixture of lights is an *additive* process. The mixture of pigments is *subtractive.* Figure 4.7 shows mixtures of lights and pigments of various colors.

Pigments gain their colors by absorbing light from certain segments of the spectrum and reflecting the rest. For example, we see most plant life as green because the pigment in chlorophyll absorbs most of the red, blue, and violet wavelengths of light. The remaining green is reflected. A red pigment absorbs most of the spectrum but reflects red. White pigments reflect all colors equally. Black pigments reflect very little light.

In *Sunday Afternoon on the Island of La Grande Jatte* (Figure 4.8), French painter Georges Seurat molded his figures and forms from dabs of color. Instead of mixing his pigments, he placed points of pure color next to one another. When the painting is viewed from very close (see the detail), the sensations are of pure color. But from a distance the juxtaposition of pure colors creates the impression of mixtures of color.

FIGURE 4.8 *Sunday Afternoon on the Island of La Grande Jatte*

The French painter Georges Seurat molded his figures and forms from dabs of color. Instead of mixing his pigments, he placed points of pure color next to one another. When the viewer is close to the canvas (see the detail), the points of color are apparent. But from a distance, they create the impression of color mixtures.

AFTERIMAGES Before reading on, why don't you try a mini-experiment? Look at the strangely colored American flag in Figure 4.9 for at least half a minute. Try not to blink as you are doing so. Then look at a sheet of white or gray paper. What has happened to the flag? If your color vision is working properly, and if you looked at the miscolored flag long enough, you should see a flag composed of the familiar red, white, and blue. The flag you perceive on the white sheet of paper is an **afterimage** of the first. (If you didn't look at the green, black, and yellow flag long enough the first time, try it again.) In afterimages, persistent sensations of color are followed by perception of the complementary color when the first color is removed. The same holds true for black and white. Staring at one will create an afterimage of the other. The phenomenon of afterimages has contributed to one of the theories of color vision, as we will see.

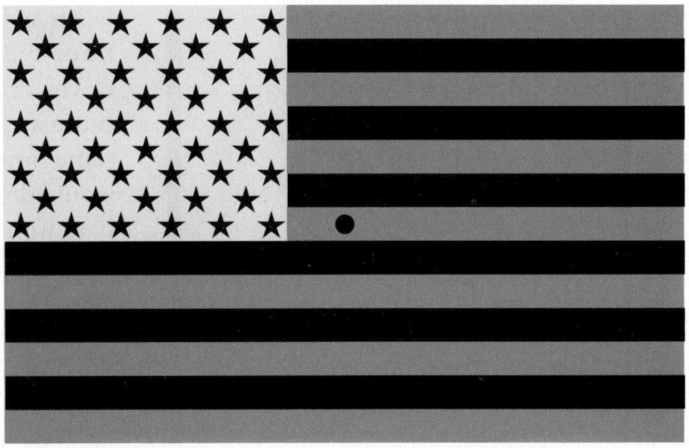

FIGURE 4.9 Three Cheers for the . . . Green, Black, and Yellow?
Don't be concerned. We can readily restore Old Glory to its familiar hues. Place a sheet of white paper beneath the book, and stare at the black dot in the center of the flag for at least 30 seconds. Then remove the book. The afterimage on the paper beneath will look familiar.

Theories of Color Vision: How Colorful?

Adults with normal color vision can discriminate many thousands of colors across the visible spectrum. Different colors have different wavelengths. Although we can vary the physical wavelengths of light in a continuous manner from shorter to longer, many changes in color are discontinuous. For example, our perception of a color shifts suddenly from blue to green, even though the change in wavelength may be smaller than that between two blues.

Question: How do we perceive color? Our ability to perceive color depends on the eye's transmission of different messages to the brain when lights with different wavelengths stimulate the cones in the retina.

CONTROVERSY IN PSYCHOLOGY

What happens in the eye and in the brain when lights with different wavelengths stimulate the retina? How many kinds of color receptors are there?

In this section we explore this controversy by discussing two theories of color vision: the *trichromatic theory* and the *opponent-process theory*.

Trichromatic theory is based on an experiment conducted by the British scientist Thomas Young in the early 1800s. As in Figure 4.7, Young projected three lights of different colors onto a screen so that they partly overlapped. He found that he could create any color from the visible spectrum by simply varying the intensities of the lights. When all three lights fell on the same spot, they created white light, or the appearance of no color at all. The three lights manipulated by Young were red, green, and blue-violet.

The German physiologist Hermann von Helmholtz saw in Young's discovery an explanation of color vision. Helmholtz suggested that the retina in the eye must have three different types of color photoreceptors or cones. Some cones must be sensitive to red light, some to green, and some to blue. We see other colors when two different types of color receptors are stimulated. The perception of yellow, for example, would result from the simultaneous stimulation of receptors for red and green. The trichromatic theory is also known as the Young–Helmholtz theory.

In 1870, another German physiologist, Ewald Hering, proposed the **opponent-process theory** of color vision: There are three types of color receptors; however, they are not sensitive just to the simple hues of red, green, and blue as Helmholtz claimed. Hering suggested instead that afterimages

Afterimage The lingering visual impression made by a stimulus that has been removed.

Trichromatic theory The theory that color vision is made possible by three types of cones, some of which respond to red light, some to green, and some to blue. (From the Greek roots *treis*, meaning "three," and *chroma*, meaning "color.")

Opponent-process theory The theory that color vision is made possible by three types of cones, some of which respond to red or green light, some to blue or yellow, and some only to the intensity of light.

(such as that of the American flag shown in Figure 4.9) are made possible by three types of color receptors: red–green, blue–yellow, and a type that perceives differences in brightness (see Figure 4.10). According to Hering, because a red–green cone could not transmit messages for red and green at the same time, if you stare at the green, black, and yellow flag for 30 seconds, that would disturb the balance of neural activity. The afterimage of red, white, and blue would represent the eye's attempt to reestablish a balance.

Research suggests that each theory of color vision is partially correct—in fact, this might simply be a two-stage process in which the cones are as Helmhotz says, and the transmission signals to the brain are as Hering proposes. For example, research shows that some cones are sensitive to blue, some to green, and some to red (Solomon et al., 2002). But studies of the bipolar and ganglion neurons suggest that messages from cones are transmitted to the brain and relayed by the thalamus to the occipital lobe in an opponent-process fashion (DeValois & Jacobs, 1984; Suttle et al., 2002). Some opponent-process cells that transmit messages to the visual centers in the brain are excited ("turned on") by green light but inhibited ("turned off") by red light. (They fire when you look at the green needles of a fir tree.) Others can be excited by red light but are inhibited by green light. (They fire when you are looking at the red ornaments on the fir tree during the holiday season.) A second set of opponent-process cells responds in an opposite manner to blue and yellow. A third set responds in an opposite manner to light and dark.

A neural rebound effect apparently helps explain the occurrence of afterimages. That is, a green-sensitive ganglion that had been excited by green light for half a minute or so might switch briefly to inhibitory activity when the light is shut off. The effect would be to perceive red even though no red light is present. Imagine looking at a green fir tree with red ornaments for a minute or so during the holidays, then turning your gaze to a white brick fireplace nearby. You might just see an image of a red tree with green ornaments!

These theoretical updates allow for the afterimage effects with the green, black, and yellow flag and are also consistent with Young's experiments in mixing lights of different colors.

FIGURE 4.10 **The Perception of Color**
Perception of color actually requires elements of both trichromatic and opponent-process theory. Cones in the retina are sensitive to either blue, green, or red. Color mixtures (such as yellow) require the simultaneous firing of groups of cones (in this case, green and red). But higher levels of visual processing occur in opponent-process fashion, explaining the occurrence of afterimages.

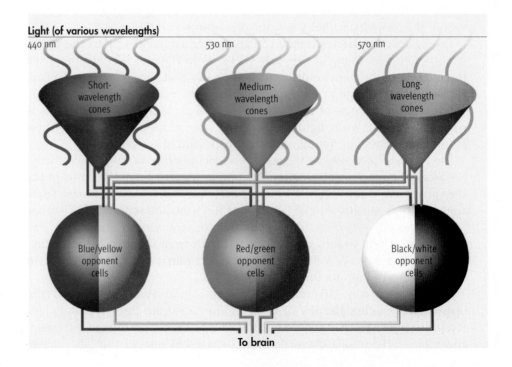

Color Blindness: What Kind of "Chromat" Are You?

If you can discriminate among the colors of the visible spectrum, you have normal color vision and are labeled a **trichromat.** This means that you are sensitive to red–green, blue–yellow, and light–dark. **Questions: What is color blindness? Why are some people color-blind?** People who are totally color-blind, called **monochromats,** are sensitive only to lightness and darkness. Total color blindness is rare. Fully color-blind individuals see the world as trichromats would on a black-and-white TV set or in a black-and-white movie.

Partial color blindness is a sex-linked trait that mostly affects males. Partially color-blind people are called **dichromats.** They can discriminate only between two colors—red and green or blue and yellow—and the colors that are derived from mixing these colors.

A dichromat might put on one red sock and one green sock, but would not mix red and blue socks. Monochromats might put on socks of any color. They would not notice a difference as long as the socks' colors did not differ in intensity—that is, brightness.

Your Turn: Now that we have discussed vision, enhance your mastery of the material with the nearby "Learning Connections." Review the material by filling in the blanks, reflect on the material by relating it to other things you know, and think critically about it.

Trichromat A person with normal color vision.

Monochromat A person who is sensitive to black and white only and hence color-blind.

Dichromat A person who is sensitive to black–white and either red–green or blue–yellow and hence partially color-blind.

Learning Connections — VISION: LETTING THE SUN SHINE IN

ACTIVE REVIEW (6) Visible light is part of a spectrum of _____ energy. (7) The color of visible light is determined by its _____. (8) Light enters the eye through the _____. (9) The muscle called the _____ determines the amount of light that is let in. (10) The _____ accommodates to an image by changing thickness and focusing light onto the retina. (11) The retina is made up of photoreceptors called _____ and _____. (12) The axons of ganglion cells make up the _____ nerve, which conducts visual information to the brain. (13) Rods transmit sensations of light and dark, and cones permit perception of _____.

REFLECT AND RELATE Try a mini-experiment. Take a watch with a second hand and enter a walk-in closet that allows just the merest sliver of light to pass under the door. Close the door. How long does it take until you can see the objects in the closet?

CRITICAL THINKING What is the evidence for the different theories of color vision?

 Go to **http://psychology.wadsworth.com/ rathus_pcc9e** for an interactive version of this Learning Connections unit.

Visual Perception: How Perceptive?

What do you see in Figure 4.11? Do you see meaningless splotches of ink or a rider on horseback? If you perceive a horse and rider, it is not just because of the visual sensations provided by the drawing. Each of the blobs is meaningless in and of itself, and the pattern is vague. Despite the lack of clarity, however, you may still perceive a horse and rider.

Visual perception is the process by which we organize or make sense of the sensory impressions caused by the light that strikes our eyes. Visual perception involves our knowledge, expectations, and motivations. Whereas sensation may be thought of as a mechanical process (e.g., light stimulating the rods and cones of our retina), perception is an active process through which we interpret the world around us. **Question: How do we organize bits of visual information into meaningful wholes?** The answer has something to do with your general knowledge and your desire to fit incoming bits and pieces of information into familiar patterns.

FIGURE 4.11 Closure

Meaningless splotches of ink, or a horse and rider? This figure illustrates the Gestalt principle of closure.

In the case of the horse and rider, your integration of disconnected pieces of information into a meaningful whole also reflects what Gestalt psychologists (see Chapter 1) refer to as the principle of **closure,** or the tendency to perceive a complete or whole figure even when there are gaps in the sensory input. Put another way, in perception the whole can be very much more than the mere sum of the parts. A collection of parts can be meaningless. It is their configuration that matters.

Perceptual Organization: Getting It Together

Early in the 20th century, Gestalt psychologists noted certain consistencies in the way we integrate bits and pieces of sensory stimulation into meaningful wholes. They attempted to identify the rules that govern these processes. Max Wertheimer, in particular, discovered many such rules. As a group, these rules are referred to as the laws of **perceptual organization.** We examine several of them, beginning with those concerning figure–ground perception. Then we consider top-down and bottom-up processing.

FIGURE–GROUND PERCEPTION If you look out your window, you may see people, buildings, cars, and streets, or perhaps grass, trees, birds, and clouds. All these objects tend to be perceived as figures against backgrounds. Individual cars seen against the background of the street are easier to pick out than cars piled on top of one another in a junkyard. Birds seen against the sky are more likely to be perceived than birds seen "in the bush."

When figure–ground relationships are **ambiguous,** or capable of being interpreted in various ways, our perceptions tend to be unstable, shifting back and forth (Bull et al., 2003). As an example, look for a while at Figure 4.12. How many people, objects, and animals can you find? If your eye is drawn back and forth, so that sometimes you are perceiving light figures on a dark background and at other time

FIGURE 4.12 Figure and Ground

How many animals and demons can you find in this Escher print? Do we have white figures on a black background or black figures on a white background? Figure–ground perception is the tendency to perceive geometric forms against a background.

Closure The tendency to perceive a broken figure as being complete or whole.

Perceptual organization The tendency to integrate perceptual elements into meaningful patterns.

Ambiguous Having two or more possible meanings.

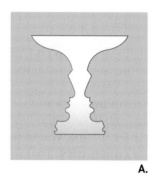 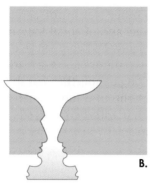 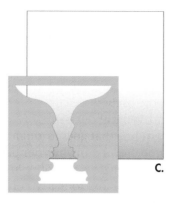

A.   B.   C.

FIGURE 4.13 **The Rubin Vase**
This is a favorite drawing used by psychologists to demonstrate figure–ground perception. Part A is ambiguous, with neither the vase nor the profiles clearly the figure or the ground. In part B, the vase is the figure; in part C, the profiles are.

Go to **http://psychology.wadsworth. com/rathus_pcc9e** to access an interactive version of this figure.

dark figures on a light background, you are experiencing figure–ground reversals. In other words, a shift is occurring in your perception of what is figure and what is ground, or background. The artist was able to have some fun with us because of our tendency to try to isolate geometric patterns or figures from a background. However, in this case the "background" is as meaningful and detailed as the "figure." Therefore, our perceptions shift back and forth.

Figure 4.13 shows a Rubin vase, one of psychologists' favorite illustrations of figure–ground relationships. The figure–ground relationship in part A of the figure is ambiguous. There are no cues that suggest which area must be the figure. For this reason, our perception may shift from seeing the vase to seeing two profiles. There is no such problem in part B. Because it seems that a white vase has been brought forward against a colored ground, we are more likely to perceive the vase than the profiles. In part C, we are more likely to perceive the profiles than the vase because the profiles are whole and the vase is broken against the background. Of course, if we wish to, we can still perceive the vase in part C, because experience has shown us where it is. Why not have some fun with friends by covering up parts B and C and asking them what they see? (They'll catch on quickly if they can see all three drawings at once.)

The Necker cube (Figure 4.14) is another ambiguous drawing that can lead to perceptual shifts. Hold this page at arm's length and stare at the center of the figure for 30 seconds or so. Try to allow your eye muscles to relax. (The feeling is of your eyes "glazing over.") After a while you will notice a dramatic shift in your perception of the box. What was once a front edge is now a back edge, and vice versa. The perceptual shift is made possible by the fact that the outline of the drawing permits two interpretations.

OTHER GESTALT RULES FOR ORGANIZATION In addition to the law of closure, Gestalt psychologists have noted that our perceptions are guided by rules or laws of *proximity, similarity, continuity,* and *common fate.*

Let's try a mini-experiment. Without reading further, describe part A of Figure 4.15. Did you say it consists of six lines or of three groups of two parallel lines? If you said three sets of lines, you were influenced by the **proximity,** or nearness, of

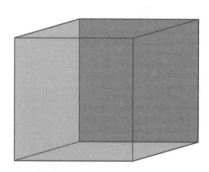

FIGURE 4.14 **The Necker Cube**
Ambiguity in the drawing of the cube makes perceptual shifts possible. Therefore, the darker tinted surface can become either the front or back of the cube.

 Go to **http://psychology.wadsworth. com/rathus_pcc9e** to access an interactive version of this figure.

Proximity Nearness. The perceptual tendency to group together objects that are near one another.

A. Proximity

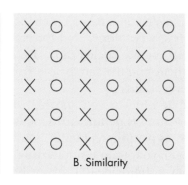

B. Similarity

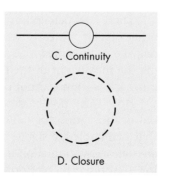

C. Continuity

D. Closure

FIGURE 4.15 **Some Gestalt Laws of Perceptual Organization**
These drawings illustrate the Gestalt laws of proximity, similarity, continuity, and closure.

some of the lines. There is no other reason for perceiving them in pairs or sub-groups: All of the lines are parallel and of equal length.

Now describe part B of the figure. Did you perceive the figure as a 6 × 6 grid, or as three columns of x's and three columns of o's? According to the law of **similarity,** we perceive similar objects as belonging together. For this reason, you may have been more likely to describe part B in terms of columns than in terms of rows or a grid.

What about part C? Is it a circle with two lines stemming from it, or is it a (broken) line that goes through a circle? If you saw it as a single (broken) line, you were probably organizing your perceptions according to the rule of **continuity.** That is, we perceive a series of points or a broken line as having unity.

According to the law of **common fate,** elements seen moving together are perceived as belonging together. A group of people running in the same direction appears unified in purpose. Birds that flock together seem to be of a feather. (Did I get that right?) Part D of Figure 4.15 provides another example of the law of closure. The arcs tend to be perceived as a circle (or circle with gaps) rather than as just a series of arcs.

TOP-DOWN VERSUS BOTTOM-UP PROCESSING Imagine that you are trying to put together a thousand-piece jigsaw puzzle—a task I usually avoid, despite the cajoling of my children. Now imagine that you are trying to accomplish it after someone has walked off with the box showing the picture formed by the completed puzzle.

When you have the box—when you know what the "big picture" or pattern looks like—cognitive psychologists refer to the task of assembling the pieces as **top-down processing.** The "top" of the visual system refers to the image of the pattern in the brain, and the top-down strategy for putting the puzzle together implies that you use the larger pattern to guide subordinate perceptual motor tasks such as hunting for particular pieces. Without knowledge of the pattern (without the box), the assembly process is referred to as **bottom-up processing.** You begin with bits and pieces of information and become aware of the pattern formed only after you have worked at it for a while (Wilson & Farah, 2003).

Top-down and bottom-up processing can be applied to many cognitive matters, even politics. If you consider yourself to be a liberal or a conservative, you can "fill in" your attitude toward many specific issues by applying the liberal or conservative position. That is top-down processing. But many people do not label themselves liberal or conservative. They look at issues and form positions on an issue-by-issue basis. Eventually they may discover an overall pattern that places them more or less in the liberal or conservative camp. That is bottom-up processing.

Perception of Motion: Life on the Move

Moving objects—people, animals, cars, or boulders plummeting down a hillside—are vital sources of sensory information. Moving objects even capture the attention of newborn infants. **Question: How do we perceive movement?** To understand how we perceive movement, recall what it is like to be on a train that has begun to pull out of the station while the train on the adjacent track remains stationary. If your own train does not lurch as it accelerates, you might think at first that the other train is moving. Or you might not be certain whether your train is moving forward or the other train is moving backward.

The visual perception of movement is based on change of position relative to other objects. To early scientists, whose only tool for visual observation was the naked eye, it seemed logical that the sun circled Earth. You have to be able to imagine the movement of the earth around the sun as seen from a theoretical point in outer space—you cannot observe it directly.

How, then, do you determine which train is moving when your train is pulling out of the station (or the other train is pulling in)? One way is to look for objects that you know are stable, such as platform columns, houses, signs, or trees. If you are stationary in relation to them, your train is not moving. Observing people walking on the station platform may not provide the answer, however, because they are

Similarity The perceptual tendency to group together objects that are similar in appearance.

Continuity The tendency to perceive a series of points or lines as having unity.

Common fate The tendency to perceive elements that move together as belonging together.

Top-down processing The use of contextual information or knowledge of a pattern in order to organize parts of the pattern.

Bottom-up processing The organization of the parts of a pattern to recognize, or form an image of, the pattern they compose.

also changing their position relative to stationary objects. You might also try to sense the motion of the train in your body. You know from experience how to do these things quite well, although it may be difficult to phrase explanations for them.

We have been considering the perception of real movement. Psychologists have also studied several types of apparent movement, or **illusions** of movement. These include the *autokinetic effect, stroboscopic motion,* and the *phi phenomenon.*

THE AUTOKINETIC EFFECT If you were to sit quietly in a dark room and stare at a point of light projected onto the far wall, after a while it might appear that the light had begun to move, even if it actually remained quite still. The tendency to perceive a stationary point of light as moving in a dark room is called the **autokinetic effect.**

Over the years, psychologists have conducted interesting experiments in which they have asked people, for example, what the light is "spelling out." The light has spelled out nothing, of course, and the words perceived by subjects reflect their own cognitive processes, not external sensations.

STROBOSCOPIC MOTION Stroboscopic motion makes motion pictures possible. In **stroboscopic motion,** the illusion of movement is provided by the presentation of a rapid progression of images of stationary objects.

So-called motion pictures do not really consist of images that move. Rather, the audience is shown 16 to 22 pictures, or *frames,* per second. Each frame differs slightly from the preceding one. Showing the frames in rapid succession provides the illusion of movement. At the rate of at least 16 frames per second, the "motion" in a film seems smooth and natural. With fewer than 16 or so frames per second, the movement looks jumpy and unnatural. That is why slow motion is achieved by filming perhaps 100 or more frames per second. When they are played back at about 22 frames per second, the movement seems slowed down, yet still smooth and natural.

THE PHI PHENOMENON Have you seen news headlines spelled out in lights that rapidly wrap around a building? Have you seen an electronic scoreboard in a baseball or football stadium? When the home team scores, some scoreboards suggest explosions of fireworks. What actually happens is that a row of lights is switched on and then off. As the first row is switched off, a second row is switched on, and so on for dozens, perhaps hundreds of rows. When the switching occurs rapidly, the **phi phenomenon** occurs: the on–off process is perceived as movement.

Like stroboscopic motion, the phi phenomenon is an example of apparent motion. Both appear to occur because of the law of continuity. We tend to perceive a series of points as having unity, so each series of lights (points) is perceived as a moving line.

Depth Perception: How Far Is Far?

Think of the problems you might have if you could not judge depth or distance. You might bump into other people, believing them to be farther away. An outfielder might not be able to judge whether to run toward the infield or the fence to catch a fly ball. You might give your front bumper a workout in stop-and-go traffic. **Question: How do we perceive depth?** It happens that *monocular* and *binocular cues* both help us perceive the depth of objects—that is, their distance from us.

Illusions Sensations that give rise to misperceptions.

Autokinetic effect The tendency to perceive a stationary point of light in a dark room as moving.

Stroboscopic motion A visual illusion in which the perception of motion is generated by a series of stationary images that are presented in rapid succession.

Phi phenomenon The perception of movement as a result of sequential presentation of visual stimuli.

■ **Stroboscopic Motion** In a motion picture, viewing a series of stationary images at the rate of about 16 to 22 frames per second provides an illusion of movement termed *stroboscopic motion.* The actual movement that is occurring is the rapid switching of stationary images.

© Abe Rezny/The Image Works

FIGURE 4.16 **What Is Wrong with This Picture?**
How does English artist William Hogarth use monocular cues for depth perception to deceive the viewer?

FRONTISPIECE TO KERBY.

Monocular cues Stimuli suggestive of depth that can be perceived with only one eye.

Perspective A monocular cue for depth based on the convergence (coming together) of parallel lines as they recede into the distance.

Interposition A monocular cue for depth based on the fact that a nearby object obscures a more distant object behind it.

Shadowing A monocular cue for depth based on the fact that opaque objects block light and produce shadows.

Texture gradient A monocular cue for depth based on the perception that closer objects appear to have rougher (more detailed) surfaces.

FIGURE 4.17 **The Effects of Interposition**
The four circles are all the same size. Which circles seem closer? The complete circles or the circles with chunks bitten out of them?

MONOCULAR CUES Now that you have considered how difficult it would be to navigate through life without depth perception, ponder the problems of the artist who attempts to portray three-dimensional objects on a two-dimensional surface. Artists use a type of **monocular cue**—pictorial cues—to create an illusion of depth. These are cues that can be perceived by one eye (*mono-* means "one"). They include perspective, relative size, clearness, interposition, shadows, and texture gradient, and they cause certain objects to appear more distant from the viewer than others.

Distant objects stimulate smaller areas on the retina than nearby ones. The amount of sensory input from them is smaller, even though they may be the same size. The distances between far-off objects also appear to be smaller than equivalent distances between nearby objects. For this reason, the phenomenon known as **perspective** occurs. That is, we tend to perceive parallel lines as coming closer together, or converging, as they recede from us. However, as we will see when we discuss *size constancy,* experience teaches us that distant objects that look small are larger when they are close. In this way, their relative size also becomes a cue to their distance.

The engraving in Figure 4.16 represents an impossible scene in which the artist uses principles of perspective to fool the viewer. Artists normally use *relative size*—the fact that distant objects look smaller than nearby objects of the same size—to suggest depth in their works. The paradoxes in *Frontispiece to Kerby* are made possible because more distant objects are *not* necessarily depicted as smaller than nearby objects. Thus, what at first seems to be background suddenly becomes foreground, and vice versa.

The *clearness* of an object also suggests its distance. Experience teaches us that we sense more details of nearby objects. For this reason, artists can suggest that objects are closer to the viewer by depicting them in greater detail. Note that the "distant" hill in the Hogarth engraving (Figure 4.16) is given less detail than the nearby plants at the bottom of the picture. Our perceptions are mocked when a man "on" the distant hill in the background is shown conversing with a woman leaning out a window in the middle ground.

We also learn that nearby objects can block our view of more-distant objects. Overlapping, or **interposition,** is the placing of one object in front of another. Experience teaches us that partly covered objects are farther away than the objects that obscure them (Figure 4.17). In the Hogarth engraving (Figure 4.16), which looks closer: the row of trees in the "background" or the moon sign hanging from the building (or is it buildings?) to the right? How does the artist use interposition to confuse the viewer?

Additional information about depth is provided by **shadowing** and is based on the fact that opaque objects block light and produce shadows. Shadows and highlights give us information about an object's three-dimensional shape and its relationship to the source of light. For example, the left part of Figure 4.18 is perceived as a two-dimensional circle, but the right part tends to be perceived as a three-dimensional sphere because of the highlight on its surface and the shadow underneath. In the "sphere," the highlighted central area is perceived as closest to us, with the surface receding to the edges.

Another monocular cue is **texture gradient.** (A gradient is a progressive change.) Closer objects are perceived as having rougher textures. In the Hogarth engraving (Figure 4.16), the building just behind the large fisherman's head has a rougher texture and therefore seems to be closer than the building with the window from which the woman is leaning. And how can the moon sign be hanging from both buildings?

Motion cues also indicate depth. If you have ever driven in the country, you have probably noticed that distant objects such as mountains and stars appear to move along with you. Objects at an intermediate distance seem to be stationary, but nearby objects such as roadside markers, rocks, and trees seem to go by quite rapidly. The tendency of objects to seem to move backward or forward as a function of their distance is known as **motion parallax.** We learn that objects that seem to move with us are farther away.

BINOCULAR CUES **Binocular cues** involve both eyes and help us perceive depth. Two binocular cues are *retinal disparity* and *convergence*.

Try an experiment. Hold your right index finger at arm's length. Now hold your left index finger about a foot closer, but in a direct line. If you keep your eyes relaxed as you do so, you will see first one finger, then the other. An image of each finger will be projected onto the retina of each eye, and each image will be slightly different because the finger will be seen from different angles. The difference between the projected images is referred to as **retinal disparity.** In the case of the closer finger, the "two fingers" look farther apart. Closer objects have greater retinal disparity.

If we try to maintain a single image of the closer finger, our eyes must turn inward, or converge on it, making us cross-eyed. **Convergence** causes feelings of tension in the eye muscles. The binocular cues of retinal disparity and convergence are strongest when objects are close.

Why are psychologists concerned about depth perception? On a fundamental level, sources of food and danger lie beyond, near or far. Evolutionary psychologists

FIGURE 4.18 **Shadowing as a Cue for Depth**
Shadowing makes the circle on the right look three-dimensional.

Motion parallax A monocular cue for depth based on the perception that nearby objects appear to move more rapidly in relation to our own motion.

Binocular cues Stimuli suggestive of depth that involve simultaneous perception by both eyes.

Retinal disparity A binocular cue for depth based on the difference in the image cast by an object on the retinas of the eyes as the object moves closer or farther away.

Convergence A binocular cue for depth based on the inward movement of the eyes as they attempt to focus on an object that is drawing nearer.

Concept Review MONOCULAR CUES FOR DEPTH PERCEPTION

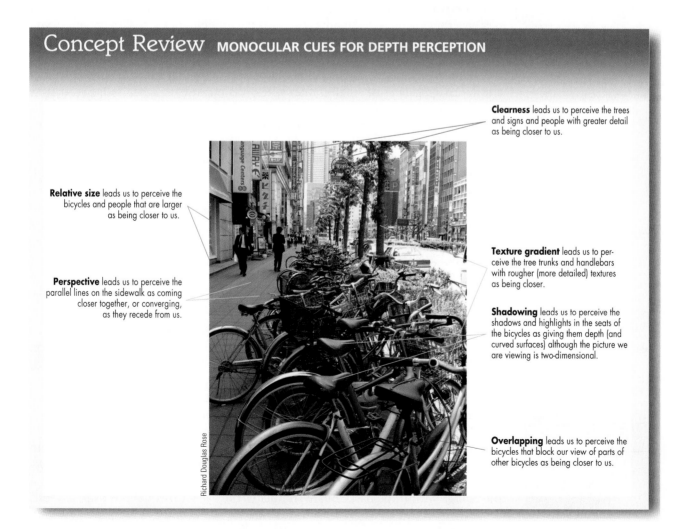

Clearness leads us to perceive the trees and signs and people with greater detail as being closer to us.

Relative size leads us to perceive the bicycles and people that are larger as being closer to us.

Perspective leads us to perceive the parallel lines on the sidewalk as coming closer together, or converging, as they recede from us.

Texture gradient leads us to perceive the tree trunks and handlebars with rougher (more detailed) textures as being closer.

Shadowing leads us to perceive the shadows and highlights in the seats of the bicycles as giving them depth (and curved surfaces) although the picture we are viewing is two-dimensional.

Overlapping leads us to perceive the bicycles that block our view of parts of other bicycles as being closer to us.

Richard Douglas Rose

Size constancy The tendency to perceive an object as being the same size even as the size of its retinal image changes according to the object's distance.

Color constancy The tendency to perceive an object as being the same color even though lighting conditions change its appearance.

Brightness constancy The tendency to perceive an object as being just as bright even though lighting conditions change its intensity.

Video Connections—The Ames Room The Ames Room shown here creates an illusion because (1) the room looks cubic when viewed with one eye but it is actually trapezoidal, and (2) people or objects seem to grow or decrease in size when they move from one corner to the other. To understand how the Ames Room works go to your companion website and click on "The Ames Room" video.

FIGURE 4.19 Brightness Constancy

The orange squares within the blue squares are the same hue, yet the orange within the dark blue square is perceived as brighter. Why?

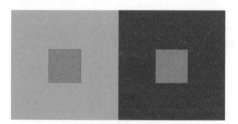

would note that organisms that have sophisticated systems for perceiving distance are more likely to survive into adulthood and reproduce, thus making these systems a stable element in their species. In the following section you will see that our methods of perception also help us keep the world a stable place, even though the shapes and colors and other properties of objects are perpetually shifting.

Perceptual Constancies: Keeping the World a Stable Place

The world is a constantly shifting display of visual sensations. Think how confusing it would be if you believed that a door was a trapezoid and not a rectangle because it is ajar. Or what if we perceived a doorway to be a different doorway when seen from 6 feet away as compared to 4 feet? As we neared it, we might think it was larger than the door we were seeking and become lost. Or consider the problems of the pet owner who recognizes his dog from the side but not from above because its shape is different when seen from above. Fortunately, these problems tend not to occur—at least with familiar objects—because perceptual constancies enable us to recognize objects even when their apparent shape or size differs. **Questions: What are perceptual constancies? Why do we perceive a door to be a rectangle even when it is partly open?**

SIZE CONSTANCY There are a number of perceptual constancies, including that of **size constancy.** We may say that people "look like ants" when viewed from the top of a tall building, but because of size constancy, we know they remain full-sized people even if the details of their forms are lost in the distance. We can thus say that we *perceive* people to be the same size, even when viewed from different distances.

The image of a dog seen from 20 feet away occupies about the same amount of space on your retina as an inch-long insect crawling on your hand. Yet you do not perceive the dog to be as small as the insect. Through your visual experiences you have acquired size constancy—that is, the tendency to perceive an object as the same size even though the size of its image on your retina varies as a function of its distance. Experience teaches us about perspective—that the same object seen at a distance appears to be smaller than when it is nearby.

A cross-cultural case study suggests that a person from another culture might indeed perceive people and cars to be insects from the vantage point of an airplane. It also emphasizes the role of experience in the development of size constancy. Anthropologist Colin Turnbull (1961) found that an African Pygmy, Kenge, thought that buffalo perceived across an open field were some form of insect. Turnbull had to drive Kenge down to where the animals were grazing to convince him that they were not insects. During the drive, as the buffalo gradually grew in size, Kenge muttered to himself and moved closer to Turnbull in fear. Even after Kenge saw that these animals were, indeed, familiar buffalo, he still wondered how they could grow large so quickly. Kenge, you see, lived in a thick forest and normally did not view large animals from great distances. For this reason, he had not developed size constancy for distant objects. However, Kenge had no difficulty displaying size constancy with objects placed at various distances in his home.

COLOR CONSTANCY **Color constancy** is the tendency to perceive objects as retaining their color even though lighting conditions may alter their appearance. Your bright yellow car may edge toward gray as the hours wend their way through twilight. But when you finally locate the car in the parking lot, you may still think of it as yellow. You expect to find a yellow car and still judge it to be "more yellow" than the (twilight-faded) red and green cars on either side of it.

Brightness constancy is similar to color constancy. Consider Figure 4.19. The orange squares within the blue squares are equally bright, yet the one within the dark blue square is perceived as brighter. Why? Again, consider the role of experience. If it were nighttime, we would expect orange to fade to gray. The fact that the orange within the dark square stimulates the eye with equal intensity suggests that it must be much brighter than the orange within the lighter square.

SHAPE CONSTANCY **Shape constancy** is the tendency to perceive objects as maintaining their shape, even if we look at them from different angles so that the shape of their image on the retina changes dramatically. You perceive the top of a coffee cup or a glass to be a circle even though it is a circle only when seen from above. When seen from an angle, it is an ellipse. When the cup or glass is seen on edge, its retinal image is the same as that of a straight line. So why do you still describe the rim of the cup or glass as a circle? Perhaps for two reasons: First, experience has taught you that the cup will look circular when seen from above. Second, you may have labeled the cup as circular or round. Experience and labels help make the world a stable place. Can you imagine the chaos that would prevail if we described objects as they appear as they stimulate our sensory organs with each changing moment?

Let us return to the door that "changes shape" when it is ajar. The door is a rectangle only when viewed straight on (Figure 4.20). When we move to the side or open it, the left or right edge comes closer and appears to be larger, changing the retinal image to a trapezoid. Yet we continue to think of doors as rectangles.

Visual Illusions: Is Seeing Believing?

The principles of perceptual organization make it possible for our eyes to "play tricks" on us. Psychologists, like magicians, enjoy pulling a rabbit out of a hat now and then. Let me demonstrate how the perceptual constancies trick the eye through *visual illusions.*

The Hering–Helmholtz and Müller–Lyer illusions (Figure 4.21, parts A and B) are named after the people who devised them. In the Hering–Helmholtz illusion, the horizontal lines are straight and parallel. However, the radiating lines cause them to appear to be bent outward near the center. The two lines in the Müller–Lyer illusion are the same length, but the line on the right, with its reversed arrowheads, looks longer.

Let us try to explain these illusions. Because of our experience and life-long use of perceptual cues, we tend to perceive the Hering–Helmholtz drawing as three-dimensional. Because of our tendency to perceive bits of sensory information as figures against grounds, we perceive the white area in the center as a circle in front of a series of radiating lines, all of which lie in front of a white

A.

Enamul Hoque/Getty Images

B.

FIGURE 4.20 **Size Constancy and Shape Constancy**
(A) Size Constancy. Although this woman's hand looks as though it is larger than her head, we recognize that this is an illusion created by the fact that her hand is closer to us than her head.
(B) Shape Constancy. When closed, the door is a rectangle. When open, the retinal image is trapezoidal. But because of shape constancy, we still perceive it as rectangular.

Shape constancy The tendency to perceive an object as being the same shape although the retinal image varies in shape as it rotates.

FIGURE 4.21 **The Hering–Helmholtz and Müller–Lyer Illusions**
In the Hering–Helmholtz illusion, are the horizontal lines straight or curved? In the Müller–Lyer illusion, are the vertical lines equal in length?

Go to **http://psychology.wadsworth.com/ rathus_pcc9e** to access an interactive version of this figure.

The Hering-Helmholtz Illusion

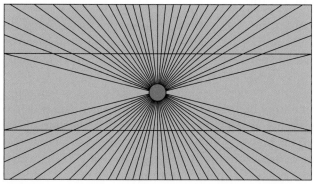

A.

The Müller-Lyer Illusion

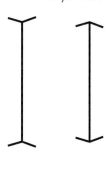

B.

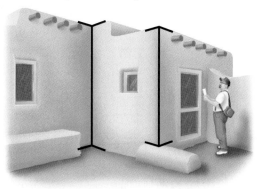

FIGURE 4.22 **A Monstrous Illusion**
The two monsters in this drawing are exactly the same height and width. Yet the top one appears to be much larger. Can you use the principle of size constancy to explain why?

Source: Ponzo illusion illustration from Mind Sights by Roger N. Shepard, © 1990 by Roger N. Shepard. Reprinted by permission of Henry Holt and Company, LLC

ground. Next, because of our experience with perspective, we perceive the radiating lines as parallel. We perceive the two horizontal lines as intersecting the "receding" lines, and we know that they would have to appear bent out at the center if they were to be equidistant at all points from the center of the circle.

Experience probably compels us to perceive the vertical lines in the Müller–Lyer illusion as the corners of a building (see Figure 4.21, part B). We interpret the length of the lines based on our experience with corners of buildings.

Figure 4.22 represents the Ponzo illusion. In this illusion, the two monsters are the same length. However, do you perceive the top monster as being bigger? The rule of size constancy may give us some insight into this illusion as well. Perhaps the converging lines again strike us as being lines receding into the distance. Again, the rule of size constancy tells us that if two objects appear to be the same size and one is farther away, the object that looks farther away must be larger. So we perceive the top monster as being larger.

Your Turn: Now that we have discussed visual perception, enhance your mastery of the material with the nearby "Learning Connections." Review the material by filling in the blanks, reflect on the material by relating it to other things you know, and think critically about it.

Learning Connections | VISUAL PERCEPTION: HOW PERCEPTIVE?

ACTIVE REVIEW (14) Perceptual organization concerns the grouping of bits of sensory stimulation into a meaningful _____. (15) Gestalt rules of perceptual organization refer to _____–ground relationships, proximity, similarity, continuity, common fate, and closure. (16) When we are putting puzzle pieces together, a picture of the result enables us to engage in _____ processing; otherwise we must solve the puzzle by bottom-up processing. (17) We perceive movement by sensing motion across the _____ and change of position in relation to other objects. (18) _____ motion, used in films, is an illusion of motion caused by the rapid presentation of a series of still images.

REFLECT AND RELATE Have you had the experience of being in a train and not knowing whether your train or one on the next track was moving? How do you explain your confusion? How did you figure out which one was really moving?

CRITICAL THINKING How do creators of visual illusions use laws of perception to trick the eye? How do research findings concerning visual perception demonstrate the difference between sensation and perception?

 Go to **http://psychology.wadsworth.com/ rathus_pcc9e** for an interactive version of this Learning Connections unit.

Hearing: Making Sense of Sound

Consider the advertising slogan for the classic science fiction film *Alien:* "In space, no one can hear you scream." It's true. Space is an almost perfect vacuum. Hearing requires a medium through which sound can travel, such as air or water. **Question: What is sound?**

Sound, or **auditory** stimulation, travels through the air like waves. If you could see them, they would look something like the ripples in a pond when you toss in a pebble. You hear the splash even if you can't see the sound of it. The sound of the splash is caused by changes in air pressure. The air is alternately compressed and expanded like the movements of an accordion. If you were listening under water, you would also hear the splash because of changes in the pressure of the water. In

Auditory Having to do with hearing.

either case, the changes in pressure are vibrations that approach your ears in waves. These vibrations—sound waves—can also be created by a ringing bell (Figure 4.23), your vocal cords, guitar strings, or the slam of a book thrown down on a desk. A single cycle of compression and expansion is one wave of sound. Sound waves can occur many (many!) times in 1 second. The human ear is sensitive to sound waves with frequencies of from 20 to 20,000 cycles per second.

Pitch and Loudness: All Sorts of Vibes

Pitch and loudness are two psychological dimensions of sound. The pitch of a sound is determined by its frequency, or the number of cycles per second as expressed in the unit **hertz (Hz).** One cycle per second is 1 Hz. The greater the number of cycles per second (Hz), the higher the pitch of the sound.

The pitch of women's voices is usually higher than that of men's voices because women's vocal cords are usually shorter and therefore vibrate at a greater frequency. Also, the strings of a violin are shorter than those of a viola or bass viol. Pitch detectors in the brain allow us to tell differences in pitch.

The loudness of a sound roughly corresponds to the height, or amplitude, of sound waves. Figure 4.24 shows records of sound waves that vary in frequency and amplitude. Frequency and amplitude are independent. That is, both high- and low-pitched sounds can be either high or low in loudness. The loudness of a sound is expressed in **decibels (dB).** Zero dB is equivalent to the threshold of hearing—the lowest sound that the typical person can hear. How loud is that? It's about as loud as the ticking of a watch 20 feet away in a very quiet room.

The decibel equivalents of many familiar sounds are shown in Figure 4.25. Twenty-five dB is equivalent in loudness to a whisper at 5 feet. Thirty dB is roughly the limit of loudness at which your librarian would like to keep your college library. You may suffer hearing damage if you are exposed to sounds of 85 to 90 dB for very long periods. This is why (careful) carpenters wear ear covers while they are hammering away, and why young people risk permanent damage to their hearing when they attend loud rock concerts, which reach levels of above 140 dB. (Bring ear plugs.) Now let us turn our attention to the human ear—the marvelous instrument that senses all these different "vibes."

The Ear: The Better to Hear You With

The human ear is good for lots of things—including catching dust, combing your hair around, and hanging jewelry from. It is also well suited to sensing sounds. **Question: How does the ear work?** The ear is shaped and structured to capture sound waves, vibrate in sympathy with them, and transmit them to centers in the brain. In this way, you not only hear something, you can also figure out what it is. The ear has three parts: the outer ear, middle ear, and inner ear (see Figure 4.26).

The outer ear is shaped to funnel sound waves to the **eardrum,** a thin membrane that vibrates in response to sound waves and thereby transmits them to the middle and inner ears. The middle ear contains the eardrum and three small bones—the hammer, the anvil, and the stirrup—which also transmit sound by vibrating. These bones were given their names (actually the Latin *malleus, incus,* and *stapes* [pronounced STAY-peas], which translate as hammer, anvil, and stirrup)

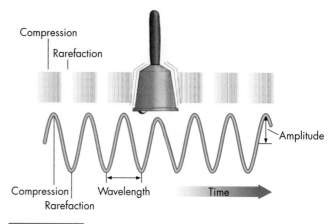

FIGURE 4.23 **Creation of Sound Waves**
The ringing of a bell compresses and expands (rarifies) air molecules, sending forth vibrations that stimulate the sense of hearing and are called sound waves.

Hertz (Hz) A unit expressing the frequency of sound waves. One hertz equals one cycle per second.

Decibel (dB) A unit expressing the loudness of a sound.

Eardrum A thin membrane that vibrates in response to sound waves, transmitting the waves to the middle and inner ears.

FIGURE 4.24 **Sound Waves of Various Frequencies and Amplitudes**
Which sounds have the highest pitch? Which are loudest?

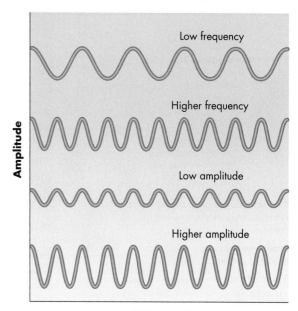

0.1 second

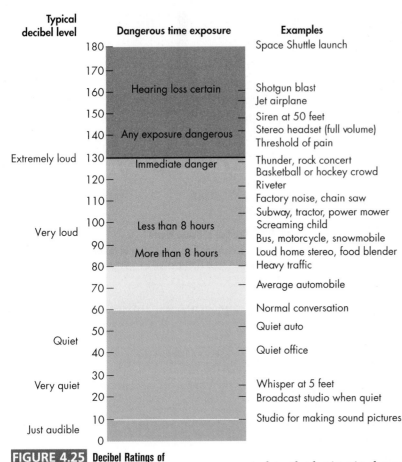

FIGURE 4.25 **Decibel Ratings of Familiar Sounds**
Zero dB is the threshold of hearing. You may suffer hearing loss if you incur prolonged exposure to sounds of 85 to 90 dB.

because of their shapes. The middle ear functions as an amplifier, increasing the pressure of the air entering the ear.

The stirrup is attached to another vibrating membrane, the *oval window.* This oval window works in conjunction with the round window, which balances the pressure in the inner ear (Figure 4.26). The round window pushes outward when the oval window pushes in, and is pulled inward when the oval window vibrates outward.

The oval window transmits vibrations into the inner ear, the bony tube called the **cochlea** (from the Greek word for "snail"). The cochlea, which is shaped like a snail shell, contains two longitudinal membranes that divide it into three fluid-filled chambers. One of the membranes that lies coiled within the cochlea is called the **basilar membrane.** Vibrations in the fluids within the chambers of the inner ear press against the basilar membrane.

The **organ of Corti,** sometimes referred to as the "command post" of hearing, is attached to the basilar membrane. There are some 16,000 receptor cells—called hair cells because they project like hair from the organ of Corti—in each ear (Larkin, 2000). Hair cells "dance" in response to the vibrations of the basilar membrane. Their up-and-down movements generate neural impulses, which are transmitted to the brain via the **auditory nerve.** Auditory input is then projected onto the hearing areas of the temporal lobes of the cerebral cortex.

Locating Sounds: Up, Down, and Around

How do you balance the loudness of a stereo set? You sit between the speakers and adjust the volume until the sound seems to be equally loud in each ear. If the sound to the right is louder, the musical instruments are perceived as being to the right rather than in front. **Question: How do we locate sounds?** There is a resemblance between balancing a stereo set and locating sounds. A sound that is louder in the right ear is perceived as coming from the right. A sound coming from the right also reaches the right ear first. Both loudness and the sequence in which the sounds reach the ears provide directional cues.

But it may not be easy to locate a sound coming from directly in front or in back of you or overhead. Such sounds are equally distant from each ear and equally loud. So what do we do? Simple—usually we turn our head slightly to determine in which ear the sound increases. If you turn your head a few degrees to the right and the loudness increases in your left ear, the sound must be coming from in front of you. Of course, we also use vision and general knowledge in locating the source of sounds. If you hear the roar of jet engines, most of the time you can bet that the airplane is overhead.

Perception of Loudness and Pitch

Sounds are heard because they cause vibration in parts of the ear and information about these vibrations is transmitted to the brain. **Question: How do we perceive loudness and pitch?** The loudness and pitch of sounds appear to be related to the number of receptor neurons on the organ of Corti that fire and how often they fire. Psychologists generally agree that sounds are perceived as louder when more of these sensory neurons fire.

Cochlea The inner ear; the bony tube that contains the basilar membrane and the organ of Corti.

Basilar membrane A membrane that lies coiled within the cochlea.

Organ of Corti The receptor for hearing that lies on the basilar membrane in the cochlea.

Auditory nerve The axon bundle that transmits neural impulses from the organ of Corti to the brain.

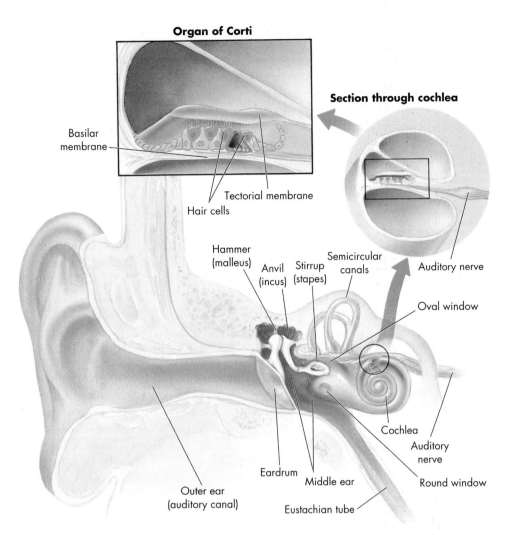

Organ of Corti

Basilar membrane

Tectorial membrane

Hair cells

Section through cochlea

Hammer (malleus)

Anvil (incus)

Stirrup (stapes)

Semicircular canals

Auditory nerve

Oval window

Cochlea

Auditory nerve

Round window

Eardrum

Middle ear

Outer ear (auditory canal)

Eustachian tube

FIGURE 4.26 **The Human Ear**
The outer ear funnels sound to the eardrum. Inside the eardrum, vibrations of the hammer, anvil, and stirrup transmit sound to the inner ear. Vibrations in the cochlea transmit the sound to the auditory nerve by way of the basilar membrane and the organ of Corti.

Go to **http://psychology.wadsworth.com/rathus_pcc9e** to access an interactive version of this figure.

CONTROVERSY IN PSYCHOLOGY

How do we explain pitch perception? What happens when the basilar membrane runs out of places to vibrate? What happens when it cannot vibrate fast enough?

It takes two processes to explain perception of color: *trichromatic theory* and *opponent-process theory.* Similarly, it takes at least two processes to explain pitch perception—that is, perception of sound waves with frequencies that vary from 20 to 20,000 cycles per second: *place theory* and *frequency theory.*

Hermann von Helmholtz helped develop the place theory of pitch discrimination as well as the Young–Helmholtz (trichromatic) theory of color vision. **Place theory** holds that the pitch of a sound is sensed according to the place along the basilar membrane that vibrates in response to it. In classic research with guinea pigs and cadavers that led to the award of a Nobel prize, Georg von Békésy (1957) found evidence for place theory. He determined that receptors at different sites along the membrane fire in response to tones of differing frequencies. Receptor neurons appear to be lined up along the basilar membrane like piano keys. The higher the pitch of a sound, the closer the responsive neurons lie to the oval window (Larkin, 2000). However, place theory appears to apply only to pitches that are at least as high as 4,000 Hz. But what about lower pitches? That's where frequency theory comes in.

Place theory The theory that the pitch of a sound is determined by the section of the basilar membrane that vibrates in response to the sound.

Frequency theory notes that for us to perceive these lower pitches, we need the stimulation of neural impulses that match the frequency of the sound waves. That is, in response to low pitches—pitches of about 20 to 1,000 cycles per second—hair cells on the basilar membrane fire at the same frequencies as the sound waves. However, neurons cannot fire more than 1,000 times per second. Therefore, frequency theory can account only for perception of pitches between 20 and 1,000 cycles per second. In actuality, frequency theory appears to account only for pitch perception between 20 and a few hundred cycles per second.

I noted that it takes *at least two processes* to explain how people perceive pitch. The *volley principle* is the third, and it accounts for pitch discrimination between a few hundred and 4,000 cycles per second (Matlin & Foley, 1995). In response to sound waves of these frequencies, groups of neurons take turns firing, in the way that one row of soldiers used to fire rifles while another row knelt to reload. Alternating firing—that is, volleying—appears to transmit sensory information about pitches in the intermediate range.

Deafness: Navigating a World of Silence

More than 1 in 10 Americans has a hearing impairment, and 1 in 100 cannot hear at all (Canalis & Lambert, 2000). Deaf people are deprived of a key source of information about the world around them. In recent years, however, society has made greater efforts to bring them into the mainstream of sensory experience. People are usually on hand to convert political and other speeches into hand signs (such as those of American Sign Language) for hearing-impaired members of the audience. Many TV shows are "closed-captioned" so that they can be understood by people with hearing problems. Special decoders render the captions visible. Also, as mentioned earlier, advocates for deaf people have emphasized the positive aspects of dwelling in a world of silence. **Questions: What is deafness? What can we do about it?**

The two major types of deafness are conductive deafness and sensorineural deafness. **Conductive deafness** stems from damage to the structures of the middle ear—either to the eardrum or to the three bones that conduct (and amplify) sound waves from the outer ear to the inner ear (Canalis & Lambert, 2000). This is the hearing impairment often found among older people. People with conductive deafness often profit from hearing aids, which provide the amplification that the middle ear does not. Surgical treatment can be successful as well.

Sensorineural deafness usually stems from damage to the structures of the inner ear, most often the loss of hair cells, which normally do not regenerate. (However, researchers are attempting to stimulate production of new hair cells by means of gene therapy and other measures; see Larkin, 2000.) Sensorineural deafness can also stem from damage to the auditory nerve, caused by such factors as disease or acoustic trauma (prolonged exposure to very loud sounds). In sensorineural deafness, people tend to be more sensitive to some pitches than to others. In the hearing impairment called Hunter's notch, the loss is limited to particular frequencies—in this case, the frequencies of the sound waves generated by a gun firing. Prolonged exposure to 85 dB can cause hearing loss. People who attend rock concerts, where sounds may reach 140 dB, risk permanently damaging their ears, as do workers who run pneumatic drills or drive noisy vehicles. The ringing sensation that often follows exposure to loud sounds probably means that hair cells in the inner ear have been damaged. If you find yourself suddenly exposed to loud sounds, remember that your fingertips serve as good emergency ear protectors.

Cochlear implants, or "artificial ears," contain microphones that sense sounds and electronic equipment that transmits sounds past damaged hair cells to stimulate the auditory nerve directly. Such implants have helped many people with sen-

Frequency theory The theory that the pitch of a sound is reflected in the frequency of the neural impulses that are generated in response to the sound.

Conductive deafness The forms of deafness in which there is loss of conduction of sound through the middle ear.

Sensorineural deafness The forms of deafness that result from damage to hair cells or the auditory nerve.

sorineural deafness (Geers et al., 2002). However, they cannot assume the functions of damaged auditory nerves.

Your Turn: Now that we have discussed hearing, enhance your mastery of the material with the nearby "Learning Connections." Review the material by filling in the blanks, reflect on the material by relating it to other things you know, and think critically about it.

 Learning Connections — **HEARING: MAKING SENSE OF SOUND**

ACTIVE REVIEW (19) Sound waves alternately _____ and expand molecules of a medium like air. (20) The human ear can hear sounds varying in frequency from 20 to _____ cycles per second (Hz). (21) The frequency of sound waves determines their _____. (22) Loudness is measured in _____ (dB). (23) The middle ear contains three bones—the "hammer," "_____," and "stirrup." (24) The cochlea contains fluids that vibrate against the _____ membrane. (25) The "command post" of hearing—called the _____—is attached to the basilar membrane. (26) Sound waves travel from the organ of Corti to the brain by the _____ nerve.

REFLECT AND RELATE Do you know anyone with hearing problems? What is the source of the impairment? How does the person cope with the impairment?

CRITICAL THINKING Are you familiar with the violin, viola, cello, and bass fiddle? How do their sounds differ? How can you use the information in this section to explain the differences?

Go to **http://psychology.wadsworth.com/ rathus_pcc9e** for an interactive version of this Learning Connections unit.

The Chemical Senses: Smell and Taste

Smell and taste are the chemical senses. In the cases of vision and hearing, physical energy strikes our sensory receptors. With smell and taste, we sample molecules of the substances being sensed.

Smell: Sampling Molecules in the Air

People are underprivileged when it comes to the sense of smell. Dogs, for instance, devote about seven times as much of the cerebral cortex as we do to the sense of smell. Male dogs sniff in order to determine where the boundaries of other dogs' territories leave off and whether female dogs are sexually receptive. Dogs have been selectively bred to enhance their sense of smell. Some now earn a living by sniffing out explosive devices or illegal drugs in suitcases.

Smell also has an important role in human behavior. It makes a crucial contribution to the **flavor** of foods, for example. If you did not have a sense of smell, an onion and an apple might taste the same to you! People's sense of smell may be deficient when we compare them to those of a dog, but we can detect the odor of 1 one-millionth of a milligram of vanilla in a liter of air.

Question: How does the sense of smell work? Smell is the sense that detects odors. An *odor* is a sample of the substance being sensed. Odors are detected by sites on receptor neurons in the **olfactory** membrane high in each nostril. Receptor neurons fire when a few molecules of the substance in gaseous form come into contact with them. Their firing transmits information about odors to the brain via the **olfactory nerve.** That is how the substance is smelled.

It is unclear how many basic kinds of odors there are. In any event, olfactory receptors may respond to more than one kind of odor. Mixtures of smell sensations also help produce the broad range of odors that we can perceive.

The sense of smell adapts rapidly to odors, such that you lose awareness of them, even obnoxious ones. This might be fortunate if you are in a locker room or an outhouse. It might not be so fortunate if you are exposed to paint fumes or

■ **An Acute Sense of Smell** Compared with humans, dogs devote much more of their cerebral cortex to the sense of smell. Dogs have been trained to sniff out drugs, explosives, and in this case, human beings.

Flavor A complex quality of food and other substances that is based on their odor, texture, and temperature as well their taste.

Olfactory Having to do with the sense of smell.

Olfactory nerve The nerve that transmits information concerning odors from olfactory receptors to the brain.

secondhand smoke, because you may lose awareness of them while danger remains. Also, one odor can mask another, which is how air fresheners work.

In many species, odors trigger instinctive responses. An experiment by one research group reveals how sex recognition in various species of lizards relies either on color or odor (López et al., 2002). The group aimed to determine whether color or odor, or a combination of the two, stimulated aggressive responses or sexual advances from males of the Spanish lizard, *P. hispanicus*. They experimentally manipulated the color and odor of male lizards, creating groups with all combinations of color and odor of males and females. They found that males reacted significantly more aggressively to intruders with male odors regardless of their color, whereas intruders with female odors were courted, regardless of their actual sex and coloring.

 A Closer Look | **HOW DID THE ANIMALS KNOW THE TSUNAMI WAS COMING?**

The tsunami that hit the southern coast of south central Asia—in countries from Indonesia to Sri Lanka to India—killed as many as one quarter of a million people. The people were caught off guard. But not the animals.

Along the western coast of Thailand, elephants giving rides to tourists began to trumpet agitatedly hours before the tsunami, just about when the earthquake that frac-

■ **Do Elephants Sense What Humans Can't** Research indicates that elephants can sense vibrations in the ground over vast distances. This might be one way they can detect an earthquake or a tsunami before a human becomes aware of it. Other animals use other senses to detect tsunamis, earthquakes, and other impending disasters.

tured the ocean floor sent the big waves rushing toward the shore. An hour before the waves slammed into the area, the elephants began wailing. Just before the waves struck, they trooped off to higher ground. Earthquakes cause vibrations on land and in the water, and storms make electromagnetic changes in the air. Elephants are particularly sensitive to ground vibrations and probably sensed, in their feet and trunks, the earthquake that caused the tsunami.

Some dogs refused to go outdoors. Others sought higher ground. A survivor in Thailand said, "Dogs are smarter than all of us. . . . [They] started running away up to the hilltops long before we even realized what was coming" (Oldenburg, 2005).

Flamingos usually breed in low-lying areas at this time of year, but on the day of the tsunami, they abandoned their sanctuary on the coast of India and headed into

safer forests before the waves hit shore (Oldenburg, 2005).

The Yala National Park in Sri Lanka was hit hard by the waves, but wildlife officials were surprised to find that hundreds of elephants, tigers, leopards, deer, wild boar, water buffalo, monkeys, and reptiles had escaped the tsunami unharmed.

Do animals have a "sixth sense" for detecting earthquakes, hurricanes, volcanic eruptions, and tsunamis before the earth starts shaking? Some birds, dogs, tigers, and elephants can detect sound waves whose frequencies are too low for humans to hear ("infrasound"). Dogs' superior sense of smell might detect subtle chemical changes in the air. Other animals are apparently supersensitive to temperature, touch, or vibration, which gives them advance warning. Many animals can apparently detect subtle or abrupt changes in the environment. Some animals apparently have acute senses of smell and hearing that warn them of something coming toward them before humans sense anything (Mott, 2005).

Michelle Heupel of the Mote Marine Laboratory in Florida concludes that many animals are highly attuned to their environment. They may not understand why changes are taking place, but some changes apparently trigger an instinct to move to a safer place (Oldenburg, 2005).

Taste: Yes, You've Got Taste

Your cocker spaniel may jump at the chance to finish off your bowl of sherbet, but your Siamese cat may turn up her nose at the opportunity. Why? Dogs can perceive the taste quality of sweetness, as can pigs, but cats cannot. But when it comes to the sense of taste, the lowly catfish may well be the champ. According to Joseph Brand (2000) of the Monell Chemical Senses Center in Philadelphia, catfish are "swimming tongues." They can detect food through murky water and across long distances because their bodies are studded with nearly 150,000 taste buds. **Truth or Fiction Revisited:** It is true that the bodies of catfish are covered with taste buds.

Taste is an extremely important sense because animals, including humans, use the sense of taste in acquiring nutrients and avoiding poisons. A food may look good from a distance. It may trigger fond memories. It may even smell good, but if it tastes bad, we are likely not to swallow it (Scott, 2001).

Question: How does the sense of taste work? As in the case of smell, taste involves sampling molecules of a substance. Taste is sensed through **taste cells**—receptor neurons located on **taste buds.** You have about 10,000 taste buds, most of which are located near the edges and back of your tongue. Taste buds tend to specialize a bit. Some, for example, are more responsive to sweetness, whereas others react to several tastes. Other taste receptors are found in the roof, sides, and back of the mouth, and in the throat. Some taste buds are even found in the stomach, although we only perceive tastes in the mouth and top of the throat. Buds deep in the mouth are evolutionarily adaptive because they can warn of poisonous food as it is about to be swallowed (Brand, 2000).

Researchers generally agree on at least four primary taste qualities: sweet, sour, salty, and bitter. Some argue for a fifth basic taste, which is termed *umami* in Japanese and means "meaty" or "savory." And others, including Susan Schiffman (2000), suggest that there may be still other basic tastes. Regardless of how many basic tastes there are, the flavor of a food involves its taste but is more complex. Although apples and onions are similar in taste, their flavors differ greatly. After all, you wouldn't chomp into a nice cold onion on a warm day, would you? The flavor of a food depends on its odor, texture, and temperature as well as on its taste. If it were not for odor, heated tenderized shoe leather might pass for steak.

Just as some people see better than others, some people taste better than others—but their superiority may be limited to one or more basic tastes. Those of us with low sensitivity for the sweet taste may require twice the sugar to sweeten our food as others who are more sensitive to sweetness. Those of us who claim to enjoy very bitter foods may actually be taste blind to them. Sensitivities to different tastes apparently have a strong genetic component (Bartoshuk, 2000).

By eating hot foods and scraping your tongue with forks and rough pieces of food, you regularly kill off many taste cells. But you need not be alarmed at this inadvertent oral aggression. Taste cells are the rabbits of the sense receptors. They reproduce rapidly enough to completely renew themselves about once a week.

Although older people often complain that their food has little or no "taste," they are more likely to experience a decline in the sense of smell. Because the flavor of a food represents both its tastes and its odors or aromas, older people experience loss in the *flavor* of their food. Therefore, older people often spice their food heavily to enhance its flavor.

Your Turn: Now that we have discussed the chemical senses, enhance your mastery of the material with the nearby "Learning Connections." Review the material by filling in the blanks, reflect on the material by relating it to other things you know, and think critically about it.

Taste cells Receptor cells that are sensitive to taste.

Taste buds The sensory organs for taste. They contain taste cells and are located on the tongue.

■ **Sensational?** The flavors of foods are determined not only by their taste, but also by their odor, texture, and temperature.

Learning Connections — THE CHEMICAL SENSES: SMELL AND TASTE

ACTIVE REVIEW (27) A(n)_____ is a sample of molecules of the substance being smelled. (28) Odors are detected by the _____ membrane in each nostril. (29) There are four primary taste qualities: sweet, sour, salty, and _____. (30) The receptor neurons for taste are called _____ cells, which are located in taste buds on the tongue.

REFLECT AND RELATE Has food ever seemed to lose its flavor when you had a cold or an allergy attack? Why did it happen? Have you had the experience of growing accustomed to a noxious odor so that you have lost awareness of it?

CRITICAL THINKING Critical thinkers pay close attention to definitions. What is the difference between the *taste* and the *flavor* of food?

 Go to **http://psychology.wadsworth.com/ rathus_pcc9e** for an interactive version of this Learning Connections unit.

The Skin Senses (Yes, It Does)

The skin is much more than a protective coating for your body. As you may know from lying on the sand beneath a broiling sun, and perhaps from touching the person lying next to you, the skin also discriminates among many kinds of sensations. **Truth or Fiction Revisited:** It is true that the skin is a sensory organ as well as a protective coating for the body. **Questions: What are the skin senses? How do they work?** The skin senses include touch, pressure, warmth, cold, and pain. We have distinct sensory receptors for pressure, temperature, and pain, but some nerve endings may receive more than one type of sensory input. Here let's focus on touch, pressure, and temperature. We consider pain—and what to do about it—in the "Life Connections" section at the end of the chapter.

Touch and Pressure: Making Contact

Sensory receptors embedded in the skin fire when the surface of the skin is touched. There may be several kinds of receptors for touch, some that respond to constant pressure, some that respond to intermittent pressure, as in tapping the skin. *Active touching* means continually moving your hand along the surface of an object so that you continue to receive sensory input from the object (O'Dell & Hoyert, 2002). You may have noticed that if you are trying to "get the feel of" a fabric or the texture of a friend's hair, you must move your hand over it. Otherwise the sensations quickly fade. If you pass your hand over the fabric or hair and then hold it still, again the sensations of touching will fade. Active touching receives information concerning not only touch per se but also pressure, temperature, and feedback from the muscles involved in movements of our hands.

Your can assess the sensitivity of your sense of touch by trying a mini-experiment suggested by Cynthia O'Dell and Mark Hoyert (2002): Set out a series of cookie-cutter outlines, close your eyes, and see how many you can identify from your sense of touch alone.

Different parts of the body are more sensitive to touch and pressure than others. If you take another look at Figure 2.15 on page 71, you'll see that the parts of the body that "cover" more than their fair share of somatosensory cortex are most sensitive to touch. These parts include the hands, face, and some other regions of the body. Psychophysicists use methods such as the **two-point threshold** to assess sensitivity to pressure. This method determines the smallest distance by which two rods touching the skin must be separated before the (blindfolded) individual reports that there are two rods rather than one. With this method, psychophysicists have found that our fingertips, lips, noses, and cheeks are more sensitive than our shoulders, thighs, and calves. That is, the rods can be closer together but perceived as distinct when they touch the lips more than when they touch the shoulders. Why the difference in sensitivity? First, nerve endings are more densely packed in the fingertips and face than in other locations. Second, more sensory cortex is devoted to the perception of sensations in the fingertips and face (see Figure 2.14 on page 70).

The sense of pressure, like the sense of touch, undergoes rapid adaptation. For example, you may have undertaken several minutes of strategic movements to wind up with your hand on the arm or leg of your date, only to discover that adaptation to this delightful source of pressure reduces the sensation.

Temperature: Sometimes Everything Is Relative

The receptors for temperature are neurons located just beneath the skin. When skin temperature increases, the receptors for warmth fire. Decreases in skin temperature cause receptors for cold to fire.

Sensations of temperature are relative. When we are at normal body temperature, we might perceive another person's skin as warm. When we are feverish, though, the other person's skin might seem cool. We also adapt to differences in temperature. When we walk out of an air-conditioned house into the July sun, we feel intense heat at first. Then the sensations of heat tend to fade (although we may

Two-point threshold The least distance by which two rods touching the skin must be separated before the person will report that there are two rods, not one, on 50% of occasions.

still be uncomfortable because of high humidity). Similarly, when we first enter a swimming pool, the water may seem cool or cold because it is below our body temperature. Yet after a few moments an 80°F pool may seem quite warm. In fact, we may chide a newcomer for not diving right in.

Your Turn: Now that we have discussed the skin senses, enhance your mastery of the material with the nearby "Learning Connections." Review the material by filling in the blanks, reflect on the material by relating it to other things you know, and think critically about it.

 Learning Connections | **THE SKIN SENSES (YES, IT DOES)**

ACTIVE REVIEW (31) The _____ threshold method allows psychophysicists to assess sensitivity to pressure by determining the distance by which two rods touching the skin must be separated before a person will report that there are two rods, not one. (32) Our lips are (*More* or *Less?*) sensitive to touch than our shoulders.

Go to **http://psychology.wadsworth.com/ rathus_pcc9e** for an interactive version of this Learning Connections unit.

REFLECT AND RELATE Have you ever entered a swimming pool and felt cold even though the water temperature was in the 70s? How can you explain the experience?

CRITICAL THINKING Does it seem strange to think of the skin as a sensory organ? If it does, be my guest and check out the discussion of "functional fixedness" in Chapter 8.

Kinesthesis and the Vestibular Sense

Try this mini-experiment. Close your eyes, and then touch your nose with your finger. If you weren't right on target, I'm sure you came close. But how? You didn't see your hand moving, and you didn't hear your arm swishing through the air. Humans and many other animals have senses that alert them to their movements and body position without relying on vision, including *kinesthesis* and the *vestibular sense*.

Kinesthesis: How Moving?

Question: What is kinesthesis? Kinesthesis is the sense that informs you about the position and motion of parts of the body. The term is derived from the ancient Greek words for "motion" (*kinesis*) and "perception" (*aisthesis*). In kinesthesis, sensory information is fed back to the brain from sensory organs in the joints, tendons, and muscles. You were able to bring your finger to your nose easily by employing your kinesthetic sense. When you make a muscle in your arm, the sensations of tightness and hardness are also provided by kinesthesis.

Imagine going for a walk without kinesthesis. You would have to watch the forward motion of each leg to be certain you had raised it high enough to clear the curb. And if you had tried the nose-to-finger brief experiment without the kinesthetic sense, you would have had no sensory feedback until you felt the pressure of your finger against your nose (or cheek, or eye, or forehead), and you probably would have missed dozens of times.

Are you in the mood for another mini-experiment? Close your eyes again. Then "make a muscle" in your right arm. Could you sense the muscle without looking at it or feeling it with your left hand? Of course you could. Kinesthesis also provides information about muscle contractions.

The Vestibular Sense: How Upright?

Truth or Fiction Revisited: It is true that you have a sense that keeps you an upright person. It is your **vestibular sense,** which provides your brain with information as to whether or not you are upright (physically, not morally). **Question: How does the vestibular sense work?** Sensory organs located in the **semicircular canals** and elsewhere in the ears monitor your body's motion and position in relation to gravity.

■ **Kinesthesis** This young acrobat receives information about the position and movement of the parts of his body through the sense of kinesthesis. Information is fed to his brain from sensory organs in the joints, tendons, and muscles. This allows him to follow his own movements without looking at himself.

Kinesthesis The sense that informs us about the positions and motion of parts of our bodies.

Vestibular sense The sense of equilibrium that informs us about our bodies' positions relative to gravity.

Semicircular canals Structures of the inner ear that monitor body movement and position.

They tell you whether you are falling and provide cues to whether your body is changing speed, such as when you are in an accelerating airplane or automobile. It is thus the vestibular sense that keeps us physically upright. Now, you may recall episodes when you have been spun around blindfolded at a party or in the spinning "Teacups" amusement park ride. Afterward, it might have been difficult for you to locate yourself in space (if you remained blindfolded) or to retain your balance. The reason is that the fluid in the semicircular canals was tossed about so fiercely that you lost your ability to monitor or control your position in relation to gravity.

Your Turn: Now that we have discussed kinesthesis and the vestibular sense, enhance your mastery of the material with the nearby "Learning Connections." Review the material by filling in the blanks, reflect on the material by relating it to other things you know, and think critically about it. The nearby Concept Review summarizes key points about the senses.

Learning Connections | KINESTHESIS AND THE VESTIBULAR SENSE

ACTIVE REVIEW (33) Kinesthesis is the sensing of bodily _____ and movement. (34) Kinesthesis relies on sensory organs in the joints, tendons, and _____. (35) The vestibular sense informs us as to whether we are in a(n) _____ position or changing speeds. (36) The vestibular sense is housed mainly in the _____ _____ of the ears.

REFLECT AND RELATE Can you touch your nose when your eyes are closed? How do you manage this feat?

CRITICAL THINKING Why are some people "natural athletes"? Might there be genetic factors related to kinesthesis and the vestibular sense that contribute to their abilities?

 Go to **http://psychology.wadsworth.com/ rathus_pcc9e** for an interactive version of this Learning Connections unit.

Sensation and Perception on the Edge: Virtual Reality and ESP

Sensation is the peripheral device that feeds information into our central processing unit—the brain. A number of fascinating topics on the edge of psychology explore the types of things that might happen if the sensations we perceive do not represent reality, or if sensation were bypassed altogether and we directly perceived things in the world outside. Make no mistake: These topics are indeed on the edge. For the time being there is little chance of mistaking virtual reality and, well, real reality. Also, research evidence fails to support perception in the absence of sensation. Nevertheless, these topics arouse a good deal of interest among the public and are worthy of our attention.

Sensation, Perception, and Virtual Reality

"Seeing is believing," or so goes the saying. But can we always believe what we see—or smell or hear or taste or feel? Not necessarily.

In *The Matrix* science-fiction films, we envision a world in which all of us are deceived into believing the world we sense every day is real, when it is actually a vanished dream. *The Matrix* is science fiction on the theme of virtual reality. **Question: What is virtual reality?** Virtual reality is the perception of events that are fed directly into the senses via electronic technology.

Virtual reality may sound purely like the stuff of science fiction, but it is in use today, employing computer-generated imagery. Although few would be fooled into believing a virtual visual world is real, psychologists are now using computer-generated images to help people overcome phobias such as fear of public speaking (Harris et al., 2002), spiders (Garcia-Palacios et al., 2002), flying (Maltby et al., 2002; Muehlberger et al., 2001), and heights (Rothbaum & Hodges, 1999). In the case of fear of heights, individuals view images in which they perceive themselves as gradually ris-

Concept Review THE SENSES

Sense	What We Sense	Receptor Organs	Nature of Sensory Receptors
Vision	Visible light (part of the spectrum of electromagnetic energy; different colors have different wavelengths)	Eyes	Photoreceptors in the retinas (*rods,* which are sensitive to the intensity of light; and *cones,* which are sensitive to color)
Hearing	Changes in air pressure (or in another medium, such as water) that result from vibrations called *sound waves*	Ears	"Hair cells" in the organ of Corti, which is attached to a membrane (the *basilar membrane*) within the inner ear (the *cochlea*)
Smell	Molecules of the substance	Nose	Receptor neurons in the olfactory membrane high in each nostril
Taste	Molecules of the substance	Tongue	Taste cells located on taste buds on the tongue
Touch, pressure	Pushing or pulling of the surface of the body	Skin	Nerve endings in the skin, some of which are located around the hair follicles
Kinesthesis	Muscle contractions	Sensory organs in joints, tendons, and muscles	Receptor cells in joints, tendons, and muscles
Vestibular sense	Movement and position in relation to gravity	Sensory organs in the ears (e.g., in the *semicircular canals*)	Receptor cells in the ears

© 1990 Andy Levin/ Photo Researchers, Inc.

Go to **http://psychology.wadsworth.com/ rathus_pcc9e** to access a drag-and-drop version of this Concept Review designed to help you test yourself on the major topics provided here.

■ **Virtual Reality or "Real" Reality?**
In *The Matrix* film series, the characters enter our world by being "plugged in." Computer technology—fortunately or unfortunately—has not yet advanced to the point where we cannot distinguish what is real from what is virtual.

ing to greater heights, even though they are remaining still. Because the images are computer generated rather than real, they are referred to as *virtual reality*. Children also use virtual reality—often in the form of virtual reality goggles or helmets—to feel that they are participating more fully in computer games.

CYBERSEX Also consider what some futurists refer to as *cybersex* or *virtual sex* (DeAngelis, 2000). You don headphones, 3-D glasses, and a light bodysuit with miniature detectors that follow your movements, as well as tiny stimulators for your skin. The detectors and stimulators are connected to computers that record your responses and create the impression of being touched by textures such as virtual satin, virtual wool, or virtual skin. The information superhighway allows you either to interact online with another person who is outfitted with similar gear or to be connected with a "canned" program.

What are some of the psychological implications of virtual sex? If we could electronically dress up as movie stars, would our sense of self and our dignity as individuals suffer? If we could at a moment's notice access a satisfying virtual sexual encounter with an appealing person (or program) who was concerned only with meeting our needs, would we become less sensitive to the needs of our real-life romantic partners? Would virtual sex provide additional outlets for people whose needs were not being fully met by others? Or would they become the preferred sexual outlets? What would be the implications for the family? For children?

Will the courts consider a virtual sex interaction to be adultery? What will the future bring? Your guess is as good as mine.

Extrasensory Perception: Is There Perception without Sensation?

Using our familiar computer analogy, sensation is the peripheral device that feeds information into our central processing unit—the brain. Our second topic on the edge of psychology asks the question: What if there were such a thing as extrasensory perception (ESP)? What if sensation were bypassed, and we directly perceived things in the world outside? Although the hard research evidence comes down hard against perception in the absence of sensation, 60% of the American public believes that some people have psychic powers or ESP (National Science Foundation, 2002). Therefore, we need to understand what the topic is about and to examine the type of research psychologists conduct to determine whether there is any validity to it. Let us begin by defining precognition and other topics in ESP.

PRECOGNITION, PSYCHOKINESIS, TELEPATHY, AND CLAIRVOYANCE Imagine the wealth you could amass if you had *precognition,* that is, if you were able to perceive future events in advance. Perhaps you would check the next week's stock market reports and know what to buy or sell. Or you could bet with confidence on who would win the next Super Bowl or World Series. Or think of the power you would have if you were capable of *psychokinesis,* that is, of mentally manipulating or moving objects. You may have gotten a glimpse of the possibilities in films like *The Matrix, The Sixth Sense,* and *Star Wars.* Precognition and psychokinesis are two concepts associated with ESP. Two other theoretical forms of ESP are *telepathy,* or direct transmission of thoughts or ideas from one person to another, and *clairvoyance,* or the perception of objects that do not stimulate the sensory organs. An example of clairvoyance is "seeing" what card will be dealt next, even though it is still in the deck and unseen even by the dealer.

Extrasensory perception (ESP)—also referred to as parapsychological or psi phenomenon—refers to the perception of objects or events through means other than sensory organs. As suggested by the root "para," meaning alongside, *parapsy-*chological (psi) means standing alongside psychology, not actually a part of psychology. Psychological communication occurs verbally or by means of body language. Psi communication refers to the transfer of information through an irregular or unusual process—not through the usual senses.

Now that we have made some definitions, let us note that many psychologists do not believe that ESP is an appropriate area for scientific inquiry. Scientists study natural events, but ESP smacks of the supernatural, even the occult. ESP also has the flavor of a nightclub act in which a blindfolded "clairvoyant" calls out the contents of an audience member's pocketbook. Other psychologists, however, believe that there is nothing wrong with investigating ESP. The issue for them is not whether ESP is sensationalistic but whether its existence can be demonstrated in the laboratory. **Question: Is there really such a thing as extrasensory perception (ESP)?**

Perhaps the best known of the ESP researchers was Joseph Banks Rhine of Duke University. Rhine studied ESP for several decades, beginning in the late 1920s. In a typical experiment in clairvoyance, Rhine would use a pack of 25 cards, which contained 5 sets of the cards shown in Figure 4.27. Pigeons pecking patterns at random to indicate which one was about to be turned up would be "correct" 20% of the time. Rhine found that some people guessed correctly significantly more often than the 20% chance rate. He concluded that these individuals might have some degree of ESP.

A more current method for studying telepathy is the *ganzfeld procedure* (Dalkvist, 2001; Parker, 2001). In this method, one person acts as a "sender" and the other as a "receiver." The sender views randomly selected visual stimuli such as photographs or videotapes, while the receiver, who is in another room and whose eyes are covered and ears are blocked, tries to mentally tune in to the sender. After a session, the receiver is shown four visual stimuli and asked to select the one transmitted by the sender. A person guessing which stimulus was "transmitted" would be correct 25% of the time (1 time in 4) by chance alone. An analysis of 28 experiments using the ganzfeld procedure, however, found that receivers correctly identified the visual stimulus 38% of the time (Honorton, 1985), a percentage unlikely to be due to chance. A series of 11 more studies with the ganzfeld procedure obtained similar results (Bem & Honorton, 1994; Honorton et al., 1990).

Overall, however, there are many reasons for skepticism of ESP. First is the *file-drawer problem.* Buyers of supermarket magazines tend to forget "psychics'" predictions when they fail to come true (that is, they have "filed" them away). Similarly, ESP researchers are less likely to report research results that show failure. Therefore, we would expect unusual findings (for example, a subject with a high success rate at psi-communication tasks over a period of several days) to appear in the research literature. In other words, if you flip a coin indefinitely, eventually you will flip 10 heads in a row. The odds against this are high, but if you report your eventual success and do not report the weeks of failure, you give the impression that you have unique coin-flipping ability. (You may even fool yourself.)

Then, too, it has not been easy to replicate experiments in ESP. People who have "demonstrated" ESP with one researcher have failed to do so with another researcher or have refused to participate in other studies. Also, the findings in one study are usually noticeably absent in follow-ups or under careful analysis. For

FIGURE 4.27 **Zener Cards**
Joseph Banks Rhine used these Zener cards in research on clairvoyance. Participants are asked to predict which card will be turned up.

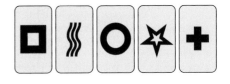

CORBIS Sygma

■ **The Sixth Sense?**
In the fictional film of that name, Bruce Willis portrays a psychologist who treats a boy who has a "sixth sense." Why are psychologists skeptical about the existence of ESP?

example, Julie Milton and Richard Wiseman (1999) reviewed the research reported by Bem and Honorton (1994). They weighed the results of 30 ganzfeld ESP studies from 7 laboratories. They found no evidence—zero—that subjects in these studies scored above chance levels on the ESP task. Follow-ups to the Milton and Wiseman (1999) review once more present conflicting conclusions (Bem et al., 2001; Storm & Ertel, 2001, 2002).

Let's make one point clearly: From all of these studies, *not one person has emerged who can reliably show ESP from one occasion to another and from one researcher to another.* **Truth or Fiction Revisited:** There is no adequate scientific evidence that people can read other people's minds. Research has not identified one single indisputable telepath or clairvoyant. In sum, most psychologists do not grant ESP research much credibility. They prefer to study perception that involves sensation. After all, what is life without sensation?

Your Turn: Now that we have discussed virtual reality and ESP, enhance your mastery of the material with the nearby "Learning Connections." Review the material by filling in the blanks, reflect on the material by relating it to other things you know, and think critically about it.

Learning Connections | SENSATION AND PERCEPTION ON THE EDGE: VIRTUAL REALITY AND ESP

ACTIVE REVIEW (37) _____ reality uses electronic media to feed in false information about the world outside through the senses. (38) _____ refers to perception of objects or events through means other than sensory organs. (39) The ganzfeld procedure is currently used to study _____. (40) One reason for skepticism about ESP is the _____ problem; that is, researchers are less likely to report research results that show failure.

REFLECT AND RELATE Does anyone you know believe that some people are "psychics"? What kind of evidence is

required to support the existence of ESP? Why do you think that many readers of this textbook will continue to believe in ESP despite the lack of scientific evidence?

CRITICAL THINKING Should psychologists conduct research into ESP? Why or why not?

Go to **http://psychology.wadsworth.com/ rathus_pcc9e** for an interactive version of this Learning Connections unit.

Life Connections

Pain, Pain, Go Away—Don't Come Again Another Day

For most people, pain is a frequent visitor. Headaches, backaches, toothaches—these are only a few of the types of pain that most of us encounter from time to time. According to a national Gallup survey of 2,002 adults in the United States (Arthritis Foundation, 2000), 89% experience pain at least once a month. More than half (55%) of people aged 65 and above say they experience pain daily. Sad to say, people aged 65 and above are most likely to attribute pain to getting older (88%), with a sense that they can do nothing about disabilities such as arthritis. By contrast, people aged 18 to 34 are more likely to attribute pain to tension or stress (73%), to overwork (64%), or to their lifestyle (51%). When we assume that there is nothing we can do about pain, we are less likely to try. Yet 43% of Americans say that pain curtails their activities, and 50% say that pain puts them in a bad mood. There are also a number of gender differences in the experiencing of, and response to, pain, as shown in Table 4.1. What is pain? What can we do about it?

Pain results when neurons called *nociceptors* in the skin are stimulated. Evolutionary psychologists would point out that pain is adaptive, if unpleasant, because it motivates us to do something about it. For some of us, however, chronic pain—pain that lasts once injuries or illnesses have cleared—saps our vitality and interferes with the pleasures of everyday life (Turk & Okifuji, 2002).

We can sense pain throughout most of the body, but pain is usually sharpest where nerve endings are densely packed, as in the fingers and face. Pain can also be felt deep within the body, as in the cases of abdominal pain and back pain. Even though headaches may seem to originate deep inside the head, there are no nerve endings for pain in the brain. In fact, brain surgery can be done with a local anesthetic that prevents the patient from feeling the drilling of a small hole through the skull.

Pain usually originates at the point of contact, as when you bang a knee (see Figure 4.28). But its reverberations throughout the nervous system are

extensive. The pain message to the brain is initiated by the release of chemicals, including prostaglandins, bradykinin, and a chemical called P (yes, P stands for "pain"). Prostaglandins facilitate transmission of the pain message to the brain and heighten circulation to the injured area, causing the redness and swelling that we call inflammation. Inflammation serves the biological function of attracting infection-fighting blood cells to the affected area to protect it against invading germs. Pain-relieving drugs such as aspirin and ibuprofen work by inhibiting the production of prostaglandins.

The pain message is relayed from the spinal cord to the thalamus and then projected to the cerebral cortex, making us aware of the location and intensity of the damage. Ronald Melzack (1999) speaks of a "neuromatrix" that includes these chemical reactions but involves other aspects of our physiology and psychology in our reaction to pain. For example, visual and other sensory inputs tell us what is happening and influence the cognitive interpretation of the situation. Our emotional response affects the degree of pain, and so do the ways in which we respond to stress. For example, if the pain derives from an object we fear, perhaps a knife or needle, we may experience more pain. If we perceive that there is nothing we can do to change the situation, perception of pain may increase. If we have self-confidence and a history of successful responding to stress, the perception of pain may diminish.

One of the more intriguing topics within the study of pain is that of phantom limb pain.

Phantom Limb Pain

Truth or Fiction Revisited: Many people experience pain in limbs that have been amputated. The fact that many people experience pain in limbs that are no longer there is one of the more fascinating phenomena of psychology. About 2

TABLE 4.1 GENDER DIFFERENCES IN EXPERIENCING AND RESPONDING TO PAIN		
Percent Who Report . . .	**Women**	**Men**
Experiencing daily pain	46	37
Feeling they have a great deal of control over their pain	39	48
Feeling that tension and stress are their leading causes of pain	72	56
Going to see the doctor about pain only when other people urge them to do it	27	38
Balancing the demands of work and family life to be the key cause of their pain	35	24
Frequent headaches	17	8
Frequent backaches	24	19
Arthritis	20	15
Sore feet	25	17

Why do you think that women are more likely than men to experience pain? What is the gender difference in willingness to see the doctor about pain? How would you explain the gender difference in willingness to see the doctor?

Source of data: Arthritis Foundation (2000, April 6). Pain in America: Highlights from a Gallup survey. http://www.arthritis.org

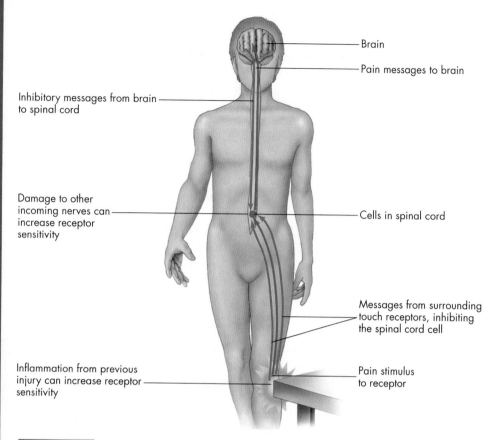

Brain

Pain messages to brain

Inhibitory messages from brain to spinal cord

Damage to other incoming nerves can increase receptor sensitivity

Cells in spinal cord

Messages from surrounding touch receptors, inhibiting the spinal cord cell

Inflammation from previous injury can increase receptor sensitivity

Pain stimulus to receptor

FIGURE 4.28 Perception of Pain

Pain originates at the point of contact, and the pain message to the brain is initiated by the release of prostaglandins, bradykinin, and substance *P*.

out of 3 combat veterans with amputated limbs report feeling pain in such missing, or "phantom," limbs (Kooijman et al., 2000). Although the pain occurs in the absence of the limb, it is real enough. It sometimes involves activation of nerves in the stump of the missing limb, but local anesthesia does not always eliminate the pain. Researchers have found that many people who experience phantom limb pain have also undergone reorganization of the motor and somatosensory cortex that is consistent with the reported pain (Karl et al., 2001).

Gate Theory

Simple remedies like rubbing a banged knee frequently help relieve pain. Why? One possible answer lies in the *gate theory* of pain originated by researchers including Ronald Melzack and Patrick Wall. From this perspective, the nervous system can process only a limited amount of stimulation at a time. Rubbing the knee transmits sensations to the brain that, in a sense, compete for the attention of neurons. Many nerves are thus prevented from transmitting pain messages to the brain. The mechanism is analogous to shutting down a "gate" in the spinal cord. It is like a switchboard being flooded with calls. The flooding prevents any of the calls from getting through.

Acupuncture

Thousands of years ago, the Chinese began mapping the body to learn where pins might be placed to deaden pain. Acupuncture has remained largely unknown in the West. But the practice got some wider attention in the 1970s when *New York Times* columnist James Reston wrote about his appendectomy in China. He reported no discomfort although acupuncture was his primary anesthetic. More recently, TV journalist

Bill Moyers's report (1993) on current usage of acupuncture in China received much attention. For example, one woman underwent brain surgery to remove a tumor after receiving anesthesia that consisted of a mild sedative, a small dose of narcotics, and six needles placed in her forehead, calves, and ankles. The surgery itself and the use of a guiding CAT scan were consistent with contemporary American practices, and the woman reported little discomfort from the surgery.

Traditional acupuncturists believe that the practice balances the body's flow of energy, but research has shown that it stimulates nerves that reach the hypothalamus and may also result in the release of *endorphins* (Reaney, 1998). Endorphins are naturally occurring chemical messengers that are similar to the narcotic morphine in their chemical structure and effects. The drug *naloxone* blocks both the painkilling effects of morphine and of acupuncture. Therefore, the analgesic effects of acupuncture may be due to the morphinelike endorphins.

Modern Psychological Methods for Coping with Pain

Coping with that age-old enemy—pain—has traditionally been a medical issue. The primary treatment has been chemical, as in the use of painkilling drugs. However, psychology has dramatically expanded our arsenal of weapons for fighting pain.

Accurate Information One irony of pain management is that giving people accurate and thorough information about their condition often helps them manage pain (Jacox et al., 1994; Ross & Berger, 1996). Most people in pain try *not* to think about why things hurt during the early phases of an illness (Moyers, 1993). Physicians, too, often neglect the human aspects of relating to their patients. That is, they focus on diagnosing and treating the causes of pain, but they often fail to discuss with patients the meaning of the pain and what the patient can expect.

Yet when uncomfortable treatment methods are used, such as cardiac catheterization or chemotherapy for cancer, knowledge of the details of the treatment, including how long it will last and how much pain there will be, can help people cope with the pain (Ludwick-Rosenthal & Neufeld, 1993). Knowledge of medical procedures reduces stress by helping people maintain control over their situation. Some people, on the other hand, do not *want* information about painful medical procedures. Their attitude is, "Do what you have to do and get it over with." It may be most helpful to match the amount of information provided with the amount desired (Ludwick-Rosenthal & Neufeld, 1993).

Distraction and Fantasy: The Nintendo Approach to Coping With Pain? Diverting attention from pain helps many people cope with it (Cohen, 2002). Psychologists frequently recommend that people use distraction or fantasy as ways of coping with pain. For example, imagine that you've injured your leg and you're waiting to see the

■ **The Nintendo Approach to Coping with Pain?**
Psychologists have found that distraction and fantasy help individuals cope with pain. Yes, it may hurt, but perhaps we can deploy our attention elsewhere.

© Cassy Cohen/PhotoEdit

doctor in an emergency room. You can distract yourself by focusing on details of your environment. You can count ceiling tiles or the hairs on the back of a finger. You can describe (or criticize) the clothes of medical personnel or passersby. Playing video games also distracts people from the pain and discomfort of medical procedures (Kolko & Rickard-Figueroa, 1985; Redd et al., 1987; Robbins, 2000). For example, child cancer patients can become wrapped up in video games while they receive injections of nausea-producing chemicals. Other distraction methods that help children deal with pain include combing one's hair and blowing on a noisemaker (Adler, 1990).

Hypnosis In 1842 London physician W. S. Ward amputated a man's leg after using a rather strange anesthetic: hypnosis. According to reports, the man experienced no discomfort. Several years later, operations were being performed routinely under hypnosis at his infirmary. Today hypnosis is often used to reduce chronic pain (Gay et al., 2002; Mamtani & Cimino, 2002) and as an anesthetic in dentistry, childbirth, even in some forms of surgery (Montgomery et al., 2000).

In using hypnosis to manage pain, the hypnotist usually instructs the person that he or she feels nothing or that the pain is distant and slight. Hypnosis can also aid in the use of distraction and fantasy. For example, the hypnotist can instruct the person to imagine that he or she is relaxing on a warm, exotic shore. We will learn more about hypnosis in Chapter 5.

Relaxation Training When we are in pain, we often tense up. Tensing muscles is uncomfortable in itself, arouses the sympathetic nervous system, and focuses our attention on the pain. Relaxation counteracts these self-defeating behavior patterns (Ross & Berger, 1996). Some psychological methods of relaxation focus on relaxing muscle groups (Gay et al., 2002). Some involve breathing exercises. Others use relaxing imagery: The imagery distracts

the person and deepens feelings of relaxation. Relaxation training may be as effective as most medications for migraine headaches (Martin, 2002) and for chronic pain in the lower back and jaw (Flor & Birbaumer, 1993).

Coping with Irrational Beliefs Irrational beliefs can heighten pain (Turk & Okifuji, 2002.) For example, telling oneself that the pain is unbearable and that it will never cease increases discomfort (Turk & Okifuji, 2002). Some people seem to feel obligated to focus on things that distress them. They may be unwilling to allow themselves to be distracted from pain and discomfort. Thus, cognitive methods aimed at changing irrational beliefs hold some promise (Jensen et al., 1994; Stroud et al., 2000).

Other Methods Pain is a source of stress, and psychologists have uncovered many factors that seem to moderate the effects of stress. One is a sense of commitment. For example, if we are undergoing a painful medical procedure to diagnose or treat an illness, it might help if we recall that we *chose* to participate, rather than see ourselves as helpless victims. Thus, we are in control of the situation, and a sense of control enhances the ability to cope with pain (Turk & Okifuji, 2002).

Supportive social networks help as well. The benefits of having friends visit us—or visiting friends who are unwell—are as consistent with psychological findings as they are with folklore.

And don't forget gate theory. When you feel pain in a toe, squeeze all your toes. When you feel pain in your calf, rub your thighs. People around you may wonder what you're doing, but you're entitled to try to "flood the switchboard" so that some pain messages don't get through.

Recite—An Active Summary™

Want to study on the go? Go to your companion website and download an audio version of this review section to your media player.

1. What are sensation and perception?

Sensation is a mechanical process that involves the stimulation of sensory receptors (neurons) and the transmission of sensory information to the central nervous system. Perception is not mechanical. Perception is the active organization of sensations into a representation of the outside world, and it reflects learning and expectations.

2. How do we know when something is there? How do we know when it has changed?

We know something is there when the intensity of the stimulus, such as a light, exceeds the absolute threshold for that stimulus. The absolute threshold is the lowest intensity at which the stimulus can be detected. We know that something has changed when the change in intensity exceeds the difference threshold. The difference threshold is the minimum difference in intensity that can be discriminated. Difference thresholds are expressed in Weber's constants.

3. What is signal-detection theory?

Signal-detection theory explains the ways in which stimulus characteristics and psychological factors—for example, motivation, familiarity with a stimulus, and attention—interact to influence whether a stimulus will be detected.

4. What are feature detectors?

Feature detectors are neurons that fire in response to specific features of sensed stimuli. For example, detectors in the visual cortex fire in response to particular features of visual input, such as lines sensed at various angles or specific colors.

5. How do our sensory systems adapt to a changing environment?

We become more sensitive to stimuli of low magnitude and less sensitive to stimuli that remain the same (such as the background noises outside the window). Growing more sensitive to stimulation is termed sensitization, or positive adaptation. Growing less sensitive to continuous stimulation is called desensitization, or negative adaptation.

6. What is light?

Visible light is the part of the range of electromagnetic energy that triggers visual sensations. Light is made up of waves of energy; the color violet has the shortest wavelength, and red has the longest. White sunlight can be broken down into the colors of the rainbow by means of a prism.

7. How does the eye work?

The eye senses and transmits visual stimulation to the occipital lobe of the cerebral cortex. After light passes through the cornea, the size of the pupil determines the amount that can pass through the lens. The lens focuses light onto the retina, which is composed of photoreceptors (neurons) called rods and cones. Cones permit perception of color. Rods transmit sensations of light and dark only. Light is transmitted from the retina to the brain via the optic nerve, which is made up of the axons of retinal ganglion cells. Visual acuity is connected with the shape of the eye and age. As we age the lenses grow brittle, making it difficult to focus; the condition is called presbyopia. Rods are more sensitive than cones to lowered lighting and continue to adapt to darkness once cones have reached their peak adaptation.

8. What are some perceptual dimensions of color?

These include hue, value, and saturation. The wavelength of light determines its hue. Yellow-orange-red colors are considered to be warm. Greens and blues are considered to be cool. Colors across from one another on the color wheel are complementary. In afterimages, persistent sensations of color are followed by perception of the complementary color when the first color is removed.

9. How do we perceive color?

There are two theories as to how we perceive color. According to the trichromatic theory, there are three types of cones—some sensitive to red, others to green, and still others to blue-violet. The opponent-process theory proposes three types of color receptors: red–green, blue–yellow, and light–dark. Opponent-process theory is supported by the appearance of afterimages. These two theories may actually reflect a two-step process.

Recite—An Active Summary™

10. What is color blindness? Why are some people color-blind?

People with normal color vision are called trichromats. Monochromats see no color, and dichromats are blind to some parts of the spectrum. Partial color blindness is a sex-linked trait that impairs the working of cones sensitive to red–green.

11. How do we organize bits of visual information into meaningful wholes?

Perceptual organization involves recognizing patterns and processing information about relationships between parts and the whole. Gestalt rules of perceptual organization involve figure–ground relationships, proximity, similarity, continuity, common fate, and closure. Perception of a whole followed by perception of parts is termed top-down processing. Perception of the parts that leads to perception of a whole is termed bottom-up processing.

12. How do we perceive movement?

We visually perceive movement when the light reflected by moving objects moves across the retina and also when objects shift in relation to one another. Distant objects appear to move more slowly than nearby objects, and objects in the middle ground may give the illusion of moving backward. Stroboscopic motion, responsible for the illusion of motion pictures, occurs through the presentation of a rapid progression of images of stationary objects (frames).

13. How do we perceive depth?

Depth perception involves monocular and binocular cues. Monocular cues include pictorial cues such as perspective, clearness, interposition, shadows, and texture gradient, and motion cues such as motion parallax. Binocular cues include retinal disparity and convergence.

14. What are perceptual constancies? Why do we perceive a door to be a rectangle even when it is partly open?

Perceptual constancies are acquired through experience and make the world a stable place. For example, we learn to assume that objects retain their size, shape, brightness, and color despite their distance from us, their position, or changes in lighting conditions.

15. What is sound?

Sound waves require a medium such as air or water in order to be transmitted. Sound waves alternately compress and expand molecules of the medium, creating vibrations. The human ear can hear sounds varying in frequency from 20 to 20,000 cycles per second (Hz). The greater the frequency, the higher the sound's pitch. The loudness of a sound roughly corresponds to the amplitude of sound waves measured in decibels (dB). We can experience hearing loss if we are exposed to protracted sounds of 85 to 90 dB or more.

16. How does the ear work?

The ear captures sound waves, vibrates in sympathy with them, and transmits auditory information to the brain. The outer ear funnels sound waves to the eardrum, which vibrates in sympathy with them and transmits the auditory information through the bones of the middle ear to the cochlea of the inner ear. The basilar membrane of the cochlea transmits those stimuli to the organ of Corti. From there, sound travels to the brain via the auditory nerve.

17. How do we locate sounds?

We locate sounds by determining in which ear they are louder. We may turn our heads to pin down that information.

18. How do we perceive loudness and pitch?

Sounds are perceived as louder when more sensory neurons fire. The place theory of pitch perception holds that the pitch of a sound is sensed according to the place along the basilar membrane that vibrates in response to it; it accounts for sounds whose frequencies exceed 4,000 Hz. Frequency theory states that pitch perception depends on the stimulation of neural impulses that match the frequency of the sound waves and accounts for frequencies of 20 to 1,000 Hz. The volley principle accounts for pitch discrimination between a few hundred and 4,000 cycles per second.

Recite—An Active Summary™

19. What is deafness? What can we do about it?

Conductive deafness—common among older people—is caused by damage to the middle ear and is often ameliorated by hearing aids, which amplify sounds. Sensorineural deafness is usually caused by damage to neurons in the inner ear and can sometimes be corrected by cochlear implants.

20. How does the sense of smell work?

The sense of smell is chemical. It samples molecules of substances called odors through the olfactory membrane in each nostril. Smell makes a key contribution to the flavor of foods.

21. How does the sense of taste work?

There are four primary taste qualities: sweet, sour, salty, and bitter. Flavor involves the odor, texture, and temperature of food, as well as its taste. Taste is sensed through taste cells, which are located in taste buds on the tongue.

22. What are the skin senses? How do they work?

The skin senses include touch, pressure, warmth, cold, and pain. Touches and pressure are sensed by receptors located around the roots of hair cells below the surface of the skin. We have separate receptors for warmth and cold beneath the skin.

23. What is kinesthesis?

Kinesthesis is the sensation of body position and movement. It relies on sensory organs in the joints, tendons, and muscles.

24. How does the vestibular sense work?

The vestibular sense is mostly housed in the semicircular canals of the ears and tells us whether we are in an upright position.

25. What is virtual reality?

Virtual reality is the perception of events that are fed directly into the senses via electronic technology. Psychologists are applying virtual reality in the treatment of fears and the creation of virtually immersive environments.

26. Is there really such a thing as extrasensory perception (ESP)?

ESP, or psi communication, refers to the perception of objects or events through means other than sensory organs. Many psychologists do not believe that ESP is an appropriate area for scientific inquiry. The ganzfeld procedure studies telepathy by having one person (the sender) try to mentally transmit visual information to a receiver in another room. Because of the file-drawer problem and lack of replication of positive results, there is no reliable evidence for the existence of ESP.

 Go to **http://psychology.wadsworth. com/rathus_pcc9e** to access an interactive version of this active summary.

Key Terms

Sensation (p. 142)
Perception (p. 143)
Absolute threshold
 (p. 143)
Psychophysicist (p. 143)
Pitch (p. 143)
Difference threshold
 (p. 144)
Weber's constant (p. 144)
Just noticeable difference
 (jnd) (p. 144)
Signal-detection theory
 (p. 145)
Feature detectors (p. 146)
Sensory adaptation
 (p. 146)
Sensitization (p. 146)
Desensitization (p. 146)
Visible light (p. 147)
Hue (p. 148)
Cornea (p. 148)
Iris (p. 148)
Pupil (p. 148)
Lens (p. 148)
Retina (p. 149)
Photoreceptors (p. 149)

Bipolar cells (p. 149)
Ganglion cells (p. 149)
Optic nerve (p. 149)
Rods (p. 149)
Cones (p. 149)
Fovea (p. 149)
Blind spot (p. 149)
Visual acuity (p. 149)
Presbyopia (p. 150)
Dark adaptation (p. 150)
Complementary (p. 151)
Afterimage (p. 153)
Trichromatic theory
 (p. 153)
Opponent-process theory
 (p. 153)
Trichromat (p. 155)
Monochromat (p. 155)
Dichromat (p. 155)
Closure (p. 156)
Perceptual organization
 (p. 156)
Ambiguous (p. 156)
Proximity (p. 157)
Similarity (p. 158)
Continuity (p. 158)

Common fate (p. 158)
Top-down processing
 (p. 158)
Bottom-up processing
 (p. 158)
Illusions (p. 159)
Autokinetic effect (p. 159)
Stroboscopic motion
 (p. 159)
Phi phenomenon (p. 159)
Monocular cues (p. 160)
Perspective (p. 160)
Interposition (p. 160)
Shadowing (p. 160)
Texture gradient (p. 160)
Motion parallax (p. 161)
Binocular cues (p. 161)
Retinal disparity (p. 161)
Convergence (p. 161)
Size constancy (p. 162)
Color constancy (p. 162)
Brightness constancy
 (p. 162)
Shape constancy (p. 163)
Auditory (p. 164)
Hertz (Hz) (p. 165)

Decibel (dB) (p. 165)
Eardrum (p. 165)
Cochlea (p. 166)
Basilar membrane
 (p. 166)
Organ of Corti (p. 166)
Auditory nerve (p. 166)
Place theory (p. 167)
Frequency theory (p. 168)
Conductive deafness
 (p. 168)
Sensorineural deafness
 (p. 168)
Flavor (p. 169)
Olfactory (p. 169)
Olfactory nerve (p. 169)
Taste cells (p. 171)
Taste buds (p. 171)
Two-point threshold
 (p. 172)
Kinesthesis (p. 173)
Vestibular sense (p. 173)
Semicircular canals
 (p. 173)

ACTIVE LEARNING RESOURCES

Visit your Companion Website for Video, Quizzing, and Self-Assessment!

http://psychology.wadsworth.com/rathus_pcc9e
On this site you can access The Ames Room video highlighted by the Video Connections icon on p. 162. In addition there are many quizzing opportunities including interactive versions of the fill-in-the-blank Active Review sections in your book.

Study on the Go!

Don't have time to study right now? You can study on the go! Visit your companion website and download an audio version of the Recite—An Active Summary section to your media player.

ThomsonNOW

http://www.thomsonedu.com
Need help studying? This site is your one-stop study shop. Take a Pre-Test and Thomson NOW will generate a Personalized Study Plan based on your test results. The Study Plan will identify the topics you need to review and direct you to online resources to help you master those topics. You can then take a Post-Test to determine the concepts you have mastered and what you still need to work on.

Author Blog

What does your author have to say about the state of psychology? Visit your companion website every Tuesday and click on "Author Blog," where he'll talk about the most recent controversies and hot topics in psychology.

Truth or Fiction?

T F We act out our forbidden fantasies in our dreams.

T F Many people have insomnia because they try too hard to fall asleep at night.

T F It is dangerous to awaken a sleepwalker.

T F You can be hypnotized against your will.

T F The effects of hypnotism are due to a special trance state.

T F You can teach a rat to raise or lower its heart rate.

T F A drink a day is good for you.

T F Heroin was once used as a cure for addiction to morphine.

T F Many health professionals calm down hyperactive children by giving them a stimulant.

T F Coca-Cola once "added life" to its signature drink through the use of a powerful—but now illegal—stimulant.

T F The number of people who die from smoking-related causes is greater than the number lost to motor vehicle accidents, abuse of alcohol and all other drugs, suicide, homicide, and AIDS *combined*.

 Go to **http://psychology.wadsworth.com/ rathus_pcc9e** to answer and score this Truth or Fiction quiz.

David Epperson/Getty Images

Consciousness

Preview

I fired up the computer, logged on, and immediately aimed my browser at the Alta Vista search engine on the Web. I entered in the keyword "Self" and hit the search button. In a matter of seconds, . . . the engine came back with a reply . . . 2.5 million hits! Looks like the self is everywhere! Maybe that meant something. Or maybe I just needed to narrow my search. So I entered in the keywords "True Self." This time I got 11,000 hits. Better. . . . How about "Essence of Self?" The search engine hummed away and returned 245 hits. Now I was definitely zooming in on the target. I could tell this was the right path because a lot of the hits included web sites devoted to philosophy, spirituality, and poetry—although it also turned up the American Legion Magazine and a web page called "Understanding Diarrhea in Travelers." No, really! . . . Finally, I entered in the keywords "The True and Essential Self." . . . Once again Alta Vista went out into the vast netherworld of global electronified knowledge and came back with . . . zero hits. Nothing! The void! The True and Essential Self was nowhere to be found, well at least not in cyberspace.

So psychologist John Suler (2005) describes one of his journeys into cyberspace. Thinking that his search engine was a bit slow, I thought I'd Google "self." It took Google 0.17 seconds to find 215 million hits. "True self"? I got 702,000 hits in 0.19 seconds. There were 54 hits for "true and essential self," but it did take Google nearly one second to come up with them. So, the True and Essential Self is now to be found in cyberspace. I wonder where it is in the real world.

The Many Meanings of Consciousness

Psychologists are quite interested in the self, which is one aspect of consciousness. Psychologists are also becoming more and more interested in people's experiences on the Internet, which some psychologists consider to create an altered state of consciousness. Consciousness, altered states of consciousness . . . let us begin this most intriguing area of psychology by posing this question: **What *is* consciousness?**

Consciousness as Awareness

One meaning of consciousness is *sensory awareness* of the environment. The sense of vision enables us to see, or be *conscious* of, the sun gleaming on the snow. Yet sometimes we are not aware of sensory stimulation. We may be unaware, or unconscious, of sensory stimulation when we do not pay attention to it. The world is abuzz with signals, yet you are conscious of, or focusing on, only the words on this page (I hope).

Therefore, another aspect of consciousness is **selective attention.** Selective attention means focusing one's consciousness on a particular stimulus. To keep your car on the road, you must pay more attention to driving conditions than to your hunger pangs.

Adaptation to our environment involves learning which stimuli must be attended to and which ones can be safely ignored. Selective attention makes our senses keener (Basic Behavioral Science Task Force, 1996b). This is why we can pick out the speech of a single person across a room at a cocktail party, a phenomenon suitably termed the *cocktail party effect.*

Although we can decide where and when we will focus our attention, various kinds of stimuli also tend to capture attention. Among them are these:

◆ Sudden changes, as when a cool breeze enters a sweltering room or we receive a particularly high or low grade on an exam.

◆ Novel stimuli, as when a dog enters the classroom or a person shows up with an unusual hairdo.

◆ Intense stimuli, such as bright colors, loud noises, sharp pain, or extremely attractive people.

Selective attention The focus of one's consciousness on a particular stimulus.

Direct inner awareness Knowledge of one's own thoughts, feelings, and memories without use of sensory organs.

◆ Repetitive stimuli, as when the same TV commercial is played a dozen times throughout the course of a football game.

How do advertisers use these facts to get "into" our consciousness and our pocketbooks? Think of some TV commercials that captured your attention. What kinds of stimuli made them front and center in your awareness?

Yet another meaning of consciousness is that of **direct inner awareness.** Close your eyes and imagine spilling a can of bright red paint across a black tabletop. Watch it spread across the black, shiny surface and then spill onto the floor. Although this image may be vivid, you did not "see" it literally. Neither your eyes nor any other sensory organs were involved. You were *conscious* of the image through direct inner awareness.

We are conscious of—or have direct inner awareness of—thoughts, images, emotions, and memories. However, we may not be able to measure direct inner awareness scientifically. Nevertheless, many psychologists argue "It is detectable to anyone that has it" (Miller, 1992, p. 180).

Conscious, Preconscious, Unconscious, and Nonconscious

Sigmund Freud, the founder of psychoanalysis, differentiated between the thoughts and feelings we are conscious, or aware, of and those that are preconscious and unconscious. **Preconscious** material is not currently in awareness but is readily available. For example, if you answer the following questions, you will summon up "preconscious" information: What did you eat for dinner yesterday? About what time did you wake up this morning? What is your phone number? You can make these preconscious bits of information conscious by directing your inner awareness, or attention, to them.

According to Freud, still other mental events are **unconscious.** This means that they are unavailable to awareness under most circumstances. Freud believed that some painful memories and sexual and aggressive impulses are unacceptable to us, so we *automatically* (unconsciously) eject them from our awareness. In other words, we *repress* them. **Repression** of these memories and impulses allows us to avoid feelings of anxiety, guilt, or shame.

People can also *choose* to stop thinking about unacceptable ideas or distractions. When we consciously eject unwanted mental events from awareness, we are engaging in **suppression.** We may, for example, suppress thoughts of an upcoming party when we need to study for a test. We may also try to suppress thoughts of a test while we are at the party!

Some bodily processes, such as the firings of neurons, are **nonconscious.** They cannot be experienced through sensory awareness or direct inner awareness. The growing of hair and the carrying of oxygen in the blood are nonconscious. We can see that our hair has grown, but we have no sense receptors that give us sensations of growing. We can feel the need to breathe but do not directly experience the exchange of carbon dioxide and oxygen.

Let us now journey all the way back to the most conscious aspect of our being—our sense of self.

Consciousness as Personal Unity: The Sense of Self

As we develop, we differentiate ourselves from that which is not us. We develop a sense of being persons, individuals. There is a totality to our impressions, thoughts, and feelings that makes up our conscious existence—our continuing sense of self in a changing world. In this usage of the word, consciousness *is* self.

Consciousness as the Waking State

The word *conscious* also refers to the waking state as opposed, for example, to sleep. From this perspective, sleep, meditation, the hypnotic "trance," and the distorted

Preconscious In psychodynamic theory, descriptive of material that is not in awareness but can be brought into awareness by focusing one's attention.

Unconscious In psychodynamic theory, descriptive of ideas and feelings that are not available to awareness.

Repression In psychodynamic theory, the automatic (unconscious) ejection of anxiety-evoking ideas, impulses, or images from awareness.

Suppression The deliberate, or conscious, placing of certain ideas, impulses, or images out of awareness.

Nonconscious Descriptive of bodily processes such as the growing of hair, of which we cannot become conscious. We may "recognize" that our hair is growing but cannot directly experience the biological process.

■ **Consciousness as the Sense of Self** The concept of *consciousness* has many meanings in psychology and in general usage. One is the sense of self, as we see here. The concept of consciousness also refers to sensory awareness, the selective aspect of attention, direct inner awareness, and the waking state.

© Reg Charity/CORBIS

A Closer Look   TERRI SCHIAVO, CONSCIOUSNESS, AND BIOLOGICAL FUNCTIONING

In 1990, 25-year-old Terri Schiavo collapsed from cardiac arrest, stopped breathing, and suffered brain damage due to lack of oxygen. For the next 15 years, she lay in what her doctors diagnosed as a vegetative state. An electroencephalogram (EEG) showed that her cerebral cortex, the seat of consciousness, was largely inactive (see Table 5.1). After the collapse, Terri began breathing on her own again, but she was sustained by a feeding tube. In 2005, Terri's doctors removed the feeding tube, following a protracted court battle between her husband, who had custody and wanted the tube removed, and her parents, who wanted her to remain alive. The battle reached state and federal courts, and even led to the passing of a special law involving only Terri by the United States Congress. Nevertheless, the tube was removed and within two weeks, Terri's life functions had ceased.

Many issues are involved in the Terri Schiavo case: medical, psychological, legal, religious, and philosophical. We will address a few of them here.

First, the medical: As you can see in Table 5.1, Terri's state was considered to be unconscious ("persistently vegetative") by the majority of the medical profession (Annas, 2005; Quill, 2005). If that diagnosis was correct, Terri had no real chance of regaining consciousness after 15 years. But if, as a few doctors suggested, Terri might instead be suffering from a "minimally conscious state," there was some possibility of recovery, even

at this late stage. An auto mechanic named Terry Wallis regained awareness from a minimally conscious state more than 18 years after he fell unconscious due to an auto accident. A Kansas resident named Sarah Scantlin, another crash victim, emerged from a minimally conscious state after 19 years.

From a psychological perspective, it would appear that Terri's EEG argued in favor of the diagnosis of vegetative state. Wallis's and Scantlin's brains showed nearly normal activity on occasion when they were socially stimulated. Terri's did not. Terri's continued breathing and conduct of other bodily functions could be explained by the continued functioning of lower parts of her brain. These parts could also explain intermittent reflexive smiling and other behaviors that gave some hope to people who cared for her.

Legally speaking, Terri's husband had custody, and state and federal courts found no reason why custody should be removed from him. He argued that Terri would not have wanted to remain indefinitely in such a state.

Now, the difficult religious and philosophical issues: Terri's parents and the Catholic Church, to which Terri belonged, believe that every human life is precious and sacred, regardless of how disabled. The church's view is also consistent with the teachings of the Greek philosopher Aristotle, who believed that no person's existence should ever be violated (Leland, 2005). Those who supported Ms. Schiavo's husband in

■ **Terri Schiavo** Terri Schiavo lay in what most health professionals labeled a vegetative state for 15 years before her feeding tube was disconnected. Her case touched off a conflict that polarized the nation into opposing camps.

effect agreed with the French philosopher Descartes, who argued that psychological self-awareness or consciousness was more important than biological functioning (Annas, 2005; Leland, 2005).

Critical thinkers will have to weigh the issues and decide for themselves where they stand on the Terri Schiavo case. Certainly, it's an issue we hope we'll never have to personally face.

perceptions that can accompany use of consciousness-altering drugs are considered *altered states of consciousness.*

In the remainder of this chapter, we explore various types of altered states of consciousness. They include sleep, dreams, and daydreams; hypnosis, meditation, and biofeedback; and finally, the effects of psychoactive drugs.

Learning Connections   THE MANY MEANINGS OF CONSCIOUSNESS

ACTIVE REVIEW (1) John B. Watson argued that only observable _____ should be studied by psychologists. (2) *Consciousness* has several meanings, including sensory awareness, the selective aspect of attention, direct inner _____, personal unity, and the waking state. (3) Sigmund _____ differentiated among ideas that are conscious, preconscious, and unconscious.

REFLECT AND RELATE Are *you* conscious, or aware, of yourself and the world around you? How do you know?

CRITICAL THINKING Why do behaviorists object to studying consciousness? Why do cognitive psychologists pursue the study of consciousness?

 Go to **http://psychology.wadsworth.com/ rathus_pcc9e** for an interactive version of this Learning Connections unit.

TABLE 5.1 CONSCIOUS, PARTIALLY CONSCIOUS, AND UNCONSCIOUS STATES

State	Conscious	Asleep**	Minimally Conscious	Comatose*	Vegetative*
Awareness	Full	Little to none	Partial	None	None
Motor functions	Full range of voluntary movements and reflexes available	Variable: May be still, may move limbs, occasionally walks	Reaches for object; may grasp objects and hold them	Variable: Some reflexes available; may withdraw from pain	May make random movements; may withdraw from pain
Hearing	Normal hearing	Little to none	May respond to commands to grasp objects, blink, etc.	None	Shows startle reflex to sudden loud noises
Vision	Normal vision	Eyes may wince at bright light or when startled	May track moving objects with eyes	None	Eyes may wince at bright light or when startled
Communication	Full range of language and body language available	May talk or shout during dreams	May produce understandable sounds or gestures	None	None
Emotional response	Full range of emotional responses available	May show horror at nightmare	May smile or cry in response to visitor's behavior	None	May show reflexive or random smiling or crying
Brain activity	High level of activity in cortex and elsewhere; memory functions	Varies from high during REM sleep to low during deep sleep; little memory	Voice of loved one may spur almost normal cortical activity; may remember surroundings	Control of primitive basic life functions by parts of the hindbrain such as the pons and the medulla	Minimal, random activity in the cortex
Cause	(Normal waking state)	Normal variation in consciousness	Brain injury; lack of oxygen	Brain injury; lack of oxygen	Brain injury; lack of oxygen
Comments	(Normal waking state)	Movements and utterances may reflect dream content; can be awakened	May recover rapidly or after many years; may be aware of surroundings	Most people recover in 2–3 weeks	May regain some awareness in few months; after 2 years, none recover

*Unconscious states. **Variable: Unconscious–partially conscious states.

Sleep, Dreams, and Daydreams: Other Worlds Within?

Sleep is a fascinating topic. After all, we spend about one-third of our adult lives asleep. Sleep experts recommend that adults get eight hours of sleep a night, but according to the National Sleep Foundation (2003), adults in the United States typically get a bit less than seven. About one-third get six hours or less of sleep a night during the work week. One-third admit that lack of sleep impairs their ability to function during the day, and nearly one in five admits to falling asleep at the wheel.

Yes, we spend one-third of our lives in sleep—or would if we could. As you can see in Figure 5.1, however, some animals get much more sleep than we do, and some obtain much less. Why? It might have something to do with evolutionary forces. Animals who are most at risk of being hunted by predators tend to sleep less—an adaptive response to the realities of life, and death.

Biological and Circadian Rhythms

We and other animals are subject to rhythms, and they are related to the rotation and revolutions of the planet. Many birds (and people who can afford it!) migrate south in the fall and north in the winter. A number of animals hibernate for the winter and emerge when buds again are about to blossom.

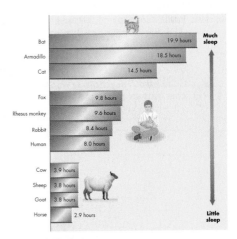

FIGURE 5.1 Sleep Times for Mammals
Different mammals require different amounts of sleep. Reasons remain uncertain, but evolution apparently plays a role: Animals more prone to being attacked by predators sleep less.

Circadian rhythm Referring to cycles that are connected with the 24-hour period of the earth's rotation. (From the Latin *circa*, meaning "about," and *dia*, meaning "day.")

Our alternating periods of wakefulness and sleep provide an example of an internally generated **circadian rhythm. Question: What is a circadian rhythm?** A circadian rhythm is a cycle that is connected with the 24-hour period of the earth's rotation. A cycle of wakefulness and sleep is normally 24 hours long. However, when people are removed from cues that signal day or night, a cycle tends to become extended to about 25 hours, and people sleep nearly 10 of them (National Sleep Foundation, 2000b). Why? We do not know. And within our periods of sleep we typically undergo a number of 90-minute cycles during which we run through five stages of sleep.

Some of us function optimally in the morning, others in the afternoon. Some of us are "night owls," who are at our best when most of our neighbors are sleeping soundly.

Why do we sleep? Why do we dream? What are daydreams? Let us explore the nature of sleep, dreams, sleep disorders, and daydreams and fantasies.

The Stages of Sleep: How Do We Sleep?

When we sleep, we slip from consciousness to unconsciousness. When we are conscious, our brains emit waves characterized by certain *frequencies* (numbers of waves per second) and *amplitudes* (heights—an index of strength). Brain waves are rough indicators of the activity of large numbers of neurons. The strength or energy of brain waves is expressed in volts (an electrical unit). Likewise, when we sleep our brains emit waves that differ from those emitted when we are conscious. The electroencephalograph, or EEG, has helped researchers identify the different brain waves during the waking state and when we are sleeping. Figure 5.2 shows EEG patterns that reflect the frequency and strength of brain waves that occur during the waking state, when we are relaxed, and when we are in the various stages of sleep. Brain waves, like other waves, are cyclical. The printouts in Figure 5.2 show what happens during a period of 15 seconds or so. **Question: How do we describe the various stages of sleep?**

High-frequency brain waves are associated with wakefulness. When we move deeper into sleep, their frequency decreases and their amplitude (strength) increases. When we close our eyes and begin to relax before going to sleep, our

FIGURE 5.2 **The Stages of Sleep**
This figure illustrates typical EEG patterns for the stages of sleep. During REM sleep, EEG patterns resemble those of the waking state. For this reason, REM sleep is often termed *paradoxical sleep.* As sleep progresses from stage 1 to stage 4, brain waves become slower, and their amplitude increases. Dreams, including normal nightmares, are most vivid during REM sleep. More disturbing sleep terrors tend to occur during deep stage 4 sleep.

 Go to **http://psychology.wadsworth.com/rathus_pcc9e** to access an interactive version of this figure.

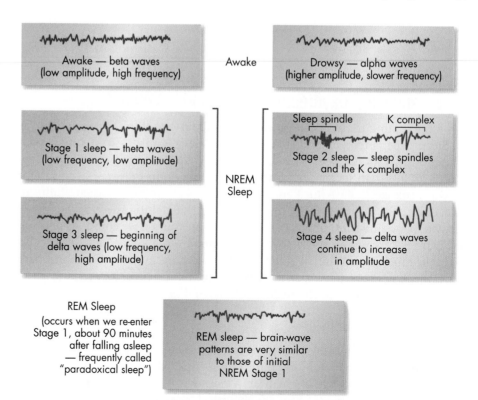

Awake — beta waves (low amplitude, high frequency)

Awake

Drowsy — alpha waves (higher amplitude, slower frequency)

Stage 1 sleep — theta waves (low frequency, low amplitude)

NREM Sleep

Sleep spindle   K complex

Stage 2 sleep — sleep spindles and the K complex

Stage 3 sleep — beginning of delta waves (low frequency, high amplitude)

Stage 4 sleep — delta waves continue to increase in amplitude

REM Sleep (occurs when we re-enter Stage 1, about 90 minutes after falling asleep — frequently called "paradoxical sleep")

REM sleep — brain-wave patterns are very similar to those of initial NREM Stage 1

brains emit many **alpha waves.** Alpha waves are low-amplitude brain waves of about 8 to 13 cycles per second.

Figure 5.2 shows five stages of sleep. The first four sleep stages are considered **non-rapid-eye-movement (NREM)** sleep. These contrast with the fifth stage, which is called **rapid-eye-movement (REM)** sleep because our eyes dart back and forth quickly beneath our closed lids.

As we enter stage 1 sleep, our brain waves slow down from the alpha rhythm and enter a pattern of **theta waves.** Theta waves, with a frequency of about 6 to 8 cycles per second, are accompanied by slow, rolling eye movements. The transition from alpha waves to theta waves may be accompanied by a **hypnagogic state** during which we may experience brief dreamlike images that resemble vivid photographs. Stage 1 sleep is the lightest stage of sleep. If we are awakened from stage 1 sleep, we may deny that we were asleep or feel that we have not slept at all.

After 30 to 40 minutes of stage 1 sleep, we undergo a rather steep descent into stages 2, 3, and 4 (see Figure 5.3). During stage 2, brain waves are medium in amplitude with a frequency of about 4 to 7 cycles per second, but these are punctuated by *sleep spindles*. Sleep spindles have a frequency of 12 to 16 cycles per second.

During deep sleep stages 3 and 4, our brains produce slower **delta waves,** which reach relatively great amplitude compared with other brain waves. During stage 3, the delta waves have a frequency of 1 to 3 cycles per second. Stage 4 is the deepest stage of sleep, from which it is the most difficult to be awakened. During stage 4 sleep, the delta waves slow to about 0.5 to 2 cycles per second, and their amplitude is greatest.

After perhaps half an hour of deep stage 4 sleep, we begin a relatively rapid journey back upward through the stages until we enter REM sleep (Figure 5.3). REM sleep derives its name from the *rapid eye movements*, observable beneath the closed eyelids, that characterize this stage. During REM sleep we produce relatively rapid, low-amplitude brain waves that resemble those of light stage 1 sleep. REM sleep is also called *paradoxical sleep* because the EEG patterns observed suggest a level of arousal similar to that of the waking state (Figure 5.3). However, it is difficult to awaken a person during REM sleep. When people are awakened during REM sleep, as is the practice in sleep research, about 80% of the time they report that they have been dreaming. (We also dream during NREM sleep, but less frequently. People report dreaming only about 20% of the time when awakened during NREM sleep.)

Each night we tend to undergo five trips through the stages of sleep (see Figure 5.3). These trips include about five periods of REM sleep. Our first journey through stage 4 sleep is usually longest. Sleep tends to become lighter as the night wears on. Our periods of REM sleep tend to become longer, and toward morning our last period of REM sleep may last close to half an hour.

The Functions of Sleep: Why Do We Sleep?

Question: Why do we sleep? Researchers do not have all the answers as to why we sleep, but sleep seems to serve a number of purposes: It rejuvenates the body, helps us recover from stress, helps us consolidate learning and memories, and, in infants, it may even promote the development of the brain.

Consider the hypothesis that sleep helps rejuvenate a tired body. Most of us have had the experience of going without sleep for a night and feeling "wrecked" or "out of it" the following day. Perhaps the next evening we went to bed early in order to "catch up on our sleep." What happens to you if you do not sleep for one night? For several nights?

Many students can pull "all-nighters" in which they cram for a test through the night and then perform reasonably well the following day (Webb, 1993). But they tend to show deficits in psychological functions such as attention, learning, and memory, especially if they go sleepless for more than one night (Ohno et al., 2002; Taylor & McFatter, 2003). Sleep deprivation makes for dangerous driving (Stutts

Alpha waves Rapid low-amplitude brain waves that have been linked to feelings of relaxation.

Non-rapid-eye-movement (NREM) sleep Stages of sleep 1 through 4.

Rapid-eye-movement (REM) sleep A stage of sleep characterized by rapid eye movements, which have been linked to dreaming.

Theta waves Slow brain waves produced during the hypnagogic state.

Hypnagogic state The drowsy interval between waking and sleeping, characterized by brief, hallucinatory, dreamlike experiences.

Delta waves Strong, slow brain waves usually emitted during stage 4 sleep.

| Sleep stage | A | 1 | 2 | 3 | 4 | 3 | 2 | REM | 1 | 2 | 3 | 4 | 3 | 2 | 3 | 2 | REM |

FIGURE 5.3 Sleep Cycles

This figure illustrates the alternation of REM and non-REM sleep for the typical sleeper. There are about five periods of REM sleep during an eight-hour night. Sleep is deeper earlier in the night, and REM sleep tends to become prolonged toward morning.

et al., 2003). The National Sleep Foundation (2003) estimates that sleep deprivation is connected with 100,000 vehicular crashes and 1,500 deaths each year. The Foundation also found that some 60% of Americans aged 18 through 54 admit to having driven a vehicle while feeling tired. A Swedish study of more than 10,000 traffic accidents concluded that early morning driving—particularly at 4:00 A.M. — is many times more dangerous than driving during the later morning or afternoon. The researchers controlled for the effects of alcohol consumption and darkness and attributed the greater number of accidents to sleepiness (Akerstedt et al., 2001). To combat sleep deprivation that occurs during the week, many people sleep late or nap on their days off (National Sleep Foundation, 2003).

WHY DO YOU NEED THE AMOUNT OF SLEEP YOU NEED? The amount of sleep we need seems to be in part genetically determined (Webb, 1993). People also tend to need more sleep during periods of stress, such as a change of job, an increase in workload, or an episode of depression (Maas, 1998). In fact, sleep seems to help us recover from stress.

Newborn babies may sleep 16 hours a day, and teenagers may sleep 12 hours or more ("around the clock"). It is widely believed that older people need less sleep than younger adults do, but sleep in older people is often interrupted by physical discomfort or the need to go to the bathroom. To make up for sleep lost at night, older people will often "nod off" during the day.

SLEEP, LEARNING, AND MEMORY REM sleep and deep sleep are both connected with the consolidation of learning and memory (Maquet, 2001; Ohno et al., 2002; Poe et al., 2000; Stickgold et al., 2000, 2001). In some studies, animals or people have been deprived of REM sleep. In fact, fetuses have periods of waking and sleeping, and REM sleep may foster the development of the brain before birth (McCarley, 1992). REM sleep may also help maintain neurons in adults by "exercising" them at night. Deprivation of REM sleep is accomplished by monitoring EEG records and eye movements and waking the person during REM sleep. Under these conditions animals and people learn more slowly and forget what they have learned more rapidly (Kennedy, 2002; Le Marec et al., 2001). In any event, people and other animals that are deprived of REM sleep tend to show *REM rebound,* meaning that they spend more time in REM sleep during subsequent sleep periods. In other words, they catch up. It is mostly during REM sleep that we dream. Let us now consider dreams, a mystery about which philosophers, poets, and scientists have theorized for centuries.

Dreams: What Is the "Stuff" of Dreams?

To quote from Shakespeare's *The Tempest,* just what is the "stuff" of dreams? What are they "made on"? **Question: What are dreams?** Like memories and fantasies, dreams involve imagery in the absence of external stimulation and can seem very real. In college I often had "anxiety dreams" the night before a test. I dreamed repeatedly that I had taken the test and it was all over. (Imagine the disappointment when I awakened and realized that the test still lay before me!)

| 3 A.M. | | | 4 A.M. | | | 5 A.M. | | 6 A.M. | | | 7 A.M. |

| 2 | 3 | 2 | REM | 1 | 2 | 3 2 A 1 | REM | A 1 A | 2 | REM |

Dreams are most likely to have vivid imagery during REM sleep, whereas images are vaguer and more fleeting during NREM sleep. Also, you tend to dream every time you are in REM sleep. Therefore, if you sleep for eight hours and undergo five sleep cycles, you may have five dreams. Dreams may compress time the way a movie does, by skipping over hours or days to a future time, but the actual action tends to take place in "real time." Fifteen minutes of events fill about 15 minutes of dreaming. Furthermore, your dream theater is quite flexible. You can dream in black and white or in full color.

Some dreams are nightmares. One common nightmare is that something heavy is sitting on your chest and watching you as you breathe. Another is that you are trying to run away from a terrible threat but cannot gain your footing or coordinate your leg muscles. Nightmares, like most pleasant dreams, are generally products of REM sleep.

Question: Why do we dream what we dream? There are many theories as to why we dream what we dream. Some are psychological and others are more biologically oriented. The nearby "A Closer Look" affords insight into beliefs about dreaming that have been discovered through anthropological research.

DREAMS AS REFLECTIONS OF "THE RESIDUE OF THE DAY" You may recall dreams involving fantastic adventures, but most dreams involve memories of the activities and problems of the day (Domhoff, 2001, 2003). If we are preoccupied with illness or death, sexual or aggressive urges, or moral dilemmas, we are likely to dream about them. The characters in our dreams are more likely to be friends and neighbors than spies, monsters, and princes—subjects that have been referred to, poetically, as "the residue of the day."

 ## A Closer Look   DREAMS ACROSS CULTURES: FROM FORESTS TO RAIN SHOWERS TO "THE DREAMING"

Anthropological research sheds fascinating light on the ways in which dreams relate to a culture's way of life (Hearne, 2003). Animals are dreamt of extensively in hunting cultures. Oceanic peoples dream of fish. These cultures respect dreams as coming from an honored source and containing knowledge that can help the dreamer. Dreams of the future are accepted as omens.

The Pagiboti of Zaire believe that their ancestors send them dreams. Dreams signal success or failure at the hunt. A dream of meeting an animal in the forest is a good omen, suggesting a good kill on the following day.

The Malaysian natives find symbolism in their dreams. A gale means sorrow is approaching. Hail means poverty. Bathing in a rain shower means that the person will escape danger. Flies, like mosquitoes, mean that an enemy nears.

In Central American pre-Mayan and Mayan cultures, dreams and visions were valued as omens of the future. People would fast, force themselves to remain awake, and chew coca leaves (laced with cocaine) to bring on visions. Dreams that followed a first puberty fast were believed to hold keys to the person's future. These people would occasionally sacrifice an animal and wrap it tightly around the person's neck, half strangling him, until lack of oxygen produced a vision. Professional diviners ("listeners") were revered because they helped steer society through natural and other disasters.

People in some ancient societies believed that the soul traveled during sleep. Dreams were given as much credence as waking experiences. When such peoples reported flying or slaying monsters, they were not lying; rather, they were reporting dreams,

which they believed to be as accurate as events that occurred while they were awake.

The wandering soul left the sleeper vulnerable. The body would die if it did not return due to an accident or ensnarement. Sorcerers of the Danger Islands might set up such snares. One could not change the appearance of the sleeper, as by shaving him, because the returning soul might not recognize him, and he would die.

The Australian aborigines believed that the earth was formed and beings created during "Dreamtime"—also known as World Dawn, or The Dreaming. Here is where the spirits of the dead return. It is a place that is still believed to provide power for healers.

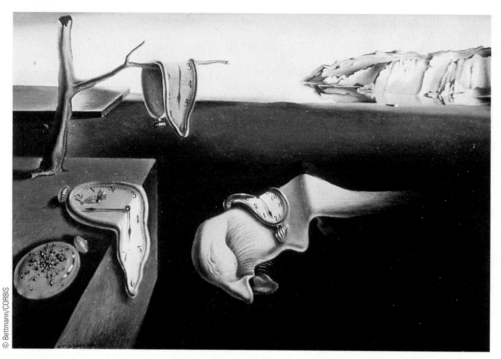

© Bettmann/CORBIS

■ **Dream Images?** In *The Persistence of Memory*, Salvador Dali seems to depict images born in dreams. What is "such stuff as dreams are made on"? "Where" do dreams come from? Why do they contain what they contain? Are most dreams exciting adventures or dull recurrences of the events of the day?

However, traumatic events can spawn nightmares, as reported in studies of the aftermath of the terrorist attacks on the World Trade Center and Pentagon in 2001 (Gorman, 2001; Singareddy & Balon, 2002). People who suffer frequent nightmares are more likely than other people to also suffer from anxieties, depression, and other kinds of psychological discomfort (Berquier & Ashton, 1992).

DREAMS AS THE EXPRESSION OF UNCONSCIOUS DESIRES "A dream is a wish your heart makes," is a song lyric from the Disney film *Cinderella*. Freud theorized that dreams reflect unconscious wishes and urges. He argued that through dreams we can express impulses we would censor during the day. Moreover, he said that the content of dreams is symbolic of unconscious fantasized objects such as the genitals. A key part of Freud's method of psychoanalysis involved interpretation of his clients' dreams. **Truth or Fiction Revisited:** However, there is no evidence that we act out forbidden fantasies in our dreams.

DREAMS AS PROTECTING SLEEP Freud also believed that dreams "protect sleep" by providing imagery that helps keep disturbing, repressed thoughts out of awareness. The theory that dreams protect sleep has been challenged by the observation that disturbing events tend to be followed by disturbing dreams on the same theme—not by protective imagery (Reiser, 2001). Our behavior in dreams is also generally consistent with our waking behavior. Most dreams, then, are unlikely candidates for the expression of repressed urges (even disguised). A person who leads a moral life tends to dream moral dreams.

THE ACTIVATION–SYNTHESIS MODEL OF DREAMS There are also biological views of the "meanings" of dreams (Domhoff, 2003). According to the **activation–synthesis model,** acetylcholine (a neurotransmitter) and the pons (a structure in the lower part of the brain) stimulate responses that lead to dreaming (Hobson, 1999, 2003). One effect is *activation* of the reticular activating system (RAS), which arouses us, but not to waking. During the waking state, firing of these cells in the reticular formation is linked to movement, particularly the movements involved in walking, running, and other physical acts. During REM sleep, however, neurotransmitters generally inhibit activity so we usually do not thrash about as we dream (Bassetti et al., 2000). In this way, we save ourselves (and our bed partners) some wear and tear. But the eye muscles are stimulated and thus show the rapid eye movement associated with dreaming. The RAS also stimulates neural activity in the parts of the cortex involved in memory. The cortex then *synthesizes,* or puts together, these sources of stimulation to some degree to yield the stuff of dreams. Yet research with the PET scan shows that the frontal lobes of the brain, which seem to be where we make sense of experience, are relatively inactive during sleep (Wade, 1998). Dreams are therefore more likely to be emotionally gripping than coherent in plot.

DREAMS AS HELPING US CONSOLIDATE MEMORIES Another view of dreams is that with the brain cut off from the world outside, learning experiences and memories are replayed and consolidated during sleep, although the evidence for this hypothesis is somewhat contradictory (Siegel, 2002; Stickgold et al., 2001). Still

Activation–synthesis model The view that dreams reflect activation of cognitive activity by the reticular activating system and synthesis of this activity into a pattern by the cerebral cortex.

another possibility is that REM activity is a way of testing whether the individual has benefitted from the restorative functions of sleep (Wade, 1998). When restoration is adequate, the brain awakens. According to this view, dreams are just the by-products of the testing.

There may be no absolute agreement on the origins of the functions of sleep or the content of dreams, but many—perhaps most—of us either live with or encounter sleep disorders now and then.

Sleep Disorders

Although nightmares are unpleasant, they do not qualify as sleep disorders. The term *sleep disorders* is reserved for other problems that can seriously interfere with our functioning. **Question: What kinds of sleep disorders are there?** Some sleep disorders, like insomnia, are all too familiar, experienced by at least half of American adults. Others, like apnea (pauses in breathing) affect fewer than 10% of us (National Sleep Foundation, 2003). In this section we discuss insomnia and less common sleep disorders: narcolepsy, apnea, and the so-called *deep-sleep disorders*—sleep terrors, bed-wetting, and sleepwalking.

 A Closer Look | **WHEN RATS DREAM, IT SEEMS, IT'S AFTER A DAY AT THE MAZES[1]**

Elephants dream of munching sweet grass under a starry savannah sky. Dogs, paws aquiver, tails thumping faintly in slumber, chase squirrels in the park. And cats, of course, dream of mice. Or so humans, prone to anthropomorphic conjecture about the four-legged world, have long suspected. Yet what animals dream about—or indeed, whether they dream at all—has remained resistant to scientific scrutiny, if only because animals cannot describe their closed-eye experiences in words.

Now, however, two researchers studying memory have offered compelling evidence that the brains of sleeping animals are at work in a way irresistibly suggestive of dreaming. And the animals in question—four pink-eared, black-and-white laboratory rats—appeared to be dreaming about something very specific: the maze they were learning to run.

Kenway Louie and Matthew Wilson (2001), who reported their findings in the journal *Neuron*, found that patterns of brain activity identified when the rats ran a circular maze—receiving a reward of chocolate-flavored sprinkles—were exactly duplicated when the rats were sleeping. In particular, the patterns, detected in the firing of clusters of cells in the hippocampus, an area involved with memory formation and storage, were reproduced during phases of sleep that in humans are strongly linked to dreaming. And they were so precise the scientists could tell where in the maze the rat would be if it were awake, and whether it would be moving or standing still.

"The animal is certainly recalling memories of those events as they occurred during the awake state, and it is doing so during dream sleep," said Dr. Matthew Wilson, the senior author of the report and an associate professor of brain and cognitive sciences at the Massachusetts Institute of Technology. Dr. Wilson added that the research was not proof, in the purest sense, that animals dream, because the dreaming experience is subjective and "our ability to ask the animal to report the content of these states is limited."

Scientists familiar with the work said the research was important not only for the glimpse it offered of the sleeping animal brain, but also because it lent support to the idea that sleep played a critical role in the encoding and storage of memories. The study demonstrates, for the first time, that complex, episodic memories are replayed or "rehearsed" in the hippocampus during sleep, perhaps representing a process by which memory is gradually consolidated and passed to other parts of the brain, a model championed by several researchers.

"I am delighted," said Dr. John Allan Hobson, a professor of psychiatry at Harvard, "because it suggests that, as we have long suspected, sleep has a lot of functional significance for learning and memory."

The relationship between sleep and memory is still debated within the field, but studies by Dr. Robert Stickgold, of Dr. Hobson's laboratory, and others indicate that when people learn new skills, their performance is dependent on how much they get of two types of sleep: nondreaming or slow-wave sleep, early in the night; and so-called rapid-eye-movement sleep, or REM sleep, later in the night. In humans, REM sleep is when most dreaming occurs.

Like humans, slumbering animals pass through different stages of sleep, and most mammals exhibit periods of REM sleep, characterized by intense activity in the brain similar to that during waking, and rapid movements of the eye. The rat, Dr. Wilson said, which has a 12-hour sleep cycle, generally passes through REM about every 20 minutes, with each REM episode lasting an average of 2 minutes.

In the study, Louie and Wilson first trained the rats to run through the maze, receiving rewards when they reached a point three-fourths of the way around it. Electrophysiological activity from clusters of neurons in the hippocampus was then recorded using multiple electrodes, made from fine wire, implanted in the rats' brains. Recordings were taken while the rats ran through the maze and during periods of sleep before and afterward.

In previous work, Dr. Wilson and other researchers had found that while rats ran a maze, hippocampal neurons fired in specific patterns, producing, as they wrote, a "unique signature of the behavioral experience." The pattern was distinct from that produced when the rats ran a different maze, ran the same maze under different conditions, or engaged in random activity.

[1] From "When Rats Dream, It Seems, It's After a Day at the Mazes," by Erica Goode, *The New York Times* (1/25/2001). Copyright © 2001 by The New York Times Co. Reprinted with permission.

TABLE 5.2 GENDER DIFFERENCES IN FACTORS THAT DISRUPT SLEEP

Factor	Percent of women reporting factor	Percent of men reporting factor
Stress (e.g., restlessness, muscle tension): 22% of adults overall	26	20
Pain: 20% of adults overall	25	13
Children: 17% of adults overall	21	12
Partner's snoring: 16% of adults overall	22	7
Pauses in partner's breathing: 8% of adults overall	11	2

Source: Based on data reported by the National Sleep Foundation, 2000b.

INSOMNIA According to the National Sleep Foundation (2003), more than half of American adults (58%) and about two-thirds of older adults are affected by insomnia in any given year. Women complain of insomnia more often than men do, by 61% to 53% (National Sleep Foundation, 2000b). Table 5.2 shows a number of factors that contribute to insomnia.

Truth or Fiction Revisited: It is true that many people have insomnia because they try too hard to fall asleep at night. People with insomnia tend to compound their sleep problems when they try to force themselves to fall asleep. Their concern heightens autonomic activity and muscle tension (Edinger et al., 2001). You cannot force or will yourself to go to sleep. You can only set the stage for sleep by lying down and relaxing when you are tired. If you focus on sleep too closely, it will elude you.

You will find strategies for tackling insomnia—and winning—in this chapter's "Life Connections" feature.

NARCOLEPSY A person with **narcolepsy** falls asleep suddenly and irresistibly. Narcolepsy afflicts as many as 100,000 people in the United States and seems to run in families. The "sleep attack" may last about 15 minutes, after which the person awakens feeling refreshed. Nevertheless, these sleep episodes are dangerous and frightening. They can occur while a person is driving or working with sharp tools. They also may be accompanied by the sudden collapse of muscle groups or even of

Narcolepsy A "sleep attack" in which a person falls asleep suddenly and irresistibly.

■ **Narcolepsy** In an experiment on narcolepsy, the dog barks, nods it head, and then falls suddenly asleep.

the entire body—a condition called *sleep paralysis*. In sleep paralysis, the person cannot move during the transition from the waking state to sleep, and hallucinations (such as of a person or object sitting on the chest) occur.

Although the causes are unknown, narcolepsy is thought to be a disorder of REM-sleep functioning. Stimulants and antidepressant drugs have helped many people with narcolepsy (Littner et al., 2001).

APNEA **Apnea** is a dangerous sleep disorder in which the air passages are obstructed. People with apnea stop breathing periodically, up to several hundred times per night (National Sleep Foundation, 2003). Obstruction may cause the sleeper to suddenly sit up and gasp for air, before falling back asleep. People with apnea are stimulated nearly, but not quite, to waking by the buildup of carbon dioxide. Some 10 million Americans have apnea, and it is associated with obesity and chronic loud snoring. Apnea is more than a sleep problem. It can lead to high blood pressure, heart attacks, and strokes (Flemons, 2002).

Causes of apnea include anatomical deformities that clog the air passageways, such as a thick palate, and problems in the breathing centers in the brain. Apnea is treated by such measures as weight loss, surgery, and *continuous positive airway pressure,* which is supplied by a mask that provides air pressure that keeps the airway open during sleep.

DEEP-SLEEP DISORDERS: SLEEP TERRORS, BED-WETTING, AND SLEEPWALKING
Sleep terrors, bed-wetting, and sleepwalking all occur during deep (stage 3 or 4) sleep, are more common among children, and may reflect immaturity of the nervous system (Vgontzas & Kales, 1999). **Sleep terrors** are similar to, but more severe than, nightmares. They usually occur during deep sleep, whereas nightmares take place during REM sleep. Sleep terrors usually occur during the first two sleep cycles of the night, whereas nightmares are more likely to occur during later sleep cycles in the night. Experiencing a surge in the heart and respiration rates, the person may suddenly sit up, talk incoherently, and move about wildly. He or she is never fully awake, returns to sleep, and may recall a vague image as of someone pressing on his or her chest. (Memories of nightmares tend to be more vivid.) Sleep terrors are often decreased by taking a minor tranquilizer at bedtime. The drug reduces the amount of time spent in stage 4 sleep.

Bed-wetting is often seen as a stigma that reflects parental harshness or the child's attempt to punish the parents, but this disorder, too, may stem from immaturity of the nervous system. In most cases it resolves itself before adolescence, often by age 8. Behavior-therapy methods that condition children to awaken when

Apnea Temporary absence or cessation of breathing. (From Greek and Latin roots meaning "without" and "breathing.")

Sleep terrors Frightening dreamlike experiences that occur during the deepest stage of NREM sleep. Nightmares, in contrast, occur during REM sleep.

Learning Connections — SLEEP, DREAMS, AND DAYDREAMS: OTHER WORLDS WITHIN?

ACTIVE REVIEW (4) EEG research shows that different stages of sleep are characterized by different _____ waves. (5) Because EEG patterns during REM sleep resemble those of the waking state, REM sleep is also called _____ sleep. (6) During a typical eight-hour night, we undergo about _____ trips through the different stages of sleep. (7) Dreams are most vivid during (*REM or NREM?*) sleep. (8) According to the _____–synthesis model, dreams reflect neural activity. (9) Sleep terrors, bed-wetting, and sleepwalking all occur during _____ sleep.

REFLECT AND RELATE How much sleep do you need? (How do you know?) Did you ever "pull an all-nighter"? What were the effects?

The next time you pull an all-nighter, why not keep a diary of your feelings the following day? This could help you the next time you are faced with the decision of whether to stay awake and study or get some sleep.

CRITICAL THINKING What do you dream about? Has anyone tried to interpret your dreams? Is the interpretation consistent with any of the theories of dreams discussed in the chapter? Why are many modern psychologists critical of Freud's theory of dreams?

 Go to **http://psychology.wadsworth.com/ rathus_pcc9e** for an interactive version of this Learning Connections unit.

they are about to urinate have been helpful (Kainz, 2002; Mellon & McGrath, 2000). The drug imipramine often helps, although the reason for its effectiveness is not fully understood. Sometimes all that is needed is reassurance that no one is to blame for bed-wetting and that most children "outgrow" it.

Perhaps half of all children occasionally talk in their sleep. Surveys suggest that some 7% to 15% walk in their sleep (Mindell, 1993; Neveus et al., 2002). Only about 2% of a random sample of nearly 5,000 people aged 15 to 100 did so (Ohayon et al., 1999). Sleepwalkers may roam about almost nightly while their parents fret about the accidents that could befall them. Sleepwalkers typically do not remember their excursions, although they may respond to questions while they are up and about.

Truth or Fiction Revisited: Contrary to myth, there is no evidence that sleepwalkers become violent if they are awakened, although they may be confused and upset. Mild tranquilizers and maturity typically put an end to sleepwalking.

Altering Consciousness by Going Online

Entering "cyberspace" alters the normal relationship between the person and the environment. Cyberspace is a psychological space, one with unique psychological features (Suler, 2005). Going online alters one's sensory experiences and allows one to exceed his or her spatial boundaries—to visit casinos, stores, chat rooms, business meetings, and other environments. It allows one to hide or change identities, to develop and access numerous relationships simultaneously, and to "save" one's experiences. Many people say and do things in the virtual world that they would not do in the real world. "As a virtual reality," writes Suler, the virtual world "stretches across a wide range from the simulated true-to-life experiences of webcams to the highly imaginative environments of avatar communities." **Avatars** are virtual bodies you "wear." You can use them to merge with your character in a video game or to chat with others. Perhaps you will not be surprised that people tend to choose avatars that are more powerful or attractive than they are (Lee & Shin, 2004).

Cyberspace is akin to an altered state of consciousness. It is a dreamlike world that enables people to experience reality and themselves from a different perspective. Cyberspace becomes an extension of one's consciousness.

You can access the great works of art and the great museums online. You can observe busy highways through webcams 6,000 miles away. You can explore resources that you can use to write papers and learn more about academic topics, reference libraries (encyclopedias, thesauruses), and the like. This virtual library makes visiting the real library optional for most students. You can play games joined in by millions of other people. You also have the opportunity to interact with other students or new acquaintances in forums or chat rooms. Changing your sex in the real world requires hormone treatments and surgery. In the virtual world, you need only misrepresent your sex.

The Concept of "Flow"

"Going with the flow" is more than just a saying. The word **flow** is used to refer to an altered state of consciousness that people may experience when they are deeply involved in a pleasant activity (Pace, 2004). If you're carrying out assignments or writing a paper, flow is a good thing. But flow is also one of the factors that keeps people returning to cyberspace when they have little time to spare. Flow tends to develop when people are experiencing challenges—such as those involved in video games or making online stock trades—and mastering them. Flow can lessen self-awareness and become motivating for its own sake. Many people want to keep going with the flow, whether they are e-mailing friends, playing games, exploring, gambling, or even shopping (Koufaris, 2002; Waterman et al., 2003).

Some online game players adopt the virtual world as a key part of their lives (Meerkerk et al., 2006; Ng & Wiemer-Hastings, 2005). Millions of people, for exam-

Avatar A virtual body worn by an online user in cyberspace while playing a video game or visiting a chat room.

Flow An altered state of consciousness experienced when one is deeply involved in a pleasant activity.

ple, spend hours each day playing the online game *Lineage*. Their lifestyle in cyberspace assumes great importance. Can the quest for flow be addictive?

Internet "Addiction"

We will see that when we speak of being addicted to drugs, we are referring to bodily changes that make having the drug in one's body the normal state of affairs. The concept of **Internet addiction** refers to a self-defeating behavior pattern in which one is so preoccupied with going online that it disrupts one's functioning in the real world (Beard, 2005). As with drug addiction, people who are addicted to the Internet may perceive it as an extremely important part of their lives, use it excessively, experience lack of control over going online, and neglect their studies or work as well as their flesh-and-blood social lives (Chou et al., 2005).

Some Internet addictions involve gaming and competition (Ng & Wiemer-Hastings, 2005). Others seek to meet social or sexual needs (Campbell et al., 2006; Meerkerk et al., 2006). Loneliness and boredom in the real world seem to increase the risk that one might become trapped online (Chak & Leung, 2004; Nichols & Nicki, 2004). Other forms of Internet gratification include belonging to a virtual community, aesthetic experience, diversion from problems in the real world, and the status gained by adding fictional assets to one's true identity (Campbell et al., 2006).

Handling Addiction to the Internet

Are you concerned that you go online too often, or spend too much time online, or that the urge to go online is too strong? Here are things you can do if you are concerned that you have become addicted to the Internet:

◆ Strictly limit the amount of time you allow yourself to spend online for recreational use. Reward yourself for sticking to the limit by putting some money toward something you really want—like a camera or an iPod. Punish yourself for going over the limit by removing money from the fund.

◆ Shut your computer off (don't just put it on standby) after you have spent your allotted amount of time online. Then you will have to reboot it before you go online again.

◆ Do something else rather than go online or visit a website that consumes too much time or encourages you to waste money. Read a book, go for a walk, check your assignments, or chat (offline!) with a friend.

◆ Go online only in a public place, so that you're reluctant to visit "adult" websites. For example, use the library or the student center or the cafeteria.

◆ Spend time you would have spent at adult websites in developing interpersonal relationships.

Internet addiction A preoccupation with going online that disrupts one's functioning in the real world.

Learning Connections | ALTERING CONSCIOUSNESS BY GOING ONLINE

ACTIVE REVIEW (10) The word _____ is used to refer to an altered state of consciousness that people may experience when they are deeply involved in a pleasant activity.

REFLECT & RELATE How often do you go online? For what purposes? Are you at all concerned about the amount of time you spend online? Explain.

CRITICAL THINKING How would one judge whether or not going online is harmful to an individual?

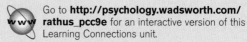 Go to **http://psychology.wadsworth.com/ rathus_pcc9e** for an interactive version of this Learning Connections unit.

Hypnosis A condition in which people appear to be highly suggestible and behave as though they are in a trance.

Altering Consciousness through Hypnosis, Meditation, and Biofeedback

Perhaps you have seen films in which Count Dracula hypnotized resistant victims into a stupor. Then he could give them a bite in the neck with no further nonsense. Perhaps you have watched a fellow student try to place a friend in a "trance" after reading a book on hypnosis. Or perhaps you have seen an audience member hypnotized in a nightclub act. If so, chances are the person acted as if he or she had returned to childhood, imagined that a snake was about to have a nip, or lay rigid between two chairs for a while. In this section we deal with what has been referred to as some of the "oddities" of psychology: hypnosis, meditation, and biofeedback. Each of these is an altered state of consciousness in that they involve focusing on stimuli that are not common parts of our daily lives.

Hypnosis: On Being Entranced

Of these altered states, perhaps the one we hear of most is hypnosis. **Question: What is hypnosis? Hypnosis,** a term derived from the Greek word for sleep, is an altered state of consciousness in which people appear to be highly suggestible and behave as though they are in a trance. Hypnosis has only recently become a respectable subject for psychological inquiry. Modern hypnosis has evolved from the ideas of Franz Mesmer in the 18th century. Mesmer asserted that everything in the universe was connected by forms of magnetism—which actually may not be far from the mark. However, he incorrectly claimed that people, too, could be drawn to one another by "animal magnetism." (No bull's-eye here.) Mesmer used bizarre props to bring people under his "spell" and managed a respectable cure rate for minor ailments. Scientists now attribute his successes to the placebo effect, not to animal magnetism.

In Profile FRANZ ANTON MESMER

He was the rage of Paris and Vienna. His clients paid a fortune to be "mesmerized." Imagine him dressed in a flowing purple robe, grandly entering mirrored rooms in palaces while music was played by an instrument called a glass harmonica. He commands one man, *"Dormez"* ("Sleep"), and the man's head drops to his chest while others gasp. He points an iron rod at a woman, and she shrieks that she feels tingling sensations running through her body. Thus did the Austrian Franz Anton Mesmer (1734–1815) use his theory of animal magnetism to "cure" afflictions ranging from paralysis to "vapors."

Mesmer was trained as a physician, and his marriage to an older, wealthy woman gained him entrance to Viennese society. A music lover, he became skillful with the glass harmonica, which had been invented by Benjamin Franklin. Wolfgang Amadeus Mozart's first opera, *Bastien und Bastienne*, debuted in Mesmer's home when Mozart was 12 years old.

Mesmer's theory held that illnesses could be cured through realignment of the magnetic forces in the body. Although his theory is nonsense, he seems to have sincerely believed in it. Mesmer's life work has contributed to our knowledge of the power of suggestion, to modern hypnotism, and, of course, to dramatic nightclub acts.

Go to **http://psychology.wadsworth.com/ rathus_pcc9e** to access more information about Franz Anton Mesmer.

Today hypnotism retains its popularity in nightclubs, but it is also used as an anesthetic in dentistry, childbirth, and various medical procedures, even surgery (Montgomery et al., 2000; Shenefelt, 2003). Some psychologists use hypnosis to teach clients how to reduce anxiety or overcome fears (Pinnell & Covino, 2000). A study with 241 surgery patients in a Boston hospital shows how hypnosis can help people deal with pain and anxiety. The patients underwent procedures in which only local anesthetics were used (Lang et al., 2000). They could use as much pain medication as they desired by means of an intravenous tube. Patients who were hypnotized during these procedures needed less additional medication for pain and experienced less anxiety as measured by blood pressure and heart rate. The hypnotized patients focused on pleasant imagery rather than the details of the surgery. Hypnosis as an aid in relaxation training also helps people cope with stress and enhance the functioning of their immune systems (Kiecolt-Glaser et al., 2001). Research also shows that hypnosis can be a useful supplement to other forms of therapy, especially in helping people control their weight and stop smoking (Lynn et al., 2003). Police also use hypnosis to prompt the memories of witnesses.

The state of consciousness called the *hypnotic trance* has traditionally been induced by asking people to narrow their attention to a small light, a spot on the wall, an object held by the hypnotist, or the hypnotist's voice. The hypnotist usually suggests that the person's limbs are becoming warm, heavy, and relaxed. People may also be told that they are becoming sleepy or falling asleep. Hypnosis is *not* sleep, however. This is shown by differences between EEG recordings for the hypnotic trance and the stages of sleep. But the word *sleep* is understood by subjects to suggest a hypnotic trance. It is also possible to induce hypnosis through instructions that direct subjects to remain active and alert (Alarcon et al., 1999; Winter, 2001). So the effects of hypnosis probably cannot be attributed to relaxation. The key appears to be that the induction procedure encourages the subject to go along with the instructions of the hypnotist (Barber, 2000).

People who are readily hypnotized are said to have *hypnotic suggestibility*. Part of "suggestibility" is knowledge of what is expected during the "trance state." Generally speaking, suggestible people are prone to fantasy, can compartmentalize unwanted memories, and want to cooperate with the hypnotist (Barber, 2000). As a result, they pay close attention to the hypnotist's instructions. **Truth or Fiction Revisited:** It is therefore extremely unlikely that someone could be hypnotized against his or her will. However, in a nightclub act, the social pressure of the audience may further encourage the subject to play along with the suggestions of the hypnotist (Barber, 2000). Hypnotists and people who have been hypnotized report that hypnosis can bring about the changes shown in Table 5.3.

TABLE 5.3 CHANGES IN CONSCIOUSNESS ATTRIBUTED TO HYPNOSIS*

Change	Comments
Passivity	Awaiting instructions and suspending planning.
Narrowed attention	Focusing on the hypnotist's voice or a spot of light and not attending to background noise or intruding thoughts.
Pseudomemories and hypermnesia	Reporting pseudomemories (false memories) or highly detailed memories (hypermnesia). Police hypnotists attempt to heighten witnesses' memories by instructing them to focus on details of a crime and reconstruct the scene. Some studies challenge the accuracies of such memories.
Suggestibility	Responding to suggestions that an arm is becoming lighter and will rise or that the eyelids are becoming heavier and must close.
Playing unusual roles	Playing roles calling for increased strength or alertness, such as riding a bicycle with less fatigue than usual. In *age regression*, people may play themselves as infants or children. A person may speak a language forgotten since childhood.
Perceptual distortions	Acting as though hypnotically induced hallucinations and delusions are real. Behave as though one cannot hear loud noises, smell odors, or feel pain.
Posthypnotic amnesia	Acting as though one cannot recall events that take place under hypnosis.
Posthypnotic suggestion	Following commands given "under" hypnosis after one "awakens," such as falling quickly into a deep trance when given the command "Sleep!" or—in the case of a would-be quitter of smoking—finding cigarette smoke aversive.

*Research evidence in support of these changes in consciousness is mixed.

Sources: Barber, 2000; Bowers & Woody, 1996; Green & Lynn, 2000; Lancaster et al., 2000; Loftus, 1994; Miller & Bowers, 1993; Weekes et al., 1992; Woody & Szechtman, 2000.

Role theory A theory that explains hypnotic events in terms of the person's ability to act *as though* he or she were hypnotized. Role theory differs from faking in that subjects cooperate and focus on hypnotic suggestions instead of pretending to be hypnotized.

Response set theory The view that response expectancies play a key role in the production of the experiences suggested by the hypnotist.

Neodissociation theory A theory of hypnotic events as the splitting of consciousness.

CONTROVERSY IN PSYCHOLOGY

How do psychologists explain hypnosis?

Hypnotism is no longer explained in terms of animal magnetism, but psychodynamic and learning theorists have offered explanations. According to Freud, hypnotized adults permit themselves to return to childish modes of responding that emphasize fantasy and impulse rather than fact and logic. Modern views of hypnosis are quite different. **Question: How do modern psychologists explain the effects of hypnosis?**

ROLE THEORY Theodore Sarbin offers a **role theory** view of hypnosis (Sarbin & Coe, 1972). He points out that the changes in behavior attributed to the hypnotic trance can be successfully imitated when people are instructed to behave *as though* they were hypnotized. For example, people can lie rigid between two chairs whether they are hypnotized or not. Also, people cannot be hypnotized unless they are familiar with the hypnotic "role"—the behavior that constitutes the trance. Sarbin is not saying that subjects *fake* the hypnotic role. Research evidence suggests that most people who are hypnotized are not faking (Kinnunen et al., 1994). Instead, Sarbin is suggesting that people *allow* themselves to enact this role under the hypnotist's directions.

RESPONSE SET THEORY The **response set theory** of hypnosis is closely related to role theory. It suggests that response expectancies (the things we know we are expected to do) play a key role in the production of personal experiences and also in experiences suggested by the hypnotist (Kirsch, 2000). A positive response to each suggestion of the hypnotist sets the stage—creates a *response set*—in which the subject is more likely to follow subsequent suggestions (Barrios, 2001).

Truth or Fiction Revisited: It has not been shown that the effects of hypnotism are due to a special trance state. Role theory and response set theory appear to be supported by research evidence that "suggestible" people want to be hypnotized, are good role players, have vivid and absorbing imaginations, and also know what is expected of them (Barber, 2000; Kirsch, 2000). The fact that the behaviors shown by hypnotized people can be mimicked by people who know what is expected of them means that we need not resort to the concept of the "hypnotic trance"—an unusual and mystifying altered state of awareness—to explain hypnotic events.

NEODISSOCIATION THEORY Runners frequently get through the pain and tedium of long-distance races by *dissociating*—by imagining themselves elsewhere, doing other things. (My students inform me that they manage the pain and tedium of *other* instructors' classes in the same way.) Ernest Hilgard (1904–2001) similarly explained hypnotic phenomena through **neodissociation theory** (Hilgard, 1994). This is the view that we can selectively focus our attention on one thing (like hypnotic suggestions) and dissociate ourselves from the things going on around us—just as the surgery patients in the Boston study focused on pleasant thoughts and not on the surgery itself (Lang et al., 2000).

Subjects in one study of neodissociation theory were hypnotized and instructed to submerge their arms in ice water—causing "cold pressor pain" (Miller et al., 1991). Subjects were given suggestions to the effect that they were not in pain, however. Highly hypnotizable people reported dissociative experiences that allowed them to avoid the perception of pain, such as imagining that they were at the beach or that their limbs were floating in air above the ice water.

Although hypnotized people may be focusing on the hypnotist's suggestions and perhaps imagining themselves to be somewhere else, they still tend to perceive their actual surroundings peripherally. In a sense, we do this all the time. We are not fully conscious, or aware, of everything going on about us. Rather, at any given moment we selectively focus on events such as tests, dates, or television shows that seem important or relevant. Yet, while taking a test we may be peripherally aware of the color of the wall or the sound of rain.

Role theory, response set theory, and neodissociation theory do not suggest that the phenomena of hypnosis are phony. Instead, they suggest that we do not need to explain these events through an altered state of awareness called a trance. Hypnosis may not be special at all. Rather, it is *we* who are special—through our imagination, our role-playing ability, and our capacity to divide our consciousness—concentrating now on one event that we deem important and concentrating on another event later.

Let us now consider two other altered states of consciousness that involve different ways of focusing our attention: meditation and biofeedback.

Transcendental meditation (TM) The simplified form of meditation brought to the United States by the Maharishi Mahesh Yogi and used as a method for coping with stress.

Meditation: On Letting the World Fade Away

Question: What is meditation? The dictionary defines *meditation* as the act or process of thinking. But the concept usually suggests thinking deeply about the universe or about one's place in the world, often within a spiritual context. As the term is commonly used by psychologists, however, meditation refers to various ways of focusing one's consciousness to alter one's relationship to the world. As used by psychologists, ironically, *meditation* can also refer to a process in which people seem to suspend thinking and allow the world to fade away.

The kinds of meditation that psychologists and other kinds of helping professionals speak of are *not* the first definition you find in the dictionary. Rather, they tend to refer to rituals, exercises, and even passive observation—activities that alter the normal relationship between the person and her or his environment. They are various methods of suspending problem solving, planning, worries, and awareness of the events of the day. These methods alter consciousness—that is, the normal focus of attention—and help people cope with stress by inducing feelings of relaxation.

Let us consider one common form of meditation. **Transcendental meditation (TM)** is a simplified form of Far Eastern meditation that was brought to the United States by the Maharishi Mahesh Yogi in 1959. Hundreds of thousands of Americans practice TM by repeating and concentrating on *mantras*—words or sounds that are claimed to help the person achieve an altered state of consciousness. TM has a number of goals that cannot be assessed scientifically, such as expanding consciousness so that it encompasses spiritual experiences, but there are also measurable goals, such as reducing anxiety and normalizing blood pressure.

Question: What are the effects of meditation? In early research, Herbert Benson (1975) found that TM lowered the heart and respiration rates and also produced what he labeled a *relaxation response*. The blood pressure of people with hypertension—a risk factor in cardiovascular disease—decreased. In fact, people who meditated twice daily tended to show more normal blood pressure through the day. Meditators produced more frequent alpha waves—brain waves associated with feelings of relaxation. Meditation increases nighttime concentrations of the hormone melatonin, which is relaxing and helps people get to sleep (Tooley et al., 2000). Research in brain imaging also shows that meditation

■ **Meditation** People use many forms of meditation to try to expand their inner awareness and experience inner harmony. Although practitioners of some forms of meditation claim that it has spiritual effects, research does suggest that meditation can have healthful effects on the blood pressure and other health-related bodily functions.

Yellow Dog Productions/Getty Images

activates neural structures involved in attention and control of the autonomic nervous system, helping produce feelings of relaxation (Lazar et al., 2000).

In more recent years, an apparently careful research program has been conducted at the College of Maharishi Vedic Medicine in Fairfield, Iowa (Ready, 2000). It has focused on older African Americans because African Americans are more prone to hypertension than European Americans. Two studies compared the effects of TM, progressive relaxation (a muscle relaxation technique), and a "health education" placebo on high blood pressure (Alexander et al., 1996; Schneider et al., 1995). They both found that TM was significantly more effective at reducing high blood pressure than progressive relaxation or the placebo. A third study reported that TM practiced by African Americans aged 20 and above for 6 to 9 months was significantly more likely than the health education placebo to reduce the progression of atherosclerosis (hardening of the arteries) (Castillo-Richmond et al., 2000).

Biofeedback: On Getting in Touch with the Untouchable

Let us begin our discussion of biofeedback by recounting some remarkable experiments in which psychologist Neal E. Miller (1909–2002) trained laboratory rats to increase or decrease their heart rates. His procedure was simple but ingenious. As discovered by psychologists James Olds and Peter Milner (1954), there is a "pleasure center" in the rat's hypothalamus. A small burst of electricity in this center is strongly reinforcing: Rats learn to do what they can, such as pressing a lever, to obtain this stimulus.

Miller (1969) implanted electrodes in the rats' pleasure centers. Then some rats were given a burst of electricity in their brain's pleasure center whenever their heart rate happened to increase. Other rats received the stimulus when their heart rate went lower. In other words, one group of rats was consistently "rewarded" (that is, their pleasure center stimulated) when their heart rate showed an increase. The other group was consistently rewarded for a decrease in heart rate. After a single 90-minute training session, the rats learned to alter their heart rates by as much as 20% in the direction for which they had been rewarded. **Truth or Fiction Revisited:** It is true that you can teach a rat to raise or lower its heart rate.

Miller's research was an early example of **biofeedback training (BFT). Question: What is biofeedback training?** Biofeedback is a system that provides, or "feeds back," information about a bodily function. Miller used electrical stimulation of the brain to feed back information to rats when they had engaged in a targeted bodily response (in this case, raised or lowered their heart rates). Somehow the rats then used this information to raise or lower their heart rates voluntarily.

Similarly, people have learned to change various bodily functions voluntarily, including heart rate, that were once considered to be beyond their control. However, electrodes are not implanted in people's brains. Rather, people hear a "blip" or observe some other signal that informs them when the targeted response is being displayed.

Question: How is biofeedback training used? BFT has been used in many ways, including helping people combat stress, tension, and anxiety. For example, people can learn to emit alpha waves (and feel somewhat more relaxed) through feedback from an EEG. A blip may increase in frequency whenever alpha waves are being emitted. The psychologist's instructions are simply to "make the blip go faster." An **electromyograph (EMG)** monitors muscle tension. The EMG can be used to help paralyzed people who have lost afferent but not efferent nerves to limbs regain some control over those limbs. The EMG is also commonly used to help people become more aware of muscle tension in the forehead, fingers, and elsewhere and to learn to lower the tension (Martin, 2002). Through the use of other instruments, people have learned to lower their heart rate, their blood pressure, and the amount of sweat in the palm of the hand (Nagourney, 2002). All of these changes are relaxing. Biofeedback is widely used by sports psychologists to teach athletes

Biofeedback training (BFT) The systematic feeding back to an organism information about a bodily function so that the organism can gain control of that function.

Electromyograph (EMG) An instrument that measures muscle tension.

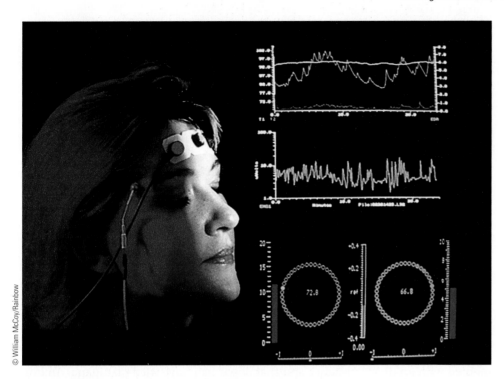

■ **Biofeedback** Biofeedback is a system that provides, or "feeds back," information about a bodily function to an organism. Through biofeedback training, people have learned to gain voluntary control over a number of functions that are normally automatic, such as heart rate and blood pressure.

how to relax muscle groups that are unessential to the task at hand so that they can control anxiety and tension.

Sleep, hypnosis, meditation, and biofeedback training all involve "natural" ways of deploying our attention or consciousness. Some altered states depend on the ingestion of psychoactive chemical substances we call "drugs." Let us now deploy our attention to the effects of alcohol and other drugs.

Your Turn: Now that we have discussed hypnosis, meditation, and biofeedback, enhance your mastery of the material with the nearby "Learning Connections." Review the material by filling in the blanks, reflect on the material by relating it to other things you know, and think critically about it.

Learning Connections — ALTERING CONSCIOUSNESS THROUGH HYPNOSIS, MEDITATION, AND BIOFEEDBACK

ACTIVE REVIEW (11) Franz Mesmer explained the hypnotic "trance" through his concept of animal _____. (12) Hypnosis typically brings about the following changes in consciousness: passivity, narrowed attention, _____ (detailed memory), suggestibility, assumption of unusual roles, perceptual distortions, posthypnotic amnesia, and posthypnotic suggestion. (13) According to _____ set theory, knowledge of what one is expected to do is a key component of being hypnotized. (14) In meditation, one focuses "passively" on a _____ in order to alter the normal person–environment relationship. (15) Investigators have shown that meditation can reduce high _____ pressure. (16) Neal Miller taught rats to increase or decrease their _____ rates by giving them an electric shock in their "pleasure centers" when they performed the targeted response.

(17) Through biofeedback training, people and lower animals have learned to control _____ functions like the heart rate.

REFLECT AND RELATE Has anybody ever tried to hypnotize you or someone you know? How did he or she do it? What were the results? How do the results fit with the theories of hypnosis discussed in this section?

CRITICAL THINKING Is it possible to explain the behavior of the rats in Miller's research on biofeedback by referring to what the animals were "thinking" when they learned to increase or decrease their heart rates? Explain.

 Go to **http://psychology.wadsworth.com/ rathus_pcc9e** for an interactive version of this Learning Connections unit.

Psychoactive substances Drugs that have psychological effects such as stimulation or distortion of perceptions.

Depressant A drug that lowers the rate of activity of the nervous system.

Stimulant A drug that increases activity of the nervous system.

Altering Consciousness through Drugs

The world is a supermarket of **psychoactive substances,** or drugs. The United States is flooded with drugs that distort perceptions and change mood—drugs that take you up, let you down, and move you across town. Some of these drugs are legal, others illegal. Some are used recreationally, others medically. Some are safe if used correctly and dangerous if they are not. Some people use drugs because their friends do or because their parents tell them not to. Some are seeking pleasure; others are seeking inner truth or escape.

For better or worse, drugs are part of American life. Young people often become involved with drugs that impair their ability to learn at school and are connected with reckless behavior (Wills et al., 2002). Alcohol is the most popular drug on high school and college campuses (Johnston et al., 2003). More than 40% of college students have tried marijuana, and 1 in 6 or 7 smokes it regularly (Johnston et al., 2003). Many Americans take **depressants** to get to sleep at night and **stimulants** to get going in the morning. Karl Marx charged that "religion . . . is the opium of the people," but heroin is the real "opium of the people." Cocaine was once a toy of the well-to-do, but price breaks have brought it into the lockers of high-school students.

Table 5.4 shows the lifetime and 30-day prevalence of use of drugs by high school seniors in the United States. Note that the majority have at least experimented with an illicit substance and that about half have tried marijuana. Among this group, European Americans are more likely to smoke cigarettes than African Americans or Latino and Latina Americans.

TABLE 5.4 **ETHNIC COMPARISONS OF LIFETIME AND 30-DAY PREVALENCE OF USE OF VARIOUS DRUGS AMONG HIGH SCHOOL SENIORS (PERCENTS)**

Drug	Ever Use Drug?			Use Drug in Past 30 Days?		
	European American	African American	Latino/Latina American	European American	African American	Latino/Latina American
Any illicit drug	54.8%	48.7%	60.0%	25.9%	20.3%	27.4%
Marijuana	49.4	45.7	55.5	22.7	19.0	24.6
Inhalants	16.7	4.6	15.4	2.1	1.3	3.1
LSD	13.2	1.7	13.1	2.3	0.8	2.4
MDMA (Ecstasy)	10.5	1.6	13.3	3.3	0.9	4.5
Cocaine	9.9	1.9	13.3	2.5	0.8	3.6
Crack	4.4	0.8	6.3	1.0	0.4	2.1
Heroin	0.9	0.4	2.6	0.5	0.2	1.2
Amphetamines	18.2	4.9	15.1	5.3	1.2	4.5
Barbiturates	10.3	2.4	8.1	3.2	0.8	2.2
Alcohol	82.0	70.3	84.3	55.1	30.0	51.2
Cigarettes	67.2	45.5	66.1	37.9	14.3	27.7
Steroids	2.8	1.3	3.4	0.8	0.4	1.5

Source of data: Johnston, L. D., O'Malley, P. M., & Bachman, J. G. (2001). *Monitoring the Future national survey results on drug use, 1975–2000. Volume I: Secondary school students* (NIH Publication No. 01-4924). Bethesda, MD: National Institute on Drug Abuse, Table 4-9.

Substance Abuse and Dependence: Crossing the Line

Where does drug use end and abuse begin? **Question: What are substance abuse and dependence?** The American Psychiatric Association (2000) defines **substance abuse** as repeated use of a substance despite the fact that it is causing or compounding social, occupational, psychological, or physical problems. If you are missing school or work because you are drunk or "sleeping it off," you are abusing alcohol. The amount you drink is not as crucial as the fact that your pattern of use disrupts your life.

Dependence is more severe than abuse, having both behavioral and biological aspects (American Psychiatric Association, 2000). Behaviorally, dependence is often characterized by loss of control over one's use of the substance. Dependent people may organize their lives around getting and using a substance. For example, biological or physiological dependence is typified by tolerance, withdrawal symptoms, or both. **Tolerance** is the body's habituation to a substance so that, with regular usage, higher doses are required to achieve similar effects. There are characteristic withdrawal symptoms, or an **abstinence syndrome,** when the level of usage suddenly drops off. The abstinence syndrome for alcohol includes anxiety, tremors, restlessness, weakness, rapid pulse, and high blood pressure.

When doing without a drug, people who are *psychologically* dependent show signs of anxiety (such as shakiness, rapid pulse, and sweating) that may be similar to abstinence syndromes. Because of these signs, they may believe that they are physiologically dependent on—or addicted to—a drug when they are actually psychologically dependent. But symptoms of abstinence from some drugs are unmistakably physiological. One symptom is **delirium tremens** ("the DTs"), experienced by some chronic alcoholics when they suddenly lower their intake of alcohol. The DTs are characterized by heavy sweating, restlessness, general disorientation, and terrifying hallucinations—often of crawling animals.

Causal Factors in Substance Abuse and Dependence

Question: What are the causes of substance abuse and dependence? Substance abuse and dependence usually begin with experimental use in adolescence (Chassin et al., 2000; Lewinsohn et al., 2000a). People experiment with drugs for various reasons, including curiosity, conformity to peer pressure, parental use, rebelliousness, escape from boredom or pressure, and the seeking of excitement or pleasure (Andrews et al., 2002; Chassin et al., 2001; Finn et al., 2000; Unger et al., 2001a; Wills et al., 2002).

A CDC survey of more than 15,000 teenagers across the United States found that use of drugs and cigarettes has increased over the past decade, despite public-education campaigns about the risks (Centers for Disease Control and Prevention, 2000b). Cigarette smoking was up slightly, with 35% of teenagers reporting lighting up in the previous month. The number of teens who reported smoking marijuana in the previous month nearly doubled from about 15% in 1991 to 27% at the turn of the millennium. Self-reported cocaine use also doubled in the same period, from about 2% to 4%. Alcohol use (within the past month) remained steady at about 50%. However, drinking in early adolescence is a risk factor for alcohol abuse later on (D. J. De Wit et al., 2000). Let us have a look at some theories of substance abuse.

PSYCHOLOGICAL VIEWS Social–cognitive theorists suggest that people commonly try tranquilizing agents such as Valium (the generic name is diazepam) and alcohol on the basis of a recommendation or observation of others. Expectations about the effects of a substance are powerful predictors of its use (Cumsille et al., 2000). In one study, researchers studied a diary of stress, expectations about alcohol, and drinking (Armeli et al., 2000). They found that men who expected that alcohol would lessen feelings of stress were more likely to drink on stressful days. But men who expected that alcohol would impair their coping ability drank *less* on stressful days.

Substance abuse Persistent use of a substance even though it is causing or compounding problems in meeting the demands of life.

Tolerance Habituation to a drug, with the result that increasingly higher doses of the drug are needed to achieve similar effects.

Abstinence syndrome A characteristic cluster of symptoms that results from sudden decrease in an addictive drug's level of usage.

Delirium tremens A condition characterized by sweating, restlessness, disorientation, and hallucinations. The DTs occur in some chronic alcohol users when there is a sudden decrease in usage.

Use of a substance may be reinforced by peers or by the drug's positive effects on mood and its reduction of unpleasant sensations such as anxiety, fear, and stress (Unger et al., 2001b; Wills et al., 2002). Many people use drugs as a form of self-medication for anxiety and depression, even for feelings of low self-esteem (Beitchman et al., 2001; Dierker et al., 2001). Substance abuse is also often found in the same people who have problems such as eating disorders and impulsiveness, but it is difficult to tease out cause and effect in these cases (Moeller et al., 2001; Stice & Bearman, 2001).

For people who are physiologically dependent, avoidance of withdrawal symptoms is also reinforcing. Carrying a supply of the substance is reinforcing because one need not worry about going without it.

Parents who use drugs may increase their children's knowledge of drugs. They also, in effect, show their children when to use them—for example, when drinking alcohol to reduce tension or to "lubricate" social interactions (Stacy & Newcomb, 1999).

BIOLOGICAL VIEWS Certain people may have a genetic predisposition toward physiological dependence on various substances, including alcohol, opioids, cocaine, and nicotine (Ellenbroek et al., 2000; Kalivas, 2003; Kendler et al., 2000a, 2000d; Wall et al., 2003). For example, the biological children of alcoholics who are reared by adoptive parents seem more likely to develop alcohol-related problems than the natural children of the adoptive parents. An inherited tendency toward alcoholism may involve greater sensitivity to alcohol (that is, greater enjoyment of it) and greater tolerance of it (Pihl et al., 1990; Schuckit et al., 2001). College students with alcoholic parents exhibit better muscular control and visual–motor

 A Closer Look | **WITH NO ANSWERS ON RISKS, STEROID USERS STILL SAY "YES"[2]**

Patrick Keogan wanted to be big, like the men with the ripped muscles he saw at the gym. "I was training like an animal," he said, working out seven days a week. But he seemed to have reached his biological limit: 5 feet 8 inches tall, 150 pounds.

"Finally, it dawned on me," he said. Those huge men at his gym who insisted they were simply lifting weights were dissembling. "There was something they were not telling me," Mr. Keogan said. Thus Mr. Keogan, a 30-year-old salesman who lives near Boston, entered the world of anabolic steroids—testosterone and other drugs that act like it, which can build muscle, fast.

He soon was taking 4,000 milligrams of testosterone a week, which he bought from dealers at his gym. (A man his age normally produces about 35 milligrams a week.) Within 20 weeks, he weighed 200 pounds. "People would look at me," he said, and ask, "What did you do?"

Now, as more and more men, and some women, are seeking large, chiseled bodies, more are learning the bitter secret of that look: It almost always takes some chemical assistance, from drugs that are often illegal but are readily available.

Use of steroid drugs has spread over the years from weight lifters to bodybuilders

to elite athletes to high school and college athletes and to groups who simply want to improve their appearance.

'ROID RAGE?

There are stories that the drugs can sometimes turn placid people violent. There are concerns that, in some sports, those who want to compete have little choice but to take them.

"The average guy will tell you that he hasn't had any problems and doesn't know anyone who does," said Dr. Harrison G. Pope Jr., a Harvard Medical School psychiatrist who studies bodybuilding culture. Yet, he said, there are rare individuals who "have almost a Jekyll and Hyde personality change," becoming aggressive and violent.

That was what worried Mr. Keogan—he quit after jumping out of his car to argue with another driver in a fit of rage, leaving his car to drift away. Now his body has shrunk to its former size, and he struggles to lift weights that were once a warm-up to his real lifting.

Testosterone also produces characteristic body changes, Dr. Pope said, with the most marked muscle growth in the upper body and the biceps. Dr. Pope has published photographs of men who did not use anabolic steroids and grew as big as possible without them, and of men who used them.

His goal, he says, is to show what a steroid-enhanced body looks like as a way to discourage use of the drug.

"It's the lying that really gets to me," Dr. Pope said. "I'll give a lecture and show a photograph of some huge bodybuilder and someone will say, 'Do you think he took steroids?' I'll say, 'Do you think World War II really happened?'"

But scientists say their ignorance about the array of anabolic drugs and their effects remains huge. Some of the drugs can lower levels of HDL cholesterol, the type that normally protects against heart disease. A lower HDL level may lead to an increased risk of heart attack and stroke. They may fuel the growth of some cancers, particularly those of the prostate. They suppress the body's own sex hormone production, which can cause infertility in people who are taking the drugs. But no one has done a long-term study of people who took huge doses of anabolic drugs; and, for the most part, no one knows what medical problems the drugs may cause or how likely they are.

[2]From "With No Answer on Risks, Steroid Users Still Say 'Yes.'" by Gina Kolata, *The New York Times* (12/2/2002). Copyright © 2002 by The New York Times Co. Reprinted with permission.

coordination when they drink than do college students whose parents are not alcoholics. They also feel less intoxicated when they drink (Pihl et al., 1990).

Now that we have learned about substance abuse and dependence, let us turn to a discussion of the different kinds of psychoactive drugs. Some are depressants, others stimulants, and still others hallucinogenics. Steroids, the drugs used to build strength and shape the body by so many athletes and bodybuilders, can also have psychological effects, as noted in the nearby "A Closer Look." Let us consider the effects of these drugs on consciousness, beginning with depressants.

Depressants

Depressant drugs generally act by slowing the activity of the central nervous system. There are also effects that are specific to each depressant drug. In this section we consider the effects of alcohol, opiates, and barbiturates.

ALCOHOL—THE SWISS ARMY KNIFE OF PSYCHOACTIVE SUBSTANCES No drug has meant so much to so many as alcohol. Alcohol is our dinnertime relaxant, our bedtime sedative, our cocktail-party social facilitator. We use alcohol to celebrate holy days, applaud our accomplishments, and express joyous wishes. The young assert their maturity with alcohol. Alcohol is used at least occasionally by the majority of high school and college students (Johnston et al., 2003; Wilgoren, 2000). Alcohol even kills germs on surface wounds.

People use alcohol like a Swiss Army knife. It does it all. Alcohol is the all-purpose medicine you can buy without prescription. It is the relief from anxiety, depression, or loneliness that you can swallow in public without criticism or stigma (Bonin et al., 2000; Swendsen et al., 2000). A man who takes a Valium tablet may look weak. A man who downs a bottle of beer may be perceived as "macho."

But the army knife also has a sharp blade. No drug has been so abused as alcohol. Ten million to 20 million Americans are alcoholics. In contrast, 750,000 to 1 million use heroin regularly, and about 800,000 use cocaine regularly (O'Brien, 1996). Excessive drinking has been linked to lower productivity, loss of employment, and downward movement in social status. Yet half of all Americans use alcohol regularly. Experiments with rats (Feola et al., 2000) and humans (H. de Wit et al., 2000) show that alcohol lowers inhibitions.

What of alcohol on campus? A study by the National Institute of Alcohol Abuse and Alcoholism (Hingson et al., 2002) found that about four college students die each day due to alcohol-related causes, another 1,300 to 1,400 have alcohol-related injuries, and nearly 200 are raped by their dates after drinking. Binge drinking—defined as having five or more drinks in a row for a male, or four or more for a female (Naimi et al., 2003b)—is connected with aggressive behavior, poor grades, sexual promiscuity, and serious accidents (Abbey et al., 2001; MacDonald et al., 2000; Vik et al., 2000). Nevertheless, binge drinking is on the rise in the United States (Naimi et al., 2003a). Forty-four percent of college students binge at least twice a month, and half this number binge three or more times every two weeks (Hingson et al., 2002). The media seem to pay more attention to deaths due to heroin and cocaine overdoses, but many more college students die each year from causes related to drinking, including accidents and alcohol overdoses (Hingson et al., 2002; Li et al., 2001). (Yes, a person can die from drinking too much at one sitting.) Despite widespread marijuana use, alcohol remains the drug of choice among adolescents.

Question: What are the effects of alcohol? The effects of alcohol vary with the dose and the duration of use. Low doses of alcohol may be stimulating because alcohol dilates blood vessels, which ferry sugars through the body. But higher doses of alcohol have a clear sedative effect, which is why alcohol is classified as a depressant. Alcohol relaxes people and deadens minor aches and pains. Alcohol also intoxicates: It impairs cognitive functioning, slurs the speech, and reduces motor coordination. Alcohol is involved in about half of the fatal automobile accidents in the United States.

Self-Assessment   Why Do You Drink?

Do you drink? If so, why? To enhance your pleasure? To cope with your problems? To help you in social interaction? Because you will feel withdrawal symptoms if you don't? The great majority of college students use alcohol, and as many as one American in ten is an alcoholic.

Directions: To gain insight into your reasons for using alcohol, respond to the following items by circling the *T* if an item is true or mostly true for you or the *F* if an item is false or mostly false for you. Then check the answer key in Appendix B.

T   F   1. I find it painful to go without alcohol for any period of time.

T   F   2. It's easier for me to relate to other people when I have been drinking.

T   F   3. I drink so that I will look more mature and sophisticated.

T   F   4. My future prospects seem brighter when I have been drinking.

T   F   5. I enjoy the taste of beer, wine, or hard liquor.

T   F   6. I don't feel disturbed or uncomfortable in any way if I go for a long time without having a drink.

T   F   7. When I drink, I feel calmer and less edgy about things.

T   F   8. I drink in order to fit in better with the crowd.

T   F   9. When I am drinking, I worry less about things.

T   F   10. I have a drink when I'm together with my family.

T   F   11. Drinking is a part of my religious ceremonies.

T   F   12. I'll have a drink to help deaden the pain of a toothache or some other physical problem.

T   F   13. I feel that I can do almost anything when I'm drinking.

T   F   14. You really can't blame people for the things they do when they have been drinking.

T   F   15. I'll have a drink before a big exam or a big date so that I feel less concerned about how things will go.

T   F   16. I like to drink for the taste of it.

T   F   17. There have been times when I've found a drink in my hand even though I can't remember placing it there.

T   F   18. I tend to drink when I feel "down" or when I want to take my mind off my troubles.

T   F   19. I find that I do better both socially and sexually after I've had a drink or two.

T   F   20. I have to admit that drinking sometimes makes me do reckless and asinine things.

T   F   21. I have missed classes or work because of having a few too many.

T   F   22. I feel that I am more generous and sympathetic when I have been drinking.

T   F   23. One of the reasons I drink is that I like the look of a drinker.

T   F   24. I like to have a drink or two on festive occasions and special days.

T   F   25. My friends and I are likely to go drinking when one of us has done something well, like "aced out" a tough exam or made some great plays on the team.

T   F   26. I'll have a drink or two when some predicament is gnawing away at me.

T   F   27. Drinking gives me pleasure.

T   F   28. Frankly, one of the lures of drinking is getting "high."

T   F   29. Sometimes I'm surprised to find that I've poured a drink when another one is still unfinished.

T   F   30. I find that I'm better at getting other people to do what I want them to do when I've been drinking.

T   F   31. Having a drink keeps my mind off my problems at home, at school, or at work.

T   F   32. I get a real gnawing hunger for a drink when I haven't had one for a while.

T   F   33. One or two drinks relax me.

T   F   34. Things tend to look better when I've been drinking.

T   F   35. I find that my mood is much improved when I've had a drink or two.

T   F   36. I can usually see things more clearly when I've had a drink or two.

T   F   37. One or two drinks heightens the pleasure of food and sex.

T   F   38. When I run out of alcohol, I buy more right away.

T   F   39. I think that I would have done better on some things if it hadn't been for the alcohol.

T   F   40. When I'm out of alcohol, things are practically unbearable until I can obtain some more.

T   F   41. I drink at fraternity or sorority parties.

T   F   42. When I think about the future and what I'm going to do, I often go and have a drink.

T   F   43. I like to go out for a drink when I've gotten a good grade.

T   F   44. I usually have a drink or two with dinner.

T   F   45. There have been times when it's been rough to get through a class, work, or practice because I wanted a drink.

Because alcohol lessens inhibitions, drinkers may do things they would not do if they were sober, such as engage in sexual activity or have unprotected sex (Cooper, 2002; MacDonald et al., 2000; Vik et al., 2000). Why? Perhaps alcohol impairs the thought processes needed to inhibit impulses (Steele & Josephs, 1990). When drunk, people may be less able to foresee the consequences of their behavior. They may also be less likely to summon up their moral beliefs. Then, too, alcohol induces feelings of elation and euphoria that may wash away doubts. Alcohol is also associated with a liberated social role in our culture. Drinkers may place the blame on alcohol ("It's the alcohol, not me"), even though they choose to drink.

Adolescent involvement with alcohol has repeatedly been linked to poor school grades and other stressors (Wills et al., 2002). Drinking can, of course, contribute to poor grades and other problems, but adolescents may drink to reduce academic and other stresses.

Men are more likely than women to become alcoholics. Why? A cultural explanation is that tighter social constraints are usually placed on women. A biological explanation is that alcohol hits women harder, discouraging them from overindulging. If you have the impression that alcohol "goes to women's heads" more quickly than to men's, you are probably right. Women seem to be more affected by alcohol because they metabolize very little of it in the stomach. Women have less of an enzyme that metabolizes alcohol in the stomach than men do (Lieber, 1990). Thus alcohol reaches women's bloodstream and brain relatively intact. Women metabolize it mainly in the liver. According to one health professional, for women "drinking alcohol has the same effect as injecting it intravenously" (Lieber, 1990). Strong stuff indeed.

Ethnicity is connected with alcohol abuse. Native Americans and Irish Americans have the highest rates of alcoholism in the United States. Jewish Americans have relatively low rates of alcoholism, a fact for which a cultural explanation is usually offered. Jewish Americans tend to expose children to alcohol (wine) early in life, but they do so within a strong family or religious context. Wine is offered in small quantities, with consequent low blood alcohol levels. Alcohol therefore is not connected with rebellion, aggression, or failure in Jewish culture.

There are also biological explanations for low levels of drinking among some ethnic groups. Asians and Asian Americans are more likely than Europeans and European Americans to show a "flushing response" to alcohol, as evidenced by redness of the face, rapid heart rate, dizziness, and headaches (Ellickson et al., 1992). Such sensitivity to alcohol may inhibit immoderate drinking among Asian Americans as well as women in general.

Regardless of how or why one starts drinking, regular drinking can lead to physiological dependence. People are then motivated to drink to avoid withdrawal symptoms. Still, even when alcoholics have "dried out"—withdrawn from alcohol—many return to drinking (Schuckit, 1996). Perhaps they still want to use alcohol as a way of coping with stress or as an excuse for failure.

CONTROVERSY IN PSYCHOLOGY

Is a drink a day good for you?

What are the physical and cognitive effects of drinking? The effects of alcohol on health are complex. Light drinking can be beneficial. One effect of having a drink or two a day is to increase levels of high-density lipoprotein (HDL, or "good" cholesterol) in the bloodstream and thus decrease the risk of cardiovascular disorders (Mukamal et al., 2001). Another positive effect is cognitive: A study of 400 older adults by researchers at the Institute of Psychiatry in London found that those who had been having a drink a day from before the age of 60 were less likely to see their cognitive abilities decline with age

Cirrhosis of the liver A disease caused by protein deficiency in which connective fibers replace active liver cells, impeding circulation of the blood. Alcohol does not contain protein; therefore, persons who drink excessively may be prone to this disease.

Wernicke–Korsakoff syndrome A cluster of symptoms associated with chronic alcohol abuse and characterized by confusion, memory impairment, and filling in gaps in memory with false information (confabulation).

Opiates A group of narcotics derived from the opium poppy that provide a euphoric rush and depress the nervous system.

Narcotics Drugs used to relieve pain and induce sleep. The term is usually reserved for opiates.

Opioids Chemicals that act on opiate receptors but are not derived from the opium poppy.

(Cervilla et al., 2000). A drink or two a day may even cut the risk of Alzheimer's disease (Norton, 2000). According to the London researchers (Cervilla et al., 2000), the path to positive cognitive results from alcohol may be through the heart: Small doses of alcohol may help maintain a healthful flow of oxygen-laden blood to the brain. On the other hand, the positive effects of alcohol tend to disappear among people who drink heavily (Cervilla et al., 2000; Xin et al., 2001). Also, there is the danger that people who drink lightly to achieve positive effects may run into problems with self-control.

Now, for the negative. As a food, alcohol is fattening. Even so, chronic drinkers may be malnourished. Although it is high in calories, alcohol does not contain nutrients such as vitamins and proteins. Moreover, it can interfere with the body's absorption of vitamins, particularly thiamine, a B vitamin. Thus chronic drinking can lead to a number of disorders such as **cirrhosis of the liver,** which has been linked to protein deficiency, and **Wernicke–Korsakoff syndrome,** which has been linked to vitamin B deficiency. Chronic heavy drinking has been linked to cardiovascular disorders and cancer. In particular, heavy drinking places women at risk for breast cancer (American Cancer Society, 2003; Singletary & Gapstur, 2001). Drinking by a pregnant woman may also harm the embryo.

Truth or Fiction Revisited: So, is a drink a day good for you? Apparently, yes. However, most health professionals are reluctant to advise that people drink regularly, though lightly. One cause for concern is that regular drinkers may lose control of the quantity of alcohol they ingest, become physiologically dependent and then suffer the effects of heavy drinking.

Alcoholics Anonymous (AA) is the most widely used program to treat alcoholism, yet research suggests that other approaches work as well for most people (Arroyo et al., 2003; Day et al., 2003). The National Institute on Alcohol Abuse and Alcoholism funded an eight-year study in which more than 1,700 problem drinkers were randomly assigned to AA's 12-step program, cognitive–behavioral therapy, or "motivational-enhancement therapy." The cognitive–behavioral treatment taught problem drinkers how to cope with temptations and how to refuse offers of drinks. Motivational enhancement was designed to enhance drinkers' desires to help themselves. The treatments worked equally well for most people, with some exceptions. For example, people with psychological problems fared somewhat better with cognitive–behavioral therapy.

Research is also under way on the use of medicines in treating problem drinking, including naltrexone, nalmefene, acamprosate (unavailable in the United States), and disulfiram. People who take disulfiram experience symptoms such as nausea and vomiting if they drink (Schuckit, 1996), but it apparently only decreases the frequency of drinking, thus leading many users to focus on finding ways around it rather than returning to a non-alcoholic lifestyle (Hunt, 2002). Naltrexone and acamprosate are apparently more effective in that they reduce the craving for alcohol (Anton, 2001; Hunt, 2002).

OPIATES **Opiates** are a group of **narcotics** that are derived from the opium poppy, from which they obtain their name. **Opioids** are similar in chemical structure but are synthesized in a laboratory. The ancient Sumerians gave the opium poppy its name: It means "plant of joy." Opiates include morphine, heroin, codeine, Demerol, and similar drugs. **Question: What are the effects of opiates?** The major medical application of this group of drugs is relief from pain.

Heroin can provide a strong euphoric "rush." Users claim that it is so pleasurable it can eradicate any thought of food or sex. Although regular users develop tolerance for heroin, high doses can cause drowsiness and stupor, alter time perception, and impair judgment. With regular use of opiates, such as morphine and heroin, the brain stops producing the neurotransmitters that are chemically similar to opiates—that is, the pain-relieving endorphins. As a result, people can become physiologically dependent on opiates, such that going without them can be an agonizing experience. Withdrawal syndromes may begin with flu-like symptoms and progress through tremors, cramps, chills alternating with sweating, rapid pulse, high blood pressure, insomnia, vomiting, and diarrhea. Because of their addictive properties, the nonmedical use of opiates has been criminalized. Penalties for possession or sale are high, so they are also expensive as street drugs. For this reason, many physiologically dependent people support their habit through dealing (selling heroin), prostitution, or selling stolen goods. This information seems to have gotten through to high school students; the great majority disapprove of using heroin (Johnston et al., 2003).

Heroin, by the way, was so named because it made people feel "heroic." It was also hailed as the "hero" that would cure physiological dependence on morphine. **Truth or Fiction Revisited:** Ironically, heroin was in fact once used as a cure for addiction to morphine.

Methadone is a synthetic opioid. It has been used to treat physiological dependence on heroin in the same way that heroin was once used to treat physiological dependence on morphine. Methadone is slower acting than heroin and does not provide the thrilling rush, but it does prevent experiencing of withdrawal symptoms. Some people must be maintained on methadone for many years before they can be gradually withdrawn from it (Fiellin et al., 2001). Some are maintained on methadone indefinitely because they are unwilling to undergo any withdrawal symptoms. However, many lead productive lives on methadone.

Many people who obtain prescriptions for opiates for pain relief neither experience a euphoric rush nor become psychologically dependent on them (Joranson et al., 2000). If they no longer need opiates for pain but have become physiologically dependent on them, they can usually quit with few, if any, side effects by gradually decreasing their dosage (Joranson et al., 2000). Thus, difficulty or ease of withdrawal may be connected with one's motives for using psychoactive drugs. Those who are seeking habitual relief from psychological pain seem to become more dependent on them than people who are seeking time-limited relief from physical pain.

BARBITURATES Question: What are the effects of barbiturates? **Barbiturates** like Nembutal and Seconal are depressants with several medical uses, including relief of anxiety and tension, relief from pain, and treatment of epilepsy, high blood pressure, and insomnia. With regular use, barbiturates lead rapidly to physiological and psychological dependence. Physicians therefore must provide these substances with care.

Barbiturates are popular as street drugs because they are relaxing and produce mild euphoria. High doses of barbiturates result in drowsiness, motor impairment, slurred speech, irritability, and poor judgment. A highly physiologically dependent person who is withdrawn abruptly from barbiturates may experience convulsions and die. Because of additive effects, it is dangerous to mix alcohol and other depressants.

Stimulants

All stimulants increase the activity of the nervous system. Some of their effects can be positive. For example, amphetamines stimulate cognitive activity and apparently help rats (Feola et al., 2000) and humans (H. de Wit et al., 2000) control impulses. The depressant alcohol, by contrast, can lower the inhibition of

Barbiturate An addictive depressant used to relieve anxiety or induce sleep.

impulses. These drugs can be appealing as street drugs because many contribute to feelings of euphoria and self-confidence. But they also have their risks—sometimes quite serious risks. In this section we discuss amphetamines, cocaine, and nicotine.

AMPHETAMINES AND RELATED STIMULANTS Question: What are the effects of amphetamines? **Amphetamines** are a group of stimulants that were first used by soldiers during World War II to help them remain alert through the night. Truck drivers have also used them to stay awake all night. Amphetamines have become perhaps more widely known through students, who have used them for all-night cram sessions, and through dieters, who use them because they reduce hunger.

Called speed, uppers, bennies (for Benzedrine), and dexies (for Dexedrine), these drugs are often abused for the euphoric rush they can produce in high doses. Some people swallow amphetamines in pill form or inject liquid Methedrine, the strongest form, into their veins. As a result, they may stay awake and high for days on end. However, such highs must end. People who have been on prolonged highs sometimes "crash," or fall into a deep sleep or depression. Some people commit suicide when crashing. On the other hand, physicians frequently prescribe stimulants in an effort to help hyperactive children control their behavior.

Truth or Fiction Revisited: It is therefore true that many health professionals calm hyperactive children by giving them a stimulant. The stimulant methylphenidate (Ritalin) is widely used to treat **attention-deficit/hyperactivity disorder (ADHD)** in children. Although some critics believe that Ritalin is prescribed too freely (Pear, 2000), Ritalin has been shown to increase the attention span, decrease aggressive and disruptive behavior, and lead to academic gains (Evans et al., 2001; Pelham et al., 2002). Why should Ritalin, a stimulant, calm children? Hyperactivity may be connected with immaturity of the cerebral cortex, and Ritalin may stimulate the cortex to exercise control over more primitive centers in the brain.

Tolerance for amphetamines develops rapidly, and users can become dependent on them, especially when they use them to self-medicate themselves for depression. Regular use of the powerful amphetamine called methamphetamine may well be physically addictive (Volkow et al., 2001a, 2001b), but the extent to which amphetamines cause physical addiction has been a subject of controversy. It is widely accepted, however, that high doses of amphetamines may cause restlessness, insomnia, loss of appetite, hallucinations, paranoid delusions (e.g., false ideas that others are eavesdropping or intend to harm one), and irritability.

Let us now discuss some of the most widely abused stimulants.

COCAINE Cocaine is derived from coca leaves—the plant from which the soft drink took its name. Do you recall the commercials claiming that "Coke adds life"? Given its caffeine and sugar content, "Coke"—Coca-Cola, that is—should provide quite a lift. **Truth or Fiction Revisited:** It is true that Coca-Cola once "added life" through the use of a powerful, then legal but now illegal, stimulant: cocaine. But Coca-Cola hasn't been "the real thing" since 1906, when the company discontinued the use of cocaine in its formula.

Question: What are the effects of cocaine? Cocaine is a stimulant that produces euphoria, reduces hunger, deadens pain, and bolsters self-confidence. Only about 4% of adolescents aged 15 to 19 have used cocaine within the past month (CDC, 2000b), and most high school students believe that use of cocaine is harmful (Johnston et al., 2003).

Cocaine may be brewed from coca leaves as a "tea," "snorted" in powder form, or injected in liquid form. Repeated snorting constricts blood vessels in the nose, drying the skin and sometimes exposing cartilage and perforating the nasal septum. These problems require cosmetic surgery. The potent cocaine derivatives known as "crack" and "bazooka" are inexpensive because they are unrefined.

© David Young-Wolff/PhotoEdit

■ **Snorting Cocaine** Cocaine is a powerful stimulant that boosts self-confidence. However, health professionals have become concerned about its physical effects, including sudden rises in blood pressure, constriction of blood vessels, and acceleration of heart rate. Several athletes have died from cocaine overdoses.

Amphetamines Stimulants derived from alpha-methyl-beta-phenyl-ethyl-amine, a colorless liquid consisting of carbon, hydrogen, and nitrogen.

Attention-deficit/hyperactivity disorder A disorder that begins in childhood and is characterized by a persistent pattern of lack of attention, with or without hyperactivity and impulsive behavior.

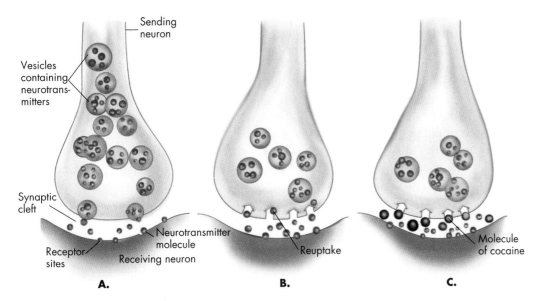

FIGURE 5.4 How Cocaine Produces Euphoria and Why People "Crash"

A. In the normal functioning of the nervous system, neurotransmitters are released into the synaptic cleft by vesicles in terminal buttons of sending neurons. Many are taken up by receptor sites in receiving neurons.
B. In the process called reuptake, sending neurons typically reabsorb excess molecules of neurotransmitters.
C. Molecules of cocaine bind to the sites on sending neurons that normally reuptake molecules of neurotransmitters. As a result, molecules of norepinephrine, dopamine, and serotonin remain longer in the synaptic cleft, increasing their typical mood-altering effects and providing a euphoric "rush." When the person stops using cocaine, the lessened absorption of neurotransmitters by receiving neurons causes his or her mood to "crash."

Biologically speaking, cocaine stimulates sudden rises in blood pressure, constricts the coronary arteries and thickens the blood (both of which decrease the oxygen supply to the heart), therefore quickening the heart rate (Kollins & Rush, 2002). These events occasionally result in respiratory and cardiovascular collapse (Moliterno et al., 1994). The sudden deaths of a number of athletes have been caused in this way. Overdoses can lead to restlessness and insomnia, tremors, headaches, nausea, convulsions, hallucinations, and delusions. Use of crack has been connected with strokes.

Cocaine—also called *snow* and *coke*—has been used as a local anesthetic since the early 1800s. In 1884 it came to the attention of a young Viennese neurologist named Sigmund Freud, who used it to fight his own depression and published an article about it titled "Song of Praise." Freud's early ardor was tempered when he learned that cocaine is habit-forming and can cause hallucinations and delusions. Cocaine causes physiological as well as psychological dependence.

NICOTINE

> *Smoking: a "custome lothesome to the Eye, hatefull to the Nose, harmefull to the Braine, dangerous to the Lungs."*
>
> King James I, 1604

Nicotine is the stimulant found in cigarettes and cigars. **Question: What are the effects of nicotine?** Nicotine stimulates discharge of the hormone adrenaline and the release of many neurotransmitters, including dopamine and acetylcholine (Arnold et al., 2003). Adrenaline creates a burst of autonomic activity that disrupts normal heart rhythms (Wang et al., 2000), accelerates the heart rate, and pours sugar into the blood. Acetylcholine is vital in memory formation, and nicotine appears to enhance memory and attention; improve performance on simple, repetitive tasks; and enhance the mood (Gentry, 2000; Rezvani & Levin, 2001). Despite its stimulative properties, it also appears to relax people and reduce stress (O'Brien, 1996).

Video Connections—Why Is Nicotine So Addictive? Go to your companion website and click on the "Why is Nicotine So Addictive?" video link. This video focuses on the role of reinforcement and how understanding cues may help people quit smoking.

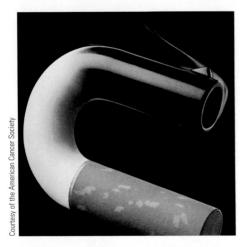

■ **Cigarettes: Smoking Guns?** The perils of cigarette smoking are widely known today. One Surgeon General declared that cigarette smoking is the chief preventable cause of death in the United States. The numbers of Americans who die from smoking are comparable to the number of lives that would be lost if two jumbo jets crashed *every day*. If flying were that unsafe, would the government ground all flights? Would the public continue to make airline reservations?

Nicotine depresses the appetite and raises the metabolic rate. Thus, some people smoke cigarettes in order to control their weight (Jeffery et al., 2000). People also tend to eat more when they stop smoking (Jeffery et al., 2000), causing some to return to the habit.

Nicotine, which may be as addictive as heroin or cocaine (MacKenzie et al., 1994), is the agent that creates physiological dependence on tobacco products (American Lung Association, 2000; Baker et al., 2000). Regular smokers adjust their smoking to maintain fairly even levels of nicotine in their bloodstream (Shiffman et al., 1997). Symptoms of withdrawal from nicotine include nervousness, drowsiness, loss of energy, headaches, irregular bowel movements, lightheadedness, insomnia, dizziness, cramps, palpitations, tremors, and sweating. Because many of these symptoms resemble those of anxiety, it was once thought that they might reflect the anxiety of attempting to quit smoking, rather than addiction.

It's no secret. Cigarette packs sold in the United States carry messages like "Warning: The Surgeon General Has Determined That Cigarette Smoking Is Dangerous To Your Health." Cigarette advertising has been banned on radio and television. Nearly 430,000 Americans die from smoking-related illnesses each year (American Lung Association, 2003). This is greater than the equivalent of two jumbo jets colliding in midair each day with all passengers lost. **Truth or Fiction Revisited:** It is higher than the number of people who die from motor vehicle accidents, alcohol and drug abuse, suicide, homicide, and AIDS *combined*.

The carbon monoxide in cigarette smoke impairs the blood's ability to carry oxygen, causing shortness of breath. The **hydrocarbons** ("tars") in cigarette and cigar smoke lead to lung cancer (American Lung Association, 2003). Smoking is responsible for about 87% of cases of lung cancer (American Lung Association, 2003). Cigarette smoking also stiffens arteries (Mahmud & Feely, 2003) and is linked to death from heart disease, chronic lung and respiratory diseases, and other health problems. Women who smoke show reduced bone density, increasing the risk of fracture of the hip and back (Hopper & Seeman, 1994). Pregnant women who smoke have a higher risk of miscarriage, preterm births, low-birth-weight babies, and stillborn babies (American Lung Association, 2003).

Passive smoking is also connected with respiratory illnesses, asthma, and other health problems. Prolonged exposure to household tobacco smoke during childhood is a risk factor for lung cancer (American Cancer Society, 2003). Because of the noxious effects of secondhand smoke, smoking has been banished from many public places such as airplanes, restaurants, and elevators.

Why, then, do people smoke? For many reasons—such as the desire to look sophisticated (although these days smokers may be more likely to be judged foolish than sophisticated), to have something to do with their hands, and—of course—to take in nicotine.

The percentage of American adults who smoke cigarettes declined from more than 40% in the mid-1960s to about 25% in recent years, but there have been increases among women, African Americans, and 8th to 12th graders (American Lung Association, 2000). The incidence of smoking is connected with gender and level of education (see Table 5.5) (American Lung Association, 2000). Better-educated people are less likely to smoke (Cavelaars et al., 2000). They are also more likely to quit smoking (Rose et al., 1996).

Nancy Rigotti and her colleagues (2000) polled more than 14,000 students from 119 nationally representative four-year colleges and universities. Sixty percent of the students responded to the survey. Among college students, European Americans were most likely to smoke cigarettes, and African Americans were least likely to smoke (corresponding to the findings in Table 5.3). In addition to smoking cigarettes, many men reported using cigars, pipes, and smokeless tobacco, all of which are also associated with health risks. Athletes and more achievement-oriented students were less likely to smoke than students whose priorities were

Hydrocarbons Chemical compounds consisting of hydrogen and carbon.

Passive smoking Inhaling of smoke from the tobacco products and exhalations of other people; also called *secondhand smoking*.

TABLE 5.5 SNAPSHOT, U.S.A.: GENDER, LEVEL OF EDUCATION, AND SMOKING		
Factor	**Group**	**Percent Who Smoke**
Gender	Women	22
	Men	27
Level of education	Fewer than 12 years	38
	16 years and above	14

Source: American Heart Association © (2000a). 2000 Heart and Stroke Statistical Update, http://www.americanheart.org; American Lung Association (2000). Smoking Fact Sheet, http://www.lungusa.org.

more social. Thus many students experiment with tobacco in college, and many become dependent on nicotine—a dependence that can haunt them for a lifetime.

Hallucinogenics

Hallucinogenic drugs are so named because they produce hallucinations—that is, sensations and perceptions in the absence of external stimulation. But hallucinogenic drugs may also have additional effects such as relaxation, euphoria, or, in some cases, panic.

MARIJUANA **Marijuana** is a substance that is produced from the *Cannabis sativa* plant, which grows wild in many parts of the world. **Question: What are the effects of marijuana?** Marijuana helps some people relax and can elevate their mood. It also sometimes produces mild hallucinations, which is why we discuss it in the section on **psychedelic,** or hallucinogenic, drugs. The major psychedelic substance in marijuana is delta-9-tetrahydrocannabinol, or THC. THC is found in the branches and leaves of the plant, but it is highly concentrated in the sticky resin. **Hashish,** or "hash," is derived from the resin and is more potent than marijuana.

In the 19th century, marijuana was used much as aspirin is used today for headaches and minor aches and pains. It could be bought without a prescription in any drugstore. Today marijuana use and possession are illegal in most states. Marijuana also carries a number of health risks. For example, it impairs the perceptual–motor coordination used in driving and operating machines. It impairs short-term memory and slows learning (Ashton, 2001). Although it causes positive mood changes in many people, there are also disturbing instances of anxiety and confusion and occasional reports of psychotic reactions (Johns, 2001).

Some people report that marijuana helps them socialize at parties. Moderate to strong intoxication is linked to reports of heightened perceptions and increases in self-insight, creative thinking, and empathy for the feelings of others. Time seems to pass more slowly for people who are strongly intoxicated. A song might seem to last an hour rather than a few minutes. There is increased awareness of bodily sensations such as heartbeat. Marijuana smokers also report that strong intoxication heightens sexual sensations. Visual hallucinations are not uncommon, and strong intoxication may cause smokers to experience disorientation. If the smoker's mood is euphoric, loss of a sense of personal identity may be interpreted as being in harmony with the universe.

Some marijuana smokers have negative experiences. An accelerated heart rate and heightened awareness of bodily sensations leads some smokers to fear that their heart will "run away" with them. Some smokers find disorientation threatening and are afraid that they will not regain their identity. Strong intoxication sometimes causes nausea and vomiting.

People can become psychologically dependent on marijuana, but use of marijuana had not been thought to lead to physiological dependence. Recent research, however, suggests that regular users of marijuana may experience tolerance and withdrawal symptoms (American Psychiatric Association, 2000; Johns, 2001).

Hallucinogenic Giving rise to hallucinations.

Marijuana The dried vegetable matter of the *Cannabis sativa* plant.

Psychedelic Causing hallucinations, delusions, or heightened perceptions.

Hashish A drug derived from the resin of *Cannabis sativa.* Often called "hash."

Is marijuana harmful? Should it be available as a medicine?

There are many controversies concerning marijuana. One is the issue as to whether marijuana should be made available as a medicine to those who could benefit from it. Marijuana has been used to treat health problems, including glaucoma and the nausea experienced by cancer patients undergoing chemotherapy (Robson, 2001). Psychiatrist Lester Grinspoon (2000), a long-time supporter of marijuana for medical uses, refers to it as an inexpensive, versatile, and reasonably safe medicine. Other medical researchers agree that marijuana has some positive effects, but the action of THC also has its negatives (Nahas et al., 2000). THC binds to a membrane receptor, 7TM, which is found in every cell. THC displaces the natural substance that would bind with the receptor and disrupts the receptor's signaling. As a result, the functioning of the brain, the immune system, and the cardiovascular and reproductive systems (e.g., it interferes with development of sperm and conception) are impaired to some degree.

Marijuana smoke also contains more hydrocarbons than tobacco smoke—a risk factor in cancer. Smokers of marijuana often admit that they know that marijuana smoke can be harmful, but they counter that compared with cigarette smokers, they smoke very few "joints" per day. Yet, as noted, marijuana elevates the heart rate and, in some people, the blood pressure. This higher demand on the heart and circulation poses a threat to people with hypertension and cardiovascular disorders. One study found that middle-aged men were five times more likely to have a heart attack within an hour of smoking marijuana (Middleman, 2000).

Another issue is whether researchers and public figures exaggerate the dangers of marijuana to discourage people from using it. Does the information about marijuana in this textbook seem to be biased? Why or why not?

Marijuana has been with us for decades, but new research on its effects continues—with more sophisticated methods. And the findings are mixed. For example, some research has suggested that marijuana usage impairs learning, memory, and attention (Solowij et al., 2002), but it was assumed by many that the reason was that marijuana distracted people from learning tasks. Other laboratory research suggests a biological reason—that marijuana reduces the release of neurotransmitters involved in the consolidation of learning (J. M. Sullivan, 2000). Yet consider the results of a synthesis of 15 previously published studies on the long-term effects of marijuana on the cognitive performance of adults. The synthesis compared 704 long-term cannabis users with 484 nonusers (Grant et al., 2003). The cognitive measures included reaction time, attention, use of language, abstract thinking, perceptual-motor skills, and learning and forgetting. The only significant difference was that long-term marijuana users showed a small comparative deficit in learning new information. The importance of this difference is open to debate.

Then there are the brain imaging studies. MRI and PET scan studies suggest that marijuana usage may have little or no effect on the size or composition of the brains of adults (Block et al., 2000). But other studies suggest that males who began using marijuana before the age of 17 may have smaller brains and less gray matter than other males (Wilson et al., 2000). Both males and females who started using marijuana early may be generally smaller in height and weight than other people. William Wilson and his colleagues (2000) suggest that these differences may reflect the effect of marijuana on pituitary and sex hormones.

More research is needed on the effects of marijuana. While some of the horror stories of the 1960s and 1970s may have been exaggerated, a number of questions about potential harm remain. More research evidence—not more speculation—is needed.

LSD AND OTHER HALLUCINOGENICS **LSD** is the abbreviation for lysergic acid diethylamide, a synthetic hallucinogenic drug. **Question: What are the effects of LSD and other kinds of hallucinogenic drugs?** Users of "acid" claim that it "expands consciousness" and opens up new worlds to them. Sometimes people believe they have achieved great insights while using LSD, but when it wears off they often cannot apply or recall these discoveries. As a powerful hallucinogenic, LSD produces vivid and colorful hallucinations.

Some LSD users have **flashbacks**—distorted perceptions or hallucinations that mimic the LSD "trip" but occur days, weeks, or longer after usage. The experiencing of flashbacks is more technically termed hallucinogen persisting perception disorder (HPPD) by the American Psychiatric Association (2000), although some writers distinguish between the two (Smith & Seymour, 1994). Over the years, both psychological and physiological explanations of HPPD have appeared. The psychological explanation of "flashbacks," in a nutshell, is that people who would use LSD regularly are also more likely to allow flights of fancy. Yet research with 38 people with HPPD suggests that following extensive use of LSD, the brain may fail to inhibit certain internal sources of visionlike experiences, especially when the eyes are closed (Abraham & Duffy, 2001). Such visionlike experiences are also apparently more likely to occur in the presence of excessive sympathetic nervous system activity—that is, anxiety (Lerner et al., 2000).

Other hallucinogenic drugs include **mescaline** (derived from the peyote cactus) and **phencyclidine (PCP).** Phencyclidine (PCP) was developed as an anesthetic and a large animal tranquilizer, and it goes by the street names "angel dust," "ozone," "wack," and "rocket fuel." The street terms "killer joints" and "crystal supergrass" refer to PCP that is combined with marijuana.

Regular use of hallucinogenics may lead to tolerance and psychological dependence. But hallucinogenics are not known to lead to physiological dependence. High doses may induce frightening hallucinations, impaired coordination, poor judgment, mood changes, and paranoid delusions.

Your Turn: Now that we have discussed drugs, enhance your mastery of the material with the nearby "Learning Connections." Review the material by filling in the blanks, reflect on the material by relating it to other things you know, and think critically about it. The Concept Review on page 222 summarizes information about drugs.

■ **An LSD Trip?** This hallucinogenic drug can give rise to a vivid parade of colors and visual distortions. Some users claim to have achieved great insights while "tripping," but typically they have been unable to recall or apply them afterward.

LSD Lysergic acid diethylamide. A hallucinogenic drug.

Flashbacks Distorted perceptions or hallucinations that occur days or weeks after LSD usage but mimic the LSD experience.

Mescaline A hallucinogenic drug derived from the mescal (peyote) cactus.

Phencyclidine (PCP) Another hallucinogenic drug whose name is an acronym for its chemical structure.

 Learning Connections — ALTERING CONSCIOUSNESS THROUGH DRUGS

ACTIVE REVIEW (18) Substance _____ is characterized by repeated use of a substance although it is impairing functioning. (19) Physiological dependence is evidenced by tolerance or by an _____ syndrome when one discontinues use of the substance. (20) Women seem to be (*More* or *Less?*) affected by alcohol than men. (21) Opiates are used in medicine to reduce _____, but they are bought "on the street" because of the euphoric rush they provide. (22) Barbiturates are used medically to treat _____. (23) Ritalin is used to treat _____-deficit/hyperactivity disorder in children. (24) _____ is a stimulant that boosts self-confidence but also triggers rises in blood pressure and constricts the coronary arteries. (25) Tobacco contains the stimulant _____. (26) _____ substances distort perceptions. (27) _____ often produces feelings of

relaxation and empathy, the feeling that time is slowing down, and reports of new insights. (28) LSD produces vivid _____.

REFLECT AND RELATE The next time you are at a social occasion, note the behavior of people who are drinking and those who are not. What do you think are individuals' motives for drinking? Does drinking visibly affect their behavior? If you drink, how does it affect your behavior?

CRITICAL THINKING Does this textbook's presentation of information about the effects of drugs seem to be straightforward or biased? What is the evidence for your view?

Go to **http://psychology.wadsworth.com/ rathus_pcc9e** for an interactive version of this Learning Connections unit.

Concept Review PSYCHOACTIVE DRUGS AND THEIR EFFECTS

Drug	Type	How Taken	Desired Effects	Tolerance	Abstinence Syndrome	Side Effects
Alcohol	Depressant	By mouth	Relaxation, euphoria, lowered inhibitions	Yes	Yes	Impaired coordination, poor judgment, hangover
Opiates	Depressants	Injected, smoked, by mouth	Relaxation, euphoria, relief from anxiety and pain	Yes	Yes	Impaired coordination and mental functioning, drowsiness, lethargy
Barbiturates	Depressants	By mouth, injected	Relaxation, sleep, euphoria, lowered inhibitions	Yes	Yes	Impaired coordination and mental functioning, drowsiness, lethargy
Amphetamines	Stimulants	By mouth, injected	Alertness, euphoria	Yes	?	Restlessness, loss of appetite, psychotic symptoms
Cocaine	Stimulant	By mouth, snorted, injected	Euphoria, self-confidence	Yes	Yes	Restlessness, loss of appetite, convulsions, strokes, psychotic symptoms
Nicotine	Stimulant	By tobacco (smoked, chewed, or sniffed)	Relaxation, stimulation, weight control	Yes	Yes	Cancer, heart disease, lung and respiratory diseases
Marijuana	Hallucinogenic	Smoked, by mouth	Relaxation, perceptual distortions, enhancement of experience	?	?	Impaired coordination, learning, respiratory problems, panic
LSD, Mescaline, PCP	Hallucinogenics	By mouth	Perceptual distortions, vivid hallucinations	Yes	No	Impaired coordination, psychotic symptoms, panic

 Go to **http://psychology.wadsworth.com/ rathus_pcc9e** to access a drag-and-drop version of this Concept Review designed to help you test yourself on the major topics provided here.

Life Connections
Getting to Sleep—and Elsewhere—without Drugs

Where do you want to go? Do you want to go to sleep? Do you want to go on a psychological trip searching for inner truth? Do you want to go on a stimulating trip that will drench your bloodstream with adrenaline? There are ways to do all these things—ways that rely on you rather than on drugs.

Check it out. There are ideas here for getting to sleep without sleeping pills. There are suggestions for thinking helpful thoughts rather than blowing the situation out of proportion. There are ways of relaxing that let you do your own mellowing out—again, drug-free. These methods are largely cognitive–behavioral (Edinger et al., 2001).

Getting to Sleep without Drugs

Do you have a problem with insomnia? The nearby self-assessment, "Are You Getting Your Z's?", may offer some insight. If you decide that you do, what can you do about it?

No question about it: The most common medical method for getting to sleep in the United States is taking pills (Edinger et al., 2001). Sleeping pills may work—for a while. So may tranquilizers. They generally work by reducing arousal and also distract you from trying to *get* to sleep. Expectations of success may also help.

But there are problems with sleeping pills. First, many may attribute success to the pill and not to themselves and come to depend on the pill. Second, a person may develop tolerance for many kinds of sleeping pills and, with regular use, need higher doses to achieve the same effects. Third, high doses of these chemicals can be dangerous, especially if mixed with alcohol. Fourth, sleeping pills do not enhance your skills at handling insomnia. Thus, when you stop taking them, insomnia is likely to return (Morin et al., 1999).

There are excellent psychological methods for coping with insomnia, which can be effective alternatives for many. Some methods like muscle relaxation exercises reduce tension directly.

Self-Assessment Sleep Quiz: Are You Getting Your Z's?[3]

This questionnaire can help you learn whether you are getting enough sleep. Circle the *T* if an item is true or mostly true, or the *F* if an item is false or mostly false for you. Then check the meaning of your answers in Appendix B.

T F

__ __ 1. I need an alarm clock in order to wake up at the appropriate time.

__ __ 2. It's a struggle for me to get out of bed in the morning.

__ __ 3. Weekday mornings I hit the snooze button several times to get more sleep.

__ __ 4. I feel tired, irritable, and stressed out during the week.

__ __ 5. I have trouble concentrating and remembering.

__ __ 6. I feel slow with critical thinking, problem solving, and being creative.

__ __ 7. I often fall asleep watching television.

__ __ 8. I often fall asleep after heavy meals or after a low dose of alcohol.

__ __ 9. I often fall asleep while relaxing after dinner.

__ __ 10. I often fall asleep within five minutes of getting into bed.

__ __ 11. I often feel drowsy while driving.

__ __ 12. I often sleep extra hours on weekend mornings.

__ __ 13. I often need a nap to get through the day.

__ __ 14. I have dark circles around my eyes.

[3]*Source:* From *Power Sleep* by James B. Maas, copyright © 1998 by James B. Maas, Ph.D. Used by permission of Villard Books, a division of Random House, Inc.

Psychological methods also divert us from the "task" of trying somehow to *get* to sleep, which, ironically, is one of the ways in which we keep ourselves awake (Mimeault & Morin, 1999). You can try any or all of the following psychological methods:

- *Relax:* Take a hot bath at bedtime or try meditating. Releasing muscle tension has been shown to reduce the amount of time needed to fall asleep and the incidence of waking up during the night (Murtagh & Greenwood, 1995).
- *Challenge exaggerated fears:* You need not be a sleep expert to realize that convincing yourself that the day will be ruined unless you get to sleep *right now* may increase, rather than decrease, bedtime tension. However, cognitive–behavioral psychologists note that we often exaggerate the problems that will befall us if we do not sleep (Edinger et al., 2001; Morin et al., 1999). Table 5.6 shows some beliefs that increase bedtime tension and some alternatives.
- *Don't ruminate in bed:* Don't plan or worry about tomorrow while in bed (National Sleep Foundation, 2000a). When you lie down for sleep, you may organize your thoughts for the next day for a few minutes, but then allow yourself to relax or engage in a soothing fantasy. If an important idea comes to you, jot it down on a handy pad so that you won't worry about forgetting it. If thoughts or inspirations persist, however, get up and think about them elsewhere. Let your bed be a place for relaxation and sleep—not your second office. A

bed—even a waterbed—should not be a think tank.

- *Establish a regular routine:* Sleeping late can end up causing problems falling asleep (sleep-onset insomnia). Set your alarm for the same time each morning and get up, regardless of how long you have slept (Mimeault & Morin, 1999; National Sleep Foundation, 2000a). By rising at a regular time, you'll encourage yourself to fall asleep at a regular time.
- *Try fantasy:* Fantasies or daydreams are almost universal and may occur naturally as we fall asleep. You can allow yourself to "go with" soothing, relaxing fantasies that occur at bedtime, or purposefully use pleasant fantasies to get to sleep. You may be able to ease yourself to sleep, for example, by focusing on a sun-drenched beach with waves lapping on the shore or on a walk through a mountain meadow on a summer day. You can construct your own "mind trips" and paint in the details.

Above all: Accept the idea that it really doesn't matter if you don't get to sleep early *this night*. You will survive. In fact, you'll do just fine.

Strategies for Gaining Self-Control and Maintaining Self-Control

> *I can resist everything except temptation.*
> Oscar Wilde (*Lady Windermere's Fan*)

With a little bit of help, you probably *can* resist temptation. There are physiological and psychological aspects to coping with the temptation of drugs. People who regularly use many of the substances discussed in this chapter can become

dependent on them. In the cases of alcohol, nicotine, cocaine, opiates, and sedatives, serious physiological dependence can develop. In some cases, as with nicotine and marijuana, users can stop using the substance on their own despite the discomforts of doing so. Going "cold turkey" is safe enough. This may not be so with other substances, particularly alcohol. Going cold turkey can be dangerous. So-called alcohol "detoxification" is a complex procedure that takes a week or so and is best carried out under medical supervision, often in a hospital.

Even when someone is no longer physiologically dependent, the battle is not over. Avoiding temptation can mean maintaining a deep personal commitment to changing one's lifestyle, sometimes including choosing a different set of friends or different leisure activities.

Cognitive–behavioral approaches to substance abuse and dependence focus on modifying abusive and dependent ideas and behavior patterns (Niaura & Abrams, 2002; Waldron et al., 2001). They teach abusers either to avoid temptation or to change their behavior when they are faced with temptation. For example, people can learn to avoid socializing with others with substance abuse problems (Latimer et al., 2000). They can avoid situations linked to abuse—bars, clubs, parties, and so on. They can learn to frequent substance-free environments such as gyms, school-sponsored activities or lectures, or cafes and coffee shops. They can learn to use competing responses when they are tempted—taking a bath or shower, walking the dog, walking around the block, taking a drive, calling a friend, or exercising. The cognitive–behavioral method of social skills training helps people develop effective social behavior in situations that are connected with substance abuse (Blake et al., 2001). They may teach individuals how to fend off social pressures to drink or have a cigarette. Many people learn how to say "no, thanks" without getting into an argument or having to leave the situation.

The cognitive–behavioral strategies outlined in Table 5.7 can help readers maintain commitment to do without drugs and deal with temptations. In the

TABLE 5.6 BELIEFS THAT INCREASE TENSION AND ALTERNATIVES

Beliefs That Increase Tension	Alternatives
If I don't get to sleep, I'll feel wrecked tomorrow.	Not necessarily. If I'm tired, I can go to bed early tomorrow night.
It's unhealthy for me not to get more sleep.	Not necessarily. Some people do very well on only a few hours of sleep.
I'll wreck my sleeping schedule for the whole week if I don't get to sleep very soon.	Not at all. If I'm tired, I'll just go to bed a bit earlier. I'll get up about the same time with no problem.
If I don't get to sleep, I won't be able to concentrate on that big test/conference tomorrow.	Possibly, but my fears may be exaggerated. I may just as well relax or get up and do something enjoyable for a while.

TABLE 5.7 GETTING THERE WITHOUT DRUGS: COGNITIVE–BEHAVIORAL STRATEGIES FOR PUTTING AN END TO SUBSTANCE ABUSE

	Strategy	Examples of Use of the Strategy
Strategies Aimed at the Stimuli That Trigger Substance Abuse	**Restriction of the stimulus field**	Gradually exclude the problem behavior from more environments. At first, make smoking off limits in the car; then make it off limits in the home.
	Avoidance of powerful stimuli that trigger habits	Avoid obvious sources of temptation. (People who go window-shopping often wind up buying more than windows.) Walk briskly through the market; don't linger by the packs of cigarettes or the alcohol section. Sit in nonsmokers' sections of restaurants and trains. Go on a smoke-ending vacation to get away from places and situations in which you're used to smoking. Don't go to the bar with people you drink heavily with.
	Stimulus control	Place yourself in an environment in which desirable behavior is likely to occur. Fill your days with novel activities–things that won't remind you of smoking or having that extra beer. Beat insomnia by using your bed only as a place for sleeping–no more studying or eating snacks in bed. In that way your bed will come to "mean" sleep to you.
Strategies Aimed at the Abusive Behavior Itself	**Response prevention**	Make unwanted behavior difficult or impossible. You cannot smoke the cigarettes or drink the beer you left on the shelf at the corner store.
	Competing responses	Engage in behaviors that are incompatible with the problem behavior. Stuff your mouth with sugar-free mints, not cigarettes. Consider nicotine replacement therapy in the form of a nicotine gum or skin patch. The use of nicotine replacements helps to avert withdrawal symptoms when dependent smokers discontinue cigarettes. Or use sugar-free mints or gum as substitutes for cigarettes. (Don't light them!)
	Chain breaking	Interfere with unwanted habitual behavior by complicating the process of engaging in it. Break the chain of reaching for a readily available cigarette and placing it in your mouth by wrapping the pack in aluminum foil and placing it on the top shelf of a closet. Rewrap the pack after taking one cigarette. Hold your cigarettes with your nondominant hand only. Put the cigarette out before you reach the end. (No more eating the filter.) Put your cigarette in the ashtray between puffs.
	Successive approximations	Gradually approach targets through a series of relatively painless steps. Decrease smoking by pausing for a minute when the cigarette is smoked halfway, or by putting it out a minute before you would wind up eating the filter.
Strategies Aimed at the Reinforcers That Maintain Abusive Behavior	**Reinforcement of desired behavior**	Why give yourself something for nothing? Make pleasant activities such as going to films, walking on the beach, or reading a new novel contingent on meeting reasonable daily behavioral goals. Each day you remain abstinent from cigarettes or limit your alcohol intake to one drink, sock away a dollar toward that camera or vacation trip you have been dreaming of.
	Response cost	Heighten awareness of the long-term reasons for dieting or cutting down on smoking by punishing yourself for not meeting a daily goal or for engaging in a bad habit. For example, if you light up, make out a check to a cause you oppose and mail it at once.
	"Grandma's method"	How did Grandma persuade children to eat their vegetables? Simple: No veggies, no dessert. In this method, desired behaviors such as quitting smoking can be encouraged by insisting that you read cards such as the following before leaving the house or the apartment: "Every day it becomes a little easier," and "Your lungs will turn pink again."
	Covert sensitization[†]	Create imaginary horror stories about problem behavior. Psychologists have successfully reduced overeating and smoking by having clients imagine that a cigarette is made from vomit. Some horror stories are not "imaginary." Deliberately focusing on heart strain and diseased lungs every time you overeat or smoke, rather than ignoring these long-term consequences, might also promote self-control.
	Covert reinforcement[‡]	Create rewarding imagery for desired behavior. Interpret withdrawal symptoms from stopping smoking or going without that beer as a sign that you're winning and getting healthier. After all, you wouldn't have withdrawal symptoms if you were smoking or drinking.

[†]Imagining punishing consequences for engaging in undesirable behavior. *Covert* means "hidden," and you use this strategy by imagining scenarios. Because you imagine them, they are hidden from the outside world and perceptible to you alone.
[‡]Imagining rewarding consequences for engaging in desirable behavior. This strategy, like covert sensitization, is used by imagining various scenarios.

case of smoking cigarettes, some suggestions are of use in cutting down and others in going cold turkey (Niaura & Abrams, 2002). In the case of alcohol, the suggestions largely have to do with controlling the amount being used. However, many health professionals believe that it is wisest for people who have been physiologically dependent on alcohol to avoid drinking altogether.

Cognitive–behavioral psychologists note that much of the "cure" for substance abuse lies in what we tell ourselves and other people about our behavior. For example, if you're going to quit smoking, why not tell your family and friends that you're quitting? By making a public commitment to do so, you shore up your resolve. Also plan a target date for quitting, perhaps a date

when you will be on vacation or away from the usual settings in which you smoke. You can use a nicotine substitute like a skin patch to help cut down before the target date and to prove to yourself that you can survive on fewer cigarettes (and, ultimately, on no cigarettes). You can plan specific things to tell yourself when you feel the urge to smoke: how you'll be stronger, free of fear of cancer,

© Ariel Skelley/CORBIS

■ **Coping with Boredom, Depression, and Other Negative Feelings—and Remaining Drug-Free** Look for a new activity or interest. Become involved in a political campaign or social cause. Find a student organization that appeals to you.

ready for the marathon, and so on, and so on. Once you have stopped, you can remind yourself repeatedly that the first few days are the hardest. After that, withdrawal symptoms weaken dramatically. And don't forget to pat yourself on the back by reminding yourself that you are accomplishing something that many millions of others find to be out of reach.

The suggestions in Table 5.6 can be generalized to nearly any substance. The following suggestions involve alternatives to substance abuse.

Getting There without Drugs: Don't Just Say No, *Do* Something Else All of us feel depressed, tense, or just plain bored from time to time. Many are intrigued by the possibility of exploring the still dark reaches of their inner selves. Many feel inadequate to face the challenges of college life now and then. Some of us see our futures as bleak and unrewarding. A vast wilderness or desert seems to lie before us.

So we all have feelings like these now and then. Then what? If you are wavering on whether or not to get involved with drugs, here are some drug-free alternatives to consider.

If you are:

- Feeling tense or anxious, try practicing self-relaxation or meditation, or exercise, or listen to relaxing music.
- Feeling bored, find a new activity or interest. Start an exercise program or get involved in athletics. Take up a hobby. Become involved in a political campaign or social cause. There are many student organizations on campus. Find one that appeals to you.
- Feeling angry, write down your feelings or channel your anger into constructive pursuits aimed at solving what has angered you or pursuits that allow you time to cool off.
- Feeling worthless, hopeless, or depressed, or putting yourself down, seek assistance from a friend or loved one. Focus on your abilities and accomplishments, not on your deficits. If that doesn't help, visit the college counseling center or health center. They may have suggestions for organizations you can become involved in, helping you feel that you can make a difference or have a "direction." You may also be suffering from a treatable case of depression.
- Wanting to probe the inner depths of your consciousness, try meditation or yoga. Or seek the advice of a counselor or minister, priest, or rabbi.
- Pressured into using drugs by friends, learn how to say "no" politely but firmly. If you need help saying no, read a self-help book on self-assertion or go to the college counseling center for advice. If necessary, get new

friends. (A real friend will not push you into doing anything that makes you feel uncomfortable, including using drugs.)

- Seeking to heighten your sensations, try dancing, jogging, parachuting, snow-boarding, Rollerblading, or mountain climbing. There are many ways to get your adrenaline flowing that do not involve chemical stimulants.
- Feeling stressed out to the point where you can't take it anymore, sit down to figure out the pressures acting upon you. List your priorities. What must be done *right now*? What can wait? If this approach fails, see your academic advisor or visit the college counseling center or health center. If you can afford the time, you may choose to take a day or two off. Sometimes the key is to establish more reasonable expectations of yourself. No drug will help you do that.
- Wanting to discover new insights on the human condition, take classes or workshops on philosophy and theology. Attend lectures by prominent thinkers. Read great works of literature. Ponder great works of art. Attend the symphony. Visit a museum. Let your mind connect with the great minds of the past and present.
- Searching for deeper personal meaning in life, become more involved in spiritual activity in your church or synagogue. Do volunteer work in hospitals or charitable organizations. Get involved in a cause you believe in. Or seek personal counseling to get in touch with your inner self.

We are all different, all unique. We have different desires, interests, and needs. Take the time to get in touch with your own and to do things that you will find fulfilling.

Want to study on the go? Go to your companion website and download an audio version of this review section to your media player.

Recite—An Active Summary™

1. What is consciousness?

The term *consciousness* has several meanings, including sensory awareness, direct inner awareness of cognitive processes, the selective aspect of attention, the sense of self, and the waking state.

2. What is a circadian rhythm?

A circadian rhythm is a cycle that is connected with the 24-hour period of the earth's rotation, such as the sleep–wake cycle.

3. How do we describe the various stages of sleep?

We undergo several stages of sleep. According to electroencephalograph (EEG) records, each stage of sleep is characterized by a different type of brain wave. There are four stages of non-rapid-eye-movement (NREM) sleep and one stage of REM sleep. Stage 1 sleep is the lightest, and stage 4 is the deepest.

4. Why do we sleep?

Sleep apparently serves a restorative function, but we do not know exactly how sleep restores us or how much sleep we need. Animals and people who have been deprived of REM sleep learn more slowly and forget what they have learned more rapidly. Nightmares are dreams that tend to occur during REM sleep.

5. What are dreams?

Dreams are a form of cognitive activity that occurs mostly while we are sleeping. Most dreaming occurs during REM sleep.

6. Why do we dream what we dream?

Freud believed that dreams reflected unconscious wishes and "protected sleep" by keeping unacceptable ideas out of awareness. The activation-synthesis hypothesis suggests that dreams largely reflect automatic biological activity by the pons and the synthesis of subsequent sensory stimulation by the frontal part of the brain. The content of most dreams is an extension of the events of the previous day.

7. What kinds of sleep disorders are there?

A common sleep disorder is insomnia, which is most often encountered by people who are anxious and tense. Deep sleep disorders include sleep terrors, bed-wetting, and sleepwalking.

8. What is hypnosis?

Hypnosis is an altered state of consciousness in which people are suggestible and behave as though they are in a trance. People who are hypnotized may show passivity, narrowed attention, hypermnesia (heightened memory), suggestibility, assumption of unusual roles, perceptual distortions, posthypnotic amnesia, and posthypnotic suggestion.

9. How do modern psychologists explain the effects of hypnosis?

Current theories of hypnosis deny the existence of a special trance state. Rather, they emphasize people's ability to role-play the "trance" (role theory), to do what is expected of them (response set theory), and to divide their consciousness (neodissociation theory) as directed by the hypnotist.

10. What is meditation?

In meditation, one focuses "passively" on an object or a mantra in order to alter the normal relationship between oneself and the environment. In this way, consciousness (that is, the normal focuses of attention) is altered.

11. What are the effects of meditation?

Meditation often has the effect of inducing relaxation. TM appears to reduce the blood pressure of hypertensive individuals.

12. What is biofeedback training?

Biofeedback is a method for increasing consciousness of bodily functions. In biofeedback, the organism is continuously provided with information about a targeted biological response such as heart rate or emission of alpha waves.

13. How is biofeedback training used?

People and lower animals can learn to control involuntary functions such as heart rate, blood pressure, even the emission of certain brain waves through biofeedback training.

Recite—An Active Summary™

14. What are substance abuse and dependence?

Substance abuse is use of a substance that persists even though it impairs one's functioning. Dependence has behavioral and physiological aspects. It may be characterized by organizing one's life around getting and using the substance and by the development of tolerance, withdrawal symptoms, or both.

15. What are the causes of substance abuse and dependence?

People usually try drugs out of curiosity, but usage can be reinforced by anxiety reduction, feelings of euphoria, and other positive sensations. People are also motivated to avoid withdrawal symptoms once they become physiologically dependent on a drug. People may have genetic predispositions to become physiologically dependent on certain substances.

16. What are the effects of alcohol?

Alcohol, the most widely used drug, is a depressant. It belongs to the group of substances that act by slowing the activity of the central nervous system. Alcohol is also intoxicating and can lead to physiological dependence. It provides an excuse for failure or for antisocial behavior, but it has not been shown to induce such behavior directly.

17. What are the effects of opiates?

The opiates morphine and heroin are depressants that reduce pain, but they are also bought on the street because of the euphoric "rush" they provide. Opiate use can lead to physiological dependence.

18. What are the effects of barbiturates?

Barbiturates are depressants. Barbiturates have medical uses, including relaxation, pain management, and treatment of epilepsy, high blood pressure, and insomnia. Barbiturates lead rapidly to physiological and psychological dependence.

19. What are the effects of amphetamines?

Stimulants are substances that act by increasing the activity of the nervous system. Amphetamines are stimulants that produce feelings of euphoria when taken in high doses. But high doses may also cause restlessness, insomnia, psychotic symptoms, and a "crash" upon withdrawal. Amphetamines and a related stimulant, Ritalin, are commonly used to treat hyperactive children.

20. What are the effects of cocaine?

The stimulant cocaine provides feelings of euphoria and bolsters self-confidence. Physically, it causes spikes in blood pressure and constricts blood vessels. Overdoses can lead to restlessness, insomnia, psychotic reactions, and cardiorespiratory collapse.

21. What are the effects of nicotine?

Nicotine is the addictive stimulant in cigarettes that can paradoxically help people relax. Cigarette smoke also contains carbon monoxide and hydrocarbons. Smoking has been linked to death from heart disease and cancer and to other health problems.

22. What are the effects of marijuana?

Marijuana is a hallucinogenic substance whose active ingredients, including THC, may produce relaxation, heightened and distorted perceptions, feelings of empathy, and reports of new insights. Marijuana elevates the heart rate and the smoke is harmful. Although it has some medical uses, it impairs learning and memory and may affect the growth of adolescents.

23. What are the effects of LSD and other kinds of hallucinogenic drugs?

LSD and other hallucinogenic drugs produce hallucinations. Some LSD users have "flashbacks" to earlier experiences. "Ecstasy" often combines a stimulant with a hallucinogenic drug.

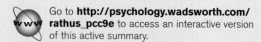

Go to **http://psychology.wadsworth.com/ rathus_pcc9e** to access an interactive version of this active summary.

Key Terms

Selective attention (p. 188)
Direct inner awareness (p. 188)
Preconscious (p. 189)
Unconscious (p. 189)
Repression (p. 189)
Suppression (p. 189)
Nonconscious (p. 189)
Circadian rhythm (p. 192)
Alpha waves (p. 193)
Non-rapid-eye-movement (NREM) sleep (p. 193)
Rapid-eye-movement (REM) sleep (p. 193)
Theta waves (p. 193)
Hypnagogic state (p. 193)

Delta waves (p. 193)
Activation–synthesis model (p. 196)
Narcolepsy (p. 198)
Apnea (p. 199)
Sleep terrors (p. 199)
Avatar (p. 200)
Flow (p. 200)
Internet addiction (p. 201)
Hypnosis (p. 202)
Role theory (p. 204)
Response set theory (p. 204)
Neodissociation theory (p. 204)
Transcendental meditation (TM) (p. 205)

Biofeedback training (BFT) (p. 206)
Electromyograph (EMG) (p. 206)
Psychoactive substances (p. 208)
Depressant (p. 208)
Stimulant (p. 208)
Substance abuse (p. 209)
Tolerance (p. 209)
Abstinence syndrome (p. 209)
Delirium tremens (p. 209)
Cirrhosis of the liver (p. 214)
Wernicke–Korsakoff syndrome (p. 214)
Opiates (p. 214)

Narcotics (p. 214)
Opioids (p. 214)
Barbiturate (p. 215)
Amphetamines (p. 216)
Attention-deficit/ hyperactivity disorder (p. 216)
Hydrocarbons (p. 218)
Passive smoking (p. 218)
Hallucinogenic (p. 219)
Marijuana (p. 219)
Psychedelic (p. 219)
Hashish (p. 219)
LSD (p. 221)
Flashbacks (p. 221)
Mescaline (p. 221)
Phencyclidine (PCP) (p. 221)

ACTIVE LEARNING RESOURCES

Visit your Companion Website for Video, Quizzing, and Self-Assessment!

http://psychology.wadsworth.com/rathus_pcc9e
On this site you can access the Why Is Nicotine So Addictive? video highlighted by the Video Connections icon on p. 217. In addition there are many quizzing opportunities including interactive versions of the fill-in-the-blank Active Review sections in your book. You can also fill out and score the Self-Assessments on p. 212 and p. 223.

Study on the Go!

Don't have time to study right now? You can study on the go! Visit your companion website and download an audio version of the Recite—An Active Summary section to your media player.

ThomsonNOW

http://www.thomsonedu.com
Need help studying? This site is your one-stop study shop. Take a Pre-Test and Thomson NOW will generate a Personalized Study Plan based on your test results. The Study Plan will identify the topics you need to review and direct you to online resources to help you master those topics. You can then take a Post-Test to determine the concepts you have mastered and what you still need to work on.

Author Blog

What does your author have to say about the state of psychology? Visit your companion website every Tuesday and click on "Author Blog," where he'll talk about the most recent controversies and hot topics in psychology.

Truth or Fiction?

T F A single nauseating meal can give rise to a taste aversion that lasts for years.

T F Psychologists helped a young boy overcome his fear of rabbits by having him eat cookies while a rabbit was brought closer and closer.

T F Psychologists have devised a way to teach children while they are sleeping.

T F During World War II, a psychologist created a guided missile that would use pigeons to take the missile to its target.

T F Punishment is ineffective at stopping unwanted behavior.

T F You can train a rat to climb a ramp, cross a bridge, climb a ladder, pedal a toy car, and do several other tasks—all in proper sequence.

T F You have to make mistakes in order to learn.

T F Despite all the media hoopla, no scientific connection has been established between TV violence and real-life aggression.

 Go to **http://psychology.wadsworth.com/ rathus_pcc9e** to answer and score this Truth or Fiction quiz.

© Michael Newman/PhotoEdit

Learning

ylan Klebold and Eric Harris were engrossed in violent video games for hours at a time. They were particularly keen on a game named *Doom*. Harris had managed to reprogram *Doom* so that he, the player, became invulnerable and had an endless supply of weapons. He would "mow down" all the other characters in the game. His program caused some of the characters to ask God why they had been shot as they lay dying. Later on, Klebold and Harris asked some of their shooting victims at Columbine High School in Colorado whether they believed in God. One of the killers also referred to his shotgun as Arlene, the name of a character in *Doom* (Saunders, 2003).

In the small rural town of Bethel, Alaska, Evan Ramsey would play *Doom, Die Hard,* and *Resident Evil* for endless hours. Ramsey shot four people, killing two and wounding two. Afterward, he said the video games taught him that being shot would reduce a player's "health factor" but probably not be lethal.

Michael Carneal was also a fan of *Doom*—and another video game, *Redneck Rampage*. He showed up at school one morning with a semiautomatic pistol, two shotguns, and two rifles. He aimed them at people in a prayer group. Before he was finished, three of them lay dead and five were wounded. Although Carneal had had no appreciable experience with firearms, authorities noted that his aim was uncannily accurate. He fired just once at each person's head, as one would do to rack up points in a video game—especially a game that offers extra points for head shots.

The debate as to whether violence in media such as films, television, and video games fuels violence in the real world has been going on for more than 40 years. However, research strongly suggests that media violence is a risk factor for increasing emotional arousal, aggressive behavior, and violent thoughts (Anderson, 2003, 2004; Arriaga et al., 2006; Weber et al., 2006).

One reason to be particularly concerned about violent video games is that they require audience participation (Anderson et al., 2004). Players don't just watch; they *participate*. Violent games like *Grand Theft Auto* have grown increasingly popular. Some games reward players for killing police, prostitutes, and bystanders.

■ **What Are the Effects of Playing Violent Video Games?** Do violent video games provide a safe outlet for aggressive impulses? Do they encourage aggressive behavior? Do they teach players aggressive skills? Do they do some or all of the above?

Midway Games/Getty Images

Virtual weapons include guns, knives, flamethrowers, swords, clubs, cars, hands, and feet. Sometimes the player assumes the role of a hero, but it is also common for the player to assume the role of a criminal.

What do we *learn* from video games and other media, such as television, films, and books? The research suggests that we learn a great deal—not only aggressive skills, but also the idea that violence is the normal state of affairs.

We will return to this controversial issue later in the chapter. This is the chapter that deals with the psychology of learning. Most of what we learn may be helpful and adaptive. But there are exceptions, as in the case of violent video games.

Question: What *is* learning? Learning as defined in psychology is more than listening to teachers, honing skateboard jumps, or mastering use of an iPod. From the behaviorist perspective, **learning** is a relatively permanent change in behavior that arises from practice or experience. The behavioral perspective plays down the roles of cognition and choice. It suggests that players of violent video games went on rampages because they had been rewarded or reinforced for similar behavior in games.

Cognitive psychologists define learning as a mental change that may or may not be associated with changes in behavior. These mental changes may affect, but do not directly cause, changes in behavior. From this perspective, the participants in the video games had acquired skills that enabled them to attack people, but they had then chosen to attack others. Learning, for cognitive psychologists, may be *shown* by changes in behavior, but learning itself is a mental process. Cognitive psychologists suggest that people choose whether or not to imitate the aggressive and other behaviors they observe, and that people are most likely to imitate behaviors that are consistent with their values.

In many animals, much behavior is instinctive, or inborn, rather than learned. For example, tadpoles start out life swimming but, after they develop legs, they hop on land in appropriate frog fashion—without taking hopping lessons. Salmon instinctively use the sense of smell to find, and return to spawn in, the stream where they were hatched after they have spent years roaming the seas. Robins instinctively know how to sing the song of their species and to build nests.

Among humans, however, the variety and complexity of behavior patterns are largely products of experience. We learn to read, to compute numbers, and to surf the Internet. It is natural to experience hunger, but humans learn to seek out the foods that are preferred in their culture. We learn which behavior patterns are deemed socially acceptable and which are considered wrong. We also unfortunately learn prejudices and stereotypes and negative behaviors such as using violence to deal with conflict. Our families and communities use verbal guidance, set examples, and apply rewards and punishments to teach us and transmit cultural values.

Sometimes learning experiences are direct, as when we are praised for doing something properly. But we can also learn from the experiences of others. We learn about the past, other peoples, and how to put things together from other people, books, and audiovisual media. In this chapter we consider various kinds of learning, including conditioning and learning in which cognition plays a more central role.

Learning (1) According to behaviorists, a relatively permanent change in behavior that results from experience. (2) According to cognitive theorists, the process by which organisms make relatively permanent changes in the way they represent the environment because of experience. These changes influence the organism's behavior but do not fully determine it.

■ **Instinct** The bird builds a nest on the basis of its genetic code. It is an example of instinctive behavior, which is not learned through experience.

Getty Images/Image Bank

Classical Conditioning: Learning What Is Linked to What

Classical conditioning involves some of the ways in which we learn to associate events with other events. Consider this: We have a distinct preference for a grade of A rather than F. We are also (usually) more likely to stop for a red light than for a green light. Why? We are not born with instinctive attitudes toward the letters *A* and *F*. Nor are we born knowing that red means "stop" and green means "go." We

Classical conditioning A simple form of learning in which an organism comes to associate or anticipate events. A neutral stimulus comes to evoke the response usually evoked by another stimulus by being paired repeatedly with the other stimulus. (Cognitive theorists view classical conditioning as the learning of relationships among events so as to allow an organism to represent its environment.) Also referred to as *respondent conditioning* or *Pavlovian conditioning*.

Reflex A simple unlearned response to a stimulus.

Stimulus An environmental condition that elicits a response.

Unconditioned stimulus (UCS) A stimulus that elicits a response from an organism prior to conditioning.

Unconditioned response (UCR) An unlearned response to an unconditioned stimulus.

Orienting reflex An unlearned response in which an organism attends to a stimulus.

Conditioned stimulus (CS) A previously neutral stimulus that elicits a conditioned response because it has been paired repeatedly with a stimulus that already elicited that response.

Conditioned response (CR) In classical conditioning, a learned response to a conditioned stimulus.

FIGURE 6.1 **Pavlov's Demonstration of Conditioned Reflexes in Laboratory Dogs**
From behind a one-way mirror, a laboratory assistant sounds a tone and then places meat on the dog's tongue. After several pairings, the dog salivates in response to the tone alone. A tube collects saliva and passes it to a vial. The quantity of saliva is taken as a measure of the strength of the animal's response.

■ **Ivan Pavlov**

learn the meanings of these symbols because they are associated with other events. A's are associated with instructor approval and the likelihood of getting into graduate school. Stopping at red lights is associated with avoiding accidents and traffic citations.

Question: What is classical conditioning? Classical conditioning is a simple form of associative learning that enables organisms to anticipate events. If the name Ivan Pavlov rings a bell with us, it is most likely because of his research in learning with dogs. **Question: What is the contribution of Ivan Pavlov to the psychology of learning?** Ivan Pavlov (1927) made his great contribution to the psychology of learning by accident. Pavlov was actually attempting to identify neural receptors in the mouth that triggered a response from the salivary glands. But his efforts were hampered by the dogs' annoying tendency to salivate at undesired times, such as when a laboratory assistant was clumsy and banged the metal food trays.

Just as you salivate after you've taken a big bite of cake, a dog salivates if meat powder is placed on its tongue. Pavlov was dosing his dogs with meat powder for his research because he knew that salivation in response to meat powder is a reflex. Reflexes are unlearned and evoked by certain stimuli. Pavlov discovered that reflexes can also be learned, or *conditioned,* by association. His dogs began salivating in response to clanging food trays because clanging, in the past, had been repeatedly paired with arrival of food. The dogs would also salivate when an assistant entered the laboratory. Why? In the past, the assistant had brought food.

Pavlov at first viewed the extra salivation of his dogs as a hindrance to his research. But then it dawned on him that this "problem" might be worth looking into. He found out that he could train, or condition, his dogs to salivate in response to any stimulus.

In his initial experiments, Pavlov trained dogs to salivate when he sounded a tone. Pavlov termed these trained salivary responses "conditional reflexes." They were *conditional* upon the repeated pairing of a previously neutral stimulus (such as the clanging of a food tray) and a stimulus (in this case, food) that evoked the target response (in this case, salivation). Today, conditional reflexes are generally referred to as *conditioned responses*.

Pavlov demonstrated conditioned responses by strapping a dog into a harness like the one shown in Figure 6.1. When meat powder was placed on the dog's tongue, it salivated. Pavlov repeated the process several times, with one difference. He preceded the meat powder by half a second or so with the sounding of a tone on each occasion. After several pairings of the meat powder and the tone, Pavlov sounded the tone but did *not* follow it with the meat powder. Still the dog salivated. It had learned to salivate in response to the tone.

Stimuli and Responses in Classical Conditioning

In Pavlov's experiment, the meat powder is an unlearned or **unconditioned stimulus (UCS).** Salivation in response to the meat powder is an unlearned or **unconditioned response (UCR).** The tone was at first a meaningless or neutral stimulus; it might have caused the dog to look in the direction of the sound—an **orienting reflex.** But the tone was not yet associated with food. Then, through repeated association with the meat powder, the tone became a learned or **conditioned stimulus (CS)** for the salivation response. Salivation in response to the tone (or conditioned stimulus) is a learned or **conditioned response (CR).** Therefore, salivation can be either a conditioned response or an unconditioned response, depending on the method used to evoke the response (see Figure 6.2).

Here is a mini-experiment that many adults have tried. They smile at infants, say something like "kitchie-coo" (don't ask me why) and then tickle the infant's foot. Perhaps the infant laughs; it also usually curls or retracts the foot. After a few repetitions—which psychologists call "trials"—the adult's simply saying "kitchie-coo" is likely to be enough to cause the infant to laugh and retract its foot.

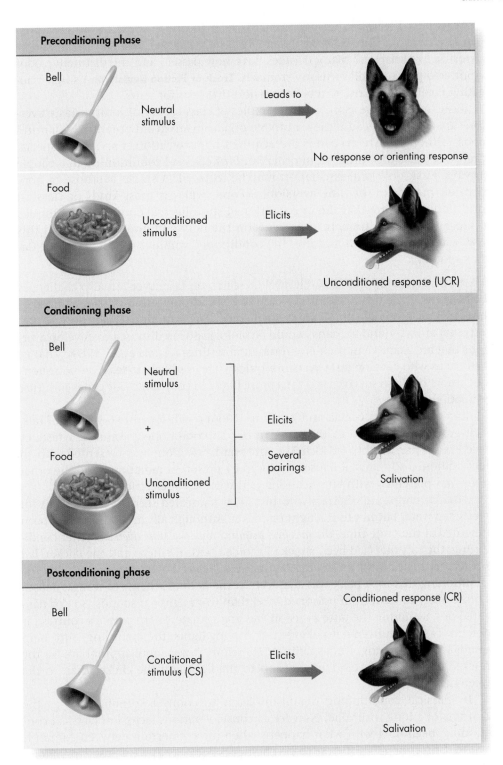

Preconditioning phase

Bell — Neutral stimulus — Leads to — No response or orienting response

Food — Unconditioned stimulus — Elicits — Unconditioned response (UCR)

Conditioning phase

Bell — Neutral stimulus

+

Food — Unconditioned stimulus — Elicits / Several pairings — Salivation

Postconditioning phase

Bell — Conditioned stimulus (CS) — Elicits — Conditioned response (CR) / Salivation

FIGURE 6.2 **A Schematic Representation of Classical Conditioning**

Prior to conditioning, food elicits salivation. The tone, a neutral stimulus, elicits either no response or an orienting response. During conditioning, the tone is rung just before meat is placed on the dog's tongue. After several repetitions, the tone, now a CS, elicits salivation, the CR.

Go to **http://psychology.wadsworth. com/rathus_pcc9e** to access an interactive version of this figure.

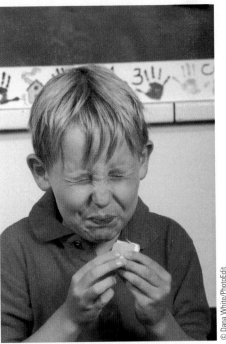

© Dana White/PhotoEdit

■ **Formation of a Taste Aversion?** Taste aversions can be acquired by means of a single pairing of the UCS and the CS. Evolutionary psychologists point out that the rapid acquisition of a taste aversion would make it more likely that an animal would survive and reproduce.

Taste Aversion: Are All Stimuli Created Equal?

When I was a child in The Bronx, my friends and I would go to the movies on Saturday mornings. One day my friends dared me to eat two huge containers of buttered popcorn by myself. I had no problem with the first enormous basket of buttered popcorn. More slowly—much more slowly—I forced down the second basket. I felt bloated and nauseated. The taste of the butter, corn, and salt lingered in my mouth and nose, and my head spun. It was obvious to me that no one could talk me into even another handful of popcorn that day. But I was surprised that I couldn't face buttered popcorn again for a year.

Years later I learned that psychologists refer to my response to buttered popcorn as a *taste aversion*. **Questions: What are taste aversions? Why are they of special interest to psychologists?** Many decades have now passed, and the distinctive odor of buttered popcorn still turns my stomach. **Truth or Fiction Revisited:** A single nauseating meal can give rise to a taste aversion that lasts for years.

Taste aversions are fascinating examples of classical conditioning. Taste aversions are adaptive because they motivate organisms to avoid potentially harmful foods. Although taste aversions are acquired by association, they are of special interest because they differ from other kinds of classical conditioning in a couple of ways. First, only one association may be required. A single overdose of popcorn left me with a lifetime aversion. Second, whereas most kinds of classical conditioning require that the unconditioned stimulus and conditioned stimulus be close together in time, in taste aversion the unconditioned stimulus (in this case, nausea) can occur hours after the conditioned stimulus (in this case, the flavor of food).

THE EVOLUTION OF TASTE AVERSION Research on taste aversion also challenges the behaviorist view that organisms learn to associate any stimuli that are linked in time. In reality, not all stimuli are created equal. The evolutionary perspective suggests that animals (and humans) would be biologically predisposed to develop aversions that are adaptive in their environmental settings (Garcia et al., 1989). That is, those of us who develop taste aversions quickly are less likely to feast on poisonous food, more likely to survive, and thus more likely to contribute our genes to future generations.

In a classic study, Garcia and Koelling (1966) conditioned two groups of rats. Each group was exposed to the same three-part conditioned stimulus: a taste of sweetened water, a light, and a clicker. Afterward, one group was presented with an unconditioned stimulus of nausea (induced by poison or radiation), and the other group was presented with an unconditioned stimulus of electric shock.

After conditioning, the rats who had been nauseated showed an aversion for sweetened water but not to the light or clicker. Although all three stimuli had been presented at the same time, *the rats had acquired only the taste aversion.* After conditioning, the rats that had been shocked avoided both the light and the clicker, *but they did not show a taste aversion to the sweetened water.* For each group of rats, the conditioning that took place was adaptive. In the natural scheme of things, nausea is more likely to stem from poisoned food than from lights or sounds. So, for nauseated rats, acquiring the taste aversion was appropriate. Sharp pain, in contrast, is more likely to stem from natural events involving lights (fire, lightning) and sharp sounds (twigs snapping, things falling). Therefore, it was more appropriate for the shocked animals to develop an aversion to the light and the clicker than to the sweetened water.

In classical conditioning organisms learn to connect stimuli, such as the sounding of a tone with food. Now let us consider various factors in classical conditioning, beginning with what happens when the connection between stimuli is severed. This is of great interest to psychologists because, as we will see, psychologists have used extinction to help people overcome fears.

Extinction and Spontaneous Recovery

Extinction and spontaneous recovery are aspects of conditioning that help us adapt by updating our expectations or revising our thinking about (representations of) the changing environment. For example, a dog may learn to associate a new scent (a conditioned stimulus) with the appearance of a dangerous animal. It can then take evasive action when it catches a whiff of that scent. A child may learn to connect hearing a car pull into the driveway (a conditioned stimulus) with the arrival of his or her parents (an unconditioned stimulus). Thus, the child may begin to squeal with delight (squealing is a conditioned response) when the car is heard.

EXTINCTION Question: What is the role of extinction in classical conditioning?
Extinction enters the picture when the times—and the relationships between
events—change. The once-dangerous animal may no longer be a threat. (What a
puppy perceives to be a threat may lose its fearsomeness once the dog matures.)
After moving to a new house, the child's parents may commute by means of public transportation. The sound of a car in a nearby driveway may signal a neighbor's,
not a parent's, homecoming. When conditioned stimuli (such as the scent of a dog
or the sound of a car) are no longer followed by unconditioned stimuli (a dangerous animal, a parent's homecoming), they lose their ability to elicit conditioned
responses. In this way the organism adapts to a changing environment.

In classical conditioning, extinction is the process by which conditioned stimuli lose the ability to elicit conditioned responses, because the conditioned stimuli
are no longer associated with unconditioned stimuli. That is, the puppy loses its
fear of the scent of the neighbor's dog, or the toddler is no longer gleeful at the
sounds of the car in the driveway. From the cognitive perspective, extinction
changes the animal's mental representation of its environment, because the conditioned stimulus no longer allows it to make the same prediction.

In experiments on the extinction of conditioned responses, Pavlov found that
repeated presentations of the conditioned stimulus (in this case, the tone) without
the unconditioned stimulus (in this case, meat powder) led to extinction of the conditioned response (salivation in response to the tone). Basically, the dog stopped
salivating at the sound of the tone. Interestingly, Figure 6.3 shows that a dog was
conditioned to begin to salivate in response to a tone after two or three pairings of
the tone with meat powder. Continued pairings of the stimuli led to increased salivation (measured in number of drops of saliva). After seven or eight trials, salivation
leveled off at 11 to 12 drops.

In the next series of experiments, salivation in response to the tone was extinguished through several trials in which the tone was presented without the meat
powder. After about 10 extinction trials, the animal no longer salivated. That is, it no
longer showed the conditioned response when the tone was sounded.

Extinction An experimental procedure in which
stimuli lose their ability to evoke learned
responses because the events that had followed
the stimuli no longer occur. (The learned
responses are said to be *extinguished*.)

FIGURE 6.3 Learning and Extinction Curves

Actual data from Pavlov (1927) compose the jagged line, and the curved lines are idealized. In the acquisition phase, a dog salivates (shows a CR)
in response to a tone (CS) after a few trials in which the tone is paired with meat powder (the UCS). Afterward, the CR is extinguished in about
ten trials during which the CS is not followed by the UCS. After a rest period, the CR recovers spontaneously. A second series of extinction trials
leads to more rapid extinction of the CR.

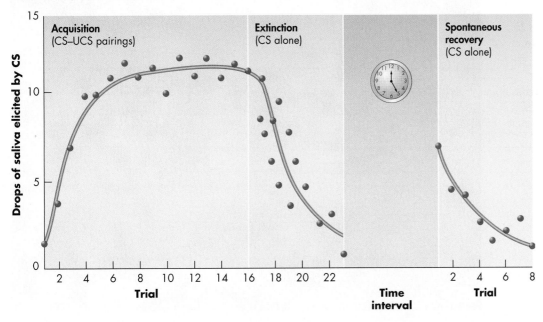

Now, what will happen if we allow a couple of days to pass and then sound the tone again? **Question: What is the role of spontaneous recovery in classical conditioning?**

SPONTANEOUS RECOVERY We asked what would happen if we were to allow a day or two to pass after we had extinguished salivation in Pavlov's dog and then again sounded he tone? Where would you place your bet? Would the dog salivate or not?

If you bet that the dog would again show the conditioned response (in this case, salivation in response to the tone), you were correct. Organisms tend to show **spontaneous recovery** of extinguished conditioned responses merely as a function of the passage of time. For this reason, the term *extinction* may be a bit misleading. When a species of animal becomes extinct, all the members of that species capable of reproducing have died. The species vanishes. But the experimental extinction of conditioned responses does not lead to their permanent eradication. Rather, it seems that they *inhibit* the response. The response remains available for future performance under the "right" conditions.

Evolutionary psychologists note that spontaneous recovery, like extinction, is adaptive. What would happen if the child heard no car in the driveway for several months? It could be that the next time a car entered the driveway, the child would associate the sounds with a parent's homecoming (rather than with the arrival of a neighbor). This expectation could be appropriate. After all, *something* had changed when no car entered the nearby driveway for so long. In the wild, a water hole may contain water for only a couple of months during the year. But evolution would favor the survival of animals that associate the water hole with the thirst drive from time to time so that they will return to it when it again holds water.

As time passes and the seasons change, things sometimes follow circular paths and arrive where they were before. Spontaneous recovery seems to function as a mechanism whereby organisms can adapt successfully to situations that recur from time to time.

Generalization and Discrimination

No two things are exactly alike. Traffic lights are hung at slightly different heights, and shades of red and green differ a little. The barking of two dogs differs, and the sound of the same animal differs slightly from one bark to the next. Rustling sounds in the undergrowth differ, but evolution would favor the survival of rabbits and deer that flee when they perceive any one of many possible rustling sounds.

■ **Spontaneous Recovery of the Tendency to Visit a Water Hole after Time Has Passed** If a water hole dries up, animals' tendencies to go to the water hole in a given season may be extinguished. However, when another season rolls around, the tendency to visit the water hole may spontaneously recover. Evolution would favor the survival of animals that associate the water hole with reduction of the thirst drive from time to time so that they are likely to return to it when it again holds water.

Adaptation requires us to respond similarly (or *generalize*) to stimuli that are equivalent in function and to respond differently to (or *discriminate* between) stimuli that are not. **Question: What is the role of generalization in classical conditioning?**

GENERALIZATION Pavlov noted that responding to different stimuli as though they are functionally equivalent—*generalizing*—is adaptive for animals. **Generalization** is the tendency for a conditioned response to be evoked by stimuli that are similar to the stimulus to which the response was conditioned. Pavlov demonstrated generalization by getting his dog to salivate when it was shown a circle. Then later the dog salivated in response to being shown closed geometric figures—even squares! The more closely the figure resembled a circle, however, the greater the *strength* of the response (as measured by drops of saliva).

But what happens if food follows the presentation of a circle but not a square? **Question: What is the role of discrimination in classical conditioning?**

DISCRIMINATION Organisms must also learn that (1) many stimuli perceived as being similar are functionally different and (2) they must respond adaptively to each. During the first couple of months of life, for example, babies can discriminate their mother's voice from those of other women. They often stop crying when they hear their mother but not when they hear a stranger.

Pavlov showed that a dog conditioned to salivate in response to circles could be trained *not* to salivate in response to ellipses. After a while, the dog no longer salivated in response to the ellipses. Instead, it showed **discrimination:** It salivated only in response to circles. Pavlov found that increasing the difficulty of the discrimination task apparently tormented the dog. After the dog was trained to salivate in response to circles but not ellipses, Pavlov showed it a series of progressively rounder ellipses. Eventually the dog could no longer distinguish the ellipses from circles. The animal was so stressed that it urinated, defecated, barked profusely, and snapped at laboratory personnel.

How do we explain the dog's belligerent behavior? In a classic work written more than 65 years ago, titled *Frustration and Aggression,* a group of behaviorally oriented psychologists suggested that frustration induces aggression (Dollard et al., 1939). Why is failure to discriminate circles from ellipses frustrating? For one thing, in such experiments, rewards—such as food—are usually contingent on correct discrimination. That is, if the dog errs, it doesn't get fed. Cognitive theorists, however, disagree (Rescorla, 1988). They would say that in Pavlov's experiment, the dog lost the ability to adjust its mental map of the environment as the ellipses grew more circular. Thus it was frustrated.

Daily living requires appropriate generalization and discrimination. No two hotels are alike, but when we travel from one city to another it is adaptive to expect to stay in a hotel. It is encouraging that a green light in Washington has the same meaning as a green light in Paris. But returning home in the evening requires the ability to discriminate between our home and those of others. And imagine the confusion that would occur if we could not discriminate our friends, mates, or coworkers from other people!

Higher-Order Conditioning

Consider a child who is burned by touching a hot stove. After this experience, the sight of the stove may evoke fear. And because hearing the word *stove* may evoke a mental image of the stove, just hearing the word may evoke fear.

Do you recall the mini-experiment in which an adult smiles, says "kitchie-coo," and then tickles an infant's foot? After a few repetitions, just smiling at the infant may cause the infant to retract its foot. In fact, just walking into the room may have the same effect! The experiences with touching the hot stove and tickling the infant's foot are examples of higher-order conditioning. **Question: What is higher-order conditioning?**

Generalization In conditioning, the tendency for a conditioned response to be evoked by stimuli that are similar to the stimulus to which the response was conditioned.

Discrimination In conditioning, the tendency for an organism to distinguish between a conditioned stimulus and similar stimuli that do not forecast an unconditioned stimulus.

■ **Generalization at the Crossroads** Chances are that you have never seen this particular traffic light in this particular setting. Because of generalization, however, we can safely bet that you would know what to do—stop or go—if you were to drive up to it.

© Robert T. Nowitz/CORBIS

In **higher-order conditioning,** a previously neutral stimulus (for example, hearing the word "stove" or seeing the adult who had done the tickling enter the room) comes to serve as a learned or conditioned stimulus after being paired repeatedly with a stimulus that has already become a learned or conditioned stimulus (for example, seeing the stove or hearing the phrase "kitchie-coo"). Pavlov demonstrated higher-order conditioning by first conditioning a dog to salivate in response to a tone. He then repeatedly paired the shining of a light with the sounding of the tone. After several pairings, shining the light (the higher-order conditioned stimulus) came to evoke the response (salivation) that had been elicited by the tone (the first-order conditioned stimulus).

Your Turn: Now that we have discussed classical conditioning, enhance your mastery of the material with the nearby "Learning Connections." Review the material by filling in the blanks, reflect on the material by relating it to other things you know, and think critically about it.

 Learning Connections | CLASSICAL CONDITIONING: LEARNING WHAT COMES AFTER WHAT

ACTIVE REVIEW (1) Behaviorists define learning in terms of a change in _____. (2) Cognitive psychologists define learning in terms of a change in the way organisms mentally _____ the environment. (3) A _____ is an environmental condition that evokes a response from an organism. (4) A response to an unconditioned stimulus (UCS) is called an _____ response (UCR). (5) A response to a conditioned stimulus (CS) is termed a _____ response (CR). (6) In conditioning a taste aversion, (*Only one* or *Several?*) association(s) is/are usually required. (7) Repeated presentation of a CS (e.g., a tone) without the UCS (e.g., meat) will _____ the CR (salivation). (8) Extinguished responses often show _____ recovery as a function of the passage of time. (9) In stimulus _____, organisms show a conditioned response in response to a range of stimuli similar to the conditioned stimulus. (10) In stimulus _____, organisms learn to show a conditioned response in response to a more limited range of stimuli. (11) In _____-order conditioning, a previously neutral stimulus comes to serve as a conditioned stimulus after being paired repeatedly with another conditioned stimulus.

REFLECT AND RELATE Had you heard or used the expression "That rings a bell"? If so, what did you think it meant? Did you know where the expression came from? Is the phrase historically accurate?

CRITICAL THINKING Critical thinkers pay attention to the definitions of terms. Psychologists disagree on the definition of learning. Behaviorists define learning as a relatively permanent change in behavior that arises from experience. Cognitive psychologists define learning as a matter of experience changing the way in which an organism represents the environment. Why do they have these different approaches?

Would behaviorists say that after a few pairings of a tone with food that a dog "knows" that the tone "means" food is on its way? Why or why not?

 Go to **http://psychology.wadsworth.com/ rathus_pcc9e** for an interactive version of this Learning Connections unit.

Higher-order conditioning (1) According to behaviorists, a classical conditioning procedure in which a previously neutral stimulus comes to elicit the response brought forth by a *conditioned* stimulus by being paired repeatedly with that conditioned stimulus. (2) According to cognitive psychologists, the learning of relationships among events, none of which evokes an unlearned response.

Counterconditioning A fear-reduction technique in which pleasant stimuli are associated with fear-evoking stimuli so that the fear-evoking stimuli lose their aversive qualities.

Applications of Classical Conditioning

In the nearby "In Profile," we meet one of the celebrities of the science of psychology, "Little Albert." Albert did not seek his fame; after all, he was under a year old at the time. At that tender age he was conditioned by John B. Watson to fear rats, and, by generalization, furry animals. Soon afterward, a protégé of Watson carried out a well-known experiment in **counterconditioning** of fears. Unfortunately, it didn't do Albert any good. Albert's mother, distraught at the events that had occurred, removed her son from the laboratory. Even if Albert didn't benefit from counterconditioning, psychologists have helped other people use it to reduce fears. Let us consider counterconditioning and other applications of classical conditioning.

In Profile   "LITTLE ALBERT"

If you happen across a gentleman in his 80s who cringes at the sight of a fur coat, he may not be concerned about animal rights. Perhaps he is "Little Albert," who was conditioned to fear furry objects before he reached his first birthday.

In 1920 the behaviorist John B. Watson and his future wife, Rosalie Rayner, published a report of their demonstration that emotional reactions can be acquired through classical conditioning. The subject of their demonstration was a lad who has become known as "Little Albert" (a counterpart to

Freud's famous case study of "Little Hans"—see Chapter 15). At the age of 11 months, Albert was a phlegmatic fellow. He wasn't given to ready displays of emotion. But he did enjoy playing with a laboratory rat. Using a method that many psychologists have criticized as unethical, Watson startled Little Albert by clanging steel bars behind his head whenever the infant played with the rat. After repeated pairings, Albert showed fear of the rat even when the clanging was halted. Albert's fear also generalized to objects that were similar in appearance to the rat, such as a rabbit and the fur collar on a woman's coat. This study has become a hallmark in psychology, although Watson has also been criticized for not attempting to *countercondition* Albert's fear.

 Go to **http://psychology.wadsworth.com/ rathus_pcc9e** to access more information about "Little Albert."

Archives of the History of American Psychology

Counterconditioning

The reasoning behind counterconditioning is this: If fears, as Watson had shown, could be conditioned by painful experiences, perhaps fears could be *counterconditioned* by substituting pleasant experiences. In 1924, Watson's protégé Mary Cover Jones attempted counterconditioning with a two-year-old boy called Peter as a method of counteracting fear.

Peter had an intense fear of rabbits. Jones arranged for a rabbit to be gradually brought closer to Peter while he engaged in some of his favorite activities, such as munching on candy and cookies. **Truth or Fiction Revisited:** Thus, it is true that psychologists helped a young boy overcome his fear of rabbits by having him eat cookies while a rabbit was brought progressively closer. Jones first placed the rabbit in a far corner of the room while Peter munched and crunched. Peter cast a wary eye, but he continued to consume the treat. Gradually the animal was brought closer until eventually Peter ate treats and touched the rabbit at the same time. Jones theorized that the joy of eating was incompatible with fear and thus counterconditioned it.

Flooding and Systematic Desensitization

If Mary Cover Jones had simply plopped the rabbit on Peter's lap rather than bring it gradually closer, she would have been using the method of **flooding.** Had she done so, the cookies on the plate, not to mention those already eaten, might have decorated the walls—even if the method eventually worked.

Flooding and systematic desensitization, like counterconditioning, are behavior therapy methods for reducing fears. They are based on the classical conditioning principle of extinction (Wolpe & Plaud, 1997). In flooding, the client is exposed to the fear-evoking stimulus until the fear response is extinguished. Little Albert, for example, might have been placed in close contact with a rat until his fear had become fully extinguished. In extinction, the conditioned stimulus (in this case, the rat) is presented repeatedly in the absence of the unconditioned stimulus (the clanging of the steel bars) until the conditioned response (fear) is no longer evoked.

A German study of 75 people aged 18 to 54 evaluated the effectiveness of a flooding-type treatment for agoraphobia (fear of being out in busy, open areas) (Fischer et al., 1998). Agoraphobic participants were exposed persistently—for two to three weeks, all day long—to densely populated, open places. Participants were assessed immediately after, six months after, and as much as 53 months after treatment, and they showed significant reductions in anxiety and in avoidance of busy, open places.

Video Connections—Little Albert Click on the "Little Albert" video link on your companion website and you can watch the historic albeit unethical video of John B. Watson and Rosalie Rayner conditioning Little Albert. You will learn more about the process of classical conditioning and have the opportunity to decide how you would go about reversing Albert's fear of rats.

Flooding A behavioral fear-reduction technique based on principles of classical conditioning. Fear-evoking stimuli (CSs) are presented continuously in the absence of actual harm so that fear responses (CRs) are extinguished.

■ **Will Fear of Busy, Open Places Be Extinguished by Persistent Exposure?** Research results are encouraging. It seems that persistent exposure of agoraphobic individuals to busy, open areas reduces their anxiety and their avoidance of such places.

Annabella Bluesky/Photo Researchers, Inc.

Although flooding is usually effective, it is unpleasant. (When you are fearful of rats, being placed in a small room with one is no picnic.) For this reason, behavior therapists frequently prefer to use **systematic desensitization,** in which the client is gradually exposed to fear-evoking stimuli under circumstances in which he or she remains relaxed. For example, while feeling relaxed, Little Albert might have been given an opportunity to look at photos of rats or to see live rats from a distance before they were brought closer to him. Systematic desensitization takes longer than flooding but is not as unpleasant.

The Bell-and-Pad Treatment for Bed-Wetting

By the age of 5 or 6, children normally awaken in response to the sensation of a full bladder. They inhibit the urge to urinate immediately, which is an automatic or reflexive response to bladder tension, and instead go to the bathroom to do so. However, some children tend not to respond to bladder tension while asleep. They remain asleep and frequently wet their beds.

By means of the bell-and-pad method, children are taught to wake up in response to bladder tension. They sleep on a special sheet or pad that has been placed on the bed. When the child starts to urinate, the water content of the urine causes an electrical circuit in the pad to close. The closing of the circuit triggers a bell or buzzer, and the child is awakened. (Similar buzzer circuits have been built into training pants as an aid to toilet training.) In terms of classical conditioning, the bell is an unconditioned stimulus that wakes the child (waking up is the unconditioned response). By means of repeated pairings, a stimulus that precedes the bell becomes associated with the bell and also gains the capacity to awaken the child. What is that stimulus? The sensation of a full bladder. **Truth or Fiction Revisited:** In this way, bladder tension gains the capacity to awaken the child *even though the child is asleep during the classical conditioning procedure.*

The bell-and-pad method is a superb example of why behaviorists prefer to explain the effects of classical conditioning in terms of the pairing of stimuli and not in terms of what the learner knows. The behaviorist may argue that we cannot assume a sleeping child "knows" that wetting the bed will cause the bell to ring. We can only note that by repeatedly pairing bladder tension with the bell, the child eventually *learns* to wake up in response to bladder tension alone. *Learning* is demonstrated by the change in the child's behavior. One can only speculate on what the child *knows* about the learning process.

Systematic desensitization A behavioral fear-reduction technique in which a hierarchy of fear-evoking stimuli is presented while the person remains relaxed.

In any event, it appears that humans are capable of learning by means of simple association. In terms of the evolutionary perspective, it would appear that organisms that can learn by means of several routes—including conditioning and conscious reflection—would have a greater chance of survival than organisms whose learning is limited to a single route.

Your Turn: Now that we have explored various applications of classical conditioning, enhance your mastery of the material with the nearby "Learning Connections." Review the material by filling in the blanks, reflect on the material by relating it to other things you know, and think critically about it.

 Learning Connections | **APPLICATIONS OF CLASSICAL CONDITIONING**

ACTIVE REVIEW (12) John B. Watson and Rosalie Rayner used conditioning to teach "Little _____" to fear rats. (13) Mary Cover Jones taught a little boy to overcome his fear of rabbits by means of _____. (14) In the behavior-therapy method of _____, a client is continuously exposed to a fear-evoking stimulus until the fear response is extinguished. (15) In systematic _____, the client is gradually exposed to fear-evoking stimuli under circumstances in which he or she remains relaxed. (16) In the _____-and-pad treatment for bed-wetting, a child is taught to awaken in the night when he or she has to urinate.

REFLECT AND RELATE Can you think of an instance in your childhood when a caregiver used a method similar to counterconditioning, flooding, or systematic desensitization to encourage you to overcome a fear?

CRITICAL THINKING What concepts of learning can we use to explain the effects of the bell-and-pad treatment for bed-wetting? (Is it possible to explain the effectiveness of the method in terms of what a child "knows"?)

Go to **http://psychology.wadsworth.com/ rathus_pcc9e** for an interactive version of this Learning Connections unit.

Operant Conditioning: Learning What Does What to What

Through classical conditioning, we learn to associate stimuli so that a simple, usually passive, response made to one stimulus is then made in response to the other. In the case of Little Albert, clanging noises were associated with presentation of a rat. As a result, the rat came to elicit the fear response caused by the clanging. However, classical conditioning is only one kind of learning that occurs in these situations. After Little Albert acquired his fear of the rat, his voluntary behavior changed. He avoided the rat as a way of reducing his fear. Thus, Little Albert engaged in another kind of learning—*operant conditioning.* In operant conditioning, organisms learn to do things—or *not* to do things—because of the consequences of their behavior. For example, I avoided buttered popcorn in order to prevent nausea. But we also seek fluids when we are thirsty, sex when we are aroused, and an ambient temperature of 68° to 70° F when we feel too hot or too cold. *Classical conditioning focuses on how organisms form anticipations about their environments. Operant conditioning focuses on what they* do *about them.*

We begin this section with the historic research of psychologist Edward L. Thorndike. Then we will examine the more recent work of B. F. Skinner.

Edward L. Thorndike and the Law of Effect

In the 1890s stray cats were mysteriously disappearing from the streets and alleyways of Harlem. Some of them, it turned out, were being brought to the quarters of Columbia University doctoral student Edward Thorndike. Thorndike was using the cats as subjects in experiments on the effects of rewards and punishments on learning.

Thorndike placed the cats in so-called "puzzle boxes." If the animal managed to pull a dangling string, a latch would be released, allowing it to jump out and reach a

In Profile "ROGER MOORE"

Who is the real Roger Moore? The British actor who played James Bond in a number of films, or the octopus of the same name? Researchers at England's Brighton University found that octopi (or, if you prefer, octopuses) are capable of learning to get into a jam—a jam jar, that is—more efficiently over time as a result of a crabby reward—crab meat, that is (Octopus, 2000). They dubbed their star octopus Roger Moore, apparently because Moore had played Bond in one film named *Octopussy.*

"We lowered a jam jar into his tank," explained biologist Tim Fullford. "We put a crab inside the jam jar. The first recorded time for opening the jar was 21 minutes. In three days, he got down to a minute." But how soon they forget! After a day or two without crabbing the response is no longer shown. Crabbing again becomes a matter of trial and error.

bowl of food. When first placed in a puzzle box, a cat would try to squeeze through any opening and would claw and bite at the confining bars and wire. It would claw at anything it could reach. Through such random behavior, it might take 3 to 4 minutes for the cat to chance upon the response of pulling the string. Pulling the string would open the cage and allow the cat to reach the food. When placed back in the cage, it might again take several minutes for the animal to pull the string. But with repetition, it took progressively less time for the cat to pull the string. After seven or eight repetitions, the cat might pull the string immediately when placed back in the box.

THE LAW OF EFFECT Thorndike explained the cat's learning to pull the string in terms of his **law of effect.** According to this law, a response (such as string pulling) is—to use Thorndike's term— "stamped in" (that is, strengthened)—in a particular situation (such as being inside a puzzle box) by a reward (escaping from the box and eating). Rewards, that is, "stamp in" S–R (stimulus–response) connections. Punishments—using Thorndike's terminology once again—"stamp out" stimulus–response connections. That is, organisms would learn *not* to engage in behavior that brings on punishment. Later we shall see that the effects of punishment on learning are not so certain.

B. F. Skinner and Reinforcement

Law of effect Thorndike's principle that responses are "stamped in" by rewards and "stamped out" by punishments.

When it comes to unusual war stories, few will top that of B. F. Skinner. One of Skinner's wartime efforts was "Project Pigeon." **Question: What is the contribution of B. F. Skinner to the psychology of learning?**

In Profile BURRHUS FREDERIC SKINNER

During his first TV appearance, the psychologist B. F. Skinner (1904–1990) was asked, "Would you, if you had to choose, burn your children or your books?" He said with a wry smile that he would have chosen to burn his children, because his contribution to the future lay more in his writings than in his genes. Skinner delighted in controversy and enjoyed shocking TV viewers with his irreverent wit.

Skinner was born into a middle-class Pennsylvania family. As a youth he was always building things—scooters, sleds, wagons, rafts, slides, and merry-go-rounds. Later he would become famous for building the so-called Skinner box, which improved on Thorndike's puzzle box as a way of studying operant behavior. He earned an undergraduate degree in English and turned to psychology only after failing to make his mark as a writer in New York's Greenwich Village.

A great popularizer of his own views, Skinner used reinforcement to teach pigeons to play basketball and the piano—sort of. On a visit to his daughter's grammar school class, it occurred to him that similar techniques might work with children. Thus he developed *programmed learning.* Although he had earlier failed at writing, he gathered a cultish following when he published *Walden Two* (1948), a novel in which children are socialized to *want* to behave prosocially.

Skinner and his followers have applied his principles not only to programmed learning but also to behavior modification programs for helping people with disorders ranging from substance abuse to phobias to sexual dysfunctions. He died in 1990, eight days after receiving an unprecedented Lifetime Contribution to Psychology award from the American Psychological Association.

Go to **http://psychology.wadsworth.com/ rathus_pcc9e** to access more information about Burrhus Frederic Skinner.

© Christopher Johnson/Stock, Boston Inc./Picture Quest

Truth or Fiction Revisited: During World War II Skinner proposed that pigeons be trained to guide missiles to their targets. In their training, the pigeons would be **reinforced** with food pellets for pecking at targets projected onto a screen (see Figure 6.4). Once trained, the pigeons would be placed in missiles. Their pecking at similar targets displayed on a screen would correct the missile's flight path, resulting in a "hit" and a sacrificed pigeon. However, plans for building the necessary missile—for some reason called the *Pelican* and not the *Pigeon*—were scrapped. The pigeon equipment was too bulky and, Skinner lamented, his suggestion was not taken seriously. Might one conclude that the Defense Department decided that Project Pigeon was—forgive me—for the birds?

Project Pigeon may have been scrapped, but the principles of learning that Skinner applied to the project have found wide application. Project Pigeon also affords insight into the inventiveness of B. F. Skinner. Not only did Skinner make contributions to the understanding of learning, we will see that he also made technological innovations such as the "Skinner box" and the cumulative recorder. In operant conditioning, an animal learns to *do* something because of the effects or consequences of that behavior.

Skinner taught pigeons and other animals to engage in **operant behavior,** behavior that operates on, or manipulates, the environment. In classical conditioning, involuntary responses such as salivation or eyeblinks are often conditioned. In operant conditioning, *voluntary* responses such as pecking at a target, pressing a lever, or many of the skills required for playing tennis are acquired, or conditioned. **Question: What is operant conditioning?**

Operant conditioning is defined as a simple form of learning in which an organism learns to engage in certain behavior because of the effects of that behavior. In operant conditioning, we learn to engage in operant behaviors, also known simply as **operants,** that result in presumably desirable consequences such as food, a hug, an A on a test, attention, or social approval. Some children learn to conform their behavior to social rules to earn the attention and approval of their parents and teachers. Other children, ironically, may learn to "misbehave," because misbehavior also gets attention from other people. In particular, children may learn to be "bad" when their "good" behavior is routinely ignored. Some children who do not do well in school, in fact, seek reinforcement from deviant peers (Patterson et al., 2000).

Reinforce To follow a response with a stimulus that increases the frequency of the response.

Operant behavior Voluntary responses that are reinforced.

Operant conditioning A simple form of learning in which an organism learns to engage in behavior because it is reinforced.

Operant The same as an operant behavior.

Methods of Operant Conditioning

In his most influential work, *The Behavior of Organisms,* Skinner (1938) made many theoretical and technological innovations. Among them was his focus on discrete behaviors such as lever pressing as the *unit,* or type, of behavior to be studied (Glenn et al., 1992). Other psychologists might focus on how organisms think or "feel." Skinner focused on measurable things that they do. Many psychologists have found these kinds of behavior inconsequential, especially when it comes to explaining and predicting human behavior. But Skinner's supporters point out that focusing on discrete behavior creates the potential for helpful changes. For example, in helping people combat depression, one psychologist might focus on their

FIGURE 6.4 **Project Pigeon**
During World War II, B. F. Skinner suggested using operant conditioning to train pigeons to guide missiles to their targets. The pigeons would first be reinforced for pecking targets projected on a screen. Afterward, in combat, pecking the on-screen target would keep the missile on course.

 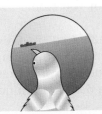    

FIGURE 6.5 **The Effects of Reinforcement**

One of the celebrities of modern psychology, a laboratory rat, earns its keep in a Skinner box. The animal presses a lever because of reinforcement—in the form of food pellets—delivered through the feeder. The habit strength of this operant is the frequency of lever pressing.

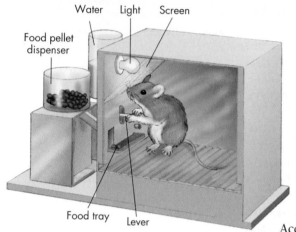

Water   Light   Screen

Food pellet dispenser

Food tray   Lever

"feelings." A Skinnerian psychologist would focus on cataloguing (and modifying) the types of things that depressed people actually *do*. Directly modifying depressive behavior might also brighten clients' self-reports about their "feelings of depression." The "Life Connections" section in the chapter on Methods of Therapy (Chapter 15) explains how people can use this principle in their own lives.

To study operant behavior efficiently, Skinner devised an animal cage (or "operant chamber") that has been dubbed the *Skinner box*. (Skinner himself repeatedly requested that his operant chamber *not* be called a Skinner box. History has thus far failed to honor his wishes, however.) Such a box is shown in Figure 6.5. The cage is ideal for laboratory experimentation because experimental conditions can be carefully introduced and removed, and the effects on laboratory animals (defined as changes in rates of lever pressing) can be carefully observed. The operant chamber (or Skinner box) is also energy-efficient—in terms of the energy of the experimenter. In contrast to Thorndike's puzzle box, a "correct" response does not allow the animal to escape and have to be recaptured and placed back in the box. According to psychologist John Garcia, Skinner's "great contribution to the study of behavior was the marvelously efficient operant methodology" (1993, p. 1158).

The rat in Figure 6.5 was deprived of food and placed in a Skinner box with a lever at one end. At first it sniffed its way around the cage and engaged in random behavior. When an animal behaves in a random manner, responses that have favorable consequences tend to occur more frequently. Responses that do not have favorable consequences are performed less frequently.

The rat's first pressing of the lever was inadvertent. However, because of this action, a food pellet dropped into the cage. The arrival of the food pellet increased the probability that the rat would press the lever again. The pellet is thus said to have *reinforced* lever pressing.

Skinner further mechanized his laboratory procedure by making use of a turning drum, or **cumulative recorder,** a tool that had previously been used by physiologists. The cumulative recorder provides a precise measure of operant behavior. Therefore, the experimenter need not even be present to record the number of correct responses.

Skinner's operant methodology even works when pigeons can fly in and out of "Skinner boxes" in the wild. Japanese researcher Ken'ichi Fuji (2002) poured commercial grain into the feeder, and several hundred pigeons flew in and out of the box over a three-month period. Although the pigeons generally learned to peck a key to obtain the grain, one pair of pigeons showed a fascinating variation on the theme. One of them always did the pecking, while the other always ate the grain!

In operant conditioning, it matters little how the first response that is reinforced comes to be made. The animal can happen on it by chance, as in random learning. The animal can also be physically guided to make the response. You may command your dog to "Sit!" and then press its backside down until it is in a sitting position. Finally you reinforce sitting with food or a pat on the head and a kind word. Animal trainers use physical guiding or coaxing to bring about the first "correct" response. Can you imagine how long it would take to train your dog if you waited for it to sit or roll over and then seized the opportunity to command it to sit or roll over? Both of you would age significantly in the process.

People, of course, can be verbally guided into desired responses when they are learning tasks such as spelling, adding numbers, or operating a machine. But they need to be informed when they have made the correct response. Knowledge of results often is all the reinforcement people need to learn new skills.

Cumulative recorder An instrument that records the frequency of an organism's operants (or "correct" responses) as a function of the passage of time.

Types of Reinforcers

Any stimulus which increases the probability that responses preceding it—whether pecking a button in a Skinner box or studying for a quiz—will be repeated serves as a reinforcer. **Question: What are the various kinds of reinforcers?** Reinforcers include food pellets when an animal has been deprived of food, water when it has been deprived of liquid, the opportunity to mate, and the sound of a tone that has previously been associated with eating. Skinner distinguished between positive and negative reinforcers.

POSITIVE AND NEGATIVE REINFORCERS **Positive reinforcers** increase the probability that a behavior will occur when they are applied. Food and approval usually serve as positive reinforcers. **Negative reinforcers** increase the probability that a behavior will occur when the reinforcers are *removed* (see Figure 6.6). People often learn to plan ahead so that they need not fear that things will go wrong. In such cases fear acts as a negative reinforcer, because *removal* of fear increases the probability that the behaviors preceding it (such as planning ahead) will be repeated.

Some reinforcers have more impact than others. For example, pigeons who learn that one food tray has more food than another choose the tray with more food (Olthof & Roberts, 2000). Similarly, you would probably choose a job that paid $1,000 over a similar job that paid $10. (If not, get in touch with me—I have some chores for you.) With sufficient reinforcement, operants become *habits*. They have a high probability of recurrence in certain situations.

IMMEDIATE VERSUS DELAYED REINFORCERS Immediate reinforcers are more effective than delayed reinforcers. Therefore, the short-term consequences of behavior often provide more of an incentive than the long-term consequences.

Some students socialize when they should be studying because the pleasure of socializing is immediate. Studying may not pay off until the final exam or graduation. (This is why younger students do better with frequent tests.) It is difficult to quit smoking cigarettes because the reinforcement of nicotine is immediate and the health hazards of smoking more distant. Focusing on short-term reinforcement is also connected with risky sexual behavior, such as engaging in sexual activity with someone who may be a stranger or failing to use devices to prevent pregnancy and sexually transmitted infections (Caffray & Schneider, 2000; Fuertes et al., 2002). One of the aspects of being human is the ability to foresee the long-range consequences of one's behavior and choices. But immediate reinforcers—such as those cookies staring in the face of the would-be dieter—can be powerful temptations indeed.

Positive reinforcer A reinforcer that when *presented* increases the frequency of an operant.

Negative reinforcer A reinforcer that when *removed* increases the frequency of an operant.

Procedure	Behavior	Consequence	Change in behavior
Use of positive reinforcement	Behavior (Studying)	Positive reinforcer (Teacher approval) is *presented* when student studies	Frequency of behavior *increases* (Student studies more)
Use of negative reinforcement	Behavior (Studying)	Negative reinforcer (Teacher disapproval) is *removed* when student studies	Frequency of behavior *increases* (Student studies more)

FIGURE 6.6 **Positive versus Negative Reinforcers**

All reinforcers *increase* the frequency of behavior. However, negative reinforcers are aversive stimuli that increase the frequency of behavior when they are *removed*. In these examples, teacher approval functions as a positive reinforcer when students study harder because of it. Teacher *disapproval* functions as a negative reinforcer when its *removal* increases the frequency of studying. Can you think of situations in which teacher approval might function as a negative reinforcer?

 Go to **http://psychology.wadsworth. com/rathus_pcc9e** to access an interactive version of this figure.

PRIMARY AND SECONDARY REINFORCERS We can also distinguish between primary and secondary, or conditioned, reinforcers. **Primary reinforcers** are effective because of the organism's biological makeup. Food, water, warmth (positive reinforcers), and pain (a negative reinforcer) all serve as primary reinforcers. **Secondary reinforcers** acquire their value through being associated with established reinforcers. For this reason they are also termed **conditioned reinforcers.** We may seek money because we have learned that it may be exchanged for primary reinforcers. Part of understanding others lies in being able to predict what they will find reinforcing.

Extinction and Spontaneous Recovery in Operant Conditioning

Keisha's teacher writes "Good" on all of her homework assignments before returning them. One day, her teacher no longer writes anything on the assignments—the reinforcement ends. Reinforcers are used to strengthen responses. What happens when reinforcement stops? **Question: What is the role of extinction in operant conditioning?**

In Pavlov's experiment, the meat powder was the event that followed and confirmed the appropriateness of salivation. In operant conditioning, the ensuing events are reinforcers. In operant conditioning the extinction of learned responses results from the repeated performance of operant behavior without reinforcement. If you go for a month without mail, you may stop checking the mailbox because the mail served as reinforcement. In other words, reinforcers maintain operant behavior or strengthen habitual behavior in operant conditioning.

Question: What is the role of spontaneous recovery in operant conditioning? Spontaneous recovery of learned responses occurs in operant conditioning as well as in classical conditioning. That is, checking the mailbox again after going without letters for a while is spontaneous recovery of checking the mailbox. Spontaneous recovery is adaptive in operant conditioning as well as in classical conditioning. Reinforcers may once again become available after time elapses, just as there are new tender sprouts on twigs when the spring arrives.

Reinforcers versus Rewards and Punishments

Reinforcers are defined as stimuli that increase the frequency of behavior. **Question: Why did Skinner make a point of distinguishing between reinforcers on the one hand and rewards and punishments on the other?** Reinforcers are known by their effects, whereas rewards and punishments are known by how they feel. It may be that most reinforcers—food, hugs, having the other person admit to starting the argument, and so on—feel good, or are pleasant events. Yet things that we might assume would feel bad, such as a slap on the hand, disapproval from a teacher, even suspensions and detention may be positively reinforcing to some—perhaps because such experiences confirm negative feelings toward teachers or one's belonging within a deviant subculture (Atkins et al., 2002).

Skinner preferred the concept of reinforcement to that of **reward** because reinforcement does not suggest trying to "get inside the head" of an organism (whether a human or lower animal) to guess what it would find pleasant or unpleasant. A list of reinforcers is arrived at scientifically, *empirically*—that is, by observing what sorts of stimuli increase the frequency of the behavior.

Punishments are defined as aversive events that suppress or decrease the frequency of the behavior they follow (see Figure 6.7). Punishment can rapidly suppress undesirable behavior (Gershoff, 2002) and may be warranted in "emergencies," such as when a child tries to run into the street. **Truth or Fiction Revisited:** Actually, punishment can work—that is, it can decrease the frequency of unwanted behavior.

Question: Why do many psychologists disapprove of punishment? However, many psychologists argue that punishment—especially corporal punishment—often fails to achieve the goals of parents, teachers, and others. Psychologist Elizabeth Gershoff

Primary reinforcer An unlearned reinforcer.

Secondary reinforcer A stimulus that gains reinforcement value through association with established reinforcers.

Conditioned reinforcer Another term for a secondary reinforcer.

Reward A pleasant stimulus that increases the frequency of the behavior it follows.

Punishment An unpleasant stimulus that suppresses the behavior it follows.

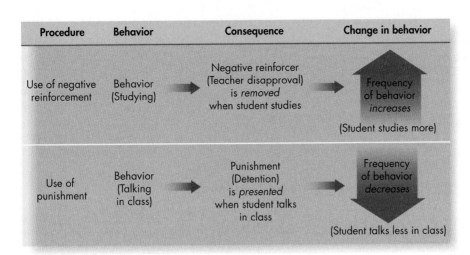

Procedure	Behavior	Consequence	Change in behavior
Use of negative reinforcement	Behavior (Studying)	Negative reinforcer (Teacher disapproval) is *removed* when student studies	Frequency of behavior *increases* (Student studies more)
Use of punishment	Behavior (Talking in class)	Punishment (Detention) is *presented* when student talks in class	Frequency of behavior *decreases* (Student talks less in class)

FIGURE 6.7 Negative Reinforcers versus Punishments

Negative reinforcers and punishments both tend to be aversive stimuli. However, reinforcers *increase* the frequency of behavior. Punishments *decrease* the frequency of behavior. Negative reinforcers increase the frequency of behavior when they are *removed*. Punishments decrease or suppress the frequency of behavior when they are *applied*. Can you think of situations in which punishing students might have effects other than those desired by the teacher?

 Go to **http://psychology.wadsworth.com/rathus_pcc9e** to access an interactive version of this figure.

(2002) analyzed 88 studies of more than 36,000 children and found connections between physical punishment (e.g., spanking) and various behavior patterns in childhood and adulthood. For example:

◆ Children who are physically punished are less likely to develop internal moral standards.
◆ Physical punishment is connected with poorer parent–child relationships.
◆ Physically punished children are more likely to be aggressive toward other children and to engage in criminal behavior later on.
◆ Physically punished children are more likely to abuse their spouses or their own children as adults.

Gershoff (2002) adds that punishment tends to suppress undesirable behavior only under circumstances in which its delivery is guaranteed. It does not take children long to learn that they can "get away with murder" with one parent or teacher but not with another. Moreover, punishment does not in itself suggest an alternative acceptable form of behavior.

There are some other reasons for not using physical punishment:

◆ It hurts.
◆ Punished individuals may withdraw from the situation. Severely punished children may run away, cut class, or drop out of school.
◆ Children also *learn* responses that are punished. Whether or not children choose to perform punished responses, punishment rivets their attention on them.

Gershoff's research findings have not gone unchallenged. Diana Baumrind and her colleagues (2002) point out, for example, that most of the studies examined by Gershoff were correlational, not experimental. Therefore, we cannot be certain about cause and effect. Consider the connection between parental punishment and childhood aggression. Does parental punishment contribute to childhood aggression, or are more aggressive children likely to frustrate their parents, leading their parents to use physical punishment? In any event, most psychologists tend to prefer rewarding children for desirable behavior to punishing them for unwanted behavior. By ignoring misbehavior, or by using **time out** from positive reinforcement, one can avoid reinforcing misbehavior.

To reward or positively reinforce children for desired behavior takes time and care. Avoiding the use of punishment is not enough. First, we must pay attention to children when they are behaving well. If we take their desirable behavior for granted and respond to them only when they misbehave, we may be encouraging

Time out Removal of an organism from a situation in which reinforcement is available when unwanted behavior is shown.

■ **A Discriminative Stimulus** You might not think that pigeons are very discriminating, yet they readily learn that pecking will not bring food in the presence of a discriminative stimulus such as a red light.

misbehavior. Second, we must be certain that children are aware of, and capable of performing, desired behavior. It is harmful and fruitless merely to punish children for unwanted behavior. We must also carefully guide them, either physically or verbally, into making the desired responses, and then reward them. We cannot teach children table manners by waiting for them to exhibit proper responses at random and then reinforcing them for their responses. Try holding a reward of ice cream behind your back and waiting for a child to exhibit proper manners. You will have a slippery dining room floor long before the child develops good table manners.

Discriminative Stimuli: Do You Step on the Accelerator when the Light Is Green or Red?

B. F. Skinner might not have been able to get his pigeons into the drivers' seats of missiles, but he had no problem training them to respond to traffic lights. Imagine yourself trying the following experiment.

You find a pigeon. Or you sit on a park bench, close your eyes, and one finds you. You place it in a Skinner box with a button on the wall. You drop a food pellet into the cage whenever the pigeon pecks the button. (Soon it will learn to peck the button whenever it has not eaten for a while.) Now you place a small green light in the cage and turn it on and off intermittently throughout the day. Reinforce button pecking with food whenever the green light is on, but not when the light is off. It will not take long for this clever city pigeon to learn that it will gain as much by grooming itself or cooing and flapping around as it will by pecking the button when the light is off.

The green light has become a discriminative stimulus. **Question: What are discriminative stimuli? Discriminative stimuli,** such as green or red lights, act as signals or cues. They provide information about when an operant (in the case of the pigeon, pecking a button) will be reinforced (by a food pellet being dropped into the cage).

Operants that are not reinforced tend to be extinguished. For the pigeon in our experiment, the behavior of pecking the button *when the light is off* is extinguished.

A moment's reflection will suggest many ways in which discriminative stimuli influence our behavior. Isn't it more efficient to answer the telephone when it is ringing? Do you think it is wise to ask someone for a favor when she or he is displaying anger and disapproval toward you?

We noted that a pigeon learns to peck a button if food drops into its cage when it does so. What if you want the pigeon to continue to peck the button, but you're running out of food? Do not despair. (Worse things have happened.) As we see in the following section, you can keep that bird pecking away indefinitely, even as you hold up on most of the food.

Schedules of Reinforcement: How Often? Under What Conditions?

In operant conditioning, some responses are maintained by means of **continuous reinforcement.** You probably become warmer every time you put on heavy clothing. You probably become less thirsty every time you drink water. Yet if you have ever watched people toss their money down the maws of slot machines, you know that behavior can also be maintained by means of **partial reinforcement. Questions: What are the various schedules of reinforcement? How do they affect behavior?**

Folklore about gambling is based on solid learning theory. You can get a person "hooked" on gambling by fixing the game so as to allow heavy winnings at first. Then you gradually space out the winnings (reinforcements) until gambling is maintained by infrequent winning—or even no winning at all. Partial reinforcement schedules can maintain gambling, like other behavior, for a great deal of time, even though it goes unreinforced (Pulley, 1998).

New operants or behaviors are acquired most rapidly through continuous reinforcement or, in some cases, through "one-trial learning" that meets with great

Discriminative stimulus In operant conditioning, a stimulus that indicates that reinforcement is available.

Continuous reinforcement A schedule of reinforcement in which every correct response is reinforced.

Partial reinforcement One of several reinforcement schedules in which not every correct response is reinforced.

reinforcement. People who cannot control their gambling often had big wins at the racetrack or casino or in the lottery in their late teens or early 20s (Greene, 1982). But once the operant has been acquired, it can be maintained by tapering off to a schedule of partial reinforcement.

Responses that have been maintained by partial reinforcement are more resistant to extinction than responses that have been maintained by continuous reinforcement (Rescorla, 1999). From the cognitive perspective, we could suggest that organisms that have experienced partial reinforcement do not expect reinforcement every time they engage in a response. Therefore, they are more likely to persist in the absence of reinforcement.

There are four basic types of reinforcement schedules. They are determined by changing either the *interval* of time that must elapse between correct responses before reinforcement occurs or the *ratio* (number) of responses that must occur before reinforcement is provided. If reinforcement of responses is immediate (zero seconds), the reinforcement schedule is continuous. A larger interval of time, such as 1 or 30 seconds, is one kind of partial-reinforcement schedule. A one-to-one (1:1) ratio of correct responses to reinforcements is also a continuous-reinforcement schedule. A higher ratio such as 2:1 or 5:1 creates another kind of partial-reinforcement schedule.

More specifically, the four basic reinforcement schedules are *fixed-interval, variable-interval, fixed-ratio,* and *variable-ratio* schedules, which we will discuss below.

INTERVAL SCHEDULES In a **fixed-interval schedule,** a fixed amount of time—say, a minute—must elapse before the correct response will result in a reinforcer. With a fixed-interval schedule, an organism's response rate falls off after each reinforcement and then picks up again as the time when reinforcement will occur approaches. For example, in a 1-minute fixed-interval schedule, a rat is reinforced with, say, a food pellet for the first operant—for example, the first pressing of a lever—that occurs after a minute has elapsed. After each reinforcement, the rat's rate of lever pressing slows down, but as the end of the 1-minute interval draws near, lever pressing increases in frequency, as suggested in Figure 6.8. It is as if the rat has learned that it must wait a while before it is reinforced. The resultant record on the cumulative recorder shows a series of characteristic upward-moving waves, or scallops, which are referred to as *fixed-interval scallops.*

Car dealers use fixed-interval reinforcement schedules when they offer incentives for buying up the remainder of the year's line every summer and fall. In a sense, they are suppressing buying at other times, except for consumers whose current cars are in their death throes or those with little self-control. Similarly, you learn to check your e-mail only at a certain time of day if your correspondent writes at that time each day.

Reinforcement is more unpredictable in a **variable-interval schedule.** Therefore, the response rate is steadier but lower. If the boss calls us in for a weekly report, we probably work hard to pull things together just before the report is to be given, just as we might cram the night before a weekly quiz. But if we know that the boss might call us in for a report on the progress of a certain project at any time (variable-interval schedule), we are likely to keep things in a state of reasonable readiness at all times. However, our efforts are unlikely to have the intensity they would in a fixed-interval schedule (for example, a weekly report). Similarly, we are less likely to cram for unpredictable pop quizzes than we are to study for regularly scheduled quizzes. But we are likely to do at least some studying on a regular basis. Likewise, if you receive e-mail from your correspondent irregularly, you are likely to check your e-mail regularly, but with less eagerness.

RATIO SCHEDULES In a **fixed-ratio schedule,** reinforcement is provided after a fixed number of correct responses have been made. In a **variable-ratio schedule,** reinforcement is provided after a variable number of correct responses have been made. In a 10:1 variable-ratio schedule, the mean number of correct responses

Fixed-interval schedule A schedule in which a fixed amount of time must elapse between the previous and subsequent times that reinforcement is available.

Variable-interval schedule A schedule in which a variable amount of time must elapse between the previous and subsequent times that reinforcement is available.

Fixed-ratio schedule A schedule in which reinforcement is provided after a fixed number of correct responses.

Variable-ratio schedule A schedule in which reinforcement is provided after a variable number of correct responses.

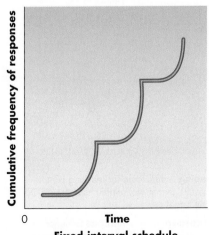

FIGURE 6.8 The "Fixed-Interval Scallop"
Organisms who are reinforced on a fixed-interval schedule tend to slack off responding after each reinforcement. The rate of response picks up as they near the time when reinforcement will become available. The results on the cumulative recorder look like upward-moving waves, or scallops.

Fixed-interval schedule

Daniel Allan/Getty Images

■ **Slot Machines Pay Off on Unpredictable Variable-Ratio Schedules**
Because "one-armed bandits" make unpredictable payoffs, people tend to maintain a high response rate—that is, to drop coins into them in rapid succession.

that would have to be made before a subsequent correct response would be reinforced is 10, but the ratio of correct responses to reinforcements might be allowed to vary from, say, 1:1 to 20:1 on a random basis.

Fixed- and variable-ratio schedules maintain a high response rate. With a fixed-ratio schedule, it is as if the organism learns that it must make several responses before being reinforced. It then "gets them out of the way" as rapidly as possible. Consider the example of piecework. If a worker must sew five shirts to receive $10, he or she is on a fixed-ratio (5:1) schedule and is likely to sew at a uniformly high rate, although there might be a brief pause after each reinforcement. With a variable-ratio schedule, reinforcement can come at any time. This unpredictability also maintains a high response rate. Slot machines tend to pay off on variable-ratio schedules, and players can be seen popping coins into them and yanking their "arms" with barely a pause. I have seen players who do not even stop to pick up their winnings. Instead, they continue to pop in the coins, whether from their original stack or from the winnings tray.

Shaping

If you are teaching hip-hop to people who have never danced, do not wait until they have performed it precisely before telling them they're on the right track. The foxtrot will be back in style before they have learned a thing.

We can teach complex behaviors by **shaping. Question: How can we use shaping to teach complex behavior patterns?** Shaping reinforces progressive steps toward the behavioral goal. At first, for example, it may be wise to smile and say, "Good," when a reluctant newcomer gathers the courage to get out on the dance floor, even if your feet are flattened by his initial clumsiness. If you are teaching someone to drive a car with a standard shift, at first generously reinforce the learner simply for shifting gears without stalling.

But as training proceeds, we come to expect more before we are willing to provide reinforcement. We reinforce **successive approximations** of the goal. If you want to train a rat to climb a ladder, first reinforce it with a food pellet when it turns toward the ladder. Then wait until it approaches the ladder before giving it a pellet. Then do not drop a pellet into the cage until the rat touches the ladder. In this way, the rat will reach the top of the ladder more quickly than if you had waited for the target behavior to occur at random. **Truth or Fiction Revisited:** Through use of shaping, one can indeed train a rat to climb a ramp, cross a bridge, climb a ladder, and so on in a desired sequence.

Learning to drive a new standard-shift automobile to a new job also involves a complex sequence of operant behaviors. At first we actively seek out all the discriminative stimuli or landmarks that give us cues for when to turn—signs, buildings, hills, valleys. We also focus on shifting to a lower gear as we slow so the car won't stall. After many repetitions, these responses, or chains of behavior chains, become habitual, and we need to pay very little attention to them.

Have you ever driven home and suddenly realized that you couldn't recall exactly how you got there? Your entire trip may seem "lost." Were you in great danger? How could you allow such a thing to happen? Actually, your driving and your responses to the demands of the route may have become so habitual that you did not have to focus on them. As you drove, you were able to think about dinner, work, or the weekend. But if something unusual had occurred on the way, such as an engine problem or a rainstorm, you would have devoted as much attention to your driving as was needed to arrive home. Your trip was probably quite safe after all.

Shaping A procedure for teaching complex behaviors that at first reinforces approximations of the target behavior.

Successive approximations Behaviors that are progressively closer to a target behavior.

Your Turn: Now that we have discussed operant conditioning, enhance your mastery of the material with the nearby "Learning Connections." Review the material by filling in the blanks, reflect on the material by relating it to other things you know, and think critically about it.

Learning Connections — OPERANT CONDITIONING: LEARNING WHAT DOES WHAT TO WHAT

ACTIVE REVIEW (17) Thorndike originated the law of _____ in learning. (18) He believed that _____ stamp in behavior and punishments stamp it out. (19) Skinner developed the concept of _____ as an alternative to the concepts of reward and punishment. (20) _____ reinforcers increase the probability that operants will occur when they are applied. (21) _____ reinforcers increase the probability that operants will occur when they are removed. (22) _____ reinforcers such as food have their value because of the biological makeup of the organism. (23) _____ reinforcers, such as money, acquire their value through association with established reinforcers. (24) In operant conditioning, repeated performance of a learned response in the absence of reinforcement leads to _____ of that response. (25) _____ are aversive stimuli that suppress the frequency of behavior. (26) A _____ stimulus indicates when an operant will be reinforced. (27) In a(n) _____ schedule, a specific amount of time must elapse since a previous correct response before reinforcement again becomes available. (28) In a(n) _____ schedule, the number of correct responses that must be performed before reinforcement becomes available is allowed to vary. (29) In shaping, we reinforce _____ approximations to the goal.

REFLECT AND RELATE Did you ever train an animal, such as a dog? If so, did you use principles of operant conditioning? Explain how.

CRITICAL THINKING Every time I tell my classes that many psychologists frown on the use of punishment, many students chide me for being unrealistic and "goody-goody." Let's try some critical thinking: What are the effects of punishment? Does it stop undesirable behavior? If so, when? Are there other ways of encouraging desirable behavior? Which is preferable? How can we judge?

Go to **http://psychology.wadsworth.com/ rathus_pcc9e** for an interactive version of this Learning Connections unit.

Applications of Operant Conditioning

Operant conditioning, like classical conditioning, is more than a laboratory procedure. We use it every day to influence other people. Parents and peers induce children to acquire so-called gender-appropriate behavior patterns through rewards and punishments. Peers influence peers by playing with peers who are generous and nonaggressive and by avoiding those who are not (Warman & Cohen, 2000). Adults often reward children for expressing attitudes that coincide with their own and punish or ignore them for expressing contradictory attitudes.

Biofeedback training (BFT) is based on operant conditioning. BFT has enabled people and lower animals to learn to control autonomic responses to attain reinforcement (Miller, 1969; Vernon et al., 2003). In BFT, people receive reinforcement in the form of *information*. For example, we can learn to emit alpha waves—the kind of brain wave associated with relaxation—through feedback from an electroencephalograph, which measures brain waves. People use other instruments to learn to lower muscle tension, heart rates, and blood pressure.

Remember that reinforcers are defined not as pleasant events but rather as stimuli that increase the frequency of behavior. Ironically, adults frequently reinforce undesirable behavior in children by paying attention to them, or punishing them, when they misbehave but ignoring them when they behave in desirable ways. Similarly, teachers who raise their voices when children misbehave may be unintentionally conferring hero status on those pupils in the eyes of their peers. To the teacher's surprise, some children may then go out of their way to earn disapproval. But teachers can learn to use behavior modification to reinforce children when they are behaving appropriately and, when possible, to extinguish misbehavior by ignoring it.

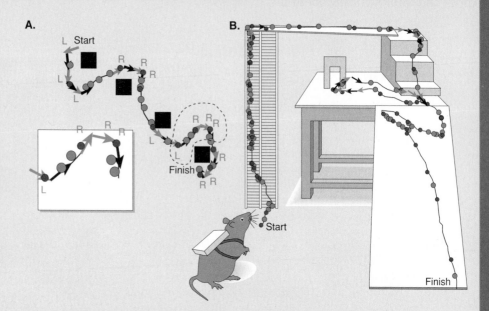

A Closer Look

ROBO RATS? USING OPERANT CONDITIONING TO TEACH RATS HOW TO SEARCH FOR SURVIVORS OF DISASTERS

City dwellers know that rats rustle through garbage, but will we one day be using rats to search through rubble where people cannot go to find survivors of disasters? The results of a study carried out in Brooklyn, New York, suggest that this is a real possibility.

Sanjiv Talwar and his colleagues (2002) used operant conditioning to guide rats through mazes by means of "remote control." They were inspired to test out the method by an earthquake in India and the terrorist attacks of September 11, 2001. The tsunami of 2004 provides an additional incentive for this type of experimentation.

The researchers outfitted five rats with electrodes in their brains and backpacks containing various electronic devices. One goal was to inform the rats whether they should turn right or left. Another was to reinforce them for doing so. To point the rats in the right direction, the team sent electric signals to brain regions that receive sensations from whiskers. The researchers inserted electrodes in the animals' pleasure centers to provide reinforcement.

The researchers placed the rats in a maze. As the animals approached a choice point where they could turn left or right, the researchers stimulated their brains as would a whisker touch on the left or right side of the head. When the animals turned in the direction of the "virtual touches," the researchers zapped their brains' pleasure centers.

Not only did the bursts of electricity teach the rats which way to turn, but they also apparently motivated the rats to move faster, even if it meant climbing steps or hopping from a shelf. The rat is apparently seeking the next burst. Talwar says that "the rats figure it out in 5 or 10 minutes" (Milius, 2002). The researchers steered the rats across a jagged pile of concrete, an area that was so brightly lit that rats would normally avoid it, even up a tree.

Robin Murphy, who is developing search-and-rescue robots in Florida, is skeptical. She admits that the rats seem to work out in experiments, but she wonders how people can guide a rat that is out of sight (a small video camera strapped to the animal's head?) and whether bursts of electricity will keep the rat going through areas with high temperatures and little or no oxygen. Murphy also worries about sending animals, even rats, into such environments. "One of the reasons many of us are in robotics is because robots can reduce the risk to living things," she says (Milius, 2002).

What do you think?

■ **Robo-Rat?** Part A of the figure shows how Talwar and his colleagues guided a rat through a zigzag course. They cued the rat to turn left (L) or right (R), then reinforced it with a burst of electricity in the rat's pleasure center for doing so. Part B shows a more complex 3-D course through which a rat was guided. The goal is to shape rats to rustle through rubble to help find survivors of a disaster.

Source: "Behavioural neuroscience: Rat navigation guided by remote control" by Sanjiv K. Talwar et al., *Nature 417* (2002), fig. 1, p. 37. Reprinted by permission of Nature Publishing Group.

Teachers also frequently use "time out" from positive reinforcement to discourage misbehavior. In this method, children are placed in a drab environment for a specified period, usually about 10 minutes, when they are disruptive. While isolated, they cannot earn the attention of peers or teachers.

B. F. Skinner developed an educational method called *programmed learning* that is based on operant conditioning. This method assumes that any complex task can be broken down into a number of small steps. These steps can be shaped individually and then combined in sequence to form the correct behavioral chain. Programmed learning does not punish errors. Instead, correct responses are reinforced. **Truth or Fiction Revisited:** Actually, one can learn *without* making mistakes.

Your Turn: Now that we have explored various applications of operant conditioning, enhance your mastery of the material with the nearby "Learning Connections." Review the material by filling in the blanks, reflect on the material by relating it to other things you know, and think critically about it.

Learning Connections | APPLICATIONS OF OPERANT CONDITIONING

ACTIVE REVIEW (30) _____ training enables organisms to gain control of autonomic responses in order to attain reinforcement. (31) In using behavior _____, teachers reinforce desired behavior and extinguish undesired behavior by ignoring it. (32) _____ learning breaks down learning tasks into small steps and reinforces correct performance of each step.

REFLECT AND RELATE How have teachers in your own experience maintained—or failed to maintain—control over their classrooms?

CRITICAL THINKING We can demonstrate that an operant conditioning technique, behavior modification, can affect the behavior of students. Does this mean that all of students' behavior can be explained according to principles of operant conditioning?

 Go to **http://psychology.wadsworth.com/ rathus_pcc9e** for an interactive version of this Learning Connections unit.

Cognitive Factors in Learning

Classical and operant conditioning were originally conceived of as relatively simple forms of learning. Much of conditioning's appeal is that it can be said to meet the behaviorist objective of explaining behavior in terms of observable events—in this case, laboratory conditions. Building on this theoretical base, some psychologists have suggested that the most complex human behavior involves the summation of a series of instances of conditioning. However, many psychologists believe that conditioning is too mechanical a process to explain all instances of learned behavior, even in laboratory rats (Weiner, 1991). They turn to cognitive factors to describe and explain additional findings in the psychology of learning. **Question: How do we explain what happens during classical conditioning from a cognitive perspective?**

In addition to concepts such as *association* and *reinforcement*, cognitive psychologists use concepts such as *mental structures, schemas, templates,* and *information processing.* Cognitive psychologists see people as searching for information, weighing evidence, and making decisions. Let us consider some classic research that points to cognitive factors in learning, as opposed to mechanical associations. These cognitive factors are not necessarily limited to humans—although, of course, people are the only species that can talk about them.

Stephen Johnson/Getty Images

■ **How Do They Learn Their Way around the Mall?** Have these shoppers simply been conditioned to turn left or right at various choice points like so many rats in a maze, or have they learned to mentally represent the mall? (And do rats also learn to mentally represent mazes?)

Latent Hidden or concealed.

Contingency theory The view that learning occurs when stimuli provide information about the likelihood of the occurrence of other stimuli.

Latent Learning: Forming Cognitive Maps

I'm all grown up. I know the whole mall.
The author's daughter Jordan at age 7

Many behaviorists argue that organisms acquire only responses, or operants, for which they are reinforced. E. C. Tolman, however, showed that rats also learn about their environment in the absence of reinforcement. In doing so, he demonstrated that rats must form cognitive maps of their surroundings. **Question: What is the evidence that people and lower organisms form cognitive maps of their environments?**

Tolman trained some rats to run through mazes for standard food goals. Other rats were permitted to explore the same mazes for several days without food goals or other rewards. After the unrewarded rats had been allowed to explore the mazes for 10 days, food rewards were placed in a box at the far end of the maze. The previously unrewarded rats reached the food box as quickly as the rewarded rats after only one or two reinforced trials (Tolman & Honzik, 1930).

Tolman concluded that rats learned about mazes in which they roamed even when they were unrewarded for doing so. He distinguished between *learning* and *performance*. Rats would acquire a cognitive map of a maze; and, even though they would not be motivated to follow an efficient route to the far end, they would learn rapid routes from one end to the other just by roaming about within the maze. Yet this learning might remain hidden, or **latent,** until they were motivated to follow the rapid routes to obtain food goals.

 A Closer Look | CONTINGENCY THEORY

Behaviorists and cognitive psychologists interpret the conditioning process in different ways. Behaviorists explain it in terms of the pairing of stimuli. Cognitive psychologists explain classical conditioning in terms of the ways in which stimuli provide information that allows organisms to form and revise mental representations of their environment (Basic Behavioral Science Task Force, 1996b). Robert Rescorla conducted research in an effort to demonstrate which view is more accurate. His viewpoint, **contingency theory,** suggests that learning occurs only when the conditioned stimulus provides *information* about the unconditioned stimulus.

In classical conditioning experiments with dogs, Rescorla (1967) obtained some results that are difficult to explain without reference to cognitive concepts. Each phase of his work paired a tone (a conditioned stimulus) with an electric shock (an unconditioned stimulus), but in different ways. With one group of animals, the shock was consistently presented after the tone. That is, the unconditioned stimulus followed on the heels of the conditioned stimulus, as in Pavlov's studies.

The dogs in this group learned to show a fear response when the tone was presented.

A second group of dogs heard an equal number of tones and received an equal number of electric shocks, but the shock never immediately followed the tone. In other words, the tone and the shock were not paired. Now, from the behaviorist perspective, the dogs should not have learned to associate the tone and the shock because one did not predict the other. Actually, the dogs learned quite a lot: They learned that they had nothing to fear when the tone was sounded! They showed vigilance and fear when the laboratory was quiet—for the shock could apparently come at any time—but they were calm in the presence of the tone.

The third group of dogs also received equal numbers of tones and shocks, but the stimuli were presented at purely random intervals. Occasionally they were paired, but most often they were not. According to Rescorla, behaviorists might argue that intermittent pairing of the tones and shocks should have brought about some learning. Yet it did not. The animals showed no fear in

response to the tone. Rescorla suggests that the animals in this group learned nothing because the tones did not allow them to make predictions about electric shock.

Rescorla concluded that contiguity—that is, the co-appearance of unconditioned stimulus and the conditioned stimulus—cannot in itself explain classical conditioning. Learning occurs only when the conditioned stimulus (in this case, the tone) provides information about the unconditioned stimulus (in this case, the shock). According to contingency theory, learning occurs because a conditioned stimulus indicates that the unconditioned stimulus is likely to follow.

Behaviorists might counter, of course, that for the second group of dogs the *absence* of the tone became the signal for the shock. Shock may be a powerful enough event that the fear response becomes conditioned to the laboratory environment. For the third group of dogs, the shock was as likely to occur in the presence of the neutral stimulus as in its absence. Therefore, many behaviorists would expect no learning to occur.

Observational Learning: Monkey See, Monkey May *Choose* to Do?

How many things have you learned from watching other people in real life, in films, and on television? From films and television, you may have gathered vague ideas about how to skydive, ride a surfboard, climb sheer cliffs, run a pattern to catch a touchdown pass in the Super Bowl, and dust for fingerprints, even if you have never tried these activities yourself. **Question: How do people learn by observing others?**

In their studies of social learning, Albert Bandura and his colleagues conducted experiments (e.g., Bandura et al., 1963) that show that we can acquire operants by observing the behavior of others. We may need some practice to refine the operants, but we can learn them through observation alone. We may also allow these operants or skills to remain latent. For example, we may not imitate aggressive behavior unless we are provoked and believe that we are more likely to be rewarded than punished for it.

Observational learning may account for most human learning. It occurs when, as children, we watch our parents cook, clean, or repair a broken appliance. Observational learning takes place when we watch teachers solve problems on the blackboard or hear them speak in a foreign language. Observational learning is not mechanically acquired through reinforcement. We can learn through observation without engaging in overt responses at all. It appears sufficient to pay attention to the behavior of others.

In the terminology of observational learning, a person who engages in a response to be imitated is a **model.** When observers see a model being reinforced for displaying an operant, the observers are said to be *vicariously* reinforced. Display of the operant thus becomes more likely for the observer as well as for the model.

Your Turn: Now that we have discussed cognitive factors in learning, enhance your mastery of the material with the nearby "Learning Connections." Review the material by filling in the blanks, reflect on the material by relating it to other things

Observational learning The acquisition of knowledge and skills through the observation of others (who are called *models*) rather than by means of direct experience.

Model An organism that engages in a response that is then imitated by another organism.

Concept Review KINDS OF LEARNING

Kind of Learning		What Is Learned	How It Is Learned
Classical conditioning Major proponents: Ivan Pavlov (known for basic research with dogs) John B. Watson (known as originator of behaviorism)		Association of events; anticipations, signs, expectations; automatic responses to new stimuli	A neutral stimulus is repeatedly paired with a stimulus (an unconditioned stimulus, or UCS) that elicits a response (an unconditioned response, or UCR) until the neutral stimulus produces a response (conditioned response, or CR) that anticipates and prepares for the unconditioned stimulus. At this point, the neutral stimulus has become a conditioned stimulus (CS).
Operant conditioning Major proponent: B. F. Skinner		Behavior that operates on, or affects, the environment to produce consequences	A response is rewarded or reinforced so that it occurs with greater frequency in similar situations.
Observational learning Major proponents: Albert Bandura Julian Rotter Walter Mischel		Expectations (if–then relationships), knowledge, and skills	A person observes the behavior of another person (live or through media such as films, television, or books) and its effects.

Go to **http://psychology.wadsworth.com/ rathus_pcc9e** to access a drag-and-drop version of this Concept Review designed to help you test yourself on the major topics provided here.

you know, and think critically about it. The nearby Concept Review summarizes various kinds of learning.

It would be of little use to discuss how we learn if we were not capable of remembering what we learn from second to second, from day to day, or in many cases for a lifetime. In the next chapter we turn our attention to the subject of memory. In Chapters 7 and 8 we will see how learning is intertwined with thinking, language, and intelligence.

Learning Connections | COGNITIVE FACTORS IN LEARNING

ACTIVE REVIEW (33) Tolman's work with rats suggests that they develop _____ maps of the environment. (34) Tolman labels learning without performing _____ learning. (35) Bandura believes that observational learning (*Is* or *Is not?*) a mechanical process. (36) According to _____ theory, learning occurs because a CS indicates that the UCS is likely to follow.

REFLECT AND RELATE Have you ever studied an atlas, a road map, a cookbook, or a computer manual for the

pleasure of doing so? What kind of learning were you engaging in?

CRITICAL THINKING How do the results of research into cognitive factors in learning challenge behaviorist principles? Refer to contingency theory, latent learning, and observational learning in your answer.

 Go to **http://psychology.wadsworth.com/ rathus_pcc9e** for an interactive version of this Learning Connections unit.

Life Connections
Violence in the Media and Aggression

Much human learning occurs through observation. We learn by observing parents and peers, attending school, reading books, and watching media such as television and films. Nearly all of us have been exposed to television, videotapes, and films in the classroom. Children in day care centers often watch *Sesame Street*. There are filmed and electronic versions of great works of literature such as Orson Welles's *Macbeth* or Laurence Olivier's *Hamlet*. Nearly every school shows films of laboratory experiments. Sometimes we view "canned lectures" by master teachers.

But what of our exposure to these media *outside* the classroom? Television is one of our major sources of informal observational learning. Children are routinely exposed to scenes of murder, beating, and sexual assault—

just by turning on the TV set (Huesmann et al., 2003; Wilson, 1997). If a child watches two to four hours of TV a day, she or he will have seen 8,000 murders and another 100,000 acts of violence *by the time she or he has finished elementary school* (Eron, 1993). Are kids

■ **What Are the Effects of Media Violence?** Preschool children in the United States watch TV an average of four hours a day. Schoolchildren spend more hours at the TV set than in the classroom. Is it any wonder that psychologists, educators, and parents express concern about the effects of media violence?

less likely to be exposed to violence by going to the movies? No. One study found that virtually all G-rated animated films have scenes of violence, with a mean duration of 9 to 10 minutes per film (Yokota & Thompson, 2000).[1] Other media that contain violence include movies, music, music videos, advertising, video games, the Internet—even comic books (Kirsh & Olczak, 2002; Villani, 2001).

Bandura's Classic Research on the Effects of Violence in the Media

A classic experiment by Bandura, Ross, and Ross (1963) suggests the powerful influence of televised models on children's aggressive behavior. One

[1]Technically speaking, the word *mean* signifies "average" here. However, in this particular case, *mean* could be interpreted as a pun, because violence even in children's films tends to be quite mean.

group of preschool children observed a film of an adult model hitting and kicking an inflated Bobo doll, while a control group saw an aggression-free film. The experimental and control children were then left alone in a room with the same doll, as hidden observers recorded their behavior. The children who had observed the aggressive model showed significantly more aggressive behavior toward the doll themselves (see Figure 6.9). Many children imitated bizarre attack behaviors devised for the model in this experiment—behaviors that they would not have thought up themselves. **Truth or Fiction Revisited:** Actually, a scientific connection has been established between violence in the media and real-life aggression.

The children exposed to the aggressive model also showed aggressive behavior patterns that had not been modeled. Observing the model, therefore, not only led to imitation of modeled behavior patterns, but also apparently disinhibited previously learned aggressive responses. The results were similar whether children observed human or cartoon models on film.

Violence tends to be glamorized in the media. For example, in one cartoon show, superheroes battle villains who are trying to destroy or take over the world. Violence is often shown to have only temporary or minimal effects. (How often has Wile E. Coyote fallen from a cliff and been pounded into the ground by a boulder, only to bounce back and pursue the Road Runner once more?) In the great majority of violent TV shows, there is no remorse, criticism, or penalty for violent behavior (Seppa, 1997). Few TV programs show harmful long-term consequences of aggressive behavior. Seeing the perpetrator of the violence go unpunished increases the chances that the child will act aggressively (Krcmar & Cooke, 2001). Children may not even view death as much of a problem. How many

times do video-game characters "die"— only to be reborn to fight again because the children have won multiple lives?

Why all this violence? Simple: Violence sells. But does violence do more than sell? That is, does media violence *cause* real violence? If so, what can parents and educators do to prevent the fictional from spilling over into the real world?

Consensus on the Effects of Violence in the Media?

In any event, most organizations of health professionals agree that media violence does contribute to aggression (Holland, 2000; Villani, 2001). This relationship has been found for girls and boys of different ages, social classes, ethnic groups, and cultures (Huesmann et al., 2003). Consider a number of ways in which depictions of violence make such a contribution:

- *Observational learning:* Children learn from observation (Holland, 2000). TV violence supplies *models* of aggressive "skills," which children may acquire. In fact, children are more likely to imitate what their parents do than to heed what they say. If adults say that they disapprove of aggression but smash furniture or slap each other when frustrated, children are likely to

develop the notion that aggression is the way to handle frustration. Classic experiments show that children tend to imitate the aggressive behavior they see on the media (Bandura et al., 1963). Media violence also provides viewers with aggressive *scripts*—that is, ideas about how to behave in situations like those they have observed (Huesmann et al., 2003).

- *Disinhibition:* Punishment inhibits behavior. Conversely, media violence may disinhibit aggressive behavior, especially when media characters "get away" with violence or are rewarded for it (Haridakis, 2002).
- *Increased emotional arousal:* Media violence and aggressive video games increase viewers' level of emotional arousal. That is, television "works them up." We are more likely to be aggressive when we are highly aroused.
- *Priming of aggressive thoughts and memories:* Media violence "primes" or arouses aggressive ideas and memories (Bushman, 1998).
- *Habituation:* We become "habituated to," or used to, repeated stimuli. Repeated exposure to TV violence may decrease viewers' sensitivity to real violence. If children come to perceive violence as the norm, they may become more tolerant of it and place less value on restraining aggressive urges (Holland, 2000; Huesmann & Guerra, 1997).

A joint statement issued by the American Medical Association, the American Academy of Pediatrics, the American Psychological Association, and the American Academy of Child and Adolescent Psychiatry (Holland, 2000) made some additional points:

- Children who see a lot of violence are more likely to view violence as an effective way of settling conflicts. Children exposed to violence are more likely to assume that violence is acceptable.

FIGURE 6.9 **Classic Research on the Imitation of Aggressive Models**

Albert Bandura and his colleagues showed that children frequently imitate the aggressive behavior that they observe. In the top row, an adult model strikes a clown doll. The lower rows show a boy and a girl imitating the aggressive behavior.

© Albert Bandura

- Viewing violence can decrease the likelihood that one will take action on behalf of a victim when violence occurs.
- Viewing violence may lead to real-life violence. Children exposed to violent programming at a young age are more likely to be violent themselves later on in life.

On the other hand, longitudinal research suggests that individuals are more likely to imitate media violence when they identify with the characters and when the portrayal of violence is realistic (Huesmann et al., 2003). Therefore, viewers may be more likely to imitate violence when the perpetrator looks like them and lives in a similar environment than when it is perpetrated by Wile E. Coyote.

Violent video games are also connected with aggressive behavior. Craig Anderson and Karen Dill (2000) found that playing violent video games increases aggressive thoughts and behavior in the laboratory. It is also connected with a history of juvenile delinquency. However, males are relatively more likely than females to act aggressively after playing violent video games and are more likely to see the world as a hostile place. Students who obtain higher grades are also less likely to behave aggressively following exposure to violent media games. Thus, cultural stereotyping of males and females, possible biological gender differences, and moderating variables like academic achievement also come into play when we are talking about the effects of media violence. There is no simple one-to-one connection between media violence and violence in real life.

There seems to be a circular relationship between exposure to media violence and aggressive behavior (Anderson & Dill, 2000; Eron, 1982; Funk et al., 2000; Haridakis, 2002). Yes, TV violence and violent video games contribute to aggressive behavior, but aggressive youngsters are also more likely to seek out this kind of

"entertainment." Figure 6.10 explores the possible connections between TV violence and aggressive behavior among viewers.

Aggressive children are frequently rejected by age-mates who are not aggressive—at least in middle-class culture (Eron, 1982; Warman & Cohen, 2000). Aggressive children may watch more television because their peer relationships are less fulfilling and because the high incidence of TV violence tends to confirm their view that aggressive behavior is normal (Eron, 1982). Media violence interacts with other contributors to violence. The family also affects the likelihood that children will imitate the violence they see on TV. Studies find that parental substance abuse, paternal physical punishments, and single motherhood contribute to the likelihood of aggression in early childhood (Brook et al., 2001; Gupta et al., 2001). Parental rejection and use of physical punishment further increase the likelihood of aggression in children (Eron, 1982). These family factors suggest that the parents of aggressive children are absent or unlikely to help young children understand that the kinds of socially inappropriate behaviors they see in the media are not for them. A harsh home life may also confirm the TV viewer's vision of the world as a violent place

FIGURE 6.10 What Are the Connections between Media Violence and Aggressive Behavior?

Does media violence cause aggressive behavior? Do aggressive children prefer to tune into violent shows? Or do third factors, such as personality traits that create a disposition toward aggression, contribute both to aggressive behavior and the observation of violent shows?

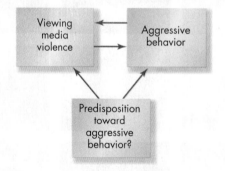

and further encourage reliance on television for companionship.

Teaching Children *Not* to Imitate Media Violence

Children are going to be exposed to media violence—if not in Saturday morning cartoon shows, then in evening dramas and in the news. Or they'll hear about violence from friends, watch other children get into fights, or read about violence in the newspapers. If all those sources of violence were somehow hidden from view, they would learn about violence in *Hamlet, Macbeth,* and even the Bible. The notion of preventing children from being exposed to violent models may be impractical.

What, then, should be done? Parents and educators can do many things to tone down the impact of media violence (Broder, 2000; Huesmann et al., 2003). Children who watch violent shows act less aggressively when they are informed that:

- The violent behavior they observe in the media does *not* represent the behavior of most people.
- The apparently aggressive behaviors they watch are not real. They reflect camera tricks, special effects, and stunts.
- Most people resolve conflicts by nonviolent means.
- The real-life consequences of violence are harmful to the victim and, often, the aggressor.

Despite our history of evolutionary forces, and despite the fact that in most species, successful aggression usually wins individuals the right to transmit their genes to future generations, humans are thinking beings. If children consider violence to be inappropriate for them, they will be less likely to act aggressively, even when they have acquired aggressive skills from exposure to the media or other sources.

Want to study on the go? Go to your companion website and download an audio version of this review section to your media player.

Recite—An Active Summary™

1. What is learning?

Learning is the process by which experience leads to modified representations of the environment (the cognitive perspective) and relatively permanent changes in behavior (the behavioral perspective).

2. What is classical conditioning?

Classical conditioning is a simple form of associative learning in which a previously neutral stimulus (the conditioned stimulus, or CS) comes to elicit the response evoked by a second stimulus (the unconditioned stimulus, or UCS) as a result of repeatedly being paired with the second stimulus.

3. What is the contribution of Ivan Pavlov to the psychology of learning?

The Russian physiologist Ivan Pavlov happened upon conditioning by chance, as he was studying salivation in laboratory dogs. Pavlov discovered that reflexes can be learned, or *conditioned,* through association.

4. What are taste aversions? Why are they of special interest to psychologists?

Taste aversions are examples of classical conditioning in which organisms learn that a food is noxious on the basis of a nauseating experience. Taste aversions are of special interest because learning may occur on the basis of a single association and because the unconditioned stimulus (in this case, nausea) can occur hours after the conditioned stimulus (in this case, the flavor of food). Taste aversions apparently provide organisms with an evolutionary advantage.

5. What is the role of extinction in classical conditioning?

Extinction and spontaneous recovery help organisms adapt to environmental changes. After a UCS–CS association has been learned, for example, repeated presentation of the CS (for example, a tone) without the UCS (meat powder) extinguishes the CR (salivation).

6. What is the role of spontaneous recovery in classical conditioning?

Extinguished responses may show spontaneous recovery as a function of the time that has elapsed since extinction occurred. Spontaneous recovery is adaptive in that environmental conditions may have reverted to what they were before.

7. What is the role of generalization in classical conditioning?

Generalization and discrimination are also adaptive. Generalization helps organisms adapt to new events by responding to a range of stimuli similar to the CS.

8. What is the role of discrimination in classical conditioning?

In discrimination, organisms learn to show a CR in response to a more limited range of stimuli by pairing only the limited stimulus with the UCS.

9. What is higher-order conditioning?

In higher-order conditioning, a previously neutral stimulus comes to serve as a CS after being paired repeatedly with a stimulus that has already become a CS.

10. What is the contribution of B. F. Skinner to the psychology of learning?

Skinner developed the concept of reinforcement, encouraged the study of discrete behaviors such as lever pressing by rats, and innovated many techniques for studying operant conditioning such as the "Skinner box" and the cumulative recorder. He was also involved in the development of behavior modification and programmed learning.

11. What is operant conditioning?

Operant conditioning is a simple form of learning in which organisms learn to engage in behavior that is reinforced. Reinforced responses occur with greater frequency.

12. What are the various kinds of reinforcers?

These include positive, negative, primary, and secondary reinforcers. Positive reinforcers increase the probability that operants will occur when they are applied. Negative reinforcers increase the probability that operants will occur when they are removed. Primary reinforcers have their value because of the organism's biological makeup. Secondary reinforcers such as money and approval acquire their value through association with established reinforcers.

Recite — An Active Summary™

13. What is the role of extinction in operant conditioning?

Extinction and spontaneous recovery are also adaptive in operant conditioning. In operant conditioning, learned responses are extinguished as a result of repeated performance in the absence of reinforcement. (Why continue to engage in a response that goes unreinforced?)

14. What is the role of spontaneous recovery in operant conditioning?

As in classical conditioning, spontaneous recovery occurs as a function of the passage of time, which is adaptive because things may return to the way they once were.

15. Why did Skinner make a point of distinguishing between reinforcers on the one hand and rewards and punishments on the other?

Rewards and punishments are defined, respectively, as pleasant and aversive events that affect behavior. Skinner preferred the concept of *reinforcement* because its definition does not rely on getting inside the head of the organism. Instead, lists of reinforcers are obtained empirically, by observing their effects on behavior.

16. Why do many psychologists disapprove of punishment?

Many psychologists recommend not using punishment because it hurts, it does not suggest acceptable behavior, it may create feelings of hostility, it may only suppress behavior in the specific situation in which it is used, it may generalize to the suppression of wide varieties of behavior, and it may suggest that recipients punish others as a way of coping with stress.

17. What are discriminative stimuli?

Discriminative stimuli (such as green lights) indicate when operants (such as pecking a button) will be reinforced (as with food).

18. What are the various schedules of reinforcement? How do they affect behavior?

Continuous reinforcement leads to the most rapid acquisition of new responses, but operants are maintained most economically through partial reinforcement. There are four basic schedules of reinforcement. In a fixed-interval schedule, a specific amount of time must elapse after a previous correct response before reinforcement again becomes available. In a variable-interval schedule, the amount of time is allowed to vary. In a fixed-ratio schedule, a fixed number of correct responses must be performed before one is reinforced. In a variable-ratio schedule, this number is allowed to vary. Ratio schedules maintain high response rates.

19. How can we use shaping to teach complex behavior patterns?

In shaping, successive approximations of the target response are reinforced, leading to the performance of a complex sequence of behaviors.

20. How do we explain what happens during classical conditioning from a cognitive perspective?

According to contingency theory, organisms learn associations between stimuli only when stimuli provide new information about each other. From this perspective, classical conditioning does not occur mechanically but because it provides information.

21. What is the evidence that people and lower organisms form cognitive maps of their environments?

Some evidence is derived from Tolman's research on latent learning. He demonstrated that rats can learn—that is, they can modify their cognitive map of the environment—in the absence of reinforcement.

22. How do people learn by observing others?

Bandura has shown that people can learn to do things simply by observing others; it is not necessary that they emit responses that are reinforced in order to learn. Learners may then choose to perform the behaviors they have observed "when the time is ripe"—that is, when they believe that the learned behavior is appropriate or is likely to be rewarded.

 Go to **http://psychology.wadsworth.com/ rathus_pcc9e** to access an interactive version of this active summary.

Key Terms

Learning (p. 233)
Classical conditioning
(p. 234)
Reflex (p. 234)
Stimulus (p. 234)
Unconditioned stimulus
(UCS) (p. 234)
Unconditioned response
(UCR) (p. 234)
Orienting reflex (p. 234)
Conditioned stimulus (CS)
(p. 234)
Conditioned response (CR)
(p. 234)
Extinction (p. 237)
Spontaneous recovery
(p. 238)
Generalization (p. 239)

Discrimination (p. 239)
Higher-order conditioning
(p. 240)
Counterconditioning
(p. 240)
Flooding (p. 241)
Systematic desensitization
(p. 242)
Law of effect (p. 244)
Reinforce (p. 245)
Operant behavior (p. 245)
Operant conditioning
(p. 245)
Operant (p. 245)
Cumulative recorder
(p. 246)
Positive reinforcer
(p. 247)

Negative reinforcer
(p. 247)
Primary reinforcer
(p. 248)
Secondary reinforcer
(p. 248)
Conditioned reinforcer
(p. 248)
Reward (p. 248)
Punishment (p. 248)
Time out (p. 249)
Discriminative stimulus
(p. 250)
Continuous reinforcement
(p. 250)
Partial reinforcement
(p. 250)

Fixed-interval schedule
(p. 251)
Variable-interval schedule
(p. 251)
Fixed-ratio schedule
(p. 251)
Variable-ratio schedule
(p. 251)
Shaping (p. 252)
Successive approximations
(p. 252)
Latent (p. 256)
Contingency theory
(p. 256)
Observational learning
(p. 257)
Model (p. 257)

ACTIVE LEARNING RESOURCES

Visit your Companion Website for Video, Quizzing, and Self-Assessment!

http://psychology.wadsworth.com/rathus_pcc9e
On this site you can access the Little Albert video highlighted by the Video Connections icon on p. 241. In addition there are many quizzing opportunities including interactive versions of the fill-in-the-blank Active Review sections in your book.

Study on the Go!

Don't have time to study right now? You can study on the go! Visit your companion website and download an audio version of the Recite—An Active Summary section to your media player.

ThomsonNOW

http://www.thomsonedu.com
Need help studying? This site is your one-stop study shop. Take a Pre-Test and Thomson NOW will generate a Personalized Study Plan based on your test results. The Study Plan will identify the topics you need to review and direct you to online resources to help you master those topics. You can then take a Post-Test to determine the concepts you have mastered and what you still need to work on.

Author Blog

What does your author have to say about the state of psychology? Visit your companion website every Tuesday and click on "Author Blog," where he'll talk about the most recent controversies and hot topics in psychology.

Truth or Fiction?

T F A woman who could not remember who she was automatically dialed her mother's number when the police gave her a telephone.

T F Oh say, can you see? If the answer is yes, you have a photographic memory.

T F Learning must be meaningful if we are to remember it.

T F It may be easier for you to recall the name of your first-grade teacher than the name of someone you just met at a party.

T F All of our experiences are permanently imprinted on the brain, so the proper stimulus can cause us to remember them exactly.

T F You may always recall where you were and what you were doing on the morning of September 11, 2001.

T F If you study with the stereo on, you would probably do better to take the test with the stereo on.

T F Learning Spanish can make it harder to remember French—and vice versa.

T F After part of his hippocampus was surgically removed, a man could not form new memories. Each time he was reminded of his uncle's dying, he grieved as he had when he first heard of it.

T F You may improve your memory by sniffing antiduretic hormone.

 Go to **http://psychology.wadsworth.com/ rathus_pcc9e** to answer and score this Truth or Fiction quiz.

J Price/Getty Images

Memory: Remembrance of Things Past— and Future

Preview

Jeff would never forget his sudden loss of memory. He watched in horror as his cell phone slipped from his pocket and fell to the floor of the Blockbuster store in Boston. Before he could grab it, it shattered into pieces. A New York college student, Jeff experienced the trauma of phone loss on his winter break.

Why was the loss traumatic? Why was it a memory problem? Simple: There was no way for Jeff to retrieve his phone book. "I was at the store and it was snowing out and I suddenly realized that I had no way of getting in touch with anyone," he explains (Metz, 2005). The worst part of the loss was that Jeff had been seeing someone in New York, and because her cell phone was her only phone, he now had no way to contact her. A day later he showed up on her doorstep, hoping she wouldn't think he had been avoiding her calls. She forgave him but had him write her number down—*on paper*. Still, Jeff would not forget the day his cell phone lost its memory. After all, he also had his family, his friends, his pizza-delivery service, his tutor, and his mother's pet groomer in it.

Jeff now copies every cell-phone entry into a little black book—made of paper. Other people back up their phone books—and their pictures and downloads—on servers provided by cellular telephone operating companies or cell-phone manufacturers. Verizon Wireless, for example, offers "Backup Assistant." Motorola's brand is "MyBackup." Most people transfer their memories from their old cell phone to the new one when they make a change.

Jeff's cell-phone memory is electronic. Information is stored on a chip smaller than a fingernail. His own memory is much more complex—involving biological structures as well as chemical and electrical processes.

This chapter is all about the "backup assistant" in your brain—your memory. Without your memory, there is no past. Without your memory, experience is trivial and learning is lost. Let us see what psychologists have learned about the ways in which we remember things—other than keying them into a cell phone's memory chip. However, first try to meet the challenges to your memory we pose in the Self-Assessment on page 267. We'll be talking about your responses throughout the chapter.

Kinds of Memory: Pressing the "Rewind" and "Fast-Forward" Buttons

Jeff remembered things he had personally done, like dropping his cell phone in Boston and showing up at his girlfriend's doorstep on a blustery day in January. Remembering a dropped cell phone is an *episodic memory*—a memory of an event in one's life. According to psychologists who have extensively researched memory, episodic memory is one kind of memory system (Dobbins et al., 2004; Schacter, 2000; Zola et al., 2003). And when I learned of Jeff's experience, I tried to remind myself repeatedly not to forget to jot down notes about it and write it up as soon as I could. (I was trying to jog my *prospective memory*—remembering to do something in the future.) Let us consider several memory systems.

Explicit versus Implicit Memories

Question: What is meant by explicit memory? **Explicit memory**—also referred to as *declarative memory*—is memory for specific information. Things that are explicit are clear, or clearly stated or explained. The use of the term *declarative* indicates that these memories state or reveal (i.e., declare) specific information. The information may be autobiographical or refer to general knowledge. ("Well, I declare!")

Implicit memory—also referred to as *nondeclarative memory*—is memory of how to perform a task; it is the act itself, *doing* something (Schacter, 1992). First let us talk more about two kinds of explicit memories described by psychologist Endel

Explicit memory Memory that clearly and distinctly expresses (explicates) specific information.

Implicit memory Memory that is suggested (implied) but not plainly expressed, as illustrated in the things that people *do* but do not state clearly.

 **Self-Assessment   Five Challenges to Your Memory**

Let's challenge your memory. This is not an actual memory test of the sort used by psychologists to determine whether people's memory functioning is within normal limits. Instead, it will provide you with some insight into how your memory works and may also be fun.

Directions: Find four sheets of blank paper and number them 1 through 4. Also use a watch with a second hand. Then follow these instructions:

1. Following are ten letters. Look at them for 15 seconds. Later in the chapter, I will ask you if you can write them on sheet number 1. (No cheating! Don't do it now.)

THUNSTOFAM

2. Look at these nine figures for 30 seconds. Then try to draw them in the proper sequence on sheet number 2. (Yes, right after you've finished looking at them. We'll talk about your drawings later, on page 279.)

3. Okay, here's another list of letters, 17 this time. Look at the list for 60 seconds and then see whether you can reproduce it on sheet number 3. (I'm being generous this time—a full minute.)

GMC–BSI–BMA–TTC–IAF–BI

4. Which of these pennies is an accurate reproduction of the Lincoln penny you see every day? This time there's nothing to draw on another sheet; just circle or put a checkmark by the penny that you think resembles the ones you throw in the back of the drawer.

5. Examine the following drawings for 1 minute. Then copy the names of the figures on sheet number 4. When you're finished, just keep reading. Soon I'll be asking you to draw those figures.

   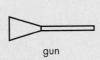

eyeglasses   hourglass   seven   gun

That's it. You'll find out about the results of this self-assessment as you read through the chapter.

Tulving (1985; Tulving & Markowitsch, 1998): episodic and semantic. They are identified according to the type of information they hold.

EPISODIC MEMORY   Question: What is meant by episodic memory? Episodic memories are kinds of explicit memories. They are memories of the things that happen to us or take place in our presence (Eichenbaum & Fortin, 2003). Episodic memory is also referred to as *autobiographical memory.* Your memories of what you ate for breakfast and of what your professor said in class this afternoon are examples of episodic memory.

It is common for us to build or "reconstruct" inaccurate memories that have a bit of this and that—something that might reflect autobiographical experience, things we hear about from family members and others, the stuff we read about or see in the media, and even things that other people suggest might have happened to us. These memories are fiction, as we see in novels, but we may believe that they are truly autobiographical (Clancy et al., 2000).

Episodic memory Memories of events experienced by a person or that take place in the person's presence.

SEMANTIC MEMORY: ON *NOT* GETTING PERSONAL **Question: What is meant by semantic memory?** General knowledge is referred to as **semantic memory.** *Semantics* concerns meanings. You can "remember" that the United States has 50 states without visiting them and personally adding them up. You "remember" who authored *Hamlet,* although you were not looking over Shakespeare's shoulder as he did so. These, too, are examples of semantic memory.

Your future recollection that there are several kinds of memory is more likely to be semantic than episodic. In other words, you are more likely to "know" that there are several types of memory than to recall the date on which you learned about them, where you were, how you were sitting, and whether you were also thinking about dinner at the time. We tend to use the phrase "I remember . . ." when we are referring to episodic memories, as in "I *remember* the blizzard of 1998." But we are more likely to say "I know . . ." in reference to semantic memories, as in "I *know* about—" (or, "I heard about—") "—the blizzard of 1898." Put it another way: You may *remember* that you wrote your mother, but you *know* that Shakespeare wrote *Hamlet.*

IMPLICIT MEMORY: WHEN REMEMBERING IS DOING Now let us think more about implicit memory. **Question: What is meant by implicit memory?** As the term *implicit* implies (should I start this sentence again?), implicit memories are suggested (or implied) but not plainly stated or expressed (not declared). Implicit memories are illustrated by the things that people *do* but not by the things they state clearly. Implicit memories involve skills, both cognitive and physical; they reveal habits; and they involve the effects of conditioning. My taste aversion to buttered popcorn—which I described in Chapter 6—is an implicit memory. Because I was once nauseated by buttered popcorn, I still feel somewhat queasy when I smell it. It's a conditioned response. I don't have to think about it. (And I don't want to think about it, to tell you the truth. I wrote about it here because of my deep commitment to you.)

Here are some other examples of implicit memories: You have learned and now remember how to speak at least one language, how to ride a bicycle, how to swim or swing a bat, how to type, how to turn on the lights, and how to drive a car. It is said that you never "forget" how to ride a bicycle. This is because implicit memories can persist even when we have not used them for many years. Getting to class "by habit"—without paying attention to landmarks or directions—is another instance of implicit memory. If someone asked you what 2 times 2 is, the number 4 would probably "jump" into your mind without much thinking about it or conscious calculation. After going over the alphabet or multiplication tables hundreds of times, our memory of them becomes automatic or implicit. We don't have to pay conscious attention to them in order to remember them.

Your memory of the alphabet or the multiplication tables is the result of a great deal of repetition that makes associations automatic, a phenomenon which psychologists refer to as **priming.** Studies involving brain imaging reveal that priming makes it possible for people to carry out a mental task with less neural activity (Savage et al., 2001; Schacter & Badgaiyan, 2001). Years of priming helps people make complete words out of the word fragments (Roediger et al., 1992; Schacter et al., 1999). Even though the perceptual cues in the following word fragments are limited, you may very well make them into words:

PYGY   MRCA   TXT   BUFL

Semantic memory General knowledge, as opposed to episodic memory.

Priming The activation of specific associations in memory, often as a result of repetition and without making a conscious effort to access the memory.

(Sample answers would be "pygmy," "merchant," "text," and "buffalo.") Let us jump ahead to the next chapter ("Thinking and Language") to mention a couple of factors that will be involved in how many words you can make out of these fragments. One is your expertise with the English language. If English is your second language, you will probably make fewer associations to these fragments than if

English is your first language. In fact, you might not perceive any complete words. Another factor could be creativity. Can you think of other factors?

Daniel Schacter (1992) also illustrates implicit memory with the story of a woman with amnesia who was wandering the streets. The police picked her up and discovered that she could not remember who she was or any other fact about her life and that she had no identification. After extensive fruitless interviewing, the police hit on the idea of asking her to dial phone numbers—just any number at all. Even though the woman did not "know" what she was doing, she dialed her mother's number. **Truth or Fiction Revisited:** It is true that a woman who could not remember who she was automatically dialed her mother's number when the police gave her a telephone. When asked for the phone numbers of people she knew, the woman had had no answer. She could not *declare* her mother's phone number. She could not make the number *explicit*. She could not even remember her mother's name, or whether she had a mother. All this explicit information was gone. But dialing her mother's phone number was apparently a habit, and she did it "on automatic pilot." We can assume that she had been *primed* for this task by dialing the number hundreds of times, perhaps many thousands of times. Implicit memory reveals the effects of experience when we are not specifically trying to recall information.

Retrospective Memory versus Prospective Memory

Retrospective memory is the recalling of information that has been previously learned. *Episodic, semantic,* and *implicit memories* all involve remembering things that were learned. **Question: What is the difference between retrospective memory and prospective memory?**

Prospective memory involves remembering to do things in the future. Tasks that depend on prospective memory include remembering to brush your teeth before going out, to pay your bills (yuck), to take out some cash, and to make the list of things to do so that you won't forget what to do! And if one does make a list of things to do, one must remember to use it. Most of us have had failures of prospective memory in which we have the feeling that we were supposed to do something, but we can't remember what. Prospective memory tends to fail when we are preoccupied (caught up in surfing the Net or fantasizing about you-know-who), distracted (we get a phone call just as we are about to get going on something), or feeling the stress of time pressure (Schacter, 1999).

There are various kinds of prospective memory tasks. For example, *habitual tasks* such as getting to class on time are easier to remember than occasional tasks such as meeting someone for coffee at an arbitrary time (d'Ydewalle et al., 1999). But motivation also plays a role. You are more likely to remember the coffee date if the person you are meeting is extremely attractive and someone whom you are interested in getting to know better. Psychologists also distinguish between event-based and time-based prospective memory tasks (Fortin et al., 2002). *Event-based tasks* are triggered by events, such as remembering to take one's medicine at breakfast or to brush one's teeth after eating. *Time-based tasks* are to be performed at a certain time or after a certain amount of time has elapsed between occurrences, such as tuning in to a favorite news program at 7:30 PM or taking a pill very four hours (d'Ydewalle et al., 1999).

There is an age-related decline in both retrospective and prospective memory (Brigman & Cherry, 2002; Reese & Cherry, 2002). Generally speaking, the decline in older adults often appears to be related to the speed of cognitive processing rather than "loss" of memory per se. In the case of prospective memory, older adults appear to be about as aware of specific cues or reminders as young adults; however, it takes them longer to respond to the cues or reminders (West & Craik, 1999). That is, if they meet with a friend, they are likely to remember that they were supposed to ask something, but it may take longer for them to remember the particular question.

Retrospective memory Memory for past events, activities, and learning experiences, as shown by explicit (episodic and semantic) and implicit memories.

Prospective memory Memory to perform an act in the future, as at a certain time or when a certain event occurs.

However, older adults with greater verbal ability and occupational status are better able to keep their intentions in mind (Reese & Cherry, 2002).

Moods and attitudes have an effect on prospective memory (Villa & Abeles, 2000). For example, negative emotional states such as depression also impair prospective memory. Depressed people are less likely to push to remind themselves to do what they intend to do (Rude et al., 1999). On the other hand, older people who are confident in their ability to remember to carry out tasks are more likely to actually remember to do them (McDonald-Miszczak et al., 1999). Yet the same confidence in one's memory does not appear to be associated with better performance at *retrospective* memory tasks (recalling the past) (McDonald-Miszczak et al., 1999). The various kinds of memory are summarized in the nearby Concept Review.

Before proceeding to the next section, why don't you turn to the piece of paper on which you wrote the names of the four figures—that is, sheet number 4—and draw them from memory as exactly as you can. Hold on to the drawings. We'll talk about them a bit later.

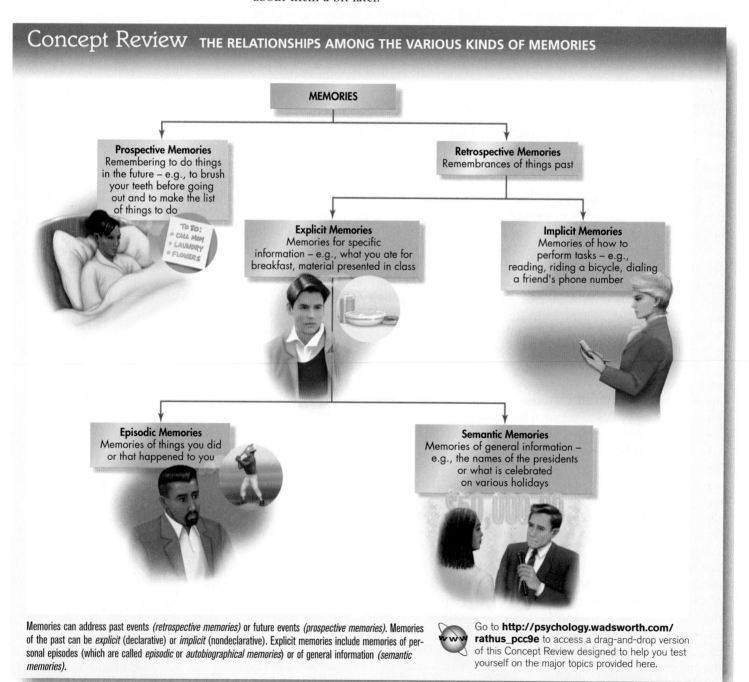

Concept Review THE RELATIONSHIPS AMONG THE VARIOUS KINDS OF MEMORIES

MEMORIES

Prospective Memories
Remembering to do things in the future – e.g., to brush your teeth before going out and to make the list of things to do

TO DO:
• CALL MOM
• LAUNDRY
• FLOWERS

Retrospective Memories
Remembrances of things past

Explicit Memories
Memories for specific information – e.g., what you ate for breakfast, material presented in class

Implicit Memories
Memories of how to perform tasks – e.g., reading, riding a bicycle, dialing a friend's phone number

Episodic Memories
Memories of things you did or that happened to you

Semantic Memories
Memories of general information – e.g., the names of the presidents or what is celebrated on various holidays

Memories can address past events *(retrospective memories)* or future events *(prospective memories)*. Memories of the past can be *explicit* (declarative) or *implicit* (nondeclarative). Explicit memories include memories of personal episodes (which are called *episodic* or *autobiographical memories*) or of general information *(semantic memories)*.

Go to **http://psychology.wadsworth.com/ rathus_pcc9e** to access a drag-and-drop version of this Concept Review designed to help you test yourself on the major topics provided here.

Your Turn: Now that we have discussed various kinds of memory, enhance your mastery of the material with the nearby "Learning Connections." Review the material by filling in the blanks, reflect on the material by relating it to other things you know, and think critically about it.

Learning Connections — KINDS OF MEMORY: PRESSING THE "REWIND" AND "FAST-FORWARD" BUTTONS

ACTIVE REVIEW (1) _____ memories are memories of specific information. (2) Memories of the events that happen to a person are _____ memories. (3) _____ memories concern generalized knowledge.

REFLECT AND RELATE Try a mini-experiment. Take out a pen or pencil and write your name. (Or, if you are using a keyboard, type your name.) Now reflect: You remembered how to hold and write with the pen or pencil, or how to type. Did you have to "think" about how to do these

things? Did you have to dredge the methods out from deep somewhere in the storage bins of your memory, or were they "right there"?

CRITICAL THINKING Definitions matter. Should this chapter be called *Memory* or *Memories?* You have retrospective versus prospective memories, implicit versus explicit memories, and so on. Do they represent different *systems* of memory, or are they just different examples of memory?

 Go to **http://psychology.wadsworth.com/ rathus_pcc9e** for an interactive version of this Learning Connections unit.

Processes of Memory: Processing Information in Our Most Personal Computers

Both psychologists and computer scientists speak of processing information. Think of using a computer to write a term paper. Once the system is up and operating, you begin to enter information. You can enter information into the computer's memory by, for example, typing letters on a keyboard or—in the case of voice recognition technology—speaking. If you were to do some major surgery on your computer (which I am often tempted to do) and open up its memory, however, you wouldn't find these letters or sounds inside it. This is because the computer is programmed to change the letters or sounds—that is, the information you have entered—into a form that can be placed in its electronic memory. Similarly, when we perceive information, we must convert it into a form that can be remembered if we are to place it in our memory.

Encoding: The Memory's "Transformer"

Information about the outside world reaches our senses in the form of physical and chemical stimuli. The first stage of information processing is changing information so that we can place it in memory: **encoding. Question: What is the role of encoding in memory?** When we encode information, we transform it into psychological formats that can be represented mentally. To do so, we commonly use visual, auditory, and semantic codes.

Let us illustrate the uses of coding by referring to the list of letters you first saw in the section on challenges to memory. Try to write the letters on sheet number 1. Go on, take a minute and then come back.

Okay, now: If you had used a **visual code** to try to remember the list, you would have mentally represented it as a picture. That is, you would have maintained—or attempted to maintain—a mental image of the letters. Some artists and art historians seem to maintain marvelous visual mental representations of works of art. This enables them to quickly recognize whether a work is authentic.

You may also have decided to read the list of letters to yourself—that is, to silently say them in sequence: "t," "h," "u," and so on. By so doing, you would have been using an **acoustic code,** or representing the stimuli as a sequence of sounds. You may also have read the list as a three-syllable word, "thun-sto-fam." This is an acoustic code, but it also involves the "meaning" of the letters, in the

Encoding Modifying information so that it can be placed in memory; the first stage of information processing.

Visual code Mental representation of information as a picture.

Acoustic code Mental representation of information as a sequence of sounds.

sense that you are interpreting the list as a word. This approach has elements of a semantic code.

Semantic codes represent stimuli in terms of their meaning. Our ten letters were meaningless in and of themselves. However, they can also serve as an acronym—a term made up of the first letters of a phrase—for the familiar phrase "THe UNited STates OF AMerica." This observation lends them meaning.

Storage: The Memory's "Save" Function

The second memory process is **storage. Question: What is the role of storage in memory?** Storage means maintaining information over time. If you were given the task of storing the list of letters—that is, told to remember it—how would you attempt to place it in storage? One way would be by **maintenance rehearsal**—by mentally repeating the list, or saying it to yourself. Our awareness of the functioning of our memory, referred to by psychologists as **metamemory,** becomes more sophisticated as we develop.

You could also have condensed the amount of information you were rehearsing by reading the list as a three-syllable word; that is, you could have rehearsed three syllables (said "thun-sto-fam" over and over again) rather than ten letters. In either case, repetition would have been the key to memory. (We talk more about such condensing, or "chunking," very soon.)

However, you could also encode the list of letters by relating it to something that you already know. This coding is called **elaborative rehearsal.** You are "elaborating" or extending the semantic meaning of the letters you are trying to remember. For example, did you recognize that the list of ten letters is an acronym for "The United States of America"? (That is, you take the first two letters of each of the words in the phrase and string them together to make up the 10 letters of THUNSTOFAM.) If you had recognized this, storage of the list of letters might have been almost instantaneous, and it would probably have been permanent.

However, adequate maintenance rehearsal can do the job. **Truth or Fiction Revisited:** Therefore, it is not true that learning must be meaningful if we are to remember it.

Retrieval: The Memory's "Find" Function

The third memory process is **retrieval. Question: What is the role of retrieval in memory?** The retrieval of stored information means locating it and returning it to consciousness. With well-known information such as our names and occupations, retrieval is effortless and, for all practical purposes, immediate. But when we are trying to remember massive quantities of information, or information that is not perfectly understood, retrieval can be tedious and not always successful. It is easiest to retrieve information stored in a computer by using the name of the file. Similarly, retrieval of information from our memories requires knowledge of the proper cues.

If you had encoded THUNSTOFAM as a three-syllable word, your retrieval strategy would involve recollection of the word and rules for decoding. In other words, you would say the "word" *thun-sto-fam* and then decode it by spelling it out. You might err in that "thun" sounds like "thumb" and "sto" could also be spelled "stow." However, using the semantic code, or recognition of the acronym for "The United States of America," could lead to flawless recollection.

I stuck my neck out by predicting that you would immediately and permanently store the list if you recognized it as an acronym. Here, too, there would be recollection (of the name of our country) and rules for decoding. That is, to "remember" the ten letters, you would have to envision the phrase ("The United States of America") and read off the first two letters of each word. Because using this semantic code is more complex than simply seeing the entire list (using a visual code), it may take a while to recall (actually, to reconstruct) the list of ten letters. But by using the phrase, you are likely to remember the list of letters permanently.

Semantic code Mental representation of information according to its meaning.

Storage The maintenance of information over time; the second stage of information processing.

Maintenance rehearsal Mental repetition of information in order to keep it in memory.

Metamemory Self-awareness of the ways in which memory functions, allowing the person to encode, store, and retrieve information effectively.

Elaborative rehearsal The kind of coding in which new information is related to information that is already known.

Retrieval The location of stored information and its return to consciousness; the third stage of information processing.

Now, what if you were not able to remember the list of ten letters? What would have gone wrong? In terms of the three processes of memory, it could be that you had (1) not encoded the list in a useful way, (2) not entered the encoded information into storage, or (3) stored the information but lacked the proper cues for remembering it—such as the phrase "The United States of America" or the rule for decoding the phrase.

By now you may have noticed that I have discussed three kinds of memory and three processes of memory, but I have not yet *defined* memory. No apologies—we weren't ready for a definition yet. Now that we have explored some basic concepts, let us give it a try: **Memory** is the processes by which information is encoded, stored, and retrieved.

Memory The processes by which information is encoded, stored, and retrieved.

Your Turn: Now that we have discussed processes of memory, enhance your mastery of the material with the nearby "Learning Connections." Review the material by filling in the blanks, reflect on the material by relating it to other things you know, and think critically about it.

 ## Learning Connections | PROCESSES OF MEMORY: PROCESSING INFORMATION IN OUR MOST PERSONAL COMPUTERS

ACTIVE REVIEW (4) _____ is the transforming of information so that we can remember it. (5) One way of storing information is by _____ rehearsal, or by mentally repeating it. (6) Another way of storing information is by _____ rehearsal, in which we relate new information to things we already know. (7) _____ of information from storage requires knowledge of the proper cues.

REFLECT AND RELATE As you read this page, are you using acoustic coding to transform the sensory

stimulation? Are you surprised that you "know" how to do this? How do you remember how to spell the words *receive* and *retrieve*?

CRITICAL THINKING Why would an author—like me—compare the functioning of memory to the functioning of a computer? Do you find the comparison to be useful or misleading?

Go to **http://psychology.wadsworth.com/rathus_pcc9e** for an interactive version of this Learning Connections unit.

Stages of Memory: Making *Sense* of the *Short* and the *Long* of It

William James (1890) was intrigued by the fact that some memories are unreliable, "going in one ear and out the other," while others could be recalled for a lifetime. He wrote:

> The stream of thought flows on, but most of its elements fall into the bottomless pit of oblivion. Of some, no element survives the instant of their passage. Of others, it is confined to a few moments, hours, or days. Others, again, leave vestiges which are indestructible, and by means of which they may be recalled as long as life endures.

Yes, the world is a constant display of sights and sounds and other sources of sensory stimulation, but only some of these things are remembered. James was correct in observing that we remember various "elements" of thought for different lengths of time, and many we do not remember at all. Psychologists Richard Atkinson and Richard Shiffrin (1968) suggested a model for how some stimuli are lost immediately, others held briefly, and still others for a lifetime. **Question: What is the Atkinson–Shiffrin model of memory?** Atkinson and Shiffrin proposed that there are three stages of memory and suggested that the progress of information through these stages determines whether (and how long) it is retained (see Figure 7.1). These stages are *sensory memory, short-term memory (STM),* and *long-term memory (LTM).*

There is a saying that when you cover a topic completely, you are talking about "the long and short of it." In the case of the stages of memory, we could say that we are trying to "make *sense* of the *short* and the *long* of it."

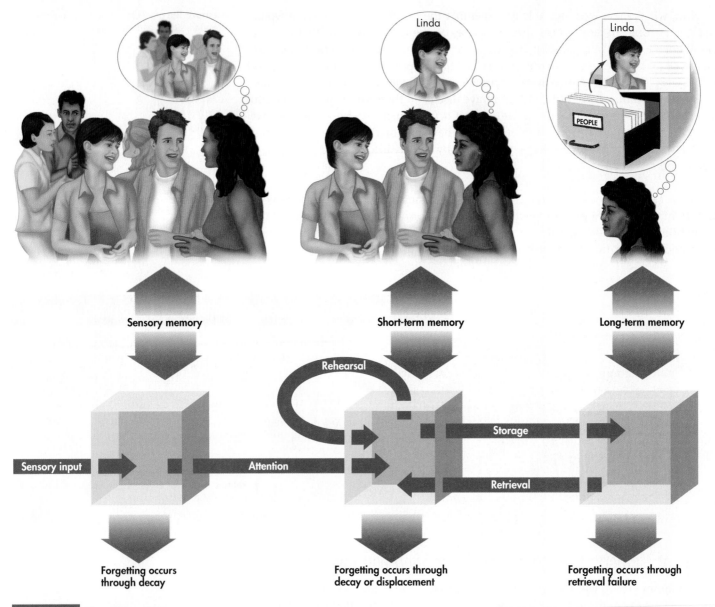

FIGURE 7.1 **Three Stages of Memory**
The Atkinson–Shiffrin model proposes that there are three distinct stages of memory. Sensory information impacts upon the registers of sensory memory, where memory traces are held briefly before decaying. If we attend to the information, much of it is transferred to short-term memory (STM). Information in STM may decay or be displaced if it is not transferred to long-term memory (LTM). We can use rehearsal or elaborative strategies to transfer memories to LTM. If information in LTM is organized poorly, or if we cannot find cues to retrieve it, it may be lost.

Go to **http://psychology.wadsworth. com/rathus_pcc9e** to access an interactive version of this figure.

Sensory Memory: Flashes on the Mental Monitor

William James (1890) also wrote about the stream of thought, or consciousness:

> Consciousness . . . does not appear to itself chopped up in bits. A "river" or a "stream" are the metaphors by which it is most naturally described. In talking of it hereafter, let us call it the stream of thought, of consciousness, or of subjective life.

When we look at a visual stimulus, our impressions may seem fluid enough. Actually, however, they consist of a series of eye fixations referred to as **saccadic eye movements.** These movements jump from one point to another about four times each second. Yet the visual sensations seem continuous, or streamlike, because of **sensory memory.** Sensory memory is the type or stage of memory that is first encountered by a stimulus. Although sensory memory holds impressions briefly, it is long enough so that a series of perceptions seem to be connected. **Question: How does sensory memory function?**

Saccadic eye movement The rapid jumps made by a person's eyes as they fixate on different points.

Sensory memory The type or stage of memory first encountered by a stimulus. Sensory memory holds impressions briefly, but long enough so that series of perceptions are psychologically continuous.

To explain the functioning of sensory memory, let us return to our list of letters: THUNSTOFAM. If the list were flashed on a screen for a fraction of a second, the visual impression, or **memory trace,** of the stimulus would also last for only a fraction of a second afterward. Psychologists speak of the memory trace of the list as being held in a visual **sensory register.**

If the letters had been flashed on a screen for, say, 1/10th of a second, your ability to remember them on the basis of sensory memory alone would be limited. Your memory would be based on a single eye fixation, and the trace of the image would vanish before a single second had passed. A century ago, psychologist William McDougall (1904) engaged in research in which he showed people one to 12 letters arranged in rows—just long enough to allow a single eye fixation. Under these conditions, people could typically remember only four or five letters. Thus recollection of THUNSTOFAM, a list of 10 letters arranged in a single row, would probably depend on whether one had encoded it so that it could be processed further.

George Sperling (1960) modified McDougall's experimental method and showed that there is a difference between what people can see and what they can report. McDougall had used a *whole-report procedure,* in which people were asked to report every letter they saw in the array. Sperling used a modified *partial-report procedure,* in which people were asked to report the contents of one of three rows of letters. In a typical procedure, Sperling flashed three rows of letters like the following on a screen for 50 milliseconds (1/20th of a second):

A G R E
V L S B
N K B T

Using the whole-report procedure, people could report an average of four letters from the entire display (one out of three). But if immediately after presenting the display Sperling pointed an arrow at a row he wanted viewers to report, they usually reported most of the letters in the row successfully.

If Sperling presented six letters arrayed in two rows, people could usually report either row without error. If people were flashed three rows of four letters each—a total of twelve—they reported correctly an average of three of four letters in the designated row, suggesting that about nine of the twelve letters had been perceived.

Sperling found that the amount of time that elapsed before indicating the row to be reported was crucial. If he delayed pointing the arrow for a few fractions of a second after presenting the letters, people were much less successful in reporting the letters in the target row. If he allowed a full second to elapse, the arrow did not aid recall at all. From these data, Sperling concluded that the memory trace of visual stimuli *decays* within a second in the visual sensory register (see Figure 7.1). With a single eye fixation, people can *see* most of a display of 12 letters clearly, as shown by their ability to immediately read off most of the letters in a designated row. Yet as the fractions of a single second are elapsing, the memory trace of the letters is fading. By the time a second has elapsed, the trace has vanished.

ICONIC MEMORY Psychologists believe we possess a sensory register for each one of our senses. The mental representations of visual stimuli are referred to as **icons.** The sensory register that holds icons is labeled **iconic memory.** Iconic memory is one kind of sensory memory. Iconic memories are accurate, photographic memories. **Truth or Fiction Revisited:** Those of us who see and mentally represent visual stimuli do have "photographic memories." However, these memories are brief. What most of us usually think of as a photographic memory—the ability to retain exact mental representations of visual stimuli over long periods of time—is technically termed **eidetic imagery.** Although all people who can see have photographic memories (that is, icons), only a few have the capacity for eidetic imagery.

Memory trace An assumed change in the nervous system that reflects the impression made by a stimulus. Memory traces are said to be "held" in sensory registers.

Sensory register A system of memory that holds information briefly, but long enough so that it can be processed further. There may be a sensory register for every sense.

Icon A mental representation of a visual stimulus that is held briefly in sensory memory.

Iconic memory The sensory register that briefly holds mental representations of visual stimuli.

Eidetic imagery The maintenance of detailed visual memories over several minutes.

© Jacques M. Chenet/CORBIS

■ **Echoic Memory: Memorizing a Script by Rehearsing Echoic Memories** As actor Bill Cosby works on memorizing a script, he first encodes visual information (printed words) as echoes (their corresponding sounds within his brain). Then he commits the echoes to memory by rehearsing (repeating) them. He refers to the visual information as frequently as necessary.

ICONIC MEMORY AND SACCADIC EYE MOVEMENTS Iconic memory smooths out the bumps in the visual ride. Saccadic eye movements occur about four times every second. Iconic memory, however, holds icons for up to a second. As a consequence, the flow of visual information seems smooth and continuous. Your impression that the words you are reading flow across the page, rather than jumping across in spurts, is a product of your iconic memory. Similarly, motion pictures present 16 to 22 separate frames, or still images, each second. Iconic memory allows you to perceive the imagery in the film as being seamless (G. R. Loftus, 1983).

ECHOIC MEMORY Mental representations of sounds, or auditory stimuli, are called **echoes.** The sensory register that holds echoes is referred to as **echoic memory.**

The memory traces of auditory stimuli (that is, echoes) can last for several seconds, many times longer than the traces of visual stimuli (icons). The difference in the duration of traces is probably based on biological differences between the eye and the ear. This difference is one of the reasons that acoustic codes aid in the retention of information that has been presented visually—or why saying the letters or syllables of THUNSTOFAM makes the list easier to remember.

Yet echoes, like icons, fade with time. If they are to be retained, we must pay attention to them. By selectively attending to certain stimuli, we sort them out from the background noise. For example, in studies on the development of patterns of processing information, young children have been shown photographs of rooms full of toys and then been asked to recall as many of the toys as they can. One such study found that 2-year-old boys are more likely to attend to and remember toys such as cars, puzzles, and trains. Two-year-old girls are more likely to attend to and remember dolls, dishes, and teddy bears (Renninger & Wozniak, 1985). Even by this early age, the things that children attend to frequently fall into stereotypical patterns.

Short-Term Memory: Keeping Things "In Mind"

Imagine that you are completing a writing assignment and you keyboard or speak words and phrases into your word-processing program. They appear on your monitor as a sign that your computer has them in *memory*. Your word-processing program allows you to add words, delete words, see if they are spelled correctly, add images, and move whole paragraphs from place to place. So you can manipulate the information in your computer's memory, but it isn't saved. It hasn't been entered into storage. If the program or the computer crashes, the information is gone. The computer's memory is a short-term affair. To maintain a long-term connection with the information, you have to save it. Saving it means giving it a name—hopefully a name that you will remember so that you can later find and retrieve the information—and instructing your computer to save it (keep it in storage until told otherwise).

If you focus on a stimulus in the sensory register, you will tend to retain it in your own **short-term memory**—also referred to as **working memory**—for a minute or so after the trace of the stimulus decays. **Question: How does short-term**

Echo A mental representation of an auditory stimulus (sound) that is held briefly in sensory memory.

Echoic memory The sensory register that briefly holds mental representations of auditory stimuli.

Short-term memory The type or stage of memory that can hold information for up to a minute or so after the trace of the stimulus decays. Also called *working memory.*

Working memory Same as *short-term memory.*

memory function? As one researcher describes it, "Working memory is the mental glue that links a thought through time from its beginning to its end" (Goldman-Rakic, 1995). When you are given a phone number by the information operator and write it down or immediately dial the number, you are retaining the number in your short-term memory. When you are told the name of someone at a party and then use that name immediately in addressing that person, you are retaining the name in short-term memory. In short-term memory, the image tends to fade significantly after 10 to 12 seconds if it is not repeated or rehearsed. It is possible to focus on maintaining a visual image in the short-term memory, but it is more common to encode visual stimuli as sounds, or auditory stimuli. Then the sounds can be rehearsed, or repeated.

Most of us know that one way of retaining information in short-term memory—and possibly storing it permanently—is to rehearse it. When an information operator tells me a phone number, I usually rehearse it continuously while I am dialing it or running around frantically searching for a pencil and a scrap of paper so that I can "save" it. The more times we rehearse information, the more likely we are to remember it. We have the capacity (if not the will or the time) to rehearse information and thereby keep it in short-term memory indefinitely.

Once information is in our short-term memories, we can work on it. Like the information in the word-processing program, we can manipulate it. But it isn't necessarily saved. If we don't do something to save it (like write down that telephone number on a scrap of paper or in a personal digital assistant), it can be gone forever. We can try to reconstruct it, but it may never be the same. Getting most of the digits in someone's phone number right doesn't get you a date for the weekend—at least not with the person you were thinking of!

Truth or Fiction Revisited: It is true that it may be easier for you to recall the name of your first-grade teacher than the name of someone you just met at a party. You need to rehearse new information in order to "save" it, but you may only need the proper cue to retrieve information from long-term memory.

KEEPING THUNSTOFAM IN SHORT-TERM MEMORY Let us now return to the task of remembering the first list of letters in the challenges to memory at the beginning of the chapter. If you had encoded the letters as the three-syllable word THUN-STO-FAM, you would probably have recalled them by mentally rehearsing (saying to yourself) the three-syllable "word" and then spelling it out from the sounds. A few minutes later, if someone asked whether the letters had been uppercase (THUNSTOFAM) or lowercase (thunstofam), you might not have been able to answer with confidence. You used an acoustic code to help recall the list, and uppercase and lowercase letters sound alike.

Because it can be pronounced, THUNSTOFAM is not too difficult to retain in short-term memory. But what if the list of letters had been TBXLFNTSDK? This list of letters cannot be pronounced as it is. You would have to find a complex acronym to code these letters, and do so within a fraction of a second—most likely an impossible task. To aid recall, you would probably choose to try to repeat the letters rapidly—to read each one as many times as possible before the memory trace fades. You might visualize each letter as you say it and try to get back to it (that is, to run through the entire list) before it decays.

Let us assume that you encoded the letters as sounds and then rehearsed the sounds. When asked to report the list, you might mistakenly say T-V-X-L-F-N-T-S-T-K. This would be an understandable error because the incorrect V and T sounds are similar, respectively, to the correct B and D sounds.

THE SERIAL-POSITION EFFECT If asked to recall the list of letters TBXLFNTSDK, you would also be likely to recall the first and last letters in the series, T and K, more accurately than the others. **Question: Why are we most likely to remember the first and last items in a list?** The tendency to recall the first and last items in a series is known as the **serial-position effect.** This effect may occur because we pay more attention

Serial-position effect The tendency to recall more accurately the first and last items in a series.

Primacy effect The tendency to recall the initial items in a series of items.

Recency effect The tendency to recall the last items in a series of items.

Chunk A stimulus or group of stimuli that is perceived as a discrete piece of information.

to the first and last stimuli in a series. They serve as the visual or auditory boundaries for the other stimuli. It may also be that the first items are likely to be rehearsed more frequently (repeated more times) than other items. The last items are likely to have been rehearsed most recently and hence are most likely to be retained in short-term memory.

According to cognitive psychologists, the tendency to recall the initial items in a list is referred to as the **primacy effect.** Social psychologists have also noted a powerful primacy effect in our formation of impressions of other people. In other words, first impressions tend to last. The tendency to recall the last items in a list is referred to as the **recency effect.** If we are asked to recall the last items in a list soon after we have been shown the list, they may still be in short-term memory. As a result, they can be "read off." Earlier items, in contrast, may have to be retrieved from long-term memory.

CHUNKING Rapidly rehearsing ten meaningless letters is not an easy task. With TBXLFNTSDK there are 10 discrete elements, or **chunks,** of information that must be kept in short-term memory. When we encode THUNSTOFAM as three syllables, there are only three chunks to swallow at once—a memory task that is much easier on the digestion.

George Miller (1956) wryly noted that the average person is comfortable with digesting about seven integers at a time, the number of integers in a telephone number: "My problem is that I have been persecuted by an integer [the number *seven*]. For seven years this number has followed me around, has intruded in my most private data, and has assaulted me from the pages of our most public journals" (1956). **Question: Is seven a magic number, or did the phone company get lucky?**

It may sound as if Miller was being paranoid or magical, but he was actually talking about research findings. Research shows that most people have little trouble recalling five chunks of information, as in a zip code. Some can remember nine, which is, for all but a few, an upper limit. So seven chunks, plus or minus one or two, is a "magic" number in the sense that the typical person can manage to remember that many chunks of information and not a great deal more.

So how, you ask, do we manage to include area codes in our recollections of telephone numbers, hence making them ten digits long? The truth of the matter is that we usually don't. We tend to recall the area code as a single chunk of information derived from our general knowledge of where a person lives. So we are more likely to remember (or "know") the ten-digit numbers of acquaintances who reside in locales with area codes that we use frequently.

Businesses pay the phone company hefty premiums so that they can attain numbers with two or three zeroes or repeated digits—for example, 592-2000 or 277-3333. These numbers include fewer chunks of information and hence are easier to remember. Customer recollection of business phone numbers increases sales. One financial services company uses the toll-free number CALL-IRA, which reduces the task to two chunks of information that also happen to be meaningfully related (semantically coded) to the nature of the business. Similarly, a clinic that helps people quit smoking arranged for a telephone number that can be reached by dialing the letters NO SMOKE.

Return to the third challenge to memory presented earlier. Were you able to remember the six groups of letters? Would your task have been simpler if you had grouped them differently? How about moving the dashes forward by a letter, so that they read GM-CBS-IBM-ATT-CIA-FBI? If we do this, we have the same list of letters, but we also have six chunks of information that can be coded semantically (according to what they mean). You may have also been able to generate the list by remembering a rule, such as "big corporations and government agencies."

If we can recall seven or perhaps nine chunks of information, how do children remember the alphabet? The alphabet contains 26 discrete pieces of information. How do children learn to encode the letters of the alphabet, which are visual symbols, as spoken sounds? There is nothing about the shape of an A that suggests its sound. Nor does the visual stimulus B sound "B-ish." Children learn to associate letters with their spoken names by **rote.** It is mechanical associative learning that takes time and repetition. If you think that learning the alphabet by rote is a simple task, try learning the Russian alphabet.

If you had recognized THUNSTOFAM as an acronym for the first two letters of each word in the phrase "THe UNited STates OF AMerica," you would also have reduced the number of chunks of information that had to be recalled. You could have considered the phrase to be a single chunk of information. The rule that you must use the first two letters of each word of the phrase would be another chunk.

Reconsider the second challenge to memory presented earlier. You were asked to remember nine chunks of visual information. Perhaps you could have used the acoustic codes "L" and "Square" for chunks 3 and 5, but no obvious codes are available for the seven other chunks. Now look at Figure 7.2. If you had recognized that the elements in the challenge could be arranged as the familiar tic-tac-toe grid, remembering the nine elements might have required two chunks of information. The first would have been the mental image of the grid, and the second would have been the rule for decoding: Each element corresponds to the shape of a section of the grid if read like words on a page (from upper left to lower right). The number sequence 1 through 9 would not in itself present a problem, because you learned this series by rote many years ago and have rehearsed it in countless calculations since then.

INTERFERENCE IN SHORT-TERM MEMORY I mentioned that I often find myself running around looking for a pencil and a scrap of paper to write down a telephone number that has been given to me. If I keep on rehearsing the number while I'm looking, I'm okay. But I have also often cursed myself for failing to keep a pad and pencil by the telephone, and sometimes this has interfered with my recollection of the number. (The moral of the story? Avoid self-reproach.) It has also happened that I have actually looked up a phone number and been about to dial it when someone has asked me for the time or where I said we were going to dinner. Unless I say, "Hold on a minute!" and manage to jot down the number on something, it's back to the phone book. Attending to distracting information, even briefly, prevents me from rehearsing the number, so it falls through the cracks of my short-term memory.

In an experiment with college students, Lloyd and Margaret Peterson (1959) demonstrated how prevention of rehearsal can wreak havoc with short-term memory. They asked students to remember three-letter combinations such as HGB—normally, three easy chunks of information. They then had the students count backward from an arbitrary number, such as 181, by threes (that is, 181, 178, 175, 172, and so on). The students were told to stop counting and to report the letter sequence after the intervals of time shown in Figure 7.3. The percentage of letter combinations that were recalled correctly fell precipitously within seconds. After 18 seconds of interference, counting had dislodged the letter sequences in almost all of these bright students' memories.

Psychologists say that the appearance of new information in short-term memory **displaces** the old information. Remember: Only a few bits of information can be retained in short-term memory at the same time. (Unfortunately we cannot upgrade our human memories from, say, 128 megabytes to 512 or 1024 megabytes.) Think of short-term memory as a shelf or workbench. Once it is full, some things fall off it when new items are shoved onto it. Here we have another possible explanation for the recency effect: The most recently learned bit of information is least likely to be displaced by additional information.

Displacement occurs at cocktail parties, and I'm not referring to jostling by the crowd. The point is this: When you meet Linda or Latrell at the party, you should have little trouble remembering the name. But then you may meet Tamara or Timothy and,

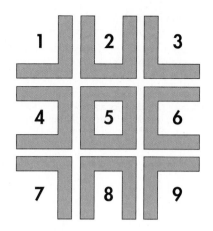

FIGURE 7.2 **A Familiar Grid**
The nine drawings in the second challenge to memory form this familiar tic-tac-toe grid when the numbers are placed inside them and they are arranged in order. This method for recalling the shapes collapses nine chunks of information into two. One is the tic-tac-toe grid. The second is the rule for decoding the drawings from the grid.

Rote Mechanical associative learning that is based on repetition.

Displace In memory theory, to cause information to be lost from short-term memory by adding new information.

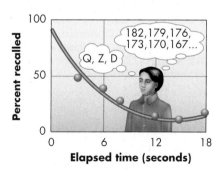

FIGURE 7.3 **The Effect of Interference on Short-Term Memory**
In this experiment, college students were asked to remember a series of three letters while they counted backward by threes. After just three seconds, retention was cut by half. Ability to recall the words was almost completely lost by 15 seconds.

Long-term memory The type or stage of memory capable of relatively permanent storage.

Repression In Freud's psychodynamic theory, the ejection of anxiety-evoking ideas from conscious awareness.

Schema A way of mentally representing the world, such as a belief or an expectation, that can influence perception of persons, objects, and situations.

still later, Keith or LaToya. By that time you may have a hard time dredging up Jennifer or Jonathan's name—unless, of course, you were very, very attracted to one of them. A passionate response would set a person apart and inspire a good deal of selective attention. According to signal-detection theory, if you were enamored enough, you might "detect" the person's name (sensory signals) with a vengeance, and the other names would dissolve into background noise.

Long-Term Memory: Your Memory's "Hard Drive"

Long-term memory is the third stage of information processing. Think of your long-term memory as a vast storehouse of information containing names, dates, places, what Johnny did to you in second grade, and what Susan said about you when you were 12. **Question: How does long-term memory function?**

Some psychologists (Freud was one) used to believe that nearly all of our perceptions and ideas are stored permanently. We might not be able to retrieve all of them. Some memories might be "lost" because of lack of proper cues, or they might be kept unconscious by the forces of **repression.** Adherents to this view often pointed to the work of neurosurgeon Wilder Penfield (1969). When parts of their brains were electrically stimulated, many of Penfield's patients reported the appearance of images that had something of the feel of memories.

Today most psychologists view this notion as exaggerated. Memory researcher Elizabeth Loftus, for example, notes that the "memories" stimulated by Penfield's probes lacked detail and were sometimes incorrect (Loftus & Loftus, 1980; Loftus, 1983). **Truth or Fiction Revisited:** It has therefore *not* been shown that all of our experiences are permanently imprinted on the brain. Now let us consider some other questions about long-term memory.

HOW ACCURATE ARE LONG-TERM MEMORIES? Psychologist Elizabeth Loftus notes that memories are distorted by our biases and needs—by the ways in which we conceptualize our worlds. We represent much of our world in the form of **schemas.**

To understand what is meant by the term *schema,* consider the problems of travelers who met up with Procrustes, the legendary highwayman of ancient Greece. Procrustes had a quirk. He was interested not only in travelers' pocketbooks but also in their height. He had a concept—a schema—of how tall people should be, and when people did not fit his schema, they were in trouble. You see, Procrustes also had a bed, the famous "Procrustean bed." He made his victims lie down in the bed, and if they were too short for it, he stretched them to make them fit. If they were too long for the bed, he practiced surgery on their legs.

FIGURE 7.4 **Memory as Reconstructive**
In their classic experiment, Carmichael, Hogan, and Walter (1932) showed people the figures in the left-hand box and made remarks as suggested in the other boxes. For example, the experimenter might say, "This drawing looks like eyeglasses [or a dumbbell]." When people later reconstructed the drawings, they were influenced by the labels. What did *your* drawings look like?

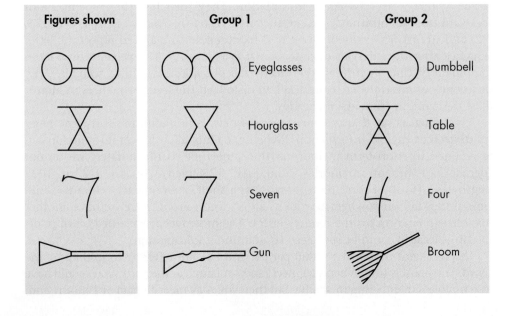

Figures shown	Group 1	Group 2
○—○	○○ Eyeglasses	○—○ Dumbbell
⋈	⋈ Hourglass	⋈ Table
7	7 Seven	4 Four
▭—	▭— Gun	🧹 Broom

Although the myth of Procrustes may sound absurd, it reflects a quirky truth about each of us. We all carry our cognitive Procrustean beds around with us—our unique ways of perceiving the world—and we try to make things and people fit them. Let me give you an example. "Retrieve" the fourth sheet of paper you prepared according to the Self-Assessment in the beginning of the chapter. You drew the figures "from memory" according to instructions on page 270. Now look at Figure 7.4. Are your drawings closer in form to those in group 1 or to those in group 2? I wouldn't be surprised if they were more like those in group 1—if, for example, your first drawing looked more like eyeglasses than a dumbbell. After all, they were labeled like the drawings in group 1. The labels serve as *schemas* for the drawings—ways of organizing your knowledge of them—and these schemas may have influenced your recollections.

■ **How Fast Were These Cars Going when They Collided?** Our schemas influence our processing of information. When shown pictures such as these, people who were asked how fast the cars were going when they *smashed* into each other offer higher estimates than people who were told that the cars *hit* each other.

Consider another example of the power of schemas in processing information. Loftus and Palmer (1974) showed people a film of a car crash and then asked them to fill out questionnaires that included a question about how fast the cars were going at the time. The language of the question varied in subtle ways, however. Some people were asked to estimate how fast the cars were going when they "hit" each other. Others were asked to estimate the cars' speed when they "smashed into" each other. On average, people who reconstructed the scene on the basis of the cue "hit" estimated a speed of 34 mph. People who watched the same film but reconstructed the scene on the basis of the cue "smashed" estimated a speed of 41 mph! In other words, the use of the word *hit* or *smashed* caused people to organize their knowledge about the crash in different ways. That is, the words served as diverse schemas that fostered the development of very different ways of processing information about the crash.

Subjects in the same study were questioned again a week later: "Did you see any broken glass?" Because there was no broken glass shown in the film, an answer of "yes" would be wrong. Of those who had earlier been encouraged to process information about the accident in terms of one car "hitting" the other, 14% incorrectly answered yes. But 32% of the subjects who had processed information about the crash in terms of one car "smashing into" the other reported, incorrectly, that they had seen broken glass.

Another experiment reported by Elizabeth Loftus (1979) shows that people may reconstruct their experiences according to their prejudices. Subjects in the study were shown a picture that contained an African American man who was holding a hat and a European American man who was holding a razor. Later, when they were asked what they had seen, many subjects erroneously recalled the razor as being in the hands of the African American. The subjects recalled information that was consistent with their schemas, but it was wrong.

Can we trust eyewitness testimony?

Jean Piaget, the investigator of children's cognitive development, distinctly remembered an attempt to kidnap him from his baby carriage as he was being wheeled along the Champs Élysées. He recalled the excited throng, the abrasions on the face of the nurse who rescued him, the police officer's white baton, and the flight of the assailant. Although they were graphic, Piaget's memories were false. Years later, the nurse admitted that she had made up the tale.

■ **Eyewitness Testimony?** How trustworthy is eyewitness testimony? Memories are reconstructive rather than photographic. The wording of questions also influences the content of the memory. Attorneys therefore are sometimes instructed not to phrase questions in such a way that they "lead" the witness.

Can eyewitness testimony be trusted? Is there reason to believe that the statements of eyewitnesses are any more factual than Piaget's? Legal professionals are concerned about the accuracy of our long-term memories as reflected in eyewitness testimony (Wells & Olson, 2003). Misidentifications of suspects "create a double horror: The wrong person is devastated by this personal tragedy, and the real criminal is still out on the streets" (Loftus, 1993, p. 550). Let us consider what can go wrong—and what can go right—with eyewitness testimony.

One problem with eyewitness testimony is that the words chosen by an experimenter—and those chosen by a lawyer interrogating a witness—have been shown to influence the reconstruction of memories (Wells & Olson, 2003). For example, as in the experiment described earlier, an attorney for the plaintiff might ask the witness, "How fast was the defendant's car going when it *smashed into* the plaintiff's car?" In such a case, the car might be reported as going faster than if the question had been: "How fast was the defendant's car going when the accident occurred?" (Loftus & Palmer, 1974). Could the attorney for the defendant claim that use of the word *smashed* biased the witness? What about jurors who heard the word *smashed*? Would they be biased toward assuming that the driver had been reckless?

Children tend to be more suggestible witnesses than adults, and preschoolers are more suggestible than older children (Ceci & Bruck, 1993; Erskine et al., 2001). But when questioned properly, even young children may be able to provide accurate and useful testimony (Ceci & Bruck, 1993; Gordon et al., 2001).

There are cases in which the memories of eyewitnesses have been "refreshed" by hypnosis. Sad to say, hypnosis does more than amplify memories; it can also distort them (Loftus, 1994). One problem is that witnesses may accept and embellish suggestions made by the hypnotist. Another is that hypnotized people may report fantasized occurrences as compellingly as if they were real (Loftus, 1994).

There are also problems in the identification of criminals by eyewitnesses. For one thing, witnesses may pay more attention to the suspect's clothing than to more meaningful characteristics such as facial features, height, and weight. In one experiment, viewers of a videotaped crime incorrectly identified a man as the criminal because he wore the eyeglasses and T-shirt that had been worn by the perpetrator on the tape. The man who had actually committed the crime was identified less often (Sanders, 1984).

Other problems with eyewitness testimony include the following:

◆ Identification is less accurate when suspects belong to ethnic or racial groups that differ from that of the witness (Wells & Olson, 2003).

◆ Identification of suspects is confused when interrogators make misleading suggestions (Loftus, 1997).

◆ Witnesses are seen as more credible when they claim to be certain in their testimony, but there is little evidence that claims of certainty are accurate (Wells & Olson, 2003).

There are thus many problems with eyewitness testimony. Yet even Elizabeth Loftus (1993), who has extensively studied the accuracy of eyewitness testimony, agrees that it is a valuable tool in the courtroom. After all, identifications made by eyewitnesses are frequently correct, and what, Loftus asks, would be the alternative to the use of eyewitnesses? If we were to prevent eyewitnesses from testifying, how many criminals would go free?

In Profile   ELIZABETH LOFTUS[1]

Elizabeth Loftus is a psychologist much in the public eye. Her research on memory is so widely recognized that the April 2002 issue of *The Review of General Psychology* ranked her as the number-one woman on the list of the top 100 psychologists of the 20th century. Loftus has also been embroiled in one controversy after another.

For three decades Loftus has been demonstrating that memories are not snapshots but instead are changeable and susceptible to bias and suggestion. In her research with people in the laboratory, she has actually implanted "memories" of seeing barns in barren fields or of being lost in a mall as a child. After the implanting, the people painted in "recalled" details of the days that never happened.

To Loftus's credit, the view of memory as porous and susceptible to distortion has become widely accepted. But Loftus then helped create what *Science News* and *Psychology Today* referred to as "Memory Wars" over the specific issue as to whether memories of traumatic sexual childhood events could be repressed and then recovered in therapy in adulthood (see the discussion of repression on page 293). Loftus argued that such "memories" can be implanted by the therapists themselves, which set her against the more "politically correct" view that such "recovered memories" are accurate. As of now, Loftus has provided expert testimony for the defense in more than 250 cases in which parents have been accused of incest on the basis of "memories" suddenly "recalled" in the office of a therapist.

Loftus's research on the malleability of memory has also brought eyewitness testimony in general into question. Loftus has aided in the defense of people ranging from serial killer Ted Bundy, O. J. Simpson, and the Hillside Stranglers to the McMartin Preschool workers (who were accused of sexually abusing children in their care). Because expert witnesses are paid to testify, one prosecutor called Loftus a whore. We doubt that the same epithet would have occurred to him if the expert witness had been male.

One case she didn't take was that of John Demjanjuk. A retired auto worker, Demjanjuk had been accused by survivors of Nazi concentration camps of being the sadistic "Butcher of Treblinka," also referred to as "Ivan the Terrible." The daughter of Jewish parents, Loftus struggled with her conscience about whether to testify in the Demjanjuk case. She declined. Later, when she was asked whether she personally believed that Demjanjuk was in fact Ivan the Terrible, Loftus replied, "Of course not" (Wilson, 2002).

[1]This profile is largely based on Amy Wilson, "War & remembrance," *Orange County Register* (Sunday, November 3, 2002).

 Go to **http://psychology.wadsworth.com/ rathus_pcc9e** to access more information about Elizabeth Loftus.

Photo by William Calvin

HOW MUCH INFORMATION *CAN* BE STORED IN LONG-TERM MEMORY? How many gigabytes of storage are there in your most personal computer—your brain? Unlike a computer, the human ability to store information is, for all practical purposes, unlimited (Goldman-Rakic, 1995). Even the largest hard drives fill up quickly when we save Web pages from the Internet, pictures, or movies. Yet how many "movies" of the past have you saved in your own long-term memory? How many thousands of scenes and stories can you rerun at will? And assuming that you have an intact sensory system, the movies in your personal storage bins not only have color and sound, but also aromas, tactile sensations, and much more. *Your long-term memory is a biochemical "hard drive" with no known limits on the gigabytes of information it can store.*

Yes, new information may replace older information in short-term memory, but there is no evidence that long-term memories—those in "storage"—are lost by displacement. Long-term memories may endure for a lifetime. Now and then it may seem that we have forgotten, or "lost," a long-term memory such as the names of our elementary or high-school classmates. Yet it may be that we cannot find the proper cues to help us retrieve them. It is like forgetting a file name when working with a computer. If long-term memories are lost, they may be lost in the same way that a misplaced object or computer file is lost. It is "lost," but we sense that it is still somewhere in the room or on the hard drive. For example, you may drive by your elementary school and suddenly recall the long-lost names of elementary school teachers and of the streets in your old neighborhood.

TRANSFERRING INFORMATION FROM SHORT-TERM TO LONG-TERM MEMORY: USING THE "SAVE" FUNCTION How can you transfer information from short-term to long-term memory? By and large, the more often chunks of information are rehearsed, the more likely they are to be transferred to long-term memory. Repeating information over and over to prevent it from decaying or being displaced is termed *maintenance rehearsal.* But maintenance rehearsal does not give meaning to information by linking it to past learning. Thus it is not considered the best way to permanently store information (Simpson et al., 1994).

A more effective method is to make information more meaningful—to purposefully relate new information to things that are already well known (Woloshyn et al., 1994). For example, to better remember the components of levers, physics students might use seesaws, wheelbarrows, and oars as examples (Scruggs & Mastropieri, 1992). The nine chunks of information in our second challenge to memory were made easier to reconstruct once they were associated with the familiar tic-tac-toe grid in Figure 7.2. Relating new material to well-known material is known as elaborative rehearsal. For example, have you seen this word before?

FUNTHOSTAM

Say it aloud. Do you know it? If you had used an acoustic code alone to memorize THUNSTOFAM, the list of letters you first saw on page 267, it might not have been easy to recognize FUNTHOSTAM as an incorrect spelling. Let us assume, however, that by now you have used elaborative rehearsal and encoded THUNSTOFAM semantically (according to its "meaning") as an acronym for "The United States of America." Then you would have been able to scan the spelling of the words in the phrase "The United States of America" to determine that FUNTHOSTAM is an incorrect spelling.

Rote repetition of a meaningless group of syllables, such as *thun-sto-fam,* relies on maintenance rehearsal for permanent storage. The process might be tedious (continued rehearsal) and unreliable. Elaborative rehearsal—tying THUNSTOFAM to the name of a country—might make storage instantaneous and retrieval practically foolproof.

LEVELS OF PROCESSING INFORMATION People who use elaborative rehearsal to remember things are *processing information at a deeper level* than people who use maintenance rehearsal. **Question: What is the levels-of-processing model of memory?** Fergus Craik and Robert Lockhart (1972) pioneered the levels-of-processing model of memory, which holds that memories tend to endure when information is processed *deeply*—attended to, encoded carefully, pondered, and related to things we already know. Remembering relies on how *deeply* people process information, not on whether memories are transferred from one *stage* of memory to another.

Evidence for the importance of levels of processing information is found in an experiment with three groups of college students, all of whom were asked to study a picture of a living room for one minute (Bransford et al., 1977). The groups' examination of the picture entailed different approaches. Two groups were informed that small x's were imbedded in the picture. The first of these groups was asked to find the x's by scanning the picture horizontally and vertically. The second group was informed that the x's could be found in the edges of the objects in the room and was asked to look for them there. The third group was asked, instead, to think about how it would use the objects pictured in the room. As a result of the divergent sets of instructions, the first two groups (the x hunters) processed information about the objects in the picture superficially. But the third group rehearsed the objects elaboratively—that is, members of this group thought about the objects in terms of their meanings and uses. It should not be surprising that the third group remembered many times more objects than the first two groups.

In another experiment, researchers asked subjects to indicate whether they recognized photos of faces they had been shown under one of three conditions: (1) being asked to recall the gender of the person in the photo, (2) being asked to recall the width of the person's nose, or (3) being asked to judge whether the person is honest (Bloom & Mudd, 1991). Subjects asked to form judgments about the persons' honesty recognized more faces. Asking people to judge other people's honesty may stimulate deeper processing of the facial features. That is, subjects may study each face in detail to see if they can relate what they see to their ideas about human nature.

Video Connections—Reconstructive Memory How might a false memory of being separated from your parents when you were a child be planted? Click on the "Reconstructive Memory" video link from your companion website and learn why reconstructive memory is not like viewing a snapshot of an event.

Language arts teachers encourage students to use new vocabulary words in sentences to process them more deeply. Each new usage is an instance of elaborative rehearsal. Usage helps build semantic codes that make it easier to retrieve the meanings of words in the future. When I was in high school, teachers of foreign languages told us that learning classical languages "exercises the mind" so that we would understand English better. Not exactly. The mind is not analogous to a muscle that responds to exercise. However, the meanings of many English words are based on foreign ones. A person who recognizes that *retrieve* stems from roots meaning "again" *(re-)* and "find" *(trouver* in French) is less likely to forget that *retrieval* means "finding again" or "bringing back."

Think, too, of all the algebra and geometry problems we were asked to solve in high school. Each problem is an application of a procedure and, perhaps, of certain formulas and theorems. By repeatedly applying the procedures, formulas, and theorems in different contexts, we rehearse them elaboratively. As a consequence, we are more likely to remember them. Knowledge of the ways in which a formula or an equation is used helps us remember the formula. Also, by building one geometry theorem on another, we relate new theorems to ones that we already understand. As a result, we process information about them more deeply and remember them better.

There is also a good deal of biologically oriented research that connects deep processing with activity in certain parts of the brain, notably the prefrontal area of the cerebral cortex (Constantinidis et al., 2001). Fergus Craik and his colleagues (e.g., Grady et al., 1999) are discovering that one reason that older adults show memory loss is that they tend not to process information quite as deeply as younger people do. Deep processing requires sustained attention, and older adults, along with people who have suffered brain injuries and strokes, are apparently not capable of focusing their attention as well as they had previously (Iidaka et al., 2000; Winocur et al., 2000).

Before proceeding to the next section, cover the preceding paragraph with your hand. Which of the following words is spelled correctly: *retrieval* or *retreival?* The spellings sound alike, so an acoustic code for reconstructing the correct spelling would fail. Yet a semantic code, such as the spelling rule "i before e except after c," would allow you to reconstruct the correct spelling: retri*e*val.

FLASHBULB MEMORIES: "TO LEAVE A SCAR UPON THE CEREBRAL TISSUES"

> *The attention which we lend to an experience is proportional to its vivid or interesting character; and it is a notorious fact that what interests us most vividly at the time is, other things equal, what we remember best. An impression may be so exciting emotionally as almost to leave a scar upon the cerebral tissues.*

> William James

Truth or Fiction Revisited: It is true that many of us will never forget where we were or what we were doing when we learned of the attacks on the World Trade Center and the Pentagon on September 11, 2001. Some of us will similarly recall where we were and what we were doing when we learned that John F. Kennedy Jr.'s airplane had crashed into the ocean in 1999—or that his father had been assassinated in 1963. Others will recall the day in 1997 when Britain's Princess Diana died in an automobile accident. We may also have a detailed memory of what we were doing when we learned of a loved one's death.

Question: Why is it that some events, like the attack of September 11, 2001, can be etched in memory for a lifetime? It appears that we tend to remember events that are surprising, important, and emotionally stirring more clearly. Such events can create "flashbulb memories," which preserve

■ **Flashbulb Memories** Where were you and what were you doing on the morning of September 11, 2001? Many older Americans never forgot where they were and what they were doing when they learned about the attack on Pearl Harbor on December 7, 1941. Major events can illuminate everything about them so that we recall everything that was happening at the time.

experiences in detail (Conway et al., 1994; Finkenauer et al., 1998), even if those details are sometimes reconstructed, as is the case with other memories (Neisser, 1991). Why is the memory etched when the "flashbulb" goes off? One factor is the distinctness of the memory. It is easier to discriminate stimuli that stand out. Such events are striking in themselves. The feelings caused by them are also special. It is thus relatively easy to pick them out from the storehouse of memories. Major events such as the assassination of a president or the loss of a close relative also tend to have important effects on our lives. We are likely to dwell on them and form networks of associations. That is, we are likely to rehearse them elaboratively. Our rehearsal may include great expectations, or deep fears, for the future.

Biology is intimately connected with psychology. Strong feelings are connected with the secretion of stress hormones, and stress hormones help etch events into our memory—"as almost to leave a scar upon the cerebral tissues," poetically speaking.

ORGANIZATION IN LONG-TERM MEMORY The storehouse of long-term memory is usually well organized. Items are not just piled on the floor or thrown into closets. **Question: How is knowledge organized in long-term memory?** We tend to gather information about rats and cats into a certain section of the storehouse, perhaps the animal or mammal section. We put information about oaks, maples, and eucalyptus into the tree section. Such categorization of stimuli is a basic cognitive function. It allows us to make predictions about specific instances and to store information efficiently.

We tend to organize information according to a *hierarchical structure,* as shown in Figure 7.5. A *hierarchy* is an arrangement of items (or chunks of information) into

A Closer Look | LIFE IS PLEASANT—AND MEMORY HELPS TO KEEP IT THAT WAY![2]

Surveys conducted in the United States and around the world consistently show that people are generally happy with their lives, even for those with physical and mental disabilities and people without much money. Researchers reviewing several studies on autobiographical memory and happiness have found that human memory is biased toward happiness and that mild depression can disrupt this bias for good over bad. The findings are published in the June 2003 issue of *Review of General Psychology.*

In their article "Life Is Pleasant—and Memory Helps to Keep It That Way!", W. Richard Walker of Winston-Salem State University, John J. Skowronski of Northern Illinois University, and Charles P. Thompson of Kansas State University find two causes for people's recollection of the past to be positively biased. The first cause, according to their review of the research, seems to be due to the simple fact that pleasant events do in fact outnumber unpleasant events because people seek out positive experiences and avoid negative ones. Across 12 studies conducted by five different research

teams, people of different racial and ethnic backgrounds and participants who ranged in age from late teens to early 50s consistently reported experiencing more positive events in their lives than negative events.

The other process at work involves our memory system treating pleasant emotions differently from unpleasant emotions. Seven studies reviewed by the researchers provide support for a fading affect for negative emotions. Pleasant emotions have been found to fade more slowly from our memory than unpleasant emotions. One mechanism for this uneven fading may involve a process known as minimization. In order to return to our normal level of happiness, we try to minimize the impact of life events. This minimization process—which occurs biologically, cognitively and socially—is usually stronger for negative events than for positive events.

"This implies that there is a tendency to 'deaden' the emotional impact of negative events relative to the impact of positive events," according Dr. Walker. "Such deadening occurs directly because people are motivated to view their life events in a relatively positive light."

The research shows that this fading affect bias represents genuine emotional fading rather than a retrospective error in memory, and it should be viewed as evidence of healthy coping processes operating in

memory, according to the authors. They add that this should not be confused with repression, a theory proposed by Sigmund Freud. This research suggests that people do remember negative events; they just remember them less negatively.

Of course, life is not pleasant for everyone. Of the 229 participants involved in eight reviewed studies where diary entries were tracked, 17 reported more unpleasant than pleasant events, indicating that the fading affect does not work for everyone. Among those with mild depression, unpleasant and pleasant emotions tend to fade evenly. In a new study to be published by the review authors, 330 participants recalled six emotionally intense memories from their lives and provided a series of ratings for each event. The participants were also assessed on depression levels. The researchers found increased levels of depression were associated with a greater disruption of the fading affect bias.

But for those not suffering from depression, the authors say the bias "suggests that autobiographical memory represents an important exception to the theoretical claim that bad is stronger than good and allows people to cope with tragedies, celebrate joyful moments, and look forward to tomorrow."

[2]Adapted from David Partenheimer (2003, June 8). "Remembering the Good Times, Putting the Bad Times in Perspective—How Our Memory Helps Make Life Pleasant: Research Explains Why Most People Are Happy with Their Lives." Washington, DC: APA Press Release. Public Affairs Office.

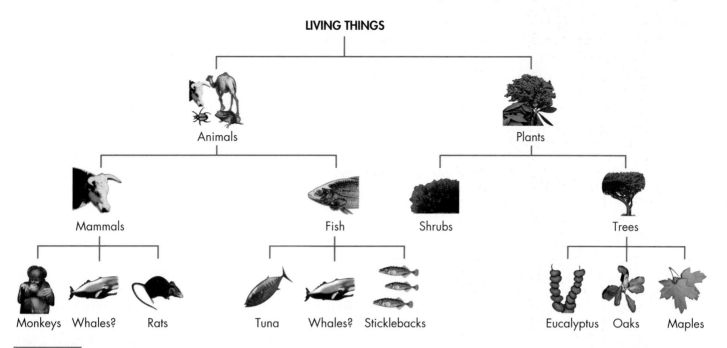

LIVING THINGS

Animals — Plants

Mammals — Fish — Shrubs — Trees

Monkeys — Whales? — Rats — Tuna — Whales? — Sticklebacks — Eucalyptus — Oaks — Maples

FIGURE 7.5 The Hierarchical Structure of Long-Term Memory

Where are whales filed in the hierarchical cabinets of your memory? Your classification of whales may influence your answers to these questions: Do whales breathe underwater? Are they warm-blooded? Do they nurse their young? A note to biological purists: This figure is not intended to represent phyla, classes, orders, and so on accurately. Rather, it shows how an individual's classification scheme might be organized.

groups or classes according to common or distinct features. As we work our way up the hierarchy shown in Figure 7.5, we find more encompassing, or *superordinate,* classes to which the items below them belong. For example, all mammals are animals, but there are many types of animals other than mammals.

When items are correctly organized in long-term memory, you are more likely to recall—or know—accurate information about them. For instance, do you "remember" whether whales breathe underwater? If you did not know that whales are mammals (or, in Figure 7.5, *subordinate* to mammals), or if you knew nothing about mammals, a correct answer might depend on some remote instance of rote learning. That is, you might be depending on chancy episodic memory rather than on reliable semantic memory. For example, you might recall some details from a TV documentary on whales. If you *did* know that whales are mammals, however, you would also know—or remember—that whales do not breathe underwater. How? You would reconstruct information about whales from knowledge about mammals, the group to which whales are subordinate. Similarly, you would know, or remember, that because they are mammals, whales are warm-blooded, nurse their young, and are a good deal more intelligent than, say, tunas and sharks, which are fish. Had you incorrectly classified whales as fish, you might have searched your memory and constructed the incorrect answer that they do breathe underwater.

Your memory is thus organized according to a remarkably complex filing system that has a certain internal logic. If you place a piece of information into the wrong file, it is probably not the fault of the filing system itself. Nevertheless, you may "lose" the information in the sense of not being able to find the best cues to retrieve it.

THE TIP-OF-THE-TONGUE PHENOMENON Having something on the tip of your tongue can be a frustrating experience. It is like reeling in a fish but having it drop off the line just before it breaks the surface of the water. Psychologists term this experience the **tip-of-the-tongue (TOT) phenomenon,** or the **feeling-of-knowing experience. Question: Why do we sometimes feel that the answer to a question is on the tip of our tongue?**

Tip-of-the-tongue (TOT) phenomenon The feeling that information is stored in memory although it cannot be readily retrieved. Also called the *feeling-of-knowing experience.*

Feeling-of-knowing experience Same as *tip-of-the-tongue phenomenon.*

Context-dependent memory Information that is better retrieved in the context in which it was encoded and stored, or learned.

Research provides insight into the TOT phenomenon (Brown & McNeill, 1966; James & Burke, 2000). In classic research, Brown and McNeill (1966) defined some rather unusual words for students, such as *sampan*, a small riverboat used in China and Japan. The students were then asked to recall the words they had learned. Some of the students often had the right word "on the tip of their tongue" but reported words with similar meanings such as *junk, barge,* or *houseboat.* Still other students reported words that sounded similar, such as *Saipan, Siam, sarong,* and *sanching.* Why?

To begin with, the words were unfamiliar, so elaborative rehearsal did not take place. The students did not have an opportunity to relate the words to other things they knew. Brown and McNeill also suggested that our storage systems are indexed according to cues that include both the sounds and the meanings of words—that is, according to both acoustic and semantic codes. By scanning words similar in sound and meaning to the word on the tip of the tongue, we sometimes find a useful cue and retrieve the word for which we are searching.

The feeling-of-knowing experience also seems to reflect incomplete or imperfect learning. In such cases, our answers may be "in the ballpark" if not on the mark. In some feeling-of-knowing experiments, people are often asked trivia questions. When they do not recall an answer, they are then asked to guess how likely it is that they will recognize the right answer if it is among a group of possibilities. People turn out to be very accurate in their estimations about whether or not they will recognize the answer. Similarly, Brown and McNeill found that the students in their TOT experiment proved to be very good at estimating the number of syllables in words that they could not recall. The students often correctly guessed the initial sounds of the words. They sometimes recognized words that rhymed with them.

Sometimes an answer seems to be on the tip of our tongue because our learning of the topic is incomplete. We may not know the exact answer, but we know something. (As a matter of fact, if we have good writing skills, we may present our incomplete knowledge so forcefully that we earn a good grade on an essay question on the topic!) At such times, the problem lies not in retrieval but in the original processes of learning and memory—that is, encoding and storage.

CONTEXT-DEPENDENT MEMORY: BEEN THERE, DONE THAT?

> *It's* déjà vu *all over again.*
>
> Yogi Berra

The context in which we acquire information can also play a role in retrieval. I remember walking down the halls of the apartment building where I had lived as a child. Cooking odors triggered a sudden assault of images of playing under the staircase, of falling against a radiator, of the shrill voice of a former neighbor calling for her child at dinnertime. Have you ever walked the halls of an old school building and been assaulted by memories of faces and names that you had thought would be lost forever? Odors, it turns out, are particularly likely to trigger related memories (Pointer & Bond, 1998).

My experience was an example of a **context-dependent memory.** My memories were particularly clear in the context in which they were formed. **Question: Why may it be useful to study in the room in which we will be tested?** One answer is that being in the proper context—for example, studying in the exam room or under the same conditions—can dramatically enhance recall (Isarida & Isarida, 1999). **Truth or Fiction Revisited:** Therefore, if you study with the stereo on, you would probably do better to take the test with the stereo on. One fascinating experiment in context-dependent memory included a number of people who were "all wet." Members of a university swimming club were

■ **Should This Student Bring the TV to Class to Take the Test?** Research on context-dependent memory suggests that we remember information better when we attempt to recall it in the context in which we learned it. If we study with the TV or stereo on, should we also take the test within the "context" of the TV or stereo?

asked to learn lists of words either while they were submerged or while they were literally high and dry (Godden & Baddeley, 1975). Students who learned the list underwater showed superior recall of the list when immersed. Similarly, those who had rehearsed the list ashore showed better retrieval on terra firma.

According to a study with 20 bilingual Cornell students, the "context" for memory extends to language (Marian & Neisser, 2000). The students emigrated from Russia at an average age of 14 and were an average of about 22 years old at the time of the experiment. They were asked to recall the details of experiences in Russia and the United States. When they were interviewed in Russian, they were better able to retrieve experiences from their lives in Russia. Similarly, when they were interviewed in English, they were better able to recall events that had happened in the United States.

Other studies have found that students do better on tests when they study under the same conditions—either in silence or with the stereo on (Grant et al., 1998). When police are interviewing witnesses to crimes, they ask the witnesses to paint the scene verbally as vividly as possible, or they visit the scene of the crime with the witnesses. People who mentally place themselves in the context in which they encoded and stored information frequently retrieve it more accurately.

One of the more eerie psychological experiences is the *déjà vu* (French for "already seen"). Sometimes we meet someone new or find ourselves in a strange place, yet we have the feeling that we know this person or have been there before. All in all, about 60% of us believe we have had a *déjà vu* experience (Brown, 2003). The *déjà vu* experience seems to occur when we are in a context similar to one we have been in before—or when we meet someone who has a way of talking or moving similar to that of someone we know or once knew. Yet we do not recall the specific place or person. Nevertheless, familiarity with the context leads us to think, "I've been here before." Other explanations for the *déjà vu* experience run from the neurological (for example, a disruption in normal neural transmission) to the cognitive (for example, dual cognitive processes that are temporarily out of synchrony) (Brown, 2003). In any event, the sense that one has been there before, or done this thing before, can be so strong that one just stands back and wonders.

STATE-DEPENDENT MEMORY **State-dependent memory** is an extension of context-dependent memory. It sometimes happens that we retrieve information better when we are in a physiological or emotional state that is similar to the one in which we encoded and stored the information. Feeling the rush of love may trigger images of other times when we fell in love. The grip of anger may prompt memories of incidents of frustration and rage. The research in this area even extends to states in which we are sober or inebriated!

Gordon Bower (1981) ran experiments in which happy or sad moods were induced by hypnotic suggestion. The subjects then learned lists of words. People who learned a list while in a happy mood showed better recall when a happy state was induced again. But people who had learned the list while in a sad mood showed superior recall when they were saddened again.

Studies of this kind are usually run with normal subjects. However, one study was carried out with people with bipolar disorder (also known as manic-depressive disorder). In this psychological disorder, moods swing from the heights of elation to the depths of depression and back, with no apparent external cause. The researchers found that the participants in the study had better recall of events that occurred when they were "up" or "down" when they were in the same mood (Eich et al., 1997).

Psychologists suggest that in day-to-day life a happy mood influences us to focus on positive events (Eich, 1995; Matt et al., 1992). As a result, we have better recall of these events in the future. A sad mood, unfortunately, leads us to focus on and recall the negative. Happiness may feed on happiness; but, under extreme circumstances, sadness can develop into a vicious cycle and lead to depression.

State-dependent memory Information that is better retrieved in the physiological or emotional state in which it was encoded and stored, or learned.

Your Turn: Now that we have discussed stages of memory and related issues concerning memory, enhance your mastery of the material with the nearby "Learning Connections." Review the material by filling in the blanks, reflect on the material by relating it to other things you know, and think critically about it.

Learning Connections | STAGES OF MEMORY: MAKING *SENSE* OF THE *SHORT* AND THE *LONG* OF IT

ACTIVE REVIEW (8) The Atkinson–Shiffrin model hypothesizes three stages of memory: _____, _____, and _____. (9) The mental representations of visual stimuli are referred to as _____. (10) The ability to retain exact mental representations of visual stimuli over long amounts of time is termed _____ imagery. (11) The mental representations of _____ stimuli are called *echoes*. (12) According to the _____-position effect, we are most likely to recall the first and last items in a series. (13) The Petersons showed that information can be displaced from short-term memory by means of _____. (14) Elizabeth Loftus and other psychologists have shown that we _____ our memories according to our schemas. (15) We need the proper _____ to retrieve information in long-term memory. (16) Detailed memories of surprising, important, and emotional events are termed "_____ memories." (17) Information in long-term memory is organized in a(n) _____ structure. (18) The _____-of-the- tongue phenomenon is most likely due to incomplete learning. (19) _____-dependent memory refers to information that is better retrieved under the circumstances in which it was encoded and stored.

REFLECT AND RELATE Try another mini-experiment. Pause the next time you experience the tip-of-the-tongue phenomenon or a *déjà vu* experience. In the case of the tip-of-the-tongue phenomenon, note all the words or ideas that come to mind as you are attempting to recall a piece of information. What do they have in common? If you eventually recall the "missing" information, consider how the words and ideas that came to mind relate to it. In the case of the *déjà vu* experience, jot down where you are, what you are doing, and all the sensory impressions that come to mind. Then, with these factors in mind, allow your thought to wander and see if you can identify the source of the *déjà vu*.

CRITICAL THINKING Were you ever convinced that you were remembering something accurately, only to discover, later, that your memory was incorrect? How do you account for the distorted memory? Can we know whether our own memories are accurate? Is it possible to function in a world of uncertain memory? (Do you have a choice?)

 Go to **http://psychology.wadsworth.com/rathus_pcc9e** for an interactive version of this Learning Connections unit.

Forgetting: Will You Remember How We Forget?

What do DAL, RIK, BOF, and ZEX have in common? They are all **nonsense syllables.** Nonsense syllables are meaningless sets of two consonants with a vowel sandwiched in between. They were first used by Hermann Ebbinghaus to study memory and forgetting (see the nearby "In Profile" feature on Hermann Ebbinghaus). Because nonsense syllables are intended to be meaningless, remembering them should depend on simple acoustic coding and maintenance rehearsal rather than on elaborative rehearsal, semantic coding, or other ways of making learning meaningful. They are thus well-suited for use in the measurement of forgetting. **Question: What types of memory tasks are used in measuring forgetting?**

Memory Tasks Used in Measuring Forgetting

Three basic memory tasks have been used by psychologists to measure forgetting: recognition, recall, and relearning. Nonsense syllables have been used in studying each of them. The study of these memory tasks has led to several conclusions about the nature of forgetting.

RECOGNITION One aspect of forgetting is failure to recognize something we have experienced. There are many ways of measuring **recognition.** In many studies, psychologists ask subjects to read a list of nonsense syllables. The subjects then read a second list of nonsense syllables and indicate whether they recognize any of the

Nonsense syllables Meaningless sets of two consonants, with a vowel sandwiched in between, that are used to study memory.

Recognition In information processing, the easiest memory task, involving identification of objects or events encountered before.

In Profile | HERMANN EBBINGHAUS

Wilhelm Wundt claimed that higher mental functions such as memory could not be studied scientifically. Hermann Ebbinghaus (1850–1909) took Wundt's argument as a challenge, not a statement of fact.

Ebbinghaus earned degrees in history and philosophy at the University of Bonn. Then he fought in the Franco-Prussian War. He spent the next seven years in independent study, traveling and tutoring to earn his keep. He was deeply affected by Fechner's *Elements of Psychophysics*, which he picked up secondhand in a London bookshop. Fechner's book showed how it was possible to study sensation and perception scientifically. Ebbinghaus was convinced that he could accomplish the same thing for his own pet topic—memory.

While teaching at the University of Berlin, Ebbinghaus constructed some 2,300 non-

sense syllables to be used as tools in studying memory. He used himself as his main subject and read through lists of 12 to 16 nonsense syllables repeatedly until he had memorized them. Then he would test himself. He noted that his memory deteriorated as time passed. He would have to reread the lists to memorize them again, but the second time around it might take 14 minutes to memorize a list that had initially taken 21 minutes. There was thus a *savings* of one-third. Ebbinghaus also discovered that he did most of his forgetting immediately after he learned a list. In other words, there was a quick initial drop-off in his *forgetting curve.* Then the curve tapered off.

Ebbinghaus was so dedicated to his research that on one occasion he rehearsed 420 lists of 16 nonsense syllables 34 times each. His immense labors led to the commonly used concepts of savings and the forgetting curve and also demonstrated that it is possible to study memory scientifically.

 Go to **http://psychology.wadsworth.com/ rathus_pcc9e** to access more information about Hermann Ebbinghaus.

---

syllables as having appeared on the first list. Forgetting is defined as failure to recognize a syllable that has been read before.

In another kind of recognition study, Harry Bahrick and his colleagues (1975) studied high-school graduates who had been out of school for various lengths of time. They interspersed photos of the graduates' classmates with four times as many photos of strangers. Recent graduates correctly recognized former classmates 90% of the time. Those who had been out of school for 40 years recognized former classmates 75% of the time. A chance level of recognition would have been only 20% (1 photo in 5 was of an actual classmate). Thus even older people showed rather solid long-term recognition ability.

Recognition is the easiest type of memory task. This is why multiple-choice tests are easier than fill-in-the-blank or essay tests. We can recognize correct answers more easily than we can recall them unaided.

RECALL In his own studies of **recall,** another kind of memory task, Ebbinghaus would read lists of nonsense syllables aloud to the beat of a metronome and then see how many he could produce from memory. After reading through a list once, he usually would be able to recall seven syllables—the typical limit for short-term memory.

Psychologists also often use lists of pairs of nonsense syllables, called **paired associates,** to measure recall. A list of paired associates is shown in Figure 7.6. Subjects read through the lists pair by pair. Later they are shown the first member of each pair and asked to recall the second. Recall is more difficult than recognition. In a recognition task, one simply indicates whether an item has been seen before or which of a number of items is paired with a stimulus (as in a multiple-choice test). In a recall task, the person must retrieve a syllable, with another syllable serving as a cue.

Retrieval is made easier if the two syllables can be meaningfully linked—that is, encoded semantically—even if the "meaning" is stretched a bit. Consider the first pair of nonsense syllables in Figure 7.6. The image of a WOMan smoking a CEG-arette may make CEG easier to retrieve when the person is presented with the cue WOM.

It is easier to recall vocabulary words from foreign languages if you can construct a meaningful link between the foreign and English words (Atkinson, 1975). The *peso,* pronounced *pay-so,* is a unit of Mexican money. A link can be formed by

FIGURE 7.6 **Paired Associates**

Psychologists often use paired associates to measure recall. Retrieving CEG in response to the cue WOM is made easier by an image of a WOMan smoking a "CEG-arette."

Recall Retrieval or reconstruction of learned material.

Paired associates Nonsense syllables presented in pairs in experiments that measure recall.

Relearning A measure of retention. Material is usually relearned more quickly than it is learned initially.

Method of savings A measure of retention in which the difference between the number of repetitions originally required to learn a list and the number of repetitions required to relearn the list after a certain amount of time has elapsed is calculated.

Savings The difference between the number of repetitions originally required to learn a list and the number of repetitions required to relearn the list after a certain amount of time has elapsed.

Interference theory The view that we may forget stored material because other learning interferes with it.

finding a part of the foreign word, such as the *pe-* (pronounced *pay*), and constructing a phrase such as "You pay with money." When you read or hear the word *peso* in the future, you recognize the *pe-* and retrieve the link or phrase. From the phrase, you then reconstruct the translation, "a unit of money."

RELEARNING: IS LEARNING EASIER THE SECOND TIME AROUND? Relearning is a third method of measuring retention. Do you remember having to learn all of the state capitals in grade school? What were the capitals of Wyoming and Delaware? Even when we cannot recall or recognize material that had once been learned, such as Cheyenne for Wyoming and Dover for Delaware, we can relearn it more rapidly the second time. Similarly, as we go through our 30s and 40s we may forget a good deal of our high-school French or geometry. Yet the second time around we could learn what previously took months or years much more rapidly.

To study the efficiency of relearning, Ebbinghaus (1885/1913) devised the **method of savings.** First he recorded the number of repetitions required to learn a list of nonsense syllables or words. Then he recorded the number of repetitions required to relearn the list after a certain amount of time had elapsed. Next he computed the difference in the number of repetitions to determine the **savings.** If a list had to be repeated 20 times before it was learned, and 20 times again after a year had passed, there were no savings. Relearning, that is, was as tedious as the initial learning. However, if the list could be learned with only 10 repetitions after a year had elapsed, half the number of repetitions required for learning had been saved.

Figure 7.7 shows Ebbinghaus's classic curve of forgetting. As you can see, there was no loss of memory as measured by savings immediately after a list had been learned. However, recollection dropped quite a bit, by half, during the first hour after learning a list. Losses of learning then became more gradual. It took a month (31 days) for retention to be cut in half again. In other words, forgetting occurred most rapidly right after material was learned. We continue to forget material as time elapses, but at a slower pace.

Before leaving this section, I have one question for you: What are the capitals of Wyoming and Delaware?

Interference Theory

When we do not attend to, encode, and rehearse sensory input, we may forget it through decay of the trace of the image. Material in short-term memory, like material in sensory memory, can be lost through decay. It can also be lost through displacement, as may happen when we try to remember several new names at a party.

Question: Why can learning Spanish make it harder to remember French? The answer may be found in **interference theory.** According to this view, we also forget material in short-term and long-term memory because newly learned material interferes with it. The two basic types of interference are retroactive interference (also called *retroactive inhibition*) and proactive interference (also called *proactive inhibition*).

FIGURE 7.7 **Ebbinghaus's Classic Curve of Forgetting**

Recollection of lists of words drops precipitously during the first hour after learning. Losses of learning then become more gradual. Retention drops by half within the first hour. However, it takes a month (31 days) for retention to be cut in half again.

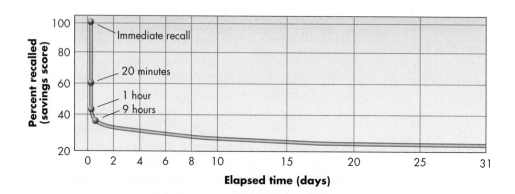

RETROACTIVE INTERFERENCE In **retroactive interference,** new learning interferes with the retrieval of old learning. For example, a medical student may memorize the names of the bones in the leg through rote repetition. Later he or she may find that learning the names of the bones in the arm makes it more difficult to retrieve the names of the leg bones, especially if the names are similar in sound or in relative location on each limb.

PROACTIVE INTERFERENCE In **proactive interference,** older learning interferes with the capacity to retrieve more recently learned material. High-school Spanish may pop in when you are trying to retrieve college French or Italian words. All three are Romance languages, with similar roots and spellings. Previously learned Japanese words probably would not interfere with your ability to retrieve more recently learned French or Italian, because the roots and sounds of Japanese differ considerably from those of the Romance languages. **Truth or Fiction Revisited:** It is therefore true that learning Spanish can make it harder to remember French— and vice versa.

Consider motor skills. You may learn to drive a standard shift on a car with three forward speeds and a clutch that must be let up slowly after shifting. Later you may learn to drive a car with five forward speeds and a clutch that must be released rapidly. For a while, you may make errors on the five-speed car because of proactive interference. (Old learning interferes with new learning.) If you return to the three-speed car after driving the five-speed car has become natural, you may stall it a few times. This is because of retroactive interference (new learning interfering with the old).

Repression: Ejecting the Unwanted from Consciousness

According to Sigmund Freud, we are motivated to forget painful memories and unacceptable ideas because they produce anxiety, guilt, and shame. **Question: What is the Freudian concept of repression?** Repression, according to Freud, is the automatic ejection of painful memories and unacceptable urges from conscious awareness. It is motivated by the desire to avoid facing painful memories and emotions. Psychoanalysts believe that repression is at the heart of disorders such as **dissociative amnesia** (see Chapter 14). There is a current controversy in psychology as to whether repression (motivated forgetting) exists and, if it does, how it works.

Retroactive interference The interference of new learning with the ability to retrieve material learned previously.

Proactive interference The interference by old learning with the ability to retrieve material learned recently.

Dissociative amnesia Amnesia thought to stem from psychological conflict or trauma.

■ **Interference** In retroactive interference, new learning interferes with the retrieval of old learning. In proactive interference, older learning interferes with the capacity to retrieve material learned more recently. For example, high-school French vocabulary may "pop in" when you are trying to retrieve words you have learned for a Spanish test in college.

© Robert Finken/Index Stock Imagery

One interesting finding is that stress hormones—the kind we secrete when we experience extremes of anxiety, guilt, and shame—*heighten* memory formation (Clayton & Williams, 2000; McGaugh et al., 2002). But supporters of the concept of repression do not claim that repressed memories were ill-formed; they say, rather, that we do not focus on them.

There is much research on repression, often in the form of case studies that are found in psychoanalytic journals (e.g., Eagle, 2000). Much has been made of case studies in which veterans have supposedly forgotten traumatic battlefield experiences, developed posttraumatic stress disorder (once called "battlefield neurosis"), and then "felt better" once they recalled and discussed the traumatic events (Karon & Widener, 1998). Critics argue that the evidence for such repression and recovery of memories is weak and that this kind of "memory" can be implanted by the suggestions of interviewers (Loftus, 2001; Thomas & Loftus, 2002; van de Wetering et al., 2002). The issue remains controversial, as we see next.

CONTROVERSY IN PSYCHOLOGY

Do people really recover repressed memories of childhood sexual abuse, or are these "memories" implanted by interviewers?

There is apparently little doubt that the memory of traumatic events can be repressed. But, as we see in this section, there is also little doubt that many so-called recovered memories, particularly memories of childhood sexual abuse, are sometimes induced by a therapist.[3]

A young woman in psychotherapy recovered the memory that at age 13 she was raped by her teacher, became pregnant, and underwent an abortion. No corroborating evidence for this event existed. In fact, the woman had not reached menarche until 15, so the pregnancy was medically impossible. Still, she filed criminal charges against the teacher, who had to spend his life savings to defend himself against the false accusation. Eventually, the court ruled that recovery of a repressed memory lacked sufficient scientific foundation to be admissible evidence.

There is apparently little question that the memory of traumatic events is sometimes repressed. For example, an otherwise law-abiding man who in a fit of rage committed a heinous crime might report it to police as if someone else had done it and make no attempt to escape or to defend himself when he is accused of the crime. Or a woman who was violently raped may afterward be unable to explain her bruises or shock until perhaps she returns to the crime scene.

But there is also little question that many so-called recovered memories, particularly those involving allegations of childhood sexual abuse by a parent or other close relative, teacher, or friend, are sometimes fictions induced by the concerted efforts of a therapist who fosters a belief that becomes so deeply held it seems like a real memory. This "false memory syndrome" has resulted in many family tragedies: alienation of children from their parents, loss of jobs, ostracism, and divorces.

"We don't know what percent of these recovered memories are real and what percent are pseudomemories," said psychiatrist Harold Lief, who was one of the first to question these induced memories. "But we do know there are hundreds, maybe thousands of cases of pseudomemories and that many families have been destroyed by them. We also know that many therapists who track down these memories and focus on them fail to deal with the patient's real problems." Indeed, many adults who had in treatment recov-

[3]From "Memories of Things That Never Were," by Jane E. Brody, *The New York Times* (4/15/2000). Copyright © 2000 by The New York Times Co. Reprinted by permission.

ered a memory of childhood sexual abuse and accused the supposed perpetrator later retracted the claim.

For example, Gail Macdonald, the author of *Making of an Illness,* had seen a social worker who used hypnosis and guided imagery to convince her that prior sexual abuse by her father was the cause of her current emotional problems. The social worker said she had dissociative identity disorder, a diagnosis he inflicted, she said, on "120 people in my little community."

As a result of the false memory, Ms. Macdonald said she divorced herself from her family, suffered horrible nightmares, wrote compulsively in journals about the abuses her father had supposedly committed, and lost so much weight she was described as corpselike until she sought the help of a psychiatrist who said she had developed "post-traumatic stress disorder as a direct result of therapy" and helped her realize that her recovered memory was false.

How can someone tell if a recovered memory is false? Serious questions should be raised when corroborating evidence is lacking, when the so-called memory occurs before a child is able to remember, and when details of the memory are preposterous (like a rape by aliens), said psychiatrist Paul McHugh. McHugh also questioned the reliability of methods typically used to elicit these "memories." Among the most common are hypnosis and guided imagery, during which a therapist may introduce the notion that sexual abuse had occurred and ask the patient to try to remember the circumstances and who the perpetrator might have been. Sometimes patients participate in a recovered memory group where other members pressure the newcomer to recall prior sexual abuse and even suggest how it may have occurred.

Psychologist Elizabeth Loftus cited numerous studies that demonstrated how easy it was to implant a false memory. By asking a series of leading questions and by having a supposed "witness" talk about the made-up experience, it is often possible to convince someone that the event actually happened. In one study, researchers easily convinced half the adult participants that they had been hospitalized in severe pain as children or that they had been lost in a shopping mall at age 5. Several people with these false memories provided detailed embellishments.

This is especially true for young children. In a study conducted by psychologist Stephen J. Ceci, preschool children were asked weekly about whether a fictitious event had ever happened to them. By the tenth week, more than half reported that it had happened and provided cogent details about it.

In one experiment, interviewers told the children: "Think real hard. Did you get your hand caught in a mousetrap and go to the hospital to get it off?" Ceci reported: "So compelling did the children's narrative appear that we suspected that some of the children had come to truly believe they had experienced the fictitious events. Neither parents nor researchers were able to convince 27% of the children that the events never happened."

Based on his research, Ceci concluded, "It is exceedingly, devilishly difficult for professionals to tell fact from fiction when a child has been repeatedly suggestively interviewed over a long period of time. They look and act the way children do when they are trying to be accurate and honest."

Infantile Amnesia: Why Can't Johnny Remember?

Question: Can children remember events from the first couple of years of life? When he interviewed people about their early experiences, Freud discovered that they could not recall episodes that had happened prior to the age of 3 or so and that recall was cloudy through the age of 5. This phenomenon is referred to as **infantile amnesia.**

Infantile amnesia has little to do with the fact that the episodes occurred in the distant past. Middle-aged and older people have vivid memories from the ages of 6

Infantile amnesia Inability to recall events that occurred prior to the age of 2 or 3. Also termed *childhood amnesia.*

and 10, yet the events happened many decades ago. But 18-year-olds show steep declines in memory when they try to recall episodes that occurred earlier than the age of 6, even though they happened less than 18 years earlier (Wetzler & Sweeney, 1986).

Freud believed that young children have aggressive impulses and perverse lusts toward their parents. He attributed infantile amnesia to repression of these impulses. However, the episodes lost to infantile amnesia are not weighted in the direction of such "primitive" impulses. In fact, infantile amnesia probably reflects the interaction of physiological and cognitive factors. For example, a structure of the limbic system (the **hippocampus**) that is involved in the storage of memories does not become mature until we are about 2 years old (Squire, 1993, 1996). Also, myelination of brain pathways is incomplete for the first few years, contributing to the inefficiency of information processing and memory formation.

There are also cognitive explanations for infantile amnesia:

◆ Infants are not particularly interested in remembering the past (Neisser, 1993).

◆ Infants, in contrast to older children, tend not to weave episodes together into meaningful stories of their own lives. Information about specific episodes thus tends to be lost. Research shows that when parents reminisce about the past with children, infants memories are strengthened (Harley & Reese, 1999; Peterson, 2002; Wang, 2003). (Of course, one could question the accuracy of some of these reminiscences.)

◆ Infants do not make reliable use of language to symbolize or classify events (Wang, 2003). Their ability to *encode* sensory input—that is, to apply the auditory and semantic codes that facilitate memory formation—is therefore limited. Yet research shows that young infants can recall events throughout the period when infantile amnesia is presumed to occur if they are now and then exposed to objects they played with or photos of events (Rovee-Collier, 1999).

In any event, we are unlikely to remember episodes from the first two years of life unless we are reminded of them from time to time as we develop. Many of the early childhood memories that seem clear today are likely to be reconstructed, and they may hold many inaccuracies. They might also be memories of events that occurred later than the period to which we attribute them. Yet there is no evidence that such early memories are systematically repressed.

Adults also experience amnesia, although usually for biological reasons, as in the cases of anterograde and retrograde amnesia (Kopelman, 2002).

Anterograde and Retrograde Amnesia

Question: Why do people frequently have trouble recalling being in accidents? In so-called **anterograde amnesia,** there are memory lapses for the period following a trauma such as a blow to the head, an electric shock, or an operation. In some cases the trauma seems to interfere with all the processes of memory. The ability to pay attention, the encoding of sensory input, and rehearsal are all impaired. A number of investigators have linked certain kinds of brain damage—such as damage to the hippocampus—to amnesia (Eichenbaum & Fortin, 2003; Spiers et al., 2001).

Consider the classic case of a man with the initials H. M. Parts of the brain are sometimes lesioned to help people with epilepsy. In H. M.'s case, a section of the hippocampus was removed (Milner, 1966). Right after the operation, H. M.'s mental functioning appeared normal. As time went on, however, it became clear that he had problems processing new information. For example, two years after the operation, H. M. believed he was 27—his age at the time of the operation. When his family moved to a new address, H. M. could not find his new home or remember the new address. He responded with appropriate grief to the death of his uncle, yet he then began to ask about his uncle and why he did not visit. **Truth or Fiction Revisited:** It is true that a man could not form new memories after part of his hippocampus was surgically removed (Figure 7.8). Each time he was reminded of his uncle's passing, he

Hippocampus A structure in the limbic system that plays an important role in the formation of new memories.

Anterograde amnesia Failure to remember events that occurred after physical trauma because of the effects of the trauma.

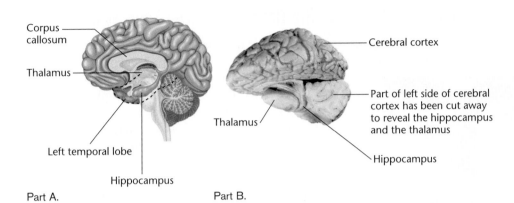

Corpus callosum
Thalamus
Left temporal lobe
Hippocampus

Part A.

Thalamus
Part of left side of cerebral cortex has been cut away to reveal the hippocampus and the thalamus
Cerebral cortex
Hippocampus

Part B.

FIGURE 7.8 The Hippocampus

The hippocampus is essential to the formation of new memories. Part A shows the location of the hippocampus in the brain. Part B is a photo of a human brain as seen from above. The upper part of the left side of the cerebral cortex has been cut away, revealing the hippocampus. The hippocampus loops over the thalamus, runs behind it, and then underneath it.

Courtesy of Dana Copeland

grieved as if he were hearing it for the first time. H. M.'s operation apparently prevented him from transferring information from short-term to long-term memory.

In **retrograde amnesia,** the source of trauma prevents people from remembering events that took place before the accident (Wheeler & McMillan, 2001). A football player who is knocked unconscious or a person in an auto accident may be unable to recall events that occurred for several minutes prior to the trauma. The football player may not recall taking the field. The person in the accident may not recall entering the car. It also sometimes happens that the individual cannot remember events that occurred for several years prior to the trauma.

In one well-known case of retrograde amnesia, a man received a head injury in a motorcycle accident (Baddeley, 1982). When he regained consciousness, he had lost memory for all events that had occurred after the age of 11. In fact, he appeared to believe that he was still 11 years old. During the next few months he gradually recovered more knowledge of his past. He moved toward the present year by year, up until the critical motorcycle ride. But he never did recover the events just prior to the accident. The accident had apparently prevented the information that was rapidly unfolding before him from being transferred to long-term memory. In terms of stages of memory, it may be that our perceptions and ideas need to consolidate, or rest undisturbed for a while, if they are to be transferred to long-term memory (Nader et al., 2000).

Your Turn: Now that we have discussed forgetting, enhance your mastery of the material with the nearby "Learning Connections." Review the material by filling in the blanks, reflect on the material by relating it to other things you know, and think critically about it.

Retrograde amnesia Failure to remember events that occurred prior to physical trauma because of the effects of the trauma.

Learning Connections — FORGETTING: WILL YOU REMEMBER HOW WE FORGET?

ACTIVE REVIEW (20) The German psychologist Hermann Ebbinghaus originated the use of _____ syllables in the study of memory and forgetting. (21) According to Ebbinghaus's classic curve of forgetting, recollection drops (*Gradually* or *Sharply?*) during the first hour after learning a list. (22) In _____ interference, new learning interferes with the retrieval of old learning. (23) In _____ interference, older learning interferes with the capacity to retrieve more recently learned material. (24) Infantile amnesia probably reflects immaturity of the brain structure called the _____ and lack of language. (25) In _____ amnesia there are memory lapses for the period following a traumatic event. (26) In _____ amnesia the source of trauma prevents people from remembering events that took place beforehand.

REFLECT AND RELATE Are multiple-choice test questions easier for you than fill-in-the-blanks? If so, why? Why does this text use "Active Reviews" rather than multiple-choice items to help students master the material?

CRITICAL THINKING Critical thinkers avoid overgeneralizing. According to the concept of infantile amnesia, children remember little or nothing from the first two years of life. But is this view of children's memory an overgeneralization? Don't children remember (recognize) their caregivers? Don't they acquire and remember language? Don't they remember how to crawl and sit up and walk? To what kinds of memories, then, does the concept of infantile amnesia apply?

 Go to **http://psychology.wadsworth.com/ rathus_pcc9e** for an interactive version of this Learning Connections unit.

The Biology of Memory: The Brain as a Living Time Machine

Joel and Clementine didn't meet on **www.match.com.** In fact, they are anything but well-matched. In the film *Eternal Sunshine of the Spotless Mind,* Joel (Jim Carrey)

is a sort of cautious, depressed male who runs into Clementine (Kate Winslet), a volatile and offbeat book clerk. Clementine divides her time between dying her hair blue and blood orange. When the relationship fails, Clementine is miserable. She visits a doctor who erases all memory of Joel from her mind—making it "spotless"—so that she will feel the warmth of the sun once more rather than the lonely dread of darkness. Joel is dumbfounded by Clementine's failure to recognize him. He learns of the process she underwent and decides to have Clementine erased from his mind as well.

The main part of the film follows the erasing process that takes place inside Joel's mind. One image of Clementine after another dissolves as the world around them dissolves as well. Erasure is possible because the doctor has "mapped" Joel's memories of Clementine. They are all interconnected, and he can follow their paths through the brain and sort of zap them.

■ **Would You Want to Erase Troublesome Memories?** Kate Winslet and Jim Carrey play a pair of mismatched lovers in *Eternal Sunshine of the Spotless Mind.* When the relationship doesn't work out, Winslet has memories of Carrey mapped and then erased from her brain. Carrey follows suit. Can memories be mapped? Can they be erased?

Are memories in fact interconnected in the brain? Psychologists know that mental processes such as the encoding, storage, and retrieval of information—that is, memory—are accompanied by changes in the brain (Kandel, 2006). Early in the twentieth century, many psychologists used the concept of the **engram** in their study of memory. Engrams were viewed as electrical circuits in the brain that corresponded to memory traces—neurological processes that paralleled experiences. Yet biological psychologists such as Karl Lashley (1950) spent many fruitless years searching for such circuits or the structures of the brain in which they might be housed. Much current research on the biology of memory focuses on the roles of stimulants, neurons, neurotransmitters, hormones, and structures in the brain.

Neural Activity and Memory: "Better Living through Chemistry"

Question: What neural events are connected with memory? The story of Joel and Clementine is fictional but may hold a kernel of truth. Rats who are reared in stimulating environments provide some answers. The animals develop more dendrites and synapses in the cerebral cortex than rats reared in impoverished environments (Neisser, 1997a). Moreover, visually stimulating rats increases the number of synapses in their visual cortex (Battaglia et al., 2004; Bilkey, 2004). Therefore, the storage of experience does involve avenues of communication among brain cells.

Information received through other senses is just as likely to lead to corresponding changes in the cortical regions that represent them. For example, sounds may similarly cause changes in the auditory cortex. Experiences perceived by several senses are apparently stored in numerous parts of the cortex. The recall of sensory experiences evidently involves neural activity in related regions of the brain.

Research with sea snails such as *Aplysia* and *Hermissenda* offers more insight into the biology of memory. *Aplysia* has only some 20,000 neurons compared with humans' *billions*. As a result, researchers have been able to study how experience is reflected at the synapses of specific neurons. The sea snail will reflexively withdraw its gills when it receives electric shock, in the way a person will reflexively withdraw a hand from a hot stove or a thorn. In one kind of experiment, researchers precede the shock with a squirt of water. After a few repetitions, the sea snail becomes conditioned to withdraw its gills when squirted with the water. When sea snails are conditioned, they release more serotonin at certain synapses. As a consequence, transmission at these synapses becomes more efficient as trials (learning) progress (Kandel, 2001, 2006). This greater efficiency is termed **long-term potentiation** (LTP). As shown in Figure 7.9, dendrites can also participate in LTP by

Engram (1) An assumed electrical circuit in the brain that corresponds to a memory trace. (2) An assumed chemical change in the brain that accompanies learning. (From the Greek *en-*, meaning "in," and *gramma*, meaning "something that is written or recorded.")

Long-term potentiation (LTP) Enhanced efficiency in synaptic transmission that follows brief, rapid stimulation.

sprouting new branches that attach to the transmitting axon. Rats that are given substances that enhance LTP learn mazes with fewer errors; that is, they are less likely to turn down the wrong alley (Uzakov et al., 2005).

Serotonin and many other naturally occurring chemical substances—including adrenaline, noradrenaline, acetylcholine, glutamate, antidiuretic hormone, and even the sex hormone estrogen—have been shown to play roles in memory:

◆ *Serotonin.* This neurotransmitter increases the efficiency of conditioning in sea snails (Kandel, 2006). It is released when stimuli are paired repeatedly, increasing the efficiency of neural transmission (LPT) at certain synapses and creating neural circuits that contain the information.

◆ *Acetylcholine (ACh).* This neurotransmitter is vital in memory formation; low levels of ACh are connected with Alzheimer's disease. Increased levels of ACh promote conditioning in mice (Farr et al., 2000a).

◆ *Glutamate.* Glutamate, like serotonin, increases the efficiency of conditioning. Agents that increase the action of glutamate promote conditioning in mice (Farr et al., 2000a, 2000b).

◆ *Adrenaline and noradrenaline (also called epinephrine and norepinephrine).* The hormone adrenaline and the related hormone and neurotransmitter noradrenaline both strengthen memory when they are released into the bloodstream following learning. Stressful events stimulate release of stress hormones from the adrenal glands—adrenaline and steroids—which, in turn, stimulate a structure in the limbic system (the amygdala) to release noradrenaline. The hormones and neurotransmitter, acting together, heighten memory for stressful events (McGaugh, 2005).

◆ *Vasopressin.* Also known as *antidiuretic hormone,* vasopressin affects fluid retention. Like many other chemical substances in the body, it has multiple tasks, one of which is facilitating memory functioning, particularly working memory (Paban et al., 2003). **Truth or Fiction Revisited:** Sniffing vasopressin in the form of a nasal spray generally benefits memory functioning (Perras et al., 1997).

◆ *Estrogen and testosterone.* The sex hormones estrogen and testosterone boost working memory in females and males, respectively (Janowsky et al., 2000). Estrogen replacement may help older, postmenopausal women retain cognitive functioning.

Brain Structures and Memory

Question: What structures in the brain are connected with memory? Memory does not reside in a single structure of the brain. As suggested in *Eternal Sunshine of the Spotless Mind,* it relies on complex neural networks that draw on various parts of the brain (Nyberg et al., 2000).

But some parts of the brain play more specific roles in memory. The hippocampus is vital for storing new information even if we can retrieve old information without it (Fields, 2005). But the hippocampus is not a storage bin. Rather, it is involved in relaying sensory information to parts of the cortex.

Where are the storage bins? The brain stores parts of memories in the appropriate areas of the sensory cortex. Sights are stored in the visual cortex, sounds in the auditory cortex, and so on. The limbic system is largely responsible for integrating these pieces of information when we recall an event. However, the frontal lobes apparently store information about where and when events occur (Chafee & Goldman-Rakic, 2000; Goldman-Rakic et al., 2000a).

But what of the decision to try to recall something? What of the spark of consciousness that drives us to move backward in time or to strive to remember to do something in the future? The prefrontal cortex is the executive center in memory (Buckner et al., 2001; Wheeler & Treisman, 2002). It appears to empower people with consciousness—the ability to mentally represent and become aware of experiences

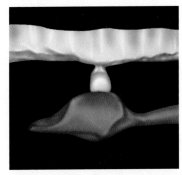

Part A.

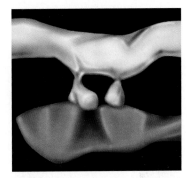

Part B.

FIGURE 7.9 One Avenue to Long-Term Potentiation (LTP)

LTP can occur via the action of neurotransmitters such as serotonin and glutamate at synapses. Structurally, LTP can also occur as shown in Parts A and B, when dendrites sprout new branches that connect with transmitting axons, increasing the amount of stimulation they receive.

that occur in the past, present, and future. It enables people to mentally travel back in time to reexperience the personal, autobiographical past. It enables people to focus on the things they intend to do in the future, such as mail a letter on the way to class or brush their teeth before going to bed (Fuster, 2000; McDaniel et al., 1999).

The hippocampus is also involved in the where and when of things (Eichenbaum & Fortin, 2003). The hippocampus does not become mature until we are about 2 years old. Immaturity may be connected with infantile amnesia. Adults with hippocampal damage may be able to form new procedural memories, even though they cannot form new episodic ("where and when") memories (Fields, 2005). They can develop new skills even though they cannot recall the practice sessions (Reed & Squire, 1997).

The thalamus (see Figure 7.8) is involved in the formation of verbal memories. Part of the thalamus of an Air Force cadet known as N. A. was damaged in a fencing accident. Afterward, N. A. could no longer form verbal memories but he could form visual memories (Squire, 2004). (One might measure visual memory by showing people pictures, allowing time to pass, and then asking them to point out those they have been shown.)

The encoding, storage, and retrieval of information thus involve biological activity. As we learn, new synapses are developed and changes occur at existing synapses. Parts of the brain are also involved in the formation of memories. In the next chapter, we see how people manipulate information they have stored to adapt to the environment or create new environments.

Your Turn: Now that we have discussed the biology of memory, enhance your mastery of the material with the nearby "Learning Connections." Review the material by filling in the blanks, reflect on the material by relating it to other things you know, and think critically about it.

Learning Connections — THE BIOLOGY OF MEMORY: THE BRAIN AS A LIVING TIME MACHINE

ACTIVE REVIEW (27) Experience enhances the avenues of communication among brain cells by development of dendrites and _____. (28) Conditioning of sea snails causes more of the neurotransmitter _____ to be released at certain synapses, making transmission at these synapses more efficient. (29) The hippocampus appears vital to the storage of (*New* or *Old?*) information. (30) The _____ seems to be involved in the formation of verbal memories.

REFLECT AND RELATE Think about the evidence concerning the relationships between various kinds of chemicals—including stimulants, neurotransmitters, and hormones—and memory. How would you design an experiment to explore whether or not a chemical had an effect on memory functioning? How would you determine a safe dose of the chemical? How would you measure memory functioning? How might your research differ if you were using people or other animals?

CRITICAL THINKING This is a *psychology* course. Why do you think we discuss the *biology* of memory?

 Go to **http://psychology.wadsworth.com/ rathus_pcc9e** for an interactive version of this Learning Connections unit.

Life Connections
Using the Psychology of Memory to Enhance Your Memory

Humans have survived the Ice Age, the Stone Age, the Iron Age, and, a bit more recently, the Industrial Revolution. Now we are trying to cope with the so-called Age of Information, in which there has been an explosion of information. Computers have been developed to process it. Humans, too, process information, and there is more of it to process than ever before. We can always add more memory to our computers, but how can people improve their memory? Fortunately, psychologists have helped devise methods for improving memory. Let us consider some of them.

Drill and Practice: "A, B, C, D . . ."
Repetition (rote maintenance rehearsal) helps transfer information from short-term to long-term memory. Does maintenance rehearsal seem too mechanical for you as a college student? If so, don't forget that this is how you learned the

alphabet and how to count! School-children write spelling words over and over to remember them. Athletes repeat motions so that they will become an implicit memory. When you have memorized formulas, during a test you can use your time to think about when to apply them, rather than using up valuable time trying to recall them.

Some students use flash cards to help them remember facts. For example, they might write "The originator of modern behaviorism is _____" on one side of the card and "John Broadus Watson" on the flip side.

In his book *Super Memory*, Douglas Herrmann (1991) recommends the following methods for remembering a person's name:

1. Say the name out loud.
2. Ask the person a question, using her or his name.
3. Use the person's name as many times as you can during your conversation.
4. Write down the name when the conversation has ended.

Relate New Information to What Is Already Known

Relating new information to what is already known is a form of elaborative rehearsal (Willoughby et al., 1994). Herrmann (1991) suggests that you can better remember the name of a new acquaintance by thinking of a rhyme for it. Now you have done some thinking about the name, and you also have two tags for the person, not one. If you are trying to retrieve the spelling of the word *retrieve,* do so by retrieving the rule "i before e except after c." There are exceptions, of course: Remember that "weird" doesn't follow the rule because it's a "weird" word.

We normally expand our knowledge base by relating new items to things already known. Children learn that a cello is like a violin, only bigger. A bass fiddle is also like a violin, but bigger yet. We remember information about whales by relating whales to other mammals. Similarly, we are better able to recall information about porpoises and dolphins if we think of them

as small whales (and not as big or smart fish).

The media are filled with stories about people who exhibit psychological disorders of one kind or another. To help remember the disorders discussed when you get to Chapter 14, think of film or TV characters with those disorders. How were the characters' behaviors consistent (or inconsistent) with the descriptions in the text (and those offered by your professor)? You will remember the subject matter better *and* become a good critic of media portrayals of psychological problems if you use this technique.

Form Unusual, Exaggerated Associations

Psychologist Charles L. Brewer uses an interesting method to teach psychology students the fundamentals of shaping:

> Dr. Brewer first danced on his desk, then bleated like a sheep and finally got down on "all fours and oinked like a pig," he said. His antics were in response to a session he teaches on "successive approximation"—shaping behavior into a desired response.
>
> To get students to "shape" him, he told them he would try to figure out what they wanted him to do. If he guessed wrong, they'd "boo and hiss," while if he did what they wanted, they'd applaud him—which is why he eventually acted like a pig. "I'll do anything to get them to learn," he said. (DeAngelis, 1994a, p. 40)

It is easier to recall stimuli that stand out from the crowd. We pay more attention to them. Sometimes, therefore, we are better able to remember information when we create unusual, exaggerated associations.

Assume that you are trying to remember the geography of the cerebral cortex, as shown in Figure 2.15 on page 71. Why not think of what you look like in right profile? (Use your left profile if it is better.) Then imagine a new imaging technique in which we can see through your skull and find four

brightly colored lobes in the right hemisphere of your cerebral cortex. Not only that, but there are little people (let's call them "homunculi") who are flapping about in the sensory and motor areas (see Figure 2.15 again). In fact, imagine that you're in a crowded line and someone steps on your toe. As a result, the homunculus (a "homunculus" is a single member of the homunculi clan) in the sensory cortex has a throbbing toe. This is communicated to the association areas of the cortex, where you decide that you are annoyed. The language areas of the cortex think up some choice words that are relayed to the throat and mouth of the homunculus in the motor cortex. Then they are sent into your throat and mouth. You also send some messages through the motor cortex that ready your muscles to attack.

Then you see that the perpetrator of the crime is a very attractive and apologetic stranger! What part of the occipital lobe is flashing the wonderful images?

Use the Method of Loci: Meat Loaf in the Pocket

Another way to form unusual associations is the *method of loci* (pronounced LOW-sigh). Select a series of related images such as the parts of your body or the furniture in your home. Then imagine an item from your shopping list, or another list you want to remember, as being attached to each image. Consider this meaty application: Remember your shopping list by imagining meat loaf in your jacket pocket and balancing a breakfast plate on your head.

By placing meat loaf or a favorite complete dinner in your pocket, rather than a single item such as ground beef, you can combine several items into one chunk of information (Figure 7.8). At the supermarket, you recall the ingredients for meat loaf and consider whether you need each one. The breakfast plate can remind you whether you need juice, bread for toast, eggs, cereals, fruit for the cereals, coffee or tea, milk for the coffee or lemons for the tea, and so on.

FIGURE 7.8 **The Method of Loci**
By imagining meat loaf in your jacket pocket, you can combine several items into a single chunk of information. Once at the supermarket, recall the ingredients for meat loaf and ask yourself which ones you need to buy.

Use Mediation: Build a Conceptual Bridge

The method of mediation also relies on forming associations: You link two items with a third one that ties them together. What if you are having difficulty remembering that John's wife's name is Tillie? You can mediate between John and Tillie as follows. Reflect that *john* is a slang term for bathroom. Bathrooms often have ceramic *tiles. Tiles,* of course, sounds like *Tillie.* So it goes: John → bathroom tiles → Tillie.

I used a combination of mediation and formation of unusual associations to help me remember foreign vocabulary words in high school. For example, the Spanish word *mujer* (pronounced moo-hair [almost]), means "woman" in English. Women have mo' hair than I do. Woman → mo' hair → mujer. This particular example would no longer work for me because now most men also have more hair than I, but the association was so outlandish that it stuck with me.

Use Mnemonic Devices: "Soak Her Toe"

Broadly speaking, methods for jogging memory can all be termed *mnemonics,* or systems for remembering information. But so-called *mnemonic* devices usually combine chunks of information into a format such as an acronym, jingle, or phrase. (By the way, the word *mnemonic*

is derived from Mnemosyne, the Greek goddess of memory. Her name is pronounced *Nee-MOS-uh-nee.* How can you remember the pronunciation? Why not think of the goddess getting down on her two knees *[nee-nee]* to worship? End of commercial for mnemonic devices.) For example, recalling the phrase "Every Good Boy Does Fine" has helped many people remember the lines in the musical staff: E, G, B, D, F. In Chapter 3, we saw that the acronym *SAME* serves as a mnemonic device for distinguishing between afferent and efferent neurons. In Chapter 5, we noted that most psychology students use the acronym *Roy G. Biv* to remember the colors of the rainbow.

Acronyms have found applications in many disciplines. Consider geography. The acronym *HOMES* stands for the Great Lakes: *Huron, Ontario, Michigan, Erie,* and *Superior.* In astronomy, the phrase "Mercury's *v*ery *e*ager *m*other *j*ust *s*erved *u*s *n*ine *p*otatoes" helps students recall the order of the planets Mercury, Venus, Earth, Mars, Jupiter, Saturn, Uranus, Neptune, and Pluto. What about biology? You can remember that Dromedary camels have one hump while Bactrian camels have two by turning the letters D and B on their sides. Table 7.1 lists some of my favorite mnemonic devices.

And how can you math students ever be expected to remember the reciprocal of pi (that is, 1 divided by 3.14)? Simple: Just remember the question "Can I remember the reciprocal?" and count the number of letters in each word. The reciprocal of pi, it turns out, is 0.318310. (Remember the last two digits as 10, not as 1 and 0.)

Finally, how can you remember how to spell *mnemonics*? Easy—be willing to grant "aMNesty" to those who cannot.

TABLE 7.1 **MNEMONIC DEVICES**

Mnemonic Device	Encoded Information
HOMES	The names of the Great Lakes: Huron, Ontario, Michigan, Erie, and Superior
No Plan Like Yours to Study History Wisely	The royal houses of England: Norman, Plantagenet, Lancaster, York, Tudor, Stuart, Hanover, Windsor
X shall stand for playmates Ten. V for Five stalwart men. I for One, D for Five. M for a Thousand soldiers true. And L for Fifty, I'll tell you.	The value of the Roman numerals. "D for Five" means D = 500.
Mary Eats Peanut Butter.	The first four hydrocarbons of the alkane class: methane, ethane, propane, and butane, in ascending order of the number of carbon atoms in their chains
These Ten Valuable Amino Acids Have Long Preserved Life in Man.	Ten vital amino acids: threonine, tryptophan, valine, arginine, histidine, lysine, phenylalanine, leucine, isoleucine, methionine
All Hairy Men Will Buy Razors.	Constituents of soil: air, humus, mineral salts, water, bacteria, rock particles
Soak Her Toe.	Translates into SOHCAHTOA, or: Sine = Opposite/Hypotenuse Cosine = Adjacent/Hypotenuse Tangent = Opposite/Adjacent
Krakatoa Positively Casts Off Fumes; Generally Sulfurous Vapors.	Biological classifications in descending order: kingdom, phylum, class, order, family, genus, species, variety
Never Lower Tillie's Pants; Mother Might Come Home.	The eight bones of the wrist: navicular, lunate, triangular, pisiform, multangular greater, multangular lesser, capitate, hamate
Roy G. Biv	The colors of the spectrum: red, orange, yellow, green, blue, indigo, violet
Lazy French Tarts Sit Naked In Anticipation.	The nerves that pass through the superior orbital fissure of the skull: lachrymal, frontal, trochlear, superior, nasal, inferior, abducent

Want to study on the go? Go to your companion website and download an audio version of this review section to your media player.

Recite—An Active Summary™

1. What is meant by explicit memory?

Explicit memories contain specific information—information that can be clearly stated or declared. The information can be autobiographical or general.

2. What is meant by episodic memory?

An episodic memory is a memory of a specific event that one has observed or participated in.

3. What is meant by semantic memory?

Semantic memory is general knowledge, as in remembering that the United States has 50 states or that Shakespeare wrote *Hamlet*.

4. What is meant by implicit memory?

Implicit or procedural memory means knowing how to do things like write with a pencil or ride a bicycle. It is also called *skill memory*.

5. What is the difference between retrospective memory and prospective memory?

Retrospective memories concern events in the past that can be explicit or implicit. Prospective memories involve remembering to do things in the future. Prospective memory is affected by factors such as distraction, mood, and age.

6. What is the role of encoding in memory?

Encoding information means transforming it so that we can place it in memory. We commonly use visual, auditory, and semantic codes to convert physical and chemical stimulation into psychological formats that can be remembered.

7. What is the role of storage in memory?

Storage means the maintenance of information over time. The main methods of storing information are maintenance rehearsal (rote repetition) and elaborative rehearsal (relating it to things we already know).

8. What is the role of retrieval in memory?

Retrieval means locating stored information and bringing it back into consciousness. Retrieval requires use of the proper cues (just as to retrieve information stored on a hard drive, we need to know the file name.) Memory is defined as the processes by which information is encoded, stored, and retrieved.

9. What is the Atkinson–Shiffrin model of memory?

Atkinson and Shiffrin propose that there are three stages of memory—sensory memory, short-term memory, and long-term memory—and that the progress of information through these stages determines whether and how long it is remembered.

10. How does sensory memory function?

Each sense is believed to have a sensory register that briefly holds the *memory traces* of stimuli in sensory memory. The traces then *decay*. Visual sensory memory makes discrete visual sensations—produced by saccadic eye movements—seem continuous. McDougall used the whole-report procedure to demonstrate that visual stimuli are maintained in sensory memory for only a fraction of a second. Sperling used the partial-report procedure to show that we can see more objects than we can report afterward. Icons are mental representations of visual stimuli. Some people, usually children, can maintain icons over long periods of time and are said to have eidetic imagery. Echoes are representations of auditory stimuli (sounds). Echoes can be held in sensory memory for several seconds.

11. How does short-term memory function?

Focusing on a stimulus allows us to maintain it in short-term memory—also called *working memory*—for a minute or so after the trace decays. Rehearsal allows us to maintain information indefinitely. Miller showed that we can hold seven chunks of information (plus or minus two) in short-term memory. The appearance of new information in short-term memory *displaces* the old information.

12. Why are we most likely to remember the first and last items in a list?

This phenomenon is referred to as the serial-position effect. We tend to remember the initial items in a list because they are rehearsed most often (the primacy effect). We tend to remember the final items in a list because they are least likely to have been displaced by new information (the recency effect).

13. Is seven a magic number, or did the phone company get lucky?

Seven may not be a magic number, but it seems that the typical person can remember about seven chunks of information (juggle that many pieces of information in short-term memory).

Recite — An Active Summary™

14. How does long-term memory function?

There is no known limit to the amount of information that can be stored in long-term memory, and memories can be stored for a lifetime. However, long-term memories have not been shown to be perfectly accurate. They are frequently biased because they are reconstructed according to our schemas—that is, our ways of mentally organizing our experiences. The memories of eyewitnesses can also be distorted by leading questions. Information is usually transferred from short-term to long-term memory by one of two paths: maintenance rehearsal (rote repetition) and elaborative rehearsal (relating information to things that are already known).

15. What is the levels-of-processing model of memory?

This model views memory in terms of a single dimension—not three stages. It is hypothesized that we encode, store, and retrieve information more efficiently when we have processed it more deeply.

16. Why is it that some events, like the attack of September 11, 2001, can be etched in memory for a lifetime?

So-called *flashbulb memories,* as of the terrorist attack of September 11, 2001, or the death of a public figure like Princess Diana or JFK, Jr., tend to occur within a web of unusual and emotionally arousing circumstances. We may elaborate them extensively—that is, relate them to many things.

17. How is knowledge organized in long-term memory?

We tend to organize information according to a hierarchical structure. That is, we classify or arrange chunks of information into groups or classes according to common features.

18. Why do we sometimes feel that the answer to a question is on the tip of our tongue?

Research suggests that the tip-of-the-tongue phenomenon often reflects incomplete learning.

19. Why may it be useful to study in the room in which we will be tested?

This is because memories are frequently dependent on the context in which they were formed. That is, context dependence refers to the finding that we often retrieve information more efficiently when we are in the same context we were in when we acquired it. State dependence refers to the finding that we often retrieve information better when we are in the same state of consciousness or mood we were in when we learned it.

20. What types of memory tasks are used in measuring forgetting?

Nonsense syllables were developed by Ebbinghaus in the 19th century as a way of measuring the functions of memory. Retention is often tested through three types of memory tasks: recognition, recall, and relearning.

21. Why can learning Spanish make it harder to remember French?

This is an example of retroactive interference, in which new learning interferes with old learning. In proactive interference, on the other hand, old learning interferes with new learning. According to interference theory, people can forget because learning can cause cues (such as English words) to be connected with the wrong information (perhaps a Spanish word when a French word is sought).

22. What is the Freudian concept of repression?

Repression refers to Freud's concept of motivated forgetting. Freud suggested that we are motivated to forget threatening or unacceptable material. Research on the recovery of repressed memories is quite controversial.

23. Can children remember events from the first couple of years of life?

Probably not. This phenomenon is referred to as infantile amnesia. Freud believed that infantile amnesia is due to repression, but modern psychologists believe that infantile amnesia reflects factors such as immaturity of the hippocampus and failure to use acoustic and semantic codes to help remember information.

24. Why do people frequently have trouble recalling being in accidents?

Physical trauma can interfere with memory formation. Two kinds of amnesia are caused by physical trauma. In anterograde amnesia, a traumatic event such as damage to the hippocampus prevents the formation of new memories. In retrograde amnesia, shock or other trauma prevents previously known information from being retrieved.

Recite—An Active Summary™

25. What neural events are connected with memory?

Learning is apparently connected with the proliferation of dendrites and synapses in the brain. Learning and memory are also connected with the release of the neurotransmitters serotonin and acetylcholine and the hormones adrenaline and vasopressin.

26. What structures in the brain are connected with memory?

The hippocampus relays sensory information to the cortex and is therefore vital in formation of new memories. Visual memories appear to be stored in the visual cortex, auditory memories in the auditory cortex, and so on. The thalamus is connected with the formation of visual memories.

Go to **http://psychology.wadsworth.com/ rathus_pcc9e** to access an interactive version of this active summary.

Key Terms

Explicit memory (p. 266)
Implicit memory (p. 266)
Episodic memory (p. 267)
Semantic memory (p. 268)
Priming (p. 268)
Retrospective memory (p. 269)
Prospective memory (p. 269)
Encoding (p. 271)
Visual code (p. 271)
Acoustic code (p. 271)
Semantic code (p. 272)
Storage (p. 272)
Maintenance rehearsal (p. 272)
Metamemory (p. 272)
Elaborative rehearsal (p. 272)

Retrieval (p. 272)
Memory (p. 273)
Saccadic eye movement (p. 274)
Sensory memory (p. 274)
Memory trace (p. 275)
Sensory register (p. 275)
Icon (p. 275)
Iconic memory (p. 275)
Eidetic imagery (p. 275)
Echo (p. 276)
Echoic memory (p. 276)
Short-term memory (p. 276)
Working memory (p. 276)
Serial-position effect (p. 277)
Primacy effect (p. 278)
Recency effect (p. 278)
Chunk (p. 278)

Rote (p. 279)
Displace (p. 279)
Long-term memory (p. 280)
Repression (p. 280)
Schema (p. 280)
Tip-of-the-tongue (TOT) phenomenon (p. 287)
Feeling-of-knowing experience (p. 287)
Context-dependent memory (p. 288)
State-dependent memory (p. 289)
Nonsense syllables (p. 290)
Recognition (p. 290)
Recall (p. 291)
Paired associates (p. 291)
Relearning (p. 292)

Method of savings (p. 292)
Savings (p. 292)
Interference theory (p. 292)
Retroactive interference (p. 293)
Proactive interference (p. 293)
Dissociative amnesia (p. 293)
Infantile amnesia (p. 295)
Hippocampus (p. 296)
Anterograde amnesia (p. 296)
Retrograde amnesia (p. 297)
Engram (p. 298)
Long-term potentiation (LTP) (p. 298)

ACTIVE LEARNING RESOURCES

Visit your Companion Website for Video, Quizzing, and Self-Assessment!

http://psychology.wadsworth.com/rathus_pcc9e
On this site you can access the Reconstructive Memory video highlighted by the Video Connections icon on p. 284. In addition there are many quizzing opportunities including interactive versions of the fill-in-the-blank Active Review sections in your book. You can also fill out and score the Self-Assessment on p. 267.

Study on the Go!

Don't have time to study right now? You can study on the go! Visit your companion website and download an audio version of the Recite—An Active Summary section to your media player.

ThomsonNOW

http://www.thomsonedu.com
Need help studying? This site is your one-stop study shop. Take a Pre-Test and Thomson NOW will generate a Personalized Study Plan based on your test results. The Study Plan will identify the topics you need to review and direct you to online resources to help you master those topics. You can then take a Post-Test to determine the concepts you have mastered and what you still need to work on.

Author Blog

What does your author have to say about the state of psychology? Visit your companion website every Tuesday and click on "Author Blog," where he'll talk about the most recent controversies and hot topics in psychology.

Truth or Fiction?

T F The most efficient way to solve a problem is to use the tried-and-true formula.

T F Only humans can solve problems by means of insight.

T F You are most likely to find the answer to a frustrating problem by continuing to plug away at it.

T F If a couple has five sons, the sixth child is likely to be a daughter.

T F People change their opinions when they are shown to be wrong.

T F Sparrows that have been reared in isolation produce songs that are very similar to those produced by birds that have been reared with other sparrows in the wild.

T F Children's first use of language is crying.

T F Young children say things like "Daddy goed away" and "Mommy sitted down" because they *do* understand rules of grammar.

T F The majority of people around the world speak at least two languages.

T F Most people in the United States who grew up speaking another language in the home do not speak English very well.

 Go to **http://psychology.wadsworth.com/ rathus_pcc9e** to answer and score this Truth or Fiction quiz.

© Peter Johnson/CORBIS

Cognition and Language

Preview

When she was 9, my daughter Jordan stumped me with a problem about a bus driver that she had heard in school. Because I firmly believe in exposing students to the kinds of torture I have undergone, see what you can do with her problem:

> You're driving a bus that's leaving from Pennsylvania. To start off with, there were 32 people on the bus. At the next bus stop, 11 people got off and 9 people got on. At the next bus stop, 2 people got off, and 2 people got on. At the next bus stop, 12 people got on, and 16 people got off. At the next bus stop, 5 people got on, and 3 people got off. What color are the bus driver's eyes?

I was not about to be fooled when I was listening to this problem. Although it seemed clear that I should be keeping track of how many people were on the bus, I had an inkling that a trick was involved. Therefore, I told myself to remember that the bus was leaving from Pennsylvania. Being clever, I also kept track of the number of stops rather than the number of people getting on and off the bus. When I was finally hit with the question about the bus driver's eyes, I was at a loss. I protested that Jordan had said nothing about the bus driver's eyes, but she insisted that she had given me enough information to answer the question.

One of the requirements of problem solving is paying attention to relevant information (de Jong & Das-Smaal, 1995). To do that, you need some familiarity with the type of problem you are dealing with. I immediately classified the bus driver problem as a trick question and paid attention to information that apparently was superfluous. But I wasn't good enough.

Cognition: The Most Human Aspect of Our Psychology

The Greek philosopher Aristotle pointed out that people differ from lower organisms in their capacity for rational thinking. Thinking enables us to build skyscrapers, create computers, and scan the interior of the body without surgery. Some people even manage to keep track of their children and balance their checkbooks.

Question: What is cognition? Cognition may be defined as the mental activity involved in understanding, processing, and communicating information. Cognition—also referred to as **thinking**—entails attending to information, representing it mentally, reasoning about it, and making judgments and decisions about it. The term *thinking* generally refers to conscious, planned attempts to make sense of and change our world. Other aspects of cognition—for example, dreaming and daydreaming—may be unplanned and seem to proceed more or less on their own.

In this chapter we explore cognition and the closely related topic of language. We begin with concepts, which provide building blocks for cognition. But before we proceed, I have one question for you: What color were the bus driver's eyes?

Concepts: Building Blocks of Cognition

I began the chapter with Jordan's problem. Let me proceed with an oral riddle from my own childhood: "What's black and white and read all over?" Because this riddle was spoken, not written, and involved the colors black and white, you would probably assume that "read" meant "red." Thus, in seeking an answer, you might scan your memory for an object that was red although it also somehow managed to be black and white. The answer to the riddle, "newspaper," was usually met with a groan.

The word *newspaper* is a **concept.** *Red, black,* and *white* are also concepts—color concepts. Concepts are mental categories used to group together objects, relations, events, abstractions, or qualities that have common properties. **Question: How do concepts function as building blocks of cognition?** Concepts are crucial to cognition. Concepts can represent objects, events, and activities—and visions of things that never were or cannot be measured, such as "Middle Earth" in Tolkien's *Lord of the*

Cognition Mental activity involved in understanding, processing, and communicating information.

Thinking Paying attention to information, mentally representing it, reasoning about it, and making decisions about it.

Concept A mental category that is used to class together objects, relations, events, abstractions, or qualities that have common properties.

OBJECTS THAT STORE INFORMATION

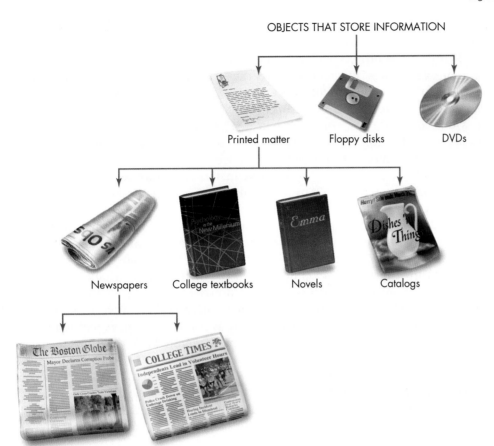

Printed matter   Floppy disks   DVDs

Newspapers   College textbooks   Novels   Catalogs

FIGURE 8.1 **Organization of Concepts into Hierarchies**

People may have a concept, "Objects that store information." This concept may include concepts such as floppy disk, DVD, and printed matter. Within the concept of printed matter, people may include newspapers, college textbooks (certainly the most important object that stores information!), novels, and catalogs. The concept of newspaper may include one's school newspaper and various commercial newspapers.

Rings novels, the land of Oz in *The Wizard of Oz,* or the "dark energy" that astronomers believe makes up much or most of the universe (96% of Cosmos Puzzles Astronomers, 2003).

Labels for objects tend to depend on recent experience with them and on our cultural setting (Sloman et al., 2002). Concepts such as *square, circle,* and *triangle* are not all that common in nature, and some peoples such as the Himba of Northern Namibia have no words for them (Roberson et al., 2002). However, these concepts are basic to the science of geometry. Much thinking has to do with categorizing new concepts and manipulating relationships among concepts, as in geometric proofs.

We tend to organize concepts in *hierarchies* (Figure 8.1). The newspaper category includes objects such as your school paper and the *Los Angeles Times.* Newspapers, college textbooks, novels, and merchandise catalogs can be combined into higher-order categories such as *printed matter* or *printed devices that store information.* If you add floppy disks and DVDs, you can create a still higher category, *objects that store information.* Now consider a question that requires categorical thinking: How are a newspaper and a DVD alike? Answers to such questions entail supplying the category that includes both objects. In this case, we can say that both objects store information. That is, their functions are similar, even if their technology differs.

Prototypes are examples that best match the essential features of categories. In less technical terms, prototypes are good examples. When new stimuli closely match people's prototypes of concepts, they are readily recognized as examples (Sloman, 1996). Which animal seems more birdlike to you, a robin or an ostrich? Why? Which of the following better fits the prototype of a fish—a sea horse or a tuna? Both self-love and maternal love may be forms of love, but more people readily agree that maternal love is a kind

Prototype A concept of a category of objects or events that serves as a good example of the category.

■ **Words and Concepts, Concepts and Words**
Circles, squares, and triangles are found only rarely in nature and not among the Himba of Northern Namibia. It is not surprising, then, that they have no words for these concepts.

Exemplar A specific example.

■ **A Goat or a Dog?** Yes, yes, you know the answer, but little children may at first include goats, horses, and other four-legged animals within the *dog* concept until they understand the differences among the animals.

of love. Apparently maternal love better fits their prototype of love (Fehr & Russell, 1991).

Many simple prototypes, such as *dog* and *red*, are taught by means of examples, or **exemplars.** Research suggests that it is more efficient for most of us to learn what *fruits* and *vegetables* are from experience with exemplars of each, rather than by working from definitions of them (Smits et al., 2002). We point to a dog and say "dog" or "This is a dog" to a child. Dogs represent *positive instances* of the dog concept. *Negative instances*—that is, things that are not dogs—are then shown to the child while we say, "This is *not* a dog." Negative instances of one concept may be positive instances of another. So, in teaching a child, we may be more likely to say, "This is not a dog—it's a cat" than simply, "This is not a dog."

Children may at first include horses and other four-legged animals within the dog schema or concept until the differences between dogs and horses are pointed out. (To them, the initial category could be more appropriately labeled "fuzzy-wuzzies.") In language development, such overinclusion of instances in a category (reference to horses as dogs) is labeled *overextension*. Children's prototypes become refined after children are shown positive and negative instances and given explanations. Abstract concepts such as *bachelor* or *square root* tend to be formed through verbal explanations that involve more basic concepts.

Your Turn: Now that we have defined cognition and discussed concepts, enhance your mastery of the material with the nearby "Learning Connections." Review the material by filling in the blanks, reflect on the material by relating it to other things you know, and think critically about it.

Learning Connections — COGNITION: THE MOST HUMAN ASPECT OF OUR PSYCHOLOGY

ACTIVE REVIEW (1) _____ is defined as mental activity involved in understanding, processing, and communicating information. (2) _____ are mental categories used to class objects, relations, or events with common properties. (3) A(n) _____ is an example that best matches the essential features of a category. (4) Simple concepts are frequently taught by presenting positive and negative _____.

REFLECT AND RELATE What examples best fit your prototypes for professors and students? How do the individuals in your classes fit with these prototypes?

CRITICAL THINKING Critical thinkers pay close attention to definitions of terms. How are the terms cognition and thinking alike? How do they differ?

 Go to **http://psychology.wadsworth.com/ rathus_pcc9e** for an interactive version of this Learning Connections unit.

Problem Solving: Getting from Here to There

Now I would like to share something personal with you. One of the pleasures I derived from my own introductory psychology course lay in showing friends the textbook and getting them involved in the problems in the section on problem solving. First, of course, I struggled with them myself. Now it's your turn. Get some scrap paper, take a breath, and have a go at the problems in the nearby Self-Assessment. The answers will be discussed in the following pages, but don't peek. *Try* the problems first.

Question: How do people go about solving problems? To answer this question, begin by considering the steps you used to try to solve parts a and b of problem 1. Did you first make sure you understood the problem by rereading the instructions? Or did you dive right in as soon as you saw them on the page? Perhaps the solutions to 1a and 1b came easily, but I'm sure you studied 1c very carefully. Let's review what you may have been thinking when you attempted to solve these problems and how your cognitive processes might have led you to or away from solutions.

Self-Assessment · Puzzles, Problems, and Just Plain Fun

Are you ready for some mind benders? Following are a number of problems I came across in my own psychology courses. They were challenging and mostly enjoyable, except that I think I scratched my head a bit too hard over a couple of them. (The hair still hasn't grown back, although people unfamiliar with my past attribute it to male-pattern baldness.)

Have some fun with them. If the answer doesn't come immediately, why not stand back from the problem for a while and see if the answer comes to you in a "flash of insight." (I confess that I was suffering from a deficiency of insight when I tried to solve them.)

You will find the answers to Problems 1a and b and 4 as you read along in the text. You will find the answers to Problems 1c, 2, and 3 in the figure on page A-19 of Appendix B.

1. Provide the next two letters in the series for each of the following:

   a. ABABABAB??

   b. ABDEBCEF??

   c. OTTFFSSE??

2. Draw straight lines through all the points in part A of Figure 8.2, using only *four* lines. Do not lift your pencil from the paper or retrace your steps. (See page A-19 for answer.)

FIGURE 8.2 Two Problems

Draw straight lines through all the points in Part A, using only four lines. Do not lift your pencil or retrace your steps. Move three matches in Part B to make four squares equal in size. Use all the matches. See page A–19 for the answers.

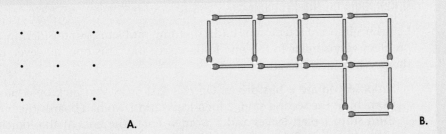

A.

B.

3. Move three matches in part B of Figure 8.2 to make four squares of the same size. You must use *all* the matches. (See page A-19 for answer.)

4. You have three jars—A, B, and C—which hold the amounts of water, in ounces, shown in Table 8.1. For each of the seven problems in Table 8.1, use the jars in any way you wish in order to arrive at the indicated amount of water. Fill or empty any jar as often as you wish. How do you obtain the desired amount of water in each problem?

TABLE 8.1 WATER-JAR PROBLEMS; THREE JARS ARE PRESENT WITH THE LISTED CAPACITY (IN OUNCES)

Problem	Jar A	Jar B	Jar C	Goal
1	21	127	3	100
2	14	163	25	99
3	18	43	10	5
4	9	42	6	21
5	20	59	4	31
6	23	49	3	20
7	10	36	7	3

For each problem, how can you use some combination of the three jars given and a tap to obtain precisely the amount of water shown?

Source: Adapted from *Rigidity of Behavior,* by Abraham S. Luchins & Edith H. Luchins, p. 109. Copyright 1959 Abraham Luchins.

After you believed you understood what was required in each problem, you probably tried to discover the structure of the cycles in each series. Series 1a has repeated cycles of two letters: *AB, AB,* and so on. Series 1b may be seen as having four cycles of two consecutive letters: *AB, DE, BC,* and so on.

Again, did you solve 1a and 1b in a flash of insight, or did you try to find rules that govern each series? In series 1a, the rule is simply to repeat the cycle. Series 1b is more complicated, and different sets of rules can be used to describe it. One correct set of rules is that odd-numbered cycles (*1* and *3,* or *AB* and *BC*) simply repeat the last letter of the previous cycle (in this case *B*) and then advance by one letter in the alphabet. The same rule applies to even-numbered cycles (*2* and *4,* or *DE* and *EF*).

If you found rules for problems 1a and 1b, you used them to produce the next letters in the series: *AB* in series 1a and *CD* in series 1b. Perhaps you then evaluated the effectiveness of your rules by checking your answers against the solutions in the preceding paragraphs.

Now, the question is whether your solutions to problems 1a and 1b helped you to understand 1c or whether they interfered with your ability to solve 1c. Let us consider what psychologists mean by "understanding" a problem. Then let us see whether you applied an *algorithm* to solve 1a and 1b. As we read on, we'll also consider the roles of *heuristics, insight,* and *mental sets,* among other cognitive processes. You'll see that solving 1a and 1b might have made it more difficult rather than less difficult to solve 1c.

Understanding the Problem

Let us begin our discussion of understanding problems by considering a bus driver problem very similar to the one Jordan gave me. This one, however, appeared in the psychological literature:

> Suppose you are a bus driver. On the first stop, you pick up 6 men and 2 women. At the second stop, 2 men leave and 1 woman boards the bus. At the third stop, 1 man leaves and 2 women enter the bus. At the fourth stop, 3 men get on and 3 women get off. At the fifth stop, 2 men get off, 3 men get on, 1 woman gets off and 2 women get on. What is the bus driver's name? (Halpern, 1989, p. 392)

Both versions of the bus driver problem demonstrate that a key to understanding a problem is focusing on the right information. If we assume it is crucial to keep track of the numbers of people getting on and off the bus, we focus on information that turns out to be unessential. In fact, it distracts us from the important information.

When we are faced with a novel problem, how can we know which information is relevant and which is not? Background knowledge helps. If you are given a chemistry problem, it helps if you have taken courses in chemistry. If Jordan gives you a problem, it is helpful to expect the unexpected. (In case you still haven't gotten it, the critical information you need to solve both bus driver problems is provided in the first sentence.)

Successful understanding of a problem generally requires three features:

1. *The parts or elements of our mental representation of the problem relate to one another in a meaningful way.* If we are trying to solve a problem in geometry, our mental triangles should have angles that total 180 degrees, not 360 degrees.

2. *The elements of our mental representation of the problem correspond to the elements of the problem in the outer world.* If we are meeting a patient in the emergency room of a hospital, we want to arrive at a diagnosis of what might be wrong before we make a treatment plan. In order to do so, we take the patient's "vital signs," including heart rate, temperature, and blood pressure, so that our mental picture of the patient begins to conform with what is going on in his or her body. The elements of our mental representations must include the key elements for solving the problem, such as the information in the first sentence

of the bus driver problem. We prepare ourselves to solve a problem by familiarizing ourselves with its elements and defining our goals.

3. *We have a storehouse of background knowledge that we can apply to the problem.* We have taken the necessary courses to solve problems in algebra and chemistry. When given a geometry problem involving a triangle, for example, we may think, "Is this problem similar to problems I've solved by using the quadratic equation?"

The Use of Algorithms: Finding the Right Formula

An **algorithm** is a specific procedure for solving a type of problem. An algorithm invariably leads to the solution—if it is used properly, that is. Mathematical formulas like the Pythagorean theorem are examples of algorithms. They yield correct answers to problems *as long as the right formula is used*. Finding the right formula to solve a problem may require scanning one's memory for all formulas that contain variables that represent one or more of the elements in the problem. The Pythagorean theorem, for example, concerns triangles with right angles. Therefore, it is appropriate to consider using this formula for problems concerning right angles, but not for others.

If you are going to be meeting someone for the first time and want to make a good impression, you consider the nature of the encounter (for example, a job interview or a "blind date") and then consider how to dress and behave for the encounter. If it's a job interview, the algorithm may be to dress neatly (possibly wearing a suit), be well-groomed, and not to wear too much cologne or perfume. If it's a date, you may ditch the suit but still be well-groomed and hike up the cologne or perfume a notch. In either case, smile and make eye contact—it's all part of the formula, as you will see in Chapter 14.

Anagrams are scrambled words. *Korc* is an anagram for *rock* (or *cork*). The task in anagram problems is to try to reorganize jumbles or groups of letters into words. Some anagram problems require us to use every letter from the pool of letters; others allow us to use only some of the letters. How many words can you make from the pool of letters *DWARG?* If you were to use the **systematic random search** algorithm, you would list every possible letter combination, using from one to all five letters. You could use a dictionary or a spell-checking program to see whether each result is, in fact, a word. Such a method might be time-consuming, but it would work.

The Use of Heuristic Devices: If It Works, Just Do It?

Question: Is it best to use a tried-and-true formula to solve a problem? Sometimes people use shortcuts that enable them to jump to conclusions—including the correct conclusion. These shortcuts are called heuristics, or heuristic devices. **Heuristics** are rules of thumb that help us simplify and solve problems. Heuristic processes are often based on problem-solving strategies that worked in the past (Klaczynski, 2001).

In contrast to algorithms, heuristics do not guarantee a correct solution. But when they work, they permit more rapid solutions. A heuristic device for solving the anagram problem would be to look for familiar letter combinations and then check the remaining letters for words that include these combinations. In *DWARG*, for example, we can find the familiar combinations *dr* and *gr*. We may then quickly find *draw, drag,* and *grad*. The drawback to this method, however, is that we might miss some words.
Truth or Fiction Revisited: It is not true that the most efficient way to solve a problem is to use the tried-and-true formula. Sometimes heuristic devices are faster.

One type of heuristic device is the **means–end analysis.** In using this heuristic device, we assess the difference between our current situation and our goals and then do what we can to reduce this discrepancy. Let's say that you are out in your car and have gotten lost. One heuristic device based on analysis of what you need to do to get to where you want to go might be to ask for directions. This approach requires no "sense of direction." An algorithm might be more complicated and require some geographical knowledge. For example, let us say that you know your

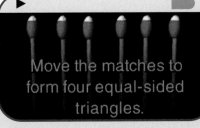

Video Connections—Problem Solving
Can you solve these riddles and explain the psychological processes behind them? Go to your companion website and click on "Problem Solving" to view the riddles and the role of insight in problem solving.

Algorithm A systematic procedure for solving a problem that works invariably when it is correctly applied.

Systematic random search An algorithm for solving problems in which each possible solution is tested according to a particular set of rules.

Heuristics Rules of thumb that help us simplify and solve problems.

Means–end analysis A heuristic device in which we try to solve a problem by evaluating the difference between the current situation and the goal.

destination is west of your current location and on the other side of the railroad tracks. You might therefore drive toward the setting sun (west) and, at the same time, watch for railroad tracks. If the road comes to an end and you must turn left or right, you can scan in both directions for tracks. If you don't see any, turn right or left, but at the next major intersection turn toward the setting sun. Eventually you should get there. If not, you can always ask for directions.

The Use of Analogies: This Is Just Like . . . ?

An *analogy* is a partial similarity among things that are different in other ways. During the Cold War, some people in the United States believed in the so-called domino theory. Seeing the nations of Southeast Asia as analogous to dominoes, they argued that if one nation were allowed to fall to communism, its neighbor would be likely to follow. They were wrong. In the late 1980s, the opposite domino effect actually occurred as communism collapsed in one Eastern European nation after another. When communism collapsed in one nation, it became more likely to collapse in neighboring nations as well.

The analogy heuristic applies the solution of an earlier problem to the solution of a new one. We use the analogy heuristic whenever we try to solve a new problem by referring to a previous problem (Halpern et al., 1990). Consider the water jar problems in Table 8.1. Problem 2 is analogous to problem 1. Therefore, the approach to solving problem 1 works with problem 2. (Later we consider what happens when the analogy heuristic fails.)

Let us see whether you can use the analogy heuristic to your advantage in the following number series problem: To solve problems 1a, 1b, and 1c on page 311, you had to figure out the rules that govern the order of the letters. Scan the following series of numbers and find the rule that governs their order:

$$8, 5, 4, 9, 1, 7, 6, 3, 2, 0$$

Hint: The problem is somewhat analogous to problem 1c.[1]

This is rather abstract and mathematical. Actually, you use the analogy heuristic regularly. For example, when you begin a new term with a new instructor, you probably try to ask yourself whom the instructor seems to remind you of. Then, perhaps, you recall the things that helped you get along with the analogous instructor and try them on the new one. We tend to look for things that helped us in the past in any new situation that looks similar.

Factors That Affect Problem Solving: Making Ruts, Climbing Out

The way you approach a problem is central to how effective you are at solving it. Other factors also influence your effectiveness at problem solving. **Question: What factors make it easier or harder to solve problems?** Three such factors—your level of expertise, whether you fall prey to a mental set, and whether you develop insight into the problem—reside within you. A couple of characteristics of problems also affect your ability to solve them effectively: the extent to which the elements of the problem are fixed in function and the way the problem is defined.

EXPERTISE To appreciate the role of expertise in problem solving, unscramble the following anagrams, taken from Novick and Coté (1992). In each case use all of the letters to form an actual English word:

DNSUO

RCWDO

IASYD

How long did it take you to unscramble each anagram ("sound," "crowd," and "daisy")? Would a person whose native language is English—that is, an "expert"—

---

[1] The analogous element is that there is a correspondence between these numbers and the first letter in the English word that spells them out.

unscramble each anagram more efficiently than a bilingual person who spoke another language in the home? Why or why not?

Experts solve problems more efficiently and rapidly than novices do. Generally speaking, people who are experts at solving a certain kind of problem share the following characteristics:

◆ They know the particular area well.

◆ They have a good memory for the elements in the problems.

◆ They form mental images or representations that facilitate problem solving (Szala, 2002).

◆ They relate the problem to similar problems (Gorodetsky & Klavir, 2003).

◆ They are more goal-directed have efficient methods for problem solving (Gorodetsky & Klavir, 2003).

These factors are interrelated. Art historians, for example, acquire a database that permits them to understand the intricacies of paintings. As a result, their memory for paintings—and who painted them—expands vastly.

Novick and Coté (1992) found that the solutions to the anagram problems seemed to "pop out" in under two seconds among experts. The experts apparently used more efficient methods than the novices. Experts seemed to use *parallel processing*. That is, they dealt simultaneously with two or more elements of the problems. In the case of DNSUO, for example, they may have played with the order of the vowels (*UO* or *OU*) at the same time that they tested which consonant (*D*, *N*, or *S*) was likely to precede them, arriving quickly at *sou* and *sound*. Novices were more likely to engage in *serial processing*—that is, to handle one element of the problem at a time.

MENTAL SETS Jordan hit me with another question: "A farmer had 17 sheep. All but 9 died. How many sheep did he have left?" Being a victim of a mental set, I assumed that this was a subtraction problem and gave the answer 8. She gleefully informed me that she hadn't said "9 died." She had said "*all but* 9 died." Therefore, the correct answer was 9. (Get it?) Put it another way: I had not *understood* the problem. My mental representation of the problem did not correspond to the actual elements of the problem.

Return to problem 1, part c in the Self-Assessment (page 311). To try to solve this problem, did you seek a pattern of letters that involved cycles and the alphabet? If so, it may be because this approach worked in solving parts a and b.

The tendency to respond to a new problem with the same approach that helped solve similar problems is termed a **mental set.** Mental sets usually make our work easier, but they can mislead us when the similarity between problems is illusory, as it was in part c of problem 1. Here is a clue: Part c is not an alphabet series. Each of the letters in the series *stands for* something. If you can discover what they stand for (that is, if you can discover the rule), you will be able to generate the 9th and 10th letters. (See page A-19 for the answer.) Similarly, the series of numbers on page 314 is not organized by a mathematical principle. *Hint:* The number 8 begins with an e when spelled out.[2]

INSIGHT: AHA! To gain **insight** into the role of insight in problem solving, consider the following problem, posed by Janet Metcalfe (1986):

A stranger approached a museum curator and offered him an ancient bronze coin. The coin had an authentic appearance and was marked with the date 544 BCE. The curator had happily made acquisitions from suspicious sources before, but this time he promptly called the police and had the stranger arrested. Why?

I'm not going to give you the answer to this problem just yet. (You'll find it in Appendix B on page A-19 under Puzzles, Problems, and Just Plain Fun.) But I'll make a guarantee. When you arrive at the solution, it will hit you all at once. You'll think "Of course!" (or something less polite). It will seem as though the pieces of information in the problem

Mental set The tendency to respond to a new problem with an approach that was successfully used with similar problems.

Insight In Gestalt psychology, a sudden perception of relationships among elements of the "perceptual field," permitting the solution of a problem.

---

[2]Yes, the numbers are organized alphabetically—good for you!

FIGURE 8.3 **Bismarck Uses a Cognitive Map to Claim His Just Desserts**
Bismarck has learned to reach dinner by climbing ladder A. But now the food goal (F) is blocked by a wire mesh barrier B. Bismarck washes his face for a while, but then, in an apparent flash of insight, he runs back down ladder A and up new ladder N to reach the goal.

Incubation In problem solving, a hypothetical process that sometimes occurs when we stand back from a frustrating problem for a while and the solution "suddenly" appears.

Functional fixedness The tendency to view an object in terms of its name or familiar usage.

have suddenly been reorganized so that the solution leaps out at you—in a flash.

Bismarck, one of University of Michigan psychologist N. R. F. Maier's rats, provided evidence of insight in laboratory rats (Maier & Schneirla, 1935). Bismarck had been trained to climb a ladder to a tabletop where food was placed. On one occasion Maier used a mesh barrier to prevent the rat from reaching his goal. But, as shown in Figure 8.3, a second ladder was provided and was clearly visible to the animal. At first Bismarck sniffed and scratched and made every effort to find a path through the mesh barrier. Then he spent some time washing his face, an activity that apparently signals frustration in rats. Suddenly he jumped into the air, turned, ran down the familiar ladder and around to the new ladder, ran up the new ladder, and claimed his just desserts. It seems that Bismarck suddenly perceived the relationships between the elements of his problem so that the solution occurred by insight. He seems to have had what Gestalt psychologists have termed an "Aha! experience." **Truth or Fiction Revisited:** It therefore appears that not only humans can solve problems by means of insight.

INCUBATION Let us return to the problems at the beginning of the section. How did you do with problem 1, part c, and problems 2 and 3? Students tend to fiddle around with them for a while. The solutions, when they come, appear to arrive in a flash. Students set the stage for the flash of insight by studying the elements in the problems carefully, repeating the rules to themselves, and trying to imagine what a solution might look like. If you tried out solutions that did not meet the goals, you may have become frustrated and thought, "The heck with it! I'll come back to it later." **Truth or Fiction Revisited:** Standing back from the problem, rather than continuing to plug away at it, may allow for the **incubation** of insight. An incubator warms chicken eggs so that they will hatch. Incubation in problem solving refers to standing back from the problem for a while as some process within may continue to work on it. Later, the answer may come to us in a flash of insight. Standing back from the problem may help by distancing us from unprofitable but persistent mental sets (Azar, 1995b).

Have another look at the role of incubation in helping us overcome mental sets. Consider the seventh water jar problem in Table 8.1. What if we had tried several solutions involving the three water jars and none had worked? We could distance ourselves from the problem for a day or two. At some point we might recall a 10, a 7, and a 3—three elements of the problem—and suddenly realize that we can arrive at the correct answer by using only two water jars!

FUNCTIONAL FIXEDNESS **Functional fixedness** may hinder problem solving. For example, first ask yourself what a pair of pliers is. Is it a tool for grasping, a paperweight, or a weapon? A pair of pliers could function as any of these, but your tendency to think of it as a grasping tool is fostered by your experience with it. You have probably used pliers only for grasping things. Functional fixedness is the tendency to think of an object in terms of its name or its familiar function. It can be similar to a mental set in that it makes it difficult to use familiar objects to solve problems in novel ways.

Now that you know what functional fixedness is, let's see if you can overcome it by solving the Duncker candle problem. You enter a room that has the following objects on a table: a candle, a box of matches, and some thumbtacks (see Figure 8.4). Your task is to use the objects on the table to attach the candle to the wall of the room so that it will burn properly. (See the Answer Key on page B.nn.)

FIGURE 8.4 **The Duncker Candle Problem**
Can you use the objects shown on the table to attach the candle to the wall of the room so that it will burn properly?

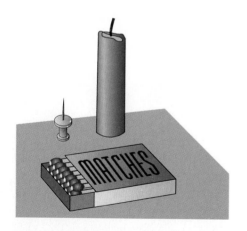

Your Turn: Now that we have problem solving, solve any problems in mastering the material with the nearby "Learning Connections." Review the material by filling in the blanks, reflect on the material by relating it to other things you know, and think critically about it.

Learning Connections — PROBLEM SOLVING: GETTING FROM HERE TO THERE

ACTIVE REVIEW (5) A(n) _____ is a specific procedure for solving a type of problem. (6) _____ devices are rules of thumb that serve as shortcuts to rapid solutions. (7) In using _____-_____ analysis, people assess the difference between their current situation and their goals and then do what they can to reduce this discrepancy. (8) We use the _____ heuristic when we solve a new problem by referring to a previous problem. (9) A(n) _____ set is the tendency to respond to a new problem with the same approach that helped solve similar problems. (10) Some problems are solved by rapid "perception of relationships" among the elements of the problem, which is called _____.

REFLECT AND RELATE Have you ever gotten lost and asked for directions? Is asking for directions an algorithm or a heuristic device?

CRITICAL THINKING Research evidence suggests that Bismarck, a laboratory rat, showed insight in solving a problem. How does a researcher determine whether rats or other laboratory animals show "insight"?

Go to **http://psychology.wadsworth.com/ rathus_pcc9e** for an interactive version of this Learning Connections unit.

Judgment and Decision Making

Decisions, decisions. Should you go to breakfast before classes begin or catch a few extra winks? Should you get married or remain single? Should you take a job or go on for advanced training when you complete your college program? If you opt for the job, cash will soon be jingling in your pockets. Yet later you may wonder if you have enough education to reach your full potential. By furthering your education, you may have to delay independence and gratification, but you may find a more fulfilling position later on. Ah, decisions, decisions.

Other kinds of decisions are judgments about the nature of the world. We make judgments about which route to school or work will be the least crowded. We make judgments about where it will be safe and convenient to live. We make judgments about what political candidates to vote for and which brand of ice cream to buy.

Question: How do people go about making judgments and decisions? You might like to think that people are so rational that they carefully weigh all the pros and cons when they make judgments or decisions. Or you might think that they insist on finding and examining all the relevant information. Actually, people make most of their decisions on the basis of limited information. They take shortcuts. They use heuristic devices—rules of thumb—in their judgments and decision making, just as they do in problem solving. For example, they may let a financial adviser select stocks for them rather than research the companies themselves. Or they may see a doctor recommended by a friend rather than examine the doctor's credentials. In this section we consider various factors in judgment and decision making.

Heuristics in Decision Making: If It Works, Must It Be Logical?

Let us begin by asking you to imagine that you flip a coin six times. In the following three possible outcomes, H stands for head and T for tail. Circle the most likely sequence:

H H H H H H

H H H T T T

T H H T H T

Did you select T H H T H T as the most likely sequence of events? Most people do. Why? There are two reasons. First, people recognize that the sequence of six heads in a row is unlikely. (The probability of achieving it is $\frac{1}{2} \times \frac{1}{2} \times \frac{1}{2} \times \frac{1}{2} \times \frac{1}{2} \times \frac{1}{2}$, or 1/64th.) Three heads and three tails are more likely than six heads (or six tails). Second, people recognize that the sequence of heads and tails ought to appear random. T H H T H T has a random look to it, whereas H H H T T T does not.

People tend to select T H H T H T because of the **representativeness heuristic.** According to this decision-making heuristic, people make judgments about events (samples) according to the populations of events that they appear to represent (Kosonen & Winne, 1995). In this case, the sample of events is six coin tosses. The "population" is an infinite number of random coin tosses. But guess what? *Each* of the sequences is equally likely (or unlikely). If the question had been whether six heads or three heads and three tails had been more likely, the correct answer would have been three and three. If the question had been whether heads and tails would be more likely to be consecutive or in random order, the correct answer would have been random order.

But each of the three sequences shown is a *specific* sequence. What is the probability of attaining the specific sequence T H H T H T? The probability that the first coin toss will result in a tail is $\frac{1}{2}$. The probability that the second will result in a head is $\frac{1}{2}$, and so on. Thus, the probability of attaining the exact sequence T H H T H T is identical to that of achieving any other specific sequence: $\frac{1}{2} \times \frac{1}{2} \times \frac{1}{2} \times \frac{1}{2} \times \frac{1}{2} \times \frac{1}{2}$ = 1/64th. (Don't just sit there. Try this out on a friend.)

Or consider this question: If a couple has five children, all of whom are boys, is their sixth child more likely to be a boy or a girl? Use of the representativeness heuristic might lead us to imagine that the couple is due for a girl. That is, five boys and one girl is closer to the assumed random distribution that accounts for roughly equal numbers of boys and girls in the world. But people with some knowledge of reproductive biology might predict that another boy is actually more likely because five boys in a row may be too many to be a random biological event. **Truth or Fiction Revisited:** Therefore, it is not true that the sixth child of a couple with five sons is likely to be a daughter. If the couple's conception of a boy or girl were truly random, however, what would be the probability of conceiving another boy? Answer: $\frac{1}{2}$.

Another heuristic device used in decision making is the **availability heuristic.** According to this heuristic, our estimates of frequency or probability are based on how easy it is to find examples of relevant events. Let me ask you whether there are more art majors or sociology majors at your college. Unless you are familiar with the enrollment statistics, you will probably answer on the basis of the numbers of art majors and sociology majors that you know personally.

The **anchoring and adjustment heuristic** suggests that there can be a good deal of inertia in our judgments. In forming opinions or making estimates, we have an initial view, or presumption. This is the anchor. As we receive additional information, we make adjustments, sometimes grudgingly. That is, if you grow up believing that one religion or one political party is the "right" one, that belief serves as a cognitive anchor. When inconsistencies show up in your religion or political party, you may adjust your views of them, but perhaps not very willingly.

Let us illustrate further by means of a math problem. Write each of the following multiplication problems on a separate piece of paper:

A. $8 \times 7 \times 6 \times 5 \times 4 \times 3 \times 2 \times 1$
B. $1 \times 2 \times 3 \times 4 \times 5 \times 6 \times 7 \times 8$

Show problem A to a few friends. Give them each 5 seconds to estimate the answer. Show problem B to some other friends and give them 5 seconds to estimate the answer.

The answers to the multiplication problems are the same because the order of the quantities being multiplied does not change the outcome. However, when

Representativeness heuristic A decision-making heuristic in which people make judgments about samples according to the populations they appear to represent.

Availability heuristic A decision-making heuristic in which our estimates of frequency or probability of events are based on how easy it is to find examples.

Anchoring and adjustment heuristic A decision-making heuristic in which a presumption or first estimate serves as a cognitive anchor. As we receive additional information, we make adjustments but tend to remain in the proximity of the anchor.

Tversky and Kahneman (1982) showed these problems to high school students, the average estimate given by students who were shown version A was significantly higher than that given by students who were shown version B. Students who saw 8 in the first position offered an average estimate of 2,250. Students who saw 1 in the first position gave an average estimate of 512. That is, the estimate was larger when 8 served as the anchor. By the way, what is the correct answer to the multiplication problems? Can you use the anchoring and adjustment heuristic to explain why both groups of students were so far off?

The Framing Effect: Say That Again?

If you were on a low-fat diet, would you be more likely to choose an ice cream that is 97% fat free or one whose fat content makes up 10% of its calorie content? On one shopping excursion I was impressed with an ice cream package's claims that the product was 97% fat free. Yet when I read the label closely, I noticed that a 4-ounce serving had 160 calories, 27 of which were contributed by fat. Fat, then, accounted for 27/160ths, or about 17%, of the ice cream's calorie content. But fat accounted only for 3% of the ice cream's *weight*. The packagers of the ice cream knew all about the *framing effect*. They understood that labeling the ice cream as "97% fat free" would make it sound more healthful than "Only 17% of calories from fat." This is an example of the framing effect.

    Question: How do people frame information in order to persuade others? The **framing effect** refers to the way in which wording, or the context in which information is presented, can influence decision making. Political groups are as aware as advertisers of the role of the framing effect and choose their words accordingly. For example, proponents of legalized abortion refer to themselves as "pro-choice" and opponents refer to themselves as "pro-life." Thus each group frames itself in a way that is positive ("pro" something) and refers to a value (freedom, life) with which it would be difficult to argue.

    Parents are also aware of the framing effect. My 3-year-old, Taylor, was invited to a play date at Abigail's house. I asked Taylor, "Would you like to play with Abigail at her house?" The question met with a resounding no. I thought things over and reframed the question: "Would you like to play at Abigail's house and have a real fun time? She has lots of toys and games, and I'll pick you up real soon." This time Taylor's decision was yes. Being aware of the framing effect helps us think critically about the claims of advertisers and to form more effective arguments of our own.

Overconfidence: Is Your Hindsight 20–20?

Whether our decisions are correct or incorrect, most of us tend to be overconfident about them (Lundeberg et al., 1994). Overconfidence applies to judgments as wide-ranging as whether one will be infected by the virus that causes AIDS (Goldman & Harlow, 1993), predicting the outcome of elections (Hawkins & Hastie, 1990), asserting that one's answers to test items are correct (Lundeberg et al., 1994), and selecting stocks. **Truth or Fiction Revisited:** It is not true that people change their opinions when they are shown to be wrong. Many people refuse to alter their judgments even in the face of contradictory evidence. (Have you ever known someone to maintain unrealistic confidence in a candidate who was far behind in the polls?)

    We also tend to view our situations with 20–20 hindsight. When we are proven wrong, we frequently find a way to show that we "knew it all along." We also become overconfident that we would have known the actual outcome if we had had access to the information that became available after the event (Hawkins & Hastie, 1990). For example, if we had known that a key player would pull a hamstring muscle, we would have predicted a different outcome for the football game. If we had known that it would be blustery on Election Day, we would have predicted a smaller voter turnout and a different outcome.

Framing effect The influence of wording, or the context in which information is presented, on decision making.

Question: Why do people tend to be convinced that they are right, even when they are dead wrong? There are several reasons for overconfidence, even when our judgments are wrong. Here are some of them:

◆ We tend to be unaware of how flimsy our assumptions may be.

◆ We tend to focus on examples that confirm our judgments and ignore those that do not.

◆ Because our working memories have limited space, we tend to forget information that runs counter to our judgments.

◆ We work to bring about the events we believe in, so they sometimes become self-fulfilling prophecies.

◆ Even when people are told that they tend to be overconfident in their decisions, they usually ignore this information (Gigerenzer et al., 1991).

Before leaving the section on thinking, I have a final problem for you:

You're driving a bus that's leaving from Pennsylvania. To start off with, there were 32 people on the bus. At the next bus stop, 11 people got off and 9 people got on. At the next bus stop, 2 people got off and 2 people got on. At the next bus stop, 12 people got on and 16 people got off. At the next bus stop, 5 people got on and 3 people got off. How many people are now on the bus?

Your Turn: Now that we have discussed judgment and decision making, why not show good judgment by deciding to enhance your mastery with the nearby "Learning Connections"? Review the material by filling in the blanks, reflect on the material by relating it to other things you know, and think critically about it.

Learning Connections JUDGMENT AND DECISION MAKING

ACTIVE REVIEW (11) According to the _____ heuristic, people make judgments about events according to the populations of events that they appear to represent. (12) According to the _____ heuristic, people's estimates of frequency or probability are based on how easy it is to find examples of relevant events. (13) In forming opinions or making estimates, our initial view serves as a(n) _____ anchor. (14) The _____ effect refers to the fact that wording, or the context in which information is presented, can influence decision making.

REFLECT AND RELATE Have you or anyone you know used the framing effect in an argument? Which term is more appealing, "pro-life" or "anti-choice"? Why?

CRITICAL THINKING Research suggests that people are reluctant to change their views, even when they are shown to be incorrect. What are the implications of these research findings for professors who desire to encourage their students to become critical thinkers? How does this color your perception of your own attitudes?

 Go to **http://psychology.wadsworth.com/ rathus_pcc9e** for an interactive version of this Learning Connections unit.

Language: "Of Shoes and Ships and Sealing Wax . . . and Whether Pigs Have Wings"

"The time has come," the Walrus said,
"To talk of many things
Of shoes—and ships—and sealing wax—
Of cabbages—and kings—
And why the sea is boiling hot—
And whether pigs have wings."

Lewis Carroll, *Through the Looking-Glass*

Lewis Carroll wasn't quite telling the truth. The sea is not boiling hot. At the risk of alienating walrus fans across the land, let me assert, most boldly, that walruses neither speak nor use other forms of language to communicate.

On the other hand, the time has come indeed to talk of how talking—of how language—permits us to communicate about shoes and ships and . . . you get the idea. When I was in high school, I was taught that humans differ from other creatures that run, swim, or fly because only we can use tools and language. Then I learned that lower animals also use tools. Otters use rocks to open clam shells. Leaf-cutting ants engage in agriculture (Wade, 2003) Chimpanzees toss rocks as weapons and use sticks to dig out grubs for food.

Going Ape over Language?

In recent years our exclusive claim to language has also been questioned because apes have been taught to use symbols to communicate. (*Symbols* such as words stand for or represent other objects, events, or ideas.) Chimpanzees and gorillas have been taught to communicate by making signs with their hands.

Chimpanzees are our closest genetic relatives, sharing an estimated 98.42% of their genetic code with humans (Zimmer, 2002–2003). MRI studies with chimpanzees and other apes shows that they, like humans, show some enlargement in the left hemisphere of the cerebral cortex, in part of Broca's area (Cantalupo & Hopkins, 2001) (see Figure 8.5). The differences that remain between humans and chimpanzees are apparently associated with capabilities such as fine control of the mouth and larynx that are not found in chimpanzees and other apes (Enard et al., 2002). The genetic differences between chimpanzees and humans probably explain why chimpanzees cannot articulate speech but also apparently give chimpanzees and other apes some meaningful ability to use language (Gibson, 2002; Mazur, 2002).

DO APES REALLY USE LANGUAGE? Apes do not speak, but they have been taught to use American Sign Language and other symbol systems. For example, a chimpanzee named Washoe, who was a pioneer in the effort to teach apes to use language, was using 181 signs by the age of 32. A baby chimp adopted by Washoe, Loulis, gained the ability to use signs just by observing Washoe and some other chimps who had been trained in sign language (Fouts, 1997). Other chimpanzees have used plastic symbols or pressed keys on a computer keyboard to communicate.

Sue Savage-Rumbaugh and her colleagues (2005; Brakke & Savage-Rumbaugh, 1996; Shanker et al., 1999) believe that pygmy chimpanzees can understand some of the semantic subtleties of language. She claims that one chimp, Kanzi, picked up language from observing another chimp being trained and has the grammatical abilities of a 2½-year-old child. Kanzi also understands several spoken words (spoken by humans, that is). Kanzi held a toy snake to a toy dog's mouth when asked to make the dog bite the snake.

Critics of the view that apes can learn to produce language, such as Herbert Terrace (1979) and Steven Pinker (1994a), note that:

◆ Apes can string together signs in a given sequence to earn rewards, but animals lower on the evolutionary ladder, such as pigeons, can also peck buttons in a certain sequence to obtain a reward.

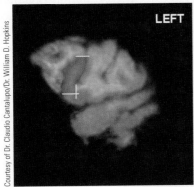
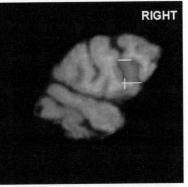

LEFT / RIGHT

Courtesy of Dr. Claudio Cantalupo/Dr. William D. Hopkins

FIGURE 8.5 **MRI Results of the Left and Right Hemispheres of the Cerebral Cortexes of a Great Ape**

In their MRI study of the brains of 25 chimpanzees and 2 gorillas, Cantalupo and Hopkins found that the great majority, 20, showed larger areas similar to Broca's area in the left hemisphere. So do most humans. Six apes showed larger areas in the right hemisphere. Only one showed no difference. It would thus appear that chimpanzees and gorillas have some rudimentary language structures in their brains, even if they are not "wired" for speech.

■ **A Chimpanzee Uses Signs to Communicate**
We share more than 98% of our genetic codes with chimpanzees and apparently also some ability to communicate using symbols. Although chimpanzees and other apes cannot articulate speech, they have enlarged areas on the left side of the brain that correspond to Broca's area in humans. There is no question that chimpanzees learn signs for objects and actions; however, many psychologists and linguists question whether they share the inborn human ability to order them according to rules of grammar.

◆ It takes apes longer to learn new signs than it takes children to learn new words.

◆ Apes are unreliable in their sequencing of signs, suggesting that by and large they do not comprehend basic rules of grammar—even the reliable sequencing of two-word phrases.

◆ People observing apes sign may be subject to *observer bias*—that is, they may be seeing what they want to see. It is sort of politically correct, especially to conservationists and animal-rights supporters, to try to humanize apes as much as possible. But we can appreciate and preserve the rights and habitats of animals, including apes, without claiming that they can use language in a meaningful way.

Scientists will continue to debate how well chimpanzees and gorillas understand and produce language, but there is little doubt that they have learned to use symbols to communicate (Hixon, 1998; Savage-Rumbaugh & Fields, 2000). Moreover, it is clear that chimpanzees understand many of the subtleties of communication. For example, when they are behind a human, they apparently understand that they must make noises to get the person's attention. Yet as soon as the person is facing them, they begin to make signs (Bodamar & Gardner, 2002). Although most researchers continue to consider that language emerges spontaneously only in people (Enard et al., 2002), perhaps we should not underestimate the abilities of apes to make use of language. **Question: Just how do we define language?**

What Is Language?

Language is the communication of thoughts and feelings by means of symbols that are arranged according to rules of grammar. Language makes it possible for one person to communicate knowledge to another and for one generation to communicate to another. It creates a vehicle for recording experiences. It allows us to put ourselves in the shoes of other people, to learn more than we could ever learn from direct experience. Language also provides many of the basic units of thinking.

In the ongoing struggle for existence, language is one of the human assets that has enabled us to survive and prosper. Other species may be stronger, run faster, smell more keenly, even live longer, but only humans have produced literature, music, mathematics, and science. Language is intricately involved with these achievements.

Do not confuse the complexities of language with the simplicity of the communications systems of many animals. Dogs may communicate their possession of a territory by barking at an intruder, but they are not saying "Excuse me, but you are too close for comfort." Birds warn other birds of predators. And, through particular types of chirps and shrieks, they communicate that they have taken possession of a certain tree or bush. The waggle dances of bees inform other bees of the location of a food source or a predator. Vervet monkeys make sounds that signal the distance and species of predators. But these are all instinctive communication patterns. **Truth or Fiction Revisited:** In another example of instinctive behavior, it is also true that swamp sparrows that have been reared in isolation produce songs that are similar—although deficient—as compared to those produced by birds that have been reared naturally in the wild. But we humans are ahead of the birds and the bees in communicating, and even the vervet monkeys and walruses. Let us see how.

Question: What are the properties of a "true" language as opposed to an inborn communication system? True language is distinguished from the communication systems of lower animals by properties such as semanticity, infinite creativity, and displacement (Ratner & Gleason, 1993).

Semanticity refers to the fact that the sounds (or signs) of a language have meaning. Words serve as symbols for actions, objects, relational concepts (*over, in,*

Language The communication of information by means of symbols arranged according to rules of grammar.

Semanticity Meaning. The quality of language in which words are used as symbols for objects, events, or ideas.

more, and so on), and other ideas. The communications systems of the birds and the bees lack semanticity. Specific sounds and—in the case of bees—specific waggles do *not* serve as symbols.

Infinite creativity refers to the capacity to create rather than imitate sentences. To produce original sentences, children must have a basic understanding of *syntax,* or the structure of grammar. Two-year-old children string signs (words) together in novel combinations.

Displacement is the capacity to communicate information about events and objects in another time or place. Language makes it possible to transmit knowledge from one person to another and from one generation to another. Therefore, people transmit not only traits from one generation to another, but also information. Information can thus accumulate in the human species, which is another feature of the human capacity to adapt.

Language and Cognition: Do We Need Words to Think?

Let us discuss language in terms of the broader picture: **Question: What are the relationships between language and thinking?** The relationships between language and thinking are complex and not always obvious. For example, can you think *without* using language? (The answer seems to be yes, but of course you would not be able to use thoughts that entail symbols that are arranged according to rules of grammar.) Would you be able to solve problems without using words or sentences? (That depends on the problem.)

Jean Piaget believed that language reflects knowledge of the world but that much knowledge can be acquired without language. For example, it is possible to understand the concepts of roundness or redness even when we do not know or use the words *round* or *red.*

Language and Culture

Different languages have different words for the same concepts, and concepts do not necessarily fully overlap. As we noted in our discussion of the Himba of Northern Namibia, concepts expressed in our own language (such as *square* and *triangle*) may also not exist in the language of another culture—and vice versa. **Question: Is it possible for English speakers to share the thoughts experienced by people who speak other languages?** The answer is probably yes in many or most cases, but in some cases, no. In any event, the question brings us to the linguistic-relativity hypothesis.

The Linguistic-Relativity Hypothesis

The **linguistic-relativity hypothesis** was proposed by Benjamin Whorf (1956). Whorf believed that language structures the way we perceive the world. That is, the categories and relationships we use to understand the world are derived from our language. Therefore, speakers of various languages conceptualize the world in different ways.

Thus most English speakers' ability to think about snow may be limited compared with that of the Inuit (Eskimos). We have only a few words for snow. The Inuit have many words. They differ according to whether the snow is hard-packed, falling, melting, covered by ice, and so on. When we think about snow, we have fewer words to choose from and have to search for descriptive adjectives. The Inuit, however, can readily find a single word that describes a complex weather condition. It might therefore be easier for them to think about this variety of snow in relation to other aspects of their world. Similarly, the Hanunoo people of the Philippines use 92 words for rice, depending on whether the rice is husked or unhusked and on how it is prepared. And whereas we have one word for camel, Arabs have more than 250.

In English, we have hundreds of words to describe different colors. There is about a 95% overlap in perception and labeling of colors among English speakers and

Infinite creativity The capacity to combine words into original sentences.

Displacement The quality of language that permits one to communicate information about objects and events in another time and place.

Linguistic-relativity hypothesis The view that language structures the way in which we view the world.

Chinese people (Moore et al., 2002). However, people who speak Shona use only three words for colors. People who speak Bassa use only two words for colors; these correspond to light and dark. It may be that at least part of our tendency to separate, say, blues from greens is learned within a cultural setting (Wierzbicka, 1999).

The Hopi Indians had two words for flying objects, one for birds and an all-inclusive word for anything else that might be found traveling through the air. Does this mean that the Hopi were limited in their ability to think about bumblebees and airplanes? Are English speakers limited in their ability to think about skiing conditions? Are people who speak Shona and Bassa "color-blind" for practical purposes? Probably not. People who use only a few words to distinguish among colors seem to perceive the same color variations as people with dozens of words. For example, the Dani of New Guinea, like the Bassa, have just two words for colors: one that refers to yellows and reds and one that refers to greens and blues. Yet performance on matching and memory tasks shows that the Dani can discriminate the many colors of the spectrum when they are motivated to do so. English-speaking skiers who are concerned about different skiing conditions have developed a comprehensive vocabulary about snow, including the terms *powder, slush, ice, hardpack,* and *corn snow,* that allows them to communicate and think about snow with the facility of the Inuit. When a need to expand a language's vocabulary arises, the speakers of that language apparently have little difficulty meeting the need.

Modern cognitive scientists generally do not accept the linguistic-relativity hypothesis (Pinker, 1990). For one thing, adults use images and abstract logical propositions, as well as words, as units of thought. Infants, moreover, display considerable intelligence before they have learned to speak. Another criticism is that a language's vocabulary suggests the range of concepts that the speakers of the language have traditionally found important, not their cognitive limits. For example, people who were magically lifted from the 19th century and placed inside an airplane probably would not think they were flying inside a bird or a large insect, even if their language lacked a word for airplane.

Your Turn: Now that we have discussed the nature of language and the role of language in cognition, enhance your mastery of the material with the nearby "Learning Connections." Review the material by filling in the blanks, reflect on the material by relating it to other things you know, and think critically about it.

Learning Connections — LANGUAGE: "OF SHOES AND SHIPS AND SEALING WAX ... AND WHETHER PIGS HAVE WINGS"

ACTIVE REVIEW (15) Apes (*Have* or *Have not?*) been taught to use symbols to communicate. (16) Language is the communication of thoughts and feelings by means of symbols that are arranged according to rules of _____. (17) According to the _____-relativity hypothesis, language structures (and limits) the way in which we perceive the world.

REFLECT AND RELATE Have you ever known someone to claim that a pet could "speak" or understand English or another language? *Did* the pet really "speak"? *Did* the pet "understand" language? What was the nature of the evidence? What is your conclusion?

CRITICAL THINKING Critical thinkers pay close attention to the definitions of terms: How do scientists distinguish true language from the communication systems of lower animals? What are the key issues in deciding whether apes can be taught to use language?

 Go to **http://psychology.wadsworth.com/ rathus_pcc9e** for an interactive version of this Learning Connections unit.

Language Development: The Two-Year Explosion

Question: How does language develop? Languages around the world develop in a specific sequence of steps, beginning with the *prelinguistic* vocalizations of crying, cooing, and babbling. These sounds are not symbols. That is, they do not represent objects or events. Therefore, they are *prelinguistic,* not linguistic.

Prelinguistic Vocalizations: Sounds without Meaning?

As parents are well aware, newborn children have one inborn, highly effective form of verbal expression: crying—and more crying. **Truth or Fiction Revisited:** But crying does not represent language; it is a prelinguistic event. During the second month, babies begin *cooing,* another form of prelinguistic expression which appears to be linked to feelings of pleasure. By the fifth or sixth month, children begin to *babble.* Children babble sounds that occur in many languages, including the throaty German *ch,* the clicks of certain African languages, and rolling *r*'s. Babies' babbling frequently combines consonants and vowels, as in "ba," "ga," and, sometimes, the much-valued "dada." "Dada" at first is purely coincidental (sorry, dads), despite the family's delight over its appearance.

Babbling, like crying and cooing, is inborn and prelinguistic. Deaf children babble, and children from cultures whose languages sound very different all seem to babble the same sounds (Gleason & Ratner, 1993). But children single out the sounds used in the home within a few months. By the age of 9 or 10 months they are repeating them regularly, and foreign sounds are dropping out. In fact, early experience in acquiring the phonemes native to one's own language can make it difficult to pronounce and even discriminate the phonemes used in other languages later in life (Iverson et al., 2003).

Children tend to utter their first word at about 1 year of age, but many parents miss it, often because it is not pronounced clearly or because pronunciation varies from one usage to the next (Nelson et al., 1993). The growth of vocabulary is slow at first. It may take children 3 to 4 months to achieve a 10-word vocabulary after they have spoken their first word. By about 18 months, children are producing a couple of dozen words.

Development of Grammar: Speaking by the Rules

The first linguistic utterances of children around the globe are single words that can express complex meanings. These initial utterances of children are called **holophrases.** For example, *mama* may be used by the child to signify meanings as varied as "There goes Mama," "Come here, Mama," and "You are my Mama." Similarly, *cat* can signify "There is a cat," "That stuffed animal looks just like my cat," or "I want you to give me my cat right now!" Most children readily teach their parents what they intend by augmenting their holophrases with gestures, intonations, and reinforcers. That is, they act delighted when parents do as requested and howl when they do not.

Toward the end of the second year, children begin to speak two-word sentences. These sentences are termed *telegraphic speech* because they resemble telegrams. Telegrams cut out the "unnecessary" words. "Home Tuesday" might stand for "I expect to be home on Tuesday." Two-word utterances seem to appear at about the same time in the development of all languages (Slobin, 1983). Two-word utterances are brief but grammatically correct. The child says, "Sit chair" to tell a parent to sit in a chair, not "Chair sit." The child says, "My shoe," not "Shoe my," to show possession. "Mommy go" means Mommy is leaving. "Go Mommy" expresses the wish for Mommy to go away.

There are different kinds of two-word utterances. Some, for example, contain nouns or pronouns and verbs ("Daddy sit"). Others contain verbs and objects ("Hit ball"). The sequence of emergence of the various kinds of two-word utterances is also apparently the same in all languages—languages diverse as English, Luo (an African tongue), German, Russian, and Turkish (Slobin, 1983). The invariance of this sequence has implications for theories of language development, as we will see.

OVERREGULARIZATION An important development for understanding the roles of nature and nurture in language is **overregularization.** Consider the formation of the past tense and of plurals in English. We add *d* or *ed* to make the past

Holophrase A single word used to express complex meanings.

Overregularization The application of regular grammatical rules for forming inflections (e.g., past tense and plurals) to irregular verbs and nouns.

tense of regular verbs and *s* or *z* sounds to make regular nouns plural. Thus, *walk* becomes *walked,* and *look* becomes *looked. Cat* becomes *cats,* and *doggy* becomes *doggies.* There are also irregular verbs and nouns. For example, *see* becomes *saw, sit* becomes *sat,* and *go* becomes *went. Sheep* remains *sheep* (plural), and *child* becomes *children.*

At first children learn a small number of these irregular verbs by imitating their parents. Two-year-olds tend to form them correctly—at first! Then they become aware of the grammatical rules for forming the past tense and plurals. As a result, they tend to make charming errors (Pinker, 1997). A 3- to 5-year-old, for example, may be more likely to say "I seed it" than "I saw it," and more likely to say "Mommy sitted down" than "Mommy sat down." They are likely to talk about the "gooses" and "sheeps" they "seed" on the farm and about all the "childs" they ran into at the playground. This tendency to regularize the irregular is what is meant by overregularization. **Truth or Fiction Revisited:** It is true that young children say things like "Daddy goed away" and "Mommy sitted down" because they understand rules of grammar.

Some parents recognize that at one point their children were forming the past tense of irregular verbs correctly and that they later began to make errors. The thing to remember is that overregularization reflects knowledge of grammar, not faulty language development. In another year or two, *mouses* will be boringly transformed into *mice,* and Mommy will no longer have *sitted* down. Parents might as well enjoy overregularization while they can.

OTHER DEVELOPMENTS By the age of 6, children's vocabularies have expanded to 10,000 words, give or take a few thousand. By 7 to 9, most children realize that words can have more than one meaning, and they are entertained by riddles and jokes that require some sophistication with language ("What's black and white, but read all over?").

Between the elementary school and high school years, language grows more complex, and children rapidly add on to their vocabularies. Vocabulary, in fact, can grow for a lifetime, especially in one's fields of specialization and interest.

Your Turn: Now that we have discussed the explosion of language in young children, enhance your mastery of the material with the nearby "Learning Connections." Review the material by filling in the blanks, reflect on the material by relating it to other things you know, and think critically about it.

Learning Connections   LANGUAGE DEVELOPMENT: THE TWO-YEAR EXPLOSION

ACTIVE REVIEW (18) Crying, cooing, and babbling are (*Prelinguistic* or *Linguistic?*) events. (19) Children babble sounds heard (*Only in their own languages* or *In all languages?*). (20) _____ are one-word utterances that have the meanings of sentences. (21) The kinds of two-word utterances used by children develop in (*A different* or *The same?*) order in different languages. (22) Children's use of sentences such as "I standed up" and "Mommy sitted down" are examples of _____.

REFLECT AND RELATE Do you know parents who were highly concerned with exactly when their children began

to talk? Did you know that Einstein did not talk until the age of 3? What does the case of Einstein suggest about language development expectations?

CRITICAL THINKING How is it possible that using the sentence "Mommy sitted down" can suggest that the child is *more* advanced in grammar than using the sentence "Mommy sat down"?

 Go to **http://psychology.wadsworth.com/ rathus_pcc9e** for an interactive version of this Learning Connections unit.

Nature and Nurture in Language Development: Don't Bother Making Threats–Houseplants Won't Talk

Since all normal humans talk but no house pets or house plants do, no matter how pampered, heredity must be involved in language. But since a child growing up in Japan speaks Japanese whereas the same child brought up in California would speak English, the environment is also crucial. Thus, there is no question about whether heredity or environment is involved in language, or even whether one or the other is "more important." Instead . . . our best hope [might be] finding out how *they interact.*

Steven Pinker (1994a)

Billions of children have acquired the languages spoken by their parents and passed them down, with minor changes, from generation to generation. Language development, like many other areas of development, apparently reflects the interactions between the influences of heredity (nature) and the environment (nurture). **Question: What are the roles of nature and nurture in language development?**

Learning Theory and Language Development: Infant Hear, Infant Say?

Learning theorists see language as developing according to laws of learning (Gleason & Ratner, 1993). They usually refer to the concepts of imitation and reinforcement. From a social–cognitive perspective, parents serve as *models*. Children learn language, at least in part, through observation and imitation. It seems likely that many words, especially nouns and verbs (including irregular verbs), are learned by imitation.

At first children accurately repeat the irregular verb forms they observe. This repetition can probably be explained in terms of modeling, but modeling does not explain all the events involved in learning. Children later begin to overregularize irregular verb forms *because of* their knowledge of rules of grammar, not through imitation. Nor does imitative learning explain how children come to utter phrases and sentences that they have *not* observed. Parents, for example, are unlikely to model utterances such as "bye-bye sock" and "allgone Daddy," but children do say them.

Learning theory cannot account for the unchanging sequence of language development and the spurts in children's language acquisition. Even the types of two-word utterances emerge in a consistent pattern in diverse cultures. Although timing differs from one child to another, the types of questions used, passive versus active sentences, and so on, all emerge in the same order.

The Nativist Approach to Language Development: Speaking from Within?

The nativist theory of language development holds that innate or inborn factors—which make up children's *nature*—cause children to attend to and acquire language in certain ways. From this perspective, children bring neurological "prewiring" to language learning (Baker, 2001; Newport, 1998; Pinker, 1994a, 1999).

According to **psycholinguistic theory,** language acquisition involves the interaction of environmental influences—such as exposure to parental speech and reinforcement—and an inborn tendency to acquire language. Noam Chomsky (1980, 1991) refers to the inborn tendency as a **language acquisition device**

Psycholinguistic theory The view that language learning involves an interaction between environmental factors and an inborn tendency to acquire language.

Language acquisition device (LAD) In psycholinguistic theory, neural "prewiring" that facilitates the child's learning of grammar.

In Profile | NOAM CHOMSKY

Courtesy Dr. Noam Chomsky, Massachusetts Institute of Technology

If you were casting a film about an intellectual, you might choose Noam Chomsky for the role. He is your stereotypical "shaggy-haired, bespectacled, rumpled genius" (Hunt, 1993). Chomsky grew up in New York during the Great Depression and was influenced by liberal politics. He planned to leave the University of Pennsylvania after two years of undergraduate study to join a leftist group in the newly born nation of Israel when a professor—Zellig Harris—got him more excited about linguistics.

If you think about it, the liberal view of language would be that environmental factors have the greatest influence on language learning. (Similarly, the liberal view of the determinants of intelligence would be that early exposure to a rich learning environment is more important than genetic factors.) Chomsky worked diligently, in fact, trying to find evidence for precisely this point of view. But he could not satisfy himself. Instead, he came to believe that the key to language ability is inborn—an innate language acquisition device. This device allows children to perceive deep grammatical relationships in sentences and to produce original sentences as a result.

Chomsky illustrates his idea, tongue in cheek, by noting that the following sentence makes sense (sort of): "Colorless green ideas sleep furiously." It is surely nonsensical but seems much more correct to an English speaker than, say, "Sleep green colorless furiously ideas." Why is the first sentence more familiar and comfortable? Go to **http://psychology.wadsworth.com/ rathus_pcc9e** to access more information about Noam Chomsky.

(LAD). Evidence for an LAD is found in the universality of human language abilities and in the specific sequence of language development (Baker, 2001).

The LAD prepares the nervous system to learn grammar. On the surface, languages differ a great deal. However, the LAD serves children all over the world because languages share what Chomsky refers to as a "universal grammar"—an underlying set of rules for turning ideas into sentences (Pinker, 1994a). Consider an analogy with computers: According to psycholinguistic theory, the universal grammar that resides in the LAD is the same as a computer's basic operating system (Baker, 2001). The particular language that a child learns to use is the same as a word-processing program.

Your Turn: Now that we have discussed two key theories of language development, enhance your mastery of the material with the nearby "Learning Connections." Review the material by filling in the blanks, reflect on the material by relating it to other things you know, and think critically about it.

In the following chapter we see that some aspects of language development—particularly vocabulary development—are strongly related to intelligence.

Learning Connections | NATURE AND NURTURE IN LANGUAGE DEVELOPMENT: DON'T BOTHER MAKING THREATS—HOUSEPLANTS WON'T TALK

ACTIVE REVIEW (23) From a social–cognitive perspective, children learn language, at least in part, through _____ and imitation. (24) According to _____ theory, language acquisition involves the interaction of environmental influences and an inborn tendency to acquire language. (25) Chomsky refers to the inborn tendency to develop language as a language _____ _____ device (LAD). (26) The LAD prepares the nervous system to learn _____. (27) According to Chomsky, languages share a(n) _____ grammar.

REFLECT AND RELATE Have you ever spoken very carefully to a pet, like a dog or a cat? Has the animal seemed to pay attention to your words? Has the animal used language to reply? Why or why not?

CRITICAL THINKING Does the nativist view of language development explain why (most) children who grow up in the United States speak English and why (most) children growing up in Japan speak Japanese? Explain. (*Hint:* The answer may be more complex than you initially think!)

 Go to **http://psychology.wadsworth.com/ rathus_pcc9e** for an interactive version of this Learning Connections unit.

Life Connections

Bilingualism and Ebonics: Making Connections or Building Walls?

It may be surprising to Americans, most of whom speak only English, but **(Truth or Fiction Revisited)** most people throughout the world do speak two or more languages. Bilingualism makes it possible to connect with people in other cultures. Lack of ability to speak other peoples' languages can build walls between them. Most countries, in fact, have minority populations whose languages differ from the national tongue. Nearly all Europeans are taught English and the languages of neighboring nations. Consider the Netherlands. Dutch is the native tongue, but all children are also taught French, German, and English and are expected to become fluent in each of them.

For more than 30 million people in the United States, English is a second language (Barringer, 1993). Spanish, French, Chinese, Russian, or Hebrew is spoken in the home and, perhaps, the neighborhood.

Bilingualism and Intellectual Development

A century ago it was widely believed that children reared in bilingual homes were retarded in their intellectual and language development. The theory was that cognitive capacity is limited, so people who store two linguistic systems are crowding their mental abilities. It is true that there is some "mixing" of languages by bilingual children (Patterson, 2000), but they can generally separate the two languages from an early age (Mueller & Hulk, 2001). Moreover, studies in the United States with children of Spanish-speaking parents who also learning English in the home or who picked it up later showed that they were generally proficient in both languages (Hammer et al., 2003; Pena et al., 2003).

Truth or Fiction Revisited: Speaking more broadly, the U.S. Bureau of the

■ **Bilingualism** Throughout the world most people speak two or more languages, and most countries have minority populations whose languages differ from that of the dominant population. It was once thought that children reared in bilingual homes were retarded in their cognitive and language development, but today most linguists consider it advantageous for children to be bilingual. Knowledge of more than one language certainly expands people's awareness of diverse cultures and broadens their perspectives.

Census reports that the majority—actually more than 75%—of Americans who first spoke another language in the home also speak English "well" or "very well" (Barringer, 1993). Moreover, a careful analysis of older studies in bilingualism shows that the bilingual children observed often lived in families with low socioeconomic status and little education. Yet these bilingual children were compared to middle-class monolingual children. In addition, achievement and intelligence tests were conducted in the monolingual child's language, which was the second language of the bilingual child (Reynolds, 1991). Lack of education and inadequate testing methods, rather than bilingualism per se, accounted for the apparent differences in achievement and intelligence.

Today most linguists consider it advantageous for children to be bilingual. For one thing, knowledge of more than one language expands their awareness of different cultures and broadens their perspectives (Cavaliere, 1996). Bilingualism apparently contributes to the complexity of the child's cognitive processes (Bialystock, 1999).

For example, bilingual children are more likely to understand that the symbols used in language are arbitrary. Monolingual children are more likely to think—erroneously—that the word *dog* is somehow intertwined with the nature of the beast. Bilingual children may thus have more cognitive flexibility. Second, learning a second language does not crowd children's available "cognitive space." Instead, learning a second language has been shown to increase children's expertise in their first (native) language. Research evidence reveals that learning French enhances knowledge of the structure of English among Canadian children whose native language is English (Lambert et al., 1991).

Ebonics

The term *Ebonics* is derived from the words *ebony* and *phonics*. It was coined by psychologist Robert Williams (Burnette, 1997). Ebonics was previously called Black English or Black Dialect (Pinker, 1994a). Williams explains that a group of African American scholars convened "to name our language, which had always been named by White scholars in the past" (Burnette, 1997, p. 12).

According to linguists, Ebonics is rooted in the remnants of the West African dialects used by slaves. It reflects attempts by the slaves, who were denied formal education, to imitate the speech of the dominant European American culture. Some observers believe that Ebonics uses verbs haphazardly, downgrading standard English. As a result, some school systems react to the concept of Ebonics with contempt—which is hurtful to the child who speaks Ebonics. Other observers say that Ebonics has different grammatical rules than standard

In Profile ROBERT WILLIAMS

He wasn't supposed to become a psychologist. He wasn't even supposed to go to college. His guidance counselor told him he had obtained a score of 82 on an IQ test (a score of 100 is considered average), and that perhaps he might be better off as a manual laborer.

So, after he graduated from high school, Robert Williams obtained work as a waiter in his hometown of Little Rock, Arkansas. But when he helped a friend solve an algebra problem, the friend encouraged him to go back to school. Williams followed the advice, enrolling in a local junior college and eventually receiving his doctorate in clinical psychology from St. Louis's Washington University.

Williams's own experience with intelligence tests led him to wonder whether they are culturally biased. He hypothesized that African American children would fare better on them if they were sensitive to African American culture. To demonstrate his point, Williams devised the *BITCH*—the Black Intelligence Test of Cultural Homogeneity. One question asked children to select a synonym for *blood* from the following choices: (a) a vampire, (b) a dependent individual, (c) an injured person, (d) a brother of color. The correct choice is *d*, and African American students proved to be more "intelligent" than European American students, according to the *BITCH*.

Williams is retired, but he has remained an active voice in the Ebonics debate and on the issue of cultural bias in intelligence testing.

 Go to **http://psychology.wadsworth.com/ rathus_pcc9e** to access more information about Robert Williams.

Courtesy of Robert Williams

English, but that the rules are consistent and allow for complex thought (Pinker, 1994a). A few years ago, the Oakland, California, school board recognized Ebonics as the primary language of African American students, just as Spanish had been recognized as the primary language of Latino and Latina American students. "I was honored," said Williams. "And truthfully, I was shocked. It was like the truth that had been covered up in the ground for so long just exploded one day" (Burnette, 1997, p. 12).

"To Be or Not to Be": Use of Verbs in Ebonics There are differences between Ebonics and standard English in the use of verbs. For example, the Ebonics usage "She-ah touch us" corresponds to the standard English "She will touch us." The Ebonics "He be gone" is the equivalent of the standard English "He has been gone for a long while." "He gone" is the same as "He is not here right now" in standard English.

Consider use of the verb *to be* in Ebonics. In standard English, *be* is part of the infinitive form of the verb and is used to form the future tense, as in "I'll be busy tomorrow." Thus, "I *be* busy" is incorrect. But in Ebonics *be* refers to a continuing state of being. The Ebonics sentence "I be busy" is the same as the standard "I have been busy for a while" and is grammatically correct.

Ebonics leaves out *to be* in cases in which standard English would use a contraction. For example, the standard "She's the one I'm talking about" could be "*She* the one *I* talking about" in Ebonics. Ebonics also often drops *ed* from the past tense and lacks the possessive *'s.*

"Not to Be" or "Not to Be Nothing": Negation in Ebonics Consider the sentence "I don't want no dinner," which is, of course, commendable. Middle-class European American children would be corrected for using double negation (do*n't* along with *no*) and would be encouraged to say "I don't want *any* dinner." Yet double negation is acceptable in Ebonics (Pinker, 1994a). Nevertheless, many teachers who use standard English have demeaned African American children who speak this way.

Many African Americans are "bilingual." They use standard English in a conference with a teacher or on the job but switch to Ebonics among friends.

Want to study on the go? Go to your companion website and download an audio version of this review section to your media player.

Recite—An Active Summary™

1. What is cognition?

Cognition is mental activity that is involved in the understanding, processing, and communicating of information. *Thinking* refers to conscious, planned attempts to make sense of the world.

2. How do concepts function as building blocks of cognition?

Concepts provide mental categories that allow for the grouping together of objects, events, or ideas with common properties. We tend to organize concepts in hierarchies. Prototypes are good examples of particular concepts. Simple prototypes are usually taught by means of exemplars, or positive and negative instances of the concept. Abstract concepts are usually formed through explanations involving more basic concepts.

3. How do people go about solving problems?

People first attempt to understand the problem. Then they use various strategies for attacking the problem, including algorithms, heuristic devices, and analogies. Algorithms are specific procedures for solving problems (such as formulas) that invariably work as long as they are applied correctly.

4. Is it best to use a tried-and-true formula to solve a problem?

Not necessarily. Heuristic devices often help us "jump" to correct conclusions. Heuristics are rules of thumb that help us simplify and solve problems. Heuristics are less reliable than algorithms, but when they are effective, they allow us to solve problems more rapidly. One commonly used heuristic device is means–end analysis, in which we assess the difference between our current situation and our goals and do what we can to reduce the discrepancy. The analogy heuristic applies the solution of an earlier problem to the solution of a new, similar problem.

5. What factors make it easier or harder to solve problems?

Key factors include one's level of expertise, whether one falls prey to a mental set, whether one develops insight into a problem, incubation, and functional fixedness.

6. How do people go about making judgments and decisions?

People sometimes make decisions by carefully weighing the pluses and minuses, but most make decisions on the basis of limited information. Decision makers frequently use rules of thumb or heuristics, which are shortcuts that are correct (or correct enough) most of the time. According to the representativeness heuristic, people make judgments about events according to the populations of events that they appear to represent. According to the availability heuristic, people's estimates of frequency or probability are based on how easy it is to find examples of relevant events. According to the anchoring and adjustment heuristic, we adjust our initial estimates as we receive additional information—but we often do so unwillingly.

7. How do people frame information in order to persuade others?

People frequently phrase or frame arguments in ways to persuade others. For example, people on both sides of the abortion issue present themselves as being in favor of an important value—either pro-life or pro-choice.

8. Why do people tend to be convinced that they are right, even when they are dead wrong?

People tend to retain their convictions, even when proven false, because they are unaware of the flimsiness of their assumptions, focus on events that confirm their judgments, and work to bring about results consistent with their judgments.

9. How do we define language?

Language is the communication of thoughts and feelings by means of symbols that are arranged according to rules of grammar.

10. What are the properties of a "true" language as opposed to an inborn communication system?

True language is distinguished from the communication systems of lower animals by properties such as semanticity, infinite creativity, and displacement. Semanticity means that the symbols of a language have meaning. Infinite creativity is the capacity to combine words into original sentences. Displacement is the ability to communicate information about events and objects from another time or place.

Recite—An Active Summary™

11. What are the relationships between language and thinking?	Language is not necessary for thinking, but language makes possible cognitive activity that involves use of symbols arranged according to rules of grammar.
12. Is it possible for English speakers to share the thoughts experienced by people who speak other languages?	Perhaps it is. According to the linguistic-relativity hypothesis, the concepts we use to understand the world are derived from our language. Therefore, speakers of various languages would think about the world in different ways. However, modern cognitive scientists suggest that the vocabulary of a language suggests the range of concepts that the users have traditionally found to be useful, not their cognitive limits.
13. How does language develop?	Children make the prelinguistic sounds of crying, cooing, and babbling before true language develops. Single-word utterances occur at about 1 year of age; two-word utterances by the age of 2. Early language is characterized by overextension of familiar words and concepts to unfamiliar objects (calling horses *doggies*), and by overregularization of verbs ("She *sitted* down"). As children develop, their vocabulary grows larger, and their sentence structure grows more complex.
14. What are the roles of nature and nurture in language development?	The two main theories of language development are learning theories and nativist theories. Learning theories focus on the roles of reinforcement and imitation. Nativist theories assume that innate factors cause children to attend to and perceive language in certain ways.

 Go to **http://psychology.wadsworth.com/ rathus_pcc9e** to access an interactive version of this active summary.

Key Terms

Cognition (p. 308)
Thinking (p. 308)
Concept (p. 308)
Prototype (p. 309)
Exemplar (p. 310)
Algorithm (p. 313)
Systematic random search (p. 313)
Heuristics (p. 313)

Means–end analysis (p. 313)
Mental set (p. 315)
Insight (p. 315)
Incubation (p. 316)
Functional fixedness (p. 316)
Representativeness heuristic (p. 318)

Availability heuristic (p. 318)
Anchoring and adjustment heuristic (p. 318)
Framing effect (p. 319)
Language (p. 322)
Semanticity (p. 322)
Infinite creativity (p. 323)
Displacement (p. 323)

Linguistic-relativity hypothesis (p. 323)
Holophrase (p. 325)
Overregularization (p. 325)
Psycholinguistic theory (p. 327)
Language acquisition device (LAD) (p. 327)

ACTIVE LEARNING RESOURCES

Visit your Companion Website for Video, Quizzing, and Self-Assessment!

http://psychology.wadsworth.com/rathus_pcc9e
On this site you can access the Problem Solving video highlighted by the Video Connections icon on p. 313. In addition there are many quizzing opportunities including interactive versions of the fill-in-the-blank Active Review sections in your book. You can also fill out and score the Self-Assessment on p. 311.

Study on the Go!

Don't have time to study right now? You can study on the go! Visit your companion website and download an audio version of the Recite—An Active Summary section to your media player.

ThomsonNOW

http://www.thomsonedu.com
Need help studying? This site is your one-stop study shop. Take a Pre-Test and Thomson NOW will generate a Personalized Study Plan based on your test results. The Study Plan will identify the topics you need to review and direct you to online resources to help you master those topics. You can then take a Post-Test to determine the concepts you have mastered and what you still need to work on.

Author Blog

What does your author have to say about the state of psychology? Visit your companion website every Tuesday and click on "Author Blog," where he'll talk about the most recent controversies and hot topics in psychology.

Truth or Fiction?

T F "Street smarts" are a sign of intelligence.

T F Creative people are highly intelligent.

T F Highly intelligent people are creative.

T F Alfred Binet, the originator of a widely used intelligence test, once used magnets to try to shift an action (such as lifting an arm) from one side of the body to the other.

T F An IQ is a score on a test.

T F Two children can answer exactly the same items on an intelligence test correctly, yet one child can be above average in IQ, and the other can be below average.

T F Gifted children tend to be physically and socially awkward.

T F Intelligence tests test a good deal more than intelligence.

T F Adopted children are more similar in intelligence to their adoptive parents than to their biological parents.

T F Head Start programs have raised children's IQs.

 Go to **http://psychology.wadsworth.com/rathus_pcc9e** to answer and score this Truth or Fiction quiz.

Intelligence and Creativity

Preview

Science has brought us many artificial objects—artificial sweeteners, designer drugs, and artificial limbs, to name a few. But one of the major scientific achievements lies in the realm of artificial intelligence. Artificial intelligence, or *AI,* is the duplication of human intellectual functioning in computers.

The concept of AI has a long history both in science fiction and in practice. The robot C3PO in *Star Wars* not only mimics human intelligence but also displays human anxieties and self-doubts. The programming in the artificial combination of flesh and metal portrayed by Arnold Schwarzenegger in the *Terminator* films presented him with options that enabled him to size up any situation and efficiently curse, kill, or utter Arnoldisms such as "I'll be back."

So much for Hollywood. The idea that human intelligence could be copied in computer form originated half a century ago. It was predicted that machines with AI would "one day" be able to understand spoken language, decipher bad handwriting, search their memories for information, reason, solve problems, make decisions, write books, and explain themselves out loud. At the time, these predictions were visionary. No longer. "One day" is today.

In some ways, AI goes beyond human intelligence. "Deep Blue," the IBM computer that defeated Russian grandmaster Garry Kasparov in chess, examined 200 million possible chess moves a *second.* Yet in 2003, Kasparov played an even more powerful computer, "Deep Junior," to a draw. But, said Kasparov, "I give us only a few years. Then they'll win every match, and we may have to struggle to win even a single game" (cited in Hoffman, 2003).

Artificial intelligence can solve problems that would take people years to solve, if they could solve them at all. Given clear direction and the right formulas, computers can carry out complex intellectual functions in a flash. "Who," asks University of Illinois professor Patrick Hayes, "can keep track of 10,000 topics like a computer?"

■ **Russian Chess Champion Garry Kasparov** Kasparov has played against computers that can analyze millions of possible moves per second and held his own. How "intelligent" are computers? What is "intelligence"?

Mario Tama/Getty Images

Moreover, when a computer learns something it can rapidly share the information with other computers. But when you learn Spanish or calculus, other people cannot readily "download" the information from you. If they could (as in the science-fiction *The Matrix* film series), education as we know it would vanish.

Even so, Deep Blue and Deep Junior are baby steps. Despite their skill at chess, in other ways they are much less than human. They do not have human insight, intuition, or creativity. Although Ray Kurzweil (2004; Kurzweil & Keklak, 2003) is developing artificial intelligence that can write poetry and create art, the sparks of brilliance we find in today's computers turn into dense wood when we compare them to Shakespeare and Picasso. (I hope my computer's not reading this.)

Some futurists speak of the merging of human and computer intelligence. They speak of things like "chipping" the human brain (installing microchips that would boost our knowledge and processing power) or of microscopic robots ("nanobots") that could set up shop at synapses and boost communication among neurons or supplant it with virtual realities that would have the immediacy of true experience.

It's all stimulating and somewhat scary. We're making computers that think more like people, and we may use computers to boost our own intellectual powers. What the worlds of natural and artificial intelligence will look like a century from now is anybody's guess. But for the moment at least, the qualities that make our psychological processes fully human have not been captured by computer science. That thought doesn't bother me a byte.

Question: Just what is intelligence? The concept of intelligence is closely related to the concept of thinking. Whereas thinking is the understanding and manipulating of information, **intelligence** is more broadly thought of as the underlying ability to understand the world and cope with its challenges. Intelligence is seen as making thinking possible.

Psychologists tend to be concerned with *how* we think, but laypeople and psychologists are often concerned with *how much* intelligence we have. At an early age, we gain impressions of how intelligent or bright we are compared with other people.

Intelligence provides the cognitive basis for academic achievements. Intelligence allows people to think—to understand complex ideas, reason, and solve problems—and to learn from experience and adapt effectively to the environment (Neisser et al., 1996). As we see in architecture, in the creation of mechanisms for heating and cooling, and in travel through space and under water, intelligence even permits people to create new environments. Although intelligence, like thinking, cannot be directly seen or touched, psychologists tie the concept to predictors such as school performance and occupational status (Luo et al., 2006; Pind et al., 2003).

Theories of Intelligence: The Most Controversial Concept in Psychology?

It may come as something as a surprise that psychologists do not agree on just what intelligence is. So now we discuss various theories about the nature of intelligence. Then we see how intelligence is measured and discuss group differences in intelligence. Finally, we examine the determinants of intelligence: heredity and the environment. Along the way, you will see why intelligence may just be the most controversial concept in the science of psychology. **Question: What are the various theories of intelligence?**

Factor Theories of Intelligence

Many investigators have viewed intelligence as consisting of one or more *factors*. Factor theories argue that intelligence is made up of a number of mental abilities, ranging from one kind of ability to hundreds.

In 1904, British psychologist Charles Spearman suggested that the behaviors we consider intelligent have a common underlying factor. He labeled this factor **g,** for "general intelligence" or broad reasoning and problem-solving abilities. Spearman supported his view by noting that people rarely score very high in one area (such as knowledge of the meaning of words) and very low in another (such as the ability to compute numbers). People who excel in one area are also likely to excel in others. But he also noted that even the most capable people are relatively superior in some areas—such as music or business or poetry. For this reason, he suggested that specific, or **s,** factors account for specific abilities.

To test his views, Spearman developed **factor analysis.** Factor analysis is a statistical technique that allows researchers to determine which items on tests seem to be measuring the same things. When he compared relationships among test scores of verbal, mathematical, and spatial reasoning, Spearman repeatedly found evidence supporting the existence of *s* factors. The evidence for *g* was more limited. Interestingly, recent research continues to find a key role for *g* in performance on intelligence tests. A number of cognitive psychologists (e.g., Colom et al., 2003) find evidence that connects *g* with *working memory*—that is, the ability to keep various elements of a problem in mind at once. Contemporary psychologists continue to use the term *g* in their research while speaking, for example, of the extent to which they believe a particular kind of test measures *g* (Gignac, 2006; Pyryt, 2000; Rushton et al., 2003).

American psychologist Louis Thurstone (1938) used factor analysis with ability tests and found only limited evidence for the existence of *g*. Thurstone concluded that Spearman had oversimplified the concept of intelligence. Thurstone's data suggested the presence of nine specific factors, which he labeled **primary mental abilities** (see Table 9.1).

Intelligence A complex and controversial concept. According to David Wechsler (1975), the "capacity . . . to understand the world [and] resourcefulness to cope with its challenges."

g Spearman's symbol for general intelligence, which he believed underlay more specific abilities.

s Spearman's symbol for *specific* factors, or *s factors*, which he believed accounted for individual abilities.

Factor analysis A statistical technique that allows researchers to determine the relationships among large number of items such as test items.

Primary mental abilities According to Thurstone, the basic abilities that make up intelligence.

TABLE 9.1 PRIMARY MENTAL ABILITIES, ACCORDING TO THURSTONE	
Ability	**Definition**
Visual and spatial abilities	Visualizing forms and spatial relationships
Perceptual speed	Grasping perceptual details rapidly, perceiving similarities and differences between stimuli
Numerical ability	Computing numbers
Verbal meaning	Knowing the meanings of words
Memory	Recalling information (words, sentences, etc.)
Word fluency	Thinking of words quickly (rhyming, doing crossword puzzles, etc.)
Deductive reasoning	Deriving examples from general rules
Inductive reasoning	Inferring general rules from examples

Over the years, psychologist J. P. Guilford (1988) expanded the numbers of factors found in intellectual functioning to hundreds. The problem with this approach seems to be that the more factors we generate, the more overlap we find among them. For example, several of his "factors" deal with solving math problems and computing numbers. Nevertheless, Guilford made a contribution by helping to catalogue the kinds of mental activities that are considered to be signs of intelligence.

The Theory of Multiple Intelligences

Psychologists like Thurstone and Guilford wrote about various factors or components of intelligence. Howard Gardner (1983/1993), instead, proposes that there are actually a number of *intelligences,* not just one. **Question: What is meant by multiple intelligences?** Gardner refers to each kind of intelligence in his theory as "an intelligence" because they can be so different from one another (see Figure 9.1).

FIGURE 9.1 Gardner's Theory of Multiple Intelligences

According to Gardner, there are several *intelligences,* not one, each based in a different area of the brain. Language ability and logic are familiar aspects of intelligence. But Gardner also refers to bodily talents, musical ability, spatial-relations skills, and two kinds of personal intelligence–sensitivity to one's own feelings (intrapersonal sensitivity) and sensitivity to the feelings of others (interpersonal sensitivity) as *intelligences.* Gardner's critics ask whether such special talents are truly "intelligences" or specific talents.

He also believes that each kind of intelligence has its neurological base in a different area of the brain. Two of these "intelligences" are familiar ones: language ability and logical–mathematical ability. However, Gardner also refers to bodily–kinesthetic talents (of the sort shown by dancers, mimes, and athletes), musical talent, spatial-relations skills, and two kinds of personal intelligence: awareness of one's own inner feelings and sensitivity to other people's feelings. Gardner (2001) has recently added "naturalist intelligence" and "existential intelligence." Naturalist intelligence refers to the ability to look at natural events, such as various kinds of animals and plants, or the stars above, and to develop insights into their nature and the laws that govern their behavior. Existential intelligence involves dealing with the larger philosophical issues of life. According to Gardner, one can compose symphonies or advance mathematical theory yet be average in, say, language and personal skills. (Are not some academic "geniuses" foolish in their personal lives?)

Critics of Gardner's view agree that people function more intelligently in some aspects of life than in others. They also agree that many people have special talents, such as bodily–kinesthetic talents, even if their overall intelligence is average. But they question whether such special intellectual skills are really "intelligences" or special talents (Neisser et al., 1996). Language skills, reasoning ability, and ability to solve math problems seem to be more closely related than musical or gymnastic talent to what most people mean by intelligence. If people have no musical ability, do we really think of them as *unintelligent?* You begin to see how difficult it is to define intelligence in a way that everyone can agree on.

The Triarchic Theory of Intelligence

Psychologist Robert Sternberg (2000; Sternberg et al., 2003) has constructed yet another theory of intelligence. His three-pronged, or *triarchic,* theory of intelligence, is reminiscent of a view proposed by the Greek philosopher Aristotle (Tigner & Tigner, 2000). **Question: What is Sternberg's triarchic model of intelligence?** The theory asserts that there are three types of intelligence: *analytical, creative,* and *practical* (see Figure 9.2).

FIGURE 9.2 **Sternberg's Theory of Intelligence**

According to Robert Sternberg, there are three types of intelligence: analytical (academic ability), creative, and practical ("street smarts"). Psychologists discuss the relationships between intelligence and creativity, but within Sternberg's model, creativity is a *type* of intellectual functioning.

Analytical intelligence
(Academic ability)
Abilities to solve problems,
compare and contrast, judge,
evaluate, and criticize

Creative intelligence
(Creativity and insight)
Abilities to invent, discover,
suppose, or theorize

Practical intelligence
("Street smarts")
Abilities to adapt to the demands
of one's environment, apply
knowledge in practical situations

Analytical intelligence is similar to Aristotle's "theoretical intelligence" and may be defined as what we generally think of as academic ability. It enables us to solve problems and to acquire new knowledge, and it is the type of intelligence best measured by standard intelligence tests. Problem-solving skills include encoding information, combining and comparing pieces of information, and generating a solution. Consider Sternberg's analogy problem:

Washington is to *1* as *Lincoln* is to (a) 5, (b) 10, (c) 15, (d) 50?

To solve the analogy, we must first correctly *encode* the elements—*Washington, 1,* and *Lincoln*—by identifying them and comparing them to other information. We can first encode *Washington* and *Lincoln* as the names of presidents and then try to combine *Washington* and *1* in a meaningful manner. (There are other possibilities: Both are also the names of memorials and cities, for example.) If we do encode the names as presidents, two possibilities quickly come to mind. Washington was the first president, and his picture is on the $1 bill. We can then generate two possible solutions and try them out. First, was Lincoln the 5th, 10th, 15th, or 50th president? Second, on what bill is Lincoln's picture found? (Do you need to consult a history book or peek into your wallet at this point?) The answer is (a) 5, because Lincoln's likeness is found on the $5 bill. (He was the nation's 16th president, not 15th president.)

Creative intelligence is similar to Aristotle's "productive intelligence" and defined by the abilities to cope with novel situations, profit from experience, and generate many possible solutions to problems. The ability to quickly relate novel situations to familiar situations (that is, to perceive similarities and differences) fosters adaptation. Moreover, experience teaches us to solve problems more rapidly. Psychologists who consider creativity to be separate from analytical intelligence or academic ability note that there is only a moderate relationship between academic ability and creativity (Simonton, 2000). However, to Sternberg, creativity *is* a basic type of intelligence.

Aristotle and Sternberg both speak of practical intelligence, or "street smarts." **Truth or Fiction Revisited:** It is therefore true that street smarts are a sign of intelligence—at least according to Aristotle and Sternberg. Practical intelligence enables people to adapt to deal with people, including difficult people, and to meet the demands of their environment. For example, keeping a job by adapting one's behavior to the employer's requirements is adaptive. But if the employer is making unreasonable demands, reshaping the environment (by changing the employer's attitudes) or selecting an alternate environment (by finding a more suitable job) is also adaptive (Sternberg, 1997b). Street smarts appear to help people get by in the real world, especially with other people, but are not particularly predictive of academic success (Heng, 2000).

CONTROVERSY IN PSYCHOLOGY

Is "emotional intelligence" a form of intelligence? Should it be taught in school?

Psychologists Peter Salovey and John Mayer developed the theory of emotional intelligence, which was popularized by the *New York Times* writer Daniel Goleman (1995). The theory holds that social and emotional skills are a form of intelligence, just as academic skills are. **Question: Just what is "emotional intelligence"?** Emotional intelligence bears more than a little resemblance to two of Gardner's "intelligences"—intrapersonal skills and interpersonal skills (including insight into the feelings of other people). It is also involved with self-insight and self-control—the ability to recognize and regulate one's moods (Salovey et al., 2002).

The theory suggests that self-awareness and social awareness are best learned during childhood (Richburg & Fletcher, 2002). Failure to develop emotional intelligence is connected with poor ability to cope with stress, depression, and aggressive behavior (Salovey et al., 2002; Wang, 2002). Moreover, childhood experiences may even mold the brain's emotional responses to life's challenges. Therefore, it is useful for schools to teach skills related to emotional intelligence as well as academic ability. "I can foresee a day," wrote Goleman (1995), "when education will routinely include [teaching] essential human competencies such as self-awareness, self-control and empathy, and the arts of listening, resolving conflicts and cooperation."

No one argues that self-awareness, self-control, empathy, and cooperation are unimportant. But critics of the theory of emotional intelligence argue that schools may not have the time (or the competence) to teach these skills, and that emotional intelligence may not really be a kind of intelligence at all. *Should* emotional intelligence be taught in the schools? Some psychologists believe that "emotional literacy" is as important as literacy in reading. However, psychologist Robert McCall (1997) echoes the views of many psychologists when he says:

> There are so many hours in a day, and one of the characteristics of American schools is we've saddled them with teaching driver's education, sex education, drug education and other skills, to the point that we don't spend as much time on academics as other countries do. There may be consequences for that.

Is emotional intelligence a form of intelligence? Psychologist Ulric Neisser (1997b) says that "The skills that Goleman describes . . . are certainly important for determining life outcomes, but nothing is to be gained by calling them forms of intelligence." Indian psychologist Nutankumar Thingujam (2002) is not as generous as Neisser. Thingujam argues that there is little agreement among psychologists on exactly what emotional intelligence is, and that the quality of tests designed to measure emotional intelligence is "questionable" at best. Two things seem certain: We will be hearing more about emotional intelligence as the years go on, and disagreements as to its usefulness will continue.

There are thus many views of intelligence—what intelligence is and how many kinds of intelligence there may be. We do not yet have the final word on the nature of intelligence, but I would like to share with you David Wechsler's definition of intelligence. Wechsler is the originator of the most widely used series of contemporary intelligence tests, and he defined intelligence as the "capacity of an individual to understand the world [and the] resourcefulness to cope with its challenges" (1975, p. 139). To Wechsler, intelligence involves accurate representation of the world and effective problem solving—adapting, profiting from experience, selecting the appropriate strategies, and so on. He leaves room for others to consider the kinds of resourcefulness—academic, practical, emotional, perhaps bodily—that are considered intelligent. We will return to Wechsler later and examine his intelligence tests.

Your Turn: Now that we have attempted to define intelligence and have explored various theories of intelligence, enhance your mastery of the material with the nearby "Learning Connections." Review the material by filling in the blanks, reflect on the material by relating it to other things you know, and think critically about it.

Learning Connections · INTELLIGENCE: THE MOST CONTROVERSIAL CONCEPT IN PSYCHOLOGY?

ACTIVE REVIEW (1) _____ may be defined as the underlying ability to understand the world and cope with its challenges. (2) Spearman suggested that intelligent behaviors have a common underlying factor, which he labeled _____, and specific factors that account for specific abilities. (3) Thurstone suggested that there are nine _____ mental abilities. (4) _____ proposes the existence of multiple intelligences, each of which is based in a different area of the brain. (5) Sternberg constructed a "triarchic" model of intelligence, including analytical, creative, and _____ intelligence.

REFLECT AND RELATE When did you form an impression of how intelligent you are? Has this impression helped you or hurt you? Explain.

CRITICAL THINKING Do the talents of dancers, gymnasts, artists, and musicians strike you as kinds of intelligences? Why or why not?

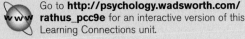

Go to **http://psychology.wadsworth.com/ rathus_pcc9e** for an interactive version of this Learning Connections unit.

Creativity and Intelligence

Think of artists, musicians, poets, scientists who innovate research methods, and other creative individuals. **Questions: What is creativity? What are the connections between creativity and intelligence?**

The concept of creativity has been difficult to define, just as the concept of intelligence. Just one of the many issues has been whether creativity is distinct from intelligence, or as Sternberg suggests, a type of intelligence. For example, we would not ask the question "Do creative people tend to be intelligent?" unless we saw creativity as something apart from intelligence. **Truth or Fiction Revisited:** The answer to whether an intelligent person is creative or a creative person is intelligent thus partly depends on definitions. If you consider creativity to be an aspect of intelligence, then the two concepts—intelligence and creativity—overlap. But if you think of intelligence as more closely related to academic ability, it is not always true that a highly intelligent person is creative or that a creative person is highly intelligent.

Within his triarchic theory, Sternberg defines **creativity** as the ability to do things that are novel and useful (Sternberg, 2001). Other psychologists note that creative people can solve problems to which there are no preexisting solutions, no tried and tested formulas (Simonton, 2000). Still other people think of creative people in terms of the arts rather than problem solving—for example, as painters or poets or musicians.

According to Sternberg and Lubart (1995, 1996), creative people share several characteristics:

◆ They take chances.
◆ They refuse to accept limitations and try to do the impossible.
◆ They appreciate art and music.
◆ They use the materials around them to make unique things.
◆ They challenge social norms.
◆ They take unpopular stands.
◆ They examine ideas that other people accept at face value.

A professor of mine remarked that there is nothing new under the sun, only new combinations of existing things. Many psychologists agree. They see creativity as the ability to make unusual, sometimes remote, associations to the elements of a problem to generate new combinations. An essential aspect of a creative response is the leap from the elements of the problem to the novel solution.

Creativity The ability to generate novel and useful solutions to problems.

Creative problem solving demands divergent rather than convergent thinking. In **convergent thinking,** thought is limited to present facts; the problem solver narrows his or her thinking to find the best solution. (You use convergent thinking to arrive at the right answer to a multiple-choice question.) In **divergent thinking,** the problem solver associates freely to the elements of the problem, allowing "leads" to run a nearly limitless course. (You may use divergent thinking when you are trying to generate ideas to answer an essay question on a test.) Problem solving can involve both kinds of thinking. At first divergent thinking helps generate many possible solutions. Convergent thinking is then used to select likely solutions and reject others. The nearby Remote Associates Test may afford you insight into your creativity.

Let's return to the connections between creativity and academic ability. Remember that Aristotle and Sternberg viewed creativity as one aspect of intelligence. To them creativity *is* intelligence, or at least one factor in intelligence. But many, perhaps most, psychologists view creativity as somewhat distinct from the kind of academic ability that is measured by intelligence tests. These psychologists would suggest that many highly creative people do not do all that well on intelligence tests, or in school, and that many brilliant individuals have little interest in art, music, and other creative endeavors. Research findings do suggest that the relationship between intelligence test scores and standard measures of creativity is only moderate (Simonton, 2000; Sternberg & Williams, 1997).

Intelligence test questions usually require analytical, convergent thinking to focus in on the one right answer. Tests of creativity determine how flexible a person's thinking is (Simonton, 2000). Try a mini-experiment yourself—or on others—to afford some additional insight into the nature of creativity. Here is an item from a test used by Getzels and Jackson (1962) to measure associative ability, a factor in creativity: "Write as many meanings as you can for each of the following words: (a) duck; (b) sack; (c) pitch; (d) fair." Those who write several meanings for each word, rather than only one, are rated as potentially more creative.

Here are some other types of mini-experiments: Another measure of creativity might ask people to produce as many words as possible that begin with T and end with N within a minute. Still another item might give people a minute to classify a list of names in as many ways as possible. How many ways can you classify the following group of names?

MARTHA   PAUL   JEFFRY   SALLY   PABLO   JOAN

Convergent thinking A thought process that narrows in on the single best solution to a problem.

Divergent thinking A thought process that attempts to generate multiple solutions to problems.

Self-Assessment   The Remote Associates Test

One aspect of creativity is the ability to associate freely to all aspects of a problem. Creative people take far-flung ideas and piece them together in novel combinations. Following are items from the Remote Associates Test, which measures the ability to find words that are distantly related to stimulus words. For each set of three words, try to think of a fourth word that is related to all three words. For example, the words *rough, resistance,* and *beer* suggest the word *draft,* as in the phrases *rough draft, draft resistance,* and *draft beer.* The answers are given in Appendix B.

1. charming	student	valiant	6. tug	gravy	show
2. food	catcher	hot	7. attorney	self	spending
3. hearted	feet	bitter	8. magic	pitch	power
4. dark	shot	sun	9. arm	coal	peach
5. Canadian	golf	sandwich	10. type	ghost	story

One way would be to classify them as men's names or women's names. Another would be English names versus Spanish names. Still another would be six-letter names, five-letter names, and four-letter names. The ability to do well on these kinds of items is connected with scores on standard intelligence tests, but only moderately so.

Your Turn: Now that we have attempted to define creativity, enhance your mastery of the material with the nearby "Learning Connections." Review the material by filling in the blanks, reflect on the material by relating it to other things you know, and think critically about it.

And now that we have begun speaking of scores on intelligence tests, let's see how psychologists go about measuring intelligence. We will see the kinds of mental activities that they have found to be useful in measuring intelligence. We will also see how psychologists attempt to *validate* their measures of intelligence—that is, how they try to demonstrate that they are in fact measuring intelligence and not other things. Later in the chapter we will also see that many psychologists believe that their efforts, to date, are filled with biases and fall short of scientific standards. As I noted at the outset of the chapter, intelligence is probably the most controversial concept in psychology.

Learning Connections CREATIVITY AND INTELLIGENCE

ACTIVE REVIEW (6) _____ has been defined as the ability to do things that are novel and useful. (7) Creative people make unusual, sometimes _____, associations to the elements of a problem. (8) Creativity appears to involve _____ thinking rather than convergent thinking.

REFLECT AND RELATE Do you know any highly creative people? Do they often challenge social norms and take unpopular stands? Are they "conformists"? How does your personal experience fit the discussion in the text?

CRITICAL THINKING Critical thinkers pay close attention to definitions of terms. Do you know some brilliant people who aren't very creative? Do you know some creative people who are not necessarily brilliant? How do you define "brilliance"? What assumptions do we make about the connection between intelligence and creativity just by posing these questions?

 Go to **http://psychology.wadsworth.com/ rathus_pcc9e** for an interactive version of this Learning Connections unit.

The Measurement of Intelligence

Although there are disagreements about the nature of intelligence, lay people and psychologists are concerned with "how much" intelligence people have, because the question has important implications for their ability to profit from experiences, such as education. Thousands of intelligence tests are administered by psychologists and educators every day. In this section we examine two of the most widely used intelligence tests.

The Stanford–Binet Intelligence Scale

Many of the concepts of psychology have their origins in common sense. The commonsense notion that academic achievement depends on children's intelligence led Alfred Binet and Theodore Simon to invent measures of intelligence.

Question: What is the Stanford–Binet Intelligence Scale? Early in the 20th century, the French public school system was looking for a test that could identify children who were unlikely to benefit from regular classroom instruction. If these children were identified, they could be given special attention. The first version of that test, the Binet–Simon scale, came into use in 1905. Since that time it has undergone

In Profile | ALFRED BINET

You never would have guessed that Alfred Binet (1857–1911) would invent the method that transformed the testing of intelligence from nonsense into science. It's not that he wasn't, well, intelligent enough. It's that he wasn't quite focused enough.

Binet, the only child of separated parents, was reared by his mother and grew up a loner. He got a degree in law, then transferred to medical school until he got bored and dropped out. He turned to psychology, but because he was independently wealthy he saw no need to earn a degree. In 1883, a former classmate, Joseph Babinski (who would go on to describe the *Babinski reflex*), introduced Binet to Jean Martin Charcot, the director of the Salpêtrière hospital. Charcot, who would also influence Sigmund Freud, gave Binet a position practicing hypnosis.

Binet and a colleague conducted some bad experiments in hypnosis. **Truth or Fiction Revisited:** Binet did use magnets to try to shift an action (such as lifting an arm) from one side of the body to the other. He also believed he had shown that he could use magnets to transform an emotion into its opposite. He was criticized for this silliness and later admitted that his "findings" could all be attributed to the power of suggestion. He resigned from the hospital and began writing and producing plays that wallowed in terror, mental illness, and murder. (Dare we wonder if he was simply ahead of his time in these particular undertakings?)

He later earned a doctorate in natural science and enthusiastically dove into craniometry–skull measurement–as a way of measuring intelligence. But his own data showed him the error of his ways. Only in middle age would he develop a method that he had first used with his own children to assess intelligence for the Ministry of Public Instruction. (For example, he had asked his children to point to parts of their bodies, to explain how things were used, and to show that they understood concepts such as *more* and *less*.) The result was the Binet–Simon scale.

You never would have guessed that it would be Binet.

 Go to **http://psychology.wadsworth.com/ rathus_pcc9e** to access more information about Alfred Binet.

---

extensive revision and refinement. The current version is the Stanford–Binet Intelligence Scale (SBIS).

Binet assumed that intelligence increases with age, so older children should get more items right than younger children. Binet therefore included a series of age-graded questions, as in Table 9.2, arranged in order of difficulty.

The Binet–Simon scale yielded a score called a **mental age,** or **MA.** The MA shows the intellectual level at which a child is functioning. For example, a child with an MA of 6 is functioning intellectually like the average 6-year-old. In taking the test, children earned "months" of credit for each correct answer. Their MA was determined by adding up the years and months of credit they attained.

Louis Terman adapted the Binet–Simon scale for use with children in the United States. The first version of the *Stanford*–Binet Intelligence Scale (SBIS) was published in 1916. (The test is so named because Terman carried out his work at Stanford University.) The SBIS included more items than the original test and was used with children aged 2 to 16. The SBIS also yielded an **intelligence quotient (IQ)** rather than an MA. As a result, American educators developed interest in learning the IQs of their pupils. The SBIS is used today with children from the age of 2 upward and with adults.

The IQ reflects the relationship between a child's mental age and his or her actual or chronological age (CA). Use of this ratio reflects the fact that the same MA score has different implications for children of different ages. That is, an MA of 8 is an above-average score for a 6-year-old but below average for a 10-year-old. In 1912 the German psychologist Wilhelm Stern suggested the IQ as a way to deal with this problem. Stern computed IQ using the formula

$$IQ = \frac{\text{Mental Age (MA)}}{\text{Chronological Age (CA)}} \times 100$$

According to this formula, a child with an MA of 6 and a CA of 6 would have an IQ of 100. Children who can handle intellectual problems as well as older children

Mental age (MA) The accumulated months of credit that a person earns on the Stanford–Binet Intelligence Scale.

Intelligence quotient (IQ) (1) Originally, a ratio obtained by dividing a child's score (or mental age) on an intelligence test by chronological age. (2) Generally, a score on an intelligence test.

TABLE 9.2 ITEMS SIMILAR TO THOSE ON THE STANFORD–BINET INTELLIGENCE SCALE

Level (Years)	Item
2	1. Children show knowledge of basic vocabulary words by identifying parts of a doll, such as the mouth, ears, and hair.
	2. Children show counting and spatial skills along with visual–motor coordination by building a tower of four blocks to match a model.
4	1. Children show word fluency and categorical thinking by filling in the missing words when they are asked questions such as: "Father is a man; mother is a _____?" "Hamburgers are hot; ice cream is _____?"
	2. Children show comprehension by answering correctly when they are asked questions such as: "Why do people have automobiles?" "Why do people have medicine?"
9	1. Children can point out verbal absurdities, as in this question: "In an old cemetery, scientists unearthed a skull which they think was that of George Washington when he was only 5 years of age. What is silly about that?"
	2. Children display fluency with words, as shown by answering these questions: "Can you tell me a number that rhymes with snore?" "Can you tell me a color that rhymes with glue?"
Adult	1. Adults show knowledge of the meanings of words and conceptual thinking by correctly explaining the differences between word pairs like "sickness and misery," "house and home," and "integrity and prestige."
	2. Adults show spatial skills by correctly answering questions like: "If a car turned to the right to head north, in what direction was it heading before it turned?"

do have IQs above 100. For instance, an 8-year-old who does as well on the SBIS as the average 10-year-old would attain an IQ of 125. Children who do not answer as many items correctly as other children of the same age attain MAs lower than their CAs. Thus, their IQ scores are below 100. **Truth or Fiction Revisited:** Therefore, it is true than an IQ is a score on a test.

IQ scores on the SBIS today are derived by comparing their results to those of other people of the same age. People who answer more items correctly than the average for people of the same age attain IQ scores above 100. People who answer fewer items correctly than the average for their age attain scores below 100. **Truth or Fiction Revisited:** Therefore, two children can answer exactly the same items on an intelligence test correctly, yet one can be above average and the other below average in IQ. This is because the ages of the children may differ. The more intelligent child would be the younger of the two.

The SBIS uses many different types of test items to arrive at an IQ score. As we see in the following section, the Wechsler scales are made up of different types of subtests, each of which tells the examiner something about the child or adult, allowing for an assessment of an individual's intellectual strengths and weaknesses.

The Wechsler Scales

In contrast to the SBIS, David Wechsler developed a series of scales for use with children and adults. **Question: What is different about the Wechsler scales of intelligence?** The Wechsler scales group test questions into a number of separate subtests, such as those shown in the nearby Concept Review on Items Similar to Those on the Wechsler Adult Intelligence Scale. Each subtest measures a different

Concept Review   ITEMS SIMILAR TO THOSE ON THE WECHSLER ADULT INTELLIGENCE SCALE

Verbal Subtests

1. *Information:* "What is the capital of the United States?" "Who was Shakespeare?"

2. *Comprehension:* "Why do we have ZIP codes?" "What does 'A stitch in time saves 9' mean?"

3. *Arithmetic:* "If 3 candy bars cost 25 cents, how much will 18 candy bars cost?"

4. *Similarities:* "How are good and bad alike?" "How are peanut butter and jelly alike?"

5. *Digit span:* Repeating a series of numbers forwards and backwards.

6. *Vocabulary:* "What does *canal* mean?"

Performance Subtests

7. *Digit Symbol:* Learning and drawing meaningless figures that are associated with numbers. The faster a person memorizes the correlations, the higher he or she scores on this subtest.

Answer key:

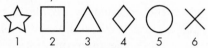

Test: (fill in the corresponding number)

8. *Picture completion:* Pointing to the missing part of a picture.

Picture Completion

What part is missing from this picture?

9. *Block design:* Copying pictures of geometric designs using multicolored blocks.

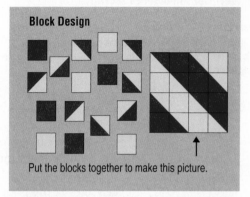

Block Design

Put the blocks together to make this picture.

10. *Picture arrangement:* Arranging cartoon pictures in sequence so that they tell a meaningful story.

Picture Arrangement

These pictures tell a story, but they are in the wrong order. Put them in the right order so that they tell a story.

11. *Object assembly:* Putting pieces of a puzzle together so that they form a meaningful object.

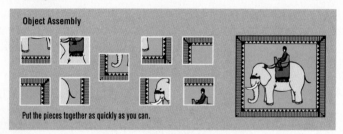

Object Assembly

Put the pieces together as quickly as you can.

type of intellectual task. For this reason, the test shows how well a person does on one type of task (such as defining words) as compared with another (such as using blocks to construct geometric designs). In this way, the Wechsler scales highlight children's relative strengths and weaknesses, as well as measure overall intellectual functioning.

Wechsler described some of his scales as measuring *verbal* tasks and others as assessing *performance* tasks. In general, verbal subtests require knowledge of verbal

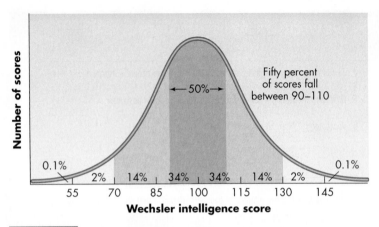

FIGURE 9.3 Approximate Distribution of IQ Scores

Wechsler defined the deviation IQ so that 50% of scores fall within the broad average range of 90 to 110. This bell-shaped curve is referred to as a *normal curve* by psychologists. It describes the distribution of many traits, including height.

concepts, whereas performance subtests require familiarity with spatial-relations concepts. But it is not that easy to distinguish between the two groupings. For example, associating to the name of the object being pieced together in subtest 11—a sign of word fluency and general knowledge as well as of spatial-relations ability—helps the person construct it more rapidly. In any event, Wechsler's scales permit the computation of verbal and performance IQs. It is not unusual for nontechnically oriented college students to attain higher verbal than performance IQs. And it is not uncommon for less-well-educated people to obtain higher performance IQs than verbal IQs.

Wechsler also introduced the concept of the deviation IQ. Instead of dividing mental by chronological age to compute an IQ, he based IQ scores on how a person's answers compared with those attained by people in the same age group. The average test result at any age level is defined as an IQ score of 100. Wechsler distributed IQ scores so that the middle 50% of them were defined as the "broad average range" of 90 to 110.

As you can see in Figure 9.3, most IQ scores cluster around the average. Only 4% of the population have IQ scores of above 130 or below 70. Table 9.3 indicates the labels that Wechsler assigned to various IQ scores and the approximate percentages of the population who attain IQ scores at those levels.

Group Tests

The SBIS and Wechsler scales are administered to one person at a time. This one-to-one ratio is considered optimal. It allows the examiner to facilitate performance (within the limits of the standardized directions) and to observe the test taker closely. Examiners thus are alerted to factors that impair performance, such as language difficulties, illness, or a noisy or poorly lit room. But large institutions with few trained examiners, such as the public schools and armed forces, require tests that can be administered simultaneously to large groups of people.

Group tests for children, first developed during World War I, were administered to 4 million children by 1921, a couple of years after the war had ended. At first these tests were heralded as remarkable instruments because they helped school administrators place children. However, as the years passed, group tests came under increasing attack, because many administrators relied on them exclu-

TABLE 9.3 VARIATIONS IN IQ SCORES

Range of Scores	Percentage of Population	Interpretation
130 and above	2	Very superior
120–129	7	Superior
110–119	16	Above average
100–109	25	High average
90–99	25	Low average
80–89	16	Slow learner
70–79	7	Borderline
Below 70	2	Intellectually deficient

sively and did not seek other sources of information about children's abilities and achievements.

At their best, intelligence tests provide just one source of information about individual children. Numbers alone, and especially IQ scores, cannot adequately reflect children's special abilities and talents.

Your Turn: Now that we have discussed methods of measuring intelligence, enhance your mastery of the material with the nearby "Learning Connections." Review the material by filling in the blanks, reflect on the material by relating it to other things you know, and think critically about it.

Learning Connections — THE MEASUREMENT OF INTELLIGENCE

ACTIVE REVIEW (9) Alfred _____ is considered to be the originator of modern intelligence testing. (10) The Stanford–Binet Intelligence Scale yields a score called a(n) _____ _____ (IQ). (11) The _____ scales have verbal and performance subtests. (12) Wechsler's test results are referred to as a(n) _____ IQ, which is based on how one's scores compare with scores of one's age-mates. (13) The mean (average) IQ is defined as a score of _____. (14) Approximately _____ percent of the population obtain IQ scores within the broad average range (90–110).

REFLECT AND RELATE Here's a mini-experiment: The next time you take a test with a large group of people, notice the factors that affect your performance. Do you feel rushed or doubt your ability or knowledge if others finish before you? Do noises or the room temperature affect your concentration?

CRITICAL THINKING Answering many of the questions we find on intelligence tests requires a solid fund of general information. Because intelligence is supposed to be the underlying ability that makes it possible to acquire information—and not information itself—does it make sense to find this type of item on an intelligence test? Explain.

Go to **http://psychology.wadsworth.com/ rathus_pcc9e** for an interactive version of this Learning Connections unit.

Differences in Intelligence

The average IQ score in the United States is very close to 100. Yet for some socioeconomic and ethnic groups in the United States, the average is higher, and for others, it is lower. Results of IQ tests have thus been seen as divisive and as maintaining a class system or social order that is at least partly based on the results of these and related tests, such as the Scholastic Assessment Tests (SATs).

In this section we first discuss these socioeconomic and ethnic differences in intelligence. Then we turn to differences in intelligence within groups—to intellectual deficiency and to intellectual giftedness.

Socioeconomic and Ethnic Differences in Intelligence Test Scores

There is a body of research suggestive of differences in intelligence—or, more precisely, intelligence test scores—between socioeconomic and ethnic groups. **Question: What are the socioeconomic and ethnic differences in intelligence in the United States?** Lower-class U.S. children obtain IQ scores some 10 to 15 points lower than those obtained by middle- and upper-class children. African American children tend to obtain IQ scores some 15 points lower than those obtained by their European American age-mates (Neisser et al., 1996). Latino and Latina American and Native American children also tend to score below the norms for European American children (Neisser et al., 1996).

Several studies of IQ have confused the factors of social class and ethnicity because disproportionate numbers of African Americans, Latino and Latina Americans, and Native Americans are found among the lower socioeconomic classes (Neisser et al., 1996). When we limit our observations to particular ethnic

■ **Who's Smart?** Asian children and Asian American children frequently outperform European American children on tests of cognitive skills. Sue and Okazaki suggest that Asian Americans place great value on education because they have been discriminated against in careers that do not require advanced education.

groups, however, we still find an effect for social class. That is, middle-class European Americans outscore lower-class European Americans. Middle-class African Americans, Latino and Latina Americans, and Native Americans also outscore lower-class members of their own ethnic groups.

There may also be cognitive differences between Asians and Caucasians. Asian Americans, for example, frequently outscore European Americans on the math portion of the Scholastic Aptitude Test. Students in China (Taiwan) and Japan also outscore European Americans on standardized achievement tests in math and science (Stevenson et al., 1986). In the United States, moreover, people of Asian Indian, Korean, Japanese, Filipino, and Chinese descent are more likely to graduate from high school and complete four years of college than European Americans, African Americans, and Latino and Latina Americans (Sue & Okazaki, 1990). Asian Americans are vastly overrepresented in competitive colleges and universities in the United States.

There are differences in mathematics ability between high school students in Germany and Japan. Japanese students, who are Asian, outscore their German counterparts, who are Caucasian (Randel et al., 2000). Most psychologists believe that ethnic differences such as these reflect cultural attitudes toward education rather than inborn racial differences in cognitive ability per se (Neisser et al., 1996). That is, the Asian children may be more motivated to work hard in school. Research shows that Chinese and Japanese students and their mothers tend to attribute academic successes to hard work (Randel et al., 2000). American mothers are more likely to attribute their children's academic successes to "natural" ability (Basic Behavioral Science Task Force, 1996b). Asian students are more likely to believe that they can make good scores happen, and they work to do so.

Sue and Okazaki (1990) agree. They note that the achievements of Asian students reflect their values in the home, the school, or the culture at large. They note that Asian Americans have been discriminated against in blue-collar careers. Therefore, they have come to emphasize the importance of education. Looking to other environmental factors, Steinberg and his colleagues (1996) claim that parental encouragement and supervision in combination with peer support for academic achievement partially explain the superior performances of European Americans and Asian Americans as compared with African Americans and Latino and Latina Americans.

Extremes in Intelligence

About 50% of U.S. children obtain IQ scores in the broad average range from 90 to 110. Nearly 95% obtain scores between 70 and 130. But what about the other 5%? Children who obtain IQ scores below 70 are generally labeled as intellectually deficient. Children who obtain scores of 130 or above are usually labeled as gifted. Both of these labels create certain expectations. Both can place heavy burdens on children and their parents.

INTELLECTUAL DEFICIENCY Question: What is intellectual deficiency? According to the American Psychiatric Association (2000), intellectual deficiency—also commonly referred to as *mental retardation*—refers to substantial limitations in general intellectual functioning that are accompanied by limitations in at least two or more areas of adaptive skills: communication, self-care, maintaining a home life, interpersonal skills, use of community resources, and organization of one's academic life, vocational life, health and safety needs, and leisure activities. Table 9.4 describes levels of intellectual deficiency. Most people who are deficient are mildly deficient. They are capable of adjusting to the demands of educational institutions

TABLE 9.4 **DEGREES OF SEVERITY OF INTELLECTUAL DEFICIENCY**

Severity of Intellectual Deficiency	IQ Level	Percent of Persons with Intellectual Deficiency	Characteristic Behaviors and Abilities
Mild	50–55 to 70	About 85%	Develop social and communication skills during preschool years. By late teens, often acquire skills up to sixth-grade level. Usually achieve social and vocational skills that permit minimal self-support.
Moderate	35–40 to 50–55	About 10%	Acquire communication skills during early childhood, profit from vocational training, and maintain self-care. Usually do not progress beyond second-grade skills. Can usually perform unskilled or semiskilled work with supervision.
Severe	20–25 to 35–40	3–4%	May learn to talk and engage in elementary self-care. May perform simple work tasks with supervision.
Profound	Below 20–25	1–2%	Impaired sensorimotor development, self-care, and communication skills. May perform simple tasks with close supervision.

Source of information: American Psychiatric Association. (2000). *Diagnostic and statistical manual of mental disorders, 4th ed., text revision (DSM–IV–TR).* Washington, DC: American Psychiatric Association.

and, eventually, to society at large. Mildly intellectually deficient children are often taught in regular classrooms, as opposed to being placed in special needs classes. This approach is intended to give them the best possible education and encourage socialization with children at all intellectual levels.

Children with Down syndrome are most likely to fall within the moderately deficient range. Moderately intellectually deficient children can learn to speak; to dress, feed, and clean themselves; and eventually to engage in work under supportive conditions, as in sheltered workshops. However, they usually do not learn how to read or compute numbers. Severely and profoundly deficient children may not acquire speech and self-help skills and are likely to remain highly dependent on others throughout their lives.

Some of the causes of intellectual deficiency, especially profound intellectual deficiency, are biological. Intellectual deficiency can stem from chromosomal abnormalities such as Down syndrome, from genetic disorders such as phenylketonuria, or from brain damage. Brain damage may have many origins, including accidents during childhood and problems during pregnancy. Maternal alcohol abuse, malnutrition, or diseases during pregnancy can all lead to intellectual deficiency in the infant.

GIFTEDNESS Question: What does it mean to be gifted? Giftedness involves more than excellence in the tasks provided by standard intelligence tests. Most educators include children who have outstanding abilities, are capable of high performance in a specific academic area such as language arts or mathematics, or who show creativity or leadership, distinction in the visual or performing arts, or talent in physical activities such as gymnastics and dancing. This view of giftedness exceeds the realm of intellectual ability alone and is consistent with Gardner's view that there are multiple intelligences, not just one.

Much of our knowledge of the progress of children who are gifted in overall intellectual functioning stems from Louis Terman's classic longitudinal studies of genius (Janos, 1987). In 1921, Terman began to track the progress of some 1,500 California schoolchildren who had attained IQ scores of 135 or above. The average score was 150, which places these children in a very superior group.

There is a stereotype that extremely bright—gifted—children tend to be "geeky," that is, physically and socially awkward. **Truth or Fiction Revisited:** But Terman found that gifted individuals tended to be taller, better physically developed, healthier, and superior in both social adaptability and leadership skills. As adults, the group was extremely successful, compared with the general population, in terms of level of education (nearly 10% had earned doctoral degrees), socioeconomic status, and creativity (the group had published more than 90 books and many more shorter pieces). Boys were much more likely than girls to climb the corporate ladder or distinguish themselves in science, literature, or the arts. But we must keep in mind that the Terman study began in the 1920s, when it was generally agreed that a woman's place was in the home. As a result, more than two-thirds of the girls became full-time homemakers or office workers (Lips, 1993). Some of the women later expressed regret that they had not fulfilled their potential. But both the women and men in the study were well-adjusted, with rates of psychological disorders and suicide below those of the national average.

CONTROVERSY IN PSYCHOLOGY

Just what do intelligence tests measure?

It is no secret that during the 1920s intelligence tests were used to prevent many Europeans and others from immigrating to the United States. For example, testing pioneer H. H. Goddard assessed 178 newly arrived immigrants at Ellis Island and claimed that the great majority of Hungarians, Italians, and Russians were "feeble-minded." Apparently it was of little concern to Goddard that these immigrants, by and large, did not understand English—the language in which the tests were administered!

It is now recognized that intelligence tests cannot be considered valid when they are used with people who do not understand the language. But what of cultural differences? **Question: Do intelligence tests contain cultural biases against ethnic minority groups and immigrants?** Are the tests valid when used with ethnic minority groups or people who are poorly educated? A survey of psychologists and educational specialists by Mark Snyderman and Stanley Rothman (1987) found that most consider intelligence tests to be **culturally biased** against African Americans and members of the lower classes. Elementary and secondary schools may also place too much emphasis on them in making educational placements.

Truth or Fiction Revisited: Some psychologists and social critics argue that intelligence tests measure many things other than intelligence—including familiarity with the dominant middle-class culture in the United States and motivation to perform well.

Is It Possible to Develop Culture-Free Intelligence Tests?

It is widely accepted that children reared in African American or Latino and Latina American neighborhoods could be at a disadvantage in intelligence testing—and in school and society in general!—not because of inborn capacity but because of cultural differences and economic deprivation (Helms, 1992; Kwate, 2001). Many psychologists, including Raymond B. Cattell (1949) and Florence Goodenough (1954), have tried to construct culture-free intelligence tests.

Cattell's Culture-Fair Intelligence Test evaluates reasoning ability through the child's ability to comprehend the rules that govern a progression of geometric designs, as shown in Figure 9.4. Goodenough's Draw-A-Person test is based on the premise that children from all cultural backgrounds have had the opportunity to observe people and note the relationships between the parts and the whole. Her instructions simply require children to draw a picture of a man or woman.

Cultural bias A factor that provides an advantage for test takers from certain cultural backgrounds, such as using test items that are based on middle-class culture in the United States.

Culture-free tests have not lived up to their promise, however. European American children still outperform African American children (Rushton et al., 2003), perhaps because they are more likely to be familiar with materials such as blocks and pencils and paper. They are more likely than disadvantaged children to have arranged blocks into various designs (practice relevant to the Cattell test) and more likely to have sketched animals, people, and inanimate objects (practice relevant to the Goodenough test). Too, culture-free tests do not predict academic success as well as other intelligence tests. For example, a study of several hundred children in Iceland found that the Raven's Standard Progressive Matrices test, which is highly similar to the test developed by Cattell, predicted scholastic achievement in mathematics much more successfully than verbal achievements (Pind et al., 2003).

All in all, intelligence tests measure traits that are required in developed, high-tech societies. The vocabulary and arithmetic subtests on the Wechsler scales, for example, reflect achievements in language skills and computational ability. The broad achievements measured by these tests reflect intelligence, but they also reflect familiarity with the cultural concepts required to answer test questions correctly. In particular, the tests seem to reflect middle-class European American culture. The irony is that they may be biased but also reasonably valid at the same time. That is, although they may discriminate against African American children, they may predict success in a culture dominated by European Americans.

Your Turn: Now that we have discussed differences in intelligence, enhance your mastery of the material with the nearby "Learning Connections." Review the material by filling in the blanks, reflect on the material by relating it to other things you know, and think critically about it.

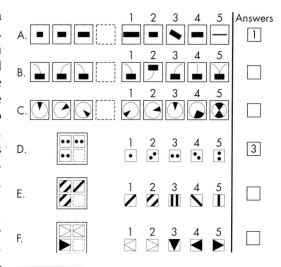

FIGURE 9.4 **Sample Items from Cattell's Culture-Fair Intelligence Test**

Culture-fair tests attempt to use items that do not discriminate against ethnic groups on the basis of their cultural background. For each item above, which answer (1, 2, 3, 4, or 5) completes the series? Answers are shown in Appendix B.

Source: Copyright © 1949, 1960 by the Institute for Personality and Ability Testing, Inc., Champaign, Illinois, USA. All rights reserved. Reproduced from Culture Fair Scale 2, Test A by R. B. Cattell and A. K. S. Cattell.

 Learning Connections   **DIFFERENCES IN INTELLIGENCE**

ACTIVE REVIEW (15) _____ _____ tend to obtain the highest scores on intelligence tests. (16) Lower-class U.S. children obtain IQ scores some _____ points lower than those obtained by middle- and upper-class children. (17) Children who obtain IQ scores below _____ are labeled intellectually deficient. (18) Children who obtain scores of _____ or above are labeled gifted. (19) Most psychologists and educational specialists (*Do* or *Do not?*) consider intelligence tests to be biased against African Americans and individuals of lower socioeconomic status.

REFLECT AND RELATE Have you known individuals who are intellectually deficient or gifted? How have people in

their lives reacted to their intellectual abilities? Did their deficiency or giftedness strongly affect their social and emotional development? Explain.

CRITICAL THINKING If intelligence tests such as the Stanford–Binet and Wechsler scales predict academic and vocational success, why do so many psychologists consider them to be invalid methods of testing children from certain minority groups and of lower socioeconomic status?

Go to **http://psychology.wadsworth.com/ rathus_pcc9e** for an interactive version of this Learning Connections unit.

Nature and Nurture in Intelligence: Where Does Intelligence Come From?

When I was in graduate school, a professor remarked that many people think of intelligence as "a knob in the head. Some people have a bigger knob and some people have a smaller one." That is, many people see intelligence as a fixed commodity. From this perspective, some people have more intelligence, some people less, and nothing much can be done about it.

In recent years this view of intelligence—as a sort of knob in the head—has been expressed most controversially by psychologist Richard Herrnstein and political theorist Charles Murray (1994) in their book *The Bell Curve*. The book made the following assertions:

1. Intelligence tests are valid indicators of intelligence (that is, *IQ* is an accurate measure of intelligence).

2. A person's intelligence is mainly due to heredity.

3. People with less intelligence (smaller "knobs in the head") are having more children than people with more intelligence ("bigger knobs"), so that the overall intelligence of the population of the United States is declining.

4. The United States is becoming divided in two, with a large lower class of people with low intelligence and a smaller class of wealthier people who are higher in intelligence.

5. Education can do little to affect intelligence (the size of the "knob").

The Bell Curve poured oil onto the fires of controversy over social class, race, and intelligence. Of course, it is true that poorer people tend to obtain lower IQ scores than wealthier people do. It is also true that African Americans are poorer than the average American, and that the IQ scores of African Americans are lower, on the average, than those of European Americans.

As pointed out by Herrnstein and Murray's critics, however, intelligence is *not* a knob in the head. Nor has it been demonstrated that intelligence is mainly heritable. Critics of *The Bell Curve* argue that IQ is affected by early learning experiences, academic and vocational motivation, and formal education (Andrews & Nelkin, 1996; Gottfredson, 1997).

Let us now discuss the roles of heredity and environmental influences on intelligence more fully. If different ethnic groups tend to score differently on intelligence tests, psychologists—like educators and other people involved in public life—want to know why. We will see that this is one debate that can make use of key empirical findings. Psychologists can point with pride to a rich mine of contemporary research on the roles of nature (genetic influences) and nurture (environmental influences) in the development of intelligence.

Genetic Influences on Intelligence

Question: What are the genetic influences on intelligence? Research on the genetic influences on human intelligence has employed several basic strategies. These include kinship studies, twin studies, and adoptee studies (Neisser et al., 1996). Let us consider each of them to see how genes may affect intellectual functioning.

We can examine the IQ scores of closely and distantly related people who have been reared together or apart. If heredity is involved in human intelligence, closely related people ought to have more similar IQs than distantly related or unrelated people, even when they are reared separately.

Figure 9.5 is a composite of the results of more than 100 studies of IQ and heredity in human beings (Bouchard et al., 1990). The IQ scores of identical (monozygotic, or MZ) twins are more alike than scores for any other pairs, even when the twins have been reared apart. There are moderate correlations between the IQ scores of fraternal (dizygotic, or DZ) twins, between those of siblings, and between those of parents and their children. Correlations between the scores of children and their foster parents and between those of cousins are weak.

The results of large-scale twin studies are consistent with the data in Figure 9.5. For instance, a study of 500 pairs of MZ and DZ twins in Louisville, Kentucky (Wilson, 1983) found that the correlations in intelligence between MZ twins were about the same as those for MZ twins in Figure 9.5. The correlations in intelligence between DZ twin pairs were the same as those between other siblings. In the MacArthur Longitudinal Twin Study, Robert Emde (1993) and his colleagues examined the intellectual abilities of 200 primarily European American, healthy 14-month-old pairs of twins. They found that identical (MZ) twins were more similar than fraternal (DZ) twins in spatial memory, ability to categorize things, and word comprehension. Emde and his colleagues concluded that genes tend to account for about 40% to 50% of differences in children's cognitive skills.

All in all, studies generally suggest that the **heritability** of intelligence is between 40% and 60% (Bouchard et al., 1990; Neisser et al., 1996). In other words, about half of the variations (the technical term is *variance*) in IQ scores can be accounted for by heredity. This is *not* the same as saying that you inherited about half of your intelligence. The implication of such a statement would be that you "got" the other half of your intelligence somewhere else. It means, rather, that about half of the difference between your IQ score and the IQ scores of other people can be explained in terms of genetic factors.

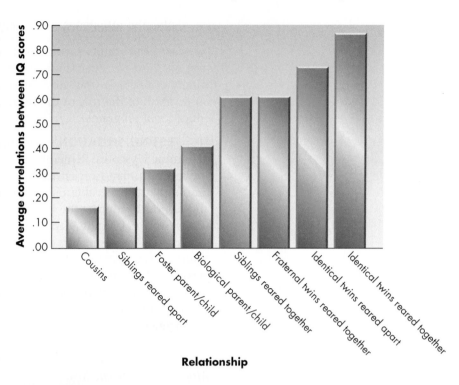

FIGURE 9.5 Findings of Studies of the Relationship between IQ Scores and Heredity
The data are a composite of studies summarized in *Science*. By and large, correlations are greater between pairs of people who are more closely related. Yet people who are reared together also have more similar IQ scores than people who are reared apart. Such findings suggest that both genetic and environmental factors contribute to IQ scores.

Note, too, that genetic pairs (such as MZ twins) who were reared together show higher correlations in their IQ scores than similar genetic pairs (such as other MZ twins) who were reared apart. This finding holds for DZ twins, siblings, parents and their children, and unrelated people. Being reared together is therefore related with similarities in IQ. *For this reason, the same group of studies used to demonstrate a role for the heritability of IQ scores also suggests that the environment plays a role in determining IQ scores.*

Another strategy for exploring genetic influences on intelligence is to compare the correlations between the IQ scores of adopted children and those of their biological and adoptive parents. When children are separated from their biological parents at an early age, one can argue that strong relationships between their IQs and those of their natural parents reflect genetic influences. Strong relationships between their IQs and those of their adoptive parents might reflect environmental influences.

Several studies with 1- and 2-year-old children in Colorado (Baker et al., 1983), Texas (Horn, 1983), and Minnesota (Scarr & Weinberg, 1983) have found a stronger relationship between the IQ scores of adopted children and those of their biological parents than between the children's scores and those of their adoptive parents. **Truth or Fiction Revisited:** Therefore, adopted children are *not* more similar in intelligence to their adoptive parents than to their biological parents. The Scarr and Weinberg report concerns African American children reared by European American adoptive parents. We return to its findings in the section on environmental influences on intelligence.

In sum, genetic factors (nature) may account for about half of the variation in intelligence test scores among individuals. This research evidence contradicts the view expressed in *The Bell Curve* that intelligence is *mainly* due to heredity. In the following section, we will see that the argument of *The Bell Curve* is an overgeneralization, and good critical thinkers do not overgeneralize. Next we see that environmental factors (nurture) also affect scores on intelligence tests.

Heritability The degree to which the variations in a trait from one person to another can be attributed to, or explained by, genetic factors.

Environmental Influences on Intelligence

Question: What are the environmental influences on intelligence? To answer this question we must consider studies of environmental influences, which also employ a variety of research strategies. These include manipulation of the testing situation, observation of the role of the home environment, and evaluation of the effects of educational programs.

THE TESTING SITUATION One approach focuses on the situational factors that determine IQ scores. Remember that an IQ is a score on a test. Thus, in some cases the testing situation itself can explain part of the social-class difference in IQ. In one study the experimenters (Zigler et al., 1992) simply made children as comfortable as possible during the test. Rather than being cold and impartial, the examiner was warm and friendly. Care was also taken to see that the children understood the directions. One result was that the children's test anxiety was markedly reduced. Another was that their IQ scores were 6 points higher than those for a control group of children who were treated in a more indifferent manner. Disadvantaged children made relatively greater gains from the modified testing procedure.

The argument of *The Bell Curve* that intelligence tests are valid indicators of intelligence is damaged by research that shows that the nature of the testing situation makes a difference. *By doing nothing more than making testing conditions more optimal for all children, we might narrow the IQ gap between European American and African American children.*

 STEREOTYPE VULNERABILITY AND INTELLIGENCE TEST SCORES Stereotype vulnerability is another aspect of the testing situation that affects test scores. Psychologist Claude Steele (1996, 1997) suggests that African American students carry an extra burden in performing scholastic tasks: They believe that they risk confirming their group's negative stereotype by doing poorly on such tasks. This concern creates performance anxiety. In turn, performance anxiety can distract African American students from the tasks; as a result, they perform more poorly than European American students.

In an experiment designed to test this view, Steele and Aronson (1995) gave two groups of African American and European American Stanford undergraduates the most difficult verbal skills test questions from the GRE. One group was told that the researchers were attempting to learn about the "psychological factors involved in solving verbal problems." The other group was told that the items were "a genuine test of your verbal abilities and limitations." African American students who were given the first message performed as well as European American students.

In Profile   CLAUDE STEELE

"His research may shed fresh light on why many [African Americans] do poorly on standardized tests," writes Ethan Watters (1995). Claude Steele has noted that African Americans experience a feeling of racial vulnerability when, for example, they see Band-Aids tinted to match pink skin. This concept of *stereotype vulnerability* describes what African Americans can feel when they see standardized tests, such as intelligence tests, that seem to be designed to be taken by students with "pink" skin. He argues that the sense of vulnerability is hard to overcome, and that society as well as individuals must change.

Claude Steele, a Stanford University psychologist, began developing his ideas in the 1980s when he took a teaching position at the University of Michigan and became aware of the greater dropout rate of African American students. He helped create the 21st Century Program, which maintains racially integrated dormitories and requires that dorm members take some classes with other dorm members.

Interestingly, Shelby Steele (Claude's twin brother and well-known conservative essayist) has been very outspoken against his brother's views. In fact, Shelby has argued that African Americans need willpower to achieve despite the odds, not affirmative action as Claude suggests. Claude reported that his 21st Century Program reduced the grade gap between African and European American students. It remains to be seen whether the 21st century will also reduce the gap between Claude and Shelby Steele.

 Go to **http://psychology.wadsworth.com/ rathus_pcc9e** to access more information about Claude Steele.

African American students who were given the second message—that proof of their abilities was on the line—performed significantly more poorly than the European American students. Apparently the second message triggered their stereotype vulnerability, which led them to perform poorly on the test. Steele's findings are further evidence of the limits of intelligence tests as valid indicators of intelligence.

THE HOME ENVIRONMENT AND STYLES OF PARENTING The home environment and styles of parenting also affect IQ scores (Molfese et al., 2003; Steinberg et al., 1996; Suzuki & Valencia, 1997). Children of parents who are emotionally and verbally responsive, furnish appropriate play materials, are involved with their children, encourage independence, and provide varied daily experiences during the early years obtain higher IQ scores later on (Gottfried et al., 1994; Molfese et al., 1997). Organization and safety in the home have also been linked to higher IQs and achievement test scores at later ages (Bradley et al., 1989).

 A Closer Look | THE MOZART EFFECT: WILL MUSIC PROVIDE CHILDREN WITH THE SWEET SOUNDS OF SUCCESS?

Technological innovations are overleaping themselves in the new millennium. Parents are concerned about what they can do to help their children grasp the new technologies. Whatever environmental factors are found to enhance children's intellectual functioning may well be music to parents' ears. But it may also turn out that music will be spatial reasoning to children's ears.

Research suggests that listening to and studying music may enhance at least one aspect of intellectual functioning—spatial reasoning. In 1993, the research team of Frances Rauscher, Gordon Shaw, and

■ **The Sweet Sounds of Success?** Some research suggests that training in music enhances children's intellectual functioning, particularly in visual-spatial areas. Perhaps perception of music and spatial relations occupy overlapping neural pathways. However, it should be noted that this field of research is in its infancy and that psychologists disagree as to its implications.

Katherine Ky published an intriguing article in *Nature* on the effects of exposure to Mozart's music. They claimed that listening to 10 minutes of a Mozart piano sonata enhanced college students' scores on spatial reasoning tasks. For example, they were better able to perceive the design of a "snowflake," after mentally cutting and folding a piece of paper, and they were better able to rotate and compare objects in space (Hershenson, 2000).

At the 1994 meeting of the American Psychological Association, a research team headed by Rauscher reported the results of a follow-up study with preschoolers in a paper titled "Music and spatial task performance: A causal relationship." They recruited 19 preschool children aged from 3 years to 4 years 9 months and gave them 8 months of music lessons, including singing and use of a keyboard. After the lessons the children's scores on an object assembly task significantly exceeded those of 15 preschoolers who did not receive the musical training.

Cognitive psychologist Lois Hetland (2000) reports that children given keyboard lessons perform better on spatial reasoning tests. She also analyzed research with college students and concluded that they scored higher on spatial-reasoning tests after hearing the music of Mozart, Schubert, and Mendelssohn but not the music of Philip Glass (a contemporary composer of classical-style music) or of Pearl Jam and other rock groups. That is, music with complex structure and rhythm apparently had more beneficial cognitive benefits.

How might listening to music or training in music affect spatial reasoning? It may be that neural pathways involved in processing music overlap those involved in other cognitive functions—such as spatial reasoning (Rauscher, 1998). Musical training thus

develops the neural firing patterns used in spatial reasoning, which may eventually help children solve geometry problems, design skyscrapers, navigate ships, perhaps even fit suitcases into the trunk of a car.

The researchers caution that their findings should be considered preliminary. Attempts to replicate the Rauscher studies have met with mixed success (McKelvie & Low, 2002; Rauscher & Shaw, 1998). Moreover, it is unclear exactly what aspects of the "treatment" may have influenced students (Nantais & Schellenberg, 1999). Is it the music itself, or could it be related factors like the spatial patterns made by the black and white keys on the keyboard, or even a mood change caused by the music (Hershenson, 2000; Husain, 2003)? University of Toronto psychologist Gariela Husain (2003) argues that music affects performance by affecting the mood; gay music enhances performance, including intellectual performance, whereas funeral dirges are, well, somewhat detrimental. It all remains somewhat speculative (Schellenberg, 2000).

Stephanie Jones and Edward Zigler (a pioneer in Head Start programs) (2002) write that the lure of the Mozart Effect seems to be part of the historic search for "quick fixes." Yes, there are things we can do to enhance children's cognitive abilities skills, but they take time, effort, and money. Intensive preschool education such as we find in Head Start programs is an example. Certainly there is nothing wrong with encouraging children to listen to Mozart, or in giving them musical training. But long-term, proven, and more expensive methods for helping children are probably more useful.

© Larry Kolvoord/The Image Works

■ **Head Start** Preschoolers who are placed in Head Start programs have shown dramatic improvements in readiness for elementary school and in IQ scores.

FIGURE 9.6 The Complex Web of Factors That Appears to Affect Intellectual Functioning

Intellectual functioning appears to be influenced by the interaction of genetic factors, health, personality, and sociocultural factors.

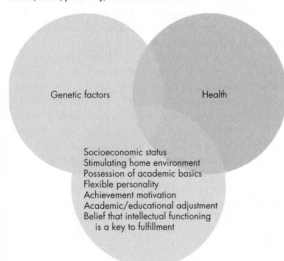

Other studies support the view that children's early environment is linked to IQ scores and academic achievement. For example, Victoria Molfese and her colleagues (1997) found that the home environment was the single most important predictor of scores on IQ tests among children aged 3 to 8.

EDUCATION Although intelligence is viewed as permitting people to profit from education, education also apparently contributes to intelligence. For example, government-funded efforts to provide preschoolers with enriched early environments have led to measurable intellectual gains. Head Start programs, for example, enhance the IQ scores, achievement test scores, and academic skills of disadvantaged children (Barnett, 1998; Zigler, 1999) by exposing them to materials and activities that middle-class children take for granted. These include letters and words, numbers, books, exercises in drawing, pegs and pegboards, puzzles, toy animals, and dolls. Head Start also helps poor children get medical and dental care, serves nutritious meals, and helps children develop the social skills necessary to succeed in school (Zigler, 1999). **Truth or Fiction Revisited:** It is therefore true that Head Start programs have raised children's IQs.

Preschool intervention programs can have long-term positive effects on children. During the elementary and high school years, graduates of preschool programs are less likely to be left back or placed in classes for slow learners. They are more likely to graduate from high school, go on to college, and earn higher incomes.

Schooling at later ages also contributes to intelligence test scores. When children of about the same age start school a year apart because of admissions standards related to their date of birth, children who have been in school longer obtain higher IQ scores (Neisser et al., 1996). Moreover, IQ test scores tend to decrease during the summer vacation (Neisser et al., 1996).

The findings on intelligence, the home environment, and educational experiences show that much indeed can be done to enhance intellectual functioning in children. Now let us return to research on the intellectual development of adopted children.

ADOPTEE STUDIES The Minnesota adoption studies reported by Scarr and Weinberg suggest a genetic influence on intelligence. But the same studies (Scarr & Weinberg, 1976, 1977) also suggest a role for environmental influences. African American children who were adopted during their first year by European American parents with above-average income and education obtained IQ scores some 15 to 25 points higher than those obtained by African American children reared by their natural parents (Scarr & Weinberg, 1976). There are two cautions regarding these findings. One is that the adoptees' average IQ score, about 106, remained below those of their adoptive parents' natural children—117 (Scarr & Weinberg, 1977). The second is that follow-up studies of the adopted children at the age of 17 found that the mean IQ score of the adopted African American children had decreased by 9 points, to 97 (Weinberg et al., 1992). The meaning of the change remains to be unraveled (Neisser, 1997a).

All in all, intellectual functioning appears to reflect the interaction of a complex web of genetic, physical, personal, and sociocultural factors (Bartels et al., 2002; Bishop et al., 2003), as suggested by Figure 9.6. The views of *The Bell Curve*—that intelligence is largely heritable and that little can be done to affect intellectual functioning—are contradicted by evidence that clearly supports a more balanced view.

Perhaps we need not be so concerned with whether we can sort out exactly how much of a person's IQ is due to heredity and how much is due to environmental influences. A majority of psychologists and educators believe that IQ reflects the complex interaction of heredity, early childhood experiences, sociocultural factors and expectations, and even the atmosphere in which intelligence tests are conducted. Psychology has traditionally supported the dignity of the individual. It might be more appropriate for us to try to identify children *of all ethnic groups* whose environments place them at risk for failure and do what we can to enrich their environments. As noted by Paul Ehrlich (2000), professor of biology and population studies at Stanford University:

> There is no such thing as a fixed human nature, but rather an interaction between our genotypes—the genetic information we have—and the different environments we live in, with the result that all our natures are unique.

Your Turn: Now that we have explored the roles of nature and nurture in the development of intelligence, enhance your mastery of the material with the nearby "Learning Connections." Review the material by filling in the blanks, reflect on the material by relating it to other things you know, and think critically about it.

 ## Learning Connections   **NATURE AND NURTURE IN INTELLIGENCE: WHERE DOES INTELLIGENCE COME FROM?**

ACTIVE REVIEW (20) When children are separated from their biological parents at an early age, strong relationships between their IQs and those of their biological parents probably reflect (*Genetic* or *Environmental?*) influences. (21) Estimates place the heritability of intelligence at about _____. (22) African American children who are adopted early by European American parents with above-average income and education obtain IQ scores that are (*Higher* or *Lower?*) than those obtained by African American children reared by their natural parents.

REFLECT AND RELATE Does your own family seem to be generally similar in overall intellectual functioning? Are there one or more family members who appear to stand out from the others because of intelligence? If so, in what ways? How do you account for the difference?

CRITICAL THINKING Why are people so concerned about "how much" of intelligence is inherited?

 Go to **http://psychology.wadsworth.com/ rathus_pcc9e** for an interactive version of this Learning Connections unit.

 ## Life Connections
Enhancing Intellectual Functioning

Does enhancing intellectual functioning sound like an impossible dream? Only if you believe that intelligence is a fixed commodity—a sort of "knob in the head." Actually, intelligence—or intellectual functioning—changes with age, experiences in the home, education, and many other factors, including day-to-day differences in responding to items on intelligence tests. Research into the effects of the home environment and early educational experiences suggests that there are many things you can do to enhance your children's intellectual functioning—*and your own:*

- Provide a safe, organized home for your children.
- Be emotionally and verbally responsive to your children. Provide appropriate and stimulating play materials. Get involved in their play.
- Provide a variety of experiences. Take your children to local museums and cultural events. Do whatever traveling your budget and time will allow.
- Encourage your children to be independent, to try to solve their own problems, to do as much of their schoolwork on their own as they can. (But make yourself available to

offer a helping hand when they need it.) Note that restrictiveness and punishment in the home environment are linked to *lower* IQ scores.
- Make sure your children know the educational basics. Expose them to materials and activities that include letters and words, numbers, books, exercises in drawing, pegs and pegboards, puzzles, toy animals, and dolls.
- Consider giving your children training in music. Not only will music broaden their intellectual horizons, but it may also enhance their spatial relations skills.

And what about you? It is not too late to enhance your own intellectual functioning, even if you are a grandparent. Psychologist Walter Schaie and his colleagues (Schaie, 1994) have been studying the cognitive development of adults for four decades and discovered factors that contribute to intellectual functioning across the life span:

- *General health.* People in good health tend to retain higher levels of intellectual functioning into late adulthood. Therefore, paying attention to one's diet, exercising, and having regular medical checkups contribute to intellectual functioning as well as physical health.
- *Socioeconomic status (SES).* People with high SES tend to maintain intellectual functioning more adequately than people with low SES. High SES is also connected with above-average income and levels of education, a history of stimulating occupational pursuits, maintenance of intact families, and better health.
- *Stimulating activities.* Cultural events, travel, participation in professional organizations, and extensive reading contribute to intellectual functioning.
- *Marriage to a spouse with a high level of intellectual functioning.* The spouse whose level of intellectual functioning is lower at the beginning of a marriage tends to increase in intellectual functioning as time goes by. Perhaps that partner is continually challenged by the other.
- *Openness to new experience.* Being open to new challenges of life apparently helps keep us young—at any age.

How can you apply Schaie's research findings? In a number of ways:

- *Take care of your health.* As we will see in the chapter on Stress and Health, good health is not simply a matter of luck. We can all do things to maximize our own health, including eating properly, exercising, and having regular medical checkups. And there is a relationship between one's intellectual functioning and general health.
- *Choose intellectually challenging companions.*
- *Remain (or become) flexible.* Be open to new experiences. Try new things. Be willing to consider evidence and change your opinions, even on political issues.

None of these measures is a guarantee, of course. But regardless of how they affect intelligence, they will certainly lead to a more stimulating life—both for your children and for you.

Recite—An Active Summary™

Want to study on the go? Go to your companion website and download an audio version of this review section to your media player.

1. Just what is intelligence?

Intelligence underlies (provides the cognitive basis for) thinking and academic achievement. Wechsler defined it as the "capacity . . . to understand the world . . . and . . . resourcefulness to cope with its challenges."

2. What are the various theories of intelligence?

Spearman and Thurstone believed that intelligence is composed of a number of factors. Spearman believed that a common factor, g, underlies all intelligent behavior but that people also have specific abilities, or s factors. Thurstone suggested that there are several primary mental abilities, including word fluency and numerical ability.

3. What is meant by multiple intelligences?

Gardner believes that people have several intelligences, not one, and that each is based in a different area of the brain. Two such "intelligences" are language ability and logical–mathematical ability, but Gardner also includes bodily–kinesthetic intelligence and others.

4. What is Sternberg's triarchic model of intelligence?

Sternberg's triarchic theory proposes three kinds of intelligence: analytical (academic ability), creative, and practical ("street smarts"). Analytical intelligence is not always the best predictor of success.

5. Just what is "emotional intelligence"?

The theory of emotional intelligence holds that social and emotional skills are a form of intelligence that helps children avert violence and depression. The theory suggests that emotional skills are best learned during childhood.

6. What is creativity? What are the connections between creativity and intelligence?

Creativity is the ability to solve problems without preexisting solutions. Creative people take chances, defy limits, and appreciate art and music. Creative problem solving involves divergent thinking. Many highly creative people do not do all that well on intelligence tests, or in school, and many brilliant people have little interest in art, music, and other creative endeavors.

7. What is the Stanford–Binet Intelligence Scale?

This is the test originated by Binet in France and developed by Terman at Stanford University. It includes age-graded questions and yields an IQ score by comparing a mental age score with chronological age.

Recite—An Active Summary™

8. What is different about the Wechsler scales of intelligence?	The Wechsler scales use deviation IQs, which compare a person's performance with that of age-mates. The Wechsler scales contain verbal and performance subtests that measure information, comprehension, similarities, vocabulary, mathematics, block design, and object assembly.
9. What are the socioeconomic and ethnic differences in intelligence in the United States?	Middle- and upper-class children outscore lower-class children by 10 to 15 points on intelligence tests. Asian Americans tend to outscore European Americans, and European Americans tend to outscore African Americans and Latino and Latina Americans.
10. What is intellectual deficiency?	Intellectual deficiency is characterized by an IQ score of no more than 70 to 75 and problems in adaptive skills. Most people who are intellectually deficient are mildly deficient.
11. What does it mean to be gifted?	Giftedness combines high scores on IQ along with ability in a specific academic area, creativity, leadership, or special talents.
12. Do intelligence tests contain cultural biases against ethnic minority groups and immigrants?	Intelligence tests were used historically to prevent many people from immigrating to the United States. Many psychologists believe that they are biased against African Americans and people in the lower classes because they require familiarity with concepts that reflect middle-class European American culture.
13. What are the genetic influences on intelligence?	Kinship studies find a stronger relationship between the IQ scores of adopted children and those of their biological parents than between the children's scores and those of their adoptive parents. Studies generally suggest that the heritability of intelligence is between 40% and 60%.
14. What are the environmental influences on intelligence?	Environmental influences on intelligence include the home environment, including styles of parenting; education, including Head Start programs; and, among adults, lifestyle, such as cultural activities. Most psychologists and educators believe that intelligence reflects the interaction of genetics, childhood experiences, and cultural factors.

 Go to **http://psychology.wadsworth. com/rathus_pcc9e** to access an interactive version of this active summary.

Key Terms

Intelligence (p. 337)
g (p. 337)
s (p. 337)
Factor analysis (p. 337)
Primary mental abilities
   (p. 337)

Creativity (p. 342)
Convergent thinking
   (p. 342)
Divergent thinking
   (p. 343)

Mental age (MA) (p. 345)
Intelligence quotient (IQ)
   (p. 345)

Cultural bias (p. 352)
Heritability (p. 355)

ACTIVE LEARNING RESOURCES

Visit your Companion Website for Quizzing and Self-Assessment!

http://psychology.wadsworth.com/rathus_pcc9e
On this site there are many quizzing opportunities including interactive versions of the fill-in-the-blank Active Review sections in your book. You can also fill out and score the Self-Assessment on p. 343.

Study on the Go!

Don't have time to study right now? You can study on the go! Visit your companion website and download an audio version of the Recite—An Active Summary section to your media player.

ThomsonNOW

http://www.thomsonedu.com
Need help studying? This site is your one-stop study shop. Take a Pre-Test and Thomson NOW will generate a Personalized Study Plan based on your test results. The Study Plan will identify the topics you need to review and direct you to online resources to help you master those topics. You can then take a Post-Test to determine the concepts you have mastered and what you still need to work on.

Author Blog

 What does your author have to say about the state of psychology? Visit your companion website every Tuesday and click on "Author Blog," where he'll talk about the most recent controversies and hot topics in psychology.

Truth or Fiction?

T F Siamese fighting fish who have been reared without ever seeing another fish assume stereotypical threatening stances and attack other males when they are introduced into their tanks.

T F Getting away from it all by going on a vacation from all sensory input for a few hours is relaxing.

T F People feel hunger due to contractions ("pangs") in the stomach.

T F You can never be too rich or too thin.

T F Checking out the Victoria's Secret catalogue can contribute to eating disorders among women.

T F A good way to prevent harmful aggression is to encourage the venting of aggressive impulses through activities such as cheering on a football team or attending a prize fight.

T F Money can't buy you happiness.

T F You may be able to fool a lie detector by squiggling your toes.

T F More than half of adult Americans are overweight.

 Go to **http://psychology.wadsworth.com/ rathus_pcc9e** to answer and score this Truth or Fiction quiz.

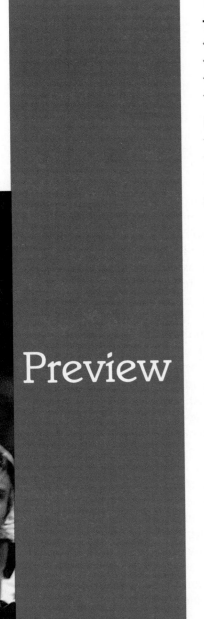

CHAPTER 10

Motivation and Emotion

Preview

The Psychology of Motivation: The *Whys* of Why

Theories of Motivation: Which Why Is Which?
- The Evolutionary Perspective: The Fish, the Spiders, and the Bees
- Drive-Reductionism and Homeostasis: "Steady, Steady . . ."
- The Search for Stimulation: Is Downtime a Downer?
- Humanistic Theory: "I've Got to Be Me"?

Hunger: Do You Go by "Tummy-Time"?
- Biological Influences on Hunger
- Psychological Influences on Hunger
- Eating Disorders: Is It True That "You Can Never Be Too Rich or Too Thin"?

Aggression: Of Australopithecines, Humans, Robins, and Testosterone
- Biology, Chemistry, and Aggression
- Psychological Aspects of Aggression
- Situational Factors and Aggression: When the Heat Is On

Achievement Motivation: "Just Do It"?
- What Flavor Is Your Achievement Motivation?

Emotion: Adding Color to Life
- The Expression of Emotions: The Smile Seen around the World?
- "Is Evvvvrybody Happy?" An Excursion into Positive Psychology
- The Facial-Feedback Hypothesis: Does Smiling Make You Happy?
- Theories of Emotion: "*How* Do You Feel?"

Life Connections: Obesity: A Serious and Pervasive Problem
- Origins of Obesity
- The Skinny on Weight Control

Recite—An Active Summary

Key Terms

Active Learning Resources

© Mango Productions/CORBIS

Cassie e-mailed me:

From: Cassie
To: Prof Rathus
Subject: **%-)**

Hey Prof! **:-V**

Sorry I couldn't make it to Intro Psych yesterday. **:-(**

You may have heard that that big retaining wall on the Henry Hudson collapsed. **8-o** It was a mean slide and I was stuck behind a thousand cars and nobody could move. **}:-[** I wasn't hurt but do you need a note from my doctor? **%-6** Just kidding.

Did I miss anything important? **:\'(**

CU L8R! **:^D**

Cassie

If I had not been a psychologist, I would just have clicked Reply and written, "Glad you weren't hurt, but every class is important. Drop by during office hours in the morning. CU tomorrow **:-).**" But being a psychologist, I had to ask myself *why* Cassie had written this e-mail in the way she had. The first answer that came to mind was that she wanted to stay in my "good graces."

That didn't sound very scientific. I had to get to the bottom of her motivation. Did the evolutionary perspective suggest that she might have recognized that students who show their professors they are trying to meet their course requirements are more likely to survive and pass their genes along to the next generation? Or that Cassie had a "keep Dr. Rathus on my side" instinct? Perhaps not. Did drive-reduction theory suggest that Cassie experienced fear when she missed class and that fear drove her to do something—namely, e-mail me—that would reduce the discomforting emotion? Perhaps. Did Cassie thrive on the exciting stimulation of introductory psychology and wish to make certain that nothing would prevent her from returning to class so she could experience that stimulation again? Knowing full well the joy (another emotion, but very different from fear) of psychology, I figured there might be something to that. Now, humanistic theory might suggest that Cassie was attempting to meet various needs, such as the need to survive introductory psychology. Or what of the need to belong to the class? The need to have the approval of her professor? The need to experience the cognitive stimulation of psychology? The need to actualize herself fully as a human being, which nothing but psychology could do so well?

As a psychologist, I also noted her methods of expressing her emotions: for example, **:-(}:-[** and **:^D** (don't look at me; you can translate these for yourself).

Perhaps I was getting too embroiled in this train of thought.

I clicked Reply, wrote "Glad you weren't hurt, but every class is important. Drop by during office hours in the morning. CU tomorrow **:-)**", and clicked Send.

She had obviously wanted to remain in my good graces—whatever those are.

All of this quite naturally leads to an exploration of the psychology of motivation and emotion. Let us begin our journey with some definitions.

The Psychology of Motivation: The *Whys* of Why

The psychology of motivation concerns the *whys* of behavior. Why do people do this or that? **Question: What are motives, needs, drives, and incentives? Motives** are hypothetical states that activate behavior, propelling one toward goals. We call

Motive A hypothetical state within an organism that propels the organism toward a goal. (From the Latin *movere*, meaning "to move.")

them "hypothetical states" because motives are not seen and measured directly; they are inferred from behavior. We may infer that Cassie was motivated to stay in my good graces by observing her behavior. Motives can take the form of *needs, drives,* and *incentives,* which are also inferred from behavior.

Psychologists speak of physiological and psychological **needs**. We must meet physiological needs to survive. Examples include the needs for oxygen, food, drink, pain avoidance, proper temperature, and elimination of waste products. Some physiological needs, such as hunger and thirst, are states of physical deprivation. When we have not eaten or drunk for a while, we develop needs for food and water. Psychological needs include needs for achievement, power, self-esteem, social approval, and belonging. Many psychological needs might have fed into Cassie's construction of her e-mail, including needs for social approval and good grades. Psychological needs may be acquired through experience, or learned, whereas physiological needs reside in the physical makeup of the organism. People share similar physiological needs, but we are also influenced by our social and cultural settings. All of us need food, but some prefer a vegetarian diet whereas others prefer meat.

Needs give rise to **drives.** Depletion of food gives rise to the hunger drive, and depletion of liquids gives rise to the thirst drive. Physiological drives are the counterparts of physiological needs. When we have gone without food and water, our body may *need* these substances. However, our *experience* of drives is psychological. Drives arouse us to action. Drives tend to be stronger when we have been deprived longer. Psychological needs for approval, achievement, and belonging also give rise to drives. We can have a drive to get ahead in the business world just as we have a drive to eat. We can also be driven to obtain *incentives.*

An **incentive** is an object, person, or situation that is viewed as capable of satisfying a need or as desirable for its own sake. Money, food, a sexually attractive person, social approval, and attention can all act as incentives that motivate behavior.

Need A state of deprivation.

Drive A condition of arousal in an organism that is associated with a need.

Physiological drives Unlearned drives with a biological basis, such as hunger, thirst, and avoidance of pain.

Incentive An object, person, or situation perceived as being capable of satisfying a need.

Learning Connections | THE PSYCHOLOGY OF MOTIVATION: THE WHYS OF WHY

ACTIVE REVIEW (1) _____ are hypothetical states that activate behavior and direct organisms toward goals. (2) Physiological needs generally reflect states of physical _____. (3) A(n) _____ is an object, person, or situation that is perceived as being capable of satisfying a need.

REFLECT AND RELATE What are some of the key motives in your own life? What are your needs? What drives you? What incentives do you work for? Can you think of any needs or drives that motivate you but might not motivate other people?

CRITICAL THINKING If we observe a person to be behaving in a certain way, are we justified in assuming that the person is *motivated* to behave in that way? For example, if we see one person acting aggressively toward another, can we assume that the motive is aggression or that the person is an aggressive individual?

 Go to **http://psychology.wadsworth.com/ rathus_pcc9e** for an interactive version of this Learning Connections unit.

Theories of Motivation: Which Why Is Which?

Although psychologists agree that it is important to understand why humans and lower animals do things, they do not agree about the precise nature of motivation. Let us consider various theoretical perspectives on motivation.

The Evolutionary Perspective: The Fish, the Spiders, and the Bees

The evolutionary perspective notes that many animals are neurally "prewired"— that is, born with preprogrammed tendencies—to respond to certain situations in certain ways. **Truth or Fiction Revisited:** It is true that Siamese fighting fish reared in isolation from other fish assume stereotypical threatening stances and attack other males when they are introduced into their tank. Spiders spin webs instinctively. Bees "dance" instinctively to communicate the location of food to other bees.

© 1987 Comstock

■ **A Fixed-Action Pattern** In the presence of another male, Siamese fighting fish assume threatening stances in which they extend their fins and gills and circle each other. If neither male retreats, there will be a conflict.

These instinctive behaviors are found in particular species. They are *species-specific*. **Question: What is meant by species-specific behaviors?** Species-specific behaviors are also called **instincts,** or *fixed-action patterns* (FAPs). Such behavior patterns are inborn. That is, they are genetically transmitted from generation to generation.

Psychologists have asked whether humans have instincts, and if so, how many. A century ago, psychologists William James (1890) and William McDougall (1908) argued that humans have instincts that foster survival and social behavior. James numbered love, sympathy, and modesty among his social instincts. McDougall compiled 12 "basic" instincts, including hunger, sex, and self-assertion. Other psychologists have made longer lists, and still others deny that people have any instincts. The question as to whether people have instincts—and which ones—remains unresolved.

Drive-Reductionism and Homeostasis: "Steady, Steady . . ."

Sigmund Freud believed that tension motivates us to behave in ways that restore us to a resting state. His views are similar to those of the **drive-reduction theory** of learning, as set forth by psychologist Clark Hull in the 1930s. **Question: What is drive-reduction theory?**

According to Hull, **primary drives** such as hunger, thirst, and pain trigger arousal (tension) and activate behavior. We learn to engage in behaviors that reduce the tension. We also acquire drives through experience. These drives are called **acquired drives.** We may acquire a drive for money because money enables us to obtain food, drink, and homes, which protect us from predators and extremes of temperature. We might acquire drives for social approval and affiliation because other people, and their good will, help us reduce primary drives, especially when we are infants. In all cases, reduction of tension is the goal. Yet some people appear to acquire what could be considered excessive drives for money or affiliation. They gather money long after their material needs have been met, and some people find it difficult to be alone, even briefly.

Primary drives like hunger are triggered when we are in a state of deprivation. Sensations of hunger motivate us to act in ways that will restore the bodily balance. This tendency to maintain a steady state is called **homeostasis.** Homeostasis works much like a thermostat. When the temperature in a room drops below the set point, the heating system is triggered. The heat stays on until the set point is reached. Similarly, most animals eat until they are no longer hungry.

The Search for Stimulation: Is Downtime a Downer?

Physical needs give rise to drives like hunger and thirst. In such cases, we are motivated to *reduce* the tension or stimulation that impinges on us. **Question: Are all motives aimed at the reduction of tension?** No, in the case of *stimulus motives,* organisms seek to *increase* stimulation.

For example, a classic study conducted at McGill University in Montreal during the 1950s suggests the importance of sensory stimulation and activity. Some "lucky" students were paid $20 a day (which, with inflation, would now be well above $100) for doing nothing—literally. Would you like to "work" by doing nothing for $100 a day? Don't answer too quickly. According to the results of classic research on sensory deprivation, you might not like it at all.

In that experiment, student volunteers were placed in quiet cubicles and blindfolded (Bexton et al., 1954). Their arms were bandaged; they could hear nothing but the dull, continuous hum of air conditioning. Many slept for a while, but after a few hours of sensory-deprived wakefulness, most felt bored and irritable. As time went on, many grew more uncomfortable. Many students quit the experiment during the first day despite the financial incentive. **Truth or Fiction Revisited:** Therefore, it is not true that getting away from it all by going on a vacation from all sensory input for a few hours is relaxing. Many of those who remained for a few days found it hard to concentrate on simple problems days

Instinct An inherited disposition to activate specific behavior patterns that are designed to reach certain goals.

Drive-reduction theory The view that organisms learn to engage in behaviors that have the effect of reducing drives.

Primary drives Unlearned, or physiological, drives.

Acquired drives Drives acquired through experience, or learned.

Homeostasis The tendency of the body to maintain a steady state.

afterward. For many, the experiment did not provide a relaxing vacation. Instead, it produced boredom and disorientation.

Lower animals and humans appear motivated to seek novel stimulation. Even when they have been deprived of food, rats may explore unfamiliar arms of mazes rather than head straight for the spot where they have learned to expect food. Animals that have just copulated and thereby reduced their primary sex drives often show renewed interest in sexual behavior when presented with a new sex partner—a novelty. People (and lower animals) tend to take in more calories at buffets and smorgasbords than when they have fewer kinds of food available (Raynor & Epstein, 2001). Children spend hour after hour manipulating the controls of video games for the pleasure of zapping video monsters. Similarly, infants prolong their play with "busy boxes"—boxes filled with objects that honk, squeak, rattle, and buzz when manipulated in certain ways.

Stimulus motives provide an evolutionary advantage. Animals that are active and motivated to learn about and manipulate their environment are more likely to survive. If you know where the nearest tall tree is, you're more likely to be able to escape from a lion. If you've explored where to find food and water, you're more likely to pass your genes to future generations.

But note that survival is more or less a question of defending oneself or one's group against dangers of one kind or another. In the following section we see that many psychologists believe that people are also motivated to develop their unique potentials, even in the absence of any external threat.

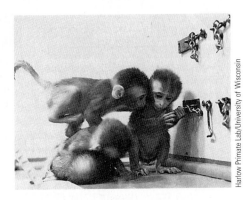

■ **Monkeying Around** Do organisms have innate drives to obtain sensory stimulation, manipulate objects (like these young rhesus monkeys), and explore the environment? The monkeys appear to monkey around with gadgets just for the fun of it. No external incentives are needed. Children similarly enjoy manipulating gadgets that honk, squeak, rattle, and buzz, even though the resultant honks and squeaks do not satisfy physiological drives such as hunger or thirst.

Self-actualization According to Maslow and other humanistic psychologists, self-initiated striving to become what one is capable of being. The motive for reaching one's full potential, for expressing one's unique capabilities.

Humanistic Theory: "I've Got to Be Me"?

Humanistic psychologists, particularly Abraham Maslow (1908–1970), suggest that human behavior is not just mechanical and aimed toward survival and reduction of tension. **Question: How does humanistic theory differ from other theories of motivation?** As a humanist, Maslow believed that people are also motivated by the conscious desire for personal growth. Humanists note that people tolerate pain, hunger, and many other sources of tension to obtain personal fulfillment.

Maslow believed that we are separated from so-called lower animals by our capacity for **self-actualization,** or self-initiated striving to become whatever we believe we are capable of being. Maslow considered self-actualization to be as important a need in humans as hunger. The need for self-actualization pushes people to strive to become concert pianists, chief executive officers, or best-selling authors—even when a person has plenty of money to live on.

Maslow (1970) organized human needs into a hierarchy. **Question: What is Maslow's hierarchy of needs?** Maslow's hierarchy ranges from physiological needs such as hunger and thirst, through self-actualization (see Figure 10.1). He believed that we naturally strive to travel up through this hierarchy.

FIGURE 10.1 **Maslow's Hierarchy of Needs**
Maslow believed we progress toward higher psychological needs once basic survival needs have been met. Where do you fit in this picture?

 Go to **http://psychology. wadsworth.com/rathus_pcc9e** to access an interactive version of this figure.

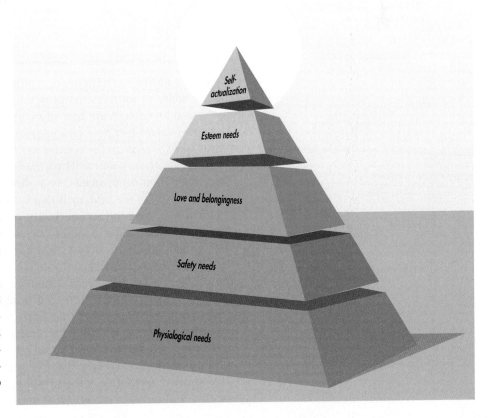

- Self-actualization
- Esteem needs
- Love and belongingness
- Safety needs
- Physiological needs

Self-Assessment  The Sensation-Seeking Scale

Some people seek higher levels of stimulation and activity than others. John is a couch potato, content to sit by the TV set all evening. Marsha doesn't feel right unless she's out on the tennis court or jogging. Cliff isn't content unless he has ridden his motorcycle over back trails at breakneck speeds, and Janet feels exuberant when she's catching the big wave or free-fall diving from an airplane.

What about you? Are you content to read or watch television all day? Or must you catch the big wave or bounce the bike across the dunes of the Mojave Desert? Sensation-seeking scales measure the level of stimulation or arousal a person will seek.

Marvin Zuckerman and his colleagues have identified four factors that are involved in sensation seeking: (1) seeking thrill and adventure, (2) disinhibition (that is, tendency to express impulses), (3) seeking experience, and (4) susceptibility to boredom. People who are high in sensation seeking are also less tolerant of sensory deprivation. They are more likely to use drugs and become involved in sexual experiences, to be drunk in public, and to volunteer for high-risk activities and unusual experiments (Pihl & Peterson, 1992; Stacy, 1997).

A shortened version of one of Zuckerman's scales follows. To gain insight into your own sensation-seeking tendencies, circle the choice, A or B, that best describes you. Then compare your answers to those in the answer key in Appendix B.

1. A. I would like a job that requires a lot of traveling.
   B. I would prefer a job in one location.

2. A. I am invigorated by a brisk, cold day.
   B. I can't wait to get indoors on a cold day.

3. A. I get bored seeing the same old faces.
   B. I like the comfortable familiarity of everyday friends.

4. A. I would prefer living in an ideal society in which everyone is safe, secure, and happy.
   B. I would have preferred living in the unsettled days of our history.

5. A. I sometimes like to do things that are a little frightening.
   B. A sensible person avoids activities that are dangerous.

6. A. I would not like to be hypnotized.
   B. I would like to have the experience of being hypnotized.

7. A. The most important goal in life is to live it to the fullest and experience as much as possible.
   B. The most important goal in life is to find peace and happiness.

8. A. I would like to try parachute jumping.
   B. I would never want to try jumping out of a plane, with or without a parachute.

9. A. I enter cold water gradually, giving myself time to get used to it.
   B. I like to dive or jump right into the ocean or a cold pool.

10. A. When I go on a vacation, I prefer the change of camping out.
    B. When I go on a vacation, I prefer the comfort of a good room and bed.

11. A. I prefer people who are emotionally expressive even if they are a bit unstable.
    B. I prefer people who are calm and even tempered.

12. A. A good painting should shock or jolt the senses.
    B. A good painting should give one a feeling of peace and security.

13. A. People who ride motorcycles must have some kind of unconscious need to hurt themselves.
    B. I would like to drive or ride a motorcycle.

Source: From M. Zuckerman, "Sensation Seeking" in *Dimensions of Personality*, H. London and J. Exner, eds., © 1980 John Wiley & Sons. Reprinted by permission.

Critics of Maslow's theory argue that there is too much individual variation for the hierarchy of motives to apply to everyone. Some people whose physiological, safety, and love needs are met show little interest in achievement and recognition. And some visual and performing artists devote themselves fully to their craft, even if they have to pass up the comforts of a warm home, live in an unsafe part of town, and alienate their friends. Thus many people seek distant, self-actualizing goals, even while their other needs, as outlined by Maslow, have not yet been met.

You can now see that each theory of motivation may have something to offer. For example, drive-reduction theory may explain why we drink when thirsty, but stimulus motive might explain why we go out to a club and drink alcohol. Each theory might apply to certain aspects of behavior. As the chapter progresses, we will describe research that lends support to each theory. Let us first describe research on the hunger drive. Hunger is based on physiological needs, and drive reduction would appear to explain some—although not all—eating behavior. Then we consider two powerful motives that push us ahead in life and sometimes to the front of the line: aggression and achievement. Psychologist Henry Murray (1938) called aggression and achievement *social motives* and felt that people learned them to meet psychological needs. But evolutionary psychologists believe that "genetic whisperings" also influence aggression and achievement and other aspects of personality and social behavior (Buss et al., 1998; Filley et al., 2001; Plomin, 2002).

Your Turn: Now that we have discussed various theories of motivation, enhance your mastery of the material with the nearby "Learning Connections." Review the material by filling in the blanks, reflect on the material by relating it to other things you know, and think critically about it.

Learning Connections — THEORIES OF MOTIVATION: WHICH WHY IS WHICH?

ACTIVE REVIEW (4) According to the _____ perspective, animals are born with instinctive tendencies to behave in certain ways. (5) Drives help the body maintain a steady state, a tendency that is called _____. (6) Studies in sensory _____ show that lack of stimulation is aversive and irritating. (7) Humanistic psychologist Maslow argued that people have a hierarchy of needs, the highest of which is the need for _____.

REFLECT AND RELATE Do you enjoy roller coasters? If so, why? Where would you place yourself in Maslow's hierarchy? Where do you see yourself as being headed? Why?

CRITICAL THINKING How does rearing an animal in isolation from others of its kind help researchers learn about what behaviors are instinctive? Would it be possible to run such an experiment with humans? Why or why not?

 Go to **http://psychology.wadsworth.com/ rathus_pcc9e** for an interactive version of this Learning Connections unit.

Hunger: Do You Go by "Tummy-Time"?

I go by tummy-time and I want my dinner.
Sir Winston Churchill

We need food to survive, but to many of us food means more than survival. Food is a symbol of family togetherness and caring. We associate food with the nurturance of the parent–child relationship, with visits home during holidays. Friends and relatives offer us food when we enter their homes, and saying no may be viewed as a personal rejection. Bacon and eggs, coffee with cream and sugar, meat and mashed potatoes—all seem to be part of sharing American values and abundance.

Biological Influences on Hunger

Questions: What bodily mechanisms regulate the hunger drive? What psychological processes are at work? In considering the bodily mechanisms that regulate hunger, let us begin with the mouth. (After all, we are talking about eating.) We also get signals of **satiety** from the digestive tract, although it takes longer for these signals to reach the brain. Therefore, if we did not receive signals of satiety from chewing and swallowing, we might eat for a long time after we had taken in enough food.

In classic "sham feeding" experiments with dogs, researchers implanted a tube in the animals' throats so that any food swallowed fell out of the body. Even though no food reached the stomach, the animals stopped feeding after a while (Janowitz & Grossman, 1949). Thus sensations of chewing and swallowing must provide some feelings of satiety. However, the dogs in the study resumed feeding sooner than animals whose food did reach the stomach. Let us proceed to the stomach, too, as we seek further regulatory factors in hunger.

An empty stomach leads to stomach contractions, which we call *hunger pangs*. Classic research suggested that stomach contractions are crucial to hunger. A man (A. L. Washburn) swallowed a balloon that was inflated in his stomach. His stomach contractions squeezed the balloon, so the contractions could be recorded by observers. Washburn also pressed a key when he felt hungry, and the researchers found a correspondence between his stomach contractions and his feelings of hunger (Cannon & Washburn, 1912).

Truth or Fiction Revisited: It is true that pangs in the stomach are connected with feelings of hunger, *but* stomach contractions are not as influential as formerly thought. (We apparently go by more than "tummy-time.") Medical observations and classic research also find that people and animals whose stomachs have been

Satiety The state of being satisfied; fullness.

© Dr. Neal Miller/Yale University

FIGURE 10.2 **A Hyperphagic Rat**

This rodent winner of the basketball look-alike contest went on a binge after it received a lesion in the ventromedial nucleus (VMN) of the hypothalamus. It is as if the lesion pushed the "set point" for body weight up several notches; the rat's weight is now about five times normal. But now it eats only enough to maintain its pleasantly plump figure, so you need not be concerned that it will eventually burst. If the lesion had been made in the lateral hypothalamus, the animal might have become the Calista Flockhart of the rat world.

removed still regulate food intake so as to maintain their normal weight (Tsang, 1938). (Food is absorbed through their intestines.) This finding led to the discovery of many other mechanisms that regulate hunger, including the hypothalamus, blood sugar level, and even receptors in the liver. When we are deprived of food, the level of sugar in the blood drops. The drop in blood sugar is communicated to the hypothalamus and apparently indicates that we have been burning energy and need to replenish it by eating.

If you were just reviving from a surgical operation, fighting your way through the fog of the anesthesia, food would probably be the last thing on your mind. But when a researcher uses a probe to destroy the **ventromedial nucleus (VMN)** of a rat's hypothalamus, the rat will grope toward food as soon as its eyes open. Then it eats vast quantities of Purina Rat Chow or whatever.

The VMN seems to be able to function like a "stop-eating center" in the rat's brain. If the VMN is electrically stimulated—that is, "switched on"—the rat stops eating until the current is turned off. When the VMN is destroyed, the rat becomes **hyperphagic** (Figure 10.2). That is, it continues to eat until it has about doubled its normal weight. Then it will level off its eating rate and maintain the higher weight. It is as if the set point of the stop-eating center has been raised to a higher level, like turning up the thermostat in a house from 65°F degrees to 70°F. Hyperphagic rats are also more finicky. They eat more fats or sweet-tasting food, but if their food is salty or bitter they actually eat less. Some people develop tumors near the base of the brain, damaging the VMN and apparently causing them to overeat and grow obese (Miller, 1995).

The **lateral hypothalamus** may function like a "start-eating center." If you electrically stimulate the lateral hypothalamus, the rat starts to eat (Miller, 1995). If you destroy the lateral hypothalamus, the rat may stop eating altogether—that is, become **aphagic.** If you force-feed an aphagic rat for a while, however, it begins to eat on its own and levels off at a relatively low body weight. It is as if you have lowered the rat's set point. It is like turning down the thermostat from, say, 70°F to 40°F.

Psychological Influences on Hunger

Although many areas of the body work in concert to regulate the hunger drive, this is only part of the story. In human beings, the hunger drive is more complex. Psychological as well as physiological factors play an important role. How many times have you been made hungry by the sight or aroma of food? How many times have you eaten not because you were hungry but because you were at a relative's home or hanging around in a cafeteria? Or because you felt anxious or depressed? Or simply because you were bored?

As we see in this chapter's "Life Connections" section, millions upon millions of Americans are eating too much and putting on more weight than is healthful for them. But now let us turn our attention to the hundreds of thousands of people—mainly adolescent girls and young women, but boys and men as well—who are eating less than is healthful for them. Some eat too much and then purposefully throw it up. Eating has become a traumatic experience for many Americans, a continuous test of willpower—or won't-power. Dieting has become the "normal"—at least in the statistical sense of the word—way of eating for women in the United States today. But for some people, especially young women, dieting becomes so extreme that their health is in jeopardy, as we see in the following section on eating disorders. **Question: What are the eating disorders?**

Ventromedial nucleus (VMN) A central area on the underside of the hypothalamus that appears to function as a stop-eating center.

Hyperphagic Characterized by excessive eating.

Lateral hypothalamus An area at the side of the hypothalamus that appears to function as a start-eating center.

Aphagic Characterized by undereating.

Eating Disorders: Is It True That "You Can Never Be Too Rich or Too Thin"?

The **eating disorders** are characterized by persistent, gross disturbances in eating patterns. In this section we focus on an eating disorder in which individuals are too thin, *anorexia nervosa,* and one in which the person may be normal in weight, but certainly not in the methods used to maintain that weight—*bulimia nervosa.*

ANOREXIA NERVOSA The Duchess of Windsor once said, "You can never be too rich or too thin." **Truth or Fiction Revisited:** Most people make no objection to having a fat bank account, but the fact is that one can most certainly be too skinny, as in the case of **anorexia nervosa.** Anorexia nervosa is a life-threatening eating disorder characterized by extreme fear of being too heavy, dramatic weight loss, a distorted body image, and resistance to eating enough to reach or maintain a healthful weight, as we see in the nearby "Closer Look" on the case of Rachel.

Rachel, like other people with anorexia nervosa, weighed less than 85% of her desirable body weight, and "desirable" body weights are already too slender for many individuals. By and large, anorexia nervosa afflicts women during adolescence and young adulthood (Winzelberg et al., 2000; Zagar & Rubenstein, 2002). The typical person with anorexia is a young European American female of higher socioeconomic status (McLaren, 2002). A study of 985 European American women and 1,061

Eating disorders A group of disorders marked by persistent, gross disturbances in eating patterns.

Anorexia nervosa A life-threatening eating disorder characterized by dramatic weight loss and a distorted body image.

A Closer Look — ANOREXIA NERVOSA: THE CASE OF RACHEL[2]

I wanted to be a runner. Runners were thin and I attributed this to dieting, not training. So I began restricting my diet: No butter, red meat, pork, dessert, candy, or snacking. If I ate any of the forbidden items I obsessed about it and felt guilty for days.

As a high school freshman, I wanted to run with the fastest girls so I trained hard, really hard and ate less. Lunch was lettuce sandwiches, carrots, and an apple. By my senior year, I was number three on the team and lunch was a bagel and an orange.

I maintained a rigid schedule—running cross country and track, having a seat on student council, volunteering, and maintaining a 3.9 GPA throughout high school—while starving myself (1,000 calories per day), trying to attain the impossible perfection I thought couldn't be far away if I only slimmed down a little bit more.

Several teammates were concerned, but I shrugged them off saying family members were tall and slender; I was a health nut, I didn't like fatty foods; I was a vegetarian; I didn't like sweets; I wasn't hungry; I wasn't starving.

A psychiatrist didn't help at all. I went in, sat on the couch and told her what she wanted to hear: I would eat more, run less, stop restricting myself, and quit obsessing about being thin. I was very good at knowing exactly what to tell others.

I dropped 10 pounds my freshman year—from 125 to 115 lbs. I was 5'8" tall and wore a size five. I hated my body so I starved myself and ran like a mad woman.

In quiet moments, I was sad and worried about what might be going on inside me.

I was already taking birth control to regain my menstrual cycle; my weight was 15% below what was recommended for my height; I was always cold; I had chest pains and an irregular heartbeat; my hair was limp and broke off; my skin was colorless.

It wasn't until I came to the University of Iowa and joined the varsity women's cross country team that I began to see what I was doing to myself. A teammate had an eating problem. Every time I saw her, I felt sick to my stomach. She had sunken cheeks, eyes so big they swallowed her face. She was an excellent student and a college-level varsity athlete. Many people wondered at her determination, but I understood. She used the same excuses I did.

For one sick instant, I wondered if I would be happier if I were that thin. That is when I started to realize I was slowly killing myself.

At the urging of my coach, I saw the team nutritionist who recommended a psychiatrist who felt no pity for me and made me take a brutally honest look at who I was and why I was starving myself. She didn't accept any of my excuses. She helped me realize that there are other things to think about besides food and body image. About this time I decided to quit the cross country team. The pressure I felt to be thin and competition at the college level were too much when I needed to focus on getting well.

After two months of therapy, my weight had dropped again. I'm not sure how far because I refused to step on a scale, but my size five pants were falling off. My psychiatrist required weekly weigh-ins.

I wasn't putting into practice any of the things my nutritionist and counselor suggested. They told me that if I wanted to have children someday I needed to eat. They warned me of osteoporosis at age 30. Then my psychiatrist scared me to death. She told me I needed to start eating more or I would be checked into the hospital and hooked up to an IV. That would put me on the same level as my Iowa teammate. I had looked at her with such horror and never realized that I was in the same position.

My psychiatrist asked how my family would feel if they had to visit me in the hospital because I refused to eat. It was enough to make me think hard the next time I went through the food service lines.

Of course, I didn't get better the next day. But it was a step in the right direction. It's taken me three years to get where I am now. At 5'8¾" (I even grew as I got healthier) and 145 lbs, I look and feel healthier, have better eating and exercise habits, and I don't obsess about food as much as I used to. On rare occasions, I think about controlling my food intake. My eating disorder will haunt me for the rest of my life. If I'm not careful, it could creep back.

[2]Source: *Well&Good.* (2002). A publication of University of Iowa Health Care. Used with permission.

TABLE 10.1 INCIDENCE OF ANOREXIA NERVOSA AND BULIMIA NERVOSA AMONG AFRICAN AMERICAN WOMEN AND EUROPEAN AMERICAN WOMEN

In their study of 985 European American women and 1,062 African American women who had participated in the 10-year National Heart, Lung, and Blood Institute (NHLBI) Growth and Health Study, Ruth Striegel-Moore and her colleagues (2003) found that the incidence of eating disorders was higher among European Americans than African Americans.

	Anorexia Nervosa	Bulimia Nervosa
African Americans	0%	0.4%
European Americans	1.5%	2.3%

Video Connections—Anorexia Nervosa
Eating disorders affect many Americans, especially women. Why? Go to your companion website and click on "Anorexia Nervosa" to listen to this woman's story of battling her eating disorder.

Bulimia nervosa An eating disorder characterized by repeated cycles of binge eating and purging.

African American women found that 1.5% of the European Americans and none of the African Americans had met the diagnostic standards for anorexia nervosa at some time during their lives (Striegel-Moore et al., 2003; see Table 10.1). Affluent females have greater access to fitness centers and health clubs and are more likely to read the magazines which idealize slender bodies and shop in the boutiques that cater to females with svelte figures. All in all, they are regularly confronted with unrealistically high standards of slimness that make them extremely unhappy with their own physiques (McLaren, 2002; Neumark-Sztainer et al., 2002a). The incidences of anorexia nervosa and bulimia nervosa have increased markedly in recent years. Women with these disorders greatly outnumber the men who have them by more than six to one, but we lack precise data on their prevalence because so many people deny their disorder (Goode, 2000; Striegel-Moore & Cachelin, 2001).

We also find eating disorders among some males, particularly among males who are compelled by their chosen activities—for example, wrestling or dancing—to keep their weight within a certain range or to remain very slender (Bailey, 2003a; Goode, 2000).

Females with anorexia nervosa can drop 25% or more of their weight within a year. Severe weight loss triggers abnormalities in the endocrine system (that is, with hormones) that prevent ovulation (Treasure & Serpell, 2001). General health deteriorates. Nearly every system in the body is affected. There are problems with the respiratory system (Key et al., 2001) and with the cardiovascular system (Eidem et al., 2001). Females with anorexia are also at risk for premature development of osteoporosis, a condition characterized by loss of bone density that usually afflicts people in late adulthood (Geiser et al., 2001; Treasure & Serpell, 2001). Given all these problems, it is not surprising that the mortality rate for females with anorexia nervosa is approximately 5%.

In one common pattern, the girl sees that she has gained some weight after reaching puberty, and she resolves that she must lose it. But even after the weight is gone, she maintains her pattern of dieting and, in many cases, exercises at a fever pitch. This pattern continues as she plunges below her "desirable" weight—according to standardized weight charts—and even after those who care about her tell her that she is becoming all skin and bones. Denial is a huge part of anorexia nervosa. Girls with the disorder tragically tend to deny that they are losing too much weight. They are in denial about any health problems, pointing to their feverish exercise routines as evidence of their strength. Distortion of the body image is a major feature of the disorder (Winzelberg et al., 2000). In one study, researchers recruited women who weighed an average of 31% below their desirable weight according to Metropolitan Life Insurance Company charts (Penner et al., 1991). They found that the women overestimated the size of their bodies by exactly 31%! Friends, coworkers, and families see females with anorexia nervosa as skin and bones. Meanwhile, the women fix their gaze into the mirror and believe that they are looking at a body shape that is too heavy.

Ironically, individuals with anorexia do not literally distance themselves from food. They may become as preoccupied with food as they are with their own body shape. They may develop a fascination with cookbooks, shop for their families, and prepare gourmet feasts—for other people, that is.

BULIMIA NERVOSA **Bulimia nervosa** is sort of a companion disorder to anorexia nervosa. It entails repeated cycles of binge eating and purging. Binge eating often follows on the heels of food restriction—as in dieting (Corwin, 2000). There are various methods of purging. Some people vomit. Other avenues include strict dieting or fasting, the use of laxatives, and engaging in demanding, prolonged exercise regimes. Individuals with eating disorders engaging in, tend to be perfectionist about their bodies. They will not settle for less than their idealized body shape and weight (Halmi et al., 2000; Santonastaso et al., 2001). Bulimia, like anorexia, triggers hormonal imbalances: One study found that nearly half of the females with bulimia nervosa have irregular menstrual cycles (Gendall et al., 2000).

Bulimia nervosa, like anorexia nervosa, tends to afflict women during adolescence and young adulthood (Lewinsohn et al., 2000b; Winzelberg et al., 2000). The study by Striegel-Moore and her colleagues (2003) found that 2.4% of the European American women in their sample reported symptoms of bulimia nervosa, as compared with 0.4% of the African Americans.

Eating disorders are upsetting and dangerous in themselves, of course, but they are also often connected with deep depression (Stice et al., 2000b). However, it seems that depression is more likely to co-occur with eating disorders than to be caused by them (Wade et al., 2000).

ORIGINS OF THE EATING DISORDERS Question: What are the origins of the eating disorders? Health professionals have done a great deal of research into the origins of eating disorders. Yet they will be the first to admit that many questions about these disorders remain unanswered (Striegel-Moore & Cachelin, 2001).

According to some psychoanalysts, anorexia nervosa may symbolize a young woman's efforts to cope with sexual fears, especially the possibility of becoming pregnant. Keep in mind that anorexia is connected with *amenorrhea* (lack of menstruation). Some psychoanalysts interpret the behavior pattern as a female's attempt to regress to her lifestyle prior to puberty. Anorexia nervosa prevents some adolescents from separating from their families and assuming adult responsibilities. Their breasts and hips flatten once more due to the loss of fatty tissue. In the adolescent's fantasies, perhaps, she remains a sexually undifferentiated child.

Many parents are obsessed with getting their children—especially their infants—to eat. Thus some psychoanalysts suggest that children now and then refuse to eat as a way of engaging in warfare with their parents. ("You have to eat something!" "I'm not hungry!") It often seems that warfare does occur in the families of adolescents with eating disorders. Parents in such families are often unhappy with the family's functioning. They frequently have issues with eating and dieting themselves. They also "act out" against their daughters—letting them know that they consider them unattractive, and, prior to the development of the eating disorder, letting them know that they think they should lose weight (Baker et al., 2000; Cooper et al., 2001).

A particularly disturbing risk factor for eating disorders in adolescent females is a history of child abuse, particularly sexual abuse (Ackard et al., 2001; K. P. Anderson et al., 2000; Leonard et al., 2003; Nagata et al., 2001). One study found a history of childhood sexual abuse in about half of women with bulimia nervosa, as opposed to a rate of about 7% among women without the disorder (Deep et al., 1999). Another study compared 45 pairs of sisters, one of whom was diagnosed with anorexia nervosa (Karwautz et al., 2001). Those with anorexia were significantly more likely to be exposed to high parental expectations *and* to sexual abuse.

Also consider the sociocultural features of eating disorders. Slimness is idealized in the United States, but when you check out *Cosmopolitan, Glamour,* or the Victoria's Secret catalogue, you are looking at models who, on average, are 9% taller and 16% thinner than the typical female—and who still manage to have ample bustlines. Miss America, the annually renewed American role model, has also been slenderizing herself across the years. The pageant began in 1922. Over the past 80 years, the winner has added only 2% in height but has lost 12 lbs in weight. In the early days of the 1920s, Miss America's weight relative to her height yielded a Body Mass Index (BMI) of 20 to 25, which is considered normal by the World Health Organization (WHO). WHO labels people as malnourished when their BMIs are lower than 18.5. However, recent Miss Americas come in at a BMI near 17 (Rubinstein & Caballero, 2000). So Miss America adds to the woes of "normal" young women, and even to those of young women who hover near the WHO "malnourished" borderline.

Truth or Fiction Revisited: Thus it is true that checking out the Victoria's Secret catalogue can contribute to eating disorders among women. As the cultural ideal slenderizes, women with desirable body weights according to the health charts feel overweight, and overweight women feel gargantuan (Utter et al., 2003; Winzelberg et al., 2000).

A survey of 4,746 junior high and high school students by Dianne Neumark-Sztainer (2002b) and her colleagues found that 57% of the girls had made serious efforts to lose weight—for example, dieting, using food substitutes like Slim-Fast, or upping their cigarette usage. Twelve percent had used more extreme measures: vomiting, using diet pills, or taking laxatives or diuretics. Even one-third of the boys had attempted to lose weight, although their tactics were usually not as severe as the girls'.

Many individuals with eating disorders, like Rachel, are involved in activities that demand weight limits, such as dancing, acting, and modeling. Male wrestlers also feel the pressure to stay within an "acceptable" weight range (Goode, 2000). Men, like women, experience pressure to create an ideal body, one with power in the upper torso and a trim abdomen (Goode, 2000).

Eating disorders tend to run in families, which raises the possibility of the involvement of genetic factors (Bergen et al., 2003; DeAngelis, 2002; Strober et al., 2000). As noted earlier, a genetic mutation might be involved in binge eating in some people (Farooqi et al., 2003). Genetic factors might also be involved in the obsessionistic and perfectionist personality traits that often accompany the need to be superthin (Bellodi et al., 2001; Halmi et al., 2000; Kaye et al., 2000; Speranza et al., 2001). We can note that perfectionists are likely to be disappointed in themselves, giving rise to feelings of depression. But it may also be that both disorders share genetic factors. Genetically inspired perfectionism, cultural emphasis on slimness, self-absorption, and family conflict may create a perfect recipe for development of eating disorders (Baker et al., 2000).

In Chapter 15, "Methods of Therapy," we will see how health professionals treat the eating disorders. We will find that there are roles for both psychotherapy and medicines.

Your Turn: Now that we have discussed the hunger drive, enhance your mastery of the material with the nearby "Learning Connections." Review the material by filling in the blanks, reflect on the material by relating it to other things you know, and think critically about it.

Learning Connections — HUNGER: DO YOU GO BY "TUMMY-TIME"?

ACTIVE REVIEW (8) Biological factors in hunger include stomach contractions, the blood _____ level, and the hypothalamus. (9) The _____ nucleus (VMN) of the hypothalamus functions as a stop-eating center. (10) As time passes after a meal, the _____ sugar level drops and fat is drawn from fat cells to provide nourishment. (11) The _____ disorders are characterized by persistent, gross disturbances in eating patterns. (12) _____ nervosa is a life-threatening eating disorder characterized by dramatic weight loss and a distorted body image. (13) The typical person with anorexia is a young, affluent _____ American female. (14) _____ nervosa involves repeated cycles of binge eating and purging. (15) One risk factor for eating disorders in adolescent females is a history of _____ abuse. (16) Eating disorders (*Do* or *Do not?*) tend to run in families.

REFLECT AND RELATE Why do *you* eat? How do you experience the hunger drive? Have you ever eaten because you were anxious or bored or because you passed a bakery window with some enticing pastries? What are the effects on your health?

CRITICAL THINKING It is possible that genetic factors are involved in the development of eating disorders. If they are, is there any purpose to trying to challenge the cultural idealization of the extremely thin female? Explain.

 Go to **http://psychology.wadsworth.com/ rathus_pcc9e** for an interactive version of this Learning Connections unit.

■ **A Speculative View of the Primate Past, from the film *2001*** Researchers have unearthed evidence that the ancestors and relatives of humans used weapons against each other as well as prey. In the film *2001*, a fictitious primate–similar in appearance to a relative but not an ancestor of humans–uses a bone from an antelope as a weapon.

Aggression: Of Australopithecines, Humans, Robins, and Testosterone

A murder trial took place in the library of anthropologist Raymond Dart. His guest, Robert Ardrey, held the evidence in his hand—the smashed jawbone of an adolescent. Dart had deduced that the adolescent had been struck in the head with the humerus bone of an antelope—a weapon derived from the animal's leg. The angle of the blow, its intensity—these and other pieces of evidence swept aside any possibility that the death had been by accident.

What was stunning to Ardrey was that the murder had taken place more than 500,000 years ago. The victim was an *australopithecine,* an early hominid who had grown to something over four feet, weighed 90 pounds, and walked upright. Though not a direct ancestor of humans, this primate shared a branch on the evolutionary tree with humans. The murderer would also have been an australopithecine. And here in a flash, to Ardrey, was an explanation of human aggression: Murder and warfare were not the products of modern society and the state. Rather, they were instinctive. Here in the dawn of time, close relatives of humans had stalked antelopes, baboons, and each other with weapons.

There were those who argued that social deprivation and inequality lay at the root of human aggression. If people were to remove poverty, inequality, and social injustice, went the litany, there would be an end to crime, aggression, and war. Ardrey (1961) dubbed this view the romantic fallacy. It was founded, in part, by the French philosopher Jean-Jacques Rousseau, who had argued that people were "noble savages" who had been corrupted by twin inventions: private property and the state. Yet Ardrey asserted that *Australopithecus* was undoubtedly savage but was not noble. Long before the invention of the state, australopithecines bore weapons and used them to brutally take the lives of not only animals, but also other australopithecines.

Critical thinking teaches us to search for rival explanations for the behavior we observe—whether we observe it in the present or its record from the distant past, and whether we observe it in humans or other species. What kinds of rival explanations might there be for aggression and even murder? One possibility is that aggressive behavior among humans (and perhaps among australopithecines) is and was learned—at one time, perhaps, by trial and error, but frequently by observing others. In Chapter 6, for example, we noted evidence that observing violence in the media is connected with violent behavior among viewers. The idea of an instinct also suggests that a behavior pattern occurs automatically, without thinking, without decision-making. Many—perhaps most—psychologists believe that violence between people is not automatic but involves evaluation of one's situation and possible patterns of behavior.

Still, we cannot ignore the fact that humans are aggressive—today. There are armed conflicts of one kind or another on nearly every continent of planet earth. There is murder and battering, often by people's most intimate partners. There is rape. Ardrey's evidence for a killer instinct is flawed, but there is evidence of a role for biology in aggression, even among humans. **Question: What have psychologists and other scientists learned about the biological and psychological origins of aggressive behavior?**

Biology, Chemistry, and Aggression

Numerous biological structures and chemicals appear to be involved in aggression. In response to certain stimuli, many lower animals show instinctive aggressive reactions. This behavior is automatic, although it can be modified somewhat by learning. For example, the male robin responds aggressively to the red breast of another robin. The hypothalamus appears to be involved in this inborn reaction pattern. Electrical stimulation of part of the hypothalamus triggers stereotypical aggressive behaviors in many lower animals. However, in humans, whose brains are more complex, other brain structures apparently moderate possible aggressive instincts.

Chemistry is also involved in aggression, especially in the form of the male sex hormone testosterone. Testosterone appears to affect the tendencies to dominate and control other people. Men have higher testosterone levels than women do and are also (usually) more aggressive than women, especially with male strangers (Pope et al., 2000). For example, aggressive boys and adolescents are likely to have higher testosterone levels than their less aggressive peers (A. Booth et al., 2003; Chance et al., 2000). Members of so-called "rambunctious" fraternities have higher testosterone levels, on average, than members of more "well-behaved" fraternities (Dabbs et al., 1996). Testosterone levels also vary with the occasion: Men's testosterone levels tend to be higher when they are "winning"—whether in athletic competitions such as football or even in chess (Bernhardt et al., 1998).

Yet all is not biological. Testosterone levels are linked with levels of risk-taking among children and adolescents, but the strength of the relationship declines as the quality of the parent–child relationship increases (A. Booth et al., 2003). Human relationships—psychosocial factors—can thus have moderating influences on levels of aggression and risk-taking. Let us look more deeply into psychological aspects of aggression.

Psychological Aspects of Aggression

Psychologists have recognized the importance of understanding (and curbing) human aggressiveness for many generations. Let us consider various psychological views of aggression.

PSYCHODYNAMIC THEORY AND AGGRESSION Sigmund Freud, the originator of psychodynamic theory, like Ardrey, believed that aggression is natural and instinctive. But Freud viewed aggressive impulses as inevitable reactions to the frustrations of daily life. He was not thinking so much in terms of the evolutionary history of humans. According to Freud, children (and adults) naturally desire to vent aggres-

A Closer Look — CROSS-CULTURAL ASPECTS OF AGGRESSION

Anthropological research shows that the stereotype of the aggressive male is not universal. Margaret Mead's (1935) research on the South Pacific island of New Guinea revealed that the sociocultural milieu influences motives such as aggressiveness and nurturance. Among the Mundugumor, a tribe of headhunters and cannibals, both women and men were warlike and aggressive. The women felt that motherhood sidetracked them from more important activities, such as butchering inhabitants of neighboring villages. In contrast, both women and men of the Arapesh tribe were gentle and nurturant of children. Then there were the Tchambuli. In that tribe the women earned a living while the men spent most of their time nurturing the children, primping, and gossiping.

As noted in Chapter 2, there is a 99.9% overlap among people in the genetic code. There is no reason to believe that significant differences in that other 0.1% account for differences in aggressiveness among the Mundugumor, the Arapesh, and the Tchambuli. Is it not more likely that the people within the various tribes had arrived at a consensus as to proper behavior over the generations, and that they taught their children to behave accordingly?

■ **What Does Cross-Cultural Research Suggest about Aggressiveness?** Margaret Mead's anthropological research in New Guinea found wide variety in the incidence of aggressiveness. Among a tribe of headhunters and cannibals, both women and men were warlike. In another tribe, both women and men were gentle and nurturant. A third tribe found reversal of the masculine and feminine stereotypes: Women earned a living while the men nurtured the children and spent time primping.

sive impulses on other people, including parents, because even the most attentive parents cannot gratify all of their demands immediately. Yet children also fear punishment and loss of love, so they repress most aggressive impulses and store them in the unconscious recesses of the mind. Instinctive behavior is thus modified by experience.

As we see in the following Controversy in Psychology, the Freudian perspective, in a sense, sees humans as "steam engines." By holding in steam rather than venting it, we set the stage for future explosions. Pent-up aggressive impulses demand an outlet. They may be expressed toward parents in roundabout ways, such as destroying furniture; later in life they may be expressed toward strangers.

CONTROVERSY IN PSYCHOLOGY

The Catharsis Controversy

Does watching violent sports such as football, boxing, and pro wrestling makes viewers more or less likely to engage in violent behavior themselves?

According to psychodynamic theory, the best way to prevent harmful aggression may be to encourage less harmful aggression. In the steam engine analogy, verbal aggression (through wit, sarcasm, or expression of negative feelings) may vent some of the aggressive steam in a person's unconscious mind. So might cheering on a football team or attending a prize fight. Psychoanalysts refer to the venting of aggressive impulses as *catharsis*. Thus, catharsis is viewed as a safety valve.

But research findings on the usefulness of catharsis are mixed. Some studies suggest that catharsis leads to pleasant reductions in tension and reduced likelihood of future aggression (e.g., Doob & Wood, 1972). Other studies, however, suggest that "venting" some steam actually encourages more aggression later on (e.g., Bushman et al., 1999). **Truth or Fiction Revisited:** Research evidence does *not* support the view that "venting" aggressive impulses through activities such as cheering on a football team or attending a prize fight is a good way of preventing harmful aggression. Research evidence has been hard on the psychodynamic perspective, yielding partial support for Freud's views at best. Most psychologists believe that Freud's views on aggression remain highly speculative. In the next section we see that there is reason to believe that people *choose* to act aggressively.

COGNITIVE PSYCHOLOGY AND AGGRESSION Cognitive psychologists assert that it is natural for people to attempt to understand their environments and make decisions. From this perspective, our behavior is influenced by our values, by how we interpret situations, and by choice. From this perspective, people who believe that aggression is necessary and justified—as during wartime—are likely to act aggressively. People who believe that a particular war or act of aggression is unjust, or who oppose aggression regardless of the circumstances, are less likely to behave aggressively (Huesmann & Guerra, 1997).

One cognitive theory suggests that frustration and discomfort trigger unpleasant feelings (Rule et al., 1987). These feelings, in turn, prompt aggression.

© Monika Graff/The Image Works

■ **Catharsis?** Are these football fans harmlessly venting aggressive impulses, or are they building the likelihood of behaving aggressively themselves? What does Freudian theory say about "catharsis"? Does the research support Freud's theory?

Aggression is *not* automatic, however. Cognitive factors intervene (Berkowitz, 1994). People *decide*—sometimes making split-second decisions—whether they will strike out or not on the basis of factors such as their previous experiences with aggression and their interpretation of the other person's motives.

But researchers find that many individuals who act aggressively distort other people's motives for their behavior. For example, they assume that other people wish them harm when they actually do not (Crick & Dodge, 1994; Dodge et al., 2002). Cognitive therapists note that we are more likely to respond aggressively to a provocation when we magnify the importance of the "insult" or otherwise stir up feelings of anger (e.g., Lochman & Dodge, 1994). How do you respond when someone bumps into you? If you view it as an intentional insult to your honor, you may respond with aggression. If you view it as an accident, or as a social problem in need of a solution, you are less likely to act aggressively.

From the cognitive perspective, in sum, it is natural for people to appraise their situations. Whether or not they behave aggressively depends on the outcome of that appraisal.

LEARNING AND AGGRESSION What do the behavioral and the social cognitive perspectives have to say about aggression? From the behavioral perspective, learning is acquired through reinforcement. Organisms that are reinforced for aggressive behavior are more likely to behave aggressively in situations similar to those in which reinforcement occurs. Environmental consequences make it more likely that an animal will be rewarded for aggression if it "picks on" a smaller, weaker animal. Strong, agile organisms are likely to be reinforced for aggressive behavior.

Among lower animals, reinforcement is usually physical, for example, food, mating, or escaping a predator. Humans respond to such reinforcements but also to other reinforcers, like social approval. Research shows that children are less likely to behave aggressively when teachers and fellow students communicate strong disapproval of aggressive behavior (Henry et al., 2000).

The behavioral perspective would describe aggressive behaviors as being instinctive, as in the case of many lower animals, or as acquired by means of reinforcement. From the social cognitive perspective, aggressive skills are mainly acquired by the observation of other people acting aggressively. Most behaviorists would see aggressive behavior as being mechanical even in humans, either because it is inborn or because the learning of aggressive behaviors is controlled by reinforcements. However, social cognitive theorists—like other cognitive theorists—believe that consciousness and choice play key roles in aggressive behavior among humans. Social cognitive theorists believe that we are not likely to act aggressively unless we believe that aggression is appropriate under the circumstances and likely to be reinforced.

Situational Factors and Aggression: When the Heat Is On

Situational factors can contribute to aggression. For example, aggression sometimes takes place within the context of a mob. When people act as individuals, fear of consequences and awareness of their moral values tend to prevent them from hurting other people. But in a mob, they may experience *deindividuation,* which is a state of reduced self-awareness and focusing on one's values. Factors that lead to deindividuation include anonymity, sharing of responsibility for aggressive behavior (also called *diffusion of responsibility*), a high level of emotional arousal due to noise and crowding, and a focus on the group's norms rather than on one's own concepts of right and wrong (Baron & Byrne, 2004). Under these circumstances, crowd members behave more aggressively than they would as individuals.

Environmental factors also contribute to the likelihood of aggressive behavior. Bad-smelling pollutants decrease feelings of attraction and heighten aggression (Baron & Byrne, 2004). Extremes of noise can also trigger violence. If you and your date have had a fight and are then exposed to a tire blowout, look out.

Angry people are more likely to behave aggressively when exposed to a sudden noise of 95 dB than one of 55 dB (Donnerstein & Wilson, 1976).

Extreme heat also apparently makes some people hot under the collar (Anderson, 2001). That is, high temperatures are connected with aggression. The frequency of honking at traffic lights in Phoenix increases with the temperature (Kenrick & MacFarlane, 1986). In Houston, murders and rapes are most likely to occur when the temperature is in the nineties Fahrenheit (Anderson & DeNeve, 1992). In Raleigh, North Carolina, the incidence of rape and aggravated assault rises with the average monthly temperature (Cohn, 1990; Simpson & Perry, 1990).

Some psychologists (e.g., Anderson & DeNeve, 1992) suggest that the probability of aggressive behavior continues to increase as the temperature soars. Others argue that once temperatures become extremely aversive, people tend to avoid aggressive behavior so that they will not be doubly struck by hot temper and hot temperature (Bell, 1992; Rotton & Cohn, 2000). The evidence does not absolutely eliminate either view, so the issue remains, well, heated.

The overall message seems to be something like this: Yes, some of the foundations of aggression may be embedded in our genes, but that does not mean that aggressive behavior is instinctive in humans. Moreover, human survival on planet earth no longer requires physical aggressiveness in the way it once may have. Yes, aggression may be affected by testosterone levels and other biological factors, but that does not mean that human aggression is mechanical or automatic. Yes, aggressive behaviors may be learned, but people make decisions about whether or not to act aggressively based on their appraisal of their situations. People's cultural milieus are one source of information people use in making these decisions. When aggression is valued within a culture, or seen as being "normal," people are more likely to choose to act aggressively. Situational factors such as being part of a mob, unpleasant odors, sudden noises, and extremes of temperature also affect the likelihood that a human will behave aggressively.

Your Turn: Now that we have discussed various theories of aggression, enhance your mastery of the material with the nearby "Learning Connections." Review the material by filling in the blanks, reflect on the material by relating it to other things you know, and think critically about it.

Learning Connections — AGGRESSION: OF AUSTRALOPITHECINES, HUMANS, ROBINS, AND TESTOSTERONE

ACTIVE REVIEW (17) Electrical stimulation of part of the brain structure called the _____ triggers stereotypical aggressive behaviors in many lower animals. (18) The male sex hormone _____ affects tendencies to dominate and control other people. (19) Cognitive psychologists assert that our behavior is influenced by our values, by how we _____ situations, and by choice. (20) When individuals are part of an aggressive mob, they may experience _____. (21) Bad odors and extreme heat (*Increase* or *Decrease?*) the likelihood of aggressive behavior.

REFLECT AND RELATE Consider people whom you would label "explosive." Do you believe that they actually explode or that they *decide* where and when to behave violently? Explain.

CRITICAL THINKING As members of the jury, what can we deduce about humans from the murder trial in Dart's library? Yes, one australopithecine may have killed another and used a weapon to do so. People have also killed other people and used weapons to do so. But do these incidents provide evidence that aggressive behavior is instinctive in humans, or in australopithecines, for that matter? Does it show whether killing and the use of weapons is hard-wired into our nervous systems or learned? Does the "evidence" presented by Dart and Ardrey answer this question?

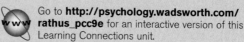

Go to **http://psychology.wadsworth.com/ rathus_pcc9e** for an interactive version of this Learning Connections unit.

Achievement Motivation: "Just Do It"?

Many students persist in studying despite being surrounded by distractions. Many people strive relentlessly to get ahead, to "make it," to earn large sums of money, to invent, to accomplish the impossible. **Question: Why do some people strive to get ahead?** Psychological research has pointed to these people having something called *achievement motivation.*

Psychologist David McClelland (1958) helped pioneer the assessment of achievement motivation through evaluation of fantasies. One method involves the Thematic Apperception Test (TAT), developed by Henry Murray. The TAT contains cards with pictures and drawings that are subject to various interpretations. Individuals are shown one or more TAT cards and asked to construct stories about the pictured theme: to indicate what led up to it, what the characters are thinking and feeling, and what is likely to happen.

One TAT card is similar to that in Figure 10.3. The meaning of the card is ambiguous—unclear. Is the girl sleeping, thinking about the book, wishing she were out with friends? Consider two stories that could be told about this card:

Story 1: "She's upset that she's got to read the book because she's behind in her assignments and doesn't particularly like to work. She'd much rather be out with her friends, and she may very well sneak out to do just that."

Story 2: "She's thinking, 'Someday I'll be a great scholar. I'll write books like this, and everybody will be proud of me.' She reads all the time."

The second story suggests the presence of more achievement motivation than the first. Classic studies find that people with high achievement motivation earn higher grades than people with comparable learning ability but lower achievement motivation. They are more likely to earn high salaries and be promoted than less motivated people with similar opportunities (Aronoff & Litevin, 1971; Orpen, 1995).

McClelland (1965) used the TAT to sort college students into groups—students with high achievement motivation and students with low achievement motivation. He found that 83% of college graduates with high achievement motivation found jobs in occupations characterized by risk, decision making, and the chance for great success, such as business management, sales, or self-employment. Most (70%) of the graduates who chose nonentrepreneurial positions showed low achievement motivation. People with high achievement motivation seem to prefer challenges and are willing to take moderate risks to achieve their goals.

What Flavor Is Your Achievement Motivation?

Do you want to do well in this course? If you do, why? Carol Dweck (1997) finds that achievement motivation can be driven by different forces. Are you motivated mainly by performance goals? That is, is your grade in the course of most importance? If it is, it may be in part because your motives concern tangible rewards such as getting into graduate school, landing a good job, reaping approval from parents or your instructor, or avoiding criticism. Performance goals are usually met through extrinsic rewards such as prestige and income. Parents of children who develop performance goals are likely to respond to good grades with tangible rewards such as toys or money and to respond to poor grades with anger and removal of privileges.

FIGURE 10.3 **Tapping Fantasies in Personality Research**
This picture is similar to a Thematic Apperception Test card used to measure the need for achievement. What is happening in this picture? What is the person thinking and feeling? What is going to happen? Your answers to these questions reflect your own needs as well as the content of the picture itself.

Or do learning goals mainly motivate you to do well? That is, is your central motive the enhancing of your knowledge and skills—your ability to understand and master the subject matter? Learning goals usually lead to intrinsic rewards, such as satisfaction with oneself. Students who develop learning goals often have parents with strong achievement motivation, parents who encourage their children to think and act independently from an early age. They help their children develop learning goals by showing warmth and praising them for their efforts to learn, exposing them to novel and stimulating experiences, and encouraging persistence (Dweck, 1997; Ginsburg & Bronstein, 1993; Gottfried et al., 1994). Children of such parents frequently set high standards for themselves, associate their achievements with self-worth, and attribute their achievements to their own efforts rather than to chance or to the intervention of others.

Many of us strive to meet both performance and learning goals in our courses as well as in other areas of life. Grades are important because they are connected with (very) tangible benefits, but learning for its own sake is also of value.

Your Turn: Now that we have discussed achievement motivation, enhance your mastery of the material with the nearby "Learning Connections." Review the material by filling in the blanks, reflect on the material by relating it to other things you know, and think critically about it.

Learning Connections — ACHIEVEMENT MOTIVATION: "JUST DO IT"

ACTIVE REVIEW (22) Individuals with (*High* or *Low?*) achievement motivation are more likely to earn high salaries and be promoted on the job. (23) McClelland used the Thematic _____ Test to measure achievement motivation. (24) Students with _____ goals are mainly motivated by factors such as good grades, rewards from parents, and the prospect of landing a good job. (25) Students with _____ goals are usually more motivated by intrinsic rewards like self-satisfaction.

REFLECT AND RELATE Do you seem to be driven mainly by performance goals or learning goals in this course and in your other courses? Explain.

CRITICAL THINKING Some people strive harder to get ahead than others. Is it circular reasoning to "explain" the difference in terms of more or less achievement motivation?

 Go to **http://psychology.wadsworth.com/ rathus_pcc9e** for an interactive version of this Learning Connections unit.

Emotion: Adding Color to Life

Emotions color our lives. We are green with envy, red with anger, blue with sorrow. Positive emotions such as love and desire can fill our days with pleasure. Negative emotions such as fear, depression, and anger can fill us with dread and make each day a chore.

Question: Just what is an emotion? An emotion can be a response to a situation, in the way that fear is a response to a threat. An emotion can motivate behavior (e.g., anger can motivate us to act aggressively). An emotion can also be a goal in itself. We may behave in ways that will lead us to experience happiness or feelings of love. Emotions are thus intertwined with motivation. We are driven by emotions and meeting—or failing to meet—our needs can have powerful emotional results.

Emotions are feeling states with physiological, cognitive, and behavioral components (Carlson & Hatfield, 1992). In terms of physiology, strong emotions arouse the autonomic nervous system (LeDoux, 1997) (see Chapter 2). The greater the arousal, the more intense the emotion. It also appears that the type of arousal affects the emotion being experienced. Although the word *emotion* might seem to be about feeling and not about thinking, cognitions—particularly interpretations of the meanings of events—are important aspects of emotions. *Fear,* which usually occurs in response to a threat, involves cognitions that one is in danger as well as arousal of the **sympathetic nervous system** (rapid heartbeat and breathing, sweating, mus-

Emotion A state of feeling that has cognitive, physiological, and behavioral components.

Sympathetic nervous system The branch of the autonomic nervous system that is most active during processes that spend body energy from stored reserves, such as in a fight-or-flight reaction to a predator or when you are anxious about a big test. When people experience fear, the sympathetic nervous system accelerates the heart rate, raises the blood pressure, tenses muscles, and so on.

TABLE 10.2 COMPONENTS OF EMOTIONS

Emotion	Physiological	Cognitive	Behavioral
Fear	Sympathetic arousal	Belief that one is in danger	Avoidance tendencies
Anger	Sympathetic and parasympathetic arousal	Frustration or belief that one is being mistreated	Attack tendencies
Depression	Parasympathetic arousal	Thoughts of helplessness, hopelessness, worthlessness	Inactivity, possible self-destructive tendencies

cle tension). Emotions also involve behavioral tendencies. Fear is connected with behavioral tendencies to avoid or escape from a particular situation (see Table 10.2). As a response to a social provocation, *anger* involves cognitions that the provocateur should be paid back, arousal of both the sympathetic and **parasympathetic nervous systems,** and tendencies to attack. *Depression* usually involves cognitions of helplessness and hopelessness, parasympathetic arousal, and tendencies toward inactivity—or, sometimes, self-destruction. *Happiness, grief, jealousy, disgust, embarrassment, liking*—all have cognitive, physiological, and behavioral components.

Parasympathetic nervous system The branch of the autonomic nervous system that is most active during processes that restore reserves of energy to the body, such as relaxing and eating. When people relax, the parasympathetic nervous system decelerates the heart rate, normalizes the blood pressure, relaxes muscles, and so on. The parasympathetic division also stimulates digestion.

The Expression of Emotions: The Smile Seen around the World?

Happiness and sadness are found in all cultures, but, **Question: How can we tell when other people are happy or sad?** It turns out that the expression of many emotions may be universal (Ekman, 2003). Smiling is apparently a universal sign of friendliness and approval. Baring the teeth, as noted by Charles Darwin (1872) in the 19th century, may be a universal sign of anger. As the originator of the theory of evolution, Darwin believed that the universal recognition of facial expressions would have survival value. For example, in the absence of language, facial expressions could signal the approach of enemies (or friends).

Most investigators (e.g., Buss, 1992; Ekman, 2003; Izard, 1994) concur that certain facial expressions suggest the same emotions in all people. Moreover, people in diverse cultures recognize the emotions manifested by certain facial expressions. In a classic study, Paul Ekman (1980) took photographs of people exhibiting anger, disgust, fear, happiness, sadness, and surprise (see Figure 10.4.) He then asked people around the world to indicate what emotions were being depicted. Those queried ranged from European college students to members of the Fore, a tribe that dwells in the New Guinea highlands. All groups, including the Fore, who had almost no contact with Western culture, agreed on the emotions being portrayed.

FIGURE 10.4 Photographs Used in Research by Paul Ekman

Ekman's research suggests that the facial expressions connected with several important emotions such as happiness, anger, surprise, and fear are universally recognized.

 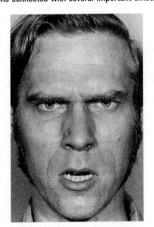  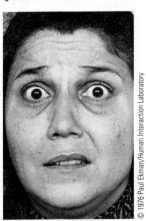

Positive psychology The field of psychology that is about personal well-being and satisfaction; joy, sensual pleasure, and happiness; and optimism and hope for the future.

The Fore also displayed familiar facial expressions when asked how they would respond if they were the characters in stories that called for basic emotional responses. Ekman and his colleagues (1987) obtained similar results in a study of ten cultures. In that study, participants were allowed to identify more than one emotion in facial expressions. The participants generally agreed on which two emotions were being shown and which emotion was more intense.

An interesting study found that women's college yearbook pictures predicted life outcomes as much as 30 years later. LeeAnne Harker and Dacher Keltner (2001) found that women who showed more positive emotions in yearbook photos—as by smiling—were more likely to show social competence, personal well-being, and even happier marriages as the years went by. By the way, their physical attractiveness did not seem to matter; it was the display of positive emotions that told the lifelong tale.

On the other hand, there is no perfect one-to-one relationship between facial expressions and emotions. Facial expressions sometimes occur in the absence of the emotion they are thought to accompany (Camras, 2000). As noted by psychologist Joseph Campos (2000), the voice, posture, and gestures also provide clues as to what people are feeling and about to do.

Many psychologists help individuals cope with negative emotions such as fear, anger, and depression. But psychologists have also studied positive emotions, such as happiness, and considered ways in which you might increase your own feelings of happiness.

■ **Christopher Reeve** The actor, who played *Superman* in several films, turned out not to be invulnerable when he was thrown from a horse. The accident paralyzed Reeve but did not destroy his fighting spirit or his general tendency toward happiness. Researchers into *positive psychology* have learned much about the origins of happiness and other positive emotions (Aspinwall & Staudinger, 2003; Keyes & Haidt, 2003).

"Is Evvvrybody Happy?" An Excursion into Positive Psychology

Ted Lewis, the Great Depression–era bandleader, used to begin his act by asking, "Is evvvvrybody happy?" Well, everybody is not happy, but surveys do suggest that the majority of people in developed nations are satisfied with their lives (Cummins & Nistico, 2002). Many people might think that psychologists are only interested in negative emotions such as anxiety, depression, and anger. Not at all. An area of psychology called **positive psychology** deals with positive emotions such as happiness and love, optimism and hope, and joy and sensual pleasures (Aspinwall & Staudinger, 2003; Hendrick & Hendrick, 2002; Keyes & Haidt, 2003).

Question: What factors contribute to happiness? Are some people just "born happy" or do life experiences determine happiness? What factors interfere with happiness? Some psychologists, such as David Lykken (Lykken & Csikszentmihalyi, 2001), believe that genetic factors play a powerful role in happiness. They note that happiness tends to run in families and that we tend to have a more or less stable level of happiness throughout much of our lives (Easterlin, 2002). Positive events such as learning that the person we love also loves us, or recognition for our work, can certainly raise the level of happiness we experience at the moment. Similarly, negative life events, such as the loss of a loved one, financial reverses, or injuries can depress us—and understandably so. Yet we may tend to bounce back to a more or less characteristic level of happiness, as did the actor Christopher Reeve following the accident—being thrown from a horse—that paralyzed him.

Which life experiences contribute to happiness? **Truth or Fiction Revisited:** Despite the saying that "Money can't buy you happiness," surveys in the United States, Russia, China, and Latin America suggest that people tend to be happier when they live in affluent societies and earn decent incomes (Frey & Stutzer, 2000; Graham & Pettinato, 2001; Schyns, 2001; Tsou & Liu, 2001). It may not be that money makes people happy in itself, but when we have enough money, at least we don't have to worry about money (Cummins, 2000).

U.S. surveys reveal more evidence for a role for social and socioeconomic factors in happiness. For example, European Americans tend to be happier than African Americans, and more educated people tend to be happier than less well educated people (Easterlin, 2001). The persistence of differences according to race and education suggests that socioeconomic circumstances are in fact important contributors to happiness (Easterlin, 2001).

People who are married (Tsou & Liu, 2001) and who have social support (Lu, 1999) tend to be happier than "loners." There is a difference, of course, between loneliness and solitude, and it could be that people who are extraverted (Cheng & Furnham, 2001) and who have the skills to maintain social relationships are generally more capable of finding life satisfaction. Happy people also tend to be open to new experiences; they are more willing to risk becoming involved in new relationships (Rath, 2002).

Research has also suggested that religious people are happier than those who are not, as was found to be the case in a recent study of American and Chinese people (Swinyard et al., 2001). Although having enough money to get by comfortably contributes to life satisfaction, this study found that materialism per se did not contribute to happiness. One's inner life—one's feeling of connectedness to important things outside oneself—was found to be a greater contributor to happiness than material possessions. Chinese college students tend to think about happiness in terms of feelings of contentment, inner harmony, personal achievement, physical wellness, spiritual enrichment, hopefulness about the future, generosity, and self-development (Lu, 2001).

Then there are the attitudinal aspects of happiness (Cheng & Furnham, 2001; Cummins & Nistico, 2002). Numerous studies have shown that people at any income level can make themselves miserable when they compare their incomes to those who bring in more (Schyns, 2001). Happiness also tends to be accompanied by optimism—a cognitive bias toward assuming that things will work out (Aspinwall & Staudinger, 2003; Diener et al., 2000; Keyes & Haidt, 2003). But the "bias" is not groundless, because happy people often believe in their ability to effect change. Thus they try harder. They are also willing to pat themselves on the back for their successes and are not quick to blame themselves when things go wrong. These attitudes contribute to self-esteem, yet another factor in happiness.

"COME ON! GET HAPPY!" A POSSIBLE OR IMPOSSIBLE DREAM? Are there lessons for you in these research findings on happiness? Perhaps. But keep in mind that the studies are correlational; for example, not one of them provided individuals with money to determine whether affluence would affect their mood. Nor did any of them manipulate people's attitudes toward life and measure the outcomes. Still, there might be no harm in placing oneself within the groups of people who are more likely to be happy. Here are some suggestions:

◆ Take advantage of your education to develop knowledge and skills that can help you be free from want. Even if money does not make you happy in itself, it is good not to have to worry about money.

◆ Do not let the fact that other people have more impair your ability to appreciate and enjoy what you have.

◆ Value friendships and other social relationships. Be open to developing new relationships.

◆ Think about the meaning of your life and whether you can make your life more meaningful to yourself.

◆ Consider whether you are generally optimistic or pessimistic about your future. If you are pessimistic, examine the reasons for your pessimism and work to overcome them. If you cannot find reasons for your pessimism, challenge yourself to change your outlook.

◆ Consider whether you blame yourself too much when things go wrong or give yourself too little credit when things go right.

In the following section on the facial-feedback hypothesis, we see that you may also find it worthwhile to "put on a happy face."

Facial-feedback hypothesis The view that stereotypical facial expressions can contribute to stereotypical emotions.

The Facial-Feedback Hypothesis: Does Smiling Make You Happy?

The face has a special place among visual stimuli. Social animals like humans need to be able to differentiate and recognize members of their group and, in people, the face is the most distinctive key to identity (Parr et al., 2000). Faces are also a key to social communication. Facial expressions reflect emotional states, and our ability to "read" these expressions enables us to interact appropriately with other people.

It is known that various emotional states give rise to certain patterns of electrical activity in the facial muscles and in the brain (Cacioppo et al., 1988). But can it work the other way around? The **facial-feedback hypothesis** argues that facial expressions can also affect our emotional state, that the causal relationship between emotions and facial expressions can work in the opposite direction. **Questions: Can smiling give rise to feelings of goodwill? Can frowning produce anger?** Perhaps they can.

Psychological research has yielded some interesting findings concerning the facial-feedback hypothesis. Inducing people to smile, for example, leads them to report more positive feelings and to rate cartoons as more humorous (Basic Behavioral Science Task Force, 1996c; Soussignan, 2002). When induced to frown, they rate cartoons as more aggressive. When they exhibit pain through facial expressions, they rate electric shocks as more painful.

What are the possible links between facial feedback and emotion? One is arousal. Intense contraction of facial muscles such as those used in signifying fear heightens arousal, which, in turn, boosts emotional response. Feedback from the contraction of facial muscles may also induce emotions. Engaging in the "Duchenne smile," characterized by "crow's feet wrinkles around the eyes and a subtle drop in the eye cover fold so that the skin above the eye moves down slightly toward the eyeball" (Ekman, 2003), can induce pleasant feelings (Soussignan, 2002).

You may have heard the British expression "Keep a stiff upper lip" as a recommendation for handling stress. It might be that a "stiff" lip suppresses emotional response—as long as the lip is relaxed rather than quivering with fear or tension. But when the lip is stiffened through strong muscle tension, facial feedback may heighten emotional response.

■ **Is Smiling Caused by Feeling Good, or Does Smiling Cause Us to Feel Good?** Smiling is usually a response to feeling good within, but research into the facial-feedback hypothesis suggests that the act of smiling can also enhance our moods.

Theories of Emotion: "*How* Do You Feel?"

David, 32, is not sleeping well. He wakes before dawn and cannot get back to sleep. His appetite is off, his energy level is low, he has started smoking again. He has a couple of drinks at lunch and muses that it's lucky that any more alcohol makes him sick to his stomach—otherwise, he'd probably be drinking too much, too. Then he thinks, "So what difference would it make?" Sometimes he is sexually frustrated; at other times he wonders whether he has any sex drive left. Although he's awake, each day it's getting harder to drag himself out of bed in the morning. This week he missed one day of work and was late twice. His supervisor has suggested in a nonthreatening way that he "do something about it." David knows that her next warning will not be unthreatening. It's been going downhill since Sue walked out. Suicide has even crossed David's mind. He wonder's if he's going crazy.

David is experiencing the emotion of depression, seriously so. Depression is to be expected following a loss, such as the end of a relationship, but David's feelings have lingered. His friends tell him that he should get out and do things, but David is so down that he hasn't the motivation to do much of anything at all. After much prompting by family and friends, David consults a psychologist who, ironically, also pushes him to get out and do things—the things he used to enjoy. The psychologist also shows David that part of his problem is that sees himself as a failure who cannot make meaningful changes.

Question: How do the physiological, situational, and cognitive components of emotions interact to produce feelings and behavior? Some psychologists argue that physiological arousal is a more basic component of emotional response than cognition and that the type of arousal we experience strongly influences our cognitive appraisal and our labeling of the emotion (e.g., Izard, 1984). For these psychologists, the body takes precedence over the mind. Do David's bodily reactions—for example, his loss of appetite and energy—take precedence over his cognitions? Other psychologists argue that cognitive appraisal and physiological arousal are so strongly intertwined that cognitive processes may determine the emotional response. Are David's ideas that he is helpless to make meaningful changes more at the heart of his feelings of depression?

The "commonsense theory" of emotions is that something happens (a situation) that is cognitively appraised (interpreted) by the person, and the feeling state (a combination of arousal and thoughts) follows. For example, you meet someone new, appraise that person as delightful, and feelings of attraction follow. Or, as in the case of David, a social relationship comes to an end, you recognize your loss, feel powerless to change it, and feel down in the dumps.

However, both historic and contemporary theories of how the components of emotions interact are at variance with this commonsense view. Let us consider a number of theories and see whether we can arrive at some useful conclusions.

THE JAMES–LANGE THEORY A century ago, William James suggested that our emotions follow, rather than cause, our behavioral responses to events. At about the same time this view was also proposed by the Danish physiologist Karl G. Lange. It is therefore termed the James–Lange theory of emotion.

According to James and Lange, certain external stimuli instinctively trigger specific patterns of arousal and action, such as fighting or fleeing (see Figure 10.5, part A). We then become angry *because* we are acting aggressively or become afraid *because* we are running away. Emotions are simply the cognitive representations (or byproducts) of automatic physiological and behavioral responses.

The James–Lange theory is consistent with the facial-feedback hypothesis. That is, smiling apparently can induce

■ **Fear, and Behavior, and Cognitive Appraisal, and . . . Fear!** Yes, this film still from *Godzilla* (1998) may look sort of silly, but it raises the question as to how we experience fear. Do we run from a dangerous stimulus and feel fear as a result? Does a dangerous stimulus trigger fear and running simultaneously? Or do we appraise our situation, decide that it is dangerous, and then feel fear and choose to run away?

CORBIS/SYGMA

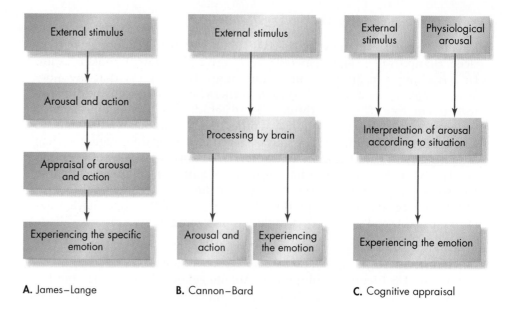

FIGURE 10.5 Theories of Emotion

Several theories of emotion have been advanced, each of which proposes a different role for the components of emotional response. According to the James–Lange theory (part A), events trigger specific arousal patterns and actions. Emotions result from our appraisal of our body responses. According to the Cannon–Bard theory (part B), events are first processed by the brain. Body patterns of arousal, action, and our emotional responses are then triggered simultaneously. According to the theory of cognitive appraisal (part C), events and arousal are appraised by the individual. The emotional response stems from the person's appraisal of the situation and his or her level of arousal.

 Go to **http://psychology.wadsworth. com/rathus_pcc9e** to access an interactive version of this figure.

pleasant feelings, even if the effect may not be strong enough to overcome feelings of sadness (Ekman, 1993). The theory also suggests that we may be able to change our feelings by changing our behavior. Changing one's behavior to change one's feelings is one aspect of behavior therapy. When David's psychologist urges him to get out and do things, she is assuming that by changing his behavior, David can have a positive effect on the way he feels.

Walter Cannon (1927) criticized the James–Lange assertion that each emotion has distinct physiological correlates. He argued that the physiological arousal associated with emotion A is not as distinct from the arousal associated with emotion B as the theory asserts. Note that the James–Lange view downplays the importance of human cognition; it denies the roles of cognitive appraisal, personal values, and personal choice in our behavioral and emotional responses to events.

THE CANNON–BARD THEORY Cannon (1927) was not content to criticize the James–Lange theory. Along with Philip Bard (1934), he suggested that an event might *simultaneously* trigger bodily responses (arousal and action) and the experience of an emotion. As shown in Figure 10.5 (part B), when an event is perceived (processed by the brain), the brain stimulates autonomic and muscular activity (arousal and action) *and* cognitive activity (experience of the emotion). Thus, according to the Cannon–Bard theory, emotions *accompany* bodily responses. They are not *produced by* bodily changes, as in the James–Lange theory.

The central criticism of the Cannon–Bard theory focuses on whether bodily responses (arousal and action) and emotions are actually stimulated simultaneously. For example, pain or the perception of danger may trigger arousal before we begin to feel distress or fear. Also, many of us have had the experience of having a "narrow escape" and becoming aroused and shaky afterward, when we have had time to consider the damage that might have occurred. What is needed is a theory that allows for an ongoing interaction of external events, physiological changes (such as autonomic arousal and muscular activity), and cognitive activities.

THE THEORY OF COGNITIVE APPRAISAL More recent theoretical approaches to emotion have stressed cognitive factors. Among those who argue that thinking comes first are Gordon Bower, Richard Lazarus, Stanley Schachter, Jerome Singer, and Robert Zajonc.

Stanley Schachter asserts that emotions are associated with similar patterns of bodily arousal that may be weaker or stronger, depending on the level of arousal. The label we give to an emotion depends largely on our cognitive appraisal of the situation. Cognitive appraisal is based on many factors, including our perception of external events and the ways in which other people seem to respond to those events (see Figure 10.5, part C). Given the presence of other people, we engage in social comparison to arrive at an appropriate response.

In a classic experiment, Schachter and Singer (1962) showed that arousal can be labeled quite differently, depending on the situation. The investigators told participants that they wanted to determine the effects of a vitamin on vision. Half of the participants received an injection of adrenaline, a hormone that increases the arousal of the sympathetic branch of the autonomic nervous system. A control group received an injection of an inactive solution. Those who had been given adrenaline then received one of three "cognitive manipulations," as shown in Table 10.3. Group 1 was told nothing about possible emotional effects of the "vitamin." Group 2 was deliberately misinformed; members of this group were led to expect itching, numbness, or other irrelevant symptoms. Group 3 was informed accurately about the increased arousal they would experience. Group 4 was a control group injected with an inactive substance and given no information about its effects.

After receiving injections and cognitive manipulations, the participants were asked to wait in pairs while the experimental apparatus was being set up. The participants did not know that the person with whom they were waiting was a confederate of the experimenter. The confederate's purpose was to exhibit a response that the individual would believe was caused by the injection.

Some of those who took part in the experiment waited with a confederate who acted in a happy-go-lucky manner. He flew paper airplanes about the room and tossed paper balls into a wastebasket. Other participants waited with a confederate who acted angry. He complained about the experiment, tore up a questionnaire, and left the waiting room in a huff. As the confederates worked for their Oscar awards, the real participants were observed through a one-way mirror.

The people in groups 1 and 2 were likely to imitate the behavior of the confederate. Those who were exposed to the happy-go-lucky confederate acted jovial and content. Those who were exposed to the angry confederate imitated that person's complaining, aggressive behavior. But those in groups 3 and 4 were less influenced by the confederate's behavior.

Schachter and Singer concluded that participants in groups 1 and 2 were in an ambiguous situation. Members of these groups felt arousal from the adrenaline injection but couldn't label their arousal as any specific emotion. Social comparison with a confederate led them to attribute their arousal either to happiness or to anger. Members of group 3 expected arousal from the injection, with no particular emotional consequences. These participants did not imitate the confederate's display of happiness or anger because they were not in an ambiguous situation; they knew they felt arousal because of the shot of adrenaline. Members of group 4 had no physiological arousal for which they needed an attribution, except perhaps for some arousal induced by observing the confederate. They also did not imitate the behavior of the confederate.

Now, happiness and anger are quite different emotions. Happiness is a positive emotion, whereas anger, for most of us, is a negative emotion. Yet Schachter and

TABLE 10.3 INJECTED SUBSTANCES AND COGNITIVE MANIPULATIONS IN THE SCHACHTER–SINGER STUDY

Group	Substance	Cognitive Manipulation
1	Adrenaline	No information given about effects
2	Adrenaline	Misinformation given: itching, numbness, etc.
3	Adrenaline	Accurate information given: physiological arousal
4	Inactive	None

Source: Schachter & Singer (1962).

Singer suggest that any physiological differences between these two emotions are so slight that different views of the situation can lead one person to label arousal as happiness and another person to label it as anger. The Schachter–Singer view could not be further removed from the James–Lange theory, which holds that each emotion is associated with specific and readily recognized body sensations. The truth, it happens, may lie somewhere in between.

In science, it must be possible to replicate experiments and attain identical or similar results; otherwise, a theory cannot be considered valid. The Schachter and Singer study has been replicated, but with *different* results (Ekman, 1993). For instance, a number of studies found that participants were less likely to imitate the behavior of the confederate and were likely to perceive unexplained arousal in negative terms, attributing it to nervousness, anger, even jealousy (Zimbardo et al., 1993).

EVALUATION What can we make of all this? Research by Paul Ekman (1993) suggests that the patterns of arousal connected with various emotions are more specific than suggested by Schachter and Singer—although less so than suggested by James and Lange. Research with brain imaging suggests that different emotions, such as happiness and sadness, involve different structures within the brain (Goleman, 1995). Moreover, lack of control over our emotions and lack of understanding of what is happening to us are disturbing experiences (Zimbardo et al., 1993). Thus our cognitive appraisals of situations apparently do affect our emotional responses, even if not quite in the way envisioned by Schachter.

In sum, various components of an experience—cognitive, physiological, and behavioral—contribute to our emotional responses. Our bodies may become aroused in a given situation, but as we saw in the classic research of Schachter and Singer, people also appraise those situations so that arousal alone does not appear to directly cause one emotion or another. The fact that none of the theories of emotion we have discussed applies to all people in all situations is comforting. Apparently our emotions are not quite as easily understood, manipulated, or—as in the case of the polygraph—even detected as some theorists have suggested.

Let us now consider a controversy concerning the polygraph or, as it is more commonly know, the lie detector.

CONTROVERSY IN PSYCHOLOGY

Just what do lie detectors detect?

The connection between autonomic arousal and emotions has led to the development of many kinds of lie detectors. Such instruments detect something, but do they detect specific emotional responses that signify lies? Let us take a closer look at the problem of lying.

Lying—for better or worse—is a part of life. A *New York Times* poll found that 60% of American adults believe that it is sometimes necessary to lie, especially to protect people's feelings (Smiley, 2000). Political leaders lie to get elected. Some students lie about why they have not completed assignments (Saxe, 1991). The great majority of people lie to their lovers—most often about other relationships (Rowatt et al., 1999; Saxe, 1991). People also lie about their qualifications to obtain jobs, and, of course, some people lie in denying guilt for crimes. Although we are unlikely to subject political leaders, students, and lovers to lie detector tests, such tests are frequently used in hiring and in police investigations.

Facial expressions often offer clues to deceit, but some people can lie with a straight face—or a smile. As Shakespeare pointed out in *Hamlet,* "One may smile, and smile, and be a villain." The use of devices to detect lies has a long, if not laudable, history:

The Bedouins of Arabia . . . until quite recently required conflicting witnesses to lick a hot iron; the one whose tongue was burned was thought to be lying. The Chinese, it is said, had a similar method for detecting lying: Suspects were forced to chew rice powder and spit it out; if the powder was dry, the suspect was guilty. A variation of this test was used during the Inquisition. The suspect had to swallow a "trial slice" of bread and cheese; if it stuck to the suspect's palate or throat he or she was not telling the truth. (Kleinmuntz & Szucko, 1984, pp. 766–767)

These methods may sound primitive, even bizarre, but they are broadly consistent with modern psychological knowledge. Anxiety about being caught in a lie is linked to arousal of the sympathetic division of the autonomic nervous system. One sign of sympathetic arousal is lack of saliva, or dryness in the mouth. The emotions of fear and guilt are also linked to sympathetic arousal and, hence, to dryness in the mouth.

Questions: How do lie detectors work? How reliable are they? Modern lie detectors, or polygraphs, monitor indicators of sympathetic arousal while a witness or suspect is being examined. These indicators include heart rate, blood pressure, respiration rate, and electrodermal response (sweating) (Figure 10.6). Questions have been raised about the validity of assessing truth or fiction in this way, however (Saxe & Ben-Shakhar, 1999).

The American Polygraph Association claims that use of the polygraph is 85% to 95% accurate. Critics find polygraph testing to be less accurate and claim that it is sensitive to more than lies (Saxe & Ben-Shakhar, 1999). Factors such as tense muscles, drugs, and previous experience with polygraph tests can significantly reduce their accuracy rate. In one experiment, people were able to reduce the accuracy of polygraph-based judgments to about 50% by biting their tongue (to produce pain) or by pressing their toes against the floor (to tense muscles) while being interviewed (Honts et al., 1985). You might thus give the examiner the impression that you are lying even when you are telling the truth, throwing off the test's results. **Truth or Fiction Revisited:** Thus it is true that you might be able to fool a lie detector by wiggling your toes.

Iacono and Lykken (1997) conducted a mail survey of members of the Society for Psychophysiological Research and the General Psychology division of the American Psychological Association. Response rates were high—91% and 74%, respectively. Most respondents replied that polygraph lie detection was not theoretically sound, that claims for its validity were overstated, that people can easily learn to beat the test, and that polygraph results should not be admitted as evidence in courts of law.

It appears that no identifiable pattern of bodily responses pinpoints lying (Fiedler et al., 2002; Saxe & Ben-Shakhar, 1999). Because of validity problems, results of polygraph examinations are no longer admitted as evidence in many courts. Even if

FIGURE 10.6 **What Do "Lie Detectors" Detect?**

The polygraph monitors heart rate, blood pressure, respiration rate, and sweat in the palms of the hands. Is the polygraph sensitive to lying only? Is it foolproof? Because of the controversy surrounding these questions, many courts no longer admit polygraph evidence.

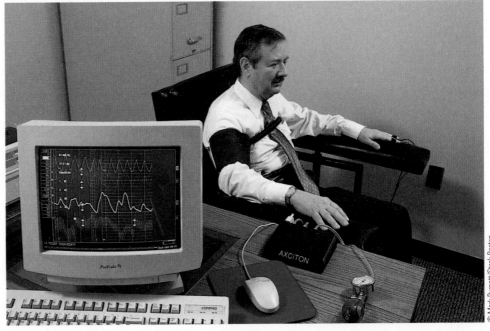

the polygraph is fallible, other research is under way in the development of techniques that could measure certain brain waves to determine whether or not a subject recognizes a photo, a name, or another stimulus, without even asking a question (Miller et al., 2002; Soskins et al., 2001).

Your Turn: Now that we have discussed the psychology of emotion, enhance your mastery of the material with the nearby "Learning Connections." Review the material by filling in the blanks, reflect on the material by relating it to other things you know, and think critically about it.

Learning Connections | EMOTION: ADDING COLOR TO LIFE

ACTIVE REVIEW (26) A(n) _____ is a feeling state. (27) The emotion of anxiety mainly involves arousal of the _____ division of the autonomic nervous system (ANS). (28) The expression of emotions such as anger, fear, happiness, and surprise appears to be (*Culture-specific* or *Universal?*). (29) Genetic factors (*Do* or *Do not?*) appear to be involved in happiness. (30) According to the James–Lange theory, emotions have specific patterns of arousal and _____. (31) According to the theory of _____ appraisal, the emotion a person will experience reflects his or her appraisal of the situation. (32) Polygraphs assess heart rate, blood _____, respiration rate, and electrodermal response (sweating).

REFLECT AND RELATE Have you ever been able to change the way you feel by *doing* something? For example, have you ever purposefully worked yourself up into a rage? Or have you ever done something enjoyable to elevate your mood? How do your personal experiences relate to the various theories of emotion?

CRITICAL THINKING Should lie detectors be used in screening candidates for mortgages or jobs?

 Go to **http://psychology.wadsworth.com/ rathus_pcc9e** for an interactive version of this Learning Connections unit.

- Substitute low-calorie foods for high-calorie foods. Fill your stomach with celery rather than cheesecake and enchiladas. Eat preplanned low-calorie snacks instead of binge eating peanuts or ice cream.
- Take a five-minute break between helpings. Ask yourself "Am I still hungry?" If not, stop eating.
- Avoid temptations that have side-tracked you in the past. Shop at the mall with the Alfalfa Sprout Café, not the Cheesecake Factory. Plan your meal before entering a restaurant. (Avoid ogling that tempting full-color menu.) Attend to your own plate, not to the sumptuous dish at the next table. (Your salad probably looks greener to them, anyhow.) Shop from a list. Walk briskly through the supermarket, preferably after dinner when you're no longer hungry. Don't be sidetracked by pretty packages (fattening things may come in them). Don't linger in the kitchen. Study, watch TV, or write letters elsewhere. Don't bring

fattening foods into the house. Prepare only enough food to keep within your calorie goals.
- Exercise to burn more calories and increase your metabolic rate. Reach for your mate, not your plate (to coin a phrase). Take a brisk walk instead of eating an unplanned snack. Build exercise routines by adding a few minutes each week.
- Reward yourself for meeting calorie goals (but not with food). Imagine how great you'll look in that new swimsuit next summer. Do not go to the latest movie unless you have met your weekly calorie goal. When you meet your weekly calorie goal, put cash in the bank toward a vacation or a new camera.
- Use imagery to help yourself lose weight. Tempted by a fattening dish? Imagine that it's rotten, that you would be nauseated by it and have a sick taste in your mouth for the rest of the day.
- Mentally walk through solutions to problem situations. Consider what you

will do when cake is handed out at the office party. Rehearse your next visit to relatives who tell you how painfully thin you look and try to stuff you with food. Imagine how you will politely (but firmly) refuse seconds and thirds, despite their objections.
- Above all, if you slip from your plan for a day, don't blow things out of proportion. Dieters are often tempted to binge, especially when they rigidly see themselves either as perfect successes or as complete failures or when they experience powerful emotions—either positive or negative. Consider the weekly or monthly trend, not just a single day. Credit yourself for the long-term trend. If you do binge, resume dieting the next day.

Losing weight—and keeping it off—is not easy, but it can be done. Making a commitment to losing weight and establishing a workable plan for doing so are two of the keys.

Want to study on the go? Go to your companion website and download an audio version of this review section to your media player.

Recite—An Active Summary™

1. What are motives, needs, drives, and incentives?

The psychology of motivation is concerned with why people behave in certain ways. Motives are hypothetical states within an organism that propel the organism toward goals. Physiological needs include those for oxygen and food. Psychological needs include those for achievement and self-esteem. Needs give rise to drives; for example, depletion of food gives rise to the hunger drive. An incentive is a desirable object, person, or situation.

2. What is meant by species-specific behaviors?

According to the evolutionary perspective, organisms are born with preprogrammed tendencies—called instincts, species-specific behaviors, or fixed-action patterns (FAPs)—to behave in certain ways in certain situations. FAPs occur in the presence of stimuli called releasers. Psychologists debate whether humans have instincts, and if so, what they are.

3. What is drive-reduction theory?

According to drive-reduction theory, we are motivated to engage in behavior that reduces drives. Primary drives such as hunger and pain are based on the biological makeup of the organism. Acquired drives such as the drive for money are learned. We learn to do what reduces drives. The body has a tendency called homeostasis to maintain a steady state; food deprivation thus leads to the hunger drive and eating, which reduces hunger.

4. Are all motives aimed at the reduction of tension?

Apparently not. Stimulus motives aim to increase rather than decrease the amount of stimulation acting on the organism. Sensory-deprivation studies suggest that inactivity and lack of stimulation are aversive in humans. People and many lower animals have needs for stimulation, activity, exploration, and manipulation. Many psychologists believe that exploration is reinforcing in itself.

5. How does humanistic theory differ from other theories of motivation?

Instincts and drives are mainly defensive, aimed at survival and reproduction. Humanistic psychologists argue that people are self-aware and that behavior can be growth-oriented; people are motivated to strive for self-actualization.

Recite—An Active Summary™

6. What is Maslow's hierarchy of needs?

Maslow hypothesized that people have a hierarchy of needs. Once lower-level needs such as physiological and safety needs are met, people strive to meet needs for love, esteem, and self-actualization.

7. What bodily mechanisms regulate the hunger drive? What psychological processes are at work?

Hunger is regulated by several internal factors, including stomach contractions, blood sugar level, receptors in the mouth and liver, and the hypothalamus. The ventromedial nucleus the hypothalamus functions as a stop-eating center. Damage to the area leads to hyperphagia in rats (gross overweight). The lateral hypothalamus may function as a start-eating center. External stimuli such as the aroma of food can also trigger hunger. Chewing and swallowing provide some satiety.

8. What are the eating disorders?

The eating disorders, anorexia nervosa and bulimia nervosa, involve gross disturbances in normal patterns of eating. Anorexia is characterized by refusal to eat and extreme thinness. Bulimia is characterized by cycles of binge eating and purging, which frequently takes the form of vomiting. Women are more likely than men to develop these disorders.

9. What are the origins of the eating disorders?

The major psychodynamic explanation of the eating disorders is that a conflicted—usually adolescent—female is attempting to remain prepubescent. However, most psychologists look to cultural idealization of the slender female—and the pressure that such idealization places on young women—as the major contributor. Yet we also find that many females with eating disorders have a history of child sexual abuse, and that eating disorders may have a genetic component—perhaps involving perfectionistic personality traits that are expressed through patterns of eating.

10. What have psychologists and other scientists learned about the biological and psychological origins of aggressive behavior?

Many lower animals show instinctive aggressive reactions. Electrical stimulation of part of the hypothalamus triggers stereotypical aggressive behaviors in many animals. Testosterone appears to affect the tendencies to dominate and control other people and is also involved in aggression. Freud believed that accumulating frustrations could trigger explosions, but that catharsis would help prevent them. Cognitive psychologists assert that our behavior is influenced by our values, our interpretation of our situations, and by choice. From the social cognitive perspective, aggressive skills are mainly acquired by the observation. Situational factors that contribute to aggression include membership in a mob and aversive environmental stimuli.

11. Why do some people strive to get ahead?

One reason may be that they have more achievement motivation than others. McClelland studied achievement motivation by means of responses to TAT cards. People with high achievement motivation earn higher grades and more money than people of comparable ability but less achievement motivation. Academic achievement may be motivated by performance or learning goals. Performance goals are tangible rewards, such as getting into graduate school. Learning goals involve the enhancement of knowledge or skills

12. What is an emotion?

An emotion is a state of feeling with physiological, cognitive, and behavioral components. Emotions motivate behavior and also serve as goals. Fear, for example, is connected with arousal of the sympathetic division of the autonomic nervous system, cognitions that one is in danger, and behavioral tendencies to escape.

13. How can we tell when other people are happy or sad?

Facial expressions are one factor in the expression of emotion. According to Ekman, the expression of several basic emotions is recognized in cultures around the world. Darwin believed that universal recognition of facial expressions had survival value.

14. What factors contribute to happiness?

Happiness may have a genetic component, but environmental and attitudinal factors also make their contributions. Affluence helps, and so do social relationships, a sense of meaning, optimism, and self-esteem.

Recite – An Active Summary™

15. Can smiling give rise to feelings of good will? Can frowning produce anger?

Facial expressions might influence one's experience of emotion. The contraction of facial muscles might be influential.

16. How do the physiological, situational, and cognitive components of emotions interact to produce feelings and behavior?

According to the James–Lange theory, emotions are associated with specific patterns of arousal and action that are triggered by certain external events. The emotion follows the behavioral response. The Cannon–Bard theory proposes that processing of events by the brain gives rise simultaneously to feelings and bodily responses; that is, feelings accompany bodily responses. According to Schachter and Singer's theory of cognitive appraisal, emotions are associated with similar patterns of arousal. The emotion a person experiences reflects a person's appraisal of the situation. Research evidence suggests that patterns of arousal are more specific than suggested by the theory of cognitive appraisal, but that cognitive appraisal plays a role in determining our responses to events.

17. How do lie detectors work? How reliable are they?

Lie detectors—also called polygraphs—monitor indicators of sympathetic arousal: heart rate, blood pressure, respiration rate, and sweating while a person is being questioned. These responses are presumed to indicate the presence of emotions—anxiety and/or guilt—that might be caused by lying. Critics find polygraph testing to be unreliable.

 Go to **http://psychology.wadsworth.com/ rathus_pcc9e** to access an interactive version of this active summary.

Key Terms

Motive (p. 364)
Need (p. 365)
Drive (p. 365)
Physiological drives (p. 365)
Incentive (p. 365)
Instinct (p. 366)
Drive-reduction theory (p. 366)
Primary drives (p. 366)

Acquired drives (p. 366)
Homeostasis (p. 366)
Self-actualization (p. 367)
Satiety (p. 369)
Ventromedial nucleus (VMN) (p. 370)
Hyperphagic (p. 370)
Lateral hypothalamus (p. 370)
Aphagic (p. 370)

Eating disorders (p. 371)
Anorexia nervosa (p. 371)
Bulimia nervosa (p. 372)
Emotion (p. 382)
Sympathetic nervous system (p. 382)
Parasympathetic nervous system (p. 383)

Positive psychology (p. 384)
Facial-feedback hypothesis (p. 386)

ACTIVE LEARNING RESOURCES

Visit your Companion Website for Video, Quizzing, and Self-Assessment!

http://psychology.wadsworth.com/rathus_pcc9e
On this site you can access the Anorexia Nervosa video highlighted by the Video Connections icon on p. 372. In addition there are many quizzing opportunities including interactive versions of the fill-in-the-blank Active Review sections in your book. You can also fill out and score the Self-Assessment on p. 368.

Study on the Go!

Don't have time to study right now? You can study on the go! Visit your companion website and download an audio version of the Recite—An Active Summary section to your media player.

ThomsonNOW

http://www.thomsonedu.com
Need help studying? This site is your one-stop study shop. Take a Pre-Test and Thomson NOW will generate a Personalized Study Plan based on your test results. The Study Plan will identify the topics you need to review and direct you to online resources to help you master those topics. You can then take a Post-Test to determine the concepts you have mastered and what you still need to work on.

Author Blog

 What does your author have to say about the state of psychology? Visit your companion website every Tuesday and click on "Author Blog," where he'll talk about the most recent controversies and hot topics in psychology.

Truth or Fiction?

T F Biting one's fingernails or smoking cigarettes as an adult is a sign of conflict experienced during early childhood.

T F Bloodletting and vomiting were once recommended as ways of coping with depression.

T F 2,500 years ago, a Greek physician devised a way of looking at personality that—with a little "tweaking"—remains in use today.

T F Actually, there are no basic personality traits. We are all conditioned by society to behave in certain ways.

T F The most well-adjusted immigrants are those who abandon the language and customs of their country of origin and become like members of the dominant culture in their new host country.

T F Psychologists can determine whether a person has told the truth on a personality test.

T F There is a psychological test made up of inkblots, and test-takers are asked to say what the blots look like to them.

T F You can inherit self-esteem.

 Go to **http://psychology.wadsworth.com/ rathus_pcc9e** to answer and score this Truth or Fiction quiz.

Personality: Theory and Measurement

Preview

College & Career Planning—
Take a Personality Assessment
Explore Suggested Careers & Majors
[The College Board]

Ultimate Personality Test
The Real You: A Scientific Analysis
It's Fun, Accurate & Free!
[From a website called "Tickle"]

Know your Personality—
The Most Detailed Personality Test on the
Internet!

R U HOT?
Does your personality make you Hot?
Take this fun test to find out!

R U NORMAL?
A fun test to see how your personality compares to the rest!

Online testing:
Free information and resources on online testing.

Employment Testing:
Hire right with Brainbench skills, aptitude & personality assessments.

Your Name Is No Accident!
See Why the Amazing Truth of Your Numerology Chart Cannot Tell a Lie

Personality The distinct patterns of behavior, thoughts, and feelings that characterize a person's adaptation to life.

■ **R U Hot?** Because people may want to check out whether they're "hot" now and then, entrepreneurs have posted tests that they claim will give people the answer online. Is "hotness" a common personality trait? Are the tests that measure "hotness" reliable and valid? Stay tuned to this chapter for some answers and speculations.

As a psychologist, almost all of my research in the area of personality involves reading, analyzing, and referencing articles in professional journals. But I, like you, often surf the net—sometimes for useful information, sometimes just for fun. So one day I Googled "personality tests online." I retrieved 27 million hits in 0.28 seconds, a fine indicator that personality assessment is a hot topic. But what about the instruments themselves? There was certainly quantity, but what about quality?

Consider the eight sponsored links shown here. It tickled my funny bone to see the College Board, administrator of the beloved SATs and author of many personality tests that help students choose majors and careers, in the same cyberspace as a website called "Tickle," which offered its own brand. The "ticklish" test consisted of 50 multiple-choice questions. I answered them, but when I had to submit personal info to get the results, I decided to stop there. The website quotes "Mark" of Boston as saying, "I could not believe that the results of my personality test were, 'Mark, you're a rock star.' I've been writing songs on my guitar my entire adult life. How did you know?!" I'll never know whether "Tickle" would have branded me a psychologist–rock star.

Then I checked out the test that promised to answer whether or not I was hot because it was advertised as a "fun test." I completed the multiple-choice questions, one of which asked me whether I'd prefer to meet Ashlee Simpson or Jennifer Aniston. But then the website refused to tell me whether I was steaming hot or just tepid unless I provided my e-mail address. Not. I didn't investigate the test that promised to tell me whether I was normal. It might not have given me the answer I wanted.

Just about every website listed on the first few pages of hits was a dot-com (.com, short for commercial) Web site. They all wanted money but I didn't want any of their information badly enough to pay.

There can be entertainment value in some of these tests and you might even learn a few things about yourself, but later in the chapter we will see that personality tests are not useful unless they can be demonstrated to be *reliable* and *valid*. For now, we will consider the meaning of the term *personality* and the various psychological theories of personality.

Question: Just what is personality? People do not necessarily agree on what the word **personality** means. Many equate personality with liveliness, as in "She's got a lot of personality." Others characterize a person's personality as consisting of one's most striking traits, as in a "shy personality" or a "happy-go-lucky personality." Psychologists define personality as the reasonably stable patterns of emotions, motives, and behavior that distinguish one person from another.

In this chapter, we lay the foundations for the understanding of personality. We see how psychologists seek to explain the development of personality—that is, why some (people) are sad or glad or bad—and to predict how people with certain personality traits respond to life's demands. We explore five perspectives on personality: the psychodynamic, trait, learning, humanistic–existential, and sociocultural perspectives. We also discuss personality tests—the methods used to measure whether people are sad, glad, bad, and lots of other things.

In Chapter 12 we extend our discussion of personality to gender differences in personality and their origins. In Chapter 13 we see how various personality factors help us—or hinder us—in our efforts to cope with stress. In Chapter 14 we consider the connections between personality and psychological disorders.

In Profile **SIGMUND FREUD**

Sigmund Freud (1856–1939) was a mass of contradictions. He has been lauded as one of the greatest thinkers of the 20th century; he has been criticized as overrated. He preached liberal views of sexuality but was himself a model of sexual restraint. He invented a popular form of psychotherapy but experienced lifelong psychologically related problems such as migraine headaches, bowel problems, fainting under stress, hatred of the telephone, and an addiction to cigars. He smoked 20 cigars a day and could not (or would not) break the habit even after he developed cancer of the jaw.

Although he was rejected by his fellow students because of his religion, Freud excelled in medical school at the University of Vienna. His interests lay in neurology and then in psychotherapy. He first practiced hypnotherapy and then developed the method that has had a profound influence on psychology and the arts—psychoanalysis.

Freud saw himself as an outsider. He was born in a small town in the Austro-Hungarian empire at a time when Jews were prevented from holding high offices or practicing most professions. He spent nearly all of his adult life in Vienna, fleeing to England to escape the Nazi threat only a year before his death.

Go to **http://psychology.wadsworth.com/ rathus_pcc9e** to access more information about Sigmund Freud.

© Bettmann/CORBIS

The Psychodynamic Perspective: Excavating the Iceberg

There are several **psychodynamic theories** of personality, each of which owes its origin to the thinking of Sigmund Freud. These theories have a number of features in common. Each teaches that personality is characterized by conflict—by a dynamic struggle. At first the conflict is external: Drives like sex, aggression, and the need for superiority come into conflict with laws, social rules, and moral codes. But at some point laws and social rules are brought inward, or *internalized*. After that the conflict is between opposing *inner* forces. At any given moment our behavior, thoughts, and emotions represent the outcome of these inner contests. **Question: What is Freud's theory of psychosexual development?**

Psychodynamic theory Sigmund Freud's perspective, which emphasizes the importance of unconscious motives and conflicts as forces that determine behavior. *Dynamic* refers to the concept of (psychological) forces being in motion.

Conscious Self-aware.

Preconscious Capable of being brought into awareness by the focusing of attention.

Unconscious In psychodynamic theory, not available to awareness by simple focusing of attention.

Sigmund Freud's Theory of Psychosexual Development

Sigmund Freud was trained as a physician. Early in his practice, Freud was astounded to find that some people apparently experience loss of feeling in a hand or paralysis of the legs in the absence of any medical disorder. These odd symptoms often disappear once the person has recalled and discussed stressful events and feelings of guilt or anxiety that seem to be related to the symptoms. For a long time, these events and feelings have lain hidden beneath the surface of awareness. Even so, they have the capacity to influence behavior.

From this sort of clinical evidence, Freud concluded that the human mind is like an iceberg. Only the tip of an iceberg rises above the surface of the water; the great mass of it is hidden in the depths (see Figure 11.1). Freud came to believe that people, similarly, are aware of only a small portion of the ideas and impulses that dwell within their minds. He argued that a much greater portion of the mind—our deepest images, thoughts, fears, and urges—remains beneath the surface of conscious awareness, where little light illumines them.

Freud labeled the region that pokes through into the light of awareness the **conscious** part of the mind. He called the regions below the surface the *preconscious* and the *unconscious*. The **preconscious** mind contains elements of experience that are out of awareness but can be made conscious simply by focusing on them. The **unconscious** mind is shrouded in mystery. It contains biological instincts such as sex and aggression. Some unconscious urges cannot be experienced consciously because mental images and words could not portray them in all their color and fury. Other unconscious urges may be kept below the surface through repression.

FIGURE 11.1 **The Human Iceberg According to Freud**

According to psychodynamic theory, only the tip of human personality rises above the surface of the mind into conscious awareness. Material in the preconscious can become conscious if we direct our attention to it. Unconscious material tends to remain shrouded in mystery.

Repression is the automatic ejection of anxiety-evoking ideas from awareness. Research evidence suggests that many people repress bad childhood experiences (Myers & Brewin, 1994). Perhaps "something shocking happens, and the mind pushes it into some inaccessible corner of the unconscious" (Loftus, 1993). Repression may also protect us from perceiving morally unacceptable impulses.

In the unconscious mind, primitive drives seek expression, while internalized values try to keep them in check. The conflict can arouse emotional outbursts and psychological problems. To explore the unconscious mind, Freud engaged in a form of mental detective work called **psychoanalysis.** For this reason, his theory of personality is also referred to as *psychoanalytic theory.* In psychoanalysis, people are prodded to talk about anything that pops into their mind while they remain comfortable and relaxed.

THE STRUCTURE OF PERSONALITY Freud spoke of mental or **psychic structures** to describe the clashing forces of personality. Psychic structures cannot be seen or measured directly, but their presence is suggested by behavior, expressed thoughts, and emotions. Freud believed that there are three psychic structures: the id, the ego, and the superego.

The **id** is present at birth. It represents physiological drives and is entirely unconscious. Freud described the id as "a chaos, a cauldron of seething excitations" (1927/1964, p. 73). The conscious mind might find it inconsistent to love and hate the same person, but Freud believed that conflicting emotions could dwell side by side in the id. In the id, one can feel hatred for one's mother for failing to gratify immediately all of one's needs, while also feeling love for her. The id follows what Freud termed the **pleasure principle.** It demands instant gratification of instincts without consideration of law, social custom, or the needs of others.

The **ego** begins to develop during the first year of life, largely because a child's demands for gratification cannot all be met immediately. The ego stands for reason and good sense, for rational ways of coping with frustration. It curbs the appetites of the id and makes plans that fit social conventions. Thus, a person can find gratification yet avoid social disapproval. The id informs you that you are hungry, but the ego decides to microwave enchiladas. The ego is guided by the **reality principle.** It takes into account what is practical along with what is urged by the id. The ego also provides the person's conscious sense of self.

Although most of the ego is conscious, some of its business is carried out unconsciously. For instance, the ego also acts as a censor that screens the impulses of the id. When the ego senses that improper impulses are rising into awareness, it may use psychological defenses to prevent them from surfacing. Repression is one such psychological defense, or **defense mechanism.** Several defense mechanisms are described in Table 11.1.

The **superego** develops throughout early childhood as the child incorporates the moral standards and values of parents and important members of the community. The child does so through **identification,** that is, by trying to become like these people. The superego functions according to the **moral principle.** It holds forth shining examples of an ideal self and also acts like the conscience, an internal moral guardian. Throughout life, the superego monitors the intentions of the ego and hands out judgments of right and wrong. It floods the ego with feelings of guilt and shame when the verdict is negative.

The ego hasn't an easy time of it. It stands between the id and the superego, striving to satisfy the demands of the id and the moral sense of the superego. From the Freudian perspective, a healthy personality has found ways to gratify most of the id's remaining unfulfilled demands without seriously offending the superego. Most of the these demands are contained or repressed. If the ego is not a good problem solver or if the superego is too stern, the ego will have a hard time of it.

According to psychodynamic theory, identification is a means by which people usually incorporate the moral standards and values of parents and important

Repression A defense mechanism that protects the person from anxiety by ejecting anxiety-evoking ideas and impulses from awareness.

Psychoanalysis In this usage, Freud's method of exploring human personality.

Psychic structure In psychodynamic theory, a hypothesized mental structure that helps explain different aspects of behavior.

Id The psychic structure, present at birth, that represents physiological drives and is fully unconscious.

Pleasure principle The governing principle of the id—the seeking of immediate gratification of instinctive needs.

Ego The second psychic structure to develop, characterized by self-awareness, planning, and delay of gratification.

Reality principle Consideration of what is practical and possible in gratifying needs; the governing principle of the ego.

Defense mechanism In psychodynamic theory, an unconscious function of the ego that protects it from anxiety-evoking material by preventing accurate recognition of this material.

Superego The third psychic structure, which functions as a moral guardian and sets forth high standards for behavior.

Identification In psychodynamic theory, the unconscious adoption of another person's behavior.

Moral principle The governing principle of the superego, which sets moral standards and enforces adherence to them.

TABLE 11.1 DEFENSE MECHANISMS

Defense Mechanism	Definition	Examples
Repression	Ejection of anxiety-evoking ideas from awareness.	• A student forgets that a difficult term paper is due. • A person in therapy forgets an appointment when anxiety-evoking material is to be discussed.
Regression	The return, under stress, to a form of behavior characteristic of an earlier stage of development.	• An adolescent cries when forbidden to use the family car. • An adult becomes highly dependent on his parents after the breakup of his marriage.
Rationalization	The use of self-deceiving justifications for unacceptable behavior	• A student blames her cheating on her teacher's leaving the room during a test. • A man explains his cheating on his income tax by saying "Everyone does it."
Displacement	The transfer of ideas and impulses from threatening or unsuitable objects to less threatening objects.	• A worker picks a fight with her spouse after being sharply criticized by her supervisor.
Projection	The thrusting of one's own unacceptable impulses onto others so that others are assumed to have those impulses.	• A hostile person perceives the world as a dangerous place. • A sexually frustrated person interprets innocent gestures as sexual advances.
Reaction formation	Engaging in behavior that opposes one's genuine impulses in order to keep those impulses repressed.	• A person who is angry with a relative behaves in a "sickly sweet" manner toward that relative. • A sadistic individual becomes a physician.
Denial	The refusal to face the true nature of a threat.	• Belief that one will not contract cancer or heart disease even though one smokes heavily. • "It can't happen to me."
Sublimation	The channeling of primitive impulses into positive, constructive efforts.	• A person paints nudes for the sake of "beauty" and "art." • A hostile person becomes a tennis star.

■ **The Oral Stage?** According to Sigmund Freud, during the first year the child is in the oral stage of development. If it fits, into the mouth it goes. What, according to Freud, are the effects of insufficient or excessive gratification during the oral stage? Is there evidence to support his views?

© Laura Dwight/CORBIS

members of the community. As we see in the nearby "Closer Look," "important members of the community" can have a way of including athletic teams.

STAGES OF PSYCHOSEXUAL DEVELOPMENT Freud stirred controversy by arguing that sexual impulses are a central factor in personality development, even among children. Freud believed that sexual feelings are closely linked to children's basic ways of relating to the world, such as sucking on their mother's breasts and moving their bowels.

Freud believed that a major instinct, which he termed **eros,** is aimed at preserving and perpetuating life. Eros is fueled by psychological, or psychic, energy, which Freud labeled **libido.** Libidinal energy involves sexual impulses, so Freud considered it to be *psychosexual*. As the child develops, libidinal energy is expressed through sexual feelings in different parts of the body, or **erogenous zones.** To Freud, human development involves the transfer of libidinal energy from one erogenous zone to another. He hypothesized five periods of **psychosexual development:** oral, anal, phallic, latency, and genital.

During the first year of life a child experiences much of his or her world through the mouth. If it fits, into the mouth it goes. This is the **oral stage.** Freud argued that oral activities such as sucking and biting give the child sexual gratification as well as nourishment.

Freud believed that children encounter conflict during each stage of psychosexual development. During the oral stage, conflict centers on the nature and extent of oral gratification. Early weaning (cessation of breast feeding) could lead to frustration. Excessive gratification, on the other hand, could lead an infant to

Eros In psychodynamic theory, the basic instinct to preserve and perpetuate life.

Libido (1) In psychodynamic theory, the energy of eros; the sexual instinct. (2) Generally, sexual interest or drive.

Erogenous zone An area of the body that is sensitive to sexual sensations.

Psychosexual development In psychodynamic theory, the process by which libidinal energy is expressed through different erogenous zones during different stages of development.

Oral stage The first stage of psychosexual development, during which gratification is hypothesized to be attained primarily through oral activities.

Fixation In psychodynamic theory, arrested development. Attachment to objects of an earlier stage.

Anal stage The second stage of psychosexual development, when gratification is attained through anal activities.

Phallic stage The third stage of psychosexual development, characterized by a shift of libido to the phallic region. (From the Greek *phallos*, referring to an image of the penis. However, Freud used the term *phallic* to refer both to boys and girls.)

Clitoris An external female sex organ that is highly sensitive to sexual stimulation.

expect that it will routinely be given anything it wants. Insufficient or excessive gratification in any stage could lead to **fixation** in that stage and to the development of traits that are characteristic of that stage. Oral traits include dependency, gullibility, and excessive optimism or pessimism.

Freud theorized that adults with an *oral fixation* could experience exaggerated desires for "oral activities," such as smoking, overeating, alcohol abuse, and nail biting. Like the infant whose very survival depends on the mercy of an adult, adults with oral fixations may be disposed toward clinging, dependent relationships.

During the **anal stage,** sexual gratification is attained through contraction and relaxation of the muscles that control elimination of waste products from the body. Elimination, which was controlled reflexively during most of the first year of life, comes under voluntary muscular control, even if such control is not reliable at first. The anal stage is said to begin in the second year of life.

During the anal stage children learn to delay the gratification that comes from eliminating as soon as they feel the urge. The general issue of self-control may become a source of conflict between parent and child. *Anal fixations* may stem from this conflict and lead to two sets of traits in adulthood. So-called *anal-retentive* traits involve excessive use of self-control. They include perfectionism, a strong need for order, and exaggerated neatness and cleanliness. *Anal-expulsive* traits, on the other hand, "let it all hang out." They include carelessness, messiness, even sadism.

Children enter the **phallic stage** during the third year of life. During this stage the major erogenous zone is the phallic region (the penis in boys and the **clitoris** in girls). Parent–child conflict is likely to develop over masturbation, to which parents may respond with threats or punishment. During the phallic stage children may develop strong sexual attachments to the parent of the other sex and begin to view the parent of the same sex as a rival for the other parent's affection.

A Closer Look | WHO'S REALLY "NUMBER ONE"? ON THE "PERSISTENT AMERICAN ITCH TO CREATE HEROES"

Who are the NASCAR fans? Are they us, with "our insatiable craving for celebrity and our ache for fable and our need to live vicariously in the glamour and accomplishment of others and our persistent American itch to create heroes?" (MacGregor, 2005). Or are they, as described in Steve Rushin's pointedly humorous and acerbic *Sports Illustrated* column, "tattooed, shirtless, sewer-mouthed drunks; and their husbands" (Miles, 2005)?

Rushin is being clever, but what, we might ask, have psychologists learned about the appeal of celebrities and especially sports celebrities? Many people form deep and enduring bonds of attachment with athletes and sports teams. Once they identify with a team, their self-esteem rises and falls with the team's wins and losses (Wann et al., 2000). Wins lead to a surge of testosterone in males (Bernhardt et al., 1998), which is connected with aggressiveness and self-confidence. Wins increase the optimism of both males and females.

George Tiedemann/NewSport/CORBIS

■ **NASCAR Hero Dale Earnhardt, Jr.** Why do fans idolize sports heroes and heroines? How do we explain the "persistent American itch to create heroes"?

Psychoanalytic theory suggests that children identify with parents and other "big" people in their lives because big people seem to hold the keys to the resources they need for sustenance and stimulation or excitement. Athletes and entertainers—the rich and famous—have their fan clubs, filled with people who tie their own lights to the brilliant suns of their stars.

Teams and sports heroes provide both entertainment and the kind of gutsy competition that evolutionary psychologists believe whisper to us from our genes, pushing us toward aggression and dominance. If we can't do it on our own, we can do it *through* someone else. In some kind of psychological sense, we can *be* someone who is more effective at climbing the heap of humankind into the sun. Evolutionary psychologists also connect adoration of sports heroes to a time when humans lived in tribes and their warrior-protectors were their true genetic representatives. Today, college and professional athletes may differ from fans in a genetic sense, but fans can still identify with and worship their heroes even while recognizing that it's sort of silly. "Our sports heroes are our warriors," notes Arizona State psychologist Robert Cialdini (2000), who has deeply studied fans' identification with athletes. "The self is centrally involved in the outcome of the event. Whoever you root for represents you."

Children have difficulty dealing with feelings of lust and jealousy. Home life would be tense indeed if they were aware of them. These feelings, therefore, remain unconscious, but their influence is felt through fantasies about marriage with the parent of the other gender and hostility toward the parent of the same gender. In boys, this conflict is labeled the **Oedipus complex,** after the legendary Greek king who unwittingly killed his father and married his mother. Similar feelings in girls give rise to the **Electra complex.** According to Greek legend, Electra was the daughter of the king Agamemnon. She longed for him after his death and sought revenge against his slayers—her mother and her mother's lover.

The Oedipus and Electra complexes are resolved by about the ages of 5 or 6. Children then repress their hostilities toward the parent of the same gender and begin to identify with her or him. Identification leads them to play the social and gender roles of that parent and to internalize his or her values. Sexual feelings toward the parent of the other gender are repressed for a number of years. When the feelings emerge again during adolescence, they are **displaced,** or transferred, to socially appropriate members of the other gender.

Freud believed that by the age of 5 or 6, children have been in conflict with their parents over sexual feelings for several years. The pressures of the Oedipus and Electra complexes cause them to repress all sexual urges. In so doing, they enter a period of **latency,** during which their sexual feelings remain unconscious. During the latency phase it is not uncommon for children to prefer playmates of their own gender.

Freud believed that we enter the final stage of psychosexual development, the **genital stage,** at puberty. Adolescent males again experience sexual urges toward their mother and adolescent females experience such urges toward their father. However, the **incest taboo** causes them to repress these impulses and displace them onto other adults or adolescents of the other gender. Boys might seek girls "just like the girl that married dear old Dad." Girls might be attracted to boys who resemble their fathers.

People in the genital stage prefer to find sexual gratification through intercourse with a member of the other gender. In Freud's view, oral or anal stimulation, masturbation, and sexual activity with people of the same gender all represent *pregenital* fixations and immature forms of sexual conduct. They are not consistent with the life instinct, eros.

Other Psychodynamic Theorists

Several personality theorists are among Freud's intellectual heirs. Their theories, like his, include dynamic movement of psychological forces, conflict, and defense mechanisms. In other respects, their theories differ considerably. **Questions: Who are some other psychodynamic theorists? What are their views on personality?**

CARL JUNG Carl Jung (1875–1961) was a Swiss psychiatrist who had been a member of Freud's inner circle. He fell into disfavor with Freud when he developed his own psychodynamic theory—**analytical psychology.** In contrast to Freud (for whom, he said, "the brain is viewed as an appendage of the genital organs"), Jung downplayed the importance of the sexual instinct. He saw it as just one of several important instincts.

Jung, like Freud, was intrigued by unconscious processes. He believed that we not only have a *personal* unconscious that contains repressed memories and impulses but also an inherited **collective unconscious.** The collective unconscious contains primitive images, or **archetypes,** that reflect the history of our species. Examples of archetypes are the all-powerful God, the young hero, the fertile and nurturing mother, the wise old man, the hostile brother—even fairy godmothers, wicked witches, and themes of rebirth or resurrection. Archetypes themselves remain unconscious, but Jung declared that they influence our thoughts and emotions and cause us to respond to cultural themes in stories and films.

Oedipus complex A conflict of the phallic stage in which the boy wishes to possess his mother sexually and perceives his father as a rival in love.

Electra complex A conflict of the phallic stage in which the girl longs for her father and resents her mother.

Displaced Transferred.

Latency A phase of psychosexual development characterized by repression of sexual impulses.

Genital stage The mature stage of psychosexual development, characterized by preferred expression of libido through intercourse with an adult of the other gender.

Incest taboo The cultural prohibition against marrying or having sexual relations with a close blood relative.

Analytical psychology Jung's psychodynamic theory, which emphasizes the collective unconscious and archetypes.

Collective unconscious Jung's hypothesized store of vague racial memories.

Archetypes Basic, primitive images or concepts hypothesized by Jung to reside in the collective unconscious.

Inferiority complex Feelings of inferiority hypothesized by Adler to serve as a central motivating force.

Drive for superiority Adler's term for the desire to compensate for feelings of inferiority.

Creative self According to Adler, the self-aware aspect of personality that strives to achieve its full potential.

Individual psychology Adler's psychodynamic theory, which emphasizes feelings of inferiority and the creative self.

ALFRED ADLER Alfred Adler (1870–1937), another follower of Freud, also felt that Freud had placed too much emphasis on sexual impulses. Adler believed that people are basically motivated by an **inferiority complex.** In some people, feelings of inferiority may be based on physical problems and the need to compensate for them. Adler believed, however, that all of us encounter some feelings of inferiority because of our small size as children, and that these feelings give rise to a **drive for superiority.** For instance, the English poet Lord Byron, who had a crippled leg, became a champion swimmer. As a child, Adler was crippled by rickets and suffered from pneumonia, and it may be that his theory developed in part from his own childhood striving to overcome repeated bouts of illness.

Adler believed that self-awareness plays a major role in the formation of personality. He spoke of a **creative self,** a self-aware aspect of personality that strives to overcome obstacles and develop the individual's potential. Because each person's potential is unique, Adler's views have been termed **individual psychology.**

KAREN HORNEY Karen Horney (1885–1952) was drummed out of the New York Psychoanalytic Institute because she took issue with the way in which psychoanalytic theory portrayed women. Early in the century, psychoanalytic theory taught that a woman's place was in the home. Women who sought to compete with men in the business world were assumed to be suffering from unconscious penis envy. Psychoanalytic theory taught that little girls feel inferior to boys when they learn that boys have a penis and they do not. Horney argued that little girls do *not* feel inferior to boys and that these views were founded on Western cultural prejudice, not scientific evidence.

Horney was born in Germany and emigrated to the United States before the outbreak of World War II. Trained in psychoanalysis, she agreed with Freud that childhood experiences are important factors in the development of adult personality. Like other neoanalysts, however, she asserted that unconscious sexual and aggressive impulses are less important than social relationships in children's development. She also believed that genuine and consistent love can alleviate the effects of even the most traumatic childhood.

ERIK ERIKSON Like many other modern psychoanalysts, Erik Erikson (1902–1994) believed that Freud had placed undue emphasis on sexual instincts. He asserted that social relationships are more crucial determinants of personality than sexual urges. To Erikson, the nature of the mother–infant relationship is more important than the details of the feeding process or the sexual feelings that might be stirred by contact with the mother. Erikson also argued that to a large extent we are the

© UPI/Bettmann/CORBIS

■ **Karen Horney** Horney, like many of Freud's intellectual descendants, took issue with Freud on many issues. For one thing, Horney did not believe that little girls had penis envy or felt inferior to boys in any other way. She also believed that children's social relationships are more important in their development than unconscious sexual and aggressive impulses.

In Profile   ERIK ERIKSON

Erik Erikson's (1902–1994) natural father deserted his mother before his birth, and the boy was reared by his mother and step-father, a physician named Theodor Homburger. They did not want Erik to feel different, so he was not told about his father for many years. Though his mother and his stepfather were Jewish, Erikson resembled his father, a Dane with blond hair and blue eyes. In his stepfather's synagogue, he looked Christian. To his classmates, he was a Jew. He began to feel different from other children and alienated from his family. He fantasized he was the child of special parents who had abandoned him. The question "Who am I?" permeated his adolescent quest for identity. As he matured, Erikson faced another identity issue: "What am I to do in life?" His stepfather encouraged him to attend medical school, but Erikson sought his own path. As a youth he studied art and traveled through Europe, leading a Bohemian life. Erikson came to label this period of soul-searching an *identity crisis.* As a result of his own search for identity, he became oriented toward his life's work–psychotherapy. He left his wanderings and plunged into psychoanalytic training under the supervision of Sigmund Freud's daughter, Anna Freud.

Despite his grueling search for identity, Erikson appears to have denied his own children information about their family. He and his wife institutionalized their fourth child, Neil, who was born with Down syndrome. But his biographer (Friedman, 1999) writes that the Eriksons told their older children that Neil had died after birth. Perhaps Erikson's upbeat view of life did not prepare him to handle harsh reality, so he pushed it away (Edmundson, 1999).

 Go to **http://psychology.wadsworth.com/ rathus_pcc9e** to access more information about Erik Erikson.

© UPI/Bettmann/CORBIS

conscious architects of our own personalities. His view grants more powers to the ego than Freud did. In Erikson's theory, it is possible for us to make real choices. In Freud's theory, we may think that we are making choices but may actually be merely rationalizing the compromises forced upon us by internal conflicts.

Erikson, like Freud, is known for devising a comprehensive theory of personality development. But whereas Freud proposed stages of psycho*sexual* development, Erikson proposed stages of psycho*social* development. Rather than label stages for various erogenous zones, Erikson labeled them for the traits that might be developed during them (see the Concept Review on page 107 in Chapter 3). Each stage is named according to its possible outcomes. For example, the first stage of **psychosocial development** is labeled the stage of trust versus mistrust because of its two possible outcomes: (1) A warm, loving relationship with the mother (and others) during infancy might lead to a sense of basic trust in people and the world. (2) On the other hand, a cold, ungratifying relationship might generate a pervasive sense of mistrust. Erikson believed that most people would wind up with some blend of trust and mistrust—hopefully more trust than mistrust. A basic sense of mistrust could interfere with the formation of relationships unless it was recognized and challenged.

For Erikson, the goal of adolescence is the attainment of **ego identity,** not genital sexuality. The focus is on who we see ourselves as being and what we stand for, not on sexual interests.

Evaluation of the Psychodynamic Perspective

Psychodynamic theories have tremendous appeal. They involve many concepts and explain many varieties of human behavior and traits. **Question: What are the strengths and weaknesses of the psychodynamic perspective?**

Although today concepts such as "the id" and "libido" strike many psychologists as unscientific, Freud fought for the idea that human personality and behavior are subject to scientific analysis. He developed his theories at a time when many people still viewed psychological problems as signs of possession by the devil or evil spirits, as they had during the Middle Ages. Freud argued that psychological disorders stem from problems within the individual—not evil spirits. His thinking contributed to the development of compassion for people with psychological disorders and methods for helping them.

Psychodynamic theory has also focused attention on the far-reaching effects of childhood events. Freud and other psychodynamic theorists are to be credited for suggesting that personality and behavior *develop* and that it is important for parents to be aware of the emotional needs of their children. **Truth or Fiction Revisited:** However, there is no adequate evidence that biting one's nails in adulthood or smoking cigarettes is a sign of an oral fixation.

Freud has helped us recognize that sexual and aggressive urges are common and that admitting to them is not the same thing as acting on them. As W. Bertram Wolfe put it, "Freud found sex an outcast in the outhouse, and left it in the living room an honored guest."

Freud also noted that people have defensive ways of looking at the world. His defense mechanisms have become part of everyday speech. Whether or not we attribute these cognitive distortions to unconscious ego functioning, our thinking may be distorted by our efforts to avert anxiety and guilt. Because defense mechanisms are unconscious, they have been difficult to assess and were rejected by academic psychologists in the 1950s and 1960s. However, the cognitive revolution of more recent years has again made them the subject of scientific investigation, and cognitive, developmental, and personality psychologists have found some evidence for their existence (Cramer, 2000; Somerfield & McCrae, 2000). The debate is unresolved.

A number of critics note that "psychic structures" such as the id, ego, and superego are too vague to measure scientifically (Hergenhahn, 2001). Nor can they

Psychosocial development Erikson's theory of personality and development, which emphasizes social relationships and eight stages of growth.

Ego identity A firm sense of who one is and what one stands for.

be used to predict behavior with precision. They are little more than useful fictions—poetic ways to express inner conflict.

Nor have the stages of psychosexual development escaped criticism. Children begin to masturbate as early as the first year, not in the phallic stage. As parents know from discovering their children play "doctor," the latency stage is not as sexually latent as Freud believed. Much of Freud's thinking about the Oedipus and Electra complexes remains little more than speculation. The evidence for some of Erikson's developmental views seems somewhat sturdier. For example, people who fail to develop ego identity in adolescence seem to encounter problems developing intimate relationships later on.

Freud's method of gathering evidence from clinical sessions is also suspect (Hergenhahn, 2001). In subtle ways, therapists may influence clients to produce memories and feelings they expect to find. Therapists may also fail to separate what they are told from their own interpretations. Also, Freud and many other psychodynamic theorists restricted their evidence gathering to case studies with individuals who sought help for psychological problems. Their clients were also mostly European and European American and from the middle and upper classes. People who seek therapy differ from the general population.

Your Turn: Now that we have discussed the psychodynamic perspective, enhance your mastery of the material with the nearby "Learning Connections." Review the material by filling in the blanks, reflect on the material by relating it to other things you know, and think critically about it.

Learning Connections THE PSYCHODYNAMIC PERSPECTIVE: EXCAVATING THE ICEBERG

ACTIVE REVIEW (1) Psychodynamic theories of personality teach that personality is characterized by _____ between primitive drives and laws, social rules, and moral codes. (2) According to Freud, the unconscious psychic structure called the _____ is present at birth and operates according to the pleasure principle. (3) The _____ is the sense of self and operates according to the reality principle. (4) The ego uses _____ mechanisms such as repression to protect itself from anxiety. (5) The _____ is the moral sense and develops by internalizing the standards of parents and others. (6) The stages of psychosexual development include the oral, _____, phallic, latency, and genital stages. (7) _____ in a stage may lead to the development of traits associated with the stage. (8) In the Oedipus and Electra complexes, children long to possess the parent of the (*Same* or *Other?*) gender and resent the parent of the same gender. (9) Jung believed that in addition to a personal unconscious mind, people also have a(n) _____ unconscious. (10) Adler believed that people are motivated by a(n) _____ complex. (11) Karen _____, like Freud, saw parent–child relationships as paramount in importance. (12) Erikson extended Freud's five developmental stages to (*How many?*).

REFLECT AND RELATE If you were fixated in a stage of psychosocial development, which stage would it be? Explain.

CRITICAL THINKING If Freud's theory is riddled with scientific shortcomings, why do you think it remains popular in the general population?

 Go to **http://psychology.wadsworth.com/ rathus_pcc9e** for an interactive version of this Learning Connections unit.

The Trait Perspective: The Five-Dimensional Universe

In most of us by the age of thirty, the character has set like plaster, and will never soften again.

William James

The notion of **traits** is very familiar. If I asked you to describe yourself, you would probably do so in terms of traits such as bright, sophisticated, and witty. (That is you, is it not?) We also describe other people in terms of traits. **Question: What are traits?** Traits are reasonably stable elements of personality that are inferred from behavior. If you describe a friend as "shy," it may be because you have observed

Trait A relatively stable aspect of personality that is inferred from behavior and assumed to give rise to consistent behavior.

social anxiety or withdrawal in that person's encounters with others. Traits are assumed to account for consistent behavior in diverse situations. You probably expect your "shy" friend to be retiring in most social confrontations—"all across the board," as the saying goes. The concept of traits is also found in other approaches to personality. Freud linked the development of certain traits to children's experiences in each stage of psychosexual development.

From Hippocrates to the Present

Question: What is the history of the trait perspective? The trait perspective dates back to the Greek physician Hippocrates (ca. 460–377 BCE) and could be even older (Maher & Maher, 1994). It has generally been assumed that traits are embedded in people's bodies, but *how?* Hippocrates believed that traits are embedded in bodily fluids, which give rise to certain types of personalities. In his view, an individual's personality depends on the balance of four basic fluids, or "humors," in the body. Yellow bile is associated with a choleric (quick-tempered) disposition; blood with a sanguine (warm, cheerful) one; phlegm with a phlegmatic (sluggish, calm, cool) disposition; and black bile with a melancholic (gloomy, pensive) temperament. Disease was believed to reflect an imbalance among the humors. Methods such as bloodletting and vomiting were recommended to restore the balance (Maher & Maher, 1994). **Truth or Fiction Revisited:** Therefore, it is true that bloodletting and vomiting were recommended as ways of coping with depression. Although Hippocrates' theory was speculative, the terms *choleric, sanguine,* and so on are still used in descriptions of personality.

More enduring trait theories assume that traits are heritable and are embedded in the nervous system. They rely on the mathematical technique of factor analysis, developed by Charles Spearman to study intelligence (see Chapter 9), to help determine which traits are basic.

Sir Francis Galton was among the first scientists to suggest that many of the world's languages use single words to describe fundamental differences in personality. Nearly 70 years ago, Gordon Allport and a colleague (Allport & Oddbert, 1936) catalogued some 18,000 human traits from a search through word lists like dictionaries. Some were physical traits such as *short, black,* and *brunette.* Others were behavioral traits such as *shy* and *emotional.* Still others were moral traits such as *honest.* This exhaustive list has served as the basis for personality research by many other psychologists. **Question: How have contemporary psychologists reduced the universe of traits to more manageable lists?**

Hans Eysenck's Trait Theory: A Two-Dimensional View

British Psychologist Hans J. Eysenck (1916–1997) developed the first English training program for clinical psychologists and focused much of his research on the relationships between two personality traits: **introversion–extraversion** and emotional stability–instability (Eysenck & Eysenck, 1985). (Emotional *insta*bility is also known as **neuroticism**). Carl Jung was first to distinguish between introverts and extraverts. Eysenck added the dimension of emotional stability–instability to introversion–extraversion. He catalogued various personality traits according to where they are situated along these dimensions or factors (see Figure 11.2). For instance, an anxious person would be high in both introversion and neuroticism—that is, preoccupied with his or her own thoughts and emotionally unstable.

Eysenck acknowledged that his scheme is similar to Hippocrates' system. According to Eysenck's dimensions, the choleric type would be extraverted and unstable; the sanguine type, extraverted and stable; the phlegmatic type, introverted and

Introversion A trait characterized by intense imagination and the tendency to inhibit impulses.

Extraversion A trait characterized by tendencies to be socially outgoing and to express feelings and impulses freely.

Neuroticism Eysenck's term for emotional instability.

■ **Extraverted Individuals?** Hans Eysenck based much of his research on the relationships between two personality traits: introversion–extraversion and emotional stability–instability. Extraversion is characterized by tendencies to be socially outgoing and to freely express feelings and impulses. Some people are mostly extraverted, others mostly introverted, and some are balanced—both outgoing (extraverted) and reflective (introverted).

Denis Felix/Getty Images

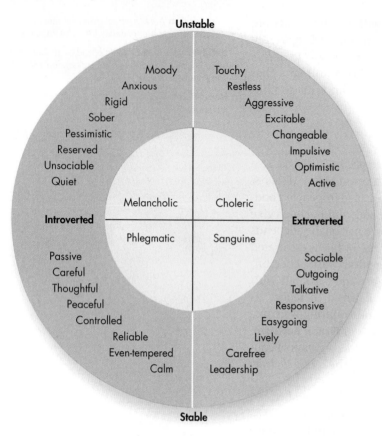

FIGURE 11.2 Eysenck's Personality Dimensions and Hippocrates' Personality Types

Various personality traits shown in the outer ring fall within the two major dimensions of personality suggested by Hans Eysenck. The inner circle shows how Hippocrates' four major personality types–choleric, sanguine, phlegmatic, and melancholic–fit within Eysenck's dimensions.

stable; and the melancholic type, introverted and unstable. **Truth or Fiction Revisited:** It is therefore true that some 2,500 years ago, Hippocrates, the Greek physician, devised a way of looking at personality that could be said to remain in use today.

The "Big Five": The Five-Factor Model

More recent research suggests that there may be five basic personality factors, not two. These include the two found by Eysenck—extraversion and neuroticism—along with conscientiousness, agreeableness, and openness to experience (see Table 11.2). Many personality theorists, especially Robert McCrae and Paul T. Costa, Jr., have played a role in the development of the five-factor model. Cross-cultural research has found that these five factors appear to define the personality structure of American, German, Portuguese, Hebrew, Chinese, Korean, Japanese, and Philippine people (Katigbak et al., 2002; McCrae & Costa, 1997). A study of more than 5,000 German, British, Spanish, Czech, and Turkish people suggests that the factors are related to people's basic temperaments, which are considered to be largely inborn (McCrae et al., 2000). The researchers interpret the results to suggest that our personalities tend to mature rather than be shaped by environmental conditions, although the expression of personality traits is certainly affected by culture. (A person who is "basically" open to new experience is likely to behave less openly in a restrictive society than in an open society.)

The five-factor model—also known as the "Big Five" model—is hot right now. There are hundreds of studies correlating scores on the five factors, according to a psychological test constructed by Costa and McCrae (the *NEO Five-Factor Inventory*), with various behavior patterns, psychological disorders, and kinds of "personalities." Consider driving. Significant negative correlations have been found between the numbers of tickets people get and accidents people get into, on the one hand, and the factor of agreeableness on the other (Cellar et al., 2000). As we have long suspected, it's safer to share the freeway with agreeable people. People who are not judgmental—who will put up with your every whim, like puppy dogs—tend to score low on conscientiousness (they don't examine you too closely) and high on agreeableness (you can be yourself; that's cool) (Bernardin et al., 2000). A firm handshake is positively correlated with extraversion and negatively correlated with neuroticism (Chaplin et al., 2000).

TABLE 11.2 THE "BIG FIVE": THE FIVE-FACTOR MODEL

Factor	Name	Traits
I	Extraversion	Contrasts talkativeness, assertiveness, and activity with silence, passivity, and reserve
II	Agreeableness	Contrasts kindness, trust, and warmth with hostility, selfishness, and distrust
III	Conscientiousness	Contrasts organization, thoroughness, and reliability with carelessness, negligence, and unreliability
IV	Neuroticism	Contrasts nervousness, moodiness, and sensitivity to negative stimuli with coping ability
V	Openness to experience	Contrasts imagination, curiosity, and creativity with shallowness and lack of perceptiveness

 A Closer Look | VIRTUOUS TRAITS—POSITIVE PSYCHOLOGY AND TRAIT THEORY

Curious. Open-minded. Persistent. Zestful. Kind. Fair. Modest. Hopeful. Humorous. That's you, isn't it?

Trait theory has recently found applications within positive psychology, a field that studies character strengths and virtues such as those just listed—how they come into being and how they are related to life satisfaction. Psychologists are also developing psychological methods that help people increase their happiness and life satisfaction.

Christopher Peterson and Martin E. P. Seligman (2004) summarized many of these research findings in their book, *Character Strengths and Virtues: A Handbook and Classification* (the *CSV*). The handbook lists six major virtues that were found in 40 different countries as different as Azerbaijan and Venezuela, along with the United States and other developed nations.

◆ *Wisdom and knowledge:* Creativity, curiosity, open-mindedness, love of learning, perspective (ability to provide other people with sound advice)
◆ *Courage:* Authenticity (speaking one's mind), bravery, persistence, zest
◆ *Humanity:* Kindness, love, social intelligence
◆ *Justice:* Fairness, leadership, teamwork
◆ *Temperance:* Forgiveness, modesty, prudence, self-regulation
◆ *Transcendence:* Appreciation of beauty and excellence, gratitude (when appropriate), hope, humor, religiosity (having a belief system about the meaning of life)

These virtues were traitlike in that they were reasonably stable individual differences (Seligman et al., 2005). Research has also found that these virtues are related to life satisfaction and personal fulfillment (Peterson et al., 2005). These virtues are also defined by a number of character strengths. The strengths of zest, gratitude, hope, and love were most closely related to life satisfaction. Although the researchers did not isolate the causes of the development of these virtues, they did find that they were widely recognized and valued, despite cultural and religious differences, and that they were generally promoted by institutions in the cultures studied (Park et al., 2005).

Evaluation of the Trait Perspective

Trait theories, like psychodynamic theories, have their pluses and minuses. **Question: What are the strengths and weaknesses of trait theory?** Trait theorists have focused much attention on the development of personality tests. They have also given rise to theories about the fit between personality and certain kinds of jobs (Holland, 1996). The qualities that suit a person for various kinds of work can be expressed in terms of abilities, personality traits, and interests.

One limitation of trait theory is that it has tended to be more descriptive than explanatory. It has historically focused on describing traits rather than on tracing their origins or finding out how they may be modified.

Your Turn: Now that we have discussed the trait perspective, enhance your mastery of the material with the nearby "Learning Connections." Review the material by filling in the blanks, reflect on the material by relating it to other things you know, and think critically about it.

Video Connections—Personality Theory and Measurement The "person-in-the-situation" phenomenon offers one explanation of why we may be shy in one situation and uninhibited in another. Go to your student website and click on "Personality Theories and Measurement" to watch a video that discusses patterns of behavior, personality traits, and how to understand "if-then" signatures.

 Learning Connections | THE TRAIT PERSPECTIVE: THE FIVE-DIMENSIONAL UNIVERSE

ACTIVE REVIEW (13) _____ are personality elements that endure and account for behavioral consistency. (14) Eysenck used factor analysis to derive two basic traits: introversion–extraversion and emotional _____. (15) Five-factor theory suggests that there are five basic personality factors: introversion–extraversion, emotional stability, _____, agreeableness, and openness to experience.

REFLECT AND RELATE How would you describe yourself in terms of traits? Where would you place yourself in

Eysenck's two-dimensional scheme? Where would you stand, according to the five-factor model? Are you pleased with your self-evaluation? Why or why not?

CRITICAL THINKING The trait theories of Hippocrates and Eysenck are similar. Is one more scientific than the other?

 Go to **http://psychology.wadsworth.com/ rathus_pcc9e** for an interactive version of this Learning Connections unit.

Learning-Theory Perspectives: All the Things You Do

Trait theory focused on enduring personality characteristics that were generally presumed to be embedded in the nervous system. Learning theorists tend not to theorize in terms of traits. They focus, instead, on behaviors and presume that those behaviors are largely learned. That which is learned is also, in principle, capable of being unlearned. As a result, learning theory and personality theory may not be a perfect fit. Nevertheless, learning theorists—both behaviorists and social cognitive theorists—have contributed to the discussion of personality. **Question: What does behaviorism contribute to our understanding of personality?**

Behaviorism: On Being Easy in One's Harness?

In 1924, at Johns Hopkins University, John B. Watson raised the battle cry of the behaviorist movement:

> Give me a dozen healthy infants, well-formed, and my own specified world to bring them up in and I'll guarantee to take any one at random and train him to become any type of specialist I might suggest—doctor, lawyer, merchant-chief and, yes, even beggar-man and thief, regardless of his talents, penchants, tendencies, abilities, vocations, and the race of his ancestors. (p. 82)

This proclamation underscores the behaviorist view that personality is plastic—that situational variables or environmental influences, not internal, individual variables, are the key shapers of human preferences and behaviors. In contrast to the psychoanalysts and structuralists of his day, Watson argued that unseen, undetectable mental structures must be rejected in favor of that which can be seen and measured. Furthermore, Watson's view is extreme and inconsistent with evidence that suggests that personality traits are to some degree heritable. Nevertheless, in the 1930s Watson's battle cry was taken up by B. F. Skinner, who agreed that psychologists should avoid trying to see into the "black box" of the organism and instead emphasized the effects that reinforcements have on behavior.

The views of Watson and Skinner largely ignored the notions of personal freedom, choice, and self-direction. Most of us assume that our wants originate within us. Watson and Skinner suggested that environmental influences such as parental approval and social custom shape us into *wanting* certain things and *not wanting* others.

In his novel *Walden Two,* Skinner (1948) described a Utopian society in which people are happy and content because they are allowed to do as they please. However, from early childhood, they have been trained or conditioned to be cooperative. Because of their reinforcement histories, they *want* to behave in decent, kind, and unselfish ways. They see themselves as free because society makes no effort to force them to behave in particular ways. The American poet Robert Frost wrote "You have freedom when you're easy in your harness." Society in Skinner's Walden Two made children "easy" in their "harnesses," but the harnesses existed.

Some object to behaviorist notions because they play down the importance of consciousness and choice. Others argue that humans are not blindly ruled by pleasure and pain. In some circumstances people have rebelled against the so-called necessity of survival by choosing pain and hardship over pleasure, or death over life. Many people have sacrificed their own lives to save those of others. The behaviorist defense might be that the apparent choice of pain or death is forced on altruistic individuals just as conformity to social custom is forced on others. The altruist is also shaped by external influences, even if those influences differ from those that affect most people.

■ **What Does This Child Want, and Why Does He Want It?**
According to B. F. Skinner, societies socialize individuals into *wanting* what is good for society. Are the music, the color, and all the excitement socializing this child into wanting to belong to the group?

© Ariel Skelley/CORBIS

Social Cognitive Theory: Is Determinism a Two-Way Street?

Social cognitive theory[1] is a contemporary view of learning developed by Albert Bandura (1986, 1999, 2002) and other psychologists (e.g., Mischel & Shoda, 1995). It focuses on the importance of learning by observation and on the cognitive processes that underlie individual differences. **Question: How does social cognitive theory differ from the behaviorist view?** Social cognitive theorists differ from behaviorists in that they see people as influencing their environment just as their environment influences them. Bandura terms this mutual pattern of influence **reciprocal determinism.** Social cognitive theorists agree with behaviorists and other empirical psychologists that discussions of human nature should be tied to observable experiences and behaviors. They assert, however, that variables within people—which they call **person variables**—must also be considered if we are to understand them.

One goal of psychological theories is the prediction of behavior. We cannot predict behavior from situational variables alone. Whether a person will behave in a certain way also depends on the person's **expectancies** about the outcomes of that behavior and the perceived or **subjective values** of those outcomes.

To social cognitive theorists, people are not simply at the mercy of the environment. Instead, they are self-aware and purposefully engage in learning. They seek to learn about their environment and to alter it in order to make reinforcers available.

OBSERVATIONAL LEARNING Observational learning (also termed **modeling** or *cognitive learning*) is one of the foundations of social cognitive theory. It refers to acquiring knowledge by observing others. For operant conditioning to occur, an organism must first engage in a response, and that response must then be reinforced. But observational learning occurs even when the learner does not perform the observed behavior. Therefore, direct reinforcement is not required either. Observing others extends to reading about them or seeing what they do and what happens to them in books, TV, radio, and film.

Our expectations stem from our observations of what happens to ourselves and other people. For example, teachers are more likely to call on males and are more accepting of "calling out" in class by males than by females (Sadker & Sadker, 1994). As a result, many males expect to be rewarded for calling out. Females, however, may learn that they will be reprimanded for behaving in what some might term an "unladylike" manner.

Social cognitive theorists believe that behavior reflects person variables and situational variables. Person variables include competencies, encoding strategies, expectancies, emotions, and self-regulatory systems and plans (Bandura & Locke, 2003; Mischel & Shoda, 1995; see Figure 11.3).

COMPETENCIES: WHAT CAN YOU DO? **Competencies** include knowledge of rules that guide conduct, concepts about ourselves and other people, and skills. Knowledge of the physical world and of cultural codes of conduct are important competencies. So are academic skills such as reading and writing, physical skills such as swimming and tossing a football, social skills such as knowing how to ask someone out, and many others. Individual differences in competencies reflect genetic variation, learning opportunities, and other environmental factors.

Social cognitive theory A cognitively oriented learning theory in which observational learning and person variables such as values and expectancies play major roles in individual differences.

Reciprocal determinism Bandura's term for the social cognitive view that people influence their environment just as their environment influences them.

Person variables Factors within the person, such as expectancies and competencies, that influence behavior.

Expectancies Personal predictions about the outcomes of potential behaviors.

Subjective value The desirability of an object or event.

Model In social cognitive theory, an organism that exhibits behaviors that others will imitate or acquire through observational learning.

Competencies Knowledge and skills.

FIGURE 11.3 **Person Variables and Situational Variables in Social Cognitive Theory**
According to social cognitive theory, person variables and situational variables interact to influence behavior.

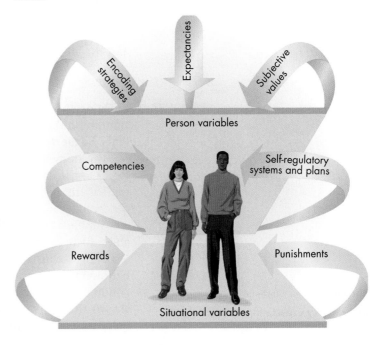

[1]The name of this theory is in flux. It was formerly referred to as social–learning theory. Today it is also sometimes referred to as *cognitive social theory* (Miller et al., 1996).

© Dimitri lundt/CORBIS

■ **How Do Competencies Contribute to Performance?** What factors contribute to this girl's performance? Individual differences in competencies stem from variations in genetic endowment, nutrition, and learning opportunities.

ENCODING STRATEGIES: HOW DO YOU SEE IT? Different people **encode** (symbolize or represent) similar stimuli in different ways. Encoding strategies affect their feelings and behavior. One person might encode a tennis game as a chance to have some fun. Another might encode the game as a demand to perfect his or her serve. Some people make themselves miserable by encoding events in self-defeating ways, as in encoding an unsuccessful date as a sign of their social incompetence. Others might encode the date as simply showing that not all people are "made for each other." Cognitive therapists foster adjustment by challenging people to view life in more optimistic ways.

EXPECTANCIES: WHAT WILL HAPPEN? There are various kinds of expectancies. Some are predictions about what will follow various stimuli or signs. For example, some people predict other people's behavior on the basis of signs such as "tight lips" or "shifty eyes" (Ross & Nisbett, 1991). Other expectancies involve what will happen if we engage in certain behaviors. **Self-efficacy expectations** are beliefs that we can accomplish certain things, such as speaking before a group, doing a backflip into a swimming pool, or solving math problems (Bandura et al., 2001; Bandura & Locke, 2003).

People with positive self-efficacy expectations have higher self-esteem (Sanna & Meier, 2000) and are more likely to try difficult tasks than people who do not believe that they can master those tasks (Heimpel et al., 2002). Lack of self-efficacy may be associated with depression and hopelessness (Bandura et al., 1999, 2001). Psychotherapy often motivates people to try new things by changing their self-efficacy expectations from "I can't" to "Perhaps I can" (Bandura, 1999).

EMOTIONS: HOW DOES IT FEEL? Because of our experiences, situations arouse various feelings in us—anxiety, depression, fear, hope, and delight. What frightens one person may entice another. What bores one person may excite another. From the social cognitive perspective, in contrast to the behaviorist perspective, we are not controlled by stimuli. Instead, stimuli arouse feelings in us, and feelings affect our behavior. For example, hearing Chopin may make one person weep and another person switch to a rock 'n' roll station.

SELF-REGULATORY SYSTEMS AND PLANS: HOW CAN YOU ACHIEVE IT? We tend to regulate our own behavior, even in the absence of observers and external constraints. We set our own goals and standards. We make plans to achieve them. We congratulate or criticize ourselves, depending on whether or not we succeed (Bandura & Locke, 2003). We can select the situations to which we expose ourselves and the arenas in which we will compete.

Evaluation of the Learning Perspective

Learning theorists have made monumental contributions to the scientific understanding of behavior, but they have left some psychologists dissatisfied. **Question: What are the strengths and weaknesses of learning theories as they apply to personality?**

Psychodynamic theorists and trait theorists propose the existence of psychological structures that cannot be seen and measured directly. Learning theorists—particularly behaviorists—have dramatized the importance of referring to publicly observable variables, or behaviors, if psychology is to be accepted as a science.

Similarly, psychodynamic theorists and trait theorists focus on internal variables such as unconscious conflict and traits to explain and predict behavior. Learning theorists emphasize the importance of environmental conditions, or situational variables, as determinants of behavior. They have also elaborated on the conditions that foster learning—even automatic kinds of learning. They have shown that we can learn to do things because of reinforcements and that many behavior patterns are acquired by observing others.

Encode Interpret; transform.

Self-efficacy expectations Beliefs to the effect that one can handle a task.

Self-Assessment — Will You Be a Hit or a Miss? The Expectancy for Success Scale

Life is filled with opportunities and obstacles. What happens when you are faced with a difficult challenge? Do you rise to meet it, or do you back off? Social cognitive theorists note that our self-efficacy expectancies influence our behavior. When we believe that we are capable of succeeding through our own efforts, we marshal our resources and apply ourselves.

The following scale, created by Fibel and Hale (1978) can give you insight as to whether you believe that your own efforts are likely to meet with success. You can compare your own expectancies for success with those of other undergraduates taking psychology courses by turning to the scoring key in the appendix.

Directions: Indicate the degree to which each item applies to you by circling the appropriate number, according to this key:

1 = highly improbable
2 = improbable
3 = equally improbable and probable, not sure
4 = probable
5 = highly probable

IN THE FUTURE I EXPECT THAT I WILL:

1. Find that people don't seem to understand what I'm trying to say — 1 2 3 4 5
2. Be discouraged about my ability to gain the respect of others — 1 2 3 4 5
3. Be a good parent — 1 2 3 4 5
4. Be unable to accomplish my goals — 1 2 3 4 5
5. Have a stressful marital relationship — 1 2 3 4 5
6. Deal poorly with emergency situations — 1 2 3 4 5
7. Find my efforts to change situations I don't like are ineffective — 1 2 3 4 5
8. Not be very good at learning new skills — 1 2 3 4 5
9. Carry through my responsibilities successfully — 1 2 3 4 5
10. Discover that the good in life outweighs the bad — 1 2 3 4 5
11. Handle unexpected problems successfully — 1 2 3 4 5
12. Get the promotions I deserve — 1 2 3 4 5
13. Succeed in the projects I undertake — 1 2 3 4 5
14. Not make any significant contributions to society — 1 2 3 4 5
15. Discover that my life is not getting much better — 1 2 3 4 5
16. Be listened to when I speak — 1 2 3 4 5
17. Discover that my plans don't work out too well — 1 2 3 4 5
18. Find that no matter how hard I try, things just don't turn out the way I would like — 1 2 3 4 5
19. Handle myself well in whatever situation I'm in — 1 2 3 4 5
20. Be able to solve my own problems — 1 2 3 4 5
21. Succeed at most things I try — 1 2 3 4 5
22. Be successful in my endeavors in the long run — 1 2 3 4 5
23. Be very successful working out my personal life — 1 2 3 4 5
24. Experience many failures in my life — 1 2 3 4 5
25. Make a good first impression on people I meet for the first time — 1 2 3 4 5
26. Attain the career goals I have set for myself — 1 2 3 4 5
27. Have difficulty dealing with my superiors — 1 2 3 4 5
28. Have problems working with others — 1 2 3 4 5
29. Be a good judge of what it takes to get ahead — 1 2 3 4 5
30. Achieve recognition in my profession — 1 2 3 4 5

Source: "The Generalized Expectancy for Success Scale," B. Fibel and W. D. Hale, *Journal of Consulting and Clinical Psychology*, Vol. 46, 1978, pp. 924–931. Copyright © 1978 by the American Psychological Association. Reprinted by permission.

On the other hand, behaviorism is limited in its ability to explain personality. Behaviorism does not describe, explain, or suggest the richness of inner human experience. We experience thoughts and feelings and browse our inner maps of the world, but behaviorism does not deal with these. To be fair, the limitations of behaviorism are self-imposed. Personality theorists have traditionally dealt with thoughts, feelings, and behavior, whereas behaviorism, which studies only that which is observable and measurable, deals with behavior alone.

Critics of social cognitive theory cannot accuse its supporters of denying the importance of cognitive activity and feelings. But they often contend that social cognitive theory has not come up with satisfying statements about the development of traits or accounted for self-awareness. Also, social cognitive theory—like its intellectual forebear, behaviorism—may not pay enough attention to genetic variation in explaining individual differences in behavior. Learning theories have done very little to account for the development of traits or personality types. **Truth or Fiction Revisited:** Actually, there may be some basic personality traits, as suggested by trait theory. We may be conditioned by society to behave in certain ways, but conditioning is unlikely to fully explain individual differences in personality.

Your Turn: Now that we have discussed learning-theory perspectives, enhance your mastery of the material with the nearby "Learning Connections." Review the material by filling in the blanks, reflect on the material by relating it to other things you know, and think critically about it.

Learning Connections: LEARNING-THEORY PERSPECTIVES: ALL THE THINGS YOU DO

ACTIVE REVIEW (16) The behaviorists John B. Watson and B. F. Skinner argued that _____ contingencies shape people into wanting to do the things that are required of them. (17) _____ cognitive theory argues that people can shape the environment and learn by intention. (18) Social cognitive theorists believe that we must consider situational and _____ variables to predict behavior. (19) _____ variables include competencies, which refer to knowledge and skills; encoding strategies; expectancies; emotions; and self-regulatory systems and plans.

REFLECT AND RELATE Self-efficacy is a key concept in social cognitive theory. Do you expect that you will succeed? Do you believe in your abilities? How do your attitudes toward yourself affect your self-esteem and your behavior?

CRITICAL THINKING In *Walden Two,* children are conditioned to *want* what is good for the group. Given the cultural and social conditioning we experience as we develop, do you think that true freedom is possible? Could it be that free will is merely an illusion? Explain your views.

 Go to **http://psychology.wadsworth.com/ rathus_pcc9e** for an interactive version of this Learning Connections unit.

The Humanistic–Existential Perspective: How Becoming?

You are unique, and if that is not fulfilled, then something has been lost.
Martha Graham

Humanists and existentialists dwell on the meaning of life. Self-awareness is the hub of the humanistic–existential search for meaning. **Questions: What is humanism? What is existentialism?**

The term **humanism** has a long history and many meanings. It became a third force in American psychology in the 1950s and 1960s, partly in response to the predominant psychodynamic and behavioral models. Humanism puts people and self-awareness at the center of consideration and argues that they are capable of free choice, self-fulfillment, and ethical behavior. Humanism also represented a reaction to the "rat race" spawned by industrialization and automation. Humanists felt that work on assembly lines produced "alienation" from inner sources of meaning. The humanistic views of Abraham Maslow and Carl Rogers emerged from these concerns.

Existentialism in part reflects the horrors of mass destruction of human life through war and genocide, frequent events in the 20th century. The European existentialist philosophers Jean-Paul Sartre and Martin Heidegger saw human life as trivial in the grand scheme of things. But psychiatrists like Viktor Frankl, Ludwig Binswanger, and Medard Boss argued that seeing human existence as meaningless could give rise to withdrawal and apathy—even suicide. Psychological salvation therefore requires giving personal meaning to things and making personal choices.

Humanism The view that people are capable of free choice, self-fulfillment, and ethical behavior.

Existentialism The view that people are completely free and responsible for their own behavior.

Yes, there is pain in life, and yes, sooner or later life ends, but people can see the world for what it is and make genuine choices.

Freud argued that defense mechanisms prevent us from seeing the world as it is. Therefore, the concept of free choice is meaningless. Behaviorists view freedom as an illusion determined by social forces. Social cognitive theorists also speak of external or situational forces that influence us. To existentialists, we are really and painfully free to do what we choose with our lives. Moreover, the meaning of our lives is the meaning that we give to our lives.

Abraham Maslow and the Challenge of Self-Actualization

Humanists see Freud as preoccupied with the "basement" of the human condition. Freud wrote that people are basically motivated to gratify biological drives and that their perceptions are distorted by their psychological needs. **Question: How do humanistic psychologists differ from psychodynamic theorists?** The humanistic psychologist Abraham Maslow argued that people also have a conscious need for **self-actualization**—to become all that they can be—and that people can see the world as it is. Because people are unique, they must follow unique paths to self-actualization. People are not at the mercy of unconscious, primitive impulses. Rather, one of the main threats to individual personality development is control by other people. We must each be free to get in touch with and actualize our selves. But self-actualization requires taking risks.

Manchau/Getty Images

■ **Being Unique** According to humanistic psychologists like Carl Rogers, each of us views the world from a unique frame of reference. What matters to one person may mean little to another.

Self-actualization In humanistic theory, the innate tendency to strive to realize one's potential.

Many people prefer to adhere to the tried and . . . what may be untrue for them. But people who adhere to the "tried and true" may find their lives degenerating into monotony and predictability.

Let us learn more about the nature of the self by examining Carl Rogers's self theory. Rogers offers insights into the ways in which the self develops—or fails to develop—in the real social world.

Carl Rogers's Self Theory

The humanistic psychologist Carl Rogers (1902–1987) wrote that people shape themselves through free choice and action. **Question: What is your self?** Rogers defined the *self* as the center of experience. Your self is your ongoing sense of who and what you are, your sense of how and why you react to the environment and how you choose to act on the environment. Your choices are made on the basis of your values, and your values are also part of your self. **Question: What is self theory?** Rogers's self theory focuses on the nature of the self and the conditions that allow the self to develop freely. Two of his major concerns are the self-concept and self-esteem.

THE SELF-CONCEPT AND FRAMES OF REFERENCE Our self-concepts consist of our impressions of ourselves and our evaluations of our adequacy. It may be helpful to think of us as rating ourselves according to various scales or dimensions such as good–bad, intelligent–unintelligent, strong–weak, and tall–short.

Rogers believed that we all have unique ways of looking at ourselves and the world—that is, unique **frames of reference.** It may be that we each use a different set of dimensions in defining ourselves and that we judge ourselves according to different sets of values. To one person, achievement–failure may be the most important dimension. To another person, the most important dimension may be decency–indecency. A third person may not even think in terms of decency.

SELF-ESTEEM AND POSITIVE REGARD Rogers assumed that we all develop a need for self-regard, or self-esteem, as we develop and become aware of ourselves. At first, self-esteem reflects the esteem in which others hold us. Parents help children develop self-esteem when they show them **unconditional positive regard**—that is, when they accept them as having intrinsic merit regardless of their behavior at the moment. But when parents show children **conditional positive regard**—that is, when they accept them only when they behave in a desired manner—children may develop **conditions of worth.** Therefore, children may come to think that they have merit only if they behave as their parents wish them to behave. The chapter's "Life Connections" section has more information on the origins of self-esteem along with suggestions as to how you can raise your own self-esteem.

Because each individual is thought to have a unique potential, children who develop conditions of worth must be somewhat disappointed in themselves. We cannot fully live up to the wishes of others and remain true to ourselves. This does not mean that the expression of the self inevitably leads to conflict. Rogers was optimistic about human nature. He believed that we hurt others or act in antisocial ways only when we are frustrated in our efforts to develop our potential. But when parents and others are loving and tolerant of our differentness, we, too, are loving—even if some of our preferences, abilities, and values differ from those of our parents.

However, children in some families learn that it is bad to have ideas of their own, especially about sexual, political, or religious matters. When they perceive their caregivers' disapproval, they may come to see themselves as rebels and label their feelings as selfish, wrong, or evil. If they wish to retain a consistent self-concept and self-esteem, they may have to deny many of their feelings or disown aspects of themselves. In this way the self-concept becomes distorted. According to Rogers, anxiety often stems from recognition that people have feelings and desires that are inconsistent with their distorted self-concept. Because anxiety is unpleasant, people may deny the existence of their genuine feelings and desires.

According to Rogers, the path to self-actualization requires getting in touch with our genuine feelings, accepting them, and acting on them. This is the goal of

Frame of reference One's unique patterning of perceptions and attitudes according to which one evaluates events.

Unconditional positive regard A persistent expression of esteem for the value of a person, but not necessarily an unqualified acceptance of all of the person's behaviors.

Conditional positive regard Judgment of another person's value on the basis of the acceptability of that person's behaviors.

Conditions of worth Standards by which the value of a person is judged.

Rogers's method of psychotherapy, *client-centered therapy.* Rogers also believed that we have mental images of what we are capable of becoming. These are termed **self-ideals.** We are motivated to reduce the discrepancy between our self-concepts and our self-ideals.

Self-ideal A mental image of what we believe we ought to be.

Evaluation of the Humanistic–Existential Perspective

Question: What are the strengths and weaknesses of humanistic–existential theory? Humanistic–existential theories have tremendous appeal for college students because of their focus on the importance of personal experience. We tend to treasure our conscious experiences (our "selves") and those of the people we care about. For lower organisms, to be alive is to move, to process food, to exchange oxygen and carbon dioxide, and to reproduce. But for human beings, an essential aspect of life is conscious experience—the sense of oneself as progressing through space and time.

Psychodynamic theories see individuals largely as victims of their childhood. Learning theories, to some degree, see people as "victims of circumstances"—or at least as victims of situational variables. But humanistic–existential theorists see humans as free to make choices. Psychodynamic theorists and learning theorists wonder whether our sense of freedom is merely an illusion. Humanistic–existential theorists, in contrast, begin by assuming personal freedom.

Ironically, the primary strength of the humanistic–existential approaches—their focus on conscious experience—is also their main weakness. Conscious experience is private and subjective. Therefore, the validity of formulating theories in terms of consciousness has been questioned. On the other hand, some psychologists (e.g., Bevan & Kessel, 1994) believe that the science of psychology can afford to loosen its methods somewhat if this will help it address the richness of human experience.

Self-actualization, like trait theory, yields circular explanations for behavior. When we see someone engaging in what seems to be positive striving, we gain little insight by attributing this behavior to a self-actualizing force. We have done nothing to account for the origins of the force. And when we observe someone who is not engaging in growth-oriented striving, it seems arbitrary to "explain" this outcome by suggesting that the self-actualizing tendency has been blocked or frustrated.

Humanistic–existential theories, like learning theories, have little to say about the development of traits and personality types. They assume that we are all unique, but they do not predict the sorts of traits, abilities, and interests we will develop.

Your Turn: Now that we have discussed the humanistic–existential perspective, enhance your mastery of the material with the nearby "Learning Connections." Review the material by filling in the blanks, reflect on the material by relating it to other things you know, and think critically about it.

 Learning Connections ▪ THE HUMANISTIC–EXISTENTIAL PERSPECTIVE: HOW BECOMING?

ACTIVE REVIEW (20) The humanistic view argues that people (*Are* or *Are not?*) capable of free choice and self-fulfillment. (21) Maslow argued that people have growth-oriented needs for self-_____. (22) Rogers's theory begins with the assumption of the existence of the _____. (23) According to Rogers, we see the world through unique frames of _____.

REFLECT AND RELATE Try a mini-experiment: Think of how your own frame of reference is unique, how it even differs from those of family members, friends, and,

perhaps, love interests. Then consider some of the things that earn the approval or disapproval of these important people in your life. Can you explain their responses to you in terms of their frames of reference?

CRITICAL THINKING If humanistic–existential theory is less scientific than some other views of personality, how do we explain its enduring popularity?

Go to **http://psychology.wadsworth.com/ rathus_pcc9e** for an interactive version of this Learning Connections unit.

The Sociocultural Perspective: Personality in Context

Thirteen-year-old Hannah brought her lunch tray to the table in the cafeteria. Her mother, Julie, eyed with horror the french fries, the plate of mashed potatoes in gravy, the bag of potato chips, and the large paper cup brimming with soda. "You can't eat that!" she said. "It's garbage!"

"Oh come on, Mom! Chill, okay?" Hannah rejoined before taking her tray to sit with some friends rather than with us.

I used to spend Saturdays with my children at the Manhattan School of Music. Not only do they study voice and piano. They—and I—have widened our cultural perspective by relating to families and students from all parts of the world.

Julie and Hannah are Korean Americans. Flustered, Julie shook her head and said, "I've now been in the United States longer than I was in Korea, and I still can't get used to the way children act here." Dimitri, a Russian American parent, chimed in. "I never would have spoken to my parents the way Michael speaks to me. I would have been . . . whipped or beaten."

"I try to tell Hannah she is part of the family," Julie continued. "She should think of other people. When she talks that way, it's embarrassing."

"Over here children are not part of the family," said Ken, an African American parent. "They are either part of their own crowd or they are 'individuals.'"

"Being an individual does not mean you have to talk back to your mother," Julie said. "What do you think, Spencer? You're the psychologist."

I think I made some unhelpful comments about the ketchup on the french fries having antioxidants and some slightly helpful comments about what is typical of teenagers in the United States. But I'm not sure, because I was thinking deeply about Hannah at the time. Not about her lunch, but about the formation of her personality and the influences on her behavior.

Question: Why is the sociocultural perspective important to the understanding of personality? As I thought about Hannah, I realized that in our multicultural society, personality cannot be understood without reference to the **sociocultural perspective.** According to a *New York Times* poll, 91% of people in the United States agree that "being an American is a big part" of who they are (Powers, 2000). Seventy-nine percent say that their religion has played a big role or some role in making them who they are, and 54% say that their race has played a big role or some role (Powers, 2000). Different cultural groups within the United States have different attitudes, beliefs, norms, self-definitions, and values (Bandura, 2002; Phinney, 2000).

Back to Hannah. Perhaps there were some unconscious psychodynamic influences operating on her. Her traits included exceptional academic ability and musical talent, which were at least partly determined by her heredity. Clearly, she was consciously striving to become a great violinist. But one could not fully understand her personality without also considering the sociocultural influences acting on her.

Here was a youngster who was strongly influenced by her peers—she was completely at home with blue jeans and french fries. She was also a daughter in an Asian American immigrant group that views education as the key to success in our culture (Leppel, 2002). Belonging to this ethnic group had certainly contributed to her ambition. But being a Korean American had not prevented her from becoming an outspoken American teenager. (Would she have been outspoken if she had been reared in Korea? I wondered. Of course, this question cannot be answered with certainty.) Her outspoken behavior had struck her mother as brazen and inappropriate. Julie was deeply offended by behavior that I consider acceptable in my own children. She reeled off the things that were "wrong" with Hannah from her Korean American perspective. I listed some things that were very right with Hannah and encouraged Julie to worry less.

Let us consider how sociocultural factors can affect one's sense of self.

Sociocultural perspective The view that focuses on the roles of ethnicity, gender, culture, and socioeconomic status in personality formation, behavior, and mental processes.

Individualism versus Collectivism: Who Am I (in This Cultural Setting)?

One could say that Julie's complaint was that Hannah saw herself as an individual and an artist to a greater extent than as a family member and a Korean girl. **Questions: What does it mean to be individualistic? What is meant by individualism and collectivism?** Cross-cultural research reveals that people in the United States and many northern European nations tend to be individualistic. **Individualists** tend to define themselves in terms of their personal identities and to give priority to their personal goals (Triandis, 2001). When asked to complete the statement "I am . . . ," they are likely to respond in terms of their personality traits ("I am outgoing," "I am artistic") or their occupations ("I am a nurse," "I am a systems analyst") (Triandis & Suh, 2002). In contrast, many people from cultures in Africa, Asia, and Central and South America tend to be collectivistic (Basic Behavioral Science Task Force, 1996c). **Collectivists** tend to define themselves in terms of the groups to which they belong and to give priority to the group's goals (Bandura, 2002; Triandis, 2001). They feel complete in terms of their relationships with others (Markus & Kitayama, 1991; see Figure 11.4). They are more likely than individualists to conform to group norms and judgments (Okazaki, 1997; Triandis & Suh, 2002). When asked to complete the statement "I am. . . ," they are more likely to respond in terms of their families, gender, or nation ("I am a father," "I am a Buddhist," "I am a Japanese") (Triandis, 2001).

The seeds of individualism and collectivism are found in the culture in which a person grows up. The capitalist system fosters individualism to some degree. It assumes that individuals are entitled to amass personal fortunes and that the process of doing so creates jobs and wealth for large numbers of people. The individualist perspective is found in the self-reliant heroes and antiheroes of Western literature and mass media—from Homer's Odysseus to Clint Eastwood's gritty cowboys and Walt Disney's Pocahontas. The traditional writings of the East have exalted people who resist personal temptations to do their duty and promote the welfare of the group.

Another issue from the sociocultural perspective is acculturation. Just how much acculturation is good for you? **Question: How does acculturation affect the psychological well-being of immigrants and their families?**

Individualist A person who defines herself or himself in terms of personal traits and gives priority to her or his own goals.

Collectivist A person who defines herself or himself in terms of relationships to other people and groups and gives priority to group goals.

Acculturation The process of adaptation in which immigrants and native groups identify with a new, dominant culture by learning about that culture and making behavioral and attitudinal changes.

Acculturation, Adjustment, and Self-Esteem: Just How Much Acculturation Is Enough?

Should Hindu women who emigrate to the United States surrender the sari in favor of California Casuals? Should Russian immigrants try to teach their children English at home? Should African American children be acquainted with the music and art of African peoples or those of Europe? Such activities are examples of **acculturation,** the process by which immigrants become acclimated to the customs and behavior patterns of their new host culture.

Self-esteem has been shown to be connected with patterns of acculturation among immigrants (Phinney et al., 1997). Those patterns take various forms. Some immigrants are completely assimilated by the dominant culture. They lose the language and customs of their country of origin and become like the dominant culture in the new host country. Others maintain almost complete separation. They retain the language and customs of their country of origin and never acclimate to those of the new country. Still others become bicultural (Ryder et al., 2000).

FIGURE 11.4 **The Self in Relation to Others From the Individualist and Collectivist Perspectives**

To an individualist, the self is separate from other people (part A). To a collectivist, the self is complete only in terms of relationships to other people (part B). (Based on Markus & Kitayama, 1991).

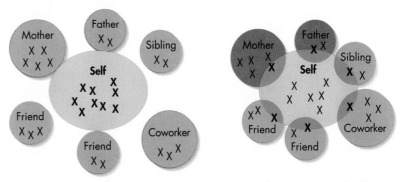

A. Independent View of Self

B. Interdependent View of Self

Concept Review PERSPECTIVES OF PERSONALITY

	Psychodynamic Perspective	**Trait Perspective**

Perspective

Preconscious and unconscious elements drive personality.

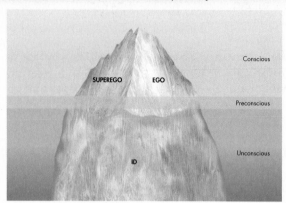

Personality is determined by a limited number of fundamental inherent traits. Hippocrates divides these traits into four types (inner circle), while Eysenck groups them into two major dimensions—extraversion/introversion and neuroticism (unstable/stable).

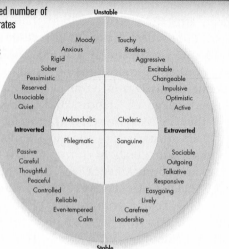

The current five-factor theory includes the two factors found by Eysenck, along with conscientiousness, agreeableness, and openness to experience.

THE BIG FIVE

Extraversion
Neuroticism
Conscientiousness
Agreeableness
Openness to Experience

Key Theorists

Sigmund Freud (1856–1939)
Carl Jung (1875–1961)
Alfred Adler (1870–1937)
Karen Horney (1885–1952)
Erik Erikson (1902–1994)
Margaret Mahler (1897–1985)

Hippocrates (460–377 BCE)
Hans Eysenck (1916–1997)
Paul T. Costa, Jr.
Robert McCrae

Focus of Research

■ Unconscious conflict
■ Drives such as sex, aggression, and the need for superiority come into conflict with laws, social rules, and moral codes

■ Use of mathematical techniques to catalogue and organize basic human personality traits

View of Personality

■ Three structures of personality–id, ego, superego
■ Five stages of psychosexual development–oral, anal, phallic, latency, genital
■ Ego analysts–or *neoanalysts*–focus more on the role of the ego in making meaningful, conscious decisions

■ Based on theory of Hippocrates and work of Gordon Allport
■ Eysenck's two-dimensional model–Introversion–extraversion and emotional stability–instability
■ Current emphasis on the five-factor model (the "Big Five")–Extraversion, agreeableness, conscientiousness, neuroticism, openness to experience

Learning-Theory Perspective

Situational and personal variables mold personality.

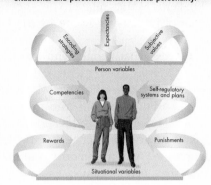

Humanistic-Existential Perspective

Maslow believed we progress toward higher psychological needs once basic survival needs have been met.

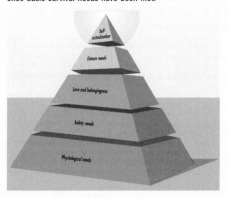

Sociocultural Perspective

To a collectivist, the self is complete only in terms of relationships to other people.

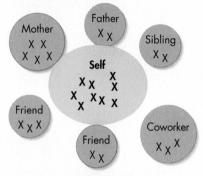

A. Independent View of Self

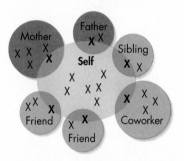

B. Interdependent View of Self

John B. Watson (1878–1958)
B. F. Skinner (1904–1990)
Albert Bandura

Abraham Maslow (1908–1970)
Carl Rogers (1902–1987)

Martha Bernal
Jean Phinney
Harry Triandis
Lillian Comas-Diaz
Stanley Sue
Richard Suinn

■ Behaviorist focus on situational factors that determine behavior
■ Social cognitive emphasis on observational learning and person variables—competencies, encoding strategies, expectancies, emotions, and self-regulation

■ The experiences of being human and developing one's unique potential within an often hostile environment

■ The roles of ethnicity, gender, culture, and socioeconomic status in personality formation and behavior

■ Watson saw personality as plastic and determined by external, situational variables
■ Skinner believed that society conditions individuals into wanting what is good for society
■ Bandura believes in reciprocal determinism—that people and the environment influence one another, and in the role of making conscious choices

■ People have inborn drives to become what they are capable of being
■ Unconditional positive regard leads to self-esteem, which facilitates individual growth and development

■ Development differs in individualistic and collectivist societies
■ Discrimination, poverty, and acculturation affect the self-concept and self-esteem

Go to **http://psychology.wadsworth.com/ rathus_pcc9e** to access a drag-and-drop version of this Concept Review designed to help you test yourself on the major topics provided here.

For example, they remain fluent in the language of their country of origin but also become conversant in the language of their new country. They also blend the customs and values of both cultures. They can switch "mental gears." That is, they apply the values of one culture under some circumstances and apply the values of the other culture under others (Hong et al., 2000). Perhaps they relate to other people in one way at work or in school, and in another way at home or in the neighborhood.

Truth or Fiction Revisited: Research evidence suggests that people who identify with the bicultural pattern, and not those who surrender their traditional backgrounds, have the highest self-esteem (Phinney et al., 1997; Phinney & Devich-Navarro, 1997). For example, Mexican Americans and Asian Americans who are more proficient in English are less likely to be anxious and depressed than less-proficient Mexican and Asian Americans (Kim et al., 2003; Salgado de Snyder et al., 1990). The ability to adapt to the ways of the new society, combined with a supportive cultural tradition and a sense of ethnic identity, apparently helps people adjust.

Evaluation of the Sociocultural Perspective

The sociocultural perspective provides valuable insights into the roles of ethnicity, gender, culture, and socioeconomic status in personality formation. When we ignore sociocultural factors, we deal only with the core of the human being—the potentials that allow the person to adapt to external forces. Sociocultural factors are external forces that are internalized. They run through us deeply, touching many aspects of our cognitions, motives, emotions, and behavior. Without reference to sociocultural factors, we may be able to understand generalities about behavior and cognitive processes. However, we will not be able to understand how individuals think, behave, and feel about themselves within a given cultural setting. The sociocultural perspective enhances our sensitivity to cultural differences and expectations and allows us to appreciate the richness of human behavior and mental processes.

Your Turn: Now that we have discussed the sociocultural perspective, enhance your mastery of the material with the nearby "Learning Connections." Review the material by filling in the blanks, reflect on the material by relating it to other things you know, and think critically about it. The nearby Concept Review summarizes the various theories of personality.

Learning Connections — THE SOCIOCULTURAL PERSPECTIVE: PERSONALITY IN CONTEXT

ACTIVE REVIEW (24) The _____ perspective considers the influences of ethnicity, gender, and socioeconomic status on personality. (25) _____ define themselves in terms of their personal identities and give priority to their personal goals. (26) _____ define themselves in terms of the groups to which they belong and to give priority to group goals. (27) Immigrants who identify with the bicultural pattern of assimilation have the (*Highest* or *Lowest?*) self-esteem.

REFLECT AND RELATE Do you see yourself as individualistic or collectivistic? Explain.

CRITICAL THINKING Can one "believe in" more than one theory of personality? For example, could one accept the sociocultural perspective *along with* another perspective?

 Go to **http://psychology.wadsworth.com/rathus_pcc9e** for an interactive version of this Learning Connections unit.

Measurement of Personality

Methods of personality assessment take a sample of behavior to predict future behavior. Standardized interviews are often used. Some psychologists use computers to conduct routine interviews. **Behavior-rating scales** assess behavior in settings such as classrooms or mental hospitals. With behavior-rating scales, trained observers usually check off each occurrence of a specific behavior within a certain time frame—say, 15

Behavior-rating scale A systematic means for recording the frequency with which target behaviors occur.

minutes. Behavior-rating scales are growing in popularity, especially for use with children (Kamphaus et al., 2000). However, standardized objective and projective tests are used more frequently, and we focus on them in this section.

Question: How are personality measures used? Measures of personality are used to make important decisions, such as whether a person is suited for a certain type of work, a particular class in school, or a drug to reduce agitation. As part of their admissions process, graduate schools often ask professors to rate prospective students on scales that assess traits such as intelligence, emotional stability, and cooperation. Students may take tests to measure their **aptitudes** and interests to gain insight into whether they are suited for certain occupations. It is assumed that students who share the aptitudes and interests of people who function well in certain positions are also likely to function well in those positions.

Let us consider the two most widely used types of personality tests: objective tests and projective tests.

Objective Tests

Question: What are objective personality tests? **Objective tests** present respondents with a **standardized** group of test items in the form of a questionnaire. Respondents are limited to a specific range of answers. One test might ask respondents to indicate whether items are true or false for them. Another might ask respondents to select the preferred activity from groups of three.

Some tests have a **forced-choice format,** in which respondents are asked to indicate which of two statements is more true for them or which of several activities they prefer. The respondents are not usually given the option of answering "none of the above." Forced-choice formats are frequently used in interest inventories, which help predict whether the person would function well in a certain occupation. The following item is similar to those found in occupational interest inventories:

I would rather

a.   be a forest ranger.
b.   work in a busy office.
c.   play a musical instrument.

The Minnesota Multiphasic Personality Inventory (MMPI[2]) contains hundreds of items presented in a true–false format. The MMPI is designed to be used by clinical and counseling psychologists to help diagnose psychological disorders. Accurate measurement of an individual's problems should point to appropriate treatment. The MMPI is the most widely used psychological test in clinical work and the most widely used instrument for personality measurement in psychological research.

The MMPI is usually scored for the 4 **validity scales** and 10 **clinical scales** described in Table 11.3. The validity scales suggest whether answers actually represent the person's thoughts, emotions, and behaviors. **Truth or Fiction Revisited:** However, psychologists cannot guarantee that deception on a personality test will be disclosed.

The validity scales in Table 11.3 assess different **response sets,** or biases, in answering the questions. People with high L scores, for example, may be attempting to present themselves as excessively moral and well-behaved individuals. People with high F scores may be trying to seem bizarre or are answering haphazardly. Many personality measures have some kind of validity scale. The clinical scales of the MMPI assess the problems shown in Table 11.3, as well as stereotypical masculine or feminine interests and introversion.

The MMPI scales were constructed *empirically*—that is, on the basis of actual clinical data rather than on the basis of psychological theory. A test-item bank of

[2]Currently the updated MMPI-2.

Aptitude A natural ability or talent.

Objective tests Tests whose items must be answered in a specified, limited manner. Tests whose items have concrete answers that are considered correct.

Standardized test A test that is given to a large number of respondents so that data concerning the typical responses can be accumulated and analyzed.

Forced-choice format A method of presenting test questions that requires a respondent to select one of a number of possible answers.

Validity scales Groups of test items that indicate whether a person's responses accurately reflect that individual's traits.

Clinical scales Groups of test items that measure the presence of various abnormal behavior patterns.

Response set A tendency to answer test items according to a bias—for instance, to make oneself seem perfect or bizarre.

■ **Is this Test Taker Telling the Truth?** How can psychologists determine whether or not people answer test items honestly? What are the validity scales of the MMPI?

Photodisc Collection/Getty Images

TABLE 11.3 MINNESOTA MULTIPHASIC PERSONALITY INVENTORY (MMPI) SCALES

	Scale	Abbreviation	Possible Interpretations
Validity Scales	Question	?	Corresponds to number of items left unanswered
	Lie	L	Lies or is highly conventional
	Frequency	F	Exaggerates complaints or answers items haphazardly; may have bizarre ideas
	Correction	K	Denies problems
Clinical Scales	Hypochondriasis	Hs	Has bodily concerns and complaints
	Depression	D	Is depressed; has feelings of guilt and helplessness
	Hysteria	Hy	Reacts to stress by developing physical symptoms; lacks insight
	Psychopathic deviate	Pd	Is immoral, in conflict with the law; has stormy relationships
	Masculinity/femininity	Mf	High scores suggest interests and behavior considered stereotypical of the other gender
	Paranoia	Pa	Is suspicious and resentful, highly cynical about human nature
	Psychasthenia	Pt	Is anxious, worried, high-strung
	Schizophrenia	Sc	Is confused, disorganized, disoriented; has bizarre ideas
	Hypomania	Ma	Is energetic, restless, active, easily bored
	Social introversion	Si	Is introverted, timid, shy; lacks self-confidence

several hundred items was derived from questions that are often asked in clinical interviews. Here are some examples of the kinds of items that were used:

My father was a good man.	T F
I am very seldom troubled by headaches.	T F
My hands and feet are usually warm enough.	T F
I have never done anything dangerous for the thrill of it.	T F
I work under a great deal of tension.	T F

The items were administered to people with previously identified symptoms, such as depressive or schizophrenic symptoms. Items that successfully set these people apart were included on scales named for these conditions. Confidence in the MMPI has developed because of its extensive use.

Now that we have defined objective tests and surveyed the MMPI, we may ask— **Questions: How do projective tests differ from objective tests? What are some of the more widely used projective tests?**

Projective Tests

In **projective tests** there are no clear, specified answers. People are shown ambiguous stimuli such as inkblots or ambiguous drawings and asked to say what they look like or to tell stories about them. There is no one correct response. It is assumed that people *project* their own personalities into their responses. The meanings they attribute to these stimuli are assumed to reflect their personalities as well as the drawings or blots themselves.

Projective test A psychological test that presents ambiguous stimuli onto which the test-taker projects his or her own personality in making a response.

THE RORSCHACH INKBLOT TEST **Truth or Fiction Revisited:** There are actually a number of psychological tests made up of inkblots, and test-takers are indeed asked to say what the blots look like to them. The best known of these is the Rorschach inkblot test, named after its originator, Hermann Rorschach.

People are given the inkblots, one by one, and are asked what they look like or what they could be. A response that reflects the shape of the blot is considered a sign of adequate **reality testing.** A response that richly integrates several features of the blot is considered a sign of high intellectual functioning. Supporters of the Rorschach believe that it provides insight into a person's intelligence, interests, cultural background, personality traits, psychological disorders, and many other variables. Critics argue that there is little empirical evidence to support the test's validity (Goode, 2001a; Hunsley & Bailey, 1999; Wood et al., 2001).

Although there is no single "correct" response to the Rorschach inkblot shown in Figure 11.5, some responses are not in keeping with the features of the blots. Figure 11.5 could be a bat or a flying insect, the pointed face of an animal, the face of a jack-o'-lantern, or many other things. But responses like "an ice cream cone," "diseased lungs," or "a metal leaf in flames" are not suggested by the features of the blot and may indicate personality problems.

THE THEMATIC APPERCEPTION TEST The Thematic Apperception Test (TAT) was developed in the 1930s by Henry Murray and Christiana Morgan. It consists of drawings, like the one shown in Figure 10.3 (see p. 381), that are open to a variety of interpretations. Individuals are given the cards one at a time and asked to make up stories about them.

The TAT is widely used in research on motivation and in clinical practice (Watkins et al., 1995). The notion is that we are likely to project our own needs into our responses to ambiguous situations, even if we are unaware of them or reluctant to talk about them. The TAT is also widely used to assess attitudes toward other people, especially parents, lovers, and spouses.

Your Turn: Now that we have discussed the measurement of personality, enhance your mastery of the material with the nearby "Learning Connections." Review the material by filling in the blanks, reflect on the material by relating it to other things you know, and think critically about it.

FIGURE 11.5 **A Rorschach Inkblot**
The Rorschach is the most widely used projective personality test. What does this inkblot look like to you? What could it be?

Reality testing The capacity to perceive one's environment and oneself according to accurate sensory impressions.

 Learning Connections   **MEASUREMENT OF PERSONALITY**

ACTIVE REVIEW (28) Personality tests sample _____ to predict future behavior. (29) _____ tests present standardized sets of test items in the form of questionnaires. (30) Projective tests present _____ stimuli and permit the respondent a broad range of answers. (31) The MMPI is an objective test that uses a(n) _____–false format to assess psychological disorders. (32) The foremost projective technique is the _____ inkblot test.

REFLECT AND RELATE Have you ever taken a personality test? What were the results? Do you believe that the results were valid? Why or why not?

CRITICAL THINKING Do you think that personality tests should be required as part of completing an application for a job? Why or why not?

 Go to **http://psychology.wadsworth.com/ rathus_pcc9e** for an interactive version of this Learning Connections unit.

Life Connections
Understanding and Enhancing Self-Esteem

Few of us are as attractive as the models in the Abercrombie's and Victoria's Secret catalogues. Should that disturb our self-esteem? Our physical attributes are only part of the story, and most of us realize that the individuals in these ads are rare indeed, and that it is pointless for us to compare ourselves with them. But research shows that one of the psychological boulders that can crush our self-esteem is self-comparison to people who are superior to us in a way that matters to us. For some of us the crusher may be superior intellectual ability (Isobe & Ura, 2002). For others it is athletic ability (Ryska, 2001–2002). For still others it is physical appearance (Paxton & Phythian, 1999).

Our self-esteem is the value or worth that we attach to ourselves. A positive self-image is one of the keys to psychological adjustment (Chen et al., 2001; Feinberg et al., 2000; Southall & Roberts, 2002). For example, high self-esteem can buffer the effects of stress and help provide the courage to deal with it (Southall & Roberts, 2002). Low self-esteem, on the other hand, makes people more vulnerable to stress. It is connected with feelings of helplessness and hopelessness, and may contribute to feelings of depression and suicidal thoughts (Bifulco et al., 2002; Bongar, 2002; Southall & Roberts, 2002).

Developmental Factors and Self-Esteem

Learning theorists might suggest that our self-esteem reflects our ability to obtain reinforcements. Social cognitive theorists would tie self-esteem to self-efficacy; they would see self-efficacy as based on successes and, in a circular manner, as leading to further successes by encouraging us to make efforts to obtain what we want (Bandura & Locke, 2003). Rogers's self theory argues that our self-esteem reflects the esteem of others, and when we are young, especially the regard of our parents. According to the five-factor model,

certain personality traits will correlate positively with self-esteem. Apparently, they are all correct.

Research does show that children's self-worth is connected with their being "good at doing things" (feelings of self-efficacy that are connected with obtaining reinforcers) and with whether they are accepted by adults and other children (obtain positive regard) (Lane et al., 2002; Tassi et al., 2001). Research with the five-factor model shows that self-esteem is predicted to some degree by the traits of emotional stability, extraversion, and agreeableness.

In keeping with gender-role stereotypes, girls tend to have more positive self-concepts regarding reading and general academics than boys during the school years. Boys tend to have more positive self-concepts in math, physical ability, and physical appearance (Quatman & Watson, 2001). Cross-cultural studies in China (Dai, 2001), Finland (Lepola et al., 2000), and Germany (Tiedemann, 2000) also find that girls tend to have higher self-concepts in writing and boys to have higher self-concepts in math.

Research suggests that authoritative parenting, as described in Chapter 3, contributes to high self-esteem in children (Baumrind, 1991a, 1991b; Furnham & Cheng, 2000; Hickman et al., 2000). That is, children with a favorable self-image tend to have parents who are strict but also involved and loving. Parental demands for mature, skillful behavior may encourage the development of these behaviors; these behaviors, in turn, may lead to social approval.

Truth or Fiction Revisited: Self-esteem also appears to have a genetic component, which would contribute to its stability (McGuire et al., 1999; Neiss et al., 2002). In any event, self-esteem, once established, seems to endure. Most of us will encounter failure in something at one time or another, but high self-esteem may contribute to a

continuing belief that they can master adversity.

Enhancing Self-Esteem

There are many things you can do to enhance your self-esteem. Broadly speaking, they involve changing the things you can change and having the wisdom to accept those you cannot change.

Improve Yourself. For example, are you miserable because of excess dependence on another person? Perhaps you can enhance your social skills or your vocational skills in an effort to become more independent. Are you too heavy? Perhaps you can follow some of the suggestions for losing weight, presented in Chapter 9.

When it comes to self-improvement, there may or may not be things you can do about your facial features, your hair, and your body. It is not a good idea to compete with the cultural ideal as exemplified by chiseled facial features and a tight, slender body, but there may be some minor adjustments you can make. One "minor" but important change is to smile more often. As you will see in Chapter 12, people are perceived as being more attractive when they are smiling.

Challenge the Realism of Your Ideal Self. Cognitive psychologists note that our internal list of "oughts" and "shoulds" can create perfectionistic standards. We constantly fall short of these standards and experience frustration. Challenge your perfectionistic demands on yourself and, when appropriate, revise them. It may be harmful to abolish worthy and realistic goals, even if we do have trouble measuring up now and then. However, some of our goals or values may not stand up to scrutiny. It is useful to consider them objectively.

Stop Comparing Yourself to Others! The research clearly shows a self-defeating cognitive aspect to self-esteem: comparing ourselves to other people who surpass us in traits or achievements that we deem to be important (Isobe & Ura, 2002; Martinot et al., 2002; Ryska, 2001–2002). You can be a respectable scientist without being an Einstein or a Madame Curie. You can be a good writer without being a Maya Angelou or a Shakespeare. You can be a worthy athlete without being a Serena Williams or a Michael Jordan. You can also make a good appearance without landing work for print ads in clothing catalogues. You can earn a decent living even if you are not making as much money as _____ (you fill in the blank). Which leads us to our next point . . .

Substitute Realistic Goals for Unattainable Goals. Perhaps we will never be as artistic, as tall, or as graceful as we would like to be. We can work to enhance our drawing skills, but if it becomes clear that we will not become Michelangelos, perhaps we can enjoy our scribblings for what they are and also find satisfaction elsewhere. We cannot make ourselves taller (except by wearing elevator shoes or high heels), but we can take off five pounds and cut our time for running the mile by a few seconds. We can also learn to whip up a great fettuccine Alfredo.

Build Self-Efficacy Expectations. Our self-efficacy expectations define the degree to which we believe that our efforts will bring about a positive outcome. They affect our willingness to take on challenges and persist in efforts to meet them. We can build self-efficacy expectations by selecting tasks that are consistent with our interests and abilities and then working at those tasks. Psychologists have devised many tests to help people focus in on their interests and abilities. They are probably available at your college testing and counseling center. But we can also build self-efficacy expectations by working at athletics or hobbies or charitable causes.

Realistic self-assessment, realistic goals, and a reasonable schedule for improvement are the keys to building self-efficacy expectations. Perhaps you will never be able to run a four- or five-minute mile, but after a few months of reasonably taxing workouts under the advice of a skilled trainer, you might be able to put a few eight- to ten-minute miles back to back. (You might even enjoy them.)

Recite—An Active Summary™

Want to study on the go? Go to your companion website and download an audio version of this review section to your media player.

1. What *is* personality?

Personality is defined as the reasonably stable patterns of behavior, including thoughts and emotions, that distinguish one person from another.

2. What is Freud's theory of psychosexual development?

Freud's theory is termed psycho*dynamic* because it assumes that we are driven largely by unconscious motives and by the movement of unconscious forces within our minds. People experience conflict as basic instincts of hunger, sex, and aggression come up against social pressures to follow laws, rules, and moral codes. At first this conflict is external; but, as we develop, it is internalized. The unconscious id represents psychological drives and seeks instant gratification. The ego, or the sense of self or "I," develops through experience and takes into account what is practical and possible in gratifying the impulses of the id. Defense mechanisms such as repression protect the ego from anxiety by repressing unacceptable ideas or distorting reality. The superego is the conscience and develops largely through the Oedipus complex and identification with others. People undergo psychosexual development as psychosexual energy, or libido, is transferred from one erogenous zone to another during childhood. There are five stages of development: oral, anal, phallic, latency, and genital. Fixation in a stage leads to development of traits associated with the stage.

3. Who are some other psychodynamic theorists? What are their views on personality?

Carl Jung's theory, analytical psychology, features a collective unconscious and numerous archetypes, both of which reflect the history of our species. Alfred Adler's theory, individual psychology, features the inferiority complex and the compensating drive for superiority. Karen Horney's theory focuses on parent–child relationships and the possible development of feelings of anxiety and hostility. Erik Erikson's theory of psychosocial development highlights the importance of early social relationships rather than the gratification of childhood sexual impulses. Erikson extended Freud's five developmental stages to eight, including stages that occur in adulthood.

4. What are the strengths and weaknesses of the psychodynamic perspective?

Freud fought for the idea that personality is subject to scientific analysis at a time when many people still viewed psychological problems as signs of possession. He also focused attention on the importance of sexuality, the effects of child rearing, and the fact that people distort perceptions according to their needs. On the other hand, there is no evidence for the existence of psychic structures, and his theory is fraught with inaccuracies about child development.

5. What are traits?

Traits are personality elements that are inferred from behavior and that account for behavioral consistency. Trait theory adopts a descriptive approach to personality.

6. What is the history of the trait perspective?

Hippocrates, the ancient Greek physician, believed that personality reflects the balance of liquids ("humors") in the body. Galton in the 19th century and Allport in the 20th century surveyed traits by studying words that referred to them in dictionaries.

7. How have contemporary psychologists reduced the universe of traits to more manageable lists?

Hans Eysenck used factor analysis to arrive at two broad, independent personality dimensions: introversion–extraversion and emotional stability–instability (neuroticism). More recent mathematical analyses point to the existence of five key factors (five-factor theory): extraversion, agreeableness, conscientiousness, emotional stability, and openness to experience.

8. What are the strengths and weaknesses of trait theory?

Trait theorists have helped develop personality tests and used them to predict adjustment in various lines of work. Critics argue that trait theory is descriptive, not explanatory.

9. What does behaviorism contribute to our understanding of personality?

Behaviorists believe that we should focus on observable behavior rather than hypothesized unconscious forces, and that we should emphasize the situational determinants of behavior. John B. Watson, the "father" of modern behaviorism, rejected notions of mind and personality altogether. He also argued that he could train any child to develop into a professional or a criminal by controlling the child's environment. B. F. Skinner, like Watson, opposed the idea of personal freedom. In *Walden Two,* Skinner argued that environmental contingencies can shape people into wanting to do the things that are required of them.

Recite—An Active Summary™

10. How does social cognitive theory differ from the behaviorist view?

Social cognitive theory has a cognitive orientation and focuses on learning by observation. To predict behavior, social cognitive theorists consider situational variables (rewards and punishments) and person variables (competencies, encoding strategies, expectancies, emotions, and self-regulatory systems and plans).

11. What are the strengths and weaknesses of learning theories as they apply to personality?

Learning theorists have highlighted the importance of referring to publicly observable behaviors in theorizing. However, behaviorism does not describe, explain, or suggest the richness of inner human experience. Critics of social cognitive theory note that it does not address self-awareness or adequately account for the development of traits. It may also not pay enough attention to genetic variation in explaining individual differences in behavior.

12. What is humanism? What is existentialism?

Humanism argues that we are capable of free choice, self-fulfillment, and ethical behavior. Existentialists argue that our lives have meaning when we give them meaning.

13. How do humanistic psychologists differ from psychodynamic theorists?

Whereas Freud wrote that people are motivated to gratify unconscious drives, humanistic psychologists believe that people have a conscious need for self-actualization.

14. What is your *self*?

According to Rogers, the self is an organized and consistent way in which a person perceives his or her "I" in relation to others.

15. What is self theory?

Self theory begins by assuming the existence of the self and each person's unique frame of reference. The self attempts to actualize (develop its unique potential) and best does so when the person receives unconditional positive regard. Conditions of worth may lead to a distorted self-concept, to disowning of parts of the self, and to anxiety.

16. What are the strengths and weaknesses of humanistic–existential theory?

Humanistic–existential theory is appealing because of its focus on self-awareness and freedom of choice, but critics argue that concepts such as conscious experience and self-actualization are unscientific.

17. Why is the sociocultural perspective important to the understanding of personality?

One cannot fully understand the personality of an individual without understanding the cultural beliefs and socioeconomic conditions that have affected that individual. The sociocultural perspective encourages us to consider the roles of ethnicity, gender, culture, and socioeconomic status in personality formation, behavior, and mental processes.

18. What does it mean to be individualistic? What is meant by individualism and collectivism?

Individualists define themselves in terms of their personal identities and give priority to their personal goals. Collectivists define themselves in terms of the groups to which they belong and give priority to the group's goals. Many Western societies are individualistic and foster individualism in personality. Many Eastern societies are collectivist and foster collectivism in personality.

19. How does acculturation affect the psychological well-being of immigrants and their families?

Immigrants who retain the customs and values of their country of origin but who also learn those of their new host country, and blend the two, tend to have higher self-esteem than immigrants who either become completely assimilated or who maintain complete separation from the new dominant culture.

20. How are personality measures used?

Personality measures are used in many ways, including assessing psychological disorders, predicting the likelihood of adjustment in various lines of work, measuring aptitudes, and determining academic placement.

21. What are objective personality tests?

Objective tests present test takers with a standardized set of test items to which they must respond in specific, limited ways (as in multiple-choice or true–false tests). A forced-choice format asks respondents to indicate which of two or more statements is true for them or which of several activities they prefer. The Minnesota Multiphasic Personality Inventory (MMPI) is widely used in the assessment of psychological disorders.

Recite—An Active Summary™

22. How do projective tests differ from objective tests? What are some of the more widely used projective tests?

Projective tests do not have specific correct answers. They present ambiguous stimuli and allow the test-taker to give a range of responses that reflect individual differences. Examples include the Rorschach inkblot test and the Thematic Apperception Test.

Go to **http://psychology.wadsworth.com/ rathus_pcc9e** to access an interactive version of this active summary.

Key Terms

Personality (p. 400)
Psychodynamic theory (p. 401)
Conscious (p. 401)
Preconscious (p. 401)
Unconscious (p. 401)
Repression (p. 402)
Psychoanalysis (p. 402)
Psychic structure (p. 402)
Id (p. 402)
Pleasure principle (p. 402)
Ego (p. 402)
Reality principle (p. 402)
Defense mechanism (p. 402)
Superego (p. 402)
Identification (p. 402)
Moral principle (p. 402)
Eros (p. 403)
Libido (p. 403)
Erogenous zone (p. 403)
Psychosexual development (p. 403)
Oral stage (p. 403)

Fixation (p. 404)
Anal stage (p. 404)
Phallic stage (p. 404)
Clitoris (p. 404)
Oedipus complex (p. 405)
Electra complex (p. 405)
Displaced (p. 405)
Latency (p. 405)
Genital stage (p. 405)
Incest taboo (p. 405)
Analytical psychology (p. 405)
Collective unconscious (p. 405)
Archetypes (p. 405)
Inferiority complex (p. 406)
Drive for superiority (p. 406)
Creative self (p. 406)
Individual psychology (p. 406)
Psychosocial development (p. 407)

Ego identity (p. 407)
Trait (p. 408)
Introversion (p. 409)
Extraversion (p. 409)
Neuroticism (p. 409)
Social cognitive theory (p. 413)
Reciprocal determinism (p. 413)
Person variables (p. 413)
Expectancies (p. 413)
Subjective value (p. 413)
Model (p. 413)
Competencies (p. 413)
Encode (p. 414)
Self-efficacy expectations (p. 414)
Humanism (p. 416)
Existentialism (p. 416)
Self-actualization (p. 417)
Frame of reference (p. 418)
Unconditional positive regard (p. 418)

Conditional positive regard (p. 418)
Conditions of worth (p. 418)
Self-ideal (p. 419)
Sociocultural perspective (p. 420)
Individualist (p. 421)
Collectivist (p. 421)
Acculturation (p. 421)
Behavior-rating scale (p. 424)
Aptitude (p. 425)
Objective tests (p. 425)
Standardized test (p. 425)
Forced-choice format (p. 425)
Validity scales (p. 425)
Clinical scales (p. 425)
Response set (p. 425)
Projective test (p. 426)
Reality testing (p. 427)

ACTIVE LEARNING RESOURCES

Visit your Companion Website for Video, Quizzing, and Self-Assessment!

http://psychology.wadsworth.com/rathus_pcc9e

On this site you can access the Personality Theory and Measurement video highlighted by the Video Connections icon on p. 411. In addition there are many quizzing opportunities including interactive versions of the fill-in-the-blank Active Review sections in your book. You can also fill out and score the Self-Assessments on p. 415 and p. 417.

Study on the Go!

Don't have time to study right now? You can study on the go! Visit your companion website and download an audio version of the Recite—An Active Summary section to your media player.

ThomsonNOW

http://www.thomsonedu.com

Need help studying? This site is your one-stop study shop. Take a Pre-Test and Thomson NOW will generate a Personalized Study Plan based on your test results. The Study Plan will identify the topics you need to review and direct you to online resources to help you master those topics. You can then take a Post-Test to determine the concepts you have mastered and what you still need to work on.

Author Blog

What does your author have to say about the state of psychology? Visit your companion website every Tuesday and click on "Author Blog," where he'll talk about the most recent controversies and hot topics in psychology.

Truth or Fiction?

T F Men are more aggressive than women.

T F Beauty is in the eye of the beholder.

T F When you're smiling, people perceive you as being more attractive.

T F Opposites attract.

T F Not only the sex organs but also the earlobes swell when people are sexually aroused.

T F Education has a liberating influence on sexual behavior.

T F Most Americans believe that some women like to be talked into sex.

T F Women say no to sex when they really want to have sex.

T F The majority of college women who have been victims of date rape do not report the assault to police or campus authorities.

 Go to **http://psychology.wadsworth.com/ rathus_pcc9e** to answer and score this Truth or Fiction quiz.

Gender and Sexuality

Preview

Off the misty coast of Ireland lies the small island of Inis Beag. From the air it is a green jewel, warm and inviting. At ground level, things are somewhat cooler.

For example, the residents of Inis Beag do not believe that women experience orgasm. The woman who chances to find pleasure in sex is considered deviant. Premarital sex is all but unknown. Women engage in sexual relations to conceive children and to appease their husbands' carnal cravings. They need not worry about being called on for frequent performances, however, because the men of Inis Beag believe, erroneously, that sex saps their strength. Sex on Inis Beag is carried out in the dark—both literally and figuratively—and with nightclothes on. The man lies on top in the so-called missionary position. In accordance with local concepts of masculinity, he ejaculates as fast as he can. Then he rolls over and falls asleep.

If Inis Beag does not sound like your cup of tea, you may find the atmosphere of Mangaia more congenial. Mangaia is a Polynesian pearl of an island, lifting lazily from the blue waters of the Pacific. It is on the other side of the world from Inis Beag—in more ways than one.

From an early age, Mangaian children are encouraged to get in touch with their sexuality through masturbation. Mangaian adolescents are expected to engage in sexual intercourse. They may be found on secluded beaches or beneath the swaying fronds of palms, diligently practicing techniques learned from village elders. Mangaian women are expected to reach orgasm several times before their partners do. Young men want their partners to reach orgasm, and they compete to see who is more effective at bringing young women to multiple orgasms.

On the island of Inis Beag, a woman who has an orgasm is considered deviant. On Mangaia, multiple orgasms are the norm (Rathus et al., 2005). If we take a quick tour of the world of sexual diversity, we also find that

♦ Nearly every society has an incest taboo, but some societies believe that a brother and sister who eat at the same table are engaging in a mildly sexual act and forbid it.

♦ What is considered sexually arousing varies enormously among different cultures. Women's breasts and armpits stimulate a sexual response in some cultures, but not in others.

♦ Kissing is nearly universal in the United States but unpopular in Japan and unknown in some cultures in Africa and South America. Upon seeing European visitors kissing, a member of an African tribe remarked, "Look at them—they eat each other's saliva and dirt."

♦ In Iran's conservative Islamic republic, flirting or holding hands in public can get one arrested or beaten (Riot, 2000; Sciolino, 2000). Nevertheless, many couples obtain officially sanctioned temporary marriages, called *sigheh,* that enable them to live together and engage in sexual relations without being disturbed by the state. A *sigheh* can last from a few minutes to 99 years.

♦ Sexual exclusiveness in marriage is valued highly in most parts of the United States, but among the people of Alaska's Aleutian Islands it is considered good manners for a man to offer his wife to a houseguest.

What turns people on? What makes the sex drive click? What springs people's hearts into their mouths, tightens their throats, and stirs feelings of desire? Is it the sight of a lover undressing, a .jpg file on a Web site, a sniff of some velvety perfume, a sip of wine? Some people become aroused by remembrances of lovers past. Some are stimulated by fantasies of flings with strangers.

People vary greatly in the cues that excite them sexually and in the frequency with which they experience sexual thoughts and feelings. Many factors contribute to the sex drive. Later we will see that sex hormones play their part in sexual arousal. In adolescence, when we are flooded with sex hormones, we may seem perpetually aroused or arousable. Yet some people rarely or never entertain sexual thoughts or fantasies. A person's cultural setting affects his or her sex drive as much as hormones. For example, the residents of Inis Beag and Mangaia have similar anatomical features and endocrine systems but vastly different attitudes toward sex. Cultural beliefs influence their sexual behavior and the pleasure they find—or do not find—in sex. Sexual motivation may be natural, but this natural function is strongly influenced by religious and moral beliefs, cultural tradition, folklore, and superstition.

Despite our cultural backgrounds, the human world—with few exceptions—is made up of women and men. We therefore begin our discussion of gender and sexuality by asking what it means to be a woman or a man, and how it is that (most) children develop behavior patterns that most societies label as feminine or masculine. We will then discuss interpersonal attraction and explore the various factors that lead us to be romantically attracted to males or females (or, sometimes, to both). The directionality of our feelings of attraction—toward females or males—is termed our *sexual orientation*. We will examine the research concerning why most but not all of us are attracted to individuals of the other sex. We will see that our sex drives are connected with sex hormones and that our bodies—whether female or male—tend to respond in more or less similar ways to sexual stimulation. Finally, we turn our attention to a couple of negative but important areas of human sexuality: sexual coercion and sexually transmitted infections. It is important that we understand forms of sexual coercion like rape and sexual harassment and what we can do about them. This chapter's "Life Connections" feature is about "Understanding and Preventing HIV/AIDS and Other Sexually Transmitted Infections" (STIs). For most people throughout the world, HIV/AIDS remains a lethal issue, and for millions of the rest of us—surprisingly large numbers of us—STIs cause distressing illnesses that too frequently leave us incapable of conceiving and bearing children.

But let us begin our tale with some fascinating questions, such as what, if anything, is masculine about being male or feminine about being female? These may sound like trick questions, but very soon you will see that they are quite serious. In fact, I sometimes think that the more questions we try to answer, the more puzzles we create.

■ **How Powerful Is the Sex Drive?** The sex drive is quite powerful among late adolescents and young adults, when sex hormones are at their peak. However, the modes of sexual expression they choose–and whether they express sexual impulses at all–are greatly influenced by cultural factors.

Gender Stereotypes and Differences: What Does It Mean to Be Female or to Be Male?

"Why Can't a Woman Be More Like a Man?" You may recognize this song title from the musical *My Fair Lady*. In the song, Henry Higgins laments that women are emotional and fickle whereas men are logical and dependable.

The excitable woman is a **stereotype. Question: What are gender-role stereotypes?** Stereotypes are fixed, conventional ideas about a group of people that can give rise to prejudice and discrimination. A **gender** stereotype is a fixed, conventional idea about how men and women ought to behave. Higgins's stereotypes reflect cultural beliefs. Cultural beliefs about men and women involve clusters of stereotypes called **gender roles.** The logical man is a gender-role stereotype. Gender-role stereotypes define the ways in which men and women are expected to behave within a given culture.

Sandra Lipsitz Bem (1993) writes that three beliefs about women and men have prevailed throughout the history of Western culture:

1. Women and men have basically different psychological and sexual natures.
2. Men are the superior, dominant sex.
3. Gender differences and male superiority are "natural."

Stereotype A fixed, conventional idea about a group.

Gender The psychological state of being male or female.

Gender role A cluster of behaviors that characterizes traditional female or male behaviors within a cultural setting.

In Profile | SANDRA LIPSITZ BEM

She doesn't buy into gender-role stereotypes, nor into traditional distinctions among heterosexuals, gay people, and bisexuals. "Although I lived monogamously with a man I loved for over 27 years," writes Cornell professor Sandra Bem in the preface of her book *The Lenses of Gender*, "I am not now and never have been a 'heterosexual.' But neither have I ever been a 'lesbian' or a 'bisexual.' What I am—and have been for as long as I can remember—is someone whose sexuality and gender have never seemed to mesh with the available cultural categories" (1993, p. vii). Since earliest childhood, she adds, her temperament and behavior have fallen outside the traditional categories of masculine and feminine. She has never been particularly tough-minded or nurturant.

In the early 1970s, much of Bem's research focused on *psychological androgyny*—the notion that both males and females can possess a combination of masculine and feminine personality traits. At the time many theorists thought that psychological androgyny was a good thing because it freed women to engage in traditionally masculine behaviors (e.g., being self-assertive) and freed men to engage in traditionally feminine behaviors (e.g., being nurturant). But critics of this research argued that the concept of androgyny lends reality to gender polarization. If we say that someone has both masculine and feminine traits, are we not suggesting that masculinity and femininity are "givens"—fixed and natural personality structures rather than cultural inventions?

Bem's interests then turned to gender polarization and resultant gender inequalities. She argues that viewing men and women as opposites reinforces male dominance. She looks forward to the day when "biological sex [will] no longer be at the core of individual identity and sexuality" (1993, p. 196).

 Go to **http://psychology.wadsworth.com/ rathus_pcc9e** to access more information about Sandra Lipsitz Bem.

These beliefs have tended to polarize our views of women and men. It is thought that gender differences in power and psychological traits are natural, but what does "natural" mean? Throughout most of history, people viewed naturalness in terms of religion, or God's scheme of things (Bem, 1993). For the past century or so, naturalness has been seen in biological, evolutionary terms—at least by most scientists. But these views ignore cultural influences.

How do males and females differ? How are they alike? The anatomical differences between women and men are obvious and are connected with the biological aspects of reproduction. To reproduce, women and men have to be biologically different. Biologists have a relatively easy time of it describing and interpreting physical sex differences.

Throughout history and in many cultures, it has also been assumed that women and men must be different in personality in order to fulfill different roles in the family and society (Bem, 1993). But the task of psychologists who would explore these differences is more complex and is wrapped up with cultural and political issues. Psychological gender differences are not as obvious as biological sex differences. In fact, women and men may well be more alike than different psychologically. On the other hand, stereotypes of what it means to be masculine and feminine are widespread (see Table 12.1). For example, in their survey of 30 countries, John Williams and Deborah Best (1994) found that the traits *active, adventurous, aggressive, arrogant,* and *autocratic* are more likely to be ascribed to men. Women are more likely to be seen as *fearful, affectionate, appreciative,* and *emotional.*

The study of gender differences directly connects with students. Students are female or male, and there are key questions about what it means to be female or to be male. **Question: Are there psychological differences between females and males?** If so, what are they? We will see that psychologists search out such gender differences in terms of research into cognitive skills, personality, and social behavior.

Gender Differences in Cognitive Skills

 It was once a dominant myth in Western culture that males were more intelligent than females because of their greater knowledge of world affairs and their skill in science and industry. However, that apparent greater male knowledge and skill did not reflect differences in cognitive ability. Rather, it reflected the systematic exclusion of females from world affairs, science, and industry. For example, assessments of intelligence do not show overall gender differences in cognitive abilities (Halpern & LaMay, 2000). However, reviews of the research suggest that girls are

TABLE 12.1 GENDER-ROLE STEREOTYPES AROUND THE WORLD

Stereotypes of Males		Stereotypes of Females	
Active	Opinionated	Affectionate	Nervous
Adventurous	Pleasure-seeking	Appreciative	Patient
Aggressive	Precise	Cautious	Pleasant
Arrogant	Quick	Changeable	Prudish
Autocratic	Rational	Charming	Self-pitying
Capable	Realistic	Complaining	Sensitive
Coarse	Reckless	Complicated	Sentimental
Conceited	Resourceful	Confused	Sexy
Confident	Rigid	Dependent	Shy
Courageous	Robust	Dreamy	Softhearted
Cruel	Sharp-witted	Emotional	Sophisticated
Determined	Show-off	Excitable	Submissive
Disorderly	Steady	Fault-finding	Suggestible
Enterprising	Stern	Fearful	Superstitious
Hardheaded	Stingy	Fickle	Talkative
Individualistic	Stolid	Foolish	Timid
Inventive	Tough	Forgiving	Touchy
Loud	Unscrupulous	Frivolous	Unambitious
Obnoxious		Fussy	Understanding
		Gentle	Unstable
		Imaginative	Warm
		Kind	Weak
		Mild	Worrying
		Modest	

Psychologists John Williams and Deborah Best (1994) found that people in 30 nations around the world tended to agree on the nature of masculine and feminine gender-role stereotypes. Men are largely seen as more adventurous and hardheaded than women. Women are generally seen as more emotional and dependent.

Source: From "Cross-Cultural Views of Women and Men," by J. E. Williams and D. L. Best in *Psychology and Culture*, eds. W. J. Lonner and R. Malpass. Published by Allyn and Bacon, Boston, MA. © 1994 by Pearson Education. Reprinted by permission of the publisher.

somewhat superior to boys in verbal abilities, such as vocabulary, ability to generate sentences and words that are similar in meaning to other words, spelling, knowledge of foreign languages, and pronunciation (Halpern, 1997). Girls seem to acquire language somewhat faster than boys do. Also, in the United States far more boys than girls have reading problems, ranging from reading below grade level to severe disabilities (Halpern, 1997; Neisser et al., 1996).

Males seem to be somewhat superior in the ability to manipulate visual images in working memory. Males as a group excel in visual–spatial abilities of the sort used in math, science, and reading maps (Collaer & Nelson, 2002; Grön et al., 2000; Halpern & LaMay, 2000). One study compared the navigation strategies of 90 male and 104 female university students (Dabbs et al., 1998). In giving directions, men more often referred to miles and directional coordinates (north, south, east, and west). Women were more likely to refer to landmarks and turning right or left. Psychological tests of spatial ability assess skills such as mentally rotating figures in space (see Figure 12.1) and finding figures embedded within larger designs (see Figure 12.2).

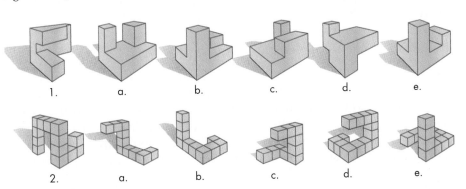

1.   a.   b.   c.   d.   e.

2.   a.   b.   c.   d.   e.

FIGURE 12.1 Rotating Figures in Space

In this test, individuals are asked which of the figures, a through e, would look like the first figure if it were rotated. Males as a group tend to outperform females on spatial relations tasks such as these. However, females do about as well as males when they receive training in the task.

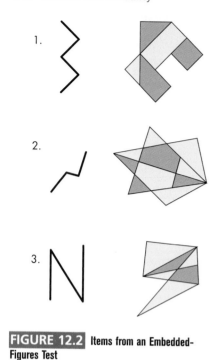

1.

2.

3.

FIGURE 12.2 Items from an Embedded-Figures Test

Studies in the United States and elsewhere find that males generally obtain higher scores on math tests than do females (Beller & Gafni, 2000; Gallagher et al., 2000; Halpern & LaMay, 2000; Leahey & Guo, 2001). Females tend to excel in computational ability in elementary school, however. Males tend to excel in mathematical problem solving in high school and college. Boys largely outperform girls on the math section of the Scholastic Assessment Test.

However, Hyde and Plant (1995) assert that in most cases, differences in cognitive skills are small. They add that differences in verbal, math, and visual–spatial abilities also appear to be narrowing as more females pursue course work in fields that had been typically reserved for males. On the other hand, psychologist J. Michael Bailey (2003a) of Northwestern University argues that these differences are more robust than Hyde and Plant would have us believe, and that the "politically correct" effort to minimize them may not reflect scientific truth.

We can, however, note that reported gender differences are *group* differences. There is greater variation in these skills between individuals *within* the groups than between males and females (Maccoby, 1990). That is, there may be a greater difference in, say, verbal skills between two women than between a woman and a man. Millions of females outdistance the "average" male in math and spatial abilities. Men have produced their verbally adept Shakespeares. Women have produced their scientific Marie Curies.

Some gender differences in cognitive skills may also reflect cultural influences rather than inborn differences (Fredricks & Eccles, 2002). In our culture spatial and math abilities are stereotyped as masculine. But when women are trained in spatial skills for just a few hours—for example, rotating geometric figures or studying floor plans—they perform about as well men on tests of these skills (Baenninger & Elenteny, 1997; Lawton & Morrin, 1999). Moreover, research suggests that girls may experience stereotype threat or vulnerability when they take math tests. In one study, girls performed more poorly on a difficult math test when they were told that the test was known to result in gender differences in scores—an experimental manipulation that apparently made them quite anxious about their performance (O'Brien & Crandall, 2003).

Gender Differences in Personality

There are differences in personality between males and females. In analyses that average the results of multiple studies in gender differences, Alan Feingold (1994, 1998) has found that women are perceived as exceeding men in sociability, happiness, anxiety, trust, and nurturance. Men are perceived as exceeding women in social dominance and tough-mindedness.

According to a survey of 565 university students, men's friendships with other men tend to be shallower and less supportive than women's friendships (Bank & Hansford, 2000). Despite the Western stereotype of women as talkative, research in communication styles suggests that in many situations men spend more time talking than women do. Men are more likely to introduce new topics and to interrupt (Hall, 1984). An analysis of 205 studies involving 23,702 participants found that women are generally more willing to discuss feelings and personal experiences (Dindia & Allen, 1992).

Gender Differences in Social Behavior

There are key gender differences in areas of social behavior such as sex and aggression. According to various measures, men show more interest in sex than women do (Peplau, 2003). Women are more likely to want to combine sex with a romantic relationship (Fisher, 2000; Peplau, 2003). A survey of more than 1,000 undergraduates by David Schmitt and his colleagues (2001) found that men reported being more interested than women in casual sex and in multiple sex partners.

Although there are exceptions, in most cultures it is the males who march off to war and battle for glory (and sneaker commercials). **Truth or Fiction Revisited:** Generally speaking, the research evidence seems to show that males behave more aggressively than females (Felson, 2002; Hines & Saudino, 2003; Zeichner et al., 2003). But as we will see in the controversy below, the answer is not quite that simple. In her classic review of the experimental research on gender differences in aggression, Ann Frodi and her colleagues (1977) found that females behave as aggressively as males when they have the means to do so and believe that aggression is justified. The Frodi group also found that:

◆ Females are more likely to feel anxious or guilty about aggression. Such feelings inhibit aggressive behavior.

◆ Females are more likely to empathize with the victim—to put themselves in the victim's place. Empathy encourages helping behavior, not aggression.

◆ Gender differences in aggression tend to decrease when the victim is anonymous. Anonymity may prevent females from empathizing with their victims.

CONTROVERSY IN PSYCHOLOGY

Are men really more aggressive than women?

Despite the stereotype of male aggressiveness, the research reveals that women are actually somewhat more likely to hit, kick, or use a weapon against their mates or dating partners (Archer, 2000; Felson, 2002). Even so, the women are more likely to be injured.

How do we interpret the data? For one thing, the findings were limited to intimate partners. Men remain more likely to act violently toward strangers and other people of the same sex (Frieze, 2000). The difference in injury rate is also instructive. Men on average are stronger than women, choose more harmful weapons, and may be more likely to intend injury. Therefore, even if women engage in aggressive acts more often with their intimate partners, men remain more dangerous. Skeptics of this research note that the incidence of injury should be the focus of the data, and not the frequency of violent acts (O'Leary, 2000; J. W. White et al., 2000).

But critical thinkers do not ignore research findings because they stir controversy. They suggest that women, like men, can turn to violence when they are frustrated. To be human is . . . to be human. Another part of being human is seeking a partner or a mate, as we see in the following section.

Gender Differences in Mate Selection

Your Daddy's rich
And your Ma is good lookin',
So hush, little baby,
Don't you cry.

From "Summertime" (from the opera *Porgy & Bess*)

How important to you is your partner's physical appearance? Cross-cultural reviews of the research on strategies for mate selection find that women tend to place greater emphasis than men on traits such as professional status, consideration, dependability, kindness, and fondness for children. Men tend to place relatively greater emphasis on physical allure, cooking ability (can't they turn on the

How willing would you be to marry someone who . . .

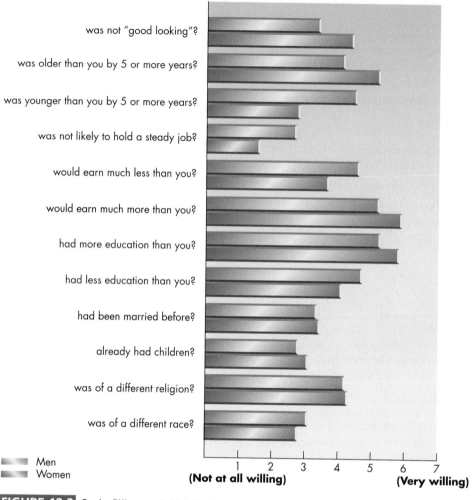

was not "good looking"?

was older than you by 5 or more years?

was younger than you by 5 or more years?

was not likely to hold a steady job?

would earn much less than you?

would earn much more than you?

had more education than you?

had less education than you?

had been married before?

already had children?

was of a different religion?

was of a different race?

Men
Women

1 2 3 4 5 6 7
(Not at all willing)   (Very willing)

FIGURE 12.3 **Gender Differences in Mate Preferences**
Susan Sprecher and her colleagues found that men are more willing than women to marry someone who is several years younger and less well educated. Women, on the other hand, are more willing than men to marry someone who is not good looking and who earns more money than they do.

microwave oven themselves?), even thrift (Buss, 1994; Feingold, 1992a). A study of about 300 male and 350 female university students in China also found that females place relatively more emphasis on earning potential in selecting a mate, and males place more emphasis on physical attractiveness (Chuang, 2002).

Susan Sprecher and her colleagues (1994) surveyed more than 13,000 Americans, attempting to represent the ethnic diversity we find in the United States. They asked how willing their subjects would be to marry someone who was older, younger, of a different religion, unlikely to hold a steady job, not good looking, and so on. Each item was answered by checking off a 7-point scale in which 1 meant "not at all" and 7 meant "very willing." Women were more willing than men to marry someone who was not good-looking (see Figure 12.3). But they were less willing to marry someone who was unlikely to hold a steady job.

There are thus some intriguing patterns of gender differences. The process by which these differences develop is termed *gender-typing*. In the following section we explore several possible sources of gender-typing: evolution, the organization of the brain, sex hormones, and experience.

Your Turn: Now that we have discussed gender stereotypes and differences, enhance your mastery of the material with the nearby "Learning Connections." Review the material by filling in the blanks, reflect on the material by relating it to other things you know, and think critically about it.

Learning Connections — GENDER STEREOTYPES AND DIFFERENCES: WHAT DOES IT MEAN TO BE FEMALE OR TO BE MALE?

ACTIVE REVIEW (1) _____ are fixed, conventional ideas about a group of people. (2) _____-role stereotypes define behavioral expectations of men and women. (3) Throughout Western history, women and men have been seen as having (*Similar* or *Different?*) psychological and sexual natures. (4) Gender polarization has historically worked mostly to the disadvantage of (*Women* or *Men?*). (5) (*Girls* or *Boys?*) are somewhat superior in verbal abilities. (6) (*Girls* or *Boys?*) are somewhat superior in visual–spatial abilities and math. (7) (*Women* or *Men?*) tend to be more interested in sex and aggressive.

REFLECT AND RELATE Do you think of males and females as being the "opposite" of one another? If so, in what ways? Why is the phrase "other sex" more appropriate than "opposite sex"?

CRITICAL THINKING Why do you think some psychologists believe that it is "politically correct" to minimize gender differences in cognitive skills and personality?

 Go to **http://psychology.wadsworth.com/ rathus_pcc9e** for an interactive version of this Learning Connections unit.

Gender-Typing: On Becoming a Woman or a Man

We find the nature–nurture controversy alive and well in the area of **gender-typing**—that is, the issue of how (most) girls develop to behave in a stereotypically feminine manner and (most) boys develop to behave in a stereotypical masculine manner. Before entering this discussion, we should note that many scholars find the very existence of the debate to be invalid because it begins with the assumption that there *are* stereotypical feminine and masculine patterns of behavior. We will keep that criticism in mind, but we also need to review the body of literature that psychologists and other scientists have created on the issue of gender-typing. That literature addresses the roles of nature and nurture in gender-typing.

Nature and Gender-Typing

Question: What is the role of nature in gender-typing? We will begin this discussion with an overview of nature in gender-typing—that is, evolution, the organization of the brain, and sex hormones.

THE ROLES OF EVOLUTION AND HEREDITY According to evolutionary psychologists like David Buss (2000) and David Schmitt (2003), gender differences were fashioned by natural selection in response to problems in adaptation that were repeatedly encountered by humans over thousands of generations. The evolutionary process is expressed through structural differences between males and females, as are found in the brain, and through differences in body chemistry, as are found in the endocrine system.

Why do males tend to place relatively more emphasis than females on physical appearance in mate selection? Why do females tend to place relatively more emphasis on personal factors such as financial status and reliability? Evolutionary psychologists believe that evolutionary forces favor the survival of women who desire status in their mates and men who emphasize physical allure because these preferences provide reproductive advantages. Some physical features such as cleanliness, good complexion, clear eyes, strong teeth and healthy hair, firm muscle tone, and a steady gait are found to be universally appealing to both males and females (Buss, 1999). Perhaps such traits have value as markers of better reproductive potential in prospective mates. According to the "parental investment model," a woman's appeal is more strongly connected with her age and health, both of which are markers of reproductive capacity. The value of men as reproducers, however, is more intertwined with factors that contribute to a stable environment for child rearing—such as social standing and reliability (Schmitt, 2003). For such reasons, evolutionary psychologists speculate that these qualities may have grown relatively more alluring to women over the millennia (Schmitt, 2003).

This theory is largely speculative, however, and not fully consistent with all the evidence. Women, like men, are attracted to physically appealing partners, and women tend to marry men similar to them in physical attractiveness and socio-economic standing. Aging men are more likely than younger men to die from natural causes. The wealth they accrue may not always be transmitted to their spouses and children, either. Many women may be more able to find reproductive success by mating with a fit, younger male than with an older, higher-status male. Even evolutionary psychologists allow that despite any innate predispositions, many men desire older women.

But evolution has also led to the development of the human brain. As we see in the following section, the organization of the brain also apparently plays a role in gender-typing.

THE ROLE OF THE ORGANIZATION OF THE BRAIN Researchers have also found sex differences in the functioning and organization of the brain. Males and females have the same structures in the brain, but they seem to use them somewhat differently. For example, Matthias Riepe and his colleagues (Grön et al., 2000) found that

Gender-typing The process by which people acquire a sense of being female or male and acquire the traits considered typical of females or males within a cultural setting.

men use the hippocampus in both hemispheres when they are trying to navigate through mazes, whereas women use only the hippocampus in the right hemisphere along with the right prefrontal cortex. It has also been found that most women tend to rely on landmarks to navigate ("Turn right at the drugstore, then left at the grocery"), whereas men use geometry, as in deriving information from a map ("The museum should be two blocks to the north") (Ritter, 2000). Riepe (2000) speculates that the women's activity in the cortex might be due to processing landmark cues, whereas the hippocampal activity in men might reflect the more geometric approach. Riepe (2000) has found the same sex difference in brain functioning in rats that are navigating mazes.

Then too, some psychological activities, such as language, seem to be controlled largely by the left side of the brain. Other psychological activities, such as aesthetic and emotional responses, seem to be controlled largely by the right side. Research with brain-imaging techniques suggests that the brain hemispheres may be more specialized in males than in females (Shaywitz et al., 1995). For example, men with damage to the left hemisphere are more likely to experience difficulties in verbal functioning than women with similar damage. Men with damage to the right hemisphere are more likely to have problems with spatial relations than women with similar injuries. Women appear to be able to use both sides of their brains for these functions and hence have a greater chance of recovery.

Sex differences in brain organization might explain, in part, why women tend to excel in verbal skills that require some spatial organization, such as reading, spelling, and crisp articulation of speech. Men, however, tend to excel at more specialized spatial-relations tasks such as interpreting road maps and visualizing objects in space.

THE ROLE OF SEX HORMONES Sex hormones and other chemical substances are responsible for the prenatal differentiation of sex organs (Davis et al., 2000). These substances may also "masculinize" or "feminize" the brain by creating predispositions consistent with some gender-role tendencies (Collaer & Hines, 1995; Crews, 1994). Evidence for the possible role of hormonal influences has been obtained from studies with lower animals (Collaer & Hines, 1995; Crews, 1994). For example, male rats are generally superior to females in maze-learning ability, a task that requires spatial skills. Female rats that are exposed to androgens in the uterus (e.g., because they have several male siblings in the uterus with them) or soon after birth learn maze routes as rapidly as males, however. They also roam larger distances and mark larger territories than most females do (Vandenbergh, 1993).

Men are generally more aggressive than women, and aggressiveness appears to be at least in part connected with testosterone (Pope et al., 2000; A. Sullivan, 2000). However, cognitive psychologists argue that boys (and girls) can choose whether or not to act aggressively, regardless hormone levels in the blood.

■ **Why Don't Male Rats Ask for Directions while Navigating Mazes?** Although the title of this caption is meant to be humorous, we can note that rats ask nothing because they cannot use language. On the other hand, research shows that male rats are generally superior to females in maze-learning ability, a task that relies on visual–spatial skills. However, female rats that are exposed to male sex hormones during prenatal development (e.g., because they have several male siblings in the uterus with them) tend to learn maze routes as quickly as males. They also roam larger distances and mark larger territories than most females—again, as male rats do. How far can we generalize from research findings with rats to humans?

Nurture and Gender-Typing

Question: What is the role of nurture in gender-typing? Just as there is no single view of nature and gender-typing, so is there no single view of nurture and gender-typing. Let us see what three psychological theories have to say about the topic: psychodynamic theory, learning theory, and gender-schema theory.

PSYCHODYNAMIC THEORY AND GENDER-TYPING The two current most prominent psychological perspectives on gender-typing are social cognitive theory and gender-schema theory. Both suggest that people—even in early childhood—attempt to understand the world around them and to behave in ways that are consistent with that understanding. However, we begin with psychodynamic theory because of its historic interest.

Sigmund Freud explained the acquisition of gender roles in terms of identification. He believed that gender-related behaviors remain flexible until the age of 5 or 6. Freud argued that it was natural for boys to want to possess their mothers and view their fathers as rivals in love. It was natural for girls to wish they had a penis. In Freud's speculative theme, appropriate gender-typing requires that boys identify with their fathers and give up the wish to possess their mothers. Girls have to surrender the wish to have a penis and identify with their mothers.

But research evidence reveals that boys and girls are inclined to develop gender-typed preferences for toys and activities earlier than predicted by psychodynamic theory. Even within the first year, boys tend to be more explorative and active than girls (Rathus, 2003). A Canadian study of 77 infants found that infants showed preferences for gender-stereotyped toys by the age of 18 months (Serbin et al., 2001). Girls gazed longer at photos of dolls, and boys gazed longer at photos of transportation toys. More recent theories of gender-typing allow for the earlier ages of gender-related preferences. They note that all that is necessary is for children to understand whether they are boys or girls and what boys and girls "do."

LEARNING THEORIES AND GENDER-TYPING The two key learning theories are behaviorism and social cognitive theory. Behaviorists explain gender-typing in terms of the selective reinforcement of behavior patterns deemed appropriate for boys and girls within a given culture. But there is no evidence that boys and girls "try out" all possible behavior patterns, nor that they are accurately reinforced.

Social cognitive theorists do not agree that reinforcement mechanically induces gender-typed behaviors. They assert, instead, that experience helps the individual create concepts of gender-appropriate behavior (Bussey & Bandura, 1999). Reinforcement helps—but by providing information as to what other people consider to be proper behavior for girls and boys.

According to social cognitive theory, children learn much of what is considered masculine or feminine by observational learning. Whom do young children observe most frequently? Usually, their parents. Research evidence shows that children's views of what is masculine and feminine are related to those of their parents (Tenenbaum & Leaper, 2002). This finding is consistent with social cognitive theory and, as we will see, also with gender-schema theory.

The importance of observational learning is also supported by the findings of experiments such as a classic experiment conducted by David Perry and Kay Bussey (1979). In this study, children learned how behaviors are gender-typed by observing the *relative frequencies* with which men and women performed them. The adult role models expressed arbitrary preferences for one item from each of 16 pairs of items—pairs such as oranges versus apples and toy cows versus toy horses—while 8- and 9-year-old boys and girls watched them. The children were then asked to show their own preferences. Boys selected an average of 14 of 16 items that agreed with the "preferences" of the men. Girls selected an average of only 3 of 16 items that agreed with the choices of the men. In other words, boys and girls learned gender-typed preferences even though those preferences were completely arbitrary.

Socialization also plays a role within social cognitive theory. Parents and other adults—even other children—inform children about how they are expected to behave. They reinforce or reward children for behavior they consider appropriate for their sex. They punish (or fail to reinforce) children for behavior they consider inappropriate. Girls, for example, are given dolls while they are still sleeping in their cribs. They are encouraged to use the dolls to rehearse caretaking behaviors in preparation for traditional feminine adult roles.

Social cognitive theory outlines ways in which experience leads to concepts of gender and how people try to regulate their own behavior to conform to what they believe is appropriate. Gender-schema theory suggests that it is human nature to

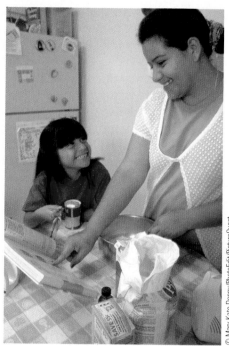

■ **Acquiring Gender Roles** How do gender roles develop? What contributions are made by evolutionary and genetic factors? What is the role of experience? Social cognitive theory notes that children obtain information as to what kinds of preferences and behaviors are considered masculine or feminine in their cultures. This information plus some use of rewards and punishments by family members and others apparently encourages most children to imitate the behavior of people of the same sex. But is learning the whole story, or does learning interact with evolutionary and genetic factors to fashion likes and dislikes and patterns of behavior?

assume gender-appropriate behavior by blending one's self-concept with cultural expectations.

GENDER-SCHEMA THEORY AND GENDER-TYPING You have probably heard the expression, "looking at the world through rose-colored glasses." According to Sandra Bem (1993), the originator of **gender-schema theory,** people look at the social world through "the lenses of gender." Bem argues that cultures tend to break males and females into opposing groups because social life is organized around exclusive gender roles. For example, girls often accept their roles as nurturant (playing with dolls). Unless parents or unusual events encourage them to challenge the validity of gender polarization, children attempt to construct identities that are consistent with the "proper" script. Most children reject behavior—in others and in themselves—that deviates. Children's self-esteem becomes wrapped up in the ways in which they measure up to the gender schema. For example, most boys tie their self-esteem to prowess in sports.

Once children understand the labels *boy* and *girl,* they have a basis for blending their self-concepts with the gender schema of their culture. The desire to do so is natural. No external pressure is required. Children who have developed a sense of being male or being female, which usually occurs by the age of 3, actively seek information about their gender schema. As in social cognitive theory, children seek to learn what is considered appropriate for them by observing other people.

Research shows that once boys and girls learn what is expected of them, they even distort their memories to fit their intended roles. For example, researchers in one study showed 5- and 6-year-old boys and girls pictures of people engaged in "gender-consistent" or "gender-inconsistent" activities (Bowes & Goodnow, 1996). The gender-consistent pictures showed boys playing with trains or sawing wood. Girls were shown cooking and cleaning. Gender-inconsistent pictures showed people of the other sex engaged in these gender-typed activities. A week later, the children were asked who had engaged in each activity, a male or a female. Both boys and girls gave wrong answers more often when the picture they had seen showed gender-*inconsistent* activity. In other words, they distorted what they had seen to conform to the gender schema of their culture.

In sum, the organization of the brain and sex hormones appear to contribute to gender-typed behavior and play roles in verbal ability, math skills, and aggres-

Gender-schema theory The view that gender identity plus knowledge of the distribution of behavior patterns into feminine and masculine roles motivate and guide the gender-typing of the child.

sion. Gender-typed behavior patterns are unlikely to result from the resolution of deep-seated conflict as Freudians would assert, or from the mechanical reinforcement of selected behaviors. Social cognitive theory assumes that children actively seek information about the environment and outlines ways in which children obtain information about which behaviors are considered masculine or feminine. Gender-schema theory focuses on how children blend their self-identities with the gender schema of their culture. Today, most scholars would agree that both nature and nurture affect most areas of behavior and mental processes—including the complex processes in gender-typing.

Your Turn: Now that we have discussed gender-typing, enhance your mastery of the material with the nearby "Learning Connections." Review the material by filling in the blanks, reflect on the material by relating it to other things you know, and think critically about it. The nearby Concept Review summarizes some of the key points about the various approaches to gender-typing.

When we speak of sex, we are not only referring to a person's anatomic sex—that is, her or his being female or being male. We are also referring to sexual behavior. In the following section we explore what motivates sexual behavior—what fuels it and the directions it takes.

Learning Connections — GENDER-TYPING: ON BECOMING A WOMAN OR A MAN

ACTIVE REVIEW (8) According to _____ theory, gender differences were fashioned by means of natural selection. (9) Research in brain-imaging suggests that the brain hemispheres are more specialized in (*Males* or *Females?*). (10) Behaviors such as maze learning and aggression appear to be connected with exposure to the hormone _____. (11) Social cognitive theorists note that children learn what is considered masculine or feminine by means of _____ learning. (12) According to _____-schema theory, children accept their culture's roles for them without realizing it. (13) Children's self-_____ then becomes wrapped up in how well they fit the gender schema of their culture.

REFLECT AND RELATE Did your parents or caregivers expose you to any particular early learning experiences in order to ensure that you would develop to be a "proper" woman or man? Would you feel comfortable giving your son a doll to play with? Why or why not?

CRITICAL THINKING Evaluate the evidence. Does the research evidence suggest that there is a role for nature in gender-typing? Does it show that there is a role for nurture?

 Go to **http://psychology.wadsworth.com/ rathus_pcc9e** for an interactive version of this Learning Connections unit.

Sexual Motivation: Pressing the "On" Button and Finding Direction

In a TV situation comedy, a mother referred to her teenage son as "a hormone with feet." She recognized that her son had become obsessed with sex, which is normal enough for adolescents in our culture. It is also now widely understood that the adolescent preoccupation with sex is strongly related to the surge in sex hormones that occurs at puberty. The phrase "a hormone with feet" implies movement as well as motivation, and movement means direction. We will see that sex hormones tend to propel us in certain directions as well as provide the driving force. **Question: How do sex hormones affect sexual motivation?**

Hormones and Sexual Motivation: Adding Fuel to the Fire

Sex hormones can be said to fuel the sex drive. Research with men who produce little testosterone—due to age or health problems—shows that their sex drive is increased when they receive testosterone replacement therapy (A. Sullivan, 2000; Yates, 2000). The most common sexual problem among women is lack of sexual desire or interest, and the sex drive in women is also connected with testosterone levels (Friedrich, 2000). Although men produce 10 to 20 times the testosterone produced by women, women produce androgens ("male" sex hormones) in the adrenal

Concept Review GENDER-TYPING

Perspective		Key Points	Comments
Nature and Gender-Typing Deals with the roles of evolution, heredity, and biology in gender-typing	**Evolution and heredity**	Psychological gender differences were fashioned by natural selection in response to problems in adaptation that were repeatedly encountered by humans over thousands of generations. The evolutionary process is expressed, for example, through gender differences in mate selection.	Evolutionary psychologists suggest that evolutionary forces favor the survival of women who desire status in their mates and men who emphasize physical allure because these preferences provide reproductive advantages. A woman's allure is more strongly connected with her age and health, both of which are markers of reproductive capacity. But the value of men as reproducers is more connected with factors that contribute to a stable environment for child rearing—such as social status and dependability.
	Organization of the brain	Brain-imaging research suggests that the hemispheres of the brain may be more specialized in males than in females. Use of language is usually based in the left hemisphere, and men with damage to the left hemisphere are more likely to experience language difficulties than women with similar damage. Spatial relations is usually more based in the right than the left hemisphere, but men with damage to the right hemisphere are more likely to have problems with spatial relations than women with similar injuries.	Sex differences in brain organization might help explain why women tend to excel in language skills that require some spatial organization, such as reading, spelling, and articulation. It may also partly explain why men tend to excel at more specialized spatial-relations tasks such as reading road maps and mentally rotating objects.
	Sex hormones	Sex hormones may "masculinize" or "feminize" the brain during prenatal development by creating predispositions consistent with some gender-role tendencies.	Male rats are generally superior to females in maze-learning ability, a task that requires spatial skills. Female rats that are exposed to androgens in the uterus (e.g., because they have several male siblings in the uterus with them) or soon after birth learn maze routes as rapidly as males, however. They also roam larger distances and mark larger territories than most females do. Men are generally more aggressive than women, and aggressiveness appears to be at least in part connected with testosterone.
Nurture and Gender-Typing Deals with theories in psychology—e.g., psychodynamic theory, learning theory, and cognitive theory—and related research	**Psychodynamic theory**	The acquisition of gender roles is explained in terms of identification. Gender-related behaviors remain flexible until the age of 5 or 6, but resolution of the Oedipus and Electra complexes at those ages leads to adoption of the preferences and behaviors of parent figures of the same sex.	Research evidence reveals that boys and girls are inclined to develop gender-typed preferences for toys and activities earlier than predicted by psychodynamic theory.
	Learning theories	Behaviorists explain gender-typing in terms of the selective reinforcement of behavior patterns deemed appropriate for boys and girls within a given culture. Social cognitive theory asserts that reinforcement encourages gender-typing by providing information as to what other people deem to be appropriate behavior and that children learn much of what is considered masculine or feminine by observational learning.	Parents, especially fathers, tend to reinforce or reward children for what they see as gender-appropriate behavior. Research in favor of the role of observational learning evidence shows that children's views of what is masculine and feminine are related to those of their parents. Moreover, research shows that children learn how behaviors are gender-typed by observing the *relative frequencies* with which males and females perform them.
	Gender-schema theory	Cultures tend to polarize females and males by organizing social life around mutually exclusive gender roles. Children come to accept the polarizing scripts and attempt to construct identities that are consistent with the "proper" script. Children develop a sense of being male or being female by about the age of 3 and seek information about what is considered appropriate for them. Children's self-esteem becomes wrapped up in the ways in which they measure up to the gender schema.	Most boys in our culture learn early to hold a high opinion of themselves if they excel in sports. Research evidence suggests that polarized female–male scripts serve as cognitive anchors within Western culture. For example, children tend to distort their memories of their observations to conform to the gender schema of their cultures.

Go to **http://psychology.wadsworth.com/rathus_pcc9e** to access a drag-and-drop version of this Concept Review designed to help you test yourself on the major topics provided here.

glands. Testosterone injections, patches, or pills can heighten the sex drive in women who do not produce enough of it (Tuiten et al., 2000).

Sex hormones promote the development of male and female sex organs and regulate the menstrual cycle. They also have activating and organizing effects on sexual behavior. They affect the sex drive and promote sexual response; these are

activating effects. Female mice, rats, cats, and dogs are receptive to males only during **estrus,** when female sex hormones are plentiful. During estrus, female rats respond to males by hopping, wiggling their ears, and arching their backs with their tails to one side, thus enabling males to penetrate them. But, as noted by Kimble (1988),

> . . . if we were to observe this same pair of animals one day [after estrus], we would see very different behaviors. The male would still be interested (at least at first), but his advances would not be answered with hopping, ear wiggling, and [arching of the back]. The female would be much more likely to "chatter" her teeth at the male (a sure sign of hostility if you are a rat). If the male were to be slow to grasp her meaning, she might turn away from him and kick him in the head, mule fashion. Clearly, it is over between them. (p. 271)

The following Controversy in Psychology suggests that pheromones, like hormones, may play a role in human sexual behavior.

Is the human sex drive affected by pheromones?

For centuries people have searched for a love potion—a magical formula that could make other people fall in love with you or be strongly attracted to you. Some scientists suggest that such potions may already exist in the form of chemical secretions known as **pheromones. Question: What are pheromones?** Pheromones are odorless chemicals that are detected through a "sixth sense"—the *vomeronasal organ (VNO)*. People possess such an organ, located in the mucous lining of the nose (Rodriguez et al., 2000). During the embryonic period, the VNO acts as a pathway for sex hormones into the brain, aiding in sexual differentiation (Rodriguez et al., 2000). But prior to birth, the VNO in humans shrinks, and some researchers believe that it stops working (Kouros-Mehr et al., 2001). If it does continue to work, it might detect pheromones and communicate information about them to the hypothalamus, where certain pheromones might affect sexual response (Cutler, 1999). People might also use pheromones in many ways. Infants might use them to recognize their mothers, and adults might respond to them in seeking a mate. Research clearly shows that lower animals use pheromones to stimulate sexual response, organize food gathering, maintain pecking orders, sound alarms, and mark territories (Curtis et al., 2001; Leinders-Zufall et al., 2000).

So what about humans? In a typical study, Winnifred Cutler and her colleagues (1998) had men wear a suspected male pheromone, whereas a control group wore a placebo. At the end of the study, the men using the pheromone increased their frequency of sexual intercourse with their female partners but did not increase the frequency of masturbation. The researchers conclude that the substance increased the sexual attractiveness of the men to their partners, although because the study was not conclusive, they do not claim that it directly stimulated sexual behavior.

Even so, some other studies are also of interest. Consider a couple of double-blind studies that exposed men and women to certain steroids (androstadienone produced by males and estratetraenol produced by females) suspected of being pheromones. They found that both steroids enhanced the moods of women but not of men; the substances also apparently reduced feelings of nervousness and tension in women, but again, not in men (Grosser et al., 2000; Jacob & McClintock, 2000). The findings about estratetraenol are not terribly surprising. This substance is related to estrogen, and women tend

Activating effect The arousal-producing effects of sex hormones that increase the likelihood of sexual behavior.

Estrus The periodic sexual excitement of many mammals, as governed by levels of sex hormones.

Pheromone A chemical secretion detected by other members of the same species that stimulates stereotypical behaviors.

to function best during the time of the month when estrogen levels are highest (Ross et al., 2000).

If current studies stand up to the scrutiny of replication and time, we might conclude that certain substances enhance the moods of women and thus make them more receptive to sexual advances. Still, the substances do not directly stimulate sexual behavior, as do pheromones with lower animals. If pheromones with such effects on humans exist, they have not yet been isolated. And they may not exist, because the higher we go up the evolutionary ladder, the less important is the role of instinctive behavior.

Sexual Orientation: Which Way Is Love?

Sex hormones have not only activating effects, but also directional or **organizing effects.** That is, they predispose lower animals toward masculine or feminine mating patterns. Sex hormones are thus likely candidates for influencing the development of sexual orientation (Lalumière et al., 2000). **Question: What is meant by sexual orientation?**

One's **sexual orientation** refers to the direction of his or her sexual and romantic interests—toward people of the other sex or toward people of the same sex. The great majority of people have a *heterosexual* orientation. That is, they are sexually attracted to, and interested in forming romantic relationships with, people of the other sex. However, some people have a **homosexual** orientation. They are attracted to and interested in forming romantic relationships with people of their own sex. Males with a homosexual orientation are referred to as *gay males.* Females with a homosexual orientation are referred to as *lesbians. Bisexual* people are attracted to both females and males.

The concept of sexual orientation differs from that of *sexual activity.* Engaging in sexual activity with people of one's own sex does not necessarily mean that one has a homosexual orientation. Sexual activity between males sometimes reflects limited sexual opportunities. Adolescent males may manually stimulate one another while fantasizing about girls. Male Sambian adolescents in New Guinea engage in oral sex with older males because of the cultural belief that they must drink "men's milk" to achieve the fierce manhood of the headhunter (Bailey, 2003b). But once they marry, they engage in sexual activity with females only.

THE ORIGINS OF SEXUAL ORIENTATION Surveys find that about 3% of the males and 2% of the females in the United States identify themselves as being gay (Bailey, 2003a; Laumann et al., 1994). Theories of the origins of sexual orientation look both at nature and nurture—the biological makeup of the individual and environmental factors. Some theories bridge the two. **Question: What do we know about the origins of gay male and lesbian sexual orientations?**

Let us begin our search for the psychological roots of sexual orientation with psychodynamic theory because of its historic importance. Freudian theory attributes the individual's sexual orientation to identification with male or female figures, particularly one's father or mother. Freud believed that homosexuality represented an abnormal resolution of the Oedipus and Electra complexes at the ages of 5 or 6 (Downey & Friedman, 1998). Many psychoanalysts attributed faulty resolution of the Oedipus complex to a "classic pattern" of family life which involves a "close-binding" mother and a "detached–hostile" father. In such a setting, boys are more likely to identify with their mothers than their fathers. Evidence for this view is sketchy, however, relying on a number of case studies. Also, many gay males show a pattern of "gender nonconformity"—for example, interest in playthings associated with girls—long before the ages of 5 or 6 (K. Cohen, 2002; Rahman & Wilson, 2003). Another sticking point is that many gay males have good relationships with both parents. Besides, many heterosexuals develop in homes that seem to fit the "classic pattern."

■ Randy Gregory holds daughter Laura Jewel Gregory, 1, with life partner Kevin Boynton outside their home.

© Michael Mulvey/Dallas Morning News,/CORBIS

Learning theorists look for the roles of factors such as reinforcement and observational learning. From this perspective, reinforcement of sexual behavior with members of one's own sex—as in reaching orgasm with them when members of the other sex are unavailable—might affect one's sexual orientation. Similarly, childhood sexual abuse by someone of the same sex could lead to a pattern of sexual activity with people of one's own sex and affect sexual orientation. Observation of others engaged in enjoyable male–male or female–female sexual encounters could also affect the development of sexual orientation. But critics point out that most individuals become aware of their sexual orientation before they experience sexual contacts with other people of either sex (Bailey, 2003a; Rahman & Wilson, 2003). Moreover, in a society that generally condemns homosexuality, young people are unlikely to believe that male–male or female–female relationships will have positive effects for them.

There is evidence for genetic factors in sexual orientation (Bailey, 2003a; Bailey et al., 2000; Kendler et al., 2000c; Rahman & Wilson, 2003). About 52% of identical (MZ) twin pairs are "concordant" (in agreement) for a gay male sexual orientation, as compared with 22% for fraternal (DZ) twins and 11% for adoptive brothers (Bailey, 2003a; Bailey & Pillard, 1991). Monozygotic (MZ) twins fully share their genetic heritage, whereas dizygotic (DZ) twins, like other pairs of siblings, overlap 50%.

RESEARCH WITH NONHUMAN ANIMALS In many species, there is little room for thinking about sex and deciding whether an individual will pursue sexual relationships with males or females. Sexual motivation comes under the almost complete governance of sex hormones (Crews, 1994). Furthermore, much sexual motivation is determined by whether the brains and sex organs of fetuses are bathed in large doses of testosterone in the uterus. In male fetuses, testosterone is normally produced by the developing testes. Yet female fetuses may also be exposed to testosterone. They can be flooded with testosterone naturally if they share the uterus with many male siblings. Researchers can also inject male sex hormones into the uterus. When female embryos are bathed in testosterone, the sex organs become masculinized in appearance, and their brains become organized in the male direction, creating a tendency toward female–female mating efforts and other masculine-typed behavior patterns at maturity (Crews, 1994). Basically, the rodents become male, although they are infertile.

In other experiments with laboratory animals, prenatal exposure to stress or to stress combined with alcohol decreases prenatal exposure to testosterone (I. L. Ward et al., 2003). As a result, male embryos are less likely to engage in stereotypical male reproductive behavior patterns when they mature.

It has been demonstrated repeatedly that sex hormones predispose lower animals toward stereotypical masculine or feminine mating patterns. Does this research suggest that gay males and lesbians differ from heterosexuals in their levels of sex hormones? Among gay male and lesbian adolescents and adults, the answer is apparently not. Sexual orientation has not been reliably connected with adolescent or adult levels of sex hormones (Friedman & Downey, 1994).

BACK TO HUMANS But do sex hormones influence the developing human embryo and fetus in the way that they affect rodents? The evidence is somewhat mixed and this possibility continues to receive intensive study (Dessens et al., 1999; I. L. Ward et al., 2003). And if prenatal hormone levels affect the sexual orientation of the fetus, what causes the fluctuation in hormone levels? We're not sure. Hormone levels in utero are affected by genetic factors, maternal stress, drinking alcohol, along with other factors—some suspected, many completely unknown. Is it possible that the brains of some gay males were feminized and the brains of some lesbians masculinized in utero (Collaer & Hines, 1995; Friedman & Downey, 1994)?

We have to conclude by confessing that much about the development of sexual orientation remains speculative. There are possible roles for prenatal exposure to certain hormones. Exposure to these hormones, in turn, may be related to

Organizing effect The directional effect of sex hormones—for example, along stereotypically masculine or feminine lines.

Sexual orientation The directionality of one's sexual and romantic interests; that is, whether one is sexually attracted to, and desires to form a romantic relationship with, members of the other sex or of one's own sex.

Homosexual Referring to people who are sexually aroused by, and interested in forming romantic relationships with, people of the same sex. (Derived from the Greek *homos*, meaning "same," not from the Latin *homo*, meaning "man.")

genetic factors, use of drugs (prescribed and illicit), even maternal stress. Moreover, the possibility that childhood experiences play a role has not been ruled out. But the interactions among these factors largely remain a mystery. Nor is there any reason to believe that the development of sexual orientation will follow precisely the same pattern for all individuals (Garnets, 2002).

 # A Closer Look   PHEROMONES AND SEXUAL ORIENTATION

Vision is normally the dominant sense in humans. We tend to gather more information about other people by looking at them than by smelling them or touching them (Wade, 2005). However, in the film *Scent of a Woman,* Al Pacino played a blind man who was drawn to women by their odor. Are there odors that are characteristic of the other sex? If so, how important are they in determining sexual attraction?

Some answers are suggested in a study by Swedish researchers (Savic et al., 2005) who used PET scans to show that gay and heterosexual men respond differently to smelling chemicals that may affect sexual arousal and that the gay men respond similarly to women (see Figure 12.4). The study involved suspected pheromones, which are chemicals emitted by a member of a species to evoke a response in another member of the species. Previously, researchers had found that pheromones may enhance people's moods, have effects on fertility, and

provide a basis for sexual communication at a level below conscious awareness.

The Swedish study investigated the effects of two chemicals: a testosterone derivative produced in men's sweat and an estrogen-like compound found in women's urine. Most odors activate neurons in specific regions of the brain, increasing the blood flow to these regions and causing them to "light up" when imaged by the PET scan. The estrogen-like compound activated the usual smell-related areas in women, but it lit up the hypothalamus—a structure involved in sexual behavior—in heterosexual men. The chemical extracted from male sweat, in contrast, did the opposite; it activated the hypothalamus in women and the usual smell-related areas in men. Each chemical seemed to be just another odor with one sex but a pheromone with the other. However, gay men in the study responded to the chemicals as women did. That is, their hypothalamus was lit up by the chemical drawn from male

sweat. Lesbians were also studied, but the data were complex and not ready for publication (Wade, 2005).

It must be noted that the Swedish study does not reveal cause and effect. A "snapshot" was taken of brain functioning at one moment in time. The snapshot did not show how the brain's responses develop. Were the activity patterns in heterosexual and gay men a cause or rather an effect of their sexual orientation? If sexual orientation has a genetic basis or is influenced by hormones in the womb or at puberty, then it might be that the neurons in the hypothalamus become hardwired in a way that shapes sexual orientation. Conversely, the findings could mean that experience leads straight and gay men to respond in different ways.

In any event, the study does suggest a role for pheromones in human sexual response and lays the groundwork for further research.

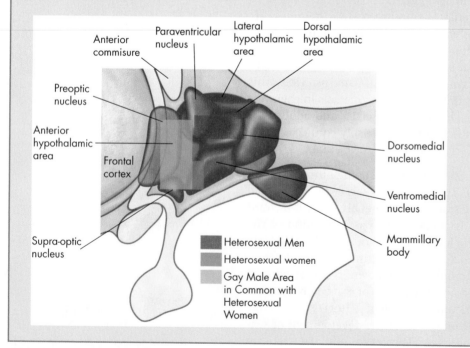

FIGURE 12.4 Who Lights Up Your Hypothalamus?
Certain areas of the hypothalamus "light up" when heterosexual males smell an estrogen-like compound (estratetraenol) found in women's urine, when heterosexual women smell an androgen-like compound (androstadienone), and when gay males smell the androstadienone. The hypothalamus of gay males responds similarly to that of heterosexual women when the person is presented with the odor of androstadienone. Note the locations of the ventromedial nucleus and the lateral hypothalamus, which are relevant to the chapter's earlier discussion of the hunger drive.

Source: Savic et al., "Brain response to putative pheromones in homosexual men," *Proceedings of the National Association of Science, 102,* fig. 3, p. 7539. Reprinted by permission.

Learning Connections

ACTIVE REVIEW (14) The hormone _____ is connected with sex drive in both males and females. (15) Sex hormones have activating and _____ effects on sexual behavior. (16) A person's sexual _____ involves whether he or she is sexually attracted to, and interested in forming romantic relationships with, people of the same or the other sex. (17) According to _____ theory, one's sexual orientation is tied to one's early history of reinforcement for sexual activity. (18) Twin studies (*Do* or *Do not?*) support a role for genes in sexual orientation. (19) Sex hormones (*Do* or *Do not?*) predispose lower animals toward stereotypical masculine or feminine mating patterns. (20) _____ are odorless chemicals that are detected through the vomeronasal organ.

REFLECT AND RELATE Have you heard the term *sexual preference?* The term implies that people choose their sexual orientation. Do you believe that people decide whether to be heterosexual or gay? Have you changed your opinion as a result of reading the text?

CRITICAL THINKING In general, people who attribute sexual orientation to biological causes are more accepting of gay male and lesbian sexual orientations. Why do you think this is so?

Go to **http://psychology.wadsworth.com/ rathus_pcc9e** for an interactive version of this Learning Connections unit.

Interpersonal Attraction: On Liking and Loving

Sexual interactions usually take place within relationships. Feelings of **attraction** can lead to liking and perhaps to love, and to a more lasting relationship. **Question: What factors contribute to attraction in our culture?** Among the factors contributing to attraction are physical appearance, similarity, and reciprocity.

Physical Appearance: How Important Is Looking Good?

Physical appearance is a key factor in attraction and in the consideration of romantic partners (Langlois et al., 2000; Sangrador & Yela, 2000). What determines physical allure? Are our standards subjective—that is, "in the eye of the beholder"? Or is there general agreement on what is appealing?

Truth or Fiction Revisited: Although there may be individual preferences, it does not seem that standards for beauty are so flexible that they are fully "in the eye of the beholder." Many standards for beauty appear to be cross-cultural (Langlois et al., 2000; Little & Perrett, 2002). For example, a study of people in England and Japan found that both British and Japanese men consider women with large eyes, high cheekbones, and narrow jaws to be most attractive (Perret, 1994). In his research, Perret created computer composites of the faces of 60 women and, as shown in part A of Figure 12.5, of the 15 women who were rated the most attractive. He then used computer enhancement to exaggerate the differences between the composite of the 60 and the composite of the 15 most attractive women. He arrived at the image shown in part B of Figure 12.5. Part B, which shows higher cheekbones and a narrower jaw than part A, was rated as the most attractive image. Similar results were found for the image of a Japanese woman. Works of art suggest that the ancient Greeks and Egyptians favored similar facial features.

In our society, tallness is an asset for men (Hensley, 1994; Pierce, 1996). Although women may be less demanding than men concerning a variety of physical feature, height—that is, tallness—is more important to women in the selection of dates and mates than it is to men.

Although preferences for facial features may transcend time and culture, preferences for body weight and shape may be more culturally determined. For example, plumpness has been valued in many cultures. Grandmothers who worry that their granddaughters are starving themselves often come from cultures in which stoutness is acceptable or desirable. In contemporary Western society, there is pres-

Attraction In social psychology, an attitude of liking or disliking (negative attraction).

FIGURE 12.5 What Features Contribute to Facial Attractiveness?

In both England and Japan, features such as large eyes, high cheekbones, and narrow jaws contribute to perceptions of the attractiveness of women. Part A shows a composite of the faces of 15 women rated as the most attractive of a group of 60. Part B is a composite in which the features of these 15 women are exaggerated—that is, developed further in the direction that separates them from the average of the entire 60.

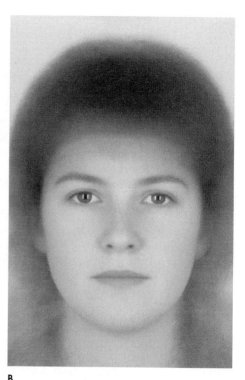

A.

B.

■ **"Looking Good"** Models like these are among those who set the standards for beauty in contemporary American culture. How important is physical attractiveness in interpersonal attraction and social and vocational success?

Matching hypothesis The view that people tend to choose persons similar to themselves in attractiveness and attitudes in the formation of interpersonal relationships.

sure on both males and females to be slender (Goode, 2000; Wade et al., 2000). Women generally favor men with a V-taper—broad shoulders and a narrow waist.

"PRETTY IS AS PRETTY DOES?" **Truth or Fiction Revisited:** Both men and women are perceived as more attractive when they are smiling (Reis et al., 1990). When you're smiling, observers expect to have positive social interactions with you (Harker & Keltner, 2001). There is thus ample reason to, as the song goes, "put on a happy face" when you are meeting people or looking for a date.

Other aspects of behavior also affect interpersonal attraction. Women who are shown videotapes of prospective dates or asked to describe ideal partners tend to prefer men who are outgoing, self-assertive, and self-confident (Burger & Cosby, 1999).

The Matching Hypothesis: Do "Opposites Attract" or Do "Birds of a Feather Flock Together"?

Although we may rate highly attractive people as most desirable, most of us are not left to blend in with the wallpaper. According to the **matching hypothesis,** we tend to date people who are similar to ourselves in physical attractiveness rather than the local Will Smith or Sandra Bullock look-alike. One motive for asking out "matches" seems to be fear of rejection by more attractive people (Bernstein et al., 1983). **Truth or Fiction Revisited:** Despite the familiar saying "opposites attract," it seems that people who are similar are more likely than opposites to be attracted to one another.

The quest for similarity extends beyond physical attractiveness. Our marital and sex partners tend to be similar to us in race/ethnicity, age, level of education, and religion. Consider some findings of the National Health and Social Life Survey (Michael et al., 1994, pp. 45–47):

◆ Nearly 94% of single European American men have European American women as their sex partners; 2% are partnered with Latina Americans, 2% with Asian American women, and less than 1% with African American women.

■ **The Matching Hypothesis** Do opposites attract, or do we tend to pair off with people who look and think the way we do? As suggested by these photographs, similarity often runs at least skin-deep.

◆ About 82% of African American men have African American women as their sex partners; nearly 8% are partnered with European American women and almost 5% with Latina Americans.

◆ About 83% of the women and men in the study chose partners within five years of their own age and of the same or a similar religion.

◆ Of nearly 2,000 women in the study, not one with a graduate college degree had a partner who had not finished high school.

Why do most people have partners from the same background as their own? One reason is that marriages are made in the neighborhood and not in heaven (Michael et al., 1994). We tend to live among people who are similar to us in background, and we therefore come into contact with them more often than with people from other backgrounds. Another reason is that we are drawn to people whose attitudes are similar to ours (Michinov & Michinov, 2001; Singh & Ho, 2000; Watson et al., 2000). People from similar backgrounds are more likely to have similar attitudes.

Other Factors in Attraction: Reciprocity and the Nearness of You?

Has anyone told you how good-looking, brilliant, and mature you are? That your taste is refined? That all in all, you are really something special? If so, have you been impressed by his or her fine judgment? **Reciprocity** is a powerful determinant of attraction (Bruce & Sanders, 2001; Sprecher, 1998). We tend to return feelings of admiration. We tend to be more open, warm, and helpful when we are interacting with strangers who seem to like us (Curtis & Miller, 1986).

Deb Levine (2000), writing in the journal *CyberPsychology and Behavior,* compares attraction online ("virtual attraction") with attraction in the real world. She notes that proximity, or nearness, is a factor online and offline, but proximity online can mean visiting the same chat room a number of times even though individuals live thousands of miles apart. Self-disclosure and reciprocity occur more quickly online, perhaps because people think they are operating from a safe distance. It is more difficult, she asserts, to check out similarities in interests because people are more or less free to present themselves as they wish. She suggests that people exchange biographies and photos within a month or so of when they meet online and meet in person, if possible, in order to dispel unrealistic expectations.

Whether online of offline, feelings of attraction are influenced by factors such as physical appearance and similarity. Let us explore what we mean when we say that feelings of attraction have blossomed into love.

Love: The Emotion That Launched a Thousand Ships?

Love—the ideal for which we make great sacrifice. Love—the sentiment that launched a thousand ships and led to the Trojan War in Homer's epic poem *The Iliad.* Through the millennia, poets have sought to capture love in words. Dante, the Italian poet, wrote of "the love that moves the sun and the other stars." The

Reciprocity In interpersonal attraction, the tendency to return feelings and attitudes that are expressed about us.

Triangular model of love Sternberg's view that love involves combinations of three components: intimacy, passion, and decision/commitment.

Intimacy Close acquaintance and familiarity; a characteristic of a relationship in which partners share their inmost feelings.

Passion Strong romantic and sexual feelings.

Consummate love The ideal form of love within Sternberg's model, which combines passion, intimacy, and commitment.

Romantic love An intense, positive emotion that involves sexual attraction, feelings of caring, and the belief that one is in love.

Affective shift hypothesis The view that men and women tend to experience different shifts in the emotions following initiation of sexual activity, such that women feel more love and commitment, and many men experience less love and commitment.

Scottish poet Robert Burns wrote that his love was like "a red, red rose." Love is beautiful and elusive. Passion and romantic love are also lusty, surging with sexual desire. **Questions: Just what is love? What is romantic love?**

There are a number of theories about the nature of love. We will discuss Robert Sternberg's (1988) **triangular model of love,** which can be thought of as a love triangle. This love triangle does not refer to two men wooing the same woman. It refers to Sternberg's view that love can include combinations of three components: intimacy, passion, and commitment (see Figure 12.6).

Intimacy refers to a couple's closeness, to their mutual concern and sharing of feelings and resources. **Passion** means romance and sexual feelings. Commitment means deciding to enhance and maintain the relationship. Passion is most crucial in short-term relationships. Intimacy and commitment are more important in enduring relationships. The ideal form of love combines all three: **consummate love.** Consummate love is made up of romantic love plus commitment.

Romantic love is characterized by passion and intimacy. Passion involves fascination (preoccupation with the loved one); sexual craving; and the desire for exclusiveness (a special relationship with the loved one). Intimacy involves caring—championing the interests of the loved one, even if it entails sacrificing one's own. People are cognitively biased toward evaluating their dating partners positively (Loving & Agnew, 2001). In plain English, we idealize the people we love. People tend to pay attention to information that confirms their romantic interests. Romantic lovers often magnify each other's positive features and overlook their flaws.

To experience romantic love, in contrast to attachment or sexual arousal, one must be exposed to a culture that idealizes the concept. In Western culture, romantic love blossoms in fairy tales about Sleeping Beauty, Cinderella, Snow White, and all their princes charming. It matures with romantic novels, television tales and films, and the personal accounts of friends and relatives about dates and romances.

THE AFFECTIVE SHIFT HYPOTHESIS Men are generally more reluctant than women to make commitments in their romantic relationships (Peplau, 2003). The **affective shift hypothesis,** developed by evolutionary psychologist David Buss and his colleagues (Haselton & Buss, 2001), offers one possible explanation of

FIGURE 12.6 The Triangular Model of Love

According to this model, love has three components: intimacy, passion, and commitment. The ideal of consummate love consists of romantic love plus commitment.

Source: From *The Psychology of Love,* R. J. Sternberg and M. J. Barnes, eds. Copyright © 1988 Yale University Press. Reprinted by permission.

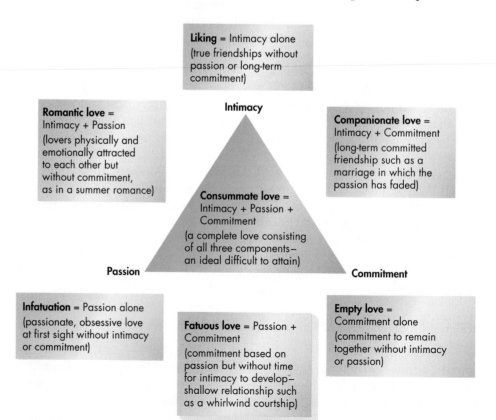

Liking = Intimacy alone (true friendships without passion or long-term commitment)

Romantic love = Intimacy + Passion (lovers physically and emotionally attracted to each other but without commitment, as in a summer romance)

Companionate love = Intimacy + Commitment (long-term committed friendship such as a marriage in which the passion has faded)

Intimacy

Consummate love = Intimacy + Passion + Commitment (a complete love consisting of all three components—an ideal difficult to attain)

Passion

Commitment

Infatuation = Passion alone (passionate, obsessive love at first sight without intimacy or commitment)

Fatuous love = Passion + Commitment (commitment based on passion but without time for intimacy to develop—shallow relationship such as a whirlwind courtship)

Empty love = Commitment alone (commitment to remain together without intimacy or passion)

Self-Assessment — Sternberg's Triangular Love Scale

Which are the strongest components of your love relationship? Intimacy? Passion? Commitment? All three components? Two of them?

To complete the following scale, fill in the blank spaces with the name of the person you love or care about deeply.

Then rate your agreement with each of the items by using a 9-point scale in which 1 = "not at all," 5 = "moderately," and 9 = "extremely." Use points in between to indicate intermediate levels of agreement between these values. Then consult the scoring key in Appendix B.

Intimacy Component

____ 1. I am actively supportive of _____'s well-being.

____ 2. I have a warm relationship with _____.

____ 3. I am able to count on _____ in times of need.

____ 4. _____ is able to count on me in times of need.

____ 5. I am willing to share myself and my possessions with _____.

____ 6. I receive considerable emotional support from _____.

____ 7. I give considerable emotional support to _____.

____ 8. I communicate well with _____.

____ 9. I value _____ greatly in my life.

____10. I feel close to _____.

____11. I have a comfortable relationship with _____.

____12. I feel that I really understand _____.

____13. I feel that _____ really understands me.

____14. I feel that I can really trust _____.

____15. I share deeply personal information about myself with _____.

Passion Component

____16. Just seeing _____ excites me.

____17. I find myself thinking about _____ frequently during the day.

____18. My relationship with _____ is very romantic.

____19. I find _____ to be very personally attractive.

____20. I idealize _____.

____21. I cannot imagine another person making me as happy as _____ does.

____22. I would rather be with _____ than anyone else.

____23. There is nothing more important to me than my relationship with _____.

____24. I especially like physical contact with _____.

____25. There is something almost "magical" about my relationship with _____.

____26. I adore _____.

____27. I cannot imagine life without _____.

____28. My relationship with _____ is passionate.

____29. When I see romantic movies and read romantic books, I think of _____.

____30. I fantasize about _____.

Commitment Component

____31. I know that I care about _____.

____32. I am committed to maintaining my relationship with _____.

____33. Because of my commitment to _____, I would not let other people come between us.

____34. I have confidence in the stability of my relationship with _____.

____35. I could not let anything get in the way of my commitment to _____.

____36. I expect my love for _____ to last for the rest of my life.

____37. I will always feel a strong responsibility for _____.

____38. I view my commitment to _____ as a solid one.

____39. I cannot imagine ending my relationship with _____.

____40. I am certain of my love for _____.

____41. I view my relationship with _____ as permanent.

____42. I view my relationship with _____ as a good decision.

____43. I feel a sense of responsibility toward _____.

____44. I plan to continue my relationship with _____.

____45. Even when _____ is hard to deal with, I remain committed to our relationship.

Source: From *The Psychology of Love* by R. J. Sternberg. Copyright © 1989 Yale University Press. Reprinted by permission of the publisher and author.

■ **Uh, Oh—What Will Happen if They Make Love?**
According to the "affective shift hypothesis," most women experience stronger feelings of love and commitment toward their partners after they make love for the first time. The picture is mixed for men. Men with few dating partners may, like most women, experience greater love and commitment. But the feelings of men with many dating partners often turn negative. That is, they want out.

men's lesser willingness to commit themselves to relationships. In a study of nearly 200 subjects, the psychologists found that women tend to experience greater feelings of love and commitment—a positive affective shift—after first-time sex than men do. But not all men are alike. (Really.) As a group, men are more likely than women to be interested in short-term relationships and multiple sex partners. In fact, it seems accurate to say that men with high numbers of sex partners tend to experience a negative affective shift following first-time sex. The negative shift in feelings motivates them to end the relationship and curbs tendencies toward making a commitment. However, men with fewer sex partners and more of an interest in developing long-term relationships also tend to experience the positive affective shift after first-time sex.

Evolutionary psychologists also suggest that men may be naturally more promiscuous than women because they are the genetic heirs of ancestors whose reproductive success was connected with the number of women they could impregnate (Buss, 1999; Schmitt, 2003; Schmitt et al., 2001). But women can produce relatively few children in their lifetimes. Thus, the theory suggests, women need to be more selective with respect to their mating partners. This controversial theory suggests that a man's "roving eye" and a woman's selectivity are embedded in their genes.

Your Turn: Now that we have discussed interpersonal attraction, enhance your mastery of the material with the nearby "Learning Connections." Review the material by filling in the blanks, reflect on the material by relating it to other things you know, and think critically about it.

Learning Connections — INTERPERSONAL ATTRACTION: ON LIKING AND LOVING

ACTIVE REVIEW (21) Physical attractiveness (*Is* or *Is not?*) a key factor in the selection of dates and mates. (22) Cross-cultural research suggests that in many cultures men find women with (*High* or *Low?*) cheekbones to be more attractive. (23) According to the _____ hypothesis, we tend to date people who are similar to ourselves. (24) According to the principle of _____, we tend to return feelings of attraction and admiration. (25) According to the triangular model of love, love can include combinations of intimacy, _____, and commitment. (26) _____ love is characterized by a combination of intimacy and passion.

REFLECT AND RELATE Could you maintain a relationship with a partner whose attitudes toward religion, politics,

education, and child rearing differed significantly from your own? Would you want to? How does your answer relate to the matching hypothesis? Does it support the view that "opposites attract" or that "birds of a feather flock together?"

CRITICAL THINKING How might the features found attractive by males and females provide humans with an evolutionary advantage? Can you think of alternative explanations as to why people tend to find these features attractive?

 Go to **http://psychology.wadsworth.com/ rathus_pcc9e** for an interactive version of this Learning Connections unit.

The Four S's: Sexual Response, Sexual Behavior, Sexual Dysfunctions, and Sex Therapy

Actually, there is a group referred to as the "four s's": The Society for the Scientific Study of Sexuality (www.sexscience.org). Their aim, like the aim of this chapter, is "the advancement of knowledge about sexuality." Do we need such knowledge? Apparently so. Although we may consider ourselves sophisticated about sex, it is surprising how little we know about sexual biology. For example, how many male readers know that women have different orifices for urination and sexual intercourse? How many readers know that the erect penis—sometimes referred to by the slang term "boner"—contains no bones? What are the dangers of being ignorant about the process of conception and about sexually transmitted infections (STIs)? In this section we fill in some gaps in knowledge. We first consider how females and males respond to sexual stimulation—that is, the so-called sexual response cycle. Then we discuss some forms of sexual behavior in the United States today. Next we consider some of the things that can go wrong during sexual behavior: problems in becoming sexually aroused or reaching orgasm that are known as *sexual dysfunctions*. Finally, we consider approaches to helping individuals overcome sexual dysfunctions, which are known collectively as *sex therapy*. In the following section we consider the problems that occur when people become physically or verbally aggressive in their interactions with other people: sexual coercion. The chapter's "Life Connections" unit will help readers understand and prevent STIs.

The Sexual Response Cycle

Although we may be more culturally attuned to focus on gender differences rather than similarities, William Masters and Virginia Johnson (1966) found that the biological responses of males and females to sexual stimulation—that is, their sexual response cycles—are quite similar. **Question: What is the sexual response cycle?** Masters and Johnson use the term *sexual response cycle* to describe the changes that occur in the body as men and women become sexually aroused (Figure 12.7). Masters and Johnson divide the **sexual response cycle** into four phases: *excitement, plateau, orgasm,* and *resolution.*

The sexual response cycle is characterized by *vasocongestion* and *myotonia.* **Vasocongestion** is the swelling of the genital tissues with blood. It causes erection of the penis and swelling of the area surrounding the vaginal opening. The testes, the nipples, and—**Truth or Fiction Revisited**—even the earlobes swell as blood vessels dilate in these areas. **Myotonia** is muscle tension. It causes facial grimaces, spasms in the hands and feet, and then the spasms of orgasm.

Erection, vaginal lubrication, and orgasm are all reflexes. That is, they occur automatically in response to adequate sexual stimulation. (Of course, the decision to enter a sexual relationship is voluntary, as are the decisions to kiss and pet and so on.)

EXCITEMENT PHASE Vasocongestion during the **excitement phase** can cause erection in young men within a few seconds after sexual stimulation begins. The scrotal skin thickens, becoming less baggy. The testes increase in size and become elevated.

In the female, excitement is characterized by vaginal lubrication, which may start 10 to 30 seconds after sexual stimulation begins. Vasocongestion swells the **clitoris** and flattens and spreads the vaginal lips. The inner part of the vagina expands. The breasts enlarge, and blood vessels near the surface become more prominent. The nipples may become erect in both men and women. Heart rate and blood pressure increase.

Sexual Response Cycle Masters and Johnson's model of sexual response, which consists of four stages or phases.

Vasocongestion Engorgement of blood vessels with blood, which swells the genitals and breasts during sexual arousal.

Myotonia Muscle tension.

Excitement phase The first phase of the sexual response cycle, which is characterized by muscle tension, increases in the heart rate, and erection in the male and vaginal lubrication in the female.

Clitoris The female sex organ that is most sensitive to sexual sensation; a smooth, round knob of tissue that is situated above the urethral opening.

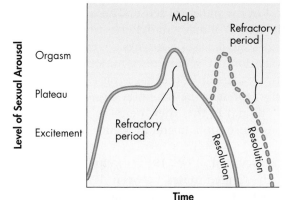
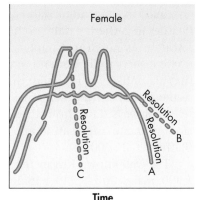

FIGURE 12.7 **Levels of Sexual Arousal during the Phases of the Sexual Response Cycle**

Masters and Johnson divide the sexual response cycle into four phases: excitement, plateau, orgasm, and resolution. During the resolution phase, the level of sexual arousal returns to the prearoused state. For men there is a refractory period following orgasm. As shown by the broken line, however, men can become rearoused to orgasm once the refractory period is past and their levels of sexual arousal have returned to preplateau levels. Pattern A for women shows a typical response cycle, with the broken line suggesting multiple orgasms. Pattern B shows the cycle of a woman who reaches the plateau phase but for whom arousal is "resolved" without reaching the orgasmic phase. Pattern C shows the possibility of orgasm in a highly aroused woman who passes quickly through the plateau phase.

PLATEAU PHASE The level of sexual arousal remains somewhat stable during the **plateau phase** of the cycle. Because of vasocongestion, men show some increase in the circumference of the head of the penis, which also takes on a purplish hue. The testes are elevated into position for **ejaculation** and may reach one and a half times their unaroused size.

In women, vasocongestion swells the outer part of the vagina, contracting the vaginal opening in preparation for grasping the penis. The inner part of the vagina expands further. The clitoris withdraws beneath the clitoral hood and shortens.

Breathing becomes rapid, like panting. Heart rate may increase to 100 to 160 beats per minute. Blood pressure continues to rise.

ORGASMIC PHASE During **orgasm** in the male, muscle contractions propel the ejaculate out of the body. Sensations of pleasure tend to be related to the strength of the contractions and the amount of seminal fluid present. The first three to four contractions are generally most intense and occur at 0.8-second intervals (five contractions every four seconds). Additional contractions occur more slowly.

Orgasm in the female is manifested by 3 to 15 contractions of the pelvic muscles that surround the vaginal barrel. The contractions first occur at 0.8-second intervals. As in the male, they produce release of sexual tension. Weaker and slower contractions follow.

Blood pressure and heart rate reach a peak, with the heart beating up to 180 times per minute. Respiration may increase to 40 breaths per minute.

RESOLUTION PHASE After orgasm, the body returns to its unaroused state. This is called the **resolution phase.** After ejaculation, blood is released from engorged areas, so that the erection disappears. In women orgasm also triggers the release of blood from engorged areas. Blood pressure, heart rate, and breathing return to normal levels. Both partners may feel relaxed and satisfied.

Unlike women, men enter a **refractory period** during which they cannot experience another orgasm or ejaculate. The refractory period of adolescent males may last only minutes, whereas that of men age 50 and above may last from several minutes to a day. Women do not undergo a refractory period and therefore can become quickly rearoused to the point of repeated (multiple) orgasm if they desire and receive continued sexual stimulation.

The sexual response cycle describes what happens when females and males are exposed to sexual stimulation. But what kinds of sexual experiences do people seek? How many sex partners do they have? Who are their partners? Let us begin to answer some of these questions by reporting the results of some key surveys of sexual behavior.

Some Surveys of Sexual Behavior: Peering into Private Lives

What is normal in Inis Beag is incredibly restrained in Mangaia. What is normal is Mangaia is loose, indecent, even "out of control" in Inis Beag. The kinds of sexual behaviors that are considered "normal" depend on the society in which one lives. **Question: What do we know about the sex lives of people in the United States?** What is "normal" in the United States, at least in the statistical sense? There are many difficulties in gathering data, such as the refusal of many individuals to participate in research. As noted in Chapter 1, large-scale magazine surveys of sexual behavior invite readers to fill out and return questionnaires, but only a minority do so, and they are unlikely to represent the entire readership of the magazine. (Nor would the readership of the magazine necessarily represent the nation at large.) People who return surveys differ from those who do not in that they are more willing to disclose intimate information and possibly also more liberal in their sexual behavior (Rathus et al., 2005).

The well-known Kinsey reports (Kinsey et al., 1948, 1953) carefully interviewed 5,300 males and 5,940 females in the United States between 1938 and 1949. Interviewers asked about sexual experiences including masturbation, oral sex, and

Plateau phase The second phase of the sexual response cycle, which is characterized by increases in vasocongestion, muscle tension, heart rate, and blood pressure in preparation for orgasm.

Ejaculation The process of propelling seminal fluid (semen) from the penis.

Orgasm The height or climax of sexual excitement, involving involuntary muscle contractions, release of sexual tensions, and, usually, subjective feelings of pleasure.

Resolution phase The fourth phase of the sexual response cycle, during which the body gradually returns to its prearoused state.

Refractory period In the sexual response cycle, a period of time following orgasm during which an individual is not responsive to sexual stimulation.

premarital sex. The nation was astounded to be informed that the majority of males masturbated and had engaged in sexual intercourse prior to marriage. Moreover, 20% to 50% of females reported engaging in these behaviors. But Kinsey had not obtained a random sample of the population either. He chose not to try to do so because he expected a high refusal rate. Thus he recruited participants from organizations and community groups, such as college fraternities and sororities. In general, he secured a high rate of participation. Still, his samples underrepresented people of color, people in rural areas, older people, poor people, and Catholics and Jews. There is thus no way of knowing whether or not Kinsey's results accurately mirrored American sexual behavior in general at the time. But the *relationships* Kinsey uncovered, such as the positive link between level of education and premarital sex, may be generalizable and seem to have held up over time.

A more recent and more accurate survey—The National Health and Social Life Survey (NHSLS; Laumann et al., 1994)—interviewed 3,432 people and may offer the most accurate information we have. Of this number, 3,159 were English-speaking adults aged 18 to 59. The other 273 respondents were obtained by purposefully oversampling African American and Hispanic American households in order to obtain more information about these ethnic groups. While the sample probably represents the overall U.S. population aged 18 to 59 quite well, it may include too few Asian Americans, Native Americans, and Jews to offer much information about these groups. The NHSLS team identified sets of households in various locales and obtained an overall participation rate of close to 80%.

The NHSLS considered the sociocultural factors of sex, level of education, religion, and race/ethnicity in many aspects of people's sexual behavior, including their number of sex partners (see Table 12.2). Males in the survey report having higher numbers of sex partners than females do. For example, one male in three (33%) reports having 11 or more sex partners since the age of 18. This compares with fewer than one woman in 10 (9%). One the other hand, most people in the United States appear to limit their numbers of sex partners to a handful or fewer. This finding has been corroborated by many surveys over the years.

Level of education is connected with sexual behavior. **Truth or Fiction Revisited:** Generally speaking, it would appear that education is a liberating influence on sexual behavior. People with some college education, or who have completed college, are likely to report having more sex partners than those who attended grade school or high school only. But if education has a liberating influence on sexuality, conservative religious experience appears to be a restraining factor. Liberal Protestants (for example, Methodists, Lutherans, Presbyterians, Episcopalians, and United Churches of Christ) and people who say they have no religion report higher numbers of sex partners than Catholics and conservative Protestants (for example, Baptists, Pentecostals, Churches of Christ, and Assemblies of God).

Ethnicity is also connected with sexual behavior. The research findings in Table 12.2 suggest that European Americans and African Americans have the highest numbers of sex partners. Latino and Latina Americans, who report having fewer partners, are mostly Catholic. Perhaps Catholicism provides a restraint on sexual behavior. Asian Americans would appear to be the most sexually restrained ethnic group. However, the sample sizes of Asian Americans and Native Americans are relatively small, and thus the information about the sexual behavior of these groups is limited.

Sexual Dysfunctions

Now that we have described common patterns of sexual behavior, we should note that not everyone becomes sexually aroused by the same kinds of stimulation. In fact, a number of people experience serious sexual problems or "dysfunctions." **Question: What are sexual dysfunctions?**

Sexual dysfunctions are persistent problems in becoming sexually aroused or reaching orgasm. Many people will be troubled by a sexual dysfunction at one

Sexual dysfunction A persistent or recurrent problem in becoming sexually aroused or reaching orgasm.

TABLE 12.2 **NUMBER OF SEX PARTNERS SINCE AGE 18 AS FOUND IN THE NHSLS* STUDY**

Sociocultural Factors	Number of Sex Partners					
	0	1	2–4	5–10	11–20	21+
	Percents					
Sex						
Male	3%	20%	21%	23%	16%	17%
Female	3	32	36	20	6	3
Education						
Less than high school	4	27	36	19	9	6
High school graduate	3	30	29	20	10	7
Some college	2	24	29	23	12	9
College graduate	2	24	26	24	11	13
Advanced degree	4	25	26	23	10	13
Religion						
None	3	16	29	20	16	16
Liberal, moderate Protestant	2	23	31	23	12	8
Conservative Protestant	3	30	30	20	10	7
Catholic	4	27	29	23	8	9
Race/Ethnicity						
European American	3	26	29	22	11	9
African American	2	18	34	24	11	11
Latino and Latina American	3	36	27	17	8	9
Asian American**	6	46	25	14	6	3
Native American**	5	28	35	23	5	5

*National Health and Social Life Survey, conducted by a research team centered at the University of Chicago.
**These sample sizes are quite small.

Source: Adapted from *The Social Organization of Sexuality: Sexual Practices in the United States* (Table 5.1C, p. 179), by E. O. Laumann, J. H. Gagnon, R. T. Michael, & S. Michaels, 1994, Chicago: University of Chicago Press.

time or another. Let's take a look at the main types of sexual dysfunctions and their causes.

TYPES OF SEXUAL DYSFUNCTIONS The sexual dysfunctions include hypoactive sexual desire disorder, female sexual arousal disorder, male erectile disorder, orgasmic disorder, premature ejaculation, dyspareunia, and vaginismus. The frequencies of these problems in the general population are suggested in Table 12.3.

In **hypoactive sexual desire disorder,** a person lacks interest in sexual activity and frequently reports a lack of sexual fantasies. This diagnosis exists because it is assumed that sexual fantasies and interests are normal responses that may be blocked by anxiety or other factors.

In women, sexual arousal is characterized by lubrication of the vaginal walls. Sexual arousal in men is characterized by erection. Almost all women sometimes have difficulty becoming or remaining lubricated. Almost all men have occasional difficulty attaining or maintaining an erection through intercourse. When these events are persistent or recurrent, they are considered dysfunctions **(female sexual arousal disorder** and **male erectile disorder).**

In **orgasmic disorder,** the man or woman, though sexually excited, takes a long time to reach orgasm or does not reach it at all. Orgasmic disorder is more common among women than among men. In **premature ejaculation,** the male ejaculates after minimal sexual stimulation, too soon to permit his partner or himself to enjoy sexual relations fully. Other dysfunctions include **dyspareunia** (painful sexual activity) and **vaginismus** (involuntary contraction of the muscles surrounding the vaginal opening, which makes entry painful and/or difficult).

Hypoactive sexual desire disorder A sexual dysfunction in which people lack sexual desire.

Female sexual arousal disorder A sexual dysfunction in which females fail to become adequately sexually aroused to engage in sexual intercourse.

Male erectile disorder A sexual dysfunction in which males fail to obtain erections that are adequate for sexual intercourse.

Orgasmic disorder A sexual dysfunction in which people have persistent or recurrent problems in reaching orgasm.

Premature ejaculation Ejaculation that occurs before the couple are satisfied with the length of sexual relations.

Dyspareunia A sexual dysfunction characterized by persistent or recurrent pain during sexual intercourse. (From roots meaning "badly paired.")

Vaginismus A sexual dysfunction characterized by involuntary contraction of the muscles surrounding the vagina, preventing entry by the penis or making entry painful.

Because not everyone experiences sexual dysfunctions, researchers have sought to determine why some do and some do not. **Question: What are the origins of sexual dysfunctions?**

CAUSES OF SEXUAL DYSFUNCTIONS Some sexual dysfunctions reflect biological problems. Lack of desire, for example, can be due to diabetes or to diseases of the heart and lungs. Fatigue can reduce sexual desire and inhibit orgasm. Depressants such as alcohol, narcotics, and tranquilizers can also impair sexual response. For example, Eric Rimm (2000) of the Harvard School of Public Health studied 2,000 men and found that erectile dysfunction was connected with a large waist, physical inactivity, and drinking too much alcohol (or not having any alcohol!). The common condition among these men may be high cholesterol levels. Cholesterol can impede the flow of blood to the penis just as it impedes the flow of blood to the heart. Antidepressant medication and antipsychotic drugs may also impair erectile functioning and cause orgasmic disorders (Ashton et al., 2000; Michelson et al., 2000).

Physically or psychologically painful sexual experiences, such as rape, can block future sexual response (Hensley, 2002; Laumann et al., 1999). Moreover, a sexual relationship is usually no better than other aspects of a relationship or marriage. Couples who have difficulty communicating are at a disadvantage in expressing their sexual desires.

Cognitive psychologists point out that irrational beliefs and attitudes can contribute to sexual dysfunctions. If we believe that we need a lover's approval at all times, we may view a disappointing sexual episode as a catastrophe. If we demand that every sexual encounter be perfect, we set ourselves up for failure.

In most cases of sexual dysfunction, the physical and psychological factors we have outlined lead to yet another psychological factor—**performance anxiety,** or fear of not being able to perform sexually. People with performance anxiety may focus on past failures and expectations of another disaster rather than enjoying present erotic sensations and fantasies. Performance anxiety can make it difficult for a man to attain erection, yet also spur him to ejaculate prematurely. It can prevent a woman from becoming adequately lubricated and can contribute to vaginismus.

Performance anxiety Anxiety concerning one's ability to perform, especially when performance may be evaluated by other people.

TABLE 12.3 CURRENT SEXUAL DYSFUNCTIONS ACCORDING TO THE NHSLS STUDY (PERCENT OF RESPONDENTS REPORTING THE PROBLEM WITHIN THE PAST YEAR)	Men	Women
Pain during sex *(dyspareunia)*	3.0	14.4
Sex not pleasurable	8.1	21.2
Unable to reach orgasm *(orgasmic disorder)*	8.3	24.1
Lack of interest in sex *(hypoactive sexual desire)*	15.8	33.4
Anxiety about performance*	17.0	11.5
Reaching climax too early *(premature ejaculation,* in the male)	28.5	10.3
Unable to keep an erection *(male erectile disorder,* also called *erectile dysfunction,* or *"ED")***	10.4	–
Having trouble lubricating *(female sexual arousal disorder)*	–	18.8

*Anxiety about performance is not itself a sexual dysfunction. However, it figures prominently in sexual dysfunctions.
**Other studies show that as many as half or more of men in middle and late adulthood have difficulty obtaining or maintaining an erection.

Source: Adapted from Tables 10.8A and 10.8B, pages 370 and 371, in Laumann, E. O., Gagnon, J. H., Michael, R. T., & Michaels, S. (1994). *The social organization of sexuality: Sexual practices in the United States.* Chicago: University of Chicago Press.

Sex therapy A collective term for short-term cognitive–behavioral models for treatment of sexual dysfunctions.

Sex Therapy

Question: How are sexual dysfunctions treated? Sexual dysfunctions are generally treated by means of **sex therapy**, which refers to a collection of mainly cognitive and behavior therapy techniques. Sex therapy is largely indebted to the pioneering work of Masters and Johnson (1970), although other therapists have also developed important techniques. Sex therapy generally focuses on:

1. *Reducing performance anxiety.* Therapists frequently prescribe that clients engage in activities such as massage or petting under "nondemand" circumstances for a while to reduce performance anxiety. Nondemand activity means sexual arousal and intercourse are not expected at first. Lessened anxiety allows natural reflexes such as erection, lubrication, and orgasm to occur.

2. *Changing self-defeating attitudes and expectations.* Clients are shown how expectations of failure can raise anxiety levels and become self-fulfilling prophecies.

3. *Teaching sexual skills.* Clients may be taught how to provide each other with adequate sexual stimulation. In the case of premature ejaculation, they may also be shown how to delay ejaculation by means such as the stop-and-go method (pausing when the male becomes too aroused).

4. *Enhancing sexual knowledge.* Some problems are connected with ignorance or misinformation about biological and sexual functioning.

5. *Improving sexual communication.* Partners are taught ways of showing each other what they like and do not like.

Moreover, biological treatments are available for various problems. For example, the drugs Viagra and Levitra help men attain erection by relaxing the muscles surrounding the blood vessels in the penis, allowing more blood to flow in and the erection to harden. Uprima facilitates erection by acting on the erection center in the brain. Several drugs are under development to facilitate sexual arousal and orgasm in both males and females, but some women also use Viagra today. Antidepressant drugs, which can impede orgasm, are sometimes prescribed to help men with premature ejaculation (Procacciante et al., 2001). Readers interested in learning more about sex therapy are advised to consult a human sexuality textbook, contact their state's psychological association, or ask their professors or college counseling centers.

Sexual dysfunctions are one category of problems in sexual interaction. Let us now consider a darker side of human interaction: sexual coercion. In sexual dysfunctions, individuals and couples generally wish to remove obstacles to having a fulfilling sexual relationship. In the case of sexual coercion, individuals—usually women—need effective barriers to prevent other people from damaging their physical and psychological well-being.

Your Turn: Now that we have discussed sexual response, sexual behavior, sexual dysfunctions, and sex therapy, enhance your mastery of the material with the nearby "Learning Connections." Review the material by filling in the blanks, reflect on the material by relating it to other things you know, and think critically about it.

![ ] Learning Connections | **THE FOUR S's: SEXUAL RESPONSE, SEXUAL BEHAVIOR, SEXUAL DYSFUNCTIONS, AND SEX THERAPY**

ACTIVE REVIEW (27) According to Masters and Johnson, human sexual response overall is characterized by vasocongestion and _____. (28) Masters and Johnson divide the sexual response cycle into four phases: _____, _____, _____, and _____.

(29) The results of surveys of sexual behavior are suspect because people who return them differ from those who do not in that they are probably more (*Liberal* or *Conservative?*) in their sexual behavior. (30) The Kinsey reports found that (*Men* or *Women?*) were more likely to

report masturbating and engaging in sexual intercourse prior to marriage. (31) Surveys suggest that a high level of education has a (*Liberating* or *Constraining?*) effect on premarital sex. (32) Women with female sexual _____ disorder have difficulty lubricating. (33) Men with persistent difficulty attaining or maintaining an erection have male _____ disorder. (34) Males who ejaculate too quickly are diagnosed with _____ ejaculation. (35) Sex therapy generally focuses on reducing _____ anxiety, changing self-defeating attitudes, teaching sexual skills, enhancing sexual knowledge, and improving communication.

REFLECT AND RELATE What do you experience when you become sexually aroused? Do your own experiences match the description of Masters and Johnson?

CRITICAL THINKING Erectile disorder is extremely disturbing to many men who experience it. What cultural attitudes and expectations heighten the stress of this dysfunction?

 Go to **http://psychology.wadsworth.com/ rathus_pcc9e** for an interactive version of this Learning Connections unit.

Sexual Coercion: Confounding Sex and Aggression

Sexual coercion includes rape and other forms of sexual pressure. It also includes *any* sexual activity between an adult and a child. Even when children cooperate, sexual relations with children are coercive because of the power adults wield over children and because children are below the legal age of consent. In this section we focus on rape and sexual harassment.

Rape: A Crime of Violence

As many as 1 in 4 women in the United States has been raped (Koss, 1993, 2003). Parents regularly encourage their daughters to be wary of strangers and strange places—places where they could fall prey to rapists. Certainly the threat of rape from strangers is real enough. Yet four out of five rapes are committed by acquaintances (Laumann et al., 1994; Rozee & Koss, 2001).

Date rape is a pressing concern on college campuses, where thousands of women have been victimized and there is much controversy over what exactly constitutes rape. More than one out of three of a sample of college men from California and Ohio admitted to coercing women into sexual activity by means of arguments, pressure, or force (Hall et al., 2000). About one man in seven had coerced a woman into sexual intercourse by means of arguments, pressure, or force. Consider one woman's account of date rape from the author's files:

> I first met him at a party. He was really good looking, and he had a great smile. I wanted to meet him, but I wasn't sure how. I didn't want to appear too forward. Then he came over and introduced himself. We talked and found we had a lot in common. I really liked him. When he asked me over to his place for a drink, I thought it would be OK. He was such a good listener, and I wanted him to ask me out again.
>
> When we got to his room, the only place to sit was on the bed. I didn't want him to get the wrong idea, but what else could I do? We talked for awhile, and then he made his move. I was so startled. He started by kissing. I really liked him, so the kissing was nice. But then he pushed me down on the bed. I tried to get up, and I told him to stop. He was so much bigger and stronger. I got scared, and I started to cry. I froze, and he raped me.
>
> It took only a couple of minutes, and it was terrible, he was so rough. When it was over he kept asking me what was wrong, like he didn't know. He had just forced himself on me, and he thought that was OK. He drove me home and said he wanted to see me again. I'm so afraid to see him. I never thought it would happen to me.

Rape is common—far too common. **Question: Why do men rape women?**

Why do men rape women?

Why do men force women into sexual activity? Sex is not the only reason. Many social scientists argue that rape is often a man's way of expressing social dominance over, or anger toward, women (Hall & Barongan, 1997). With some rapists, violence appears to enhance sexual arousal. They therefore seek to combine sex and aggression (Barbaree & Marshall, 1991).

Evolutionary psychologists suggest that prior to civilization, males who were more sexually aggressive were more likely to transmit their genes to future generations (Fisher, 2000; Koss, 2003; Thornhill & Palmer, 2000). There thus remains a tendency for males to be more sexually aggressive than females. Although the evolutionary perspective may view sexual coerciveness in men as "natural," evolutionary psychologists generally agree that rape is inexcusable and criminal in modern society, and that males can *choose* not to be aggressive.

However, many social critics contend that American culture also *socializes* men into becoming rapists by reinforcing males for aggressive and competitive behavior (Koss & Kilpatrick, 2001). The date rapist could be said to be asserting culturally expected dominance over women.

There are also powerful cognitive contributors to rape. For example, research shows that college men frequently perceive a date's protests as part of an adversarial sex game (Bernat et al., 1999). One male undergraduate said "Hell, no" when asked whether a date had consented to sex. He added, ". . . but she didn't say no, so she must have wanted it, too. . . . It's the way it works" (Celis, 1991). Consider the comments of the man who victimized the woman whose story appeared earlier in the section:

I first met her at a party. She looked really hot, wearing a sexy dress that showed off her great body. We started talking right away. I knew that she liked me by the way she kept smiling and touching my arm while she was speaking. She seemed pretty relaxed so I asked her back to my place for a drink. . . . When she said yes, I knew that I was going to be lucky!

When we got to my place, we sat on the bed kissing. At first, everything was great. Then, when I started to lay her down on the bed, she started twisting and saying she didn't want to. Most women don't like to appear too easy, so I knew that she was just going through the motions. When she stopped struggling, I knew that she would have to throw in some tears before we did it.

She was still very upset afterwards, and I just don't understand it! If she didn't want to have sex, why did she come back to the room with me? You could tell by the way she dressed and acted that she was no virgin, so why she had to put up such a big struggle I don't know.

Another cognitive factor in rape is belief in stereotypical myths about rape.

MYTHS ABOUT RAPE You would not be blamed if somebody shot you when you were walking down the street or punched you when you were sitting in class. These behaviors would be recognized as the crimes of violence they are. Yet women are frequently blamed when they are raped, and rape is also a crime of violence. Women are especially likely to be blamed for whatever happens to them if they dress provocatively or use "bad" language.

Most people in the United States believe in a number of myths about rape—myths that blame the victim and have the effect of supporting rape. These people include those from whom the rape victim might seek support (Filipas & Ullman, 2001), including clergy (Sheldon & Parent, 2002) and, perhaps most surprisingly, other women (Cowan, 2000).

For example, most Americans aged 50 and above believe that the woman is partly responsible for rape if she dresses provocatively (Gibbs, 1991). They are unlikely to be sympathetic if such a "bold" woman complains of being raped. **Truth or Fiction Revisited:** It is also true that most Americans believe that some women like to be talked into sex. In fact, a majority of Americans—including a majority of American *women*—share this belief (Gibbs, 1991). Does the existence of this widespread belief encourage men to pressure their dates into sex? If so, it is a harmful belief indeed.

Other myths include the notions that "women say no when they mean yes" and "rapists are crazed by sexual desire" (Powell, 1996, p. 139). Still another myth is that deep down inside, women *want* to be raped. **Truth or Fiction Revisited:** *It is not true that women say no when they mean yes.* Myths such as this foster a social climate that encourages rape. Such myths deny the impact of the assault and transfer blame onto the victim. Men, including the most fundamentalist clergy, who support traditional, rigidly defined gender roles are more likely to blame the victims of rape (Raichle & Lambert, 2000; Sheldon & Parent, 2002). The myths contribute to a social climate that can be lenient toward rapists and unsympathetic toward victims. Moreover, the myths lead to hostility toward women, which in turn can lead to rape (Hall et al., 2000; see Figure 12.8). **Truth or Fiction Revisited:** Because of the tendency to blame the victim, most college victims of date rape do *not* inform police or campus authorities of the assault (Fisher et al., 2003).

If you want to learn whether you harbor some of the more common myths about rape, complete the nearby self-assessment on cultural myths that create a climate that supports rape.

PREVENTING RAPE The aftermath of rape can include physical harm, anxiety, depression, sexual dysfunction, sexually transmitted infection, and/or pregnancy (Hensley, 2002; Koss et al., 2003). **Question: How can we prevent rape?** From a sociocultural perspective, prevention of rape involves publicly examining and challenging the widely held cultural attitudes and ideals that contribute to rape. The traditions of male dominance and rewards for male aggressiveness take a daily toll on women. One thing we can do is encourage colleges and universities to require students to attend lectures and seminars on rape (Shultz et al., 2000). The point is to debunk myths about rape and for men to learn that "No" means "No," despite the widespread belief that some women like to be talked into sex. Research evidence suggests that college programs with male students can modify attitudes toward women and myths about rape (Davis & Liddell, 2002; Holcomb et al., 2002; O'Donohue et al., 2003).

On a personal level, there are things that women can do to protect themselves. *The New Our Bodies, Ourselves* (Boston Women's Health Book Collective, 1992) includes the following suggestions for preventing rape by strangers:

◆ Establish signals and arrangements with other women—such as ringing an entry buzzer a few times—in an apartment building or neighborhood.

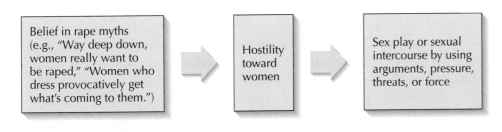

FIGURE 12.8 **A Common Pathway to Sexual Aggression**

A statistical technique called path analysis reveals the powerful cognitive aspects of sexual aggression. Belief in rape myths, such as the idea that women really want to be raped or that women who dress provocatively get what's coming to them, increases hostility toward women. Hostility toward women, in turn, is a common characteristic of rapists.

Self-Assessment | Cultural Myths That Create a Climate That Supports Rape

The following statements are based on a questionnaire by Martha Burt (1980). Read each statement and indicate whether you believe it to be true or false by circling the T or the F. Then turn to the key in Appendix B to learn about the implications of your answers.

T F 1. A woman who goes to the home or apartment of a man on their first date implies that she is willing to have sex.

T F 2. Any female can get raped.

T F 3. One reason why women falsely report a rape is because they need to call attention to themselves.

T F 4. Any healthy woman can successfully resist a rapist if she really wants to.

T F 5. When women go around braless or wearing short skirts and tight tops, they are just asking for trouble.

T F 6. In the majority of rapes, the victim is promiscuous or has a bad reputation.

T F 7. If a girl engages in necking or petting and she lets things get out of hand, it is her own fault if her partner forces sex on her.

T F 8. Women who get raped while hitchhiking get what they deserve.

T F 9. A woman who is stuck-up and thinks she is too good to talk to guys on the street deserves to be taught a lesson.

T F 10. Many women have an unconscious wish to be raped and may then unconsciously set up a situation in which they are likely to be attacked.

T F 11. If a woman gets drunk at a party and has intercourse with a man she's just met there, she should be considered "fair game" to other males at the party who want to have sex with her too, whether she wants to or not.

T F 12. Many women who report a rape are lying because they are angry and want to get back at the man they accuse.

T F 13. Many, if not most, rapes are merely invented by women who discovered they were pregnant and wanted to protect their reputation.

◆ List only first initials in the telephone directory or on the mailbox.

◆ Use dead-bolt locks.

◆ Keep windows locked and obtain iron grids for first-floor windows.

◆ Keep entrances and doorways brightly lit.

◆ Have keys ready for the front door or the car.

◆ Do not walk alone in the dark.

◆ Avoid deserted areas.

◆ Never allow a strange man into your apartment or home without checking his credentials.

◆ Drive with the car windows up and the door locked.

◆ Check the rear seat of the car before entering.

◆ Avoid living in an unsafe building.

◆ Do not pick up hitchhikers (including women).

◆ Do not talk to strange men in the street.

◆ Shout "Fire!" not "Rape!" People crowd around fires but avoid scenes of violence.

Powell (1996) adds the following suggestions for avoiding date rape:

◆ Communicate your sexual limits to your date. Tell your partner how far you would like to go so that he will know what the limits are. For example, if your partner starts fondling you in ways that make you uncomfortable, you might say, "I'd prefer if you didn't touch me there. I really like you, but I prefer not getting so intimate at this point in our relationship."

◆ Meet new dates in public places, and avoid driving with a stranger or a group of people you've just met. When meeting a new date, drive in your own car and meet your date at a public place. Don't drive with strangers or offer rides to strangers or groups of people. In some cases of date rape, the group disappears just prior to the assault.

◆ State your refusal in definitive terms. Be firm in refusing a sexual overture. Look your partner straight in the eye. The more definite you are, the less likely your partner will be to misinterpret your wishes.

◆ Become aware of your fears. Take notice of any fears of displeasing your partner that might stifle your assertiveness. If your partner is truly respectful of you, you need not fear an angry or demeaning response. But if your partner is not respectful, it is best to become aware of it early and end the relationship right away.

◆ Pay attention to your "vibes." Trust your gut-level feelings. Many victims of acquaintance rape said afterward that they had had a strange feeling about the man but failed to pay attention to it.

◆ Be especially cautious if you are in a new environment, such as college or a foreign country. You may be especially vulnerable to exploitation when you are becoming acquainted with a new environment, different people, and different customs.

◆ If you have broken off a relationship with someone you don't really like or feel good about, don't let him into your place. Many so-called date rapes are committed by ex-lovers and ex-boyfriends.

Sexual Harassment

Question: What is sexual harassment? **Sexual harassment** involves deliberate or repeated unwanted comments, gestures, or physical contact of a sexual nature (Powell, 1996). It occurs frequently on college campuses, in the business world, and in the military. The great majority of victims are female, and nearly half of the women in college and the workforce report being victimized (American Psychological Association, 1998; Jorgenson & Wahl, 2000). Even the highest-ranking female officer in the Army was not immune. In 2000, Lt. Gen. Claudia J. Kennedy alleged that another general "groped" her in her office (Myers, 2000).

If it is sometimes difficult to draw the line between sexual persuasion and attempted rape, it can be even *more* difficult to distinguish between a legitimate (if unwelcome) sexual invitation and sexual harassment. People accused of sexual harassment often claim that the charges are exaggerated. They say that the victim "overreacted" to normal male–female interaction. Or "she took me too seriously." However, sexual harassment *is* a serious problem, and most harassers know very well what they are doing (Powell, 1996).

Where does "normal male–female interaction" end and sexual harassment begin? Consider some examples:

◆ Verbal abuse.
◆ Unwelcome sexual overtures or advances.
◆ Pressure to engage in sexual activity.
◆ Remarks about a person's body, clothing, or sexual activities.
◆ Leering at, or ogling, someone.
◆ Telling unwanted "dirty" jokes in mixed company.
◆ Unnecessarily touching, patting, or pinching.
◆ Whistles and catcalls.
◆ Brushing up against someone.
◆ Demands for sex that are accompanied by threats, such as being fired from a job or not getting a promotion.

Your college may publish guidelines about sexual harassment. Check with the dean of students or the president's office.

Sexual harassment Deliberate or repeated unwanted comments, gestures, or physical contact of a sexual nature.

College students are sexually harassed by other students and sometimes by professors (Matchen & DeSouza, 2000; van Roosmalen & McDaniel, 1998). Professors are sometimes harassed by students. Some cases are so serious that women switch major fields, schools, or jobs to avoid it (Munson et al., 2000; van Roosmalen & McDaniel, 1998). Ironically, as with rape, society often blames the victim of sexual harassment for being provocative or for not saying no firmly enough.

RESISTING SEXUAL HARASSMENT Question: What can you do if you are sexually harassed on campus or in the workplace? Here are some suggestions:

1. Behave in a professional manner. Harassment often can be stopped cold if you respond to the harasser in a curt, businesslike manner.

2. Discourage harassment and promote the kind of social behavior you want. Speak up. If your supervisor or professor asks you to come to the office after hours, say that you would rather talk during office hours. Stick to business. If the harasser does not take this suggestion, be more direct: "Mr. Smith, I'd like to keep our relationship purely business, OK?"

3. Don't get into a situation in which you are alone with someone who might harass you. Have a coworker around when you consult your supervisor. Or see your professor before or after class, when other people are around.

4. Keep a record of incidents to document them in case you decide to lodge an official complaint.

5. Put the harasser on direct notice that you recognize the harassment for what it is and that you want it to stop.

6. Confide about harassment to reliable friends, school counselors or advisers, union representatives, or parents or relatives. Harassment is stressful, and social support helps us cope with stress. Other people may also have helpful advice.

7. Many places of business and campuses have offices where complaints about sexual harassment are filed and acted on. Check with the dean of students or the president's office.

8. See a lawyer. Sexual harassment is illegal, and you can stop it.

Your Turn: Now that we have discussed sexual coercion, enhance your mastery of the material with the nearby "Learning Connections." Review the material by filling in the blanks, reflect on the material by relating it to other things you know, and think critically about it.

 Learning Connections   **SEXUAL COERCION: CONFOUNDING SEX AND AGGRESSION**

ACTIVE REVIEW (36) Most rapes are committed by (*Strangers* or *Acquaintances?*). (37) Many social scientists argue that rape mainly has to do with (*Sexual desire* or *Power?*). (38) Sexual harassment (*Is* or *Is not?*) illegal.

REFLECT AND RELATE Some evolutionary psychologists speculate that rape—or at least some forms of sexual coerciveness—may be "natural" for men. If they are correct, should society then condone sexual aggressiveness or rape? Or does society have a right to expect that men will control harmful behavior, even if it "goes against the grain" of their genes? What do you think?

CRITICAL THINKING How do American cultural beliefs have the effect of supporting rape?

 Go to **http://psychology.wadsworth.com/ rathus_pcc9e** for an interactive version of this Learning Connections unit.

Life Connections

Understanding and Preventing HIV/AIDS and Other Sexually Transmitted Infections

Sexual relationships can be sources of pleasure and personal fulfillment. They also carry some risks and responsibilities. One of the risks is that of contracting HIV/AIDS or other sexually transmitted infections (STIs). Although media attention usually focuses on HIV/AIDS, other STIs are more widespread. Nearly 4 million new chlamydia infections occur each year, with the incidence among college students especially high (CDC, 2001). Chlamydia is a major cause of pelvic inflammatory disease, which often leads to infertility.

Most college students are informed about HIV transmission and AIDS, yet many are unaware that chlamydia can go undetected for years. A survey of first-year college students found a great deal of ignorance about human papilloma virus (HPV) and genital warts (Baer et al., 2000). The findings were ironic: Although nearly all (96% of the males and 95% of the females) had heard of genital warts, only 4% of the males and 12% of the females knew that HPV caused them. Moreover, the students were generally ignorant of the modes of transmission of HPV. Ignorance in this case is danger rather than bliss because HPV infection is linked to cervical cancer (Josefsson et al., 2000). Yet as many as 1 million new cases of HPV infection occur each year in the United States—more than syphilis, genital herpes, and AIDS combined.

Women experience the effects of most STIs disproportionately (Garcia-Moreno, 2000; Glynn et al., 2001). They are more likely to develop infertility if an STI spreads through the reproductive system. STIs are believed to account for 15 to 30% of cases of infertility among American women.

One of the reasons for discussing STIs in a psychology textbook involves psychological risk factors, which are cognitive and behavioral:

- *Cognitive:* People tend to deny or underestimate their risk of infection. For example, HIV in the United States has been characterized as mainly transmitted by anal intercourse and the sharing of contaminated needles (CDC, 2003). Therefore, many Americans who do not engage in anal sex or use these drugs dismiss the threat of HIV/AIDS. Yet transmission of HIV via male–female sexual intercourse accounts for the majority of cases around the world (UNAIDS, 2003).
- *Behavioral:* Despite their knowledge of the effects of infection by HIV and other disease organisms, many people do not change their behavior in an effort to prevent infection (Dailard, 2001; Santelli et al., 2000).

HIV/AIDS

AIDS is a fatal condition in which the person's immune system is so weakened that he or she falls prey to so-called opportunistic diseases. It is caused by the human immunodeficiency virus (HIV).

Transmission. HIV is transmitted by infected blood, semen, vaginal and cervical secretions, and breast milk. The first three fluids may enter the body through vaginal, anal, or oral sex with an infected partner. Other means of infection include sharing a hypodermic needle with an infected person, as is common among people who inject illicit drugs, and transfusion with contaminated blood. There need be no concern about closed-mouth kissing. Note, too, that saliva has never been shown to transmit HIV. *However,* transmission through deep kissing is theoretically possible if blood in an infected person's mouth (e.g., from toothbrushing or gum disease) enters cuts (again, as from toothbrushing or gum disease) in the other person's mouth. HIV may also be transmitted from mother to child through childbirth or breast-feeding. There is no evidence that public toilets, insect bites, or holding, hugging, living with, or attending school with an infected person transmits HIV. People today are unlikely to be infected by means of blood transfusions because blood supplies are routinely screened for HIV.

What HIV Does. HIV kills white blood cells called *CD4 lymphocytes*[1] (or, more simply, *CD4 cells*) that are found in the immune system. CD4 cells recognize viruses and "instruct" other white blood cells—called *B lymphocytes*—to make antibodies, which combat disease. (See Chapter 13.) Eventually, however, CD4 cells are depleted and the body is left vulnerable to opportunistic diseases.

AIDS is characterized by fatigue, fever, unexplained weight loss, swollen lymph nodes, diarrhea, and, in many cases, impairment of learning and memory. Among the opportunistic infections that may take hold are Kaposi's sarcoma, a cancer of the blood cells that occurs in many males who contract AIDS; PCP (pneumocystis carinii pneumonia), a kind of pneumonia; and, in women, invasive cancer of the cervix.

Diagnosis and Treatment. Infection by HIV is generally diagnosed by means of blood, saliva, or urine tests. For many years researchers were frustrated in their efforts to develop effective vaccines and treatments for HIV infection and AIDS. There is still no safe, effective vaccine, but recent developments in drug therapy have raised hopes about treatment.

AZT and similar antiviral drugs inhibit reproduction of HIV by targeting

---

[1]Also called *T₄ cells* or *helper T cells*.

the enzyme called *reverse transcriptase*. *Protease inhibitors* target the *protease* enzyme, which is involved in the reproductive cycle of HIV. A "cocktail" of antiviral drugs such as AZT and protease inhibitors has become the more or less standard treatment and has reduced HIV to below detectable levels in many infected people (Penedo et al., 2003). New drugs such as "fusion inhibitors" that attack HIV at a different point in their reproductive cycle are becoming available as time goes on.

Many physicians also treat people who fear that they have been exposed to HIV with antiviral drugs to reduce the likelihood of infection. *If you think that you may have been exposed to HIV, talk to your doctor about it immediately.*

Current drug therapy has given rise to the hope that AIDS will become increasingly manageable, a chronic disease but not a terminal illness. However, treatment is expensive, and many who could benefit from it cannot afford it. In addition, some people with AIDS do not respond to the drug cocktail, and HIV levels bounce back. *Therefore, the most effective way of dealing with AIDS is prevention* (Antoni & Pitts, 2003; Brown et al., 2003).

More information about STIs is found in Table 12.4. For the latest on HIV/AIDS, you can call the National AIDS Hotline at 1-800-342-AIDS. Call 1-800-344-SIDA for information in Spanish. Or go to the CDC Web site: www.cdc.gov. Once you're there, click on "Health Topics A–Z," then on "AIDS/HIV."

Preventing HIV/AIDS and Other STIs

Prevention is the primary weapon against STIs. People need to learn about the transmission, symptoms, and effects of STIs. They need to learn about "safer sex" techniques, including abstinence, and, if they are sexually active, the use of condoms. Educating people to use condoms is associated with lower levels of infection (Ford et al., 2000; Fylkesnes et al., 2001).

But there remains what social psychologists call the A–B problem (see Chapter 16); that is, people do not always behave (B) in accord with their attitudes (A). Thus knowledge may not be enough to change behavior (Parsons et al., 2000). For example, many female adolescents lack power in their relationships. Males are likely to pressure females into unwanted sexual relations or to pressure them into unprotected sexual relations (Friedman et al., 2001; Garcia-Moreno & Watts, 2000). In many cases, that is, prevention involves the empowerment of adolescent females (United Nations Special Session on AIDS, 2001).

What can *you* do to prevent the transmission of HIV and other STI-causing organisms? A number of things.

1. *The first aspect of prevention is psychological: Don't ignore the threat of STIs.* Don't simply assume that your partner is uninfected or believe it would hurt the relationship to ask about STIs.

2. *Remain abstinent.* One way to curb the sexual transmission of HIV and other organisms that cause STIs is sexual abstinence. But what does "abstinence" mean? Does it mean avoiding sexual intercourse (yes) or any form of sexual activity with another person (not necessarily)? Kissing, hugging, and petting to orgasm (without coming into contact with semen or vaginal secretions) are generally considered safe in terms of HIV transmission. However, kissing can transmit oral herpes (as shown by cold sores) and some bacterial STIs.

3. *Engage in a monogamous relationship with someone who is not infected.* Sexual activity within a monogamous relationship with an uninfected person is safe.

Readers who do not abstain from sexual relationships or limit themselves to a monogamous relationship can do some things to make sex safer—if not perfectly safe:

4. *Be selective.* Engage in sexual activity only with people you know well. Consider whether they are likely to have engaged in the kinds of behaviors that transmit HIV or other STIs.

5. *Inspect your partner's genitals.* People who have STIs often have a variety of symptoms. Examining your partner's genitals for blisters, discharges, chancres, rashes, warts, lice, and unpleasant odors during foreplay may reveal signs of such diseases.

6. *Wash your own genitals before and after contact.* Washing beforehand helps protect your partner. Washing promptly afterward with soap and water helps remove germs.

7. *Use condoms.* *Latex* condoms (but not condoms made from animal membrane) protect the woman from having HIV-infected semen enter the vagina and the man from contact with HIV-infected vaginal secretions. Condoms also prevent transmission of bacterial STIs.

8. *If you fear that you have been exposed to HIV or another infectious organism, talk to your doctor about it.* Early treatment is usually more effective than later treatment. There is a difference between exposure to HIV and infection by HIV; early treatment may prevent infection.

9. *When in doubt, stop.* If you are not sure that sex is safe, stop and think things over or seek expert advice.

If you think about it, the last item is rather good general advice. When in doubt, why not stop and think, regardless of whether the doubt is about your sex partner, your college major, or a financial investment?

TABLE 12.4 CAUSES, TRANSMISSION, SYMPTOMS, DIAGNOSIS, AND TREATMENT OF SEXUALLY TRANSMITTED INFECTIONS (STIs)

STI and Cause	Methods of Transmission	Symptoms	Diagnosis	Treatment
Acquired immune deficiency syndrome (AIDS): *Human immunodeficiency virus (HIV)*	■ Sexual intercourse ■ Injection of contaminated blood ■ From mother to child during childbirth or breast-feeding	■ Flulike symptoms ■ Chronically swollen lymph nodes and intermittent weight loss, fever, fatigue, and diarrhea ■ May be asymptomatic for many years ■ "Opportunistic" infections	■ Blood, saliva, and urine tests can detect HIV antibodies in the bloodstream ■ Other tests detect the virus itself	A "cocktail" of antiviral drugs including protease inhibitors reduces the amount of HIV in the blood
Bacterial vaginosis: *Gardnerella vaginalis* bacterium and others	■ Sexual contact	■ In women, a vaginal discharge, genital irritation, and mild pain during urination ■ In men, inflammation of the penis, urethritis, and cystitis ■ May be asymptomatic	■ Culture and examination of bacterium	Oral treatment with metronidazole (Flagyl)
Candidiasis (moniliasis, thrush, "yeast infection"): *Candida albicans*–a yeastlike fungus	■ Sexual contact ■ Sharing a washcloth or towel with an infected person	■ In women, vulval itching, discharge, soreness or swelling of genital tissues ■ In men, itching and burning on urination, or inflammation of the penis	■ Diagnosis usually made on basis of symptoms	Vaginal suppositories, creams, or tablets containing miconazole, clotrimazole, or teraconazole
Chlamydia and non-gonococcal urethritis (NGU): *Chlamydia trachomatis* bacterium in women, and several in men	■ Vaginal, oral, or anal sexual activity	■ In women, frequent and painful urination, abdominal pain and inflammation, and vaginal discharge ■ In men, burning or painful urination, slight discharge; may be asymptomatic	■ The Abbott Testpack analyzes a cervical smear in women	Antibiotics
Genital herpes: *Herpes simplex virus–type 2 (HSV-2)*	■ Vaginal, oral, or anal sexual activity ■ Most contagious during outbreaks	■ Painful, reddish bumps around the genitals ■ Bumps become blisters or sores that fill with pus and break, shedding viral particles ■ Burning urination, fever, aches and pains, swollen glands, and vaginal discharge possible	■ Clinical inspection of sores ■ Culture and examination of fluid drawn from sore	Antiviral drugs may provide relief and prompt healing but are not cures
Genital warts (venereal warts): *Human papilloma virus (HPV)*	■ Sexual contact ■ Other forms of contact, as with infected towels or clothing	■ Painless warts resembling cauliflowers on the genitals or anus or in the rectum	■ Clinical inspection ■ Pap tests	Removal by freezing, podophyllin, burning, and surgery
Gonorrhea ("clap," "drip"): Gonococcus bacterium *(Neisseria gonorrhoeae)*	■ Vaginal, oral, or anal sexual activity	■ In men, thick discharge, burning urination ■ In women, may be symptom-free or there may be increased discharge, burning urination, irregular menstruation	■ Clinical inspection ■ Culture of sample discharge	Antibiotics
Pubic lice ("crabs"): *Pthirus pubis* (an insect, not a crab)	■ Sexual contact ■ Contact with infested towel, sheet, or toilet seat	■ Intense itching in pubic area and other hairy regions to which lice can attach	■ Clinical examination	Drugs containing pyrethrins or piperonal butoxide (e.g., NIX, A200, RID, Triple X)
Syphilis: *Treponema pallidum*	■ Vaginal, oral, or anal sexual activity	■ Hard, round, painless chancre (sore) appears at site of infection within 2 to 4 weeks ■ May progress through additional stages if not treated ■ Potentially lethal	■ Clinical examination or examination of fluid from a chancre ■ Blood test (the VDRL)	Antibiotics
Trichomoniasis ("trich"): *Trichomonas vaginalis*–a protozoan (one-celled animal)	■ Almost always transmitted sexually	■ In women, a discharge, itching or burning in vulva ■ Mild urethritis in men ■ May be asymptomatic	■ Microscopic examination of vaginal secretions ■ Examination of culture of sample	Metronidazole (Flagyl)

Recite—An Active Summary™

Want to study on the go? Go to your companion website and download an audio version of this review section to your media player.

1. What are gender-role stereotypes?

Cultures have broad expectations of men and women that are termed *gender-role stereotypes*. In our culture women are expected to be gentle, dependent, kind, helpful, patient, and submissive. Men are expected to be tough, competitive, gentlemanly, and protective.

2. Are there psychological differences between females and males?

Boys have historically been seen as excelling in math and spatial relations skills, whereas girls have been viewed as excelling in language skills. However, these differences are small and growing narrower. Females are more extraverted and nurturant than males. Males are more tough-minded and aggressive than females. Men are more interested than women in casual sex and multiple sex partners. Women are more willing than men to marry someone who is not good-looking but less willing to marry someone who is unlikely to hold a steady job.

3. What is the role of nature in gender-typing?

Biological views of gender-typing focus on the roles of evolution, genetics, and prenatal influences in predisposing men and women to sex-linked behavior patterns. According to evolutionary psychologists, gender differences were fashioned by natural selection in response to problems in adaptation that were repeatedly encountered by humans over thousands of generations. Testosterone in the brains of male fetuses spurs greater growth of the right hemisphere of the brain, which may be connected with the ability to manage spatial-relations tasks. Testosterone is also connected with aggressiveness.

4. What is the role of nurture in gender-typing?

Psychologists have looked at nurture and gender-typing in terms of psychodynamic, social cognitive, and gender-schema theories. Freud explained gender-typing in terms of identification with the parent of the same sex through resolution of the Oedipus complex. Social cognitive theorists explain gender-typing in terms of the ways in which experience helps the individual create concepts of gender-appropriate behavior, and how the individual is motivated to engage in such behavior. Social cognitive theorists use terms such as observational learning, identification, and socialization. Research shows that women can behave as aggressively as men when they are provoked, have the means, and believe that the social climate will tolerate their aggression. Gender-schema theory proposes that once children learn the gender schema of their culture, their self-esteem becomes tied up in how well they express the traits considered relevant to their gender.

5. How do sex hormones affect sexual motivation?

Sex hormones have activating and organizing effects on behavior. "Male" sex hormones appear to fuel the sex drive, even in women, who produce much less of them. Many female animals are receptive to males only during estrus, when female sex hormones are plentiful.

6. What are pheromones?

Pheromones are chemical secretions that are detected through a vomeronasal organ. Pheromones trigger sexual and other behaviors in many mammals, but their role in human sexuality is controversial.

7. What is meant by *sexual orientation*?

Sexual orientation refers to the direction of one's erotic interests. Heterosexual people are sexually attracted to people of the other sex and interested in forming romantic relationships with them. Homosexual people are sexually attracted to people of their own sex and interested in forming romantic relationships with them.

8. What do we know about the origins of gay male and lesbian sexual orientations?

Psychodynamic theory connects sexual orientation with improper resolution of the Oedipus and Electra complexes. Learning theorists focus on the role of reinforcement of early patterns of sexual behavior. Evidence of a genetic contribution to sexual orientation is accumulating. Sex hormones are known to have both organizing and activating effects, but research has failed to connect sexual orientation with differences in adult levels of sex hormones. However, sex hormones may play a role in determining sexual orientation during prenatal development.

9. What factors contribute to attraction in our culture?

Men seem to find large eyes and narrows jaws to be attractive in women. In our culture, slenderness is considered attractive in both men and women, and tallness is valued in men. Women tend to see themselves as being heavier than the cultural ideal. We are more

Recite—An Active Summary™

attracted to good-looking people. Similarity in attitudes and sociocultural factors (ethnicity, education, and so on), and reciprocity in feelings of admiration, also enhance attraction. According to the matching hypothesis, we tend to seek dates and mates at our own level of attractiveness, largely because of fear of rejection.

10. Just what is love? What is romantic love?

Sternberg's theory suggests that love has three components: intimacy, passion, and commitment. Different kinds of love combine these components in different ways. Romantic love is characterized by the combination of passion and intimacy. Consummate love has all three factors.

11. What is the sexual response cycle?

The sexual response cycle describes the body's response to sexual stimulation. It is generally characterized by vasocongestion and myotonia and consists of four phases: excitement, plateau, orgasm, and resolution. Excitement is characterized by erection in the male and lubrication in the female. Orgasm is characterized by muscle contractions and release of sexual tension. Following orgasm, males enter a refractory period during which they are temporarily unresponsive to sexual stimulation.

12. What do we know about the sex lives of people in the United States?

Males are generally more likely than females to masturbate, engage in premarital sex, and have a large number of sex partners. Education appears to have a liberating influence on sexual behavior, whereas conservative religious beliefs appear to have a constraining effect.

13. What are sexual dysfunctions?

Sexual dysfunctions are persistent or recurrent problems in becoming sexually aroused or reaching orgasm. They include hypoactive sexual desire disorder (lack of interest in sex), female sexual arousal disorder and male erectile disorder (characterized by inadequate vasocongestion), orgasmic disorder, premature ejaculation, dyspareunia (pain during sex), and vaginismus (involuntary contraction of the muscles surrounding the vagina, impeding intercourse).

14. What are the origins of sexual dysfunctions?

Sexual dysfunctions may be caused by physical problems, negative attitudes toward sex, lack of sexual knowledge and skills, problems in the relationship, and performance anxiety.

15. How are sexual dysfunctions treated?

Sexual dysfunctions are treated by sex therapy, which focuses on reducing performance anxiety, changing self-defeating attitudes and expectations, teaching sexual skills, enhancing sexual knowledge, and improving sexual communication. There are also biological treatments that can help enhance the physical aspects of sexual response.

16. Why do men rape women?

Social critics argue that men are socialized into sexual aggression by being generally reinforced for aggressiveness and competitiveness. Social attitudes such as gender role stereotyping, seeing sex as adversarial, and myths that tend to blame the victim all help create a climate that encourages rape.

17. How can we prevent rape?

Rape can be prevented by social change and by cautionary measures such as avoiding deserted areas and—in dating—by dating in groups and being assertive in expressing one's sexual intentions and limits.

18. What is sexual harassment?

Sexual harassment consists of gestures, verbal comments, or physical contact of a sexual nature that is unwelcome to the recipient.

19. What can you do if you are sexually harassed on campus or in the workplace?

Sexual harassment is often stopped by means such as imparting a professional attitude, avoiding being alone with the harasser, keeping a record of incidents, notifying the harasser that you recognize the harassment for what it is and that you want it to stop, filing complaints with appropriate campus offices, and consulting a lawyer about the problem.

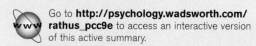

Go to **http://psychology.wadsworth.com/ rathus_pcc9e** to access an interactive version of this active summary.

Key Terms

Stereotype (p. 437)

Gender (p. 437)

Gender role (p. 437)

Gender-typing (p. 443)

Gender-schema theory (p. 446)

Activating effect (p. 449)

Estrus (p. 449)

Pheromone (p. 449)

Organizing effect (p. 451)

Sexual orientation (p. 451)

Homosexual (p. 451)

Attraction (p. 453)

Matching hypothesis (p. 454)

Reciprocity (p. 455)

Triangular model of love (p. 456)

Intimacy (p. 456)

Passion (p. 456)

Consummate love (p. 456)

Romantic love (p. 456)

Affective shift hypothesis (p. 456)

Sexual response cycle (p. 459)

Vasocongestion (p. 459)

Myotonia (p. 459)

Excitement phase (p. 459)

Clitoris (p. 459)

Plateau phase (p. 460)

Ejaculation (p. 460)

Orgasm (p. 460)

Resolution phase (p. 460)

Refractory period (p. 460)

Sexual dysfunction (p. 461)

Hypoactive sexual desire disorder (p. 462)

Female sexual arousal disorder (p. 462)

Male erectile disorder (p. 462)

Orgasmic disorder (p. 462)

Premature ejaculation (p. 462)

Dyspareunia (p. 462)

Vaginismus (p. 462)

Performance anxiety (p. 463)

Sex therapy (p. 464)

Sexual harassment (p. 469)

ACTIVE LEARNING RESOURCES

Visit your Companion Website for Quizzing and Self-Assessment!

http://psychology.wadsworth.com/rathus_pcc9e

On this site there are many quizzing opportunities including interactive versions of the fill-in-the-blank Active Review sections in your book. You can also fill out and score the Self-Assessments on p. 457 and p. 468.

Study on the Go!

Don't have time to study right now? You can study on the go! Visit your companion website and download an audio version of the Recite—An Active Summary section to your media player.

ThomsonNOW

http://www.thomsonedu.com

Need help studying? This site is your one-stop study shop. Take a Pre-Test and Thomson NOW will generate a Personalized Study Plan based on your test results. The Study Plan will identify the topics you need to review and direct you to online resources to help you master those topics. You can then take a Post-Test to determine the concepts you have mastered and what you still need to work on.

Author Blog

 What does your author have to say about the state of psychology? Visit your companion website every Tuesday and click on "Author Blog," where he'll talk about the most recent controversies and hot topics in psychology.

Truth or Fiction?

T F Because variety is the spice of life, the more change the better.

T F Going on vacation is stressful.

T F Searching for social approval or perfection is an excellent way of making yourself miserable.

T F "A merry heart doeth good like a medicine."

T F At any given moment, countless microscopic warriors within our bodies are carrying out search-and-destroy missions against foreign agents.

T F Blowing things out of proportion can give you a headache.

T F African Americans are more likely than European Americans to contract cancer and more likely to die from it when they do.

T F People who exercise regularly live two years longer, on average, than their sedentary counterparts.

T F Ketchup (ketchup?) is a health food.

 Go to **http://psychology.wadsworth.com/ rathus_pcc9e** to answer and score this Truth or Fiction quiz.

© Duomo/CORBIS

Stress, Health, and Adjustment

Preview

Katrina came through the door of a home in a New Orleans suburb at 10 o'clock on Monday morning. She didn't knock. She flowed underneath the door and then she began to come in through the windows, the rising waters of a tempest whose winds had tossed torrents against the shore at close to 150 miles per hour.

Gail, a nurse, and her husband Earl, a machinist, had socked away some money for the future and nearly owned their one-story brick home free and clear. They had been looking forward to spending more time with their grandchildren.

But in minutes Katrina changed their lives forever. Before they fully comprehended what was happening, water was sloshing up against their waists. The front door normally opened out, but Katrina held it shut. Gail and Earl managed to climb out a window against Katrina's onrushing fury.

Gail and Earl, like many of their neighbors, owned a boat—a 17-foot Sunbird. They slogged through the sudden river and the pouring rain to where the boat was parked under the roof of their carport. They pulled themselves up onto it, and then they realized that the keys to the engine were still in the house.

Gail and Earl looked at each other. Earl knew what he had to do. He slid back into the water. There was no more reaching the ground to walk through it. He swam back to the house. Once he was in the house, the water continued to rise.

■ **Katrina.** Hurricane Katrina flooded some 80% of New Orleans by means of rain, the storm surge, and the breaking of levees. Natural disasters such as Katrina expose people to countless life changes in addtion to the danger itself. For many, life will never be the same. For hundreds who were caught in the storm surge or in collapsing buildings, life ended permaturely.

"The boat was just about touching the roof of the carport," Gail said. "I'm screaming for him to hurry up. Because if we got stuck under there, you know, we would have died" (Herbert, 2005).

Somehow Earl found the keys and worked his way back to the boat, and they got the engine going. By the time they left the carport, the water was up to the roof of the house. They could barely see through the rain much less maneuver, but they managed to move the boat two blocks to the shelter of the roof of the drive-through lane of a bank. But about an hour later they had to return to the storm because the boat was bouncing up against the roof of the drive-through.

Fortunately, the rain eased and Gail and Earl piloted the Sunbird out across the alien waterscape. There was no refilling the engine with gasoline. The gas stations were underwater. Even locating themselves was an eerie experience, since the street signs were underwater. Cars and trucks bobbed by like strange logs in a stream.

Then it dawned on them that people around them were screaming for help. Drenched people stood on rooftops or leaned out of upper story windows, waving and yelling. Gail and Earl took as many as they could in the Sunbird and found their way to a shelter in a local high school.

Then they turned about and went out for more people. Others—police, firefighters, civilians—were also out in boats doing their part. Local officials managed to find them gasoline. They rode the waters and ferried people to the shelter for two days, bringing in 150. Hungry, unwashed despite the flooding, and exhausted, Gail and Earl themselves were then evacuated to Baton Rouge, where they rested for a couple of days before making their way to relatives in Florida. It never occurred to them that they were heroes.

Their home is gone. So, too, are their jobs. They lost a car and a truck. Yet they were lucky. "If we did not have family," Gail said, "we'd be living under a bridge."

When asked how the ordeal had affected her psychologically, Gail said, "Don't ask me now. It's too early." Later she added, "Listen, everybody's depressed and kind of still in shock. Everybody who's been through this thing. It's hard to believe it happened" (Herbert, 2005).

Disasters like Katrina take an emotional toll as well as a physical one (Carey, 2005; Leitch, 2005). Studies of communities devastated by fires, earthquakes, tsunamis, hurricanes, and other disasters suggest that most survivors eventually come to live with their memories and their grief. But many have lingering nightmares, flashbacks, depression, and irritability that suggest deeper effects of stress.

This chapter is about stress—its origins, its psychological and physical effects, and ways of coping. **Question: What is stress?**

Stress: What It Is, Where It Comes From

In physics, stress is defined as a pressure or force exerted on a body. Tons of rock pressing on the earth, one car smashing into another, a rubber band stretching—all are types of physical stress. Psychological forces, or stresses, also press, push, or pull. We may feel "crushed" by the weight of a big decision, "smashed" by adversity, or "stretched" to the point of snapping. In the case of the victims of Katrina, physical events had both psychological and physical consequences. As we will see throughout the chapter, those psychological consequences can also affect our health.

Psychologists define **stress** as the demand made on an organism to adapt, cope, or adjust. Some stress is healthful and necessary to keep us alert and occupied. Stress researcher Hans Selye (1980) referred to such healthful stress as **eustress.** We may experience eustress when we begin a sought-after job or are trying to choose the color of an iPod. But intense or prolonged stress, such as that caused by Hurricane Katrina or by social or financial problems, can overtax our adjustive capacity, affect our moods, impair our ability to experience pleasure, and harm the body (Baker et al., 2006; Critchley et al., 2005; Hammerfald et al., 2006; Strike & Steptoe, 2005).

Stress is one of the key topics in health psychology. **Question: What is health psychology? Health psychology** studies the relationships between psychological factors and the prevention and treatment of physical health problems. Health psychologists investigate how

◆ psychological factors such as stress, behavior patterns, and attitudes can lead to or aggravate illness;

◆ people can cope with stress;

◆ stress and **pathogens** (disease-causing organisms such as bacteria and viruses) interact to influence the immune system;

◆ people decide whether or not to seek health care;

◆ psychological interventions such as health education (concerning nutrition, smoking, and exercise, for example) and behavior modification can contribute to physical health.

In this chapter we consider sources of stress, factors that moderate the impact of stress, and the body's response to stress. We consider various physical health issues that overlap with the science of psychology, including headaches, heart disease, and cancer. We have seen how disasters create stress. Let us consider less severe but more common sources of stress: daily hassles, life changes, conflict, irrational beliefs, and Type A behavior.

Stress The demand that is made on an organism to adapt.

Eustress (YOU-stress). Stress that is healthful.

Health psychology The field of psychology that studies the relationships between psychological factors (e.g., attitudes, beliefs, situational influences, and behavior patterns) and the prevention and treatment of physical illness.

Pathogen A microscopic organism (e.g., bacterium or virus) that can cause disease.

Daily hassles Notable daily conditions and experiences that are threatening or harmful to a person's well-being.

Uplifts Notable pleasant daily conditions and experiences.

Daily Hassles: The Stress of Everyday Life

Which straw will break the camel's back? The last straw, according to the saying. Similarly, stresses can pile up until we can no longer cope with them. Some of these stresses are **daily hassles. Question: What are daily hassles?** Daily hassles are regularly occurring conditions and experiences that can threaten or harm our well-being. Others are life changes. Lazarus and his colleagues (1985) analyzed a scale that measures daily hassles and their opposites—termed **uplifts**—and found that hassles could be grouped as follows.

1. *Household hassles:* preparing meals, shopping, and home maintenance.
2. *Health hassles:* physical illness, concern about medical treatment, and side effects of medication.
3. *Time-pressure hassles:* having too many things to do, too many responsibilities, and not enough time.
4. *Inner concern hassles:* being socially isolated, lonely (Cacioppo et al., 2003).
5. *Environmental hassles:* crime, neighborhood deterioration, and traffic noise.
6. *Financial responsibility hassles:* concern about owing money such as mortgage payments and loan installments.
7. *Work hassles:* job dissatisfaction, not liking one's duties at work, and problems with coworkers.
8. *Security hassles:* concerns about job security, terrorism, taxes, property investments, stock market swings, and retirement.

An Israeli study of Israeli Jews and Arabs found that uplifts were related to family satisfaction among both groups and to general life satisfaction among Jews (Lavee & Ben-Ari, 2003). Daily hassles, by contrast, are linked to variables such as nervousness, worrying, inability to get started, feelings of sadness, and feelings of loneliness.

Life Changes: Variety May Be the Spice of Life, But Does Too Much Spice Leave a Bad Taste?

You might think that marrying Mr. or Ms. Right, finding a good job, and moving to a better neighborhood all in the same year would propel you into a state of bliss. It might. **Truth or Fiction Revisited:** Although variety adds spice to life, too much variety might lead to physical illness. **Question: How can too much of a good thing make you ill?** It is because the events that add variety to life are changes. Even pleasant changes require adjustment. Piling one atop the other, even positive changes can lead to headaches, high blood pressure, and other health problems.

Life changes differ from daily hassles in two key ways.

1. Many life changes are positive and desirable; hassles, by definition, are negative.
2. Hassles occur regularly; life changes occur at irregular intervals.

Peggy Blake and her colleagues (1984) constructed a scale to measure the impact of life changes among college students. Surveys with students revealed that death of a spouse or parent were considered the most stressful life changes (94 and 88 life-change units, respectively; see Table 13.1). Academic failure (77 units) and graduation from college (68 units) were also considered highly stressful, even though graduation from college is a positive event—considering the alternative. Positive life changes such as an outstanding personal achievement (49 units) and going on vacation (30 units) also made the list. **Truth or Fiction Revisited:** Although

Richard Douglas Rose

■ **A Daily Hassle** Daily hassles are notable daily conditions and experiences that are threatening or harmful to a person's well-being. Here we see a daily hassle for some commuters in the Philippines. What are some of the daily hassles in your life?

TABLE 13.1 LIFE-CHANGE UNITS CONNECTED WITH VARIOUS EVENTS

Event	Life-Change Units
1. Death of a spouse, lover, or child	94
2. Death of a parent or sibling	88
3. Beginning formal higher education	84
4. Jail sentence	82
5. Divorce or marital separation	82
6. Unwanted pregnancy of self, spouse, or lover	80
7. Abortion of unwanted pregnancy of self, spouse, or lover	80
8. Academic failure	77
9. Marrying or living with lover against parents' wishes	75
10. Change in love relationship or important friendship	74
11. Change in marital status of parents	73
12. Hospitalization of a parent or sibling	70
13. Graduation from college	68
14. Major personal injury or illness	68
15. Wanted pregnancy of self, spouse, or lover	67
16. Preparing for an important exam or writing a major paper	65
17. Major financial difficulties	65
18. Change in academic status	64
19. Change in relationship with members of your immediate family	62
20. Hospitalization of yourself or a close relative	61
21. Change in course of study, major field, vocational goals, or work status	60
22. Change in own financial status	59
23. Beginning or ceasing service in the armed forces	57
24. Change in living arrangements, conditions, or environment	55
25. Change in frequency or nature of sexual experiences	55
26. Change in degree of interest in college or attitudes toward education	55
27. Academic success	54
28. Change to a new college or university	54
29. Change in number or type of arguments with roommate	52
30. Change in responsibility at work	50
31. Change in amount or nature of social activities	50
32. Change in routine at college or work	49
33. Change in amount of leisure time	49
34. Outstanding personal achievement	49
35. Improvement of own health	47
36. Change in study habits	46
37. Change in religious affiliation	44
38. Change in address or residence	43
39. Change in weight or eating habits	39
40. Vacation or travel	30

Source: Adapted from *Self-Assessment and Behavior Change Manual* (pp. 43–47), by Peggy Blake, Robert Fry, and Michael Pesjack, 1984, McGraw-Hill. Reprinted by permission of McGraw-Hill Companies.

vacations can be good for your health (Gump & Matthews, 2000), they remain a life change that requires adjustment.

HASSLES, LIFE CHANGES, AND HEALTH PROBLEMS Hassles and life changes—especially negative life changes—affect us psychologically. They can cause us to worry and affect our moods (Harkness & Luther, 2001). Stressors such as hassles and life changes also predict health problems such as heart disease and cancer, even athletic injuries (Perna et al., 2003). Holmes and Rahe (1967) found that people who "earned" 300 or more life-change units within a year, according to their scale, were at greater risk for health problems. Eight of 10 developed health problems, compared with only 1 of 3 people whose totals of life-change units for the year were below 150.

Moreover, people who remain married to the same person live longer than people who experience marital breakups and remarry (Tucker et al., 1996). Apparently the life changes of divorce and remarriage—or the instability associated with them—can be harmful to health.

CONTROVERSY IN PSYCHOLOGY

Just how are daily hassles and life changes connected with health problems?

The links between daily hassles, life changes, and health problems are supported by research. But what leads to what? Although it may appear obvious that hassles and life changes should *cause* health problems, what is obvious can be incomplete, even wrong. In this case, researchers are not even certain that stress causes illness. Let us consider a number of limitations in the research on the connections between daily hassles, life changes, and health problems:

1. *The nature of the links.* The nature of the links between hassles, life changes, and illness are open to question. It may seem logical that the hassles and life changes caused the disorders, but other explanations of the data are also possible (Figure 13.1). One possible explanation is that people who are *predisposed* toward medical or psychological problems encounter more hassles and amass more life-change units (Harkness & Luther, 2001). For example, undiagnosed medical disorders may contribute to sexual problems, arguments with spouses or in-laws, changes in living conditions and personal habits, and changes in sleeping habits.

2. *Positive versus negative life changes.* Other aspects of the research on the relationship between life changes and illness have also been challenged. For instance, positive life changes may be less disturbing than hassles and negative life changes, even though the number of life-change units assigned to them is high (Lefcourt et al., 1981). Consider item number 33 in Table 13.1: "Change in amount of leisure time." It apparently requires as much adaptation to obtain more leisure time as to lose leisure time, but would you personally find both outcomes to be equally stressful?

3. *Personality differences.* People with different personalities respond to stress in different ways. People who are easygoing or psychologically hardy are less likely to become ill under the impact of stress. Optimism also helps people cope with stress. An optimistic outlook helps people marshal social support and find other ways of coping with stress (Brissette et al., 2002).

4. *Cognitive appraisal.* The stress of an event reflects the meaning of the event to the individual (Folkman & Moskowitz, 2000a; Kiecolt-Glaser et al., 2002a). Pregnancy, for example, can be a positive or negative life change, depending on whether one wants and is prepared to have a child. We

FIGURE 13.1 **What Are the Relationships among Daily Hassles, Life Changes, and Physical Illness?**
Do daily hassles and life events cause illness, or do people who are predisposed toward medical or psychological problems encounter or generate more hassles and amass more life-change units?

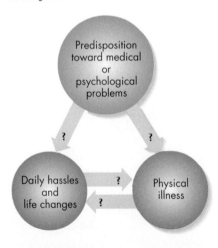

appraise the hassles, traumatic experiences, and life changes that we encounter. In responding to them, we take into account their perceived danger, our values and goals, our beliefs in our coping ability, our social support, and so on. The same event will be less taxing to someone with greater coping ability and support than to someone who lacks these advantages.

Despite these methodological flaws, hassles and life changes require adjustment. It seems wise to be aware of hassles and life changes and how they may affect us.

Conflict: Darned if You Do, Darned if You Don't

Should you eat dessert or try to stick to your diet? Should you live on campus, which is more convenient, or should you rent an apartment, where you may have more independence? Choices like these can place us in **conflict. Question: What is conflict?** In psychology, conflict is the feeling of being pulled in two or more directions by opposing motives. Conflict is frustrating and stressful. Psychologists often classify conflicts into four types: approach–approach, avoidance–avoidance, approach–avoidance, and multiple approach–avoidance.

Classic experimental research by Neal E. Miller (1944) and others suggests that the **approach–approach conflict** (Figure 13.2, Part A) is the least stressful type of conflict. Here, each of two goals is desirable, and both are within reach. You may not be able to decide between pizza or tacos, or a trip to Nassau or Hawaii. I recently had such a conflict in which I was "forced" to choose between triple-chocolate fat-free

Conflict Being torn in different directions by opposing motives. Feelings produced by being in conflict.

Approach–approach conflict A type of conflict in which the goals that produce opposing motives are positive and within reach.

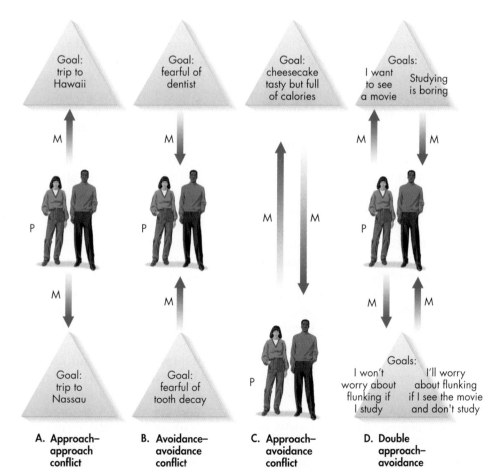

FIGURE 13.2 Models for Conflict

Part A shows an approach–approach conflict, in which a person (P) has motives (M) to reach two goals (G) that are desirable, but approach of one requires exclusion of the other. Part B shows an avoidance–avoidance conflict in which both goals are negative, but avoiding one requires approaching the other. Part C shows an approach–avoidance conflict, in which the same goal has desirable and undesirable properties. Part D shows a double approach–avoidance conflict, which is the simplest kind of *multiple* approach–avoidance conflict. In a multiple approach–avoidance conflict, two or more goals have mixed properties.

A. Approach–approach conflict ("Where should I vacation?")

B. Avoidance–avoidance conflict ("Should I see the dentist?")

C. Approach–avoidance conflict ("Should I eat the cheesecake?")

D. Double approach–avoidance conflict ("Should I study or go to a movie?")

frozen yogurt and coffee-chocolate-chip fat-free frozen yogurt. Such conflicts are usually resolved by making a decision (I took the triple chocolate!). Those who experience this type of conflict may vacillate until they make a decision, as shown by college students who do not make decisions but spend a great deal of time thinking about their conflicting goals (Emmons & King, 1988).

Avoidance–avoidance conflict (Figure 13.2, Part B) is more stressful because you are motivated to avoid each of two negative goals. However, avoiding one of them requires approaching the other. You may be fearful of visiting the dentist but also afraid that your teeth will decay if you do not make an appointment and go. You may not want to contribute to the Association for the Advancement of Lost Causes, but you fear that your friends will consider you cheap or uncommitted if you do not. Each potential outcome in an avoidance–avoidance conflict is undesirable. When an avoidance–avoidance conflict is highly stressful and no resolution is in sight, some people withdraw from the conflict by focusing on other matters or doing nothing. Highly conflicted people have been known to refuse to get up in the morning and start the day.

When the same goal produces both approach and avoidance motives, we have an **approach–avoidance conflict** (Figure 13.2, Part C). People and things have their pluses and minuses, their good points and their bad points. Cheesecake may be delicious, but oh, the calories! Goals that produce mixed motives may seem more attractive from a distance but undesirable from up close (Miller, 1944). Many couples repeatedly break up and then reunite. When they are apart and lonely, they may recall each other fondly and swear that they could make the relationship work if they got together again. But after they spend time together again, they may find themselves thinking, "How could I ever have believed that this so-and-so would change?"

The most complex form of conflict is the **multiple approach–avoidance conflict,** in which each of several alternative courses of action has pluses and minuses. An example with two goals is shown in Figure 13.2, Part D. This sort of conflict might arise on the eve of an examination, when you are faced with the choice of studying or, say, going to a film. Each alternative has both positive and negative aspects: "Studying's a bore, but I won't have to worry about flunking. I'd love to see the movie, but I'd just be worrying about how I'll do tomorrow."

All forms of conflict entail motives that aim in opposite directions. When one motive is much stronger than the other—such as when you feel starved and are only slightly concerned about your weight—it will probably not be too stressful to act in accordance with the powerful motive—in this case, to eat. When each conflicting motive is powerful, however, you may experience stress and confusion about the proper course of action. At such times you need to make a decision. Yet decision making can also be stressful, especially when there is no clear correct choice.

Research by Robert Emmons and Laura King has connected internal conflict with various health problems. In one study (Emmons & King, 1988), the researchers enlisted 88 college undergraduates and surveyed their personal goals and the degree of conflict experienced between them. They used diaries to assess the students' emotional lives and physical symptoms. Students who reported more conflict and more ambivalence about conflict more often reported feeling anxious and depressed, reported more physical complaints, and made significantly more visits to the college health center over the course of two years.

In other studies, King and Emmons assessed the psychological and physical well-being of people who were self-rated and rated by spouses as being in conflict over expressing their feelings. One study (King & Emmons, 1990) found that ambivalence (approach–avoidance conflict) over expressing feelings was connected with psychological distress (anxiety and depression) and physical complaints (headaches, nausea, and the like). The second study (King & Emmons, 1991) focused on 50 married couples and found that ambivalence over expressing feelings and attempts to control one's emotions were negatively correlated with psychological and physical well-being. That is, rather than vacillate and dwell on internal conflict, it was often apparently healthier to express one's genuine feelings.

Avoidance–avoidance conflict A type of conflict in which the goals are negative, but avoidance of one requires approaching the other.

Approach–avoidance conflict A type of conflict in which the same goal produces approach and avoidance motives.

Multiple approach–avoidance conflict A type of conflict in which each of a number of goals produces approach and avoidance motives.

Irrational Beliefs: Ten Doorways to Distress

Psychologist Albert Ellis notes that our beliefs about events, as well as the events themselves, can be stressors (Ellis, 2002; Ellis & Dryden, 1996). Consider a case in which a person is fired from a job and is anxious and depressed about it. It may seem logical that losing the job is responsible for the misery, but Ellis points out how the individual's beliefs about the loss compound his or her misery.

Question: How do irrational beliefs create or compound stress? Let us examine this situation according to Ellis's A ➡ B ➡ C approach: Losing the job is an *activating event* (A). The eventual outcome, or *consequence* (C), is misery. Between the activating event (A) and the consequence (C), however, lie *beliefs* (B), such as these: "This job was the most important thing in my life," "What a no-good failure I am," "My family will starve," "I'll never find a job as good," "There's nothing I can do about it." Beliefs such as these compound misery, foster helplessness, and divert us from planning and deciding what to do next. The belief that "There's nothing I can do about it" fosters helplessness. The belief that "I am a no-good failure" internalizes the blame and may be an exaggeration. The belief that "My family will starve" may also be an exaggeration.

Let's diagram the situation like this:

$$\text{Activating events} \Rightarrow \text{Beliefs} \Rightarrow \text{Consequences}$$

or

$$A \Rightarrow B \Rightarrow C$$

Anxieties about the future and depression over a loss are normal and to be expected. However, the beliefs of the person who lost the job tend to **catastrophize** the extent of the loss and contribute to anxiety and depression—and thus raise the blood pressure (Dunkley et al., 2003; Melmed, 2003). By heightening the individual's emotional reaction to the loss and fostering feelings of helplessness, these beliefs also impair coping ability. They lower the person's self-efficacy expectations.

Ellis proposes that many of us carry with us the irrational beliefs shown in Table 13.2. They are our personal doorways to distress. In fact, they can give rise to problems in themselves. When problems assault us from other sources, these beliefs can magnify their effect.

Catastrophize To interpret negative events as being disastrous; to "blow out of proportion."

TABLE 13.2 IRRATIONAL BELIEFS: COGNITIVE DOORWAYS TO DISTRESS

Irrational Belief 1: You must have sincere love and approval almost all the time from the people who are important to you.

Irrational Belief 2: You must prove yourself to be thoroughly competent, adequate, and achieving at something important.

Irrational Belief 3: Things must go the way you want them to go. Life is awful when you don't get your first choice in everything.

Irrational Belief 4: Other people must treat everyone fairly and justly. When people act unfairly or unethically, they are rotten.

Irrational Belief 5: When there is danger or fear in your world, you must be preoccupied with and upset by it.

Irrational Belief 6: People and things should turn out better than they do. It's awful and horrible when you don't find quick solutions to life's hassles.

Irrational Belief 7: Your emotional misery stems from external pressures that you have little or no ability to control. Unless these external pressures change, you must remain miserable.

Irrational Belief 8: It is easier to evade life's responsibilities and problems than to face them and undertake more rewarding forms of self-discipline.

Irrational Belief 9: Your past influenced you immensely and must therefore continue to determine your feelings and behavior today.

Irrational Belief 10: You can achieve happiness by inertia and inaction, or by just enjoying yourself from day to day.

Source: From *Self-Assessment and Behavioral Change Manual* by Peggy Blake, Robert Fry, and Michael Pesjack, pp 43–47. Copyright © 1984 by Peggy Blake. Reprinted by permission of McGraw-Hill Companies.

■ **Type A Behavior** The Type A behavior pattern is characterized by a sense of time urgency, competitiveness, and hostility.

Ellis finds it understandable that we would want the approval of others but irrational to believe that we cannot survive without it. It would be nice to be competent in everything we do, but it's unreasonable to *expect* it. Sure, it would be nice to be able to serve and volley like a tennis pro, but most of us haven't the time or natural ability to perfect the game. Demanding perfection prevents us from going out on the court on weekends and batting the ball back and forth just for fun (Ellis, 2002). Belief number 5 is a prescription for perpetual emotional upheaval. Beliefs numbers 7 and 9 lead to feelings of helplessness and demoralization. Sure, Ellis might say, childhood experiences can explain the origins of irrational beliefs, but it is our own cognitive appraisal—here and now—that causes us to be miserable.

Truth or Fiction Revisited: Research findings confirm the connections between irrational beliefs (e.g., excessive dependence on social approval and perfectionism) and feelings of anxiety and depression (Chang & Sanna, 2001; Rice & Dellwo, 2001; Wiebe & McCabe, 2002).

The Type A Behavior Pattern: Burning Out from Within?

Some people create stress for themselves through the **Type A behavior** pattern. **Question: What is Type A behavior?** Type A people are highly driven, competitive, impatient, and aggressive—so much so that they are prone to getting into auto accidents (Ben-Zur, 2002; Karlberg et al., 1998; Magnavita et al., 1997). They feel rushed and under pressure all the time and keep one eye firmly glued to the clock (Conte et al., 2001). They are not only prompt for appointments but often early. They eat, walk, and talk rapidly and become restless when others work slowly. They attempt to dominate group discussions. Type A people find it difficult to give up control or share power. They are often reluctant to delegate authority in the workplace, and because of this they increase their own workloads.

Type A people find it difficult just to go out on the tennis court and bat the ball back and forth. They watch their form, perfect their strokes, and strive for continual self-improvement. They demand to be perfectly competent and achieving in everything they undertake.

TYPE B If there is a Type A, there is bound to be a Type B. Type B people, in contrast to Type A people, relax more readily and focus more on the quality of life. They are less ambitious and less impatient, and they pace themselves. Type A people earn higher grades and more money than Type Bs who are equal in intelligence.

Your Turn: Now that we have discussed sources of stress, enhance your mastery of the material with the nearby "Learning Connections." Review the material by filling in the blanks, reflect on the material by relating it to other things you know, and think critically about it.

Type A behavior Behavior characterized by a sense of time urgency, competitiveness, and hostility.

Learning Connections — STRESS: WHAT IT IS, WHERE IT COMES FROM

ACTIVE REVIEW (1) Daily _____ are regularly occurring conditions and experiences that threaten or harm our well-being. (2) Life changes, even pleasant ones, are stressful because they require _____. (3) The feeling of being pulled in two or more directions by opposing motives is called _____. (4) Albert _____ notes that our beliefs about events, as well as the events themselves, can be stressors. (5) Type A behavior is characterized by a sense of time _____, competitiveness, and aggressiveness.

REFLECT AND RELATE How many daily hassles do you experience? Are they temporary or permanent? How many are connected with your role as a student? What can you do about them?

CRITICAL THINKING Life changes are stressful. Should people therefore avoid life changes?

Go to **http://psychology.wadsworth.com/ rathus_pcc9e** for an interactive version of this Learning Connections unit.

Self-Assessment | Are You Type A or Type B?

Complete the questionnaire by placing a check mark under Yes if the behavior pattern described is typical of you and under No if it is not. Try to work rapidly and leave no items blank. Then read the section on Type A behavior and turn to the scoring key in Appendix B.

Yes No   Do You:

___ ___   1. Strongly accent key words in your everyday speech?

___ ___   2. Eat and walk quickly?

___ ___   3. Believe that children should be taught to be competitive?

___ ___   4. Feel restless when watching a slow worker?

___ ___   5. Hurry other people to get on with what they're trying to say?

___ ___   6. Find it highly aggravating to be stuck in traffic or waiting for a seat at a restaurant?

___ ___   7. Continue to think about your own problems and business even when listening to someone else?

___ ___   8. Try to eat and shave, or drive and jot down notes at the same time?

___ ___   9. Catch up on your work while on vacations?

___ ___   10. Bring conversations around to topics of concern to you?

___ ___   11. Feel guilty when you spend time just relaxing?

___ ___   12. Find that you're so wrapped up in your work that you no longer notice office decorations or the scenery when you commute?

___ ___   13. Find yourself concerned with getting more things rather than developing your creativity and social concerns?

___ ___   14. Try to schedule more and more activities into less time?

___ ___   15. Always appear for appointments on time?

___ ___   16. Clench or pound your fists or use other gestures to emphasize your views?

___ ___   17. Credit your accomplishments to your ability to work rapidly?

___ ___   18. Feel that things must be done now and quickly?

___ ___   19. Constantly try to find more efficient ways to get things done?

___ ___   20. Insist on winning at games rather than just having fun?

___ ___   21. Interrupt others often?

___ ___   22. Feel irritated when others are late?

___ ___   23. Leave the table immediately after eating?

___ ___   24. Feel rushed?

___ ___   25. Feel dissatisfied with your current level of performance?

Psychological Moderators of Stress

There is no one-to-one relationship between stress and physical or psychological health problems. Physical factors account for some of the variability in our responses: Some people inherit predispositions toward specific disorders. Psychological factors also play a role, however (Melmed, 2003). They can influence, or *moderate,* the effects of stress. In this section we discuss several psychological moderators of stress: self-efficacy expectations, psychological hardiness, humor, predictability and control, and social support.

Self-Efficacy Expectations: "The Little Engine That Could"

Self-efficacy is the ability to make things happen. Our **self-efficacy expectations** affect our ability to withstand stress (Basic Behavioral Science Task Force, 1996a; Maciejewski et al., 2000). **Question: How do our self-efficacy expectations affect our ability to withstand stress?**

A classic experiment by Albert Bandura and his colleagues (1985) shows that high self-efficacy expectations are accompanied by relatively *lower* levels of adrenaline and noradrenaline in the bloodstream when we are faced with fear-inducing objects. The Bandura group assessed subjects' self-efficacy, exposed them to fearful stimuli, and monitored the levels of adrenaline and noradrenaline in their bloodstreams as they did so. Adrenaline and noradrenaline are secreted when we are under stress. They arouse the body in several ways, such as accelerating the heart rate and releasing glucose from the liver. As a result, we may have "butterflies in the stomach" and feel nervous. Excessive arousal can also distract us from coping with the tasks at hand. People with higher self-efficacy expectations thus have biological as well as psychological reasons for remaining calmer.

People who are self-confident are less prone to be disturbed by adverse events (Kaslow et al., 2002; Lang & Heckhausen, 2001). People with higher self-efficacy expectations are more likely to lose weight or quit smoking and less likely to relapse afterward (E. S. Anderson et al., 2000, 2001; Shiffman et al., 2000). They are better able to function in spite of pain (Lackner et al., 1996). A study of Native Americans found that alcohol abuse was correlated with self-efficacy expectations (M. J. Taylor, 2000). That is, individuals with feelings of powerlessness were more likely to abuse alcohol, perhaps as a way of lessening the stresses in their lives.

People are more likely to comply with medical advice when they believe that it will work (Schwartzer & Renner, 2000). Women, for example, are more likely to engage in breast self-examination when they believe that they will really be able to detect abnormal growths (Miller et al., 1996). People are more likely to try to quit smoking when they believe that they can do so successfully (Segan et al., 2002).

Psychological Hardiness: Tough Enough?

Psychological hardiness also helps people resist stress (Richardson, 2002). Our understanding of this phenomenon is derived largely from the pioneering work of Suzanne Kobasa and her colleagues (1994). They studied business executives who seemed able to resist illness despite stress. In one phase of the research, executives completed a battery of psychological tests. Kobasa (1990) found that the psychologically hardy executives had three key characteristics. **Question: What characteristics are connected with psychological hardiness?** The characteristics include commitment, challenge, and control.

1. Kobasa found that psychologically hardy executives were high in *commitment*. They tended to involve themselves in, rather than feel alienated from, whatever they were doing or encountering.
2. They were also high in *challenge*. They believed that change, rather than stability, is normal in life. They appraised change as an interesting incentive to personal growth, not as a threat to security.
3. They were high in perceived *control* over their lives. A sense of control is one of the keys to psychological hardiness (Folkman & Moskowitz, 2000b; Tennen & Affleck, 2000). Hardy participants felt and behaved as though they were influential, rather than helpless, in facing the various rewards and punishments of life. Psychologically hardy people tend to have what Julian B. Rotter (1990) terms an internal **locus of control.** The nearby Locus of Control Scale will offer you insight as to how psychologically hardy you may be.

AP/Wide World Photos

■ **Self-Efficacy Expectations and Performance**
Outstanding athletes tend to have high self-efficacy expectations. That is, they believe in themselves. Self-efficacy expectations are one of the psychological factors that moderate the effects of stress on us.

Self-efficacy expectations Our beliefs that we can bring about desired changes through our own efforts.

Psychological hardiness A cluster of traits that buffer stress and are characterized by commitment, challenge, and control.

Locus of control The place (locus) to which an individual attributes control over the receiving of reinforcers—either inside or outside the self.

Hardy people are more resistant to stress because they *choose* to face it (Kobasa, 1990). They also interpret stress as making life more interesting. For example, they see a conference with a supervisor as an opportunity to persuade the supervisor rather than as a risk to their position.

Sense of Humor: "A Merry Heart Doeth Good Like a Medicine"

The idea that humor lightens the burdens of life and helps people cope with stress has been with us for millennia. Consider the biblical maxim "A merry heart doeth good like a medicine" (Proverbs 17:22).

Question: Is there any evidence that "A merry heart doeth good like a medicine"? Truth or Fiction Revisited: Research suggests that humor can moderate the effects of stress. In one study, students completed a checklist of negative life events and a measure of mood disturbance (Martin & Lefcourt, 1983). The measure of mood disturbance also yielded a stress score. The students also rated their sense of humor. Students were asked to try to produce humor in an experimental stressful situation, and their ability to do so was rated by the researchers. Students who had a greater sense of humor and were capable of producing humor in the stressful experimental condition were less affected by the stress than other students. In other experiments, Lefcourt (1997) found that exposing students to humorous videotapes raised the level of immunoglobulin A (a measure of the functioning of the immune system) in their saliva.

How does humor help people cope with stress? We are uncertain, but there are many possibilities. One is that laughter stimulates the output of endorphins, which might enhance the functioning of the immune system. Another is that the benefits of humor may be explained in terms of the positive cognitive shifts they entail and the positive emotions that accompany them. Then, too, students may perceive their ability to produce humor under stress as a sign of their self-efficacy, and self-confidence helps us handle stress better.

Predictability and Control: "If I Can Stop the Roller Coaster, I Don't Want to Get Off"

The ability to predict a stressor apparently moderates its impact. **Question: How do predictability and control help us cope with stress?** Predictability allows us to brace ourselves for the inevitable and, in many cases, plan ways of coping with it. Control—even the illusion of being in control—allows us to feel that we are not at the mercy of the fates (Folkman & Moskowitz, 2000b; Tennen & Affleck, 2000). There is also a relationship between the desire to assume control over one's situation and the usefulness of information about impending stressors. Predictability is of greater benefit to **"internals"**—that is, to people who wish to exercise control over their situations—than to **"externals."** People who want information about medical procedures and what they will experience cope better with pain when they undergo those procedures (Ludwick-Rosenthal & Neufeld, 1993).

Social Support: On Being in It Together

People are social beings, and social support also seems to act as a buffer against the effects of stress (Cohen et al., 2001a; Folkman & Moskowitz, 2000a).

The concept of social support has many definitions:

1. *Emotional concern:* listening to people's problems and expressing feelings of sympathy, caring, understanding, and reassurance.
2. *Instrumental aid:* the material supports and services that facilitate adaptive behavior. For example, after a disaster the government may arrange for low-interest loans so that survivors can rebuild. Relief organizations may provide foodstuffs, medicines, and temporary living quarters.
3. *Information:* guidance and advice that enhance people's ability to cope.

Internals People who perceive the ability to attain reinforcements as being largely within themselves.

Externals People who perceive the ability to attain reinforcements as being largely outside themselves.

Self-Assessment | The Locus of Control Scale

Psychologically hardy people tend to have an internal locus of control. They believe that they are in control of their own lives. In contrast, people with an external locus of control tend to see their fate as being out of their hands.

Are you "internal" or "external"? To learn more about your perception of your locus of control, respond to this questionnaire, which was developed by Nowicki and Strickland (1973). Place a check mark in either the Yes or the No column for each question. When you are finished, turn to the answer key in Appendix B.

Yes   No

___ ___ 1. Do you believe that most problems will solve themselves if you just don't fool with them?

___ ___ 2. Do you believe that you can stop yourself from catching a cold?

___ ___ 3. Are some people just born lucky?

___ ___ 4. Most of the time, do you feel that getting good grades means a great deal to you?

___ ___ 5. Are you often blamed for things that just aren't your fault?

___ ___ 6. Do you believe that if somebody studies hard enough he or she can pass any subject?

___ ___ 7. Do you feel that most of the time it doesn't pay to try hard because things never turn out right anyway?

___ ___ 8. Do you feel that if things start out well in the morning, it's going to be a good day no matter what you do?

___ ___ 9. Do you feel that most of the time parents listen to what their children have to say?

___ ___ 10. Do you believe that wishing can make good things happen?

___ ___ 11. When you get punished, does it usually seem it's for no good reason at all?

___ ___ 12. Most of the time, do you find it hard to change a friend's opinion?

___ ___ 13. Do you think cheering more than luck helps a team win?

___ ___ 14. Did you feel that it was nearly impossible to change your parents' minds about anything?

___ ___ 15. Do you believe that parents should allow children to make most of their own decisions?

___ ___ 16. Do you feel that when you do something wrong there's very little you can do to make it right?

___ ___ 17. Do you believe that most people are just born good at sports?

___ ___ 18. Are most other people your age stronger than you are?

___ ___ 19. Do you feel that one of the best ways to handle most problems is just not to think about them?

4. *Appraisal:* feedback from others about how one is doing. This kind of support involves helping people interpret, or "make sense of," what has happened to them.

5. *Socializing:* simple conversation, recreation, even going shopping with another person. Socializing has beneficial effects, even when it is not oriented specifically toward solving problems.

Question: Is there evidence that social support helps people cope with stress? Yes, research does support the value of social support. Introverts, people who lack social skills, and people who live by themselves seem more prone to developing infectious diseases such as colds under stress (Cohen & Williamson, 1991). Social support helps people cope with the stresses of cancer and other health problems (Azar, 1996b; Wilcox et al., 1994). Social support helps Mexican Americans and other

Yes   No

____ ____ 20. Do you feel that you have a lot of choice in deciding who your friends are?

____ ____ 21. If you find a four-leaf clover, do you believe that it might bring you good luck?

____ ____ 22. Did you often feel that whether or not you did your homework had much to do with what kind of grades you got?

____ ____ 23. Do you feel that when a person your age is angry with you, there's little you can do to stop him or her?

____ ____ 24. Have you ever had a good luck charm?

____ ____ 25. Do you believe that whether or not people like you depends on how you act?

____ ____ 26. Did your parents usually help you if you asked them to?

____ ____ 27. Have you ever felt that when people were angry with you, it was usually for no reason at all?

____ ____ 28. Most of the time, do you feel that you can change what might happen tomorrow by what you did today?

____ ____ 29. Do you believe that when bad things are going to happen they are just going to happen no matter what you try to do to stop them?

____ ____ 30. Do you think that people can get their own way if they just keep trying?

____ ____ 31. Most of the time do you find it useless to try to get your own way at home?

____ ____ 32. Do you feel that when good things happen, they happen because of hard work?

____ ____ 33. Do you feel that when somebody your age wants to be your enemy there's little you can do to change matters?

____ ____ 34. Do you feel that it's easy to get friends to do what you want them to do?

____ ____ 35. Do you usually feel that you have little to say about what you get to eat at home?

____ ____ 36. Do you feel that when someone doesn't like you, there's little you can do about it?

____ ____ 37. Did you usually feel it was almost useless to try in school, because most other children were just plain smarter than you were?

____ ____ 38. Are you the kind of person who believes that planning ahead makes things turn out better?

____ ____ 39. Most of the time, do you feel that you have little to say about what your family decides to do?

____ ____ 40. Do you think it's better to be smart than to be lucky?

immigrants to cope with the stresses of acculturation (Hovey, 2000). Social support helped children cope with the stresses of Hurricane Andrew (Vernberg et al., 1996) and Chinese villagers cope with an earthquake (X. Wang et al., 2000). It has been found to help women cope with the aftermath of rape (Valentiner et al., 1996). Stress is also less likely to lead to high blood pressure or alcohol abuse in people who have social support (Linden et al., 1993).

How does stress contribute to the development of physical health problems? Let us gain insight into this question by examining the effects of stress on the body.

Your Turn: Now that we have discussed psychological moderators of stress, enhance your mastery of the material with the nearby "Learning Connections." Review the material by filling in the blanks, reflect on the material by relating it to other things you know, and think critically about it.

ACTIVE REVIEW (6) People with (*Higher* or *Lower?*) self-efficacy expectations tend to cope better with stress. (7) Psychologically hardy executives are high in _____, challenge, and control. (8) Being able to predict and control the onset of a stressor (*Increases* or *Decreases?*) its impact on us.

REFLECT AND RELATE Are you committed to your undertakings—including college? Do you seek or avoid challenges? Are you in control of your life? What do your answers suggest about your psychological hardiness?

CRITICAL THINKING Social support helps most people cope with stress. What does this research finding suggest about human nature?

 Go to **http://psychology.wadsworth.com/ rathus_pcc9e** for an interactive version of this Learning Connections unit.

General adaptation syndrome (GAS) Selye's term for a hypothesized three-stage response to stress.

Alarm reaction The first stage of the GAS, which is triggered by the impact of a stressor and characterized by sympathetic activity.

Fight-or-flight reaction An innate adaptive response to the perception of danger.

■ **Are Their Alarm Systems Going Off as They Take Out a Loan?** The alarm reaction of the general adaptation syndrome can be triggered by daily hassles and life changes—such as taking out a large loan—as well as by physical threats. When the stressor persists, diseases of adaptation may develop.

Keith Brofsky/Getty Images

Stress and the Body: The War Within

Stress is more than a psychological event. It is more than "knowing" it is there; it is more than "feeling" pushed and pulled. Stress also has very definite effects on the body which, as we will see, can lead to psychological and physical health problems. Stress researcher Hans Selye outlined a number of the bodily effects in his concept of the *general adaptation syndrome (GAS)*.

The General Adaptation Syndrome

Hans Selye suggested that under stress the body is like a clock with an alarm that does not shut off until the clock shakes apart or its energy has been depleted. The body's response to different stressors shows certain similarities whether the stressor is a bacterial invasion, perceived danger, or a major life change (Selye, 1976). For this reason, Selye labeled this response the **general adaptation syndrome (GAS). Question: What is the general adaptation syndrome?** The GAS is a group of bodily changes that occur in three stages: an alarm reaction, a resistance stage, and an exhaustion stage. These changes mobilize the body for action and—like that alarm that goes on ringing—can eventually wear out the body.

THE ALARM REACTION The **alarm reaction** is triggered by perception of a stressor. This reaction mobilizes or arouses the body, biologically speaking. Early in the 20th century, physiologist Walter B. Cannon (1932) argued that this mobilization was the basis for an instinctive **fight-or-flight reaction.** But contemporary psychologists question whether the fight-or-flight reaction is instinctive in humans (Updegraff et al., 2002). In any event, the alarm reaction involves bodily changes that are initiated by the brain and regulated by the endocrine system and the sympathetic division of the autonomic nervous system (ANS). Let us consider the roles of these systems.

Stress has a domino effect on the endocrine system (Bauer et al., 2003; Melmed, 2003; see Figure 13.3). The hypothalamus secretes corticotrophin-releasing hormone (CRH). CRH causes the pituitary gland to secrete adrenocorticotrophic hormone (ACTH). ACTH then causes the adrenal cortex to secrete cortisol and other corticosteroids (steroidal hormones produced by the adrenal cortex). Corticosteroids help protect the body by combating allergic reactions (such as difficulty breathing) and producing inflammation. (However, corticosteroids can be harmful to the cardiovascular system, which is one reason that chronic stress can impair one's health and why athletes who use steroids to build the muscle mass can experience cardiovascular problems.) Inflammation increases circulation to parts of the body that are injured. It ferries in hordes of white blood cells to fend off invading pathogens.

Two other hormones that play a major role in the alarm reaction are secreted by the adrenal medulla. The sympathetic division of the ANS activates

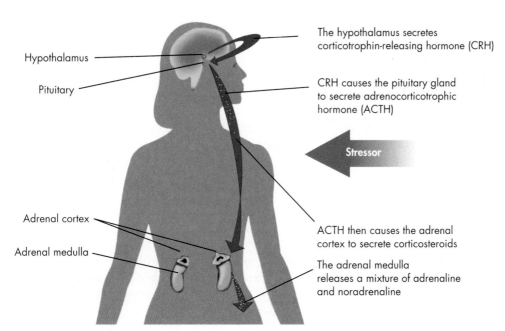

Hypothalamus

Pituitary

The hypothalamus secretes corticotrophin-releasing hormone (CRH)

CRH causes the pituitary gland to secrete adrenocorticotrophic hormone (ACTH)

Stressor

Adrenal cortex

Adrenal medulla

ACTH then causes the adrenal cortex to secrete corticosteroids

The adrenal medulla releases a mixture of adrenaline and noradrenaline

FIGURE 13.3 **Stress and the Endocrine System**
Stress has a domino effect on the endocrine system, leading to the release of corticosteroids and a mixture of adrenaline and noradrenaline. Corticosteroids combat allergic reactions (such as difficulty in breathing) and cause inflammation. Adrenaline and noradrenaline arouse the body to cope by accelerating the heart rate and providing energy for the fight-or-flight reaction.

the adrenal medulla, causing it to release a mixture of adrenaline and noradrenaline. This mixture arouses the body by accelerating the heart rate and causing the liver to release glucose (sugar). This provides the energy that fuels the fight-or-flight reaction, which activates the body so that it is prepared to fight or flee from a predator.

The fight-or-flight reaction stems from a period in human prehistory when many stressors were life threatening. It was triggered by the sight of a predator at the edge of a thicket or by a sudden rustling in the undergrowth. Today it may be aroused when you are caught in stop-and-go traffic or learn that your mortgage payments are going to increase. Once the threat is removed, the body returns to a lower state of arousal. Many of the bodily changes that occur in the alarm reaction are outlined in Table 13.3.

We noted that many contemporary theorists do not believe that the fight-or-flight reaction is universal. In the following "Controversy in Psychology," Shelley Taylor and her colleagues report evidence that many women experience a tend-and-befriend response to threats, rather than a fight-or-flight response. Margaret Kemeny and her colleagues (e.g., Updegraff et al., 2002) also observe that some people attempt to respond productively to stress by pulling back from the situation in order to better appraise it and conserve their resources while they are doing so. This response pattern to stress is described by two theories that are currently under development: "cognitive adaptation theory" and "conservation of resources theory."

TABLE 13.3 **COMPONENTS OF THE ALARM REACTION***

Corticosteroids are secreted.	Muscles tense.
Adrenaline is secreted.	Blood shifts from internal organs to the skeletal musculature.
Noradrenaline is secreted.	Digestion is inhibited.
Respiration rate increases.	Sugar is released from the liver.
Heart rate increases.	Blood coagulability increases.
Blood pressure increases.	

*The alarm reaction is triggered by various types of stressors. It is defined by the release of corticosteroids and adrenaline and by activity of the sympathetic branch of the autonomic nervous system. It prepares the body to fight or flee from a source of danger.

CONTROVERSY IN PSYCHOLOGY

"Fight or flight" or "tend and befriend"?
Do men and women respond differently to stress?

Nearly a century ago, Harvard University physiologist Walter Cannon labeled the body's response to stress the "fight-or-flight" reaction. He believed that the body was prewired to become mobilized or aroused in preparation for combat when faced with a predator or a competitor, or, if the predator was threatening enough, that "discretion"—that is, a "strategic retreat"—would sometimes be the "better part of valor." Although the biology of his day did not allow Cannon to be as precise as we can be, we now know that the fight-or-flight reaction includes bodily changes that involve the brain (perceptions, neurotransmitters), the endocrine system (hormones), and the sympathetic division of the autonomic nervous system (rapid heartbeat, rapid breathing, muscle tension). The sum of these bodily changes pumps us up to fight like demons or, when advisable, to beat a hasty retreat.

Or does it?

According to a review of the literature by UCLA psychologist Shelley E. Taylor and her colleagues (2000b), women under stress are more likely to tend to the kids or "interface" with family and friends than to fight or flee. Taylor explains that the study was prompted by an offhand remark of a student who had noticed that nearly all of the rats in studies of the effects of stress on animals were male. Taylor did an overview of the research on stress with humans and noted that prior to 1995, when federal agencies began requiring more equal representation of women if they were to fund research, only 17% of the subjects were female. Quite a gender gap—and one that had allowed researchers to ignore the question as to whether females responded to stress in the same way as males.

Taylor and her colleagues then dug more deeply into the literature and found that "Men and women do have some reliably different responses to stress," notes S. E. Taylor (2000). "I think we've really been missing the boat on one of the most important responses."

The "woman's response" to stress can be called the "tend-and-befriend" response. It involves nurturing and seeking the support of others rather than fighting or fleeing. The studies that were reviewed showed that when females faced a predator, a disaster, or even an especially bad day at the office, they often responded by caring for their children and seeking contact and support from others, particularly other women. After a bad day at the office, men are more likely to withdraw from the family or start arguments.

This response may be prewired in female humans and in females of other mammalian species. Evolutionary psychologists might suggest that the tend-and-befriend response might have become sealed in our genes because it promotes the survival of females who are tending to their offspring. (Females who choose to fight may often die or at least be separated from their offspring—no evolutionary brass ring here.)

Gender differences in behavior are frequently connected with gender differences in hormones and other biological factors. This one is no different. Taylor and her colleagues point to the effects of the pituitary hormone oxytocin. Oxytocin is connected with nurturing behaviors such as affiliating with and cuddling one's young in many mammals (Taylor et al., 2000b). The literature also shows that when oxytocin is released during stress, it tends to have a calming effect on both rats and humans. It makes them less afraid and more social.

But wait a minute! Men also release oxytocin when they are under stress. So why the gender difference? The answer may lie in the presence of other hormones, the sex hormones estrogen and testosterone. Female have more estro-

■ **"Fight-or-Flight" or "Tend-and-Befriend"?**
Walter Cannon labeled the body's response to stress the "fight-or-flight" reaction. He thought that evolution "prewired" the body to become mobilized in preparation for combat or rapid retreat when faced with a threat. It has been assumed that this reaction applies to both men and women, but research by Shelley Taylor and her colleagues suggests that women may be prewired to take care of others ("tend") or affiliate with others ("befriend") when they encounter threats.

© Bonnie Kamin/PhotoEdit

gen than males do, and estrogen appears to enhance the effects of oxytocin. Males, on the other hand, have more testosterone than females, and testosterone may mitigate the effects of oxytocin by prompting feelings of self-confidence (which may be exaggerated) and fostering aggression (Sullivan, 2000).

It is thus possible that males are more aggressive than females under stress because of the genetic balance of hormones in their bodies, while females are more affiliative and nurturant. Due to these differences, women tend to out-live men. "Men are more likely than women to respond to stressful experiences by developing certain stress-related disorders, including hypertension, aggressive behavior, or abuse of alcohol or hard drugs," Taylor added in a UCLA press release (May 2000). "Because the tend-and-befriend regulatory system may, in some ways, protect women against stress, this biobehavioral pattern may provide insights into why women live an average of seven and a half years longer than men."

Not all psychologists agree with a biological explanation. Psychologist Alice H. Eagly (2000) allows that gender differences in response to stress may be rooted in hormones but suggests an alternative: The differences may reflect learning and cultural conditioning. "I think we have a certain amount of evidence that women are in some sense more affiliative, but what that's due to becomes the question. Is it biologically hard-wired? Or is it because women have more family responsibility and preparation for that in their development? That is the big question for psychologists."

A very big question, indeed.

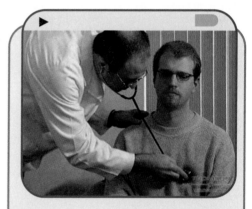

Video Connections—Health and Stress Stress is a huge problem in our society and has far-reaching effects on our health. Learn more about stress and health and how investigators study the link between them when you click on the "Health and Stress" video link on your companion website.

THE RESISTANCE STAGE According to Selye's theory, if the alarm reaction mobilizes the body and the stressor is not removed, we enter the adaptation or **resistance stage** of the GAS. Levels of endocrine and sympathetic activity are lower than in the alarm reaction but still higher than normal. (It's as if the alarm is still on, but a bit softer.) But make no mistake: The individual feels tense, and there continues to be a heavy burden on the body.

THE EXHAUSTION STAGE If the stressor is still not dealt with adequately, we may enter the **exhaustion stage** of the GAS. Individual capacities for resisting stress vary, but anyone will eventually become exhausted when stress continues indefinitely. The muscles become fatigued. The body is depleted of the resources required for combating stress. With exhaustion, the parasympathetic division of the ANS may predominate. As a result, our heartbeat and respiration rate slow down, and many aspects of sympathetic activity are reversed. It might sound as if we would profit from the respite, but remember that we are still under stress—possibly an external threat. Continued stress in the exhaustion stage may lead to what Selye terms "diseases of adaptation." These are connected with constriction of blood vessels and alteration of the heart rhythm, and can range from allergies to hives and coronary heart disease (CHD)—and, ultimately, death.

Discussion of the effects of stress on the immune system paves the way for understanding the links between psychological factors and physical illness.

Effects of Stress on the Immune System

Research shows that stress suppresses the **immune system,** as measured by the presence of various substances in the blood that make up the immune system (Cohen et al., 2001b). Psychological factors such as feelings of control and social support moderate these effects (Cohen et al., 2001a).

THE IMMUNE SYSTEM Given the complexity of the human body and the fast pace of scientific change, we often feel that we are dependent on trained professionals to cope with illness. Yet we actually do most of this coping by ourselves, by means of the immune system. **Question: How does the immune system work?**

Resistance stage The second stage of the GAS, characterized by prolonged sympathetic activity in an effort to restore lost energy and repair damage. Also called the *adaptation stage.*

Exhaustion stage The third stage of the GAS, characterized by weakened resistance and possible deterioration.

Immune system The system of the body that recognizes and destroys foreign agents (antigens) that invade the body.

Leukocytes White blood cells. (Derived from the Greek words *leukos*, meaning "white," and *kytos*, literally meaning "a hollow" but used to refer to cells.)

Antigen A substance that stimulates the body to mount an immune system response to it. (The contraction for *anti*body *gen*erator.)

Antibodies Substances formed by white blood cells that recognize and destroy antigens.

Inflammation Increased blood flow to an injured area of the body, resulting in redness, warmth, and an increased supply of white blood cells.

Psychoneuroimmunology (sigh-coe-new-row-im-you-NOLL-oh-gee). The field that studies the relationships between psychological factors (e.g., attitudes and overt behavior patterns) and the functioning of the immune system.

The immune system has several functions that combat disease (Delves & Roitt, 2000). One of these is the production of white blood cells, which engulf and kill pathogens such as bacteria, fungi, and viruses, and worn-out and cancerous body cells. The technical term for white blood cells is **leukocytes. Truth or Fiction Revisited:** Leukocytes carry on microscopic warfare. They engage in search-and-destroy missions in which they "recognize" and eradicate foreign agents and unhealthy cells.

Leukocytes recognize foreign substances by their shapes. The foreign substances are termed **antigens** because the body reacts to them by generating specialized proteins, or **antibodies.** Antibodies attach themselves to the foreign substances, deactivating them and marking them for destruction. The immune system "remembers" how to battle antigens by maintaining their antibodies in the bloodstream, often for years.[1]

Inflammation is another function of the immune system. When injury occurs, blood vessels in the area first contract (to stem bleeding) and then dilate. Dilation increases the flow of blood, cells, and natural chemicals to the damaged area, causing the redness, swelling, and warmth that characterize inflammation (Duenwald, 2002). The increased blood supply also floods the region with white blood cells to combat invading microscopic life forms such as bacteria, which otherwise might use the local damage as a port of entry into the body.

STRESS AND THE IMMUNE SYSTEM Psychologists, biologists, and medical researchers have combined their efforts in a field of study that addresses the relationships among psychological factors, the nervous system, the endocrine system, the immune system, and disease. This field is called **psychoneuroimmunology.** One of its major concerns is the effect of stress on the immune system (Kiecolt-Glaser et al., 2002a). **Question: How does stress affect the functioning of the immune system?**

One of the reasons that stress eventually exhausts us is that it stimulates the production of steroids. Steroids suppress the functioning of the immune system. Suppression has negligible effects when steroids are secreted occasionally. But persistent secretion of steroids decreases inflammation and interferes with the forma-

[1]A vaccination introduces a weakened form of an antigen (usually a bacteria or a virus) into the body to stimulate the production of antibodies. Antibodies can confer immunity for many years, in some cases for a lifetime.

■ **Microscopic Warfare** The immune system helps us to combat disease. It produces white blood cells (leukocytes), such as that shown here, which routinely engulf and kill pathogens like bacteria and viruses.

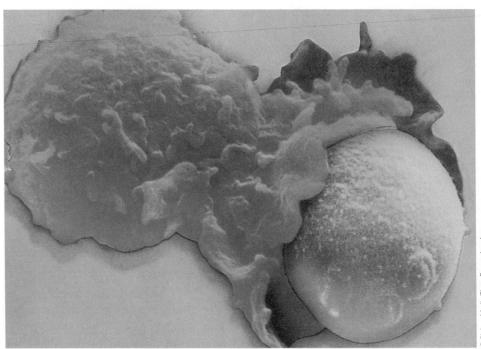

© Biology Media/Photo Researchers Inc.

tion of antibodies. As a consequence, we become more vulnerable to various illnesses, including the common cold (Cohen et al., 1993). By weakening the immune system, stress may also be connected with a more rapid progression of HIV infection to AIDS (Leserman et al., 2000).

In one study, dental students showed lower immune system functioning, as measured by lower levels of antibodies in their saliva, during stressful periods of the school year than immediately following vacations (Jemmott et al., 1983). In contrast, social support buffers the effects of stress and enhances the functioning of the immune system (Cohen et al., 2001a). In the Jemmott study, students who had many friends showed less suppression of immune system functioning than students with few friends.

Other studies with students have shown that the stress of exams depresses the immune system's response to the Epstein-Barr virus, which causes fatigue and other problems (Glaser et al., 1993). Here too, students who were lonely showed greater suppression of the immune system than students who had more social support. All in all, however, there is only modest evidence that psychological interventions enhance the functioning of the immune system. A review of the research found that hypnosis (intended to help people relax), stress management methods, and conditioning methods were of some use, but less than reliable (Miller & Cohen, 2001).

Your Turn: Now that we have discussed stress and the body, enhance your mastery of the material with the nearby "Learning Connections." Review the material by filling in the blanks, reflect on the material by relating it to other things you know, and think critically about it.

Learning Connections — STRESS AND THE BODY: THE WAR WITHIN

ACTIVE REVIEW (9) The general adaptation syndrome has three stages: _____, resistance, and exhaustion. (10) Cannon dubbed the alarm reaction the _____ reaction. (11) Women may show a tend-and-_____ response to stress rather than fight-or-flight. (12) Under stress, pituitary ACTH causes the adrenal cortex to release _____ that help the body respond to stress by fighting inflammation and allergic reactions. (13) Two hormones that play a role in the alarm reaction are secreted by the adrenal medulla: _____ and noradrenaline. (14) The immune system produces (*Red* or *White?*) blood cells, called leukocytes, that routinely engulf and kill pathogens. (15) _____ are pathogens that are recognized and destroyed by leukocytes. (16) Some leukocytes produce _____, or specialized proteins that bind to their antigens and mark them for destruction.

REFLECT AND RELATE What do you experience happening in your body when you are under stress? How do those sensations fit the description of the general adaptation syndrome?

CRITICAL THINKING Prolonged stress is connected with health problems. Must you avoid stress to remain healthy, or can you do something to become psychologically hardy?

Go to **http://psychology.wadsworth.com/ rathus_pcc9e** for an interactive version of this Learning Connections unit.

Psychology and Health

Why do people become ill? Why do some people develop cancer? Why do others have heart attacks? Why do still others seem to be immune to these illnesses? Why do some of us seem to come down with everything that is going around, while others ride out the roughest winters with nary a sniffle? **Question: What is the multifactorial approach to health?** The multifactorial approach recognizes that there is no single, simple answer to these questions. The likelihood of contracting an illness—be it a case of the flu or cancer—can reflect the interaction of many factors, including genetic factors.

Biological factors such as pathogens, inoculations, injuries, age, gender, and a family history of disease may strike us as the most obvious causes of illness. Genetics, in particular, tempts some people to assume there is little they can do about their health. It is true that there are some severe health problems that are unavoidable for people with certain genes. "There is this kind of fatalistic approach to genes that the general public seems to have now—that if your mom, dad, sister or brother had something that you're doomed to have it too," writes Dr. Robert N. Hoover (2000) of the National Cancer Institute. But in many cases, especially with cardiovascular problems and cancer, genes only create *predispositions* toward the health problem.

Genetic predispositions interact with the environment to express themselves (Kéri, 2003). A problematic family medical history is not always a portent of doom. For example, genetic factors are involved in breast cancer. However, rates of breast cancer among women who have recently immigrated to the United States from rural Asia are similar to those in their countries of origin and nearly 80% lower than the rates among third-generation Asian American women, whose rates are similar to those of European American women (Hoover, 2000). Thus factors related to one's lifestyle are also intimately connected with the risk of breast cancer—and most other kinds of cancer.

As shown in the nearby Concept Review, psychological (behavior and personality), sociocultural factors, environmental factors, and stressors all play roles in health and illness. Many health problems are affected by psychological factors, such as attitudes, emotions, and behavior (Kiecolt-Glaser et al., 2002b; Salovey et al., 2000). Table 13.4 reveals that nearly 1 million deaths each year in the United States are preventable (National Center for Health Statistics, 1996). Stopping smoking, eating right, exercising, and controlling alcohol use would prevent nearly 80% of these. Psychological states such as anxiety and depression can impair the functioning of the immune system, rendering us more vulnerable to physical disorders ranging from viral infections to cancer (McGuire et al., 2002; Salovey et al., 2000).

Let us now discuss some health problems, including headaches, heart disease, and cancer. Each of them involves biological, psychological, and environmental factors—including the social and technological environments. Although these are medical problems, we also explore ways in which psychologists have contributed to their prevention and treatment.

Headaches: When Stress Presses and Pounds

Headaches are among the most common stress-related physical ailments. Nearly 20% of people in the United States suffer severe headaches. **Question: How has psychology contributed to the understanding and treatment of headaches?** To answer this question, let us consider the common muscle-tension headache and the more severe migraine headache.

TABLE 13.4 **ANNUAL PREVENTABLE DEATHS IN THE UNITED STATES***

■ Elimination of tobacco use could prevent 400,000 deaths each year from cancer, heart and lung diseases, and stroke.

■ Improved diet and exercise could prevent 300,000 deaths from conditions like heart disease, stroke, diabetes, and cancer.

■ Control of underage and excess drinking of alcohol could prevent 100,000 deaths from motor vehicle accidents, falls, drownings, and other alcohol-related injuries.

■ Immunizations for infectious diseases could prevent up to 100,000 deaths.

■ Safer sex or sexual abstinence could prevent 20,000 deaths from sexually transmitted infections (STIs).

*Other measures for preventing needless deaths include improved worker training and safety to prevent accidents in the workplace, wider screening for breast and cervical cancer, and control of high blood pressure and elevated blood cholesterol levels.

Concept Review BIOPSYCHOSOCIAL FACTORS IN HEART DISEASE AND CANCER

Heart Disease

Cancer

Biological:
Family history
Physiological conditions:
  Obesity
  High serum cholesterol
  Hypertension

Biological:
Family history
Physiological conditions:
  Obesity

Psychological (personality and behavior):
Type A behavior
Hostility and holding in feelings of anger
Job strain
Chronic fatigue, stress, anxiety, depression,
    and emotional strain
Patterns of consumption:
  Heavy drinking (but a drink a day may be
      helpful with heart disease)
  Smoking
  Overeating
Sudden stressors
Physical inactivity

Psychological (personality and behavior):
Patterns of consumption:
  Smoking
  Drinking alcohol (especially in women)
  Eating animal fats?
Sunbathing (skin cancer)
Prolonged depression
Stress? Especially prolonged stress

Sociocultural:
African Americans are more prone to hyper-
    tension and heart disease than Euro-
    pean Americans
Access to health care
Timing of diagnosis and treatment

Sociocultural:
Socioeconomic status
Access to health care
Timing of diagnosis and treatment
Higher death rates are found in nations with
    higher rates of fat intake

MUSCLE-TENSION HEADACHE The single most frequent kind of headache is the muscle-tension headache. During the first two stages of the GAS we are likely to contract muscles in the shoulders, neck, forehead, and scalp. Persistent stress can lead to constant contraction of these muscles, causing muscle-tension headaches. **Truth or Fiction Revisited:** Psychological factors, such as the tendency to catastrophize negative events—that is, to blow them out of proportion—can bring on a tension headache (Ukestad & Wittrock, 1996). Tension headaches usually come on gradually. They are most often characterized by dull, steady pain on both sides of the head and feelings of tightness or pressure.

MIGRAINE HEADACHE The **migraine headache** usually has a sudden onset and is identified by severe throbbing pain on one side of the head. Migraines affect one American in ten (Mulvihill, 2000). They may last for hours or days. Sensory and motor disturbances often precede the pain; a warning "aura" may include vision problems and perception of unusual odors. The migraines themselves are often accompanied by sensitivity to light, loss of appetite, nausea, vomiting, sensory and motor disturbances such as loss of balance, and changes in mood. Imaging techniques suggest that when something triggers a migraine, neurons at the back of the brain fire in waves that ripple across the top of the head then down to the brainstem, the site of many pain centers.

Triggers for migraines include barometric pressure; pollen; certain drugs; monosodium glutamate (MSG), a chemical which is often used to enhance flavor; chocolate; aged cheese; beer, champagne, and red wine; and the hormonal changes connected with menstruation (Goadsby et al., 2002; Mulvihill, 2000).

The behaviors connected with migraine headaches serve as a mini-textbook in health psychology (Holroyd, 2002). For example, the Type A behavior pattern apparently contributes to migraines. In one study, 53% of people who had migraine headaches showed the Type A behavior pattern, compared with 23% of people who had muscle tension headaches (Rappaport et al., 1988). Another study compared 26 women who had regular migraines with women who had none. The migraine sufferers were more sensitive to pain, more self-critical, more likely to catastrophize stress and pain, and less likely to seek social support when under stress (Hassinger et al., 1999).

Regardless of the source of the headache, we can unwittingly propel ourselves into a vicious cycle. Headache pain is a stressor that can lead us to increase, rather than relax, muscle tension in the neck, shoulders, scalp, and face.

Coronary Heart Disease: Taking Stress to Heart

Coronary heart disease (CHD) is the leading cause of death in the United States, most often from heart attacks (American Heart Association, 2000a). **Question: What are the major risk factors for coronary heart disease?** Let us begin by considering the risk factors for CHD.

◆ *Family history:* People with a family history of CHD are more likely to develop the disease themselves (American Heart Association, 2000a; Nabel, 2003).

◆ *Physiological conditions:* Obesity, high **serum cholesterol** levels, and **hypertension** are risk factors for CHD (American Heart Association, 2000a; Stamler et al., 2000; Xin et al., 2001). Even "high normal" blood pressure increases the risk for CHD (Ramachandran et al., 2001).

About one American in five has hypertension, or abnormally high blood pressure (Blumenthal et al., 2002), which can lead to CHD. When high blood pressure has no identifiable cause, it is referred to as *essential hypertension*. This condition has a genetic component (Levy et al., 2000; S. W. Williams et al., 2000). However, blood pressure is also connected with emotions like depression and anxiety (Kazuomi Kario et al., 2001). It also rises when we inhibit the expression of strong feelings or are angry or on guard against threats (Jorgensen et al., 1996). When we are under stress, we may believe that we can feel our blood pressure "pounding through the roof," but this notion is usually false. Most people cannot recognize hypertension. Therefore it is important to check the blood pressure regularly.

◆ *Patterns of consumption:* Patterns include heavy drinking, smoking, and overeating (Stampfer et al., 2000; Xin et al., 2001). On the other hand, a little alcohol seems to be good for the heart (Blanco-Colio et al., 2000). There is a debate as to whether a low-carbohydrate diet may be as healthful, or even more healthful, than a low-fat diet. This question is reviewed in the nearby "A Closer Look."

Migraine headaches Throbbing headaches that are connected with changes in the supply of blood to the head.

Serum cholesterol Cholesterol in the blood.

Hypertension High blood pressure.

◆ *Type A behavior:* Most studies suggest that there is at least a modest relationship between Type A behavior and CHD (Le Melledo et al., 2001; Smith & Ruiz, 2002). It also seems that alleviating Type A behavior patterns may reduce the risk of *recurrent* heart attacks (Friedman & Ulmer, 1984).

◆ *Hostility and holding in feelings of anger:* Hostility seems to be the component of the Type A behavior pattern that is most harmful to physical health (Birks & Roger, 2000; Donker, 2000; Smith & Ruiz, 2002). One study that controlled for the influences of other risk factors, like high blood pressure and cholesterol levels, smoking, and obesity, found that people who are highly prone to anger are about three times as likely as other people to have heart attacks (J. E. Williams et al., 2000). The stress hormones connected with anger can constrict blood vessels to the heart, leading to a heart attack. Chronically hostile and angry people also have higher cholesterol levels (Richards et al., 2000). Highly hostile young adults—as

 ## A Closer Look | THE ATKINS "DIET REVOLUTION": PRESCRIPTION FOR HEART HEALTH OR HEART DISEASE?

Many people complain that they find it difficult to diet because they are consigned to eating "rabbit food"–vegetables, fruits, salads, and whole grains. Others balk because they are permitted to eat fish and poultry (white meat, without the skin), but urged to avoid beef and high-fat dairy products such as butter and whole milk.

When Dr. Robert C. Atkins's "diet revolution" (from the book of the same name) came along in the early 1970s, it achieved instant popularity because it argued that you could eat your fat and lose it–your fat, that is. In other words, you could eat bacon and eggs and hamburger meat (proteins and fats), so long as you cut down on the buns and the ketchup (carbohydrates). The medical community was quick to vilify the low-carbohydrate diet because fruits and vegetables, which are high in vitamins and fiber and various other substances that are believed to fight cancer and heart disease (e.g., the phytochemicals in broccoli and the lycopene in tomatoes), including whole grains, are mainly made up of carbohydrates.

Atkins's books were filled with theory as to why a low-carbohydrate diet ought to raise "good cholesterol" (HDL) and lower "bad cholesterol" (LDL), and he also had numerous anecdotes to support his views. But very little controlled research was done on the subject. Until recently.

In 2003 the respected *New England Journal of Medicine* published two studies on the effects of the Atkins low-carbohydrate diet. The first (Samaha et al., 2003) randomly assigned 132 severely obese men and women to either a low-carbohydrate or low-fat diet. Over a period of 6 months, subjects who ate the low-carbohydrate diet lost more weight (a mean of 13 pounds) than those eating the low-fat diet (a mean of about 4 pounds).

The second study (Foster et al., 2003), like the first, randomly assigned obese men and women to either a low-carbohydrate or low-fat diet, but there were only 63 participants. After 6 months, a similar advantage in weight loss was found for individuals who ate the low-carbohydrate diet. Interestingly, however, when the participants were evaluated at the end of a year, the differences in weight loss had all but vanished. Those who ate the low-carbohydrate diet showed a significant increase in HDL ("good cholesterol"), however.

There are many limitations to these studies. For example:

- There were high dropout rates of participants in both of them (for example, only 79 of the 132 participants completed the Samaha study).
- The studies were carried out with obese participants only. It is not clear that results can be generalized to people who are slightly overweight or of average weight.
- It is unclear whether differences in weight loss were due to *what* was eaten or to the total number of calories eaten.
- The studies were relatively brief in duration. There is little reason to believe that what was found after 6 months would hold at a year (remember that differences in weight loss vanished after a year in the Foster study) or at 5 years.
- The dependent variables were limited to weight change, blood levels of cholesterol, and a couple of other variables related to the health of the cardiovascular system. It remains to be seen whether a low-carbohydrate (high-fat) diet will increase the risk of several types of cancer, as many health professionals suspect.
- There is clear evidence that eating (and sticking to) a lower-fat, lower-calorie diet and

exercising can cut the risk of both heart disease and cancer.
- If the low-fat diet sounds like rabbit food, keep in mind that the low-carbohydrate diet is not so appetizing either. You can eat the steak, but hold the potatoes–they're made up mainly of carbohydrates. You can eat the bacon and eggs, but hold the toast–bread is made up mainly of carbohydrates. And for those who would like to chomp into an apple or a banana, or a cracker, or to drink a glass of beer or wine, remember that these, too, are made up mainly of carbohydrates. The following is just an anecdote, but one Atkins dieter told me that "Given the list of things I'm not allowed to eat, I've lost all interest in eating." It's not too surprising, then, that this particular individual lost weight on the diet. He did not stick to it, however, and gained back every ounce he had lost–and more.

A good deal more research will have to be done on the Atkins diet before it becomes widely accepted by the health community as beneficial–especially in terms of its effects on the risk of cancer. Nonetheless, some researchers, such as Gary Foster who headed the second study published in *The New England Journal of Medicine*, note that they have become more "open-minded" about possible benefits of the Atkins diet. And, as this book goes to press, the "South Beach Diet," which claims to combine the most healthful aspects of the Atkins diet and anticancer diets, has become "hot." Another month, another diet.

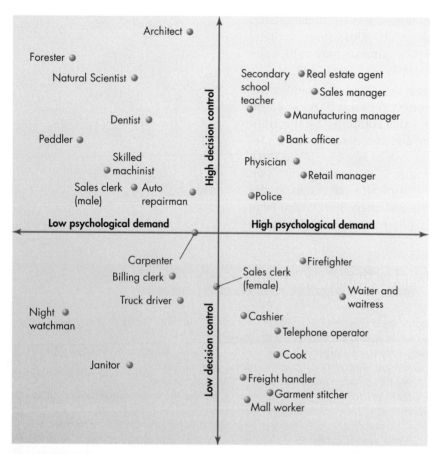

High decision control

Low psychological demand | High psychological demand

Low decision control

Architect

Forester

Natural Scientist

Dentist

Peddler

Skilled machinist

Sales clerk (male) • Auto repairman

Secondary school teacher • Real estate agent

Sales manager

Manufacturing manager

Bank officer

Physician

Retail manager

Police

Carpenter

Billing clerk

Truck driver

Night watchman

Janitor

Sales clerk (female)

Firefighter

Waiter and waitress

Cashier

Telephone operator

Cook

Freight handler

Garment stitcher

Mall worker

FIGURE 13.4 **The Job-Strain Model**

This model highlights the psychological demands made by various occupations and the amount of personal (decision) control they allow. Occupations characterized by high demand and low decision control place workers at greatest risk for heart disease.

young as 18 to 30—are already at greater risk for hardening of the arteries, which increases the risk of heart attacks (Iribarren et al., 2000).

♦ *Job strain:* Overtime work, assembly line labor, and exposure to conflicting demands can all contribute to CHD. High-strain work, which makes heavy demands on workers but gives them little personal control, puts workers at the highest risk (Bishop et al., 2003; Krantz et al., 1988; Smith & Ruiz, 2002). As shown in Figure 13.4, the work of waiters and waitresses may best fit this description.

♦ *Chronic fatigue, stress, anxiety, depression, and emotional strain* (Heinz et al., 2003; Pasic et al., 2003; Tacon et al., 2003). Depression is connected with irregularities in the heart rate and may make blood platelets "sticky," which may, in turn, cause clots (Kramer, 2003).

♦ *Sudden stressors:* For example, after the 1994 Los Angeles earthquake there was an increased incidence of death from heart attacks in people with heart disease (Leor et al., 1996).

♦ *A physically inactive lifestyle* (Stampfer et al., 2000).

African Americans are more likely than European Americans to have heart attacks and to die from them (Freeman & Payne, 2000). Figure 13.5 compares the death rates from heart disease of African American women and women from other ethnic backgrounds in the United States (Smith, 2000). Early diagnosis and treatment might help decrease the racial gap. However, African Americans with heart disease are less likely than European Americans to obtain complex procedures such as bypass surgery and simple measures such as aspirin, even when they would benefit equally from them (Freeman & Payne, 2000; Rathore et al., 2000). Moreover, when European Americans and African Americans show up in the emergency room with heart attacks and other severe cardiac problems, physicians are more likely to misdiagnose the conditions among the African Americans (J. H. Pope et al., 2000).

Cancer: Swerving Off Course

Cancer is the number-one killer of women in the United States and the number-two killer of men (American Cancer Society, 2003). Cancer is characterized by the development of abnormal, or mutant, cells that may take root anywhere in the body: in the blood, bones, digestive tract, lungs, and sex organs. If their spread is not controlled early, the cancerous cells may *metastasize*—that is, establish colonies elsewhere in the body. It appears that our bodies develop cancerous cells frequently. However, these are normally destroyed by the immune system. People whose immune system is damaged by physical or psychological factors may be more likely to develop tumors (Antoni, 2003).

Question: What are the major risk factors for cancer?

RISK FACTORS As with many other disorders, people can inherit a disposition toward cancer (American Cancer Society, 2003). Carcinogenic genes may remove the brakes from cell division, allowing cells to multiply wildly. Or they may allow mutations to accumulate unchecked. However, many behavior patterns markedly heighten the risk for cancer. These include smoking, drinking alcohol (especially in women), eating animal fats, and sunbathing (which may cause skin cancer due to exposure to ultraviolet light). Prolonged psychological conditions such as depression or stress also apparently heighten the risk of some kinds of cancer by depressing the functioning of the immune system (Bauer et al., 2003; McGuire et al., 2002; Salovey et al., 2000).

Truth or Fiction Revisited: African Americans are also more likely than European Americans to contract most forms of cancer (Freeman & Payne, 2000). Possibly because of genetic factors, the incidence of lung cancer is significantly higher among African Americans than European Americans (American Cancer Society, 2003). Once they contract cancer, African Americans are more likely than European Americans to die from it (Freeman & Payne, 2000). The results for African Americans are connected with their lower **socioeconomic status** and relative lack of access to health care (Whitfield et al., 2002).

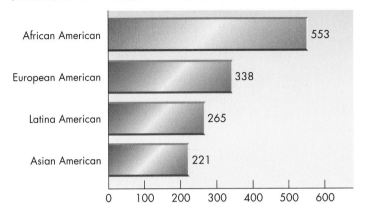

FIGURE 13.5 Deaths from Heart Disease per 100,000 Women Aged 35 and Above

African American women have experienced a higher annual death rate from heart attacks (553 per 100,000) than women from any other ethnic group in the United States.

Also consider cultural differences in health. Death rates from cancer are higher in such nations as the Netherlands, Denmark, England, Canada, and—yes—the United States, where average rates of daily fat intake are high (Cohen, 1987). Death rates from cancer are lower in such nations as Thailand, the Philippines, and Japan, where fat intake is lower. Thailand, the Philippines, and Japan are Asian nations, but do not assume that the difference is racial! The diets of Japanese Americans are similar in fat content to those of other Americans—and so are their rates of death from cancer. According to the British Heart Foundation (Reaney, 2000), it turns out that there are also significant differences among Europeans. French, Spanish, and Portuguese people enjoy the lowest death rates from coronary heart disease (CHD) and also eat diets that are relatively low in fat and high in fruits and vegetables. People in Ireland, Finland, and Britain suffer the most deaths from CHD and also eat high-fat diets and relatively fewer fruits and vegetables.

STRESS AND CANCER Researchers have uncovered possible links between stress and cancer (Heffner et al., 2003; Salovey et al., 2000). For example, Rachel Yehuda (2003) suggests that stress sometimes lowers levels of cortisol and impairs the ability of the immune system to destroy cancer cells.

Experimental research that could not be conducted with humans has been carried out using rats and other animals. In one type of study, animals are injected with cancerous cells or with viruses that cause cancer and then exposed to various conditions. In this way researchers can determine which conditions influence the likelihood that the animals' immune systems will be able to fend off the disease. Such experiments suggest that once cancer has developed, stress can influence its course. In one study, for example, rats were implanted with small numbers of cancer cells so that their own immune systems would have a chance to combat them (Visintainer et al., 1982). Some of the rats were then exposed to inescapable shocks. Others were exposed to escapable shocks or to no shock. The rats that were exposed to the most stressful condition—the inescapable shock—were half as likely as the other rats to reject the cancer and twice as likely to die from it.

PSYCHOLOGICAL FACTORS IN THE TREATMENT OF CANCER People with cancer not only must cope with the biological aspects of their illnesses; they may also face a host of psychological problems. These include feelings of anxiety and depression about treatment methods and the eventual outcome, changes in body image after the removal of a breast or testicle, feelings of vulnerability, and family problems (Azar, 1996b). For example, some families criticize members with cancer for feeling sorry for themselves or not fighting the disease hard enough (Andersen et al., 1994; Rosenthal,

Socioeconomic status One's social and financial level, as indicated by measures such as income, level of education, and occupational status. Abbreviated *SES*.

1993). Psychological stress due to cancer can weaken the immune system, setting the stage for other health problems, such as respiratory tract infections (Andersen, 2002).

There are also psychological treatments for the nausea that often accompanies chemotherapy. People undergoing chemotherapy who also obtain relaxation training and guided imagery techniques experience significantly less nausea and vomiting than patients who do not use these methods (Azar, 1996c). Distraction helps (L. L. Cohen, 2002). Studies with children find that playing video games reduces the discomfort of chemotherapy (Kolko & Rickard-Figueroa, 1985; Redd et al., 1987). Children focus on battling computer-generated enemies rather than the side effects of drugs.

Of course, cancer is a medical disorder. However, health psychologists have improved the methods used to treat people with cancer. For example, a crisis like cancer can lead people to feel that life has spun out of control (Merluzzi & Martinez Sanchez, 1997). Control is a factor in psychological hardiness. A sense of loss of control can heighten stress and impair the immune system. Health psychology therefore stresses the value of encouraging people with cancer to remain in charge of their lives (Jacox et al., 1994). Even measures such as training physicians to listen more attentively, convey warmth, and provide feedback (as opposed to saying nothing) can help (Andersen, 2002).

Cancer requires medical treatment, and in many cases, there are few treatment options. However, people with cancer can still choose how they will deal with the disease. Patients' moods are connected with the functioning of the immune system, and we know that prolonged stress, depression, and feelings of tension depress the immune system (McGuire et al., 2002). However, we should point out that the literature is mixed as to whether patients' attitudes and moods can actually affect the course of cancer (Kiecolt-Glaser et al., 2002b). Still, there are some encouraging notes. For example, one 10-year follow-up of women with breast cancer found a significantly higher survival rate for women who responded to their diagnosis with anger and a "fighting spirit" rather than with stoic acceptance (Pettingale et al., 1985). A five-year follow-up of nearly 600 women with early stage breast cancer found that the survival rate was significantly higher for women who showed a fighting spirit as compared with women who reported feeling helpless and hopeless—that is, depressed (Faller et al., 1999; Watson et al., 1999).

Psychologists are teaching coping skills to people with cancer in order to relieve psychological distress as well as pain. One study of 235 women with

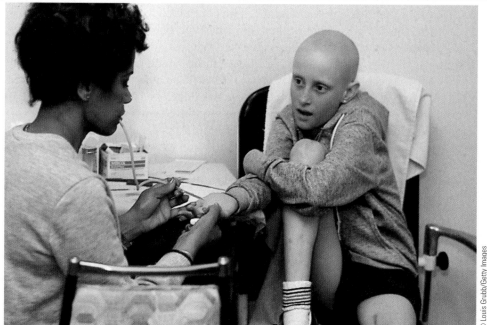

■ **How Have Health Psychologists Helped This Youngster Cope with Cancer?** Cancer is a medical disorder, but psychologists have contributed to the treatment of people with cancer. For example, psychologists help people with cancer remain in charge of their lives, combat feelings of hopelessness, manage stress, and cope with the side effects of chemotherapy.

© Louis Grubb/Getty Images

metastatic breast cancer found that group therapy aimed at providing support and helping the women express their feelings enhanced the women's moods and decreased the amount of pain they experienced (Goodwin et al., 2001). Unfortunately, the therapy did not affect their survival rate. But psychological methods such as relaxation training, meditation, biofeedback training, and exercise can all help patients cope with their disorders (Andersen, 2002).

Yet another psychological application is helping people undergoing chemotherapy keep up their strength by eating. The problem is that chemotherapy often causes nausea. Nausea then becomes associated with foods eaten during the day, causing taste aversions (Azar, 1996c). So people with cancer, who may already be losing weight because of their illness, may find that taste aversions aggravate the problems caused by lack of appetite. To combat these conditions, Bernstein (1996) recommends eating unusual foods prior to chemotherapy. If taste aversions develop, they are associated with the unusual food and not the patient's normal diet.

Your Turn: Now that we have discussed the relationships between psychology and health problems such as headaches, heart disease, and cancer, enhance your mastery of the material with the nearby "Learning Connections." Review the material by filling in the blanks, reflect on the material by relating it to other things you know, and think critically about it.

 ## Learning Connections   PSYCHOLOGY AND HEALTH

ACTIVE REVIEW (17) Psychological states such as anxiety and depression impair the functioning of the _____ system, rendering us more vulnerable to health problems. (18) The most common kind of headache is the _____ headache. (19) The _____ headache has a sudden onset and is identified by throbbing pain on one side of the head. (20) Risk factors for coronary heart disease include family history, obesity, hypertension, high levels of serum _____, heavy drinking, smoking, hostility, Type A behavior, and job strain. (21) African Americans have (*More* or *Less?*) access to health care than European Americans do. (22) African Americans are (*More* or *Less?*) likely than European Americans to have heart attacks and contract most forms of cancer. (23) Genetic factors (*Play* or *Do not play?*) a role in cancer.

REFLECT AND RELATE Do coronary heart disease or cancer run in your family? If so, what can you do about it?

CRITICAL THINKING Health problems such as headaches, coronary disorders, and cancer are usually conceptualized as medical problems. What are the roles of psychologists in understanding and treating these problems?

 Go to **http://psychology.wadsworth.com/ rathus_pcc9e** for an interactive version of this Learning Connections unit.

Life Connections

Preventing and Coping with Health Problems: Stress, Headaches, Heart Disease, and Cancer

Health psychologists have engaged in a wealth of research concerning the ways in which mental processes and behavior can help people prevent and cope with health problems. In this section, we highlight ways of preventing and coping with stress, headaches, heart disease, cancer, and sexually transmitted infections. Because stress depresses the functioning of the immune system, it may be that alleviating stress has beneficial effects on the immune system, thus making us less vulnerable to some health problems. Still, do not assume that stress-management is the cure-all. This area of research is in its infancy (Miller & Cohen, 2001). But at the very least, stress reduction reduces feelings of stress! Moreover the strategies for preventing and coping with heart disease and cancer involve significant improvements in your lifestyle. By following them, there is an excellent chance that you will live longer. It is almost a certainty that you will live *better*.

Coping with Stress

What do these things have in common: (1) telling yourself that you can live with another person's disappointment, (2) taking a deep breath and telling yourself to relax, (3) taking the scenic route to work, and (4) jogging for half an hour? These are all methods suggested by psychologists to help people cope with the stresses of modern life.

Stress takes many forms and can harm our psychological well-being and physical health. Here we highlight ways of coping with stress.

Controlling Irrational Thoughts— How to Change Your Mind for the Better People often feel pressure from their own thoughts. Consider the following experiences:

1. You have difficulty with the first item on a test and become convinced that you will flunk.

2. You want to express your genuine feelings but think that if you do so you might make another person angry or upset.

3. You haven't been able to get to sleep for 15 minutes and assume that you will lie awake all night and feel "wrecked" in the morning.

4. You're not sure what decision to make, so you try to put the problem out of your mind by going out, playing cards, or watching TV.

5. You decide not to play tennis because your form isn't perfect and you're in less than perfect condition.

If you have had these or similar experiences, it may be because you harbor some of the irrational beliefs identified by Albert Ellis (see Table 13.2). These beliefs may make you overly concerned about the approval of others (item 2 in the preceding list) or perfectionistic (item 5). They may lead you to think that you can solve problems by pretending that they do not exist (item 4) or that a minor setback will invariably lead to greater problems (items 1 and 3).

How do we change the irrational thoughts that create and compound stress? The answer is deceptively simple: We just change them. However, this may require work. Moreover, before we can change our thoughts we must become aware of them.

Cognitive–behavioral psychologists (e.g., Marks & Dar, 2000) outline a multistep procedure for controlling the irrational or catastrophizing thoughts that often accompany feelings of anxiety, conflict, or tension:

1. Develop awareness of the thoughts that seem to be making you miserable by careful self-examination. Study the examples at the beginning of this section or in Table 13.5 to see if they apply to you. (Also consider Ellis's list of irrational beliefs in Table 13.2 and ask yourself whether any of them governs your behavior.) Also: When you encounter anxiety or frustration, pay close attention to your thoughts.

2. Evaluate the accuracy of the thoughts. Are they guiding you toward a solution, or are they compounding

TABLE 13.5 CONTROLLING IRRATIONAL BELIEFS AND THOUGHTS

Irrational (Upsetting) Thoughts	Rational (Calming) Thoughts
"Oh my God, I'm going to completely lose control!"	"This is painful and upsetting, but I don't have to go to pieces over it."
"This will never end."	"This will end even if it's hard to see the end right now."
"It'll be awful if Mom gives me that look again."	"It's more pleasant when Mom's happy with me, but I can live with it if she isn't."
"How can I go out there? I'll look like a fool."	"So you're not perfect. That doesn't mean that you're going to look stupid. And so what if someone thinks you look stupid? You can live with that, too. Just stop worrying and have some fun."
"My heart's going to leap out of my chest! How much can I stand?"	"Easy–hearts don't leap out of chests. Stop and think! Distract yourself. Breathe slowly, in and out."
"What can I do? There's nothing I can do!"	"Easy–stop and think. Just because you can't think of a solution right now doesn't mean there's nothing you can do. Take it a minute at a time. Breathe easy."

Do irrational beliefs or catastrophizing thoughts compound your feelings of anxiety and tension? Cognitive psychologists suggest that you can cope with stress by becoming aware of your irrational, upsetting thoughts and replacing them with rational, calming thoughts.

your problems? Do they reflect reality or do they blow things out of proportion? Do they misplace the blame for failure or shortcomings? and so on.

3. Prepare thoughts that are incompatible with the irrational or catastrophizing thoughts and practice saying them firmly to yourself. (If nobody is nearby, why not say them firmly aloud?)

4. Reward yourself with a mental pat on the back for making effective changes in your beliefs and thought patterns.

Lowering Arousal: Turning Down the Inner Alarm Stress tends to trigger intense activity in the sympathetic branch of the autonomic nervous system—in other words, arousal. Arousal is a sign that something may be wrong. It is a message telling us to survey the situation and take appropriate action. But once we are aware that a stressor is acting upon us and have developed a plan to cope with it, it is no longer helpful to have blood pounding fiercely through our arteries.

Psychologists and other scientists have developed many methods for teaching people to reduce arousal. These include meditation, biofeedback, and progressive relaxation. In progressive relaxation, people purposefully tense a particular muscle group before relaxing it. This sequence allows them to develop awareness of their muscle tensions and also to differentiate between feelings of tension and relaxation.

The following instructions will help you to try meditation as a means for lowering the arousal connected with stress:

1. Begin by meditating once or twice a day for 10 to 20 minutes.

2. In meditation, what you *don't* do is more important than what you *do* do. Adopt a passive, "what happens, happens" attitude.

3. Create a quiet, nondisruptive environment. For example, don't face a light directly.

4. Do not eat for an hour beforehand; avoid caffeine for at least two hours.

5. Assume a comfortable position. Change it as needed. It's okay to scratch or yawn.

6. As a device to aid concentrating, you may focus on your breathing or seat yourself before a calming object such as a plant or burning incense. Benson suggests "perceiving" (rather than mentally saying) the word *one* on every out-breath. This means thinking the word, but "less actively" than usual (good luck). Others suggest thinking or perceiving the word *in* as you are inhaling and *out,* or *ah-h-h,* as you are exhaling.

7. If you are using a mantra (like the syllable "om," pronounced *oammm*), you can prepare for meditation and say the mantra out loud several times. Enjoy it. Then say it more and more softly. Close your eyes and only think the mantra. Allow yourself to perceive, rather than actively think, the mantra. Again, adopt a passive attitude. Continue to perceive the mantra. It may grow louder or softer, disappear for a while, and then return.

8. If disruptive thoughts enter your mind as you are meditating, you can allow them to "pass through." Don't get wrapped up in trying to squelch them, or you may raise your level of arousal.

9. Allow yourself to drift. (You won't go too far.) What happens, happens.

10. Above all, take what you get. You cannot force the relaxing effects of meditation. You can only set the stage for it and allow it to happen.

Exercising: Run for Your Life?

I like long walks, especially when they are taken by people who annoy me.
Fred Allen

Exercise, particularly aerobic exercise, enhances the functioning of the immune system, contributes to our psychological well-being, and helps us cope with stress (Jonsdottir et al., 2000; Tkachuk & Martin, 1999). *Aerobic exercise* refers to exercise that requires a sustained increase in consumption of oxygen. Aerobic exercise promotes cardiovascular fitness. Aerobic exercises include, but are not limited to, running and jogging, running in place, walking (at more than a leisurely pace), aerobic dancing, jumping rope, swimming, bicycle riding, basketball, racquetball, and cross-country skiing.

Anaerobic exercises, in contrast, involve short bursts of muscle activity. Examples of anaerobic exercises are weight training, calisthenics (which usually allow rest periods between exercises), and sports such as baseball, in which there are infrequent bursts of strenuous activity. Anaerobic exercises can strengthen muscles and improve flexibility.

Exercise helps people cope by enhancing their physical fitness, or "condition." Fitness includes muscle strength; muscle endurance; suppleness or flexibility; cardiorespiratory, or aerobic, fitness; and a higher ratio of muscle to fat (usually due to both building muscle and reducing fat). Fitness also enhances our natural immunity and boosts our levels of endorphins (Jonsdottir et al., 2000). Cardiovascular fitness, or "condition," means that the body can use more oxygen during vigorous activity and pump more blood with each heartbeat. Because conditioned athletes' hearts pump more blood with each beat, they usually have a slower pulse rate—that is, fewer heartbeats per minute. However, during aerobic exercise they may double or triple their resting heart rate for minutes at a time.

Sustained physical activity does more than promote fitness. It reduces hypertension (Blumenthal et al., 2002; Taylor-Tolbert et al., 2000) and the risk of heart attacks (Stampfer et al., 2000) and strokes (Hu et al., 2000). Exercise has been shown to keep the arteries more supple, even among older adults (Mackey et al., 2002); that is, it counters hardening of the arteries.

In one research program, Ralph Paffenbarger and his colleagues (1993; Lee et al., 2000; Sesso et al., 2000) have been tracking several thousand Harvard University alumni by means of university records and questionnaires. They have correlated the incidence of heart attacks in this group with their levels of physical activity. As shown in Figure 13.6, the incidence of heart attacks declines as physical activity rises to a level at which about 2,000 calories are used per week—the equivalent of jogging about 20 miles a week. Inactive alumni have the highest risk of heart attacks. **Truth or Fiction Revisited:**

Alumni who burn at least 2,000 calories a week through exercise live two years longer, on the average, than their less active counterparts.

Of course, there is an important limitation to Paffenbarger's research: It does not show that a sedentary lifestyle causes CHD or that aerobic exercise prevents CHD. It is also possible that people who are in better health *choose* to engage in higher levels of physical activity. If such is the case, then their lower incidence of heart attacks and their lower mortality rates would be attributable to their initial superior health, not to their physical activity.

Aerobic exercise raises blood levels of high-density lipoproteins (HDL, or "good cholesterol") (Stampfer et al., 2000). HDL lowers the amount of low-density lipoproteins (LDL, or "bad cholesterol") in the blood. This is another way in which exercise may reduce the risk of heart attacks.

How about you? Are you thinking of climbing onto the exercise bandwagon? If so, consider these suggestions:
1. Unless you have engaged in sustained and vigorous exercise recently, seek the advice of a medical expert. If you smoke, have a family history of heart disease, are overweight, or are over 40, get a stress test.
2. Consider joining a beginner's aerobics class. Group leaders are not usually experts in physiology, but at least they "know the steps." You'll also be among other beginners and derive the benefits of social support.
3. Get the proper equipment to facilitate performance and avert injury.
4. Read up on the activity you are considering. Books, magazines, and newspaper articles will give you ideas as to how to get started and how fast to progress.
5. Try to select activities that you can sustain for a lifetime. Don't worry about building yourself up rapidly. Enjoy yourself. Your strength and endurance will progress on their own. If you do not enjoy what you're doing, you're not likely to stick to it.
6. If you feel severe pain, don't try to exercise "through" it. Soreness is to be expected for beginners (and for old-

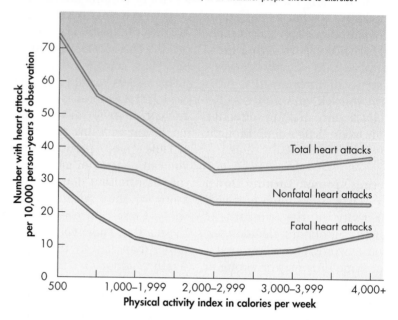

FIGURE 13.6 **Heart Attacks and Physical Activity**
Paffenbarger and his colleagues have tracked the health of 17,000 Harvard alumni and found that the incidence of heart attacks declines as the level of aerobic exercise rises to burning about 2,000 calories a week. Does aerobic exercise prevent heart attacks, or do healthier people choose to exercise?

timers now and then). In that sense, soreness, at least when it is intermittent, is normal. But sharp pain is abnormal and a sign that something is wrong.
7. Have fun!

Preventing and Coping with Headaches

Because many headaches are related to stress, one way to fight headaches is to lessen the stress in your life. All the methods mentioned here—challenging irrational beliefs, lowering the physical alarm, and exercising—may be of help. We described the method of meditation for lowering arousal. Progressive relaxation focuses on decreasing muscle tension and has been shown to be highly effective in relieving muscle tension headaches (Blanchard et al., 1990; Holden et al., 1999). Biofeedback training has also helped many people with migraine headaches (Powers et al., 2001; Scharff et al., 2002).

Aspirin, acetaminophen, ibuprofen, and many prescription drugs are also used to fight headache pain. Some inhibit the production of the prostaglandins that help initiate transmission of pain messages to the brain. Newer prescription drugs can help prevent many migraines (Bateman, 2000);

ask your doctor. People who are sensitive to MSG or red wine can request meals without MSG and switch to white wine.

Reducing the Risk of CHD through Behavior Modification

Once CHD has been diagnosed, a number of medical treatments, including surgery and medication, are available. However, people who have not had CHD (as well as those who have) can profit from behavior modification techniques designed to reduce the risk factors. These methods include:

- *Stopping smoking* (see Chapter 5).
- *Dietary change:* See Chapter 9 for strategies for maintaining a healthful body weight. However, most health experts agree on three dietary strategies that are helpful in preventing CHD (Hu & Willett, 2002; Mozaffarian et al., 2003): Substitute nonhydrogenated unsaturated fats for saturated fats; increase consumption of omega-3 fatty acids, which are found in fish, fish oil supplements, and plant sources; and eat a diet high in fruits, vegetables, nuts (unsalted), and whole grains.
- *Reducing hypertension:* There is medication for reducing hypertension, but behavioral changes, including

the dietary changes outlined above, are sometimes enough: meditation (Alexander et al., 1996; Schneider et al., 1995), aerobic exercise (Danforth et al., 1990), and consuming less salt (Sacks et al., 2001).

- *Lowering low-density lipoprotein (harmful) serum cholesterol:* There is also medication for lowering LDL, but behavioral methods involve exercise, medication, and cutting down on foods that are high in cholesterol and saturated fats (Stampfer et al., 2000). Lowering LDL is helpful at any time of life, even during older adulthood. However, even young adults should think about their LDL levels, because elevated LDL in young adulthood can establish a pattern that places one at risk for cardiovascular disease later in life (Stamler et al., 2000).
- *Modifying Type A behavior.*
- *Managing feelings of anger.*
- *Exercising:* Sustained physical activity helps protect people from CHD as well as cope with stress (Stampfer et al., 2000).

Preventing and Coping with Cancer

Cancer is a frightening disease; and, in many cases, there may be little that can be done about its eventual outcome. However, we are not helpless in the face of cancer. We can take measures like the following:

- Limit exposure to behavioral risk factors for cancer (Chlebowski, 2000).
- Modify diet by reducing intake of fats and increasing intake of fruits and vegetables (Kant et al., 2000; Mangelsdorf, 2002). **Truth or Fiction Revisited:** Tomatoes (especially cooked tomatoes, such as we find in tomato sauce and ketchup—yes,

ketchup!), broccoli, cauliflower, and cabbage appear to be especially helpful (Angier, 1994a). (Yes, Grandma was right about veggies.)

- Exercise regularly. (Yes, exercise not only helps us cope with stress. It also lowers the risk of developing CHD and cancer. Just do it.)
- Have regular medical checkups so that cancer will be detected early. Cancer is most treatable in the early stages.
- Regulate exposure to stress (Folkman & Moskowitz, 2000a).
- If we are struck by cancer, we can fight it energetically.

We conclude this section with good news for readers of this book: *Better-educated* people—that means *you*—are more likely to modify health-impairing behavior and reap the benefits of change (Pappas et al., 1993).

Recite—An Active Summary™

1. What is health psychology?

Health psychology studies the relationships between psychological factors and the prevention and treatment of physical health problems.

2. What is stress?

Stress is the demand made on an organism to adjust. Whereas some stress—called eustress—is desirable to keep us alert and occupied, too much stress can tax our adjustive capacities and contribute to physical health problems.

3. What are daily hassles?

Daily hassles are regularly occurring experiences that threaten or harm our well-being. There are several kinds of hassles, including household, health, time pressure, inner concern, environmental, financial responsibility, work, and future security hassles.

4. How is it that too much of a good thing can make you ill?

Too many positive life changes can affect one's health because life changes require adjustment, whether they are positive or negative. In contrast to daily hassles, life changes occur irregularly. Research shows that hassles and life changes are connected with health problems such as heart disease and cancer. However, the demonstrated connection between life changes and health is correlational; thus causality remains clouded.

5. What is conflict?

Conflict is the stressful feeling of being pulled in two or more directions by opposing motives. There are four kinds of conflict: approach–approach, avoidance–avoidance, approach–avoidance (in the case of a single goal), and multiple approach–avoidance, when each alternative has its pluses and minuses.

6. How do irrational beliefs create or compound stress?

Albert Ellis shows that negative activating events (A) can be made more aversive (C) when irrational beliefs (B) compound their effects. People often catastrophize negative events. Two common irrational beliefs are excessive needs for social approval and perfectionism. Both set the stage for disappointment and increased stress.

7. What is Type A behavior?

Type A behavior is connected with a sense of time urgency and characterized by competitiveness, impatience, and aggressiveness. Type B people relax more readily.

Recite—An Active Summary™

8. How do our self-efficacy expectations affect our ability to withstand stress?

Self-efficacy expectations encourage us to persist in difficult tasks and to endure discomfort. Self-efficacy expectations are also connected with lower levels of adrenaline and noradrenaline, thus having a braking effect on bodily arousal.

9. What characteristics are connected with psychological hardiness?

Kobasa found that psychological hardiness among business executives is characterized by commitment, challenge, and control.

10. Is there any evidence that "A merry heart doeth good like a medicine"?

Yes. Research evidence shows that students who produce humor under adversity experience less stress. Moreover, watching humorous videos apparently enhances the functioning of the immune system.

11. How do predictability and control help us cope with stress?

Predictability allows us to brace ourselves, and control permits us to plan ways of coping with it.

12. Is there evidence that social support helps people cope with stress?

Social support has been shown to help people resist infectious diseases such as colds. It also helps people cope with the stress of cancer and other health problems. Kinds of social support include expression of emotional concern, instrumental aid, information, appraisal, and simple socializing.

13. What is the general adaptation syndrome?

The GAS is a cluster of bodily changes triggered by stressors. The GAS consists of three stages: alarm, resistance, and exhaustion. Corticosteroids help resist stress by fighting inflammation and allergic reactions. Adrenaline arouses the body by activating the sympathetic nervous system, which is highly active during the alarm and resistance stages of the GAS. Sympathetic activity is characterized by rapid heartbeat and respiration rate, release of stores of sugar, muscle tension, and other responses that deplete the body's supply of energy. The parasympathetic division of the ANS predominates during the exhaustion stage of the GAS and is connected with depression and inactivity. Prolonged stress is dangerous.

14. How does the immune system work?

Leukocytes (white blood cells) engulf and kill pathogens, worn-out body cells, and cancerous cells. The immune system also "remembers" how to battle antigens by maintaining their antibodies in the bloodstream. The immune system also facilitates inflammation, which increases the number of white blood cells that are transported to a damaged area.

15. How does stress affect the functioning of the immune system?

Stress depresses the functioning of the immune system by stimulating the release of corticosteroids. Steroids counter inflammation and interfere with the formation of antibodies.

16. What is the multifactorial approach to health?

This view recognizes that many factors, including biological, psychological, sociocultural, and environmental factors, affect our health. Nearly 1 million preventable deaths occur each year in the United States. Measures such as quitting smoking, eating properly, exercising, and controlling alcohol intake would prevent nearly 80% of them.

17. How has psychology contributed to the understanding and treatment of headaches?

Psychologists participate in research concerning the origins of headaches, including stress and tension. Psychologists help people alleviate headaches by reducing tension. They have also developed biofeedback training methods for helping people cope with migraines.

18. What are the major risk factors for coronary heart disease?

The major risk factors for coronary heart disease include family history; physiological conditions such as hypertension and high levels of serum cholesterol; behavior patterns such as heavy drinking, smoking, eating fatty foods, and Type A behavior; work overload; chronic tension and fatigue; and physical inactivity. They help people achieve healthier cardiovascular systems by stopping smoking, controlling weight, reducing hypertension, lowering LDL levels, changing Type A behavior, reducing hostility, and exercising.

19. What are the major risk factors for cancer?

The major risk factors for cancer include family history, smoking, drinking alcohol, eating animal fats, sunbathing, and stress. The following measures can be helpful in preventing and treating cancer: controlling exposure to behavioral risk factors for cancer, having regular medical checkups, regulating exposure to stress, and vigorously fighting cancer if it develops.

 Go to **http://psychology.wadsworth. com/rathus_pcc9e** to access an interactive version of this active summary.

Key Terms

Stress (p. 481)
Eustress (p. 481)
Health psychology (p. 481)
Pathogen (p. 481)
Daily hassles (p. 482)
Uplifts (p. 482)
Conflict (p. 485)
Approach–approach conflict (p. 485)
Avoidance–avoidance conflict (p. 486)

Approach–avoidance conflict (p. 486)
Multiple approach–avoidance conflict (p. 486)
Catastrophize (p. 487)
Type A behavior (p. 488)
Self-efficacy expectations (p. 490)
Psychological hardiness (p. 490)
Locus of control (p. 490)

Internals (p. 491)
Externals (p. 491)
General adaptation syndrome (GAS) (p. 494)
Alarm reaction (p. 494)
Fight-or-flight reaction (p. 494)
Resistance stage (p. 497)
Exhaustion stage (p. 497)
Immune system (p. 497)
Leukocytes (p. 498)

Antigen (p. 498)
Antibodies (p. 498)
Inflammation (p. 498)
Psychoneuroimmunology (p. 498)
Migraine headaches (p. 502)
Serum cholesterol (p. 502)
Hypertension (p. 502)
Socioeconomic status (p. 505)

ACTIVE LEARNING RESOURCES

Visit your Companion Website for Video, Quizzing, and Self-Assessment!

http://psychology.wadsworth.com/rathus_pcc9e
On this site you can access the Health and Stress video highlighted by the Video Connections icon on p. 497. In addition there are many quizzing opportunities including interactive versions of the fill-in-the-blank Active Review sections in your book. You can also fill out and score the Self-Assessments on p. 489 and p. 492.

Study on the Go!

Don't have time to study right now? You can study on the go! Visit your companion website and download an audio version of the Recite—An Active Summary section to your media player.

ThomsonNOW

http://www.thomsonedu.com
Need help studying? This site is your one-stop study shop. Take a Pre-Test and Thomson NOW will generate a Personalized Study Plan based on your test results. The Study Plan will identify the topics you need to review and direct you to online resources to help you master those topics. You can then take a Post-Test to determine the concepts you have mastered and what you still need to work on.

Author Blog

 What does your author have to say about the state of psychology? Visit your companion website every Tuesday and click on "Author Blog," where he'll talk about the most recent controversies and hot topics in psychology.

Truth or Fiction?

T F A man shot the president of the United States in front of millions of television witnesses, yet was found not guilty by a court of law.

T F In the Middle Ages, innocent people were drowned to prove that they were not possessed by the Devil.

T F It is abnormal to feel anxious.

T F Some people have more than one identity, and each one may have different allergies and eyeglass prescriptions.

T F Feeling "up" is not always a good thing.

T F People with schizophrenia may see and hear things that are not really there.

T F Some people can kill or maim others with no feelings of guilt at all.

T F People who threaten to commit suicide are only seeking attention.

 Go to **http://psychology.wadsworth.com/ rathus_pcc9e** to answer and score this Truth or Fiction quiz.

Psychological Disorders

Dissociative identity disorder A disorder in which a person appears to have two or more distinct identities or personalities that may alternately emerge.

Multiple personality disorder The previous term for *dissociative identity disorder.*

Insanity A legal term descriptive of a person judged to be incapable of recognizing right from wrong or of conforming his or her behavior to the law.

Schizophrenia A psychotic disorder characterized by loss of control of thought processes and inappropriate emotional responses.

Psychological disorders Patterns of behavior or mental processes that are connected with emotional distress or significant impairment in functioning.

■ **Exorcism** This medieval woodcut represents the practice of exorcism, in which a demon is expelled from a person who has been "possessed."

During one long fall semester, the Ohio State campus lived in terror. Four college women were abducted, forced to cash checks or obtain money from automatic teller machines, and then raped. A mysterious phone call led to the arrest of a 23-year-old drifter—let's call him "William"—who had been dismissed from the Navy.

William was not the boy next door.

Psychologists and psychiatrists who interviewed William concluded that 10 personalities—8 male and 2 female—resided within him (Scott, 1994). His personality had been "fractured" by an abusive childhood. His several personalities displayed distinct facial expressions, speech patterns, and memories. They even performed differently on psychological tests.

Arthur, the most rational personality, spoke with a British accent. Danny and Christopher were quiet adolescents. Christine was a 3-year-old girl. Tommy, a 16-year-old, had enlisted in the Navy. Allen was 18 and smoked. Adelena, a 19-year-old lesbian personality, had committed the rapes. Who had made the mysterious phone call? Probably David, 9, an anxious child.

The defense claimed that William's behavior was caused by a psychological disorder termed **dissociative identity disorder** (also referred to as **multiple personality disorder**). Several distinct identities or personalities dwelled within him. Some of them were aware of the others. Some believed that they were unique. Billy, the core identity, had learned to sleep as a child in order to avoid his father's abuse. A psychiatrist asserted that Billy had also been "asleep," or in a "psychological coma," during the abductions. Billy should therefore be found not guilty by reason of **insanity.**

William was found not guilty. He was committed to a psychiatric institution and released six years later.

Truth or Fiction Revisited: In 1982, John Hinckley was also found not guilty of the assassination attempt on President Reagan's life, although the shooting was witnessed on television by millions. Expert witnesses testified that he should be diagnosed with **schizophrenia.** Hinckley, too, was committed to a psychiatric institution.

Dissociative identity disorder and schizophrenia are examples of **psychological disorders.** If William and Hinckley had lived in Salem, Massachusetts, in 1692, just 200 years after Columbus set foot in the New World, they might have been hanged as witches. At that time, most people assumed that the strange behaviors that were associated with psychological disorders were caused by possession by the devil. A score of people were executed in Salem that year for allegedly practicing the arts of Satan.

Throughout human history people have attributed unusual behavior and psychological disorders to demons. The ancient Greeks believed that the gods punished humans by causing confusion and madness. An exception was the physician Hippocrates, who made the radical suggestion that psychological disorders are caused by an abnormality of the brain. The notion that biology could affect thoughts, feelings, and behavior was to lie dormant for about 2,000 years.

During the Middle Ages in Europe, as well as during the early period of European colonization of Massachusetts, it was generally believed that psychological disorders were signs of possession by the devil. Possession could stem from retribution, in which God caused the devil to possess a person's soul as punishment for committing certain kinds of sins. Agitation and confusion were ascribed to such retribution. Possession was also believed to result from deals with the devil, in which people traded their souls for earthly gains. Such individuals were called witches. Witches were held responsible for unfortunate events ranging from a neighbor's infertility to a poor harvest. In Europe, as many as 500,000 accused witches were killed during the next two centuries (Hergenhahn, 2001). The goings on at Salem were trivial by comparison.

Truth or Fiction Revisited: A document authorized by Pope Innocent VIII, *The Hammer of Witches,* proposed ingenious "diagnostic" tests to identify those who were possessed. The water-float test was based on the principle that pure metals sink to the bottom during smelting. Impurities float to the surface. Suspects were thus placed in deep water. Those who sank to the bottom and drowned were judged to be pure. Those who managed to keep their heads above water were assumed to be "impure" and in league with the devil. Then they were in real trouble. This ordeal is the origin of the phrase, "damned if you do, and damned if you don't."

Few people in the United States today would argue that unusual or unacceptable behavior is caused by demons. Still, we continue to use "demonic" language. How many times have you heard the expressions "Something got into me" or "The devil made me do it"?

Throughout history, as noted, most people have explained disorders like those of William and Hinckley from a demonological perspective. Today, however, psychologists and other health professionals tend to explain psychological disorders from various psychological perspectives: the evolutionary and biological perspectives, the cognitive perspective, the humanistic–existential perspective, the psychodynamic perspective, and the learning perspective.

We will see how these various perspectives explain each of the disorders covered in the chapter. In many cases we will see that there is an *interaction* between perspectives, such as the biological perspective and the cognitive perspective, as discussed in Chapter 1. We will also frequently find an interaction between the biological *nature* of the individual and his or her life experiences, or *nurture*. The origins of psychological disorders are often complex. We cannot pretend that they are simple, but we can present them clearly.

But first let us pose and answer a key question: **Question: What, exactly, are psychological disorders?**

What Are Psychological Disorders?

Psychology is the study of behavior and mental processes. Psychological disorders are behaviors or mental processes—like those of "William" and John Hinckley—that are connected with various kinds of distress or disability. However, they are not predictable responses to specific events.

Truth or Fiction Revisited: Some psychological disorders are characterized by anxiety, but many people are anxious now and then without being considered disordered. It is appropriate to be anxious before an important date or on the eve of a midterm exam. When, then, are feelings like anxiety deemed to be abnormal or signs of a psychological disorder? For one thing, anxiety may suggest a disorder when it is not appropriate to the situation. It is inappropriate to be anxious when entering an elevator or looking out of a fourth-story window. The magnitude of the problem may also suggest disorder. Some anxiety is usual before a job interview. However, feeling that your heart is pounding so intensely that it might leap out of your chest—and then avoiding the interview—are not usual.

Behavior or mental processes are suggestive of psychological disorders when they meet some combination of the following criteria:

1. *They are unusual.* Although people with psychological disorders are a minority, uncommon behavior or mental processes are not abnormal in themselves. Only one person holds the record for running or swimming the fastest mile. That person is different from you and me but is not abnormal. Only a few people qualify as geniuses in mathematics, but mathematical genius is not a sign of a psychological disorder.

   Rarity or statistical deviance may not be sufficient for behavior or mental processes to be labeled abnormal, but it helps. Most people do not see or hear things that are not there. "Seeing things" and "hearing things," as Hinckley did, are abnormal. We must also consider the situation. Although many of us feel "panicked" when we realize that a term paper or report is due the next day, most of us do not have panic attacks "out of the blue." Unpredictable panic attacks thus are suggestive of psychological disorder.

2. *They suggest faulty perception or interpretation of reality.* Our society considers it normal to be inspired by religious beliefs but abnormal to believe that God is literally speaking to you. "Hearing voices" and "seeing things" are considered

Hallucination A perception in the absence of sensory stimulation that is confused with reality.

Ideas of persecution Erroneous beliefs that one is being victimized or persecuted.

hallucinations. Similarly, **ideas of persecution,** such as believing that the Mafia or the FBI are "out to get you," are considered signs of disorder. (Unless, of course, they *are* out to get you.) Hinckley's view, that he would be impressing a popular actress with his behavior, was delusional.

3. *They suggest severe personal distress.* Anxiety, exaggerated fears, and other psychological states cause personal distress, and severe personal distress may be considered abnormal. William and Hinckley were in distress—although, of course, they victimized other people. Anxiety, of course, may be an appropriate response to a situation, as when a big test or a big date is coming up.

4. *They are self-defeating.* Behavior or mental processes that cause misery rather than happiness and fulfillment may suggest psychological disorder. Chronic drinking that impairs work and family life and cigarette smoking that impairs health may therefore be deemed abnormal.

5. *They are dangerous.* Behavior or mental processes that are hazardous to the self or others may be considered suggestive of psychological disorders. People who threaten or attempt suicide may be considered abnormal, as may people who threaten or attack others, like William and Hinckley. Yet criminal behavior or aggressive behavior in sports need not imply a psychological disorder.

6. *The individual's behavior is socially unacceptable.* We must consider the cultural context of a behavior pattern in judging whether or not it is normal (Lopez & Guarnaccia, 2000). In the United States, it is deemed normal for males to be aggressive in sports and in combat. In other situations, warmth and tenderness are valued. Many people in the United States admire women who are self-assertive, yet Latino and Latina American, Asian American, and "traditional" European American groups may see outspoken women as disrespectful.

Classifying Psychological Disorders

Classification is at the heart of science. Without classifying psychological disorders, investigators would not be able to communicate with each other and scientific

■ **Hallucinations** Hallucinations are a feature of schizophrenia. They are perceptions that occur in the absence of external stimulation, as in "hearing voices" or "seeing things." Hallucinations cannot be distinguished from real perceptions. Are the cats in this Sandy Skoglund photograph real or hallucinatory?

© Sandy Skoglund/Janet Borden, Inc.

progress would come to a halt. The most widely used classification scheme for psychological disorders[1] is the *Diagnostic and Statistical Manual* (*DSM*) of the American Psychiatric Association (2000). **Question: How are psychological disorders classified?**

The current edition of the *DSM* is the *DSM-IV-TR* (fourth edition, text revision), and it provides information about a person's overall functioning as well as a diagnosis. People may receive diagnoses for clinical syndromes or personality disorders or both. The *DSM* also includes information about people's medical conditions and psychosocial problems as well as a global assessment of functioning. Medical conditions include physical disorders or problems that may affect people's response to psychotherapy or drug treatment. Psychosocial and environmental problems include difficulties that may affect the diagnosis, treatment, or outcome of a psychological disorder. The global assessment of functioning allows the clinician to compare the client's current level of functioning with her or his highest previous level of functioning to help set goals for restoring functioning.

Although the *DSM* is widely used, researchers have some concerns about it. Two of them concern the **reliability** and **validity** of the diagnostic standards. The *DSM* might be considered *reliable* if different interviewers or raters would make the same diagnosis when they evaluate the same people. The *DSM* might be considered *valid* if the diagnoses described in the manual correspond to clusters of behaviors observed in the real world (Nestadt et al., 2006). A specific type of validity, called **predictive validity**, means that if a diagnosis is valid then we should be able to predict what will happen to the person over time (that is, the *course* of the disorder) and what type of treatment may be of help.

The *DSM* contains various kinds of psychological disorders, many of which are discussed in this chapter. The standards for assessing these disorders are rather strict—so strict that some actual cases of disorders might be left out. Moreover, the reliability and validity of various diagnoses differs (Hilsenroth et al., 2004). For example, the diagnosis of schizophrenia might be more reliable and valid than the diagnosis of borderline personality disorder (Johansen et al., 2004). All in all, when evaluating the DSM we should consider whether it improves clinical decision making and whether it enhances the clinical outcome for people with psychological disorders. The *DSM*, now in a revised version of its fourth edition, is less than perfect but appears to be making progress toward these goals.

Reliability The consistency of a method of assessment, such as a psychological test or (in this case) a manual describing the symptoms of psychological disorders.

Validity The extent to which a method of assessment, such as a psychological test or, in this case, a manual describing the symptoms of psychological disorders, measures the traits or clusters of behavior it is supposed to assess.

Predictive validity The extent to which a diagnosis permits one to predict the course of a disorder and the type of treatment that may be of help.

---

[1]The American Psychiatric Association refers to psychological disorders as *mental disorders*.

Concept Review PSYCHOLOGICAL DISORDERS

	Anxiety Disorders	Dissociative Disorders	Somatoform Disorders

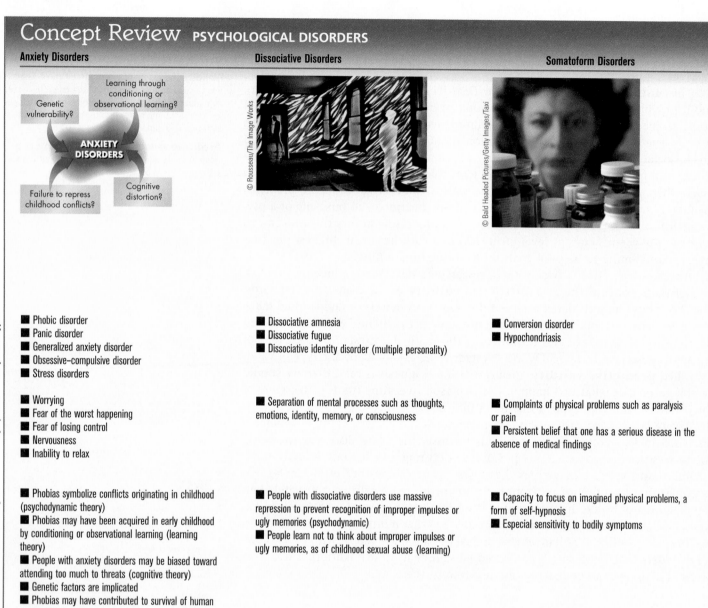

Class

Anxiety Disorders:
- Genetic vulnerability?
- Learning through conditioning or observational learning?
- ANXIETY DISORDERS
- Failure to repress childhood conflicts?
- Cognitive distortion?

Major Subtypes

Anxiety Disorders:
- Phobic disorder
- Panic disorder
- Generalized anxiety disorder
- Obsessive–compulsive disorder
- Stress disorders

Dissociative Disorders:
- Dissociative amnesia
- Dissociative fugue
- Dissociative identity disorder (multiple personality)

Somatoform Disorders:
- Conversion disorder
- Hypochondriasis

Symptoms

Anxiety Disorders:
- Worrying
- Fear of the worst happening
- Fear of losing control
- Nervousness
- Inability to relax

Dissociative Disorders:
- Separation of mental processes such as thoughts, emotions, identity, memory, or consciousness

Somatoform Disorders:
- Complaints of physical problems such as paralysis or pain
- Persistent belief that one has a serious disease in the absence of medical findings

Possible Origins

Anxiety Disorders:
- Phobias symbolize conflicts originating in childhood (psychodynamic theory)
- Phobias may have been acquired in early childhood by conditioning or observational learning (learning theory)
- People with anxiety disorders may be biased toward attending too much to threats (cognitive theory)
- Genetic factors are implicated
- Phobias may have contributed to survival of human species (evolutionary perspective)
- Receptor sites in the brain may not be sensitive enough to the neurotransmitter GABA, which quells anxiety reactions (neurological perspective)

Dissociative Disorders:
- People with dissociative disorders use massive repression to prevent recognition of improper impulses or ugly memories (psychodynamic)
- People learn not to think about improper impulses or ugly memories, as of childhood sexual abuse (learning)

Somatoform Disorders:
- Capacity to focus on imagined physical problems, a form of self-hypnosis
- Especial sensitivity to bodily symptoms

 Go to **http://psychology.wadsworth.com/ rathus_pcc9e** to access a drag-and-drop version of this Concept Review designed to help you test yourself on the major topics provided here.

Mood Disorders	Schizophrenia	Personality Disorders

■ Major depression ■ Bipolar disorder	■ Paranoid schizophrenia ■ Disorganized schizophrenia ■ Catatonic schizophrenia	■ Paranoid ■ Schizotypal ■ Schizoid ■ Antisocial ■ Avoidant
■ Disturbance in expressed emotions	■ Disturbances in language and thought (e.g., delusions, loose associations), attention and perception (e.g., hallucinations) ■ Disturbances in motor activity ■ Disturbances in mood ■ Withdrawal and absorption in daydreams or fantasy	■ Inflexible and maladaptive patterns of behavior ■ Impairment in personal or social functioning ■ Providing a source of distress to oneself or others
■ Depression may be anger turned inward due to holding in rather than expressing feelings of anger; bipolar disorder may be due to alternate domination by the ego and superego (psychodynamic) ■ In depression, people learn that they are helpless to change their situations (learning) ■ Perfectionism, rumination, and attributional style–internal, stable, and global attributions for failures and shortcomings–lead to depression (cognitive) ■ Depression connected with neuroticism, which is believed to be heritable (genetic) ■ Depression connected with underutilization of neurotransmitter serotonin (neurological)	■ Ego may be overwhelmed by the id (psychodynamic) ■ Schizophrenic behavior can be imitated in the hospital setting and reinforced by staff attention (learning) ■ Poor parenting, poverty, complications during pregnancy and birth contribute to schizophrenia (situational) ■ Schizophrenia runs in families, with a high concordance rate among MZ twins (genetic) ■ People with schizophrenia may have larger ventricles, smaller prefrontal cortexes, and fewer synapses than others; overutilization of neurotransmitter dopamine (neurological)	■ Faulty resolution of Oedipus complex (psychodynamic) ■ Children learn maladaptive ways of relating to other people (learning) ■ Antisocial individuals misinterpret other people's behavior as threatening (cognitive) ■ Exaggerated personality traits, which are partly heritable (genetic) ■ Antisocial individuals may have less gray matter, which might lower arousal and thus feelings of guilt and the effects of punishment (neurological)

Prevalence of Psychological Disorders

At first glance, psychological disorders might seem to affect only a few of us. Relatively few people are admitted to psychiatric hospitals. Most people will never seek the help of a psychologist or psychiatrist. And the insanity plea—though well publicized—is a rarity in the criminal justice system. Many of us have "eccentric" relatives or friends, but most of them are not considered to be "crazy." But the truth of the matter is that psychological disorders affect us all in one way or another.

About half of us will meet the criteria for a *DSM-IV* disorder at some time or another in our lives, with the disorder most often beginning in childhood or adolescence (Kessler et al., 2005a; see Table 14.1). Slightly more than a fourth of us will experience a psychological disorder in any given year (Kessler et al., 2005b; see Table 14.1). But if we include the problems of family members, friends, and coworkers, add in the number of those who foot the bill in terms of health insurance and taxes, and factor in increased costs due to lost productivity, then perhaps everyone is affected in one way or another.

Let us now consider the kinds of psychological disorders. Some of them, like anxiety disorders, are common. Others, like dissociative identity disorder (the disorder with which William was diagnosed), are rare.

Your Turn: Now that we have defined the nature of psychological disorders, enhance your mastery of the material with the nearby "Learning Connections." Review the material by filling in the blanks, reflect on the material by relating it to other things you know, and think critically about it.

TABLE 14.1 **PAST-YEAR AND LIFETIME PREVALENCES OF PSYCHOLOGICAL DISORDERS**

	Anxiety Disorders	Mood Disorders	Substance Use Disorders	Any Disorder
Prevalence during past year	18.1%	9.5%	3.8%	26.2%
Lifetime prevalence	28.8%	20.8%	14.6%	46.4%
Median age of onset	11 years	30 years	20 years	14 years

Sources: Kessler et al., 2005a; Kessler et al., 2005b.
The data in this table are based on a nationally representative sample of 9,282 English-speaking U.S. residents aged 18 and above. Respondents could report symptoms of more than one type of disorder. For example, anxiety and mood disorders are often "comorbid"—that is, occur together. Anxiety and mood disorders are discussed in this chapter. Substance use disorders include abuse of or dependence on alcohol or other drugs, as described in Chapter 5.

Learning Connections — WHAT ARE PSYCHOLOGICAL DISORDERS?

Anxiety Disorders: Real Life "Fear Factors"?

Imagine allowing spiders to crawl all over your body or clinging to a beam swinging hundreds of feet above the ground. These are the types of experiences to which many people have been exposed on the "reality TV" show *Fear Factor*. What makes the show so riveting to some viewers? Perhaps the fact that many of us, perhaps most of us, could not imagine participating in such activities, for nearly any amount of fame or fortune. Fear of spiders and fear of heights are examples of phobias, which are a type of anxiety disorder.

Anxiety has psychological and physical features. Psychological features include worrying, fear of the worst things happening, fear of losing control, nervousness, and inability to relax. Physical features reflect arousal of the sympathetic branch of the autonomic nervous system. They include trembling, sweating, a pounding or racing heart, elevated blood pressure (a flushed face), and faintness. Anxiety is an appropriate response to a real threat. It can be abnormal, however, when it is excessive or when it comes out of nowhere—that is, when events do not seem to warrant it. **Question: What kinds of anxiety disorders are there?** There are different kinds of anxiety disorders, but all of them are characterized by excessive or unwarranted anxiety.

Types of Anxiety Disorders

The anxiety disorders include phobias, panic disorder, generalized anxiety, obsessive–compulsive disorder, and stress disorders.

PHOBIAS There are several types of phobias, including specific phobias, social phobia, and agoraphobia. Some of them, such as social phobia, can be highly detrimental to one's quality of life (Stein & Kean, 2000). **Specific phobias** are excessive, irrational fears of specific objects or situations, such as spiders, snakes, or heights. One specific phobia is fear of elevators. Some people will not enter elevators despite the hardships they incur as a result (such as walking up six flights of steps). Yes, the cable *could* break. The ventilation *could* fail. One *could* be stuck in midair waiting for repairs. These problems are uncommon, however, and it does not make sense for most people to walk up and down several flights of stairs to elude them. Similarly, some people with a specific phobia for hypodermic needles will not have injections, even to treat profound illness. Injections can be painful, but most people with a phobia for needles would gladly suffer an even more painful pinch if it would help them fight illness. Other specific phobias include **claustrophobia** (fear of tight or enclosed places), **acrophobia** (fear of heights),

Specific phobia Persistent fear of a specific object or situation.

Claustrophobia Fear of tight, small places.

Acrophobia Fear of high places.

■ **A Person with a Phobia** Phobias are excessive, irrational fears that can interfere with the person's functioning. A phobia for needles can prevent a person from seeking needed medical assistance.

© Spencer Grant/PhotoEdit

and fear of mice, snakes, and other creepy-crawlies. (Fear of spiders is technically referred to as *arachnophobia*.) Fears of animals and imaginary creatures are common among children.

Social phobias are persistent fears of scrutiny by others or of doing something that will be humiliating or embarrassing. Fear of public speaking is a common social phobia.

Agoraphobia is also widespread among adults. Agoraphobia is derived from the Greek words meaning "fear of the marketplace," or fear of being out in open, busy areas. Persons with agoraphobia fear being in places from which it might be difficult to escape or in which help might not be available if they get upset. In practice, people who receive this diagnosis often refuse to venture out of their homes, especially by themselves. They find it difficult to hold a job or to maintain an ordinary social life.

PANIC DISORDER

> *My heart would start pounding so hard I was sure I was having a heart attack. I used to go to the emergency room. Sometimes I felt dizzy, like I was going to pass out. I was sure I was about to die.*
>
> Kim Weiner

Panic disorder is an abrupt attack of acute anxiety that is not triggered by a specific object or situation. People with panic disorder have strong physical symptoms such as shortness of breath, heavy sweating, tremors, and pounding of the heart. Like Kim Weiner (1992), they are particularly aware of cardiac sensations (Wilhelm et al., 2001). It is not unusual for them to think they are having a heart attack. Saliva levels of cortisol (a stress hormone) are elevated during attacks (Bandelow et al., 2000). Many fear suffocation. People with the disorder may also experience choking sensations; nausea; numbness or tingling; flushes or chills; and fear of going crazy or losing control. Panic attacks may last minutes or hours. Afterwards, the person usually feels drained.

Many people panic now and then. The diagnosis of panic disorder is reserved for those who undergo a series of attacks or live in fear of attacks.

Panic attacks seem to come from nowhere. Thus, some people who have had them stay home for fear of having an attack in public. They are diagnosed as having panic disorder with agoraphobia.

GENERALIZED ANXIETY DISORDER The central feature of **generalized anxiety disorder** is persistent anxiety. As with panic disorder, the anxiety cannot be attributed to a phobic object, situation, or activity. Rather, it seems to be free floating. The core of the disorder appears to be pervasive worrying about numerous stressors (Aikins & Craske, 2001). Features of the disorder include motor tension (shakiness, inability to relax, furrowed brow, fidgeting); autonomic overarousal (sweating, dry mouth, racing heart, light-headedness, frequent urinating, diarrhea); and excessive vigilance, as shown by irritability, insomnia, and a tendency to be easily distracted.

OBSESSIVE–COMPULSIVE DISORDER **Obsessions** are recurrent, anxiety-provoking thoughts or images that seem irrational and beyond control. They are so compelling and recurrent that they disrupt daily life. They may include doubts about whether one has locked the doors and shut the windows, or images such as one mother's repeated fantasy that her children had been run over on the way home from school. One woman became obsessed with the idea that she had contaminated her hands with Sani-Flush and that the chemicals were spreading to everything she touched. A 16-year-old boy found "numbers in his head" when he was about to study or take a test.

Compulsions are thoughts or behaviors that tend to reduce the anxiety connected with obsessions. They are seemingly irresistible urges to engage in specific acts, often repeatedly, such as elaborate washing after using the bathroom. The impulse is recurrent and forceful, interfering with daily life. The woman who felt contaminated by Sani-Flush spent 3 to 4 hours at the sink each day and complained, "My hands look like lobster claws."

Social phobia An irrational, excessive fear of public scrutiny.

Agoraphobia Fear of open, crowded places.

Panic disorder The recurrent experiencing of attacks of extreme anxiety in the absence of external stimuli that usually elicit anxiety.

Generalized anxiety disorder Feelings of dread and foreboding and sympathetic arousal of at least 6 months' duration.

Obsession A recurring thought or image that seems beyond control.

Compulsion An irresistible urge to repeat an act or engage in ritualistic behavior like hand washing.

STRESS DISORDERS Darla, who lives in Oregon, dreamed that she was trapped in a World Trade Center tower when it was hit by an airplane on September 11, 2001. Kelly, a Californian, dreamed of a beautiful bald eagle that was suddenly transformed into a snarling bird with glowing red eyes ("Sleepers Suffer WTC Nightmares," 2001).

The all-too-real nightmare of the events of September 11th have caused many people to have bad dreams. Such dreams are part of the experience of posttraumatic stress disorder.

Posttraumatic stress disorder (PTSD) is characterized by a rapid heart rate and feelings of anxiety and helplessness that are caused by a traumatic experience. Such experiences may include a natural or human-made disaster, a threat or assault, or witnessing a death. PTSD may occur months or years after the event. It frequently occurs among firefighters, combat veterans, and people whose homes and communities have been swept away by natural disasters or who have been victims of accidents or interpersonal violence (Blanchard et al., 2003; Vasterling et al., 2002; Waelde et al., 2001; Weinstein et al., 2001).

The traumatic event is revisited in the form of intrusive memories, recurrent dreams, and flashbacks—the sudden feeling that the event is recurring (Rutkowski, 2001; Yehuda, 2002). People with PTSD typically try to avoid thoughts and activities connected to the traumatic event. They may also find it more difficult to enjoy life (Beckham et al., 2000) and have sleep problems (Lavie, 2001), irritable outbursts, difficulty concentrating, extreme vigilance, and an intensified "startle" response (Shayley et al., 2000). The terrorist attacks of September 11, 2001, took their toll on sleep. According to a poll taken by the National Sleep Foundation (2001) two months after the attacks, nearly half of Americans had difficulty falling asleep, as compared with about one-quarter of Americans before the attacks (Figure 14.1). Women respondents were more likely than men to report sleep problems, for example, difficulty falling asleep (50% vs. 37%).

Acute stress disorder, like PTSD, is characterized by feelings of anxiety and helplessness that are caused by a traumatic event. However, PTSD can occur 6 months or more after the traumatic event and tends to persist. Acute stress disorder occurs within a month of the event and lasts from 2 days to 4 weeks. Women who have been raped, for example, experience acute distress that tends to peak in severity about 3

Posttraumatic stress disorder (PTSD) A disorder that follows a distressing event outside the range of normal human experience and that is characterized by features such as intense fear, avoidance of stimuli associated with the event, and reliving of the event.

Acute stress disorder A disorder, like PTSD, that is characterized by feelings of anxiety and helplessness and caused by a traumatic event. Acute stress disorder occurs within a month of the event and lasts from 2 days to 4 weeks.

■ **A Traumatic Experience** Traumatic experiences like the terrorist attack on the World Trade Center can lead to posttraumatic stress disorder (PTSD). PTSD is characterized by intrusive memories of the experience, recurrent dreams about it, and the sudden feeling that it is, in fact, recurring (as in "flashbacks").

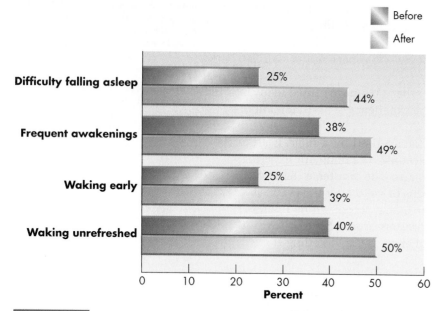

Before
After

Difficulty falling asleep — 25% / 44%

Frequent awakenings — 38% / 49%

Waking early — 25% / 39%

Waking unrefreshed — 40% / 50%

Percent

FIGURE 14.1 **Sleep Problems among Americans before and Two Months after September 11, 2001**
Insomnia is one of the symptoms of stress disorders. A poll by the National Sleep Foundation found that Americans had a greater frequency of sleep problems after the terrorist attacks of September 11.

weeks after the assault (Davidson & Foa, 1991; Rothbaum et al., 1992). Yet the same women frequently go on to experience PTSD (Koss et al., 2002; Street et al., 2003).

Mark Schuster and his colleagues (2001) conducted a telephone survey of a nationally representative sample of 560 American adults—not just those who lived near the attacks—three to five days following the terrorist attacks on September 11, 2001. They found that 90% of respondents reported at least one stress-related symptom, and 44% reported more severe symptoms of stress. Respondents coped by seeking social support, as in talking with others (98%) or participating in group activities (60%), by turning to religion (90%), and by making donations (36%). The great majority of parents of children aged 5 to 18 (84%) reported that they had talked with their children about the attacks for at least an hour, and about one-third (34%) restricted their children's exposure to television coverage of the attacks.

Theoretical Views

There are thus several kinds of anxiety disorders. **Question: What is known about the origins of anxiety disorders?**

PSYCHOLOGICAL VIEWS According to the psychodynamic perspective, phobias symbolize conflicts originating in childhood. Psychodynamic theory explains generalized anxiety as persistent difficulty in repressing primitive impulses. Obsessions are explained as leakage of unconscious impulses, and compulsions are seen as acts that allow people to keep such impulses partly repressed. For example, fixation in the anal stage is theorized to be connected with development of traits such as excessive neatness of the sort that could explain some cases of obsessive–compulsive disorder.

Some learning theorists—particularly behaviorists—consider phobias to be conditioned fears that were acquired in early childhood. Therefore, their origins are beyond memory. Avoidance of feared stimuli is reinforced by the reduction of anxiety.

Other learning theorists—social cognitive theorists—note that observational learning plays a role in the acquisition of fears (Basic Behavioral Science Task Force,

In Profile LITTLE HANS

Do you want to talk about conflict? Do you want to talk about drama? Do you want to talk about raw, unnerving fear? Well, forget about aliens from outer space. Forget about income taxes and things that go bump in the night. For there in turn of the century Vienna, that flourishing European capital of the arts, horses were biting people in the streets. Or so thought one petrified 5-year-old boy by the name of Hans.

In 1908 Hans's distraught father sought Sigmund Freud's advice. Freud went on to write one of his most famous case studies, "Analysis of a Phobia in a 5-Year-Old Boy." Freud concluded that the horses were symbols that represented Hans's father. Being bitten symbolized being castrated. In other words, Hans

unconsciously feared that his father would castrate him. Why? Because Hans was his father's rival in a contest for the affection of his mother. Hans, that is, was in the throes of the Oedipus complex.

Freud's analysis has been criticized on many grounds. For one thing, Freud carried out Hans's psychoanalysis from a distance—by mail with the boy's father! For another, other interpretations of the boy's fear of horses are possible. Historically speaking, however, the case of Little Hans laid much of the groundwork for the psychoanalytic belief that phobic objects symbolize unconscious conflicts that date from early childhood.

1996b). If parents squirm, grimace, and shudder at the sight of mice, blood, or dirt on the kitchen floor, children might assume that these stimuli are awful and imitate their parents' behavior.

Cognitive theorists suggest that anxiety is maintained by thinking that one is in a terrible situation and helpless to change it. People with anxiety disorders may be cognitively biased toward paying a good deal of attention to threats (Fox et al., 2001; Sookman et al., 2001). Psychoanalysts and learning theorists agree that compulsive behavior reduces anxiety.

Cognitive theorists note that people's appraisals of the magnitude of threats help determine whether they are traumatic and can lead to PTSD (Folkman & Moskowitz, 2000a; Koss et al., 2002). People with panic attacks tend to misinterpret bodily cues and to view them as threats. Obsessions and compulsions may serve to divert attention from more frightening issues, such as "What am I going to do with my life?" When anxieties are acquired at a young age, we may later interpret them as enduring traits and label ourselves as "people who fear _____" (you fill it in). We then live up to the labels. We also entertain thoughts that heighten and perpetuate anxiety such as "I've got to get out of here," or "My heart is going to leap out of my chest." Such ideas intensify physical signs of anxiety, disrupt planning, make stimuli seem worse than they really are, motivate avoidance, and decrease self-efficacy expectations. The belief that we will not be able to handle a threat heightens anxiety. The belief that we are in control reduces anxiety (Bandura et al., 1985).

BIOLOGICAL VIEWS Biological factors play a role in anxiety disorders. Genetic factors are implicated in most psychological disorders, including anxiety disorders (Kendler et al., 2001; Nestadt et al., 2000; Schmidt et al., 2000). For one thing, anxiety disorders tend to run in families. Twin studies find a higher **concordance** rate for anxiety disorders among identical twins than among fraternal twins (Kendler et al., 2001). Studies of adoptees who are anxious similarly show that the biological parent places the child at risk for anxiety and related traits.

Evolutionary psychologists suggest that anxiety may reflect natural selection. Susan Mineka (Oehman & Mineka, 2001) suggests that humans (and nonhuman primates) are genetically predisposed to fear stimuli that may have posed a threat to their ancestors. Evolutionary forces would have favored the survival of individuals who were predisposed toward acquiring fears of large animals, spiders, snakes, heights, entrapment, sharp objects, and strangers. Thus the individuals who fearlessly encounter potentially harmful stimuli such as we see on shows like *Fear Factor* may be at a disadvantage, evolutionarily speaking, rather than at an advantage.

Perhaps a predisposition toward anxiety—in the form of a highly reactive autonomic nervous system—can be inherited. What might make a nervous system "highly reactive"? In the case of panic disorder, faulty regulation of levels of serotonin and norepinephrine may be involved. Other anxiety disorders may involve the excitatory neurotransmitter **glutamate,** and receptor sites in the brain may not be sensitive enough to **gamma-aminobutyric acid (GABA),** an inhibitory neurotransmitter that may counterbalance glutamate (Kalin, 2003; Lydiard, 2003; Stroele et al., 2002). The **benzodiazepines,** a class of drugs that reduce anxiety, may work by increasing the sensitivity of receptor sites to GABA.

In many cases anxiety disorders may reflect the interaction of biological and psychological factors. In panic disorder, biological imbalances may initially trigger attacks. However, subsequent fear of attacks—and of the bodily cues that signal their onset—may heighten discomfort and give one the idea there is nothing one can do about them (Craske & Zucker, 2001). Feelings of helplessness increase fear. People with panic disorder therefore can be helped by psychological methods that provide ways of reducing physical discomfort—including regular breathing—and show them that there are, after all, things they can do to cope with attacks (Craske & Zucker, 2001).

Concordance Agreement.

Glutamate An excitatory neurotransmitter that is involved in anxiety reactions.

Gamma-aminobutyric acid (GABA) An inhibitory neurotransmitter that is implicated in anxiety reactions.

Benzodiazepines A class of drugs that reduce anxiety; minor tranquilizers.

Your Turn: Now that we have discussed anxiety disorders, enhance your mastery of the material with the nearby "Learning Connections." Review the material by filling in the blanks, reflect on the material by relating it to other things you know, and think critically about it.

Learning Connections ANXIETY DISORDERS: REAL LIFE "FEAR FACTORS"?

ACTIVE REVIEW (6) A _____ is an irrational, excessive fear. (7) _____ disorder is characterized by sudden attacks in which people typically fear that they may be losing control or going crazy. (8) In obsessive–_____ disorder people are troubled by intrusive thoughts or impulses to repeat some activity. (9) _____ is caused by a traumatic experience and characterized by reliving it the form of intrusive memories, recurrent dreams, and flashbacks. (10) Psychodynamic theory explains generalized anxiety as persistent difficulty in maintaining _____ of primitive impulses. (11) _____ see phobias as conditioned fears. (12) Anxiety disorders (*Do* or *Do Not?*) tend to run in families.

REFLECT AND RELATE Have you ever felt anxious? Did your anxiety strike you as being normal under the circumstances? Why or why not?

CRITICAL THINKING Critical thinkers attend to the definitions of terms. For example, is anxiety abnormal? What is the difference between run-of-the-mill anxiety and an *anxiety disorder?*

 Go to **http://psychology.wadsworth.com/ rathus_pcc9e** for an interactive version of this Learning Connections unit.

Dissociative Disorders: Splitting Consciousness

William's disorder, described at the beginning of the chapter, was a dissociative disorder. In the **dissociative disorders** there is a separation of mental processes such as thoughts, emotions, identity, memory, or consciousness—the processes that make the person feel whole. **Question: What kinds of dissociative disorders are there?**

Types of Dissociative Disorders

The *DSM* lists several dissociative disorders. Among them are dissociative amnesia, dissociative fugue, and dissociative identity disorder (also termed multiple personality).

DISSOCIATIVE AMNESIA In **dissociative amnesia** the person is suddenly unable to recall important personal information (that is, explicit episodic memories). The loss of memory cannot be attributed to organic problems such as a blow to the head or alcoholic intoxication. It is thus a psychological dissociative disorder and not an organic one. In the most common example, the person cannot recall events for a number of hours after a stressful incident, as in warfare or in the case of an uninjured survivor of an accident. In generalized amnesia, people forget their entire lives. Amnesia may last for hours or years.

DISSOCIATIVE FUGUE In **dissociative fugue,** the person abruptly leaves his or her home or place of work and travels to another place, having lost all memory of his or her past life. While at the new location the person either does not think about the past or reports a past filled with invented memories. The new personality is often more outgoing and less inhibited than the "real" identity. Following recovery, the events that occurred during the fugue are not recalled.

DISSOCIATIVE IDENTITY DISORDER Dissociative identity disorder (formerly termed *multiple personality disorder*) is the name given to William's disorder. In dissociative identity disorder, two or more identities or personalities, each with distinct traits and memories, "occupy" the same person. Each identity may or may not be aware of the others or of events experienced by the others (Huntjens et al., 2003).

Dissociative disorders Disorders in which there are sudden, temporary changes in consciousness or self-identity.

Dissociative amnesia A dissociative disorder marked by loss of memory or self-identity; skills and general knowledge are usually retained. Previously termed *psychogenic amnesia*.

Dissociative fugue A dissociative disorder in which one experiences amnesia and then flees to a new location. Previously termed *psychogenic fugue*.

■ **Dissociative Identity Disorder** In the film *The Three Faces of Eve*, Joanne Woodward played three personalities in the same woman: the shy, inhibited Eve White (lying on couch); the flirtatious, promiscuous Eve Black (in dark dress); and a third personality (Jane) who could accept her sexual and aggressive impulses and still maintain her sense of identity.

Truth or Fiction Revisited: The identities of people with dissociative identity disorder can be very different from one another. They might even have different eyeglass prescriptions (Braun, 1988). Braun reports cases in which assorted identities showed different allergic responses. In one person, an identity named Timmy was not sensitive to orange juice. But when other identities gained control over him and drank orange juice, he would break out with hives. Hives would also erupt if another identity emerged while the juice was being digested. If Timmy reappeared when the allergic reaction was present, the itching of the hives would cease and the blisters would start to subside. In other cases reported by Braun, different identities within a person might show various responses to the same medicine. Or one identity might exhibit color blindness while others have normal color vision.

A few celebrated cases of this disorder have been portrayed in the popular media. One of them became the subject of the film *The Three Faces of Eve*. A timid housewife named Eve White harbored two other identities. One was Eve Black, a sexually aggressive, antisocial personality. The third was Jane, an emerging identity who was able to accept the existence of her primitive impulses yet engage in socially appropriate behavior. Finally the three faces merged into one—Jane. Ironically, later on, Jane (Chris Sizemore in real life) reportedly split into 22 identities. Another well-publicized case is that of Sybil, a woman with 16 identities who was portrayed by Sally Field in the film *Sybil*.

Theoretical Views

The dissociative disorders are some of the odder psychological disorders. **Question: What is known about the origins of dissociative disorders?**

Psychologists of different theoretical persuasions have offered hypotheses about the origins of dissociative identity disorder and other dissociative disorders. According to psychodynamic theory, for example, people with dissociative disorders use massive repression to prevent them from recognizing improper impulses or remembering ugly events (Vaillant, 1994). In dissociative amnesia and fugue, the person forgets a profoundly disturbing event or impulse. In dissociative identity disorder, the person expresses unacceptable impulses through alternate identities.

According to learning theorists, people with dissociative disorders have learned *not to think* about bad memories or disturbing impulses in order to avoid feelings of anxiety, guilt, and shame. Both psychodynamic and learning theories suggest that dissociative disorders help people keep disturbing memories or ideas out of mind. Of what could such memories be? Research suggests that many—perhaps most—cases involve memories of sexual or physical abuse during childhood, usually by a relative or caretaker (Banyard et al., 2003; Martinez-Taboas & Bernal, 2000; Migdow, 2003). Yet some studies find no connection between dissociative disorders in adulthood and abuse in childhood (Elzinga et al., 2002).

As noted, dissociative disorders are quite odd, and it may be that some claim to have dissociative disorders in order to avoid responsibility for misbehavior. Therefore, it should come as no surprise that some professionals question whether they exist at all.

Do dissociative disorders really exist?

There is a good deal of skepticism about whether dissociative disorders exist (Thomas, 2001). For example, there were about 50 known cases of dissociative identity disorder before the public learned about "Sybil." By the 1990s, however, this number had mushroomed to more than 20,000 ("Tapes raise new doubts," 1998). Moreover, psychologists who have listened carefully to tapes of Sybil's therapy have raised the possibility that some of her psychiatrists may have "coached" her into reporting the symptoms. Sybil herself is reported to have vacillated as to whether or not her story was true ("Tapes raise new doubts," 1998). It is possible that many or even most people who are diagnosed with dissociative amnesia or dissociative identity disorder are faking. The technical term for faking in order to obtain some benefit—such as being excused from responsibility for a crime or from family obligations—is *malingering*.

Your Turn: Now that we have discussed dissociative disorders, enhance your mastery of the material with the nearby "Learning Connections." Review the material by filling in the blanks, reflect on the material by relating it to other things you know, and think critically about it.

Learning Connections — DISSOCIATIVE DISORDERS: SPLITTING CONSCIOUSNESS

ACTIVE REVIEW (13) Dissociative _____ is characterized by motivated forgetting. (14) In dissociative _____ disorder, the person behaves as if distinct personalities occupy the body. (15) According to learning theory, people learn not to _____ about disturbing acts or impulses in dissociative disorders. (16) Many people with dissociative disorders have a history of physical or sexual _____.

REFLECT AND RELATE Have you seen a film or a TV show in which a character was supposed to have dissociative

identity disorder (perhaps it was called "multiple personality")? What kind of behavior did the character display? Does the behavior seem consistent with the description of the disorder in the text? In the film or TV show, what were the supposed origins of the disorder?

CRITICAL THINKING What is malingering? Can you think of a way to determine whether someone who claims to have a dissociative disorder is malingering?

 Go to **http://psychology.wadsworth.com/ rathus_pcc9e** for an interactive version of this Learning Connections unit.

Somatoform Disorders: When the Body Expresses Stress

People with **somatoform disorders** complain of physical problems such as paralysis, pain, or a persistent belief that they have a serious disease. Yet no evidence of a physical abnormality can be found. **Question: What kinds of somatoform disorders are there?** In this section we discuss two somatoform disorders: conversion disorder and hypochondriasis.

Types of Somatoform Disorders

Conversion disorder is characterized by a major change in, or loss of, physical functioning, although there are no medical findings to explain the loss of functioning. The behaviors are not intentionally produced. That is, the person is not faking. Conversion disorder is so named because it appears to "convert" a source of stress into a physical difficulty.

Somatoform disorders Disorders in which people complain of physical (somatic) problems even though no physical abnormality can be found.

Conversion disorder A disorder in which anxiety or unconscious conflicts are "converted" into physical symptoms that often have the effect of helping the person cope with anxiety or conflict.

If you lost the ability to see at night, or if your legs became paralyzed, you would understandably show concern. But some people with conversion disorder show indifference to their symptoms, a remarkable feature referred to as **la belle indifférence.**

During World War II, some bomber pilots developed night blindness. They could not carry out their nighttime missions, although no damage to the optic nerves was found. In rare cases, women with large families have been reported to become paralyzed in the legs, again with no medical findings. More recently, a Cambodian woman who had witnessed atrocities became blind as a result.

Another more common type of somatoform disorder is **hypochondriasis** (also called *hypochondria*). People with this disorder insist that they are suffering from a serious physical illness, even though no medical evidence of illness can be found. They become preoccupied with minor physical sensations and continue to believe that they are ill despite the reassurance of physicians that they are healthy. They may run from doctor to doctor, seeking the one who will find the causes of the sensations. Fear of illness may disrupt their work or home life. **Question: What is known about the origins of somatoform disorders?**

Theoretical Views

There is evidence that people with conversion disorder are susceptible to being hypnotized. In fact, some investigators consider conversion disorder to be a form of self-hypnosis (Roelofs et al., 2002). The idea here would seem to be that individuals with conversion disorder bring themselves to focus intently on an imaginary physical problem, to the point where they exclude conflicting information.

There is research evidence that people who develop hypochondriasis are particularly sensitive to bodily sensations and tend to ruminate about them (Lecci & Cohen, 2002). However, the history of the name of the somatoform disorders affords us insight into an interesting former sexist explanation of them. Consistent with psychodynamic theory, early versions of the *DSM* labeled somatoform disorders as "hysterical neuroses."

■ **Hypochondriasis** People with hypochondriasis are irrationally concerned that they have contracted illnesses. Such people appear to be unusually sensitive to physical sensations. Do they also focus on their physical symptoms as an alternative to dealing with the social and other problems in their lives?

CONTROVERSY IN PSYCHOLOGY

Are somatoform disorders the special province of women?

"Hysterical" derives from the word *hystera*, the Greek word for uterus or womb. Like many other Greeks, Hippocrates believed that hysteria was a sort of female trouble that was caused by a wandering uterus. It was erroneously thought that the uterus could roam through the body—that it was not anchored in place! As the uterus meandered, it could cause pains and odd sensations almost anywhere. The Greeks also believed that pregnancy anchored the uterus and ended hysterical complaints. What do you think Greek physicians prescribed to end monthly aches and pains? Good guess.

Even in the earlier years of the 20th century, it was suggested that strange sensations and medically unfounded complaints were largely the province of women. Moreover, viewing the problem as a neurosis suggested that it stemmed from unconscious childhood conflicts. The psychodynamic view of conversion disorders is that the symptoms protect the individual from feelings of guilt or shame or from another source of stress. Conversion disorders, like dissociative disorders, often seem to serve a purpose. For example, the "blindness" of the World War II pilots may have enabled them to avoid feelings of fear of being literally shot down or of guilt for killing civilians. The night blindness of the pilots shows that conversion disorders are not the special province of women—whether they were once labeled hysterical or not.

La belle indifférence A French term descriptive of the lack of concern sometimes shown by people with conversion disorders.

Hypochondriasis Persistent belief that one is ill despite lack of medical findings.

Your Turn: Now that we have discussed somatoform disorders, enhance your mastery of the material with the nearby "Learning Connections." Review the material by filling in the blanks, reflect on the material by relating it to other things you know, and think critically about it.

 ## Learning Connections   SOMATOFORM DISORDERS: WHEN THE BODY EXPRESSES STRESS

ACTIVE REVIEW (17) In _____ disorders, people complain of physical problems or persist in believing they have a serious disease, even though no medical problem can be found. (18) In a(n) _____ disorder, there is a major change in or loss of physical functioning with no organic basis.

REFLECT AND RELATE Have you heard anyone referred to as being "hysterical"? What was the usage of the word

intended to mean? Now that you know the origin of the term, do you feel that it was used appropriately?

CRITICAL THINKING Why have somatoform disorders been considered "hysterical"? What are the social problems in labeling them as hysterical?

 Go to **http://psychology.wadsworth.com/ rathus_pcc9e** for an interactive version of this Learning Connections unit.

Mood Disorders: Up, Down, and Around

Mood disorders are characterized by disturbance in expressed emotions. The disruption generally involves sadness or elation. Most instances of sadness are normal, or "run-of-the-mill." If you have failed an important test, if you have lost money in a business venture, or if your closest friend becomes ill, it is understandable and fitting for you to be sad about it. It would be odd, in fact, if you were *not* affected by adversity.

Types of Mood Disorders

Question: What kinds of mood disorders are there? In this section we discuss two mood disorders: major depression and bipolar disorder.

MAJOR DEPRESSION Depression is the common cold of psychological problems. People with run-of-the-mill depression may feel sad, blue, or "down in the dumps." They may complain of lack of energy, loss of self-esteem, difficulty concentrating, loss of interest in activities and other people (Nezlek et al., 2000), pessimism, crying, and thoughts of suicide.

These feelings are more intense in people with **major depressive disorder (MDD).** According to a nationally representative sample of more than 9,000 adults in the United States, MDD affects 6% to 7% of us within any given year, and one person in six over the course of our lives (Kessler et al., 2003). About half of those with MDD experience severe symptoms such as poor appetite, serious weight loss, and agitation or **psychomotor retardation.** They may be unable to concentrate and make decisions. They may say that they "don't care" anymore and in some cases attempt suicide. A minority may display faulty perception of reality—so-called psychotic behaviors. These include delusions of unworthiness, guilt for imagined wrongdoings, even the notion that one is rotting from disease. There may also be delusions, as of the devil administering deserved punishment, or hallucinations, as of strange bodily sensations.

BIPOLAR DISORDER **Truth or Fiction Revisited:** It is true that feeling "up" is not always a good thing. People with **bipolar disorder,** formerly known as *manic–depressive disorder,* have mood swings from ecstatic elation to deep depression. The cycles seem to be unrelated to external events. In the elated, or **manic** phase, the person may show excessive excitement or silliness, carrying jokes too far.

Major depressive disorder A serious to severe depressive disorder in which the person may show loss of appetite, psychomotor retardation, and impaired reality testing.

Psychomotor retardation Slowness in motor activity and (apparently) in thought.

Bipolar disorder A disorder in which the mood alternates between two extreme poles (elation and depression). Also referred to as *manic–depression.*

Manic Elated, showing excessive excitement.

The manic person may be argumentative. He or she may show poor judgment, destroying property, making huge contributions to charity, or giving away expensive possessions. People often find manic individuals abrasive and avoid them. They are often oversexed and too restless to sit still or sleep restfully. They often speak rapidly (showing "pressured speech") and jump from topic to topic (showing **rapid flight of ideas**). It can be hard to get a word in edgewise.

Depression is the other side of the coin. People with bipolar depression often sleep more than usual and are lethargic. People with major (or unipolar) depression are more likely to have insomnia and agitation. Those with bipolar depression also exhibit social withdrawal and irritability. Some people with bipolar disorder attempt suicide when the mood shifts from the elated phase toward depression (Jamison, 2000). They will do almost anything to escape the depths of depression that lie ahead.

The Case of Women and Depression

Women are about two times more likely to be diagnosed with depression than men (Greenberger et al., 2000; Kessler, 2003). This gender difference begins to emerge during adolescence, at about the age of 13 (Hankin & Abramson, 2001).

Many people assume that biological gender differences largely explain why women are more likely to become depressed. Low levels of estrogen are widely seen as the culprit. As noted in Chapter 2, estrogen levels plummet prior to menstruation. How often do we hear degrading remarks such as "It must be that time of the month" when a woman expresses feelings of anger or irritation? But part of the gender difference may be due to the fact that men are less likely than women to admit to depression or seek treatment for depression. "I'm the John Wayne generation," admitted one man, a physician. "'It's only a flesh wound'; that's how you deal with it. I thought depression was a weakness—there was something disgraceful about it. A real man would just get over it" (cited in Wartik, 2000).

Still in any given year, about 12% of women and 7% of men in the United States are estimated to be diagnosable with depression (Depression Research, 2000). It was once assumed that depression was most likely to accompany menopause in women, because women could no longer carry out their "natural" function of childbearing. However, women are more likely to encounter severe depression during the childbearing years (Depression Research, 2000).

Yes, hormonal changes during adolescence, the menstrual cycle, and childbirth may contribute to depression in women (Cyranowski et al., 2000; McGrath et al., 1990). The bodies and brains of males, on the other hand, are stoked by testosterone during adolescence. High testosterone levels are connected with feelings of self-confidence, high activity levels, and aggressiveness, a cluster of traits and behaviors that are more connected with elation (even if sometimes misplaced) than with depression (H. G. Pope et al., 2000; Sullivan, 2000).

However, some theorists suggest that women may also have a "cognitive vulnerability" to depression as well, connected, for example, with greater tendencies than men to ruminate about stresses and other negative events (Hankin & Abramson, 2001).

A panel convened by the American Psychological Association attributed most of the gender difference to the greater stresses placed on women, which tend to be greatest when they are trying to meet the multiple demands of childbearing, child rearing, and financial support of the family (McGrath et al., 1990). Women are more likely to experience physical and sexual abuse, poverty, single parenthood, and sexism. Single mothers, in particular, have lower socioeconomic status than men, and depression and other psychological disorders are more common among poor people (Cairney & Wade, 2002). Women are also more likely than men to help other people who are under stress. Supporting other people heaps additional caregiving burdens on themselves. A part of "therapy" for depressed women, then, is

Rapid flight of ideas Rapid speech and topic changes, characteristic of manic behavior.

■ **Women and Depression** Women are much more likely than men to be diagnosed with depression. Does the gender difference reflect biases among the mental-health professionals who make the diagnoses, women's (frequent) status as second-class citizens, the fact that women are often expected to take care of the family as well as earn a living, hormonal and other biological differences between women and men, other factors—or all of the above or some of the above?

© Peter Cade/Getty Images/Stone

to modify the overwhelming demands that are placed on women today (Comas-Diaz, 1994). The pain may lie in the individual, but the cause often lies in society.

Women may be more likely than men to encounter depression, but men also become depressed. Let us now consider theoretical views of depression that apply both to men and women.

Theoretical Views

Question: What is known about the origins of mood disorders? Although the mood disorders are connected with processes within the individual, let us begin by noting that many kinds of situations are also connected with depression. For example, depression may be a reaction to losses and stress (Cowen, 2002; Mazure et al., 2000). Sources of chronic strain such as marital discord, physical discomfort, incompetence, and failure or pressure at work all contribute to feelings of depression. We tend to be more depressed by things we bring on ourselves, such as academic problems, financial problems, unwanted pregnancy, conflict with the law, arguments, and fights (Greenberger et al., 2000). However, some people recover from depression less readily than others. People who remain depressed have lower self-esteem (Andrews, 1998; Sherrington et al., 2001), are less likely to be able to solve social problems (Reinecke et al., 2001), and have less social support.

What are the origins of depression?

PSYCHOLOGICAL VIEWS Psychoanalysts suggest various explanations for depression. In one, people who are at risk for depression are overly concerned about hurting other people's feelings or losing their approval. As a result, they hold in feelings of anger rather than expressing them. Anger is turned inward and experienced as misery and self-hatred. From the psychodynamic perspective, bipolar disorder may be seen as alternating states in which the personality is first dominated by the superego and then by the ego. In the depressive phase of the disorder, the superego dominates, producing exaggerated ideas of wrongdoing and associated feelings of guilt and worthlessness. After a while the ego asserts supremacy, producing the elation and self-confidence often seen in the manic phase. Later, in response to the excessive display of ego, feelings of guilt return and plunge the person into depression once again.

Many learning theorists suggest that depressed people behave as though they cannot obtain reinforcement. For example, they appear to be inactive and apathetic. Many people with depressive disorders have an external locus of control. That is, they do not believe they can control events so as to achieve reinforcements (Tong, 2001; Weinmann et al., 2001).

Research conducted by learning theorists has also found links between depression and **learned helplessness.** In classic research, psychologist Martin Seligman taught dogs that they were helpless to escape an electric shock. The dogs were prevented from leaving a cage in which they received repeated shocks. Later, a barrier to a safe compartment was removed, offering the animals a way out. When they were shocked again, however, the dogs made no effort to escape. They had apparently learned that they were helpless. Seligman's dogs were also, in a sense, reinforced for doing nothing. That is, the shock *eventually* stopped when the dogs were showing helpless behavior—inactivity and withdrawal. "Reinforcement" might have increased the likelihood of repeating the "successful behavior"—that is, doing nothing—in a similar situation. This helpless behavior resembles that of people who are depressed.

Other cognitive factors also contribute to depression. For example, perfectionists set themselves up for depression by making irrational demands on themselves. They are likely to fall short of their (unrealistic) expectations and to feel depressed as a result (Flett & Hewitt, 2002; Flett et al., 2002).

Cognitive psychologists also note that people who ruminate about feelings of depression are more likely to prolong them (Nolen-Hoeksema, 2000; Spasojevic & Alloy, 2001; A. Ward et al., 2003). Women are more likely than men to ruminate about feelings of depression (Nolen-Hoeksema, 2001). Men seem more likely to try

Learned helplessness A model for the acquisition of depressive behavior, based on findings that organisms in aversive situations learn to show inactivity when their operants go unreinforced.

to fight off negative feelings by distracting themselves. Men are also more likely to distract themselves by turning to alcohol (Nolen-Hoeksema, 2001). They thus expose themselves and their families to further problems.

Still other cognitions involve the ways in which people explain their failures and shortcomings to themselves. Seligman (1996) suggests that when things go wrong we may think of the causes of failure as either *internal* or *external, stable* or *unstable, global* or *specific*. These various **attributional styles** can be illustrated using the example of having a date that does not work out. An internal attribution involves self-blame, as in "I really loused it up." An external attribution places the blame elsewhere (as in "Some couples just don't take to each other," or, "She was the wrong sign for me"). A stable attribution ("It's my personality") suggests a problem that cannot be changed. An unstable attribution ("It was because I had a head cold") suggests a temporary condition. A global attribution of failure ("I have no idea what to do when I'm with other people") suggests that the problem is quite large. A specific attribution ("I have problems making small talk at the beginning of a relationship") chops the problem down to a manageable size. Research has shown that people who are depressed are more likely to attribute the causes of their failures to internal, stable, and global factors—factors that they are relatively powerless to change (Lewinsohn et al., 2000b; Riso et al. 2003; Ziegler & Hawley, 2001).

Let's add one remarkable note about attributional styles and the mind–body connection. Shelley Taylor and her colleagues (2000a) found that self-blame for negative events is connected with poorer functioning of the immune system. Too much self-blame, in other words, is not only depressing; it can also make us physically ill.

BIOLOGICAL FACTORS Researchers are also searching for biological factors in mood disorders. Depression, for example, is often associated with the trait of **neuroticism,** which is heritable (Mulder, 2002). Anxiety is also connected with neuroticism, and mood and anxiety disorders are frequently found in the same person (Mulder, 2002).

Genetic factors appear to be involved in major depression and bipolar disorder (Jamison, 2000; Lewinsohn et al., 2000b; Nurnberger et al., 2001; P. F. Sullivan et al., 2000). Support for a role for genetic factors in bipolar disorder is found in twin and adoption studies (Craddock & Jones, 2001).

Research into depression focuses on underutilization of the neurotransmitter serotonin in the brain (Yatham et al., 2000; Young et al., 2003). It has been shown, for example, that learned helplessness is connected with lower serotonin levels in rats' brains (Wu et al., 1999). Moreover, people with severe depression often respond to drugs that heighten the action of serotonin.

Relationships between mood disorders and biological factors are complex and under intense study. Even if people are biologically predisposed toward depression, self-efficacy expectations and attitudes—particularly attitudes about whether one can change things for the better—may also play a role.

Your Turn: Now that we have discussed mood disorders, enhance your mastery of the material with the nearby "Learning Connections." Review the material by filling in the blanks, reflect on the material by relating it to other things you know, and think critically about it.

■ **Why Did He Miss That Tackle?** This football player is compounding his feelings of depression by attributing his shortcomings on the field to factors that he cannot change. For example, he tells himself that he missed the tackle out of stupidity and lack of athletic ability. He ignores the facts that his coaching was poor and his teammates failed to support him.

Attributional style The tendency to attribute one's behavior to internal or external factors, stable or unstable factors, and so on.

Neuroticism A personality trait characterized largely by persistent anxiety.

₥ Learning Connections　MOOD DISORDERS: UP, DOWN, AND AROUND

ACTIVE REVIEW (19) Mood disorders are characterized by disturbance in expressed _____. (20) _____ depression can reach psychotic proportions, with grossly impaired reality testing. (21) In bipolar disorder there are mood swings between _____ and depression.

(22) Manic people may have grand, delusional schemes and show rapid _____ of ideas. (23) Seligman and his colleagues have explored links between depression and learned _____. (24) Depressed people are more likely than other people to make (*Internal* or *External?*),

stable, and global attributions for failures. (25) Mood disorders (*Do* or *Do not?*) Tend to run in families. (26) Depression is connected with deficiency in the neurotransmitter _____.

REFLECT AND RELATE When you fall short of your goals, do you tend to be merciless in your self-criticism or to blame other people or "circumstances"? Do your views of

your shortcomings tend to worsen or to ease your feelings of depression?

CRITICAL THINKING Critical thinkers pay close attention to the definitions of terms. When is depression to be considered a psychological disorder? How does bipolar disorder differ from responses to the "ups and downs" of life?

 Go to **http://psychology.wadsworth.com/ rathus_pcc9e** for an interactive version of this Learning Connections unit.

Schizophrenia: When Thinking Runs Astray

Jennifer was 19. Her husband David brought her into the emergency room because she had cut her wrists. When she was interviewed, her attention wandered. She seemed distracted by things in the air, or something she might be hearing. It was as if she had an invisible earphone.

She explained that she had cut her wrists because the "hellsmen" had told her to. Then she seemed frightened. Later she said that the hellsmen had warned her not to reveal their existence. She had been afraid that they would punish her for talking about them.

David and Jennifer had been married for about one year. At first they had been together in a small apartment in town. But Jennifer did not want to be near other people and had convinced him to rent a bungalow in the country. There she would make fantastic drawings of goblins and monsters during the days. Now and then she would become agitated and act as if invisible things were giving her instructions.

"I'm bad," Jennifer would mutter. "I'm bad." She would begin to jumble her words. David would then try to convince her to go to the hospital, but she would refuse. Then the wrist-cutting would begin. David thought he had made the cottage safe by removing knives and blades. But Jennifer would always find something.

Then Jennifer would be brought to the hospital, have stitches put in, be kept under observation for a while, and medicated. She would explain that she cut herself because the hellsmen had told her that she was bad and must die. After a few days she would deny hearing the hellsmen, and she would insist on leaving the hospital. David would take her home. The pattern continued.

When the emergency room staff examined Jennifer's wrists and heard that she believed she had been following the orders of "hellsmen," they suspected that she could be diagnosed with schizophrenia. **Question: What is schizophrenia?** Schizophrenia is a severe psychological disorder that touches every aspect of a person's life. It is characterized by disturbances in thought and language, perception and attention, motor activity, and mood, and withdrawal and absorption in daydreams or fantasy.

Schizophrenia has been referred to as the worst disorder affecting human beings. It afflicts nearly 1% of the population worldwide. Its onset occurs relatively early in life, and its adverse effects tend to endure.

People with schizophrenia have problems in memory, attention, and communication. Their thinking and communication ability becomes unraveled (Kerns & Berenbaum, 2002). Unless we are allowing our thoughts to wander, our thinking is normally tightly knit. We start at a certain point, and associated thoughts tend to be logically connected. But people with schizophrenia often think illogically. Their speech may be jumbled. They may combine parts of words into new words or make meaningless rhymes. They may jump from topic to topic, conveying little useful information. They usually do not recognize that their thoughts and behavior are abnormal.

Many people with schizophrenia have **delusions**—for example, delusions of grandeur, persecution, or reference. In the case of delusions of grandeur, a person may believe that he is a famous historical figure such as Jesus, or a person on a special mission. He may have grand, illogical plans for saving the world. Delusions tend to be unshakable even in the face of evidence that they are not true. People with delusions of persecution may believe that they are sought by the Mafia, CIA, FBI, or some other group. A woman with delusions of reference said that news stories contained coded information about her. A man with such delusions complained that neighbors had "bugged" his walls with "radios." Other people with schizophrenia have had delusions that they have committed unpardonable sins, that they were rotting away from disease, or that they or the world did not exist.

Truth or Fiction Revisited: It is true that people with schizophrenia may see and hear things that are not really there. Their perceptions often include hallucinations—imagery in the absence of external stimulation that the person cannot distinguish from reality. In Shakespeare's *Macbeth*, for example, after killing King Duncan, Macbeth apparently experiences a hallucination:

> *Is this a dagger which I see before me,*
> *The handle toward my hand? Come, let me clutch thee:*
> *I have thee not, and yet I see thee still.*
> *Art thou not, fatal vision, sensible*
> *To feeling as to sight? or art thou but*
> *A dagger of the mind, a false creation,*
> *Proceeding from the heat-oppressed brain?*

Jennifer apparently hallucinated the voices of "hellsmen." Other people who experience hallucinations may see colors or even obscene words spelled out in midair. Auditory hallucinations are the most common type.

In individuals with schizophrenia, motor activity may become wild or so slowed that the person is said to be in a **stupor**—that is, a condition in which the senses, thought, and movement are inhibited. There may be strange gestures and facial expressions. The person's emotional responses may be flat or blunted, or inappropriate—as in giggling upon hearing bad news. People with schizophrenia tend to withdraw from social contacts and become wrapped up in their own thoughts and fantasies. **Question: What kinds of schizophrenia are there?**

Types of Schizophrenia

All types of schizophrenia involve a thought disorder. However, three major types of schizophrenia—paranoid, disorganized, and catatonic schizophrenia—all have distinct features.

PARANOID TYPE People with **paranoid schizophrenia** have systematized delusions and, frequently, related auditory hallucinations. They usually have delusions of grandeur and persecution, but they may also have delusions of jealousy, in which they believe that a spouse or lover has been unfaithful. They may show agitation, confusion, and fear, and may experience vivid hallucinations that are consistent with their delusions. People with paranoid schizophrenia often construct complex or systematized delusions involving themes of wrongdoing or persecution. John Nash, the character in the true story *A Beautiful Mind*, believed that the government was recruiting him to decipher coded messages by our Cold War enemies.

DISORGANIZED TYPE People with **disorganized schizophrenia** show incoherence, loosening of associations, disorganized behavior, disorganized delusions, fragmentary delusions or hallucinations, and flat or highly inappropriate emotional responses. Extreme social impairment is common. People with this type of schizophrenia may also exhibit silliness and giddiness of mood, giggling, and nonsensical speech. They may neglect their appearance and personal hygiene and lose control of their bladder and bowels.

Delusions False, persistent beliefs that are unsubstantiated by sensory or objective evidence.

Stupor A condition in which the senses, thought, and movement are dulled.

Paranoid schizophrenia A type of schizophrenia characterized primarily by delusions—commonly of persecution—and by vivid hallucinations.

Disorganized schizophrenia A type of schizophrenia characterized by disorganized delusions and vivid hallucinations.

■ **Schizophrenia in** *A Beautiful Mind* In the film *A Beautiful Mind*, Russell Crowe played the role of the mathematician John Forbes Nash, Jr. Nash struggled with schizophrenia for more than three decades and was eventually awarded a Nobel Prize for work he had done as a graduate student decades earlier.

Everett Collection

■ **Catatonic Schizophrenia** People with catatonic schizophrenia show striking motor impairment and may hold unusual positions for hours.

CATATONIC TYPE Catatonic schizophrenia is one of the most unusual psychological disorders (Taylor & Fink, 2003). People with **catatonic schizophrenia** show striking impairment in motor activity. It is characterized by a slowing of activity into a stupor that may suddenly change into an agitated phase. Catatonic individuals may maintain unusual, even difficult postures for hours, even as their limbs grow swollen or stiff. A striking feature of this condition is **waxy flexibility**, in which the person maintains positions into which he or she has been manipulated by others. Catatonic individuals may also show **mutism**, but afterward they usually report that they heard what others were saying at the time.

Schizophrenia is thus characterized by extremely unusual behavior. **Question: What is known about the origins of schizophrenia?**

Theoretical Views

Psychologists have investigated various factors that may contribute to schizophrenia. They include psychological and biological factors.

PSYCHOLOGICAL VIEWS According to the psychodynamic perspective, schizophrenia occurs because the ego is overwhelmed by sexual or aggressive impulses from the id. The impulses threaten the ego and cause intense inner conflict. Under this threat, the person regresses to an early phase of the oral stage in which the infant has not yet learned that it and the world are separate. Fantasies become confused with reality, giving rise to hallucinations and delusions. Yet critics point out that schizophrenic behavior is not the same as infantile behavior.

Most learning theorists have explained schizophrenia in terms of conditioning and observational learning. They have suggested that people engage in schizophrenic behavior when it is more likely to be reinforced than normal behavior. This may occur when a person is reared in a socially unrewarding or punitive situation. Inner fantasies then become more reinforcing than social realities. Patients in a psychiatric hospital may learn what is "expected" by observing others. Hospital staff may reinforce schizophrenic behavior by paying more attention to patients who behave bizarrely. This view is consistent with folklore that the child who disrupts the class attracts more attention from the teacher than the "good" child.

Although quality of parenting is connected with the development of schizophrenia (Buckley et al., 2000), critics note that many people who are reared in socially punitive settings are apparently immune to the extinction of socially appropriate behavior. Other people develop schizophrenic behavior without having had opportunities to observe other people with schizophrenia.

Many investigators have considered whether and how social and cultural factors such as poverty, discrimination, and overcrowding contribute to schizophrenia—especially among people who are genetically vulnerable to the disorder. Classic research in New Haven, Connecticut, showed that the rate of schizophrenia was twice as high in the lowest socioeconomic class as in the next-higher class on the socioeconomic ladder (Hollingshead & Redlich, 1958). It appears that poor-quality housing contributes to psychological disorders (Evans et al., 2000b). Some sociocultural theorists therefore suggest that treatment of schizophrenia requires alleviation of poverty and other social ills, rather than changing people whose behavior is deviant.

Critics of this view suggest that low socioeconomic status may be a result, rather than a cause, of schizophrenia. People with schizophrenia may drift toward low social status because they lack the social skills and cognitive abilities to function at higher social class levels. Thus, they may wind up in poor neighborhoods in disproportionately high numbers.

Evidence for the hypothesis that people with schizophrenia drift downward to lower socioeconomic status is mixed. Many people with schizophrenia do drift downward occupationally in comparison with their fathers' occupations. Many others, however, were reared in families in which the father came from the lowest socioeconomic class. Because the stresses of poverty may play a role in the devel-

Catatonic schizophrenia A type of schizophrenia characterized by striking motor impairment.

Waxy flexibility A feature of catatonic schizophrenia in which people can be molded into postures that they maintain for quite some time.

Mutism Refusal to talk.

opment of schizophrenia, many researchers are interested in the possible interactions between psychosocial stressors and biological factors (Buckley et al., 2000; Sawa & Snyder, 2002).

BIOLOGICAL VIEWS Schizophrenia appears to be a brain disorder (Egan et al., 2001). Many studies have been done to determine how the brains of schizophrenic people differ from those of others. Studies have focused on the amount of gray matter in the brain (see Figure 14.3), the size of ventricles (hollow spaces), activity levels in the brain, and brain chemistry (e.g., neurotransmitters).

One avenue of brain research connects the major deficits we find in schizophrenia—problems in attention, working memory, abstract thinking, and language—with dysfunction in the prefrontal cortex of the brain. Imaging of the brain has shown that people with schizophrenia have less gray matter than other people (Kasai et al., 2003). For example, they have smaller brains and, in particular, a smaller prefrontal region of the cortex (Flashman et al., 2000; Selemon et al., 2002, 2003; Staal et al., 2000). They also tend to have larger ventricles in the brain than other people (Keller et al., 2003; Wright et al., 2000). PET scans reveal that people with schizophrenia also tend to have a lower level of activity in the frontal region of the brain (Kim et al., 2000; Meyer-Lindenberg et al., 2001; Lahti, et al., 2001). Still other research connects the lower activity levels with a loss in synapses (the structures that permit communication between neurons) in the region (Glantz & Lewis, 2000; McGlashan & Hoffman, 2000; Selemon et al., 2002, 2003) or white matter (Wolkin et al., 2003).

What might account for differences in brain structure and functioning? Research evidence suggests that there are a number of biological risk factors for schizophrenia, such as heredity, complications during pregnancy and birth, and birth during winter (Andreasen, 2003; Buckley et al., 2000; Jablensky & Kalaydjieva, 2003; Sawa & Snyder, 2002). Schizophrenia, like many other psychological disorders, runs in families (Conklin & Iacono, 2002; Hwu et al., 2003). People with schizophrenia constitute about 1% of the population. Yet children with one parent who has been diagnosed with schizophrenia have about a 10% chance of being diagnosed with schizophrenia themselves. Children with two such parents have about a 35% to 40% chance of being so diagnosed (Gottesman, 1991; Straube & Oades, 1992). Twin studies also find about a 45% concordance rate for the diagnosis among pairs of identical (MZ) twins, whose genetic codes are the same, compared with a 17% rate among pairs of fraternal (DZ) twins (Plomin & Crabbe, 2000). Moreover, adoptee studies find that the biological parent typically places the child at greater risk for schizophrenia than the adoptive parent—even though the child has been reared by the adoptive parent (Gottesman, 1991). Sharing genes with relatives who have schizophrenia apparently places a person at risk of developing the disorder. Many studies have been carried out to try to isolate the gene or genes involved in schizophrenia. Some studies find locations for multiple genes on several chromosomes.

But heredity is not the only factor that creates a vulnerability to schizophrenia. It also turns out that many people with schizophrenia have undergone complications during pregnancy and birth (Rosso et al., 2000). For example, the mothers of many people with schizophrenia had the flu during the sixth or seventh month of pregnancy (Brown & Susser, 2002). Poor maternal nutrition has also been implicated (Hulshoff et al., 2000; Pol et al., 2000). Complications during childbirth, especially prolonged labor, seem to be connected with the larger ventricles we find among people with schizophrenia (McNeil et al., 2000). People with schizophrenia are also somewhat more likely to have been born during winter than would be predicted by chance (Pol et al., 2000; Suvisaari et al., 2002). Alcohol abuse may also lead to differences in brain structures among people with schizophrenia (E. V. Sullivan et al., 2000). On the other hand, research evidence is mixed as to whether viral infections in childhood are connected with schizophrenia (Suvisaari et al., 2003). But taken

Video Connections—Schizophrenia Schizophrenia is considered the most severe of the psychological disorders and afflicts about 1% of the population. Etta suffers from schizophrenia. By clicking on the "Schizophrenia" video link on your companion website you can view a conversation between Etta and a therapist. Through Etta's plight you will realize how devastating this disorder is.

together, these biological risk factors suggest that schizophrenia involves atypical development of the central nervous system. Problems in the nervous system may involve brain chemistry as well as brain structures, and research along these lines has led to the dopamine theory of schizophrenia.

THE DOPAMINE THEORY OF SCHIZOPHRENIA Numerous chemical substances have been suspected of playing a role in schizophrenia, and much research has focused on the neurotransmitter dopamine. According to the dopamine theory of schizophrenia, people with schizophrenia overutilize dopamine (use more of it than other people do) although they may not produce more of it (Gijsman et al., 2002; Tsai & Coyle, 2002). Why? Research suggests that they have increased concentrations of dopamine at the synapses in the brain and also larger numbers of dopamine receptors (Butcher, 2000). It's a sort of "double hit" of neural transmission that may be connected with the confusion that characterizes schizophrenia.

Because many psychological and biological factors have been implicated in schizophrenia, most investigators today favor a *multifactorial* model. According to this model, genetic factors create a predisposition toward schizophrenia (see Figure 14.2). Genetic vulnerability to the disorder interacts with other factors, such as complications of pregnancy and birth, stress, and quality of parenting, to give rise to the disorder (Buckley et al., 2000; Sawa & Snyder, 2002).

Because the perceptions and judgment of people with schizophrenia are impaired, the diagnosis is sometimes associated with the insanity plea in the criminal courts. The following "Controversy in Psychology" offers insight into the insanity plea.

FIGURE 14.2 **The Biopsychosocial Model of Schizophrenia**

According to the biopsychosocial model of schizophrenia, people with a genetic vulnerability to the disorder experience increased risk for schizophrenia when they encounter problems such as viral infections, birth complications, stress, and poor parenting. People without the genetic vulnerability would not develop schizophrenia despite psychological and social/sociocultural problems.

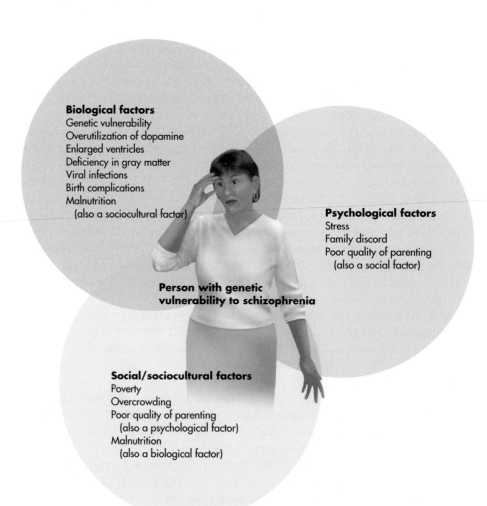

Biological factors
Genetic vulnerability
Overutilization of dopamine
Enlarged ventricles
Deficiency in gray matter
Viral infections
Birth complications
Malnutrition
    (also a sociocultural factor)

Psychological factors
Stress
Family discord
Poor quality of parenting
    (also a social factor)

Person with genetic vulnerability to schizophrenia

Social/sociocultural factors
Poverty
Overcrowding
Poor quality of parenting
    (also a psychological factor)
Malnutrition
    (also a biological factor)

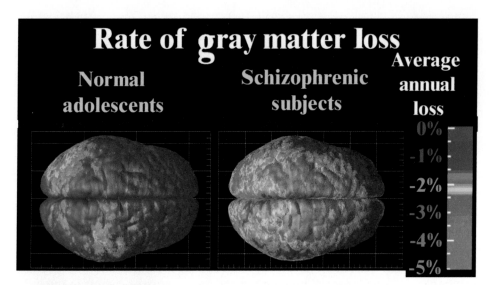

FIGURE 14.3 Average Rates of Loss of Gray Matter among Normal Adolescents and Adolescents Diagnosed with Schizophrenia.

High-resolution MRI scans show rates of gray matter loss in normal 13- to 18-year-olds and among adolescents of the same age diagnosed with schizophrenia. Maps of brain changes reveal profound, progressive loss in schizophrenia (right). Loss also occurs in normal adolescents (left), but at a slower rate.
Source: P.M. Thompson, et al. (2001). Mapping adolescent brain change reveals dynamic wave of accelerated gray matter loss in very early-onset schizophrenia. *Proceedings of the National Academy of Sciences of the USA, 98*(20), 11650–11655.

CONTROVERSY IN PSYCHOLOGY

Should we ban the insanity plea?

John Hinckley was found not guilty of a 1981 assassination attempt on President Ronald Reagan by reason of insanity. Hinckley was diagnosed with schizophrenia and was committed to a psychiatric institution rather than given a prison term.

In pleading insanity, lawyers use the M'Naghten rule, named after Daniel M'Naghten, who tried to assassinate British prime minister Robert Peel in 1843. M'Naghten had delusions that Peel was persecuting him, and he killed the minister's secretary in the attempt. The court found M'Naghten not guilty by reason of insanity. That is, the defendant did not understand what he was doing at the time of the act, did not realize it was wrong, or was giving in to an irresistible impulse. The insanity plea is still used in much the same way (Follingstad & McCormick 2002).

Many people would like to ban the insanity plea (DeAngelis, 1994). They worry that "the world is getting more violent" Bersoff (1994, p. 28) or "that people are literally getting away with murder." But the insanity plea is used in only about 1% of felony cases (DeAngelis, 1994). Moreover, people found not guilty by reason of insanity are institutionalized for indefinite terms—supposedly until they are no longer insane. Hinckley remains institutionalized more than two decades after he tried to kill President Reagan. If he had been convicted of attempted murder, he might already have served his time in jail.

Your Turn: Now that we have discussed schizophrenia, enhance your mastery of the material with the nearby "Learning Connections." Review the material by filling in the blanks, reflect on the material by relating it to other things you know, and think critically about it.

Learning Connections | SCHIZOPHRENIA: WHEN THINKING RUNS ASTRAY

ACTIVE REVIEW (27) Schizophrenic disorders are characterized by disturbances in _____ and language (as in the loosening of associations and in delusions); in perception and attention (as in hallucinations); in motor activity; in mood; and by withdrawal and autism.

(28) Paranoid schizophrenia is characterized by paranoid _____. (29) _____ schizophrenia is characterized by impaired motor activity waxy flexibility.
(30) Schizophrenia (*Does* or *Does not?*) tend to run in families. (31) The prefrontal region of the brain of people

with schizophrenia has (*More* or *Fewer?*) synapses than those of other people. (32) People with schizophrenia utilize more of the neurotransmitter _____ than other people do.

REFLECT AND RELATE There is evidence for genetic factors in schizophrenia. What would you tell the son or

daughter of a person with schizophrenia about the likelihood of his or her developing schizophrenia? Explain.

CRITICAL THINKING Agree or disagree with the following statement and support your answer: Schizophrenia is a disease of the brain.

 Go to **http://psychology.wadsworth.com/ rathus_pcc9e** for an interactive version of this Learning Connections unit.

Personality Disorders: Making Oneself or Others Miserable

Personality disorders, like personality traits, are characterized by enduring patterns of behavior. Personality disorders, however, are inflexible and maladaptive. They impair personal or social functioning and are a source of distress to the individual or to other people. **Question: What kinds of personality disorders are there?**

Types of Personality Disorders

There are a number of personality disorders. They include the paranoid, schizotypal, schizoid, antisocial, and avoidant personality disorders. The defining trait of the **paranoid personality disorder** is a tendency to interpret other people's behavior as threatening or demeaning. People with the disorder do not show the grossly disorganized thinking of paranoid schizophrenia. However, they are mistrustful of others, and their relationships suffer for it. They may be suspicious of coworkers and supervisors, but they can generally hold a job.

Schizotypal personality disorder is characterized by peculiarities of thought, perception, or behavior, such as excessive fantasy and suspiciousness, feelings of being unreal, or odd usage of words. The bizarre behaviors that characterize schizophrenia are absent, so this disorder is schizo*typal*, not schizophrenic.

The **schizoid personality** is defined by indifference to relationships and flat emotional response. People with this disorder are "loners." They do not develop warm, tender feelings for others. They have few friends and rarely maintain long-term relationships. Some people with schizoid personality disorder do very well on the job provided that continuous social interaction is not required. They do not have hallucinations or delusions.

People with **borderline personality disorder** show instability in their relationships, self-image, and mood, and lack of control over impulses (Yen et al., 2002). They tend to be uncertain of their values, goals, loyalties, careers, choices of friends, sometimes even their sexual orientations (Sokolova et al., 2002). Instability in self-image or identity may leave them with feelings of emptiness and boredom. Many cannot tolerate being alone and make desperate attempts to avoid feelings of abandonment. They may be clinging and demanding in social relationships, but clinging often pushes away the people on whom they depend. They alternate between extremes of adulation in their relationships (when their needs are met) and loathing (when they feel scorned). They tend to view other people as all good or all bad, shifting abruptly from one extreme to the other (Butler et al., 2002). As a result, they may flit from partner to partner in brief and stormy relationships. People whom they had idealized are treated with contempt when they feel the other person has failed them.

Instability of moods is a central characteristic of borderline personality disorder. Moods run the gamut from anger and irritability to depression and anxiety, with each lasting from a few hours to a few days. People with the disorder have difficulty controlling anger and are prone to fights or smashing things. They often act on impulse, like eloping with someone they have just met. This impulsive and unpredictable behavior is often self-destructive and linked to a risk of suicidal

Personality disorders Enduring patterns of maladaptive behavior that are sources of distress to the individual or others.

Paranoid personality disorder A personality disorder characterized by persistent suspiciousness but not involving the disorganization of paranoid schizophrenia.

Schizotypal personality disorder A personality disorder characterized by oddities of thought and behavior but not involving bizarre psychotic behaviors.

Schizoid personality disorder A personality disorder characterized by social withdrawal.

Borderline personality disorder A personality disorder characterized by instability in relationships, self-image, mood, and lack of impulse control.

attempts and gestures. It may involve spending sprees, gambling, drug abuse, engaging in unsafe sexual activity, reckless driving, binge eating, or shoplifting. People with the disorder may also engage in self-mutilation, such as scratching their wrists or burning cigarettes on their arms (Sachsse et al., 2002). Self-mutilation is sometimes a means of manipulating others, particularly in times of stress. Frequent self-mutilation is also associated with suicide attempts.

Truth or Fiction Revisited: It is true that some people can kill or maim others with no feelings of guilt at all. When these people also persistently violate the rights of others and are in repeated conflict with the law, they may be diagnosed with **antisocial personality disorder** (see Table 14.2). People with antisocial personality disorder often show a superficial charm and are at least average in intelligence. They fail to learn to improve their behavior from punishment, and they do not form meaningful bonds with other people (Levenston et al., 2000; Romero et al., 2001). Though they are often heavily punished by their parents and rejected by peers, they continue in their impulsive, careless styles of life. Women are more likely than men to have anxiety and depressive disorders. Men are more likely than women to have antisocial personality disorder (K. G. Anderson et al., 2001).

People with **avoidant personality disorder** are generally unwilling to enter a relationship without some assurance of acceptance because they fear rejection and criticism. As a result, they may have few close relationships outside their immediate families. Unlike people with schizoid personality disorder, however, they have some interest in, and feelings of warmth toward, other people. **Question: What is known about the origins of personality disorders?**

Theoretical Views

Many theoretical explanations of personality disorders are derived from the psychodynamic model. Traditional Freudian theory focuses on Oedipal problems as the source of many psychological disorders, including personality disorders. Faulty resolution of the Oedipus complex might lead to lack of guilt, because conscience, or superego, is thought to depend on proper resolution of the complex. Although lack of guilt may occur more often among children who are rejected and punished by parents rather than given affection (Denham et al., 2000; Hastings et al., 2000), the view that such treatment causes Oedipal problems is speculative.

Learning theorists suggest that childhood experiences can contribute to maladaptive ways of relating to others in adulthood—that is, can lead to personality disorders. Cognitive psychologists find that antisocial adolescents encode social information in ways that bolster their misdeeds. For example, they tend to interpret other people's behavior as threatening, even when it is not (Crick & Dodge, 1994; Lochman, 1992). Aggressive individuals often find it difficult to solve social problems in useful ways

■ **A Person with Borderline Personality Disorder?** Many well-known individuals such as Marilyn Monroe (seen here with her husband, playwright Arthur Miller) and Lawrence of Arabia may have had borderline personality disorder. The disorder is characterized by instability in relationships, self-image, and mood, and by problems in impulse control.

© Bettmann/CORBIS

Antisocial personality disorder The diagnosis given a person who is in frequent conflict with society, yet who is undeterred by punishment and experiences little or no guilt and anxiety.

Avoidant personality disorder A personality disorder in which the person is unwilling to enter relationships without assurance of acceptance because of fears of rejection and criticism.

TABLE 14.2	CHARACTERISTICS OF PEOPLE DIAGNOSED WITH ANTISOCIAL PERSONALITY DISORDER

Key Characteristics	Other Common Characteristics
History of delinquency and truancy	Lack of loyalty or of formation of enduring relationships
Persistent violation of the rights of others	Failure to maintain good job performance over the years
Impulsiveness	Failure to develop or adhere to a life plan
Poor self-control	Sexual promiscuity
Lack of remorse for misdeeds	Substance abuse
Lack of empathy	Inability to tolerate boredom
Deceitfulness and manipulativeness	Low tolerance for frustration
Irresponsibility	Irritability
Glibness; superficial charm	
Exaggerated sense of self-worth	

Sources: Levenston et al., 2000; Romero et al., 2001.

(McMurran et al., 2002). Cognitive therapists have encouraged some antisocial adolescents to view social provocations as problems to be solved rather than as threats to their "manhood," with some favorable initial results (Lochman, 1992).

Genetic factors are apparently involved in some personality disorders (Eaves et al., 2000; Rutter & Silberg, 2002). Personality traits are to some degree heritable (Plomin, 2000), and many personality disorders seem to be extreme variations of normal personality traits. An analysis of 51 twin and adoption studies estimated that genetic factors were the greatest influences on antisocial behavior (Rhee & Waldman, 2002). Referring to the five-factor model of personality, people with schizoid personalities tend to be highly introverted (Ross et al., 2002; Widiger & Costa, 1994). People with avoidant personalities tend to be both introverted and emotionally unstable (neurotic) (Ross et al., 2002; Widiger & Costa, 1994).

Perhaps the genetics of antisocial personality involve the prefrontal cortex of the brain, a part of the brain connected with emotional responses. There is some evidence that people with antisocial personality, as a group, have less gray matter (associative neurons) in the prefrontal cortex of the brain than other people (Damasio, 2000; Raine et al., 2000). The lesser amount of gray matter could lessen the level of arousal of the nervous system. As a result, it would be more difficult to condition fear responses (Blair & James, 2001, 2003). People with the disorder would then be unlikely to show guilt for their misdeeds and would seem to be unafraid of punishment. But a biological factor such as a lower-than-normal level of arousal might not in itself cause the development of an antisocial personality (Rutter & Silberg, 2002). Perhaps a person must also be reared under conditions that do not foster the self-concept of a law-abiding citizen.

The label of borderline personality has been applied to people as diverse as Marilyn Monroe and Lawrence of Arabia. Some theorists believe we live in fragmented and alienating times that tend to create the problems in forming a stable identity and stable relationships. "Living on the edge," or border, can be seen as a metaphor for an unstable society.

Your Turn: Now that we have discussed personality disorders, enhance your mastery of the material with the nearby "Learning Connections." Review the material by filling in the blanks, reflect on the material by relating it to other things you know, and think critically about it.

Although the causes of many psychological disorders remain in dispute, various methods of therapy have been devised to deal with them. Those methods are the focus of Chapter 15.

Learning Connections — PERSONALITY DISORDERS: MAKING ONESELF OR OTHERS MISERABLE

ACTIVE REVIEW (33) _____ disorders are inflexible, maladaptive behavior patterns that impair personal or social functioning and are a source of distress to the individual or to others. (34) The defining trait of the _____ personality is suspiciousness. (35) Social _____ is the major characteristic of the schizoid personality. (36) Persons with _____ personality disorder violate the rights of others, show little or no guilt for their misdeeds, and are undeterred by punishment. (37) Research suggests that people with antisocial personalities have (*Higher* or *Lower?*)-than-normal levels of arousal than most people. (38) Their levels of arousal may be connected with lower-than-normal levels of (*White* or *Gray?*) matter in the prefrontal cortex.

REFLECT AND RELATE Do you know anyone whom you consider to have a "bad personality"? What characteristics lead you to describe him or her in this way? What is the difference between people with "bad personalities" and people with personality disorders?

CRITICAL THINKING Sick people may be excused from school or work. If some criminals are "sick" in the sense of being diagnosed with antisocial personality disorder, does the disorder relieve them of responsibility for criminal behavior? Explain.

 Go to **http://psychology.wadsworth.com/ rathus_pcc9e** for an interactive version of this Learning Connections unit.

Life Connections
Understanding and Preventing Suicide

In January 2002, 15-year-old Charles Bishop flew his small airplane into the side of a bank building in Tampa, Florida. It was no accident. He left a suicide note expressing sympathy for what terrorists had done four months earlier, flying passenger jets into the towers of the World Trade Center in New York and the Pentagon, outside Washington, DC. His teachers and friends expressed shock and dismay.

Terrorist examples and politics aside, his teachers and friends were trying to understand how Charles could have intentionally flown into the side of an—in this case—extremely unforgiving skyscraper. After all, he, like so many people, had "so much to live for." Didn't he? Apparently Charles didn't think so. Neither do the other thousands of other Americans who take their own lives each year.

About 30,000 people each year take their lives in the United States (CDC, 2000c). Suicide is the third or fourth leading cause of death among older teenagers (National Center for Health Statistics, 2002). What prompts people to take their own lives? Who is most at risk of attempting or committing suicide?

Risk Factors in Suicide

Most suicides are linked to feelings of depression and hopelessness (Beautrais, 2003; Leslie et al., 2002; Sampaio et al., 2001). My daughter Jill Rathus and her colleagues (Miller et al., 2000; Velting et al., 2000) have found that suicidal adolescents experience four areas of psychological problems: (1) confusion about the self, (2) impulsiveness, (3) emotional instability, and (4) interpersonal problems. Some suicidal teenagers, like suicidal adults, are highly achieving, rigid perfectionists who have set impossibly high expectations for themselves (Miller et al., 2000; Wu et al., 2001). Many people throw themselves into feelings of depression and hopelessness by comparing themselves negatively with others, even when the comparisons are inappropriate (Barber, 2001). ("No, you didn't get the promotion, but you got a raise, and the person who received the promotion has been with the company longer.")

Suicide attempts are more common following stressful life events, especially "exit events" (Beautrais, 2003). Exit events entail loss of social support, as in the death of a parent or friend, divorce, or a family member's leaving home. These exit events result in what Shneidman (2001) refers to as psychological pain, or "psychache." Other contributors to suicidal behavior among adolescents include concerns over sexuality, grades in school, problems at home, and substance abuse (Beautrais, 2003; Miller et al., 2000; Wu et al., 2001). It is not always a stressful event itself that precipitates suicide but the individual's anxiety or fear of being "found out" about something, such as failing a course or getting arrested (Marttunen, 1998). Problem-solving ability—or lack of it—is connected with suicide. People who consider suicide are apparently less capable of solving problems, especially their social problems, than others (Miller et al., 2000; Townsend et al., 2001). People contemplating suicide are thus less likely to find productive ways of changing the stressful situation. They have borne the "psychache"; now they want a magical solution to problems that require work, or else a quick way out (Shneidman, 2001).

There is a tendency for suicide to run in families (Bongar, 2002; Joiner, 2002; Qin et al., 2003). Many suicide attempters have family members with serious psychological problems, and about 25% have family members who have taken their lives (Segal & Roy, 2001; Sorensen & Rutter, 1991). The causal connections are unclear, however. Do people who attempt suicide inherit disorders that can lead to suicide? Does the family environment subject family members to feelings of hopelessness? Does the suicide of a family member give a person the idea of committing suicide or create the impression that he or she is somehow fated to commit suicide? Perhaps these possibilities and others—such as poor problem-solving ability—form a complex web of contributing factors.

Sociocultural Factors in Suicide

Suicide is connected not only with feelings of depression and stressful events, but also with age, educational status, ethnicity, and gender. Consider some facts about suicide:

- Suicide is the third leading cause of death among young people aged 15 to 24 (National Center for Health Statistics, 2002). More teenagers and young adults die from suicide than from cancer, heart disease, AIDS, birth defects, stroke, pneumonia and influenza, and chronic lung disease combined (National Center for Health Statistics, 2002).

- Suicide is more common among college students than among people of the same age who do not attend college. Each year about 10,000 college students attempt suicide.

- Although teenage suicides loom large in the media spotlight, older people are actually more likely to commit suicide (National Center for Health Statistics, 2002). The suicide rate among older people who are unmarried or divorced is double that of older people who are married (CDC, 2000c).

Rates of suicide and suicide attempts also vary among different ethnic groups and according to gender. For example, about one in every six Native Americans (17%) has attempted suicide—a rate higher than that of other Americans (Blum et al., 1992). About one in eight Latino and Latina Americans has attempted suicide and three in ten have considered it (National Center for Health Statistics, 2002). European Americans are next, with 8% attempting and 28% contemplating suicide. African Americans are least likely to attempt suicide (6.5%) or to think about it (20%). The actual suicide rates for African Americans are only about two-thirds of those for European Americans, despite the fact that African Americans are more likely to live in poverty and suffer from discrimination (National Center for Health Statistics, 2002). How can we explain this "disconnect" between hope for the future and suicide rates? One possibility is that some suicidal African American males may engage in risk-taking behaviors that lead to early death by homicide or accident. Another possibility is that cultural factors such as the support offered by extended families and the important role of religion may have a protective effect. Yet another possibility is that when African Americans are feeling low, they tend to blame social circumstances, including discrimination. Many European Americans, on the other hand, may feel that there is no one to blame but themselves.

About three times as many females as males attempt suicide, but about five times as many males succeed (National Center for Health Statistics, 2002). In part, males are more likely to "succeed" because of the methods they choose. The methods preferred by males are more deadly and more rapid: Males are more likely to shoot or hang themselves; females more often use drugs, such as overdoses of tranquilizers or sleeping pills, or poisons. Females often do not take enough of these chemicals. It also takes a while for them to work, giving people the opportunity to find them and intervene.

Now let us consider some myths about suicide.

Myths about Suicide

You may have heard that individuals who threaten suicide are only seeking attention. Those who are serious just do it. **Truth or Fiction Revisited:** Actually, it is not true that people who threaten suicide are only seeking attention. Most people who commit suicide give warnings about their intentions (Jackson & Nuttall, 2001; Waters, 2000).

Some believe that those who fail at suicide attempts are only seeking attention. But many people who commit suicide have made prior attempts (Jackson & Nuttall, 2001; Waters, 2000). Contrary to widespread belief, discussing suicide with a person who is depressed does not prompt the person to attempt suicide (CDC, 1995). Extracting a promise not to commit suicide before calling or visiting a helping professional seems to prevent some suicides.

Some believe that only "insane" people (meaning people who are out of touch with reality) would take their own lives. However, suicidal thinking is not necessarily a sign of psychosis, neurosis, or personality disorder. Instead, people may consider suicide when they think they have run out of options (Nock & Kazdin, 2002; Townsend et al., 2001).

Warning Signs of Suicide

The great majority of people who commit suicide send out a variety of signals about their impending act (Bongar, 2002; Hendin et al., 2001). Sad to say, these signals often are overlooked, sometimes because other people do not recognize them, sometimes because other people do not have adequate access to health care (MacDonald, 1999; Wu et al., 2001). Sometime people do not receive help until they actually attempt suicide, and sometimes not even then (Gili-Planas et al., 2001; Wu et al., 2001). Here are some clues that a person may be at risk of committing suicide (Bongar, 2002; Hendin et al., 2001):
- Changes in eating and sleeping patterns.
- Difficulty concentrating on school or the job.
- A sharp decline in performance and attendance at school or on the job.
- Loss of interest in previously enjoyed activities.
- Giving away prized possessions.
- Complaints about physical problems when no medical basis for the problems can be found.
- Withdrawal from social relationships.

- Personality or mood changes.
- Talking or writing about death or dying.
- Abuse of drugs or alcohol.
- An attempted suicide.
- Availability of a handgun.
- A precipitating event such as an argument, a broken romantic relationship, academic difficulties, problems on the job, loss of a friend, or trouble with the law.
- In the case of adolescents, knowing or hearing about another teenager who has committed suicide (which can lead to so-called "cluster" suicides).
- Threatening to commit suicide.

What Can You Do?

Imagine that you are having a heart-to-heart talk with Jamie, one of your best friends. Things haven't been going well. Jamie's grandmother died a month ago, and they were very close. Jamie's course work has been suffering, and things have also been going downhill with the person Jamie has been seeing. But you are not prepared when Jamie looks you in the eye and says, "I've been thinking about this for days, and I've decided that the only way out is to kill myself."

If someone tells you that he or she is considering suicide, you may become frightened and flustered or feel that an enormous burden has been placed on you. You are right: It has. In such a case your objective should be to encourage the person to consult a health care provider, or to consult one yourself, as soon as possible. But if the person refuses to talk to anyone else and you feel that you can't break free for a consultation, there are a number of things you can do (Hendin et al., 2001; Omer & Elitzur, 2001; Shneidman, 2001):

1. Keep talking. Encourage the person to talk to you or to some other trusted person (Los Angeles Unified School District, 2000). Draw the person out with questions like "What's happening?" "Where do you hurt?" "What do you want to happen?" Questions like these may encourage the person to express frustrated needs and provide some relief. They also give you time to think.

2. Be a good listener. Be supportive with people who express suicidal thoughts or feel depressed, hopeless, or worthless. They may believe their condition is hopeless and will never improve, but let them know that you are there for them and willing to help them get help. Show that you understand how upset the person is. Do *not* say, "Don't be silly."

3. Suggest that something other than suicide might solve the problem, even if it is not evident at the time. Many suicidal people see only two solutions—either death or a magical resolution of their problems. Therapists try to "remove the mental blinders" from suicidal people.

4. Emphasize as concretely as possible how the person's suicide would be devastating to you and to other people who care.

5. Ask how the person intends to commit suicide. People with concrete plans and a weapon are at greater risk. Ask if you might hold on to the weapon for a while. Sometimes the answer is yes.

6. Suggest that the person go *with you* to obtain professional help *now*. The emergency room of a general hospital, the campus counseling center or infirmary, or the campus or local police station will do. Some campuses have hotlines you can call. Some cities have suicide prevention centers with hotlines that people can use anonymously.

7. Extract a promise that the person will not commit suicide before seeing you again. Arrange a specific time and place to meet. Get professional help as soon as you are apart.

8. Do *not* tell people threatening suicide that they're silly or crazy. Do *not* insist on contact with specific people, such as parents or a spouse. Conflict with these people may have led to the suicidal thinking in the first place.

Resources

You can also check out the following resources:

- The national suicide hotline: 1-800-SUICIDE (1-800-784-2433).
- American Association of Suicidology: Their Web site, www.suicidology.org, provides information on ways to prevent suicide. You will also find a list of crisis centers.
- American Foundation for Suicide Prevention: Their Web site, www.afsp.org, offers information about suicide and links to other suicide and mental health sites.

Want to study on the go? Go to your companion website and download an audio version of this review section to your media player.

Recite — An Active Summary™

1. What are psychological disorders?

Psychological disorders are characterized by unusual behavior, socially unacceptable behavior, faulty perception of reality, personal distress, dangerous behavior, or self-defeating behavior.

2. How are psychological disorders grouped or classified?

The most widely used classification scheme is found in the *Diagnostic and Statistical Manual (DSM)* of the American Psychiatric Association. The current edition of the *DSM*—the *DSM-IV-TR*—groups disorders on the basis of observable symptoms and no longer uses the category of neuroses.

3. What kinds of anxiety disorders are there?

Anxiety disorders are characterized by motor tension, feelings of dread, and overarousal of the sympathetic branch of the autonomic nervous system. These disorders include irrational, excessive fears, or phobias; panic disorder, characterized by sudden attacks in which people typically fear that they may be losing control or going crazy; generalized or pervasive anxiety; obsessive–compulsive disorder, in which people are troubled by intrusive thoughts or impulses to repeat some activity; and stress disorders, in which a stressful event is followed by persistent fears and intrusive thoughts about the event. Posttraumatic stress disorder can occur 6 months or more after the event, whereas acute stress disorder occurs within a month.

4. What is known about the origins of anxiety disorders?

The psychodynamic perspective tends to view anxiety disorders as representing difficulty in repressing primitive impulses. Many learning theorists view phobias as conditioned fears. Cognitive theorists focus on ways in which people interpret threats. Some people may also be genetically predisposed to acquire certain kinds of fears. Anxiety disorders tend to run in families. Some psychologists suggest that biochemical factors—which could be inherited—may create a predisposition toward anxiety disorders. One such factor is faulty regulation of neurotransmitters.

5. What kinds of dissociative disorders are there?

Dissociative disorders are characterized by sudden, temporary changes in consciousness or self-identity. They include dissociative amnesia; dissociative fugue, which involves forgetting plus fleeing and adopting a new identity; and dissociative identity disorder (multiple personality), in which a person behaves as if more than one personality occupies his or her body.

Recite—An Active Summary™

6. What is known about the origins of dissociative disorders?

Many psychologists suggest that dissociative disorders help people keep disturbing memories or ideas out of mind. These memories may involve episodes of childhood sexual or physical abuse.

7. What kinds of somatoform disorders are there?

People with somatoform disorders exhibit or complain of physical problems, although no medical evidence of such problems can be found. The somatoform disorders include conversion disorder and hypochondriasis. In conversion disorder, stress is converted into a physical symptom, and the individual may show la belle indifférence (indifference to the symptom).

8. What is known about the origins of somatoform disorders?

These disorders were once called "hysterical neuroses" and expected to be found more often among women. However, they are also found among men and may reflect the relative benefits of focusing on physical symptoms rather than fears and conflicts.

9. What kinds of mood disorders are there?

Mood disorders involve disturbances in expressed emotions. Major depression is characterized by persistent feelings of sadness, loss of interest, feelings of worthlessness or guilt, inability to concentrate, and physical symptoms that may include disturbances in regulation of eating and sleeping. Feelings of unworthiness and guilt may be so excessive that they are considered delusional. Bipolar disorder is characterized by dramatic swings in mood between elation and depression; manic episodes include pressured speech and rapid flight of ideas.

10. What is known about the origins of mood disorders?

Research emphasizes possible roles for learned helplessness, attributional styles, and underutilization of serotonin in depression. People who are depressed are more likely than other people to make internal, stable, and global attributions for failures. Genetic factors involving regulation of neurotransmitters may also be involved in mood disorders. For example, bipolar disorder has been linked to inappropriate levels of the neurotransmitter glutamate. Moreover, people with severe depression often respond to drugs that heighten the action of serotonin.

11. What is schizophrenia?

Schizophrenia is a most severe psychological disorder that is characterized by disturbances in thought and language, such as loosening of associations and delusions; in perception and attention, as found in hallucinations; in motor activity, as shown by a stupor or by excited behavior; in mood, as in flat or inappropriate emotional responses; and in social interaction, as in social withdrawal and absorption in daydreams or fantasy.

12. What kinds of schizophrenia are there?

The major types of schizophrenia are paranoid, disorganized, and catatonic. Paranoid schizophrenia is characterized largely by systematized delusions; disorganized schizophrenia by incoherence; and catatonic schizophrenia by motor impairment.

13. What is known about the origins of schizophrenia?

Schizophrenia is connected with smaller brains, especially fewer synapses in the prefrontal region, and larger ventricles in the brain. According to the multifactorial model, genetic vulnerability to schizophrenia may interact with other factors, such as stress, complications during pregnancy and childbirth, and quality of parenting, to cause the disorder to develop. According to the dopamine theory of schizophrenia, people with schizophrenia *use* more dopamine than other people do, perhaps because they have more dopamine in the brain along with more dopamine receptors than other people.

14. What kinds of personality disorders are there?

Personality disorders are inflexible, maladaptive behavior patterns that impair personal or social functioning and cause distress for the individual or others. The defining trait of paranoid personality disorder is suspiciousness. People with schizotypal personality disorders show oddities of thought, perception, and behavior. Social withdrawal is the major characteristic of schizoid personality disorder. People with antisocial personality disorders persistently violate the rights of others and are in conflict with the law. They show little or no guilt or shame over their misdeeds and are largely undeterred by punishment. People with avoidant personality disorder tend to avoid entering relationships for fear of rejection and criticism.

Recite—An Active Summary™

15. What is known about the origins of personality disorders?

Go to **http://psychology.wadsworth.com/rathus_pcc9e** to access an interactive version of this active summary.

Psychodynamic theory connected many personality disorders with hypothesized Oedipal problems. Genetic factors may be involved in some personality disorders. Antisocial personality disorder may develop from some combination of genetic vulnerability (less gray matter in the prefrontal cortex of the brain, which may provide lower-than-normal levels of arousal), inconsistent discipline, and cynical processing of social information.

Key Terms

Dissociative identity disorder (p. 516)
Multiple personality disorder (p. 516)
Insanity (p. 516)
Schizophrenia (p. 516)
Psychological disorders (p. 516)
Hallucination (p. 518)
Ideas of persecution (p. 518)
Reliability (p. 519)
Validity (p. 519)
Predictive validity (p. 519)
Specific phobia (p. 523)
Claustrophobia (p. 523)
Acrophobia (p. 523)
Social phobia (p. 524)
Agoraphobia (p. 524)
Panic disorder (p. 524)
Generalized anxiety disorder (p. 524)

Obsession (p. 524)
Compulsion (p. 524)
Posttraumatic stress disorder (PTSD) (p. 525)
Acute stress disorder (p. 525)
Concordance (p. 527)
Glutamate (p. 527)
Gamma-aminobutyric acid (GABA) (p. 527)
Benzodiazepines (p. 527)
Dissociative disorders (p. 528)
Dissociative amnesia (p. 528)
Dissociative fugue (p. 528)
Somatoform disorders (p. 530)
Conversion disorder (p. 530)
La belle indifférence (p. 531)

Hypochondriasis (p. 531)
Major depressive disorder (p. 532)
Psychomotor retardation (p. 532)
Bipolar disorder (p. 532)
Manic (p. 532)
Rapid flight of ideas (p. 533)
Learned helplessness (p. 534)
Attributional style (p. 535)
Neuroticism (p. 535)
Delusions (p. 537)
Stupor (p. 537)
Paranoid schizophrenia (p. 537)
Disorganized schizophrenia (p. 537)
Catatonic schizophrenia (p. 538)

Waxy flexibility (p. 538)
Mutism (p. 538)
Personality disorders (p. 542)
Paranoid personality disorder (p. 542)
Schizotypal personality disorder (p. 542)
Schizoid personality disorder (p. 542)
Borderline personality disorder (p. 542)
Antisocial personality disorder (p. 543)
Avoidant personality disorder (p. 543)

Active Learning Resources

Visit your Companion Website for Video and Quizzing!

http://psychology.wadsworth.com/rathus_pcc9e
On this site you can access the Schizophrenia video highlighted by the Video Connections icon on p. 539. In addition there are many quizzing opportunities including interactive versions of the fill-in-the-blank Active Review sections in your book.

Study on the Go!

Don't have time to study right now? You can study on the go! Visit your companion website and download an audio version of the Recite—An Active Summary section to your media player.

ThomsonNOW

http://www.thomsonedu.com
Need help studying? This site is your one-stop study shop. Take a Pre-Test and Thomson NOW will generate a Personalized Study Plan based on your test results. The Study Plan will identify the topics you need to review and direct you to online resources to help you master those topics. You can then take a Post-Test to determine the concepts you have mastered and what you still need to work on.

Author Blog

What does your author have to say about the state of psychology? Visit your companion website every Tuesday and click on "Author Blog," where he'll talk about the most recent controversies and hot topics in psychology.

Truth or Fiction?

T F Residents of London used to visit the local insane asylum for a fun night out on the town.

T F Some psychotherapists interpret clients' dreams.

T F Some psychotherapists let their clients take the lead in psychotherapy.

T F Other psychotherapists challenge their clients to make the tough choices in life.

T F Still other psychotherapists tell their clients exactly what to do.

T F Lying in a reclining chair and fantasizing can be an effective way of confronting fears.

T F Smoking cigarettes can be an effective method for helping people . . . stop smoking cigarettes.

T F You might be able to put an end to bad habits merely by keeping a record of where and when you practice them.

T F The same kind of drug is used to treat depression, panic disorder, obsessive–compulsive disorder, even eating disorders.

T F The originator of a surgical technique intended to reduce violence learned that it was not always successful . . . when one of his patients shot him.

T F People with psychological disorders should always say no to drugs.

 Go to **http://psychology.wadsworth.com/ rathus_pcc9e** to answer and score this Truth or Fiction quiz.

Methods of Therapy

Preview

Christian Witkin

■ **Firefighter Stephen King and Dr. JoAnn Difede, Who Treated Him with Virtual Therapy**
King was at the World Trade Center on September 11, 2001, and he developed PTSD.

Image and copyright by Hunter Hoffman, U.W. Virtual World programmed by Howard Abrams.

■ **A Program Containing Images of the World Trade Center Intended to Help People with Posttraumatic Stress Disorder, like Firefighter Stephen King**
After being exposed to virtual stimuli that represent sources of anxiety and stress, virtual-therapy clients are better able to be exposed to the actual stimuli.

Some things are too painful to bear. One of them, for New York Fire Chief Stephen King, was 9/11. His experiences at the World Trade Center that day led him to retire from the department, avoid bridges and tunnels, and stay out of Manhattan.

"I was in the north tower, the one that got hit first," King (2005) explains. "Where I was and what I saw that day—the many people that jumped, the magnitude of it—was just overwhelming." Many who witnessed the events of that day developed stress disorders.

But a new tool in the treatment of anxiety disorders, *virtual therapy,* has helped King face the past—and his future. Using the technology we find in video games, programs mimic traumatic settings and events, whether they be public speaking in an auditorium, flying in an airplane, spiders, or, in King's case, images of the World Trade Center.

JoAnn Difede, director of Anxiety and Traumatic Stress Studies Program at Weill Cornell Medical College, is using virtual therapy to help World Trade Center survivors cope with their memories (Difede & Hoffman, 2002). "The idea," Difede (2005) explains, "behind the treatment is to systematically expose the patient to aspects of their experience in a graded fashion so they can confront their fear of the trauma."

University of Southern California psychologist Albert Rizzo has developed scenes from classrooms and parties to help people overcome social anxieties. " 'To help people deal with their problems, you must get them exposed to what they fear most," Rizzo notes (Rizzo & Schultheis, 2002).

Drs. Difede and Rizzo use programs like 3D Studio MAX and DeepPaint to create the necessary software. Atlanta-based company Virtually Better has developed scenes of a bridge and a glass elevator to desensitize patients to fear of heights, a virtual airplane cabin for people who fear flying, and a virtual thunderstorm to help people lessen fear of tempestuous weather. The U.S. Army has asked Virtually Better to use its 3D imaging software to create programs that will help soldiers returning from Iraq and Afghanistan.

Virtually Better is working on programs to help treat addictions. Psychologists are studying whether virtual exposure to alcohol, drugs, and cigarettes can evoke cravings that patients can learn to resist. Virtually Better's contributions include scenes of a virtual crack house and a virtual bar.

Virtual therapy was also used to help desensitize Joanne Cartwright, who had a fear of spiders that impaired the quality of her life. "I washed my truck every night before I went to work in case there were webs," says Cartwright (cited in Robbins, 2000). "I put all my clothes in plastic bags and taped duct tape around my doors so spiders couldn't get in. I thought I was going to have a mental breakdown. I wasn't living." Twelve virtual therapy desensitization sessions changed her life. "I'm amazed," notes Cartwright, "because I am doing all this stuff I could never do," such as camping and hiking.

Writing in *Scientific American,* psychologist Hunter Hoffman (2004) describes an elaborate virtual environment called *SpiderWorld* that helps people with spider phobias overcome their aversion by gradually approaching virtual spiders and reaching out to touch them. A toy spider and a device that tracks the patient's hand movements provide tactile sensations akin to touching a real spider. Virtual immersion in *SpiderWorld* and similar virtual environments has also helped people cope with pain by distracting them from it.

Chief Stephen King received virtual therapy to learn to cope with his traumatic experience at the World Trade Center. If he had chosen a different kind of therapist, he might have been:

◆ Lying on a couch, talking about anything that popped into awareness, and exploring the possible meaning of his recurrent dreams.

◆ Sitting face to face with a warm, gentle therapist who expressed faith in King's ability to manage his problems.

◆ Listening to a frank, straightforward therapist assert that King was compounding his emotional problems and demanding that he be "man enough" to face the trauma of 9/11 and just move on.

◆ Taking medication.

◆ Participating in some combination of these approaches.

These methods, although different, all represent methods of therapy. In this chapter we explore various methods of psychotherapy and biological therapy. **Question: What is psychotherapy?**

■ **Dr. Hunter Hoffman of the University of Washington Uses Virtual Therapy to Treat "Miss Muffet"**
Miss Muffet is the name playfully given by Hoffman to a woman with a phobia for spiders. She is wearing virtual-reality headgear and sees the scene displayed on the monitor, which shows a large and hairy—but virtual—tarantula.

What Is Psychotherapy?

There are many kinds of psychotherapy, but they all have certain common characteristics. **Psychotherapy** is a systematic interaction between a therapist and a client that applies psychological principles to affect the client's thoughts, feelings, or behavior in order to help the client overcome psychological disorders, adjust to problems in living, or develop as an individual.

Quite a mouthful? True. But note the essentials:

1. *Systematic interaction.* Psychotherapy is a systematic interaction between a client and a therapist. The therapist's theoretical point of view interacts with the client's to determine how the therapist and client relate to each other.

2. *Psychological principles.* Psychotherapy is based on psychological theory and research in areas such as personality, learning, motivation, and emotion.

3. *Thoughts, feelings, and behavior.* Psychotherapy influences clients' thoughts, feelings, and behavior. It can be aimed at any or all of these aspects of human psychology.

4. *Psychological disorders, adjustment problems, and personal growth.* Psychotherapy is often used with people who have psychological disorders. Other people seek help in adjusting to problems such as shyness, weight problems, or loss of a life partner. Still other clients want to learn more about themselves and to reach their full potential as individuals, parents, or creative artists.

The History of Therapies

Historically speaking, "treatments" of psychological disorders often reflected the assumption that people who behaved in strange ways were possessed by demons. **Question: How, then, have people with psychological problems and disorders been treated throughout the ages?** Because of this belief, treatment tended to involve cruel practices such as exorcism and execution. Some people who could not meet the demands of everyday life were tossed into prisons. Others begged in the streets, stole food, or became prostitutes. A few found their way to monasteries or other retreats that offered a kind word and some support. Generally speaking, they died early.

Psychotherapy A systematic interaction between a therapist and a client that brings psychological principles to bear on influencing the client's thoughts, feelings, or behavior to help that client overcome abnormal behavior or adjust to problems in living.

Asylum (uh-SIGH-lum). An institution for the care of the mentally ill.

ASYLUMS Asylums originated in European monasteries. They were the first institutions meant primarily for people with psychological disorders. But their function was warehousing, not treatment. Their inmate populations mushroomed until the stresses created by noise, overcrowding, and disease aggravated the problems they were meant to ease. Inmates were frequently chained and beaten.

The word *bedlam* derives from St. Mary's of *Bethlehem,* the London asylum that opened its gates in 1547. Here unfortunate people with psychological disorders were chained, whipped, and allowed to lie in their own waste. **Truth or Fiction Revisited:** And here the ladies and gentlemen of the British upper class might stroll on a lazy afternoon to be amused by inmates' antics. The price of admission was one penny.

Humanitarian reform movements began in the 18th century. In Paris, the physician Philippe Pinel unchained the patients at La Bicêtre. Rather than run amok, as had been feared, most patients profited from kindness and freedom. Many eventually reentered society. Later movements to reform institutions were led by William Tuke in England and Dorothea Dix in America.

MENTAL HOSPITALS In the United States mental hospitals gradually replaced asylums. In the mid-1950s more than a million people resided in state, county, Veterans Administration, or private facilities. The mental hospital's function is treatment, not warehousing. Still, because of high patient populations and understaffing, many patients received little attention. Even today, with somewhat improved conditions, one psychiatrist may be responsible for the welfare of several hundred residents on the weekend when other staff members are absent.

THE COMMUNITY MENTAL HEALTH MOVEMENT Since the 1960s, efforts have been made to maintain people with serious psychological disorders in their communities. Community mental health centers attempt to maintain new patients as outpatients and to serve patients who have been released from mental hospitals. Today most people with chronic psychological disorders live in the community, not the hospital. Social critics note that many people who had resided in hospitals for decades were suddenly discharged to "home" communities that seemed foreign and forbidding to them. Many do not receive adequate follow-up care. Many join the ranks of the homeless (Drury, 2003).

Your Turn: Now that we have defined psychotherapy, enhance your mastery of the material with the nearby "Learning Connections." Review the material by filling in the blanks, reflect on the material by relating it to other things you know, and think critically about it.

Learning Connections · WHAT IS THERAPY? THE SEARCH FOR A "SWEET OBLIVIOUS ANTIDOTE"

ACTIVE REVIEW (1) Psychotherapy is a systematic interaction between a therapist and a client that applies _____ principles to influence clients' thoughts, feelings, or behavior. (2) Historic treatments of psychological disorders were based on the demonological model and included the _____ of evil spirits.

REFLECT AND RELATE Before you get deeper into the chapter, consider what you think happens in psychotherapy. Then ask yourself whether your ideas actually fit one or more of the kinds of therapy you will be reading about.

CRITICAL THINKING At the beginning of the chapter, we described four different approaches to treating Jasmine's depression. Does one of these approaches seem to you to be more effective or more scientific than the others? Explain.

Go to **http://psychology.wadsworth.com/ rathus_pcc9e** for an interactive version of this Learning Connections unit.

Psychodynamic Therapies: Digging Deep Within

Psychodynamic therapies are based on the thinking of Sigmund Freud, the founder of psychodynamic theory. They assume that psychological problems reflect early childhood experiences and internal conflicts. According to Freud, these conflicts involve the shifting of psychic, or libidinal, energy among the three psychic structures—the id, ego, and superego. These shifts of psychic energy determine our behavior. When primitive urges threaten to break through from the id or when the superego floods us with excessive guilt, defenses are established and distress is created. Freud's psychodynamic therapy method—psychoanalysis—aims to modify the flow of energy among these structures, largely to bulwark the ego against the torrents of energy loosed by the id and the superego. With impulses and feelings of guilt and shame placed under greater control, clients are freer to develop adaptive behavior. **Question: How, then, do psychoanalysts conduct a traditional Freudian psychoanalysis?**

Traditional Psychoanalysis: "Where Id Was, There Shall Ego Be"

> *Canst thou not minister to a mind diseas'd,*
> *Pluck out from the memory a rooted sorrow,*
> *Raze out the written troubles of the brain,*
> *And with some sweet oblivious antidote*
> *Cleanse the stuff'd bosom of that perilous stuff*
> *Which weighs upon the heart?*
>
> Shakespeare, *Macbeth*

In this passage, Macbeth asks a physician to help Lady Macbeth after she has gone mad. In the play, her madness is caused partly by events—namely, her role in murders designed to seat her husband on the throne of Scotland. There are also hints of mysterious, deeply rooted problems, such as conflicts about infertility.

If Lady Macbeth's physician had been a traditional psychoanalyst, he might have asked her to lie on a couch in a slightly darkened room. He would have sat behind her and encouraged her to talk about anything that came to mind, no matter how trivial, no matter how personal. To avoid interfering with her self-exploration, he might have said little or nothing for session after session. That would have been par for the course. A traditional **psychoanalysis** can extend for months, even years.

Psychoanalysis is the clinical method devised by Freud for plucking "from the memory a rooted sorrow," for razing "out the written troubles of the brain." It aims to provide *insight* into the conflicts that are presumed to lie at the roots of a person's problems. Insight means many things, including knowledge of the experiences that lead to conflicts and maladaptive behavior, recognition of unconscious feelings and conflicts, and conscious evaluation of one's thoughts, feelings, and behavior.

Psychoanalysis also aims to help the client express feelings and urges that have been repressed. By so doing, Freud believed that the client spilled forth the psychic energy that had been repressed by conflicts and guilt. He called this spilling forth **catharsis.** Catharsis would provide relief by alleviating some of the forces assaulting the ego.

Freud was also fond of saying, "Where id was, there shall ego be." In part, he meant that psychoanalysis could shed light on the inner workings of the mind. He also sought to replace impulsive and defensive behavior with coping behavior. In this way, for example, a man with a phobia for knives might discover that he had been repressing the urge to harm someone who had taken advantage of him. He might also find ways to confront the person verbally.

FREE ASSOCIATION Early in his career as a therapist, Freud found that hypnosis allowed his clients to focus on repressed conflicts and talk about them. The relaxed "trance state" provided by hypnosis seemed to allow clients to "break through" to

Psychoanalysis Freud's method of psychotherapy.

Catharsis (cuh-THAR-sis) In psychoanalysis, the expression of repressed feelings and impulses to allow the release of the psychic energy associated with them.

Free association In psychoanalysis, the uncensored uttering of all thoughts that come to mind.

Resistance The tendency to block the free expression of impulses and primitive ideas—a reflection of the defense mechanism of repression.

Interpretation An explanation of a client's utterance according to psychoanalytic theory.

Transference Responding to one person (such as a spouse or the psychoanalyst) in a way that is similar to the way one responded to another person (such as a parent) in childhood.

topics of which they would otherwise be unaware. Freud also found, however, that many clients denied the accuracy of this material once they were out of the trance. Other clients found them to be premature and painful. Freud therefore turned to **free association,** a more gradual method of breaking through the walls of defense that block a client's insight into unconscious processes.

In free association, the client is made comfortable—for example, lying on a couch—and asked to talk about any topic that comes to mind. No thought is to be censored—that is the basic rule. Psychoanalysts ask their clients to wander "freely" from topic to topic, but they do not believe that the process occurring *within* the client is fully free. Repressed impulses clamor for release.

The ego persists in trying to repress unacceptable impulses and threatening conflicts. As a result, clients might show **resistance** to recalling and discussing threatening ideas. A client about to entertain such thoughts might claim, "My mind is blank." The client might accuse the analyst of being demanding or inconsiderate. He or she might "forget" the next appointment when threatening material is about to surface.

The therapist observes the dynamic struggle between the compulsion to utter certain thoughts and the client's resistance to uttering them. Through discreet remarks, the analyst subtly tips the balance in favor of utterance. A gradual process of self-discovery and self-insight ensues. Now and then the analyst offers an **interpretation** of an utterance, showing how it suggests resistance or deep-seated feelings and conflicts.

TRANSFERENCE Freud believed that clients not only responded to him as an individual but also in ways that reflected their attitudes and feelings toward other people in their lives. He labeled this process **transference.** For example, a young woman client might respond to him as a father figure and displace her feelings toward her father onto Freud, perhaps seeking affection and wisdom. A young man could also see Freud as a father figure, but rather than wanting affection from Freud, he might view Freud as a rival, responding to Freud in terms of his own unresolved Oedipal complex.

Analyzing and working through transference has been considered a key aspect of psychoanalysis. Freud believed that clients reenact their childhood conflicts with their parents when they are in therapy. Clients might thus transfer the feelings of anger, love, or jealousy they felt toward their own parents onto the analyst.

■ **A View of Freud's Consulting Room** Freud would sit in a chair by the head of the couch while a client free-associated. The basic rule of free association is that no thought is censored. Freud did not believe that free association was really "free"; he assumed that significant feelings would rise to the surface and demand expression.

© Freud Museum, London

Childhood conflicts often involve unresolved feelings of love, anger, or rejection. A client may interpret a suggestion by the therapist as a criticism and see it as a devastating blow, transferring feelings of self-hatred that he had repressed because his parents had rejected him in childhood. Transference can also distort clients' relationships with other people here and now, such as relationships with spouses or employers. The following therapeutic dialogue illustrates the way in which an analyst may interpret a client's inability to communicate his needs to his wife as a function of transference. The purpose is to provide his client, a Mr. Arianes, with insight into how his relationship with his wife has been colored by his childhood relationship with his mother:

Arianes:	I think you've got it there, Doc. We weren't communicating. I wouldn't tell [my wife] what was wrong or what I wanted from her. Maybe I expected her to understand me without saying anything.
Therapist:	Like the expectations a child has of its mother.
Arianes:	Not my mother!
Therapist:	Oh?
Arianes:	No, I always thought she had too many troubles of her own to pay attention to mine. I remember once I got hurt on my bike and came to her all bloodied up. When she saw me she got mad and yelled at me for making more trouble for her when she already had her hands full with my father.
Therapist:	Do you remember how you felt then?
Arianes:	I can't remember, but I know that after that I never brought my troubles to her again.
Therapist:	How old were you?
Arianes:	Nine, I know that because I got that bike for my ninth birthday. It was a little too big for me still, that's why I got hurt on it.
Therapist:	Perhaps you carried this attitude into your marriage.
Arianes:	What attitude?
Therapist:	The feeling that your wife, like your mother, would be unsympathetic to your difficulties. That there was no point in telling her about your experiences because she was too preoccupied or too busy to care.
Arianes:	But she's so different from my mother. I come first with her.
Therapist:	On one level you know that. On another, deeper level there may well be the fear that people—or maybe only women, or maybe only women you're close to—are all the same, and you can't take a chance at being rejected again in your need.
Arianes:	Maybe you're right, Doc, but all that was so long ago, and I should be over that by now.
Therapist:	That's not the way the mind works. If a shock, or a disappointment is strong enough it can permanently freeze our picture of ourselves and our expectations of the world. The rest of us grows up—that is, we let ourselves learn about life from experience and from what we see, hear, or read of the experiences of others, but that one area where we really got hurt stays unchanged. So what I mean when I say you might be carrying that attitude into your relationship with your wife is that when it comes to your hopes of being understood and catered to when you feel hurt or abused by life, you still feel very much like that nine-year-old boy who was rebuffed in his need and gave up hope that anyone would or could respond to him. (Basch, 1980, pp. 29–30)

DREAM ANALYSIS **Truth or Fiction Revisited:** It is true that some therapists interpret clients' dreams. Freud often asked clients to jot down their dreams upon waking so that they could discuss them in therapy. Freud considered dreams the "royal road to the unconscious." He believed that the content of dreams is determined by unconscious processes as well as by the events of the day. Unconscious impulses tend to be expressed in dreams as a form of **wish fulfillment.**

But unacceptable sexual and aggressive impulses are likely to be displaced onto objects and situations that reflect the client's era and culture. These objects become

Wish fulfillment A primitive method used by the id to attempt to gratify basic instincts.

Phallic symbol A sign that represents the penis.

Manifest content In psychodynamic theory, the reported content of dreams.

Latent content In psychodynamic theory, the symbolized or underlying content of dreams.

Ego analyst A psychodynamically oriented therapist who focuses on the conscious, coping behavior of the ego instead of the hypothesized, unconscious functioning of the id.

symbols of unconscious wishes. For example, long, narrow dream objects might be **phallic symbols,** but whether the symbol takes the form of a spear, rifle, stick shift, or spacecraft partially reflects the dreamer's cultural background.

In Freud's theory, the perceived content of a dream is called its visible, or **manifest content.** Its presumed hidden or symbolic content is its **latent content.** If a man dreams he is flying, flying is the manifest content of the dream. Freud usually interpreted flying as symbolic of erection, so concerns about sexual potency might make up the latent content of the dream.

Modern Psychodynamic Approaches

Some psychoanalysts adhere faithfully to Freud's techniques. They engage in protracted therapy that continues to rely heavily on free association, interpretation of dreams, and other traditional methods. In recent years, however, more modern forms of psychodynamic therapy have been devised. **Question: How do modern psychodynamic approaches differ from traditional psychoanalysis?** Modern psychodynamic therapy is briefer and less intense and makes treatment available to clients who do not have the time or money for long-term therapy. Many modern psychodynamic therapists do not believe that prolonged therapy is needed or justifiable in terms of the ratio of cost to benefits.

Some modern psychodynamic therapies continue to focus on revealing unconscious material and breaking through psychological defenses. Nevertheless, they differ from traditional psychoanalysis in several ways (Prochaska & Norcross, 2003). One is that the client and therapist usually sit face to face (the client does not lie on a couch). The therapist is usually directive. That is, modern therapists often suggest helpful behavior instead of focusing on insight alone. Finally, there is usually more focus on the ego as the "executive" of personality and less emphasis on the id. For this reason, many modern psychodynamic therapists are considered **ego analysts.**

Many of Freud's followers, the "second generation" of psychoanalysts—from Jung and Adler to Horney and Erikson—believed that Freud had placed too much emphasis on sexual and aggressive impulses and underestimated the role of the ego. For example, Freud aimed to establish conditions under which clients could spill forth psychic energy and eventually shore up the ego. Erikson, in contrast, spoke to clients directly about their values and concerns, encouraging them to develop desired traits and behavior patterns. Even Freud's daughter, the psychoanalyst Anna Freud (1895–1982), was more concerned with the ego than with unconscious forces and conflicts.

Your Turn: Now that we have discussed psychodynamic therapies, enhance your mastery of the material with the nearby "Learning Connections." Review the material by filling in the blanks, reflect on the material by relating it to other things you know, and think critically about it.

Learning Connections — PSYCHODYNAMIC THERAPIES: DIGGING DEEP WITHIN

ACTIVE REVIEW (3) Freud's method of psychoanalysis attempts to shed light on _____ conflicts that are presumed to lie at the roots of clients' problems. (4) Freud believed that psychoanalysis would promote _____, that is, the spilling forth of repressed psychic energy. (5) The chief psychoanalytic method is _____ association. (6) Freud considered _____ to be the "royal road to the unconscious."

REFLECT AND RELATE Does it make you or other people you know feel good to talk with someone about your problems? Are there some "deep secrets" you are unwilling to talk about or share with others? How do you think a psychoanalyst would respond if you brought them up? Why?

CRITICAL THINKING Are "modern" psychoanalytic approaches psychodynamic? Do "Freudians" have a "right" to use different techniques?

Go to **http://psychology.wadsworth.com/ rathus_pcc9e** for an interactive version of this Learning Connections unit.

Humanistic Therapies: Strengthening the Self

Psychodynamic therapies focus on internal conflicts and unconscious processes. Humanistic therapies focus on the quality of the client's subjective, conscious experience (Cain & Seeman, 2002). Traditional psychoanalysis focuses on early childhood experiences. Humanistic therapies usually focus on what clients are experiencing "here and now."

These differences, however, are mainly a matter of emphasis. The past has a way of influencing current thoughts, feelings, and behavior. Carl Rogers, the originator of client-centered therapy, believed that childhood experiences gave rise to the conditions of worth that troubled his clients here and now. He and Fritz Perls, the originator of Gestalt therapy, recognized that early incorporation of other people's values often leads clients to "disown" parts of their own personalities.

Client-Centered Therapy: Removing Roadblocks to Self-Actualization

Question: What is Carl Rogers's method of client-centered therapy? Rogers believed that we are free to make choices and control our destinies, despite the burdens of the past. He also believed that we have natural tendencies toward health, growth, and fulfillment. Psychological problems arise from roadblocks placed in the path of self-actualization—that is, what Rogers believed was an inborn tendency to strive to realize one's potential. If, when we are young, other people only approve of us when we are doing what they want us to do, we may learn to disown the parts of ourselves to which they object. We may learn to be seen but not heard—not even by ourselves. As a result, we may experience stress and discomfort and the feeling that we—or the world—are not real.

In Profile CARL ROGERS

© Bettman/CORBIS

He spent his early years in a wealthy Chicago suburb, where he attended school with Ernest Hemingway and Frank Lloyd Wright's children. His family, with its six children, was religious and close-knit. His father viewed such activities as smoking, drinking, playing cards, and going to the movies as questionable. It was all right to be tolerant of them, but relationships with those who engaged in them were discouraged. When Carl Rogers was 12, his family moved to a farm farther from the city to protect the children from such unwholesome influences.

Rogers (1902–1987) took refuge in books and developed an interest in science. His first college major was agriculture. During a student visit to Peking in 1922, he was exposed for the first time to people from different ethnic backgrounds. He wrote his parents to proclaim his independence from their conservative views. Shortly thereafter he developed an ulcer and had to be hospitalized.

Rogers then attended New York's Union Theological Seminary with the goal of becoming a minister. At the same time he took courses in psychology and education across the street at Columbia University. After a couple of years he came to believe that psychology might be a better way of helping people, so he transferred to Columbia. Perhaps in response to his parents' efforts to "protect" him from other ways of thinking, Rogers developed a form of therapy—client-centered therapy—intended to help people get in touch with their genuine feelings and pursue their own interests, regardless of other people's wishes.

Go to **http://psychology.wadsworth.com/ rathus_pcc9e** to access more information about Carl Rogers.

Client-centered therapy aims to provide insight into the parts of us that we have disowned so that we can feel whole. It creates a warm, therapeutic atmosphere that encourages self-exploration and self-expression. The therapist's acceptance of the client is thought to foster self-acceptance and self-esteem. Self-acceptance frees the client to make choices that develop his or her unique potential.

Client-centered therapy is nondirective. **Truth or Fiction Revisited:** It is true that the client takes the lead, stating and exploring problems. An effective client-centered therapist has several qualities:

◆ **Unconditional positive regard:** Respect for clients as human beings with unique values and goals.

Client-centered therapy Carl Rogers's method of psychotherapy, which emphasizes the creation of a warm, therapeutic atmosphere that frees clients to engage in self-exploration and self-expression.

Unconditional positive regard Acceptance of the value of another person, although not necessarily acceptance of everything the person does.

■ **Client-Centered Therapy** By showing the qualities of unconditional positive regard, empathic understanding, genuineness, and congruence, client-centered therapists create an atmosphere in which clients can explore their feelings.

◆ *Empathic understanding:* Recognition of the client's experiences and feelings. Therapists view the world through the client's **frame of reference** by setting aside their own values and listening closely.

◆ *Genuineness:* Openness and honesty in responding to the client. Client-centered therapists must be able to tolerate differentness because they believe that every client is different in important ways.

The following excerpt from a therapy session shows how Carl Rogers uses empathetic understanding and paraphrases a client's (Jill's) feelings. His goal is to help her recognize feelings that she has partially disowned:

Jill:	I'm having a lot of problems dealing with my daughter. She's 20 years old; she's in college; I'm having a lot of trouble letting her go. . . . And I have a lot of guilt feelings about her; I have a real need to hang on to her.
C.R.:	A need to hang on so you can kind of make up for the things you feel guilty about. Is that part of it?
Jill:	There's a lot of that. . . . Also, she's been a real friend to me, and filled my life. . . . And it's very hard. . . . a lot of empty places now that she's not with me.
C.R.:	The old vacuum, sort of, when she's not there.
Jill:	Yes. Yes. I also would like to be the kind of mother that could be strong and say, you know, "Go and have a good life," and this is really hard for me, to do that.
C.R.:	It's very hard to give up something that's been so precious in your life, but also something that I guess has caused you pain when you mentioned guilt.
Jill:	Yeah. And I'm aware that I have some anger toward her that I don't always get what I want. I have needs that are not met. And, uh, I don't feel I have a right to those needs. You know. . . . she's a daughter; she's not my mother. Though sometimes I feel as if I'd like her to mother me . . . it's very difficult for me to ask for that and have a right to it.
C.R.:	So, it may be unreasonable, but still, when she doesn't meet your needs, it makes you mad.
Jill:	Yeah I get very angry, very angry with her.
C.R.:	*(Pauses)* You're also feeling a little tension at this point, I guess.
Jill:	Yeah. Yeah. A lot of conflict. . . . (C.R.: M-hm.) A lot of pain.
C.R:	A lot of pain. Can you say anything more about what that's about? (Farber et al., 1996, pp. 74–75)

Empathic understanding (em-PATH-ick). Ability to perceive a client's feelings from the client's frame of reference. A quality of the good client-centered therapist.

Frame of reference One's unique patterning of perceptions and attitudes, according to which one evaluates events.

Genuineness Recognition and open expression of the therapist's own feelings.

Client-centered therapy is practiced widely in college and university counseling centers, not just to help students experiencing, say, anxieties or depression but also to help them make decisions. Many college students have not yet made career

© Stephen Frisch/Stock Boston, LLC

choices or wonder whether they should become involved with particular people or in sexual activity. Client-centered therapists do not tell clients what to do. Instead, they help clients arrive at their own decisions.

Gestalt Therapy: Getting It Together

Gestalt therapy was originated by Fritz Perls (1893–1970). **Question: What is Fritz Perls's method of Gestalt therapy?** Like client-centered therapy, Gestalt therapy assumes that people disown parts of themselves that might meet with social disapproval or rejection. People also don social masks, pretending to be things that they are not. Therapy aims to help individuals integrate conflicting parts of their personality. Perls used the term *Gestalt* to signify his interest in giving the conflicting parts of the personality an integrated form or shape. He aimed to have his clients become aware of inner conflict, accept the reality of conflict rather than deny it or keep it repressed, and make productive choices despite misgivings and fears. **Truth or Fiction Revisited:** People in conflict frequently find it difficult to make choices, and Perls firmly challenged them to do so.

Although Perls's ideas about conflicting personality elements owe much to psychodynamic theory, his form of therapy, unlike psychoanalysis, focuses on the here and now. In Gestalt therapy, clients perform exercises to heighten their awareness of their current feelings and behavior, rather than exploring the past. Perls also believed, along with Rogers, that people are free to make choices and to direct their personal growth. But the charismatic and forceful Perls was unlike the gentle and accepting Rogers in temperament (Prochaska & Norcross, 2003). Thus, unlike client-centered therapy, Gestalt therapy is highly directive. The therapist leads the client through planned experiences.

There are a number of Gestalt exercises and games, including the following:

1. *The dialogue:* In this game, the client undertakes verbal confrontations between opposing wishes and ideas to heighten awareness of internal conflict. An example of these clashing personality elements is "top dog" and "underdog." One's top dog might conservatively suggest, "Don't take chances. Stick with what you have or you might lose it all." One's frustrated underdog might then rise up and assert, "You never try anything. How will you ever get out of this rut if you don't take on new challenges?" Heightened awareness of the elements of conflict can clear the path toward resolution, perhaps through a compromise of some kind.

2. *I take responsibility:* Clients end statements about themselves by adding, "and I take responsibility for it."

3. *Playing the projection:* Clients role-play people with whom they are in conflict, expressing, for example, the ideas of their parents.

Body language also provides insight into conflicting feelings. Clients might be instructed to attend to the ways in which they furrow their eyebrows and tense their facial muscles when they express certain ideas. In this way, they often find that their body language asserts feelings they have been denying in their spoken statements.

The following excerpt from a therapy session with a client named Max shows how Perls would make clients take responsibility for what they experience. One of his techniques is to show how clients are treating something they are doing (a "verb") like something that is just out there and beyond their control (a "noun"):

Max: I feel the tenseness in my stomach and in my hands.
Perls: *The* tenseness. Here we've got a noun. Now *the* tenseness is a noun. Now change the noun, the thing, into a verb.
Max: I am tense. My hands are tense.
Perls: Your hands are tense. They have nothing to do with you.

■ **Fritz Perls** Known to friends, clients, and peers alike as "Fritz," Perls put clients through structured experiences to help them understand how their feelings might be in conflict. He believed that people had to accept responsibility for making choices in their lives.

Gestalt therapy Fritz Perls's form of psychotherapy, which attempts to integrate conflicting parts of the personality through directive methods designed to help clients perceive their whole selves.

Max:	I am tense.
Perls:	You are tense. How are you tense? What are you doing?
Max:	I am tensing myself.
Perls:	That's it. (Perls, 1971, p. 115)

Once Max understands that he is tensing himself and takes responsibility for it, he can choose to stop tensing himself. The tenseness is no longer something out there that is victimizing him; it is something he is doing to himself.

Psychodynamic theory views dreams as the "royal road to the unconscious." Perls saw the content of dreams as representing disowned parts of the personality. Perls would often ask clients to role-play elements of their dreams in order to get in touch with these parts of their personality.

Your Turn: Now that we have discussed humanistic therapies, enhance your mastery of the material with the nearby "Learning Connections." Review the material by filling in the blanks, reflect on the material by relating it to other things you know, and think critically about it.

 Learning Connections | **HUMANISTIC THERAPIES: STRENGTHENING THE SELF**

ACTIVE REVIEW (7) _____ therapies focus on clients' subjective, conscious experience. (8) Client-centered therapy is a (*Directive* or *Nondirective?*) method that provides clients with an accepting atmosphere that enables them to overcome roadblocks to self-actualization. (9) The client-centered therapist shows (*Conditional* or *Unconditional?*) positive regard, empathetic understanding, and genuineness. (10) Gestalt therapy provides (*Directive* or *Nondirective?*) methods that are designed to help clients accept responsibility and integrate conflicting parts of the personality.

REFLECT AND RELATE Carl Rogers believed that our psychological well-being is connected with our freedom to develop our unique frames of reference and potentials. Do you think you can separate your "real self" from your sociocultural experiences and religious training? What would you be like if you had been reared by other people in another place?

CRITICAL THINKING Why are the therapies of Rogers and Perls placed in the same category? What do they have in common? How do they differ?

 Go to **http://psychology.wadsworth.com/ rathus_pcc9e** for an interactive version of this Learning Connections unit.

Behavior Therapy: Adjustment Is What You Do

Psychodynamic and humanistic forms of therapy tend to focus on what people think and feel. Behavior therapists tend to focus on what people do. **Question: What is behavior therapy? Behavior therapy**—also called *behavior modification*—applies principles of learning to directly promote desired behavioral changes (Rachman, 2000). Behavior therapists rely heavily on principles of conditioning and observational learning. They help clients discontinue self-defeating behavior patterns such as overeating, smoking, and phobic avoidance of harmless stimuli. They also help clients acquire adaptive behavior patterns such as the social skills required to start social relationships or say no to insistent salespeople. **Truth or Fiction Revisited:** In both cases, they may use specific procedures—telling their clients what to do.

Behavior therapists may help clients gain "insight" into maladaptive behavior in the sense of fostering awareness of the circumstances in which it occurs. They do not foster insight in the psychoanalytic sense of unearthing the childhood origins of problems and the symbolic meanings of maladaptive behavior. Behavior therapists, like other therapists, may also build warm, therapeutic relationships with clients, but they see the efficacy of behavior therapy as deriving from specific, learning-based procedures (Rachman, 2000). They insist that their methods be established by experimentation and that the outcomes be assessed in terms of

Behavior therapy Systematic application of the principles of learning to the direct modification of a client's problem behaviors.

measurable behavior. In this section we consider some frequently used behavior-therapy techniques.

Fear-Reduction Methods

Many people seek therapy because of fears and phobias that interfere with their functioning. This is one of the areas in which behavior therapy has made great inroads. **Question: What are some behavior-therapy methods for reducing fears?** These include flooding (see Chapter 6), systematic desensitization, and modeling.

SYSTEMATIC DESENSITIZATION Adam has a phobia for receiving injections. His behavior therapist treats him as he reclines in a comfortable padded chair. In a state of deep muscle relaxation, Adam observes slides projected on a screen. A slide of a nurse holding a needle has just been shown three times, 30 seconds at a time. Each time Adam has shown no anxiety. So now a slightly more discomforting slide is shown: one of the nurse aiming the needle toward someone's bare arm. After 15 seconds, our armchair adventurer notices twinges of discomfort and raises a finger as a signal (speaking might disturb his relaxation). The projector operator turns off the light, and Adam spends 2 minutes imagining his "safe scene"—lying on a beach beneath the tropical sun. Then the slide is shown again. This time Adam views it for 30 seconds before feeling anxiety.

Truth or Fiction Revisited: Adam is in effect confronting his fear while lying in a recliner and relaxing. Adam is undergoing **systematic desensitization,** a method for reducing phobic responses originated by psychiatrist Joseph Wolpe (1915–1997). Systematic desensitization is a gradual process in which the client learns to handle increasingly disturbing stimuli while anxiety to each one is being counterconditioned. About 10 to 20 stimuli are arranged in a sequence, or **hierarchy,** according to their capacity to elicit anxiety. In imagination or by being shown photos, the client travels gradually up through this hierarchy, approaching the target behavior. In Adam's case, the target behavior was the ability to receive an injection without undue anxiety.

Wolpe developed systematic desensitization on the assumption that anxiety responses, like other behaviors, are learned or conditioned (Rachman, 2000). He reasoned that they can be unlearned by means of counterconditioning or extinction. In counterconditioning, a response that is incompatible with anxiety is made to appear under conditions that usually elicit anxiety. Muscle relaxation is incompatible with

Systematic desensitization Wolpe's method for reducing fears by associating a hierarchy of images of fear-evoking stimuli with deep muscle relaxation.

Hierarchy An arrangement of stimuli according to the amount of fear they evoke.

 Use your *Connections* CD-ROM to access an animation about the behavioral treatment of phobias.

■ **Overcoming Fear of Flying** One way behavior therapists help clients overcome phobias is by having them gradually approach the feared object or situation while they remain relaxed. This woman is gradually reducing her fear of being in an airplane and flying.

Modeling A behavior-therapy technique in which a client observes and imitates a person who approaches and copes with feared objects or situations.

Aversive conditioning A behavior-therapy technique in which undesired responses are inhibited by pairing repugnant or offensive stimuli with them.

Rapid smoking An aversive conditioning method for quitting smoking in which the smoker inhales every 6 seconds, thus rendering once-desirable cigarette smoke aversive.

anxiety. For this reason, Adam's therapist is teaching him to relax in the presence of (usually) anxiety-evoking slides of needles.

Remaining in the presence of phobic imagery, rather than running away from it, is also likely to enhance self-efficacy expectations (Galassi, 1988). Self-efficacy expectations are negatively correlated with levels of adrenaline in the bloodstream (Bandura et al., 1985). Raising clients' self-efficacy expectations thus may help lower their adrenaline levels and reduce their feelings of nervousness.

MODELING **Modeling** relies on observational learning. In this method clients observe, and then imitate, people who approach and cope with the objects or situations that the clients fear. Bandura and his colleagues (1969) found that modeling worked as well as systematic desensitization—and more rapidly—in reducing fear of snakes. Like systematic desensitization, modeling is likely to increase self-efficacy expectations in coping with feared stimuli.

Aversive Conditioning

Many people also seek behavior therapy because they want to break bad habits, such as smoking, excessive drinking, nail biting, and the like. One behavior-therapy approach to helping people do so is **aversive conditioning. Question: How do behavior therapists use aversive conditioning to help people break bad habits?** Aversive conditioning is a controversial procedure in which painful or aversive stimuli are paired with unwanted impulses, such as desire for a cigarette or desire to engage in antisocial behavior, in order to make the impulse less appealing. For example, to help people control alcohol intake, tastes of different alcoholic beverages can be paired with drug-induced nausea and vomiting or with electric shock.

Aversive conditioning has been used with problems as diverse as cigarette smoking, sexual abuse, and retarded children's self-injurious behavior. **Rapid smoking** is an aversive-conditioning method designed to help smokers quit. In this method, the would-be quitter inhales every 6 seconds. In another method the hose of a hair dryer is hooked up to a chamber containing several lit cigarettes. Smoke is blown into the quitter's face as he or she also smokes a cigarette. A third method uses branching pipes so that the smoker draws in smoke from several cigarettes at the same time. In

■ **Getting Some Help from the Situation**
Principles of operant conditioning suggest that we can improve our study habits by building the amount of time we study gradually and placing ourselves in situations in which there are few distractions.

Royalty-Free/CORBIS

these methods, overexposure makes once-desirable cigarette smoke aversive. The quitter becomes motivated to avoid, rather than seek, cigarettes. **Truth or Fiction Revisited:** Therefore, smoking can be a way to stop smoking. However, interest in aversive conditioning for quitting smoking has waned because of side effects such as raising blood pressure and the availability of nicotine-replacement techniques.

In one study of aversive conditioning in the treatment of alcoholism, 63% of the 685 people treated remained abstinent for one year afterward, and about a third remained abstinent for at least 3 years (Wiens & Menustik, 1983). It may seem ironic that punitive aversive stimulation is sometimes used to stop children from punishing themselves, but people sometimes hurt themselves in order to obtain sympathy and attention. If self-injury leads to more pain than anticipated and no sympathy, it might be discontinued.

Operant Conditioning Procedures

We usually prefer to relate to people who smile at us rather than ignore us and to take courses in which we do well rather than fail. We tend to repeat behavior that is reinforced. Behavior that is not reinforced tends to become extinguished. Behavior therapists have used these principles of operant conditioning with psychotic patients as well as with clients with milder problems. **Question: How do behavior therapists apply principles of operant conditioning in behavior modification?**

The staff at one mental hospital was at a loss about how to encourage withdrawn schizophrenic patients to eat regularly. Ayllon and Haughton (1962) observed that staff members were making the problem worse by coaxing patients into the dining room and even feeding them. Staff attention apparently reinforced the patients' lack of cooperation. Some rules were changed. Patients who did not arrive at the dining hall within 30 minutes after serving were locked out. Staff could not interact with patients at mealtime. With uncooperative behavior no longer reinforced, patients quickly changed their eating habits. Then patients were required to pay one penny to enter the dining hall. Pennies were earned by interacting with other patients and showing other socially appropriate behaviors. These target behaviors also became more frequent.

Health professionals are concerned as to whether people who are, or have been, dependent on alcohol can exercise control over their drinking. One study showed that rewards for remaining abstinent from alcohol can exert a powerful effect (Petry et al., 2000). In the study, one group of alcohol-dependent veterans was given a standard treatment while another group received the treatment *plus* the chance to win prizes for remaining alcohol-free, as measured by a Breathalyzer test. By the end of the 8-week treatment period, 84% of the veterans who could win prizes remained in the program, as compared with 22% of the standard treatment group. The prizes had an average value of $200, far less than what alcohol-related absenteeism from work and other responsibilities can cost.

THE TOKEN ECONOMY Many psychiatric wards and hospitals now use **token economies** in which patients must use tokens such as poker chips to purchase TV viewing time, extra visits to the canteen, or a private room (Comaty et al., 2001). The tokens are reinforcements for productive activities such as making beds, brushing teeth, and socializing. Token economies have not eliminated all symptoms of schizophrenia but have enhanced patient activity and cooperation. Tokens have also been used to modify the behavior of children with conduct disorders.

SUCCESSIVE APPROXIMATIONS The operant conditioning method of **successive approximations** is often used to help clients build good habits. Let us use a (not uncommon!) example: You want to study 3 hours each evening but can concentrate for only half an hour. Rather than attempting to increase your study time all at once, you could do so gradually by adding, say, 5 minutes each evening. After every hour or so of studying, you could reinforce yourself with 5 minutes of people-watching in a busy section of the library.

■ **Aversive Conditioning** In aversive conditioning, unwanted behaviors take on a noxious quality as a result of being repeatedly paired with aversive stimuli. Overexposure is making cigarette smoke aversive to this smoker.

Video Connections—Virtual Reality Therapy Virtual reality therapy helps people overcome fears like that of the subway and other enclosed spaces. Go to your student companion website and click on "Virtual Reality Therapy" to learn more about how psychologists use virtual reality and why they might use different treatment methods for people with the same kind of problems.

Token economy A controlled environment in which people are reinforced for desired behaviors with tokens (such as poker chips) that may be exchanged for privileges.

Successive approximations In operant conditioning, a series of behaviors that gradually become more similar to a target behavior.

SOCIAL SKILLS TRAINING In social skills training, behavior therapists decrease social anxiety and build social skills through operant-conditioning procedures that employ **self-monitoring,** coaching, modeling, role-playing, **behavior rehearsal,** and **feedback.** Social skills training has been used to help formerly hospitalized mental patients maintain jobs and apartments in the community. For example, a worker can rehearse politely asking a supervisor for assistance or asking a landlord to fix the plumbing in an apartment.

Social skills training is effective in groups. Group members can role-play important people—such as parents, spouses, or potential dates—in the lives of other members.

BIOFEEDBACK TRAINING Through **biofeedback training (BFT),** therapists help clients become more aware of, and gain control over, various bodily functions. Therapists attach clients to devices that measure bodily functions such as heart rate. "Bleeps" or other electronic signals are used to indicate (and thereby reinforce) changes in the desired direction—for example, a slower heart rate. (Knowledge of results is a powerful reinforcer.) One device, the electromyograph (EMG), monitors muscle tension. It has been used to augment control over muscle tension in the forehead and elsewhere, thereby alleviating anxiety, stress, and headaches.

BFT also helps clients voluntarily regulate functions once thought to be beyond conscious control, such as heart rate and blood pressure. Hypertensive clients use a blood pressure cuff and electronic signals to gain control over their blood pressure. The electroencephalograph (EEG) monitors brain waves and can be used to teach people how to produce alpha waves, which are associated with relaxation. Some people have overcome insomnia by learning to produce the kinds of brain waves associated with sleep.

Self-Control Methods

Do mysterious forces sometimes seem to be at work in your life? Forces that delight in wreaking havoc on New Year's resolutions and other efforts to put an end to your bad habits? Just when you go on a diet, that juicy pizza stares at you from the TV set. Just when you resolve to balance your budget, that sweater goes on sale. **Question: How can you—yes, *you*—use behavior therapy to deal with temptation and enhance your self-control?**

FUNCTIONAL ANALYSIS OF BEHAVIOR Behavior therapists usually begin with a **functional analysis** of the problem behavior. In this way, they help determine the stimuli that trigger the behavior and the reinforcers that maintain it. Then clients are taught how to manipulate the antecedents and consequences of their behavior and how to increase the frequency of desired responses and decrease the frequency of undesired responses. You can use a diary to jot down each instance of a problem behavior. Note the time of day, location, your activity at the time (including your thoughts and feelings), and reactions (yours and others'). Functional analysis serves a number of purposes. It makes you more aware of the environmental context of your behavior and can increase your motivation to change. **Truth or Fiction Revisited:** For these reasons, keeping a record of where and when you engage in "bad habits" can help you end them and may occasionally be all that you need to end them.

Brian used functional analysis to master his nail biting. Table 15.1 shows a few items from his notebook. He discovered that boredom and humdrum activities seemed to serve as triggers for nail biting. He began to watch out for feelings of boredom as signs to practice self-control. He also made some changes in his life so that he would feel bored less often. There are numerous self-control strategies aimed at the stimuli that trigger behavior, the behaviors themselves, and reinforcers. Table 5.6 on page 225 describes some of them.

Self-monitoring Keeping a record of one's own behavior to identify problems and record successes.

Behavior rehearsal Practice.

Feedback In assertiveness training, information about the effectiveness of a response.

Biofeedback training (BFT) The systematic feeding back to an organism of information about a bodily function so that the organism can gain control of that function.

Functional analysis A systematic study of behavior in which one identifies the stimuli that trigger problem behavior and the reinforcers that maintain it.

TABLE 15.1 **EXCERPTS FROM BRIAN'S DIARY OF NAIL BITING FOR APRIL 14**

Incident	Time	Location	Activity (Thoughts, Feelings)	Reactions
1	7:45 a.m.	Freeway	Driving to work, bored, not thinking	Finger bleeds, pain
2	10:30 a.m.	Office	Writing report	Self-disgust
3	2:25 p.m.	Conference	Listening to dull financial report	Embarrassment
4	6:40 p.m.	Living room	Watching evening news	Self-disgust

Note: A functional analysis of problem behavior like nail biting increases awareness of the environmental context in which it occurs, spurs motivation to change, and, in highly motivated people, might lead to significant behavioral change.

Your Turn: Now that we have discussed behavior therapy, enhance your mastery of the material with the nearby "Learning Connections." Review the material by filling in the blanks, reflect on the material by relating it to other things you know, and think critically about it.

Learning Connections · BEHAVIOR THERAPY: ADJUSTMENT IS WHAT YOU DO

ACTIVE REVIEW (11) Behavior therapy applies principles of _____ to bring about desired behavioral changes. (12) Behavior-therapy methods for reducing fears include flooding; systematic _____, in which a client is gradually exposed to more fear-arousing stimuli; and modeling. (13) _____ conditioning associates undesired behavior with painful stimuli to decrease the frequency of the behavior. (14) _____ conditioning methods reinforce desired responses and extinguish undesired responses. (15) In self-control methods, clients first engage in a(n) _____ analysis of problem behavior. (16) Clients are then taught how to change the behavior by manipulating its antecedents and _____.

REFLECT AND RELATE Would any of the methods for reducing fears be helpful to you in your life? If so, which method would you prefer? Explain.

Do you think that aversive conditioning is an ethical form of therapy? Explain.

CRITICAL THINKING Behavior therapists argue that their methods are more scientific than those of other therapists. How do they attempt to ensure that their methods are scientific?

 Go to **http://psychology.wadsworth.com/ rathus_pcc9e** for an interactive version of this Learning Connections unit.

Cognitive Therapies: Adjustment Is What You Think (and Do)

There is nothing either good or bad, but thinking makes it so.
Shakespeare, *Hamlet*

In this line from *Hamlet,* Shakespeare did not mean to suggest that injuries and misfortunes are painless or easy to manage. Rather, he meant that our appraisals of unfortunate events can heighten our discomfort and impair our coping ability. In so doing, Shakespeare was providing a kind of motto for cognitive therapists.
Question: What is cognitive therapy?

Cognitive therapy focuses on changing the beliefs, attitudes, and automatic types of thinking that create and compound their clients' problems (Beck, 1993; Ellis & Dryden, 1996). Cognitive therapists, like psychodynamic and humanistic therapists, aim to foster self-insight, but they aim to heighten insight into *current cognitions* as well as those of the past. Cognitive therapists also aim to directly change maladaptive cognitions in order to reduce negative feelings, provide insight, and help the client solve problems.

You may have noticed that many behavior therapists incorporate cognitive procedures in their methods. For example, techniques such as systematic desensitization,

Cognitive therapy A form of therapy that focuses on how clients' cognitions (expectations, attitudes, beliefs, etc.) lead to distress and may be modified to relieve distress and promote adaptive behavior.

covert sensitization, and covert reinforcement ask clients to focus on visual imagery. Behavioral methods for treating bulimia nervosa focus on clients' irrational attitudes toward their weight and body shape as well as foster healthful eating habits. Let us look at the approaches and methods of some major cognitive therapists.

Cognitive Therapy: Correcting Cognitive Errors

Cognitive therapy is the name of a general approach to therapy as well as Aaron Beck's specific methods. Beck (1991, 1993) focuses on clients' cognitive distortions. **Question: What is Aaron Beck's method of cognitive therapy?** Beck encourages clients to become their own personal scientists and challenge beliefs that are not supported by evidence.

Beck questions people in a way that encourages them to see the irrationality of their ways of thinking. For example, depressed people tend to minimize their accomplishments and to assume that the worst will happen. Both distortions heighten feelings of depression. Cognitive distortions can be fleeting and automatic, difficult to detect (Persons et al., 2001). Beck's therapy methods help clients become aware of distortions and challenge them.

Beck notes how cognitive errors contribute to clients' miseries:

1. Clients may *selectively perceive* the world as a harmful place and ignore evidence to the contrary.
2. Clients may *overgeneralize* on the basis of a few examples. For example, they may perceive themselves as worthless because they were laid off at work or as unattractive because they were refused a date.
3. Clients may *magnify,* or blow out of proportion, the importance of negative events. They may catastrophize failing a test by assuming they will flunk out of college or catastrophize losing a job by believing that they will never find another one and that serious harm will befall their family as a result.
4. Clients may engage in *absolutist thinking,* or looking at the world in black and white rather than in shades of gray. In doing so, a rejection on a date takes on the meaning of a lifetime of loneliness; an uncomfortable illness takes on life-threatening proportions.

The concept of pinpointing and modifying errors may become clearer from the following excerpt from a case in which a 53-year-old engineer obtained cognitive therapy for severe depression. The engineer had left his job and become inactive. As reported by Beck and his colleagues, the first goal of treatment was to foster physical activity—even things like raking leaves and preparing dinner—because activity is incompatible with depression. Then:

> [The engineer's] cognitive distortions were identified by comparing his assessment of each activity with that of his wife. Alternative ways of interpreting his experiences were then considered.
>
> In comparing his wife's résumé of his past experiences, he became aware that he had (1) undervalued his past by failing to mention many previous accomplishments, (2) regarded himself as far more responsible for his "failures" than she did, and (3) concluded that he was worthless since he had not succeeded in attaining certain goals in the past. When the two accounts were contrasted, he could discern many of his cognitive distortions. In subsequent sessions, his wife continued to serve as an "objectifier."
>
> In midtherapy, [he] compiled a list of new attitudes that he had acquired since initiating therapy. These included:
>
> 1. "I am starting at a lower level of functioning at my job, but it will improve if I persist."

2. "I know that once I get going in the morning, everything will run all right for the rest of the day."

3. "I can't achieve everything at once."

4. "I have my periods of ups and downs, but in the long run I feel better."

5. "My expectations from my job and life should be scaled down to a realistic level."

6. "Giving in to avoidance [e.g., staying away from work and social interactions] never helps and only leads to further avoidance."

He was instructed to reread this list daily for several weeks even though he already knew the content. (Rush et al., 1975)

The engineer gradually became less depressed and returned to work and an active social life. Along the way, he learned to combat inappropriate self-blame for problems, perfectionist expectations, magnification of failures, and overgeneralization from failures.

Becoming aware of cognitive errors and modifying catastrophizing thoughts helps us cope with stress. Internal, stable, and global attributions of failure lead to depression and feelings of helplessness. Cognitive therapists also alert clients to cognitive errors such as these so that the clients can change their attitudes and pave the way for more effective overt behavior.

In Profile   AARON BECK AND ALBERT ELLIS

Aaron Beck and Albert Ellis are two of the preeminent cognitive therapists in the United States. Aaron Beck used cognitive and behavioral techniques on himself before he became a psychiatrist. In fact, one of the reasons Aaron Beck went into medicine was to confront his own fear of blood. He had had a series of operations as a child, and from then on the sight of blood had made him feel faint. During his first year of medical school, he forced himself to watch operations. In his second year, he became a surgical assistant. Soon the sight of blood became normal to him. Later he essentially argued himself out of an irrational fear of tunnels. He convinced himself that the tunnels did not cause the fear because the symptoms of faintness and shallow breathing would appear before he entered them.

As a psychiatrist, Beck first practiced psychoanalysis. However, he could not find scientific evidence for psychoanalytic beliefs. Psychoanalytic theory explained depression as anger turned inward, so that it is transformed into a need to suffer. Beck's own clinical experiences led him to believe that it is more likely that depressed people experience cognitive distortions such as the *cognitive triad*. That is, they expect the worst of themselves ("I'm no good"), the world at large ("This is an awful place"), and their future ("Nothing good will ever happen"). Beck's approach to therapy is active. Beck encourages clients to challenge beliefs that are not supported by evidence. Beck also challenges his own points of view. "I am a big self-doubter," Beck (2000) admits. "I always doubt what I do, which is one of the reasons I do so much research and encourage research." Beck teaches health professionals his form of therapy—and scientific skepticism—at the University of Pennsylvania.

Psychologist Albert Ellis, like Aaron Beck, was originally trained in psychoanalysis but became frustrated with the slow rate of progress made by clients. He also found himself uncomfortable with the psychoanalyst's laid-back approach and took to engaging in sometimes heated discussions with his clients about their irrational and self-defeating ways of viewing themselves and other people. Ellis can be even more argumentative than Beck with his clients. He confronts them with the ways in which their irrational beliefs, especially those that give rise to excessive needs for social approval and perfect performance, make them miserable.

Ellis has been a workaholic and a prolific writer, having the ability to connect both with professionals and the public. Just a few of his dozens of mass-market books include *A Guide to Rational Living*, *How to Live with a Neurotic*, *How to Keep People from Pushing Your Buttons*, *Optimal Aging: Getting Over Getting Older*, and *Sex without Guilt*. Never resting, Ellis recently revised his *Sex without Guilt*, which was originally written half a century ago. The 2003 version is called *Sex without Guilt in the 21st Century*.

Photograph by Michael Fenichel, www.fenichel.com

    Go to **http://psychology.wadsworth.com/ rathus_pcc9e** to access more information about Aaron Beck and Albert Ellis.

Rational emotive behavior therapy (REBT)
Albert Ellis's form of therapy that encourages clients to challenge and correct irrational expectations and maladaptive behaviors.

Rational Emotive Behavior Therapy: Overcoming "Musts" and "Shoulds"

In **rational emotive behavior therapy (REBT),** Albert Ellis (2002) points out that our beliefs *about* events, not only the events themselves, shape our responses to them. Moreover, many of us harbor a number of irrational beliefs that can give rise to problems or magnify their impact. Two of the most important ones are the belief that we must have the love and approval of people who are important to us and the belief that we must prove ourselves to be thoroughly competent, adequate, and achieving. **Question: What is Albert Ellis's method of rational emotive behavior therapy (REBT)?**

Albert Ellis, like Aaron Beck, began as a psychoanalyst. But he became disturbed by the passive role of the analyst and by the slow rate of obtaining results—if they were obtained at all. Still, Ellis finds a role for Freud's views: "One of the main things [Freud] did was point out the importance of unconscious thinking. Freud pointed out that when people are motivated to do things, that they unconsciously think, and even feel, certain things. We use that concept," Ellis (2000) admits, "although Freud, as usual, ran it into the ground."

Ellis's REBT methods are active and directive. He does not sit back like the traditional psychoanalyst and occasionally offer an interpretation. Instead, he urges clients to seek out their irrational beliefs, which can be unconscious, though not as deeply buried as Freud believed. Nevertheless, they can be hard to pinpoint without some direction. Ellis shows clients how those beliefs lead to misery and challenges clients to change them. When Ellis sees clients behaving according to irrational beliefs, he may refute the beliefs by asking "Where is it written that you must . . . ?" or "What evidence do you have that . . . ?" According to Ellis, we need less misery and less blaming in our lives, and more action.

Ellis straddles behavioral and cognitive therapies. He originally dubbed his method of therapy *rational–emotive therapy,* because his focus was on the cognitive—irrational beliefs and how to change them. However, Ellis has also always promoted behavioral changes to cement cognitive changes. In keeping with his broad philosophy, he recently changed the name of rational–emotive therapy to rational emotive *behavior* therapy.

Many theorists consider cognitive therapy to be a collection of techniques that are part of the overall approach known as behavior therapy, which is discussed in the following section. Some members of this group use the term "cognitive–behavioral therapy." Others argue that the term *behavior therapy* is broad enough to include cognitive techniques. Many cognitive therapists and behavior therapists differ in focus, however. Behavior therapists deal with client cognitions in order to change *overt* behavior. Cognitive therapists also see the value of tying treatment outcomes to observable behavior, but they believe that cognitive change is a key goal in itself.

Your Turn: Now that we have discussed cognitive therapy, enhance your mastery of the material with the nearby "Learning Connections." Review the material by filling in the blanks, reflect on the material by relating it to other things you know, and think critically about it. The nearby Concept Review summarizes several methods of therapy.

Learning Connections · COGNITIVE THERAPIES: ADJUSTMENT IS WHAT YOU THINK (AND DO)

ACTIVE REVIEW (17) _____ therapists focus on the beliefs, attitudes, and automatic thoughts that create and compound their clients' problems. (18) Aaron Beck notes four types of cognitive errors that contribute to clients' miseries: selective abstraction of the world as a harmful place; overgeneralization; magnification of the importance of negative events, and _____ thinking, or looking at the world in black and white rather than shades of gray. (19) Albert Ellis's REBT confronts clients with the ways in which _____ beliefs contribute to problems such as anxiety and depression.

REFLECT AND RELATE Do you believe that you must have the love and approval of people who are important to you? Do you believe that you must prove yourself to be thoroughly competent, adequate, and achieving? Do such beliefs make you miserable? What can you do about them?

CRITICAL THINKING Many therapists call themselves cognitive–behavioral therapists. Does it seem possible to combine behavior therapy and cognitive therapy?

 Go to **http://psychology.wadsworth.com/ rathus_pcc9e** for an interactive version of this Learning Connections unit.

Group Therapies

When a psychotherapist has several clients with similar problems—anxiety, depression, adjustment to divorce, lack of social skills—it often makes sense to treat them in a group rather than in individual sessions. The methods and characteristics of the group reflect the needs of the members and the theoretical orientation of the leader. In group psychoanalysis, clients might interpret one another's dreams. In a client-centered group, they might provide an accepting atmosphere for self-exploration. Members of behavior therapy groups might be jointly desensitized to anxiety-evoking stimuli or might practice social skills together. **Question: What are the advantages and disadvantages of group therapy?**

Group therapy has the following advantages:

1. It is economical (Prochaska & Norcross, 2003). It allows the therapist to work with several clients at once.

2. Compared with one-to-one therapy, group therapy provides more information and life experience for clients to draw upon.

3. Appropriate behavior receives group support. Clients usually appreciate an outpouring of peer approval.

4. When we run into troubles, it is easy to imagine that we are different from other people or inferior to them. Affiliating with people with similar problems is reassuring.

5. Group members who show improvement provide hope for other members.

6. Many individuals seek therapy because of problems in relating to other people. People who seek therapy for other reasons also may be socially inhibited. Members of groups have the opportunity to practice social skills in a relatively nonthreatening atmosphere. In a group consisting of men and women of different ages, group members can role-play one another's employers, employees, spouses, parents, children, and friends. Members can role-play asking one another out on dates, saying no (or yes), and so on.

But group therapy is not for everyone. Some clients fare better with individual treatment. Many prefer not to disclose their problems to a group. They may be overly shy or want individual attention. It is the responsibility of the therapist to insist that group disclosures be kept confidential, to establish a supportive atmosphere, and to ensure that group members obtain the attention they need.

Many types of therapy can be conducted either individually or in groups. Encounter groups and family therapy are conducted only in groups.

Encounter Groups

Encounter groups are not appropriate for treating serious psychological problems. Rather, they are intended to promote personal growth by heightening awareness of one's own needs and feelings and those of others. This goal is sought through intense confrontations, or encounters, between strangers. **Questions: What are encounter groups? What are their effects?**

Encounter group A type of group that aims to foster self-awareness by focusing on how group members relate to each other in a setting that encourages open expression of feelings.

Concept Review METHODS OF THERAPY

Psychodynamic Therapies	Humanistic Therapies	Behavior Therapies
Assume disorders stem from unresolved unconscious conflict	Assume that disorders reflect feelings of alienation from one's genuine beliefs and feelings.	Assume disorders reflect learning of maladaptive responses (such as maladaptive fear responses, or phobias) or failure to acquire adaptive responses (such as social skills).

Freud's consulting room.

Client-centered therapists provide a warm atmosphere in which clients feel free to explore their genuine feelings.

One way behavior therapists help clients overcome phobias is to have them gradually approach the feared object or situation while they remain relaxed.

Goals

To strengthen the ego; to provide self-insight into unconscious conflict	To help clients get in touch with parts of themselves that they have "disowned" and actualize their unique desires and abilities	To use principles of learning to help clients engage in adaptive behavior and discontinue maladaptive behavior

Methods

Traditional psychoanalysis is lengthy and nondirective and involves methods such as free association and dream analysis.	Client-centered therapy is nondirective. It provides an atmosphere of "unconditional positive regard" from the therapist in which clients can engage in self-exploration without fear. Gestalt therapy uses highly directive methods to help clients integrate conflicting parts of the personality into a healthy "Gestalt," or whole.	Behavior therapy is directive and uses fear-reduction methods (including systematic desensitization) to overcome phobias such as fear of flying, aversive conditioning (to help clients discontinue bad habits), operant conditioning procedures (e.g., social skills training), and self-control methods (beginning with functional analysis of behavior).

Comments

Most effective with verbal, "upscale" clients. Modern ego-analytic approaches are briefer and more directive than traditional psychoanalysis.	Client-centered therapy is practiced widely in college and university counseling centers to help students make academic and personal decisions.	Behavior therapists have developed treatment for problems (e.g., smoking, phobias, sexual dysfunctions) for which there previously were no effective treatment methods.
Principle proponent: Sigmund Freud (1856–1939) formulated his psychodynamic theory of personality a century ago. His method of therapy, psychoanalysis, achieved greatest prominence in the 1940s and 1950s.	**Principle proponents:** Carl Rogers (1902–1970) developed client-centered therapy in the mid-20th century. Fritz Perls (1893–1970) originated Gestalt therapy, which reached its greatest prominence in the 1960s.	**Principle proponents:** Joseph Wolpe (1915–1997) introduced systematic desensitization in the late 1950s. Albert Bandura integrated behavioral and cognitive factors in forming his therapeutic methods, such as modeling.

Sigmund Freud

Carl Rogers

Fritz Perls

Joseph Wolpe

Albert Bandura

Like ships in the night, group members come together out of the darkness, touch one another briefly, then sink back into the shadows of one another's lives. But something is gained from the passing.

Encounter groups stress interactions between group members in the here and now. Discussion of the past may be outlawed. Interpretation is out. However,

Cognitive Therapies

Assume disorders reflect cognitive errors such as excessive self-blame, pessimism, and selective focus on negative events.

The therapist seeks to guide the client to correct cognitive errors and recognize irrational beliefs.

To make clients aware of the beliefs, attitudes, and automatic types of thinking that create and compound their problems; to help them correct these kinds of thinking to reduce negative feelings and solve problems

Aaron Beck's cognitive therapy helps people recognize and correct cognitive errors such as selective perception, overgeneralization, magnification of negative events, and absolutist thinking. Rational emotive behavior therapists show clients how irrational beliefs catastrophize events and make them miserable.

Many theorists consider cognitive therapy to be part of behavior therapy, and some call it cognitive–*behavioral* therapy.

Priniciple proponents: Aaron Beck introduced his approach, "cognitive therapy," in the 1960s. Albert Ellis first developed what he called "rational–emotive therapy" (RET) in the late 1950s and 1960s. More recently, he changed the name to "rational emotive behavior therapy" (REBT).

Aaron Beck and Albert Ellis

Biological Therapies

Assume that disorders reflect the interaction of genetic vulnerability with other factors, such as imbalances of neurotransmitters or hormones or situational stressors; for example, depression may reflect interaction of genetic vulnerability with low levels of serotonin and with a personal failure.

Many drugs have been used to combat psychological disorders.

To decrease anxiety, alleviate depression, lessen mood swings in bipolar disorder, eliminate or lessen symptoms of schizophrenia

Antianxiety drugs (also known as *anxiolytic* drugs or "minor tranquilizers"), antidepressant drugs, lithium and other drugs for treatment of bipolar disorder, antipsychotic drugs ("major tranquilizers"), electroconvulsive shock therapy (ECT) for treatment of depression that is unresponsive to drug therapy, psychosurgery

Most psychologists prefer psychotherapy to biological therapies as being more helpful in developing strategies for solving problems. There is controversy as to whether cognitive therapy is as effective as biological therapy for depression. Most psychologists agree that biological therapies may be appropriate when disorders are severe and unresponsive to psychotherapy.

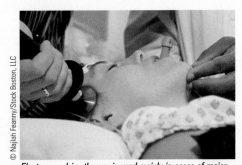

Electroconvulsive therapy is used mainly in cases of major depression where other therapies have failed

 Go to **http://psychology.wadsworth.com/ rathus_pcc9e** to access a drag-and-drop version of this Concept Review designed to help you test yourself on the major topics provided here.

expression of genuine feelings toward others is encouraged. When group members think a person's social mask is phony, they may descend en masse to rip it off.

Encounter groups can be damaging when they urge overly rapid disclosure of intimate matters or when several members attack one member. Responsible leaders do not tolerate these abuses and try to keep the group moving in a growth-enhancing direction.

Couple Therapy

Couple therapy helps couples enhance their relationship by improving their communication skills and helping them manage conflict (Prochaska & Norcross, 2003). There are often power imbalances in relationships, and couple therapy helps individuals find "full membership" in the couple. Correcting power imbalances increases happiness and can decrease the incidence of domestic violence. Ironically, in situations of domestic violence, the partner with *less* power in the relationship is usually the violent one. Violence sometimes appears to be a way of compensating for inability to share power in other aspects of the relationship (Rathus & Sanderson, 1999).

Today the main approach to couple therapy is cognitive–behavioral (Rathus & Sanderson, 1999). It teaches couples communications skills (such as how to listen and how to express feelings), ways of handling feelings like depression and anger, and ways of solving problems.

Family Therapy

Question: What is family therapy? Family therapy is a form of group therapy in which one or more families constitute the group. Family therapy may be undertaken from various theoretical viewpoints. One is the systems approach, in which family interaction is studied and modified to enhance the growth of individual family members and of the family unit as a whole (Prochaska & Norcross, 2003).

Family members with low self-esteem often cannot tolerate different attitudes and behaviors in other family members. Faulty communication within the family also creates problems. In addition, it is not uncommon for the family to present an "identified patient"—that is, the family member who has *the* problem and is *causing* all the trouble. Yet family therapists usually assume that the identified patient is a scapegoat for other problems within and among family members. It is a sort of myth: Change the bad apple—or identified patient—and the barrel—or family—will be functional once more.

The family therapist—often a specialist in this field—attempts to teach the family to communicate more effectively and encourage growth and autonomy in each family member.

Your Turn: Now that we have discussed group therapies, enhance your mastery of the material with the nearby "Learning Connections." Review the material by filling in the blanks, reflect on the material by relating it to other things you know, and think critically about it.

Family therapy A form of therapy in which the family unit is treated as the client.

 Learning Connections   **GROUP THERAPIES**

ACTIVE REVIEW (20) Group therapy is (*More* or *Less?*) economical than individual therapy. (21) _____ groups promote personal growth by heightening awareness of people's needs and feelings through intense confrontations. (22) In the _____ approach to family therapy, family interaction is modified to enhance the growth of family members and the family unit as a whole.

REFLECT AND RELATE Do you think you could share your intimate problems with a group of strangers? Can you see any advantages or disadvantages to doing so?

CRITICAL THINKING Critical thinkers avoid overgeneralization. Is it accurate to say that individual therapy is preferable to group therapy, or is the statement an overgeneralization?

Go to **http://psychology.wadsworth.com/ rathus_pcc9e** for an interactive version of this Learning Connections unit.

Does Psychotherapy Work?

In 1952, the British psychologist Hans Eysenck published a review of psychotherapy research—"The Effects of Psychotherapy"—that sent shock waves through the psychotherapy community. On the basis of his review of the research, Eysenck concluded that the rate of improvement among people in psychotherapy was no greater than the rate of "spontaneous remission"—that is, the rate of improvement that would be shown by people with psychological disorders who received no treatment at all. Eysenck was not addressing people with schizophrenia, who typically profit from biological forms of therapy, but he argued that whether or not people with problems such as anxiety and depression received therapy, two of three reported substantial improvement within two years.

That was half a century ago. Since that time, sophisticated research studies—many of them employing a statistical averaging method called **meta-analysis**—have strongly suggested that psychotherapy is, in fact, effective.

Before we report on the research dealing with the effectiveness of therapy, let us review some of the problems of this kind of research (Shadish, 2002). **Question: What kinds of problems do researchers encounter when they conduct research on psychotherapy?**

Problems in Conducting Research on Psychotherapy

It is not an easy matter to evaluate the effectiveness of psychotherapy. Many problems bedevil the effort.

PROBLEMS IN RUNNING EXPERIMENTS ON PSYCHOTHERAPY The ideal method for evaluating a treatment—such as a method of therapy—is the experiment (Chambless & Hollon, 1998; Shadish, 2002). However, experiments on therapy methods are difficult to arrange and control. The outcomes can be difficult to define and measure.

Consider psychoanalysis. In well-run experiments, people are assigned at random to experimental and control groups. A true experiment on psychoanalysis would require randomly assigning people seeking therapy to psychoanalysis and to a control group or other kinds of therapy for comparison. But a person may have to remain in traditional psychoanalysis for years to attain beneficial results. Could we create control treatments that last as long? Moreover, some people seek psychoanalysis per se, not psychotherapy in general. Would it be ethical to assign them at random to other treatments or to a no-treatment control group? Clearly not.

In an ideal experiment, subjects and researchers are "blind" with regard to the treatment the subjects receive. Blind research designs allow researchers to control for subjects' expectations. In an ideal experiment on therapy, individuals would be blind regarding the type of therapy they are obtaining—or whether they are obtaining a placebo. However, it is difficult to mask the type of therapy clients are obtaining (Seligman, 1995). Even if we could conceal it from clients, could we hide it from therapists?

PROBLEMS IN MEASURING OUTCOMES OF THERAPY Consider the problems we run into when measuring outcomes of therapy (Shadish, 2002). Behavior therapists define their goals in behavioral terms—such as a formerly phobic individual being able to obtain an injection or look out of a 20th-story window. Therefore, behavior therapists do not encounter many problems in this area. But what about the client-centered therapist who fosters insight and self-actualization? We cannot directly measure these qualities. The psychoanalytic process is educational as well as therapeutic, and some argue that different standards must be applied in evaluating what the client gains from treatment (Strupp, 2001).

ARE CLINICAL JUDGMENTS VALID? Because of problems like these, many clinicians believe that important clinical questions cannot be answered through research (Silberschatz, 1998). For them, clinical judgment is the basis for evaluating the effectiveness of therapy. Unfortunately, therapists have a stake in believing

Meta-analysis A method for combining and averaging the results of individual research studies.

that their clients profit from treatment. They are not unbiased judges, even when they try to be.

DOES THERAPY HELP BECAUSE OF THE METHOD OR BECAUSE OF "NONSPECIFIC FACTORS"? Even when psychotherapy helps, we're often not sure why (Marks, 2002). Sorting out the benefits of therapy per se from other aspects of the therapy situation is a staggering task. These other aspects are termed *nonspecific factors*. They refer to features that are found in most therapies, such as the client's relationship with the therapist. Most therapists, regardless of theoretical outlook, show warmth and empathy, encourage exploration, and instill hope (Perlman, 2001; Scaturo, 2001). People in therapy also often learn to present themselves to their therapists in a positive light, and creating favorable impressions can help boost one's self-concept in therapy as in everyday life (Arkin & Hermann, 2000; Kelly, 2000). Many of the benefits of therapy could stem from interactions such as these. In such cases, the method itself might have little more value than a "sugar pill" in combating physical ailments.

WHAT IS THE EXPERIMENTAL TREATMENT IN PSYCHOTHERAPY OUTCOME STUDIES? We may also ask, what exactly is the experimental "treatment" being evaluated? Various therapists may say that they are practicing psychoanalysis, but they differ both as individuals and in their training. It is therefore difficult to specify just what is happening in the therapeutic session.

Analyses of the Effectiveness of Psychotherapy

Despite these evaluation problems, research on the effectiveness of therapy has been encouraging (Luborsky et al., 2002; Shadish et al., 2000). Some of this research has relied on meta-analysis. Meta-analysis combines and averages the results of individual studies. Generally speaking, the studies included in the analysis address similar issues in a similar way. Moreover, the analysts judge them to have been conducted in a valid manner. **Question: What, then, do we know about the effectiveness of psychotherapy?**

In their classic early use of meta-analysis, Mary Lee Smith and Gene Glass (1977) analyzed the results of dozens of outcome studies of various types of therapies. They concluded that people who obtained psychodynamic therapy showed greater well-being, on the average, than 70% to 75% of those who did not obtain treatment. Similarly, nearly 75% of the clients who obtained client-centered therapy were better off than people who did not obtain treatment. Psychodynamic and client-centered therapies appear to be most effective with well-educated, verbal, strongly motivated clients who report problems with anxiety, depression (of light to moderate proportions), and interpersonal relationships. Neither form of therapy appears to be effective with people with psychotic disorders such as major depression, bipolar disorder, and schizophrenia. Smith and Glass (1977) found that people who obtained Gestalt therapy showed greater well-being than about 60% of those who did not obtain treatment. The effectiveness of psychoanalysis and client-centered therapy thus was reasonably comparable. Gestalt therapy fell behind.

Smith and Glass (1977) did not include cognitive therapies in their meta-analysis because at the time of their study many cognitive approaches were relatively new. Because behavior therapists also incorporate many cognitive techniques, it can be difficult to sort out which aspects—cognitive or otherwise—of behavioral treatments are most effective. However, many meta-analyses of cognitive–behavioral therapy have been conducted since the early work of Smith and Glass. Their results are encouraging.

A meta-analysis of 90 studies by William R. Shadish and his colleagues (2000) concurred that psychotherapy is generally effective. Generally speaking, the more therapy the better; that is, people who have more psychotherapy tend to fare better than people who have less of it. Therapy also appears to be more effective when the outcome measures reflect the treatment (e.g., when the effects of treatment aimed at fear-reduction are measured in terms of people's ability to approach fear-inducing objects and situations).

Studies of cognitive therapy have shown that modifying irrational beliefs of the type described by Albert Ellis helps people with problems such as anxiety and depression (Engels et al., 1993; Haaga & Davison, 1993). Modifying self-defeating beliefs of the sort outlined by Aaron Beck also frequently alleviates anxiety and depression (Butler & Beck, 2001; Frank & Kupfer, 2003). Cognitive therapy may help people with severe depression, who had been thought responsive only to biological therapies (Hollon & Shelton, 2001; Simons et al., 1995). Cognitive

A Closer Look ETHNICITY AND PSYCHOTHERAPY

The United States, they are a-changing. The numbers of African Americans, Asian Americans, and Latino and Latina Americans are growing rapidly (U. S. Bureau of the Census, 2003), yet most of the "prescriptions" for psychotherapy discussed in this chapter were originated by, and intended for use with, Europeans and European Americans (Dana, 2002).

Americans from ethnic minority groups are less likely than European Americans to seek therapy (Kim & Omizo, 2003; Sue & Sue, 2002). Reasons for their lower participation rate include:

- Unawareness that therapy would help (Sue & Sue, 2002).

- Lack of information about the availability of professional services or inability to pay for them (Dana, 2002).

- Distrust of professionals, particularly European American professionals and (for women) male professionals (Whaley, 2001; Wong et al., 2003).

- Language barriers (American Psychological Association, 1993).

- Reluctance to open up about personal matters to strangers—especially strangers who are not members of one's own ethnic group (Whaley, 2001; Wong et al., 2003).

- Cultural inclinations toward other approaches to problem solving, such as religious approaches and psychic healers (Baez & Hernandez, 2001; de Rios, 2002; Olson, 2003).

- Negative experiences with professionals and authority figures (Whaley, 2001).

There are thus many reasons that clinicians need to be sensitive to the cultural heritage, language, and values of the people they see in therapy (American Psychological Association, 1993; Comas-Diaz,

1994). That is, they need to develop *multicultural competence* (Sue & Sue, 2002). Let us consider some of the issues involved in conducting psychotherapy with African Americans, Asian Americans, Latino and Latina Americans, and Native Americans.

African Americans often are reluctant to seek psychological help because of cultural assumptions that people should manage their own problems and because of mistrust of the therapy process (Jackson & Greene, 2000; Whaley, 2001). They tend to assume that people are supposed to solve their own problems. Signs of emotional weakness such as tension, anxiety, and depression are stigmatized. Many African Americans are also suspicious of their therapists—especially when the therapist is a European American. They may withhold personal information because of the society's history of racial discrimination (Dana, 2002; Whaley, 2001).

Asian Americans tend to stigmatize people with psychological disorders. As a result, they may deny problems and refuse to seek help for them (Kim & Omizo, 2003).

© Bill Aron/PhotoEdit

■ **Is Psychotherapy for Everyone?** Why are members of some ethnic groups more willing to seek therapy than members of other ethnic groups? Do members of all ethnic groups have the same kinds of needs in therapy? Must therapists be from the same ethnic group as their clients? Can therapists from the dominant culture be sensitive to the life issues of people from ethnic minority groups?

Asian Americans, especially recent immigrants, also may not understand or believe in Western approaches to psychotherapy. For example, Western psychotherapy typically encourages people to express their feelings openly. This mode of behavior may conflict with the Asian tradition of restraint in public. Many Asians also experience and express psychological problems as physical symptoms (Kim & Omizo, 2003; Sue & Sue, 2002). Rather than thinking of themselves as being anxious, they may focus on physical features of anxiety such as a pounding heart and heavy sweating. Rather than thinking of themselves as depressed, they may focus on fatigue and low energy levels.

Therapists need to be aware of potential conflicts between the traditional Latino and Latina American value of interdependency in the family and the typical European American belief in independence and self-reliance (Baez & Hernandez, 2001; de Rios, 2002).

Many psychological disorders experienced by Native Americans involve the disruption of their traditional culture caused by European colonization (Olson, 2003). Loss of cultural identity and social disorganization have set the stage for problems such as alcoholism, substance abuse, and depression. Efforts to prevent psychological disorders should focus on strengthening Native American cultural identity, pride, and cohesion.

Psychotherapy is most effective when therapists attend to and respect people's sociocultural as well as individual differences. Although it is the individual who experiences psychological anguish, the fault often lies in the cultural setting and not the individual.

therapy has also helped people with personality disorders (Beck et al., 2001; Trull et al., 2003).

Behavioral and cognitive therapies have provided strategies for treating anxiety disorders, social skills deficits, and problems in self-control (DeRubeis & Crits-Christoph, 1998). These therapies—which are often integrated as *cognitive–behavioral therapy*—have also provided empirically supported methods for helping couples and families in distress (Baucom et al., 1998), and for modifying behaviors related to health problems such as headaches (Blanchard, 1992), smoking, chronic pain, and bulimia nervosa (Agras et al., 2000; Compas et al., 1998). Cognitive–behavioral therapists have also innovated treatments for sexual dysfunctions for which there previously were no effective treatments. One meta-analysis of psychodynamic therapy and cognitive–behavioral therapy found both treatments to be effective with personality disorders (Leichsenring & Leibing, 2003). It is perhaps of interest that of hundreds of studies reviewed, the researchers found only 14 psychodynamic studies and 11 cognitive–behavioral studies that were rigorous enough to be included in the meta-analysis.

Cognitive–behavioral therapy has been used to help anorexic and bulimic individuals challenge their perfectionism and their attitudes toward their bodies. It has also been used to systematically reinforce appropriate eating behavior. Studies that compare the effectiveness of cognitive–behavioral therapy and antidepressants find them to be comparably effective, with cognitive–behavioral therapy frequently showing a slight advantage (e.g., Jacobi et al., 2002). Drugs, after all, do not directly "attack" people's perfectionist attitudes and their distorted body images. They ease the presence of negative feelings and may help individuals enlist their own psychological resources, but pills do not contain advice or even a sympathetic ear.

Cognitive therapy has helped many people with schizophrenia (who are also using drug therapy) modify their delusional beliefs (Chadwick & Lowe, 1990). Behavior therapy has helped to coordinate the care of institutionalized patients, including people with schizophrenia and mental retardation (Spreat & Behar, 1994). However, there is little evidence that psychological therapy alone is effective in treating the quirks of thought exhibited in people with severe psychotic disorders.

Thus, it is not enough to ask which type of therapy is most effective. We must ask which type is most effective for a particular problem and a particular patient. What are its advantages? Its limitations? Clients may successfully use systematic desensitization to overcome stage fright, as measured by ability to speak to a group of people. If clients also want to know *why* they have stage fright, however, behavior therapy alone will not provide the answer.

As we see in the nearby "A Closer Look" on ethnicity and psychotherapy, we must also consider the sociocultural features of clients in determining how to make therapy most effective. Failure to do so leaves many people who would profit from therapy on the wayside. And in some cases, inappropriate methods of therapy may do more harm than good.

Your Turn: Now that we have explored the issue as to whether or not psychotherapy is effective, enhance your mastery of the material with the nearby "Learning Connections." Review the material by filling in the blanks, reflect on the material by relating it to other things you know, and think critically about it.

Learning Connections · DOES PSYCHOTHERAPY WORK?

ACTIVE REVIEW (23) Smith and Glass used the method of _____-analysis to analyze the results of dozens of outcome studies of various types of therapies.
(24) Current research shows that psychotherapy (*Is* or *Is not?*) effective in the treatment of psychological disorders.

(25) _____ therapy appears to be helpful for people with severe depression who had been thought to respond only to biological therapies. (26) African Americans may be reluctant to seek therapy because of cultural assumptions that people (*Should* or *Should not?*) manage their

own problems and because they mistrust European American professionals. (27) There may be conflict between the traditional Latino and Latina American value of _____ in the family and the typical European American belief in independence.

REFLECT AND RELATE If a medical doctor or a psychotherapist recommended a course of treatment for a problem, would you have any difficulty asking that medical doctor or psychotherapist about evidence as to whether or not

that form of treatment has been shown to be effective? Why or why not?

CRITICAL THINKING Justin swears he feels much better because of psychoanalysis. "I feel so much better now," he claims. Deborah swears by her experience with Gestalt therapy. Are these anecdotal endorsements acceptable as scientific evidence? Why or why not?

 Go to **http://psychology.wadsworth.com/ rathus_pcc9e** for an interactive version of this Learning Connections unit.

Biological Therapies

The kinds of therapy we have discussed are psychological in nature—forms of *psycho*therapy. Psychotherapies apply *psychological* principles to treatment, principles based on psychological knowledge of matters such as learning and motivation. People with psychological disorders are also often treated with biological therapies. Biological therapies apply what is known of people's *biological* structures and processes to the amelioration of psychological disorders. For example, they may work by altering events in the nervous system, as by changing the action of neurotransmitters. In this section, we discuss three biological, or medical, approaches to treating people with psychological disorders: drug therapy, electroconvulsive therapy, and psychosurgery. **Question: What kinds of drug therapy are available for psychological disorders?**

Drug Therapy: In Search of the Magic Pill?

In the 1950s Fats Domino popularized the song "My Blue Heaven." Fats was singing about the sky and happiness. Today "blue heavens" is one of the street names for the 10-milligram dose of the antianxiety drug Valium. Clinicians prescribe Valium and other drugs for people with various psychological disorders.

ANTIANXIETY DRUGS Most antianxiety drugs (also called *minor tranquilizers*) belong to the chemical class known as *benzodiazepines*. Valium (diazepam) is a benzodiazepine. Other benzodiazepines include chlordiazepoxide (for example, Librium), oxazepam (Serax), and alprazolam (Xanax). Antianxiety drugs are usually prescribed for outpatients who complain of generalized anxiety or panic attacks, although many people also use them as sleeping pills. Valium and other antianxiety drugs depress the activity of the central nervous system (CNS). The CNS, in turn, decreases sympathetic activity, reducing the heart rate, respiration rate, and feelings of nervousness and tension.

Many people come to tolerate antianxiety drugs very quickly. When tolerance occurs, dosages must be increased for the drug to remain effective.

Sedation (feelings of being tired or drowsy) is the most common side effect of antianxiety drugs. Problems associated with withdrawal from these drugs include **rebound anxiety.** That is, some people who have been using these drugs regularly report that their anxiety becomes worse than before once they discontinue them. Antianxiety drugs can induce physical dependence, as evidenced by withdrawal symptoms such as tremors, sweating, insomnia, and rapid heartbeat.

ANTIPSYCHOTIC DRUGS People with schizophrenia are often given antipsychotic drugs (also called *major tranquilizers*). In most cases these drugs reduce agitation, delusions, and hallucinations. Many antipsychotic drugs, including phenothiazines (for example, Thorazine) and clozapine (Clozaril) are thought to act by blocking dopamine receptors in the brain (Buckley et al., 2000; Sawa & Snyder, 2002). Research along these lines supports the theory that schizophrenia is connected with overactivity of the neurotransmitter dopamine.

Rebound anxiety Anxiety that can occur when one discontinues use of a tranquilizer.

ANTIDEPRESSANTS People with major depression often take so-called **antidepressant** drugs. **Truth or Fiction Revisited:** These drugs are also helpful for some people with eating disorders, panic disorder, obsessive–compulsive disorder, and social phobia (Bacaltchuk et al., 2000; Barlow et al., 2000; McElroy et al., 2000; Santonastaso et al., 2001). Problems in the regulation of noradrenaline and serotonin may be involved in eating and panic disorders as well as in depression. Antidepressants are believed to work by increasing levels of one or both of these neurotransmitters, which can affect both depression and the appetite (Schneider et al., 2003; C. L. White et al., 2000). However, as noted in the section on the effectiveness of psychotherapy, cognitive–behavioral therapy addresses irrational attitudes concerning weight and body shape, fosters normal eating habits, and helps people resist the urges to binge and purge, often making this form of therapy more effective with people with bulimia than antidepressants (Wilson et al., 2002). But when cognitive–behavioral therapy does not help people with bulimia nervosa, drug therapy may (Walsh et al., 2000).

There are various antidepressants. Each increases the concentration of noradrenaline or serotonin in the brain (Frank & Kupfer, 2003). *Monoamine oxidase (MAO) inhibitors* block the activity of an enzyme that breaks down noradrenaline and serotonin. *Tricyclic and tetracyclic antidepressants* prevent the reuptake of noradrenaline and serotonin by the axon terminals of the transmitting neurons. **Selective serotonin-reuptake inhibitors (SSRIs)** such as Prozac, Zoloft, and Effexor also block the reuptake of serotonin by presynaptic neurons. As a result, serotonin remains in the synaptic cleft longer, influencing receiving neurons. SSRIs appear to be more effective than other antidepressants (Bech et al., 2000).

Antidepressant drugs must usually build up to a therapeutic level over several weeks. Because overdoses can be lethal, some people stay in a hospital during the buildup to prevent suicide attempts. There are also side effects, some of which are temporary, such as nausea, agitation, and weight gain.

LITHIUM The ancient Greeks and Romans were among the first to use the metal lithium as a psychoactive drug. They prescribed mineral water—which contains lithium—for people with bipolar disorder. They had no inkling as to why this treatment sometimes helped. A salt of the metal lithium (lithium carbonate), in tablet form, flattens out cycles of manic behavior and depression in most people. Lithium can also be used to strengthen the effects of antidepressant medication (Bauer et al., 2000). It is not known exactly how lithium works, although it affects the functioning of neurotransmitters.

People with bipolar disorder may have to use lithium indefinitely, as a person with diabetes must use insulin to control the illness. Lithium also has been shown to have side effects such as hand tremors, memory impairment, and excessive thirst and urination (Kleindienst & Greil, 2003). Memory impairment is reported as the main reason why people discontinue lithium.

Electroconvulsive Therapy

Question: What is electroconvulsive therapy (ECT)? Electroconvulsive therapy (ECT) is a biological form of therapy for psychological disorders that was introduced by the Italian psychiatrist Ugo Cerletti in 1939. Cerletti had noted that some slaughterhouses used electric shock to render animals unconscious. The shocks also produced convulsions. Along with other European researchers of the period, Cerletti erroneously believed that convulsions were incompatible with schizophrenia and other major psychological disorders.

ECT was originally used for a variety of psychological disorders. Because of the advent of antipsychotic drugs, however, it is now used mainly for people with major depression who do not respond to antidepressants (Thase & Kupfer, 1996).

People typically obtain one ECT treatment three times a week for up to 10 sessions. Electrodes are attached to the temples and an electrical current strong

Antidepressant (ant-eye-dee-PRESS-ant). Acting to relieve depression.

Selective serotonin-reuptake inhibitors (SSRIs) Antidepressant drugs that work by blocking the reuptake of serotonin by presynaptic neurons.

Electroconvulsive therapy (ECT) Treatment of disorders like major depression by passing an electric current (that causes a convulsion) through the head.

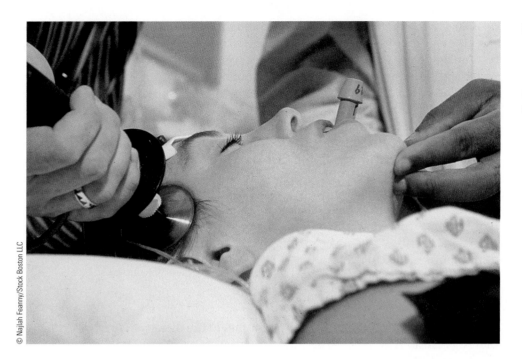

■ **Electroconvulsive Therapy** In ECT, electrodes are placed on each side of the patient's head and a current is passed between them, inducing a seizure. ECT is used mainly in cases of major depression when antidepressant drugs and psychotherapy are not sufficient.

enough to produce a convulsion is induced. The shock causes unconsciousness, so the patient does not recall it. Nevertheless, patients are given a **sedative** so that they are asleep during the treatment.

CONTROVERSY IN PSYCHOLOGY

Should health professionals use electroconvulsive therapy?

ECT is controversial for many reasons, such as the fact that many professionals are distressed by the thought of passing an electric shock through a patient's head and producing convulsions. But there are side effects, including memory problems in the form of retrograde amnesia (Lisanby et al., 2000; Weiner, 2000). (Some researchers argue that stronger shock to one side of the head may be as effective yet have fewer side effects as compared with weaker shock to both sides of the head [Sackeim et al., 2000].) However, research suggests that for most people, cognitive impairment tends to be temporary (Eranti & McLoughlin, 2003). One study followed up 10 adolescents who had received ECT an average of 3½ years earlier. Six of the 10 had complained or memory impairment immediately after treatment, but only one complained of continued problems at the follow-up. Nevertheless, psychological tests did not reveal any differences in cognitive functioning between severely depressed adolescents who had received ECT and others who had not (Cohen et al., 2000).

Psychosurgery

Psychosurgery is more controversial than ECT. **Questions: What is psychosurgery? How is it used to treat psychological disorders?** The best-known modern technique, **prefrontal lobotomy,** has been used with people with severe disorders. In this method, a picklike instrument severs the nerve pathways that link the prefrontal lobes of the brain to the thalamus. This method was pioneered by the Portuguese

Sedative A drug that relieves nervousness or agitation or puts one to sleep.

Psychosurgery Surgery intended to promote psychological changes or to relieve disordered behavior.

Prefrontal lobotomy The severing or destruction of a section of the frontal lobe of the brain.

neurologist Antonio Egas Moniz and was brought to the United States in the 1930s. The theoretical rationale for the operation was vague and misguided and Moniz's reports of success were exaggerated. Nevertheless, by 1950 prefrontal lobotomies had been performed on more than a thousand people in an effort to reduce violence and agitation. Anecdotal evidence of the method's unreliable outcomes is found in an ironic footnote to history: One of Dr. Moniz's "failures" shot the doctor, leaving a bullet lodged in his spine and paralyzing his legs. **Truth or Fiction Revisited:** It is true that the originator of a surgical technique intended to reduce violence learned that it was not always successful . . . when one of his patients shot him.

Prefrontal lobotomy also has a host of side effects, including hyperactivity and distractibility, impaired learning ability, overeating, apathy and withdrawal, epileptic-type seizures, reduced creativity, and, now and then, death. Because of these side effects, and because of the advent of antipsychotic drugs, this method has been largely discontinued in the United States.

Does Biological Therapy Work?

There are thus a number of biological approaches to the therapy of psychological disorders. **Question: What do we know about the effectiveness of biological therapies?**

There is little question that drug therapy has helped many people with severe psychological disorders. For example, antipsychotic drugs largely account for the reduced need for the use of restraint and supervision (padded cells, straitjackets, hospitalization, and so on) with people diagnosed with schizophrenia. Antipsychotic drugs have allowed hundreds of thousands of former mental hospital residents to lead largely normal lives in the community, hold jobs, and maintain family lives. Most of the problems related to these drugs concern their side effects. **Truth or Fiction Revisited:** Therefore, people with psychological disorders should *not* always say no to drugs.

But many comparisons of psychotherapy (in the form of cognitive therapy) and drug therapy for depression suggest that cognitive therapy is as effective as, or more effective than, antidepressants (Antonuccio, 1995; Muñoz et al., 1994). For one thing, cognitive therapy provides coping skills that reduce the risk of recurrence of depression once treatment ends (Hollon & Shelton, 2001). Then again, at least one study suggests that a combination of cognitive therapy and antidepressant medication is superior to either treatment alone with chronically depressed people (Keller et al., 2000). On the other hand, SSRIs may also help prevent subsequent heart attacks in depressed people who have had prior heart attacks (Writing Committee for the ENRICHD Investigators, 2003). The chapter's "Life Connections" section discusses cognitive–behavioral methods for tackling depression.

Many psychologists and psychiatrists are comfortable with the short-term use of antianxiety drugs in helping clients manage periods of unusual anxiety or tension. However, many people use antianxiety drugs routinely to dull the arousal stemming from anxiety-producing lifestyles or interpersonal problems. Rather than make the often painful decisions required to confront their problems and change their lives, they prefer to take a pill.

Despite the controversies surrounding ECT, it helps many people who do not respond to antidepressant drugs (Thase & Kupfer, 1996). ECT, that is, may be a useful "last resort" when other treatment methods are of no avail.

In sum, drug therapy and perhaps ECT seem to be effective for some disorders that do not respond to psychotherapy alone. Yet common sense and research evidence suggest that psychotherapy is preferable for problems such as anxiety and mild depression. No chemical can show a person how to change an idea or solve an interpersonal problem.

A Closer Look — EYE-MOVEMENT DESENSITIZATION AND REPROCESSING

Helping professionals are often inspired to develop therapy methods based on their personal experiences. A troubled young man named Carl Rogers discovered that his strict authoritarian father had coldly communicated values that were preventing him from becoming his own person. Rogers developed a therapy method that provides a warm atmosphere to help clients learn about and act on their genuine feelings. Aaron Beck found that he could argue himself out of his fear of driving through tunnels. Thus he developed cognitive therapy methods based on encouraging clients to recognize and challenge irrational fears and concerns.

So, too, with Francine Shapiro. As she paints it, Shapiro (1989) had troubling thoughts on her mind when she entered the park. But as her eyes darted about, taking in the scene, she found her troubled thoughts disappearing. Thus she developed a therapy method that has fad-like followers: eye-movement desensitization and reprocessing (EMDR). EMDR has joined the arsenal of therapeutic weapons against stress disorders. Shapiro has now trained thousands of helping professionals to use EMDR. In this method, the client is asked to imagine a traumatic scene while the therapist moves a finger rapidly back and forth before his or her eyes for about 20–30 seconds. The client follows the finger while keeping the troubling scene in mind. The client tells the therapist what he or she was thinking and how he or she felt during the procedure. The procedure is repeated until the client's feelings of anxiety are dissipated. Treatment takes about three 90-minute sessions.

Evidence from a number of studies suggests that EMDR helps decrease the anxiety associated with traumatic events. One study, for example, compared the effectiveness of EMDR with two alternative treatments: exposure therapy (used, e.g., with firefighter Stephen King to reduce his anxieties over the attacks of 9/11) and relaxation training (Taylor et al., 2003). Another study looked at the effectiveness of EMDR on numerous people following September 11 (Silver et al., 2005). These studies and others (such as Sikes & Sikes's [2005] study with college students and Devilly's [2002] review of the literature) suggest that EMDR is effective. But there are questions, including just how effective EMDR is and why it works (May, 2005). Devilly (2002), as noted, allows that EMDR is often effective, but his review finds other exposure therapies to be more effective. Research also challenges the idea that eye movements are a necessary part of therapy (May, 2005; Devilly, 2002). Skeptics have tried EMDR–or a cousin of it–using finger tapping rather than finger wagging or instructing clients to keep their eyes straight ahead. The results have remained the same.

It may be that the effects of EMDR can be attributed to a combination of nonspecific therapy factors and to exposure. Clients receiving EMDR may profit from a "therapeutic alliance" with the helping professional and from expectations of success. Moreover, the client *is* to some degree being exposed to the trauma that haunts him or her, and under circumstances in which the client believes he or she will be able to manage the trauma.

Conclusion? Exposure helps people cope with trauma. Eye movements are (probably) not needed.

Your Turn: Now that we have discussed biological therapies, enhance your mastery of the material with the nearby "Learning Connections." Review the material by filling in the blanks, reflect on the material by relating it to other things you know, and think critically about it.

Learning Connections — BIOLOGICAL THERAPIES

ACTIVE REVIEW (28) (*Minor* or *Major?*) tranquilizers are usually prescribed for people who complain of anxiety or tension. (29) (*Minor* or *Major?*) tranquilizers are used to reduce agitation, delusions, and hallucinations. (30) _____ have been used to treat panic disorder, obsessive–compulsive disorder, depression, and eating disorders. (31) Major tranquilizers that belong to the chemical class of phenothiazines are thought to work by blocking the action of the neurotransmitter _____. (32) Antidepressants heighten the action of the neurotransmitter _____. (33) ECT is mainly used to treat severe cases of _____. (34) The best-known psychosurgery technique is the _____ lobotomy.

REFLECT AND RELATE Consider your own sociocultural background. In your experience, do people from your background express any particular attitudes toward people who use antianxiety drugs or antidepressants? Explain.

CRITICAL THINKING Are there times when it is appropriate to prescribe medical treatment for a psychological disorder? How would you make that decision?

 Go to **http://psychology.wadsworth.com/ rathus_pcc9e** for an interactive version of this Learning Connections unit.

Life Connections

Alleviating Depression: Getting out of the Dumps

Be not afraid of life. Believe that life is worth living and your belief will help create the fact.
William James

We began the chapter with the case of a depressed college sophomore, Jasmine. We noted that various kinds of therapist might treat her depression in different ways.

Depression is characterized by inactivity, feelings of sadness, and cognitive distortions. When we suspect that our feelings may fit the picture of a major depressive episode or bipolar disorder, it may be helpful to talk things over with our instructor or visit the college counseling or health center. Some of us may also want to try to get at the deep-seated roots of our feelings of depression, and doing so in some cases might require long-term talk therapy. On the other hand, cognitive–behavioral therapists have pointed out that there are many things we can do on our own to cope with milder feelings of depression. These methods attempt to directly reverse the characteristics of depression. They include:
• Engaging in pleasant events.
• Thinking rationally.
• Exercising.
• Asserting ourselves.

Engaging in Pleasant Events

There is a relationship between our moods and what we do. Losses, failures, and tension can trigger feelings of depression. Pleasant events can generate feelings of happiness and joy. You may be able to use pleasant events to lift your mood purposefully by taking the following steps:
1. Check off items in Table 15.2 that appeal to you.
2. Engage in at least three pleasant events each day.
3. Record your activities in a diary. Add other activities and events that strike you as pleasant, even if they are unplanned.

4. Toward the end of each day, rate your response to each activity, using a scale like this one:

+3 Wonderful
+2 Very nice
+1 Somewhat nice
 0 No particular response
−1 Somewhat disappointing
−2 Rather disappointing
−3 The pits

5. After a week or so, check the items in the diary that received positive ratings.
6. Repeat successful activities and experiment with new ones.

Thinking Rationally

Public opinion is a weak tyrant compared with our own private opinion. What a man thinks of himself, that it is which determines . . . his fate.
Henry David Thoreau, *Walden*

Depressed people tend to blame themselves for failures and problems, even when they are not at fault. They *internalize* blame and see their problems as *stable* and *global*—as all but impossible to change. Depressed people also make cognitive errors such as *catastrophizing* their problems and *minimizing* their accomplishments.

Column 1 in Table 15.3 illustrates a number of irrational, depressing thoughts. How many of them have you had? Column 2 indicates the type of cognitive error being made (such as internalizing or catastrophizing), and column 3 shows examples of rational alternatives.

You can pinpoint irrational, depressing thoughts by identifying the kinds of thoughts you have when you feel low. Look for the fleeting thoughts that can trigger mood changes. It helps to jot them down. Then challenge their accuracy. Do you characterize difficult situations as impossible and hopeless? Do you expect too much from yourself and minimize your achievements? Do you internalize more than your fair share of blame?

You can use Table 15.3 to classify your cognitive errors and construct rational alternatives. Write these next to each irrational thought. Review them from time to time. When you are alone, you can read the irrational thought aloud. Then follow it by saying to yourself firmly, "No, that's irrational!" Then read the rational alternative aloud twice, *emphatically*.

After you have thought or read aloud the rational alternative, think, "That makes more sense! That's a more accurate view of things! I feel better now that I have things in perspective."

Exercising

Exercise not only fosters physical health. It can enhance psychological well-being and help us cope with depression.

■ **Tackling Depression or Just Having Fun?** Many cognitive–behavioral therapists tackle depression directly, by focusing on what depressed people do (or don't do) and think. Depressed people are often inactive, withdrawn from the activities that typically delighted them. Therefore, cognitive–behavioral therapists may prescribe such activities as part of the treatment for depression.

© Tom Stewart/CORBIS

TABLE 15.2 A CATALOG OF PLEASANT EVENTS

1. Being in the country
2. Wearing expensive or formal clothes
3. Making contributions to religious, charitable, or political groups
4. Talking about sports
5. Meeting someone new
6. Going to a rock concert
7. Playing baseball, softball, football, or basketball
8. Planning trips or vacations
9. Buying things for yourself
10. Being at the beach
11. Doing art work (painting, sculpture, drawing, moviemaking, etc.)
12. Rock climbing or mountaineering
13. Reading the Scriptures
14. Playing golf
15. Rearranging or redecorating your room or house
16. Going naked
17. Going to a sports event
18. Going to the races
19. Reading stories, novels, poems, plays, magazines, newspapers
20. Going to a bar, tavern, club
21. Going to lectures or talks
22. Creating or arranging songs or music
23. Boating
24. Restoring antiques, refinishing furniture
25. Watching television or listening to the radio
26. Camping
27. Working in politics
28. Working on machines (cars, bikes, radios, television sets)
29. Playing cards or board games
30. Doing puzzles or math games
31. Having lunch with friends or associates
32. Playing tennis
33. Driving long distances
34. Woodworking, carpentry
35. Writing stories, novels, poems, plays, articles
36. Being with animals
37. Riding in an airplane
38. Exploring (hiking away from known routes, spelunking, etc.)
39. Singing
40. Going to a party
41. Going to church functions
42. Playing a musical instrument
43. Snow skiing, ice skating
44. Wearing informal clothes, "dressing down"
45. Acting
46. Being in the city, downtown
47. Taking a long, hot bath
48. Playing pool or billiards
49. Bowling
50. Watching wild animals
51. Gardening, landscaping
52. Wearing new clothes
53. Dancing
54. Sitting or lying in the sun
55. Riding a motorcycle
56. Just sitting and thinking
57. Going to a fair, carnival, circus, zoo, amusement park
58. Talking about philosophy or religion
59. Gambling
60. Listening to sounds of nature
61. Dating, courting
62. Having friends come to visit
63. Going out to visit friends
64. Giving gifts
65. Getting massages or backrubs
66. Photography
67. Collecting stamps, coins, rocks, etc.
68. Seeing beautiful scenery
69. Eating good meals
70. Improving your health (having teeth fixed, changing diet, having a checkup, etc.)
71. Wrestling or boxing
72. Fishing
73. Going to a health club, sauna
74. Horseback riding
75. Protesting social, political, or environmental conditions
76. Going to the movies
77. Cooking meals
78. Washing your hair
79. Going to a restaurant
80. Using cologne, perfume
81. Getting up early in the morning
82. Writing a diary
83. Giving massages or backrubs
84. Meditating or doing yoga
85. Doing heavy outdoor work
86. Snowmobiling, dune buggying
87. Being in a body-awareness, encounter, or "rap" group
88. Swimming
89. Running, jogging
90. Walking barefoot
91. Playing Frisbee or catch
92. Doing housework or laundry, cleaning things
93. Listening to music
94. Knitting, crocheting
95. Making love
96. Petting, necking
97. Going to a barber or beautician
98. Being with someone you love
99. Going to the library
100. Shopping
101. Preparing a new or special dish
102. Watching people
103. Bicycling
104. Writing letters, cards, or notes
105. Talking about politics or public affairs
106. Watching attractive women or men
107. Caring for houseplants
108. Having coffee, tea, or Coke, etc., with friends
109. Beachcombing
110. Going to auctions, garage sales, etc.
111. Water skiing, surfing, diving
112. Traveling
113. Attending the opera, ballet, or a play
114. Looking at the stars or the moon
115. Surfing the Net
116. Playing videogames

Source: Adapted from D. J. MacPhillamy & P. M. Lewinsohn, *Pleasant Events Schedule, Form III-S,* University of Oregon, Mimeograph, 1971.

Depression is characterized by inactivity and feelings of helplessness. Exercise is, in a sense, the opposite of inactivity. Exercise might also help alleviate feelings of helplessness. In one experiment, 156 adult volunteers who were depressed were randomly assigned to four months of either aerobic exercise, antidepressant medication, or a combination of the two (Babyak et al., 2000). Following treatment, all three groups showed comparable relief from depression. But at a further 6-month follow-up, subjects from the exercise groups who had continued to exercise showed the greatest improvement. Other experiments also find that exercise alleviates feelings of depression (Jorm et al., 2002; Tkachuk & Martin, 1999). Exercise has also been shown to decrease anxiety and hostility and to boost self-esteem (Hansen et al., 2001; Norvell & Belles, 1993).

Asserting Ourselves: Stand Up!

We humans are social creatures, and social interactions are important to us. Unassertive behavior patterns are linked to feelings of depression. Learning to express our feelings and relate to others has been shown to alleviate feelings of depression (Hersen et al., 1984). Assertive behavior permits more effective interactions with family members, friends, coworkers, and strangers. In this way we remove sources of frustration and expand our social support. Expressions of positive feelings—saying you love someone or simply saying "Good morning" cheerfully—help reduce feelings of hostility and pave the way toward further social involvement.

Assertive behavior involves the expression of one's genuine feelings, standing up for one's legitimate rights, and refusing unreasonable requests. It means resisting undue social influences, disobeying *arbitrary* authority figures, and resisting conformity to *arbitrary* group standards. But many feelings such as love and admiration are positive, so assertive behavior also means expressing positive feelings ("That was great!" "You're wonderful!").

Assertive people also influence others to join them in worthwhile social and political activities. They may become involved in political campaigns, consumer groups, conservationist organizations, and other groups to advance their causes.

Alternatives to assertive behavior include submissive, or *unassertive*, behavior and *aggressive* behavior. When we are submissive, our self-esteem plummets. Unexpressed feelings sometimes smolder as resentments and then catch fire as socially inappropriate outbursts. Aggressive behavior includes physical and verbal attacks, threats, and insults. Sometimes we get our way through aggression, but we also earn the condemnation of others. And, unless we are unfeeling, we condemn ourselves for bullying others. You may wish to take the nearby questionnaire to gain insight into how assertive you are as part of the process of deciding whether to become more assertive.

Perhaps you can't become completely assertive overnight, but you can decide *now* that you have been unassertive long enough and plan to change. There may be times when you want to quit and revert to your unassertive ways. Expressing your genuine beliefs may lead to some immediate social disapproval. Others may have a stake in your remaining a doormat, and the people we wind up confronting are sometimes those who are closest to us: parents, spouses, supervisors, and friends.

Perhaps the strategies presented here will work for you. If they don't, why not talk things over with your professor or visit the college health or counseling center?

TABLE 15.3 IRRATIONAL, DEPRESSING THOUGHTS AND RATIONAL ALTERNATIVES

Irrational Thought	Type of Thought	Rational Alternative
"There's nothing I can do."	Catastrophizing (the size of the problem), minimizing (one's coping ability), stabilizing	"I can't think of anything to do right now, but if I work at it, I may."
"I'm no good."	Internalizing, globalizing, stabilizing	"I did something I regret, but that doesn't make me evil or worthless as a person."
"This is absolutely awful."	Catastrophizing	"This is pretty bad, but it's not the end of the world."
"I just don't have the brains for college."	Stabilizing, globalizing	"I guess I really need to go back over the basics in that course."
"I just can't believe I did something so disgusting!"	Catastrophizing	"That was a bad experience. Well, I won't be likely to try that again soon."
"I can't imagine ever feeling right."	Stabilizing, catastrophizing	"This is painful, but if I try to work it through step by step, I'll probably eventually see my way out of it."
"It's all my fault."	Internalizing	"I'm not blameless, but I wasn't the only one involved. It may have been my idea, but he went into it with his eyes open."
"I can't do anything right."	Globalizing, stabilizing, catastrophizing, minimizing	"I sure screwed this up, but I've done a lot of things well, and I'll do other things well."
"I hurt everybody who gets close to me."	Internalizing, globalizing, stabilizing	"I'm not totally blameless, but I'm not responsible for the whole world. Others make their own decisions, and they have to live with the results, too."
"If people knew the real me, they would have it in for me."	Globalizing, minimizing (the positive in yourself)	"I'm not perfect, but nobody's perfect. I have positive as well as negative features, and I am entitled to self-interests."

Many of us create or compound feelings of depression because of cognitive errors such as those in this table. Have you had any of these irrational, depressing thoughts? Are you willing to challenge them?

Self-Assessment | Do You Speak Your Mind or Do You Wimp Out? The Assertiveness Schedule

What about you? Do you enrich the pockets of every tele-marketer, or do you say no? Do you stick up for your rights, or do you allow others to walk all over you? Do you say what you feel or what you think other people want you to say? Do you initiate relationships with attractive people, or do you shy away from them?

One way to gain insight into how assertive you are is to take the following assertiveness schedule. Once you have finished, turn to Appendix B to find out how to calculate your score. A table in the appendix will also allow you to compare your assertiveness to that of a sample of 1,400 students drawn from 35 college campuses across the United States.

If you believe that you are not assertive enough, why not take the quick course in self-assertion offered here? You need not spend your life imitating a doormat.

Directions: Indicate how well each item describes you by using this code:

3 = very much like me
2 = rather like me
1 = slightly like me
−1 = slightly unlike me
−2 = rather unlike me
−3 = very much unlike me

_____ 1. Most people seem to be more aggressive and assertive than I am.*

_____ 2. I have hesitated to make or accept dates because of "shyness."*

_____ 3. When the food served at a restaurant is not done to my satisfaction, I complain about it to the waiter or waitress.

_____ 4. I am careful to avoid hurting other people's feelings, even when I feel that I have been injured.*

_____ 5. If a salesperson has gone to considerable trouble to show me merchandise that is not quite suitable, I have a difficult time saying "No."*

_____ 6. When I am asked to do something, I insist upon knowing why.

_____ 7. There are times when I look for a good, vigorous argument.

_____ 8. I strive to get ahead as well as most people in my position.

_____ 9. To be honest, people often take advantage of me.*

_____ 10. I enjoy starting conversations with new acquaintances and strangers.

_____ 11. I often don't know what to say to people who are sexually attractive to me.*

_____ 12. I will hesitate to make phone calls to business establishments and instituions*

_____ 13. I would rather apply for a job or for admission to a college by writing letters than by going through with personal interviews.*

_____ 14. I find it embarrassing to return merchandise.*

_____ 15. If a close and respected relative were annoying me, I would smother my feelings rather than express my annoyance.*

_____ 16. I have avoided asking questions for fear of sounding stupid.*

_____ 17. During an argument I am sometimes afraid that I will get so upset that I will shake all over.*

_____ 18. If a famed and respected lecturer makes a comment which I think is incorrect, I will have the audience hear my point of view as well.

_____ 19. I avoid arguing over prices with clerks and salespeople.*

_____ 20. When I have done something important or worthwhile, I manage to let others know about it.

_____ 21. I am open and frank about my feelings.

_____ 22. If someone has been spreading false and bad stories about me, I see him or her as soon as possible and "have a talk" about it.

_____ 23. I often have a hard time saying "No."*

_____ 24. I tend to bottle up my emotions rather than make a scene.*

_____ 25. I complain about poor service in a restaurant and elsewhere.

_____ 26. When I am given a compliment, I sometimes just don't know what to say.*

_____ 27. If a couple near me in a theater or at a lecture were conversing rather loudly, I would ask them to be quiet or to take their conversation elsewhere.

_____ 28. Anyone attempting to push ahead of me in a line is in for a good battle.

_____ 29. I am quick to express an opinion.

_____ 30. There are times when I just can't say anything.*

Reprinted from Rathus, 1973, pp. 398–406.

*These asterisks are explained in the answer key.

Recite—An Active Summary™

Want to study on the go? Go to your companion website and download an audio version of this review section to your media player.

1. What is psychotherapy?

Psychotherapy is a systematic interaction between a therapist and a client that uses psychological principles to help the client overcome psychological disorders or adjust to problems in living.

2. How have people with psychological problems and disorders been treated throughout the ages?

Mostly badly. It has been generally assumed that psychological disorders represented possession due to witchcraft or divine retribution, and cruel methods such as exorcism were used to try to rid the person of evil spirits. Asylums were the first institutions for people with psychological disorders, and eventually mental hospitals and the community mental health movement came into being.

3. How do psychoanalysts conduct a traditional Freudian psychoanalysis?

The goals of psychoanalysis are to provide self-insight, encourage the spilling forth (catharsis) of psychic energy, and replace defensive behavior with coping behavior. The main method is free association, but dream analysis and interpretations are used as well. For example, a psychoanalyst may help clients gain insight into the ways in which they are transferring feelings toward their parents onto a spouse or even onto the analyst.

4. How do modern psychodynamic approaches differ from traditional psychoanalysis?

Modern approaches are briefer and more directive, and the therapist and client usually sit face to face.

5. What is Carl Rogers's method of client-centered therapy?

Client-centered therapy uses nondirective methods to help clients overcome obstacles to self-actualization. The therapist shows unconditional positive regard, empathic understanding, and genuineness.

6. What is Fritz Perls's method of Gestalt therapy?

Perls's highly directive method aims to help people integrate conflicting parts of their personality. He aimed to make clients aware of conflict, accept its reality, and make choices despite fear.

7. What is behavior therapy?

Behavior therapy relies on psychological learning principles (for example, conditioning and observational learning) to help clients develop adaptive behavior patterns and discontinue maladaptive ones.

8. What are some behavior-therapy methods for reducing fears?

These include flooding, systematic desensitization, and modeling. Flooding exposes a person to fear-evoking stimuli without aversive consequences until fear is extinguished. Systematic desensitization counterconditions fears by gradually exposing clients to a hierarchy of fear-evoking stimuli while they remain relaxed. Modeling encourages clients to imitate another person (the model) in approaching fear-evoking stimuli.

9. How do behavior therapists use aversive conditioning to help people break bad habits?

This is a behavior-therapy method for discouraging undesirable behaviors by repeatedly pairing clients' self-defeating goals (for example, alcohol, cigarette smoke, deviant sex objects) with aversive stimuli so that the goals become aversive rather than tempting.

10. How do behavior therapists apply principles of operant conditioning in behavior modification?

These are behavior therapy methods that foster adaptive behavior through principles of reinforcement. Examples include token economies, successive approximation, social skills training, and biofeedback training.

11. How can you use behavior therapy to deal with temptation and enhance your self-control?

Behavior-therapy methods for adopting desirable behavior patterns and breaking bad habits begin with a functional analysis to determine the antecedents and consequences of the problem behavior, along with the details of the behavior itself. They then focus on modifying the antecedents (stimuli that act as triggers) and consequences (reinforcers) of behavior and on modifying the behavior itself.

12. What is cognitive therapy?

Cognitive therapies aim to give clients insight into irrational beliefs and cognitive distortions and replace these cognitive errors with rational beliefs and accurate perceptions.

Recite—An Active Summary™

13. What is Aaron Beck's method of cognitive therapy?

Aaron Beck notes that clients develop emotional problems such as depression because of cognitive errors that lead them to minimize accomplishments and catastrophize failures. He found that depressed people experience cognitive distortions such as the cognitive triad; that is, they expect the worst of themselves, the world at large, and the future. Beck teaches clients how to scientifically dispute cognitive errors.

14. What is Albert Ellis's method of rational emotive behavior therapy (REBT)?

Albert Ellis originated rational emotive behavior therapy, which holds that people's beliefs *about* events, not only the events themselves, shape people's responses to them. Ellis points out how irrational beliefs, such as the belief that we must have social approval, can worsen problems. Ellis literally argues clients out of irrational beliefs.

15. What are the advantages and disadvantages of group therapy?

Group therapy is more economical than individual therapy. Moreover, group members benefit from the social support and experiences of other members. However, some clients cannot disclose their problems in the group setting or risk group disapproval. They need individual attention.

16. What are encounter groups? What are their effects?

Encounter groups attempt to foster personal growth by heightening awareness of people's needs and feelings through intense confrontations between strangers. Encounter groups can be harmful when they urge too rapid disclosure of personal matters or when several members attack an individual.

17. What is family therapy?

In family therapy, one or more families make up the group. Family therapy undertaken from the "systems approach" modifies family interactions to enhance the growth of individuals in the family and the family as a whole.

18. What kinds of problems do researchers encounter when they conduct research on psychotherapy?

It is difficult and perhaps impossible to randomly assign clients to therapy methods such as traditional psychoanalysis. Moreover, clients cannot be kept blind as to the treatment they are receiving. Further, it can be difficult to sort out the effects of nonspecific therapeutic factors such as instillation of hope from the effects of specific methods of therapy.

19. What do we know about the effectiveness of psychotherapy?

Statistical analyses such as meta-analysis show that people who obtain most forms of psychotherapy fare better than people who do not. Psychodynamic and client-centered approaches are particularly helpful with highly verbal and motivated individuals. Cognitive and behavior therapies are probably most effective. Cognitive therapy appears to be as effective as drug therapy in the treatment of depression.

20. What kinds of drug therapy are available for psychological disorders?

Antipsychotic drugs help many people with schizophrenia by blocking the action of dopamine receptors. Antidepressants often help people with severe depression, apparently by raising levels of serotonin available to the brain. Lithium often helps people with bipolar disorder, apparently by regulating levels of glutamate. The use of antianxiety drugs for daily tensions and anxieties is not recommended because people who use them rapidly build tolerance for the drugs. Also, these drugs do not solve personal or social problems, and people attribute their resultant calmness to the drug and not to self-efficacy.

21. What is electroconvulsive therapy (ECT)?

In ECT an electrical current is passed through the temples, inducing a seizure and frequently relieving severe depression. ECT is controversial because of side effects such as loss of memory and because nobody knows why it works.

22. What is psychosurgery? How is it used to treat psychological disorders?

Psychosurgery is a controversial method for alleviating agitation by severing nerve pathways in the brain. The best-known psychosurgery technique, prefrontal lobotomy, has been largely discontinued because of side effects.

Recite—An Active Summary™

23. What do we know about the effectiveness of biological therapies?

There is controversy as to whether psychotherapy or drug therapy should be used with people with anxiety disorders or depression. Drugs do not teach people how to solve problems and build relationships. Having said that, antidepressants are apparently advisable when psychotherapy does not help people with depression; furthermore, ECT appears to be helpful in some cases in which neither psychotherapy nor drug therapy (antidepressants) is of help. Psychosurgery has been all but discontinued because of questions about whether it is effective and because of side effects. Most health professionals agree that antipsychotic drugs are of benefit to large numbers of people with schizophrenia.

 Go to **http://psychology.wadsworth.com/ rathus_pcc9e** to access an interactive version of this active summary.

Key Terms

Psychotherapy (p. 553)
Asylum (p. 554)
Psychoanalysis (p. 555)
Catharsis (p. 555)
Free association (p. 556)
Resistance (p. 556)
Interpretation (p. 556)
Transference (p. 556)
Wish fulfillment (p. 557)
Phallic symbol (p. 558)
Manifest content (p. 558)
Latent content (p. 558)
Ego analyst (p. 558)
Client-centered therapy
  (p. 559)

Unconditional positive
  regard (p. 559)
Empathic understanding
  (p. 560)
Frame of reference
  (p. 560)
Genuineness (p. 560)
Gestalt therapy (p. 561)
Behavior therapy (p. 562)
Systematic desensitization
  (p. 563)
Hierarchy (p. 563)
Modeling (p. 564)
Aversive conditioning
  (p. 564)

Rapid smoking (p. 564)
Token economy (p. 565)
Successive approximations
  (p. 565)
Self-monitoring (p. 566)
Behavior rehearsal
  (p. 566)
Feedback (p. 566)
Biofeedback training (BFT)
  (p. 566)
Functional analysis
  (p. 566)
Cognitive therapy
  (p. 567)
Rational emotive behavior

therapy (REBT) (p. 570)
Encounter group (p. 571)
Family therapy (p. 574)
Meta-analysis (p. 575)
Rebound anxiety (p. 579)
Antidepressant (p. 580)
Selective serotonin-
  reuptake inhibitors
  (SSRIs) (p. 580)
Electroconvulsive therapy
  (ECT) (p. 580)
Sedative (p. 581)
Psychosurgery (p. 581)
Prefrontal lobotomy
  (p. 581)

ACTIVE LEARNING RESOURCES

Visit your Companion Website for Video, Quizzing, and Self-Assessment!

http://psychology.wadsworth.com/rathus_pcc9e
On this site you can access the Virtual Reality Therapy video highlighted by the Video Connections icon on p. 565. In addition there are many quizzing opportunities including interactive versions of the fill-in-the-blank Active Review sections in your book. You can also fill out and score the Self-Assessment on p. 587.

Study on the Go!

Don't have time to study right now? You can study on the go! Visit your companion website and download an audio version of the Recite—An Active Summary section to your media player.

ThomsonNOW

http://www.thomsonedu.com
Need help studying? This site is your one-stop study shop. Take a Pre-Test and Thomson NOW will generate a Personalized Study Plan based on your test results. The Study Plan will identify the topics you need to review and direct you to online resources to help you master those topics. You can then take a Post-Test to determine the concepts you have mastered and what you still need to work on.

Author Blog

What does your author have to say about the state of psychology? Visit your companion website every Tuesday and click on "Author Blog," where he'll talk about the most recent controversies and hot topics in psychology.

Truth or Fiction?

T F People act in accord with their consciences.

T F Airing a TV commercial repeatedly turns off the audience and decreases sales.

T F Being compelled by the law to recycle can change a person's attitude toward recycling.

T F We appreciate things more when we have to work for them.

T F You should just "be yourself" in a job interview. There's no point to getting dressed up and watching your language.

T F We tend to hold others responsible for their misdeeds but to see ourselves as victims of circumstances when we misbehave.

T F Most people will torture an innocent person, just because they are ordered to do so.

T F Seeing is believing.

T F Nearly 40 people stood by and did nothing while a woman was being stabbed to death.

T F Women are less likely than men to toss garbage from the car window.

T F People have condemned billions of other people without ever meeting them or learning their names.

 Go to **http://psychology.wadsworth.com/ rathus_pcc9e** to answer and score this Truth or Fiction quiz.

Social Psychology

Consider some news from Iraq. On May 4, 2005, a suicide bomber in the Kurdish city of Erbil targets police recruits. He kills himself, along with another 60 people, and wounds 150. Victims' bodies are loaded into ambulances, pickup trucks, and on the backs of donkeys. Dozens of the wounded are taken to hospitals. Two days later, a suicide bomber detonates the explosives strapped around his torso in a crowded market at midday in a town 25 miles southeast of Baghdad. Sixteen people die and more than 40 are wounded. On July 25, a bomber wrapped in explosives ignites himself next to an oil tanker south of Baghdad, killing 59. In an orgy of a dozen suicide bombings in Baghdad on September 14, more than 160 Iraqis are killed and another 600 wounded.

As noted by political scientist Mark Danner of the University of California, "There have been suicide truck bombs, suicide tanker bombs, suicide police cars, suicide bombers on foot, suicide bombers posing as police officers, suicide bombers posing as soldiers, even suicide bombers on bicycles" (2005, p. 52). And in the United States, of course, there have been suicide terrorists using fully-fueled airplanes as bombs.

Although you might think of suicide terrorism as a recent phenomenon, it dates back thousands of years (Pastor, 2004). But we have become most recently aware of suicide terrorism by strikes throughout the Muslim world, in Israel, and—with the attacks on New York, Washington, Madrid, and London—in the Western world. The word "suicide" in the phrase "suicide bomber" leads people to turn to psychologists for understanding, with the idea that something must be very wrong psychologically with these terrorists (Pastor, 2004). But many social scientists assert that suicide terrorists have no telltale psychological profile (Consortium of Social Science Associations, 2003; Leenaars, 2006; Lester et al., 2004). Social psychologist Philip Zimbardo (2004) argues that we must look to the "situationist perspective" to understand suicide terrorism.

■ **London, July 7, 2005.** Commuters coming into London on this summer morning were accompanied by four suicide bombers, who detonated the bombs, and themselves, at the peak of rush hour on three subway trains and aboard a bus. More than 50 people died, along with the bombers, and 700 were wounded. The bombers were apparently expressing their displeasure over Britain's support of the United States in Iraq.

The **situationist perspective** studies the ways in which people can be goaded by social influences into doing things that are not necessarily consistent with their personalities. In particular, Zimbardo (2004) has investigated the relative ease with which "ordinary" men and women can be incited by social influence to behave in evil ways.

The situationist perspective is part of the field of **social psychology**. **Question: What is social psychology?** Social psychology studies the nature and causes of behavior and mental processes in social situations. The social psychological topics we discuss in this chapter include attitudes, social perception, social influence, and group behavior. As we explore each of these, we will ask what they might offer to those of us who have difficulty imagining why people would surrender their own lives to take the lives of others.

Situationist perspective The view that social influence can goad people into doing things that are inconsistent with their usual behavior.

Social psychology The field of psychology that studies the nature and causes of people's thoughts and behavior in social situations.

Attitude An enduring mental representation of a person, place, or thing that evokes an emotional response and related behavior.

A–B problem The issue of how well we can predict behavior on the basis of attitudes.

Stereotype A fixed, conventional idea about a group.

Attitudes: "The Good, the Bad, and the Ugly"

How do you feel about abortion, stem cell research, and exhibiting the Ten Commandments in courthouses? These are hot-button topics because people have strong **attitudes** toward them. They each give rise to cognitive evaluations (such as approval or disapproval), feelings (liking, disliking, or something stronger), and behavioral tendencies (such as approach or avoidance). **Question: What are attitudes?** Attitudes are behavioral and cognitive tendencies that are expressed by evaluating particular people, places, or things with favor or disfavor. Although I asked you how you "feel," attitudes are not just feelings or emotions. Many psychologists view thinking—or judgment—as more basic. Feelings and behavior follow.

Attitudes are largely learned, and they affect behavior. They can foster love or hate. They can give rise to helping behavior or to mass destruction. They can lead to social conflict or to the resolution of conflicts. Attitudes can change, but not easily. Most people do not change their religion or political affiliation without serious reflection—or force.

The A–B Problem: Do We Act in Accord with Our Beliefs?

Our definition of attitude implies that our behavior is consistent with our cognitions—that is, with our beliefs and feelings. **Questions: Do people do as they think? (For example, do people really vote their consciences?)** When we are free to do as we wish, our behavior is often consistent with our cognitions. But, as indicated by the term **A–B problem,** there are exceptions. **Truth or Fiction Revisited:** In fact, the links between attitudes (A) and behaviors (B) tend to be weak to moderate (Eagly & Chaiken, 1993). For example, research reveals that attitudes toward health-related behaviors such as use of alcohol, smoking, and drunken driving are not consistent predictors of these behaviors (Stacy et al., 1994).

It also appears that we tend to live up to our **stereotypes**—even our stereotypes of ourselves. For example, when older people are reminded that they are "elderly," they tend to walk more slowly (Wheeler & Petty, 2001).

■ **Do People Always Vote Their "Conscience"?** The A–B problem refers to the research finding that people do not always act in accord with their attitudes.

© Mark Richards/PhotoEdit

A number of factors influence the likelihood that we can predict behavior from attitudes:

1. *Specificity.* We can better predict specific behavior from specific attitudes than from global attitudes. For example, we can better predict church attendance by knowing people's attitudes toward church attendance than by knowing whether they are Christian.

2. *Strength of attitudes.* Strong attitudes are more likely to determine behavior than weak attitudes (Petty et al., 1997). A person who believes that the nation's destiny depends on Republicans taking control of Congress is more likely to vote than a person who leans toward the Republican party but does not believe that the outcome of elections makes much difference.

3. *Vested interest.* People are more likely to act on their attitudes when they have a vested interest in the outcome (Lehman & Crano, 2002). People are more likely to vote for (or against) unionization of their workplace, for example, when they believe that their job security depends on the outcome.

4. *Accessibility.* People are more likely to behave in accord with their attitudes when they are accessible—that is, when they are brought to mind (Kallgren et al., 2000; Petty et al., 1997). This is why politicians attempt to "get out the vote" by means of media blitzes just prior to an election. It does them little good to have supporters who forget them on election day. Attitudes with a strong emotional impact are more accessible, which is one reason that politicians strive to get their supporters "worked up" over the issues.

Origins of Attitudes

 You were not born a Republican or a Democrat. You were not born a Christian, a Jew, or a Muslim, although your parents may have practiced one of these religions when you came along. **Question: Where do attitudes come from?** Political, religious, and other attitudes are learned or derived from cognitive processes. In this section we describe some of the processes that result in acquiring attitudes.

Conditioning may play a role in acquiring attitudes. Experiments have shown that attitudes toward national groups can be influenced by associating them with positive words (such as *gift* or *happy*) or negative words (such as *ugly* or *failure*) (De Houwer et al., 2001). Parents often reward children for saying and doing things that agree with their own attitudes. Patriotism is encouraged by showing approval to children when they sing the national anthem or wave the flag.

Attitudes formed through direct experience may be stronger and easier to recall, but we also acquire attitudes by observing others. The approval or disapproval of peers leads adolescents to prefer short or long hair, baggy jeans, or preppie sweaters. The media inform us that body odor and bad breath are dreaded diseases—and, perhaps, that people who use harsh toilet paper are somehow un-American.

COGNITIVE APPRAISAL Despite what we have said, the acquisition of attitudes is not so mechanical. People are also motivated to have a valid understanding of reality, so that they can make predictions and exercise some control over their environment (Wood, 2000). So people also evaluate information and form or change attitudes, including stereotypes, on the basis of new information (Petty et al., 1997, 1999). For example, we may believe that a car is more reliable than we had thought if a survey by *Consumer Reports* finds that it has an excellent repair record. Even so, initial attitudes act as cognitive anchors (Wegener et al., 2001; Wood, 2000). We often judge new ideas in terms of how much they deviate from our existing attitudes. Accepting larger deviations requires more information processing—in other words, more intellectual work (Petty et al., 1997, 1999). For this reason, perhaps, great deviations—such as changes from liberal to conservative attitudes, or vice versa—are apt to be resisted.

Changing Attitudes through Persuasion: How Persuasive?

Let advertisers spend the same amount of money improving their product that they do on advertising and they wouldn't have to advertise it.
Will Rogers

Rogers's social comment sounds on the mark, but he was probably wrong. It does little good to have a wonderful product if its existence remains a secret. **Question: Can you really change people?—their attitudes and behavior, that is?**

The **elaboration likelihood model** describes the ways in which people respond to persuasive messages (Crano, 2000). Consider two routes to persuading others to change attitudes. The first, or central, route inspires thoughtful consideration of arguments and evidence. The second, or peripheral, route associates objects with positive or negative cues. When politicians avow that "This bill is supported by Jesse Jackson (or Jesse Helms)," they are seeking predictable, knee-jerk reactions, not careful consideration of a bill's merits. Other cues are rewards (such as a smile or a hug), punishments (such as parental disapproval), and such factors as the trustworthiness and attractiveness of the communicator.

Advertisements, which are a form of persuasive communication, also rely on central and peripheral routes. Some ads focus on the quality of the product (central route). Others attempt to associate the product with appealing images (peripheral route). Ads for Total cereal, which highlight its nutritional benefits, provide information about the quality of the product. So, too, did the "Pepsi Challenge" taste-test ads, which claimed that Pepsi tastes better than Coca-Cola. Marlboro cigarette ads that focus on the masculine, rugged image of the "Marlboro man"[2] offer no information about the product itself. Nor do ads that show football players heading for Disney World or choosing a brand of beer.

In this section we look at one central factor in persuasion—the nature of the message—and three peripheral factors: the messenger, the context of the message, and the audience. We also examine the foot-in-the-door technique.

THE PERSUASIVE MESSAGE: SAY WHAT? SAY HOW? SAY HOW OFTEN? How do we respond when TV commercials are repeated until we have memorized every dimple on the actors' faces? Research suggests that familiarity breeds content, not contempt (Macrae et al., 2002; Zajonc, 2001).

You might not be crazy about *zebulons* and *afworbu's* at first, but Robert Zajonc (1968) found that people began to react favorably toward these bogus foreign words on the basis of repeated exposure. **Truth or Fiction Revisited:** It appears that repeated exposure to people and things as diverse as the following enhances their appeal (Baron & Byrne, 2004):

◆ Political candidates (who are seen in repeated TV commercials).
◆ Photographs of African Americans.
◆ Photographs of college students.
◆ Abstract art.
◆ Classical music.

Classic research suggests that the more complex the stimuli, the more likely it is that frequent exposure will have favorable effects (Smith & Dorfman, 1975). The 100th playing of a Bach fugue may be less tiresome than the 100th performance of a pop tune.

Elaboration likelihood model The view that persuasive messages are evaluated (elaborated) on the basis of central and peripheral cues.

---

[2] The rugged actor in the original TV commercials died of lung cancer. Apparently cigarettes were more rugged than he was.

■ **Most Valuable Players or Most Valuable Endorsers?** Advertisers use a combination of central and peripheral cues to sell their products. What factors contribute to the persuasiveness of messages? To the persuasiveness of communicators? Why are Tiger Woods and Anna Kournikova sought-after commodities by advertisers?

When trying to persuade someone, is it helpful or self-defeating to alert them to the arguments presented by the opposition? In two-sided arguments, the communicator recounts the arguments of the opposition in order to refute them. In research concerning a mock trial, college undergraduates were presented with two-sided arguments—those of the prosecution and those of the defendant (McKenzie et al., 2002). When one argument was weak, the college "jurors" expressed more confidence in their decision than when they did not hear the other side at all. Theologians and politicians sometimes forewarn their followers about the arguments of the opposition and then refute each one. Forewarning creates a kind of psychological immunity to them (Jacks & Devine, 2000).

It would be nice to think that people are too sophisticated to be persuaded by a **fear appeal.** However, many women who are warned of the dire risk they run if they fail to be screened for breast cancer are more likely to obtain mammograms than women who are informed of the *benefits* of mammography (Ruiter et al., 2001). Interestingly, although suntanning has been shown to increase the likelihood of skin cancer, warnings against suntanning were shown to be more effective when students were warned of risks to their *appearance* (premature aging, wrinkling, and scarring of the skin) than when the warning dealt with the risk to their health (Jones & Leary, 1994). That is, students informed of tanning's cosmetic effects were more likely to say they would protect themselves from the sun than were students informed about the risk of cancer. Fear appeals are most effective when the audience believes that the risks are serious—as in causing wrinkles!—and that the audience members can change their behavior to avert the risks—as in preventing cancer or wrinkling (T. R. Schneider et al., 2001).

Audiences also tend to believe arguments that appear to run counter to the vested interests of the communicator (Lehman & Crano, 2002). If the president of Chrysler or General Motors said that Toyotas and Hondas were superior, you can bet that we would prick up our ears.

THE PERSUASIVE COMMUNICATOR: WHOM DO YOU TRUST? Would you buy a used car from a person who had been convicted of larceny? Would you leaf through fashion magazines featuring homely models? Probably not. Research shows that persuasive communicators are characterized by expertise, trustworthiness, attractiveness, or similarity to their audiences (Petty et al., 1997).

TV news anchors enjoy high prestige. One study (Mullen et al., 1987) found that before the 1984 presidential election, Peter Jennings of ABC News had shown significantly more favorable facial expressions when reporting on Ronald Reagan

Fear appeal A type of persuasive communication that influences behavior on the basis of arousing fear instead of rational analysis of the issues.

than when reporting on Walter Mondale. Tom Brokaw of NBC and Dan Rather of CBS had not shown favoritism. The researchers also found that a higher percentage of viewers of ABC News voted for Reagan than viewers of NBC or CBS News. Did Jennings subtly persuade viewers to vote for Reagan? Perhaps he did in a number of cases. But viewers do not simply absorb, spongelike, whatever the media feed them. People find it painful when they are confronted with information that discredits their own opinions (Foerster et al., 2000). Therefore, they often show **selective avoidance** and **selective exposure** (Perse, 1998). That is, they switch channels when the news coverage runs counter to their own attitudes. They also seek communicators whose outlook coincides with their own. Thus, it could be that Reagan supporters favored Jennings over Brokaw and Rather.

THE CONTEXT OF THE MESSAGE: "GET 'EM IN A GOOD MOOD" You are too shrewd to let someone persuade you by buttering you up, but perhaps someone you know would be influenced by a sip of wine, a bite of cheese, and a sincere compliment. Aspects of the immediate environment, such as music, increase the likelihood of persuasion. When we are in a good mood, we apparently are less likely to evaluate the situation carefully (Park & Banaji, 2000; Petty et al., 1997).

It is also counterproductive to call your dates fools when they differ with you—even though their ideas are bound to be foolish if they do not agree with yours. Agreement and praise are more effective ways to encourage others to embrace your views. Appear sincere, or else your compliments will look manipulative. (It seems unfair to let out this information.)

THE PERSUADED AUDIENCE Why do some people have sales resistance? Why do others enrich the lives of every door-to-door salesperson? It may be that people with high self-esteem and low social anxiety are more likely to resist social pressure (Ellickson et al., 2001).

A classic study by Schwartz and Gottman (1976) reveals the cognitive nature of the social anxiety that can make it difficult for some people to refuse requests. The researchers found that people who comply with unreasonable requests are more apt to report thoughts like the following:

◆ "I was worried about what the other person would think of me if I refused."

◆ "It is better to help others than to be self-centered."

◆ "The other person might be hurt or insulted if I refused."

People who refuse unreasonable requests reported thoughts like these:

◆ "It doesn't matter what the other person thinks of me."

Selective avoidance Diverting one's attention from information that is inconsistent with one's attitudes.

Selective exposure Deliberately seeking and attending to information that is consistent with one's attitudes.

Foot-in-the-door technique A method for inducing compliance in which a small request is followed by a larger request.

 A Closer Look — THE FOOT-IN-THE-DOOR TECHNIQUE

You might suppose that contributing money to door-to-door solicitors for charity will get you off the hook. Perhaps they'll take the cash and leave you alone for a while. Actually, the opposite is true. The next time they mount a campaign, they may call on you to go door to door on their behalf! Organizations compile lists of people they can rely on. Because they have gotten their "foot in the door," this is known as the **foot-in-the-door technique.**

Consider a classic experiment by Freedman and Fraser (1966). Groups of women received phone calls from a consumer group requesting that they let a six-person crew come to their home to catalog their household products. The job could take hours. Only 22% of one group acceded to this irksome request. But 53% of another group of women assented to a visit from this wrecking crew. Why was the second group more compliant? They had been phoned a few days earlier and had agreed to answer a few questions about the soap products they used. Thus they had been primed for the second request: The caller had gotten a foot in the door.

Research suggests that people who accede to small requests become more amenable to larger ones for a variety of reasons, including conformity and self-perception as the kind of people who help in this way (Burger, 1999). Regardless of how the foot-in-the-door technique works, if you want to say no, it may be easier to do so (and stick to your guns) the first time a request is made. Later may be too late.

◆ "I am perfectly free to say no."

◆ "This request is unreasonable."

Changing Attitudes and Behavior by Means of Cognitive Dissonance: "I Think, Therefore I Am . . . Consistent"?

The brain within its groove
Runs evenly and true . . .

Emily Dickinson

Question: What is cognitive-dissonance theory? According to **cognitive-dissonance theory,** people are thinking creatures who seek consistency in their behaviors and their attitudes—their views of the world (Albarracín & Wyer, 2000). People must apparently mentally represent the world accurately in order to predict and control events. Consistency in beliefs, attitudes, and behavior helps make the world seem like a predictable place. Therefore, if we find ourselves in the uncomfortable spot where two cherished ideas conflict, we are motivated to reduce the discrepancy— just as the Seekers in the nearby "A Closer Look" did when the flying saucers did not land on schedule.

In the first and still one of the best-known studies on cognitive dissonance, one group of participants received $1 (worth $5 to $10 today) for telling someone else that a boring task was interesting (Festinger & Carlsmith, 1959). Members of a second group received $20 (worth $100 to $200 today) to describe the chore positively. Both groups were paid to engage in **attitude-discrepant behavior**—that is, behavior that ran counter to what they actually thought. After presenting their fake

Cognitive-dissonance theory The view that we are motivated to make our cognitions or beliefs consistent.

Attitude-discrepant behavior Behavior inconsistent with an attitude that may have the effect of modifying an attitude.

A Closer Look   THE SEEKERS AND THE GUARDIANS: WHAT HAPPENS *WHEN PROPHECY FAILS?*

The Seekers were quite a group. Their brave leader, Marian Keech, dutifully recorded the messages that she believed were sent to her by the Guardians from outer space. One particular message was somewhat disturbing. It specified that the world would come to an end on December 21. A great flood would engulf Lake City, the home of Ms. Keech and many of her faithful followers.

A second message brought good news, however. Ms. Keech received word that the Seekers would be rescued from the flood. You see, Ms. Keech reported that she received messages through "automatic writing." The messengers would communicate through her: She would write down their words, supposedly without awareness. This bit of writing was perfectly clear: The Seekers would be saved by flying saucers at the stroke of midnight on the 21st.

In their classic observational study, Leon Festinger and his colleagues (1956) described how they managed to be present in Ms. Keech's household at the fateful hour by pretending to belong to the group. Their purpose was to observe the behavior of the Seekers during and following (what they assumed would be) the prophecy's failure.

Let us return to the moment of truth. Many Seekers had quit their jobs and gone on spending sprees before the anticipated end. Now they were all gathered together. As midnight approached they fidgeted, awaiting the flying saucers. Midnight came, but no saucers. Anxious glances were exchanged. Silence. Coughs. A few minutes passed, tortuously slowly. Watches were checked, more glances exchanged. At 4:00 AM a bitter and frantic Ms. Keech complained that she sensed that members of the group were doubting her. At 4:45 AM, however, she seemed suddenly relieved. A third message was arriving, and Ms. Keech was spelling it out through automatic writing! The Seekers, it turned out, had managed to save the world through their faith. The universal powers had decided to let the world travel on along its sinful way for a while longer. Why? Because of the faith of the Seekers, there was hope!

You guessed it. The faith of most of those present was renewed. They called wire services and newspapers to spread the word. The three psychologists from the University of Minnesota went home, weary but enlightened, and wrote a book entitled *When Prophecy Fails*, which serves as one of the key documents about the relationships about truth and attitude change (or lack or change).

What about Ms. Keech's husband? He was a tolerant sort. He slept through it all.

Leon Festinger, the lead author of *When Prophecy Fails*, was developing a cognitive theory of motivation called *cognitive-dissonance theory*. The theory suggested that when the prophecy failed, the Seekers would be caught between two key conflicting cognitions: (1) Ms. Keech is a prophet, and (2) Ms. Keech is wrong. Ms. Keech, as it happened, was shown to be wrong. How did the seekers resolve the conflict? One way would have been for the Seekers to lose faith in Ms. Keech—and in their own judgment in following her. But the researchers argued that such a course might be humiliating. (Who likes to admit that he or she has been a fool?) Still, according to cognitive-dissonance theory, the Seekers needed some way to resolve the conflict. Thus they apparently jumped at the "solution" of accepting the "truthfulness" of Ms. Keech's third message—the message that their faith had saved the world. It feels good to save the world now and then. The Seekers went out to spread the word and find additional converts.

enthusiasm for the boring task, the participants were asked to rate their own liking for it. Ironically, those who were paid *less* rated the task as actually more interesting than their better-paid colleagues reported. **Truth or Fiction Revisited:** Similarly, being compelled by the law to recycle can change a person's attitude toward recycling.

Learning theorists (see Chapter 6) might predict a different outcome. Learning theorists might predict that the more we are reinforced for doing something (given more money, for example), the more we should like it (not find the task quite as boring, that is). But that is not what happened here. Cognitive-dissonance theorists rightly predicted this outcome. Because the ideas (cognitions) of (a) "I was paid very little" and (b) "I told someone that this assignment was interesting" are dissonant, people will tend to engage in **effort justification.** The discomfort of cognitive dissonance motivates people to explain their behavior to themselves in such a way that unpleasant undertakings seem worth it. Participants who were paid only $1 may have justified their lie by concluding that they may not have been lying in the first place. **Truth or Fiction Revisited:** As another example of effort justification, we do tend to appreciate things more when we have to work for them.

Your Turn: Now that we have defined social psychology and discussed attitudes, enhance your mastery of the material with the nearby "Learning Connections." Review the material by filling in the blanks, reflect on the material by relating it to other things you know, and think critically about it.

Learning Connections: ATTITUDES: "THE GOOD, THE BAD, AND THE UGLY"

ACTIVE REVIEW (1) _____ psychology is the study of the nature and causes of our behavior and mental processes in social situations. (2) A(n) _____ is a behavioral and cognitive tendency that are expressed by evaluating people or things with favor or disfavor. (3) When we are free to do as we wish, our behavior (*Is* or *Is not?*) usually consistent with our attitudes. (4) Attitudes are acquired through conditioning, observational learning, and _____ appraisal. (5) Early attitudes serve as _____ anchors. (6) According to the _____ likelihood model, there are central and peripheral routes to persuasion. (7) According to the _____-in-the-door effect, people are more likely to agree to large requests after they have agreed to smaller ones. (8) According to cognitive-_____ theory, we are motivated to make our cognitions consistent with one another and with our behavior.

REFLECT AND RELATE Here's a mini-experiment: Keep a log of radio or TV commercials you hear or see for a few days. Which ones grab your attention? Why? Which ones do you believe? Why? Which ones tempted you to consider buying or trying a product? Why?

CRITICAL THINKING How can you use the information in this section to develop sales resistance? How can the information make you a more critical consumer of commercials?

 Go to **http://psychology.wadsworth.com/ rathus_pcc9e** for an interactive version of this Learning Connections unit.

Social Perception: Looking out, Looking Within

An important area of social psychology concerns the ways in which we perceive other people—for example, the importance of the first impressions they make on us. Next we explore some factors that contribute to **social perception:** the primacy and recency effects, attribution theory, and body language.

Primacy and Recency Effects: The Importance of First Impressions

Why do you wear a suit to a job interview? Why do defense attorneys make sure that their clients dress neatly and get their hair cut before they are seen by the jury? **Questions: Do first impressions really matter? What are the primacy and recency effects?** Apparently first impressions do matter—a great deal.

Whether we are talking about the business or social worlds, or even the relationship between a therapist and a client, first impressions are important (Bidell

Effort justification In cognitive-dissonance theory, the tendency to seek justification (acceptable reasons) for strenuous efforts.

Social perception A subfield of social psychology that studies the ways in which we form and modify impressions of others.

■ **First Impressions** Why is it so important to make a good first impression? What are some ways of doing so?

et al., 2002; Laungani, 2002). First impressions are an example of the primacy effect. Let's have a look at the primacy and recency effects.

When I was a teenager, a young man was accepted or rejected by his date's parents the first time they were introduced. If he was considerate and made small talk, her parents would allow the couple to stay out past curfew—perhaps even to watch submarine races at the beach during the early morning hours. If he was boorish or uncommunicative, he was seen as a cad forever after. Her parents would object to him, no matter how hard he worked to gain their favor.

My experiences demonstrated to me that first impressions often make or break us. This phenomenon is known as the **primacy effect. Truth or Fiction Revisited:** It is apparently not true that you should just "be yourself" in a job interview. Dressing down or cursing may very well cost you the job.

Why are first impressions so important? The answer may be because we infer traits from behavior. If we act considerately at first, we are labeled considerate. The *trait* of consideration is used to explain and predict our future behavior. If, after being labeled considerate, one keeps a date out past curfew, this lapse is likely to be seen as an exception to a rule—excused by circumstances or external causes. If one is first seen as inconsiderate, however, several months of considerate behavior may be perceived as a cynical effort to "make up for it."

Subjects in a classic experiment on the primacy effect read different stories about "Jim" (Luchins, 1957). The stories consisted of one or two paragraphs. The one-paragraph stories portrayed Jim as either friendly or unfriendly. These paragraphs were also used in the two-paragraph stories, but in this case the paragraphs were read in the reverse order. Of those reading only the "friendly" paragraph, 95% rated Jim as friendly. Of those who read just the "unfriendly" paragraph, 3% rated him as friendly. Seventy-eight percent of those who read two-paragraph stories in the "friendly–unfriendly" order labeled Jim as friendly. When they read the paragraphs in the reverse order, only 18% rated Jim as friendly.

How can we encourage people to pay more attention to impressions occurring after the first encounter? Abraham Luchins accomplished this by allowing time to elapse between the presentations of the two paragraphs. In this way, fading memories allowed more recent information to take precedence. This is known as the **recency effect.** Luchins found a second way to counter first impressions: He simply asked subjects to avoid making snap judgments and to weigh all the evidence.

There is some interesting research on the role of the handshake in making a first impression. In our culture, a firm handshake is a key to making a good first impression, by women as well as men. Researchers find that a firm handshake is perceived as an indication of being outgoing and open to new experience. A weak handshake was perceived as indicative of shyness and social anxiety (Chaplin et al., 2000). Thus women in the business world are well advised to shake hands of new acquaintances firmly.

Attribution Theory: You're Free to Choose, but I'm Caught in the Middle?

When she was 3 years old, one of my daughters believed that a friend's son was a boy because he *wanted* to be a boy. Since she was 3 at the time, this error in my daughter's **attribution** of the boy's gender is understandable. Adults tend to make somewhat similar attribution errors, however. Although they do not believe that people's preferences have much to do with their gender, they do tend to exaggerate the role of choice in their behavior. **Questions: What is attribution theory? Why do we assume that other people intend the mischief that they do?**

Primacy effect The tendency to evaluate others in terms of first impressions.

Recency effect The tendency to evaluate others in terms of the most recent impression.

Attribution A belief concerning why people behave in a certain way.

An attribution is an assumption about why people do things. When you assume that one child is mistreating another child because she is "mean," you are making an attribution. The process by which we make inferences about the motives and traits of others through observation of their behavior is the **attribution process.** This section focuses on *attribution theory,* or the processes by which people draw conclusions about the factors that influence one another's behavior. Attribution theory is important because attributions lead us to perceive others either as purposeful actors or as victims of circumstances.

DISPOSITIONAL AND SITUATIONAL ATTRIBUTIONS Social psychologists describe two types of attributions. **Dispositional attributions** ascribe a person's behavior to internal factors such as personality traits and free will. **Situational attributions** attribute a person's actions to external factors such as social influence or socialization. If you assume that one child is mistreating the other because her parents have given her certain attitudes toward the other child, you are making a situational attribution.

THE FUNDAMENTAL ATTRIBUTION ERROR In cultures that view the self as independent, such as ours, people tend to attribute other people's behavior primarily to internal factors such as personality, attitudes, and free will (Gilovich & Eibach, 2001; Reeder, 2001). This bias in the attribution process is known as the **fundamental attribution error.** In such individualistic societies, people tend to focus on the behavior of others rather than on the circumstances surrounding their behavior. For example, if a teenager gets into trouble with the law, individualistic societies are more likely to blame the teenager than the social environment in which the teenager lives. When involved in difficult negotiations, there is a tendency to attribute the toughness to the personalities of the negotiators on the other side rather than the nature of the process of negotiation (Morris et al., 1999). **Truth or Fiction Revisited:** Therefore, we do tend to hold others responsible for their misdeeds but to see ourselves as victims of circumstances when we misbehave.

One reason for the fundamental attribution error is that we tend to infer traits from behavior. But in collectivist cultures that stress interdependence, such as Asian cultures, people are more likely to attribute other people's behavior to a person's social roles and obligations (Basic Behavioral Science Task Force, 1996c). For example, Japanese people might be more likely to attribute a businessperson's extreme competitiveness to the "culture of business" rather than to his or her personality.

THE ACTOR–OBSERVER EFFECT When we see people (including ourselves) doing things that we do not like, we tend to see the others as willful actors but to see ourselves as victims of circumstances (Baron & Byrne, 2004). The tendency to attribute other people's behavior to dispositional factors and our own behavior to situational influences is called the **actor–observer effect.**

Consider an example. Parents and children often argue about the children's choice of friends or dates. When they do, the parents tend to infer traits from behavior and to see the children as stubborn and resistant. The children also infer traits from behavior. Thus they may see their parents as bossy and controlling. Parents and children alike attribute the others' behavior to internal causes. That is, both make dispositional attributions about other people's behavior.

Try a mini-experiment: The next time you observe friends or family members having an argument, ask one of them afterwards why the argument occurred—who had done something wrong and why. If the individual admits to having dome something wrong himself or herself, does he or she make a dispositional or a situational attribution? If he or she blames the other person, does he or she make a dispositional or a situational attribution?

Attribution process The process by which people draw inferences about the motives and traits of others.

Dispositional attribution An assumption that a person's behavior is determined by internal causes such as personal attitudes or goals.

Situational attribution An assumption that a person's behavior is determined by external circumstances such as the social pressure found in a situation.

Fundamental attribution error The assumption that others act predominantly on the basis of their dispositions, even when there is evidence suggesting the importance of their situations.

Actor–observer effect The tendency to attribute our own behavior to situational factors but to attribute the behavior of others to dispositional factors.

■ **The Actor–Observer Effect** Who is at fault here? People tend to make dispositional attributions for other people's behavior, but they tend to see their own behavior as motivated by situational factors. Thus people are aware of the external forces acting on themselves when they behave, but tend to attribute other people's behavior to choice and will.

Butch Martin/Getty Images

How do the parents and children perceive themselves? The parents probably see themselves as being forced into combat by their children's foolishness. If they become insistent, it is in response to the children's stubbornness. The children probably see themselves as responding to peer pressures and, perhaps, to sexual urges that may have come from within but seem like a source of outside pressure. The parents and the children both tend to see their own behavior as motivated by external forces. That is, they make situational attributions for their own behavior.

The actor–observer effect extends to our perceptions of both the in-group (an extension of ourselves) and the out-group. Consider conflicts between nations, for example. Both sides may engage in brutal acts of violence. Each side usually considers the other to be calculating, inflexible, and—not infrequently—sinister. Each side also typically views its own people as victims of circumstances and its own violent actions as justified or dictated by the situation. After all, we may look at the other side as being in the wrong, but can we expect them to agree with us?

THE SELF-SERVING BIAS There is also a **self-serving bias** in the attribution process. We are likely to ascribe our successes to internal, dispositional factors but our failures to external, situational influences (Duval & Silvia, 2002; Pronin et al., 2002). When we have done well on a test or impressed a date, we are likely to credit our intelligence and charm. But when we fail, we are likely to blame bad luck, an unfair test, or our date's bad mood.

We can extend the self-serving bias to sports. A study with 27 college wrestlers found that they tended to attribute their wins to stable and internal conditions such as their abilities, but their losses to unstable and external conditions such as an error by a referee (De Michele et al., 1998). Sports fans fall into the same trap. They tend to attribute their team's victories to internal conditions and their losses to external conditions (Wann & Schrader, 2000).

There are exceptions to the self-serving bias. In accord with the bias, when we work in groups, we tend to take the credit for the group's success but to pin the blame for group failure on someone else. But the outcome is different when we are friends with other group members: Then we tend to share the credit for success or the blame for failure (Campbell et al., 2000). Another exception is found in the fact that depressed people are more likely than other people to ascribe their failures to internal factors, even when external forces are mostly to blame.

Another interesting attribution bias is a gender difference in attributions for friendly behavior. Men are more likely than women to interpret a woman's smile or friendliness toward a man as flirting (Abbey, 1987; Buss, 2000). Perhaps traditional differences in gender roles still lead men to expect that a "decent" woman will be passive.

FACTORS CONTRIBUTING TO THE ATTRIBUTION PROCESS Our attribution of behavior to internal or external causes can apparently be influenced by three factors: *consensus, consistency,* and *distinctiveness* (Kelley & Michela, 1980). When few people act in a certain way—that is, when **consensus** is low—we are likely to attribute behavior to dispositional (internal) factors. Consistency refers to the degree to which the same person acts in the same way on other occasions. Highly consistent behavior can often be attributed to dispositional factors. Distinctiveness is the extent to which the person responds differently in different situations. If the person acts similarly in different situations, distinctiveness is low. We therefore are likely to attribute his or her behavior to dispositional factors.

Let us apply the criteria of consensus, consistency, and distinctiveness to the behavior of a customer in a restaurant. She takes one bite of her strawberry cheesecake and calls the waiter. She tells him that her food is inedible and demands that it be replaced. Now, has she complained as a result of internal causes (for example, because she is hard to please) or external causes (that is, because the food really is bad)? Under the following circumstances, we are likely to attribute her behavior to internal, dispositional causes: (1) No one else at the table is com-

Self-serving bias The tendency to view one's successes as stemming from internal factors and one's failures as stemming from external factors.

Consensus General agreement.

plaining, so consensus is low. (2) She has returned her food on other occasions, so consistency is high. (3) She complains in other restaurants also, so distinctiveness is low (see Table 16.1).

But under the following circumstances, we are likely to attribute the customer's behavior to external, situational causes: (1) Everyone else at the table is also complaining, so consensus is high. (2) She does not usually return food, so consistency is low. (3) She usually does not complain at restaurants, so distinctiveness is high. Given these conditions, we are likely to believe that the cheesecake really is awful and that the customer is justified in her response.

Body Language: The Body Speaks

Body language is important in social perception. **Question: What is body language?** Body language is nonverbal language; it refers to the meanings we infer from the ways in which people carry themselves and the gestures they make (Flack et al., 1999; McClave, 2000). At an early age we learn that the way people carry themselves provides cues to how they feel and are likely to behave. You may have noticed that when people are "uptight" they may also be rigid and straight-backed. People who are relaxed are more likely to "hang loose." Factors such as eye contact, posture, and the distance between two people provide cues to the individuals' moods and their feelings toward their companions. When people face us and lean toward us, we may assume that they like us or are interested in what we are saying. If we overhear a conversation between a couple and observe that the woman is leaning toward the man while the man is sitting back and toying with his hair, we are likely to infer that he is not interested in what she is saying.

Here's a mini-experiment: The next time you are out among people, look around. Can you tell whether other people are enjoying being with one another, or whether they are finding the experience annoying? How can you tell?

TOUCHING: PUT THE ARM ON PEOPLE (LITERALLY) Touching also communicates. Women are more likely than men to touch other people when they are interacting with them (Stier & Hall, 1984). In one "touching" experiment, Kleinke (1977) showed that appeals for help can be more effective when the distressed person makes physical contact with people who are asked for aid. A woman obtained more coins for phone calls when she touched the arm of the person she was asking for money. In another experiment, waitresses obtained higher tips when they touched patrons on the hand or the shoulder while making change (Crusco & Wetzel, 1984).

In these experiments, the touching was noncontroversial. It was usually gentle, brief, and done in familiar settings. However, when touching suggests greater intimacy than is desired, it can be seen as negative. A study in a nursing home found that responses to being touched depended on factors such as the status of the staff member, the type of touch, and the part of the body that was touched (Hollinger & Buschmann, 1993). Touching was considered positive when it was appropriate to the situation and did not appear to be condescending. It was seen as negative when it was controlling, unnecessary, or overly intimate.

TABLE 16.1	FACTORS LEADING TO INTERNAL OR EXTERNAL ATTRIBUTIONS OF BEHAVIOR	
	Internal Attribution	**External Attribution**
Consensus	Low: Few people behave this way.	High: Most people behave this way.
Consistency	High: The person behaves this way frequently.	Low: The person does not behave this way frequently.
Distinctiveness	Low: The person behaves this way in many situations.	High: The person behaves this way in few situations.

■ **Gazing versus Staring** Gazing into an attractive person's eyes can give rise to feelings of passion, but people interpret a hard stare as an aversive challenge.

GAZING AND STARING: THE EYES HAVE IT We usually feel that we can learn much from eye contact. When other people "look us squarely in the eye," we may assume that they are being assertive or open with us. Avoidance of eye contact may suggest deception or depression. Gazing is interpreted as a sign of liking or friend-liness (Kleinke, 1986). In one penetrating study, men and women were asked to gaze into each other's eyes for two minutes (Kellerman et al., 1989). After doing so, they reported having passionate feelings toward one another. (Watch out!)

Of course, a gaze is not the same thing as a persistent hard stare. A hard stare is interpreted as a provocation or a sign of anger. Adolescent males sometimes engage in staring contests as an assertion of dominance. The male who looks away first loses the contest. In a classic series of field experiments, Phoebe Ellsworth and her colleagues (1972) subjected drivers stopped at red lights to hard stares by riders of motor scoot-ers (see Figure 16.1). When the light changed, people who were stared at crossed the intersection more rapidly than people who were not. People who are stared at exhibit higher levels of physiological arousal than people who are not (Strom & Buck, 1979).

Your Turn: Now that we have discussed social perception, enhance your mastery of the material with the nearby "Learning Connections." Review the material by filling in the blanks, reflect on the material by relating it to other things you know, and think critically about it.

FIGURE 16.1 Diagram of an Experiment in Hard Staring and Avoidance
In the Greenbaum and Rosenfeld study, the confederate of the experimenter stared at some drivers and not at others. Recipients of the stares drove across the intersection more rapidly once the light turned green. Why?

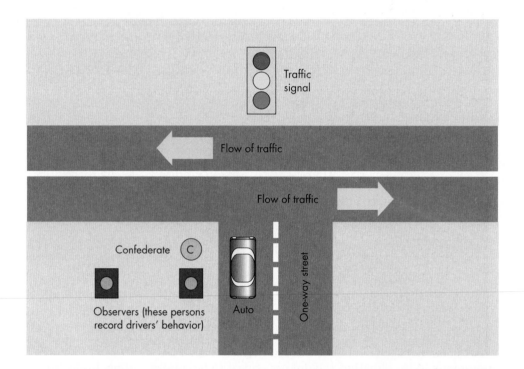

![] **Learning Connections** | **SOCIAL PERCEPTION: LOOKING OUT, LOOKING WITHIN**

ACTIVE REVIEW (9) The psychology of social _____ involves the ways in which we perceive other people and ourselves. (10) The tendency to perceive others in terms of first impressions is an example of the _____ effect. (11) Our inference of the motives and traits of others through observation of their behavior is called the _____ process. (12) People who feel (*Positively* or *Negatively*?) toward one another tend to position them-selves close together. (13) Gazing into another's eyes can be a sign of love, but a hard _____ is an aversive challenge.

REFLECT AND RELATE Did you ever try to "make a good first impression"? What was the occasion? What did you do? Was your effort successful? Explain.

CRITICAL THINKING Why is it that we tend to hold others accountable for their misdeeds but excuse ourselves for the bad things we do? How can you use this information to enhance your social relationships?

 Go to **http://psychology.wadsworth.com/ rathus_pcc9e** for an interactive version of this Learning Connections unit.

Social Influence: Are You an Individual or One of the Crowd?

Most people would be reluctant to wear blue jeans to a funeral, walk naked on city streets, or, for that matter, wear clothes at a nudist colony. This is because other people and groups can exert enormous pressure on us to behave according to their norms. **Social influence** is the area of social psychology that studies the ways in which people alter the thoughts, feelings, and behavior of others (Baron & Byrne, 2004; Crano, 2000). We already learned how attitudes can be changed through persuasion. In this section we describe a couple of classic experiments that demonstrate how people influence others to engage in destructive obedience or conform to social norms.

Obedience to Authority: Does Might Make Right?

Throughout history soldiers have followed orders—even when it comes to slaughtering innocent civilians. The Turkish slaughter of Armenians, the Nazi slaughter of Jews, the mutual slaughter of Hutus and Tutsis in Rwanda—these are all examples of the tragedies that can arise from simply following orders. We may say we are horrified by such crimes, and we cannot imagine why people engage in them. But how many of us would refuse to follow orders issued by authority figures? **Questions: Why will so many people commit crimes against humanity if they are ordered to do so? (Why don't they refuse?)**

THE MILGRAM STUDIES: SHOCKING STUFF AT YALE Yale University psychologist Stanley Milgram also wondered how many people would resist immoral requests made by authority figures. To find out, he undertook a series of classic experiments at the university that have become known as the Milgram studies on obedience.

In an early phase of his work, Milgram (1963) placed ads in New Haven (Connecticut) newspapers for people who would be willing to participate in studies on learning and memory. He enlisted 40 people ranging in age from 20 to 50— teachers, engineers, laborers, salespeople, people who had not completed elementary school, people with graduate degrees.

Let's suppose that you have answered the ad. You show up at the university in exchange for a reasonable fee ($4.50, which in the early 1960s might easily fill your gas tank) and to satisfy your own curiosity. You may be impressed. After all, Yale is a venerable institution that dominates the city. You are no less impressed by the elegant labs, where you meet a distinguished behavioral scientist dressed in a white coat and another person who has responded to the ad. The scientist explains that the purpose of the experiment is to study the *effects of punishment on learning*. The experiment requires a "teacher" and a "learner." By chance, you are appointed the teacher and the other recruit the learner.

You, the scientist, and the learner enter a laboratory room containing a threatening chair with dangling straps. The scientist straps the learner in. The learner expresses some concern, but this is, after all, for the sake of science. And this is Yale University, isn't it? What could happen to a person at Yale?

You follow the scientist to an adjacent room, from which you are to do your "teaching." This teaching promises to have an impact. You are to punish the learner's errors by pressing levers marked from 15 to 450 volts on a fearsome-looking console. Labels describe 28 of the 30 levers as running the gamut from "Slight Shock" to "Danger: Severe Shock." The last two levers are simply labeled "XXX." Just in case you have no idea what electric shock feels like, the scientist gives you a sample 45-volt shock. It stings. You pity the person who might receive more.

Your learner is expected to learn pairs of words, which are to be read from a list. After hearing the list once, the learner is to produce the word that pairs with the stimulus word from a list of four alternatives. This is done by pressing a switch that lights one of four panels in your room. If it is the correct panel, you proceed to the next stimulus word. If not, you are to deliver an electric shock. With each error, you are to increase the voltage of the shock (Figure 16.2).

Social influence The area of social psychology that studies the ways in which people influence the thoughts, feelings, and behavior of others.

FIGURE 16.2 **The Experimental Set-up in the Milgram Studies**

When the "learner" makes an error, the experimenter prods the "teacher" to deliver a painful electric shock.

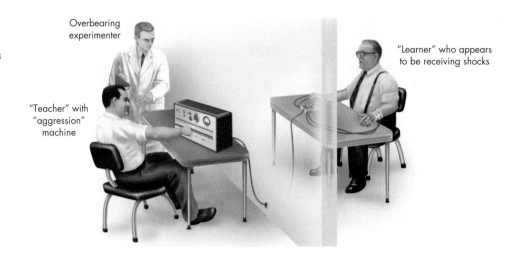

Overbearing experimenter

"Learner" who appears to be receiving shocks

"Teacher" with "aggression" machine

You probably have some misgivings. Electrodes have been strapped to the learner's wrists, and the scientist has applied electrode paste "to avoid blisters and burns." You have also been told that the shocks will cause "no permanent tissue damage," although they might be extremely painful. Still, the learner is going along. And after all, this is Yale.

The learner answers some items correctly and then makes some errors. With mild concern you press the levers up through 45 volts. You've tolerated that much yourself. Then a few more mistakes are made. You press the 60-volt lever, then 75. The learner makes another mistake. You pause and look at the scientist, who is reassuring: "Although the shocks may be painful, there is no permanent tissue damage, so please go on." The learner makes more errors, and soon you are up to a shock of 300 volts. But now the learner is pounding on the other side of the wall! Your chest tightens, and you begin to perspire. "Damn science and the $4.50!" you think. You hesitate and the scientist says, "The experiment requires that you continue." After the delivery of the next stimulus word, the learner chooses no answer at all. What are you to do? "Wait for 5 to 10 seconds," the scientist instructs, "and then treat no answer as a wrong answer." But after the next shock the pounding on the wall resumes! Now your heart is racing, and you are convinced you are causing extreme pain and discomfort. Is it possible that no lasting damage is being done? Is the experiment that important, after all? What to do? You hesitate again, and the scientist says, "It is absolutely essential that you continue." His voice is very convincing. "You have no other choice," he says, "you *must* go on." You can barely think straight, and for some unaccountable reason you feel laughter rising in your throat. Your finger shakes above the lever. *What are you to do?*

Milgram had foreseen that some "teachers" in his experiment would hesitate. He had therefore conceived standardized statements that his assistants would use when subjects balked—for example: "Although the shocks may be painful, there is no permanent tissue damage, so please go on." "The experiment requires that you continue." "It is absolutely essential that you continue." "You have no other choice, you *must* go on."

To repeat: If you are a teacher in the Milgram study, what do you do? Milgram (1963, 1974) found out what most people in his sample would do. The sample was a cross-section of the male population of New Haven. Of the 40 men in this phase of his research, only 5 refused to go beyond the 300-volt level, the level at which the learner first pounded the wall. Nine other "teachers" defied the scientist within the 300-volt range. But 65% of the subjects complied with the scientist throughout the series, believing they were delivering 450-volt, XXX-rated shocks. **Truth or Fiction Revisited:** Therefore, it appears to be true that most people will torture an innocent person, just because they are ordered to do so.

Were these subjects unfeeling? Not at all. Milgram was impressed by their signs of stress. They trembled, they stuttered, they bit their lips. They groaned, they sweated, they dug their fingernails into their flesh. Some had fits of laughter, although laughter was inappropriate. One salesperson's laughter was so convulsive that he could not continue with the experiment.

Milgram's initial research on obedience was limited to a sample of New Haven men. Could he generalize his findings to other men or to women? Would college students, who are considered to be independent thinkers, show more defiance? A replication of Milgram's study with a sample of Yale men yielded similar results. What about women, who are supposedly less aggressive than men? In subsequent research, women, too, administered shocks to the learners. All this took place in a nation that values independence and free will.

In various phases of Milgram's research, nearly half or the majority of the subjects complied throughout the series, believing that they were delivering 450-volt, XXX-rated shocks. These findings held for men from the New Haven community and for male students at Yale, and for women.

ON DECEPTION AND TRUTH AT YALE I have said that the "teachers" in the Milgram studies *believed* that they were shocking other people when they pressed the levers on the console. They weren't. The only real shock in this experiment was the 45-volt sample given to the teachers. Its purpose was to make the procedure believable.

The learners in the experiment were actually confederates of the experimenter. They had not answered the newspaper ads but were in on the truth from the start. The "teachers" were the only real subjects. They were led to believe they had been chosen at random for the teacher role, but the choosing was rigged so that newspaper recruits would always become teachers.

Milgram debriefed his subjects after the experiment was complete. He explained the purpose and methods of his research in detail. He emphasized the fact that they had not actually harmed anyone. But of course the subjects did believe that they were hurting other people as the experiment was being carried out. As you can imagine, the ethics of the Milgram studies have been debated by psychologists for four decades.

WHY DID PEOPLE IN THE MILGRAM STUDIES OBEY THE EXPERIMENTERS? In any event, many people obey the commands of others even when they are required to perform immoral tasks. But *why?* Why did Germans "just follow orders" during the Holocaust? Why did "teachers" obey the experimenter in Milgram's study? We do not have all the answers, but we can offer a number of hypotheses:

1. *Socialization.* Despite the expressed American ideal of independence, we are socialized from early childhood to obey authority figures such as parents and teachers. Obedience to immoral demands may be the ugly sibling of socially desirable respect for authority figures (Blass, 1999).

2. *Lack of social comparison.* In Milgram's experimental settings, experimenters displayed command of the situation. Teachers (subjects), however, were on the experimenter's ground and very much on their own so they did not have the opportunity to compare their ideas and feelings with those of other people in the same situation. They therefore were less likely to have a clear impression of what to do.

3. *Perception of legitimate authority.* One phase of Milgram's research took place within the hallowed halls of Yale University. Subjects might have been overpowered by the reputation and authority of the setting. An experimenter at Yale might have appeared to be a highly legitimate authority figure—as might a government official or a high-ranking officer in the military (Blass & Schmitt, 2001). Yet further research showed that the university setting contributed to compliance but was not fully responsible for it. The percentage of individuals who complied with the experimenter's demands dropped from 65% to 48% when Milgram (1974) replicated the study in a dingy storefront in a nearby town. At first glance, this finding might seem encouraging. But the main point of the Milgram studies

is that most people are willing to engage in morally reprehensible acts at the behest of a legitimate-looking authority figure. Hitler and his henchmen were authority figures in Nazi Germany. "Science" and Yale University legitimized the authority of the experimenters in the Milgram studies.

4. *The foot-in-the-door technique.* The foot-in-the-door technique might also have contributed to the obedience of the teachers. Once they had begun to deliver shocks to learners, they might have found it progressively more difficult to extricate themselves from the situation. Soldiers, similarly, are first taught to obey orders unquestioningly in unimportant matters such as dress and drill. By the time they are ordered to risk their lives, they have been saluting smartly and following commands without question for a long time.

5. *Inaccessibility of values.* People are more likely to act in accordance with their attitudes when their attitudes are readily available, or accessible. Most people believe that it is wrong to harm innocent people. But strong emotions interfere with clear thinking. As the teachers in the Milgram experiments became more aroused, their attitudes might thus have become less "accessible." As a result, it might have become progressively more difficult for them to behave according to these attitudes.

6. *Buffers.* Several buffers decreased the effect of the learners' pain on the teachers. For example, the "learners" (actually confederates of the experimenter) were in another room. When they were in the same room with the teachers, their compliance rate dropped from 65% to 40%. Moreover, when the teacher held the learner's hand on the shock plate, the compliance rate dropped to 30%. In modern warfare, opposing military forces may be separated by great distances. They may be little more than a blip on a radar screen. It is one thing to press a button to launch a missile or aim a piece of artillery at a distant troop carrier or a faraway mountain ridge. It is another to hold a weapon to a victim's throat.

Conformity: Do Many Make Right?

We are said to **conform** when we change our behavior in order to adhere to social norms. **Social norms** are widely accepted expectations concerning social behavior. Explicit social norms are often made into rules and laws such as those that require us to whisper in libraries and to slow down when driving past a school. There are also unspoken or implicit social norms, such as those that cause us to face

Conform To changes one's attitudes or overt behavior to adhere to social norms.

Social norms Explicit and implicit rules that reflect social expectations and influence the ways people behave in social situations.

■ **Conformity** In the military, individuals are taught to conform until the group functions in machine-like fashion. What pressures to conform do you experience? Do you surrender to them? Why or why not?

A. Standard line

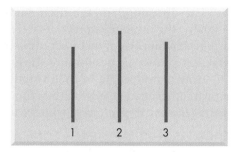

1   2   3

B. Comparison lines

FIGURE 16.3 Cards Used in the Asch Study on Conformity

Which line on card B–1, 2, or 3–is the same length as the line on card A? Line 2, right? But would you say "2" if you were a member of a group and six people answering ahead of you all said "3"? Are you sure?

the front in an elevator or to be "fashionably late" for social gatherings. Can you think of some instances in which you have conformed to social pressure? (Would you wear blue jeans if everyone else wore slacks or skirts?)

The tendency to conform to social norms is often good. Many norms have evolved because they promote comfort and survival. Group pressure can also promote maladaptive behavior, as when people engage in risky behavior because "everyone is doing it." **Question: Why do so many people tend to follow the crowd?**

To answer this question, let us look at a classic experiment on conformity conducted by Solomon Asch in the early 1950s. We then examine factors that promote conformity.

SEVEN LINE JUDGES CAN'T BE WRONG: THE ASCH STUDY Can you believe what you see with your own eyes? Seeing is believing, isn't it? Not if you were a subject in Asch's (1952) study.

You entered a laboratory room with seven other subjects, supposedly taking part in an experiment on visual discrimination. At the front of the room stood a man holding cards with lines drawn on them.

The eight of you were seated in a series. You were given the seventh seat, a minor fact at the time. The man explained the task. There was a single line on the card on the left. Three lines were drawn on the card at the right (Figure 16.3). One line was the same length as the line on the other card. You and the other subjects were to call out, one at a time, which of the three lines—1, 2, or 3—was the same length as the one on the card on the left. Simple.

The subjects to your right spoke out in order: "3," "3," "3," "3," "3," "3." Now it was your turn. Line 3 was clearly the same length as the line on the first card, so you said "3." The fellow after you then chimed in: "3." That's all there was to it. Then two other cards were set up at the front of the room. This time line 2 was clearly the same length as the line on the first card. The answers were "2," "2," "2," "2," "2," "2." Again it was your turn. You said "2," and perhaps your mind began to wander. Your stomach was gurgling a bit. The fellow after you said "2."

Another pair of cards was held up. Line 3 was clearly the correct answer. The six people on your right spoke in turn: "1," "1 . . ." Wait a second! ". . . 1," "1." You forgot about dinner and studied the lines briefly. No, line 1 was too short by a good half inch. But the next two subjects said "1" and suddenly it was your turn. Your hands had become sweaty, and there was a lump in your throat. You wanted to say "3," but was it right? There was really no time, and you had already paused noticeably. You said "1," and so did the last fellow.

Now your attention was riveted on the task. Much of the time you agreed with the other seven judges, but sometimes you did not. And for some reason beyond your understanding, they were in perfect agreement even when they were wrong—assuming you could trust your eyes. The experiment was becoming an uncomfortable experience, and you began to doubt your judgment. **Truth or Fiction Revisited:** Therefore, seeing is not always believing—especially when the group sees things differently.

The discomfort in the Asch study was caused by the pressure to conform. Actually, the other seven recruits were confederates of the experimenter. They pre-arranged a number of incorrect responses. The sole purpose of the study was to see whether you would conform to the erroneous group judgments.

How many people in Asch's study caved in? How many went along with the crowd rather than give what they thought to be the right answer? Seventy-five percent. *Three out of four agreed with the majority's wrong answer at least once.*

FACTORS THAT INFLUENCE CONFORMITY Several factors increase the tendency to conform. They include the following:

◆ Belonging to a collectivist rather than an individualistic society (Phalet & Schoenpflug, 2001).
◆ The desire to be liked by other members of the group (but valuing being right over being liked *decreases* the tendency to conform).
◆ Low self-esteem.
◆ Social shyness (Santee & Maslach, 1982).
◆ Lack of familiarity with the task.

Other factors in conformity include group size and social support. The likelihood of conformity, even to incorrect group judgments, increases rapidly as group size grows to five members, then rises more slowly as the group grows to about eight members. At about that point the maximum chance of conformity is reached. Yet finding just one other person who supports your minority opinion apparently is enough to encourage you to stick to your guns (Morris et al., 1977).

Your Turn: Now that we have discussed social influence, enhance your mastery of the material with the nearby "Learning Connections." Review the material by filling in the blanks, reflect on the material by relating it to other things you know, and think critically about it.

 Learning Connections | SOCIAL INFLUENCE: ARE YOU AN INDIVIDUAL OR ONE OF THE CROWD?

ACTIVE REVIEW (14) Most people (*Do* or *Do not*?) comply with the demands of authority figures when those demands are immoral. (15) The following factors contribute to obedience: socialization, lack of _____ comparison, perception of experimenters as legitimate authority figures, and inaccessibility of values. (16) In Asch's studies of conformity, _____% of the subjects agreed with an incorrect majority judgment at least once.

REFLECT AND RELATE There are many possible explanations for obedience, as found in the Milgram studies. Milgram's research has alerted us to a real danger—the tendency of many, if not most, people to obey the orders of an authority figure even when they run counter to moral values. It has happened before. It is happening now. What will you do to stop it?

CRITICAL THINKING Critical thinkers do not overgeneralize. Most people would probably agree that it is good for children to be obedient. But is it always good for children—and for adults—to be obedient? As an individual, how can you determine whether or not it is good for *you* to be obedient? How do we define the limits?

 Go to **http://psychology.wadsworth.com/ rathus_pcc9e** for an interactive version of this Learning Connections unit.

Group Behavior

To be human is to belong to groups. Groups have much to offer us. They help us satisfy our needs for affection, attention, and belonging. They empower us to do things we could not manage by ourselves. But groups can also pressure us into doing things we might not do if we were acting alone, such as taking great risks or attacking other people.

This section considers ways in which people behave differently as group members than they would as individuals. We begin with social facilitation.

Social Facilitation: Monkey See, Monkey Do Faster?

When you are given a group assignment, do you work harder or less hard than you would alone? Why?

One effect of groups on individual behavior is **social facilitation,** or the effects on performance that result from the presence of others. **Question: Do we run faster when we are in a group?** Apparently so. Runners and bicycle riders tend to move faster when they are members of a group. This effect is not limited to people. Dogs and cats eat more rapidly around others. Even roaches—yes, roaches—run more rapidly when other roaches are present (Zajonc, 1980).

Research suggests that the presence of other people increases our levels of arousal, or motivation (Platania & Moran, 2001; Thomas et al., 2002). At high levels of arousal, our performance of simple tasks is facilitated. Our performance of complex responses may be impaired, however. For this reason, a well-rehearsed speech may be delivered more masterfully before a larger audience. An offhand speech or a question-and-answer session may be hampered by a large audience.

Social facilitation may be influenced by **evaluation apprehension** as well as arousal (Platania & Moran, 2001; Thomas et al., 2002). Our performance before a group is affected not only by the presence of others but also by concern that they are evaluating us. When giving a speech, we may "lose our thread" if we are distracted by the audience and focus too much on its apparent reaction. If we believe that we have begun to flounder, evaluation apprehension may skyrocket. As a result, our performance may falter even more.

The presence of others can also impair performance—not when we are acting *before* a group but when we are anonymous members *of* a group (Guerin, 1999). Workers, for example, may "goof off" or engage in *social loafing* on humdrum jobs when they believe they will not be found out and held accountable. Under these conditions there is no evaluation apprehension. There may also be **diffusion of responsibility** in groups. Each person may feel less obligation to help because others are present, especially if the others are perceived as being capable of doing the job (Hart et al., 2001). Group members may also reduce their efforts if an apparently capable member makes no contribution but "rides free" on the efforts of others.

How would you perform in a tug of war? Would the presence of other people pulling motivate you to pull harder? (If so, we might attribute the result to "social facilitation," unless you personally enjoy tugging [Smith et al., 2001].) Or would the fact that no one can tell how hard you are pulling encourage you to "loaf"? (If so, should we attribute the result to "diffusion of responsibility"?)

Group Decision Making: Is a Camel a Horse Made by a Committee?

Organizations use groups such as committees or juries to make decisions in the belief that group decisions are more accurate than individual decisions (Gigone & Hastie, 1997). **Question: How do groups make decisions?** Social psychologists have discovered a number of "rules," or **social decision schemes,** that govern much of group decision making (Stasser, 1999). Here are some examples:

1. *The majority-wins scheme.* In this commonly used scheme, the group arrives at the decision that was initially supported by the majority. This scheme appears to guide decision making most often when there is no single objectively correct decision. An

Social facilitation The process by which a person's performance is increased when other members of a group engage in similar behavior.

Evaluation apprehension Concern that others are evaluating our behavior.

Diffusion of responsibility The spreading or sharing of responsibility for a decision or behavior within a group.

Social decision schemes Rules for predicting the final outcome of group decision making on the basis of the members' initial positions.

■ **Social Facilitation** Runners tend to move faster when they are members of a group. Does the presence of other people raise our levels of arousal or produce "evaluation apprehension"?

■ **How Will They Make Their Decision?** Will the majority prevail? Will someone point to a significant piece of evidence that sways the day? Will the group follow the lead of the first person to change his or her mind? What other possibilities are there?

© Royalty-Free/CORBIS

example would be a decision about which car models to build when their popularity has not been tested in the court of public opinion.

2. *The truth-wins scheme.* In this scheme, as more information is provided and opinions are discussed, the group comes to recognize that one approach is objectively correct. For example, a group deciding whether to use SAT scores in admitting students to college would profit from information about whether the scores do predict college success.

3. *The two-thirds majority scheme.* Juries tend to convict defendants when two-thirds of the jury initially favors conviction.

4. *The first-shift rule.* In this scheme, the group tends to adopt the decision that reflects the first shift in opinion expressed by any group member. If a car-manufacturing group is divided on whether to produce a convertible, it may opt to do so after one member of the group who initially was opposed to the idea changes her mind. Similarly, if a jury is deadlocked, the members may eventually follow the lead of the first juror to switch his position.

Polarization and the "Risky Shift"

We might think that a group decision would be more conservative than an individual decision. After all, shouldn't there be an effort to compromise, to "split the difference"? We might also expect that a few mature individuals would be able to balance the opinions of daredevils. **Questions: Are group decisions more risky or more conservative than those of the individual members of the group? Why?**

Groups do not always appear to work as we might expect, however. Consider the **polarization** effect. As an individual, you might recommend that your company risk an investment of $500,000 to develop or market a new product. Other company executives, polled individually, might risk similar amounts. If you were gathered together to make a group decision, however, you would probably recommend either an amount well above this figure or nothing at all (Kamalanabhan et al., 2000; Mordock, 1997). This group effect is called *polarization,* or the taking of an extreme position. If you had to gamble on which way the decision would go,

Polarization In social psychology, taking an extreme position or attitude on an issue.

however, you would do better to place your money on movement toward the higher sum—that is, to bet on a **risky shift.** Why?

One possibility is that one member of the group may reveal information that the others were not aware of. This information may clearly point in one direction or the other. With doubts removed, the group becomes polarized. It moves decisively in the appropriate direction. It is also possible that social facilitation occurs in the group setting and that the resulting greater motivation prompts more extreme decisions.

Why, however, do groups tend to take *greater* risks than those their members would take as individuals? One answer is diffusion of responsibility (Kamalanabhan et al., 2000; Mordock, 1997). If the venture flops, the blame will not be placed on you alone. Remember the self-serving bias: You can always say (and think) that the failure was the result of a group decision. You thus protect your self-esteem (Larrick, 1993). If the venture pays off, however, you can attribute the outcome to your cool analysis and boast of your influence on the group. Note that all this behavior fits right in with what is known about the self-serving bias.

Groupthink: When Smart People Think as One, Dumb Decisions May Follow

Groupthink, a concept originated by Irving Janis (1982), is a problem that sometimes arises in group decision making. **Question: What is groupthink?** In **groupthink,** group members tend to be more influenced by group cohesiveness and a dynamic leader than by the realities of the situation (Eaton, 2001; Postmes et al., 2001). Group problem solving may degenerate into groupthink when a group senses an external threat (Rempel & Fisher, 1998). Groupthink is usually fueled by a dynamic group leader. The threat heightens the cohesiveness of the group and is a source of stress. Under stress, group members tend not to consider all their options carefully. Flawed decisions are frequently made as a result.

Groupthink has been connected with fiascos such as the Bay of Pigs invasion of Cuba, the Watergate scandal, the Iran-Contra affair, and NASA's decision to launch the *Challenger* space shuttle despite engineers' warnings about the dangers created by unusually cold weather (Raven, 1998; Brownstein, 2003; Turner & Pratkanis, 1998). Janis (1982) and other researchers (Brownstein, 2003; Postmes et al., 2001; Turner & Pratkanis, 1998) note several characteristics of groupthink that contribute to such flawed group decisions:

1. *Feelings of invulnerability.* Each decision-making group might have believed that it was beyond the reach of critics or the law—in some cases, because the groups consisted of powerful people who were close to the president of the United States.

2. *The group's belief in its rightness.* These groups apparently believed in the rightness of what they were doing. In some cases, they were carrying out the president's wishes. In the case of the *Challenger* launch, NASA had a track record of successful launches.

3. *Discrediting of information contrary to the group's decision.* The government group involved in the Iran-Contra affair knowingly broke the law. Its members apparently discredited the law by (a) deciding that it was inconsistent with the best interests of the United States and (b) enlisting private citizens to do the dirty work so that the government was not directly involved.

4. *Pressures on group members to conform.* Group cohesiveness and a dynamic leader pressure group members to conform. Striving for unanimity overrides the quest for realism, and authority can trump expertise.

5. *Stereotyping of members of the out-group.* Members of the group that broke the law in the Iran-Contra affair reportedly stereotyped people who would oppose them as "communist sympathizers" and "knee-jerk liberals."

Risky shift The tendency to make riskier decisions as a member of a group than as an individual acting independently.

Groupthink A process in which group members are influenced by cohesiveness and a dynamic leader to ignore external realities as they make decisions.

A Closer Look | Who Are the Suicide Terrorists? A Case of the Fundamental Attribution Error?

Following the attacks of September 11, President George W. Bush labeled the suicide terrorists "evil cowards." Senator John Warner declared, "Those who would commit suicide in their assaults on the free world are not rational and are not deterred by rational concepts." Attempting to fend off anti-Islamic rage, some Islamic leaders advised their followers to say that "terrorists are extremist maniacs who don't represent Islam at all" (cited by Altran, 2006).

Evil. Cowardly. Irrational. Maniacal. Do such concepts begin to paint a psychological portrait of suicide terrorists? Information about them comes from people who knew them before they committed their acts and from studies of would-be suicide terrorists who were prevented from carrying out their missions.

So, what have we learned? We could say "not much" and we could say "a great deal." How do we resolve this contradiction? Perhaps with the help of social psychology. Those who have studied the nature of evil, such as Stanley Milgram, find that many, perhaps most, perpetrators of evil are "ordinary people" (Baumeister, 1996; Berkowitz, 2004; Samuels & Casebeer, 2005). The Consortium of Social Science Associations (COSSA) (2003) testified to Congress that they had to conclude there was no clear profile of the suicide terrorist. They averaged 21 or 22 years of age, but some were younger and many were older. Some were devout Muslims but most seemed to be no more devout than their communities. Most had at least some high-school education, and some had attended college.

The U.S. Council of Foreign Relations (2002) reported on a study of Palestinian suicide terrorists recruited by Hamas. Whereas suicidal people in general tend to be depressed, even desperate, the Council noted that many suicide bombers held paying jobs, even in poverty-stricken communities. They harbored strong hatred of Israel, just as the suicide bombers of 9/11 harbored strong hatred of the United States. After a bombing, Hamas gave the families of bombers several thousand dollars and assured them their sons had died as martyrs in a holy struggle ("jihad"). COSSA and the Council speculate that some of the suicide terrorists might have had "masculine self-image problems" and been seeking recognition—but not all of them.

So, in seeking a profile, are we making a fundamental attribution error? According to attribution theory, we tend to attribute too much of other people's behavior to internal factors such as attitudes and choice (Gilovich & Eibach, 2001; Reeder, 2001). Moreover, victims of crime and terrorism tend to make the fundamental attribution error in explaining what they have suffered and may overlook the situational influences that produce the act (Baumeister, 1996; Berkowitz, 2004; Zimbardo, 2004).

People tend to explain behavior in terms of personal traits and personal choice, even when significant factors are at work in the person's society (Miller, 2006). As noted by Scott Altran (2006), who has studied suicide terrorism:

> U.S. government and media characterizations of Middle East suicide bombers as craven homicidal lunatics may suffer from a fundamental attribution error: No instances of religious or political suicide terrorism stem from lone actions of cowering or unstable bombers. Psychologist Stanley Milgram found that ordinary Americans also readily obey destructive orders under the right circumstances.

If suicide terrorists are responding to group pressure and magnetic leaders, do we absolve them of guilt for their crimes? Not at all. But perhaps we need to recognize that there is little if anything that is special or extraordinary about them.

Waleed M. Alsheri · Mohammed Atta · Wail M. Alshehri · Abdulaziz Alomari · Satam M.A. al-Suqami

Ahmed Alnami · Ahmed Ibrahim A. al Haznawi · Ziad Samir al-Jarrah · Saeed Alghamdi

  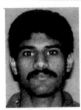  

Khalid Almihdar · Majed Moqed · Nawaf Alhazmi · Salem Alhazmi · Hani Hanjour

Marwan Alshehhi · Ahmed Alghamdi · Mohand Alshehri · Hamza Alghamdi · Fayez Rashid Ahmed Hassan al-Qadi Banihammad

■ **Why Did They Fly into the World Trade Center and the Pentagon?** Was it a matter of personality and personal choice? Was it a web of situational factors? What does social psychology have to teach us about the nature of evil?

Groupthink can be averted if group leaders encourage members to remain skeptical about options and to feel free to ask probing questions and disagree with one another.

Mob Behavior and Deindividuation: The "Beast with Many Heads"

Have you ever done something as a member of a group that you would not have done as an individual? What was it? What motivated you? How do you feel about it?

The Frenchman Gustave Le Bon (1895/1960) branded mobs and crowds as irrational, resembling a "beast with many heads." Mob actions such as race riots and lynchings sometimes seem to operate on a psychology of their own. **Questions: Do mobs bring out the beast in us? How is it that mild-mannered people commit mayhem when they are part of a mob?** In seeking an answer, let us examine a lynching.

THE LYNCHING OF ARTHUR STEVENS In their classic volume *Social Learning and Imitation,* Neal Miller and John Dollard (1941) vividly described a lynching that occurred in the South in the 1930s. Arthur Stevens, an African American, was accused of murdering his lover, a European American woman, when she wanted to break up with him. Stevens was arrested, and he confessed to the crime. Fearing violence, the sheriff moved Stevens to a town 200 miles away during the night. But his location was discovered. On the next day a mob of a hundred people stormed the jail and returned Stevens to the scene of the crime.

Outrage spread from one member of the mob to another like a plague bacillus. Laborers, professionals, women, adolescents, and law-enforcement officers alike were infected. Stevens was tortured and murdered. His corpse was dragged through the streets. The mob then went on a rampage, chasing and assaulting other African Americans. The riot ended only when troops were sent in to restore law and order.

DEINDIVIDUATION When people act as individuals, fear of consequences and self-evaluation tend to prevent them from engaging in antisocial behavior. But in a mob, they may experience **deindividuation,** a state of reduced self-awareness and lowered concern for social evaluation. Many factors lead to deindividuation. These include anonymity, diffusion of responsibility, arousal due to noise and crowding, and a focus on emerging group norms rather than on one's own values (Baron & Byrne, 2004). Under these circumstances crowd members behave more aggressively than they would as individuals.

Deindividuation The process by which group members may discontinue self-evaluation and adopt group norms and attitudes.

AP/Wide World Photos

■ **An Angry Mob Is Contained by Police** The French social thinker Gustave Le Bon branded mobs as irrational, like a "beast with many heads." Police are taught that it's useful to confront groups as early as possible, to prevent them from becoming so highly emotionally aroused that they forget their values as individuals and focus on the emerging group norms.

Police know that mob actions are best averted early by dispersing small groups that could gather into a crowd. On an individual level, perhaps we can resist deindividuation by instructing ourselves to stop and think whenever we begin to feel highly aroused in a group. If we dissociate ourselves from such groups when they are forming, we are more likely to remain critical and avoid behavior that we might later regret.

Altruism and the Bystander Effect: Some Watch while Others Die

Altruism—selfless concern for the welfare of others—is connected with some heroic and some very strange behavior throughout the animal kingdom (Zahavi, 2003). Humans have been known to sacrifice themselves to ensure the survival of their children or of comrades in battle. Primates sometimes suicidally attack the leopard to give others the opportunity to escape.

These behaviors are heroic. But consider the red spider's strange ways (Begley & Check, 2000). After depositing its sperm into a female red spider, the male of the species will do a flip into her mouth and become her dinner! Clearly, the red spider is not bothered by the spark of consciousness, and it certainly is blind to the light of reason. But evolutionary psychologists might argue that the self-sacrificing behavior of the male red spider is actually selfish from an evolutionary point of view. How, you might wonder, can individuals sacrifice themselves and at the same time be acting in their own self-interests? To answer the question, you should also know that female red spiders are promiscuous; they will mate with multiple suitors. However, eating a "lover" slows them down, increasing the probability that *his* sperm will fertilize her eggs and that his genes will survive and be transmitted to the next generation. We could thus say that the male red spider is altruistic in that he puts the welfare of future generations ahead of his own. Fatherhood ain't easy.

Red spiders, of course, do not think—at least, not in any humanly understandable sense of the concept of thinking. But people do. So how, one might ask, could the murder of 28-year-old Kitty Genovese have happened? It took place in New York City more than a generation ago. Murder was not unheard of in the Big Apple, but Kitty had screamed for help as her killer stalked her for more than half an hour and stabbed her in three separate attacks (Rosenthal, 1994). Thirty-eight neighbors heard the commotion. Twice the assault was interrupted by their voices and bedroom lights. Each time the attacker returned. Yet nobody came to the victim's aid. No one even called the police. **Truth or Fiction Revisited:** Therefore, it is true that nearly 40 people stood by and did nothing while a woman was being stabbed to death.

Why? Some witnesses said matter-of-factly that they did not want to get involved. One said that he was tired. Still others said "I don't know." As a nation, are we a callous bunch who would rather watch than help when others are in trouble?

Question: Why do people sometimes sacrifice themselves for others and, at other times, ignore people who are in trouble? Why did 38 bystanders allow Kitty Genovese to die? When do we decide to come to the aid of someone who is in trouble?

THE HELPER: WHO HELPS? It turns out that many factors are involved in helping behavior. The following are among them:

1. Observers are more likely to help when they are in a good mood (Baron & Byrne, 2004). Perhaps good moods impart a sense of personal power—the feeling that we can handle the situation (Cunningham et al., 1990; Dulin & Hill, 2003).

2. People who are empathic are more likely to help people in need (Darley, 1993). Empathic people feel the distress of others, feel concern for them, and can imagine what it must be like to be in need. Women are more likely than men to be empathic and thus more likely to help people in need (Trobst et al., 1994).

Altruism Unselfish concern for the welfare of others.

3. Bystanders may not help unless they believe that an emergency exists (Baron & Byrne, 2004). Perhaps some people who heard Kitty Genovese's calls for help were not certain as to what was happening. (But remember that others admitted they did not want to get involved.)

4. Observers must assume the responsibility to act (Baron & Byrne, 2004). It may seem logical that a group of people would be more likely to have come to the aid of Kitty Genovese than a lone person. After all, a group could more effectively have overpowered her attacker. Yet research by Darley and Latané (1968) suggests that a lone person may have been more likely to try to help her.

   In their classic experiment, male subjects were performing meaningless tasks in cubicles when they heard a (convincing) recording of a person apparently having an epileptic seizure. When the men thought that four other persons were immediately available, only 31% tried to help the victim. When they thought that no one else was available, however, 85% of them tried to help. As in other areas of group behavior, it seems that *diffusion of responsibility* inhibits helping behavior in groups or crowds. When we are in a group, we are often willing to let George (or Georgette) do it. When George isn't around, we are more willing to help others ourselves. (Perhaps some who heard Kitty Genovese thought, "Why should I get involved? Other people can hear her too.")

5. Observers must know what to do (Baron & Byrne, 2004). We hear of cases in which people impulsively jump into the water to save a drowning child and then drown themselves. Most of the time, however, people do not try to help unless they know what to do. For example, nurses are more likely than people without medical training to try to help accident victims (Cramer et al., 1988). Observers who are not sure that they can take charge of the situation may stay on the sidelines for fear of making a social blunder and being ridiculed. Or they may fear getting hurt themselves. (Perhaps some who heard Kitty Genovese thought, "If I try to intervene, I may get killed or make an idiot of myself.")

6. Observers are more likely to help people they know (Rutkowski et al., 1983). Aren't we also more likely to give to charity when asked directly by a coworker or supervisor in the socially exposed situation of the office as compared with a letter received in the privacy of our own homes?

   Evolutionary psychologists suggest that altruism is a natural aspect of human nature—even if not in the same way as in the case of the red spider! Self-sacrifice sometimes helps close relatives or others who are similar to us to survive. Self-sacrifice is "selfish" from a genetic or evolutionary point of view (Bruene & Ribbert, 2002). It helps us perpetuate a genetic code similar to our own. This view suggests that we are more likely to be altruistic with our relatives rather than strangers, however. The Kitty Genoveses of the world may remain out of luck unless they are surrounded by kinfolk or friends.

7. Observers are more likely to help people who are similar to themselves. Being able to identify with the person in need appears to promote helping behavior (Cialdini et al., 1997). Poorly dressed people are more likely to succeed in requests for a dime with poorly dressed strangers. Well-dressed people are more likely to get money from well-dressed strangers (Hensley, 1981).

THE VICTIM: WHO IS HELPED? Although women are more likely than men to help people in need, it is traditional for men to help women, particularly in the South. Women were more likely than men to receive help, especially from men, when they dropped coins in Atlanta (a southern city) than in Seattle or Columbus (northern cities) (Latané & Dabbs, 1975). Why? The researchers suggest that traditional gender roles persist more strongly in the South.

Women are also more likely than men to be helped when their cars have broken down on the highway or they are hitchhiking. Is this gallantry or are there sexual overtones to some of this "altruism"? There may be, because attractive and unaccompanied women are most likely to be helped by men (Benson et al., 1976).

© Royalty-free/CORBIS

© Werner Bokelberg/Getty Images/The Image Bank

■ **So, Which One Would You Give a Ride?** Social psychologists note that we are more willing to help people who are similar to ourselves. On the other hand, women are more likely to be helped than men. Is it because women appear to pose less of a threat or to be more in need? Is it chivalry? Or is something else at work?

Research concerning altruism and the bystander effect highlight the fact that we are members of a vast, interdependent social fabric. The next time you see a stranger in need, what will you do? Are you sure? The next section will ask you to consider what you will do to help your mother—Mother Earth, that is.

Your Turn: Now that we have discussed group behavior, enhance your mastery of the material with the nearby "Learning Connections." Review the material by filling in the blanks, reflect on the material by relating it to other things you know, and think critically about it.

 Learning Connections | **GROUP BEHAVIOR**

ACTIVE REVIEW (17) Social _____ refers to the enhancement of performance that results from the presence of others. (18) However, performance may decline when we are _____ members of a group. (19) Social-_____ schemes seem to govern group decision making: the majority-wins scheme, the truth-wins scheme, the two-thirds majority scheme, and the first-shift rule. (20) Groups are (*More* or *Less?*) likely than individuals to take extreme positions. (21) That is, people in a group are likely to experience a _____ shift. (22) Members of a group may experience _____, which is a state of reduced self-awareness and lowered concern for social evaluation. (23) Groupthink is usually (*Realistic* or *Unrealistic?*). (24) Helping behavior is also known as _____.

REFLECT AND RELATE Families, classes, religious groups, political parties, nations, circles of friends, bowling teams, sailing clubs, conversation groups, therapy groups—how many groups do you belong to? How does belonging to these groups influence your behavior? Do these groups sometimes push or pull you in different directions?

CRITICAL THINKING According to evolutionary theory, self-sacrifice can be "selfish." How does the theory explain this view? Do you agree or disagree? Explain.

Go to **http://psychology.wadsworth.com/rathus_pcc9e** for an interactive version of this Learning Connections unit.

Environmental Psychology: The Big Picture

What do you picture when you hear the phrase "the environment"? Is it vast acres of wilderness? Is it deep, rolling oceans? Or do you picture seagulls and ducks coated in gunk as a result of an oil spill? Do you think of billowing summer storm clouds and refreshing rain, or do you conjure up visions of crowded sidewalks and acid rain? All this—the beauty and the horror—is the territory of environmental psychology. **Question: What is environmental psychology?**

Environmental psychologists study the ways in which people and the physical environment influence each other. As people, we have needs that must be met if we are to remain physically and psychologically healthy. Environmental conditions such as temperature and population density affect our capacities to meet these needs. People also affect the environment. We have pushed back forests and driven many species to extinction. In recent years, our impact has mushroomed. So have the controversies over the greenhouse effect, the diminution of the ozone layer, and acid rain. Many of us have an aesthetic interest in the environment and appreciate the remaining pockets of wilderness. Protecting the environment also ultimately means protecting ourselves—for it is in the environment that we flourish or fade away.

Although most people in the United States consider themselves to be "environmentalists," only a few actually do something about it. Environmental activists are frequently spurred on by social influence. They either belong to environmental organizations or have friends or neighbors who encourage them (Werner, 2003; McFarlane & Boxall, 2003). Moreover, only about half of Americans report feelings guilty when they litter or do something else that is harmful to the environment (Hinds, 2000; Kaiser & Shimoda, 1999). There is a decided A–B problem when it comes to environmental activism. General support of environmentalism is only weakly connected with pro-environmental behaviors (Bamberg, 2003). Specific attitudes, as about recycling of glass bottles, is a better predictor of behavior.

Women are somewhat more likely to protect the environment than men are. Some psychologists (e.g., Day, 2000) attribute the gender difference to the "ethic of care," which is more characteristic of the feminine gender-role. Women, that is, are reared to put others first and to have the primary responsibility for care-giving. Care-giving in the family becomes extended to the environment at large. **Truth or Fiction Revisited:** Women are therefore less likely to toss garbage from the car window.

In this section we consider some findings of environmental psychologists concerning the effects of noise, temperature, air pollution, and crowding.

Noise: Of Muzak, Rock 'n' Roll, and Low-Flying Aircraft

Environmental psychologists apply knowledge of sensation and perception to design environments that produce positive emotional responses and contribute to human performance. They may thus suggest soundproofing certain environments or using pleasant background sounds such as music or recordings of water in natural environments (rain, the beach, brooks, and so on). Noise can be aversive, however—especially loud noise (Staples, 1996). How do you react when chalk is scraped on the blackboard or when a low-flying airplane screeches overhead? **Question: What are the effects of noise on behavior and mental processes?**

The decibel (dB) is used to express the loudness of noise. The hearing threshold is defined as zero dB. Your school library is probably about 30 to 40 dB. A freeway is about 70 dB. One hundred forty dB is painfully loud, and 150 dB can rupture your eardrums. After 8 hours of exposure to 110 to 120 dB, your hearing may be damaged (rock groups play at this level). High noise levels are stressful and can lead to health problems such as hypertension, neurological and intestinal disorders, and ulcers (Cohen et al., 1986; Staples, 1996).

High noise levels such as those imposed by traffic or low-flying airplanes also impair daily functioning. They can lead to forgetfulness, perceptual errors, even dropping things. Preschool children who are exposed to loud noise in their day care setting are less advanced in their prereading skills (Maxwell & Evans, 2000).

Couples may enjoy high noise levels at the disco, but grating noises of 80 dB seem to decrease feelings of attraction. They cause people to stand farther apart. Loud noise also reduces helping behavior. People are less likely to help pick up a dropped package when the background noise of a construction crew is at 92 dB than when it's

Environmental psychology The field of psychology that studies the ways in which people and the environment influence each other.

at 72 dB (Staples, 1996). They're even less willing to make change for a quarter. As noted in Chapter 10, sudden loud noises may also prompt aggressive behavior.

Temperature: The Perils of Getting Hot under the Collar

"Summertime," goes the song from *Porgy and Bess,* "and the livin' is easy. Fish are jumpin', and"—and if you live in Minneapolis, the rate of crime against property is high. Ellen Cohn and James Rotton (2000) studied property crime rates in that northern city over a two-year period and discovered that warm weather encourages outdoor activity, including going from house to house to steal. Outdoor activity is more difficult during Minneapolis's bitter winters, and people's property is also apparently safer.

Environmental psychologists study the ways in which temperature can facilitate or impair behavior and mental processes. **Question: What are the effects of temperature on our behavior and mental processes?**

Environmental psychologists point out that small changes in arousal—as induced by mild changes in temperature—tend to get our attention, motivate us, increase feelings of attraction, and facilitate the performance of tasks. So it is not surprising that a delightful summer day in Minneapolis might facilitate the "performance" of thieves as well as families heading for the parks and lakes. But great increments in arousal, such as those caused by major deviations from ideal temperatures, are aversive and hinder the performance of complex tasks. Extreme temperatures can sap our ability to cope. And again as noted in Chapter 10, high temperatures are connected with aggressive behavior.

A French experiment gave men and women the opportunity to change uncomfortable noise levels and uncomfortable temperatures, but only one at a time. Women in the study accepted noisier environments than men did, suggesting that women find extreme temperatures to be more aversive than high noise levels (Pellerin & Candas, 2003). Yet a Chinese study found that women who endured the noise of air conditioning in the workplace for a number of years suffered anxiety, hostility, depression, and various bodily complaints (Yunfang et al., 2000). Nobody is suggesting that the air conditioning should have been turned off, but perhaps it is useful to pay a premium—if one can—for relatively quiet machines. A British study found that a quiet workplace made it easier for workers to withstand stress on the job (Leather et al., 2003).

Of Aromas and Air Pollution: Facilitating, Fussing, and Fuming

Environmental psychologists also investigate the effects of odors ranging from perfumes to auto fumes, industrial smog, cigarette smoke, fireplaces, even burning leaves. **Question: What are the effects of air pollution on behavior and mental processes?** As an example, the lead in auto fumes may impair children's intellectual functioning in the same way that eating lead paint does.

Carbon monoxide, a colorless, odorless gas found in cigarette smoke, auto fumes, and smog, decreases the oxygen-carrying capacity of the blood. Carbon monoxide impairs learning ability and perception of the passage of time. It may also contribute to highway accidents. Residents of Los Angeles, New York, and other cities are accustomed to warnings to stay indoors or remain inactive in order to reduce air consumption when atmospheric inversions allow smog to accumulate. High levels of air pollution are connected with higher rates of respiratory illness and death (Czubaj, 2002; Dockery et al., 1993; Samet et al., 2000). Odorous pollutants, like other forms of aversive stimulation, decrease feelings of attraction and heighten aggression (Baron & Byrne, 2004).

Being told that there is an air problem also apparently has its downside. A Belgian study found that people who were warned that an environmental odor could pose dangers reported more symptoms of illness than people who received no such warning (Winters et al., 2003).

Crowding and Personal Space: "Don't Burst My Bubble, Please"

Psychologists distinguish between "density" and "crowding." *Density* refers to the number of people in an area. *Crowding* suggests an aversive high-density social situation. (In other words, *crowding* is used to mean that we are "too close for comfort.") **Questions: When are we too close for comfort? What are the effects of crowding on behavior and mental processes?**

Not all instances of density are equal. Whether we feel crowded depends on who is thrown in with us and on our interpretation of the situation (Baron & Byrne, 2004). (One student of mine reported that she had not at all minded being crowded in by the Dallas Cowboys football players who surrounded her on an airplane ride.)

PSYCHOLOGICAL MODERATORS OF THE IMPACT OF HIGH DENSITY A sense of control enhances psychological hardiness. Examples from everyday life, including shopping in crowded stores (Machleit et al., 2000), suggest that a sense of control over the situation—of being able to choose—also helps us cope with the stress of being packed in. When we are at a concert, disco, or sports event, we may encounter higher density than we do in a frustrating ticket line. But we may be having a wonderful time. Why? Because we have *chosen* to be at the concert and are focusing on our good time (unless a tall or noisy person is sitting in front of us). We feel that we are in control.

People in the navy volunteer to serve in the cramped spaces of the submarine. In that sense they are in control. On the other hand, both officers and enlistees experience a relatively high number of health problems related to their work environments, chief among them being respiratory illnesses and accidents (Thomas et al., 2003). Members of the crew tend to support one another, but a Spanish study did not find that social support eases the effects of crowding (Gomez-Jacinto & Hombrados-Mendieta, 2002).

We tend to moderate the effects of high density in subway cars and other vehicles by ignoring our fellow passengers and daydreaming, reading newspapers and books, or finding humor in the situation. Some people catch a snooze and wake up just before their stop.

SOME EFFECTS OF CITY LIFE Big city dwellers are more likely to experience stimulus overload and to fear crime than suburbanites and rural folk (Herzog & Chernick, 2000). Overwhelming crowd stimulation, bright lights, shop windows, and so on cause them to narrow their perceptions to a particular face, destination, or job. The pace of life increases—pedestrians walk faster in bigger cities (Sadalla et al., 1990). City dwellers are less willing to shake hands with, make eye contact with, or help strangers. People who move to the city from more rural areas adjust by becoming more deliberate in their daily activities. They plan ahead to take safety precautions, and they increase their alertness to potential dangers. All major population groups within the United States—African American, Asian American, European American, and Latino and Latina American—find high-density living conditions to be aversive (Evans et al., 2000a).

A study in New Delhi, India, found that women and men responded somewhat differently to living in a crowded, impoverished neighborhood (Ruback & Pandey, 2002). Consistent with traditional gender roles, the women were more likely to report being disturbed by household stressors, such as number of people living in a room and bickering. The men were relatively more likely to complain about neighborhood-level environmental stressors: traffic, garbage, crime, and air pollution.

Not all cities are the same. Cross-cultural research reveals that cities in Europe and Japan function at a faster pace than cities in undeveloped countries, as measured by the pace of walking the streets, the time taken to complete a simple task, and the accuracy of public clocks (Levine & Norenzayan, 1999). They may get more done, but people in "faster" cities are also more likely to smoke and to die from coronary heart disease (Levine & Norenzayan, 1999).

Farming, anyone?

Personal space A psychological boundary that surrounds a person and serves protective functions.

PERSONAL SPACE One adverse effect of crowding is the invasion of one's **personal space.** Personal space is an invisible boundary, a sort of bubble, that surrounds you. You are likely to become anxious and perhaps angry when others invade your space. This may happen when someone sits down across from or next to you in an otherwise empty cafeteria or stands too close to you in an elevator. Personal space appears to serve both protective and communicative functions. People usually sit and stand closer to people who are similar to themselves in race, age, or socioeconomic status. Dating couples come closer together as the attraction between them grows (Hess, 2003).

There is some interesting cross-cultural research on personal space. For example, North Americans and northern Europeans apparently maintain a greater distance between themselves and others than Southern Europeans, Asians, and Middle Easterners do (Baron & Byrne, 2004; Evans et al., 2000a). Men approached women more closely than women approached men in front of an automatic teller machine in Turkey (Kaya & Erkip, 1999).

People from relatively collectivist cultures, such as Asian Americans and Latino and Latina Americans, tend to perceive their homes as being less crowded than African Americans and European Americans do, even when the number of individuals is held constant (Evans et al., 2000a). However, cognitive perception of crowding is not the same as psychological distress. Based on their study of 464 adults from these four ethnic groups, the researchers found no evidence that Asian Americans and Latino and Latina Americans experience less psychological distress from crowding than African Americans and European Americans do (Figure 16.4).

As you complete this text, I hope that you will have decided to allow psychology to enter your personal psychological space. A professor of mine once remarked that the true measure of the success of a course is whether the student decides to take additional courses in the field. The choice is yours. *Enjoy.*

Your Turn: Now that we have discussed environmental psychology, enhance your mastery of the material with the nearby "Learning Connections." Review the material by filling in the blanks, reflect on the material by relating it to other things you know, and think critically about it.

FIGURE 16.4 Crowding and Psychological Distress among Four Ethnic Groups in the United States

According to this study of 464 adults, distress increased as did population density in the household, but there were no significant differences among ethnic groups.

Source: From G. W. Evans, S. J. Lepore, & K. M. Allen (2000). Cross-Cultural Differences in Tolerance for Crowding: Fact or Fiction? *Journal of Personality & Social Psychology,* 79(2), 204–210. Copyright © 2000 by the American Psychological Association. Reprinted with permission.

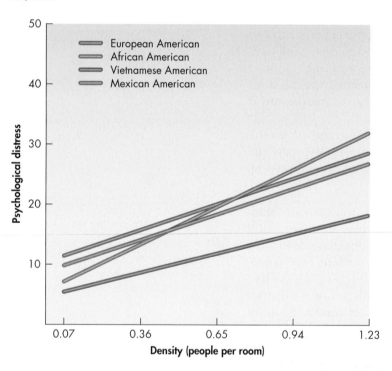

Learning Connections — ENVIRONMENTAL PSYCHOLOGY: THE BIG PICTURE

ACTIVE REVIEW (25) Environmental psychologists study the ways in which people and the _____ environment influence each other. (26) High noise levels impair learning and memory, (*Increase* or *Decrease?*) feelings of attraction, decrease helping behavior, and foster aggression. (27) Moderate shifts in temperature tend to (*Facilitate* or *Impair?*) learning and performance. (28) High heat levels (*Increase* or *Decrease?*) aggressiveness. (29) Unpleasant odors (*Increase* or *Decrease?*) feelings of attraction.

REFLECT AND RELATE As you read this book, crises loom concerning disposal of toxic wastes, industrial and

vehicular emissions, population growth, devastation of the rain forest, pollution, and other environmental issues. You dwell on planet earth. It is your home. How can you become better informed? How can you encourage people to be kinder to the environment?

CRITICAL THINKING Critical thinkers pay close attention to the definitions of terms. What is an *environmentalist?* Do you consider yourself to be an environmentalist? Why or why not?

Go to **http://psychology.wadsworth.com/ rathus_pcc9e** for an interactive version of this Learning Connections unit.

Life Connections
Understanding and Combating Prejudice

People have condemned billions of other people. Without ever meeting them. Without ever learning their names. In this section, we discuss some of the reasons for this. We will be dealing with a particularly troubling kind of attitude: prejudice.

Prejudice is an attitude toward a group that leads people to evaluate members of that group negatively—even though they have never met them. **Truth or Fiction Revisited:** Prejudiced people have in fact condemned billions of other people without ever meeting them or learning their names. On a cognitive level, prejudice is linked to expectations that members of the target group will behave poorly, say, in the workplace, or engage in criminal behavior. On an emotional level, prejudice is associated with negative feelings such as fear, dislike, or hatred. In behavioral terms, it is connected with avoidance, aggression, and discrimination. Prejudice is the most troubling kind of attitude. It is connected with the genocide of millions upon millions of people.

Discrimination
One form of behavior that results from prejudice is discrimination. Many groups in the United States have experienced discrimination—women, gay males and lesbians, older people, and ethnic groups such as African Americans, Asian Americans, Latino and Latina Americans, Irish Americans, Jewish Americans, and Native Americans. Discrimination takes many forms, including denial of access to jobs, housing, and the voting booth.

Stereotypes
Are Jewish Americans shrewd and ambitious? Are African Americans superstitious and musical? Are gay men and lesbians unfit for military service? Such ideas are *stereotypes*—prejudices about certain groups that lead people to view members of those groups in a biased fashion.

Some stereotypes are positive rather than negative, such as the cultural stereotypes about physically attractive people. By and large, we assume that "good things come in pretty packages." Attractive children and adults are judged and treated more positively than their unattractive peers (Langlois et al., 2000). We expect attractive people to be poised, sociable, popular, intelligent, mentally healthy, fulfilled, persuasive, and successful in their jobs and marriages (Eagly et al., 1991; Feingold, 1992b). Research shows that attractiveness is positively correlated with popularity, social skills, and sexual experience (Feingold, 1992b; Langlois et al., 2000).

Attractive people are even more likely to be judged innocent of crimes in mock jury experiments and observational studies (Mazzella & Feingold, 1994). When they are found guilty, they are given less severe sentences. Perhaps we assume that attractive people have less need to resort to deviant behavior to achieve their goals. Even when they have erred, perhaps they will be more likely to change their evil ways.

Sources of Prejudice
The sources of prejudice are many and varied:
1. *Dissimilarity.* We are apt to like people who share our attitudes. In forming impressions of others, we are influenced by attitudinal similarity and dissimilarity (Duckitt, 1992). People of different religions and races often have different backgrounds, however, giving rise to dissimilar attitudes. Even when people of different races share important values, they may assume that they do not.
2. *Social conflict.* There is often social and economic conflict between people of different races and religions. For example, for many decades Southern European Americans and African Americans have competed for jobs, giving rise to negative attitudes, even lynchings (Green et al., 1998).
3. *Social learning.* Children acquire some attitudes from other people, especially their parents. Children tend to imitate their parents, and parents reinforce their children for doing so (Duckitt, 1992). In this way prejudices can be transmitted from generation to generation.

The mass media also perpetuate stereotypes. TV commercials tend to portray European Americans, especially men, as being more prominent and wielding more authority than African Americans (Coltraine & Messineo, 2000). European Americans, especially women, are portrayed as being more likely to obtain romantic and domestic fulfillment. In general, European American men tend to be portrayed as powerful, European American women as sex objects, African American men as aggressive, and African American women as unimportant.

4. *Information processing.* One cognitive view is that prejudices act as cognitive filters through which we perceive the social world. The brain tends to automatically place people into categories such as "familiar" and "foreign," and "good" and "bad." Such categorization may then bias people's feelings and reactions toward others (Azar, 2002). It is also easier to attend to, and remember, instances of behavior that are consistent with our biases than it is to reconstruct our mental categories (Kashima, 2000; Sherman & Frost, 2000). If you believe that Jewish Americans are stingy, it is easier to recall a Jewish American's negotiation of a price than a Jewish American's charitable donation. If you believe that Californians are airheads, it may be easier to recall TV images of surfing than of scientific conferences at Cal Tech and Berkeley. On the other hand, people are often likely to evaluate messages from stigmatized groups such as gay males or African Americans extra carefully, in an effort to make sure that they are judging on the basis of the message and not the deliverer of the message (Petty et al., 1999).

5. *Social categorization.* A second cognitive perspective focuses on the tendency to divide our social world into

"us" and "them." People usually view those who belong to their own groups—the "in-group"—more favorably than those who do not—the "out-group" (Duckitt, 1992). Moreover, there is a tendency to assume that members of the out-group are more similar in their attitudes and behavior than members of our own groups (Mussweiler & Bodenhausen, 2002). Our isolation from the out-group makes it easier to maintain our stereotypes.

Combating Prejudice

Prejudice has been with us throughout history, and it is unlikely that a miracle cure is at hand. Yet we need not stand idly by when we witness prejudice. We can create millions of mini-miracles—changes in those of us who wish to end prejudice. Here are some things we can do to combat prejudice:

1. *Encourage intergroup contact and cooperation.* Prejudice encourages us to avoid other groups, which is unfortunate because intergroup contact is one way of breaking down prejudices (Baron & Byrne, 2004). Intergroup contact reveals that members of religious and racial groups have varying values, abilities, interests, and personalities. That is, contact heightens awareness of individual variation, and this knowledge can lead us to abandon stereotypical thinking (Hewstone & Hamberger, 2000; Sherman & Frost, 2000). Intergroup contact is especially effective when people are striving to meet common goals. Playing on the same team, working together on a joint educational project or the yearbook are examples.

2. *Present examples of admired individuals within groups that are often stigmatized.* Nilanjana Dasgupta and Anthony G. Greenwald (2001) found that they could modify negative attitudes toward African Americans by presenting photographs of admired African American individuals. Similarly, they could combat automatic preference for European Americans by presenting pictures of Europeans who were disliked. The effects of bringing admired individuals to mind will presumably work with verbal reminders as well.

■ **Intergroup Contact** Intergroup contact can reduce feelings of prejudice when people work together toward common goals.

© George Disario/CORBIS

3. *Attack discriminatory behavior.* It is sometimes easier to change people's behavior than to alter their feelings. Yet cognitive dissonance theory suggests that when we change people's behavior, their feelings may follow along. It is illegal to deny access to an education and jobs on the basis of gender, religion, race, or disability. Seek legal remedies if you have been discriminated against. Have you been denied access to living accommodations or a job because of prejudice? Talk about it to your academic advisor, the college equal opportunity office, or the dean of students. Unfortunately, many members of ethnic minority groups are reluctant to discuss instances of discrimination with members of majority groups, such as European American males (Stangor et al., 2002).

4. *Hold discussion forums.* Many campuses conduct workshops and discussion groups on gender, race, and

diversity. Talk to your dean of students about holding such workshops.

5. *Examine your own beliefs.* Prejudice isn't "out there." Prejudice dwells within us. It is easy to focus on the prejudices of others, but what about our own? Have you examined your own attitudes and rejected stereotyping and prejudice?

Even if we do not personally harbor feelings of racial or religious enmity, are we doing anything to counter such feelings in others? Do we confront people who make prejudiced remarks? Do we belong to organizations that deny access to members of other racial and religious groups? Do we strike up conversations with people from other groups or avoid them? College is meant to be a broadening experience, and we deny ourselves much of the education we could be receiving when we limit our encounters to people who share our own backgrounds.

Video Connections—Stereotype Threat
"Nobody ever takes it for granted that I am very skilled at what I do," says this young mathematician. Why would she say this? We encounter stereotypes nearly every day. Click on the video link called "Stereotype Threat" from your companion website and learn more about stereotypes and how Claude Steele induced and reduced stereotype threat in his experiments.

Want to study on the go? Go to your companion website and download an audio version of this review section to your media player.

Recite—An Active Summary™

1. What is social psychology?

Social psychology is the field of psychology that studies the factors that influence people's thoughts, feelings, and behaviors in social situations.

2. What are attitudes?

Attitudes are behavioral and cognitive tendencies expressed by evaluating particular people, places, or things with favor or disfavor.

3. Do people do as they think? (For example, do people really vote their consciences?)

When we are free to act as we wish, our behavior is often consistent with our beliefs and feelings. But as indicated by the term *A–B problem,* the links between attitudes (A) and behaviors (B) are often weak to moderate. The following strengthen the A–B connection: specificity of attitudes, strength of attitudes, whether people have a vested interest in the outcome of their behavior, and the accessibility of the attitudes.

4. Where do attitudes come from?

Attitudes are acquired (not inborn). They can be learned somewhat mechanically by means of conditioning or learning by observation. However, people also appraise and evaluate situations and often form their own judgments.

5. Can you really change people?—their attitudes and behavior, that is?

People attempt to change other people's attitudes and behavior by means of persuasion. According to the elaboration likelihood model, persuasion occurs through both central and peripheral routes. Change occurs through the central route by means of consideration of arguments and evidence. Peripheral routes involve associating the objects of attitudes with positive or negative cues, such as attractive or unattractive communicators. Repeated messages generally "sell" better than messages delivered only once. People tend to show greater response to fear appeals than to purely factual presentations. This is especially so when the appeals offer concrete advice for avoiding negative outcomes. Persuasive communicators tend to show expertise, trustworthiness, attractiveness, or similarity to the audience. In the foot-in-the-door technique, people are asked to comply with larger requests after they have complied with smaller ones.

6. What is cognitive-dissonance theory?

Cognitive-dissonance theory hypothesizes that people dislike situations in which their attitudes and behavior are inconsistent. Such situations apparently induce cognitive dissonance, which people can reduce by changing their attitudes. For example, people engage in effort justification; that is, they tend to justify boring or fruitless behavior to themselves by concluding that their efforts are worthwhile, even when they go unrewarded.

7. Do first impressions really matter? What are the primacy and recency effects?

First impressions can last (the primacy effect) because we tend to label or describe people in terms of the behavior we see initially. The recency effect appears to be based on the fact that—other things being equal—recently learned information is easier to remember.

8. What is attribution theory? Why do we assume that other people intend the mischief that they do?

The tendency to infer the motives and traits of others through observation of their behavior is referred to as the attribution process. In dispositional attributions, we attribute people's behavior to internal factors such as their personality traits and decisions. In situational attributions, we attribute people's behavior to their circumstances or external forces. According to the actor–observer effect, we tend to attribute the behavior of others to internal, dispositional factors. However, we tend to attribute our own behavior to external, situational factors. The so-called fundamental attribution error is the tendency to attribute too much of other people's behavior to dispositional factors. The self-serving bias refers to the finding that we tend to attribute our successes to internal, stable factors and our failures to external, unstable factors. The attribution of behavior to internal or external causes is influenced by three factors: consensus, consistency, and distinctiveness. For example, when few people act in a certain way—that is, when the consensus is low—we are likely to attribute behavior to internal factors.

9. What is body language?

Body language refers to the tendency to infer people's thoughts and feelings from their postures and gestures. For example, people who feel positively toward one another position

Recite—An Active Summary™

themselves closer together and are more likely to touch. Touching results in a negative reaction when it suggests more intimacy than is desired. Gazing into another's eyes can be a sign of love, but a hard stare is an aversive challenge. Women are more likely than men to touch people with whom they are interacting.

10. Why will so many people commit crimes against humanity if they are ordered to do so? (Why don't they refuse?)

The majority of subjects in the Milgram studies complied with the demands of authority figures, even when the demands required that they hurt innocent people by means of electric shock. Factors contributing to obedience include socialization, lack of social comparison, perception of legitimate authority figures, the foot-in-the-door technique, inaccessibility of values, and buffers between the perpetrator and the victim.

11. Why do so many people tend to follow the crowd?

Asch's research in which subjects judged the lengths of lines suggests that the majority of people will follow the crowd, even when the crowd is wrong. Personal factors such as desire to be liked by group members, low self-esteem, high self-consciousness, and shyness contribute to conformity. Belonging to a collectivist society and group size also contribute to conformity.

12. Do we run faster when we are in a group?

The concept of social facilitation refers to the effects on performance that result from the presence of other people. The presence of others may facilitate performance for reasons such as increased arousal and evaluation apprehension. However, when we are anonymous group members, we may experience diffusion of responsibility and task performance may fall off. This phenomenon is termed *social loafing*.

13. How do groups make decisions?

Social psychologists have identified several decision-making schemes, including the majority-wins scheme, the truth-wins scheme, the two-thirds majority scheme, and the first-shift rule.

14. Are group decisions more risky or more conservative than those of the individual members of the group? Why?

Group decisions tend to be more polarized and riskier than individual decisions, largely because groups diffuse responsibility. Group decisions may be highly productive when group members are knowledgeable, there is an explicit procedure for arriving at decisions, and there is a process of give and take.

15. What is groupthink?

Groupthink is an unrealistic kind of decision making that is fueled by the perception of external threats to the group or to those whom the group wishes to protect. It is facilitated by a dynamic group leader, feelings of invulnerability, the group's belief in its rightness, the discrediting of information that contradicts the group's decision, conformity, and the stereotyping of members of the out-group.

16. Do mobs bring out the beast in us? How is it that mild-mannered people commit mayhem when they are part of a mob?

Highly emotional crowds may induce attitude-discrepant behavior through the process of *deindividuation*, which is a state of reduced self-awareness and lowered concern for social evaluation. The high emotions are connected with arousal that makes it more difficult to access one's own values.

17. Why do people sometimes sacrifice themselves for others and, at other times, ignore people who are in trouble?

A number of factors contribute to altruism (the tendency to help others). Among them are empathy, being in a good mood, feelings of responsibility, knowledge of how to help, and acquaintance with—and similarity to—the person in need of help. According to the bystander effect, we are unlikely to aid people in distress when we are members of crowds. Crowds tend to diffuse responsibility.

18. What is environmental psychology?

Environmental psychology is the field of psychology that studies the ways in which humans and the physical environment influence each other.

19. What are the effects of noise on behavior and mental processes?

High noise levels are stressful and can lead to health problems such as hearing loss, hypertension, and neurological and intestinal disorders. High noise levels impair learning and memory. Loud noise also dampens helping behavior and heightens aggressiveness.

Recite—An Active Summary™

20. What are the effects of temperature on our behavior and mental processes?

Moderate shifts in temperature are mildly arousing and usually have positive effects such as facilitating learning and performance and increasing feelings of attraction. But extremes of temperature tax the body, are a source of stress, and impair performance. High temperatures are also connected with aggression.

21. What are the effects of air pollution on behavior and mental processes?

The lead in auto fumes may impair learning and memory. Carbon monoxide decreases the capacity of the blood to carry oxygen and thus impairs learning ability and perception and contributes to accidents. Unpleasant odors decrease feelings of attraction and heighten aggression.

22. When are we too close for comfort? What are the effects of crowding on behavior and mental processes?

Density refers to the number of people in an area. *Crowding* suggests aversive high density. A sense of control or choice—as in choosing to attend a concert or athletic contest—helps us cope with the stress of high density. Perhaps because of crowding, noise, and so on, city dwellers are less likely than people who live in small towns to interact with or help strangers.

Go to **http://psychology.wadsworth.com/ rathus_pcc9e** to access an interactive version of this active summary.

Key Terms

Situationist perspective (p. 595)
Social psychology (p. 595)
Attitude (p. 595)
A–B problem (p. 595)
Stereotype (p. 595)
Elaboration likelihood model (p. 597)
Fear appeal (p. 598)
Selective avoidance (p. 599)
Selective exposure (p. 599)
Foot-in-the-door technique (p. 599)

Cognitive-dissonance theory (p. 600)
Attitude-discrepant behavior (p. 600)
Effort justification (p. 601)
Social perception (p. 601)
Primacy effect (p. 602)
Recency effect (p. 602)
Attribution (p. 602)
Attribution process (p. 603)
Dispositional attribution (p. 603)

Situational attribution (p. 603)
Fundamental attribution error (p. 603)
Actor–observer effect (p. 603)
Self-serving bias (p. 604)
Consensus (p. 604)
Social influence (p. 607)
Conform (p. 610)
Social norms (p. 610)
Social facilitation (p. 613)
Evaluation apprehension (p. 613)

Diffusion of responsibility (p. 613)
Social decision schemes (p. 613)
Polarization (p. 614)
Risky shift (p. 615)
Groupthink (p. 615)
Deindividuation (p. 617)
Altruism (p. 618)
Environmental psychology (p. 621)
Personal space (p. 624)

ACTIVE LEARNING RESOURCES

Visit your Companion Website for Video, Quizzing, and Self-Assessment!

http://psychology.wadsworth.com/rathus_pcc9e
On this site you can access the Stereotype Threat video highlighted by the Video Connections icon on p. 626. In addition there are many quizzing opportunities including interactive versions of the fill-in-the-blank Active Review sections in your book.

Study on the Go!

Don't have time to study right now? You can study on the go! Visit your companion website and download an audio version of the Recite—An Active Summary section to your media player.

ThomsonNOW

http://www.thomsonedu.com
Need help studying? This site is your one-stop study shop. Take a Pre-Test and Thomson NOW will generate a Personalized Study Plan based on your test results. The Study Plan will identify the topics you need to review and direct you to online resources to help you master those topics. You can then take a Post-Test to determine the concepts you have mastered and what you still need to work on.

Author Blog

What does your author have to say about the state of psychology? Visit your companion website every Tuesday and click on "Author Blog," where he'll talk about the most recent controversies and hot topics in psychology.

Truth or Fiction?

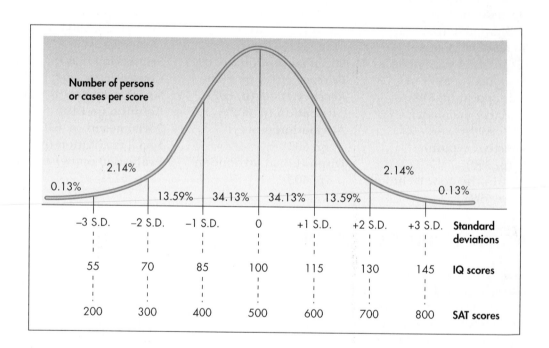

Statistics

Preview

Statistics

I magine that some visitors from outer space arrive outside Madison Square Garden in New York City. Their goal this dark and numbing winter evening is to learn all they can about planet Earth. They are drawn inside the Garden by lights, shouts, and warmth. The spotlighting inside rivets their attention to a wood-floored arena where the New York Big Apples are hosting the California Quakes in a briskly contested basketball game.

Our visitors use their sophisticated instruments to take some measurements of the players. Some interesting statistics are sent back to their planet of origin: It appears that (1) 100% of Earthlings are male and (2) the height of Earthlings ranges from 6 feet 1 inch to 7 feet 2 inches.

These measurements are called **statistics. Question: What is statistics?** Statistics is the name given the science concerned with obtaining and organizing numerical information or measurements. Our imagined visitors have sent home statistics about the gender and size of human beings that are at once accurate and misleading. Although they accurately measured the basketball players (we have translated their units of measurement into feet and inches for readers' convenience), their small **sample** of Earth's **population** was, shall we say, distorted.

Question: What are samples and populations? A population is a complete group of people, other animals, or measures from which a sample is drawn. For example, all people on Earth could be defined as the population of interest. So could all women, or all women in the United States. A sample is a group of measures drawn from a population. Fortunately for us Earthlings, about half of the world's population is female. And the **range** of heights observed by the aliens, of 6 feet 1 inch to 7 feet 2 inches, is both restricted and too high—much too high. People vary in height by more than 1 foot and 1 inch. And our **average** height is not between 6 feet 1 inch and 7 feet 2 inches; rather, it is a number of inches below.

Psychologists, like our imagined visitors, are vitally concerned with measuring human as well as animal characteristics and traits—not just physical characteristics such as height, but also psychological traits such as intelligence, sociability, aggressiveness, neatness, anxiety, and depression. By observing the central tendencies (averages) and variations in measurement from person to person, psychologists can say that one person is average or above average in intelligence, or that someone else is less anxious than, say, 60% of the population.

But psychologists, unlike our aliens, attempt to select a sample that accurately represents the entire population. Professional basketball players do not represent the entire human species. **Truth or Fiction Revisited:** Basketball players are taller, stronger, and more agile than the rest of us. They also make more sneaker commercials. Their "abnormalities" are assets to them, of course, not deficits.

In this appendix we survey some of the statistical methods used by psychologists to draw conclusions about the measurements they take in research. First we discuss *descriptive statistics* and learn what types of statements we can make about height and other human traits. Then we discuss the *normal curve* and learn why basketball players are abnormal—at least in terms of height. We explain *correlation coefficients* and provide you with some less-than-shocking news: As a group, students who study obtain higher grades than students who do not study. Finally, we have a look at *inferential statistics,* and we see why we can be bold enough to say that the difference in height between basketball players and other people is not a chance fluctuation or fluke. Basketball players are in fact *statistically significantly* taller than the general population.

Statistics Numerical facts assembled in such a manner that they provide useful information about measures or scores. (From the Latin *status*, meaning "standing" or "position.")

Sample Part of a population.

Population A complete group from which a sample is selected.

Range A measure of variability defined as the high score in a distribution minus the low score.

Average The central tendency of a group of measures, expressed either as the mean, median, or mode of a distribution.

Learning Connections   STATISTICS

Descriptive Statistics

Being told that someone is a "10" may sound great at first. However, it is not very descriptive unless you know something about how the scores on the scale are distributed and how frequently one finds a 10. Fortunately—for 10s, if not for the rest of us—one usually means that the person is a 10 on a scale of from 1 to 10, and that 10 is the highest possible score on the scale. If this is not sufficient, one will also be told that 10s are few and far between—rather unusual statistical events. **Truth or Fiction Revisited:** But note that the scale could also vary from 0 to 100, in which case a score of 10 would place one nearer to the bottom of the scale and make a score of 50 the center point of the scale. With such a scale, being a 10 would be much less impressive.

The idea of the scale from 1 to 10 may not be very scientific, but it does suggest something about **descriptive statistics. Question: What is descriptive statistics?** (Why isn't it always good to be a "10"?) Descriptive statistics is the branch of statistics that provides information about distributions of scores. We can use descriptive statistics to clarify our understanding of a distribution of scores such as heights, test grades, IQs, or even increases or decreases in measures of aggressive behavior following the drinking of alcohol. For example, descriptive statistics can help us determine measures of central tendency (averages) and to determine how much fluctuation or variability there is in the scores. Being a 10 loses much of its charm if the average score is an 11. Being a 10 is more remarkable in a distribution whose scores range from 1 to 10 than it is in a distribution whose scores range from 9 to 11.

Let us now consider some of the concerns of descriptive statistics: the frequency distribution, measures of central tendency (types of averages), and measures of variability.

The Frequency Distribution

Question: What is a frequency distribution? A **frequency distribution** takes scores or items of raw data, puts them into order as from the lowest to the highest, and indicates how often a score appears. A frequency distribution groups data according to class intervals, although the class may be a single unit (one), as in Table A.2. Table A.1 shows the rosters for a recent basketball game between the California Quakes and the New York Big Apples. The players are listed according to the numbers on their uniforms. Table A.2 shows a frequency distribution of the heights of the players, with the two teams combined. The class interval in Table A.2 is 1 inch.

It would also be possible to use other class intervals, such as 3 inches, as shown in Table A.3. In determining the size of a class interval, the researcher tries

Descriptive statistics The branch of statistics that is concerned with providing descriptive information about a distribution of scores.

Frequency distribution An ordered set of data that indicates the frequency (how often) with which scores appear.

TABLE A.1 ROSTERS OF QUAKES VERSUS BIG APPLES AT NEW YORK

California Quakes		New York Big Apples	
2 Callahan	6'7"	3 Roosevelt	6'1"
5 Daly	6'11"	12 Chaffee	6'5"
6 Chico	6'2"	13 Baldwin	6'9"
12 Capistrano	6'3"	25 Delmar	6'6"
21 Brentwood	6'5"	27 Merrick	6'8"
25 Van Nuys	6'3"	28 Hewlett	6'6"
31 Clemente	6'9"	33 Hollis	6'9"
32 Whittier	6'8"	42 Bedford	6'5"
41 Fernando	7'2"	43 Coram	6'2"
43 Watts	6'9"	45 Hampton	6'10"
53 Huntington	6'6"	53 Ardsley	6'10"

A glance at the rosters for a recent basketball game in which the New York Big Apples "entertained" the California Quakes shows that the heights of the team members, combined, ranged from 6 feet 1 inch to 7 feet 2 inches. Do the heights of the team members represent those of the general male population? What do you think?

to collapse the data into a small enough number of classes to ensure that they will be meaningful at a glance. But the researcher also tries to keep a large enough number of categories (classes) to ensure that important differences are not obscured.

TABLE A.2 FREQUENCY DISTRIBUTION OF BASKETBALL PLAYERS (QUAKES AND BIG APPLES COMBINED), WITH A ONE-INCH CLASS INTERVAL

Class Interval	Number of Players in Class
6'1"–6'1.9"	1
6'2"–6'2.9"	2
6'3"–6'3.9"	2
6'4"–6'4.9"	0
6'5"–6'5.9"	3
6'6"–6'6.9"	3
6'7"–6'7.9"	1
6'8"–6'8.9"	2
6'9"–6'9.9"	4
6'10"–6'10.9"	2
6'11"–6'11.9"	1
7'0"–7'0.9"	0
7'1"–7'1.9"	0
7'2"–7'2.9"	1

TABLE A.3 FREQUENCY DISTRIBUTION OF HEIGHTS OF BASKETBALL PLAYERS, USING A THREE-INCH CLASS INTERVAL

Class Interval	Number of Players in Class
6'1"–6'3.9"	5
6'4"–6'6.9"	6
6'7"–6'9.9"	7
6'10"–7'0.9"	3
7'1"–7'3.9"	1

Table A.3 obscures the fact that no players are 6 feet 4 inches tall. If the researcher believes that this information is extremely important, a class interval of 1 inch may be maintained.

Figure A.1 shows two methods of graphing the information in Table A.3: the **frequency histogram** and the **frequency polygon.** Students sometimes have difficulty interpreting graphs, but the purpose of graphs is to reveal key information about frequency distributions at a glance. Note that in both kinds of graph, the frequency histogram and the frequency polygon, the class intervals are usually drawn along the horizontal line. The horizontal line is also known as the *X*-axis. The numbers of cases (scores, persons, or events) in each class interval are shown along the vertical line, which is also known as the *Y*-axis. In the histogram, the number of scores in each class interval is represented by a bar—a rectangular solid—so that the graph looks like a series of steps. In the polygon, the number of scores in each class interval is plotted as a point. The points are connected to form a many-sided geometric figure (polygon). Note that empty class intervals were added at each end of the frequency polygon so that the sides of the figure could be brought down to the *X*-axis to close the geometric figure.

Measures of Central Tendency

Never try to walk across a river just because it has an average depth of four feet.
Martin Friedman

Truth or Fiction Revisited: A river with an average depth of 4 feet could be over your head in many places, so, as suggested in the quip by Martin Friedman, a measure of central tendency can sometimes be misleading. **Question: What are measures of**

Frequency histogram A graphic representation of a frequency distribution that uses rectangular solids (bars) to represent the frequency with which scores appear.

Frequency polygon A graphic representation of a frequency distribution that connects the points that show the frequencies with which scores appear, thereby creating a multisided geometric figure.

FIGURE A.1 Two Graphical Representations of the Data in Table A.3
The graph on the left is called a frequency histogram, or bar graph. The graph on the right is called a frequency polygon.

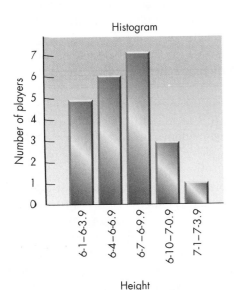

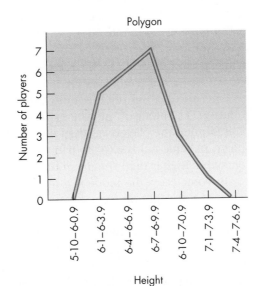

central tendency? Measures of central tendency are "averages" that show the center or balancing points of a frequency distribution. There are three commonly used types of measures of central tendency: the *mean, median,* and *mode.* Each attempts to describe something about the scores in a frequency distribution through the use of a typical or representative number.

The **mean** is what most people think of as "the average." We obtain the mean of a distribution by adding up the scores and then dividing the sum by the number of scores. In the case of the basketball players, it would be advisable to first convert the heights into a single unit, such as inches (6'1" becomes 73", and so on). If we add all the heights in inches and then divide by the number of players (22), we obtain a mean height of 78.73". If we convert that number back into units of feet and inches, we obtain 6'6.73".

The **median** is the score of the middle case in a distribution. It is the score beneath which 50% of the cases fall. In a distribution with an even number of cases, such as the distribution of the heights of the 22 basketball players as shown in Table A.2, we obtain the median by finding the mean of the two middle cases. When we list the 22 cases in ascending order (moving from lowest to highest), the 11th case is 6'6" and the 12th case is 6'7". Therefore, the median of the distribution is (6'6" + 6'7")/2, or 6'6½".

When we analyze the heights of the basketball players, we find that the mean and median are similar. Either one serves as a useful indicator of the central tendency of the data. But suppose we are trying to find the average savings of 30 families living on a suburban block. Let us assume that 29 of the 30 families have savings between $8,000 and $12,000, adding up to $294,000. But the 30th family has savings of $1,400,000! The mean savings for a family on this block would thus be $56,467. The mean can be greatly distorted by one or two extreme scores. An IQ score of 145 would similarly distort the mean of the IQ scores of a class of 20 students, among whom the other 19 IQ scores ranged from 93 to 112. Then, too, if a few basketball players signed up for one of your classes, the mean of the students' heights would be distorted in an upward direction. **Truth or Fiction Revisited:** Therefore, adding people's incomes and then dividing them by the number of people can be an awful way of showing the average income. A few extremely high incomes, or IQ scores, or heights can distort the average of a group in an upward direction.

When there are a few extreme scores in a distribution, the median is a better indicator of central tendency. The median savings on our hypothetical block would lie between $8,000 and $12,000. Thus it would be more representative of the central tendency of savings. Studies of the incomes of families in the United States usually report median rather than mean incomes just to avoid the distortion of findings that would occur if the incomes of a handful of billionaires were treated in the same way as more common incomes. On the other hand, one could argue that choosing the median as the average obscures or hides the extreme scores, which are just as "real" as the other scores. Perhaps it is best to use the median and a footnote—a rather big footnote.

The **mode** is simply the most frequently occurring score or measure in a distribution. The mode of the data in Table A.1 is 6'9" because this height occurs most often among the players on the two teams. The median class interval for the data shown in Table A.3 is 6'6½" to 6'9½". With this particular distribution, the mode is somewhat higher than the mean or median.

In some cases the mode is a more appropriate description of the central tendency of a distribution than the mean or the median. Figure A.2 shows a **bimodal** distribution—that is, a distribution with two modes. This is a hypothetical distribution of test scores obtained by a class. The mode at the left indicates the most common class interval (45 to 49) for students who did not study, and the mode to the right shows the most common class interval (65 to 69) for students who did study. (Don't be alarmed. I'm sure that the professor, who is extremely fair, will be

Mean A type of average that is calculated by adding all the scores and then dividing by the number of scores.

Median The central score in a frequency distribution; the score beneath which 50% of the cases fall.

Mode The most frequently occurring number or score in a distribution.

Bimodal Having two modes.

delighted to curve the grades so that the interval of 75 to 79 is an A+ and the interval of 65 to 69 is at least a B.) The mean and median test scores would probably lie within the 55 to 59 class interval, yet use of that interval as the measure of central tendency could obscure rather than reveal the important aspects of this distribution of test scores. It might suggest that the test was too hard, not that a number of students chose not to study. Similarly, one of the distribution's modes might be a bit larger than the other, so one could follow the exact rule for finding the mode and report just one of them. But this approach would also hide the meaning of this particular distribution of scores. All in all, it is clearly best to visualize this distribution of scores as bimodal. Even when the modes are not exactly equal, it is often most accurate to report distributions as bimodal, or, when there are three or more modes, as multimodal. One chooses one's measure or measures of central tendency to describe the essential features of a frequency distribution, not to hide them.

Measures of Variability

Our hypothetical class obtained test scores ranging from call intervals of 35 to 39 to call intervals of 75 or 79. That is, the scores *varied* from the lower class interval to the higher class interval. Now, if all the students had obtained scores from 55 to 59 or from 65 to 69, the scores would not have varied as much; that is, they would have clustered closer to one another and would have had lower variability.

Question: What are measures of variability? The measures of the variability of a distribution inform us about the spread of scores—that is, about the typical distances of scores from the average score. Two commonly used measures of variability are the *range* of scores and the *standard deviation* of scores.

The range of scores in a distribution is defined as the difference between the highest score and the lowest score. The range is obtained by subtracting the lowest score from the highest score. The range of heights in Table A.2 is obtained by subtracting 6'1" from 7'2", or 1'1". It is useful to know the range of temperatures when we move to an area with a different climate so that we may anticipate the weather and dress for it appropriately. A teacher must have some understanding of the range of abilities or skills in a class in order to teach effectively. An understanding of the range of human heights can be used to design doorways, beds, and headroom in automobiles. Even so, the typical doorway is 6'8" high; and, as we saw with the California Quakes and New York Big Apples, some people will have to duck to get through.

The range is an imperfect measure of variability because of the manner in which it is influenced by extreme scores. The range of savings of the 30 families on our suburban block is $1,400,000 minus $8,000, or $1,392,000. This is a large number, and it is certainly true. However, it tells us little about the *typical* variation of savings accounts, which lie within a more restricted range of $8,000 to $12,000.

The **standard deviation** is a statistic that does a better job of showing how the scores in a distribution are distributed (spread) about the mean. It is usually better than the range because it considers every score in the distribution, not just the extreme (highest and lowest) scores. Consider Figure A.3. Each distribution in the figure has the same number of scores, the same mean, and the same range of scores. However, the scores in the distribution on the right side cluster more closely about the mean. Therefore, the standard deviation of the distribution on the right is smaller. That is, the typical score deviates less from the mean score.

The standard deviation is usually abbreviated as S.D. It is calculated by the formula

$$\text{S.D.} = \sqrt{\frac{\text{Sum of } d^2}{N}}$$

where d equals the deviation of each score from the mean of the distribution and N equals the number of scores in the distribution.

FIGURE A.2 **A Bimodal Distribution**
This hypothetical distribution represents students' scores on a test. The mode at the left represents the central tendency of the test scores of students who did not study. The mode at the right represents the mode of the test scores of students who did study. (I'm allowed to be moralistic about studying; I wrote the book.)

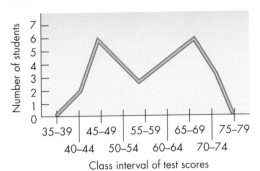

Standard deviation A measure of the variability of a distribution, obtained by the formula

$$\text{S.D.} = \sqrt{\frac{\text{Sum of } d^2}{N}}$$

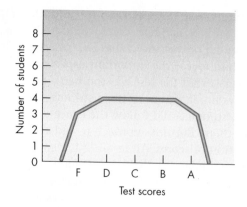

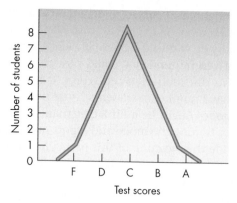

Let us find the mean and standard deviation of the IQ scores listed in column 1 of Table A.4. To obtain the mean we add all the scores, attain 1,500, and then divide by the number of scores (15) to obtain a mean of 100. We obtain the deviation score (d) for each IQ score by subtracting the score from 100. The d for an IQ score of 85 equals 100 minus 85, or 15, and so on. Then we square each d and add the squares. The S.D. equals the square root of the sum of squares (1,426) divided by the number of scores (15), or 9.75.

As an additional exercise, we can show that the S.D. of the test scores on the left (in Figure A.3) is greater than that for the scores on the right. First we assign

TABLE A.4 **HYPOTHETICAL SCORES OBTAINED FROM AN IQ TESTING**

IQ Score	d (Deviation Score)	d^2 (Deviation Score Squared)
85	15	225
87	13	169
89	11	121
90	10	100
93	7	49
97	3	9
97	3	9
100	0	0
101	−1	1
104	−4	16
105	−5	25
110	−10	100
112	−12	144
113	−13	169
117	−17	289
Sum of IQ scores = 1,500		Sum of d^2 scores = 1,426

$$\text{Mean} = \frac{\text{Sum of scores}}{\text{Number of scores}} = \frac{1,500}{15} = 100$$

$$\text{Standard Deviation (S.D.)} = \sqrt{\frac{\text{Sum of } d^2}{N}} = \sqrt{\frac{1,426}{15}} = \sqrt{95.07} = 9.75$$

the grades a number according to a 4.0 system. Let A = 4, B = 3, C = 2, D = 1, and F = 0. The S.D. for each distribution is computed in Table A.5. The larger S.D. for the distribution on the left indicates that the scores in that distribution are more variable, or tend to be farther from the mean.

TABLE A.5 COMPUTATION OF STANDARD DEVIATIONS FOR TEST-SCORE DISTRIBUTIONS IN FIGURE A.3

Distribution at Left			Distribution to the Right		
Grade	d	d^2	Grade	d	d^2
A (4)	2	4	A (4)	2	4
A (4)	2	4	B (3)	1	1
A (4)	2	4	B (3)	1	1
B (3)	1	1	B (3)	1	1
B (3)	1	1	B (3)	1	1
B (3)	1	1	C (2)	0	0
B (3)	1	1	C (2)	0	0
C (2)	0	0	C (2)	0	0
C (2)	0	0	C (2)	0	0
C (2)	0	0	C (2)	0	0
C (2)	0	0	C (2)	0	0
D (1)	-1	1	C (2)	0	0
D (1)	-1	1	C (2)	0	0
D (1)	-1	1	D (1)	-1	1
D (1)	-1	1	D (1)	-1	1
F (0)	-2	4	D (1)	-1	1
F (0)	-2	4	D (1)	-1	1
F (0)	-2	4	F (0)	-2	4

Sum of grades = 36

Mean grade = 36/18 = 2

Sum of d^2 = 32

S.D. = $\sqrt{32/18}$ = 1.33

Sum of grades = 36

Mean grade = 36/18 = 2

Sum of d^2 = 16

S.D. = $\sqrt{16/18}$ = 0.94

Learning Connections   DESCRIPTIVE STATISTICS

ACTIVE SUMMARY (4)_____ statistics provides information about distributions of scores. (5) Descriptive statistics helps us determine measures of central tendency and how much fluctuation or _____ there is in a distribution. (6) A(n) _____ distribution takes items of data, puts them into order, and indicates how often a score appears. (7) A frequency distribution groups data according to _____ intervals. (8) In the frequency histogram and polygon, the class intervals are usually drawn along the *X*-axis, or (*Horizontal* or *Vertical?*) line.

(9) The numbers of cases in each class interval are shown along the Y-axis, or (*Horizontal* or *Vertical?*) line. (10) We obtain the _____ of a distribution by adding the scores and then dividing the sum by the number of scores. (11) The _____ is the score beneath which 50% of the cases fall. (12) The _____ is the most frequently occurring measure in a distribution. (13) The range of scores is obtained by subtracting the _____ score from the highest score. (14) The standard deviation is calculated by the formula:

$$\text{S.D.} = \sqrt{\frac{\text{Sum of \_}^2}{N}}$$

REFLECT AND RELATE Would it take a 3.00, 4.00, or 5.00 grade point average for you to be a perfect student? Would yet another number be required? Explain?

CRITICAL THINKING Provide examples of distributions in which the median and mode are better measures of central tendency than the mean. Why is being a "10" more remarkable in a distribution whose scores range from 1 to 10 than in a distribution whose scores range from 9 to 11?

 Go to **http://psychology.wadsworth.com/ rathus_pcc9e** for an interactive version of this Learning Connections unit.

The Normal Curve

Many human traits and characteristics including height and intelligence seem to be distributed in a pattern known as a normal distribution. **Question: What is a normal distribution?** In a **normal distribution,** the mean, median, and mode all fall at the same data point or score. Scores cluster most heavily about the mean, fall off rapidly in either direction at first (as shown in Figure A.4), and then taper off more gradually.

The curve in Figure A.4 is bell-shaped. This type of distribution is also called a **normal curve** or bell-shaped curve. This curve is the hypothesized distribution of variables in which different scores are determined by chance variation. Height is thought to be largely determined by chance combinations of genetic material. A distribution of the heights of a random sample of the population approximates normal distributions for men and women, with the mean of the distribution for men a few inches higher than the mean for women.

Test developers traditionally assumed that intelligence was also randomly or normally distributed among the population. For that reason, they constructed intelligence tests so that scores would be distributed as close to "normal" as possible. In actuality, IQ scores are also influenced by environmental factors and chromosomal abnormalities, so that the resultant curves are not perfectly normal. The means of most IQ tests are defined as scores of 100 points. The Wechsler scales are constructed to have standard deviations of 15 points, as shown in Figure A.4. A

Normal distribution A symmetrical distribution that is assumed to reflect chance fluctuations; approximately 68% of cases lie within a standard deviation of the mean.

Normal curve Graphic presentation of a normal distribution, which shows a characteristic bell shape.

FIGURE A.4 **A Bell-Shaped or Normal Curve**
In a normal curve, approximately two out of three cases (68%) lie within a standard deviation (S.D.) from the mean. The mean, median, and mode all lie at the same score. IQ tests and the Scholastic Assessment Tests (SATs) are constructed so that their distributions approximate the normal curve.

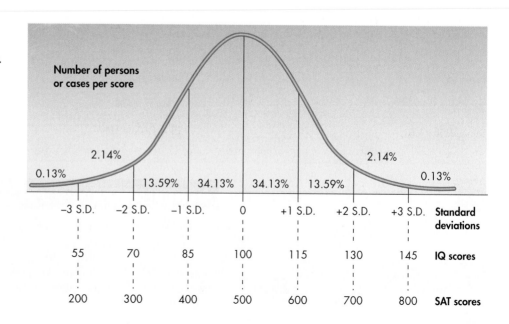

standard deviation of 15 points causes 50% of the Wechsler scores to fall between 90 and 110, which is called the "broad average" range. About 68% of scores (two out of three) fall between 85 and 115 (within a standard deviation of the mean), and more than 95% fall between 70 and 130—that is, within two standard deviations of the mean. **Truth or Fiction Revisited:** Psychologists, therefore, may express your IQ score in terms of how deviant you are. The more extreme high (and low) IQ scores deviate more from the mean score.

The Scholastic Assessment Tests (SATs) were constructed so that the mean scores would be 500 points and the S.D. would be 100 points. Thus a score of 600 would equal or excel that of some 84% to 85% of the test takers. Because of the complex interaction of variables that determine SAT scores, their distribution is not exactly normal either. Moreover, the actual mean scores and standard deviations tend to vary from year to year, and, in the case of the SAT IIs, from test to test. The normal curve is an idealized curve.

Truth or Fiction Revisited: An IQ score of 130 may therefore be more impressive than an SAT score of 500. The IQ score of 130 is two standard deviations above the mean and exceeds that of more than 97% of the population. An SAT score of 500 is the mean SAT score and thus equals or excels that of about 50% of the population.

The Correlation Coefficient

What is the relationship between intelligence and educational achievement? Between cigarette smoking and lung cancer among humans? Between the personality trait of introversion and numbers of dates among college students? We cannot run experiments to determine whether the relationships between these variables are causal, because we cannot manipulate the independent variable. That is, we cannot assign high or low intelligence at random. Nor can we (ethically) assign some people to smoke cigarettes and others not to smoke. People must be allowed to make their own decisions, so it is possible that the same factors that lead some people to smoke—or to continue to smoke after they have experimented with cigarettes—also lead to lung cancer. (Even if we were to assign a group of people to a nonsmoking condition, could we monitor them continuously to make sure that they weren't sneaking puffs?) Nor can we designate who will be introverted and who will be extraverted. True, we could encourage people to act as if they are introverted or extraverted, but behavior is not the same thing as a personality trait. We cannot run true experiments to answer any of these questions, but the **correlation coefficient** can be used to reveal whether there is a relationship between intelligence and achievement, a relationship between smoking and cancer, or a relationship between personality and dating. Correlational research shows that smoking and cancer are related but does not reveal cause and effect. However, experimental research with animals does strongly suggest that smoking will cause cancer in humans.

Correlation coefficient A number between −1.00 and +1.00 that indicates the direction (negative or positive) and extent (from none to perfect) of the relationship between two variables.

FIGURE A.5 Positive and Negative Correlations

When there is a positive correlation between variables, as there is between intelligence and achievement, one increases as the other increases. By and large, the more time students spend studying, the better their grades are likely to be, as suggested in the diagram to the left. (Each dot represents the amount of time a student spends studying each week and his or her grade point average.) But there is a negative correlation between grades and juvenile delinquency. As the number of delinquent acts per year increases, one's grade point average tends to decline. Correlational research may suggest but does not demonstrate cause and effect.

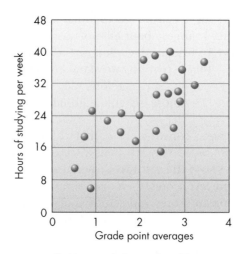

Positive correlation, as found between intelligence and academic achievment

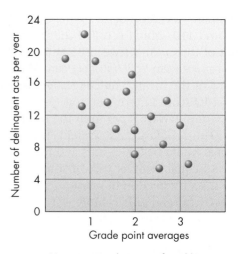

Negative correlation, as found between delinquency and academic achievment

Question: What is the correlation coefficient? The correlation coefficient is a statistic that describes the relationship between two variables. A correlation coefficient can vary from +1.00 to −1.00. A correlation coefficient of +1.00 is called a perfect positive correlation, and it describes the relationship between temperatures as measured by the Fahrenheit and Centigrade scales. A correlation coefficient of −1.00 is a perfect negative correlation, and a correlation of 0 (zero) reveals no relationship between variables.

As suggested by Figures A.5 and A.6, most correlation coefficients in psychological research are less than perfect. The left-hand graph in Figure A.5 reveals a positive relationship between time spent studying and grade point averages. Because there is a positive correlation between the variables but the relationship is not perfect, the correlation coefficient will lie between 0.00 and +1.00. Perhaps it is about +0.60 or +0.70. However, we cannot absolutely predict what a person's GPA will be if we know the hours per week that he or she spends studying (nor can we predict exactly how much time the person spends studying on the basis of his or her GPA). Nevertheless, it would seem advisable to place oneself among those who spend a good deal of time studying if one wishes to achieve a good GPA.

The right-hand drawing in Figure A.5 reveals a negative relationship between number of delinquent acts committed per year and GPA. The causal connection is less than perfectly clear. Does delinquency interfere with studying and academic achievement? Does poor achievement weaken a student's commitment to trying to get ahead through work? Do feelings of distance from "the system" contribute both to delinquent behavior and a low GPA? The answers are not to be found in Figure A.5, but the negative correlation between delinquent behavior and GPA does suggest that it is worthwhile to study the issues involved and—for a student—to distance himself or herself from delinquent behavior if he or she wishes to achieve in the academic world.

 Learning Connections **THE CORRELATION COEFFICIENT**

ACTIVE REVIEW (19) The correlation _____ is a statistic that describes the relationship between two variables. (20) Correlational research (*Does* or *Does not?*) reveal cause and effect. (21) Correlation coefficients vary from +1.00 to _____.

REFLECT AND RELATE In you own experience, how would you explain the correlation between students' test scores and the amount of time they put into studying? Is studying the only factor involved in their grades? Explain.

CRITICAL THINKING Why is the correlation between grades at your college and the price of eggs in the local supermarket likely to be close to zero?

 Go to **http://psychology.wadsworth.com/ rathus_pcc9e** for an interactive version of this Learning Connections unit.

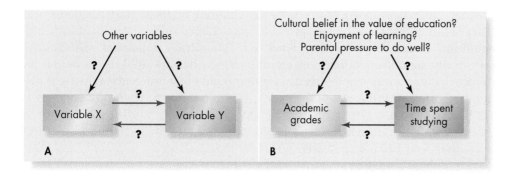

FIGURE A.6 **Correlational Relationships, Cause and Effect**

Correlational relationships may suggest but do not demonstrate cause and effect. In part A, there is a correlation between variables X and Y. Does this mean that either variable X causes variable Y or that variable Y causes variable X? Not necessarily. Other factors could affect both variables X and Y. Consider the examples of academic grades (variable X) and time spent studying (variable Y) in part B. There is a positive correlation between the two. Does this mean that studying contributes to good grades? Perhaps. Does it mean that good grades encourage studying? Again, perhaps. But there could also be other variables—such as cultural belief in the value of education, enjoyment of learning, even parental pressure to do well—that contribute both to time spent studying and good grades.

Inferential Statistics

Head Start programs have apparently raised children's intellectual functioning, as reflected in their grades and IQ scores. In one such study, children enrolled in a Head Start program obtained a mean IQ score of 99, whereas children similar in background who were not enrolled in Head Start obtained a mean IQ score of 93. Is this difference of six points in IQ *significant,* or does it represent a chance fluctuation in scores? In a study reported in Chapter 1, college students were provoked by people in league with the researchers. Some of the students believed they had drunk alcohol (in a cocktail with tonic water); others believed they had drunk tonic water only. The students were then given the opportunity to shock the individuals who had provoked them. Students who believed they had drunk alcohol chose higher levels of shock than students who believed they had drunk tonic water only. Did the mean difference in shock level chosen by the two groups of students represent actual differences between the groups, or might it have been a chance fluctuation? The individuals in the Head Start study were a sample of young children. The individuals in the alcohol study were a sample of college students. Inferential statistics help us determine whether we can conclude that the differences between such samples reflect real differences that are found in the populations that they represent.

Descriptive statistics enables us to provide descriptive information about samples of scores. **Question: What are inferential statistics? Inferential statistics** assist us in determining whether we can generalize differences among samples to the populations that they represent.

Figure A.7 shows the distribution of heights of 1,000 men and 1,000 women who were selected at random from the general U.S. population. The mean height for men is greater than the mean height for women. Can we conclude, or **infer,** that this difference in height is not just a chance fluctuation but represents an actual difference between the general populations of men and women? Or must we avoid such an inference and summarize our results by stating only that the mean height of the sample of men in the study was greater than the mean height of the sample of women in the study?

If we could not draw inferences about populations from studies of samples, our research findings would be limited indeed. We could only speak about the specific individuals studied. There would be no point to learning about any study in which you did not participate because it would not apply to you! Fortunately, that is not the case. Inferential statistics permits us to extend findings with samples to the populations from which they were drawn.

Statistically Significant Differences

We asked whether the differences in height between our samples of men and women were simply a chance fluctuation or whether they represented actual differences between the heights of men and women. Researchers tend not to talk about "real differences" or "actual differences" between groups, however. Instead, they speak of statistically significant differences. Similarly, researchers asked

Inferential statistics The branch of statistics that is concerned with confidence with which conclusions drawn about samples can be extended to the populations from which the samples were drawn.

Infer To go from the particular to the general; to draw a conclusion.

FIGURE A.7 **Distribution of Heights for Random Samples of Men and Women**

Note that the mean height of the men is greater than that of the women. Is the group mean difference in height statistically significant? Researchers use a tool called inferential statistics to determine the answer.

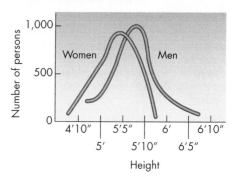

whether differences in IQ scores between children in Head Start programs and other children from similar backgrounds were chance fluctuations or statistically significant differences. **Question: What are "statistically significant" differences?** Statistically significant differences are differences that are unlikely to be due to chance fluctuation. Psychologists usually do not accept a difference as being statistically significant unless the probability *(p)* that it is due to chance fluctuation is less than 1 in 20 (i.e., $p < .05$). They are more comfortable labeling a difference as statistically significant when the probability *(p)* that it is due to chance fluctuation is less than 1 in 100 (i.e., $p < .01$).

Psychologists use formulas involving the means (e.g., mean IQ scores of 93 versus 99) and the standard deviations of sample groups to determine whether differences in means are statistically significant. As you can see in Figure A.8, the farther apart group means are, the more likely it is that they are statistically significant. In other words, if the men are on the average 5 inches taller than the women, it is more likely that the difference is statistically significant than if them men are only one-quarter of an inch taller on average. Principle 1: Everything else being equal, the greater the difference between means, the greater the probability that the difference is statistically significant. This makes common sense. After all, if you were told that your neighbor's car had gotten one-tenth of a mile more per gallon of gas than your car in the past year, you would probably attribute the difference to chance fluctuation. But if the difference were greater, say 14 miles per gallon, you would probably assume that the difference reflected an actual difference in driving habits or the efficiency of the automobile.

As you can see in Figure A.9, the smaller the standard deviations (a measure of variability) of the groups, the more likely it is that the difference between means is statistically significant. Consider the extreme example in which there is *no* variability within each group. That is, imagine that every woman in the randomly selected sample of 1,000 women is exactly 5'5" tall. Similarly, imagine that every man in the randomly selected sample of 1,000 men is exactly 5'10" tall. In such a case the heights of the men and women would not overlap at all, and it would appear that the differences were statistically significant. Consider the other extreme—one with unnaturally large variability. Imagine that the heights of the women vary from 2' to 14' and that the heights of the men vary from 2'1" to 14'3". In such a case we might be more likely to assume that the difference in group means of 5" was a chance fluctuation. Principle 2: Everything else being equal, the smaller the variability of the distributions of scores, the greater the probability that the difference in group means is statistically significant.

Therefore, we cannot conclude that men are taller than women unless we know the average heights of men and women and how much the heights within each group vary. We must know both the central tendencies (means) and variability of the two distributions of heights in order to infer that the mean heights are statistically significantly different.

FIGURE A.8 **Decreasing and Increasing the Mean Group Difference in Heights**

Everything else being equal, the greater the difference in group means, the greater the probability that the difference is statistically significant. The distribution on the right shows a greater difference in group means; therefore, there is a greater probability that the difference is statistically significant.

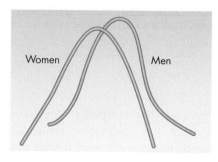
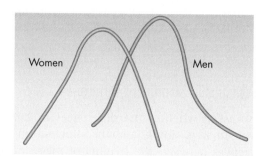

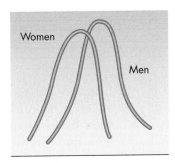
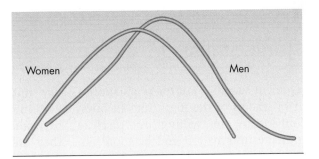

FIGURE A.9 **Decreasing and Increasing the Variability of the Distributions of Scores**
Everything else being equal, the smaller the variability in group scores, the greater the probability that the difference in groups means is statistically significant. The distribution on the right shows a greater difference in the variability of the groups; therefore, there is a *lower* probability that the difference in group means is statistically significant.

We have been "eyeballing" the data and making assumptions. We have been relying on what one professor of mine called the "Wow!" effect. As noted, psychologists and other researchers actually use mathematical techniques that take group means and standard deviations into account to determine whether group differences are statistically significant. It is often the case that eyeballing real data does not yield clear results or even good guesses.

Samples and Populations

Inferential statistics are mathematical tools that psychologists apply to samples of scores to determine whether they can generalize or extend their findings to populations of scores. They must therefore be quite certain that the samples involved actually represent the populations from which they were drawn. Sampling techniques are crucial. Random sampling is the best method, and sampling is random only if every member of the target population has an equal chance of being selected.

It matters little how sophisticated our statistical methods are if the samples studied do not represent the target populations. We could use a variety of sophisticated statistical techniques to analyze the heights of the New York Big Apples and the California Quakes, but none of these methods would tell us much about the height of the general population. Or about the height of women. (Or about the height of people who can't pass the ball, shoot, or play defense.)

Learning Connections INFERENTIAL STATISTICS

ACTIVE REVIEW (22) _____ statistics enables us to provide descriptive information about samples of scores. (23) _____ statistics help us decide whether we can generalize differences among samples to their populations. (24) Psychologists usually do not accept a difference as being statistically significant unless the probability that it is due to chance fluctuation is less than one in _____. (25) Psychologists use formulas involving the means and _____ deviations of sample groups to determine whether differences in means are statistically significant.

REFLECT AND RELATE Suppose that some aliens "borrowed" you for a while and studied you to learn about the human species. What could they correctly infer about all people from studying you? What errors would they make if they assumed that other people were just like you?

CRITICAL THINKING What does it mean to say that the difference in heights between men and women is *statistically significant?* (For example, does it mean that all men are taller than all women, or that the average height of men is at least three inches greater than the average height of women?)

 Go to **http://psychology.wadsworth.com/ rathus_pcc9e** for an interactive version of this Learning Connections unit.

Life Connections
Thinking Critically about "Junk Statistics"

When you read popular magazines or go online, you are frequently asked to participate in polls on political matters, sports, and who is the hottest new pop star. Perhaps you complete a questionnaire and mail it in, or, more likely, you click on a few answers and then send them in electronically—getting instant feedback on the results of the poll.

Statistics is an exact science, yet very often we wind up with useless or misleading results. Critical thinkers have an attitude of skepticism, and, as suggested in Chapter 1, skepticism may best be directed toward the results of magazine and online surveys of sexual behavior. These surveys sound impressive because they often obtain completed questionnaires from many thousands of readers. We can also grant that their answers are probably computed and analyzed flawlessly. Why, then, should we be skeptical of the published results? The answer, in a nutshell, is volunteer bias. That is, the respondents did not represent the American population. In fact, they might have represented no one other than themselves. In the case of research on sexual behavior, volunteers may represent subgroups of the population—or of readers of the magazines in question—who are willing to disclose intimate information and be more liberal in their sexual practices.

A case in point is a survey by *Elle* magazine (2003), which was conducted on the magazine's Web site. Nearly 60,000 people completed the online questionnaire. However, *Elle* publishes in 35 countries and polled mainly its own readership, a group of perhaps millions of fashion-conscious young adults. Also, participants were computer-savvy enough to find their ways to the specified Web site. Sixty thousand people will fill a small city, but they do not make up a high percentage of the million or more readers who were invited to participate.

What did the *Elle* survey find? To begin with, nearly 80% of the respondents said that their faces were "nice" or "very attractive," which sounds suspiciously high if we are trying to represent the population at large. But then consider that 41% of the women and 52% of the men characterized their bodies as "good" or "great." This result was reported by statistical analysis in a day and age in which most valid surveys inform us that the great majority of women in our culture believe that they are too heavy. The numbers no doubt accurately reflect the answers of the participants; the question is whom the participants reflect. The *Elle* survey may have been completed by people who are not only fashion-conscious, but also body-conscious. They do not represent the people in our culture at large. They may not even represent the general readership of *Elle*.

Social scientist Edward Laumann and his colleagues (1994), who labored to obtain a nationally representative example for the NHSLS study reported in Chapter 12, are particularly harsh in their judgment of surveys like the one conducted by *Elle*. They write that "such studies, in sum, produce junk statistics of no value whatsoever in making valid and reliable population projections" (p. 45). Numbers can look impressive, especially when statistics from large samples are generated by computers. But the critical reader will ask *who* completed the questionnaire and whom they represented.

Recite—An Active Summary™

1. What is statistics?

Statistics is the science that assembles data in such a way that they provide useful information about measures or scores. Such measures or scores include people's height, weight, and scores on psychological tests such as IQ tests.

2. What are samples and populations?

A sample is part of a population. A population is a complete group from which a sample is drawn. The example with basketball players shows that a sample must represent its population if it is to provide accurate information about the population.

3. What is descriptive statistics?

Descriptive statistics is the branch of statistics that provides information about the central tendencies and variabilities of distributions of scores.

4. What is a frequency distribution?

A frequency distribution organizes a set of data, usually from low scores to high scores, and indicates how frequently a score appears. Class intervals may be used on large sets of data to provide a quick impression of how the data tend to cluster. The histogram and frequency polygon are two ways of graphing data to help people visualize the way in which the data are distributed.

5. What are measures of central tendency?

Measures of central tendency are "averages" that show the center or balancing points of a frequency distribution. The mean—which is what most people consider the average—is obtained

Recite—An Active Summary™

by adding the scores in a distribution and dividing by the number of scores. The median is the score of the middle or central case in a distribution. The mode is the most common score in a distribution. Distributions can be bimodal (having two modes) or multimodal.

6. What are measures of variability?

Measures of variability provide information about the spread of scores in a distribution. The range is defined as the difference between the highest and lowest scores. The standard deviation is a statistic that shows how scores cluster around the mean. Distributions with higher standard deviations are more spread out.

7. What is a normal distribution?

The normal or bell-shaped curve is hypothesized to occur when the scores in a distribution occur by chance. The normal curve has one mode, and approximately two of three scores (68%) are found within one standard deviation of the mean. Fewer than 5% of cases are found beyond two standard deviations from the mean.

8. What is the correlation coefficient?

The correlation coefficient is a statistic that describes how variables such as IQ and grade point averages are related. It varies from +1.00 to –1.00. When correlations between two variables are positive, it means that one (such as school grades) tends to rise as the other (such as IQ) rises.

9. What are inferential statistics?

Inferential statistics is the branch of statistics that indicates whether researchers can extend their findings with samples to the populations from which they were drawn.

10. What are "statistically significant" differences?

Statistically significant differences are believed to represent real differences between groups, and not chance fluctuation.

Go to **http://psychology.wadsworth.com/ rathus_pcc9e** to access an interactive version of this active summary.

Key Terms

Statistics (p. A–2)
Sample (p. A–2)
Population (p. A–2)
Range (p. A–2)
Average (p. A–2)
Descriptive statistics (p. A–3)

Frequency distribution (p. A–3)
Frequency histogram (p. A–5)
Frequency polygon (p. A–5)
Mean (p. A–6)

Median (p. A–6)
Mode (p. A–6)
Bimodal (p. A–6)
Standard deviation (p. A–7)
Normal distribution (p. A–10)

Normal curve (p. A–10)
Correlation coefficient (p. A–11)
Inferential statistics (p. A–13)
Infer (p. A–13)

ACTIVE LEARNING RESOURCES

Visit your Companion Website for Video, Quizzing, and Self-Assessment!

http://psychology.wadsworth.com/rathus_pcc9e
On this site you can access the Facial Analysis video highlighted by the Video Connections icon on p. 24. In addition there are many quizzing opportunities including interactive versions of the fill-in-the-blank Active Review sections in your book.

Study on the Go!

Don't have time to study right now? You can study on the go! Visit your companion website and download an audio version of the Recite—An Active Summary section to your media player.

ThomsonNOW

http://www.thomsonedu.com
Need help studying? This site is your one-stop study shop. Take a Pre-Test and Thomson NOW will generate a Personalized Study Plan based on your test results. The Study Plan will identify the topics you need to review and direct you to online resources to help you master those topics. You can then take a Post-Test to determine the concepts you have mastered and what you still need to work on.

Author Blog

What does your author have to say about the state of psychology? Visit your companion website every Tuesday and click on "Author Blog," where he'll talk about the most recent controversies and hot topics in psychology.

Answer Keys to Self-Assessments and Active Reviews

Answer Keys to Self-Assessments

Scoring Key for the Social-Desirability Scale (Chapter 1, p. 26)

Place a check mark on the appropriate line of the scoring key each time your answer agrees with the one listed in the scoring key. Add the check marks and record the total number of check marks below.

1. T_____	10. F_____	19. F_____	28. F_____
2. T_____	11. F_____	20. T_____	29. T_____
3. F_____	12. F_____	21. T_____	30. F_____
4. T_____	13. T_____	22. F_____	31. T_____
5. F_____	14. F_____	23. F_____	32. F_____
6. F_____	15. F_____	24. T_____	33. T_____
7. T_____	16. T_____	25. T_____	
8. T_____	17. T_____	26. T_____	
9. F_____	18. T_____	27. T_____	

Interpreting Your Score

Low Scorers (0–8) About one respondent in six earns a score between 0 and 8. Such respondents answered in a socially *undesirable* direction much of the time. It may be that they are more willing than most people to respond to tests truthfully, even when their answers might meet with social disapproval.

Average Scorers (9–19) About two respondents in three earn a score from 9 through 19. They tend to show an average degree of concern for the social desirability of their responses, and it may be that their general behavior represents an average degree of conformity to social rules and conventions.

High Scorers (20–33) About one respondent in six earns a score between 20 and 33. These respondents may be highly concerned about social approval and respond to test items in such as way as to avoid the disapproval of people who may read their responses. Their general behavior may show high conformity to social rules and conventions.

Answer Key for "Symptoms of PMS" (Chapter 2, p. 83)

There are no numerical answers to this Self-Assessment. Ask yourself, rather, whether you are experiencing any moderate to disabling psychological or physical symptoms of PMS. We advise you to discuss any symptoms that are moderate or more severe with your physician, preferably a gynecologist. It is important for your health that you discuss any *"disabling"* symptoms at all with your gynecologist. Even if you have some mild symptoms, you may want to check them off and bring them to the attention of your gynecologist. Nothing is to be gained by suffering in silence.

Scoring Key for the "Why Do You Drink?" Questionnaire (Chapter 5, p. 212)

Why do you drink? Score your questionnaire by seeing how many items you answered for each of the reasons for drinking shown in Table B.1. Consider the key as *suggestive* only. For example, if you answered several items in the manner indicated on the *addiction* factor, it may be wise to examine seriously what your drinking means to you. But do not interpret a few test item scores as binding evidence of addiction.

TABLE B.1 REASONS FOR DRINKING

Addiction
1. T
6. F
32. T
38. T
40. T

Anxiety/Tension Reduction
7. T
9. T
12. T
15. T
18. T
26. T
31. T
33. T

Pleasure/Taste
2. T
5. T
16. T
27. T
28. T
35. T
37. T

Transforming Agent
2. T
4. T
19. T
22. T
28. T
30. T

34. T
36. T

Social Reward
3. T
8. T
23. T

Celebration
10. T
24. T
25. T

Religion
11. T

Social Power
2. T
13. T
19. T
30. T

Scapegoating (Using alcohol as an excuse for failure of social misconduct)
14. T
15. T
20. T
21. T
39. T

Habit
17. T
29. T

Scoring Key for the "Sleep Quiz: Are You Getting Your Z's?" (Chapter 5, p. 223)

Psychologist James Maas, the author of *Power Sleep* (HarperCollins, 1999), writes that an answer of "true" to two or more of the statements in the questionnaire may be a sign of a sleep problem.

Answer Key for "Puzzles, Problems, and Just Plain Fun" (Chapter 8, p. 311) and to the Duncker Candle Problem

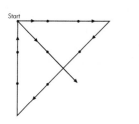

For problem 1c, note that each of the letters is the first letter of the numbers one through eight. Therefore, the two missing letters are *NT*, for *nine* and *ten*. The solutions to problems 2 and 3 and to the Duncker candle problem are shown in this illustration. To solve the Duncker candle problem, use the thumbtack to pin the matchbox to the wall. Then set the candle on top of the box. Functional fixedness prevents many people from conceptualizing the matchbox as anything more than a device to hold matches. Commonly given *wrong* answers include trying to affix the bottom of the candle to the wall with melted wax or trying to tack the candle to the wall.

And what of the coined stamped with the date 544 BCE? BCE stands for "before the common era," that is, before the birth of Jesus. Prior to the birth of Jesus, people did not know He was going to be born.

Scoring Key for the Remote Associates Test (Chapter 9, p. 343)

1. Prince
2. Dog
3. Cold
4. Glasses
5. Club
6. Boat
7. Defense
8. Black
9. Pit
10. Writer

Answers to Cattell Culture-Free Intelligence Test Items (Chapter 9, p. 353)

A. 1
B. 3
C. 1
D. 3
E. 1
F. 4

Scoring Key for the Sensation-Seeking Scale (Chapter 10, p. 368)

Because this is a shortened version of a questionnaire, no norms are available. However, answers in agreement with the following key point in the direction of sensation seeking:

1. A	6. B	11. A
2. A	7. A	12. A
3. A	8. A	13. B
4. B	9. B	
5. A	10. A	

Scoring Key for the Expectancy-for-Success Scale (Chapter 11, p. 415)

In order to calculate your total score for the expectancy-for-success scale, first reverse the scores for the following items: 1, 2, 4, 6, 7, 8, 14, 15, 17, 18, 24, 27, and 28. That is, change a 1 to a 5; a 2 to a 4; leave a 3 alone; change a 4 to a 2; and a 5 to a 1. Then add the scores.

The range of total scores can vary from 30 to 150. The higher your score, the greater your expectancy for success in the future—and, according to social cognitive theory, the more motivated you will be to apply yourself in facing difficult challenges.

Fibel and Hale administered their test to undergraduates taking psychology courses and found that women's scores ranged from 65 to 143 and men's from 81 to 138.

The average score for each gender was 112 (112.32 for women and 112.15 for men).

Key for Sternberg's Triangular Love Scale (Chapter 12, pp. 457)

First add your scores for the items on each of the three components—intimacy, passion, and decision/commitment—and divide each total by 15. This procedure will yield an average rating for each subscale. An average rating of 5 on a particular subscale indicates a moderate level of the component represented by the subscale. A higher rating indicates a greater level. A lower rating indicates a lower level. Examining your ratings on these components will give you an idea of the degree to which you perceive your love relationship to be characterized by these three components of love. For example, you might find that passion is stronger than decision/commitment, a pattern that is common in the early stages of an intense romantic relationship. You might find it interesting to complete the questionnaire a few months or perhaps a year or so from now to see how your feelings about your relationship change over time. You might also ask your partner to complete the scale so that the two of you can compare your respective scores. Comparing your ratings for each component with those of your partner will give you an idea of the degree to which you and your partner see your relationship in a similar way.

Answer Key for "Cultural Myths That Create a Climate That Supports Rape" Questionnaire (Chapter 12, p. 468)

Actually, each item, with the exception of number 2, represents a cultural myth that supports rape. These myths tend to view sex as an adversarial game, stereotype women as flirtatious and deceitful, and blame the victim.

Answer Key for the "Are You Type A or Type B?" Questionnaire (Chapter 13, p. 489)

Type A people are ambitious, hard driving, and chronically discontent with their current achievements. Type Bs, by contrast, are more relaxed, more involved with the quality of life.

Yeses suggest the Type A behavior pattern, which is marked by a sense of time urgency and constant struggle. In appraising your "type," you need not be overly concerned with the precise number of "yes" answers; we have no normative data for you. But as Friedman and Rosenman (1974, p. 85) note, you should have little trouble spotting yourself as "hard core" or "moderately afflicted"—that is, if you are honest with yourself.

Answer Key for the Locus of Control Scale (Chapter 13, pp. 492–493)

Place a check mark in the blank space in the scoring key, below, each time your answer agrees with the answer in the key. The number of check marks is your total score.

Scoring Key:

1. Yes ___	11. Yes ___	21. Yes ___	31. Yes ___
2. No ___	12. Yes ___	22. No ___	32. No ___
3. Yes ___	13. No ___	23. Yes ___	33. Yes ___
4. No ___	14. Yes ___	24. Yes ___	34. No ___
5. Yes ___	15. No ___	25. No ___	35. Yes ___
6. No ___	16. Yes ___	26. No ___	36. Yes ___
7. Yes ___	17. Yes ___	27. Yes ___	37. Yes ___
8. Yes ___	18. Yes ___	28. No ___	38. No ___
9. No ___	19. Yes ___	29. Yes ___	39. Yes ___
10. Yes ___	20. No ___	30. No ___	40. No ___

TOTAL SCORE _____

Interpreting Your Score

Low scorers (0–8). About one respondent in three earns a score of from 0 to 8. Such respondents tend to have an internal locus of control. They see themselves as responsible for the reinforcements they attain (and fail to attain) in life. *Average scorers* (9–16). Most respondents earn from 9 to 16 points. Average scorers may see themselves as partially in control of their lives. Perhaps they see themselves as in control at work, but not in their social lives—or vice versa. *High scorers* (17–40). About 15 percent of respondents attain scores of 17 or above. High scorers tend largely to see life as a game of chance, and success as a matter of luck or the generosity of others.

Scoring Key for the Rathus Assertiveness Schedule (Chapter 15, p. 587)

Tabulate your score as follows: For those items followed by an asterisk (*), change the signs (plus to minus; minus to plus). For example, if the response to an asterisked item was 2, place a minus sign (−) before the two. If the response to an asterisked item was −3, change the minus sign to a plus sign (+) by adding a vertical stroke. Then add up the scores of the 30 items.

Scores on the assertiveness schedule can vary from +90 to −90. Table B.3 will show you how your score compares to those of 764 college women and 637 men from 35 campuses across the United States. For example, if you are a woman and your score was 26, it exceeded that of 80% of the women in the sample. A score of 15 for a male exceeds that of 55 to 60% of the men in the sample.

TABLE B.3 PERCENTILES FOR SCORES ON THE RAS

Women's Scores	Percentile	Men's Scores
55	99	65
48	97	54
45	95	48
37	90	40
31	85	33
26	80	30
23	75	26
19	70	24
17	65	19
14	60	17
11	55	15
8	50	11
6	45	8
2	40	6
−1	35	3
−4	30	1
−8	25	−3
−13	20	−7
−17	15	−11
−24	10	−15
−34	5	−24
−39	3	−30
−48	1	−41

Source: Nevid, J. S., & Rathus, S. A. (1978). Multivariate and normative data pertaining to the RAS with the college population. *Behavior Therapy, 9,* 675.

Answer Keys to Active Reviews

Chapter 1 What Is Psychology?

1. Behavior
2. Predict
3. Theories
4. Pure
5. Applied
6. Psychotherapy
7. Counseling
8. School
9. Educational
10. Developmental
11. Social
12. Experimental
13. Industrial
14. Aristotle
15. Socrates
16. Wilhelm Wundt
17. Functionalism
18. John B. Watson
19. Gestalt
20. Sigmund Freud
21. Biologically
22. Evolutionary
23. Cognitive
24. Existential
25. Social
26. Sociocultural
27. Mary Whiton Calkins
28. Christine Ladd-Franklin
29. Clark
30. Robert Williams
31. Hypothesis
32. Populations
33. Random
34. Case
35. Survey
36. Naturalistic
37. Correlational
38. Cause
39. Experiment
40. Independent
41. Control
42. Blind
43. Ethical
44. Informed
45. Debriefed
46. Animals, nonhuman animals

Chapter 2 Biology and Psychology

1. Selection
2. Survival
3. Random
4. Fitted, adapted, suited
5. Environmental
6. Instincts, fixed action patterns
7. Behavioral
8. Molecular
9. Genes
10. Chromosomes
11. Down
12. Identical, monozygotic
13. Neurotransmitters
14. Axon
15. Myelin
16. Efferent
17. Firing
18. Synapse
19. Hippocampus
20. Schizophrenia
21. Serotonin
22. Peripheral
23. Autonomic
24. Electroencephalograph
25. Resonance
26. Cerebellum
27. Hypothalamus
28. Callosum
29. Occipital
30. Frontal, prefrontal
31. Left
32. More
33. Epilepsy
34. Hypothalamus
35. Prolactin
36. Thyroxin
37. Cortex
38. Medulla

Chapter 3 The Voyage through the Life Span

1. Ovulation
2. Zygote
3. Uterus
4. Embryonic
5. Five
6. Assimilation
7. Sensorimotor
8. Concrete
9. Zone
10. Three
11. Psychosocial
12. Initial-preattachment
13. Contact
14. Instinct, fixed action pattern
15. Authoritative
16. Secondary
17. Testosterone
18. Formal
19. Imaginary
20. Universal
21. Stress
22. Diffusion
23. Young
24. Programmed-senescence
25. Wear
26. Crystallized
27. Fluid
28. Is not
29. Generativity
30. Do not
31. Integrity
32. Denial
33. Fails to support
34. Terminally

Chapter 4 Sensation and Perception

1. Sensation
2. Perception
3. Absolute
4. Difference
5. Signal
6. Electromagnetic
7. Wavelength
8. Cornea
9. Iris
10. Lens
11. Rods, cones
12. Optic
13. Color
14. Whole
15. Figure
16. Top–down
17. Retina
18. Stroboscopic
19. Compress
20. 20,000
21. Pitch
22. Decibels
23. Anvil
24. Basilar
25. Organ of Corti
26. Auditory
27. Odor
28. Olfactory
29. Bitter
30. Taste
31. Two-point
32. More
33. Position
34. Muscles
35. Upright
36. Semicircular canals
37. Virtual
38. Extrasensory perception
39. Telepathy
40. File-drawer

Chapter 5 Consciousness

1. Behavior
2. Awareness
3. Freud
4. Brain
5. Paradoxical
6. Five
7. REM
8. Activation
9. Deep
10. Normal
11. Magnetism
12. Hypermnesia
13. Response
14. Mantra
15. Blood
16. Heart
17. Autonomic, automatic
18. Abuse
19. Abstinence
20. More
21. Pain
22. Anxiety, pain, epilepsy, high blood pressure, insomnia
23. Attention
24. Cocaine
25. Nicotine
26. Hallucinogenic
27. Marijuana
28. Hallucinations

Chapter 6 Learning

1. Behavior
2. Represent
3. Stimulus
4. Unconditioned
5. Conditioned
6. Only one
7. Extinguish
8. Spontaneous
9. Generalization
10. Discrimination
11. Higher
12. Albert
13. Counterconditioning
14. Flooding
15. Desensitization
16. Bell, buzzer
17. Effect
18. Rewards
19. Reinforcement
20. Positive
21. Negative
22. Primary
23. Secondary, learned, conditioned, acquired
24. Extinction
25. Punishments
26. Discriminative
27. Fixed-interval
28. Variable-ratio
29. Successive
30. Biofeedback
31. Modification
32. Programmed
33. Cognitive
34. Latent
35. Is not
36. Contingency

Chapter 7 Memory

1. Explicit
2. Episodic, autobiographical
3. Semantic
4. Encoding
5. Maintenance
6. Elaborative
7. Retrieval
8. Sensory, short-term, long-term
9. Icons
10. Eidetic
11. Auditory
12. Serial
13. Interference
14. Reconstruct
15. Cues
16. Flashbulb
17. Hierarchical, classified
18. Tip
19. Context
20. Nonsense
21. Sharply
22. Retroactive
23. Proactive
24. Hippocampus
25. Anterograde
26. Retrograde
27. Synapses
28. Serotonin
29. New
30. Thalamus

Chapter 8 Cognition and Language

1. Cognition, Thinking
2. Concepts
3. Prototype
4. Exemplars
5. Algorithm
6. Heuristic
7. Means–end
8. Analogy
9. Mental
10. Insight
11. Representativeness
12. Availability
13. Cognitive
14. Framing
15. Have
16. Grammar
17. Linguistic
18. Prelinguistic
19. In all languages
20. Holophrases
21. The same
22. Overregularization
23. Observation, modeling
24. Psycholinguistic
25. Acquisition device
26. Grammar
27. Universal

Chapter 9 Intelligence and Creativity

1. Intelligence
2. *g*
3. Primary
4. Gardner
5. Practical
6. Creativity
7. Remote
8. Divergent
9. Binet
10. Intelligence quotient
11. Wechsler
12. Deviation
13. 100
14. 50
15. Asian Americans
16. 10 to 15
17. 70
18. 130
19. Do
20. Genetic
21. 40% to 60%
22. Higher

Chapter 10 Motivation and Emotion

1. Motives
2. Deprivation
3. Incentive
4. Evolutionary, ethological
5. Homeostasis
6. Deprivation
7. Self-actualization
8. Sugar
9. Ventromedial
10. Blood
11. Eating
12. Anorexia
13. European
14. Bulimia
15. Child, sexual
16. Do
17. Hypothalamus
18. Testosterone
19. Appraise, interpret
20. Deindividuation, diffusion of responsibility
21. Increase
22. High
23. Apperception
24. Performance
25. Learning
26. Emotion
27. Sympathetic
28. Universal
29. Do
30. Action
31. Cognitive
32. Pressure

Chapter 11 Personality: Theory and Measurement

1. Conflict
2. Id
3. Ego
4. Defense
5. Superego
6. Anal
7. Fixation
8. Other
9. Collective
10. Inferiority
11. Horney
12. Eight
13. Traits
14. Stability
15. Conscientiousness
16. Situational, environmental
17. Social
18. Person
19. Person
20. Are
21. Actualization
22. Self
23. Reference
24. Sociocultural
25. Individualists
26. Collectivists
27. Highest
28. Behavior
29. Objective
30. Ambiguous
31. True
32. Rorschach

Chapter 12 Gender and Sexuality

1. Stereotypes
2. Gender
3. Different
4. Women
5. Girls
6. Boys
7. Men
8. Evolutionary
9. Males
10. Testosterone
11. Observational
12. Gender
13. Esteem
14. Testosterone
15. Organizing
16. Orientation
17. Learning
18. Do
19. Do
20. Pheromones
21. Is
22. High
23. Matching
24. Reciprocity
25. Passion
26. Romantic
27. Myotonia
28. Excitement, plateau, orgasm, and resolution
29. Liberal
30. Men
31. Liberating
32. Arousal
33. Erectile
34. Premature
35. Performance
36. Acquaintances
37. Power
38. Is

Chapter 13 Stress, Health, and Adjustment

1. Hassles
2. Adjustment, adaptation
3. Conflict
4. Ellis
5. Urgency
6. Higher
7. Commitment
8. Decreases
9. Alarm
10. Fight-or-flight
11. Befriend
12. Corticosteroids, steroids
13. Adrenaline
14. White
15. Antigens
16. Antibodies
17. Immune
18. Muscle-tension
19. Migraine
20. Cholesterol
21. Less
22. More
23. Play

Chapter 14 Psychological Disorders

1. Possession
2. *Hammer*
3. Perception
4. Psychiatric
5. Szasz
6. Phobia
7. Panic
8. Compulsive
9. Posttraumatic stress disorder
10. Repression
11. Behaviorists, learning theorists
12. Do
13. Amnesia
14. Identity
15. Think
16. Abuse
17. Somatoform
18. Conversion
19. Emotions
20. Major
21. Elation
22. Flight
23. Helplessness
24. Internal
25. Do
26. Serotonin
27. Thought
28. Delusions
29. Catatonic
30. Does
31. Fewer
32. Dopamine
33. Personality
34. Paranoid
35. Withdrawal
36. Antisocial
37. Lower
38. Gray

Chapter 15 Methods of Therapy

1. Psychological
2. Exorcism
3. Unconscious
4. Catharsis, abreaction
5. Free
6. Dreams
7. Humanistic
8. Nondirective
9. Unconditional
10. Directive
11. Learning
12. Desensitization
13. Aversive
14. Operant
15. Functional
16. Consequences
17. Cognitive, cognitive–behavioral
18. Absolutist
19. Irrational
20. More
21. Encounter
22. Systems
23. Meta
24. Is
25. Cognitive
26. Should
27. Interdependence, dependence
28. Minor
29. Major
30. Antidepressants, selective serotonin reuptake inhibitors (SSRIs), etc.
31. Dopamine
32. Serotonin
33. Depression
34. Prefrontal

Chapter 16 Social Psychology

1. Social
2. Attitude
3. Is
4. Cognitive
5. Cognitive
6. Elaboration
7. Foot
8. Dissonance
9. Perception
10. Primacy
11. Attribution
12. Positively
13. Stare
14. Do
15. Social
16. 75
17. Facilitation
18. Anonymous
19. Decision
20. More
21. Risky
22. Deindividuation
23. Unrealistic
24. Altruism
25. Physical
26. Decrease
27. Facilitate
28. Increase
29. Decrease

Appendix A Statistics

1. Statistics
2. Range
3. Central
4. Descriptive
5. Variation, variability
6. Frequency
7. Class
8. Horizontal
9. Vertical
10. Mean
11. Median
12. Mode
13. Lowest
14. d
15. Normal, bell-shaped
16. Bell
17. 100
18. 15
19. Coefficient
20. Does not
21. –1.00
22. Descriptive
23. Inferential
24. 20
25. Standard

Abbey, A. (1987). Misperceptions of friendly behavior as sexual interest. *Psychology of Women Quarterly, 11,* 173–194.

Abbey, A., et al. (2001). Alcohol and sexual assault. *Alcohol Research & Health, 25*(1), 43–51.

Abeles, N. (1997). Memory problems in later life. *APA Monitor, 28*(6), 2.

Aber, J. L., & Allen, J. P. (1987). Effects of maltreatment of young children on young children's socioemotional development. *Developmental Psychology, 23,* 406–414.

Abraham, C. (2002). *Possessing genius: The bizarre odyssey of Einstein's brain.* New York: St. Martin's Press.

Abraham, H. D., & Duffy, F. H. (2001). EEG coherence in post-LSD visual hallucinations. *Psychiatry Research: Neuroimaging, 107*(3), 151–163.

Ackard, D. M., Neumark-Sztainer, D., Hannan, P. J., French, S., & Story, M. (2001). Binge and purge behavior among adolescents: Associations with sexual and physical abuse in a nationally representative sample: The Commonwealth Fund survey. *Child Abuse & Neglect, 25*(6) 771–785.

Ader, D. N., & Johnson, S. B. (1994). Sample description, reporting, and analysis of sex in psychological research. *American Psychologist, 49,* 216–218.

Adler, T. (1990). Distraction, relaxation can help "shut off" pain. *APA Monitor, 21*(9), 11.

Agras, W. S., Walsh, T., Fairburn, C. G., Wilson, G. T., & Kraemer, H. C. (2000). A multicenter comparison of cognitive-behavioral therapy and interpersonal psychotherapy for bulimia nervosa. *Archives of General Psychiatry, 57*(5), 459–466.

Aikins, D. E., & Craske, M. G. (2001). Cognitive theories of generalized anxiety disorder. *Psychiatric Clinics of North America, 24*(1), 57–74.

Ainsworth, M. D. S., Blehar, M. C., Waters, E., & Wall, S. (1978). *Patterns of attachment: A psychological study of the strange situation.* Hillsdale, NJ: Erlbaum.

Ainsworth, M. D. S., & Bowlby, J. (1991). An ethological approach to personality development. *American Psychologist, 46,* 333–341.

Akerstedt, T., Kecklund, G., & Hoerte, L. (2001). Night driving, season, and the risk of highway accidents. *Sleep: Journal of Sleep and Sleep Disorders Research, 24*(4), 401–406.

Alarcon, A., Capafons, A., Bayot, A., & Cardena, E. (1999). Preference between two methods of active-alert hypnosis: Not all techniques are created equal. *American Journal of Clinical Hypnosis, 41*(3), 269–276.

Albarracín, D., & Wyer, Jr., R. S. (2000). The cognitive impact of past behavior: Influences on beliefs, attitudes, and future behavioral decisions. *Journal of Personality and Social Psychology, 79*(1), 5–22.

Alexander, C. N., et al. (1996). Trial of stress reduction for hypertension in older African Americans: II. Sex and risk subgroup analysis. *Hypertension, 28,* 228–237.

Allen, L. (1993, August). Integrating a sociocultural perspective into the psychology curriculum. G. Stanley Hall lecture presented to the American Psychological Association, Toronto, Canada.

Altran, S. (2006). Genesis and future of suicide terrorism. http://www.interdisciplines.org/terrorism/papers/1. Accessed May 2006.

American Association of University Women (AAUW). (1992). *How schools shortchange women: The A.A.U.W. report.* Washington, DC: American Association of University Women Educational Foundation.

American Cancer Society. (2003). http://www.cancer.org/.

American Heart Association online (2000). *2000 Heart and stroke statistical update.* http://www.americanheart.org.

American Lung Association. (2000). Smoking fact sheet, http:/www.lungusa.org.

American Lung Association. (2003). http:/www.lungusa.org.

American Psychiatric Association. (2000). *Diagnostic and statistical manual of mental disorders* (4th ed., text revision). *DSM–IV–TR.* Washington, DC: Author.

American Psychological Association. (1993). Guidelines for providers of psychological services to ethnic, linguistic, and culturally diverse populations. *American Psychologist, 48,* 45–48.

American Psychological Association. (1998, March 16). Sexual harassment: Myths and realities. APA Public Information Home Page; http://www.apa.org.

American Psychological Association. (2002). Ethical principles of psychologists and code of conduct. *American Psychologist, 57*(12), 1060–1073.

American Psychological Association Research Office. (2000). First-year (full-time) students in doctoral-level departments of psychology by race/ethnicity: 1999–2000. *Graduate Study in Psychology 2000.* Washington, DC: American Psychological Association.

Andersen, B. L. (2002). Biobehavioral outcomes following psychological interventions for cancer patients. *Journal of Consulting & Clinical Psychology, 70*(3), 590–610.

Andersen, B. L., Kiecolt-Glaser, J. K., & Glaser, R. (1994). A biobehavioral model of cancer stress and disease course. *American Psychologist, 49,* 389–404.

Anderson, C. A. (2001). Heat and violence. *Current Directions in Psychological Science, 10*(1), 33–38.

Anderson, C. A. (2003). Violent video games: Myths, facts, and unanswered questions. *Psychological Science Agenda: Science Briefs, 16*(5), 1–3.

Anderson, C. A. (2004). An update on the effects of violent video games. *Journal of Adolescence, 27,* 113–122.

Anderson, C. A., Carnagey, N. L., Flanagan, M., Benjamin, A. J., Eubanks, J., & Valentine, J. C. (2004). Violent video games: Specific effects of violent content on aggressive thoughts and behavior. *Advances in Experimental Social Psychology, 36,* 199–249.

Anderson, C. A., & DeNeve, K. M. (1992). Temperature, aggression, and the negative affect escape model. *Psychological Bulletin, 111,* 347–351.

Anderson, C. A., & Dill, K. E. (2000). Video games and aggressive thoughts, feelings, and behavior in the laboratory and in life. *Journal of Personality and Social Psychology, 78*(4), 772–790.

Anderson, E. S., Winett, R. A., & Wojcik, J. R. (2000). Social-cognitive determinants of nutrition behavior among supermarket food shoppers: A structural equation analysis. *Health Psychology, 19*(5), 479–486.

Anderson, E. S., Winett, R. A., Wojcik, J. R., Winett, S. G., & Bowden, T. (2001). A computerized social cognitive intervention for nutrition behavior: Direct and mediated effects on fat, fiber, fruits and vegetables, self-efficacy and outcome expectations among food shoppers. *Annals of Behavioral Medicine, 23*(2), 88–100.

Anderson, K. G., Sankis, L. M., & Widiger, T. A. (2001). Pathology versus statistical infrequency: Potential sources of gender bias in personality disorder criteria. *Journal of Nervous & Mental Disease, 189*(10), 661–668.

Anderson, K. P., LaPorte, D. J., & Crawford, S. (2000). Child abuse and bulimic symptomology: Review of specific abuse variables. *Child Abuse and Neglect 24*(11), 1495–1502.

Andreasen, N. C. (2003). From molecule to mind: Genetics, genomics, and psychiatry. *American Journal of Psychiatry, 160,* 613.

Andrews, B. (1998). Self-esteem. *Psychologist, 11*(7), 339–342.

Andrews, J. A., Tildesley, E., Hops, H., & Li., F. (2002). The influence of peers on young adult substance use. *Health Psychology, 21*(4), 349–357.

Andrews, L. B., & Nelkin, D. (1996). *The Bell Curve:* A statement. *Science, 271*(5245), 13–14.

Angier, N. (1994). Benefits of broccoli confirmed as chemical blocks tumors. *The New York Times,* p. C11.

Annas, G. J. "Culture of Life" politics at the bedside—The Case of Terri Schiavo. *New England Journal of Medicine, 352*(16), 1710–1715.

Anton, R. F. (2001). Pharmacologic approaches to the management of alcoholism. *Journal of Clinical Psychiatry, 62*(Suppl20), 11–17.

Antoni, M. H. (2003). Psychoneuroendocrinology and psychoneuroimmunology of cancer: Plausible mechanisms worth pursuing? *Brain, Behavior & Immunity, 17*(Suppl1), S84–S91.

Antoni, M. H., & Pitts, M. (2003). Editorial: Journal of Psychosomatic Research: Special issue. *Journal of Psychosomatic Research, 54*(3), 179–183.

Antonuccio, D. (1995). Psychotherapy for depression: No stronger medicine. *American Psychologist, 50,* 452–454.

Archer, J. (2000). Sex differences in aggression between heterosexual partners: A meta-analytic review. *Psychological Bulletin, 126*(5), 651–680.

Arendt, J. (2000). Melatonin, circadian rhythms, and sleep. *The New England Journal of Medicine online, 343*(15).

Ardrey, R. (1961). *African genesis: a personal investigation into the animal origins and nature of man.* London: Collins.

Arkin, R. M., & Hermann, A. D. (2000). Constructing desirable identities—Self-presentation in psychotherapy and daily life: Comment on Kelly (2000). *Psychological Bulletin, 126*(4), 501–504.

Armeli, S., Carney. M. A., Tennen, H., Affleck, G., & O'Neil, T. (2000). Stress and alcohol use: A daily process examination of the stressor-vulnerability model. *Journal of Personality and Social Psychology, 78*(5), 979–994.

Arnett, J. J. (1999). Adolescent storm and stress, reconsidered. *American Psychologist, 54*(5), 317–326.

Arnett, J. J. (2000). Emerging adulthood. *American Psychologist, 55*(5), 469–480.

Arnold, H. M., Nelson, C. L., Sarter, M., & Bruno, J. P. (2003). Sensitization of cortical acetylcholine release by repeated administration of nicotine in rats. *Psychopharmacology, 165*(4), 346–358.

Aronoff, J., & Litevin, G. H. (1971). Achievement motivation training and executive advancement. *Journal of Applied Behavioral Science, 7*(2), 215–229.

Arriaga, P., Esteves, F., Carneiro, P., & Monteiro, M. B. (2006). Violent computer games and their effects on state hostility and physiological arousal. *Aggressive Behavior, 32*(2), 146–158.

Arroyo, J. A., Miller, W. R., & Tonigan, J. S. (2003). The influence of Hispanic ethnicity on long-term outcome in three alcohol-treatment modalities. *Journal of Studies on Alcohol, 64*(1), 98–104.

Arthritis Foundation. (2000, April 6). Pain in America: Highlights from a Gallup survey. http://www.arthritis.org/answers/sop_factsheet.asp.

Asch, S. E. (1952). *Social psychology.* Englewood Cliffs, NJ: Prentice-Hall.

Ashton, A. K., et al. (2000). Antidepressant-induced sexual dysfunction and ginkgo biloba. *American Journal of Psychiatry, 157,* 836–837.

Ashton, C. H. (2001). Pharmacology and effects of cannabis: a brief review. *The British Journal of Psychiatry, 178,* 101–106.

Aspinwall, L. G., & Staudinger, U. M. (2003). *A psychology of human strengths: Fundamental questions and future directions for a positive psychology.* Washington, DC: American Psychological Association.

Atkins, M. S., et al. (2002). Suspensions and detention in an urban, low-income school: Punishment or reward? *Journal of Abnormal Child Psychology, 30*(4), 361–371.

Atkinson, R. C. (1975). Mnemotechnics in second-language learning. *American Psychologist, 30,* 821–828.

Atkinson, R. C., & Shiffrin, R. M. (1968). Human memory: A proposed system and its control processes. In K. Spence (ed.), *The psychology of learning and motivation, Vol. 2.* New York: Academic Press.

Austin, S. (1999). Women's aggressive fantasies: A feminist post-Jungian hermeneutic. *Harvest: Journal for Jungian Studies, 45*(2), 7–28.

Ayllon, T., & Haughton, E. (1962). Control of the behavior of schizophrenic patients by food. *Journal of the Experimental Analysis of Behavior, 5,* 343–352.

Azar, B. (1995). Breaking through barriers to creativity. *APA Monitor, 26*(8), 1, 20.

Azar, B. (1996b). Scientists examine cancer patients' fears. *APA Monitor, 27*(8), 32.

Azar, B. (1996c). Training is enhanced by virtual reality. *APA Monitor, 26*(3), 24.

Azar, B. (1997a). Poor recall mars research and treatment. *APA Monitor, 28*(1), 1, 29.

Azar, B. (1997b). Environment is key to serotonin levels. *APA Monitor, 28*(4), 26, 29.

Azar, B. (2002). At the frontier of science. *Monitor on Psychology online, 33*(1).

Babyak, M., et al. (2000). Exercise treatment for major depression: Maintenance of therapeutic benefit at 10 months. *Psychosomatic Medicine, 62*(5), 633–638.

Bacaltchuk, J., Hay, P., & Mari, J. J. (2000). Antidepressants versus placebo for the treatment of bulimia nervosa: A systematic review. *Australian & New Zealand Journal of Psychiatry, 34*(2), 310–317.

Baddeley, A. (1982). *Your memory: A user's guide.* New York: Macmillan.

Baenninger, M. A., & Elenteny, K. (1997). Cited in B. Azar (1997), Environment can mitigate differences in spatial ability. *APA Monitor, 28*(6), 28.

Baer, H., Allen, S., & Braun, L. (2000). Knowledge of human papillomavirus infection among young adult men and women: Implications for health education and research. *Journal of Community Health: The Publication for Health Promotion & Disease Prevention, 25*(1), 67–78.

Baez, A., & Hernandez, D. (2001). Complementary spiritual beliefs in the Latino community: The interface with psychotherapy. *American Journal of Orthopsychiatry, 71*(4), 408–415.

Bagley, C., & D'Augelli, A. R. (2000). Suicidal behaviour in gay, lesbian, and bisexual youth. *British Medical Journal, 320,* 1617–1618.

Bahrick, H. P., Bahrick, P. O., & Wittlinger, R. P. (1975). Fifty years of memory for names and faces. *Journal of Experimental Psychology: General, 104,* 54–75.

Bailey, J. M. (1999). Homosexuality and mental illness. *Archives of General Psychiatry, 56*(10), 883–884.

Bailey, J. M. (2003a). Personal communication.

Bailey, J. M. (2003b). *The man who would be queen: The science of gender-bending and transsexualism.* Washington, DC: Joseph Henry Press.

Bailey, J. M., Dunne, M. P., & Martin, N. G. (2000). Genetic and environmental influences on sexual orientation and its correlates in an Australian twin sample. *Journal of Personality and Social Psychology, 78*(3), 524–536.

Bailey, J. M., & Pillard, R. C. (1991). A genetic study of male sexual orientation. *Archives of General Psychiatry, 48,* 1089–1096.

Baker, C. W., Whisman, M. A., & Brownell, K. D. (2000). Studying intergenerational transmission of eating attitudes and behaviors: Methodological and conceptual questions. *Health Psychology, 19*(4), 376–381.

Baker, L. A., DeFries, J. C., & Fulker, D. W. (1983). Longitudinal stability of cognitive ability in the Colorado adoption project. *Child Development, 54,* 290–297.

Baker, M. C. (2001). *The atoms of language: The mind's hidden rules of grammar.* New York: Basic Books.

Baker, S. L., Kentner, A. C., Konkle, A. T. M., Barbagallo, L. S., & Bielajew, C. (2006). Behavioral and physiological effects of chronic mild stress in female rats. *Physiology & Behavior, 87*(2), 314–322.

Baltes, P. B. (1997). On the incomplete architecture of human ontogeny: Selection, optimization, and compensation as foundation of developmental theory. *American Psychologist, 52,* 366–380.

Baltes, P. B., & Staudinger, U. M. (2000). Wisdom: A metaheuristic (pragmatic) to orchestrate mind and virtue toward excellence. *American Psychologist, 55,* 122–136.

Bamberg, S. (2003). How does environmental concern influence specific environmentally related behaviors? A new answer to an old question. *Journal of Environmental Psychology, 23*(1), 21–32.

Bandelow, B., et al. (2000). Salivary cortisol in panic attacks. *American Journal of Psychiatry, 157*, 454–456.

Bandura, A. (1986). *Social foundations of thought and action: A social-cognitive theory.* Englewood Cliffs, NJ: Prentice-Hall.

Bandura, A. (1999). Social cognitive theory: An agentic perspective. *Asian Journal of Social Psychology, 2*(1), 21–41.

Bandura, A. (2002). Social cognitive theory in cultural context. *Applied Psychology: An International Review, 51*(2), 269–290.

Bandura, A., Barbaranelli, C., Vittorio Caprara, G., & Pastorelli, C. (2001). Self-efficacy beliefs as shapers of children's aspirations and career trajectories. *Child Development, 72*(1), 187–206.

Bandura, A., Blanchard, E. B., & Ritter, B. (1969). The relative efficacy of desensitization and modeling approaches for inducing behavioral, affective, and cognitive changes. *Journal of Personality and Social Psychology, 13*, 173–199.

Bandura, A., & Locke, E. A. (2003). Negative self-efficacy and goal effects revisited. *Journal of Applied Psychology, 88*(1), 87–99.

Bandura, A., & McDonald, F. J. (1963). Influence of social reinforcement and the behavior of models in shaping children's moral judgments. *Journal of Abnormal and Social Psychology, 67*, 274–281.

Bandura, A., Pastorelli, C., Barbaranelli, C., & Caprara, G. V. (1999). Self-efficacy pathways to childhood depression. *Journal of Personality & Social Psychology, 76*(2), 258–269.

Bandura, A., Ross, S. A., & Ross, D. (1963). Imitation of film-mediated aggressive models. *Journal of Abnormal and Social Psychology, 66*, 3–11.

Bandura, A., Taylor, C. B., Williams, S. L., Medford, I. N., & Barchas, J. D. (1985). Catecholamine secretion as a function of perceived coping self-efficacy. *Journal of Consulting and Clinical Psychology, 53*, 406–414.

Bank, B. J., & Hansford, S. L. (2000). Gender and friendship: Why are men's best same-sex friendships less intimate and supportive? *Personal Relationships, 7*(1), 63–78.

Banks, M. S., & Shannon, E. (1993). Spatial and chromatic visual efficiency in human neonates. In C. E. Granrud (ed.), *Visual perception and cognition in infancy.* Hillsdale, NJ: Erlbaum.

Banyard, V. L., Williams, L. M., Siegel, J. A., & West, C. M. (2003). Childhood sexual abuse in the lives of Black women: Risk and resilience in a longitudinal study. *Women & Therapy, 25*(3–4), 45–58.

Barbaree, H. E., & Marshall, W. L. (1991). The role of male sexual arousal in rape: Six models. *Journal of Consulting and Clinical Psychology, 59*, 621–630.

Barber, J. G. (2001). Relative misery and youth suicide. *Australian & New Zealand Journal of Psychiatry, 35*(1), 49–57.

Barber, T. X. (2000). A deeper understanding of hypnosis: Its secrets, its nature, its essence. *American Journal of Clinical Hypnosis, 42*(3–4), 208–272.

Bard, P. (1934). The neurohumoral basis of emotional reactions. In C. A. Murchison (ed.), *Handbook of general experimental psychology.* Worcester, MA: Clark University Press.

Barlow, D. H., Gorman, J. M., Shear, M. K., & Woods, S. W. (2000). Cognitive–behavioral therapy, imipramine, or their combination for panic disorder: A randomized controlled trial. *Journal of the American Medical Association, 283*, 2529–2536.

Barnett, W. S. (1998). Long-term cognitive and academic effects of early childhood education of children in poverty. *Preventive Medicine: An International Journal Devoted to Practice & Theory, 27*(2), 204–207.

Baron, R. A., & Byrne, D. (2004). *Social psychology,* 10th ed. Boston: AB Longman.

Barringer, F. (1993). For 32 million Americans, English is a second language. *The New York Times,* April 28, p. A18.

Barrios, A. A. (2001). A theory of hypnosis based on principles of conditioning and inhibition. *Contemporary Hypnosis, 18*(4), 163–203.

Bartels, M., Rietveld, M. J. H., Van Baal, G. C. M., & Boomsma, D. I. (2002). Genetic and environmental influences on the development of intelligence. *Behavior Genetics, 32*(4), 237–249.

Bartoshuk, L. M. (2000). Psychophysical advances aid the study of genetic variation in taste. *Appetite, 34*(1), 105.

Basch, M. F. (1980). *Doing psychotherapy.* New York: Basic Books.

Basic Behavioral Science Task Force of the National Advisory Mental Health Council. (1996a). Basic behavioral science research for mental health: Vulnerability and resilience. *American Psychologist, 51*, 22–28.

Basic Behavioral Science Task Force of the National Advisory Mental Health Council. (1996b). Basic behavioral science research for mental health: Perception, attention, learning, and memory. *American Psychologist, 51*, 133–142.

Basic Behavioral Science Task Force of the National Advisory Mental Health Council. (1996c). Basic behavioral science research for mental health: Sociocultural and environmental practices. *American Psychologist, 51*, 722–731.

Bassetti, C., Vella, S., Donati, F., Wielepp, P., & Weder, B. (2000). SPECT during sleepwalking. *The Lancet, 356*, 484–485.

Bateman, D. N. (2000). Triptans and migraine. *The Lancet, 355*, 860–861.

Battaglia, F. P., Sutherland, G. R., & McNaughton, B. L. (2004). Local sensory cues and place cell directionality: Additional evidence of prospective coding in the hippocampus. *Journal of Neuroscience, 24*(19), 4541–4550.

Baucom, D. H., Shoham, V., Mueser, K. T., Daiuto, A. D., & Stickle, T. R. (1998). Empirically supported couple and family interventions for marital distress and adult mental health problems. *Journal of Consulting and Clinical Psychology, 66*, 53–88.

Bauer, M., et al. (2000). Double-blind, placebo-controlled trial of the use of lithium to augment antidepressant medication in continuation treatment of unipolar major depression. *American Journal of Psychiatry, 157*, 1429–1435.

Bauer, M. E., et al. (2003). Altered glucocorticoid immunoregulation in treatment resistant depression. *Psychoneuroendocrinology, 28*(1), 49–65.

Baumeister, R. F. (1996). *Evil: Inside human cruelty and violence.* New York: W. H. Freeman/Times Books/Henry Holt & Co.

Baumrind, D. (1973). The development of instrumental competence through socialization. In A. D. Pick (ed.), *Minnesota Symposia on Child Development, Vol. 7.* Minneapolis: University of Minnesota Press.

Baumrind, D. (1991a). The influence of parenting style on adolescent competence and substance abuse. *Journal of Early Adolescence, 11*, 56–95.

Baumrind, D. (1991b). Parenting styles and adolescent development. In J. Brooks-Gunn, R. Lerner, & A. C. Petersen (eds.), *Encyclopedia of Adolescence, II.* New York: Garland.

Baumrind, D., Larzelere, R. E., & Cowan, P. A. (2002). Ordinary physical punishment: Is it harmful? Comment on Gershoff (2002). *Psychological Bulletin, 128*(4), 580–589.

Baydar, N., & Brooks-Gunn, J. (1991). Effects of maternal employment and child-care arrangements on preschoolers' cognitive and behavioral outcomes: Evidence from the Children of the National Longitudinal Survey of Youth. *Developmental Psychology, 27*, 932–945.

Baynes, K., & Gazzaniga, M. S. (2000). Callosal disconnection. In Farah, M. J., & Feinberg, T. E. (eds.). *Patient-based approaches to cognitive neuroscience. Issues in clinical and cognitive neuropsychology* (pp. 327–333). Cambridge, MA: The MIT Press.

Beard, K. W. (2005). Internet addictions: A review of current assessment techniques and potential assessment questions. *CyberPsychology & Behavior, 8*(1), 7–14.

Beautrais, A. L. (2003). Suicide and serious suicide attempts in youth: A multiple-group comparison study. *American Journal of Psychiatry, 160*, 1093–1099.

Bech, P., et al. (2000). Meta-analysis of randomised controlled trials of fluoxetine *v.* placebo and tricyclic antidepressants in the short-term treatment of major depression. *British Journal of Psychiatry, 176*, 421–428.

Beck, A. T. (1991). Cognitive therapy: A 30-year retrospective. *American Psychologist, 46*, 368–375.

Beck, A. T. (1993). Cognitive therapy: Past, present, and future. *Journal of Consulting and Clinical Psychology, 61*, 194–198.

Beck, A. T. (2000). Cited in J. Chamberlin (2000), An historic meeting of the minds. *Monitor on Psychology, 31*(9), 27.

Beck, A. T., et al. (2001). Dysfunctional beliefs discriminate personality disorders. *Behaviour Research & Therapy, 39*(10), 1213–1225.

Beckham, J. C., et al. (2000). Ambulatory cardiovascular activity in Vietnam combat veterans with and without posttraumatic stress disorder. *Journal of Consulting and Clinical Psychology, 68*, 269–276.

Begley, S., & Check, E. (2000, August 5). Sex and the single fly. *Newsweek*, pp. 44–45.

Beitchman, J. H., et al. (2001). Comorbidity of psychiatric and substance use disorders in late adolescence: A cluster analytic approach. *American Journal of Drug & Alcohol Abuse, 27*(3), 421–440.

Bekoff, M. (2002). *Minding animals: Awareness, emotions, and heart.* New York: Oxford University Press.

Bell, P. A. (1992). In defense of the negative affect escape model of heat and aggression. *Psychological Bulletin, 111*, 342–346.

Beller, M., & Gafni, N. (2000). Can item format (multiple choice vs. open-ended) account for gender differences in mathematics achievement? *Sex Roles, 42*(1–2), 1–21.

Bellodi, L., et al. (2001). Morbidity risk for obsessive–compulsive spectrum disorders in first-degree relatives of patients with eating disorders. *American Journal of Psychiatry, 158*, 563–569.

Belsky, J. (1990a). Developmental risks associated with infant day care: Attachment insecurity, noncompliance and aggression? In S. Cherazi (ed.), *Psychosocial issues in day care.* New York: American Psychiatric Press.

Belsky, J. (1990b). The "effects" of infant day care reconsidered. In N. Fox & G. G. Fein (eds.), *Infant day care: The current debate.* Norwood, NJ: Ablex.

Belsky, J. (1993). Etiology of child maltreatment. *Psychological Bulletin, 114*, 413–434.

Belsky, J., Weinraub, M., Owen, M., & Kelly, J. (2001, April). Quantity of child care and problem behavior. In J. Belsky (Chair), *Early childcare and children's development prior to school entry.* Symposium conducted at the 2001 Biennial Meetings of the Society for Research in Child Development, Minneapolis, MN.

Bem, D. J., & Honorton, C. (1994). Does psi exist? Replicable evidence for an anomalous process of information transfer. *Psychological Bulletin, 115*, 4–18.

Bem, D. J., Palmer, J., & Broughton, R. S. (2001). Updating the ganzfeld database: A victim of its own success? *Journal of Parapsychology, 65*(3), 207–218.

Bem, S. L. (1993). *The lenses of gender.* New Haven: Yale University Press.

Benda, B. B., & Corwyn, R. F. (2002). The effect of abuse in childhood and in adolescence on violence among adolescents. *Youth & Society, 33*(3), 339–365.

Benson, H. (1975). *The relaxation response.* New York: Morrow.

Benson, P. L., Karabenick, S. A., & Lerner, R. M. (1976). Pretty pleases: The effects of physical attractiveness, race, and sex on receiving help. *Journal of Experimental Social Psychology, 12*, 409–415.

Ben-Zur, H. (2002). Associations of type A behavior with the emotional traits of anger and curiosity. *Anxiety, Stress & Coping: An International Journal, 15*(1), 95–104.

Bergen, A. W., et al. (2003). Candidate genes for anorexia nervosa in the 1p33-36 linkage region: serotonin 1D and delta opioid receptor loci exhibit significant association to anorexia nervosa. *Molecular Psychiatry, 8*(4), 397–406.

Berkowitz, L. (1994). Is something missing? Some observations prompted by the cognitive-neoassociationist view of anger and emotional aggression. In L. R. Huesmann (ed.), *Aggressive behavior: Current perspectives.* New York: Plenum.

Berkowitz, L. (2004). Two views of evil: Evil is not only banal. *PsycCRITIQUES.*

Bernat, J. A., Wilson, A. E., & Calhoun, K. S. (1999). Sexual coercion history, calloused sexual beliefs and judgments of sexual coercion in a date rape analogue. *Violence and Victims, 14*(2), 147–160.

Bernardin, H. J., Cooke, D. K., & Villanova, P. (2000). Conscientiousness and agreeableness as predictors of rating leniency. *Journal of Applied Psychology, 85*(2) 232–236.

Bernhardt, P. C., Dabbs, J. M., Jr., Fielden, J. A., & Lutter, C. D. (1998). Testosterone changes during vicarious experiences of winning and losing among fans at sporting events. *Physiology & Behavior, 65*(1), 59–62.

Bernstein, I. (1996). Cited in B. Azar (1996), Research could help patients cope with chemotherapy. *APA Monitor, 27*(8), 33.

Bernstein, W. M., Stephenson, B. O., Snyder, M. L., & Wicklund, R. A. (1983). Causal ambiguity and heterosexual affiliation. *Journal of Experimental Social Psychology, 19*, 78–92.

Berquier, A., & Ashton, R. (1992). Characteristics of the frequent nightmare sufferer. *Journal of Abnormal Psychology, 101*, 246–250.

Bersoff, D. (1994). Cited in T. DeAngelis (1994), Experts see little impact from insanity plea ruling. *APA Monitor, 25*(6), 28.

Bevan, W., & Kessel, F. (1994). Plain truths and home cooking. *American Psychologist, 49*, 505–509.

Bexton, W. H., Heron, W., & Scott, T. H. (1954). Effects of decreased variation in the sensory environment. *Canadian Journal of Psychology, 8*, 70–76.

Bialystock, E. (1999). Cognitive complexity and attentional control in the bilingual mind. *Child Development, 70*(3), 636–644.

Bidell, M. P., Turner, J. A., & Casas, J. M. (2002). First impressions count: Ethnic/racial and lesbian/gay/bisexual content of professional psychology application materials. *Professional Psychology: Research & Practice, 33*(1), 97–103.

Bifulco, A., et al. (2002). Childhood adversity, parental vulnerability and disorder: Examining inter-generational transmission of risk. *Journal of Child Psychology & Psychiatry & Allied Disciplines, 43*(8), 1075–1086.

Bigelow, B. J. (2001). Relational scaffolding of school motivation: Developmental continuities in students' and parents' ratings of the importance of school goals. *Journal of Genetic Psychology, 162*(1), 75–92.

Bilkey, D. K. (2004). Neuroscience: In the place space. *Science, 305*, 1245–1246.

Birks, Y., & Roger, D. (2000). Identifying components of type-A behaviour: "Toxic" and "non-toxic" achieving. *Personality & Individual Differences, 28*(6), 1093–1105.

Bishop, E. G., et al. (2003). Development genetic analysis of general cognitive ability from 1 to 12 years in a sample of adoptees, biological siblings, and twins. *Intelligence, 31*(1), 31–49.

Bjorklund, D. F. (2000). *Children's thinking* (3rd ed.). Pacific Grove, CA: Brooks/Cole.

Blair, R., & James, R. (2001). Neurocognitive models of aggression, the antisocial personality disorders, and psychopathy. *Journal of Neurology, Neurosurgery & Psychiatry, 71*(6), 727–731.

Blair, R., & James, R. (2003). Neurobiological basis of psychopathy. *British Journal of Psychiatry, 182*, 5–7.

Blake, P., Fry, R., & Pesjack, M. (1984). *Self-assessment and behavior change manual* (pp. 43–47). New York: Random House.

Blake, S. M., Amaro, H., Schwartz, P. M., & Flinchbaugh, L. J. (2001). A review of substance abuse prevention interventions for young adolescent girls. *Journal of Early Adolescence, 21*(3), 294–324.

Blanchard, E. B. (1992). Psychological treatment of benign headache disorders. *Journal of Consulting and Clinical Psychology, 60*, 537–551.

Blanchard, E. B., et al. (1990). Placebo-controlled evaluation of abbreviated progressive muscle relaxation and of relaxation combined with cognitive therapy in the treatment of tension headache. *Journal of Consulting and Clinical Psychology, 58*, 210–215.

Blanchard, E. B., et al. (2003). A controlled evaluation of cognitive behavioral therapy for posttraumatic stress in motor vehicle accident survivors. *Behaviour Research & Therapy, 41*(1), 79–96.

Blanco-Colio, L. M., et al. (2000). Red wine intake prevents nuclear factor-B activation in peripheral blood mononuclear cells of healthy volunteers during postprandial lipemia. *Circulation, 102*, 1020–1026.

Blascovich, J. (2000). Cited in R. A. Clay (2000), Linking up online: Is the Internet enhancing interpersonal connections or leading to greater social isolation? *Monitor on Psychology online, 31*(4).

Blascovich, J., Spencer, S. J., Quinn, D., & Steele, C. (2001). African Americans and high blood pressure: The role of stereotype threat. *Psychological Science, 12*(3), 225–229.

Blass, T. (1999). The Milgram Paradigm after 35 years: Some things we now know about obedience to authority. *Journal of Applied Social Psychology, 29*(5), 955–978.

Blass, T., & Schmitt, C. (2001). The nature of perceived authority in the Milgram paradigm: Two replications. *Current Psychology: Developmental, Learning, Personality, Social, 20*(2), 115–121.

Block, R. I., et al. (2000). Effects of frequent marijuana use on brain tissue volume and composition. *Neuroreport: For Rapid Communication of Neuroscience Research, 11*(3), 491–496.

Bloom, L., & Mudd, S. A. (1991). Depth of processing approach to face recognition. *Journal of Experimental Psychology: Learning, Memory, and Cognition, 17,* 556–565.

Blum, D. (1997). *Sex on the brain: The biological differences between men and women.* New York: Viking.

Blumenthal, J. A., Sherwood, A., Gullette, E. C. D., Georgiades, A., & Tweedy, D. (2002). Biobehavioral approaches to the treatment of essential hypertension. *Journal of Consulting and Clinical Psychology, 70*(3), 569–589.

Bodamar, M. D., & Gardner, R. A. (2002). How cross-fostered chimpanzees *(Pan troglodytes)* initiate and maintain conversations. *Journal of Comparative Psychology, 116*(1), 12–26.

Bogen, J. E. (1969). The other side of the brain II: An appositional mind. *Bulletin of the Los Angeles Neurological Society, 34,* 135–162.

Bogen, J. E. (1998). My developing understanding of Roger Wolcott Sperry's philosophy. *Neuropsychologia, 36*(10), 1089–1096.

Bogen, J. E. (2000). Split-brain basics: Relevance for the concept of one's other mind. *Journal of the American Academy of Psychoanalysis, 28*(2), 341–369.

Bohlin, G., Hagekull, B., & Rydell, A. (2000). Attachment and social functioning: A longitudinal study from infancy to middle childhood. *Social Development, 9*(1), 24–39.

Bongar, B. (2002). *The suicidal patient: Clinical and legal standards of care* (2nd ed.). Washington, DC: American Psychological Association.

Bonin, M. F., McCreary, D. R., & Sadava, S. W. (2000). Problem drinking behavior in two community-based samples of adults: Influence of gender, coping, loneliness, and depression. *Psychology of Addictive Behaviors, 14*(2), 151–161.

Booth, A., Johnson, D. R., Granger, D. A., Crouter, A. C., & McHale, S. (2003). Testosterone and child and adolescent adjustment: The moderating role of parent–child relationships. *Developmental Psychology, 39*(1), 85–98.

Boskind-White, M., & White, W. C. (1983). *Bulimarexia: The binge/purge cycle.* New York: W. W. Norton.

Boston Women's Health Book Collective. (1992). *The new our bodies, ourselves.* New York: Simon & Schuster.

Bouchard, T. J., Jr., & Loehlin, J. C. (2001). Genes, evolution, and personality. *Behavior Genetics, 31*(3), 243–273.

Bouchard, T. J., Jr., Lykken, D. T., McGue, M., Segal, N. L., & Tellegen, A. (1990). Sources of human psychological differences: The Minnesota study of twins reared apart. *Science, 250,* 223–228.

Bower, G. H. (1981). Mood and memory. *American Psychologist, 36,* 129–148.

Bowers, K. S., & Woody, E. Z. (1996). Hypnotic amnesia and the paradox of intentional forgetting. *Journal of Abnormal Psychology, 105,* 381–390.

Bowes, J. M., & Goodnow, J. J. (1996). Work for home, school, or labor force. *Psychological Bulletin, 119,* 300–321.

Bowlby, J. (1988). *A secure base.* New York: Basic Books.

Boyatzis, R. E. (1974). The effect of alcohol consumption on the aggressive behavior of men. *Quarterly Journal for the Study of Alcohol, 35,* 959–972.

Bradley, R. H., et al. (1989). Home environment and cognitive development in the first 3 years of life. *Developmental Psychology, 25,* 217–235.

Brakke, K. E., & Savage-Rumbaugh, E. S. (1996).The development of language skills in pan: II. Production. *Language & Communication, 16*(4), 361–380.

Brand, J. (2000). Cited in U. L. McFarling (2000), Sniffing out genes' role in our senses of taste and smell. *The Los Angeles Times online,* August 27.

Bransford, J. D., Nitsch, K. E., & Franks, J. J. (1977). Schooling and the facilitation of knowing. In R. C. Anderson, R. J. Spiro, & W. E. Montague (eds.), *Schooling and the acquisition of knowledge.* Hillsdale, NJ: Erlbaum.

Braun, B. G. (1988). *Treatment of multiple personality disorder.* Washington, DC: American Psychiatric Press.

Brewin, C. R., Andrews, B., & Gotlib, I. H. (1993). Psychopathology and early experience. *Psychological Bulletin, 113,* 82–98.

Brigman, S., & Cherry, K. E. (2002). Age and skilled performance: Contributions of working memory and processing speed. *Brain & Cognition, 50*(2), 242–256.

Brissette, I., Scheier, M. F., & Carver, C. S. (2002). The role of optimism in social network development, coping, and psychological adjustment during a life transition. *Journal of Personality & Social Psychology, 82*(1), 102–111.

Broberg, A. G., Wessels, H., Lamb, M. E., & Hwang, C. P. (1997). Effects of day care on the development of cognitive abilities in 8-year-olds: A longitudinal study. *Developmental Psychology, 33*(1), 62–69.

Broder, S. (2000, July 29). Fighting media violence! www.Family Education.com.

Brody, J. E. (2000). Memories of things that never were. *The New York Times,* April 25, p. F8.

Brook, J. S., Zheng, L., Whiteman, M., & Brook, D. W. (2001). Aggression in toddlers: Associations with parenting and marital relations. *Journal of Genetic Psychology, 162*(2), 228–241.

Brown, A. S. (2003). A review of the déjà vu experience. *Psychological Bulletin, 129*(3), 394–413.

Brown, A. S., & Susser, E. S. (2002). In utero infection and adult schizophrenia. *Mental Retardation & Developmental Disabilities Research Reviews, 8*(1), 51–57.

Brown, L., Macintyre, K., & Trujillo, L. (2003). Interventions to reduce HIV/AIDS stigma. What have we learned? *AIDS Education & Prevention, 15*(11), 49–69.

Brown, R., & McNeill, D. (1966). The tip-of-the-tongue phenomenon. *Journal of Verbal Learning and Verbal Behavior, 5,* 325–337.

Browne, M. W. (1995). Scientists deplore flight from reason. *The New York Times,* June 6, pp. C1, C7.

Brownstein, A. L. (2003). Biased predecision processing. *Psychological Bulletin, 129*(4), 545–568.

Bruce, N. W., & Sanders, K. A. (2001). Incidence and duration of romantic attraction in students progressing from secondary to tertiary education. *Journal of Biosocial Science, 33*(2), 173–184.

Bruene, M., & Ribbert, H. (2002). Grundsaetzliches zur Konzeption einer evolutionaeren Psychiatrie. *Schweizer Archiv für Neurologie und Psychiatrie, 153*(1), 4–11.

Buchanan, C. M., Eccles, J. S., & Becker, J. B. (1992). Are adolescents the victims of raging hormones? Evidence for activational effects of hormones on moods and behavior at adolescence. *Psychological Bulletin, 111,* 62–107.

Buckley, P. F., Buchanan, R. W., Tamminga, C. A., & Schulz, S. C. (2000). Schizophrenia research. *Schizophrenia Bulletin, 26*(2), 411–419.

Buckner, R. L., Wheeler, M. E., & Sheridan, M. A. (2001). Encoding processes during retrieval tasks. *Journal of Cognitive Neuroscience, 13*(3), 406–415.

Bull, N. J., Hunter, M., & Finlay, D. C. (2003). Cue gradient and cue density interact in the detection and recognition of objects defined by motion, contrast, or texture. *Perception, 32*(1) 29–39.2

Bulman-Fleming, M. B., Bryden, M. P., & Wyse, D. M. (1996). Associations among familial sinistrality, allergies, and developmental language disorders. *International Journal of Neuroscience, 87*(3–4), 257–265.

Burger, J. M. (1999). The foot-in-the-door compliance procedure: A multiple-process analysis and review. *Personality & Social Psychology Review, 3*(4), 303–325.

Burger, J. M., & Cosby, M. (1999). Do women prefer dominant men? The case of the missing control condition. *Journal of Research in Personality, 33*(3), 358–368.

Burgess, R. L., & Drais, A. A. (2001). Explaining child maltreatment: From behavior analysis to behavioral biology. *Revista Mexicana de Analisis de la Conducta, 27*(2), 201–224.

Burnette, E. (1997). "Father of Ebonics" continues his crusade. *APA Monitor, 28*(4), 12

Burt, M. R. (1980). Cultural myths and supports for rape. *Journal of Personality and Social Psychology, 38,* 217–230.

Burt, V. K., & Stein, K. (2002). Epidemiology of depression throughout the female life cycle. *Journal of Clinical Psychiatry, 63*(Suppl7), 9–15.

Bushman, B. J. (1998). Priming effects of media violence on the accessibility of aggressive constructs in memory. *Personality & Social Psychology Bulletin, 24*(5), 537–545.

Bushman, B. J., Baumeister, R. F., & Stack, A. D. (1999). Catharsis, aggression, and persuasive influence: Self-fulfilling or self-defeating prophecies? *Journal of Personality & Social Psychology, 76*(3), 367–376.

Buss, D. M. (1992). Is there a universal human nature? *Contemporary Psychology, 37,* 1262–1263.

Buss, D. M. (1994). *The evolution of desire.* New York: Basic Books.

Buss, D. M. (1999). Adaptive individual differences revisited. *Journal of Personality, 67*(2), 259–264.

Buss, D. M. (2000). The evolution of happiness. *American Psychologist, 55,* 15–23.

Buss, D. M., Haselton, M. G., Shackelford, T. K., Bleske, A. L., & Wakefield, J. C. (1998). Adaptations, exaptations, and spandrels. *American Psychologist, 53,* 533–548.

Bussey, K., & Bandura, A. (1999). Social cognitive theory of gender development and differentiation. *Psychological Review, 106*(4), 676–713.

Butcher, J. (2000). Dopamine hypothesis gains further support. *The Lancet, 356,* 139–146.

Butler, A. C., & Beck, J. S. (2001). Cognitive therapy outcomes. A review of meta-analyses. *Tidsskrift for Norsk Psykologforening, 38*(8), 698–706.

Butler, A. C., Brown, G. K., Beck, A. T., & Grisham, J. R. (2002). Assessment of dysfunctional beliefs in borderline personality disorder. *Behaviour Research & Therapy, 40*(10), 1231–1240.

Butler, R. (1998). Cited in CD-ROM that accompanies J. S. Nevid, S. A. Rathus, & H. Rubenstein (1998), *Health in the new millennium.* New York: Worth Publishers.

Cacioppo, J. T., Hawkley, L. C., & Bernston, G. G. (2003). The anatomy of loneliness. *Current Directions in Psychological Science, 12*(3), 71–74.

Cacioppo, J. T., Martzke, J. S, Petty, R. E., & Tassinary, L. G. (1988). Specific forms of facial EMG response index emotions during an interview. *Journal of Personality and Social Psychology, 54,* 552–604.

Cado, S., & Leitenberg, H. (1990). Guilt reactions to sexual fantasies during intercourse. *Archives of Sexual Behavior, 19*(1), 49–63.

Caffray, C. M., & Schneider, S. L. (2000). Why do they do it? Affective motivators in adolescents' decisions to participate in risk behaviours. *Cogntiion & Emotion, 14*(4), 543–576.

Cain, D. J., & Seeman, J. (2002). *Humanistic psychotherapies: Handbook of research and practice.* Washington, DC: American Psychological Association.

Cairney, J., & Wade, T. J. (2002). Single parent mothers and mental health care service use. *Social Psychiatry & Psychiatric Epidemiology, 37*(5), 236–242.

Californians losing fight against flab. (2000). Reuters News Agency online, June 14.

Campbell, A. J., Cumming, S. R., & Hughes, I. (2006). Internet use by the socially fearful: Addiction or therapy? *CyberPsychology & Behavior, 9*(1), 69–81.

Campbell, W. K., Sedikides, C., Reeder, G. D., & Elliott, A. J. (2000). Among friends? An examination of friendship and the self-serving bias. *British Journal of Social Psychology, 39*(2), 229–239.

Campos, J. J. (2000). Cited in B. Azar (2000), What's in a face? *Monitor on Psychology, 31*(1), 44–45.

Campos, J. J., Hiatt, S., Ramsey, D., Henderson, C., & Svejda, M. (1978). The emergence of fear on the visual cliff. In M. Lewis & L. Rosenblum (eds.), *The origins of affect.* New York: Plenum.

Camras, L. (2000). Cited in B. Azar (2000), What's in a face? *Monitor on Psychology, 31*(1), 44–45.

Canalis, R. F., & Lambert, P. R. (2000). *The ear: Comprehensive otology.* Philadelphia: Lippincott Williams & Wilkins.

Cann, R. E. (2002). Human evolution: Tangled genetic routes. *Nature, 416,* 6876.

Canetti, L., Bachar, E., & Berry, E. M. (2002). Food and emotion. *Behavioural Processes, 60*(2), 157–164.

Cannon, W. B. (1927). The James–Lange theory of emotions: A critical examination and an alternative theory. *American Journal of Psychology, 39,* 106–124.

Cannon, W. B. (1932). *The wisdom of the body.* New York: Norton.

Cannon, W. B., & Washburn, A. (1912). An explanation of hunger. *American Journal of Physiology, 29,* 441–454.

Cantalupo, C., & Hopkins, W. D. (2001). Asymmetric Broca's area in great apes: A region of the ape brain is uncannily similar to one linked with speech in humans. *Nature, 414*(6863), 505.

Carey, B. (2005). After food and shelter, help in coping with unbearable loss. *The New York Times online,* January 4.

Carey, G., & DiLalla, D. L. (1994). Personality and psychopathology: Genetic perspectives. *Journal of Abnormal Psychology, 103,* 32–43.

Carlson, J. G., & Hatfield, E. (1992). *Psychology of emotion.* Fort Worth: Harcourt Brace Jovanovich.

Carlsson, K., et al. (2000). Tickling expectations: Neural processing in anticipation of a sensory stimulus. *Journal of Cognitive Neuroscience, 12,* 691–703.

Carmichael, L. L., Hogan, H. P., & Walter, A. A. (1932). An experimental study of the effect of language on the reproduction of visually perceived form. *Journal of Experimental Psychology, 15,* 73–86.

Carroll, D. (2004). *Psychology of language,* 4th ed. Belmont, CA: Wadsworth Publishing Company.

Carroll, M. E., & Overmier, J. B. (2001). *Animal research and human health.* Washington, DC: American Psychological Association.

Carstensen, L. (1997, August 17). The evolution of social goals across the life span. Paper presented to the American Psychological Association, Chicago.

Case, R. (1992). *The mind's staircase.* Hillsdale, NJ: Erlbaum.

Cassaday, H. J., et al. (2003). Intraventricular 5,7-dihydroxytryptamine lesions disrupt acquisition of working memory task rules but not performance once learned. *Progress in Neuro-Psychopharmacology & Biological Psychiatry, 27*(1), 147–156.

Castillo-Richmond, A., et al. (2000). Effects of stress reduction on carotid atherosclerosis in hypertensive African Americans. *Stroke, 31,* 568.

Cattell, R. B. (1949). *The culture-free intelligence test.* Champaign, IL: Institute for Personality and Ability Testing.

Caughy, M. O., DiPietro, J. A., & Strobino, D. M. (1994). Day-care participation as a protective factor in the cognitive development of low-income children. *Child Development, 65*(2), 457–471.

Cavaliere, F. (1996). Bilingual schools face big political challenges. *APA Monitor, 27*(2), 36.

Cavanaugh, J. C., & Green, E. E. (1990). I believe, therefore I can: Self-efficacy beliefs in memory aging. In E. A. Lovelace (ed.), *Aging and cognition: Mental processes, self-awareness, and interventions.* Amsterdam: North-Holland, Elsevier.

Cavelaars, A. E. J. M., et al. (2000). Educational differences in smoking: international comparison. *British Medical Journal, 320,* 1102–1107.

CDC (See Centers for Disease Control and Prevention.)

Ceci, S. J., & Bruck, M. (1993). Suggestibility of the child witness. *Psychological Bulletin, 113,* 403–439.

Celis, W. (1991). Students trying to draw line between sex and an assault. *The New York Times,* January 2, pp. 1, B8.

Cellar, D. F., Nelson, Z. C., & Yorke, C. M. (2000). The five-factor model and driving behavior: Personality and involvement in vehicular accidents. *Psychological Reports, 86*(2) 454–456.

Centers for Disease Control and Prevention. (1995). *Suicide surveillance: 1980–1990.* Washington, DC: USDHHS.

Centers for Disease Control and Prevention. (2000b, June 9). Youth risk behavior surveillance—United States, 1999. *Morbidity and Mortality Weekly Report, 49*(SS05); 1–96.

Centers for Disease Control and Prevention. (2000c). Suicide in the United States. Page updated January 28, 2000: http://www.cdc.gov/ncipc/factsheets/suifacts.htm

Centers for Disease Control and Prevention. (2000d). National and state-specific pregnancy rates among adolescents—United States, 1995–1997. *Morbidity and Mortality Weekly Report, 49*(27).

Centers for Disease Control and Prevention. (2001, December 3). Sexually transmitted disease surveillance 2000. Atlanta, GA: Division of STD Prevention, National Center for HIV, STD and TB Prevention.

Centers for Disease Control and Prevention. (2003). *HIV/AIDS surveillance report: U.S. HIV and AIDS cases reported through December 2002, 14*(2).

Cervilla, J. A., et al. (2000). Long-term predictors of cognitive outcome in a cohort of older people with hypertension. *British Journal of Psychiatry, 177,* 66–71.

Chadwick, P. D. J., & Lowe, C. F. (1990). Measurement and modification of delusional beliefs. *Journal of Consulting and Clinical Psychology, 58,* 225–232.

Chafee, M. V., & Goldman-Rakic, P. S. (2000). Inactivation of parietal and prefrontal cortex reveals interdependence of neural activity during memory-guided saccades. *Journal of Neurophysiology, 83*(3), 1550–1566.

Chak, K., & Leung, L. (2004). Shyness and locus of control as predictors of Internet addiction and Internet use. *CyberPsychology and Behavior, 7*(5), 559–570.

Chambless, D. L., & Hollon, S. D. (1998). Defining empirically supported therapies. *Journal of Consulting and Clinical Psychology, 66,* 7–18.

Chance, S. E., Brown, R. T., Dabbs, J. M., Jr., & Casey, R. (2000). Testosterone, intelligence and behavior disorders in young boys. *Personality & Individual Differences, 28*(3) 437–445.

Chang, D. F., & Sue, S. (2003). The effects of race and problem type on teachers' assessments of student behavior. *Journal of Consulting & Clinical Psychology, 71*(2), 235–242.

Chang, E. C., & Sanna, L. J. (2001). Negative attributional style as a moderator of the link between perfectionism and depressive symptoms: Preliminary evidence for an integrative model. *Journal of Counseling Psychology, 48*(4), 490–495.

Chaplin, W. F., Phillips, J. B., Brown, J. D., Clanton, N. R., & Stein, J. L. (2000). Handshaking, gender, personality, and first impressions. *Journal of Personality and Social Psychology, 79*(1), 110–117.

Chassin, L., Presson, C. C., Pitts, S. C., & Sherman, S. J. (2000). The natural history of cigarette smoking from adolescence to adulthood in a Midwestern community sample: Multiple trajectories and their psychological correlates. *Health Psychology, 19,* 223–231.

Chassin, L., Presson, C. C., Rose, J. S., & Sherman, S. J. (2001). From adolescence to adulthood: Age-related changes in beliefs about cigarette smoking in a Midwestern community sample. *Health Psychology, 20*(5), 377–386.

Chavez, M. L., & Spitzer, M. F. (2002). Herbals and other dietary supplements for premenstrual syndrome and menopause. *Psychiatric Annals, 32*(1), 61–71.

Chen, X., Chen, H., & Kaspar, V. (2001). Group social functioning and individual socioemotional and school adjustment in Chinese children. *Merrill-Palmer Quarterly, 47*(2), 264–299.

Cheng, H., & Furnham, A. (2001). Attributional style and personality as predictors of happiness and mental health. *Journal of Happiness Studies, 2*(3), 307–327.

Chlebowski, R. T. (2000). Primary care: Reducing the risk of breast cancer. *The New England Journal of Medicine online, 343*(3).

Chomsky, N. (1980). Rules and representations. *Behavioral and Brain Sciences, 3,* 1–16.

Chomsky, N. (1991). Linguistics and cognitive science. In A. Kasher (ed.), *The Chomskyan turn.* Cambridge, MA: Blackwell.

Chou, C., Condron, L., & Belland, J. C. (2005). A review of the research on Internet addiction. *Educational Psychology Review, 17*(4), 363–388.

Chuang, Y. (2002). Sex differences in mate selection preference and sexual strategy: Tests for evolutionary hypotheses. *Chinese Journal of Psychology, 44*(1), 75–93.

Cialdini, R. B. (2000). Cited in J. C. McKinley, Jr. (2000), It isn't just a game: Clues to avid rooting. *The New York Times online,* August 11.

Cialdini, R. B., et al. (1997). Reinterpreting the empathy-altruism relationship: When one into one equals oneness. *Journal of Personality & Social Psychology, 73*(3), 481–494.

Clancy, S. A., Schacter, D. L., McNally, R. J., & Pitman, R. K. (2000). False recognition in women reporting recovered memories of sexual abuse. *Psychological Science, 11*(1), 26–31.

Clarke-Stewart, K. A. (1991). A home is not a school: The effects of child care on children's development. *Journal of Social Issues, 47,* 105–123.

Clarke-Stewart, K. A., & Beck, R. J. (1999). Maternal scaffolding and children's narrative retelling of a movie story. *Early Childhood Research Quarterly, 14*(3), 409–434.

Clay, R. A. (2000). Staying in control. *Monitor on Psychology, 31*(1), 32–34.

Clayton, E. C., & Williams, C. L. (2000). Adrenergic activation of the nucleus tractus solitarius potentiates amygdala norepinephrine release and enhances retention performance in emotionally arousing and spatial memory tasks. *Behavioural Brain Research, 112*(1–2), 151–158.

Cochran, S. D., Sullivan, J. G., & Mays, V. M. (2003). Prevalence of mental disorders, psychological distress, and mental health services use among lesbian, gay, and bisexual adults in the United States. *Journal of Consulting and Clinical Psychology, 71*(1), 53–61.

Cohen, D., et al. (2000). Absence of cognitive impairment at long-term follow-up in adolescents treated with ECT for severe mood disorder. *American Journal of Psychiatry, 157,* 460–462.

Cohen, K. (2002). Relationships among childhood sex-atypical behavior, spatial ability, handedness, and sexual orientation in men. *Archives of Sexual Behavior, 31*(1), 129–143.

Cohen, L. A. (1987, November). Diet and cancer. *Scientific American,* pp. 42–48, 53–54.

Cohen, L. L. (2002). Reducing infant immunization distress through distraction. *Health Psychology, 21*(2), 207–211.

Cohen, S., Evans, G. W., Stokols, D., & Krantz, D. S. (1986). *Behavior, health, and environmental stress.* New York: Plenum.

Cohen, S., Gottlieb, B. H., & Underwood, L. G. (2001a). Social relationships and health: Challenges for measurement and intervention. *Advances in Mind–Body Medicine, 17*(2), 129–141.

Cohen, S., Miller, G. E., & Rabin, B. S. (2001b). Psychological stress and antibody response to immunization: A critical review of the human literature. *Psychosomatic Medicine, 63*(1), 7–18.

Cohen, S., Tyrrell, D. A. J., & Smith, A. P. (1993). Negative life events, perceived stress, negative affect, and susceptibility to the common cold. *Journal of Personality and Social Psychology, 64,* 131–140.

Cohen, S., & Williamson, G. M. (1991). Stress and infectious disease in humans. *Psychological Bulletin, 109,* 5–24.

Cohn, E. G. (1990). Weather and violent crime. *Environment and Behavior, 22,* 280–294.

Cohn, E. G., Rotton, J. (2000). Weather, seasonal trends, and property crimes in Minneapolis, 1987–1988. A moderator-variable time-series analysis of routine activities. *Journal of Environmental Psychology, 20*(3), 257–272.

Cohn, L. D., Macfarlane, S., Yanez, C., & Imai, W. K. (1995). Risk-perception: Differences between adolescents and adults. *Health Psychology, 14,* 217–222.

Collaer, M. L., & Hines, M. (1995). Human behavioral sex differences: A role for gonadal hormones during early development? *Psychological Bulletin, 118,* 55–107.

Collaer, M. L., & Nelson, J. D. (2002). Large visuospatial sex difference in line judgment: Possible role of attentional factors. *Brain & Cognition, 49*(1), 1–12.

Collier, G. (1994). *Social origins of mental ability.* New York: Wiley.

Colom, R., Flores-Mendoza, C., & Rebollo, I. (2003). Working memory and intelligence. *Personality & Individual Differences, 34*(1), 33–39.

Coltraine, S., & Messineo, M. (2000). The perpetuation of subtle prejudice: Race and gender imagery in 1990s television advertising. *Sex Roles, 42*(5–6), 363–389.

Comas-Diaz, L. (1994, February). Race and gender in psychotherapy with women of color. *Winter roundtable on cross-cultural counseling and psychotherapy: Race and gender.* New York: Teachers College, Columbia University.

Comas-Diaz, L. (2001). Hispanics, Latinos, or Americanos: The evolution of identity. *Cultural Diversity & Ethnic Minority Psychology, 7*(2), 115–120.

Comaty, J. E., Stasio, M., & Advokat, C. (2001). Analysis of outcome variables of a token economy system in a state psychiatric hospital: A program evaluation. *Research in Developmental Disabilities, 22*(3), 233–253.

Compas, B. E., Haaga, D. A. F., Keefe, F. J., Leitenberg, H., & Williams, D. A. (1998). Sampling of empirically supported psychological treatments from health psychology: Smoking, chronic pain, cancer, and bulimia nervosa. *Journal of Consulting and Clinical Psychology, 66,* 89–112.

Concar, D. (2002, April 20). Ecstasy on the brain. NewScientist.com.

Condon, J. T. (2001). Premenstrual syndrome in primary care: An update. *Primary Care Psychiatry, 7*(3), 85–90.

Conklin, H. M., & Iacono, W. G. (2002). Schizophrenia: A neurodevelopmental perspective. *Current Directions in Psychological Science, 11*(1), 33–37.

Consortium of Social Science Associations. (2003). McQuery testifies to Homeland Security Science Subcommittee. *Washington Update, 22*(10), 1–7.

Constantinidis, C., Franowicz, M. N., & Goldman-Rakic, P. S. (2001). Coding specificity in cortical microcircuits: A multiple-electrode analysis of primate prefontal cortex. *Journal of Neuroscience, 21*(10), 3646–3655.

Conte, J., M., Schwenneker, H. H., Dew, A. F., & Romano, D. M. (2001). Incremental validity of time urgency and other Type A subcomponents in predicting behavioral and health criteria. *Journal of Applied Social Psychology, 31*(8), 1727–1748.

Conway, M. A., et al. (1994). The formation of flashbulb memories. *Memory & Cognition, 22*(3), 326–343.

Cooper, M. L. (2002). Alcohol use and risky sexual behavior among college students and youth: Evaluating the evidence. *Journal of Studies on Alcohol,* Suppl14, 101–117.

Cooper, Z., & Fairburn, C. G. (2001). A new cognitive behavioural approach to the treatment of obesity. *Behaviour Research & Therapy, 39*(5), 499–511.

Cooper, M., Galbraith, M., & Drinkwater, J. (2001). Assumptions and beliefs in adolescents with anorexia nervosa and their mothers. *Eating Disorders: The Journal of Treatment & Prevention, 9*(3), 217–223.

Corballis, M. C. (1998). Sperry and the Age of Aquarius: Science, values and the split brain. *Neuropsychologia, 36*(10), 1083–1087.

Corballis, P. M., Funnell, M. G., & Gazzaniga, M. S. (2002). Hemispheric asymmetries for simple visual judgments in the split brain. *Neuropsychologia, 40*(4), 401–410.

Cornish, K. M. (1996). The Geschwind and Galaburda theory of cerebral lateralisation: An empirical evaluation of its assumptions. *Current Psychology: Developmental, Learning, Personality, Social, 15*(1), 68–76.

Corwin, R. L. (2000). Biological and behavioral consequences of food restriction. *Appetite, 34*(1), 112.

Cory, G. A. (2002). MacLean's evolutionary neuroscience, the CSN model and Hamilton's rule: Some developmental, clinical, and social policy implications. *Brain & Mind, 3*(1), 151–181.

Cotman, C. W. (2000, July). Amyloid toxicity. Paper presented to the World Alzheimer Congress 2000, Washington, DC.

Courtenay, W. H. (2000). Engendering health: A social constructionist examination of men's health beliefs and behaviors. *Psychology of Men & Masculinity, 1*(1), 4–15.

Cowan, G. (2000). Women's hostility toward women and rape and sexual harassment myths. *Violence Against Women, 6*(3), 238–246.

Cowen, P. J. (2002). Cortisol, serotonin and depression: All stressed out? *British Journal of Psychiatry, 180*(2), 99–100.

Crabb, P. B. (2000). The material culture of homicidal fantasies. *Aggressive Behavior, 26*(3), 225–234.

Craddock, N., & Jones, I. (2001). Molecular genetics of bipolar disorder. *British Journal of Psychiatry, 178*(Suppl41), s128–s133.

Craik, F. I. M., & Lockhart, R. S. (1972). Levels of processing. *Journal of Verbal Learning and Verbal Behavior, 11,* 671–684.

Cramer, P. (2000). Defense mechanisms in psychology today. *American Psychologist, 55*(6), 637–646.

Cramer, R. E., McMaster, M. R., Bartell, P. A., & Dragna, M. (1988). Subject competence and minimization of the bystander effect. *Journal of Applied Social Psychology, 18,* 1133–1148.

Crano, W. D. (2000) Milestones in the psychological analysis of social influence. *Group Dynamics, 4*(1), 68–80.

Craske, M. G., & Zucker, B. G. (2001). Consideration of the APA practice guideline for the treatment of patients with panic disorder: Strengths and limitations for behavior therapy. *Behavior Therapy, 32*(2), 259–281.

Crews, D. (1994). Animal sexuality. *Scientific American, 270*(1), 108–114.

Crick, F., & Koch, C. (1997). The problem of consciousness. *Scientific American mysteries of the mind, Special Issue Vol. 7,* No. 1, 18–26.

Crick, N. R., & Dodge, K. A. (1994). A review and reformulation of social information-processing mechanisms in children's social adjustment. *Psychological Bulletin, 115,* 74–101.

Critchley, H. D., et al. (2005). Mental stress and sudden cardiac death: Asymmetric midbrain activity as a linking mechanism. *Brain: A Journal of Neurology, 128*(1), 75–85.

Crowe, R. A. (1990). Astrology and the scientific method. *Psychological Reports, 67,* 163–191.

Crusco, A. H., & Wetzel, C. G. (1984). The Midas touch: The effects of interpersonal touch on restaurant tipping. *Personality and Social Psychology Bulletin, 10,* 512–517.

Cummins, R. A. (2000). Personal income and subjective well-being: A review. *Journal of Happiness Studies, 1*(2), 133–158.

Cummins, R. A., & Nistico, H. (2002). Maintaining life satisfaction: The role of positive cognitive bias. *Journal of Happiness Studies, 3*(1), 37–69.

Cumsille, P. E., Sayer, A. G., & Graham, J. W. (2000). Perceived exposure to peer and adult drinking as predictors of growth in positive alcohol expectancies during adolescence. *Journal of Consulting and Clinical Psychology, 68*(3), 531–536.

Cunningham, M. R., Shaffer, D. R., Barbee, A. P., Wolff, P. L., & Kelley, D. J. (1990). Separate processes in the relation of elation and depression to helping. *Journal of Experimental Social Psychology, 26,* 13–33.

Curnoe, S., & Langevin, R. (2002). Personality and deviant sexual fantasies: An examination of the MMPIs. *Journal of Clinical Psychology, 58*(7), 803–815.

Curtis, J. T., Liu, Y., & Wang, Z. (2001). Lesions of the vomeronasal organ disrupt mating-induced pair bonding in female prairie voles *(Microtus ochrogaster). Brain Research, 901*(1–2), 167–174.

Curtis, R. C., & Miller, K. (1986). Believing another likes or dislikes you: Behavior making the beliefs come true. *Journal of Personality and Social Psychology, 51,* 284–290.

Cutler, W. B. (1999). Human sex-attractant hormones: Discovery, research, development, and application in sex therapy. *Psychiatric Annals, 29*(1) 54–59.

Cutler, W. B., Friedmann, E., & McCoy, N. L. (1998). Pheromonal influences on sociosexual behavior in men. *Archives of Sexual Behavior, 27*(1), 1–13.

Cyranowski, J. M., Frank, E., Young, E., & Shear, M. M. (2000). Adolescent onset of the gender difference in lifetime rates of major depression: A theoretical model. *Archives of General Psychiatry, 57*(1), 21–27.

Czubaj, C. A. (2002). School indoor air quality. *Journal of Instructional Psychology, 29*(4), 317–321.

Dabbs, J. M., Jr., Chang, E-L., Strong, R. A., & Milun, R. (1998). Spatial ability, navigation strategy, and geographic knowledge among men and women. *Evolution & Human Behavior, 19*(2) 89–98.

Dabbs, J. M., Jr., Hargrove, M. F., & Heusel, C. (1996). Testosterone differences among college fraternities: Well-behaved vs rambunctious. *Personality & Individual Differences, 20*(2), 157–161.

Dai, D. Y. (2001). A comparison of gender differences in academic self-concept and motivation between high-ability and average Chinese adolescents. *Journal of Secondary Gifted Education, 13*(1), 22–32.

Dailard, C. (2001, February). Sex education: Politicians, parents, teachers and teens. *The Guttmacher Report on Public Policy.* New York: The Alan Guttmacher Institute.

Dalkvist, J. (2001). The ganzfeld method: Its current status. *European Journal of Parapsychology, 16,* 19–22.

Damasio, A. R. (2000). A neural basis for sociopathy. *Archives of General Psychiatry online, 57*(2).

Dana, R. H. (2002). Mental health services for African Americans: A cultural/racial perspective. *Cultural Diversity & Ethnic Minority Psychology, 8*(1), 3–18.

Danforth, J. S., et al. (1990). Exercise as a treatment for hypertension in low-socioeconomic-status black children. *Journal of Consulting and Clinical Psychology, 58,* 237–239.

Danner, M. (2005). Taking stock of the forever war. *The New York Times Magazine,* September 11, pp. 44–53, 68, 86–87.

Darley, J. M. (1993). Research on morality. *Psychological Science, 4,* 353–357.

Darley, J. M., & Latané, B. (1968). Bystander intervention in emergencies: Diffusion of responsibility. *Journal of Personality and Social Psychology, 8,* 377–383.

Dasgupta, N., & Greenwald, A. G. (2001). On the malleability of automatic attitudes: Combating automatic prejudice with images of admired and disliked individuals. *Journal of Personality and Social Psychology, 81*(5), 800–814.

Davidson, J. R., & Foa, E. G. (1991). Diagnostic issues in posttraumatic stress disorder. *Journal of Abnormal Psychology, 100,* 346–355.

Davis, A. M., Grattan, D. R., & McCarthy, M. M. (2000). Decreasing GAD neonatally attenuates steroid-induced sexual differentiation of the rat brain. *Behavioral Neuroscience, 114*(5) 923–933.

Davis, S. (2000). Testosterone and sexual desire in women. *Journal of Sex Education & Therapy, 25*(1), 25–32.

Davis, T. L., & Liddell, D. L. (2002). Getting inside the house: The effectiveness of a rape prevention program for college fraternity men. *Journal of College Student Development, 43*(1), 35–50.

Dawson, T. L. (2002). New tools, new insights: Kohlberg's moral judgement stages revisited. *International Journal of Behavioral Development, 26*(2), 154–166.

Day, E., Wilkes, S., & Copello, A. (2003). Spirituality is not everyone's cup of tea for treating addiction. *BMJ: British Medical Journal, 326*(7394), 881.

Day, K. (2000). The ethic of care and women's experiences of public space. *Journal of Environmental Psychology, 20*(2), 103–124.

Day, S. J., & Altman, D. G. (2000). Statistics notes: Blinding in clinical trials and other studies *British Medical Journal, 321,* 504.

DeAngelis, T. (1994a). Educators reveal keys to success in classroom. *APA Monitor, 25*(1), 39–40.

DeAngelis, T. (1994b). Experts see little impact from insanity plea ruling. *APA Monitor, 25*(6), 28.

DeAngelis, T. (2000). Is Internet addiction real? *APA Monitor, 31*(4), 24–26.

DeAngelis, T. (2002). A genetic link to anorexia. *APA Monitor, 33*(3), 34–36.

DeCasper, A. J., & Prescott, P. A. (1984). Human newborns' perception of male voices. *Developmental Psychobiology, 17,* 481–491.

Deep, A. L., et al. (1999). Sexual abuse in eating disorder subtypes and control women: The role of comorbid substance dependence in bulimia nervosa. *International Journal of Eating Disorders, 25*(1), 1–10.

DeGrandpre, R. J. (2000). A science of meaning: Can behaviorism bring meaning to psychological science? *American Psychologist, 55*(7), 721–739.

De Guerrero, M. C. M., & Villamil, O. S. (2000). Activating the ZPD: Mutual scaffolding in L2 peer revision. *Modern Language Journal, 84*(1), 51–68.

De Houwer, J., Thomas, S., & Baeyens, F. (2001). Associative learning of likes and dislikes: A review of 25 years of research on human evaluative conditioning. *Psychological Bulletin, 127*(6), 853–869.

de Jong, P. F., & Das-Smaal, E. A. (1995). Attention and intelligence. *Journal of Educational Psychology, 87,* 80–92.

Delgado, J. M. R. (1969). *Physical control of the mind.* New York: Harper & Row.

Delves, P. J., & Roitt, I. M. (2000). Advances in immunology: The immune system. *The New England Journal of Medicine online, 343*(1).

De Michele, P. E., Gansneder, B., & Solomon, G. B. (1998). Success and failure attributions of wrestlers: Further evidence of the self-serving bias. *Journal of Sport Behavior, 21*(3), 242-255.

Denham, S. A., et al. (2000). Prediction of externalizing behavior problems from early to middle childhood: The role of parental socialization and emotion expression. *Development & Psychopathology, 12*(1), 23–45.

Denmark, F. L. (1998). Women and psychology: An international perspective. *American Psychologist, 53*(4), 465–473.

Dennerstein, L. L. (2003). The sexual impact of menopause. In S. B. Levine, et al. (eds.), *Handbook of clinical sexuality for mental health professionals* (pp. 187–198). New York: Brunner-Routledge.

Dennis, H. (2000). Cited in J. Y. Stewart & E. Armet (2000), Aging in America: Retirees reinvent the concept. *Los Angeles Times online,* April 3.

Depression Research at the National Institute of Mental Health. (2000). NIH Publication No. 00-4501. http://www.nimh.nih.gov/publicat/depresfact.cfm.

de Rios, M. D. (2002). What we can learn from shamanic healing: Brief psychotherapy with Latino immigrant clients. *American Journal of Public Health, 92*(10), 1576–1578.

DeRubeis, R. J., & Crits-Christoph, P. (1998). Empirically supported individual and group psychological treatments for adult mental disorders. *Journal of Consulting and Clinical Psychology, 66,* 37–52.

Dessens, A. B., et al. (1999). Prenatal exposure to anticonvulsants and psychosexual development. *Archives of Sexual Behavior, 28*(1) 31–44.

de Toledo-Morrell, L. (2000, July). Hippocampal and entorhinal atrophy in aging and Alzheimer's disease: Relation to function. Paper presented to the World Alzheimer Congress 2000, Washington, DC.

DeValois, R. L., & Jacobs, G. H. (1984). Neural mechanisms of color vision. In I. Darian-Smith (Ed.), *Handbook of physiology* (Vol. 3). Bethesda, MD: American Physiological Society.

Devilly, G. J. (2002). Eye movement desensitization and reprocessing: A chronology of its development and scientific standing. *Scientific Review of Mental Health Practice, 1*(2), 113–138.

DeVries, R. (2000). Vygotsky, Piaget, and education: A reciprocal assimilation of theories and educational practices. *New Ideas in Psychology, 18*(2–3), 187–213.

De Wit, D. J., et al. (2000). Age at first alcohol use: A risk factor for the development of alcohol disorders. *American Journal of Psychiatry, 157,* 745–750.

de Wit, H., Crean, J., & Richards, J. B. (2000). Effects of *d*-amphetamine and ethanol on a measure of behavioral inhibition in humans. *Behavioral Neuroscience, 114*(4), 830–837.

Dickson, N., Paul, C., Herbison, P., & Silva, P. (1998). First sexual intercourse: age, coercion, and later regrets reported by a birth cohort. *British Medical Journal, 316,* 29–33.

Diener, E., Napa Scollon, C. K., Oishi, S., Dzokoto, V., Suh, E. M. (2000). Positivity and the construction of life satisfaction judgments: Global happiness is not the sum of its parts. *Journal of Happiness Studies, 1*(2), 159–176.

Dierker, L. C., et al. (2001). Association between psychiatric disorders and the progression of tobacco use behaviors. *Journal of the American Academy of Child & Adolescent Psychiatry, 40*(10), 1159–1167.

Difede, J. (2005). In Lake, M. (2005, May 2). Virtual reality heals 9/11 wounds. http://www.cnn.com/2005/TECH/04/29/spark.virtual/index.html.

Difede, J., & Hoffman, H. G. (2002). Virtual reality exposure therapy for World Trade Center post-traumatic stress disorder: A case report. *CyberPsychology & Behavior, 5*(6), 529–535.

DiLalla, D. L., Carey, G., Gottesman, I. I., & Bouchard, T. J., Jr. (1996). Heritability of MMPI personality indicators of psychopathology in twins reared apart. *Journal of Abnormal Psychology, 105,* 491–499.

DiLalla, D. L., Gottesman, I. I., Carey, G., & Bouchard, T. J., Jr. (1999). Heritability of MMPI Harris-Lingoes and Subtle-Obvious subscales in twins reared apart. *Assessment, 6*(4), 353–366.

Dill, C. A., Gilden, E. R., Hill, P. C., & Hanselka, L. L. (1982). Federal human subjects regulations. *Personality and Social Psychology Bulletin, 8,* 417–425.

Dindia, K., & Allen, M. (1992). Sex differences in self-disclosure. *Psychological Bulletin, 112,* 106–124.

Dobbins, I. G., Simons, J. S., & Schacter, D. L. (2004). fMRI evidence for separable and lateralized prefrontal memory monitoring processes. *Journal of Cognitive Neuroscience, 16*(6), 908–920.

Doblin, R. (2002). A clinical plan for MDMA (ecstasy) in the treatment of posttraumatic stress disorder (PTSD): Partnering with the FDA. *Journal of Psychoactive Drugs, 34*(2), 185–194.

Dockery, D. W., et al. (1993). An association between air pollution and mortality in six U.S. cities. *New England Journal of Medicine, 329,* 1753–1759.

Dodge, K. A., Laird, R., Lochman, J. E., Zelli, A., & Conduct Problems Prevention Research Group U.S. (2002). Multidimensional latent-construct analysis of children's social information processing patterns: Correlations with aggressive behavior problems. *Psychological Assessment, 14*(1), 60–73.

Dogil, G., et al. (2002). The speaking brain: A tutorial introduction to fMRI experiments in the production of speech, prosody and syntax. *Journal of Neurolinguistics, 15*(1), 59–90.

Dollard, J., Doob, L. W., Miller, N. E., Mowrer, O. H., & Sears, R. R. (1939). *Frustration and aggression*. New Haven, CT: Yale University Press.

Domhoff, G. W. (2001). A new neurocognitive theory of dreams. *Dreaming: Journal of the Association for the Study of Dreams, 11*(1), 13–33.

Domhoff, G. W. (2003). *The scientific study of dreams: Neural networks, cognitive development, and content analysis.* Washington, DC: American Psychological Association.

Donker, F. J. S. (2000). Cardiac rehabilitation: A review of current developments. *Clinical Psychology Review, 20*(7), 923–943.

Donnelly, D., & Fraser, J. (1998). Gender differences in sado-masochistic arousal among college students. *Sex Roles, 39*(5–6), 391–407.

Donnerstein, E. I., & Wilson, D. W. (1976). Effects of noise and perceived control on ongoing and subsequent aggressive behavior. *Journal of Personality and Social Psychology, 34*, 774–781.

Doob, A. N., & Wood, L. (1972). Catharsis and aggression. *Journal of Personality and Social Psychology, 22*, 236–245.

Downey, J. I., & Friedman, R. C. (1998). Female homosexuality: Classical psychoanalytic theory reconsidered. *Journal of the American Psychoanalytic Association, 46*(2), 471–506.

Drapkin, R. G., Wing, R. R., & Shiffman, S. (1995). Responses to hypothetical high risk situations. *Health Psychology, 14*, 427–434.

Drury, L. J. (2003). Community care for people who are homeless and mentally ill. *Journal of Health Care for the Poor & Underserved, 14*(2), 194–207.

Dubbert, P. M. (2002). Physical activity and exercise: Recent advances and current challenges. *Journal of Consulting and Clinical Psychology, 70*(3), 526–536.

Duckitt, J. (1992). Psychology and prejudice. *American Psychologist, 47*, 1182–1193.

Duenwald, M. (2002). Body's defender goes on the attack. *The New York Times,* January 22, pp. F1, F9.

Duka, T., Tasker, R., & McGowan, J. F. (2000). The effects of 3-week estrogen hormone replacement on cognition in elderly healthy females. *Psychopharmacology, 149*(2), 129–139.

Dulin, P. L., & Hill, R. D. (2003). Relationships between altruistic activity and positive and negative affect among low-income older adult service providers. *Aging & Mental Health, 7*(4), 294–299.

Duncan, J., et al. (2000). A neural basis for general intelligence. *Science, 289*(5478), 457–460.

Dunkley, D. M., Zuroff, D. C., & Blankstein, K. R. (2003). Self-critical perfectionism and daily affect: Dispositional and situational influences on stress and coping. *Journal of Personality & Social Psychology, 84*(1), 234–252.

Durbin, D. L., Darling, N., Steinberg, L., & Brown, B. B. (1993). Parenting style and peer group membership among European-American adolescents. *Journal of Research on Adolescence, 3*(1), 87–100.

Duval, T. S., & Silvia, P. J. (2002). Self-awareness, probability of improvement, and the self-serving bias. *Journal of Personality & Social Psychology, 82*(1), 49–61.

Dweck, C. (1997). Paper presented to the meeting of the Society for Research in Child Development. Cited in B. Murray (1997). Verbal praise may be the best motivator of all. *APA Monitor, 28*(6), 26.

d'Ydewalle, G., Luwel, K., & Brunfaut, E.. (1999). The importance of ongoing concurrent activities as a function of age in time- and event-based prospective memory. *European Journal of Cognitive Psychology, 11*(2), 219–237.

Eagle, M. (2000). Repression, part I of II. *Psychoanalytic Review, 87*(1), 1–38.

Eagly, A. H. (2000). Cited in E. Goode (2000), Response to stress found that's particularly female. *The New York Times,* May 19, p. A20.

Eagly, A. H., Ashmore, R. D., Makhijani, M. G., & Longo, L. C. (1991). What is beautiful is good, but . . . *Psychological Bulletin, 110*, 109–128.

Eagly, A. H., & Chaiken, S. (1993). *The psychology of attitudes*. Fort Worth: Harcourt Brace Jovanovich.

Easterlin, R. A. (2001). Life cycle welfare: Trends and differences. *Journal of Happiness Studies, 2*(1), 1–12.

Easterlin, R. A. (2002). Is reported happiness five years ago comparable to present happiness? A cautionary note. *Journal of Happiness Studies, 3*(2), 193–198.

Eaton, J. (2001). Management communication: The threat of groupthink. *Corporate Communications, 6*(4), 183–192.

Eaves, L., et al. (2000). Genetic and environmental causes of covariation in interview assessments of disruptive behavior in child and adolescent twins. *Behavior Genetics, 30*(4), 321–334.

Eberly, M. B., & Montemayor, R. (1999). Adolescent affection and helpfulness toward parents: A 2-year follow-up. *Journal of Early Adolescence, 19*(2), 226–248.

Ebbinghaus, H. (1913). *Memory: A contribution to experimental psychology.* (H. A. Roger & C. E. Bussenius, trans.). New York: Columbia University Press. (Original work published 1885).

Edinger, J. D., Wohlgemuth, W. K., Radtke, R. A., Marsh, G. R., & Quillian, R. E. (2001). Cognitive behavioral therapy for treatment of chronic primary insomnia: A randomized controlled trial. *Journal of the American Medical Association, 285*(14), 1856–1864.

Edmundson, M. (1999). Psychoanalysis, American style. *The New York Times online,* August 22.

Egan, M.. F., et al. (2001). Relative risk of neurological signs in siblings of patients with schizophrenia. *American Journal of Psychiatry, 158,* 1827–1834.

Egawa, T., et al. (2002). Impairment of spatial memory in kaolin-induced hydrocephalic rats is associated with changes in the hippocampal cholinergic and noradrenergic contents. *Behavioural Brain Research, 129*(1–2), 31–39.

Ehrlich, P. R. (2000). Cited in N. Angier (2000), A conversation with Dr. Paul R. Ehrlich—On human nature, genetics and the evolution of culture. *The New York Times online,* October 10.

Eich, E. (1995). Searching for mood dependent memory. *Psychological Science, 6,* 67–75.

Eich, E., Macaulay, D., & Lam, R. W. (1997). Mania, depression, and mood dependent memory. *Cognition & Emotion, 11*(5-6), 607–618.

Eichenbaum, H., & Fortin, N. (2003). Episodic memory and the hippocampus: It's about time. *Current Directions in Psychological Science, 12*(2), 53–57.

Eidem, B. W., et al. (2001). Early detection of cardiac dysfunction: Use of the myocardial performance index in patients with anorexia nervosa. *Journal of Adolescent Health, 29*(4), 267–270.

Ekman, P. (1980). *The face of man.* New York: Garland.

Ekman, P. (1993). Facial expression and emotion. *American Psychologist, 48,* 384–392.

Ekman, P. (2003). Cited in J. Foreman (2003), A conversation with Paul Ekman: The 43 facial muscles that reveal even the most fleeting emotions. *The New York Times online,* August 5.

Ekman, P., et al. (1987). Universals and cultural differences in the judgments of facial expressions of emotion. *Journal of Personality and Social Psychology, 53,* 712–717.

Elkind, D. (1967). Egocentrism in adolescence. *Child Development, 38,* 1025–1034.

Elkind, D. (1985). Egocentrism redux. *Developmental Review, 5,* 218–226.

Elkind, D., & Bowen, R. (1979). Imaginary audience behavior in children and adolescents. *Developmental Psychology, 15*(1), 38–44.

Elle. (2003, June). The *Elle*/MSNBC.com Sex & Body Image Survey. *Elle,* pp. 110–113.

Ellenbroek, B. A.. Sluyter, F., & Cools, A. R. (2000). The role of genetic and early environmental factors in determining apomorphine susceptibility. *Psychopharmacology, 148*(2), 124–131.

Ellickson, P. L., Hays, R. D., & Bell, R. M. (1992). Stepping through the drug use sequence. *Journal of Abnormal Psychology, 101,* 441–451.

Ellickson, P. L., Tucker, J. S., Klein, D. J., & McGuigan, K. A. (2001). Prospective risk factors for alcohol misuse in late adolescence. *Journal of Studies on Alcohol, 62*(6), 773–782.

Ellis, A. (2000). Cited in J. Chamberlin (2000), An historic meeting of the minds. *Monitor on Psychology, 31*(9), 27.

Ellis, A. (2002). The role of irrational beliefs in perfectionism. In G L. Flett & P L. Hewitt (eds.), *Perfectionism: Theory, research, and treatment*. Washington, DC: American Psychological Association.

Ellis, A., & Dryden, W. (1996). *The practice of rational emotive behavior therapy*. New York: Springer.

Ellsworth, P. C., Carlsmith, J. M., & Henson, A. (1972). The stare as a stimulus to flight in human subjects. *Journal of Personality and Social Psychology, 21*, 302–311.

Elzinga, B. M., Bermond, B., & van Dyck, R. (2002). The relationship between dissociative proneness and alexithymia. *Psychotherapy & Psychosomatics, 71*(2), 104–111.

Emde, R. (1993). Cited in T. Adler (1993), Shy, bold temperament? It's mostly in the genes. *APA Monitor, 24*(1), 7, 8.

Emmons, R. A., & King, L. A. (1988). Conflict among personal strivings: Immediate and long-term implications for psychological and physical well-being. *Journal of Personality & Social Psychology, 54*(6), 1040–1048.

Enard, W., et al. (2002). Molecular evolution of FOXP2, a gene involved in speech and language. *Nature, 418*(6900), 869–872.

Engel, J. (1996). Surgery for seizures. *New England Journal of Medicine, 334*, 647–652.

Engels, G. I., Garnefski, N., & Diekstra, R. F. W. (1993). Efficacy of rational–emotive therapy. *Journal of Consulting and Clinical Psychology, 61*, 1083–1090.

Eranti, S. V., & McLoughlin, D. M. (2003). Electroconvulsive therapy— State of the art. *British Journal of Psychiatry, 182*, 8–9.

Erel, O., Oberman, Y., & Yirmiya, N. (2000). Maternal versus nonmaternal care and seven domains of children's development. *Psychological Bulletin, 126*(5), 727–747.

Erikson, E. H. (1963). *Childhood and society*. New York: W. W. Norton.

Eron, L. D. (1982). Parent-child interaction, television violence, and aggression of children. *American Psychologist, 37*, 197–211.

Eron, L. D. (1993). Cited in T. DeAngelis (1993), It's baaack: TV violence, concern for kid viewers. *APA Monitor, 24*(8), 16.

Erskine, A., Markham, R., & Howie, P. (2001). Children's script-based inferences: Implications for eyewitness testimony. *Cognitive Development, 16*(4), 871–887.

Espasa, F. P. (2002). Considerations on depressive conflict and its different levels of intensity: Implications for technique. *International Journal of Psychoanalysis, 83*(4), 825–836.

Evans, G. W., Lepore, S. J., & Allen, K. M. (2000a). Cross-cultural differences in tolerance for crowding: Fact or fiction? *Journal of Personality & Social Psychology, 79*(2), 204–210.

Evans, G. W., Wells, N. M., Chan, H. E., & Saltzman, H. (2000b). Housing quality and mental health. *Journal of Consulting and Clinical Psychology, 68*(3), 526–530.

Evans, S. W., et al. (2001). Dose-response effects of methylphenidate on ecologically valid measures of academic performance and classroom behavior in adolescents with ADHD. *Experimental & Clinical Psychopharmacology, 9*(2), 163–175.

Eysenck, H. J. (1952). The effects of psychotherapy: An evaluation. *Journal of Consulting Psychology. 16*, 319–324

Eysenck, H. J., & Eysenck, M. W. (1985). *Personality and individual differences*. New York: Plenum.

Faller, H., Buelzebruck, H., Drings, P., & Lang, H. (1999). Coping, distress, and survival among patients with lung cancer. *Archives of General Psychiatry, 56*(8) 756–762.

Fallon, A. E., & Rozin, P. (1985). Sex differences in perceptions of desirable body shape. *Journal of Abnormal Psychology, 94*, 102–105.

Fantz, R. L. (1961). The origin of form perception. *Scientific American, 204*(5), 66–72.

Farber, B. A., Brink, D. C., & Raskin, P. M. (1996). *The psychotherapy of Carl Rogers: Cases and commentary* (pp. 74–75). New York: The Guilford Press.

Farooqi, I. S., et al. (2003). Clinical spectrum of obesity and mutations in the melanocortin 4 receptor gene. *New England Journal of Medicine, 348*(12), 1085–1095.

Farr, S. A., Flood, J. F., & Morley, J. E. (2000a). The effect of cholinergic, GABAergic, serotonergic, and glutamatergic receptor modulation on posttrial memory processing in the hippocampus. *Neurobiology of Learning & Memory, 73*(2), 150–167.

Farr, S. A., Uezu, K., Creonte, T. A., Flood, J. F., & Morley, J. E. (2000b). Modulation of memory processing in the cingulate cortex of mice. *Pharmacology, Biochemistry & Behavior, 65*(3), 363–368.

Fehr, B., & Russell, J. A. (1991). The concept of love viewed from a prototype perspective. *Journal of Personality and Social Psychology, 60*, 425–438.

Feinberg, M. E., Neiderhiser, J. M., Simmens, S., Reiss, D., & Hetherington, E. M. (2000). Sibling comparison of differential parental treatment in adolescence: Gender, self-esteem, and emotionality as mediators of the parenting-adjustment association. *Child Development, 71*(6), 1611–1628.

Feingold, A. (1992a). Gender differences in mate selection preferences. *Psychological Bulletin, 112*, 125–139.

Feingold, A. (1992b). Good-looking people are not what we think. *Psychological Bulletin, 111*, 304–341.

Feingold, A. (1994). Gender differences in personality: A meta-analysis. *Psychological Bulletin, 116*, 429–456.

Feingold, A. (1998). Gender stereotyping for sociability, dominance, character, and mental health: A meta-analysis of findings from the bogus stranger paradigm. *Genetic, Social, & General Psychology Monographs, 124*(3), 253–270.

Felson, R. B. (2002). *Violence and gender reexamined*. Washington, DC: American Psychological Association.

Feola, T. W., de Wit, H., & Richards, J. B. (2000). Effects of *d*-amphetamine and alcohol on a measure of behavioral inhibition in rats. *Behavioral Neuroscience, 114*(4), 838–848.

Festinger, L., & Carlsmith, J. M. (1959). Cognitive consequences of forced compliance. *Journal of Abnormal and Social Psychology, 58*, 203–210.

Festinger, L., Riecken, H. W., Jr., & Schachter, S. (1956). *When prophecy fails*. Minneapolis: University of Minnesota Press.

Fibel, B., & Hale, W. D. (1978). The generalized expectancy for success scale—A new measure. *Journal of Consulting and Clinical Psychology, 46*, 924–931.

Fiedler, K., Schmid, J., & Stahl, T. (2002). What is the current truth about polygraph lie detection? *Basic & Applied Social Psychology, 24*(4), 313–324.

Field, T. M. (1991). Young children's adaptations to repeated separations from their mothers. *Child Development, 62*, 539–547.

Fields, R. D. (2005). Making memories stick. *Scientific American,* February, pp. 75–81.

Fiellin, D. A., et al. (2001). Methadone maintenance in primary care: A randomized controlled trial. *Journal of the American Medical Association, 286*(14), 1724–1731.

Filipas, H. H., & Ullman, S. E. (2001). Social reactions to sexual assault victims from various support sources. *Violence & Victims, 16*(6), 673–692.

Filley, C. M., et al. (2001). Toward an understanding of violence: Neurobehavioral aspects of unwarranted physical aggression: Aspen Neurobehavioral Conference Consensus Statement. *Neuropsychiatry, Neuropsychology, & Behavioral Neurology, 14*(1), 1–14.

Finkenauer, C., et al. (1998). Flashbulb memories and the underlying mechanisms of their formation: Toward an emotional-integrative model. *Memory & Cognition, 26*(3), 516–531.

Finn, P. R., Sharkansky, E. J., Brandt, K. M., & Turcotte, N. (2000). The effects of familial risk, personality, and expectancies on alcohol use and abuse. *Journal of Abnormal Psychology, 109*(1), 122–133.

Fischer, M., Hand, I., & Angenendt, J. (1998). Langzeiteffekte von Kurzzeit-Verhaltenstherapien bei Agoraphobie. *Zeitschrift für Klinische Psychologie. Forschung und Praxis, 17*(3), 225–243.

Fisher, B. S., Daigle, L. E., Cullen, F. T., & Turner, M. G. (2003). Reporting sexual victimization to the police and others: Results from a national-level study of college women. *Criminal Justice & Behavior, 30*(1), 6–38.

Fisher, H. E. (2000). Brains do it: Lust, attraction and attachment. *Cerebrum, 2*, 23–42.

Flack, W. F., Jr., Laird, J. D., & Cavallaro, L. A. (1999). Separate and combined effects of facial expressions and bodily postures on emotional feelings. *European Journal of Social Psychology, 29*(2–3), 203–217.

Flashman, L. A., McAllister, T. W., Andreasen, N. C., & Saykin, A. J. (2000). Smaller brain size associated with unawareness of illness in patients with schizophrenia. *American Journal of Psychiatry, 157,* 1167–1169.

Flavell, J. H. (2000). Development of children's knowledge about the mental world. *International Journal of Behavioral Development, 24*(1), 15–23.

Flavell, J. H., Miller, P. H., & Miller, S. A. (2002). *Cognitive development* (4th ed.). Upper Saddle River, NJ: Prentice Hall.

Flegal, K. M., Carroll, M. D., Ogden, C. L., & Johnson, C. L. (2002). Prevalence and trends in obesity among U.S. adults, 1999–2000. *Journal of the American Medical Association, 288*(14), 1723–1727.

Flemons, W. W. (2002). Obstructive sleep apnea. *New England Journal of Medicine, 347*(7), 498–504.

Flett, G. L., & Hewitt, P. L. (2002). *Perfectionism.* Washington, DC: American Psychological Association.

Flett, G. L., Madorsky, D., Hewitt, P. L., & Heisel, M. J. (2002). Perfectionism cognitions, rumination, and psychological distress. *Journal of Rational-Emotive & Cognitive Behavior Therapy, 20*(1) 33–47.

Flor, H., & Birbaumer, N. (1993). Comparison of the efficacy of electromyographic biofeedback, cognitive–behavioral therapy, and conservative medical intervention in the treatment of chronic musculoskeletal pain. *Journal of Consulting and Clinical Psychology, 61,* 653–658.

Foerster, J., Higgins, E. T., & Strack, F. (2000). When stereotype disconfirmation is a personal threat: How prejudice and prevention focus moderate incongruency effects. *Social Cognition, 18*(2), 178–197.

Fogel, D. B. (2000, July). Paper presented at the 2000 Congress on Evolutionary Computation, San Diego.

Folkman, S., & Moskowitz, T. (2000a). Positive affect and the other side of coping. *American Psychologist, 55*(6), 647–654.

Folkman, S., & Moskowitz, J. T. (2000b). The context matters. *Personality & Social Psychology Bulletin, 26*(2), 150–151.

Follingstad, D., & McCormick, M. (2002). *Law and mental health professionals.* Washington, DC: American Psychological Association.

Fontaine, K. R., Redden, D. T., Wang, C., Westfall, A. O., & Allison, D. B. (2003). Years of life lost due to obesity. *Journal of the American Medical Association, 289*(2), 187–193.

Ford, K., Wirawan, D. N., Reed, B. D., Muliawan, P., & Sutarga, M. (2000). AIDS and STD knowledge, condom use, and HIV/STD infection among female sex workers in Bali, Indonesia. *AIDS Care, 12*(5), 523–534.

Fortin, S., Godbout, L., & Braun, C. M. J. (2002). Strategic sequence planning and prospective memory impairments in frontally lesioned head trauma patients performing activities of daily living. *Brain & Cognition, 48*(2-3), 361–365.

Foster, G. D., et al. (2003). A randomized trial of a low-carbohydrate diet for obesity. *The New England Journal of Medicine, 348*(21), 2082-2090.

Fouts, R. S. (1997). *Next of kin: What chimpanzees have taught me about who we are.* New York: Morrow.

Fox, E., Russo, R., Bowles, R., & Dutton, K. (2001). Do threatening stimuli draw or hold visual attention in subclinical anxiety? *Journal of Experimental Psychology: General, 130*(4), 681–700.

Frank, E., & Kupfer, D. J. (2003). Progress in the therapy of mood disorders: Scientific support. *American Journal of Psychiatry, 160,* 1207–1208.

Frankel, K. A., & Bates, J. E. (1990). Mother–toddler problem solving. *Child Development, 61,* 810–819.

Franklin, A. J., & Boyd-Franklin, N. (2000). Invisibility syndrome: A clinical model of the effects of racism on African-American males. *American Journal of Orthopsychiatry, 70*(1), 33–41.

Fraser, A. M., Brockert, J. E., & Ward, R. H. (1995). Association of young maternal age with adverse reproductive outcomes. *New England Journal of Medicine, 332,* 1113–1117.

Fredricks, J. A., & Eccles, J. S. (2002). Children's competence and value beliefs from childhood through adolescence: Growth trajectories in two male-sex-typed domains. *Developmental Psychology, 38*(4), 519–533.

Freedman, J. L., & Fraser, S. C. (1966). Compliance without pressure: The foot-in-the-door technique. *Journal of Personality and Social Psychology, 4,* 195–202.

Freeman, E. W., et al. (2001). Evaluation of a unique oral contraceptive in the treatment of premenstrual dysphoric disorder. *Journal of Women's Health & Gender-Based Medicine, 10*(6), 561–569.

Freeman, H. P., & Payne, R. (2000). Racial injustice in health care. *The New England Journal of Medicine, 342,* 1045–1047.

Freeman, M. S., Spence, M. J., & Oliphant, C. M. (1993, June). *Newborns prefer their mothers' low-pass filtered voices over other female filtered voices.* Paper presented at the annual convention of the American Psychological Society, Chicago.

Freese, T. E., Miotto, K., & Reback, C. J. (2002). The effects and consequences of selected club drugs. *Journal of Substance Abuse Treatment, 23*(2), 151–156.

Freud, S. (1927). A religious experience. In *Standard edition of the complete psychological works of Sigmund Freud, Vol. 21.* London: Hogarth Press, 1964.

Freund, C. S. (1990). Maternal regulation of children's problem-solving behavior and its impact on children's performance. *Child Development, 61,* 113–126.

Frey, B. S., & Stutzer, A. (2000). Happiness prospers in democracy. *Journal of Happiness Studies, 1*(3), 79–102.

Frias-Armenta, M. (2002). Long-term effects of child punishment on Mexican women: A structural model. *Child Abuse & Neglect, 26*(4), 371–386.

Friedman, L. J. (1999). *Identity's architect: A biography of Erik H. Erikson.* New York: Scribner.

Friedman, M., & Rosenman, R. H. (1974). *Type A behavior and your heart.* New York: Random House.

Friedman, M., & Ulmer, D. (1984). *Treating Type A behavior and your heart.* New York: Fawcett Crest.

Friedman, R. C., & Downey, J. I. (1994). Homosexuality. *New England Journal of Medicine, 331,* 923–930.

Friedman, S. R., et al. (2001). Correlates of anal sex with men among young adult women in an inner city minority neighborhood. *AIDS, 15*(15), 2057–2060.

Friedrich, M. J. (2000). Can male hormones really help women? *Journal of the American Medical Association online, 283*(20).

Frieze, I. H. (2000). Violence in close relationships—Development of a research area. *Psychological Bulletin, 126*(5), 681–684.

Frisch, R. (1997). Cited in N. Angier (1997), Chemical tied to fat control could help trigger puberty. *The New York Times,* pp. C1, C3.

Fritsch, G., & Hitzig, E. (1960). On the electrical excitability of the cerebrum. In G. von Bonin (Ed.), *Some papers on the cerebral cortex.* Springfield, IL: Charles C Thomas. (Original work published in 1870.)

Frodi, A. M., Macauley, J., & Thome, P. R. (1977). Are women always less aggressive than men? A review of the experimental literature. *Psychological Bulletin, 84,* 634–660.

Fuertes, A., et al. (2002). Factores asociados a las conductas sexuales de reigso en la adolencia. *Infancia y Aprendizaje, 25*(3), 347–361.

Fuji, K. (2002). Field experiments on operant conditioning of wild pigeons (Columbia livia). *Japanese Journal of Animal Psychology, 52*(1), 9–14.

Funk, J. B., Buchman, D., Myers, M., & Jenks, J. (2000, August 7). Asking the right question in research on violent electronic games. Paper presented to the annual meeting of the American Psychological Association, Washington, DC.

Furnham, A., & Cheng, H. (2000). Perceived parental behaviour, self-esteem and happiness. *Social Psychiatry & Psychiatric Epidemiology, 35*(10), 463–470.

Fuster, J. M. (2000). The prefrontal cortex of the primate: A synopsis. *Psychobiology, 28*(2), 125–131.

Fylkesnes, K., et al. (2001). Declining HIV prevalence and risk behaviours in Zambia: Evidence from surveillance and population-based surveys. *AIDS, 15*(7), 907–916.

Galambos, N. L., Barker, E. T., & Krahn, H. J. (2006). Depression, self-esteem, and anger in emerging adulthood: Seven-year trajectories. *Developmental Psychology, 42*(2), 350–365.

Galambos, N. L., & Turner, P. K. (1999). Parent and adolescent temperaments and the quality of parent–adolescent relations. *Merrill-Palmer Quarterly, 45*(3), 493–511.

Galassi, J. P. (1988). Four cognitive–behavioral approaches. *The Counseling Psychologist, 16*(1), 102–105.

Gallagher, A. M., et al. (2000). Gender differences in advanced mathematical problem solving. *Journal of Experimental Child Psychology, 75*(3), 165–190.

Gallup, G. H., & Newport, F. (1991). Belief in paranormal phenomena among adult Americans. *Skeptical Inquirer, 15*(4), 137–146.

Garcia, J. (1993). Misrepresentation of my criticism of Skinner. *American Psychologist, 48,* 1158.

Garcia, J., Brett, L. P., & Rusiniak, K. W. (1989). Limits of Darwinian conditioning. In S. B. Klein & R. R. Mowrer (Eds.), *Contemporary learning theories: Instrumental conditioning theory and the impact of biological constraints on learning.* Hillsdale, NJ: Erlbaum.

Garcia, J., & Koelling, R. A. (1966). Relation of cue to consequences in avoidance learning. *Psychonomic Science 4,* 123–124.

Garcia-Moreno, C., & Watts, C. (2000). Violence against women: Its importance for HIV/AIDS. *AIDS, 14*(Suppl3), S253–S265.

Garcia-Palacios, A., Hoffman, H., Carlin, A., Furness, T. A., & Botella, C. (2002). Virtual reality in the treatment of spider phobia: A controlled study. *Behaviour Research & Therapy, 40*(9), 983–993.

Gardner, H. (1983/1993). *Frames of mind.* New York: Basic Books.

Gardner, H. (2001). Multiple intelligence. *The New York Times,* April 5, p. A20.

Garfinkel, R. (1995). Cited in P. Margoshes (1995), For many, old age is the prime of life. *APA Monitor, 26*(5), 36–37.

Garnets, L. D. (2002). Sexual orientations in perspective. *Cultural Diversity and Ethnic Minority Psychology, 8*(2), 115–129.

Gay, M., Philippot, P., & Luminet, O. (2002). Differential effectiveness of psychological interventions for reducing osteoarthritis pain: A comparison of Erickson hypnosis and Jacobson relaxation. *European Journal of Pain, 6*(1), 1–16.

Geers, A., Spehar, B., & Sedey, A. (2002). Use of speech by children from total communication programs who wear cochlear implants. *American Journal of Speech-Language Pathology, 11*(1), 50–58.

Geiser, F., et al. (2001). Magnetic resonance spectroscopic and relaxometric determination of bone marrow changes in anorexia nervosa. *Psychosomatic Medicine, 63*(4), 631–647.

Gendall, K. A., Bulik, C. M., Joyce, P. R., McIntosh, V. V., & Carter, F. A. (2000). Menstrual cycle irregularity in bulimia nervosa: Associated factors and changes with treatment. *Journal of Psychosomatic Research, 49*(6), 409–415.

Gentry, M. V., et al. (2000). Nicotine patches improve mood and response speed in a lexical decision task. *Addictive Behaviors, 25*(4), 549–557.

Gernsbacher, M. A., & Kaschak, M. P. (2003). Neuroimaging studies of language production and comprehension. *Annual Review of Psychology, 54,* 91–114.

Gershoff, E. T. (2002). Corporal punishment by parents and associated child behaviors and experiences: A meta-analytic and theoretical review. *Psychological Bulletin, 128*(4), 539–579.

Geschwind, N., & Galaburda, A. M. (1987). *Cerebral lateralization: Biological mechanisms, associations, and pathology.* Cambridge, MA: Harvard University Press.

Getzels, J. W., & Jackson, P. W. (1962). *Creativity and intelligence.* New York: Wiley.

Gibbs, N. (1991, June 3). When is it rape? *Time,* pp. 48–54.

Gibson, K. R. (2002). Evolution of human intelligence: The roles of brain size and mental construction. *Brain, Behavior & Evolution, 59*(1–2), 10–20.

Gigerenzer, G., Hoffrage, U., & Kleinbölting, H. (1991). Probabilistic mental models. *Psychological Review, 98,* 506–528.

Gignac, G. E. (2006). Evaluating subtest "g" saturation levels via the single trait-correlated uniqueness (STCU) SEM approach: Evidence in favor of crystallized subtests as the best indicators of "g." *Intelligence, 34*(1), 29–46.

Gignac, G., & Vernon, P. A. (2003). Digit symbol rotation: A more g-loaded version of the traditional digit symbol subtest. *Intelligence, 31*(1), 1–8.

Gigone, D., & Hastie, R. (1997). Proper analysis of the accuracy of group judgments. *Psychological Bulletin, 121,* 149–167.

Gijsman, H. J., et al. (2002). A dose-finding study on the effects of branch chain amino acids on surrogate markers of brain dopamine function. *Psychopharmacology, 160*(2), 192–197.

Gili-Planas, M., Roca-Bennasar, M., Ferrer-Perez, V., & Bernardo-Arroyo, M. (2001). Suicidal ideation, psychiatric disorder, and medical illness in a community epidemiological study. *Suicide & Life-Threatening Behavior, 31*(2), 207–213.

Gill, T. M., DiPietro, L., & Krumholz, H. M. (2000). Role of exercise stress testing and safety monitoring for older persons starting an exercise program. *Journal of the American Medical Association, 284,* 342–349.

Gilligan, C. (1982). *In a different voice.* Cambridge, MA: Harvard University Press.

Gilligan, C., Ward, J. V., & Taylor, J. M. (1989). *Mapping the moral domain: A contribution of women's thinking to psychological theory and education.* Cambridge, MA: Harvard University Press.

Gilovich, T., & Eibach, R. (2001). The fundamental attribution error where it really counts. *Psychological Inquiry, 12*(1), 23–26.

Ginsburg, G., & Bronstein, P. (1993). Family factors related to children's intrinsic/extrinsic motivational orientation and academic performance. *Child Development, 64,* 1461–1474.

Glantz, L. A., & Lewis, D. A. (2000). Decreased dendritic spine density on prefrontal cortical pyramidal neurons in schizophrenia. *Archives of General Psychiatry, 57*(1), 65–73.

Glaser, R., et al. (1993). Stress and the memory T-cell response to the Epstein-Barr virus. *Health Psychology, 12,* 435–442.

Gleason, J. B., & Ratner, N. B. (1993). Language development in children. In J. B. Gleason & N. B. Ratner (eds.), *Psycholinguistics.* Fort Worth, TX: Harcourt Brace Jovanovich.

Glenn, S. S., Ellis, J., & Greenspoon, J. (1992). On the revolutionary nature of the operant as a unit of behavioral selection. *American Psychologist, 47,* 1326–1329.

Glynn, J. R., et al. (2001). Why do young women have a much higher prevalence of HIV than young men? A study of Kisumu, Kenya and Ndola Zambia. *AIDS, 15*(Suppl4), S51–S60.

Goadsby, P. J., Lipton, R. B., & Ferrari, M. D. (2002). Drug therapy: Migraine—Current understanding and treatment. *New England Journal of Medicine, 346,* 257–270.

Godden, D. R., & Baddeley, A. D. (1975). Context-dependent memory in two natural environments: On land and underwater. *British Journal of Psychology, 66,* 325–331.

Gold, P. E., & Greenough, W. T. (2001). *Memory consolidation.* Washington, DC: American Psychological Association.

Goldman, J. A., & Harlow, L. L. (1993). Self-perception variables that mediate AIDS-preventive behavior in college students. *Health Psychology, 12,* 489–498.

Goldman-Rakic, P. S. (1995). Cited in D. Goleman (1995), Biologists find site of working memory. *The New York Times,* May 2, pp. C1, C9.

Goldman-Rakic, P. S., Muly, E. C., III, & Williams, G. V. (2000). D-sub-1 receptors in prefrontal cells and circuits. *Brain Research Reviews, 31* (2–3), 295–301.

Goldschmidt, D., & Reuters. (2000). Portions, foods in a diet won't determine weight loss, study says. Web posted on www.CNN.com on October 20, 2000.

Goldsmith, H., et al. (2003). Research psychologists' roles in the genetic revolution. *American Psychologist, 58*(4), 318–319.

Goleman, D. J. (1995). *Emotional intelligence.* New York: Bantam Books.

Gomez-Jacinto, L., & Hombrados-Mendieta, I. (2002). Multiple effects of community and household crowding. *Journal of Environmental Psychology, 22*(3), 233–246.

Goodall, J (2000). *My life with the chimpanzees.* New York: Minstrel Books.

Goode, E. (2000). Thinner: The male battle with anorexia. *The New York Times,* June 25, p. MH8.

Goode, E. (2001a). What's in an inkblot? Some say, not much. *The New York Times,* February 20, pp. F1, F4.

Goode, E. (2001b). When rats dream, it seems, it's after a day at the mazes. *The New York Times online,* January 25.

Goodwin, P. J., et al. (2001). The effect of group psychosocial support on survival in metastatic breast cancer. *New England Journal of Medicine, 345*(24), 1719–1726.

Gordon, B. N., Baker-Ward, L., & Ornstein, P. A. (2001). Children's testimony: A review of research on memory for past experiences. *Clinical Child & Family Psychology Review, 4*(2), 157–181.

Gorman, J. M. (2001). A call to action: Overcoming anxiety through active coping. *American Journal of Psychiatry, 158*(12), 1953–1955.

Gorodetsky, M., & Klavir, R. (2003). What can we learn from how gifted/average pupils describe their processes of problem solving? *Learning & Instruction, 13*(3), 305–325.

Gottesman, I. I. (1991). *Schizophrenia genesis.* New York: Freeman.

Gottfredson, L. S. (1997). Mainstream science on intelligence: An editorial with 52 signatories, history and bibliography. *Intelligence, 24*(1), 13–23.

Gottfried, A. E., Fleming, J. S., & Gottfried, A. W. (1994). Role of parental motivational practices in children's academic intrinsic motivation and achievement. *Journal of Educational Psychology, 86,* 104–113.

Grady, C. L., McIntosh, A. R., Rajah, M. N., Beig, S., & Craik, F. I. M. (1999). The effects of age on the neural correlates of episodic encoding. *Cerebral Cortex, 9*(8), 805–814.

Graf, P. (1990). Life-span changes in implicit and explicit memory. *Bulletin of the Psychonomic Society, 28,* 353–358.

Graham, C., & Pettinato, S. (2001). Happiness, markets, and democracy: Latin America in comparative perspective. *Journal of Happiness Studies, 2*(3), 237–268.

Granot, D., & Mayseless, O. (2001). Attachment security and adjustment to school in middle childhood. *International Journal of Behavioral Development, 25*(6), 530–541.

Grant, H. M., et al. (1998). Context-dependent memory for meaningful material: Information for students. *Applied Cognitive Psychology, 12*(6), 617–623.

Grant, I., Gonzalez, R., Carey, C. L., Natarajan, L., & Wolfson, T. (2003, July). Minimal long-term effects of marijuana use found in central nervous system. *Journal of the International Neuropsychological Society.*

Green, D. P., Glaser, J., & Rich, A. (1998). From lynching to gay bashing: The elusive connection between economic condition and hate crime. *Journal of Personality and Social Psychology, 75,* 82–92.

Green, J. P., & Lynn, S. J. (2000). Hypnosis and suggestion-based approaches to smoking cessation: An examination of the evidence. *International Journal of Clinical & Experimental Hypnosis, 48*(2), 195–224.

Greenberger, E., Chen, C., Tally, S. R., & Dong, Q. (2000). Family, peer, and individual correlates of depressive symptomology among U.S. and Chinese adolescents. *Journal of Consulting and Clinical Psychology, 68,* 209–219.

Greene, J. (1982). The gambling trap. *Psychology Today, 16*(9), 50–55.

Griesmaier, F-P. (2003). On explaining phenomenal consciousness. *Journal of Experimental & Theoretical Artificial Intelligence, 15*(2), 227–242.

Griffin, C. (2001). Imagining new narratives of youth: Youth research, the "new Europe" and global youth culture. *Childhood: A Global Journal of Child Research, 8*(2), 147–166.

Grinspoon, L. (2000). Medical cannabis: The patient's and the doctor's dilemmas. *Addiction Research, 8*(1), 1–4.

Grön, G., Wunderlich, A. P., Spitzer, M., Tomczak, R. & Riepe, M. W. (2000). Brain activation during human navigation: gender-different neural networks as substrate of performance. *Nature Neuroscience, 3*(4), 404–408.

Grosser, B. I., Monti-Bloch, L., Jennings-White, C., & Berliner, D. L. (2000). Behavioral and electrophysiological effects of androstadienone, a human pheromone. *Psychoneuroendocrinology, 25*(3), 289–300.

Guerin, B. (1999). Social behaviors as determined by different arrangements of social consequences: Social loafing, social facilitation, deindividuation, and a modified social loafing. *Psychological Record, 49*(4), 565–578.

Guilford, J. P. (1988). Some changes in the structure-of-intellect model. *Educational and Psychological Measurement, 48,* 1–4.

Gulcur, L., Stefancic, A., Shinn, M., Tsemberis, S., & Fischer, S. N. (2003). Housing, hospitalization and cost outcomes for homeless individuals with psychiatric disabilities participating in continuum of care and housing first programmes. *Journal of Community & Applied Social Psychology, 13*(2), 171–186.

Gump, B. B., & Matthews, K. A. (2000). Are vacations good for your health? The 9-year mortality experience after the Multiple Risk Factor Intervention Trial. *Psychosomatic Medicine, 62*(5), 608–612.

Gunter, C., & Dhand, R. (2002). Human biology by proxy. Introductory article to an entire issue on the mouse genome. *Nature, 420,* 509.

Gupta, V. B., Nwosa, N. M., Nadel, T. A., & Inamdar, S. (2001). Externalizing behaviors and television viewing in children of low-income minority parents. *Clinical Pediatrics, 40*(6), 337–341.

Haaf, R. A., Smith, P. H., & Smitley, S. (1983). Infant response to face-like patterns under fixed trial and infant-control procedures. *Child Development, 54,* 172–177.

Haaga, D. A. F., & Davison, G. C. (1993). An appraisal of rational–emotive therapy. *Journal of Consulting and Clinical Psychology, 61,* 215–220.

Haden, C. A., Ornstein, P. A., Eckerman, C. O., & Didow, S. M. (2001). Mother–child conversational interactions as events unfold: Linkages to subsequent remembering. *Child Development, 72*(4), 1016–1031.

Haenen, J. (2001). Outlining the teaching–learning process: Piotr Gal'perin's contribution. *Learning & Instruction, 11*(2), 157–170.

Hakim, A. A., et al. (1998). Effects of walking on mortality among nonsmoking retired men. *New England Journal of Medicine, 338,* 94–99.

Hall, C. S. (1984). "A ubiquitous sex difference in dreams" revisited. *Journal of Personality and Social Psychology, 46,* 1109–1117.

Hall, G. C. N., & Barongan, C. (1997). Prevention of sexual aggression. *American Psychologist, 52,* 5–14.

Hall, G. C. N., Sue, S., Narang, D. S., & Lilly, R. S. (2000). Culture-specific models of men's sexual aggression: Intra- and interpersonal determinants. *Cultural Diversity & Ethnic Minority Psychology, 6*(3), 252–267.

Halmi, K. A., et al. (2000). Perfectionism in anorexia nervosa: Variation by clinical subtype, obsessionality, and pathological eating behavior. *American Journal of Psychiatry, 157,* 1799–1805.

Halpern, D. F. (1989). *Thought and knowledge.* (2nd ed.). Hillsdale, NJ: Erlbaum.

Halpern, D. F. (1997). Sex differences in intelligence: Implications for education. *American Psychologist, 52,* 1091–1102.

Halpern, D. F., Hansen, C., & Riefer, D. (1990). Analogies as an aid to understanding and memory. *Journal of Educational Psychology, 82,* 298–305.

Halpern, D. F., & LaMay, M. L. (2000). The smarter sex: A critical review of sex differences in intelligence. *Educational Psychology Review, 12*(2), 229–246.

Hamilton, M. (2001). Who believes in astrology? Effect of favorableness of astrologically derived personality descriptions on acceptance of astrology. *Personality & Individual Differences, 31*(6), 895–902.

Hammer, C. S., Miccio, A. W., & Wagstaff, D. A. (2003). Home literacy experiences and their relationship to bilingual preschoolers' developing English literacy abilities: An initial investigation. *Language, Speech, & Hearing Services in Schools, 34*(1), 20–30.

Hammerfald, K., et al. (2006). Persistent effects of cognitive-behavioral stress management on cortisol responses to acute stress in healthy subjects—A randomized controlled trial. *Psychoneuroendocrinology, 31*(3), 333–339.

Hankin, B. L., & Abramson, L. Y. (2001). Development of gender differences in depression: An elaborated cognitive vulnerability–transactional stress theory. *Psychological Bulletin, 127*(6), 773–796.

Hansell, N. K., et al. (2001). Genetic influence on ERP slow wave measures of working memory. *Behavior Genetics, 31*(6), 603–614.

Hansen, C. J., Stevens, L. C., & Coast, J. R. (2001). Exercise duration and mood state: How much is enough to feel better? *Health Psychology, 20*(4), 267–275.

Haridakis, P. M. (2002). Viewer characteristics, exposure to television violence, and aggression. *Media Psychology, 4*(4), 323–352.

Hariton, E. B., & Singer, J. L. (1974). Women's fantasies during sexual intercourse: Normative and theoretical implications. *Journal of Consulting & Clinical Psychology, 42*(3), 313–322.

Harker, L., & Keltner, D. (2001). Expressions of positive emotion in women's college yearbook pictures and their relationship to personality and life outcomes across adulthood. *Journal of Personality and Social Psychology, 80*(1), 112–124.

Harkness, K. L., & Luther, J. (2001). Clinical risk factors for the generation of life events in major depression. *Journal of Abnormal Psychology, 110*(4), 564–572.

Harley, K., & Reese, E. (1999). Origins of autobiographical memory. *Developmental Psychology, 35*(5), 1338–1348.

Harlow, H. F. (1959). Love in infant monkeys. *Scientific American, 200,* 68–86.

Harlow, H. F., & Zimmermann, R. R. (1959). Affectional responses in the infant monkey. *Science, 130,* 421–432.

Harris, S. R., Kemmerling, R. L., & North, M. M. (2002). Brief virtual reality therapy for public speaking anxiety. *CyberPsychology & Behavior, 5*(6), 543–550.

Hart, A. J., et al. (2000). Differential response in the human amygdala to racial outgroup vs. ingroup face stimuli. *NeuroReport, 11*(11), 2351–2355.

Hart, J. W., Bridgett, D. J., & Karau, S. J. (2001). Coworker ability and effort as determinants of individual effort on a collective task. *Group Dynamics, 5*(3), 181–190.

Haselton, M. G., & Buss, D. M. (2001). The affective shift hypothesis: The functions of emotional changes following sexual intercourse. *Personal Relationships, 8*(4), 357–369.

Hassinger, H. J., Semenchuk, E. M., & O'Brien, W. H. (1999). Appraisal and coping responses to pain and stress in migraine headache sufferers. *Journal of Behavioral Medicine, 22*(4), 327–340.

Hastings, P. D., Zahn-Waxler, C., Robinson, J., Usher, B., & Bridges, D. (2000). The development of concern for others in children with behavior problems. *Developmental Psychology, 36*(5), 531–546.

Hawkins, S. A., & Hastie, R. (1990). Hindsight: Biased judgments of past events after the outcomes are known. *Psychological Bulletin, 107,* 311–327.

Hayes, P. (1993). Cited in S. Chartrand (1993), A split in thinking among keepers of artificial intelligence. *The New York Times,* July 18, p. E6.

Health, United States (2002). http://www.cdc.gov/nchs. (National Center for Health Statistics).

Hearne, K. (2003). http://ourworld.compuserve.com/homepages/keithhearne/Cultural.html. Accessed July 15, 2003.

Heffner, K. L., Loving, T. J., Robles, T. F., & Kiecolt-Glaser, J. K. (2003). Examining psychosocial factors related to cancer incidence and progression: In search of the silver lining. *Brain, Behavior & Immunity, 17*(Suppl1), S109–S111.

Heim, C., et al. (2000). Pituitary-adrenal and autonomic responses to stress in women after sexual and physical abuse in childhood. *Journal of the American Medical Association, 284,* 592–597.

Heim, C., Newport, D. J., Miller, A. H., & Nemeroff, C. B. (2002). Dr. Heim and colleagues reply. *American Journal of Psychiatry, 159*(1), 157–158.

Heimpel, S. A., Wood, J. V., Marshall, M. A., & Brown, J. D. (2002). Do people with low self-esteem really want to feel better? Self-esteem differences in motivation to repair negative moods. *Journal of Personality & Social Psychology, 82*(1), 128–147.

Heinz, A., et al. (2003). Effects of acute psychological stress on adhesion molecules interleukins and sex hormones: Implications for coronary heart disease. *Psychopharmacology, 165*(2), 111–117.

Heller, D. A., de Faire, U., Pedersen, N. L., Dahlén, G., & McClearn, G. E. (1993). Genetic and environmental influences on serum lipid levels in twins. *New England Journal of Medicine, 328,* 1150–1156.

Helms, J. E. (1992). Why is there no study of cultural equivalence in standardized cognitive ability testing? *American Psychologist, 47,* 1083–1101.

Helson, R. (1993). In K. D. Hulbert & D. T. Schuster (eds.), *Women's lives through time* (pp. 190–210). San Francisco: Jossey-Bass.

Hendin, H., Maltsberger, J. T., Lipschitz, A., Pollinger H., & Kyle, J. (2001). Recognizing and responding to a suicide crisis. *Suicide & Life-Threatening Behavior, 31*(2), 115–128.

Hendrick, S., & Hendrick, C. (2002). Love. In C. R. Snyder & S. J. Lopez (eds.). *Handbook of positive psychology* (pp. 472–484). London: Oxford University Press.

Heng, M. A. (2000). Scrutinizing common sense: The role of practical intelligence in intellectual giftedness. *Gifted Child Quarterly, 44*(3), 171–182.

Henker, B., Whelen, C. K., Jammer, L. D., & Delfino, R. J. (2002). Anxiety, affect, and activity in teenagers: Monitoring daily life with electronic diaries. *Journal of the American Academy of Child and Adolescent Psychiatry, 41*(6), 660–670.

Henry, D., et al. (2000). Normative influences on aggression in urban elementary school classrooms. *American Journal of Community Psychology, 28*(1), 59–81.

Hensley, L. G. (2002). Treatment for survivors of rape: Issues and interventions. *Journal of Mental Health Counseling, 24*(4), 330–347.

Hensley, W. E. (1981). The effects of attire, location, and sex on aiding behavior. *Journal of Nonverbal Behavior, 6,* 3–11.

Herbert, B. (2005). A waking nightmare. *The New York Times online,* September 26.

Hergenhahn, B. R. (2001). *An introduction to the history of psychology* (4th ed.). Pacific Grove, CA: Brooks/Cole.

Herman-Giddens, M. E., et al. (1999). Underascertainment of child abuse mortality in the United States. *Journal of the American Medical Association, 282,* 463–467.

Herrmann, D. J. (1991). *Super memory.* Emmaus, PA: Rodale.

Herrnstein, R. J., & Murray, C. (1994). *The bell curve: Intelligence and class structure in American life.* New York: Free Press.

Hershenson, R. (2000). Debating the Mozart theory. *The New York Times Magazine online,* August 6.

Hersen, M., Bellack, A. S., Himmelhoch, J. M., & Thase, M. E. (1984). Effects of social skill training, amitriptyline, and psychotherapy in unipolar depressed women. *Behavior Therapy. 15*(1), 21–40.

Hertz-Pannier, L., et al. (2002). Late plasticity for language in a child's non-dominant hemisphere: A pre- and post-surgery fMRI study. *Brain, 125*(2), 361–372.

Herzog, T. R., & Chernick, K. K. (2000). Tranquility and danger in urban and natural settings. *Journal of Environmental Psychology, 20*(1), 29–39.

Hess, J. A. (2003). Measuring distance in personal relationships: The Relationship Distance Index. *Personal Relationships, 10*(2), 197–215.

Hetland, L. (2000). Cited in R. Hershenson (2000), Debating the Mozart theory. *The New York Times Magazine online,* August 6.

Hewstone, M., & Hamberger, J. (2000). Perceived variability and stereotype change. *Journal of Experimental Social Psychology, 36*(2), 103–124.

Hickman, G. P., Bartholomae, S., & McKenry, P. C. (2000). Influence of parenting style on the adjustment and academic achievement of traditional college freshmen. *Journal of College Student Development, 41*(1), 41–54.

Hicks, T. V., & Leitenberg, H. (2001). Sexual fantasies about one's partner versus someone else: Gender differences in incidence and frequency. *Journal of Sex Research, 38*(1), 43–50.

Hilgard, E. R. (1994). Neodissociation theory. In S. J. Lynn & J. W. Rhue. *Dissociation: Clinical, theoretical and research perspectives.* New York: Guilford Press.

Hilsenroth, M. J., Baity, M. R., Mooney, M. A., & Meyer, G. J. (2004). DSM-IV major depressive episode criteria: An evaluation of reliability and validity across three different rating methods. *International Journal of Psychiatry in Clinical Practice, 8*(1), 3–10.

Hinds, M. D. (2000). The politics of pollution. *American Demographics online,* May.

Hines, D. A., & Saudino, K. J. (2003). Gender differences in psychological, physical, and sexual aggression among college students using the Revised Conflict Tactics Scales. *Violence & Victims, 18*(2), 197–217.

Hingson, R., et al. (2002). *A call to action: Changing the culture of drinking at U.S. colleges.* Washington, DC: National Institutes of Health: National Institute of Alcohol Abuse and Alcoholism.

Hixson, M. D. (1998). Ape language research: A review and behavioral perspective. *Analysis of Verbal Behavior, 15,* 17–39.

Hobson, J. A. (1999). Arrest of firing of aminergic neurones during REM sleep: Implications for dream theory. *Brain Research Bulletin, 50*(5-6), 333–334.

Hobson, J. A. (2003). *Dreaming: An introduction to the science of sleep.* New York: Oxford University Press.

Hoffman, H. G. (2004). Virtual reality therapy. *Scientific American, 291*(2), 58–65.

Hoffman, P. (2003). Who's best at chess? For now, it's neither man nor machine. *The New York Times online,* February 8.

Holcomb, D. R., Savage, M. P., Seehafer, R., & Waalkes, D. M. (2002). A mixed-gender date rape prevention intervention targeting freshman college athletes. *College Student Journal, 36*(2), 165–179.

Holden, C. (1980). Identical twins reared apart. *Science, 207*(4437), 1323–1328.

Holden, E. W., Deichmann, M. M., & Levy, J. D. (1999). Empirically supported treatments in pediatric psychology: Recurrent pediatric headache. *Journal of Pediatric Psychology, 24*(2), 91–109.

Holland, J. J. (2000). Groups link media to child violence. The Associated Press online, July 25.

Holland, J. L. (1996). Exploring careers with a typology. *American Psychologist, 51*, 397–406.

Hollinger, L. M., & Buschmann, M. B. (1993). Factors influencing the perception of touch by elderly nursing home residents and their health caregivers. *International Journal of Nursing Studies, 30*, 445–461.

Hollingshead, A. B., & Redlich, F. C. (1958). *Social class and mental illness.* New York: Wiley.

Hollon, S. D., & Shelton, R. C. (2001). Treatment guidelines for major depressive disorder. *Behavior Therapy, 32*(2), 235–258.

Holmes, T. H., & Rahe, R. H. (1967). The social readjustment rating scale. *Journal of Psychosomatic Research, 11*, 213–218.

Holroyd, K. A. (2002). Assessment and psychological management of recurrent headache disorders. *Journal of Consulting & Clinical Psychology, 70*(3), 656–677.

Hong, Y., Morris, M. W., Chiu, C., & Benet-Martinez, V. (2000). A dynamic constructivist approach to culture and cognition. *American Psychologist, 55*(7), 709–720.

Honorton, C. (1985). Meta-analysis of psi Ganzfeld research. *Journal of Parapsychology, 49*, 51–91.

Honorton, C., et al. (1990). Psi communication in the Ganzfeld. *Journal of Parapsychology, 54*, 99–139.

Honts, C. R., Hodes, R. L., & Raskin, D. C. (1985). Effects of physical countermeasures on the physiological detection of deception. *Journal of Applied Psychology, 70*(1), 177–187.

Hoover, R. N. (2000). Cancer—Nature, nurture, or both. *New England Journal of Medicine online, 343*(2).

Hopper, J. L., & Seeman, E. (1994). The bone density of female twins discordant for tobacco use. *New England Journal of Medicine, 330*, 387–392.

Horn, J. M. (1983). The Texas adoption project. *Child Development, 54*, 268–275.

Hovey, J. D. (2000). Acculturative stress, depression, and suicidal ideation in Mexican immigrants. *Cultural Diversity and Ethnic Minority Psychology, 6*(2), 134–151.

Hu, F. B., et al. (2000). Physical activity and risk of stroke in women. *Journal of the American Medical Association, 283*, 2961–2967.

Hu, F. B., & Willett, W. C. (2002). Optimal diets for prevention of coronary heart disease. *Journal of the American Medical Association, 288*, 2569–2578.

Hubel, D. H., & Wiesel, T. N. (1979). Brain mechanisms of vision. *Scientific American, 241*, 150–162.

Huesmann, L. R., & Guerra, N. G. (1997). Children's normative beliefs about aggression and aggressive behavior. *Journal of Personality & Social Psychology, 72*(2), 408–419.

Huesmann, L. R., Moise-Titus, J., Podolski, C., & Eron, L. D. (2003). Longitudinal relations between children's exposure to TV violence and their aggressive and violent behavior in young adulthood: 1977–1992. *Developmental Psychology, 39*(2), 201–221.

Hulshoff P., et al. (2000). Prenatal exposure to famine and brain morphology in schizophrenia. *American Journal of Psychiatry, 157*(7), 1170–1172.

Hunsley, J., & Bailey, J. M. (1999). The clinical utility of the Rorschach: Unfulfilled promises and an uncertain future. *Psychological Assessment, 11*(3), 266–277.

Hunt, M. (1993). *The story of psychology.* New York: Anchor Books.

Hunt, R. R. (2002). How effective are pharmacologic agents for alcoholism? *Journal of Family Practice, 51*(6), 577.

Huntjens, R. J. C., et al. (2003). Interidentity amnesia for neutral, episodic information in dissociative identity disorder. *Journal of Abnormal Psychology, 112*(2), 290–297.

Husain, G. (2003). Cited in M. Elias (2003), Music affects mood, but it won't make kids smarter. *USA Today,* August 17.

Hvas, L., Reventlow, S., & Malterud, K. (2004). Women's needs and wants when seeing the GP in relation to menopausal issues. *Scandinavian Journal of Primary Health Care, 22*(2), 118–121.

Hwu, H., Liu, C., Fann, C. S., Ou-Yang, W., & Lee, S. F. (2003). Linkage of schizophrenia with chromosome 1q loci in Taiwanese families. *Molecular Psychiatry, 8*(4), 445–452.

Hyde, J. S., & Plant, E. A. (1995). Magnitude of psychological gender differences. *American Psychologist, 50*, 159–161.

Iacono, W. G., & Lykken, D. T. (1997). The validity of the lie detector: Two surveys of scientific opinion. *Journal of Applied Psychology, 82*(3), 426–433.

Iervolino, A. C., Hines, M., Golombok, S. E., Rust, J., & Plomin, R. (2005). Genetic and environmental influences on sex-typed behavior during the preschool years. *Child Development. 76*(4), 826–840.

Iidaka, T., Anderson, N. D., Kapur, S., Cabeza, R., & Craik, F. I. M. (2000). The effect of divided attention on encoding and retrieval in episodic memory revealed by positron emission tomography. *Journal of Cognitive Neuroscience, 12*(2), 267–280.

Insel, T. R. (2000). Toward a neurobiology of attachment. *Review of General Psychology, 4*(2), 176–185.

International Human Genome Sequencing Consortium (2006). A Global map of p53 transcription-factor binding sites in the human genome. *Cell, 124* (1), 207–219.

Iribarren, C., et al. (2000). Association of hostility with coronary artery calcification in young adults: The CARDIA study. *Journal of the American Medical Association, 283*, 2546–2551.

Isabella, R. A. (1998). Origins of attachment: The role of context, duration, frequency of observation, and infant age in measuring maternal behavior. *Journal of Social & Personal Relationships, 15*(4), 538–554.

Isarida, T., & Isarida, T. (1999). Effects of contextual changes between class and intermission on episodic memory. *Japanese Journal of Psychology, 69*(6), 478–485.

Isobe, C., & Ura, M. (2002). The effects of intergroup upward comparison and trait self-esteem on the affection and state self-esteem in upward comparison with in-group members. *Japanese Journal of Experimental Social Psychology, 41*(2), 98–110.

Iverson, P., et al. (2003). A perceptual interference account of acquisition difficulties for non-native phonemes. *Cognition, 87*(1), B47–B57.

Izard, C. E. (1984). Emotion–cognition relationships and human development. In C. E. Izard, J. Kagan, & R. B. Zajonc (eds.), *Emotions, cognition, and behavior.* New York: Cambridge University Press.

Izard, C. E. (1994). Basic emotions, relations among emotions, and emotion-cognition relations. *Psychological Bulletin, 115*, 561–565.

Jablensky, A. V., & Kalaydjieva, L. V. (2003). Genetic epidemiology of schizophrenia: Phenotypes, risk factors, and reproductive behavior. *American Journal of Psychiatry, 160*, 425–429.

Jacks, J. Z., & Devine, P. G. (2000). Attitude importance, forewarning of message content, and resistance to persuasion. *Basic & Applied Social Psychology, 22*(1) 19–29.

Jackson, H., & Nuttall, R. L. (2001). Risk for preadolescent suicidal behavior: An ecological model. *Child & Adolescent Social Work Journal, 18*(3), 189–203.

Jackson, L. C., & Greene, B. (2000). *Psychotherapy with African American women: Innovations in psychodynamic perspectives and practice.* New York: Guilford.

Jacob, S., & McClintock, M. K. (2000). Psychological state and mood effects of steroidal chemosignals in women and men. *Hormones and Behavior, 37*(1), 57–78.

Jacobi, C., Dahme, B., & Dittmann, R. (2002). Cognitive–behavioural, fluoxetine and combined treatment for bulimia nervosa: Short- and long-term results. *European Eating Disorders Review, 10*(3), 179–198.

Jacox, A., Carr, D. B., & Payne, R. (1994). New clinical-practice guidelines for the management of pain in patients with cancer. *New England Journal of Medicine, 330*, 651–655.

Jaffee, S., & Hyde, J. S. (2000). Gender differences in moral orientation. *Psychological Bulletin, 126*(5), 703–726.

James, L. E., & Burke, D. M. (2000). Phonological priming effects on word retrieval and tip-of-the-tongue experiences in young and older adults. *Journal of Experimental Psychology—Learning, Memory, and Cognition, 26*(6), 1378–1391.

James, W. (1890). *The principles of psychology.* New York: Henry Holt.

Jamison, K. R. (2000). Suicide and bipolar disorder. *Journal of Clinical Psychiatry, 61*(Suppl9), 47–51.

Janis, I. L. (1982). *Groupthink* (2nd ed.). Boston: Houghton Mifflin.

Janos, P. M. (1987). A fifty-year follow-up of Terman's youngest college students and IQ-matched agemates. *Gifted Child Quarterly, 31,* 55–58.

Janowitz, H. D., & Grossman, M. I. (1949). Effects of variations in nutritive density on intake of food in dogs and cats. *American Journal of Physiology, 158,* 184–193.

Janowsky, J. S., Chavez, B., & Orwoll, E. (2000). Sex steroids modify working memory. *Journal of Cognitive Neuroscience, 12,* 407–414.

Janus, C., et al. (2000). A peptide immunization reduces behavioural impairment and plaques in a model of Alzheimer's disease. *Nature, 408*(6815), 979–981.

Jeffery, R. W., Hennrikus, D. J., Lando, H. A., Murray, D. M., & Liu, J. W. (2000). Reconciling conflicting findings regarding postcessation weight concerns and success in smoking cessation. *Health Psychology, 19,* 242–246.

Jemmott, J. B., et al. (1983). Academic stress, power motivation, and decrease in secretion rate of salivary secretory immunoglobulin A. *Lancet, 1,* 1400–1402.

Jensen, M. P., Turner, J. A., & Romano, J. M. (1994). Correlates of improvement in multidisciplinary treatment of chronic pain. *Journal of Consulting and Clinical Psychology, 62,* 172–179.

Johansen, M., Karterud, S., Pedersen, G., Gude, T., & Falkum, E. (2004). An investigation of the prototype validity of the borderline DSM-IV construct. *Acta Psychiatrica Scandinavica, 109*(4), 289–298.

Johns, A. (2001). Psychiatric effects of cannabis. *The British Journal of Psychiatry, 178,* 116–122.

Johnson, R. L. (2002). Pathways to adolescent health: Early intervention. *Journal of Adolescent Health, 31*(Suppl6), 240–250.

Johnston, L. D., O'Malley, P. M., & Bachman, J. G. (2001). *Monitoring the Future national survey results on drug use, 1975–2000. Volume I: Secondary school students* (NIH Publication No. 01-4924). Bethesda, MD: National Institute on Drug Abuse.

Johnston, L. D., O'Malley, P. M., & Bachman, J. G. (2003). *Monitoring the Future national results on adolescent drug use: Overview of key findings 2002.* Bethesda, MD: National Institute on Drug Abuse.

Joiner, T. E., Jr. (2002). The trajectory of suicidal behavior over time. *Suicide & Life-Threatening Behavior, 32*(1), 33–41.

Jones, C. J., & Meredith, W. (2000). Developmental paths of psychological health from early adolescence to later adulthood. *Psychology and Aging, 15*(2), 351–360.

Jones, J. L., & Leary, M. R. (1994). Effects of appearance-based admonitions against sun exposure on tanning intentions in young adults. *Health Psychology, 13,* 86–90.

Jones, S. M., & Zigler, E. (2002). The Mozart effect: Not learning from history. *Journal of Applied Developmental Psychology, 23*(3), 355–372.

Jonsdottir, I. H., Hellstrand, K., Thoren, P., & Hoffman, P. (2000). Enhancement of natural immunity seen after voluntary exercise in rats. Role of central opioid receptors. *Life Sciences, 66*(13), 1231–1239.

Joranson, D. E., Ryan, K. M., Gilson, A. M., & Dahl, J. L. (2000). Trends in medical use and abuse of opioid analgesics. *Journal of the American Medical Association, 283,* 1710–1714.

Jorgenson, L. M., & Wahl, K. M. (2000). Workplace sexual harassment: Incidence, legal analysis, and the role of the psychiatrist. *Harvard Review of Psychiatry, 8*(2), 94–98.

Jorgensen, R. S., Johnson, B. T., Kolodziej, M. E., & Schreer, G. E. (1996). Elevated blood pressure and personality. *Psychological Bulletin, 120,* 293–320.

Jorm, A. F., et al. (2002). Sexual orientation and mental health: Results from a community survey of young and middle-aged adults. *British Journal of Psychiatry, 180,* 423–427.

Josefsson, A. M., et al. (2000). Viral load of human papilloma virus 16 as a determinant for development of cervical carcinoma in situ: a nested case-control study. *The Lancet, 355,* 2189–2193.

Kail, R. (2000). Speed of information processing: Developmental change and links to intelligence. *Journal of School Psychology, 38*(1), 51–61.

Kainz, K. (2002). A behavioral conditioning program for treatment of nocturnal enuresis. *Behavior Therapist, 25*(10), 185–187.

Kaiser, F. G., & Shimoda, T. A. (1999). Responsibility as a predictor of ecological behaviour. *Journal of Environmental Psychology, 19*(3), 243–253.

Kalin, N. H. (2003). Nonhuman primate studies of fear, anxiety, and temperament and the role of benzodiazepine receptors and GABA systems. *Journal of Clinical Psychiatry, 64*(Suppl3), 41–44.

Kalivas, P. W. (2003). Predisposition to addiction: Pharmacokinetics, pharmacodynamics, and brain circuitry. *American Journal of Psychiatry, 160,* 1–2.

Kallgren, C. A., Reno, R. R., & Cialdini, R. B. (2000). A focus theory of normative conduct: When norms do and do not affect behavior. *Personality & Social Psychology Bulletin, 26*(8), 1002–1012.

Kamalanabhan, T. J., Sunder, D. L., & Vasanthi, M. (2000). An evaluation of the Choice Dilemma Questionnaire as a measure of risk-taking propensity. *Social Behavior & Personality, 28*(2), 149–156.

Kamphaus, R. W., Petoskey, M. D., & Rowe, E. W. (2000). Current trends in psychological testing of children. *Professional Psychology: Research and Practice, 31*(2), 155–164.

Kandel, E. R. (2001). The molecular biology of memory storage: A dialogue between genes and synapses. *Science, 294,* 1030–1038.

Kandel, E. R. (2006). *In search of memory: The emergence of a new science of mind.* New York: W. W. Norton.

Kandel, E. R., & Hawkins, R. D. (1992). The biological basis of learning and individuality. *Scientific American, 267*(3), 78–86.

Kant, A. K., et al. (2000). A prospective study of diet quality and mortality in women. *Journal of the American Medical Association, 283,* 2109–2115.

Kapur, S. (2003). Psychosis as a state of aberrant salience: A framework linking biology, phenomenology, and pharmacology in schizophrenia. *American Journal of Psychiatry, 160*(1), 13–23.

Karl, A., Birbaumer, N., Lutzenberger, W., Cohen, L. G., & Flor, H. (2001). Reorganization of motor and somatosensory cortex in upper extremity amputees with phantom limb pain. *Journal of Neuroscience, 21*(10), 3609–3618.

Karlberg, L., et al. (1998). Is there a connection between car accidents, near accidents, and Type A drivers? *Behavioral Medicine, 24*(3), 99–106.

Karon, B. P., & Widener, A. (1998). Repressed memories: The real story. *Professional Psychology: Research & Practice, 29*(5), 482–487.

Karwautz, A., et al. (2001). Individual-specific risk factors for anorexia nervosa: A pilot study using a discordant sister-pair design. *Psychological Medicine, 31*(2), 317–329.

Kasai, K., et al. (2003). Progressive decrease of left Heschl gyrus and planum temporale gray matter volume in first-episode schizophrenia: A longitudinal magnetic resonance imaging study. *Archives of General Psychiatry, 60*(8), 766–775.

Kashima, Y. (2000). Maintaining cultural stereotypes in the serial reproduction of narratives. *Personality & Social Psychology Bulletin, 26*(5), 594–604.

Kaslow, N. J., et al., (2002). Risk and protective factors for suicidal behavior in abused African American women. *Journal of Consulting & Clinical Psychology, 70*(2), 311–319.

Kaufman, J., & Zigler, E. (1989). The intergenerational transmission of child abuse. In D. Cicchetti & V. Carlson (eds.), *Child maltreatment* (pp. 129–150). Cambridge, U.K.: Cambridge University Press.

Kawas, C. (2000, July). Estrogen and the prevention of Alzheimer's disease. Paper presented to the World Alzheimer Congress 2000, Washington, DC.

Kaya, N., & Erkip, F. (1999). Invasion of personal space under the condition of short-term crowding: A case study on an automatic teller machine. *Journal of Environmental Psychology, 19*(2), 183–189.

Kaye, W. H., Klump, K. L., Frank, G. K. W., & Strober, M. (2000). Anorexia and bulimia nervosa. *Annual Review of Medicine, 51,* 299–313.

Kazuomi Kario, J. E., et al. (2001). Gender differences in associations of diurnal blood pressure variation, awake physical activity, and sleep quality with negative affect: The Work Site Blood Pressure Study. *Hypertension, 38,* 997–1002.

Keller, A., et al. (2003). Progressive loss of cerebellar volume in child-hood-onset schizophrenia. *American Journal of Psychiatry, 160,* 128–133.

Keller, M. B., et al. (2000). A Comparison of nefazodone, the cognitive behavioral-analysis system of psychotherapy, and their combination for the treatment of chronic depression. *The New England Journal of Medicine, 342*(20), 1462–1470.

Kellerman, J., Lewis, J., & Laird, J. D. (1989). Looking and loving: The effects of mutual gaze on feelings of romantic love. *Journal of Research in Personality, 23,* 145–161.

Kelley, H. H., & Michela, J. L. (1980). Attribution theory and research. *Annual Review of Psychology, 31,* 457–501.

Kellman, P. J., & von Hofsetn, C. (1992). The world of the moving infant. In C. Rovee-Collier & L. P. Lipsitt (eds.), *Advances in Infancy Research* (Vol. 7). Norwood, NJ: Ablex.

Kelly, A. (2000). Helping construct desirable identities: A self-presentational view of psychotherapy. *Psychological Bulletin, 126*(4), 475–494.

Kenchaiah, S., et al. (2002). Obesity and the risk of heart failure. *New England Journal of Medicine online, 347*(5), 305–313.

Kendler, K. S., et al. (2000a). Illicit psychoactive substance use, heavy use, abuse, and dependence in a US population-based sample of male twins. *Archives of General Psychiatry, 57,* 261–269.

Kendler, K. S., Myers, J. M., & Neale, M. C. (2000b). A multidimensional twin study of mental health in women. *American Journal of Psychiatry, 157,* 506–513.

Kendler, K. S., Thornton, L. M., Gilman, S. E., & Kessler, R. C. (2000c). Sexual orientation in a U.S. national sample of twin and nontwin sibling pairs. *American Journal of Psychiatry, 157,* 1843–1846.

Kendler, K. S., Thornton, L. M., & Pedersen, N. L. (2000d). Tobacco consumption in Swedish twins reared apart and reared together. *Archives of General Psychiatry, 57,* 886–892.

Kendler, K. S., Myers, J., Prescott, C. A., & Neale, M. C. (2001). The genetic epidemiology of irrational fears and phobias in men. *Archives of General Psychiatry, 58*(3), 257–265.

Kennedy, C. H. (2002). Effects of REM sleep deprivation on a multiple schedule of appetitive reinforcement. *Behavioural Brain Research, 128*(2), 205–214.

Kenrick, D. T., & MacFarlane, S. W. (1986). Ambient temperature and horn honking. *Environment and Behavior, 18,* 179–191.

Keppel, B. (2002). Kenneth B. Clark in the patterns of American culture. *American Psychologist, 57*(1), 29–37.

Kéri, S. (2003). Genetics, psychology, and determinism. *American Psychologist, 58*(4), 319.

Kerns, J. G., & Berenbaum, H. (2002). Cognitive impairments associated with formal thought disorder in people with schizophrenia. *Journal of Abnormal Psychology, 111*(2), 211–224.

Kessler, R. C. (2003). Epidemiology of women and depression. *Journal of Affective Disorders, 74*(1), 5–13.

Kessler, R. C., et al. (2003). The epidemiology of major depressive disorder: Results from the National Comorbidity Survey Replication (NCS-R). *Journal of the American Medical Association, 289*(23), 3095–3105.

Kessler, R. C., et al. (2005a). Lifetime prevalence and age-of-onset distributions of DSM-IV disorders in the National Comorbidity Survey Replication. *Archives of General Psychiatry, 62*(6), 593-602.

Kessler, R. C., Chiu, W. T., Demler, O., & Walters, E. E. (2005b). Prevalence, severity, and comorbidity of 12-month DSM-IV disorders in the National Comorbidity Survey Replication. *Archives of General Psychiatry, 62*(6), 617–627.

Key, A., Lacey, J. H., & Nussey, S. (2001). Do starvation diets lead to irreversible lung changes? *European Eating Disorders Review, 9*(5), 348–353.

Keyes, C. L. M., & Haidt, J. (2003). *Flourishing: Positive psychology and the life well-lived.* Washington, DC: American Psychological Association.

Kiecolt-Glaser, J. K., Marucha, P. T., Atkinson, C., & Glaser, R. (2001). Hypnosis as a modulator of cellular immune dysregulation during acute stress. *Journal of Consulting & Clinical Psychology, 69*(4), 674–682.

Kiecolt-Glaser, J. K., McGuire, L., Robles, T. F., & Glaser, R. (2002a). Psychoneuroimmunology and psychosomatic medicine: Back to the future. *Psychosomatic Medicine, 64*(1), 15–28.

Kiecolt-Glaser, J. K., McGuire, L., Robles, T. F., & Glaser, R. (2002b). Emotions, morbidity, and mortality: New perspectives from psychoneuroimmunology. *Annual Review of Psychology, 53*(1), 83–107.

Kilshaw, D., & Annett, M. (1983). Right- and left-hand skill: Effects of age, sex, and hand preferences showing superior in left-handers. *British Journal of Psychology, 74,* 253–268.

Kim, B. S. K., Brenner, B. R., Liang, C. T. H., & Asay, P. A. (2003). A qualitative study of adaptation experiences of 1.5-generation Asian Americans. *Cultural Diversity & Ethnic Minority Psychology, 9*(2), 156–170.

Kim, B. S. K., & Omizo, M. M. (2003). Asian cultural values, attitudes toward seeking professional psychological help, and willingness to see a counselor. *Counseling Psychologist, 31*(3), 343–361.

Kim, H., et al. (2002). Oxidative damage causes formation of lipofuscin-like substances in the hippocampus of the senescence-accelerated mouse after kainate treatment. *Behavioural Brain Research, 131*(1–2), 211–220.

Kim, J., et al. (2000). Regional neural dysfunctions in chronic schizophrenia studied with positron emission tomography. *American Journal of Psychiatry, 157,* 542–548.

Kim, K., & Rohner, R. P. (2002). Parental warmth, control, and involvement in schooling: Predicting academic achievement among Korean American adolescents. *Journal of Cross-Cultural Psychology, 33*(2), 127–140.

Kimble, D. P. (1988). *Biological psychology.* New York: Holt, Rinehart and Winston.

King, L. A., & Emmons, R. A. (1990). Conflict over emotional expression: Psychological and physical correlates. *Journal of Personality & Social Psychology, 58*(5), 864–877.

King, L. A., & Emmons, R. A. (1991). Psychological, physical, and interpersonal correlates of emotional expressiveness, conflict, and control. *European Journal of Personality, 5*(2), 131–150.

King, R. (2000). Cited in L. Frazier (2000), The new face of HIV is young, black. *The Washington Post,* July 16, p. C01.

King, S. (2005). Virtual reality heals 9/11 wounds. Cited in M. Lake (2005), http://www.cnn.com/2005/TECH/04/29/spark.virtual/index.html.

Kinnunen, T., Zamansky, H. S., & Block, M. L. (1994). Is the hypnotized subject lying? *Journal of Abnormal Psychology, 103,* 184–191.

Kinsey, A. C., Pomeroy, W. B., & Martin, C. E. (1948). *Sexual behavior in the human male.* Philadelphia: W. B. Saunders.

Kinsey, A. C., Pomeroy, W. B., Martin, C. E., & Gebhard, P. H. (1953). *Sexual behavior in the human female.* Philadelphia: W. B. Saunders.

Kirsch, I. (2000). The response set theory of hypnosis. *American Journal of Clinical Hypnosis, 42*(3–4), 274–292.

Kirsh, S. J., & Olczak, P. V. (2002). The effects of extremely violent comic books on social information processing. *Journal of Interpersonal Violence, 17*(11), 1160–1178.

Kite, M. E., et al. (2001). Women psychologists in academe: Mixed progress, unwarranted complacency. *American Psychologist, 56*(12), 1080–1098.

Klaczynski, P. A. (2001). Framing effects on adolescent task representations, analytic and heuristic processing and decision making. Implications for the normative/descriptive gap. *Journal of Applied Developmental Psychology, 22*(3), 289–309.

Kleindienst, N., & Greil, W. (2003). Lithium in the long-term treatment of bipolar disorders. *European Archives of Psychiatry & Clinical Neuroscience, 253*(3), 120–125.

Kleinke, C. L. (1977). Compliance to requests made by gazing and touching experimenters in field settings. *Journal of Experimental Social Psychology, 13,* 218–223.

Kleinke, C. L. (1986). Gaze and eye contact. *Psychological Review, 100,* 78–100.

Kleinmuntz, B., & Szucko, J. J. (1984). Lie detection in ancient and modern times. *American Psychologist, 39,* 766–776.

Klüver, H., & Bucy, P. C. (1939). Preliminary analysis of functions of the temporal lobe in monkeys. *Archives of Neurology and Psychiatry, 42,* 979–1000.

Knafo, A., Iervolino, A. C., & Plomin, R. (2005). Masculine girls and feminine boys: Genetic and environmental contributions to atypical gender development in early childhood. *Journal of Personality & Social Psychology, 88*(2), 400–412.

Kobasa, S. C. O. (1990). Stress-resistant personality. In R. E. Ornstein & C. Swencionis (eds.), *The healing brain* (pp. 219–230). New York: The Guilford Press.

Kobasa, S. C. O., Maddi, S. R., Puccetti, M. C., & Zola, M. A. (1994). Effectiveness of hardiness, exercise, and social support as resources against illness. In A. Steptoe & J. Wardle (eds.), *Psychosocial processes and health* (pp. 247–260). Cambridge, U.K.: Cambridge University Press.

Kohlberg, L. (1969). *Stages in the development of moral thought and action.* New York: Holt, Rinehart and Winston.

Kohlberg, L. (1981). *The philosophy of moral development.* San Francisco: Harper & Row.

Kohout, J., & Williams, S. (1999). Far more psychology degrees are going to women. *APA Monitor online, 30*(10).

Kolata, G. (2000). True secret of fad diets: It's calories. *The New York Times,* January 18, p. F7.

Kolata, G. (2002). With no answers on risks, steroid users still say "yes." *The New York Times online,* December 2.

Kolko, D. J., & Rickard-Figueroa, J. L. (1985). Effects of video games on the adverse corollaries of chemotherapy in pediatric oncology patients. *Journal of Consulting and Clinical Psychology, 53,* 223–228.

Kollins, S. H., & Rush, C. R. (2002). Sensitization to the cardiovascular but not subject-rated effects of oral cocaine in humans. *Biological Psychiatry, 51*(2), 143–150.

Kooijman, C. M., et al. (2000). Phantom pain and phantom sensations in upper limb amputees: An epidemiological study. *Pain, 87*(1), 33–41.

Kopelman, M. D. (2002). Disorders of memory. *Brain, 125*(10), 2152–2190.

Kosonen, P., & Winne, P. H. (1995). Effects of teaching statistical laws on reasoning about everyday problems. *Journal of Educational Psychology, 87,* 33–46.

Koss, M. P. (1993). Rape. *American Psychologist, 48,* 1062–1069.

Koss, M. P. (2003). Evolutionary models of why men rape: Acknowledging the complexities. In C. B. Travis (ed). *Evolution, gender, and rape* (pp. 191–205). Cambridge, MA: MIT Press.

Koss, M. P., Bailey, J. A., Yuan, N. P., Herrera, V. M., & Lichter, E. L. (2003). Depression and PTSD in survivors of male violence: Research and training initiatives to facilitate recovery. *Psychology of Women Quarterly, 27*(2), 130–142.

Koss, M. P., Figueredo, A. J., & Prince, R. J. (2002). Cognitive mediation of rape's mental, physical and social health impact: Tests of four models in cross-sectional data. *Journal of Consulting & Clinical Psychology, 70*(4), 926–941.

Koss, M. P., & Kilpatrick, D. G. (2001). Rape and sexual assault. In E. Gerrity et al. (eds.). *The mental health consequences of torture. Plenum series on stress and coping* (pp. 177–193). Dordrecht, Netherlands: Kluwer Academic Publishers.

Kosslyn, S. M. (1994). *Image and brain.* Cambridge, MA: The MIT Press, a Bradford Book.

Kouros-Mehr, H., et al. (2001). Identification of non-functional human VNO receptor genes provides evidence for vestigiality of the human VNO. *Chemical Sciences, 26*(9), 1167–1174.

Kramer, P. D. (2003). Your Zoloft might prevent a heart attack. *The New York Times,* June 22, p. WK3.

Krantz, D. S., Contrada, R. J., Hill, D. R., & Friedler, E. (1988). Environmental stress and biobehavioral antecedents of coronary heart disease. *Journal of Consulting and Clinical Psychology, 56,* 333–341.

Krcmar, M., & Cooke, M. C. (2001). Children's moral reasoning and their perceptions of television violence. *Journal of Communication, 51*(2), 300–316.

Kroger, J. K., et al. (2002). Recruitment of anterior dorsolateral prefrontal cortex in human reasoning: A parametric study of relational complexity. *Cerebral Cortex, 12*(5), 477–485.

Kübler-Ross, E. (1969). *On death and dying.* New York: Macmillan.

Kuczmarski, R. J., et al. (2000, December 4). CDC Growth charts: United States. Advance data from vital and health statistics; no. 314. Hyattsville, MD: National Center for Health Statistics.

Kurzweil, R. (2000, June 19). Will my PC be smarter than I am? *Time Magazine,* pp. 82–83.

Kurzweil, R. C. (2004). Generating visual art. U.S. patent application #20040012590, January 22.

Kurzweil, R. C., & Keklak, J. A. (2003). Basic poetry generation. U.S. patent application #20030036040, February 20.

Kwate, N. O. A. (2001). Intelligence or misorientation? Eurocentrism in the WICS-III. *Journal of Black Psychology, 27*(2), 221–238.

Kyle, T. M., & Williams, S. (2000, May). Results of the 1998–1999 APA survey of graduate departments of psychology. APA Research Office. Washington, DC: American Psychological Association.

Lackner, J. M., Carosella, A. M., & Feuerstein, M. (1996). Pain expectancies, pain, and functional self-efficacy expectancies as determinants of disability in patients with chronic low back disorders. *Journal of Consulting and Clinical Psychology, 64,* 212–220.

Lahti, A. C., et al. (2001). Abnormal patterns of regional cerebral blood flow in schizophrenia with primary negative symptoms during an effortful auditory recognition task. *American Journal of Psychiatry, 158,* 1797–1808.

Lal, S. (2002). Giving children security: Mamie Phipps Clark and the radicalization of child psychology. *American Psychologist, 57*(1), 20–28.

Lam, A. G., & Sue, S. (2001). Client diversity. *Psychotherapy: Theory, Research, Practice, Training, 38*(4), 479–486.

Lamb, M. E., & Baumrind, D. (1978). Socialization and personality development in the preschool years. In M. E. Lamb (ed.), *Social and personality development.* New York: Holt, Rinehart and Winston.

Lambert, W. E., Genesee, F., Holobow, N., & Chartrand, L. (1991). *Bilingual education for majority English-speaking children.* Montreal, Canada: McGill University.

Lancaster, T., Stead, L., Silagy, C., & Sowden, A. (2000). Regular review: Effectiveness of interventions to help people stop smoking: Findings from the Cochrane Library. *British Medical Journal, 321,* 355–358.

Lane, A. M., Jones, L., & Stevens, M. J. (2002). Coping with failure: The effects of self-esteem and coping on changes in self-efficacy. *Journal of Sport Behavior, 25*(4), 331–345.

Lang, A. R., Goeckner, D. J., Adesso, V. J., & Marlatt, G. A. (1975). Effects of alcohol on aggression in male social drinkers. *Journal of Abnormal Psychology, 84,* 508–518.

Lang, E. V., et al. (2000). Adjunctive non-pharmacological analgesia for invasive medical procedures: a randomised trial. *The Lancet, 355,* 1486–1490.

Lang, F. R., & Heckhausen, J. (2001). Perceived control over development and subjective well-being: Differential benefits across adulthood. *Journal of Personality & Social Psychology, 81*(3), 509–523.

Langer, E. J., Rodin, J., Beck, P., Weinan, C., & Spitzer, L. (1979). Environmental determinants of memory improvement in late adulthood. *Journal of Personality and Social Psychology, 37,* 2003–2013.

Langlois, J. H., et al. (2000). Maxims or myths of beauty? A meta-analytic and theoretical review. *Psychological Bulletin, 126*(3), 390–423.

Larkin, M. (2000). Can lost hearing be restored? *The Lancet, 356,* 741–748.

Larrick, R. P. (1993). Motivational factors in decision theories. *Psychological Bulletin, 113,* 440–450.

Larson, R., & Richards, M. H. (1991). Daily companionship in late childhood and early adolescence. *Child Development, 62,* 284–300.

Lashley, K. S. (1950). In search of the engram. In *Symposium of the Society for Experimental Biology* (Vol. 4). New York: Cambridge University Press.

Latané, B., & Dabbs, J. M. (1975). Sex, group size, and helping in three cities. *Sociometry, 38,* 180–194.

Latimer, W. W., Winters, K. C., Stinchfield, R., & Traver, R. E. (2000). Demographic, individual, and interpersonal predictors of adolescent alcohol and marijuana use following treatment. *Psychology of Addictive Behaviors, 14*(2), 162–173.

Laumann, E. O., Gagnon, J. H., Michael, R. T., & Michaels, S. (1994). *The social organization of sexuality.* Chicago: University of Chicago Press.

Laumann, E. O., Paik, A., & Rosen, R. C. (1999). Sexual dysfunction in the United States. Prevalence and predictors. *Journal of the American Medical Association, 281*(6), 537–544.

Laungani, P. (2002). The counselling interview: First impressions. *Counselling Psychology Quarterly, 15*(1), 107–113.

Lavee, Y., & Ben-Ari, A. (2003). Daily stress and uplifts during times of political tension: Jews and Arabs in Israel. *American Journal of Orthopsychiatry, 73*(1), 65–73.

Lavie, P. (2001). Current concepts: Sleep disturbances in the wake of traumatic events. *New England Journal of Medicine, 345,* 1825–1832.

Lawton, C. A., & Morrin, K. A. (1999). Gender differences in pointing accuracy in computer-simulated 3D mazes. *Sex Roles, 40*(1–2), 73–92.

Lazar, S. W., et al. (2000). Functional brain mapping of the relaxation response and meditation. *Neuroreport: For Rapid Communication of Neuroscience Research, 11*(7), 1581–1585.

Lazarus, R. S., DeLongis, A., Folkman, S., & Gruen, R. (1985). Stress and adaptational outcomes. *American Psychologist, 40,* 770–779.

Leahey, E., & Guo, G. (2001). Gender differences in mathematical trajectories. *Social Forces, 80*(2), 713–732.

Leather, P., Beale, D., & Sullivan, L. (2003). Noise, psychosocial stress and their interaction in the workplace. *Journal of Environmental Psychology, 23*(2), 213–222.

Le Bon, G. (1960). *The crowd.* New York: Viking. (Original work published 1895)

Lecci, L., & Cohen, D. J. (2002). Perceptual consequences of an illness-concern induction and its relation to hypochondriacal tendencies. *Health Psychology, 21*(2), 147–156.

LeDoux, J. E. (1997). Emotion, memory, and the brain. *Scientific American mysteries of the mind, Special Issue Vol. 7,* No. 1, 68–75.

LeDoux, J. E. (1998). Fear and the brain: Where have we been, and where are we going? *Biological Psychiatry, 44*(12), 1229–1238.

Lee, I-M., Sesso, H. D., & Paffenbarger, R. S., Jr. (2000). Physical activity and coronary heart disease risk in men: Does the duration of exercise episodes predict risk? *Circulation, 102,* 981–986.

Leenaars, A. A. (2006). Altruistic suicide: Update. *Archives of Suicide Research, 10*(1), 99.

Lefcourt, H. M. (1997). Cited in R. A. Clay (1997), Researchers harness the power of humor. *APA Monitor, 28*(9), 1, 18.

Lefcourt, H. M., Miller, R. S., Ware, E. E., & Sherk, D. (1981). Locus of control as a modifier of the relationship between stressors and moods. *Journal of Personality and Social Psychology, 41,* 357–369.

Lehman, B. J., & Crano, W. D. (2002). The pervasive effects of vested interest on attitude-criterion consistency in political judgment. *Journal of Experimental Social Psychology, 38*(2), 101–112.

Leichsenring, F., & Leibing, E. (2003). The effectiveness of psychodynamic therapy and cognitive behavior therapy in the treatment of personality disorders: A meta-analysis. *American Journal of Psychiatry, 160,* 1223–1232.

Leinders-Zufall, T., et al. (2000). Ultrasensitive pheromone detection by mammalian vomeronasal neurons. *Nature, 405,* 792–796.

Leitch, M. L. (2005). Just like bodies, psyches can drown in disasters. *The New York Times online,* May 31.

Leitenberg, H., & Henning, K. (1995). Sexual fantasy. *Psychological Bulletin, 117*(3), 469–496.

Leland, J. (2005). The Schiavo case: Final moments. *The New York Times online,* March 27.

Le Marec, N., Beaulieu, I., & Godbout, R. (2001). Four hours of paradoxical sleep deprivation impairs alternation performance in a water maze in the rat. *Brain & Cognition, 46*(1–2), 195–197.

Le Melledo, J., et al. (2001). The influence of Type A behavior pattern on the response to the panicogenic agent CCK-4. *Journal of Psychosomatic Research, 51*(3), 513–520.

Lensvelt-Mulders, G., & Hettema, J. (2001). Genetic analysis of autonomic reactivity to psychologically stressful situations. *Biological Psychology, 58*(1), 25–40.

Leonard, S., Steiger, H., & Kao, A. (2003). Childhood and adulthood abuse in bulimic and nonbulimic women: Prevalences and psychological correlates. *International Journal of Eating Disorders, 33*(4), 397–405.

Leonardo, E. D., & Hen, R. (2006). Genetics of affective and anxiety disorders. *Annual Review of Psychology, 57,* 117–137.

Leor, J., Poole, K., & Kloner, R. A. (1996). Sudden cardiac death triggered by an earthquake. *New England Journal of Medicine, 334,* 413–419.

Lepola, J., Vaurus, M., & Maeki, H. (2000). Gender differences in the development of academic self-concept of attainment from the 2nd to the 6th grade: Relations with achievement and perceived motivational orientation. *Psychology: The Journal of the Hellenic Psychological Society, 7*(3), 290–308.

Leppel, K. (2002). Similarities and differences in the college persistence of men and women. *Review of Higher Education: Journal of the Association for the Study of Higher Education, 25*(4), 433–450.

Lerner, A. G., et al. (2000). LSD-induced hallucinogen persisting perception disorder treatment with clonidine: An open pilot study. *International Clinical Psychopharmacology, 15*(1), 35–37.

Leserman, J., et al. (2000). Impact of stressful life events, depression, social support, coping, and cortisol on progression to AIDS. *American Journal of Psychiatry, 157,* 1221–1228.

Leslie, M. B., Stein, J. A., & Rotheram-Borus, M. J. (2002). Sex-specific predictors of suicidality among runaway youth. *Journal of Community Psychology, 31*(1), 27–40.

Lester, D., Yang, B., & Lindsay, M. (2004). Suicide bombers: Are psychological profiles possible? *Studies in Conflict & Terrorism, 27*(4), 283–295.

Levenston, G. K., Patrick, C. J., Bradley, M. M., & Lang, P. J. (2000). The psychopath as observer: Emotion and attention in picture processing. *Journal of Abnormal Psychology, 109*(3), 373–385.

Levine, D. (2000). Virtual attraction: What rocks your boat. *CyberPsychology & Behavior, 3*(4), 565–573.

Levine, R. V., & Norenzayan, A. (1999). The pace of life in 31 countries. *Journal of Cross-Cultural Psychology, 30*(2), 178–205.

Levinson, D. J. (1996). *The seasons of a woman's life.* New York: Knopf.

Levinson, D. J., Darrow, C. N., Klein, E. B., Levinson, M. H., & McKee, B. (1978). *The seasons of a man's life.* New York: Knopf.

Levy, D., et al. (2000). Evidence for a gene influencing blood pressure on chromosome 17: Genome scan linkage results for longitudinal blood pressure phenotypes in subjects from the Framingham Heart Study. *Hypertension, 36,* 477–483.

Lewin, T. (1995). Parents poll shows higher incidence of child abuse. *The New York Times,* December 7, p. B16.

Lewinsohn, P. M., Brown, R. A., Seeley, J. R., & Ramsey, S. E. (2000a). Psychological correlates of cigarette smoking abstinence, experimentation, persistence, and frequency during adolescence. *Nicotine & Tobacco Research, 2*(2), 121–131.

Lewinsohn, P. M., Rohde, P., Seeley, J. R., Klein, D. N., & Gotlib, I. H. (2000b). Natural course of adolescent major depressive disorder in a community sample: Predictors of recurrence in young adults. *American Journal of Psychiatry, 157,* 1584–1591.

Lewis-Fernández, R., & Kleinman, A. (1994). Culture, personality, and psychopathology. *Journal of Abnormal Psychology, 103,* 67–71.

Leyton, M., et al. (2000). Acute tyrosine depletion and alcohol ingestion in healthy women. *Alcoholism: Clinical & Experimental Research, 24*(4) 459–464.

Li, G., Baker, S. P., Smialek, J. E., & Soderstrom, C. A. (2001). Use of alcohol as a risk factor for bicycling injury. *Journal of the American Medical Association, 284,* 893–896.

Lidow, M. S., et al. (2001). Antipsychotic treatment induces alterations in dendrite- and spine-associated proteins in dopamine-rich areas of the primate cerebral cortex. *Biological Psychiatry, 49*(1), 1–12.

Lieber, C. S. (1990). Cited in Barroom biology: How alcohol goes to a woman's head. *The New York Times,* January 14, p. E24.

Lillqvist, O., & Lindeman, M. (1998). Belief in astrology as a strategy for self-verification and coping with negative life-events. *European Psychologist, 3*(3), 202–208.

Lin, J., & Thompson, D. S. (2001). Treating premenstrual dysphoric disorder using serotonin agents. *Journal of Women's Health & Gender-Based Medicine, 10*(8), 745–750.

Lindeman, M. (1998). Motivation, cognition and pseudoscience. *Scandinavian Journal of Psychology, 39*(4), 257–265.

Linden, W., Chambers, L., Maurice, J., & Lenz, J. W. (1993). Sex differences in social support, self-deception, hostility, and ambulatory cardiovascular activity. *Health Psychology, 12,* 376–380.

Lips, H. (1993). *Sex and gender* (2nd ed.). Mountain View, CA: Mayfield.

Lisanby, S. H., et al. (2000). The effects of electroconvulsive therapy on memory of autobiographical and public events. *Archives of General Psychiatry, 57*(6), 581–590.

Little, A. C., & Perrett, D. I. (2002). Putting beauty back in the eye of the beholder. *Psychologist, 15*(1), 28–32.

Littner, M., et al. (2001). Practice parameters for the treatment of narcolepsy: An update for 2000. *Sleep: Journal of Sleep & Sleep Disorders Research, 24*(4), 451–466.

Lochman, J. E. (1992). Cognitive-behavioral intervention with aggressive boys. *Journal of Consulting and Clinical Psychology, 60,* 426–432.

Lochman, J. E., & Dodge, K. A. (1994). Social-cognitive processes of severely violent, moderately aggressive, and nonaggressive boys. *Journal of Consulting and Clinical Psychology, 62,* 366–374.

Loftus, E. F. (1979). The malleability of human memory. *American Scientist, 67*(3), 312–320.

Loftus, E. F. (1983). Silence is not golden. *American Psychologist, 38,* 564–572.

Loftus, E. F. (1993). Psychologists in the eyewitness world. *American Psychologist, 48,* 550–552.

Loftus, E. F. (1994). Conference on memory, Harvard Medical School. Cited in D. Goleman (1994), Miscoding is seen as the root of false memories. *The New York Times,* May 31, pp. C1, C8.

Loftus, E. F. (1997). Cited in Loftus consulting in Oklahoma City bombing trial. *APA Monitor, 28*(4), 8–9.

Loftus, E. F. (2001). Imagining the past. *Psychologist, 14*(11), 584–587.

Loftus, E. F., & Loftus, G. R. (1980). On the permanence of stored information in the brain. *American Psychologist, 35,* 409–420.

Loftus, E. F., & Palmer, J. C. (1974). Reconstruction of automobile destruction. *Journal of Verbal Learning and Verbal Behavior, 13,* 585–589.

Loftus, G. R. (1983). The continuing persistence of the icon. *Behavioral and Brain Sciences, 6,* 28.

"Longer, healthier, better." (1997). *The New York Times Magazine,* March 9, pp. 44–45.

Lonky, M. L. (2003). Human consciousness: A systems approach to the mind/brain interaction. *Journal of Mind & Behavior, 24*(1), 91–118.

López, P., Martín, J., & Cuadrado, M. (2002). Pheromone-mediated intrasexual aggression in male lizards, *Podarcis hispanicus. Aggressive Behavior, 28,* 154–163.

Lopez, S. R., & Guarnaccia, P. J. J. (2000). Cultural psychopathology: Uncovering the social world of mental illness. *Annual Review of Psychology, 51,* 571–598.

Lorenz, K. Z. (1981). *The foundations of ethology.* New York: Springer-Verlag.

Los Angeles Unified School District. (2000). Youth Suicide Prevention Information. http://www.sanpedro.com/spyc/suicide.htm

Louie, K., & Wilson, M. A. (2001). Temporally structured replay of awake hippocampal ensemble activity during rapid eye movement sleep. *Neuron, 29*(1), 145–156.

Loving, T. J., & Agnew, C. R. (2001). Socially desirable responding in close relationships: A dual-component approach and measure. *Journal of Social & Personal Relationships, 18*(4), 551–573.

Lu, L. (1999). Personal or environmental causes of happiness: A longitudinal analysis. *Journal of Social Psychology, 139*(1), 79–90.

Lu, L. (2001). Understanding happiness: A look into the Chinese folk psychology. *Journal of Happiness Studies, 2*(4) 407–432.

Luborsky, L., et al. (2002). The dodo bird verdict is alive and well—mostly. *Clinical Psychology: Science & Practice, 9*(1), 2–12.

Luchins, A. S. (1957). Primacy-recency in impression formation. In C. I. Hovland (ed.), *The order of presentation in persuasion.* New Haven, CT: Yale University Press.

Luchins, A. S., & Luchins, E. H. (1959) *Rigidity of behavior.* Eugene: University of Oregon Press.

Ludwick-Rosenthal, R., & Neufeld, R. W. J. (1993). Preparation for undergoing an invasive medical procedure. *Journal of Consulting and Clinical Psychology, 61,* 156–164.

Lundeberg, M. A., Fox, P. W., & Puncochar, J. (1994). Highly confident but wrong. *Journal of Educational Psychology, 86,* 114–121.

Luo, D., Thompson, L. A., & Detterman, D. K. (2006). The criterion validity of tasks of basic cognitive processes. *Intelligence, 34*(1), 79–120.

Lydiard, R. B. (2003). The role of GABA in anxiety disorders. *Journal of Clinical Psychiatry, 64*(Suppl3), 21–27.

Lykken, D. T., & Csikszentmihalyi, M. (2001). Happiness—stuck with what you've got? *Psychologist, 14*(9), 470–472.

Lykken, D. T., McGue, M., Tellegen, A., & Bouchard, T. J., Jr. (1992). Emergenesis: Genetic traits that may not run in families. *American Psychologist, 47,* 1565–1577.

Lynn, S. J., Shindler, K., & Meyer, E. (2003). Hypnotic suggestibility, psychopathology, and treatment outcome. *Sleep & Hypnosis, 5*(1), 2–10.

Maas, J. B. (1998). *Power sleep: Revolutionary strategies that prepare your mind and body for peak performance.* New York: Villard.

Maccoby, E. E. (1990). Gender and relationships. *American Psychologist, 45,* 513–520.

Maccoby, E. E. (1992). The role of parents in the socialization of children: An historical overview. *Developmental Psychology, 28,* 1006–1017.

MacDonald, D. J., & Standing, L. G. (2002). Does self-serving bias cancel the Barnum effect? *Social Behavior & Personality, 30*(6), 625–630.

MacDonald, K. (1992). Warmth as a developmental construct. *Child Development, 63,* 753–773.

MacDonald, T. K., MacDonald, G., Zanna, M. P., & Fong, G. T. (2000). Alcohol, sexual arousal, and intentions to use condoms in young men: Applying alcohol myopia theory to risky sexual behavior. *Health Psychology, 19,* 290–298.

Macfarlane, J. A. (1975). Olfaction in the development of social preferences in the human neonate. In M. A. Hofer (ed.), *Parent–infant interaction.* Amsterdam: Elsevier.

MacGregor, J. (2005). *Sunday money.* New York: HarperCollins.

Machleit, K. A., Eroglu, S. A., & Mantel, S. P. (2000). Perceived retail crowding and shopping satisfaction: What modifies this relationship? *Journal of Consumer Psychology, 9*(1), 29–42.

Maciejewski, P. K., Prigerson, H. G., & Mazure, C. M. (2000). Self-efficacy as a mediator between stressful life events and depressive symptoms: Differences based on history of prior depression. *British Journal of Psychiatry, 176,* 373–378.

MacKenzie, T. D., Bartecchi, C. E., & Schrier, R. W. (1994). The human costs of tobacco use. *New England Journal of Medicine, 330,* 975–980.

Mackey, R. H., et al. (2002). Correlates of aortic stiffness in elderly individuals: a subgroup of the cardiovascular health study. *American Journal of Hypertension, 15*(1), 16–23.

Macrae, C. N., Mitchell, J. P., & Pendry, L. F. (2002). What's in a forename? Cue familiarity and stereotypical thinking. *Journal of Experimental Social Psychology, 38*(2), 186–193.

Madigan, S., & O'Hara, R. (1992). Short-term memory at the turn of the century: Mary Whiton Calkins's memory research. *American Psychologist, 47*(2), 170–174.

Magnavita, N., et al. (1997). Type A behaviour pattern and traffic accidents. *British Journal of Medical Psychology, 70*(1), 103–107.

Maher, B. A., & Maher, W. B. (1994). Personality and psychopathology. *Journal of Abnormal Psychology, 103,* 72–77.

Mahmud, A., & Feely, F. (2003). Effect of smoking on arterial stiffness and pulse pressure amplification. *Hypertension, 41,* 183–187.

Maier, N. R. F., & Schneirla, T. C. (1935). *Principles of animal psychology.* New York: McGraw-Hill.

Maltby, N., Kirsch, I., Mayers, M., & Allen, G. J. (2002). Virtual reality exposure therapy for the treatment of fear of flying: A controlled investigation. *Journal of Consulting & Clinical Psychology, 70*(5), 1112–1118.

Mamtani, R., & Cimino, A. (2002). A primer of complementary and alternative medicine and its relevance in the treatment of mental health problems. *Psychiatric Quarterly, 73*(4), 367–381.

Mangelsdorf, D. (2002). Cited in Study shows how vitamin D prevents colon cancer. Reuters, May 16.

Manji, H. (2003). Depression, III: Treatments. *American Journal of Psychiatry, 160,* 24.

Maquet, P. (2001). The role of sleep in learning and memory. *Science, 294*(5544), 1048–1052.

Marian, V., & Neisser, U. (2000). Language-dependent recall of autobiographical memories. *Journal of Experimental Psychology: General, 129*(3), 361–368.

Markon, K. E., Krueger, R. F., Bouchard, T. J., Jr., & Gottesman, I. I. (2002). Normal and abnormal personality traits: Evidence for genetic and environmental relationships in the Minnesota Study of Twins Reared Apart. *Journal of Personality, 70*(5), 661–693.

Marks, I. M. (2002). The maturing of therapy: Some brief psychotherapies help anxiety/depressive disorders but mechanisms of action are unclear. *British Journal of Psychiatry, 180*(3), 200–204.

Marks, I. M., & Dar, R. (2000). Fear reduction by psychotherapies: Recent findings, future directions. *The British Journal of Psychiatry, 176,* 507–511.

Markus, H., & Kitayama, S. (1991). Culture and the self. *Psychological Review, 98*(2), 224–253.

Martin, R. A., & Lefcourt, H. M. (1983). Sense of humor as a moderator of the relation between stressors and moods. *Journal of Personality and Social Psychology, 45,* 1313–1324.

Martin, S. (2002). Easing migraine pain. *Monitor on Psychology, 33*(4), 71.

Martinez-Taboas, A., & Bernal, G. (2000). Dissociation, psychopathology, and abusive experiences in a nonclinical Latino university student group. *Cultural Diversity & Ethnic Minority Psychology, 6*(1), 32–41.

Martinot, D., Redersdorff, S., Guimond, S., & Dif, S. (2002). Ingroup versus outgroup comparisons and self-esteem: The role of group status and ingroup identification. *Personality & Social Psychology Bulletin, 28*(11), 1586–1600.

Marttunen, M. J., et al. (1998). Completed suicide among adolescents with no diagnosable psychiatric disorder. *Adolescence, 33*(131), 669–681.

Maslow, A. H. (1970). *Motivation and personality* (2nd ed.). New York: Harper & Row.

Masters, W. H., & Johnson, V. E. (1966). *Human sexual response.* Boston: Little, Brown.

Masters, W. H., & Johnson, V. E. (1970). *Human sexual inadequacy.* Boston: Little, Brown.

Matchen, J., & DeSouza, E. (2000). The sexual harassment of faculty members by students. *Sex Roles, 42*(3–4), 295–306.

Matlin, M. W., & Foley, H. J. (1995). *Sensation and perception* (4th ed.). Boston: Allyn & Bacon.

Matt, G. E., Vasquez, C., & Campbell, W. K. (1992). Mood-congruent recall of affectively toned stimuli: A meta-analytic review. *Clinical Psychology Review, 12,* 227–255.

Matthews, K. (1994). Cited in B. Azar (1994), Women are barraged by media on "the change." *APA Monitor, 25*(5), 24–25.

Matthews, K., et al. (1997). Women's Health Initiative. *American Psychologist, 52,* 101–116.

Maxwell, L. E., & Evans, G. W. (2000). The effects of noise on preschool children's pre-reading skills. *Journal of Environmental Psychology, 20*(1), 91–97.

May, R. (2005). How do we know what works? *Journal of College Student Psychotherapy, 19*(3), 69–73.

Mazur, A. (2002). Take a chimp, add language, melt the glaciers . . . *Journal for the Theory of Social Behaviour, 32*(1), 29–39.

Mazure, C. M., et al. (2000). Adverse life events and cognitive-personality characteristics in the prediction of major depression and antidepressant response. *American Journal of Psychiatry, 157,* 896–903.

Mazzella, R., & Feingold, A. (1994). The effects of physical attractiveness, race, socioeconomic status, and gender of defendants and victims on judgments of mock jurors. *Journal of Applied Social Psychology, 24*(15), 1315–1344.

McAndrew, F. T. (2002). New evolutionary perspectives on altruism: Multilevel-selection and costly-signaling theories. *Current Directions in Psychological Science, 11*(2), 79–82.

McCall, R. (1997). Cited in S. Sleek (1997), Can "emotional intelligence" be taught in today's schools? *APA Monitor, 28*(6), 25.

McCarley, R. W. (1992). Cited in S. Blakeslee (1992), Scientists unraveling chemistry of dreams. *The New York Times,* January 7, pp. C1, C10.

McClave, E. Z. (2000). Linguistic functions of head movements in the context of speech. *Journal of Pragmatics, 32*(7), 855–878.

McClelland, D. C. (1958). Methods of measuring human motivation. In J. W. Atkinson (ed.), *Motives in fantasy, action, and society.* Princeton, NJ: Van Nostrand.

McClelland, D. C. (1965). Achievement and entrepreneurship. *Journal of Personality and Social Psychology, 1,* 389–392.

McCourt, K., et al. (1999). Authoritarianism revisited: Genetic and environmental influences examined in twins reared apart and together. *Personality & Individual Differences, 27*(5), 985–1014.

McCrae, R. R., Costa, P. T., Jr., et al. (2000). Nature over nurture: Temperament, personality, and life span development. *Journal of Personality & Social Psychology, 78*(1), 173–186.

McDaniel, M. A., Glisky, E. L., Guynn, M. J., & Routhieaux, B. C. (1999). Prospective memory: A neuropsychological study. *Neuropsychology, 13*(1), 103–110.

McDermott, D. (1997). Yes, computers *can* think. *The New York Times,* May 14, p. A21.

McDonald-Miszczak, L., Gould, O. N., & Tychynski, D. (1999). Metamemory predictors of prospective and retrospective memory performance. *Journal of General Psychology, 126*(1) 37–52.

McDougall, W. (1904). The sensations excited by a single momentary stimulation of the eye. *British Journal of Psychology, 1,* 78–113.

McDougall, W. (1908). *An introduction to social psychology.* London: Methuen.

McElroy, S. L., et al. (2000). Placebo-controlled trial of sertraline in the treatment of binge eating disorder. *American Journal of Psychiatry, 157,* 1004–1006.

McFarlane, B. L., & Boxall, P. C. (2003). The role of social psychological and social structural variables in environmental activism: An example of the forest sector. *Journal of Environmental Psychology, 23*(1), 79–87.

McGaugh, J. L. .(2005) Emotional arousal and advanced amygdale activity: New evidence for the old perseveration-consolidation hypothesis. *Learning & Memory, 12*(2), 77–79.

McGaugh, J. L., McIntyre, C. K., & Power, A. E. (2002). Amygdala modulation of memory consolidation: Interaction with other brain systems. *Neurobiology of Learning & Memory, 78*(3), 539–552.

McGlashan, T. H., & Hoffman, R. E. (2000). Schizophrenia as a disorder of developmentally reduced synaptic connectivity. *Archives of General Psychiatry, 57,* 637–648.

McGovern, T. V. (1989). Task force eyes the making of a major. *APA Monitor, 20*(7), 50.

McGrath, E., Keita, G. P., Strickland, B. R., & Russo, N. F. (1990). *Women and depression.* Washington DC: American Psychological Association.

McGue, M., Pickens, R. W., & Svikis, D. S. (1992). Sex and age effects on the inheritance of alcohol problems: A twin study. *Journal of Abnormal Psychology, 101,* 3–17.

McGuire, L., Kiecolt-Glaser, J. K., & Glaser, R. (2002). Depressive symptoms and lymphocyte proliferation in older adults. *Journal of Abnormal Psychology, 111*(1), 192–197.

McGuire, S., Manke, B., Saudino, K. J., Reiss, D., Hetherington, E. M., & Plomin, R. (1999). Perceived competence and self-worth during adolescence: A longitudinal behavioral genetic study. *Child Development, 70*(6), 1283–1296.

McKee, P., & Barber, C. E. (2001). Plato's theory of aging. *Journal of Aging & Identity, 6*(2), 93–104.

McKelvie, P., & Low, J. (2002). Listening to Mozart does not improve children's spatial ability: Final curtains for the Mozart effect. *British Journal of Developmental Psychology, 20*(2), 241–258.

McKenzie, C. R. M., Lee, S. M., & Chen, K. K. (2002). When negative evidence increases confidence: Changes in belief after hearing two sides of a dispute. *Journal of Behavioral Decision Making, 15*(1), 1–18.

McKinley, J. C., Jr. (2000). It isn't just a game: Clues to avid rooting. *The New York Times online,* August 11.

McLaren, L. (2002). Cited in Wealthy women most troubled by poor body image. Reuters online, February 11.

McMurran, M., Blair, M., & Egan, V. (2002). An investigation of the correlations between aggression, impulsiveness, social problem-solving, and alcohol use. *Aggressive Behavior, 28,* 439–445.

McNeil, T. F., Cantor-Graae, E., & Weinberger, D. R. (2000). Relationship of obstetric complications and differences in size of brain structures in monozygotic twin pairs discordant for schizophrenia. *American Journal of Psychiatry, 157,* 203–212.

Mead, M. (1935). *Sex and temperament in three primitive societies.* New York: Dell.

Meerkerk, G., van den Eijnden, R. J. J. M., & Garretsen, H. F. L. (2006). Predicting compulsive Internet use: It's all about sex! *CyberPsychology & Behavior, 9*(1), 95–103.

Meijer, J., & Elshout, J. J. (2001). The predictive and discriminant validity of the zone of proximal development. *British Journal of Educational Psychology, 71*(1), 93–113.

Mellon, M. W., & McGrath, M. L. (2000). Empirically supported treatments in pediatric psychology: Nocturnal enuresis. *Journal of Pediatric Psychology, 25*(4), 193–214.

Melmed, R. N. (2003). Mind, body, and medicine: An integrative text. *American Journal of Psychiatry, 160*(3), 605–606.

Meltzoff, A. N. (1997). Cited in B. Azar (1997), New theory on development could usurp Piagetian beliefs. *APA Monitor, 28*(6), 9.

Meltzoff, A. N., & Gopnik, A. (1997). *Words, thoughts, and theories.* Cambridge, MA: MIT Press.

Melzack, R. (1999, August). From the gate to the neuromatrix. *Pain,* Suppl. 6, S121–S126.

Merluzzi, T. V., & Martinez Sanchez, M. (1997). Assessment of self-efficacy and coping with cancer. *Health Psychology, 16,* 163–170.

Metcalfe, J. (1986). Premonitions of insight predict impending error. *Journal of Experimental Psychology: Learning, Memory, and Cognition, 12,* 623–634.

Metz, R. (2005). Think of a number . . . Come on, think! *The New York Times online,* March 10.

Meyer, I. H. (2003). Prejudice, social stress, and mental health in lesbian, gay, and bisexual populations: Conceptual issues and research evidence. *Psychological Bulletin, 129*(5), 674–697.

Meyer-Lindenberg, A., et al. (2001). Evidence for abnormal cortical functional connectivity during working memory in schizophrenia. *American Journal of Psychiatry, 158,* 1809–1817.

Michael, R. T., Gagnon, J. H., Laumann, E. O., & Kolata, G. (1994). *Sex in America: A definitive survey.* Boston: Little, Brown.

Michelson, D., et al. (2000). Female sexual dysfunction associated with antidepressant administration: A randomized, placebo-controlled study of pharmacologic intervention. *American Journal of Psychiatry, 157,* 239–243.

Michinov, E., & Michinov, N. (2001). The similarity hypothesis: A test of the moderating role of social comparison orientation. *European Journal of Social Psychology, 31*(5), 549–555.

Middleman, M. A. (2000, May). Paper presented to the 40th Annual Conference on Cardiovascular Disease Epidemiology and Prevention of the American Heart Association, San Diego.

Migdow, J. (2003). The problem with pleasure. *Journal of Trauma & Dissociation, 4*(1), 5–25.

Milar, K. S. (2000). The first generation of women psychologists and the psychology of women. *American Psychologist, 55*(6), 616–619.

Miles, J. (2005). NASCAR nation. *The New York Times Book Review,* May 22, pp. 1, 10–11.

Milgram, S. (1963). Behavioral study of obedience. *Journal of Abnormal and Social Psychology, 67,* 371–378.

Milgram, S. (1974). *Obedience to authority.* New York: Harper & Row.

Miller, A. L., Wyman, S. E., Huppert, J. D., Glassman, S. L., & Rathus, J. H. (2000). Analysis of behavioral skills utilized by suicidal adolescents receiving dialectical behavior therapy. *Cognitive & Behavioral Practice, 7*(2), 183–187.

Miller, A. R., Rosenfeld, P. J., Soskins, M., & Jhee, M. (2002). P300 amplitude and topography in an autobiographical paradigm involving simulated amnesia. *Journal of Psychophysiology, 16*(1), 1–11.

Miller, G. A. (1956). The magical number seven, plus or minus two: Some limits on our capacity for processing information. *Psychological Review, 63,* 81–97.

Miller, G. E., & Cohen, S. (2001). Psychological interventions and the immune system: A meta-analytic review and critique. *Health Psychology, 20*(1), 47–63.

Miller, J. L. (1992). Trouble in mind. *Scientific American, 267*(3), 180.

Miller, L. (2006). The terrorist mind: I. A psychological and political analysis. *International Journal of Offender Therapy and Comparative Criminology, 50*(2), 121–138.

Miller, M. E., & Bowers, K. S. (1993). Hypnotic analgesia. *Journal of Abnormal Psychology, 102,* 29–38.

Miller, M. F., Barabasz, A. F., & Barabasz, M. (1991). Effects of active alert and relaxation hypnotic inductions on cold pressor pain. *Journal of Abnormal Psychology, 100,* 223–226.

Miller, N. B., Cowan, P. A., Cowan, C. P., Hetherington, E. M., & Clingempeel, W. G. (1993). Externalizing in preschoolers and early adolescents. *Developmental Psychology, 29,* 3–18.

Miller, N. E. (1944). Experimental studies of conflict. In J. McVicker Hunt (ed.). *Personality and the behavior disorders, Vol. I* (pp. 431–465). Oxford, U.K.: Ronald Press.

Miller, N. E. (1969). Learning of visceral and glandular responses. *Science, 163,* 434–445.

Miller, N. E. (1995). Clinical-experimental interactions in the development of neuroscience. *American Psychologist, 50,* 901–911.

Miller, N. E., & Dollard, J. (1941). *Social learning and imitation.* New Haven, CT: Yale University Press.

Miller, S. M., Shoda, Y., & Hurley, K. (1996). Applying cognitive-social theory to health-protective behavior: Breast self-examination in cancer screening. *Psychological Bulletin, 199,* 70–94.

Milne, R. D., Syngeniotis, A., Jackson, G., & Corballis, M. C. (2002). Mixed lateralization of phonological assembly in developmental dyslexia. *Neurocase, 8*(3), 205–209.

Milner, B. R. (1966). Amnesia following operation on temporal lobes. In C. W. M. Whitty & O. L. Zangwill (eds.), *Amnesia.* London: Butterworth.

Milstead, M., Lapsley, D., & Hale, C. (1993, March). *A new look at imaginary audience and personal fable.* Paper presented at the meeting of the Society for Research in Child Development, New Orleans, LA.

Milton, J., & Wiseman, R. (1999). Does psi exist? Lack of replication of an anomalous process of information transfer. *Psychological Bulletin, 125*(4), 387–391.

Mimeault, V., & Morin, C. M. (1999). Self-help treatment for insomnia: Bibliotherapy with and without professional guidance. *Journal of Consulting & Clinical Psychology, 67*(4), 511–519.

Mindell, J. A. (1993). Sleep disorders in children. *Health Psychology, 12,* 151–162.

Miniño, A. M., Heron, M., & Smith, B. L. (2006). Deaths: Preliminary data for 2004. http://www.cdc.gov/nchs/products/pubs/pubd/hestats/prelimdeaths04/preliminarydeaths04.htm, Figure 2.

Minton, H. L. (2000). Psychology and gender at the turn of the century. *American Psychologist, 55*(6), 613–615.

Mischel, W., & Shoda, Y. (1995). A cognitive-affective system theory of personality. *Psychological Review, 102,* 246–268.

Moeller, F. G., et al. (2001). Psychiatric aspects of impulsivity. *American Journal of Psychiatry, 158*(11), 1783–1793.

Molfese, V. J., DiLalla, L. F., & Bunce, D. (1997). Prediction of the intelligence test scores of 3- to 8-year-old children by home environment, socioeconomic status, and biomedical risks. *Merrill-Palmer Quarterly, 43*(2) 219–234.

Molfese, V. J., Modglin, A., & Molfese, D. L. (2003). The role of environment in the development of reading skills: A longitudinal study of preschool and school-age measures. *Journal of Learning Disabilities, 36*(1), 59–67.

Moliterno, D. J., et al. (1994). Coronary-artery vasoconstriction induced by cocaine, cigarette smoking, or both. *New England Journal of Medicine, 330,* 454–459.

Montgomery, G. H., DuHamel, K. N., & Redd, W. H. (2000). A meta-analysis of hypnotically induced analgesia: How effective is hypnosis? *International Journal of Clinical & Experimental Hypnosis, 48*(2), 138–153.

Moore, C. C., Romney, A. K., & Hsia, T. (2002). Cultural, gender, and individual differences in perceptual and semantic structures of basic colors in Chinese and English. *Journal of Cognition & Culture, 2*(1), 1–28.

Mordock, B. (1997). Skepticism, data, risky shift, polarization, and attitude change: Their role in implementing innovations. *Psychologist-Manager Journal, 1*(1), 41–46.

Morgan, D., et al. (2000). A peptide vaccination prevents memory loss in an animal model of Alzheimer's disease. *Nature, 408*(6815), 982–984.

Morin, C. M., Colecchi, C., Stone, J., Sood, R., & Brink, D. (1999). Behavioral and pharmacological therapies for late-life insomnia: A randomized controlled trial. *Journal of the American Medical Association, 281*(11), 991–999.

Moro, C., & Rodriguez, C. (2000). La creation des representations chez l'enfant au travers des processus de semiosis. *Enfance, 52*(3), 287–294.

Morris, M. W., Larrick, R. P., & Su, S. K. (1999). Misperceiving negotiation counterparts: When situationally determined bargaining behaviors are attributed to personality traits. *Journal of Personality & Social Psychology, 77*(1), 52–67.

Morris, W. N., Miller, R. S., & Spangenberg, S. (1977). The effects of dissenter position and task difficulty on conformity and response conflict. *Journal of Personality, 45*, 251–256.

Morrison, E. S., et al. (1980). *Growing up sexual.* New York: Van Nostrand Reinhold Co.

Moruzzi, G., & Magoun, H. W. (1949). Brain stem reticular formation and activation of the EEG. *Electroencephalography & Clinical Neurophysiology, 1*, 455–473.

Moss, D. P. (2002). Cited in R. A. Clay (2002), A renaissance for humanistic psychology. *Monitor on Psychology, 33*(8), 42–43.

Moss, E., & St-Laurent, D. (2001). Attachment at school age and academic performance. *Developmental Psychology, 37*(6), 863–874.

Mott, M. (2005). Did animals sense tsunami was coming? *National Geographic News.* Moyers, B. (1993). *Healing and the mind.* New York: Doubleday.

Mozaffarian, D., et al. (2003). Cereal, fruit, and vegetable fiber intake and the risk of cardiovascular disease in elderly individuals. *Journal of the American Medical Association, 289*, 1659–1666.

Muehlberger, A., Herrmann, M. J., Wiedemann, G., Ellgring, H., & Pauli, P. (2001). Repeated exposure of flight phobics to flights in virtual reality. *Behaviour Research & Therapy, 39*(9), 1033–1050.

Mueller, N., & Hulk, A. (2001). Crosslinguistic influence in bilingual language acquisition: Italian and French as recipient languages. *Bilingualism: Language & Cognition, 4*(1), 1–21.

Muir, G. D. (2000). Early ontogeny of locomotor behaviour: A comparison between altricial and precocial animals. *Brain Research Bulletin, 53*(5), 719–726.

Mukamal, K. J., Maclure, M., Muller, J. E., Sherwood, J. B., & Mittleman, M. A. (2001). Prior alcohol consumption and mortality following acute myocardial infarction. *Journal of the American Medical Association, 285*(15), 1965–1970.

Mulder, R. T. (2002). Personality pathology and treatment outcome in major depression: A review. *American Journal of Psychiatry, 159*(3), 359–371.

Mullen, B., et al. (1987). Newscasters' facial expressions and voting behavior of viewers. *Journal of Personality and Social Psychology, 51*(2), 291–295.

Mulnard, R. A., et al. (2000). Estrogen replacement therapy for treatment of mild to moderate Alzheimer disease. *Journal of the American Medical Association, 283*, 1007–1015.

Mulvihill, K. (2000). Many miss out on migraine remedies. *The New York Times online,* March 14.

Muñoz, R. F., Hollon, S. D., McGrath, E., Rehm, L. P., & VandenBos, G. R. (1994). On the AHCPR *Depression in Primary Care* guidelines: Further considerations for practitioners. *American Psychologist, 49*, 42–61.

Munro, G. D., & Munro, J. E. (2000). Using daily horoscopes to demonstrate expectancy confirmation. *Teaching of Psychology, 27*(2), 114–116.

Munson, L. J., Hulin, C., & Drasgow, F. (2000). Longitudinal analysis of dispositional influences and sexual harassment: Effects on job and psychological outcomes. *Personnel Psychology, 53*(1), 21–46.

Murray, H. A. (1938). *Explorations in personality.* New York: Oxford University Press.

Murtagh, D. R. R., & Greenwood, K. M. (1995). Identifying effective psychological treatments for insomnia: A meta-analysis. *Journal of Consulting and Clinical Psychology, 63*, 79–89.

Mussweiler, T., & Bodenhausen, G. V. (2002). I know you are, but what am I? Self-evaluative consequences of judging in-group and out-group members. *Journal of Personality & Social Psychology, 82*(1), 19–32.

Myers, L. B., & Brewin, C. R. (1994). Recall of early experience and the repressive coping style. *Journal of Abnormal Psychology, 103*, 288–292.

Myers, S. L. (2000). Female general in army alleges sex harassment. *The New York Times,* March 31, pp. A1, A22.

Nabel, E. G. (2003). Cardiovascular disease. *New England Journal of Medicine, 349*(1), 60–72.

Nader, K., Schafe, G. E., & Le Doux, J. E. (2000). Fear memories require protein synthesis in the amygdala for reconsolidation after retrieval. *Nature, 406*, 722–726.

Nagata, T., et al. (2001). Physical and sexual abuse histories in patients with eating disorders: A comparison of Japanese and American patients. *Psychiatry & Clinical Neurosciences, 55*(4), 333–340.

Nagourney, E. (2002). Neal E Miller is dead at 92; studied brain and behavior. *The New York Times,* April 2, p. A21.

Nagtegaal, J. E., et al. (2000). Effects of melatonin on the quality of life in patients with delayed sleep phase syndrome. *Journal of Psychosomatic Research, 48*(1), 45–50.

Nahas, G., Sutin, K., & Bennett, W. M. (2000). Review of "Marihuana and Medicine." *The New England Journal of Medicine online, 343*(7).

Naimi, T. S., et al. (2003a). Binge drinking among US adults. *Journal of the American Medical Association, 289*(1), 70–75.

Naimi, T. S., et al. (2003b). Definitions of binge drinking. *Journal of the American Medical Association, 289*(13), 1636.

Nantais, K. M., & Schellenberg, E. G. (1999). The Mozart effect: An artifact of preference. *Psychological Science, 10*(4), 370–373.

National Center for Health Statistics. (2002, April 21). Abstracted from Suicide statistics by age, race, and sex. *Monthly Vital Statistics Report, 48*(11). Atlanta: Centers for Disease Control and Prevention. http://www.cdc.gov/nchs/fastats/suicide.htm

National Science Foundation. (2002). Cited in Associated Press (2002), Study: Science literacy poor in U.S. Associated Press, April 30.

National Sleep Foundation. (2000a). Helping yourself to a good night's sleep. http://www.sleepfoundation.org/publications/goodnights.html.

National Sleep Foundation. (2000b). 2000 Omnibus Sleep in America Poll. http://www.sleepfoundation.org/publications/2000poll.html#3.

National Sleep Foundation. (2001, November 19). Events of 9-11 took their toll on Americans' sleep, particularly for women, according to new National Sleep Foundation poll. http://www.sleepfoundation.org/whatsnew/crisis_poll.html.

National Sleep Foundation. (2003). *2003 Sleep in America Poll.* Washington, DC: National Sleep Foundation. www.sleepfoundation.org.

Navarro, J. F., & Maldonado, E. (2002). Acute and subchronic effects of MDMA ("ecstasy") on anxiety in male mice tested in the elevated plus-maze. *Progress in Neuro-Psychopharmacology & Biological Psychiatry, 26*(6), 1151–1154.

Neiss, M. B., Sedikides, C., & Stevenson, J. (2002). Self-esteem: A behavioural genetic perspective. *European Journal of Personality, 16*(5), 351–368.

Neisser, U. (1991). A case of misplaced nostalgia. *American Psychologist, 46*(1), 34–36.

Neisser, U. (1993). Cited in D. J. Goleman (1993), Studying the secrets of childhood memory. *The New York Times,* April 6, pp. C1, C11.

Neisser, U. (1997a). Never a dull moment. *American Psychologist, 52,* 79–81.

Neisser, U. (1997b). Cited in S. Sleek (1997), Can "emotional intelligence" be taught in today's schools? *APA Monitor, 28*(6), 25.

Neisser, U., et al. (1996). Intelligence: Knowns and unknowns. *American Psychologist, 51,* 77–101.

Nelson, K., Hampson, J., & Shaw, L. K. (1993). Nouns in early lexicons: Evidence, explanations, and implications. *Journal of Child Language, 20,* 228.

Nestadt, G., et al. (2000). A family study of obsessive-compulsive disorder. *Archives of General Psychiatry, 57*(4), 358–363.

Nestadt, G., et al. (2006). Latent structure of the diagnostic and statistical manual of mental disorders, fourth edition personality disorder criteria. *Comprehensive Psychiatry, 47*(1), 54–62.

Neumark-Sztainer, D., et al. (2002a). Ethnic/racial differences in weight-related concerns and behaviors among adolescent girls and boys: Findings from Project EAT. *Journal of Psychosomatic Research, 53*(5), 963–974.

Neumark-Sztainer, D., Story, M., Hannan, P. J., & Croll, J. (2002b). Overweight status and eating patterns among adolescents: Where do youths stand in comparison with the Healthy People 2010 objectives? *American Journal of Public Health, 92*(5), 844–851.

Neveus, T., Cnattingius, S., Olsson, U., & Hetta, J. (2002). Sleep habits and sleep problems among a community sample of schoolchildren. *Journal of the American Academy of Child & Adolescent Psychiatry, 41*(7), 828.

Newcomb, M. D., & Locke, T. F. (2001). Intergenerational cycle of maltreatment: A popular concept obscured by methodological limitations. *Child Abuse & Neglect, 25*(9), 1219–1240.

Newport, E. L. (1998). Cited in B. Azar (1998), Acquiring sign language may be more innate than learned. *APA Monitor, 29*(4), 12.

Nezlek, J. B., Hampton, C. P., & Shean, G. D. (2000). Clinical depression and day-to-day social interaction in a community sample. *Journal of Abnormal Psychology, 109*(1), 11–19.

Ng, B. D., & Wiemer-Hastings, P. (2005). Addiction to the Internet and online gaming. *CyberPsychology & Behavior, 8*(2), 110–113.

Niaura, R., & Abrams, D. B. (2002). Smoking cessation: Progress, priorities, and prospectus. *Journal of Consulting and Clinical Psychology, 70*(3), 494–509.

Nichols, L. A., & Nicki, R. (2004). Development of a psychometrically sound Internet addiction scale: A preliminary step. *Psychology of Addictive Behaviors, 18*, 381–384.

NIMH. See National Institute of Mental Health.

96% of cosmos puzzles astronomers. (2003, June 20). Associated Press.

Nock, M. K., & Kazdin, A. E. (2002). Examination of affective, cognitive, and behavioral factors and suicide-related outcomes in children and young adolescents. *Journal of Community Psychology, 31*(1), 48–58.

Nolen-Hoeksema, S. (2000). The role of rumination in depressive disorders and mixed anxiety/depressive symptoms. *Journal of Abnormal Psychology, 109*(3), 504–511.

Nolen-Hoeksema, S. (2001). Gender differences in depression. *Current Directions in Psychological Science, 10*(5), 173–176.

Norton, A. (2000). A drink a day keeps brain in tip-top shape. Reuters News Agency online, July 21.

Norvell, N., & Belles, D. (1993). Psychological and physical benefits of circuit weight training in law enforcement personnel. *Journal of Consulting and Clinical Psychology, 61*, 520–527.

Novick, L. R., & Coté, N. (1992). The nature of expertise in anagram solution. In *Proceedings of the Fourteenth Annual Conference of the Cognitive Science Society*. Hillsdale, NJ: Erlbaum.

Nowicki, S., & Strickland, B. R. (1973). A locus of control scale. *Journal of Consulting & Clinical Psychology, 40*(1), 148–154.

Nuland, S. (2005). Do you want to live forever? *MIT Technology Review, 108*(2), 36–45.

Nurnberger, J. I., Jr., et al. (2001). Evidence for a locus on chromosome 1 that influences vulnerability to alcoholism and affective disorder. *American Journal of Psychiatry, 158*, 718–724.

Nyberg, L., et al. (2000). Large scale neurocognitive networks underlying episodic memory. *Journal of Cognitive Neuroscience, 12*(1), 163–173.

O'Brien, C. P. (1996). Recent developments in the pharmacotherapy of substance abuse. *Journal of Consulting and Clinical Psychology, 64*, 677–686.

O'Brien, L. T., & Crandall, C. S. (2003). Stereotype threat and arousal: Effects on women's math performance. *Personality & Social Psychology Bulletin, 29*(6), 782–789.

Octopus opens jam jar in one minute. (2000). Reuters News Agency online, June 1.

O'Dell, C. D., & Hoyert, M. D. (2002). Active and passive touch: A research methodology project. *Teaching of Psychology, 29*(4), 292–294.

O'Donohue, W., Yeater, E. A., & Fanetti, M. (2003). Rape prevention with college males: The roles of rape myth acceptance, victim empathy, and outcome expectancies. *Journal of Interpersonal Violence, 18*(5), 513–531.

Oehman, A., & Mineka, S. (2001). Fears, phobias, and preparedness: Toward an evolved module of fear and fear learning. *Psychological Review, 108*(3), 483–522.

Oettingen, G., Pak, H., & Schnetter, K. (2001). Self-regulation of goal-setting: Turning free fantasies about the future into binding goals. *Journal of Personality & Social Psychology, 80*(5), 736–753.

Ohayon, M. M., Guilleminault, C., & Priest, R. G. (1999). Night terrors, sleepwalking, and confusional arousals in the general population: Their frequency and relationship to other sleep and mental disorders. *Journal of Clinical Psychiatry, 60*(4), 268–276.

Ohno, H., Urushihara, R., Sei, H., & Morita, Y. (2002). REM sleep deprivation suppresses acquisition of classical eyeblink conditioning. *Sleep: Journal of Sleep Research & Sleep Medicine, 25*(8), 877–881.

Okazaki, S. (1997). Sources of ethnic differences between Asian American and white American college students on measures of depression and social anxiety. *Journal of Abnormal Psychology, 106*(1), 52–60.

Oktedalen, O., Solberg, E. E., Haugen, A. H., & Opstad, P. K. (2001). The influence of physical and mental training on plasma beta-endorphin level and pain perception after intensive physical exercise. *Stress & Health: Journal of the International Society for the Investigation of Stress, 17*(2), 121–127.

Olanow, W. M. (2000, July). Clinical and pathological perspective on Parkinsonism. Paper presented to the World Alzheimer Congress 2000, Washington, DC.

Oldenburg, D. (2005). A sense of doom: Animal instinct for disaster. *Washington Post,* January 9.

Olds, J. (1969). The central nervous system and the reinforcement of behavior. *American Psychologist, 24*, 114–132.

Olds, J., & Milner, P. (1954). Positive reinforcement produced by electrical stimulation of the septal area and other regions of the rat brain. *Journal of Comparative and Physiological Psychology, 47*, 419–427.

O'Leary, K. D. (2000). Are women really more aggressive than men in intimate relationships? *Psychological Bulletin, 126*(5), 685–689.

Olson, M. J. (2003). Counselor understanding of Native American spiritual loss. *Counseling & Values, 47*(2), 109–117.

Olthof, A., & Roberts, W. A. (2000). Summation of symbols by pigeons (*Columba livia*): The importance of number and mass of reward items. *Journal of Comparative Psychology, 114*(2), 158–166.

Omer, H., & Elitzur, A. C. (2001). What would you say to the person on the roof? A suicide prevention text. *Suicide & Life-Threatening Behavior, 31*(2), 129–139.

Orpen, C. (1995). The Multifactorial Achievement Scale as a predictor of salary growth and motivation among middle-managers. *Social Behavior & Personality, 23*(2), 159–162.

Paban, V., Soumireu-Mourat, B., & Alescio-Lautier, B. (2003). Behavioral effects of arginine-sup-8-vasopressin in the Hebb-Williams maze. *Behavioural Brain Research, 141*(1), 1–9.

Pace, S. (2004). A grounded theory of the flow experiences of Web users. *International Journal of Human-Computer Studies, 60*(3), 327–363.

Paffenbarger, R. S., Jr., et al. (1993). The association of changes in physical-activity level and other lifestyle characteristics with mortality among men. *New England Journal of Medicine, 328*, 538–545.

Page, K. (1999). The graduate. *Washington Post Magazine,* May 16, pp. 152, 18, 20.

Palmero, F., Breva, A., Diago, J. L., Diez, J. L., & Garcia, I. (2002). Funcionamiento psicofisiologico y susceptibilidad a la sintomatologia premenstrual en mujeres Tipo A y Tipo B. *Revista Internacional de Psicologia Clinica y de la Salud, 2*(1), 111–136.

Pappas, G., Queen, S., Hadden, W., & Fisher, G. (1993). The increasing disparity of mortality between socioeconomic groups in the United States, 1960 and 1986. *New England Journal of Medicine, 329*, 103–109.

Park, J., & Banaji, M. R. (2000). Mood and heuristics: The influence of happy and sad states on sensitivity and bias in stereotyping. *Journal of Personality & Social Psychology, 78*(6), 1005–1023.

Park, N., Peterson, C., & Seligman, M. E. P. (2005). *Character strengths in forty nations and fifty states.* Unpublished manuscript, University of Rhode Island.

Parker, A. (2001). The ganzfeld: Suggested improvements of an apparently successful method for psi research. *European Journal of Parapsychology, 16*, 23–29.

Parker, J. G., & Herrera, C. (1996). Interpersonal processes in friendship: A comparison of abused and nonabused children's experience. *Developmental Psychology, 32*, 1025–1038.

Parker, K. J., Kinney, L. F., Phillips, K. M., & Lee, T. M. (2001). Paternal behavior is associated with central neurohormone receptor binding patterns in meadow voles (*Microtus pennsylvanicus*). *Behavioral Neuroscience, 115*(6), 1341–1348.

Parr, L. A., Winslow, J. T., Hopkins, W. D., & de Waal, F. B. M. (2000). Recognizing facial cues: Individual discrimination by chimpanzees (*Pan troglodytes*) and Rhesus monkeys (*Macaca mulatta*). *Journal of Comparative Psychology, 114*(1), 47–60.

Parrott, A. (Ed.). (2003). Cognitive deficits and cognitive normality in recreational cannabis and ecstasy/MDMA users. *Human Psychopharmacology: Clinical & Experimental, 18*(2), 89–90.

Parsons, J. T., Halkitis, P. N., Bimbi, D., & Borkowski, T. (2000). Perceptions of the benefits and costs associated with condom use and unprotected sex among late adolescent college students. *Journal of Adolescence, 23*(4), 377–391.

Partenheimer, D. (2003, June 8). Remembering the good times, putting the bad times in perspective—How our memory helps make life pleasant: Research explains why most people are happy with their lives. Washington, DC: APA Press Release, Public Affairs Office.

Pasic, J., Levy, W. C., & Sullivan, M. D. (2003). Cytokines in depression and heart failure. *Psychosomatic Medicine, 65*(2), 181–193.

Pastor, L. H. (2004). Countering the psychological consequences of suicide terrorism. *Psychiatric Annals, 34*(9), 701–704.

Patterson, G. R., Dishion, T. J., & Yoerger, K. (2000). Adolescent growth in new forms of problem behavior: Macro- and micro-peer dynamics. *Prevention Science, 1*(1), 3–13.

Patterson, J. L. (2000). Observed and reported expressive vocabulary and word combinations in bilingual toddlers. *Journal of Speech, Language, & Hearing Research, 43*(1), 121–128.

Pavlov, I. (1927). *Conditioned reflexes.* London: Oxford University Press.

Paxton, S. J., & Phythian, K. (1999). Body image, self-esteem, and health status in middle and later adulthood. *Australian Psychologist, 34*(2), 116–121.

Pear, R. (2000). White House seeks to curb pills used to calm young. *The New York Times online,* March 20.

Pears, K. C., & Capaldi, D. M. (2001). Intergenerational transmission of abuse: A two-generational prospective study of an at-risk sample. *Child Abuse & Neglect, 25*(11), 1439–1461.

Pekala, R. J., Angelini, F., Kumar, V. K. (2001). The importance of fantasy-proneness in disassociation: A replication. *Contemporary Hypnosis, 18*(4), 204–214.

Pelham, W. E., et al. (2002). Effects of methyphenidate and expectancy on children with ADHD: Behavior, academic performance, and attributions in a summer treatment program and regular classroom settings. *Journal of Consulting & Clinical Psychology, 70*(2), 320–335.

Pellerin, N., & Candas, V. (2003). Combined effects of temperature and noise on human discomfort. *Physiology & Behavior, 78*(1), 99–106.

Pena, E., Bedore, L. M., & Rappazzo, C. (2003). Comparison of Spanish, English, and bilingual children's performance across semantic tasks. *Language, Speech, & Hearing Services in Schools, 34*(1), 5–16.

Penedo, F. J., et al. (2003). Personality, quality of life and HAART adherence among men and women living with HIV/AIDS. *Journal of Psychosomatic Research, 54*(3), 271–278.

Penfield, W. (1969). Consciousness, memory, and man's conditioned reflexes. In K. H. Pribram (ed.), *On the biology of learning.* New York: Harcourt Brace Jovanovich.

Penner, L. A., Thompson, J. K., & Coovert, D. L. (1991). Size overestimation among anorexics: Much ado about very little? *Journal of Abnormal Psychology, 100,* 90–93.

Pentney, A. R. (2001). An exploration of the history and controversies surrounding MDMA and MDA. *Journal of Psychoactive Drugs, 33*(3), 213–221.

Penton-Voak, I. S., & Perrett, D. I. (2000). Female preference for male faces changes cyclically: Further evidence. *Evolution & Human Behavior, 21*(1), 39–48.

Peplau, L. A. (2003). Human sexuality: How do men and women differ? *Current Directions in Psychological Science, 12*(2), 37–40.

Perlman, L. M. (2001). Nonspecific, unintended, and serendipitous effects of psychotherapy. *Professional Psychology: Research & Practice, 32*(3), 283–288.

Perls, F. S. (1971). *Gestalt therapy verbatim.* New York: Bantam.

Perna, F. M., Antoni, M. H., Baum, A., Gordon, P., & Schneiderman, N. (2003). Cognitive behavioral stress management effects on injury and illness among competitive athletes: A randomized clinical trial. *Annals of Behavioral Medicine, 25*(1), 66–73.

Perras, B., et al. (1997). Verbal memory after three months of intranasal vasopressin in healthy old humans. *Psychoneuroendocrinology, 22*(6), 387–396.

Perrett, D. I. (1994). *Nature.* Cited in J. E. Brody (1994). Notions of beauty transcend culture, new study suggests. *The New York Times,* March 21, p. A14.

Perry, D. G., & Bussey, K. (1979). The social learning theory of sex differences. *Journal of Personality and Social Psychology, 37,* 1699–1712.

Perse, E. M. (1998). Implications of cognitive and affective involvement for channel changing. *Journal of Communication, 48*(3), 49–68.

Persons, J. B., Davidson, J., & Tompkins, M. A. (2001). *Essential components of cognitive–behavior therapy for depression.* Washington, DC: American Psychological Association.

Peterson, C. (2002). Children's long-term memory for autobiographical events. *Developmental Review, 22*(3), 370–402.

Peterson, C., Park, N., & Seligman, M. E. P. (2005). Orientations to happiness and life satisfaction: The full life versus the empty life. *Journal of Happiness Studies, 6*(1), 25–41.

Peterson, C., & Seligman, M. E. P. (2004). *Character strengths and virtues: A handbook and classification.* Washington, DC: American Psychological Association.

Peterson, L. R., & Peterson, M. J. (1959). Short-term retention of individual verbal items. *Journal of Experimental Psychology, 58,* 193–198.

Petrov, E. S., Varlinskaya, E. I., & Spear, N. E. (2001). Self-administration of ethanol and saccharin in newborn rats: Effects on suckling plasticity. *Behavioral Neuroscience, 115*(6), 1318–1331.

Petry, N. M., Martin, B., Cooney, J. L., & Kranzler, H. R. (2000). Give them prizes and they will come: Contingency management for treatment of alcohol dependence. *Journal of Consulting and Clinical Psychology, 68,* 250–257.

Pettingale, K. W., et al. (1985). Mental attitudes to cancer. *Lancet, 1,* 750.

Petty, R. E., Fleming, M. A., & White, P. H. (1999). Stigmatized sources and persuasion: Prejudice as a determinant of argument scrutiny. *Journal of Personality & Social Psychology, 76*(1), 19–34.

Petty, R. E., Wegener, D. T., & Fabrigar, L. R. (1997). Attitudes and attitude change. *Annual Review of Psychology, 48,* 609–647.

Phalet, K., & Schoenpflug, U. (2001). Intergenerational transmission of collectivism and achievement values in two acculturation contexts: The case of Turkish families in Germany and Turkish and Moroccan families in the Netherlands. *Journal of Cross-Cultural Psychology, 32*(2), 186–201.

Phelps, E. A., O'Connor, K. J., Cunningham, W. A., Funayama, E. S., & Banaji, M. R. (2000). Performance on indirect measures of race evaluation predicts amygdala activation. *Journal of Cognitive Neuroscience, 12*(5).

Phinney, J. S. (1996). When we talk about American ethnic groups, what do we mean? *American Psychologist, 51,* 918–927.

Phinney, J. S. (2000). Identity formation across cultures: The interaction of personal, societal, and historical change. *Human Development, 43*(1), 27–31.

Phinney, J. S., Cantu, C. L., & Kurtz, D. A. (1997). Ethnic and American identity as predictors of self-esteem among African American, Latino, and white adolescents. *Journal of Youth & Adolescence, 26*(2), 165–185.

Phinney, J. S., & Devich-Navarro, M. (1997). Variations in bicultural identification among African American and Mexican American adolescents. *Journal of Research on Adolescence, 7*(1), 3–32.

Piaget, J. (1932). *The moral judgment of the child.* London: Kegan Paul.

Piaget, J. (1963). *The origins of intelligence in children.* New York: W. W. Norton.

Piaget, J., & Smith, L. (Trans.). (2000). Commentary on Vygotsky's criticisms of language and thought of the child and judgment and reasoning in the child. *New Ideas in Psychology, 18*(2-3), 241–259.

Pierce, C. A. (1996). Body height and romantic attraction: A meta-analytic test of the male-taller norm. *Social Behavior & Personality, 24*(2), 143–149.

Pihl, R. O, & Peterson, J. B. (1992). Etiology. *Annual Review of Addictions Research and Treatment, 2,* 153–175.

Pihl, R. O., Peterson, J. B., & Finn, P. (1990). Inherited predisposition to alcoholism. *Journal of Abnormal Psychology, 99,* 291–301.

Pind, J., Gunnarsdottir, E. K., & Johannesson, H. S. (2003). Raven's Standard Progressive Matrices: New school age norms and a study of the test's validity. *Personality and Individual Differences, 34*(3), 375–386.

Pinel, J. P. J., Assanand, S., & Lehman, D. R. (2000). Hunger, eating, and ill health. *American Psychologist, 55*(10), 1105–1116.

Pinker, S. (1990). Language acquisition. In D. N. Osherson & H. Lasnik (eds.), *An invitation to cognitive science: Language* (Vol. 1). Cambridge, MA: The MIT Press, a Bradford Book.

Pinker, S. (1994a). *The language instinct.* New York: William Morrow.

Pinker, S. (1994b). Building a better brain. *The New York Times Book Review,* June 19, pp. 13–14.

Pinker, S. (1997). Words and rules in the human brain. *Nature, 387*(6633), 547–548.

Pinker, S. (1999). Out of the minds of babes. *Science, 283*(5398), 40–41.

Pinnell, C. M., & Covino, N. A. (2000). Empirical findings on the use of hypnosis in medicine: A critical review. *International Journal of Clinical & Experimental Hypnosis, 48*(2), 170–194.

Pinquart, M., & Sörensen, S. (2000). Influences of socioeconomic status, social network, and competence on subjective well-being in later life: A meta-analysis. *Psychology and Aging, 15*(2), 187–224.

Plomin, R. (2000). Behavioural genetics in the 21st century. *International Journal of Behavioral Development, 24*(1), 30–34.

Plomin, R. (Ed.). (2002). *Behavioral genetics in the postgenomic era.* Washington, DC: American Psychological Association.

Plomin, R., & Asbury, K. (2005). Nature and nurture: Genetic and environmental influences on behavior. *Annals of the American Academy of Political and Social Science, 600*(1), 86–98.

Plomin, R., & Crabbe, J. (2000). DNA. *Psychological Bulletin, 126*(6), 806–828.

Plomin, R., & McGuffin, P. (2003). Psychopathology in the postgenomic era. *Annual Review of Psychology, 54,* 205–228.

Plomin, R., Owen, M. J., & McGuffin, P. (1994). The genetic basis of complex human behaviors. *Science, 264,* 1733–1739.

Plous, S. (1996). Attitudes toward the use of animals in psychological research and education. *American Psychologist, 51,* 1167–1180.

Poe, G. R., Nitz, D. A., McNaughton, B. L., & Barnes, C. A. (2000). Experience-dependent phase-reversal of hippocammpal neuron firing during REM sleep. *Brain Research, 855*(1), 176–180.

Pointer, S. C., & Bond, N. W. (1998). Context-dependent memory: Colour versus odor. *Chemical Senses, 23*(3), 359–362.

Pol, H. E. H., et al. (2000). Prenatal exposure to famine and brain morphology in schizophrenia. *American Journal of Psychiatry, 157,* 1170–1172.

Pollock, B., Prior, H., & Güntürkün, O. (2000). Development of object permanence in food-storing magpies (*Pica pica*). *Journal of Comparative Psychology, 114*(2), 148–157.

Pope, H. G., Kouri, E. M., & Hudson, J. I. (2000). Effects of supraphysiologic doses of testosterone on mood and aggression in normal men: A randomized controlled trial. *Archives of General Psychiatry, 57,* 133–140.

Porter, R. H., Makin, J. W., Davis, L. B., & Christensen, K. M. (1992). Breast-fed infants respond to olfactory cues from their own mother and unfamiliar lactating females. *Infant Behavior and Development, 15,* 85–93.

Posada, G., et al. (2002). Maternal caregiving and infant security in two cultures. *Developmental Psychology, 38*(1), 67–78.

Postmes, T., Spears, R., & Cihangir, S. (2001). Quality of decision making and group norms. *Journal of Personality & Social Psychology, 80*(6), 918–930.

Powell, E. (1996). *Sex on your terms.* Boston: Allyn & Bacon.

Powers, R. (2000). American dreaming. *The New York Times magazine,* May 7, pp. 66–67.

Powers, S. W., et al. (2001). A pilot study of one-session biofeedback training in pediatric headache. *Neurology, 56*(1), 133.

Price, L. H., & Heninger, G. R. (1994). Lithium in the treatment of mood disorders. *New England Journal of Medicine, 331,* 591–598.

Prior, S. M., & Welling, K. A. (2001). "Read in your head": A Vygotskian analysis of the transition from oral to silent reading. *Reading Psychology, 22*(1), 1–15.

Procacciante, S., Latini, A., Martin, L. S., Stasi, R., & Paulis, G. (2001). Paroxetine in the treatment of premature ejaculation: Results of a phase II study. *New Trends in Experimental & Clinical Psychiatry, 17*(1–4), 79–83.

Prochaska, J. O., & Norcross, J. C. (2003). *Systems of psychotherapy* (5th ed.). Belmont, CA: Wadsworth.

Pronin, E., Lin, D. Y., & Ross, L. (2002). The bias blind spot: Perceptions of bias in self versus others. *Personality & Social Psychology Bulletin, 28*(3), 369–381.

Pryce, C. R., Bettschen, D., Bahr, N. I., & Feldon, J. (2001). Comparison of the effects of infant handling, isolation, and nonhandling on acoustic startle, prepulse inhibition, locomotion, and HPA activity in the adult rat. *Behavioral Neuroscience, 115*(1), 71–83.

Pulido, R., & Marco, A. (2000) El efecto Barnum en estudiantes universitarios y profesionales de la psicologia en Mexico. [The Barnum effect in university students and psychology professionals in Mexico.] *Revista Intercontinental de Psicologia y Educacion, 2*(2), 59–66.

Pulley, B. (1998). Those seductive snake eyes: Tales of growing up gambling. *The New York Times,* June 16, A1, A28.

Pyryt, M. C. (2000). Finding "g": Easy viewing through higher order factor analysis. *Gifted Child Quarterly, 44*(3), 190–192.

Qin, P., Agerbo, E., & Mortensen, P. B. (2003). Suicide risk in relation to socioeconomic, demographic, psychiatric, and familial factors: A national register-based study of all suicides in Denmark, 1981–1997. *American Journal of Psychiatry, 160,* 765–772.

Quatman, T., & Watson, C. M. (2001). Gender differences in adolescent self-esteem: An exploration of domains. *Journal of Genetic Psychology, 162*(1), 93–117.

Quill, T. E. (2005). Terri Schiavo—A tragedy compounded. *New England Journal of Medicine,* http://www.nejm.org. Accessed April 4.

Rachman, S. (2000). Joseph Wolpe (1915–1997): Obituary. *American Psychologist, 55*(4), 431–432.

Rahman, Q., & Wilson, G. D. (2003). Born gay? The psychobiology of human sexual orientation. *Personality & Individual Differences, 34*(8), 1337–1382.

Raichle, K., & Lambert, A. J. (2000). The role of political ideology in mediating judgments of blame in rape victims and their assailants: A test of the just world, personal responsibility, and legitimization hypotheses. *Personality & Social Psychology Bulletin, 26*(7), 853–863.

Raine, A., et al. (2000). Reduced prefrontal gray matter volume and reduced autonomic activity in antisocial personality disorder. *Archives of General Psychiatry, 57*(2), 119–127.

Rakowski, W. (1995). Cited in P. Margoshes (1995), For many, old age is the prime of life. *APA Monitor, 26*(5), 36–37.

Ramachandran S. V., et al. (2001). Impact of high-normal blood pressure on the risk of cardiovascular disease. *New England Journal of Medicine, 345*(18), 1291–1297.

Randel, B., Stevenson, H. W., & Witruk, E. (2000). Attitudes, beliefs, and mathematics achievement of German and Japanese high school students. *International Journal of Behavioral Development, 24*(2), 190–198.

Rappaport, N. B., McAnulty, D. P., & Brantley, P. J. (1988). Exploration of the Type A behavior pattern in chronic headache sufferers. *Journal of Consulting and Clinical Psychology, 56,* 621–623.

Rathore, S. S., et al. (2000). Race, sex, poverty, and the medical treatment of acute myocardial infarction in the elderly. *Circulation, 102,* 642–648.

Rath, N. (2002). The power to feel fear and the one to feel happiness are the same. *Journal of Happiness Studies, 3*(1), 1–21.

Rathus, J. H., & Sanderson, W. C. (1999). *Marital distress: Cognitive behavioral interventions for couples.* Northvale, NJ: Jason Aronson.

Rathus, S. A. (1973). A 30-item schedule for assessing assertive behavior. *Behavior Therapy, 4,* 398–406.

Rathus, S. A. (2003). *Voyages: Childhood and adolescence.* Belmont, CA: Wadsworth Publishing Company.

Rathus, S. A., Nevid, J. S., & Fichner-Rathus, L. (2005). *Human sexuality in a world of diversity* (6th ed.). Boston: Allyn & Bacon.

Ratner, N. B., & Gleason, J. B. (1993). An introduction to psycholinguistics. In J. B. Gleason & N. B. Ratner (eds.), *Psycholinguistics.* Fort Worth, TX: Harcourt Brace Jovanovich.

Rauscher, F. H. (1998). Response to Katie Overy's paper, "Can music really 'improve' the mind?" *Psychology of Music, 26*(2), 197–199.

Rauscher, F. H., & Shaw, G. L. (1998). Key components of the Mozart effect. *Perceptual & Motor Skills, 86*(3), 835–841.

Raven, B. H. (1998). Groupthink, Bay of Pigs, and Watergate reconsidered. *Organizational Behavior & Human Decision Processes, 73*(2–3), 352–361.

Raynor, H., A., & Epstein, L. H. (2001). Dietary variety, energy regulation, and obesity. *Psychological Bulletin, 127*(3), 325–341.

Ready, T. (2000, June 7). Meditation apparently good for the heart as well as the mind. Healtheon/WebMD.

Reaney, P. (1998). Acupuncture can work but is not totally safe. Reuters News Agency online, March 16.

Reaney, P. (2000). In matters of the heart, France tops EU neighbors. Reuters News Agency online, February 14.

Redd, W. H., et al. (1987). Cognitive/attentional distraction in the control of conditioned nausea in pediatric cancer patients receiving chemotherapy. *Journal of Consulting and Clinical Psychology, 55,* 391–395.

Reed, J. M., & Squire, L. R. (1997). Impaired recognition memory in patients with lesions limited to the hippocampal formation. *Behavioral Neuroscience, 111*(4) 667–675.

Reeder, G. D. (2001). On perceiving multiple causes and inferring multiple internal attributes. *Psychological Inquiry, 12*(1), 34–36.

Reese, C. M., & Cherry, K. E. (2002). The effects of age, ability, and memory monitoring on prospective memory task performance. *Aging, Neuropsychology, & Cognition, 9*(2), 98–113.

Reid, P. T. (1994). The real problem in the study of culture. *American Psychologist, 49,* 524–525.

Reinecke, M. A., DuBois, D. L., & Schultz, T. M. (2001). Social problem solving, mood, and suicidality among inpatient adolescents. *Cognitive Therapy & Research, 25*(6), 743–756.

Reis, H. T. (2002). Virtually immersive environments. *Psychological Inquiry, 13*(2), 132–134.

Reis, H. T., et al. (1990). What is smiling is beautiful and good. *European Journal of Social Psychology, 20,* 259–267.

Reiser, M. (2001). The dream in contemporary psychiatry. *American Journal of Psychiatry, 158*(3), 351–359.

Reitzle, M. (2006). The connections between adulthood transitions and the self-perception of being adult in the changing contexts of East and West Germany. *European Psychologist, 11*(1), 25–38.

Rempel, M. W., & Fisher, R. J. (1998). Perceived threat, cohesion, and group problem solving in intergroup conflict. *International Journal of Conflict Management, 8*(3), 216–234.

Renninger, K. A., & Wozniak, R. H. (1985). Effect of interest on attentional shift, recognition, and recall in young children. *Developmental Psychology, 21,* 624–632.

Rescorla, R. A. (1967). Inhibition of delay in Pavlovian fear conditioning. *Journal of Comparative & Physiological Psychology, 64*(1), 114–120.

Rescorla, R. A. (1988). Pavlovian conditioning: It's not what you think it is. *American Psychologist, 43,* 151–160.

Rescorla, R. A. (1999). Partial reinforcement reduces the associative change produced by nonreinforcement. *Journal of Experimental Psychology: Animal Behavior Processes, 25*(4) 403–414.

Rest, J. R. (1983). Morality. In P. H. Mussen, J. Flavell, & E. Markman (eds.), *Handbook of child psychology: Vol. 3. Cognitive development.* New York: Wiley.

Reynolds, A. G. (1991). The cognitive consequences of bilingualism. In A. G. Reynolds (ed.), *Bilingualism, multiculturalism, and second language learning.* Hillsdale, NJ: Erlbaum.

Rezvani, A. H., & Levin, E. D. (2001). Cognitive effects of nicotine. *Biological Psychiatry, 49*(3), 258–267.

Rhee, S. H., & Waldman, I. D. (2002). Genetic and environmental influences on antisocial behavior: A meta-analysis of twin and adoption studies. *Psychological Bulletin, 128*(3), 490–529.

Rice, K. G., & Dellwo, J. P. (2001). Within-semester stability and adjustment correlates of the Multidimensional Perfectionism Scale. *Measurement & Evaluation in Counseling & Development, 34*(3), 146–156.

Richards, J. C., Hof, A., & Alvarenga, M. (2000). Serum lipids and their relationships with hostility and angry affect and behaviors in men. *Health Psychology, 19*(4) 393–398.

Richardson, G. E. (2002). The metatheory of resilience and resiliency. *Journal of Clinical Psychology, 58*(3), 307–321.

Richburg, M., & Fletcher, T. (2002). Emotional intelligence: Directing a child's emotional education. *Child Study Journal, 32*(1), 31–38.

Rickard, T. C., et al. (2000). The calculating brain: An fMRI study. *Neuropsychologia, 38*(3), 325–335.

Riepe, M. (2000). Cited in M. Ritter (2000), Brains differ in navigation skills. The Associated Press online, March 21.

Rigotti, N. A., Lee, J. E., & Wechsler, H. (2000). U.S. college students' use of tobacco products: Results of a national survey. *Journal of the American Medical Association, 284*(6), 699–705.

Rimm, E. (2000). Lifestyle may play role in potential for impotence. Paper presented to the annual meeting of the American Urological Association, Atlanta, May.

Riot erupts after grocer arrested for "flirting." (2000). Reuters News Agency online, July 31.

Riso, L. P., et al. (2003). Cognitive aspects of chronic depression. *Journal of Abnormal Psychology, 112*(1), 72–80.

Ritter, M. (2000). Brains differ in navigation skills. The Associated Press online, March 21.

Rizzo, A. A., & Schultheis, M. T. (2002). Expanding the boundaries of psychology: The application of virtual reality. *Psychological Inquiry, 13*(2), 134–140.

Robbins, J. (2000). Virtual reality finds a real place as a medical aid. *The New York Times online,* July 4.

Roberson, D., Davidoff, J., & Shapiro, L. (2002). Squaring the circle: The cultural relativity of good shape. *Journal of Cognition & Culture, 2*(1), 29–51.

Robins, R. W., Gosling, S. D., & Craik, K. H. (1999). An empirical analysis of trends in psychology. *American Psychologist, 54*(2), 117–128.

Robson, P. (2001). Therapeutic aspects of cannabis and cannabinoids. *The British Journal of Psychiatry, 178,* 107–115.

Rodriguez, I., Greer, C. A., Mok, M. Y., & Mombaerts, P. (2000). A putative pheromone receptor gene expressed in human olfactory mucosa. *Nature Genetics, 26*(1), 18–19.

Rodriguez, P., & Levy, W. B. (2001). A model of hippocampal activity in trace conditioning: Where's the trace? *Behavioral Neuroscience, 115*(6), 1224–1238.

Roediger, H. L., Weldon, M. S., Stadler, M.. L., & Riegler, G. L. (1992). Direct comparison of two implicit memory tests: Word fragment and word stem completion. *Journal of Experimental Psychology: Learning, Memory, & Cognition, 18*(6), 1251–1269.

Roelofs, K., et al. (2002). Hypnotic susceptibility in patients with conversion disorder. *Journal of Abnormal Psychology, 111*(2), 390–395.

Rogers, C. R. (1951). *Client-centered therapy.* Boston: Houghton Mifflin.

Romero, E., Luengo, M. A., & Sobral, J. (2001). Personality and antisocial behaviour: Study of temperamental dimensions. *Personality & Individual Differences, 31*(3), 329–348.

Roncesvalles, M. N. C., Woollacott, M. H., & Jensen, J. L. (2001). Development of lower extremity kinetics for balance control in infants and young children. *Journal of Motor Behavior, 33*(2), 180–192.

Rose, J. S., Chassin, L., Presson, C. C., & Sherman, S. J. (1996). Prospective predictors of quit attempts and smoking cessation in young adults. *Health Psychology, 15,* 261–268.

Rosenbaum, D. E. (2000). On left-handedness, its causes and costs. *The New York Times,* May 16, pp. F1, F6.

Rosenbaum, M. (2002). Ecstasy: America's new "reefer madness." *Journal of Psychoactive Drugs, 34*(2), 137–142.

Rosenstein, D., & Oster, H. (1988). Differential facial responses to four basic tastes. *Child Development, 59,* 1555–1568.

Rosenthal, A. M. (1994). The way she died. *The New York Times,* March 15, p. A23.

Rosenthal, E. (1993). Listening to the emotional needs of cancer patients. *The New York Times,* July 20, pp. C1, C7.

Ross, J. L., Roeltgen, D., Feuillan, P., Kushner, H., & Cutler, W. B. (2000). Use of estrogen in young girls with Turner syndrome: Effects on memory. *Neurology, 54*(1), 164–170.

Ross, L., & Nisbett, R. E. (1991). *The person and the situation.* New York: McGraw-Hill.

Ross, M. J., & Berger, R. S. (1996). Effects of stress inoculation training on athletes' postsurgical pain and rehabilitation after orthopedic injury. *Journal of Consulting and Clinical Psychology, 64,* 406–410.

Ross, S. R., Lutz, C. J., & Bailley, S. E. (2002). Positive and negative symptoms of schizotypy and the Five-Factor Model: A domain and facet level analysis. *Journal of Personality Assessment, 79*(1), 53–72.

Rosso, I. M., et al. (2000). Obstetric risk factors for early-onset schizophrenia in a Finnish birth cohort. *American Journal of Psychiatry, 157,* 801–807.

Roth, D. B., & Gellert, M. (2000). Cancer: New guardians of the genome. *Nature, 404,* 823–824.

Rothbart, M. K., & Ahadi, S. A. (1994). Temperament and the development of personality. *Journal of Abnormal Psychology, 103,* 55–66.

Rothbaum, B. O., Foa, E. B., Riggs, D. S., Murdock, T., & Walsh, W. (1992). A prospective examination of post-traumatic stress disorder in rape victims. *Journal of Traumatic Stress, 5,* 455–475.

Rothbaum, B. O., Hodges, L., Anderson, P. L., Price, L., & Smith, S. (2002). Twelve-month follow-up of virtual reality and standard exposure therapies for the fear of flying. *Journal of Consulting & Clinical Psychology, 70*(2), 428–432.

Rothbaum, B. O., & Hodges, L. F. (1999). The use of virtual reality exposure in the treatment of anxiety disorders. *Behavior Modification, 23*(4), 507–525.

Rothbaum, B. O., Hodges, L. F., Ready, D., Graap, K., & Alarcon, R. D. (2001). Virtual reality exposure therapy for Vietnam veterans with posttraumatic stress disorder. *Journal of Clinical Psychiatry, 62*(8), 617–622.

Rotter, J. B. (1990). Internal versus external control of reinforcement. *American Psychologist, 45,* 489–493.

Rotton, J., & Cohn, E. G. (2000). Violence is a curvilinear function of temperature in Dallas: A replication. *Journal of Personality and Social Psychology, 78*(6), 1074–1081.

Rovee-Collier, C. (1999). The development of infant memory. *Current Directions in Psychological Science, 8*(3), 80–85.

Rowatt, W. C., Cunningham, M. R., & Druen, P. B. (1999). Lying to get a date: The effect of facial physical attractiveness on the willingness to deceive prospective dating partners. *Journal of Social & Personal Relationships, 16*(2), 209–223.

Rowe, J. B., Owen, A. M., Johnsrude, I. S., & Passingham, R. E. (2001). Imaging the mental components of a planning task. *Neuropsychologia, 39*(3), 315–327.

Rozee, P. D., Koss, M. P. (2001). Rape: A century of resistance. *Psychology of Women Quarterly, 25*(4), 295–311.

Rozin, P., & Fallon, A. (1988). Body image, attitudes to weight, and misperceptions of figure preferences of the opposite sex. *Journal of Abnormal Psychology, 97,* 342–345.

Ruback, R. B., & Pandey, J. (2002). Mental distress and physical symptoms in the slums of New Delhi: The role of individual, household, and neighborhood factors. *Journal of Applied Social Psychology, 32*(11), 2296–2320.

Rubinstein, S., & Caballero, B. (2000). Is Miss America an undernourished role model? *Journal of the American Medical Association online, 283*(12).

Rude, S. S., Hertel, P. T., Jarrold, W., Covich, J., & Hedlund, S. (1999). Depression-related impairments in prospective memory. *Cognition & Emotion, 13*(3), 267–276.

Ruiter, R. A. C., Abraham, C., & Kok, G. (2001). Scary warnings and rational precautions: A review of the psychology of fear appeals. *Psychology & Health, 16*(6), 613–630.

Rule, B. G., Taylor, B. R., & Dobbs, A. R. (1987). Priming effects of heat on aggressive thoughts. *Social cognition, 5,* 131–143.

Rush, A. J., Khatami, M., & Beck, A. T. (1975). Cognitive and behavior therapy in chronic depression. *Behavior Therapy, 6,* 398-404.

Rushton, J. P., Skuy, M., & Fridjhon, P. (2003). Performance on Raven's Advanced Progressive Matrices by African, East Indian, and White engineering students in South Africa. *Intelligence, 31*(2), 123-137.

Rutkowski, G. K., Gruder, C. L., & Romer, D. (1983). Group cohesiveness, social norms, and bystander intervention. *Journal of Personality and Social Psychology, 44,* 545–552.

Rutkowski, K. (2001). Anxiety, depression and nightmares in PTSD. *Archives of Psychiatry & Psychotherapy, 3*(2), 41–50.

Rutter, M., & Silberg, J. (2002). Gene-environment interplay in relation to emotional and behavioral disturbance. *Annual Review of Psychology, 53*(1), 463–490.

Ryder, A. G., Alden, L. E., & Paulhus, D. L. (2000). Is acculturation unidimensional or bidimensional? A head-to-head comparison in the prediction of personality, self-identity, and adjustment. *Journal of Personality and Social Psychology, 79*(1), 49–65.

Ryska, T. A. (2001–2002). Self-esteem among intercollegiate athletes: The role of achievement goals and competitive orientation. *Imagination, Cognition & Personality, 21*(1), 67–80.

Sachsse, U., von der Heyde, S., & Huether, G. (2002). Stress regulation and self-mutilation. *American Journal of Psychiatry, 159*(4), 672.

Sackeim, H. A., et al. (2000). A prospective, randomized, double-blind comparison of bilateral and right unilateral electroconvulsive therapy at different stimulus intensities. *Archives of General Psychiatry, 57*(5), 425–434.

Sacks, F. M., et al. (2001). Effects on blood pressure of reduced dietary sodium and the Dietary Approaches to Stop Hypertension (DASH) Diet. *The New England Journal of Medicine, 344*(1), 3–10.

Sadalla, E. K., Kenrick, D. T., & Vershure, B. (1987). Dominance and heterosexual attraction. *Journal of Personality and Social Psychology, 52,* 730–738.

Sadalla, E. K., Sheets, V., & McCreath, H. (1990). The cognition of urban tempo. *Environment & Behavior, 22*(2), 230–254.

Sadker, M., & Sadker, D. (1994). *How America's schools cheat girls.* New York: Scribners.

Sagi, A., Koren-Karie, N., Gini, M., Ziv, Y., & Joels, T. (2002). Shedding further light on the effects of various types and quality of early child care on infant-mother attachment relationship: The Haifa Study of Early Child Care. *Child Development, 73*(4), 1166–1186.

Sagrestano, L. M., McCormick, S. H., Paikoff, R. L., & Holmbeck, G. N. (1999). Pubertal development and parent–child conflict in low-income, urban, African American adolescents. *Journal of Research on Adolescence, 9*(1), 85–107.

Salgado de Snyder, V. N., Cervantes, R. C., & Padilla, A. M. (1990). Gender and ethnic differences in psychosocial stress and generalized distress among Hispanics. *Sex Roles, 22,* 441–453.

Salovey, P., Rothman, A. J., Detweiler, J. B., & Steward, W. T. (2000). Emotional states and physical health. *American Psychologist, 55,* 110–121.

Salovey, P., Stroud, L. R., Woolery, A., & Epel, E. S. (2002). Perceived emotional intelligence, stress reactivity, and symptom reports: Further explorations using the trait meta-mood scale. *Psychology & Health, 17*(5), 611–627.

Samaha, F. F., et al. (2003). A low-carbohydrate as compared with a low-fat diet in severe obesity. *The New England Journal of Medicine, 348*(21), 2074–2081.

Samet, J. M., Dominici, F., Curriero, F. C., Coursac, I., & Zeger, S. L. (2000). Fine particulate air pollution and mortality in 20 U.S. cities, 1987–1994. *The New England Journal of Medicine, 343*(24), 1742–1749.

Sampaio, D., et al. (2000). Representacoes sociais do suicidio em estudantes do ensino secundario. *Analise Psicologica, 18*(2), 139–155.

Samuels, S. M., & Casebeer, W. D. (2005). A social psychological view of morality: Why knowledge of situational influences on behavior can improve character development practices. *Journal of Moral Education, 34*(1), 73–87.

Sanacora, G., Mason, G. F., & Krystal, J. H. (2000). Impairment of GABAergic transmission in depression: New insights from neuroimaging studies. *Critical Reviews in Neurobiology, 14*(1), 23–45.

Sanders, G. S. (1984). Effects of context cues on eyewitness identification responses. *Journal of Applied Social Psychology, 14,* 386–397.

Sandman, C., & Crinella, F. (1995) Cited in P. Margoshes (1995), For many, old age is the prime of life. *APA Monitor, 26*(5), 36–37.

Sangrador, J. L., & Yela, C. (2000). "What is beautiful is loved": Physical attractiveness in love relationships in a representative sample. *Social Behavior & Personality, 28*(3) 207–218.

Sanna, L. J., & Meier, S. (2000). Looking for clouds in a silver lining: Self-esteem, mental simulations, and temporal confidence changes. *Journal of Research in Personality, 34*(2), 236–251.

Sano, M. (2000, July). Estrogen in Alzheimer's disease: Treatment or prevention. Paper presented to the World Alzheimer Congress 2000, Washington, DC.

Santee, R. T., & Maslach, C. (1982). To agree or not to agree: Personal dissent amid social pressure to conform. *Journal of Personality & Social Psychology, 42*(4), 690–700.

Santelli, J. S., Lowry, R., Brener, N. D., & Robin, L. (2000). The association of sexual behaviors with socioeconomic status, family structure and race/ethnicity among US adolescents. *American Journal of Public Health, 90*(10), 1582–1588.

Santonastaso, P., Friederici, S., & Favaro, A. (2001). Sertraline in the treatment of restricting anorexia nervosa: An open controlled trial. *Journal of Child & Adolescent Psychopharmacology, 11*(2), 143–150.

Sapp, M. (2002). Implications of Barber's three dimensional theory of hypnosis. *Sleep & Hypnosis, 4*(2), 70–76.

Sarbin, T. R., & Coe, W. C. (1972). *Hypnosis.* New York: Holt, Rinehart and Winston.

Sarriera, J., et al. (2001). Formacao da identidade ocupacional em adolescentes. *Estudos de Psicologia, 6*(1), 27–32.

Saunders, K. W. (2003). Regulating youth access to violent video games: Three responses to First Amendment concerns. www.law.msu.edu/lawrev/2003-1/2-Saunders.pdf.

Savage, C. R., et al. (2001). Prefrontal regions supporting spontaneous and directed application of verbal learning strategies. Evidence from PET. *Brain, 124*(1), 219–231.

Savage-Rumbaugh, E. S., et al. (1993). *Monographs of the Society for Research in Child Development, 58*(3–4), v–221.

Savage-Rumbaugh, E. S., & Fields, W. M. (2000). Linguistic, cultural and cognitive capacities of bonobos *(Pan paniscus)*. *Culture & Psychology, 6*(2), 131–153.

Savage-Rumbaugh, S., Segerdahl, P., & Fields, W. M. (2005). Individual differences in language competencies in apes resulting from unique rearing conditions imposed by different first epistemologies. In L. L. Namy (ed.), *Symbol use and symbolic representation: Developmental and comparative perspectives. Emory symposia in cognition* (pp. 199–219). Mahwah, NJ: Lawrence Erlbaum Publishers.

Savic, I., Berglund, H., & Lindström, P. (2005). Brain response to putative pheromones in homosexual men. *Proceedings of the National Association of Sciences, 102*, 7356–7361.

Sawa, A., & Snyder, S. H. (2002, April 26). Schizophrenia: Diverse approaches to a complex disease. *Science,* pp. 692–695.

Saxe, L. (1991). Lying. *American Psychologist, 46*, 409–415.

Saxe, L., & Ben-Shakhar, G. (1999). Admissibility of polygraph tests: The application of scientific standards post-Daubert. *Psychology, Public Policy, & Law, 5*(1), 203–223.

Saywitz, K. J., Mannarino, A. P., Berliner, L., & Cohen, J. A. (2000). Treatment for sexually abused children and adolescents. *American Psychologist, 55*(9), 1040–1049.

Scarr, S., & Kidd, K. K. (1983). Developmental behavior genetics. In M. Haith & J. J. Campos (eds.), *Handbook of child psychology.* New York: Wiley.

Scarr, S., & Weinberg, R. A. (1976). IQ test performance of black children adopted by white families. *American Psychologist, 31*, 726–739.

Scarr, S., & Weinberg, R. A. (1977). Intellectual similarities within families of both adopted and biological children. *Intelligence, 1*, 170–191.

Scarr, S., & Weinberg, R. A. (1983). The Minnesota adoption studies: Genetic differences and malleability. *Child Development, 54*, 260–267.

Scaturo, D. J. (2001). The evolution of psychotherapy and the concept of manualization: An integrative perspective. *Professional Psychology: Research & Practice, 32*(5), 522–530.

Schacter, D. L. (1992). Understanding implicit memory: A cognitive neuroscience approach. *American Psychologist, 47*(4), 559–569.

Schacter, D. L. (1993). Understanding implicit memory: A cognitive neuroscience approach. In A. F. Collins, S. E. Gathercole, et al. (eds.), *Theories of memory,* pp. 387–412. Hillsdale, NJ: Lawrence Erlbaum Associates.

Schacter, D. L. (1999). The seven sins of memory: Insights from psychology and cognitive neuroscience. *American Psychologist, 54*(3), 182–203.

Schacter, D. L. (2000). Memory: Memory systems. In A. E. Kazdin (ed.), *Encyclopedia of psychology,* vol. 5 (pp. 169–172). Washington, DC: American Psychological Association.

Schacter, D. L., & Badgaiyan, R. D. (2001). Neuroimaging of priming: New perspectives on implicit and explicit memory. *Current Directions in Psychological Science, 10*(1), 1–4.

Schacter, D. L., Badgaiyan, R. D., & Alpert, N. M. (1999). Visual word stem completion priming within and across modalities: A PET study.

Neuroreport: For Rapid Communication of Neuroscience Research, 10(10), 2061–2065.

Schachter, S., & Singer, J. E. (1962). Cognitive, social, and physiological determinants of emotional state. *Psychological Review, 69*, 379–399.

Schaie, K. W. (1994). The course of adult intellectual development. *American Psychologist, 49*, 304–313.

Scharff, L., Marcus, D. A., & Masek, B. J. (2002). A controlled study of minimal-contact thermal biofeedback treatment in children with migraine. *Journal of Pediatric Psychology, 27*(2), 109–119.

Schellenberg, E. G. (2000). Cited in R. Hershenson (2000), Debating the Mozart theory. *The New York Times Magazine online,* August 6.

Schiffman, S. S. (2000). Taste quality and neural coding: Implications from psychophysics and neurophysiology. *Physiology and Behavior, 69*(1–2), 147–159.

Schmidt, N. B., et al. (2000). Evaluating gene x psychological risk factor effects in the pathogenesis of anxiety: A new model approach. *Journal of Abnormal Psychology, 109*(2), 308–320.

Schmitt, D. P. (2003). Universal sex differences in the desire for sexual variety: Tests from 52 nations, 6 continents, and 13 islands. *Journal of Personality and Social Psychology, 85*(1), 85–104.

Schmitt, D. P., Shackelford, T. K., Duntley, J., Tooke, W. & Buss, D. M. (2001). The desire for sexual variety as a key to understanding basic human mating strategies. *Personal Relationships, 8*(4), 425–455.

Schneider, K. J., Bugental, J. F. T., & Pierson, J. F. (eds.). (2001). *The handbook of humanistic psychology: Leading edges in theory, research, and practice.* Thousand Oaks, CA: Sage Publications.

Schneider, L. S., et al. (2003). An 8-week multicenter, parallel-group, double-blind, placebo-controlled study of sertraline in elderly outpatients with major depression. *American Journal of Psychiatry, 160*, 1277–1285.

Schneider, R. H., et al. (1995). A randomized controlled trial of stress reduction for hypertension in older African Americans. *Hypertension, 26*, 820.

Schneider, T. R., et al. (2001). Visual and auditory message framing effects on tobacco smoking. *Journal of Applied Social Psychology, 31*(4), 667–682.

Schuckit, M. A. (1996). Recent developments in the pharmacotherapy of alcohol dependence. *Journal of Consulting and Clinical Psychology, 64*, 669–676.

Schuckit, M. A., et al. (2001) A genome-wide search for genes that relate to a low level of response to alcohol. *Alcoholism: Clinical & Experimental Research, 25*(3), 323–329.

Schulz, R., & Heckhausen, J. (1996). A life span model of successful aging. *American Psychologist, 51*, 702–714.

Schupf, N. (2000, July). Epidemiology of dementia in Down syndrome. Paper presented to the World Alzheimer Congress 2000, Washington, DC.

Schuster, M. A., et al. (2001). A national survey of stress reactions after the September 11, 2001, terrorist attacks. *New England Journal of Medicine, 345*(20), 1507–1512.

Schwarts, S. J., Côté, J. E., & Arnett, J. J. (2005). Identity and agency in emerging adulthood: Two developmental routes in the individualization process. *Youth & Society, 37*(2), 201–229.

Schwartz, R. M., & Gottman, J. M. (1976). Toward a task analysis of assertive behavior. *Journal of Consulting and Clinical Psychology, 44*, 910–920.

Schwartzer, R., & Renner, B. (2000). Social-cognitive predictors of health behavior: Action self-efficacy and coping self-efficacy. *Health Psychology, 19*(5), 487–495.

Schyns, P. (2001). Income and satisfaction in Russia. *Journal of Happiness Studies, 2*(2), 173–204.

Sciolino, E. (2000). Love finds a way in Iran: "Temporary marriage." *The New York Times online,* October 4.

Scott, J. (1994). Multiple personality cases perplex legal system. *The New York Times,* May 9, pp. A1, B10, B11.

Scott, T. R. (2001). The role of taste in feeding. *Appetite, 37*(2), 111–113.

Scruggs, T. E., & Mastropieri, M. A. (1992). Remembering the forgotten art of memory. *American Educator, 16*(4), 31–37.

Segal, N. L., & Roy, A. (2001). Suicidal attempts and ideation in twins whose co-twins' deaths were non-suicides: Replication and elaboration. *Personality & Individual Differences, 31*(3), 445–452.

Segan, C. J., Borland, R., & Greenwood, K. M. (2002). Do transtheoretical model measures predict the transition from preparation to action in smoking cessation? *Psychology & Health, 17*(4), 417–435.

Selemon, L. D., Kleinman, J. E., Herman, M. M., & Goldman-Rakic, P. S. (2002). Smaller frontal gray matter volume in postmortem schizophrenic brains. *American Journal of Psychiatry, 159*(12), 1983–1991.

Selemon, L. D., Mrzljak, J., Kleinman, J. E., Herman, M. M., & Goldman-Rakic, P. S. (2003). Regional specificity in the neuropathologic substrates of schizophrenia: A morphometric analysis of Broca's area 44 and area 9. *Archives of General Psychiatry, 60*(1), 69–77.

Seligman, M. E. P. (1995). The effectiveness of psychotherapy: The *Consumer Reports* study. *American Psychologist, 50,* 965–974.

Seligman, M. E. P. (1996, August). Predicting and preventing depression. Master lecture presented to the meeting of the American Psychological Association, Toronto.

Seligman, M. E. P., Steen, T. A., Park, N., & Peterson, C. (2005). Positive psychology progress: Empirical validation of interventions. *American Psychologist, 60*(5), 410–421.

Selye, H. (1976). *The stress of life* (rev. ed.). New York: McGraw-Hill.

Selye, H. (1980). The stress concept today. In I. L. Kutash, et al. (eds.), *Handbook on stress and anxiety.* San Francisco: Jossey-Bass.

Seppa, N. (1997). Children's TV remains steeped in violence. *APA Monitor, 28*(6), 36.

Serbin, L. A., Poulin-Dubois, D., Colburne, K. A., Sen, M. G., & Eichstedt, J. A. (2001). Gender stereotyping in infancy: Visual preferences for and knowledge of gender-stereotyped toys in the second year. *International Journal of Behavioral Development, 25*(1), 7–15.

Service, R. F. (1994). Will a new type of drug make memory-making easier? *Science, 266,* 218–219.

Sesso, H. D., Paffenbarger, R. S., Jr., & Lee, I-M. (2000). Physical activity and coronary heart disease in men: The Harvard Alumni Health Study. *Circulation, 102,* 975–980.

Shadish, W. R. (2002). Revisiting field experiments: Field notes for the future. *Psychological Methods, 7*(1), 3–18.

Shadish, W. R., Matt, G. E., Navarro, A. M., & Phillips, G. (2000). The effects of psychological therapies under clinically representative conditions: A meta-analysis. *Psychological Bulletin, 126*(4), 512–529.

Shafran, R., Cooper, Z., & Fairburn, C. (2002). Clinical perfectionism: A cognitive–behavioural analysis. *Behaviour Research and Therapy, 40*(7), 773–791.

Shanker, S. G., Savage-Rumbaugh, E. S., & Taylor, T. J. (1999). Kanzi: A new beginning. *Animal Learning & Behavior, 27*(1), 24–25.

Shapiro, F. (1989). Efficacy of the eye movement desensitization procedure in the treatment of traumatic memories. *Journal of Traumatic Stress, 2,* 199–223.

Shayley, A. Y., et al. (2000). Auditory startle response in trauma survivors with posttraumatic stress disorder: A prospective study. *American Journal of Psychiatry, 157,* 255–261.

Shaywitz, B. A., et al. (1995). Sex differences in the functional organization of the brain for language. *Nature, 373,* 607–609.

Shaywitz, B. A., & Shaywitz, S., E. (2000). Estrogen and Alzheimer disease: Plausible theory, negative clinical trial. *Journal of the American Medical Association, 283*(8), 1055–1056.

Sheldon, J. P., & Parent, S. L. (2002). Clergy's attitudes and attributions of blame toward female rape victims. *Violence Against Women, 8*(2), 233–256.

Shenal, B. V., & Harrison, D. W. (2003). Investigation of the laterality of hostility, cardiovascular regulation, and auditory recognition. *International Journal of Neuroscience, 113*(2), 205–222.

Shenefelt, P. D. (2003). Hypnosis-facilitated relaxation using self-guided imagery during dermatologic procedures. *American Journal of Clinical Hypnosis, 45*(3), 225–232.

Sherman, J. W., & Frost, L. A. (2000). On the encoding of stereotype-relevant information under cognitive load. *Personality & Social Psychology Bulletin, 26*(1), 26–34.

Sherrington, J. M., Hawton, K. E., Fagg, J., Andrews, B., & Smith, D. (2001). Outcome of women admitted to hospital for depressive illness: Factors in the prognosis of severe depression. *Psychological Medicine, 31*(1), 115–125.

Sherry, J. L. (2001). The effects of violent video games on aggression: A meta-analysis. *Human Communication Research, 27*(3), 409–431.

Sherwood, N. E., & Neumark-Sztainer, D. (2001). Internalization of the sociocultural ideal: Weight-related attitudes and dieting behaviors among young adolescent girls. *American Journal of Health Promotion, 15*(4), 228–231.

Shiffman, S., et al. (1997). A day at a time: Predicting smoking lapse from daily urge. *Journal of Abnormal Psychology, 106,* 104–116.

Shiffman, S., et al. (2000). Dynamic effects of self-efficacy on smoking lapse and relapse. *Health Psychology, 19*(4), 315–323.

Shneidman, E. S. (2001). *Comprehending suicide.* Washington, DC: American Psychological Association.

Shulman, S., Blatt, S. J., & Feldman, B. (2006). Vicissitudes of the impetus for growth and change among emerging adults. *Psychoanalytic Psychology, 23*(1), 159–180.

Shultz, S. K., Scherman, A., & Marshall, L. J. (2000). Evaluation of a university-based date rape prevention program: Effect on attitudes and behavior related to rape. *Journal of College Student Development, 41*(2), 193–201.

Siegel, J. M. (2002). The REM sleep–memory consolidation hypothesis. *Science, 294*(5544), 1058–1063.

Sikes, V., & Sikes, C. (2005). A response to May's commentary on "A look at EMDR: Technique, research, and use with college students." *Journal of College Student Psychotherapy, 19*(3), 75–79.

Silberschatz, G. (1998). In Persons, J. B., & Silberschatz, G. (1998). Are results of randomized controlled trials useful to psychotherapists? *Journal of Consulting and Clinical Psychology, 66,* 126–135.

Silver, E. (1994). Cited in T. DeAngelis (1994), Experts see little impact from insanity plea ruling. *APA Monitor, 25*(6), 28.

Silver, S. M., Rogers, S., Knipe, J., & Colelli, G. (2005). EMDR therapy following the 9/11 terrorist attacks: A community-based intervention project in New York City. *International Journal of Stress Management, 12*(1), 29–42.

Simons, A. D., Gordon, J. S., Monroe, S. M., & Thase, M. E. (1995). Toward an integration of psychologic, social, and biologic factors in depression. *Journal of Consulting and Clinical Psychology, 63,* 369–377.

Simonton, D. K. (2000). Creativity: Cognitive, personal, developmental, and social aspects. *American Psychologist, 55,* 151–158.

Simpson, M., & Perry, J. D. (1990). Crime and climate. *Environment and Behavior, 22,* 295–300.

Simpson, M. L., Olejnik, S., Tam, A. Y., & Supattathum, S. (1994). Elaborative verbal rehearsals and college students' cognitive performance. *Journal of Educational Psychology, 86,* 267–278.

Singareddy, R. K., & Balon, R. (2002). Sleep in posttraumatic stress disorder. *Annals of Clinical Psychiatry, 14*(3), 183–190.

Singh, R., & Ho, S. Y. (2000). Attitudes and attraction: A new test of the attraction, repulsion and similarity–dissimilarity asymmetry hypotheses. *British Journal of Social Psychology, 39*(2), 197–211.

Singletary, K. W., & Gapstur, S. M. (2001). Alcohol and breast cancer: Review of epidemiologic and experimental evidence and potential mechanisms. *Journal of the American Medical Association, 286*(17), 2143–2151.

Skinner, B. F. (1938). *The behavior of organisms: An experimental analysis.* New York: Appleton.

Skinner, B. F. (1948). *Walden Two.* New York: Macmillan.

Skinner, B. F. (1983). Intellectual self-management in old age. *American Psychologist, 38,* 239–244.

Sleepers suffer WTC nightmares. (2001, November 22). The Associated Press.

Slobin, D. I. (1983). Crosslinguistic evidence for basic child grammar. Paper presented to the biennial meeting of the Society for Research in Child Development, Detroit.

Sloman, S. A. (1996). The empirical case for two systems of reasoning. *Psychological Bulletin, 119,* 3–22.

Sloman, S. A., Harrison, M. C., & Malt, B. C. (2002). Recent exposure affects artifact naming. *Memory & Cognition, 30*(5), 687–695.

Smetana, J., & Gaines, C. (1999). Adolescent–parent conflict in middle-class African American families. *Child Development, 70*(6), 1447–1463.

Smiley, J. (2000). The good life. *The New York Times Magazine,* May 7, pp. 58–59.

Smith, B. N., Kerr, N. A., Markus, M. J., & Stasson, M. F. (2001). Individual differences in social loafing: Need for cognition as a motivator in collective performance. *Group Dynamics, 5*(2), 150–158.

Smith, D. (2003a). 10 ways practitioners can avoid frequent ethical pitfalls. *Monitor on Psychology, 34*(1), 50–55.

Smith, D. (2003b). Five principles for research ethics. *Monitor on Psychology, 34*(1), 56–60.

Smith, D. (2003c). What you need to know about the new code: The chair of APA's Ethics Code Task Force highlights changes to the 2002 Ethics Code. *Monitor on Psychology online, 34*(1).

Smith, D. E., & Seymour, R. B. (1994). LSD: History and toxicity. *Psychiatric Annals, 24*(3), 145–147.

Smith, G. F., & Dorfman, D. (1975). The effect of stimulus uncertainty on the relationship between frequency of exposure and liking. *Journal of Personality and Social Psychology, 31*, 150–155.

Smith, M. L., & Glass, G. V. (1977). Meta-analysis of psychotherapy outcome studies. *American Psychologist, 32*, 752–760.

Smith, T. W., & Ruiz, J. M. (2002). Course of coronary heart disease: Current status and implications for research and practice. *Journal of Consulting and Clinical Psychology, 70*(3), 548–568.

Smith, V. (2000, February 16). Female heart, geography link shown. The Associated Press.

Smits, T., Storms, G., Rosseel, Y., & De Boeck, P. (2002). Fruits and vegetables categorized: An application of the generalized context model. *Psychonomic Bulletin & Review, 9*(4), 836–844.

Snyderman, M., & Rothman, S. (1987). Survey of expert opinion on intelligence and aptitude testing. *American Psychologist, 42*, 137–144.

Sokolova, E. T., Burlakova, N. S., & Leontiou, F. (2002). Connection between the diffuse gender identity phenomenon and the personal cognitive style. *Voprosy Psychologii, 3*, 41–51.

Solomon, E. P., Berg, L. R., & Martin, D. W. (2002). *Biology* (6th ed.). Pacific Grove, CA: Brooks/Cole.

Solowij, N., et al., for the Marijuana Treatment Project Research Group. (2002). Cognitive functioning of long-term heavy cannabis users seeking treatment. *Journal of the American Medical Association, 287*(9), 1123–1131.

Somerfield, M. R., & McCrae, R. R. (2000). Stress and coping research: Methodological challenges, theoretical advances, and clinical applications. *American Psychologist, 55*(6), 620–625.

Sommerfeld, J. (2000). Lifting the curse—Should monthly periods be optional? MSNBC online, April 18.

Sookman, D., Pinard, G., & Beck, A. T. (2001). Vulnerability schemas in obsessive–compulsive disorder. *Journal of Cognitive Psychotherapy, 15*(2), 109–130.

Sorensen, S. B., & Rutter, C. M. (1991). Transgenerational patterns of suicide attempt. *Journal of Consulting and Clinical Psychology, 59*, 861–866.

Soskins, M., Rosenfeld, J. P., & Niendam, T. (2001). Peak to peak measurement of P300 recorded at 0.3 Hz high pass filter settings in intra-individual diagnosis. *International Journal of Psychophysiology, 40*(2), 173–180.

Soussignan, R. (2002). Duchenne smile, emotional experience, and autonomic reactivity: A test of the facial feedback hypotheses. *Emotion, 2*(1), 52–74.

Southall, D., & Roberts, J. E. (2002). Attributional style and self-esteem in vulnerability to adolescent depressive symptoms following life stress: A 14-week prospective study. *Cognitive Therapy & Research, 26*(5), 563–579.

Spasojevic, J., & Alloy, L. B. (2001). Rumination as a common mechanism relating depressive risk factors to depression. *Emotion, 1*(1), 25–37.

Sperling, G. (1960). The information available in brief visual presentations. *Psychological Monographs, 74*, 1–29.

Speranza, M., et al. (2001). Obsessive compulsive disorders in eating disorders. *Eating Behaviors, 2*(3), 193–207.

Sperry, R. W. (1998). A powerful paradigm made stronger. *Neuropsychologia, 36*(10), 1063–1068.

Spiers, H. J., Maguire, E. A., & Burgess, N. (2001). Hippocampal amnesia. *Neurocase, 7*(5), 357–382.

Spreat, S., & Behar, D. (1994). Trends in the residential (inpatient) treatment of individuals with a dual diagnosis. *Journal of Consulting and Clinical Psychology, 61*, 43–48.

Sprecher, S. (1998). Insiders' perspectives on reasons for attraction to a close other. *Social Psychology Quarterly, 61*(4) 287–300.

Sprecher, S., Sullivan, Q., & Hatfield, E. (1994). Mate selection preferences. *Journal of Personality and Social Psychology, 66*(6), 1074–1080.

Squire, L. R. (1993). Memory and the hippocampus. *Psychological Review, 99*, 195–231.

Squire, L. R. (1996, August). Memory systems of the brain. Master lecture presented to the meeting of the American Psychological Association, Toronto.

Squire, L. R. (2004). Memory systems of the brain: A brief history and current perspective. *Neurobiology of Learning & Memory, 82*(3), 171–177.

Staal, W. G., et al. (2000). Structural brain abnormalities in patients with schizophrenia and their healthy siblings. *American Journal of Psychiatry, 157*, 416–421.

Stacy, A. W. (1997). Memory activation and expectancy as prospective predictors of alcohol and marijuana use. *Journal of Abnormal Psychology, 106*, 61–73.

Stacy, A. W., Bentler, P. M., & Flay, B. R. (1994). Attitudes and health behavior in diverse populations: Drunk driving, alcohol use, binge eating, marijuana use, and cigarette use. *Health Psychology, 13*(1), 73–85.

Stacy, A. W., & Newcomb, M. D. (1999). Adolescent drug use and adult drug problems in women: Direct, interactive, and mediational effects. *Experimental & Clinical Psychopharmacology, 7*(2), 160–173.

Stamler, J., et al. (2000). Relationship of baseline serum cholesterol levels in 3 large cohorts of younger men to long-term coronary, cardiovascular, and all-cause mortality and to longevity. *Journal of the American Medical Association, 284*, 311–318.

Stampfer, M. J., Hu, F. B., Manson, J. E., Rimm, E. B., & Willett, W. C. (2000). Primary prevention of coronary heart disease in women through diet and lifestyle. *New England Journal of Medicine, 343*(1), 16–22.

Stangor, C., Swim, J. K., Van Allen, K. L., & Sechrist, G. B. (2002). Reporting discrimination in public and private contexts. *Journal of Personality & Social Psychology, 82*(1), 69–74.

Staples, S. I. (1996). Human responses to environmental noise. *American Psychologist, 51*, 143–150.

Stasser, G. (1999). A primer of social decision scheme theory: Models of group influence, competitive model-testing, and prospective modeling. *Organizational Behavior & Human Decision Processes, 80*(1), 3–20.

Steele, C. M. (1996, August). The role of stereotypes in shaping intellectual identity. Master lecture presented to the meeting of the American Psychological Association, Toronto.

Steele, C. M. (1997). A threat in the air: How stereotypes shape intellectual identity and performance. *American Psychologist, 52*, 613–629.

Steele, C. M., & Aronson, J. (1995). Stereotype threat and the intellectual test performance of African Americans. *Journal of Personality and Social Psychology, 69*, 797–811.

Steele, C. M., & Josephs, R. A. (1990). Alcohol myopia. *American Psychologist, 45*, 921–933.

Stein, M. B., & Kean, Y. M. (2000). Disability and quality of life in social phobia: Epidemiologic findings. *American Journal of Psychiatry, 157*, 1606–1613.

Stein, R, A., & Strickland, T. L. (1998). A review of the neuropsychological effects of commonly used prescription medications. *Archives of Clinical Neuropsychology, 13*(3), 259–284.

Steinberg, L. (1996). *Beyond the classroom*. New York: Simon & Schuster.

Steinberg, L. (2001). We know some things: Parent–adolescent relationships in retrospect and prospect. *Journal of Research on Adolescence, 11*(1), 1–19.

Steinberg, L., Brown, B. B., & Dornbusch, S. M. (1996). Ethnicity and adolescent achievement. *American Educator, 20*(2), 28–35.

Steiner, M., Dunn, E., & Born, L. (2003). Hormones and mood: From menarche to menopause and beyond. *Journal of Affective Disorders, 74*(1), 67–83.

Steiner, M., & Pearlstein, T. (2000). Premenstrual dysphoria and the serotonin system pathophysiology and treatment. *Journal of Clinical Psychiatry, 61*(Suppl12), 17–21.

Sternberg, R. J. (1988). Triangulating love. In R. J. Sternberg & M. J. Barnes (eds.), *The psychology of love*. New Haven, CT: Yale University Press.

Sternberg, R. J. (1997). The concept of intelligence and its role in lifelong learning and success. *American Psychologist, 52*, 1030–1037.

Sternberg, R. J. (2000). In search of the zipperump-a-zoo. *Psychologist, 13*(5), 250–255.

Sternberg, R. J. (2001). What is the common thread of creativity? *American Psychologist, 56*(4), 360–362.

Sternberg, R. J., Lautrey, J., & Lubart, T. I. (2003). *Models of intelligence: International perspectives*. Washington, D.C.: American Psychological Association.

Sternberg, R. J., & Lubart, T. I. (1995). *Defying the crowd: Cultivating creativity in a culture of conformity*. New York: Free Press.

Sternberg, R. J., & Lubart, T. I. (1996). Investing in creativity. *American Psychologist, 51*, 677–688.

Sternberg, R. J., Wagner, R. K., Williams, W. M., & Horvath, J. A. (1995). Testing common sense. *American Psychologist, 50*, 912–927.

Sternberg, R. J., & Williams, W. M. (1997). Does the Graduate Record Examination predict meaningful success in the graduate training of psychologists? *American Psychologist, 52*, 630–641.

Stevenson, H. W., Lee, S. Y., & Stigler, J. W. (1986). Mathematics achievement of Chinese, Japanese, and American children. *Science, 231*, 693–699.

Stewart, A. J., & Ostrove, J. M. (1998). Women's personality in middle age: Gender, history, and midcourse corrections. *American Psychologist, 53*(11), 1185–1194.

Stewart, A. J., Ostrove, J. M. & Helson, R. (2001). Middle aging in women: Patterns of personality change from the 30s to the 50s. *Journal of Adult Development, 8*(1), 23–37.

Stewart, J. Y., & Armet, E. (2000). Aging in America: Retirees reinvent the concept. *Los Angeles Times online*, April 3.

Stice, E., Akutagawa, D., Gaggar, A., & Agras, W. S. (2000a). Negative affect moderates the relation between dieting and binge eating. *International Journal of Eating Disorders, 27*(2), 218–229.

Stice, E., & Bearman, S. K. (2001). Body-image and eating disturbances prospectively predict increases in depressive symptoms in adolescent girls: A growth curve analysis. *Developmental Psychology, 37*(5), 597–607.

Stice, E., Hayward, C., Cameron, R. P., Killen, J. D., & Taylor, C. B. (2000). Body-image and eating disturbances predict onset of depression among female adolescents: A longitudinal study. *Journal of Abnormal Psychology, 109*(3), 438–444.

Stickgold, R, Hobson, J. A., Fosse, R., & Fosse, M. (2001). Sleep, learning, and dreams: Off-line memory reprocessing. *Science, 294*(5544), 1052–1057.

Stickgold, R., Whidbee, D., Schirmer, B., Patel, V., & Hobson, J. A. (2000). Visual discrimination task improvement: A multi-step process occurring during sleep. *Journal of Cognitive Neuroscience, 12*(2), 246–254.

Stier, D. S., & Hall, J. A. (1984). Gender differences in touch. *Journal of Personality and Social Psychology, 47*, 440–459.

Storm, L., & Ertel, S. (2001). Does psi exist? Comments on Milton and Wiseman's (1999) meta-analysis of ganzfeld research. *Psychological Bulletin, 127*(3), 424–433.

Storm, L., & Ertle, Suitbert. (2002). The ganzfeld debate continued: A response to Milton & Wiseman (2001). *Journal of Parapsychology, 66*(1), 73–82.

Straneva, P. A., et al. (2002). Menstrual cycle, beta-endorphins, and pain sensitivity in premenstrual dysphoric disorder. *Health Psychology, 21*(4), 358–367.

Straube, E. R., & Oades, R. D. (1992). *Schizophrenia*. San Diego: Academic Press.

Strauch, I., & Lederbogen, S. (1999). The home dreams and waking fantasies of boys and girls between ages 9 and 15: A longitudinal study. *Dreaming: Journal of the Association for the Study of Dreams, 9*(2–3), 153–161.

Strauss, M. (1995). Cited in C. Collins (1995), Spanking is becoming the new don't. *The New York Times*, May 11, p. C8.

Street, A. E., King, L. A., King, D. W., & Riggs, D. S. (2003). The associations among male-perpetrated partner violence, wives' psychological distress and children's behavior problems: A structural equation modeling analysis. *Journal of Comparative Family Studies, 34*(1), 23–40.

Strickland, T. L., Miller, B. L., Kowell, A., & Stein, R. (1998). Neurobiology of cocaine-induced organic brain impairment: Contributions from functional neuroimaging. *Neuropsychology Review, 8*(1), 1–9.

Striegel-Moore, R. H., & Cachelin, F. M. (2001). Etiology of eating disorders in women. *Counseling Psychologist, 29*(5), 635–661.

Striegel-Moore, R. H., et al. (2003). Eating disorders in white and black women. *American Journal of Psychiatry, 160*, 1326–1331.

Strike, P. C., & Steptoe, A. (2005). Behavioral and emotional triggers of acute coronary syndromes: A systematic review and critique. *Psychosomatic Medicine, 67*(2), 179–186.

Strober, M., Freeman, R., Lampert, C., Diamond, J., & Kaye, W. (2000). Controlled family study of anorexia nervosa and bulimia nervosa: Evidence of shared liability and transmission of partial syndromes. *American Journal of Psychiatry, 157*, 393–401.

Stroele, A., et al. (2002). GABA-sub(A) receptor-modulating neuroactive steroid composition in patients with panic disorder before and during paroxetine treatment. *American Journal of Psychiatry, 159*(1), 145–147.

Strom, J. C., & Buck, R. W. (1979). Staring and participants' sex. *Personality and Social Psychology Bulletin, 5*, 114–117.

Strote, J., Lee, J. E., & Wechsler, H. (2002). Increasing MDMA use among college students: Results of a national survey. *Journal of the American Academy of Child & Adolescent Psychiatry, 41*(10), 1215.

Stroud, M. W., Thorn, B. E., Jensen, M. P., & Boothby, J. L. (2000). The relation between pain beliefs, negative thoughts, and psychosocial functioning in chronic pain patients. *Pain, 84*(2–3), 347–352.

Strupp, H. H. (2001). Implications of the empirically supported treatment movement for psychoanalysis. *Psychoanalytic Dialogues, 11*(4), 605–619.

Stunkard, A. J., Harris, J. R., Pedersen, N. L., & McLearn, G. E. (1990). A separated twin study of the body mass index. *New England Journal of Medicine, 322*, 1483–1487.

Stutts, J. C., Wilkins, J. W., Osberg, J. S., & Vaughn, B. V. (2003). Driver risk factors for sleep-related crashes. *Accident Analysis & Prevention, 35*(3), 321–331.

Sue, D. W., & Sue, D. (2002). *Counseling the culturally diverse: Theory and practice, 4th ed.* Hoboken, NJ: Wiley.

Sue, S., & Okazaki, S. (1990). Asian-American educational achievements. *American Psychologist, 45*, 913–920.

Suinn, R. M. (2001). The terrible twos—anger and anxiety: Hazardous to your health. *American Psychologist, 56*(1), 27–36.

Suler, J. (2005). Psychological qualities of cyberspace. http://www.rider.edu/~suler/psycyber/netself.html. Accessed March 29.

Sullivan, A. (2000). The He hormone. *The New York Times Magazine*, April 2, pp. 46–51ff.

Sullivan, E. V., et al. (2000). Contribution of alcohol abuse to cerebellar volume deficits in men with schizophrenia. *Archives of General Psychiatry, 57*, 894–902.

Sullivan, J. M. (2000) Cellular and molecular mechanisms underlying learning and memory impairments produced by cannabinoids. *Learning & Memory, 7*(3), 132–139.

Sullivan, P. F., Neale, M. C., & Kendler, K. S. (2000). Genetic epidemiology of major depression: Review and meta-analysis. *American Journal of Psychiatry, 157*, 1552–1562.

Suttle, C. M., Banks, M. S., & Graf, E. W. (2002). FPL and sweep VEP to tritan stimuli in young human infants. *Vision Research, 42*(26), 2879–2891.

Suvisaari, J. M., Haukka, J. K., & Loennqvist, J. K. (2002). "Seasonal fluctuation in schizophrenia": Dr. Suvisaari and colleagues reply. *American Journal of Psychiatry, 159*(3), 500.

Suvisaari, J., Mautemps, N., Haukka, J., Hovi, T., & Löönnqvist, J. (2003). Childhood central nervous system viral infections and adult schizophrenia. *American Journal of Psychiatry, 160*, 1183–1185.

Suzuki, L. A., & Valencia, R. R. (1997). Race-ethnicity and measured intelligence: Educational implications. *American Psychologist, 52*, 1103–1114.

Swendsen, J. D., et al. (2000). Mood and alcohol consumption: An experience sampling test of the self-medication hypothesis. *Journal of Abnormal Psychology, 109*(2), 198–204.

Swerdlow, N. R., et al. (2003). Prestimulus modification of the startle reflex: Relationship to personality and psychological markers of dopamine function. *Biological Psychology, 62*(1), 17–26.

Swinyard, W. R., Kau, A., & Phua, H. (2001). Happiness, materialism, and religious experience in the U.S. and Singapore. *Journal of Happiness Studies, 2*(1), 13–32.

Szala, M. (2002). Two-level pattern recognition in a class of knowledge-based systems. *Knowledge-Based Systems, 15*(1–2), 95–101.

Szasz, T. (1999). Medical incapacity, legal incompetence and psychiatry. *Psychiatric Bulletin, 23*(9), 517–519.

Szasz, T. (2000). Second commentary on "Aristotle's function argument." *Philosophy, Psychiatry, & Psychology, 7*(1), 3–16.

Tacon, A. M., McComb, J., Caldera, Y., & Randolph, P. (2003). Mindfulness meditation, anxiety reduction, and heart disease: A pilot study. *Family & Community Health, 26*(1), 25–33.

Taffe, M. A., et al. (2002). Cognitive performance of MDMA-treated rhesus monkeys: Sensitivity to serotonergic challenge. *Neuropsychopharmacology, 27*(6), 993–1005.

Takahashi, T., et al. (2002). Melatonin alleviates jet lag symptoms caused by an 11-hour eastward flight. *Psychiatry & Clinical Neurosciences, 56*(3), 301–302.

Talwar, S. K., et al. (2002). Rat navigation guided by remote control. *Nature, 417*, 37–38.

Tanasescu, M., et al. (2002). Exercise type and intensity in relation to coronary heart disease in men. *Journal of the American Medical Association, 288*, 1994–2000.

Tapes raise new doubts about "Sybil" personalities. (1998). *The New York Times online*, August 19.

Tassi, F., Schneider, B. H., & Richard, J. F. (2001). Competitive behavior at school in relation to social competence and incompetence in middle childhood. *Revue Internationale de Psychologie Sociale, 14*(2), 165–184.

Taylor, D. J., & McFatter, R. M. (2003). Cognitive performance after sleep deprivation: Does personality make a difference? *Personality & Individual Differences, 34*(7), 1179–1193.

Taylor, M. A., & Fink, M. (2003). Catatonia in psychiatric classification: A home of its own. *American Journal of Psychiatry, 160*, 1233–124.

Taylor, M. J. (2000). The influence of self-efficacy on alcohol use among American Indians. *Cultural Diversity and Ethnic Minority Psychology, 6*(2), 152–167.

Taylor, S. E. (2000). Cited in E. Goode (2000), Response to stress found that's particularly female. *The New York Times*, May 19, p. A20.

Taylor, S. E., Kemeny, M. E., Reed, G. M., Bower, J. E., & Gruenewald, T. L. (2000a). Psychological resources, positive illusions, and health. *American Psychologist, 55*(1), 99–109.

Taylor, S. E., et al. (2000b). Biobehavioral responses to stress in females: Tend-and-befriend, not fight-or-flight. *Psychological Review, 107*(3), 411–429.

Taylor, S., et al. (2003). Comparative efficacy, speed, and adverse effects of three PTSD treatments: Exposure therapy, EMDR, and relaxation training. *Journal of Consulting and Clinical Psychology, 71*, 330–338.

Taylor-Tolbert, N. S., et al. (2000). Exercise reduces blood pressure in heavy older hypertensive men. *American Journal of Hypertension, 13*, 44–51.

Teachout, T. (2000). For more artists, a fine old age. *The New York Times online*, April 2.

Teller, D. Y. (1998). Spatial and temporal aspects of infant color vision. *Vision Research, 38*(21), 3275–3282.

Tenenbaum, H. R., & Leaper, C. (2002). Are parents' gender schemas related to their children's gender-related cognitions? A meta-analysis. *Developmental Psychology, 38*(4), 615–630.

Teng, E., & Squire, L. R. (1999). Memory for places learned long ago is intact after hippocampal damage. *Nature, 400*(6745), 675–677.

Tennen, H., & Affleck, G. (2000). The perception of personal control: Sufficiently important to warrant careful scrutiny. *Personality & Social Psychology Bulletin, 26*(2), 152–156.

Terrace, H. S. (1979, November). How Nim Chimpsy changed my mind. *Psychology Today*, 65–76.

Thase, M. E., & Kupfer, D. J. (1996). Recent developments in the pharmacotherapy of mood disorders. *Journal of Consulting and Clinical Psychology, 64*, 646–659.

Thingujam, N. S. (2002). Emotional intelligence: What is the evidence? *Psychological Studies, 47*(1–3), 54–69.

Thom, A., Sartory, G., & Jöhren, P. (2000). Comparison between one-session psychological treatment and benzodiazepine in dental phobia. *Journal of Consulting and Clinical Psychology, 68*(3), 378–387.

Thomas, A. (2001). Factitious and malingered dissociative identity disorder: Clinical features observed in 18 cases. *Journal of Trauma & Dissociation, 2*(4), 59–77.

Thomas, A. K., & Loftus, E. F. (2002). Creating bizarre false memories through imagination. *Memory & Cognition, 30*(3), 423–431.

Thomas, S. L., Skitka, L. J., Christen, S., & Jurgena, M. (2002). Social facilitation and impression formation. *Basic & Applied Social Psychology, 24*(1), 67–70.

Thomas, T. L., et al. (2003). Health of U.S. Navy submarine crew during periods of isolation. *Aviation, Space, & Environmental Medicine, 74*(3), 260–265.

Thornhill, R., & Palmer, C. (2000). *A natural history of rape: Biological bases of sexual coercion.* Cambridge, Mass.: MIT Press.

Thurstone, L. L. (1938). Primary mental abilities. *Psychometric Monographs, 1.*

Tiedemann, J. (2000). Parents' gender stereotypes and teachers' beliefs as predictors of children's concept of their mathematical ability in elementary school. *Journal of Educational Psychology, 92*(1), 144–151.

Tigner, R. B., & Tigner, S. S. (2000). Triarchic theories of intelligence: Aristotle and Sternberg. *History of Psychology, 3*(2), 168–176.

Tkachuk, G. A., & Martin, G. L. (1999). Exercise therapy for patients with psychiatric disorders: Research and clinical implications. *Professional Psychology: Research and Practice, 30*(3), 275–282.

Tolman, E. C., & Honzik, C. H. (1930). Introduction and removal of reward, and maze performance in rats. *University of California Publications in Psychology, 4*, 257–275.

Tong, H. (2001). Loneliness, depression, anxiety, and the locus of control. *Chinese Journal of Clinical Psychology, 9*(3), 196–197.

Tooley, G. A., Armstrong, S. M., Norman, T. R., & Sali, A. (2000). Acute increases in night-time plasma melatonin levels following a period of meditation. *Biological Psychology, 53*(1) 69–78.

Townsend, E., et al. (2001). The efficacy of problem-solving treatments after deliberate self-harm: Meta-analysis of randomized controlled trials with respect to depression, hopelessness and improvement in problems. *Psychological Medicine, 31*(6), 979–988.

Treasure, J., & Serpell, L. (2001). Osteoporosis in young people: Research and treatment in eating disorders. *Psychiatric Clinics of North America, 24*(2), 359–370.

Triandis, H. C. (2001). Individualism–collectivism and personality. *Journal of Personality, 69*(6), 907–924.

Triandis, H. C., & Suh, E. M. (2002). Cultural influences on personality. *Annual Review of Psychology, 53*(1), 133–160.

Trinh, N., et al. (2003). Efficacy of cholinesterase inhibitors in the treatment of neuropsychiatric symptoms and functional impairment in Alzheimer disease. *Journal of the American Medical Association, 289*, 210–216.

Trobst, K. K., Collins, R. L., & Embree, J. M. (1994). The role of emotion in social support provision. *Journal of Social and Personal Relationships, 11*, 45–62.

Trull, T. J., Stepp, S. D., & Durrett, C. A. (2003). Research on borderline personality disorder: An update. *Current Opinion in Psychiatry, 16*(1), 77–82.

Tryon, R. C. (1940). Genetic differences in maze learning in rats. *Yearbook of the National Society for Studies in Education, 39*, 111–119.

Tsai, G., & Coyle, J. T. (2002). Glutamatergic mechanisms in schizophrenia. *Annual Review of Pharmacology & Toxicology, 42*, 165–179.

Tsang, Y. C. (1938). Hunger motivation in gastrectomized rats. *Journal of Comparative Psychology, 26*, 1–17.

Tsou, M., & Liu, J. (2001). Happiness and domain satisfaction in Taiwan. *Journal of Happiness Studies, 2*(3), 269–288.

Tucker, J. S., Friedman, H. S., Wingard, D. L., & Schwartz, J. E. (1996). Marital history at midlife as a predictor of longevity. *Health Psychology, 15*, 94–101.

Tuiten, A., et al. (2000). Time course of effects of testosterone administration on sexual arousal in women. *Archives of General Psychiatry, 57*, 149–153.

Tulving, E. (1985). How many memory systems are there? *American Psychologist, 40*, 385–398.

Tulving, E., & Markowitsch, H. J. (1998). Episodic and declarative memory: Role of the hippocampus. *Hippocampus, 8*(3), 198–204.

Turk, D. C., & Okifuji, A. (2002). Psychological factors in chronic pain: Evolution and revolution. *Journal of Consulting and Clinical Psychology, 70*(3), 678–690.

Turnbull, C. M. (1961). Some observations regarding the experiences and behavior of the BaMbuti Pygmies. *American Journal of Psychology, 74,* 304–308.

Turner, A. M., & Greenough, W. T. (1985). Differential rearing effects on rat visual cortex synapses: I. Synaptic and neuronal density and synapses per neuron. *Brain Research, 329,* 195–203.

Turner, M. E., & Pratkanis, A. R. (1998). A social identity maintenance model of groupthink. *Organizational Behavior & Human Decision Processes, 73*(2–3), 210–235.

Tversky, A., & Kahneman, D. (1982). Judgment under uncertainty. In D. Kahneman, P. Slovic, & A. Tversky (eds.), *Judgment under uncertainty: Heuristics and biases.* New York: Cambridge University Press.

Tyrka, A. R., Waldron, I., Graber, J. A., & Brooks-Gunn, J. (2002). Prospective predictors of the onset of anorexic and bulimic syndromes. *International Journal of the Eating Disorders, 32*(3), 282–290.

Ukestad, L. K., & Wittrock, D. A. (1996). Pain perception and coping in female tension headache sufferers and headache-free controls. *Health Psychology, 15,* 65–68.

Unger, J. B., Rohrbach, L. A., Howard-Pitney, B., Ritt-Olson, A., & Mouttapa, M. (2001a). Peer influences and susceptibility to smoking among Californian adolescents. *Substance Use & Misuse, 36*(5), 551–571.

Unger, J. B., et al. (2001b) Stressful life events among adolescents in Wuhan, China: Associations with smoking, alcohol use, and depressive symptoms. *International Journal of Behavioral Medicine, 8*(1), 1–18.

United Nations Special Session on AIDS. (2001, June 25–27). Preventing HIV/AIDS among young people. New York: United Nations.

Updegraff, J. A., Taylor, S. E., Kemeny, M. E., & Wyatt, G. E. (2002). Positive and negative effects of HIV infection in women with low socioeconomic resources. *Personality & Social Psychology Bulletin, 28*(3), 382–394.

USBC (U.S. Bureau of the Census). (2002). *Statistical abstract of the United States* (122nd ed.). Washington, DC: U.S. Government Printing Office.

USBC (U.S. Bureau of the Census). (2003). *Statistical abstract of the United States* (123rd ed.). Washington, DC: U.S. Government Printing Office.

U.S. Council on Foreign Relations. (2002). Terrorism. http://cfrterrorism.org/groups/hamas_print.html.

Utter, J., Neumark-Sztainer, D., Wall, M., & Story, M. (2003). Reading magazine articles about dieting and associated weight control behaviors among adolescents. *Journal of Adolescent Health, 32*(1), 78–82.

Uzakov, S., Frey, J. U., & Korz, V. (2005). Reinforcement of rat hippocampal LTP by holeboard training. *Learning & Memory, 12,* 165–171.

Vaillant, G. E. (1994). Ego mechanisms of defense and personality psychopathology. *Journal of Abnormal Psychology, 103,* 44–50.

Valentiner, D. P., Foa, E. B., Riggs, D. S., & Gershuny, B. S. (1996). Coping strategies and posttraumatic stress disorder in female victims of sexual and nonsexual assault. *Journal of Abnormal Psychology, 105,* 455–458.

Vandenbergh, J. G. (1993). Cited in N. Angier (1993). Female gerbil born with males is found to be begetter of sons. *The New York Times,* August 24, p. C4.

van de Wetering, S., Bernstein, D. M., & Loftus, E. F. (2002). Public education against false memories: A modest proposal. *International Journal of Cognitive Technology, 7*(2), 4–7.

van Roosmalen, E., & McDaniel, S. A. (1998). Sexual harassment in academia: A hazard to women's health. *Women & Health, 28*(2), 33–54.

Veenstra-Vanderweele, J., & Cook, E. H. (2003). Genetics of childhood disorders: XLVI. Autism, part 5: Genetics of autism. *Journal of the American Academy of Child and Adolescent Psychiatry, 42*(1), 116–118.

Van Raalte, J. L., & Brewer, B. W. (2002). *Exploring sport and exercise psychology* (2nd ed.). Washington, DC: American Psychological Association.

Vasterling, J. J., et al. (2002). Attention, learning, and memory performances and intellectual resources in Vietnam veterans: PTSD and no disorder comparisons. *Neuropsychology, 16*(1), 5–14.

Velting, D. M., Rathus, J. H., & Miller, A. L. (2000). MACI personality scale profiles of depressed adolescent suicide attempters: A pilot study. *Journal of Clinical Psychology, 56*(10), 1381–1385.

Vermeer, H. J., Boekaerts, M., & Seegers, G. (2000). Motivational and gender differences: Sixth-grade students' mathematical problem-solving behavior. *Journal of Educational Psychology, 92*(2), 308-315.

Vernberg, E. M., La Greca, A. M., Silverman, W. K., & Prinstein, M. J. (1996). Prediction of posttraumatic stress symptoms in children after Hurricane Andrew. *Journal of Abnormal Psychology, 105,* 237–248.

Vernon, D., et al. (2003). The effect of training distinct neurofeedback protocols on aspects of cognitive performance. *International Journal of Psychophysiology, 47*(1), 75–85.

Vgontzas, A. N., & Kales, A. (1999). Sleep and its disorders. *Annual Review of Medicine, 50,* 387–400.

Vik, P. W., Carrello, P., Tate, S. R., & Field, C. (2000). Progression of consequences among heavy-drinking college students. *Psychology of Addictive Behaviors, 14*(2), 91–101.

Villa, K. K., & Abeles, N. (2000). Broad spectrum intervention and the remediation of prospective memory declines in the able elderly. *Aging & Mental Health, 4*(1), 21–29.

Villani, S. (2001). Impact of media on children and adolescents: A 10-year review of the research. *Journal of the American Academy of Child & Adolescent Psychiatry, 40*(4), 392–401.

Visintainer, M. A., Volpicelli, J. R., & Seligman, M. E. P. (1982). Tumor rejection in rats after inescapable or escapable shock. *Science, 216*(23), 437–439.

Volkow, N. D., et al. (2001a). Association of dopamine transporter reduction with psychomotor impairment in methamphetamine abusers. *American Journal of Psychiatry, 158,* 377–382.

Volkow, N. D., et al. (2001b). Higher cortical and lower subcortical metabolism in detoxified methamphetamine abusers. *American Journal of Psychiatry, 158,* 383–389.

Volz, J. (2000). Successful aging: The second 50. *Monitor on Psychology, 30*(1), 24–28.

Von Békésy, G. (1957, August). The ear. *Scientific American,* pp. 66–78.

Voneida, T. J. (1998). Sperry's concept of mind as an emergent property of brain function and its implications for the future of humankind. *Neuropsychologia, 36*(10), 1077–1082.

Vygotsky, L. S. (1962). *Thought and language.* Cambridge, MA: MIT Press.

Vygotsky, L. (1978). *Mind in society: The development of higher psychological processes.* Cambridge, MA: Harvard University Press.

Wadden, T. A., Brownell, K. D., & Foster, G. D. (2002). Obesity: Responding to the global epidemic. *Journal of Consulting and Clinical Psychology, 70*(3), 510–525.

Wade, N. (1998). Was Freud wrong? Are dreams the brain's start-up test? *The New York Times online,* January 6.

Wade, N. (2003). Early voices: The leap to language. *The New York Times online,* July 15.

Wade, N. (2005). For gay men, an attraction to a different kind of sweat. *The New York Times online,* May 10.

Wade, T. D., Bulik, C. M., Neale, M., & Kendler, K. S. (2000). Anorexia nervosa and major depression: Shared genetic and environmental risk factors. *American Journal of Psychiatry, 157*(3), 469–471.

Waelde, L. C., Koopman, C., Rierdan, J., & Spiegel, D. (2001). Symptoms of acute stress disorder and posttraumatic stress disorder following exposure to disastrous flooding. *Journal of Trauma & Dissociation, 2*(2), 37–52.

Wagner, R. K. (1997). Intelligence, training, and employment. (1997). *American Psychologist, 52,* 1059–1069.

Waldron, H. B., Slesnick, N., Brody, J. L., & Peterson, T. R. (2001). Treatment outcomes for adolescent substance abuse at 4- and 7-month assessments. *Journal of Consulting & Clinical Psychology, 69*(5), 802–813.

Walk, R. D., & Gibson, E. J. (1961). A comparative and analytical study of visual depth perception. *Psychological Monographs, 75*(15).

Walker, W. R., Skowronski, J. J., & Thompson, C. P. (2003). Life is pleasant—and memory helps to keep it that way! *Review of General Psychology, 7*(2), 203-210.

Wall, T. L., Carr, L. G., & Ehlers, C. L. (2003). Protective association of genetic variation in alcohol dehydrogenase with alcohol dependence in Native American Mission Indians. *American Journal of Psychiatry, 160*, 41–46.

Walsh, B. T., et al. (2000). Fluoxetine for bulimia nervosa following poor response to psychotherapy. *American Journal of Psychiatry, 157*, 1332–1334.

Wang, C. (2002). Emotional intelligence, general self-efficacy, and coping style of juvenile delinquents. *Chinese Mental Health Journal, 16*(8), 565–567.

Wang, H., et al. (2000). Nicotine as a potent blocker of the cardiac A-type K$^+$ channels: Effects on cloned Kv4.3 channels and native transient outward current. *Circulation, 102*, 1165–1171.

Wang, Q. (2003). Infantile amnesia reconsidered: A cross-cultural analysis. *Memory, 11*(1), 65–80.

Wang, X., et al. (2000). Longitudinal study of earthquake-related PTSD in a randomly selected community sample in North China. *American Journal of Psychiatry, 157*, 1260–1266.

Wann, D. L., Royalty, J., & Roberts, A. (2000). The self-presentation of sports fans: Investigating the importance of team identification and self-esteem. *Journal of Sport Behavior, 23*(2), 198–206.

Wann, D. L., & Schrader, M. P. (2000). Controllability and stability in the self-serving attributions of sport spectators. *Journal of Social Psychology, 140*(2), 160–168.

Ward, A., Lyubomirsky, S., Sousa, L., & Nolen-Hoeksema, S. (2003). Can't quite commit: Rumination and uncertainty. *Personality & Social Psychology Bulletin, 29*(1), 96–107.

Ward, I. L., et al. (2003). Fetal testosterone surge: Specific modulations induced in male rats by maternal stress and/or alcohol consumption. *Hormones & Behavior, 43*(5), 531–539.

Warman, D. M., & Cohen, R. (2000). Stability of aggressive behaviors and children's peer relationships. *Aggressive Behavior, 26*(4), 277–290.

Wartik, N. (2000). Depression comes out of hiding. *The New York Times*, June 25, pp. MH1, MH4.

Waters, M. (2000). Psychologists spotlight growing concern of higher suicide rates among adolescents. *Monitor on Psychology, 31*(6), 41.

Watkins, C. E., Jr., Campbell, V. L., Nieberding, R., & Hallmark, R. (1995). Contemporary practice of psychological assessment by clinical psychologists. *Professional Psychology: Research and Practice, 26*, 54–60.

Watson, D., Hubbard, B., & Wiese, D. (2000). Self-other agreement in personality and affectivity: The role of acquaintanceship, trait visibility, and assumed similarity. *Journal of Personality & Social Psychology, 78*(3), 546–558.

Watson, J. B. (1913). Psychology as the behaviorist views it. *Psychological Review, 20*, 158–177.

Watson, J. B. (1924). *Behaviorism*. New York: W. W. Norton.

Watson, M., Haviland, J. S., Greer, S., Davidson, J., & Bliss, J. M. (1999). Influence of psychological response on survival in breast cancer: A population-based cohort study. *The Lancet, 354*(9187), 1331–1336.

Webb, W. (1993). Cited in T. Adler (1993), Sleep loss impairs attention—and more. *APA Monitor, 24*(9), 22–23.

Weber, R., Ritterfeld, U., & Mathiak, K. (2006). Does playing violent video games induce aggression? Empirical evidence of a functional magnetic resonance imaging study. *Media Psychology, 8*(1), 39–60.

Webster, J. D. (2003). An exploratory analysis of a self-assessed wisdom scale. *Journal of Adult Development, 10*(1), 13–22.

Wechsler, D. (1975). Intelligence defined and undefined. *American Psychologist, 30*, 135–139.

Weekes, J. R., Lynn, S. J., Green, J. P., & Brentar, J. T. (1992). Pseudomemory in hypnotized and task-motivated subjects. *Journal of Abnormal Psychology, 101*, 356–360.

Wegener, D. T., Petty, R. E., Detweiler-Bedell, B. T., & Jarvis, W. B. G. (2001). Implications of attitude change theories for numerical anchoring: Anchor plausibility and the limits of anchor effectiveness. *Journal of Experimental Social Psychology, 37*(1), 62–69.

Weinberg, R. A., Scarr, S., & Waldman, I. D. (1992). The Minnesota Transracial Adoption Study: A follow-up of IQ test performance at adolescence. *Intelligence, 16*, 117–135.

Weiner, B. (1991). Metaphors in motivation and attribution. *American Psychologist, 46*, 921–930.

Weiner, K. (1992). Cited in D. J. Goleman (1992), Heart seizure or panic attack? *The New York Times*, January 8, p. C12.

Weiner, R. D. (2000). Retrograde amnesia with electroconvulsive therapy. *Archives of General Psychiatry online, 57*(6).

Weinmann, M., Bader, J., Endrass, J., & Hell, D. (2001). Sind Kompetenz- und Kontrolluebeberzeugungen depressionsabhaengig? Eine Verlaufsuntersuchung. *Zeitschrift fuer Klinische Psychologie und Psychotherapie, 30*(3), 153–158.

Weinstein, C. S., Fucetola, R., & Mollica, R. (2001). Neuropsychological issues in the assessment of refugees and victims of mass violence. *Neuropsychology Review, 11*(3), 131–141.

Wells, G. L., & Olsen, E. A. (2003). Eyewitness testimony. *Annual Review of Psychology, 54*, 277–295.

Werner, C. M. (2003). Changing homeowners' use of toxic household products: A transactional approach. *Journal of Environmental Psychology, 23*(1), 33–45.

West, R., & Craik, F. I. M. (1999). Age-related decline in prospective memory: The roles of cue accessibility and cue sensitivity. *Psychology & Aging, 14*(2), 264–272.

Wetzler, S. E., & Sweeney, J. A. (1986). Childhood amnesia. In D. C. Rubin (ed.), *Autobiographical memory.* New York: Cambridge University Press.

Whaley, A. L. (2001). Cultural mistrust and mental health services for African Americans: A review and meta-analysis. *Counseling Psychologist, 29*(4), 513–531.

Wheeler, M. A., & McMillan, C. T. (2001). Focal retrograde amnesia and the episodic–semantic distinction. *Cognitive, Affective & Behavioral Neuroscience, 1*(1), 22–36.

Wheeler, M. E., & Treisman, A. M. (2002). Binding in short-term visual memory. *Journal of Experimental Psychology: General, 131*(1), 48–64.

Wheeler, S. C., & Petty, R. E. (2001). The effects of stereotype activation on behavior: A review of possible mechanisms. *Psychological Bulletin, 127*(6), 797–826.

White, A. M., Matthews, D. B., & Best, P. J. (2000). Ethanol, memory, and hippocampal function: A review of recent findings. *Hippocampus, 10*(1), 88–93.

White, J. W., Smith, P. H., Koss, M. P., & Figueredo, A. J. (2000). Intimate partner aggression—What have we learned? *Psychological Bulletin, 126*(5), 690–696.

Whitfield, K. E., Weidner, G., Clark, R., & Anderson, N. B. (2002). Sociodemographic diversity and behavioral medicine. *Journal of Consulting and Clinical Psychology, 70*(3), 463–481.

Whorf, B. (1956). *Language, thought, and reality.* New York: Wiley.

Wiebe, R. E., & McCabe, S. B. (2002). Relationship perfectionism, dysphoria, and hostile interpersonal behaviors. *Journal of Social & Clinical Psychology, 21*(1), 67–91.

Wiens, A. N., & Menustik, C. E. (1983). Treatment outcome and patient characteristics in an aversion therapy program for alcoholism. *American Psychologist, 38*, 1089–1096.

Wierzbicka, A. (1999). "Universals of colour" from a linguistic point of view. *Behavioral & Brain Sciences, 22*(4), 724–725.

Wilcox, V. L., Kasl, S. V., & Berkman, L. F. (1994). Social support and physical disability in older people after hospitalization. *Health Psychology, 13*, 170–179.

Wilgoren, J. (2000). Effort to curb binge drinking in college falls short. *The New York Times*, March 15, p. A16.

Wilhelm, F. H., Gevirtz, R., & Roth, W. T. (2001). Respiratory dysregulation in anxiety, functional cardiac, and pain disorders: Assessment, phenomenology, and treatment. *Behavior Modification, 25*(4), 513–545.

Williams, J. E., & Best, D. L. (1994). Cross-cultural views of women and men. In W. J. Lonner & R. Malpass (eds.), *Psychology and culture.* Boston: Allyn & Bacon.

Williams, J. E., et al. (2000). Anger proneness predicts coronary heart disease risk: Prospective analysis from the Atherosclerosis Risk In Communities (ARIC) study. *Circulation, 101*(17), 2034–2039.

Williams, S. M., et al. (2000). Combinations of variations in multiple genes are associated with hypertension. *Hypertension, 36*, 2–6.

Willoughby, T., Wood, E., & Khan, M. (1994). Isolating variables that impact on or detract from the effectiveness of elaboration strategies. *Journal of Educational Research, 86,* 279–289.

Wills, T. A., Sandy, J. M., & Yaeger, A. M. (2002). Moderators of the relation between substance use level and problems: Test of a self-regulation model in middle adolescence. *Journal of Abnormal Psychology, 111*(1), 3–21.

Wilson, A. (2002, November 3). War & remembrance: Controversy is a constant for memory researcher Elizabeth Loftus, newly installed at UCI. *Orange County Register.*

Wilson, B. (1997). Cited in N. Seppa (1997), Children's TV remains steeped in violence. *APA Monitor, 28*(6), 36.

Wilson, G. T., Fairburn, C. C., Agras, W. S., Walsh, B. T., & Kraemer, H. (2002). Cognitive–behavioral therapy for bulimia nervosa: Time course and mechanisms of change. *Journal of Consulting & Clinical Psychology, 70*(2), 267–274.

Wilson, K. D., & Farah, M. J. (2003). When does the visual system use viewpoint-invariant representations during recognition? *Cognitive Brain Research, 16*(3), 399–415.

Wilson, R. S. (1983). The Louisville twin study: Developmental synchronies in behavior. *Child Development, 54,* 298–316.

Wilson, W., et al. (2000). Brain morphological changes and early marijuana use: A magnetic resonance and positron emission tomography study. *Journal of Addictive Diseases, 19*(1), 1–22.

Winocur, G., et al. (2000). Cognitive rehabilitation in clinical neuropsychology. *Brain & Cognition, 42*(1), 120–123.

Winter, W. E. (2001). The use of a skill-based activity in therapeutic induction. *American Journal of Clinical Hypnosis, 44*(2), 119–126.

Winters, W., et al. (2003). Media warnings about environmental pollution facilitate the acquisition of symptoms in response to chemical substances. *Psychosomatic Medicine, 65*(3), 332–338.

Winzelberg, A. J., et al. (2000). Effectiveness of an Internet-based program for reducing risk factors for eating disorders. *Journal of Consulting and Clinical Psychology, 68,* 346–350.

Wittchen, H., Becker, E., Lieb, R., & Krause, P. (2002). Prevalence, incidence and stability of premenstrual dysphoric disorder in the community. *Psychological Medicine, 32*(1), 119–132.

Wolkin, A., et al. (2003). Inferior frontal white matter anisotropy and negative symptoms of schizophrenia: A diffusion tensor imaging study. *American Journal of Psychiatry, 160,* 572–574.

Wolkow, C. A., Kimura, K. D., Lee, M-S., & Ruvkun, G. (2000). Regulation of *C. elegans* life-span by insulinlike signaling in the nervous system. *Science, 290*(5489), 147–150.

Woloshyn, V. E., Paivio, A., & Pressley, M. (1994). Use of elaborative interrogation to help students acquire information consistent with prior knowledge and information inconsistent with prior knowledge. *Journal of Educational Psychology, 86,* 79–89.

Wolpe, J., & Plaud, J. J. (1997, September). Pavlov's contributions to behavior therapy: The obvious and the not so obvious. *American Psychologist, 52*(9), 966–972.

Wong, E. C., et al. (2003). Examining culturally based variables associated with ethnicity: Influences on credibility perceptions of empirically supported interventions. *Cultural Diversity & Ethnic Minority Psychology, 9*(1), 88–96.

Wood, W. (2000). Attitude change: Persuasion and social influence. *Annual Review of Psychology, 51,* 539–570.

Woody, E., & Szechtman, H. (2000). Hypnotic hallucinations: Towards a biology of epistemology. *Contemporary Hypnosis, 17*(1), 4–14.

Wright, I. C., et al. (2000). Meta-analysis of regional brain volumes in schizophrenia. *American Journal of Psychiatry 157,* 16–25.

Writing Committee for the ENRICHD Investigators. (2003). Effects of treating depression and low perceived social support on clinical events after myocardial infarction: The Enhancing Recovery in Coronary Heart Disease Patients (ENRICHD) Randomized Trial. *Journal of the American Medical Association, 289*(23), 3106–3116.

Wu, J., et al. (1999). Serotonin and learned helplessness: A regional study of 5-HT$_{1A}$, 5-HT$_{2A}$ receptors and the serotonin transport site in rat brain. *Journal of Psychiatric Research, 33*(1), 17–22.

Wu, P., et al. (2001). Factors associated with use of mental health services for depression by children and adolescents. *Psychiatric Services, 52*(2), 189–195.

Xin, X., et al. (2001). Effects of alcohol reduction on blood pressure: A meta-analysis of randomized controlled trials. *Hypertension, 38,* 1112–1117.

Yacoubian, G. S. (2003). Correlates of ecstasy use among high school seniors surveyed through Monitoring the Future. *Drugs: Education, Prevention & Policy, 10*(1), 65–72.

Yaffe, K., et al. (2000). Cognitive decline in women in relation to non-protein-bound oestradiol concentrations. *Lancet, 356,* 708–712.

Yang, O. S. (2000). Guiding children's verbal plan and evaluation during free play: An application of Vygotsky's genetic epistemology to the early childhood classroom. *Early Childhood Education Journal, 28*(1), 3–10.

Yanovski S. Z., & Yanovski J. A. (2002). Drug therapy: Obesity. *New England Journal of Medicine, 346,* 591–602.

Yates, W. R. (2000). Testosterone in psychiatry: Risks and benefits. *Archives of General Psychiatry, 58,* 12.

Yatham, L. N., et al. (2000). Brain serotonin$_2$ receptors in major depression: A positron emission tomography study. *Archives of General Psychiatry, 57,* 850–858.

Ybarra, G. J., Passman, R. H., & Eisenberg, C. S. L. (2000). The presence of security blankets or mothers (or both) affects distress during pediatric examinations. *Journal of Consulting and Clinical Psychology, 68,* 322–330.

Yehuda, R. (2002). Post-traumatic stress disorder. *New England Journal of Medicine, 346*(2), 108–114.

Yehuda, R. (2003). Hypothalamic-pituitary-adrenal alterations in PTSD: Are they relevant to understanding cortisol alterations in cancer? *Brain, Behavior & Immunity, 17*(Suppl1), S73–S83.

Yen, S., Zlotnick, C., & Costello, E. (2002). Affect regulation in women with borderline personality disorder traits. *Journal of Nervous & Mental Disease, 190*(10), 693–696.

Yesavage, J. A., et al. (2002). Modeling the prevalence and incidence of Alzheimer's disease and mild cognitive impairment. *Journal of Psychiatric Research, 36*(5), 281–286.

Yokota, F., & Thompson, K. M. (2000). Violence in G-rated animated films. *Journal of the American Medical Association, 283,* 2716–2720.

Young, E. A., et al. (2003). Mineralocorticoid receptor function in major depression. *Archives of General Psychiatry, 60,* 24–28.

Yunfang, L., Jingbo, H., Wenjing, W., Chenglie, Z., & Changli, L. (2000). Psychological state of female workers in air-conditioned workshop. *Homeostasis in Health & Disease, 40*(6), 213–216.

Zagar, K., & Rubenstein, A. (2002). *The inside story on teen girls.* Washington, DC: American Psychological Association.

Zahavi, A. (2003). Indirect selection and individual selection in sociobiology. *Animal Behaviour, 65,* 859–863.

Zajonc, R. B. (1968). Attitudinal effects of mere exposure. *Journal of Personality and Social Psychology, Monograph Supplement, 2*(9), 1–27.

Zajonc, R. B. (1980). Compresence. In P. Paulus (ed.), *The psychology of group influence.* Hillsdale, NJ: Erlbaum.

Zajonc, R. B. (2001). Mere exposure: A gateway to the subliminal. *Current Directions in Psychological Science, 10*(6), 224–228.

Zebrowitz, L. A. (2002). The affordances of immersive virtual environmental technology for studying social affordances. *Psychological Inquiry, 13*(2), 143–145.

Zeichner, A., Parrott, D. J., & Frey, F. C. (2003). Gender differences in laboratory aggression under response choice conditions. *Aggressive Behavior, 29*(2), 95–106.

Ziegler, D. J., & Hawley, J. L. (2001). Relation of irrational thinking and the Pessimistic Explanatory Style. *Psychological Reports, 88*(2), 483–488.

Zigler, E. (1999). Head Start is not child care. *American Psychologist, 54*(2), 142.

Zigler, E., Taussig, C., & Black, K. (1992). Early childhood intervention: A promising preventative for juvenile delinquency. *American Psychologist, 47,* 997–1006.

Zimbardo, P. G. (2004). A situationist perspective on the psychology of evil: Understanding how good people are transformed into perpetrators. In A. G. Miller (ed.), *The social psychology of good and evil* (pp. 21–50). New York: Guilford Press.

Zimbardo, P. G., LaBerge, S., & Butler, L. D. (1993). Psychophysiological consequences of unexplained arousal. *Journal of Abnormal Psychology, 102,* 466–473.

Zimmer, C. (2002–2003). Searching for your inner chimp. *Natural History, 112*(December, 2002–January, 2003).

Zimprich, D., & Martin, M. (2002). Can longitudinal changes in processing speed explain longitudinal age changes in fluid intelligence? *Psychology & Aging, 17*(4), 690–695.

Zola, S., Squire, L. R., & Lombroso, P. J. (2003). Genetics of childhood disorders: XLIX. Learning and memory, part 2: Multiple memory systems. *Journal of the American Academy of Child & Adolescent Psychiatry, 42*(4), 504–506.

Zucker, A. N., Ostrove, J. M., & Stewart, A. J. (2002). College-educated women's personality development in adulthood: Perceptions and age differences. *Psychology & Aging, 17*(2), 236–244.

Glossary

A–B problem The issue of how well we can predict behavior on the basis of attitudes.

Absolute threshold The minimal amount of energy that can produce a sensation.

Abstinence syndrome A characteristic cluster of symptoms that results from sudden decrease in an addictive drug's level of usage.

Accommodation According to Piaget, the modification of schemas so that information inconsistent with existing schemas can be integrated or understood.

Acculturation The process of adaptation in which immigrants and native groups identify with a new, dominant culture by learning about that culture and making behavioral and attitudinal changes.

Acetylcholine (ACh) A neurotransmitter that controls muscle contractions.

Acoustic code Mental representation of information as a sequence of sounds.

Acquired drives Drives acquired through experience, or learned.

Acrophobia Fear of high places.

Action potential The electrical impulse that provides the basis for the conduction of a neural impulse along an axon of a neuron.

Activating effect The arousal-producing effects of sex hormones that increase the likelihood of sexual behavior.

Activation–synthesis model The view that dreams reflect activation of cognitive activity by the reticular activating system and synthesis of this activity into a pattern by the cerebral cortex.

Actor–observer effect The tendency to attribute our own behavior to situational factors but to attribute the behavior of others to dispositional factors.

Acute stress disorder A disorder, like PTSD, that is characterized by feelings of anxiety and helplessness and caused by a traumatic event. Acute stress disorder occurs within a month of the event and lasts from 2 days to 4 weeks.

Adolescence The period of life bounded by puberty and the assumption of adult responsibilities.

Affective shift hypothesis The view that men and women tend to experience different shifts in the emotions following initiation of sexual activity, such that women feel more love and commitment, and many men experience less love and commitment.

Afferent neurons Neurons that transmit messages from sensory receptors to the spinal cord and brain. Also called sensory neurons.

Afterimage The lingering visual impression made by a stimulus that has been removed.

Age-30 transition Levinson's term for the ages from 28 to 33, which are characterized by reassessment of the goals and values of the 20s.

Agoraphobia Fear of open, crowded places.

Alarm reaction The first stage of the GAS, which is triggered by the impact of a stressor and characterized by sympathetic activity.

Algorithm A systematic procedure for solving a problem that works invariably when it is correctly applied.

All-or-none principle The fact that a neuron fires an impulse of the same strength whenever its action potential is triggered.

Alpha waves Rapid low-amplitude brain waves that have been linked to feelings of relaxation.

Altruism Unselfish concern for the welfare of others.

Alzheimer's disease (AHLTS-high-mers). A progressive form of mental deterioration characterized by loss of memory, language, problem solving, and other cognitive functions.

Ambiguous Having two or more possible meanings.

Amniotic sac A sac within the uterus that contains the embryo or fetus.

Amphetamines Stimulants derived from *alpha-methyl-beta-phenyl-ethyl-amine*, a colorless liquid consisting of carbon, hydrogen, and nitrogen.

Amygdala A part of the limbic system that apparently facilitates stereotypical aggressive responses.

Anal stage The second stage of psychosexual development, when gratification is attained through anal activities.

Analytical psychology Jung's psychodynamic theory, which emphasizes the collective unconscious and archetypes.

Anchoring and adjustment heuristic A decision-making heuristic in which a presumption or first estimate serves as a cognitive anchor. As we receive additional information, we make adjustments but tend to remain in the proximity of the anchor.

Androgens Male sex hormones.

Animism The belief that inanimate objects move because of will or spirit.

Anorexia nervosa A life-threatening eating disorder characterized by dramatic weight loss and a distorted body image.

Anterograde amnesia Failure to remember events that occurred after physical trauma because of the effects of the trauma.

Antibodies Substances formed by white blood cells that recognize and destroy antigens.

Antidepressant (ant-eye-dee-PRESS-ant). Acting to relieve depression.

Antidiuretic hormone (ADH) A pituitary hormone that conserves body fluids by increasing reabsorption of urine and is connected with paternal behavior in some mammals. Also called vasopressin.

Antigen A substance that stimulates the body to mount an immune system response to it. (The contraction for *anti*body *gen*erator.)

Antisocial personality disorder The diagnosis given a person who is in frequent conflict with society, yet who is undeterred by punishment and experiences little or no guilt and anxiety.

Aphagic Characterized by undereating.

Aphasia A disruption in the ability to understand or produce language.

Apnea Temporary absence or cessation of breathing. (From Greek and Latin roots meaning "without" and "breathing.")

Applied research Research conducted in an effort to find solutions to particular problems.

Approach–approach conflict A type of conflict in which the goals that produce opposing motives are positive and within reach.

Approach–avoidance conflict A type of conflict in which the same goal produces approach and avoidance motives.

Aptitude A natural ability or talent.

Archetypes Basic, primitive images or concepts hypothesized by Jung to reside in the collective unconscious.

Artificialism The belief that natural objects have been created by human beings.

Assimilation According to Piaget, the inclusion of a new event into an existing schema.

Asylum (uh-SIGH-lum). An institution for the care of the mentally ill.

Attachment The enduring affectional tie that binds one person to another.

Attachment-in-the-making phase The second phase in forming bonds of attachment, characterized by preference for familiar figures.

Attention-deficit/hyperactivity disorder A disorder that begins in childhood and is characterized by a persistent pattern of lack of attention, with or without hyperactivity and impulsive behavior.

Attitude An enduring mental representation of a person, place, or thing that evokes an emotional response and related behavior.

Attitude-discrepant behavior Behavior inconsistent with an attitude that may have the effect of modifying an attitude.

Attraction In social psychology, an attitude of liking or disliking (negative attraction).

Attribution A belief concerning why people behave in a certain way.

Attribution process The process by which people draw inferences about the motives and traits of others.

Attributional style The tendency to attribute one's behavior to internal or external factors, stable or unstable factors, and so on.

Auditory Having to do with hearing.

Auditory nerve The axon bundle that transmits neural impulses from the organ of Corti to the brain.

Authoritarian parents Parents who are rigid in their rules and who demand obedience for the sake of obedience.

Authoritative parents Parents who are strict and warm. Authoritative parents demand mature behavior but use reason rather than force in discipline.

Autokinetic effect The tendency to perceive a stationary point of light in a dark room as moving.

Autonomic nervous system (ANS) The division of the peripheral nervous system that regulates glands and activities such as heartbeat, respiration, digestion, and dilation of the pupils.

Autonomy Self-direction.

Availability heuristic A decision-making heuristic in which our estimates of frequency or probability of events are based on how easy it is to find examples.

Avatar A virtual body worn by an online user in cyberspace while playing a video game or visiting a chat room.

Average The central tendency of a group of measures, expressed either as the mean, median, or mode of a distribution.

Aversive conditioning A behavior-therapy technique in which undesired responses are inhibited by pairing repugnant or offensive stimuli with them.

Avoidance–avoidance conflict A type of conflict in which the goals are negative, but avoidance of one requires approaching the other.

Avoidant personality disorder A personality disorder in which the person is unwilling to enter relationships without assurance of acceptance because of fears of rejection and criticism.

Axon A long, thin part of a neuron that transmits impulses to other neurons from branching structures called terminal buttons.

Barbiturate An addictive depressant used to relieve anxiety or induce sleep.

Basilar membrane A membrane that lies coiled within the cochlea.

Behavior-rating scale A systematic means for recording the frequency with which target behaviors occur.

Behavior rehearsal Practice.

Behavior therapy Systematic application of the principles of learning to the direct modification of a client's problem behaviors.

Behavioral genetics The area of biology and psychology that focuses on the transmission of traits that give rise to behavior. Behavioral genetics also addresses individual differences in behavior.

Behaviorism The school of psychology that defines psychology as the study of observable behavior and studies relationships between stimuli and responses.

Benzodiazepines A class of drugs that reduce anxiety; minor tranquilizers.

Bimodal Having two modes.

Binocular cues Stimuli suggestive of depth that involve simultaneous perception by both eyes.

Biofeedback training (BFT) The systematic feeding back to an organism of information about a bodily function so that the organism can gain control of that function.

Bipolar cells Neurons that conduct neural impulses from rods and cones to ganglion cells.

Bipolar disorder A disorder in which the mood alternates between two extreme poles (elation and depression). Also referred to as *manic–depression.*

Blind In experimental terminology, unaware of whether or not one has received a treatment.

Blind spot The area of the retina where axons from ganglion cells meet to form the optic nerve.

Borderline personality disorder A personality disorder characterized by instability in relationships, self-image, mood, and lack of impulse control.

Bottom-up processing The organization of the parts of a pattern to recognize, or form an image of, the pattern they compose.

Brightness constancy The tendency to perceive an object as being just as bright even though lighting conditions change its intensity.

Broca's aphasia A language disorder characterized by slow, laborious speech.

Bulimia nervosa An eating disorder characterized by repeated cycles of binge eating and purging.

Case study A carefully drawn biography that may be obtained through interviews, questionnaires, and psychological tests.

Catastrophize To interpret negative events as being disastrous; to "blow out of proportion."

Catatonic schizophrenia A type of schizophrenia characterized by striking motor impairment.

Catharsis (cuh-THAR-sis) In psychoanalysis, the expression of repressed feelings and impulses to allow the release of the psychic energy associated with them.

Center According to Piaget, to focus one's attention.

Central nervous system The brain and spinal cord.

Cerebellum A part of the hindbrain involved in muscle coordination and balance.

Cerebral cortex The wrinkled surface area (gray matter) of the cerebrum.

Cerebrum The large mass of the forebrain, which consists of two hemispheres.

Chromosome A microscopic rod-shaped body in the cell nucleus carrying genes that transmit hereditary traits from generation to generation. Humans normally have 46 chromosomes.

Chunk A stimulus or group of stimuli that is perceived as a discrete piece of information.

Circadian rhythm Referring to cycles that are connected with the 24-hour period of the earth's rotation. (From the Latin *circa,* meaning "about," and *dia,* meaning "day.")

Cirrhosis of the liver A disease caused by protein deficiency in which connective fibers replace active liver cells, impeding circulation of the blood. Alcohol does not contain protein; therefore, persons who drink excessively may be prone to this disease.

Classical conditioning A simple form of learning in which an organism comes to associate or anticipate events. A neutral stimulus comes to evoke the response usually evoked by another stimulus by being paired repeatedly with the other stimulus. (Cognitive theorists view classical conditioning as the learning of relationships among events so as to allow an organism to represent its environment.) Also referred to as *respondent conditioning* or *Pavlovian conditioning.*

Claustrophobia Fear of tight, small places.

Clear-cut-attachment phase The third phase in forming bonds of attachment, characterized by intensified dependence on the primary caregiver.

Client-centered therapy Carl Rogers's method of psychotherapy, which emphasizes the creation of a warm, therapeutic atmosphere that frees clients to engage in self-exploration and self-expression.

Clinical scales Groups of test items that measure the presence of various abnormal behavior patterns.

Clitoris The external female sex organ that is most sensitive to sexual sensation; a smooth, round knob of tissue that is situated above the urethral opening.

Closure The tendency to perceive a broken figure as being complete or whole.

Cochlea The inner ear; the bony tube that contains the basilar membrane and the organ of Corti.

Cognition Mental activity involved in understanding, processing, and communicating information; the use of mental processes to perceive and mentally represent the world, think, and engage in problem solving and decision making.

Cognitive Having to do with mental processes such as sensation and perception, memory, intelligence, language, thought, and problem solving.

Cognitive-dissonance theory The view that we are motivated to make our cognitions or beliefs consistent.

Cognitive therapy A form of therapy that focuses on how clients' cognitions (expectations, attitudes, beliefs, etc.) lead to distress and may be modified to relieve distress and promote adaptive behavior.

Collective unconscious Jung's hypothesized store of vague racial memories.

Collectivist A person who defines herself or himself in terms of relationships to other people and groups and gives priority to group goals.

Color constancy The tendency to perceive an object as being the same color even though lighting conditions change its appearance.

Common fate The tendency to perceive elements that move together as belonging together.

Competencies Knowledge and skills.

Complementary Descriptive of colors of the spectrum that when combined produce white or nearly white light.

Compulsion An irresistible urge to repeat an act or engage in ritualistic behavior like hand washing.

Concept A mental category that is used to class together objects, relations, events, abstractions, or qualities that have common properties.

Concordance Agreement.

Concrete-operational stage Piaget's third stage, characterized by logical thought concerning tangible objects, conservation, and subjective morality.

Conditional positive regard Judgment of another person's value on the basis of the acceptability of that person's behaviors.

Conditioned reinforcer Another term for a secondary reinforcer.

Conditioned response (CR) In classical conditioning, a learned response to a conditioned stimulus.

Conditioned stimulus (CS) A previously neutral stimulus that elicits a conditioned response because it has been paired repeatedly with a stimulus that already elicited that response.

Conditions of worth Standards by which the value of a person is judged.

Conductive deafness The forms of deafness in which there is loss of conduction of sound through the middle ear.

Cones Cone-shaped photoreceptors that transmit sensations of color.

Confident power Feelings of self-confidence, self-efficacy.

Conflict Being torn in different directions by opposing motives. Feelings produced by being in conflict.

Conform To changes one's attitudes or overt behavior to adhere to social norms.

Conscious Self-aware.

Consensus General agreement.

Conservation According to Piaget, recognition that basic properties of substances such as weight and mass remain the same when superficial features change.

Consummate love The ideal form of love within Sternberg's model, which combines passion, intimacy, and commitment.

Contact comfort A hypothesized primary drive to seek physical comfort through contact with another.

Context-dependent memory Information that is better retrieved in the context in which it was encoded and stored, or learned.

Contingency theory The view that learning occurs when stimuli provide information about the likelihood of the occurrence of other stimuli.

Continuity The tendency to perceive a series of points or lines as having unity.

Continuous reinforcement A schedule of reinforcement in which every correct response is reinforced.

Control groups In experiments, groups whose members do not obtain the treatment, while other conditions are held constant.

Conventional level According to Kohlberg, a period during which moral judgments largely reflect social conventions. A "law and order" approach to morality.

Convergence A binocular cue for depth based on the inward movement of the eyes as they attempt to focus on an object that is drawing nearer.

Convergent thinking A thought process that narrows in on the single best solution to a problem.

Conversion disorder A disorder in which anxiety or unconscious conflicts are "converted" into physical symptoms that often have the effect of helping the person cope with anxiety or conflict.

Cornea Transparent tissue forming the outer surface of the eyeball.

Corpus callosum A thick fiber bundle that connects the hemispheres of the cortex.

Correlation An association or relationship among variables, as we might find between height and weight or between study habits and school grades.

Correlation coefficient A number between −1.00 and +1.00 that expresses the strength and direction (positive or negative) of the relationship between two variables.

Correlational method A mathematical method of determining whether one variable increases or decreases as another variable increases or decreases. For example, there is a correlation between intelligence test scores and grades in school.

Corticosteroids Steroids produced by the adrenal cortex that regulate carbohydrate metabolism and increase resistance to stress by fighting inflammation and allergic reactions. Also called cortical steroids.

Counterconditioning A fear-reduction technique in which pleasant stimuli are associated with fear-evoking stimuli so that the fear-evoking stimuli lose their aversive qualities.

Creative self According to Adler, the self-aware aspect of personality that strives to achieve its full potential.

Creativity The ability to generate novel and useful solutions to problems.

Critical period A period of time when an instinctive response can be elicited by a particular stimulus.

Crystallized intelligence One's lifetime of intellectual achievement, as shown largely through vocabulary and knowledge of world affairs.

Cultural bias A factor that provides an advantage for test takers from certain cultural backgrounds, such as using test items that are based on middle-class culture in the United States.

Cumulative recorder An instrument that records the frequency of an organism's operants (or "correct" responses) as a function of the passage of time.

Daily hassles Notable daily conditions and experiences that are threatening or harmful to a person's well-being.

Dark adaptation The process of adjusting to conditions of lower lighting by increasing the sensitivity of rods and cones.

Debrief To elicit information about a completed procedure.

Decentration Simultaneous focusing on more than one dimension of a problem, so that flexible, reversible thought becomes possible.

Decibel (dB) A unit expressing the loudness of a sound.

Defense mechanism In psychodynamic theory, an unconscious function of the ego that protects it from anxiety-evoking material by preventing accurate recognition of this material.

Deindividuation The process by which group members may discontinue self-evaluation and adopt group norms and attitudes.

Delirium tremens A condition characterized by sweating, restlessness, disorientation, and hallucinations. The DTs occur in some chronic alcohol users when there is a sudden decrease in usage.

Delta waves Strong, slow brain waves usually emitted during stage 4 sleep.

Delusions False, persistent beliefs that are unsubstantiated by sensory or objective evidence.

Dendrites Rootlike structures, attached to the cell body of a neuron, that receive impulses from other neurons.

Dependent variable A measure of an assumed effect of an independent variable.

Depolarize To reduce the resting potential of a cell membrane from about 270 millivolts toward zero.

Depressant A drug that lowers the rate of activity of the nervous system.

Descriptive statistics The branch of statistics that is concerned with providing descriptive information about a distribution of scores.

Desensitization The type of sensory adaptation in which we become less sensitive to constant stimuli. Also called *negative adaptation*.

Dichromat A person who is sensitive to black–white and either red–green or blue–yellow and hence partially color-blind.

Difference threshold The minimal difference in intensity required between two sources of energy so that they will be perceived as being different.

Diffusion of responsibility The spreading or sharing of responsibility for a decision or behavior within a group.

Direct inner awareness Knowledge of one's own thoughts, feelings, and memories without use of sensory organs.

Discrimination In conditioning, the tendency for an organism to distinguish between a conditioned stimulus and similar stimuli that do not forecast an unconditioned stimulus.

Discriminative stimulus In operant conditioning, a stimulus that indicates that reinforcement is available.

Disorganized schizophrenia A type of schizophrenia characterized by disorganized delusions and vivid hallucinations.

Displace In memory theory, to cause information to be lost from short-term memory by adding new information.

Displaced Transferred.

Displacement The quality of language that permits one to communicate information about objects and events in another time and place.

Dispositional attribution An assumption that a person's behavior is determined by internal causes such as personal attitudes or goals.

Dissociative amnesia A dissociative disorder marked by loss of memory or self-identity; skills and general knowledge are usually retained. Thought to stem from psychological conflict or trauma. Previously termed *psychogenic amnesia*.

Dissociative disorders Disorders in which there are sudden, temporary changes in consciousness or self-identity.

Dissociative fugue A dissociative disorder in which one experiences amnesia and then flees to a new location. Previously termed *psychogenic fugue*.

Dissociative identity disorder A disorder in which a person appears to have two or more distinct identities or personalities that may alternately emerge.

Divergent thinking A thought process that attempts to generate multiple solutions to problems.

Dizygotic (DZ) twins Twins that develop from two fertilized ova and who are thus as closely related as brothers and sisters in general. Also called fraternal twins.

DNA Abbreviation for deoxyribonucleic acid, the substance that forms the basic material of chromosomes. It takes the form of a double helix and contains the genetic code.

Dopamine A neurotransmitter that is involved in Parkinson's disease and that appears to play a role in schizophrenia.

Double-blind study A study in which neither the subjects nor the observers know who has received the treatment.

Down syndrome A condition caused by an extra chromosome on the 21st pair and characterized by mental deficiency, a broad face, and slanting eyes.

The dream In this usage, Levinson's term for the overriding drive of youth to become someone important, to leave one's mark on history.

Drive for superiority Adler's term for the desire to compensate for feelings of inferiority.

Drive A condition of arousal in an organism that is associated with a need.

Drive-reduction theory The view that organisms learn to engage in behaviors that have the effect of reducing drives.

Dyspareunia A sexual dysfunction characterized by persistent or recurrent pain during sexual intercourse. (From roots meaning "badly paired.")

Eardrum A thin membrane that vibrates in response to sound waves, transmitting the waves to the middle and inner ears.

Eating disorders A group of disorders marked by persistent, gross disturbances in eating patterns.

Echo A mental representation of an auditory stimulus (sound) that is held briefly in sensory memory.

Echoic memory The sensory register that briefly holds mental representations of auditory stimuli.

Efferent neurons Neurons that transmit messages from the brain or spinal cord to muscles and glands. Also called motor neurons.

Effort justification In cognitive-dissonance theory, the tendency to seek justification (acceptable reasons) for strenuous efforts.

Ego The second psychic structure to develop, characterized by self-awareness, planning, and delay of gratification.

Ego analyst A psychodynamically oriented therapist who focuses on the conscious, coping behavior of the ego instead of the hypothesized, unconscious functioning of the id.

Ego identity Erikson's term for a firm sense of who one is and what one stands for.

Ego integrity versus despair Erikson's term for the crisis of late adulthood, characterized by the task of maintaining one's sense of identity despite physical deterioration.

Egocentrism According to Piaget, the assumption that others view the world as one does oneself.

Eidetic imagery The maintenance of detailed visual memories over several minutes.

Ejaculation The process of propelling seminal fluid (semen) from the penis.

Elaboration likelihood model The view that persuasive messages are evaluated (elaborated) on the basis of central and peripheral cues.

Elaborative rehearsal The kind of coding or method for increasing retention of new information by relating it to information that is well known.

Electra complex A conflict of the phallic stage in which the girl longs for her father and resents her mother.

Electroconvulsive therapy (ECT) Treatment of disorders like major depression by passing an electric current (that causes a convulsion) through the head.

Electromyograph (EMG) An instrument that measures muscle tension.

Embryonic stage The baby from the third through the eighth weeks following conception, during which time the major organ systems undergo rapid differentiation.

Emotion A state of feeling that has cognitive, physiological, and behavioral components.

Empathic understanding (em-PATH-ick). Ability to perceive a

client's feelings from the client's frame of reference. A quality of the good client-centered therapist.

Empty-nest syndrome A sense of depression and loss of purpose felt by some parents when the youngest child leaves home.

Encode Interpret; transform.

Encoding Modifying information so that it can be placed in memory; the first stage of information processing.

Encounter group A type of group that aims to foster self-awareness by focusing on how group members relate to each other in a setting that encourages open expression of feelings.

Endocrine system The body's system of ductless glands that secrete hormones and release them directly into the bloodstream.

Endorphins Neurotransmitters that are composed of amino acids and that are functionally similar to morphine.

Engram (1) An assumed electrical circuit in the brain that corresponds to a memory trace. (2) An assumed chemical change in the brain that accompanies learning. (From the Greek *en-*, meaning "in," and *gramma*, meaning "something that is written or recorded.")

Environmental psychology The field of psychology that studies the ways in which people and the environment influence each other.

Epilepsy Temporary disturbances of brain functions that involve sudden neural discharges.

Epinephrine A hormone produced by the adrenal medulla that stimulates sympathetic ANS activity. Also called adrenaline.

Episodic memory Memories of events experienced by a person or that take place in the person's presence.

Erogenous zone An area of the body that is sensitive to sexual sensations.

Eros In psychodynamic theory, the basic instinct to preserve and perpetuate life.

Estrogen A generic term for several female sex hormones that promote

growth of female sex characteristics and regulate the menstrual cycle.

Estrus The periodic sexual excitement of many mammals, as governed by levels of sex hormones.

Ethical Moral; referring to one's system of deriving standards for determining what is moral.

Ethnic group A group characterized by common features such as cultural heritage, history, race, and language.

Ethologist A scientist who studies the characteristic behavior patterns of species of animals.

Eustress (YOU-stress). Stress that is healthful.

Evaluation apprehension Concern that others are evaluating our behavior.

Evolutionary psychology The branch of psychology that studies the ways in which adaptation and natural selection are connected with mental processes and behavior.

Excitement phase The first phase of the sexual response cycle, which is characterized by muscle tension, increases in the heart rate, and erection in the male and vaginal lubrication in the female.

Exhaustion stage The third stage of the GAS, characterized by weakened resistance and possible deterioration.

Existentialism The view that people are completely free and responsible for their own behavior.

Expectancies Personal predictions about the outcomes of potential behaviors.

Experiment A scientific method that seeks to confirm cause-and-effect relationships by introducing independent variables and observing their effects on dependent variables.

Experimental groups In experiments, groups whose members obtain the treatment.

Explicit memory Memory that clearly and distinctly expresses (explicates) specific information.

Externals People who perceive the ability to attain reinforcements as being largely outside themselves.

Extinction An experimental procedure in which stimuli lose their ability to evoke learned responses because the events that had followed the stimuli no longer occur. (The learned responses are said to be *extinguished*.)

Extraversion A trait characterized by tendencies to be socially outgoing and to express feelings and impulses freely.

Facial-feedback hypothesis The view that stereotypical facial expressions can contribute to stereotypical emotions.

Factor analysis A statistical technique that allows researchers to determine the relationships among large number of items such as test items.

Family therapy A form of therapy in which the family unit is treated as the client.

Fear appeal A type of persuasive communication that influences behavior on the basis of arousing fear instead of rational analysis of the issues.

Feature detectors Neurons in the sensory cortex that fire in response to specific features of sensory information such as lines or edges of objects.

Feedback In assertiveness training, information about the effectiveness of a response.

Feeling-of-knowing experience Same as *tip-of-the-tongue phenomenon.*

Female sexual arousal disorder A sexual dysfunction in which females fail to become adequately sexually aroused to engage in sexual intercourse.

Fetal stage The baby from the third month following conception through childbirth, during which time there is maturation of organ systems and dramatic gains in length and weight.

Fight-or-flight reaction An innate adaptive response to the perception of danger.

Fixation In psychodynamic theory, arrested development. Attachment to objects of an earlier stage.

Fixation time The amount of time spent looking at a visual stimulus.

Fixed-interval schedule A schedule in which a fixed amount of time

must elapse between the previous and subsequent times that reinforcement is available.

Fixed-ratio schedule A schedule in which reinforcement is provided after a fixed number of correct responses.

Flashbacks Distorted perceptions or hallucinations that occur days or weeks after LSD usage but mimic the LSD experience.

Flavor A complex quality of food and other substances that is based on their odor, texture, and temperature as well their taste.

Flooding A behavioral fear-reduction technique based on principles of classical conditioning. Fear-evoking stimuli (CSs) are presented continuously in the absence of actual harm so that fear responses (CRs) are extinguished.

Flow An altered state of consciousness experienced when one is deeply involved in a pleasant activity.

Fluid intelligence Mental flexibility as shown in learning rapidly to solve new kinds of problems.

Foot-in-the-door technique A method for inducing compliance in which a small request is followed by a larger request.

Forced-choice format A method of presenting test questions that requires a respondent to select one of a number of possible answers.

Formal-operational stage Piaget's fourth stage, characterized by abstract logical thought; deduction from principles.

Fovea An area near the center of the retina that is dense with cones and where vision is consequently most acute.

Frame of reference One's unique patterning of perceptions and attitudes, according to which one evaluates events.

Framing effect The influence of wording, or the context in which information is presented, on decision making.

Free association In psychoanalysis, the uncensored uttering of all thoughts that come to mind.

Frequency distribution An ordered set of data that indicates the

frequency (how often) with which scores appear.

Frequency histogram A graphic representation of a frequency distribution that uses rectangular solids (bars) to represent the frequency with which scores appear.

Frequency polygon A graphic representation of a frequency distribution that connects the points that show the frequencies with which scores appear, thereby creating a multisided geometric figure.

Frequency theory The theory that the pitch of a sound is reflected in the frequency of the neural impulses that are generated in response to the sound.

Frontal lobe The lobe of the cerebral cortex that lies to the front of the central fissure.

Functional analysis A systematic study of behavior in which one identifies the stimuli that trigger problem behavior and the reinforcers that maintain it.

Functional fixedness The tendency to view an object in terms of its name or familiar usage.

Functionalism The school of psychology that emphasizes the uses or functions of the mind rather than the elements of experience.

Fundamental attribution error The assumption that others act predominantly on the basis of their dispositions, even when there is evidence suggesting the importance of their situations.

g Spearman's symbol for general intelligence, which he believed underlay more specific abilities.

Gamma-aminobutyric acid (GABA) An inhibitory neurotransmitter that apparently helps calm anxiety.

Ganglion cells Neurons whose axons form the optic nerve.

Gender The culturally defined concepts of masculinity and femininity; the psychological state of being male or female.

Gender role A cluster of behaviors that characterizes traditional female or male behaviors within a cultural setting.

Gender-schema theory The view that gender identity plus knowledge of the distribution of behavior patterns into feminine and masculine roles motivate and guide the gender-typing of the child.

Gender-typing The process by which people acquire a sense of being female or male and acquire the traits considered typical of females or males within a cultural setting.

Gene A basic unit of heredity, which is found at a specific point on a chromosome.

General adaptation syndrome (GAS) Selye's term for a hypothesized three-stage response to stress.

Generalization In conditioning, the tendency for a conditioned response to be evoked by stimuli that are similar to the stimulus to which the response was conditioned.

Generalize To extend from the particular to the general; to apply observations based on a sample to a population.

Generalized anxiety disorder Feelings of dread and foreboding and sympathetic arousal of at least 6 months' duration.

Generativity versus stagnation Erikson's term for the crisis of middle adulthood, characterized by the task of being productive and contributing to younger generations.

Genes The basic building blocks of heredity.

Genetics The area of biology that focuses on heredity.

Genital stage The mature stage of psychosexual development, characterized by preferred expression of libido through intercourse with an adult of the other gender.

Genotype One's genetic makeup, based on the sequencing of the nucleotides we term A, C, G, and T.

Genuineness Recognition and open expression of the therapist's own feelings.

Germinal stage The first stage of prenatal development, during which the dividing mass of cells has not become implanted in the uterine wall.

Gestalt psychology The school of psychology that emphasizes the tendency to organize perceptions into wholes and to integrate separate stimuli into meaningful patterns.

Gestalt therapy Fritz Perls's form of psychotherapy, which attempts to integrate conflicting parts of the personality through directive methods designed to help clients perceive their whole selves.

Gland An organ that secretes one or more chemical substances such as hormones, saliva, or milk.

Glial cells Cells that nourish and insulate neurons, direct their growth, and remove waste products from the nervous system.

Glutamate An excitatory neurotransmitter that is involved in anxiety reactions.

Gray matter In the spinal cord, the grayish neurons and neural segments that are involved in spinal reflexes.

Groupthink A process in which group members are influenced by cohesiveness and a dynamic leader to ignore external realities as they make decisions.

Growth hormone A pituitary hormone that regulates growth.

Hallucination A perception in the absence of sensory stimulation that is confused with reality.

Hallucinogenic Giving rise to hallucinations.

Hashish A drug derived from the resin of *Cannabis sativa*. Often called "hash."

Health psychology The field of psychology that studies the relationships between psychological factors (e.g., attitudes, beliefs, situational influences, and behavior patterns) and the prevention and treatment of physical illness.

Heredity The transmission of traits from parent to offspring by means of genes.

Heritability The degree to which the variations in a trait from one person to another can be attributed to, or explained by, genetic factors.

Hertz (Hz) A unit expressing the frequency of sound waves. One hertz equals one cycle per second.

Heuristics Rules of thumb that help us simplify and solve problems.

Hierarchy An arrangement of stimuli according to the amount of fear they evoke.

Higher-order conditioning (1) According to behaviorists, a classical conditioning procedure in which a previously neutral stimulus comes to elicit the response brought forth by a *conditioned* stimulus by being paired repeatedly with that conditioned stimulus. (2) According to cognitive psychologists, the learning of relationships among events, none of which evokes an unlearned response.

Hippocampus A structure in the limbic system that plays an important role in the formation of new memories.

Holophrase A single word used to express complex meanings.

Homeostasis The tendency of the body to maintain a steady state.

Homosexual Referring to people who are sexually aroused by, and interested in forming romantic relationships with, people of the same sex. (Derived from the Greek *homos*, meaning "same," not from the Latin *homo*, meaning "man.")

Hormone A substance secreted by an endocrine gland that regulates various body functions.

Hue The color of light, as determined by its wavelength.

Humanism The philosophy and school of psychology that asserts that people are conscious, self-aware, and capable of free choice, self-fulfillment, and ethical behavior.

Hydrocarbons Chemical compounds consisting of hydrogen and carbon.

Hyperphagic Characterized by excessive eating.

Hypertension High blood pressure.

Hypnagogic state The drowsy interval between waking and sleeping, characterized by brief, hallucinatory, dreamlike experiences.

Hypnosis A condition in which people appear to be highly suggestible and behave as though they are in a trance.

Hypoactive sexual desire disorder A sexual dysfunction in which people lack sexual desire.

Hypochondriasis Persistent belief that one is ill despite lack of medical findings.

Hypothalamus A bundle of nuclei below the thalamus involved in body temperature, motivation, and emotion.

Hypothesis In psychology, a specific statement about behavior or mental processes that is tested through research.

Icon A mental representation of a visual stimulus that is held briefly in sensory memory.

Iconic memory The sensory register that briefly holds mental representations of visual stimuli.

Id The psychic structure, present at birth, that represents physiological drives and is fully unconscious.

Ideas of persecution Erroneous beliefs that one is being victimized or persecuted.

Identification In psychodynamic theory, the unconscious adoption of another person's behavior.

Identity certainty A strong and clear sense of who one is and what one stands for.

Illusions Sensations that give rise to misperceptions.

Imaginary audience An aspect of adolescent egocentrism; the belief that other people are as concerned with our thoughts and behaviors as we are.

Immune system The system of the body that recognizes and destroys foreign agents (antigens) that invade the body.

Implicit memory Memory that is suggested (implied) but not plainly expressed, as illustrated in the things that people *do* but do not state clearly.

Imprinting A process occurring during a critical period in the development of an organism, in which that organism responds to a stimulus in a manner that will afterward be difficult to modify.

Incentive An object, person, or situation perceived as being capable of satisfying a need.

Incest taboo The cultural prohibition against marrying or having sexual relations with a close blood relative.

Incubation In problem solving, a hypothetical process that sometimes occurs when we stand back from a frustrating problem for a while and the solution "suddenly" appears.

Independent variable A condition in a scientific study that is manipulated so that its effects may be observed.

Indiscriminate attachment Showing attachment behaviors toward any person.

Individual psychology Adler's psychodynamic theory, which emphasizes feelings of inferiority and the creative self.

Individualist A person who defines herself or himself in terms of personal traits and gives priority to her or his own goals.

Infantile amnesia Inability to recall events that occurred prior to the age of 2 or 3. Also termed *childhood amnesia*.

Infer To go from the particular to the general, to draw a conclusion.

Inferential statistics The branch of statistics that is concerned with confidence with which conclusions drawn about samples can be extended to the populations from which the samples were drawn.

Inferiority complex Feelings of inferiority hypothesized by Adler to serve as a central motivating force.

Infinite creativity The capacity to combine words into original sentences.

Inflammation Increased blood flow to an injured area of the body, resulting in redness, warmth, and an increased supply of white blood cells.

Informed consent A subject's agreement to participate in research after receiving information about the purposes of the study and the nature of the treatments.

Initial-preattachment phase The first phase in forming bonds of attachment, characterized by indiscriminate attachment.

Insanity A legal term descriptive of a person judged to be incapable of recognizing right from wrong or of conforming his or her behavior to the law.

Insight In Gestalt psychology, a sudden perception of relationships among elements of the "perceptual field," permitting the solution of a problem.

Instinct A stereotyped pattern of behavior that is triggered by a particular stimulus and nearly identical among members of a species, even when they are reared in isolation; an inherited disposition to activate specific behavior patterns that are designed to reach certain goals.

Instinctive An inborn pattern of behavior that is triggered by a particular stimulus.

Instrumental competence Ability to manipulate one's environment to achieve one's goals.

Intelligence A complex and controversial concept. According to David Wechsler (1975), the "capacity . . . to understand the world [and] resourcefulness to cope with its challenges."

Intelligence quotient (IQ) (1) Originally, a ratio obtained by dividing a child's score (or mental age) on an intelligence test by chronological age. (2) Generally, a score on an intelligence test.

Interference theory The view that we may forget stored material because other learning interferes with it.

Internals People who perceive the ability to attain reinforcements as being largely within themselves.

Internet addiction A preoccupation with going online that disrupts one's functioning in the real world.

Interneuron A neuron that transmits a neural impulse from a sensory neuron to a motor neuron.

Interposition A monocular cue for depth based on the fact that a nearby object obscures a more distant object behind it.

Interpretation An explanation of a client's utterance according to psychoanalytic theory.

Intimacy Close acquaintance and familiarity; a characteristic of a relationship in which partners share their inmost feelings.

Intimacy versus isolation Erikson's life crisis of young adulthood, which is characterized by the task of developing abiding intimate relationships.

Introspection Deliberate looking into one's own cognitive processes to examine one's thoughts and feelings.

Introversion A trait characterized by intense imagination and the tendency to inhibit impulses.

Iris A muscular membrane whose dilation regulates the amount of light that enters the eye.

Just noticeable difference (jnd) The minimal amount by which a source of energy must be increased or decreased so that a difference in intensity will be perceived.

Kinesthesis The sense that informs us about the positions and motion of parts of our bodies.

La belle indifférence A French term descriptive of the lack of concern sometimes shown by people with conversion disorders.

Language The communication of information by means of symbols arranged according to rules of grammar.

Language acquisition device (LAD) In psycholinguistic theory, neural "prewiring" that facilitates the child's learning of grammar.

Latency A phase of psychosexual development characterized by repression of sexual impulses.

Latent Hidden or concealed.

Latent content In psychodynamic theory, the symbolized or underlying content of dreams.

Lateral hypothalamus An area at the side of the hypothalamus that appears to function as a start-eating center.

Law of effect Thorndike's principle that responses are "stamped in" by rewards and "stamped out" by punishments.

Learned helplessness A model for the acquisition of depressive behavior, based on findings that organisms in aversive situations learn to show inactivity when their operants go unreinforced.

Learning (1) According to behaviorists, a relatively permanent change in behavior that results from experi-ence. (2) According to cognitive theorists, the process by which organisms make relatively permanent changes in the way they represent the environment because of experi-ence. These changes influence the organism's behavior but do not fully determine it.

Lens A transparent body behind the iris that focuses an image on the retina.

Lesion An injury that results in impaired behavior or loss of a function.

Leukocytes White blood cells. (Derived from the Greek words *leukos,* meaning "white," and *kytos,* literally meaning "a hollow" but used to refer to cells.)

Libido (1) In psychodynamic theory, the energy of eros; the sexual instinct. (2) Generally, sexual interest or drive.

Limbic system A group of structures involved in memory, motivation, and emotion that forms a fringe along the inner edge of the cerebrum.

Linguistic-relativity hypothesis The view that language structures the way in which we view the world.

Locus of control The place (locus) to which an individual attributes control over the receiving of rein-forcers—either inside or outside the self.

Long-term memory The type or stage of memory capable of relatively permanent storage.

Long-term potentiation (LTP) Enhanced efficiency in synaptic transmission that follows brief, rapid stimulation.

LSD Lysergic acid diethylamide. A hallucinogenic drug.

Maintenance rehearsal Mental repetition of information in order to keep it in memory.

Major depressive disorder A seri-ous to severe depressive disorder in which the person may show loss of appetite, psychomotor retardation, and impaired reality testing.

Male erectile disorder A sexual dysfunction in which males fail to obtain erections that are adequate for sexual intercourse.

Manic Elated, showing excessive excitement.

Manifest content In psychody-namic theory, the reported content of dreams.

Marijuana The dried vegetable mat-ter of the *Cannabis sativa* plant.

Matching hypothesis The view that people tend to choose persons similar to themselves in attractive-ness and attitudes in the formation of interpersonal relationships.

Maturation The process of develop-ment as guided by the unfolding of the genetic code.

Mean A type of average that is cal-culated by adding all the scores and then dividing by the number of scores.

Means–end analysis A heuristic device in which we try to solve a problem by evaluating the difference between the current situation and the goal.

Median The central score in a fre-quency distribution; the score beneath which 50% of the cases fall.

Medulla An oblong area of the hindbrain involved in regulation of heartbeat and respiration.

Melatonin A pineal hormone that helps regulate the sleep–wake cycle and may affect the onset of puberty.

Memory The processes by which information is encoded, stored, and retrieved.

Memory trace An assumed change in the nervous system that reflects the impression made by a stimulus. Memory traces are said to be "held" in sensory registers.

Menarche The beginning of menstruation.

Menopause The cessation of menstruation.

Mental age (MA) The accumulated months of credit that a person earns on the Stanford–Binet Intelligence Scale.

Mental set The tendency to respond to a new problem with an approach that was successfully used with similar problems.

Mescaline A hallucinogenic drug derived from the mescal (peyote) cactus.

Meta-analysis A method for combining and averaging the results of individual research studies.

Metamemory Self-awareness of the ways in which memory functions, allowing the person to encode, store, and retrieve information effectively.

Method of savings A measure of retention in which the difference between the number of repetitions originally required to learn a list and the number of repetitions required to relearn the list after a certain amount of time has elapsed is calculated.

Midlife crisis A crisis experienced by many people during the midlife transition when they realize that life may be more than halfway over and reassess their achievements in terms of their dreams.

Midlife transition Levinson's term for the ages from 40 to 45, which are characterized by a shift in psychological perspective from viewing ourselves in terms of years lived to viewing ourselves in terms of the years we have left.

Migraine headaches Throbbing headaches that are connected with changes in the supply of blood to the head.

Mode The most frequently occurring number or score in a distribution.

Model In social cognitive theory, an organism that exhibits behaviors that others will imitate or acquire through observational learning.

Modeling A behavior-therapy technique in which a client observes and imitates a person who approaches and copes with feared objects or situations.

Monochromat A person who is sensitive to black and white only and hence color-blind.

Monocular cues Stimuli suggestive of depth that can be perceived with only one eye.

Monozygotic (MZ) twins Twins that develop from a single fertilized ovum that divides in two early in prenatal development. MZ twins thus share the same genetic code. Also called identical twins.

Moral principle The governing principle of the superego, which sets moral standards and enforces adherence to them.

Motion parallax A monocular cue for depth based on the perception that nearby objects appear to move more rapidly in relation to our own motion.

Motive A hypothetical state within an organism that propels the organism toward a goal. (From the Latin *movere*, meaning "to move.")

Motor cortex The section of cortex that lies in the frontal lobe, just across the central fissure from the sensory cortex. Neural impulses in the motor cortex are linked to muscular responses throughout the body.

Multiple approach–avoidance conflict A type of conflict in which each of a number of goals produces approach and avoidance motives.

Multiple personality disorder The previous term for *dissociative identity disorder*.

Mutation A sudden variation in an inheritable characteristic, as distinguished from a variation that results from generations of gradual selection.

Mutism Refusal to talk.

Myelin A fatty substance that encases and insulates axons, facilitating transmission of neural impulses.

Myotonia Muscle tension.

Narcolepsy A "sleep attack" in which a person falls asleep suddenly and irresistibly.

Narcotics Drugs used to relieve pain and induce sleep. The term is usually reserved for opiates.

Natural selection A core concept of the theory of evolution that holds that adaptive genetic variations among members of a species enable individuals with those variations to survive and reproduce. As a result, such variations tend to be preserved, whereas nonadaptive variations tend to drop out.

Naturalistic observation A scientific method in which organisms are observed in their natural environments.

Nature The inborn, innate character of an organism.

Need A state of deprivation.

Negative correlation A relationship between two variables in which one variable increases as the other decreases.

Negative reinforcer A reinforcer that when *removed* increases the frequency of an operant.

Neodissociation theory A theory of hypnotic events as the splitting of consciousness.

Neonate A newly born child.

Nerve A bundle of axons from many neurons.

Neural impulse The electrochemical discharge of a nerve cell, or neuron.

Neuron A nerve cell.

Neuroticism A personality trait characterized largely by persistent anxiety; Eysenck's term for emotional instability.

Neurotransmitters Chemical substances involved in the transmission of neural impulses from one neuron to another.

Nonconscious Descriptive of bodily processes such as the growing of hair, of which we cannot become conscious. We may "recognize" that our hair is growing but cannot directly experience the biological process.

Non-rapid-eye-movement (NREM) sleep Stages of sleep 1 through 4.

Nonsense syllables Meaningless sets of two consonants, with a vowel sandwiched in between, that are used to study memory.

Norepinephrine A neurotransmitter whose action is similar to that of the hormone epinephrine and that may play a role in depression.

Normal curve Graphic presentation of a normal distribution, which shows a characteristic bell shape.

Normal distribution A symmetrical distribution that is assumed to reflect chance fluctuations; approximately 68% of cases lie within a standard deviation of the mean.

Nurture The sum total of the environmental factors that affect an organism from conception onward. (In another usage, nurture refers to the act of nourishing and otherwise promoting the development of youngsters.)

Object permanence Recognition that objects removed from sight still exist, as demonstrated in young children by continued pursuit.

Objective responsibility According to Piaget, the assignment of blame according to the amount of damage done rather than the motives of the actor.

Objective tests Tests whose items must be answered in a specified, limited manner. Tests whose items have concrete answers that are considered correct.

Observational learning The acquisition of knowledge and skills through the observation of others (who are called *models*) rather than by means of direct experience.

Obsession A recurring thought or image that seems beyond control.

Occipital lobe The lobe that lies behind and below the parietal lobe and behind the temporal lobe.

Oedipus complex A conflict of the phallic stage in which the boy wishes to possess his mother sexually and perceives his father as a rival in love.

Olfactory Having to do with the sense of smell.

Olfactory nerve The nerve that transmits information concerning odors from olfactory receptors to the brain.

Operant The same as an operant behavior.

Operant behavior Voluntary responses that are reinforced.

Operant conditioning A simple form of learning in which an organism learns to engage in behavior because it is reinforced.

Opiates A group of narcotics derived from the opium poppy that provide a euphoric rush and depress the nervous system.

Opioids Chemicals that act on opiate receptors but are not derived from the opium poppy.

Opponent-process theory The theory that color vision is made possible by three types of cones, some of which respond to red or green light,

some to blue or yellow, and some only to the intensity of light.

Optic nerve The nerve that transmits sensory information from the eye to the brain.

Oral stage The first stage of psychosexual development, during which gratification is hypothesized to be attained primarily through oral activities.

Organ of Corti The receptor for hearing that lies on the basilar membrane in the cochlea.

Organizing effect The directional effect of sex hormones—for example, along stereotypically masculine or feminine lines.

Orgasm The height or climax of sexual excitement, involving involuntary muscle contractions, release of sexual tensions, and, usually, subjective feelings of pleasure.

Orgasmic disorder A sexual dysfunction in which people have persistent or recurrent problems in reaching orgasm.

Orienting reflex An unlearned response in which an organism attends to a stimulus.

Overregularization The application of regular grammatical rules for forming inflections (e.g., past tense and plurals) to irregular verbs and nouns.

Oxytocin A pituitary hormone that stimulates labor and lactation.

Paired associates Nonsense syllables presented in pairs in experiments that measure recall.

Panic disorder The recurrent experiencing of attacks of extreme anxiety in the absence of external stimuli that usually elicit anxiety.

Paranoid personality disorder A personality disorder characterized by persistent suspiciousness but not involving the disorganization of paranoid schizophrenia.

Paranoid schizophrenia A type of schizophrenia characterized primarily by delusions—commonly of persecution—and by vivid hallucinations.

Parasympathetic The branch of the ANS that is most active during processes such as digestion that restore the body's reserves of energy.

Parasympathetic nervous system The branch of the autonomic nervous system that is most active during processes that restore reserves of energy to the body, such as relaxing and eating. When people relax, the parasympathetic nervous system decelerates the heart rate, normalizes the blood pressure, relaxes muscles, and so on. The parasympathetic division also stimulates digestion.

Parietal lobe The lobe that lies just behind the central fissure.

Partial reinforcement One of several reinforcement schedules in which not every correct response is reinforced.

Passion Strong romantic and sexual feelings.

Passive smoking Inhaling of smoke from the tobacco products and exhalations of other people; also called *secondhand smoking*.

Pathogen A microscopic organism (e.g., bacterium or virus) that can cause disease.

Perception The process by which sensations are organized into an inner representation of the world.

Perceptual organization The tendency to integrate perceptual elements into meaningful patterns.

Performance anxiety Anxiety concerning one's ability to perform, especially when performance may be evaluated by other people.

Period of the ovum Another term for the germinal stage.

Peripheral nervous system The part of the nervous system consisting of the somatic nervous system and the autonomic nervous system.

Permissive parents Parents who impose few, if any, rules and who do not supervise their children closely.

Person variables Factors within the person, such as expectancies and competencies, that influence behavior.

Personal fable Another aspect of adolescent egocentrism; the belief that our feelings and ideas are special and unique and that we are invulnerable.

Personal space A psychological boundary that surrounds a person and serves protective functions.

Personality The distinct patterns of behavior, thoughts, and feelings that characterize a person's adaptation to life.

Personality disorders Enduring patterns of maladaptive behavior that are sources of distress to the individual or others.

Perspective A monocular cue for depth based on the convergence (coming together) of parallel lines as they recede into the distance.

Phallic stage The third stage of psychosexual development, characterized by a shift of libido to the phallic region. (From the Greek *phallos,* referring to an image of the penis. However, Freud used the term *phallic* to refer both to boys and girls.)

Phallic symbol A sign that represents the penis.

Phencyclidine (PCP) Another hallucinogenic drug whose name is an acronym for its chemical structure.

Phenotype One's actual development and appearance, as based on one's genotype and environmental influences.

Pheromone A chemical secretion detected by other members of the same species that stimulates stereotypical behaviors.

Phi phenomenon The perception of movement as a result of sequential presentation of visual stimuli.

Photoreceptors Cells that respond to light.

Physiological drives Unlearned drives with a biological basis, such as hunger, thirst, and avoidance of pain.

Pitch The highness or lowness of a sound, as determined by the frequency of the sound waves.

Pituitary gland The gland that secretes growth hormone, prolactin, antidiuretic hormone, and other hormones.

Place theory The theory that the pitch of a sound is determined by the section of the basilar membrane that vibrates in response to the sound.

Placebo A bogus treatment that has the appearance of being genuine.

Placenta A membrane that permits the exchange of nutrients and waste products between the mother and her developing child but does not allow the maternal and fetal bloodstreams to mix.

Plateau phase The second phase of the sexual response cycle, which is characterized by increases in vasocongestion, muscle tension, heart rate, and blood pressure in preparation for orgasm.

Pleasure principle The governing principle of the id—the seeking of immediate gratification of instinctive needs.

Polarization In social psychology, taking an extreme position or attitude on an issue.

Polarize To ready a neuron for firing by creating an internal negative charge in relation to the body fluid outside the cell membrane.

Polygenic Referring to traits that are influenced by combinations of genes.

Pons A structure of the hindbrain involved in respiration, attention, and sleep and dreaming.

Population A complete group of organisms or events.

Positive correlation A relationship between variables in which one variable increases as the other also increases.

Positive psychology The field of psychology that is about personal well-being and satisfaction; joy, sensual pleasure, and happiness; and optimism and hope for the future.

Positive reinforcer A reinforcer that when *presented* increases the frequency of an operant.

Postconventional level According to Kohlberg, a period during which moral judgments are derived from moral principles and people look to themselves to set moral standards.

Posttraumatic stress disorder (PTSD) A disorder that follows a distressing event outside the range of normal human experience and that is characterized by features such as intense fear, avoidance of stimuli

associated with the event, and reliving of the event.

Preconscious In psychodynamic theory, descriptive of material that is not in awareness but can be brought into awareness by focusing one's attention.

Preconventional level According to Kohlberg, a period during which moral judgments are based largely on expectation of rewards or punishments.

Prefrontal lobotomy The severing or destruction of a section of the frontal lobe of the brain.

Premature ejaculation Ejaculation that occurs before the couple are satisfied with the length of sexual relations.

Preoperational stage The second of Piaget's stages, characterized by illogical use of words and symbols, spotty logic, and egocentrism.

Presbyopia A condition characterized by brittleness of the lens.

Primacy effect The tendency to recall the initial items in a series of items, or to evaluate others in terms of first impressions.

Primary drives Unlearned, or physiological, drives.

Primary mental abilities According to Thurstone, the basic abilities that make up intelligence.

Primary reinforcer An unlearned reinforcer.

Priming The activation of specific associations in memory, often as a result of repetition and without making a conscious effort to access the memory.

Proactive interference The interference by old learning with the ability to retrieve material learned recently.

Progesterone A female sex hormone that promotes growth of the sex organs and helps maintain pregnancy.

Projective test A psychological test that presents ambiguous stimuli onto which the test-taker projects his or her own personality in making a response.

Prolactin A pituitary hormone that regulates production of milk and, in lower animals, maternal behavior.

Prospective memory Memory to perform an act in the future, as at a certain time or when a certain event occurs.

Prototype A concept of a category of objects or events that serves as a good example of the category.

Proximity Nearness. The perceptual tendency to group together objects that are near one another.

Psychedelic Causing hallucinations, delusions, or heightened perceptions.

Psychic structure In psychodynamic theory, a hypothesized mental structure that helps explain different aspects of behavior.

Psychoactive substances Drugs that have psychological effects such as stimulation or distortion of perceptions.

Psychoanalysis Freud's method of psychotherapy, of exploring human personality; the school of psychology that emphasizes the importance of unconscious motives and conflicts as determinants of human behavior.

Psychodynamic theory Sigmund Freud's perspective, which emphasizes the importance of unconscious motives and conflicts as forces that determine behavior. *Dynamic* refers to the concept of (psychological) forces being in motion.

Psycholinguistic theory The view that language learning involves an interaction between environmental factors and an inborn tendency to acquire language.

Psychological disorders Patterns of behavior or mental processes that are connected with emotional distress or significant impairment in functioning.

Psychological hardiness A cluster of traits that buffer stress and are characterized by commitment, challenge, and control.

Psychology The science that studies behavior and mental processes.

Psychomotor retardation Slowness in motor activity and (apparently) in thought.

Psychoneuroimmunology (sigh-coe-new-row-im-you-NOLL-oh-gee). The field that studies the relationships between psychological factors (e.g., attitudes and overt behavior patterns) and the functioning of the immune system.

Psychophysicist A person who studies the relationships between physical stimuli (such as light or sound) and their perception.

Psychosexual development In psychodynamic theory, the process by which libidinal energy is expressed through different erogenous zones during different stages of development.

Psychosocial development Erikson's theory of personality and development, which emphasizes social relationships and eight stages of growth.

Psychosurgery Surgery intended to promote psychological changes or to relieve disordered behavior.

Psychotherapy A systematic interaction between a therapist and a client that brings psychological principles to bear on influencing the client's thoughts, feelings, or behavior to help that client overcome abnormal behavior or adjust to problems in living.

Puberty The period of physical development during which sexual reproduction first becomes possible.

Punishment An unpleasant stimulus that suppresses the behavior it follows.

Pupil The apparently black opening in the center of the iris, through which light enters the eye.

Pure research Research conducted without concern for immediate applications.

Random sample A sample drawn so that each member of a population has an equal chance of being selected to participate.

Range A measure of variability defined as the high score in a distribution minus the low score.

Rapid-eye-movement (REM) sleep A stage of sleep characterized by rapid eye movements, which have been linked to dreaming.

Rapid flight of ideas Rapid speech and topic changes, characteristic of manic behavior.

Rapid smoking An aversive conditioning method for quitting smoking in which the smoker inhales every 6 seconds, thus rendering once-desirable cigarette smoke aversive.

Rational emotive behavior therapy (REBT) Albert Ellis's form of therapy that encourages clients to challenge and correct irrational expectations and maladaptive behaviors.

Reality principle Consideration of what is practical and possible in gratifying needs; the governing principle of the ego.

Reality testing The capacity to perceive one's environment and oneself according to accurate sensory impressions.

Rebound anxiety Anxiety that can occur when one discontinues use of a tranquilizer.

Recall Retrieval or reconstruction of learned material.

Recency effect The tendency to recall the last items in a series of items, or to evaluate others in terms of the most recent impression.

Receptor site A location on a dendrite of a receiving neuron tailored to receive a neurotransmitter.

Reciprocal determinism Bandura's term for the social cognitive view that people influence their environment just as their environment influences them.

Reciprocity In interpersonal attraction, the tendency to return feelings and attitudes that are expressed about us.

Recognition In information processing, the easiest memory task, involving identification of objects or events encountered before.

Reflex A simple unlearned response to a stimulus.

Refractory period A phase following firing during which a neuron is less sensitive to messages from other neurons and will not fire; in the sexual response cycle, a period of time following orgasm during which an individual is not responsive to sexual stimulation.

Reinforce To follow a response with a stimulus that increases the frequency of the response.

Reinforcement A stimulus that follows a response and increases the frequency of the response.

Relearning A measure of retention. Material is usually relearned more quickly than it is learned initially.

Replicate Repeat, reproduce, copy.

Representativeness heuristic A decision-making heuristic in which people make judgments about samples according to the populations they appear to represent.

Repression A defense mechanism that protects the person from anxiety by ejecting anxiety-evoking ideas and impulses from awareness; in Freud's psychodynamic theory, the automatic (unconscious) ejection of anxiety-evoking ideas, impulses, or images from awareness.

Resistance The tendency to block the free expression of impulses and primitive ideas—a reflection of the defense mechanism of repression.

Resistance stage The second stage of the GAS, characterized by prolonged sympathetic activity in an effort to restore lost energy and repair damage. Also called the *adaptation stage*

Resolution phase The fourth phase of the sexual response cycle, during which the body gradually returns to its prearoused state.

Response set A tendency to answer test items according to a bias—for instance, to make oneself seem perfect or bizarre.

Response set theory The view that response expectancies play a key role in the production of the experiences suggested by the hypnotist.

Resting potential The electrical potential across the neural membrane when it is not responding to other neurons.

Reticular activating system (RAS) A part of the brain involved in attention, sleep, and arousal.

Retina The area of the inner surface of the eye that contains rods and cones.

Retinal disparity A binocular cue for depth based on the difference in the image cast by an object on the retinas of the eyes as the object moves closer or farther away.

Retrieval The location of stored information and its return to consciousness; the third stage of information processing.

Retroactive interference The interference of new learning with the ability to retrieve material learned previously.

Retrograde amnesia Failure to remember events that occurred prior to physical trauma because of the effects of the trauma.

Retrospective memory Memory for past events, activities, and learning experiences, as shown by explicit (episodic and semantic) and implicit memories.

Reversibility According to Piaget, recognition that processes can be undone, that things can be made as they were.

Reward A pleasant stimulus that increases the frequency of the behavior it follows.

Risky shift The tendency to make riskier decisions as a member of a group than as an individual acting independently.

Rods Rod-shaped photoreceptors that are sensitive only to the intensity of light.

Role diffusion Erikson's term for lack of clarity in one's life roles (due to failure to develop ego identity).

Role theory A theory that explains hypnotic events in terms of the person's ability to act *as though* he or she were hypnotized. Role theory differs from faking in that subjects cooperate and focus on hypnotic suggestions instead of pretending to be hypnotized.

Romantic love An intense, positive emotion that involves sexual attraction, feelings of caring, and the belief that one is in love.

Rooting The turning of an infant's head toward a touch, such as by the mother's nipple.

Rote Mechanical associative learning that is based on repetition.

s Spearman's symbol for *specific* factors, or *s factors,* which he believed accounted for individual abilities.

Saccadic eye movement The rapid jumps made by a person's eyes as they fixate on different points.

Sample Part of a population.

Satiety The state of being satisfied; fullness.

Savings The difference between the number of repetitions originally required to learn a list and the number of repetitions required to relearn the list after a certain amount of time has elapsed.

Scaffolding Vygotsky's term for temporary cognitive structures or methods of solving problems that help the child as he or she learns to function independently.

Schema A way of mentally representing the world, such as a belief or an expectation, that can influence perception of persons, objects, and situations; according to Piaget, a hypothetical mental structure that permits the classification and organization of new information.

Schizoid personality disorder A personality disorder characterized by social withdrawal.

Schizophrenia A psychotic disorder characterized by loss of control of thought processes and inappropriate emotional responses.

Schizotypal personality disorder A personality disorder characterized by oddities of thought and behavior but not involving bizarre psychotic behaviors.

Secondary reinforcer A stimulus that gains reinforcement value through association with established reinforcers.

Secondary sex characteristics Characteristics that distinguish the sexes, such as distribution of body hair and depth of voice, but that are not directly involved in reproduction.

Sedative A drug that relieves nervousness or agitation or puts one to sleep.

Selection factor A source of bias that may occur in research findings when subjects are allowed to choose for themselves a certain treatment in a scientific study.

Selective attention The focus of one's consciousness on a particular stimulus.

Selective avoidance Diverting one's attention from information that is inconsistent with one's attitudes.

Selective exposure Deliberately seeking and attending to information that is consistent with one's attitudes.

Selective serotonin-reuptake inhibitors (SSRIs) Antidepressant drugs that work by blocking the reuptake of serotonin by presynaptic neurons.

Self-actualization According to Maslow and other humanistic psychologists, self-initiated striving to become what one is capable of being. The motive for reaching one's full potential, for expressing one's unique capabilities.

Self-efficacy expectations Our beliefs that we can bring about desired changes through our own efforts, that one can handle a task.

Self-ideal A mental image of what we believe we ought to be.

Self-monitoring Keeping a record of one's own behavior to identify problems and record successes.

Self-serving bias The tendency to view one's successes as stemming from internal factors and one's failures as stemming from external factors.

Semantic code Mental representation of information according to its meaning.

Semantic memory General knowledge, as opposed to episodic memory.

Semanticity Meaning. The quality of language in which words are used as symbols for objects, events, or ideas.

Semicircular canals Structures of the inner ear that monitor body movement and position.

Sensation The stimulation of sensory receptors and the transmission of sensory information to the central nervous system.

Sensitization The type of sensory adaptation in which we become more sensitive to stimuli that are low in magnitude. Also called *positive adaptation.*

Sensorimotor stage The first of Piaget's stages of cognitive development, characterized by coordination of sensory information and motor activity, early exploration of the environment, and lack of language.

Sensorineural deafness The forms of deafness that result from damage to hair cells or the auditory nerve.

Sensory adaptation The processes by which organisms become more sensitive to stimuli that are low in magnitude and less sensitive to stimuli that are constant or ongoing in magnitude.

Sensory memory The type or stage of memory first encountered by a stimulus. Sensory memory holds impressions briefly, but long enough so that series of perceptions are psychologically continuous.

Sensory register A system of memory that holds information briefly, but long enough so that it can be processed further. There may be a sensory register for every sense.

Serial-position effect The tendency to recall more accurately the first and last items in a series.

Serotonin A neurotransmitter, deficiencies of which have been linked to affective disorders, anxiety, and insomnia.

Serum cholesterol Cholesterol in the blood.

Sex chromosomes The 23rd pair of chromosomes, whose genetic material determines the sex of the individual.

Sex therapy A collective term for short-term cognitive–behavioral models for treatment of sexual dysfunctions.

Sexual dysfunction A persistent or recurrent problem in becoming sexually aroused or reaching orgasm.

Sexual harassment Deliberate or repeated unwanted comments, gestures, or physical contact of a sexual nature.

Sexual orientation The directionality of one's sexual and romantic interests; that is, whether one is sexually attracted to, and desires to form a romantic relationship with, members of the other sex or of one's own sex.

Sexual Response Cycle Masters and Johnson's model of sexual response, which consists of four stages or phases.

Shadowing A monocular cue for depth based on the fact that opaque objects block light and produce shadows.

Shape constancy The tendency to perceive an object as being the same shape although the retinal image varies in shape as it rotates.

Shaping A procedure for teaching complex behaviors that at first reinforces approximations of the target behavior.

Short-term memory The type or stage of memory that can hold information for up to a minute or so after the trace of the stimulus decays. Also called *working memory.*

Signal-detection theory The view that the perception of sensory stimuli involves the interaction of physical, biological, and psychological factors.

Similarity The perceptual tendency to group together objects that are similar in appearance.

Situational attribution An assumption that a person's behavior is determined by external circumstances such as the social pressure found in a situation.

Size constancy The tendency to perceive an object as being the same size even as the size of its retinal image changes according to the object's distance.

Sleep terrors Frightening dreamlike experiences that occur during the deepest stage of NREM sleep. Nightmares, in contrast, occur during REM sleep.

Social cognitive theory A cognitively oriented learning theory in which observational learning and person variables such as values and expectancies play major roles in individual differences; includes cognitive factors in the explanation and prediction of behavior. Formerly termed social-learning theory.

Social decision schemes Rules for predicting the final outcome of group decision making on the basis of the members' initial positions.

Social facilitation The process by which a person's performance is increased when other members of a group engage in similar behavior.

Social influence The area of social psychology that studies the ways in which people influence the thoughts, feelings, and behavior of others.

Social norms Explicit and implicit rules that reflect social expectations and influence the ways people behave in social situations.

Social perception A subfield of social psychology that studies the ways in which we form and modify impressions of others.

Social phobia An irrational, excessive fear of public scrutiny.

Social psychology The field of psychology that studies the nature and causes of people's thoughts and behavior in social situations.

Sociocultural perspective The view that focuses on the roles of ethnicity, gender, culture, and socioeconomic status in personality formation, behavior, and mental processes.

Socioeconomic status One's social and financial level, as indicated by measures such as income, level of education, and occupational status. Abbreviated *SES*.

Somatic nervous system The division of the peripheral nervous system that connects the central nervous system with sensory receptors, skeletal muscles, and the surface of the body.

Somatoform disorders Disorders in which people complain of physical (somatic) problems even though no physical abnormality can be found.

Somatosensory cortex The section of cortex in which sensory stimulation is projected. It lies just behind the central fissure in the parietal lobe.

Species A category of biological classification consisting of related organisms who are capable of interbreeding. Homo sapiens—humans—make up one species.

Specific phobia Persistent fear of a specific object or situation.

Spinal cord A column of nerves within the spine that transmits messages from sensory receptors to the brain and from the brain to muscles and glands throughout the body.

Spinal reflex A simple, unlearned response to a stimulus that may involve only two neurons.

Spontaneous recovery The recurrence of an extinguished response as a function of the passage of time.

Standard deviation A measure of the variability of a distribution, obtained by the formula

$$S.D. = \sqrt{\frac{\text{Sum of } d^2}{N}}$$

Standardized test A test that is given to a large number of respondents so that data concerning the typical responses can be accumulated and analyzed.

State-dependent memory Information that is better retrieved in the physiological or emotional state in which it was encoded and stored, or learned.

Statistics Numerical facts assembled in such a manner that they provide useful information about measures or scores (From the Latin *status*, meaning "standing" or "position.")

Stereotype A fixed, conventional idea about a group.

Stimulant A drug that increases activity of the nervous system.

Stimulus An environmental condition that elicits a response.

Storage The maintenance of information over time; the second stage of information processing.

Stratified sample A sample drawn so that identified subgroups in the population are represented proportionately in the sample. How can stratified sampling be carried out to ensure that a sample represents the ethnic diversity we find in the population at large?

Stress The demand that is made on an organism to adapt.

Stroboscopic motion A visual illusion in which the perception of motion is generated by a series of sta-

tionary images that are presented in rapid succession.

Structuralism The school of psychology that argues that the mind consists of three basic elements—sensations, feelings, and images—that combine to form experience.

Stupor A condition in which the senses, thought, and movement are dulled.

Subjective moral judgment According to Piaget, moral judgment that is based on the motives of the perpetrator.

Subjective value The desirability of an object or event.

Substance abuse Persistent use of a substance even though it is causing or compounding problems in meeting the demands of life.

Successive approximations In operant conditioning, a series of behaviors that gradually become more similar to a target behavior.

Superego The third psychic structure, which functions as a moral guardian and sets forth high standards for behavior.

Suppression The deliberate, or conscious, placing of certain ideas, impulses, or images out of awareness.

Survey A method of scientific investigation in which a large sample of people answer questions about their attitudes or behavior.

Sympathetic The branch of the ANS that is most active during emotional responses, such as fear and anxiety, that spend the body's reserves of energy.

Sympathetic nervous system The branch of the autonomic nervous system that is most active during processes that spend body energy from stored reserves, such as in a fight-or-flight reaction to a predator or when you are anxious about a big test. When people experience fear, the sympathetic nervous system accelerates the heart rate, raises the blood pressure, tenses muscles, and so on.

Synapse A junction between the axon terminals of one neuron and the dendrites or cell body of another neuron.

Systematic desensitization Wolpe's behavioral fear-reduction technique in which a hierarchy of fear-evoking stimuli is presented while the person remains relaxed.

Systematic random search An algorithm for solving problems in which each possible solution is tested according to a particular set of rules.

Taste buds The sensory organs for taste. They contain taste cells and are located on the tongue.

Taste cells Receptor cells that are sensitive to taste.

Temporal lobe The lobe that lies below the lateral fissure, near the temples of the head.

Testosterone A male sex hormone produced by the testes that promotes growth of male sexual characteristics and sperm.

Texture gradient A monocular cue for depth based on the perception that closer objects appear to have rougher (more detailed) surfaces.

Thalamus An area near the center of the brain involved in the relay of sensory information to the cortex and in the functions of sleep and attention.

Theory A formulation of relationships underlying observed events.

Theta waves Slow brain waves produced during the hypnagogic state.

Thinking Paying attention to information, mentally representing it, reasoning about it, and making decisions about it.

Thyroxin The thyroid hormone that increases metabolic rate.

Time out Removal of an organism from a situation in which reinforcement is available when unwanted behavior is shown.

Tip-of-the-tongue (TOT) phenomenon The feeling that information is stored in memory although it cannot be readily retrieved. Also called the *feeling-of-knowing experience.*

Token economy A controlled environment in which people are reinforced for desired behaviors with tokens (such as poker chips) that may be exchanged for privileges.

Tolerance Habituation to a drug, with the result that increasingly higher doses of the drug are needed to achieve similar effects.

Top-down processing The use of contextual information or knowledge of a pattern in order to organize parts of the pattern.

Trait A relatively stable aspect of personality that is inferred from behavior and assumed to give rise to consistent behavior.

Transcendental meditation (TM) The simplified form of meditation brought to the United States by the Maharishi Mahesh Yogi and used as a method for coping with stress.

Transference Responding to one person (such as a spouse or the psychoanalyst) in a way that is similar to the way one responded to another person (such as a parent) in childhood.

Treatment In experiments, a condition received by subjects so that its effects may be observed.

Triangular model of love Sternberg's view that love involves combinations of three components: intimacy, passion, and decision/commitment.

Trichromat A person with normal color vision.

Trichromatic theory The theory that color vision is made possible by three types of cones, some of which respond to red light, some to green, and some to blue. (From the Greek roots *treis,* meaning "three," and *chroma,* meaning "color.")

Trust versus mistrust Erikson's first stage of psychosexual development, during which children do—or do not—come to trust that primary caregivers and the environment will meet their needs.

Two-point threshold The least distance by which two rods touching the skin must be separated before the person will report that there are two rods, not one, on 50% of occasions.

Type A behavior Behavior characterized by a sense of time urgency, competitiveness, and hostility.

Umbilical cord A tube between the mother and her developing child through which nutrients and waste products are conducted.

Unconditional positive regard A persistent expression of esteem for the value of a person, but not necessarily an unqualified acceptance of all of the person's behaviors.

Unconditioned response (UCR) An unlearned response to an unconditioned stimulus.

Unconditioned stimulus (UCS) A stimulus that elicits a response from an organism prior to conditioning.

Unconscious In psychodynamic theory, descriptive of ideas and feelings that are not available to awareness.

Uninvolved parents Parents who generally leave their children to themselves.

Uplifts Notable pleasant daily conditions and experiences.

Vaginismus A sexual dysfunction characterized by involuntary contraction of the muscles surrounding the vagina, preventing entry by the penis or making entry painful.

Validity scales Groups of test items that indicate whether a person's responses accurately reflect that individual's traits.

Variable-interval schedule A schedule in which a variable amount of time must elapse between the previous and subsequent times that reinforcement is available.

Variable-ratio schedule A schedule in which reinforcement is provided after a variable number of correct responses.

Vasocongestion Engorgement of blood vessels with blood, which swells the genitals and breasts during sexual arousal.

Ventromedial nucleus (VMN) A central area on the underside of the hypothalamus that appears to function as a stop-eating center.

Vestibular sense The sense of equilibrium that informs us about our bodies' positions relative to gravity.

Visible light The part of the electromagnetic spectrum that stimulates the eye and produces visual sensations.

Visual acuity Sharpness of vision.

Visual code Mental representation of information as a picture.

Volunteer bias A source of bias or error in research reflecting the prospect that people who offer to participate in research studies differ systematically from people who do not.

Waxy flexibility A feature of catatonic schizophrenia in which people can be molded into postures that they maintain for quite some time.

Weber's constant The fraction of the intensity by which a source of physical energy must be increased or decreased so that a difference in intensity will be perceived.

Wernicke's aphasia A language disorder characterized by difficulty comprehending the meaning of spoken language.

Wernicke–Korsakoff syndrome A cluster of symptoms associated with chronic alcohol abuse and characterized by confusion, memory impairment, and filling in gaps in memory with false information (confabulation).

White matter In the spinal cord, axon bundles that carry messages from and to the brain.

Wisdom Expert knowledge concerning the meaning of life, concern for people's welfare, and a push toward excellence.

Wish fulfillment A primitive method used by the id to attempt to gratify basic instincts.

Working memory Same as *short-term memory*.

Zone of proximal development (ZPD) Vygotsky's term for the situation in which a child carries out tasks with the help of someone who is more skilled, frequently an adult who represents the culture in which the child develops.

Zygote A fertilized ovum (egg cell).

Author Index

Subject Index

Credits

This page constitutes an extension of the copyright page. We have made every effort to trace the ownership of all copyrighted material and to secure permission from copyright holders. In the event of any question arising as to the use of any material, we will be pleased to make the necessary corrections in future printings. Thanks are due to the following authors, publishers, and agents for permission to use the material indicated.

Photo Credits

Chapter 1. **2:** C Squared Studios/Getty Images **4:** AP/Wide World Photos **7:** © Jeff Greenberg/PhotoEdit **8:** Brown Brothers **10:** top, Archives of the History of American Psychology **10:** bottom, Archives of the History of American Psychology **11:** Archives of the History of American Psychology **12:** top right, Bob and Marian Breland-Bailey, Hot Springs, AR **12:** top left, Tom McHugh/Photo Researchers, Inc. **14:** top, Archives of the History of American Psychology **14:** Archives of the History of American Psychology **14:** bottom, Archives of the History of American Psychology **14:** bottom, © Christopher Johnson/Stock,Boston Inc./PictureQuest **14:** bottom, UPI/Bettmann/CORBIS **14:** top, © Bettmann/CORBIS **14:** top, © UPI/Bettmann/CORBIS **18:** Larry Williams/CORBIS **20:** Archives of the History of American Psychology **21:** Library of Congress **23:** The Granger Collection, New York **28:** Michael K. Nicols/National Geographic Society/Getty **31:** © Annie Griffiths Belt/CORBIS **34:** © Claus Meyer/Black Star Publishing/PictureQuest **36:** Greg Mancuso/Stock, Boston LLC

Chapter 2. **42:** © Pete Saloutos/CORBIS **44:** Topham/The Image Works **45:** Topham/The Image Works **46:** © David Thompson/OSF/Animals, Animals **50:** right, The Everett Collection **50:** left, © Reuters NewMedia, Inc./CORBIS **51:** © Michael Greenlar/The Image Works **59:** AFP Photo/Stephen Jaffe **61:** Yellow Dog Productions/Getty Images **65:** Reprinted with permission from Damasio H. Gravowski T, Frank R, Galaburda AM, Damasio AR: The return of Phineas Gage: Clues about the brain from a famous patient. *Science*, 264:1102–1105, © 1994. American Association for the Advancement of Science. Photo courtesy of H. Damasio, Human Neuroanatomy and Neuroimaging Laboratory, Department of Neurology, University of Iowa. **66:** top right, Ohio Nuclear Corporation/SPL/Photo Researchers, Inc. **66:** middle right, Spencer Grant/Stock, Boston **66:** bottom right, CNRI/SPL/Photo Researchers, Inc. **69:** © William Fritsch/Brand X Pictures/PictureQuest **70:** Columbia Pictures Corporation/ZUMA/CORBIS **74:** Culver Pictures **75:** right, AP/Wide World Photos **75:** left, © Bettmann/CORBIS **81:** Science Photo Library/Photo Researchers, Inc.

Chapter 3. **88:** © Margo Granitsas/The Image Works **92:** © Fotografia, Inc./CORBIS **97:** © Farrell Grehan/CORBIS **98:** top right, Doug Goodman/Photo Researchers, Inc. **99:** (bottom) © George Zimbel **99:** top, (top) © Doug Goodman/Photo Researchers, Inc. **103:** Davidson Films, Inc. **105:** Courtesy of Harvard University Archives **108:** © Marvin S. Roberts **109:** left, left, © Martin Rogers/Stock, Boston **109:** right, right, © Martin Rogers/Stock, Boston **110:** Harlow Primate Lab, University of Wisconsin **111:** Thomas McAvoy/Time Life Pictures/Getty Images **114:** © 2002 Tony Anderson/Getty Images/FPG **116:** © Eastcott-Momatiuk/The Image Works **118:** © Ariel Skelley/CORBIS **126:** AP/Wide World Photos **128:** © Royalty-Free/CORBIS **130:** Ken Fisher/Getty Images **134:** © Bob Daemmrich/Stock, Boston/PictureQuest

Chapter 4. **140:** Erwin Redl/www.paramedia.net **142:** Warner Bros./The Kobal Collection **144:** The Granger Collection, New York **145:** The Granger Collection, New York **146:** DAVID OLIVER/Getty Images **150:** Omikron/Photo Researchers, Inc. **152:** top, © Fritz Goro/Time Life Pictures/Getty Images **152:** bottom left (left

detail and right), Geroge Seurat. "A Sunday Afternoon on La Grande Jatte." 1884–86. Oil on canvas, 81 × 120 3/8". Helen Birch Bartlett Memorial Collection, 1926.224. © 1998 The Art Institute of Chicago. All rights reserved. **156:** bottom, M.C. Escher. "Mosaic II" © 2001 M.C. Escher/Cordon Art-Baarn, Holland. All rights reserved. **159:** © Abe Rezny/The Image Works **160:** © Bettmann/CORBIS **161:** Richard Douglas Rose **163:** Enamul Hoque/Getty Images **169:** AP/Wide World Photos **170:** Paul Souders/Getty Images **171:** © Kathy Ferguson-Johnson/PhotoEdit **173:** © 1990 Andy Levin/Photo Researchers, Inc. **176:** Warner Bros./Photofest **178:** CORBIS/Sygma **181:** © Cassy Cohen/PhotoEdit

Chapter 5. **186:** © David Epperson/Getty Images **189:** © Reg Charity/CORBIS **190:** AP **196:** © Bettmann/CORBIS **198:** © 1990 Louie Psihoyos **205:** © Yellow Dog Productions/Getty Images **207:** © William McCoy/Rainbow **216:** © David Young-Wolff/PhotoEdit **218:** Courtesy of the American Cancer Society **221:** © Anne Marie Rousseau/The Image Works **226:** © Ariel Skelley/CORBIS

Chapter 6. **230:** © Michael Newman/PhotoEdit **232:** Midway Games/Getty Images **233:** Getty Images/ImageBank **234:** © Hulton-Deutsch Collection/CORBIS **235:** © Dana White/PhotoEdit **238:** © Boyd Norton/The Image Works **239:** © Robert T. Nowitz/CORBIS **241:** © Archives of the History of American Psychology **242:** Annabella Bluesky/Photo Researchers, Inc. **244:** bottom, © Christopher Johnson/Stock,Boston Inc./PictureQuest **250:** © Hank Morgan/Rainbow **252:** © Daniel Allan/Getty Images **254:** Reprinted by permission of Nature Publishing Group **254:** Courtesy of Dr. Sanjiv Talwar **256:** © Stephen Johnson/Getty Images **258:** © Tony Freeman/PhotoEdit **259:** © Albert Bandura

Chapter 7. **264:** J Price/Getty Image **276:** © Jacques M. Chenet/CORBIS **281:** © Tony Freeman/PhotoEdit **282:** © Royalty-Free/CORBIS **283:** Photo by William Calvin **285:** AP/Wide World Photos **288:** © David Young Wolff/PhotoEdit **291:** © Bettmann/CORBIS **293:** © Robert Finken/Index Stock Imagery **297:** Courtesy of Dana Copeland **298:** Steve Sands/New York Newswire/CORBIS

Chapter 8. **306:** © Peter Johnson/CORBIS **309:** © Peter Johnson/CORBIS **310:** © Gale Zucker/Stock, Boston LLC **321:** Courtesy of Dr. Claudio Cantalupo/Dr. William D. Hopkins **322:** © Susan Kulkin/Photo Researchers, Inc. **328:** Courtesy Dr. Noam Chomsky, Massachussetts Institute of Technology **329:** © A. Ramey/PhotoEdit **330:** Courtesy of Robert Williams

Chapter 9. **334:** © Andrea Pistolesi/The Image Bank/Getty Images **336:** Mario Tama/Getty Images **345:** © Culver Pictures **350:** © Paul Barton/CORBIS **356:** L.A. Cicero, Stanford University News Service **357:** © Larry Kolvoord/The Image Works **358:** © Mark Richards/PhotoEdit

Chapter 10. **362:** AP/Wide World Photos **364:** Mango Productions/CORBIS **366:** © 1987 Comstock **367:** Harlow Primate Lab, University of Wisconsin **370:** © Dr. Neal Miller/Yale University **375:** The Everett Collection **377:** Library of Congress **378:** © Monika Graff/The Image Works **383:** © 1976 Paul Ekman/Human Interaction Laboratory **384:** © Richard Ellis/The Image Works **386:** © DPA/RS3/The Image Works **387:** © CORBIS/SYGMA **391:** Mark Burnett/Stock, Boston

Chapter 11. **398:** © Jon Feingersh/CORBIS **400:** Image 100/Getty Images **401:** © Bettmann/CORBIS **403:** © Laura Dwight/CORBIS **404:** George Tiedemann/NewSport/CORBIS **406:** top, © UPI/Bettmann/CORBIS **406:** bottom, UPI/Bettmann/CORBIS **409:** Denis Felix/Getty Images **412:** © Ariel Skelley/CORBIS **414:** © Dimitri Iundt/CORBIS **417:** Manchau/Getty Images **425:** Photodisc Collection/Getty Images

Chapter 12. **434:** © Leif Skoogfors/CORBIS **437:** © Esbin-Anderson/Photo Network/PictureQuest **438:** © Harvey Ferdschnei-

Coverage of Applications, Diversity, and Evolutionary Psychology in
Psychology: Concepts and Connections, Ninth Edition